READINGS AND MATERIALS

Tax Policy

SECOND EDITION

by

Philip D. Oliver

Ben J. Altheimer Distinguished Professor of Law
William H. Bowen School of Law
University of Arkansas at Little Rock

Foundation Press

NEW YORK, NEW YORK

2004

© 1996 FOUNDATION PRESS
© 2004 By FOUNDATION PRESS
       395 Hudson Street
       New York, NY 10014
       Phone Toll Free 1–877–888–1330
       Fax (212) 367–6799
       fdpress.com
Printed in the United States of America

ISBN 1–58778–161–1

TEXT IS PRINTED ON 10% POST CONSUMER RECYCLED PAPER

For Kunky

PREFACE TO THE SECOND EDITION

Tax policy is the preeminent policy course in the curriculum of most schools. There are several reasons for this. First is the unrivaled impact of tax law. With the possible exception of criminal law, it is the most important branch of law. The Department of Commerce estimates that taxes at all levels take over 30 percent of gross domestic product.[a]

With taxes claiming nearly one dollar in three, it is hardly surprising that tax law affects almost all aspects of life. Taxes affect our employment decisions, the form of our compensation, when we retire, our decisions about savings and investments, and all manner of business decisions. Less obviously, taxes also affect such things as where we live (both the political jurisdiction and the type of housing). Taxes profoundly influence marital and family relationships as well. No other branch of law even begins to have the broad economic *and* social impact of tax law.

All these dollars mean that tax policy is a central political issue for every presidential administration, and in every Congress—and in every legislature, town hall, and county supervising board. A student of politics or government will find no better laboratories than tax policy debates, which are played out for high stakes both politically and financially. On the practical side, anyone attempting to influence politicians (as well as judges and administrators) who make tax decisions goes better armed with an understanding of policy issues. Arguments founded in self interest or client interest are more persuasive when framed with reference to broader values.

At the same time, development of tax policy is more than just a fight about dollars, or about political power. Through the decades, the debate over tax policy issues has generated the country's richest policy literature, and it continues to do so. The debate is sophisticated and nuanced, combining elements of pure theory with considerations of political practicality and public acceptance. Study of the reasoning in tax policy literature will serve a student who would attempt to reason, and to persuade, in any area.

For these reasons, the study of tax policy is not just for tax specialists, but is valuable to students plan to specialize in other areas. Tax policy issues are not simple, but this book should be fully accessible to a reader who has taken any tax course at the undergraduate, graduate, or law school level. Indeed, even a student without any formal study of taxation should be able to handle the policy issues considered, though in that case a basic undergraduate course in economics would be helpful.

*   *   *

---

a. The Department of Commerce estimates that 2002 gross domestic product amounted to $10.446 trillion, and that receipts by federal, state, and local governments totaled $3.178 trillion, or 30.4%. U.S. DEP'T. OF COM., SURV. OF CURRENT BUS., vol. 83, no. 8, August, 2003, tbl. 1.1, at D-3, tbl. 3.2, at D-9, tbl. 3.3, at D-9.

This second edition follows the same broad chapter outlines of the seventeen chapters of the first edition. Nevertheless, it will be readily apparent to anyone familiar with the first edition that the second edition is a considerably changed book. The seventeen chapters cover an additional 326 pages of text, not counting the appendices, tables, and index that were not part of the first edition. Almost every chapter includes at least one excerpt that was not part of the first edition—a total of 38 new excerpts—and in most chapters new subchapters have been added. Political considerations, and the resulting restraints on policy choice, receive additional emphasis. Increased attention has been given to the goal of making the chapters of the book function as an integral whole, a task somewhat easier for a single author than for two working together.

The five chapters of Part I address fundamental issues concerning the country's tax system, and particularly the federal income tax. Chapter One continues to focus on fiscal policy, and now offers widely differing views regarding the seriousness of our budgetary deficits. At the same time, the chapter has been reorganized to give increased consideration to reasons for taxation unrelated to fiscal policy. Chapter Two addresses timing issues and the realization rule, matters of increasingly obvious importance. The chapter has been considerably broadened by the addition of three new subchapters, one of which explores ways of achieving the economic equivalent of mark-to-market taxation while avoiding the annual appraisals and liquidity problems that taxation without realization seems to entail. Chapter Three deals with the social and economic ramifications of the nontaxation of imputed income—issues of both practical and theoretical interest. Chapter Four addresses the question of whether rates should be flat or progressive, and if progressive, the more difficult question of how to determine the *degree* of progressivity. A new subchapter explores the contribution of optimal taxation theory to the debate. Chapter Five addresses the issue of whether we should deal with taxpayers as individuals or as members of families. Two new subchapters address problems that grow with longevity and the divorce rate—the proper treatment of elderly taxpayers, and of innocent and former spouses who have filed a joint return but now seek to avoid joint and several liability. Many of the issues considered in Part I will resurface later in the book.

Part II considers an idea that has been gathering force both in the literature and in the political sphere—replacement or supplementation of the income tax with some form of broad-based consumption tax, either the value added tax used in much of the world, or a consumption-type income tax that would closely resemble our present income tax in terms of administration. While the pure form of this consumption-type income tax is largely untested, a new subchapter emphasizes the increasing tendency of our income tax to resemble such a consumption-type tax.

Part III provides an opportunity to examine in detail three aspects of the tax treatment of wealth transferred by reason of death. Two of the chapters have been considerably revised to take account of the Economic Growth and Tax Relief Reconciliation Act of 2001, which may signal a future without an estate tax and in which a form of carryover basis replaces stepped-up basis at death.

Part IV begins with a substantially revised chapter on tax expenditures, which have enjoyed political resurgence since the Tax Reform Act of 1986. New excerpts—of which the chapter includes seven—question the proposition that direct spending is to be preferred to tax expenditures (here the political theory of public choice is raised and challenged), as well as the form that tax expenditures should take. A new subchapter examines the Earned Income Tax Credit in detail. The remaining two chapters of the part consider an exclusion (for personal injury awards) and a deduction (for state and local taxes). There are other important exclusions—employer-provided health insurance, for example, the largest single item in the tax expenditure budget, dwarfs the exclusion for tort awards. The exclusion for personal injury awards is perhaps the most interesting exclusion, however, because while it *may* be a tax expenditure, it may instead merely recognize that an accident victim should not be taxed because being compensated for an injury entails no element of profit. Similarly, a chapter on any of the other major personal deductions (medical expenses, interest, or charitable contributions) could have been included—and, were space no consideration, would have been included—but the deduction for state and local taxes raises unique federalism issues.

Part V is directed to three important topics in the taxation of business and investment income. All three chapters have been substantially revised. Chapter Fourteen examines corporations and dividends, and especially the "double tax" issue. The chapter takes account of the substantial changes in 2003, and of the even broader change initially requested by the President. A new subchapter examines the politics of integration. Chapter Fifteen addresses a perennial political heavyweight that has received yet another recent statutory facelift—the proper tax treatment of capital gains and losses. The central issue of whether capital gains should be taxed at preferential rates is addressed by four new excerpts. The topic of Chapter Sixteen—what to do about inflation—has been gaining increasing attention because of its relationship to any proposal to replace the realization rule with mark-to-market taxation, an issue considered in a new subchapter.

Finally, Part VI closes the book with an expanded chapter entirely devoted to the political framework in which the tax legislative process operates. Some professors and some students will regard this chapter as tangential to a consideration of tax policy issues, while others will see it as the center ring at the circus.

As was the case in preparing the first edition, there was never a shortage of potential excerpts. Instead, the challenge was to choose from a wealth of high-quality materials, and then to trim their well-crafted presentations without losing the essence of the argument. As with the first edition, an effort has been made to include a blend of academic and non-academic pieces, and a slight preference has been extended to relatively recent materials. The principal criterion for selection, however, was an effort to compile materials that explain an issue and present a range of views to the reader, as clearly and simply as the complexity of the issue permits.

Each subchapter begins with a textual introduction to place the excerpts in context. The subchapters close with notes and questions, which serve to review and examine the ideas presented in the excerpts, as well as to present the views of other commentators whose work was not excerpted.

I suggest that the reader examine the note on Editorial Conventions, at page xlv, before beginning.

I shall appreciate any comments, suggestions for improvement, or suggestions for items that might profitably be included in a future edition (including reprints).

* * *

To some degree, work on the second edition began almost as soon as the first was published, in 1996. During this period, and particularly during the past three years, many people have made valuable contributions, which I wish to acknowledge. I am aware of the risk that I shall fail to mention some who should be mentioned, and apologize in advance.

Initial thanks go to my very good friend, Professor Emeritus Fred W. Peel, Jr., who co-authored the first edition. Fred is now 85 and in poor health, and could not participate to any degree in the work on the second edition. Obviously, however, his knowledge, language, and choices of excerpts are reflected to a considerable degree in this second edition. Less obvious is Fred's indirect influence on the book through his influence on me. Fred served as something of a mentor when I joined the faculty of the University of Arkansas at Little Rock School of Law in 1980, particularly in the years before his retirement in 1987. Up until his move to California in 1993, I regularly profited from thousands of conversations with him (including many about tax policy). At the same time, of course we could not be in total agreement in compiling the first edition, and in compiling the second I have had to follow my own judgment. Accordingly, the chapters in which Fred had the greatest hand in the first edition (1, 2, 4, 5, 11, 14, 15, 16, and 17) are the ones which have been most substantially revised.

I acknowledge with gratitude the ongoing support of the Ben J. Altheimer Charitable Foundation.

Colleagues at other schools have provided assistance for which I am grateful. Alan Schenk of Wayne State was helpful in the revision of Chapter Six (Value Added Tax), as he had been for the first edition. Larry Ward of Iowa was kind in sharing the numerical data that he had compiled concerning the present and future value of one dollar, which are found in the appendices of this book (and of the basic tax book that he and Alan Gunn co-author). Edward Spurgeon and Elizabeth Mustard of Georgia, in the course of evaluating the teaching of tax and elder law, published a helpful critique of the first edition.[b]

Here at the William H. Bowen School of Law at the University of Arkansas at Little Rock, I appreciate the support of my dean, Chuck Goldner, and of his predecessor, Rod Smith. The Law Library staff—in particular, Professor Melissa Serfass—proved unfailingly helpful. Faculty secretaries Cheryl Bigelow and Gail Harris each performed many valuable tasks.

I profited from outstanding research assistants. Over the past 20 months, Shawn Key and Lori Burrows did all that was asked, and more—indeed, all that could have been hoped. They were both pleasant and conscientious throughout a lengthy process that frequently was tedious. Both provided valuable research, and they produced most of the tables in the front and back of the book. They shared duties in the final proofreading of every word in the book. Miss Burrows assumed responsibility for obtaining approvals for the reproduction of copyrighted materials. Mr. Key and I have gotten to know each other very well indeed, meeting at all hours as he performed every manner of job, and always with such disconcerting promptness that the ball was perpetually in my court. Mr. Key had total control of the vast amount of technical work required in converting newly excerpted materials into a computerized format, and of subsequently of putting the entire book into camera-ready form. His work was substantial and extended over a long period; without exception, it was performed skillfully, creatively, and in good humor. (Part of his good humor was putting up with my Eighteenth Century level of computer skills.) At an early stage, valuable research assistance was provided by Jana Berryman, an outstanding alumna of this school, which I also acknowledge with gratitude.

---

b. Edward D. Spurgeon & Elizabeth J. Mustard, *Integrating Tax and Elder Law into Elder Law and Tax Courses*, 30 STETSON L. REV. 1375, 1403-05 (2001).

PREFACE

I hope that those who worked on this book will find the final product worthy of their efforts. Those defects that remain are entirely my responsibility.

Finally, I appreciate the support and sacrifices of my wife and colleague, Professor Ranko Shiraki Oliver, and of our daughter, Kunky.

PHILIP D. OLIVER
Little Rock, Arkansas
October, 2003

SELECTIONS AND
COPYRIGHT ACKNOWLEDGMENTS

Chapter 1: The Purposes of Taxation

Robert Eisner, *We Don't Need Balanced Budgets*, Wall Street Journal, January 11, 1995. Copyright © Dow Jones and Company, Inc. Reprinted with permission.

Daniel N. Shaviro, *The Growing US Fiscal Gap,* World Economics, Vol. 3, No. 4, Oct-Dec. 2002. Copyright © 2003 by the NTC Economic and Financial Publishing. Reprinted with permission.

Donald W. Kiefer, *Whatever Happened to Counter-Cyclical Economic Stimulus*, National Tax Association Forum, Winter 1993. Copyright © 1993 by the National Tax Association—Tax Institute of America. Reprinted with permission.

Edward M. Gramlich, *Savings, Investment, and the Tax Reform Act of 1986*, National Tax Association—Tax Institute of America 79th Annual Conference (1986). Copyright © 1986 by the National Tax Association—Tax Institute of America. Reprinted with permission.

Richard Ruggles, *Accounting for Saving and Capital Formation in the United States, 1947-1991*, 7 Journal of Economic Perspectives 3 (1993). Copyright © 1993, American Economics Association. Reprinted with permission.

Congressional Budget Office Report, Effective Federal Tax Rates, 1979-1997.

Chapter 2: When Should Income Be Taxed?

Alan Gunn & Larry D. Ward, *Federal Income Taxation*, (5th ed. 2002). Copyright © 2002 by The West Publishing Group. Reprinted with permission.

Henry C. Simons, *Personal Income Taxation* (1938). Copyright © 1938 by the University of Chicago. All rights reserved. Published February 1938. Third Impressions 1955. Composed and printed by the University of Chicago Press, Chicago, Illinois. U.S.A. Reprinted with permission.

Henry C. Simons, *Federal Tax Reform* (1950) Copyright 1950 © by the University of Chicago. All rights reserved. Published 1950. Composed and printed by the University of Chicago Press, Chicago, Illinois. U.S.A. Reprinted with permission.

Mark L. Louie, *Note, Realizing Appreciation Without Sale: Accrual Taxation of Capital Gains on Marketable Securities*, 34 Stanford Law Review 857 (1982). Reprinted with the permission of the Stanford Law Review and the Fred B. Rothman Co. Copyright © 1982 by the Board of Trustees of the Leland Stanford Junior University.

Marvin A. Chirelstein, *Federal Income Taxation* (7th ed. 1994). Copyright © 1994, Foundation Press. Reprinted with permission.

Fred W. Peel, Jr., *Capital Losses: Falling Short on Fairness and Simplicity*, 17 Baltimore Law Review 418 (1988). Copyright © 1988. University of Baltimore Law Review. Reprinted with permission.

Victor Thuronyi, *The Concept of Income*, 46 Tax Law Review 45 (1990). Copyright © 1990 by the New York University School of Law. Reprinted with permission.

J. Gregory Ballentine, *Three Failures in Economic Analysis of Tax Reform*, National Tax Association—Tax Institute of America 79th Annual Conference (1986). Copyright © 1986 by the National Tax Association—Tax Institute of America. Reprinted with permission.

David A. Weisbach, *A Partial Mark-to-Market Tax System*, 53 Tax Law Review 95 (1999). Copyright © 1999 by the New York University School of Law. Reprinted with permission.

Stephen B. Land, *Defeating Deferral: A Proposal for Retrospective Taxation,* 52 Tax Law Review 45 (1996). Copyright © 1996 by the New York University School of Law. Reprinted with permission.

Jay A. Soled, *A Proposal to Lengthen the Tax Accounting Period*, 14 American Journal of Tax Policy 35 (1997). Copyright © 1997 by the University of Alabama Law Review. Reprinted with permission.

Chapter 3:   Imputed Income

Richard Goode, *Imputed Rent of Owner-Occupied Dwellings under the Income Tax*, 15 Journal of Finance 504 (1960). Copyright © 1960 by the Journal of Finance, Stern School of Business. Reprinted with permission.

Thomas Chancellor, *Imputed Income and the Ideal Income Tax*, 67 Oregon Law Review 561 (1988). Copyright © 1988 by the University of Chicago. Reprinted with permission.

Michael J. McIntyre & Oliver Oldman, *Taxation of the Family in a Comprehensive and Simplified Income Tax*, 90 Harvard Law Review 1573 (1977). Copyright © 1977 by the Harvard Law Review Association. Reprinted with permission.

William A. Klein, *Tax Deductions for Family Care Expenses*, 14 Boston College Industrial & Commercial Law Review 917 (1973). Copyright © 1973 by Boston College Law School. Reprinted with permission.

Daniel C. Schaffer & Donald H. Berman, *Two Cheers for the Child Care Deduction*, 28 Tax Law Review 535 (1973). Copyright © 1973 by the New York University School of Law. Reprinted with permission.

Edward J. McCaffrey, *Taxation and the Family: A Fresh Look at Behavioral Gender Biases in the Code*, 40 University of California at Los Angeles Law Review 983 (1993). Copyright © 1993, the Regents of the University of California. Reprinted with permission.

Chapter 4: Progressive Tax Rates

JB McCombs, *An Historical Review and Analysis of Early United States Tax Policy Scholarship: Definition of Income and Progressive Rates,* 64 Saint John's Law Review 471 (1990). Copyright © 1990, The St. John's Law Review Association. Reprinted with permission.

Dan Throop Smith, *High Progressive Tax Rates: Inequity and Immorality?*, 20 University of Florida Law Review 451 (1968). Copyright © 1968, the University of Florida Law Review. Reprinted with permission.

Charles O. Galvin & Boris I. Bittker, *The Income Tax: How Progressive Should it Be?,* Second Lecture, by Boris I. Bittker (1969). Copyright © 1987 the American Enterprise Institute for Public Policy Research. Reprinted with permission of the American Enterprise Institute for Public Policy Research, Washington, D.C.

Jeffrey A. Schoenblum, *Tax Fairness or Unfairness? A Consideration of the Philosophical Bases for Unequal Taxation of Individuals*, 12 American Journal of Tax Policy 221 (1995). Copyright © 1995 by the University of Alabama School of Law. Reprinted with permission.

Charles E. McLure, Jr., *Comments on Fundamental Tax Reform*, National Tax Association—Tax Institute of America 78th Annual Conference (1985). Copyright © 1985 by The National Tax Association—Tax Institute of America. Reprinted with permission.

Shoup Mission, *Report on Japanese Taxation*.

U.S. Department of the Treasury, *Tax Reform for Fairness, Simplicity, and Economic Growth* (1984).

Joseph Bankman & Thomas Griffith, *Social Welfare and the Rate Structure: A New Look at Progressive Taxation*, 75 California Law Review 1906 (1987). Copyright © 1987 by the California Law Review, University of California, Berkeley. Reprinted with permission.

Lawrence Zelenak & Kemper Moreland, *Can the Graduated Income Tax Survive Optimal Tax Analysis?*, 53 Tax Law Review 51 (1999). Copyright © 1999 by New York University School of Law. Reprinted with permission.

Chapter 5:   Taxing Families

Poe v. Seaborn, 282 U.S. 101 (1930).

Staff of the Joint Committee on Taxation, *Income Tax Treatment of Married Couples and Single Persons* (1980).

Daniel R. Feenberg & Harvey S. Rosen, *Recent Developments in the Marriage Tax*, 48 National Tax Journal 91 (1995). Copyright © 1995 by the National Tax Association—Tax Institute of America. Reprinted with permission.

Marriage Penalty and Family Tax Relief Act of 2001 Report, House Report 107-29, 107th Congress, 1st Session (2001).

Boris I. Bittker, *Federal Income Taxation and the Family*, 27 Stanford Law Review 1389 (1975). Reprinted with permission of the Sanford Law Review and the Fred B. Rothman Co. Copyright © 1975 by the Board of Trustees of the Leland Stanford Junior University.

Lawrence Zelenak, *Marriage and the Income Tax*, 67 Southern California Law Review 339 (1994). Reprinted with permission of the Southern California Law Review. Copyright © 1994 Southern California Law Review.

Marjorie E. Kornhauser, *Love, Money, and the IRS: Family, Income-Sharing, and the Joint Income Tax Return*, 45 Hastings Law Journal 63 (1993). Copyright © 1993 by the University of California, Hastings College of the Law. Reprinted with permission.

Fred W. Peel, Jr., *An Approach to Income Tax Simplification*, 1 University of Arkansas at Little Rock Law Journal 1 (1978). Copyright © 1978 by the University of Arkansas of Little Rock Law Review. Reprinted with permission.

Internal Revenue Service Restructuring and Reform Act of 1998, H.R. Report 105-599 (Conference Report). 1998-3 Internal Revenue Cumulative Bulletin 747, 1003-09.

Martha W. Jordan, *The Innocent Spouse Problem: Defining a Proportionate Solution*, 24 Ohio Northern University Law Review 517 (1998). Copyright © 1998 by the Ohio Northern University Law Review. Reprinted with permission.

Lawrence Zelenak, *Children and the Income Tax*, 49 Tax Law Review 349 (1994). Copyright © 1994 by the New York University School of Law. Reprinted with permission.

Allan J. Samansky, *Tax Policy and the Obligation to Support Children*, 57 Ohio State Law Journal 329 (1996). Copyright © 1996 by the Ohio State Law Journal. Reprinted with permission.

Joseph Pechman, *Federal Tax Policy* (5th ed. 1987). Copyright © 1987 by the Brookings Institution. Reprinted with permission.

Jonathan Barry Forman, *Reconsidering the Income Tax Treatment of the Elderly: It's Time for the Elderly to Pay Their Fair Share*, 56 University of Pittsburgh Law Review 589 (1995). Copyright © 1995 by the University of Pittsburgh Law Review. Reprinted with permission.

Chapter 6:   Value Added Taxes

Richard W. Lindholm, *The Origin of the Value-Added Tax*, 6 Journal of Corporation Law 11 (1980). Copyright © 1980 by the University of Iowa. Reprinted with permission.

Alan Schenk, *Radical Tax Reform for the 21st Century: The Role for a Consumption Tax*, 2 Chapman Law Review 133 (1999). Copyright © 1999 by Chapman Law Review. Reprinted with permission.

Committee on Ways & Means, Hearing Announcement on the Tax Restructuring Act of 1979, Statement by Representative Al Ullman (D., Oregon), H.R. 5665, 96th Congress, 1st Session, Ways and Means Committee Print 96-38, at 6-12 (1979).

U.S. Department of the Treasury, *Tax Reform for Fairness, Simplicity, and Economic Growth* (1984).

American Bar Association, *Value Added Tax: A Model Statute and Commentary* (1989). Copyright © 1989 American Bar Association. Reprinted with permission.

Charles E. McLure, Jr., *The Value-Added Tax: Key to Deficit Reduction?* (1987). Copyright © 1987 the American Enterprise Institute for Public Policy Research. Reprinted with permission of the American Enterprise Institute for Public Policy Research, Washington D.C.

John F. Due, *Economics of the Value Added Tax*, 6 Journal of Corporation Law 61 (1980). Copyright © 1980 by the University of Iowa. Reprinted with permission.

Alan Schenk, *Value Added Tax: Does this Consumption Tax Have a Place in the Federal Tax System?*, 7 Virginia Tax Review 207 (1987). Copyright © 1987 by the Virginia Tax Review. Reprinted with permission.

Joseph Isenbergh, *The End of Income Taxation*, 45 Tax Law Review 283 (1990). Copyright © 1990 by the New York University School of Law. Reprinted with permission.

Michael J. Graetz, *Revisiting the Income Tax vs. Consumption Tax Debate*, 57 Tax Notes 1437 (1992). Copyright © 1992 by the Tax Analysts. Reprinted with permission.

Chapter 7: A Consumption-Type Income Tax

William D. Andrews, *A Consumption-Type or Cash Flow Personal Income Tax*, 87 Harvard Law Review 1113 (1974). Copyright © 1974 by the Harvard Law Review Association. Reprinted with permission.

Alvin Warren, *Would a Consumption Tax Be Fairer than an Income Tax?*, 89 Yale Law Journal 1081 (1980). Copyright © 1980 the Yale Law Journal Company. Reprinted by permission of the Yale Law Journal Company and the Fred B. Rothman Company.

Chapter 8: Life Insurance

Charles E. McLure, Jr., *The Income Tax Treatment of Interest Earned on Savings in Life Insurance,* in the Economics of Federal Subsidy Programs: A Compendium of Papers Submitted to the Joint Economic Committee of the Congress of the United States, Part 3 (1972).

Andrew D. Pike, *Reflections on the Meaning of Life: An Analysis of Section 7702 and the Taxation of Cash Value Life Insurance*, 42 Tax Law Review 491 (1988). Copyright © 1988 by the New York University School of Law. Reprinted with permission.

U.S. Department of the Treasury, *Tax Reform for Fairness, Simplicity, and Economic Growth* (1984).

Chapter 9: Transfer Taxes and Wealth Taxes

Louis Eisenstein, *The Rise and Decline of the Estate Tax*, 11 Tax Law Review 223 (1956). Copyright © 1990 by the New York University School of Law. Reprinted with permission.

Mark L. Ascher, *Curtailing Inherited Wealth*, 89 Michigan Law Review 69 (1990). Copyright © 1990 by the Michigan Law Review Association. Reprinted with permission.

Michael J. Graetz, *To Praise the Estate Tax, Not to Bury It*, 93 Yale Law Journal 259 (1983). Copyright © 1983 the Yale Law Journal Company. Reprinted by permission of the Yale Law Journal Company and the Fred B. Rothman Company from the Yale Law Journal, Vol. 93, pages 259-286.

Joel C. Dobris, A *Brief for the Abolition of All Transfer Taxes*, 35 Syracuse Law Review 1215 (1984). Copyright © 1984 by the Syracuse Law Review. Reprinted with permission.

Henry J. Lischer, Jr., *Incomplete Transfer Tax Repeal: Should the Gift Tax Survive?*, 56 Southern Methodist University Law Review 601 (2003). Copyright © 2003 by the Southern Methodist University Law Review. Reprinted with permission.

Harry J. Rudick, *A Proposal for an Accessions Tax*, 1 Tax Law Review 25 (1945). Copyright © 1945 by the New York University School of Law. Reprinted with permission.

John E. Donaldson, *The Future of Transfer Taxation: Repeal, Restructuring and Refinement, or Replacement*, 50 Washington & Lee Law Review 539 (1993). Copyright © 1993 by John E. Donaldson. All Rights Reserved. This article originally appeared in 50 Washington & Lee Law Review 539 (1993). Reprinted with permission.

Joseph M. Dodge, *Comparing a Reformed Estate Tax with An Accessions Tax and an Income-Inclusion System, and Abandoning The Generation-Skipping Tax*, 56 Southern Methodist University Law Review 551 (2003). Copyright © 2003 by the Southern Methodist University Law Review. Reprinted with permission.

George Cooper, *A Voluntary Tax? New Perspectives on Sophisticated Estate Tax Avoidance*, 77 Columbia Law Review 161 (1977). Copyright © 1977 by the Columbia Law Review. Reprinted with permission.

Daniel Q. Posin, *Toward a Theory of Federal Taxation: A Comment*, 50 Journal of Air Law and Commerce 907 (1985). Copyright © 1985 by the School of Law, Southern Methodist University. Reprinted with permission.

Chapter 10: Income Tax Treatment of Property Transferred at Death or by Gift

U.S. Department of the Treasury, *General Explanations of the Administration's Fiscal Year 2002 Tax Relief Proposals* (2001).

Lawrence Zelenak, *Taxing Gains at Death*, 46 Vanderbilt Law Review 361 (1993). Copyright © 1983 by the Vanderbilt Law Review, Vanderbilt University School of Law. Reprinted with permission.

Louis M. Castruccio, *Becoming More Inevitable? Death and Taxes . . . and Taxes*, 17 University of California at Los Angeles Law Review 459 (1970). Copyright © 1970, by the Regents of the University of California. Reprinted with permission.

Dan Subotnik, *On Constructively Realizing Constructive Realization: Building the Case for Death and Taxes*, 38 Kansas Law Review 1 (1989). Copyright © 1989 Kansas Law Review. Reprinted with permission.

Joseph M. Dodge, *Beyond Estate and Gift Tax Reform: Including Gifts and Bequests in Income*, 91 Harvard Law Review 1177 (1978). Copyright © 1978 by the Harvard Law Review Association. Reprinted with permission.

David M. Hudson, *Tax Policy and the Federal Income Taxation of the Transfer of Wealth*, 19 Willamette Law Review 1 (1983). Copyright © 1982 by the Willamette Law Review

Douglas A. Kahn & Jeffrey H. Kahn, *"Gifts, Gafts, and Gefts"—The Income Tax Definition and Treatment of Private and Charitable "Gifts" and a Principled Policy Justification for the Exclusion of Gifts from Income*, 78 Notre Dame Law Review 441 (2003). Copyright © 2003 by the Notre Dame Law Review. Reprinted with permission.

Chapter 11: Tax Expenditures

Office of Management and Budget, *Analytical Perspectives Budget of the United States Government Fiscal Year 2004* (2003).

Edward A. Zelinsky, *James Madison and Public Choice at Gucci Gulch: A Procedural Defense of Tax Expenditures and Tax Institutions*, 102 Yale Law Journal 1165 (1993). Reprinted with permission of the Yale Law Journal company and William S. Hein Company from The Yale Law Journal, Vol. 102, pages 1165-1207.

Douglas A. Kahn & Jeffrey S. Lehman, *Expenditure Budgets: A Critical View*, 54 Tax Notes 1661 (1992). Copyright © 1992. Tax Analysts. Reprinted with permission.

Boris I. Bittker, *Accounting for Federal "Tax Subsidies" in the National Budget*, 22 National Tax Journal 244 (1969). Copyright © 1969 by The National Tax Association—Tax Institute of America. Reprinted with permission.

Philip D. Oliver, *Section 265(2): A Counterproductive Solution to a Nonexistent Problem*, 40 Tax Law Review 351 (1985). Copyright © 1985 by the New York University School of Law. Reprinted with permission.

William H. Bradley & Philip D. Oliver, *Investment Tax Credit: The Illusory Incentive*, 2 Virginia Tax Review 267 (1983).Copyright © 1983 by the Virginia Tax Review. Reprinted with permission.

Daniel S. Goldberg, *Tax Subsidies: One-Time vs. Periodic—An Economic Analysis of the Tax Policy Alternatives*, 49 Tax Law Review 305 (1994). Copyright © 1994 by the New York University School of Law. Reprinted with permission.

Ann L. Alstott, *The Earned Income Tax Credit and the Limitations of Tax-Based Welfare Reform*, 108 Harvard Law Review 533 (1995). Copyright © 1995 by the Harvard Law Review. Reprinted with Permission.

George K. Yin, John Karl Scholz, Jonathan Barry Forman & Mark J. Mazur, *Improving the Delivery of Benefits to the Working Poor: Proposals to Reform the Earned Income Tax Credit Program*, 11 American Journal of Tax Policy 225 (1994). Copyright © 1994 by the University of Alabama Law Review. Reprinted with permission.

Chapter 12: Personal Injury Awards

J. Martin Burke & Michael K. Friel, *Tax Treatment of Employment-Related Personal Injury Awards: The Need for Limits*, 50 Montana Law Review 13 (1989). Copyright © 1989 by the Montana Law Review. Reprinted with permission.

Paul B. Stephan, III, *Federal Income Taxation and Human Capital*, 70 Virginia Law Review 1357 (1984). Copyright © 1984 by the Virginia Law Review. Reprinted with permission.

Jennifer J.S. Brooks, *Developing a Theory of Damage Recovery Taxation*, 14 William Mitchell Law Review 759 (1988). Copyright © 1988 by the William Mitchell Law Review. Reprinted with permission.

Douglas A. Kahn, *Compensatory and Punitive Damages for a Personal Injury: To Tax or Not to Tax?*, 2 Florida Tax Review 327 (1995). Copyright © 1995 by the Florida Tax Review. Reprinted with permission.

Joseph M. Dodge, *Taxes and Torts*, 77 Cornell Law Review 143 (1992). Copyright © 1992 by the Cornell Law Review, all rights reserved. Reprinted with permission.

Thomas D. Griffith, *Should "Tax Norms" Be Abandoned? Rethinking Tax Policy Analysis and The Taxation of Personal Injury Recoveries*, 1993 Wisconsin Law Review 1115. Copyright © 1993 by the Wisconsin Law Review. Reprinted with permission.

Lawrence A. Frolik, *The Convergence of I.R.C. § 104(a)(2),* Norfolk & Western Railway Co. v. Liepelt *and Structured Tort Settlements: Tax Policy "Derailed,"* 51 Fordham Law Review 565 (1983). Copyright © 1983 by the Fordham Law Review. Reprinted with permission.

Chapter 13: Federal Tax Treatment of State and Local Taxes

U.S. Department of the Treasury, *Tax Reform for Fairness, Simplicity, and Economic Growth* (1984).

Senate Committee on Finance, Senate Report No. 99-313 (1986).

Nonna A. Noto & Dennis Zimmerman, *Limiting State-Local Tax Deductibility: Effects Among the States*, 37 National Tax Journal 539 (1984). Copyright © 1984 by the National Tax Journal. Reprinted with permission.

William J. Turnier, *Evaluating Personal Deductions in an Income Tax—The Ideal*, 66 Cornell Law Review 262 (1981). Copyright © 1981 by the Cornell Law Review. Reprinted with permission.

JB McCombs, *A New Federal Tax Treatment of State and Local Taxes*, 19 Pacific Law Journal 747 (1988). Copyright © 1988 by the University of the Pacific, McGeorge School of Law. Reprinted with permission.

Walter W. Heller, *Deductions and Credits For State Income Taxes*, House Committee on Ways and Means, 1 Tax Revision Compendium 419 (1959).

Chapter 14: Corporations and Dividends

Joseph A. Pechman, *Federal Tax Policy*, (5th ed. 1987). Copyright © 1987 by The Brookings Institution. Reprinted with permission.

U.S. Department of the Treasury, *General Explanations of the Administration's Fiscal Year 2004 Revenue Proposals* (2003).

U.S. Department of the Treasury, *Tax Reform for Fairness, Simplicity, and Economic Growth* (1984).

Alvin C. Warren, Reporter, American Law Institute Reporter's Study of Corporate Tax Integration: Summary and Proposals (1993). Copyright © 1993 by the American Law Institute. Reprinted with permission.

American Institute of Certified Public Accountants, Statement of Tax Policy: Integration of the Corporate and Shareholder Tax Systems (1993). Reprinted with permission from Statement of Tax Policy: Integration of the Corporate and Shareholder Tax Systems, Copyright © 1993 by the American Institute of Certificate Public Accountants, Inc.

U.S. Department of the Treasury, *Report on Integration of the Individual and Corporate Tax Systems* (1992).

Fred W. Peel, Jr., *A Proposal for Eliminating Double Taxation of Corporate Dividends*, 39 Tax Lawyer 1 (1985). Copyright © 1985 American Bar Association. Reprinted with permission.

William D. Andrews, Reporter, American Law Institute Reporter's Study of the Taxation of Corporate Distributions, Appendix to Subchapter C Proposals (1982). Copyright © 1982 by the American Law Institute. Reprinted with permission.

Michael J. Graetz, *The Tax Aspects of Leveraged Buyouts and Other Corporate Financial Restructuring Transactions*, 42 Tax Notes 721 (1989). Reprinted with permission. Copyright © 1989. Tax Analysts.

Razeen Sappideen, *Imputation of the Corporate and Personal Income Tax: Is it Chasing One's Tail?*, 15 American Journal of Tax Policy 167 (1998). Copyright © 1998 by the University of Alabama Law Review. Reprinted with permission.

Jennifer Arlen & Deborah M. Weiss, *A Political Theory of Corporate Taxation*, 105 Yale Law Journal 325 (1995). Copyright © 1995 by the Yale Law Journal. Reprinted with permission.

Chapter 15: Capital Gains and Losses

Calvin H. Johnson, *Seventeen Culls from Capital Gains*, 48 Tax Notes 1285 (1990). Copyright © 1990 by Tax Analysts. Reprinted with permission.

Noël B. Cunningham & Deborah H. Schenk, *The Case for a Capital Gains Preference*, 48 Tax Law Review 319 (1993). Copyright © 1993 by the New York University School of Law Tax Law Review. Reprinted with permission.

Daniel Halperin, *A Capital Gains Preference Is Not EVEN a Second-Best Solution*, 48 Tax Law Review 381 (1993). Copyright © 1993 by the New York University School of Law Tax Law Review. Reprinted with permission.

Daniel N. Shaviro, *Uneasiness and Capital Gains,* 48 Tax Law Review 393 (1993). Copyright © 1993 by the New York University School of Law Tax Law Review. Reprinted with permission.

George R. Zodrow, *Economic Analyses of Capital Gains Taxation: Realizations, Revenues, Efficiency and Equity*, 48 Tax Law Review 419 (1993). Copyright © 1993 by the New York University School of Law Tax Law Review. Reprinted with permission.

Discussion by CCH Tax Advisory Board Roundtable, Vol. 79, No. 26, Pt. 2, May 27, 1992. Reproduced with permission from CCH Tax Advisory Board Roundtable published and copyrighted by CCH Incorporated, 2700 Lake Cook Road, Riverwoods, Illinois 60015.

Fred W. Peel, Jr., *Capital Gains: Falling Short on Fairness and Simplicity*, 17 University of Baltimore Law Review 418 (1988). Copyright © 1988 by the University of Baltimore Law Review. Reprinted with permission.

Congressional Budget Office, *Indexing Capital Gains* (1990).

Testimony of Michael J. Boskin, *Tax Incentives for Increasing Savings and Investments*, Hearings Before the Senate Committee on Finance, 101st Congress, 2d Session (1990).

House Report No. 84, 104th Congress, 1st Session (1995).

James M. Poterba, *Capital Gains Tax Policy Toward Entrepreneurship*, 42 National Tax Journal 375 (1989). Copyright © 1989 by the National Tax Association—Tax Institute of America. Reprinted with permission.

Chapter 16: Responding to Price Level Changes

Henry J. Aaron, ed., *Inflation and the Income Tax* (1976). Copyright © 1976 by The Brookings Institution. Reprinted with permission.

Calvin Engler & Mitchell L. Engler, *Taxation of Capital Gains—Let's Be Fair*, 50 Tax Notes 1303 (1991). Copyright © 1991 Tax Analysts. Reprinted with permission.

New York State Bar Association Section on Taxation Ad Hoc Committee, *Report on Inflation Adjustments to the Basis of Capital Assets*, 48 Tax Notes 759 (1990). Copyright © 1990 by Tax Analysts. Reprinted with permission.

U.S. Department of the Treasury, *Report on Tax Reform for Fairness, Simplicity, and Economic Growth* (1984).

Michael C. Durst, *Inflation and the Tax Code: Guidelines for Policymaking*, 73 Minnesota Law Review 1217 (1989). Copyright © 1989 by the Minnesota Law Review Foundation. Reprinted with permission.

Mitchell L. Engler, *Partial Basis Indexation: An Implicit Response to Tax Deferral*, 53 Tax Law Review 177 (2000). Copyright © 2000 by the New York University School of Law Tax Law Review. Reprinted with permission.

Reed Shuldiner, *Indexing the Tax Code,* 48 Tax Law Review 537 (1993). Copyright © 1993 by the New York University School of Law Tax Law Review. Reprinted with permission.

Chapter 17: Taxes and the Legislative Process

Kenneth W. Gideon, *Tax Policy at the Treasury Department: A 20-Year Perspective*, 57 Tax Notes 889 (1992). Copyright © 1992 by Tax Analysts. Reprinted with permission.

Ronald A. Pearlman, *The Tax Legislative Process: 1972-1992*, 57 Tax Notes 939 (1992). Copyright © 1992 by Tax Analysts. Reprinted with permission.

Michael D. Bopp, *The Roles of Revenue Estimation and Scoring in the Federal Budget Process*, 56 Tax Notes 1629 (1992). Copyright © 1992 by Tax Analysts. Reprinted with permission.

Michael J. Graetz, *Paint-by-Numbers Tax Lawmaking,* 95 Columbia Law Review 609 (1995). Copyright © 1995 by the Columbia Law Review. Reprinted with permission.

John F. Witte, *A Long View of Tax Reform*, 39 National Tax Journal 255 (1986). Copyright © 1986 by the National Tax Association—Tax Institute of America. Reprinted with permission.

Jeffrey H. Birnbaum, *Showdown at Gucci Gulch*, 40 National Tax Journal 357 (1987). Copyright © 1987 by the National Tax Association—Tax Institute of America. Reprinted with permission.

Gerard M. Brannon, *Some Economics of Tax Reform, 1986*, 39 National Tax Journal 277 (1986). Copyright © 1986 by the National Tax Association—Tax Institute of America. Reprinted with permission.

Appendices I and II

SUMMARY OF CONTENTS

PART II: CONSUMPTION TAXES

TABLE OF CONTENTS

PART II: CONSUMPTION TAXES

EDITORIAL CONVENTIONS

Each chapter is divided into subchapters. Except for the introductory subchapter, which may be entirely textual, subchapters begin with textual introduction, follow with excerpts of works originally published elsewhere, and conclude with notes and questions.

Necessarily, all excerpts have been tightly edited. Most footnotes and other citations to authority, including many cross references, are deleted without indication. Other deletions in text are indicated by three asterisks (* * *). (Only one set of asterisks is used to indicate a deletion, even where the deleted language is from more than one paragraph.) Where the excerpted work quotes yet another source, and the author of the excerpted work excised a portion of the quoted source, such deletions are differentiated by use of ellipses (. . .).

Clear errors in excerpted works have been corrected, occasionally without indication, more frequently by insertion of bracketed language. Bracketed language is used more frequently to clarify or simplify. Use of brackets implies no criticism of the authors or editors of the original sources; frequently, it was the editing for inclusion in this book that necessitated clarification.

Three types of footnotes are employed. Numbered footnotes are those used in original sources; they retain both the numbering and the style as when originally published. Authors of most materials excerpted are identified, usually by position at time of original publication, by asterisk footnotes. All other footnotes added by the editor are lettered footnotes. Lettered footnotes that fall within excerpts are further identified as editor's footnotes by adding "(Ed.)."

Unless the context indicates otherwise, references to "sections" are to the Internal Revenue Code of 1986 in effect at the date of submission for publication (October, 2003). Authors of excerpted materials frequently refer to the Internal Revenue Code in existence at the time their work was originally published; on occasion, footnotes or bracketed material indicate the state of current law, but more often it seemed that such an addition would be more distracting than valuable.

TAX POLICY

*

PROLOGUE

THE CANONS OF TAXATION

Taxes are what we pay for civilized society.[a]

A necessary consequence of the coming of civilization is the organization of some sort of government, and with it associated expenses. Bearing those expenses requires some form of taxation. Different governmental and societal structures produce different tax systems. The tax system, even of an advanced society, need not depend on objective law:

> In the old Chinese system, quotas of tax liability were parceled out to the Provinces on the basis of the Emperor's opinion of what each Province should pay. The Province did the same to the districts, which did the same to the chos (groups of 100 hos), which did the same to the hos (groups of 100 families). The ho leader assessed on each of his 100 families the tax liability he thought each should pay, based on his intimate knowledge of each.[b]

The United States, which prides itself on having a "government of laws" and not a "government of men," obviously prefers a taxing system based on laws of general application. Nevertheless, if one assumed good faith on the part of each official involved, the ancient Chinese system could be viewed as extremely just, because it allows consideration of individual factors that could not be recognized in a tax statute.

We shall not devote much attention to how taxing decisions are made or how much should be collected in taxes, although these important matters are addressed in Chapters Seventeen and One, respectively. Rather, given the assumed need for substantial revenues, we shall ask what substantive decisions about the structure of taxation should be made—what decisions would serve well our large, complex, and diverse society and economy.

The primary criteria to be applied in wisely structuring taxes are open to debate and are a central focus of this book. Perhaps the most important is equity—but, like beauty, tax equity lies in the eye of the beholder. Another factor is the effect of taxing decisions on the economic well being of individual taxpayers and of the entire society. This is likely to be tied to notions of economic efficiency versus economic distortions, and of structuring taxes so as not to encourage unproductive decisions and actions. Another important

---

a. Justice Oliver Wendell Holmes, *in* Compania General de Tabacos de Filipinas v. Collector of Internal Revenue, 275 U.S. 87, 100 (1927) (dissenting).

b. Herbert Stein, *What's Wrong with the Federal Tax System?*, *in* HOUSE COMM. ON WAYS AND MEANS, 86th Cong., 1st Sess., 1 TAX REVISION COMPENDIUM 107, 110 (1959).

criterion must be administrability. For example, a tax that in theory seems just and wise, but whose collection depends *entirely* on self assessment by taxpayers, is in practice likely to be inequitable and to raise little revenue.

The most famous set of criteria for tax policy are the canons stated in 1776 by Adam Smith in his keynote for the age of capitalism, *The Wealth of Nations*:

> Before I enter upon the examination of particular taxes, it is necessary to premise the four following maxims with regard to taxes in general.
>
> I. The subjects of every state ought to contribute towards the support of the government, as nearly as possible, in proportion to their respective abilities; that is, in proportion to the revenue which they respectively enjoy under the protection of the state. * * *
>
> II. The tax which each individual is bound to pay ought to be certain, and not arbitrary. The time of payment, the manner of payment, the quantity to be paid, ought all to be clear and plain to the contributor, and to every other person. * * *
>
> III. Every tax ought to be levied at the time, or in the manner, in which it is most likely to be convenient for the contributor to pay it. * * *
>
> IV. Every tax ought to be so contrived as both to take out and to keep out of the pockets of the people as little as possible, over and above what it brings into the public treasury of the state.[c]

Testifying before the Ways and Means Committee in 1959, Professor Neil Jacoby placed Adam Smith's call for proportional taxation in historical context, and suggested additional and competing criteria for good tax policy:

> When Smith wrote, * * * the British revenue system consisted almost entirely of customs duties, excises, and real property taxes and was highly regressive. * * * Smith's demand that taxes should be "proportional" to the revenues was quite radical for its time. * * * Of course, we have long since abandoned the view that flat proportionality in personal income is equitable. * * *
>
> John Stuart Mill [writing in 1897] was among the first of the British economists to argue explicitly for use of the tax system to mitigate great inequalities in personal income and wealth, although he was careful to note that progression should not "impair the motives upon which society depends for keeping up (not to say increasing) the produce of its labor and capital."[d]

When Professor Jacoby appeared before the Ways and Means Committee, progressive tax was at its zenith in American history: top federal income tax rates exceeded 90 percent. "Flat proportionality" has made a comeback in

---

c. ADAM SMITH, THE WEALTH OF NATIONS 777-78 (1776).

d. Neil H. Jacoby, *Guidelines of Income Tax Reform for the 1960's, in* HOUSE COMM. ON WAYS AND MEANS, 86th Cong., 1st Sess., 1 TAX REVISION COMPENDIUM 157, 158-60 (1959).

American politics, however. A recurring proposal in recent years has been the implementation of some form of proportional, or "flat," tax.

Wilbur Mills, long-time chairman of the Ways and Means Committee, provided his own list of criteria at the same 1959 hearings:

> [T]ax reform must seek, among other things, (1) a tax climate more favorable to economic growth; (2) greater equity through closer adherence to the principle that equal incomes should bear equal tax liabilities; (3) assurance that the degree of progression in the distribution of tax burdens accords as closely as possible with widely held standards of fairness; (4) an overall tax system which contributes significantly to maintaining stability in the general price level and a stable and high rate of use of human and material resources; (5) a tax system which interferes as little as possible with the operation of the free market mechanism in directing resources into their most productive uses; and (6) greater ease of compliance and administration.[e]

As Chairman Mills' formulation suggests, tax policy concerns in recent decades have brought the matter of incentives to the fore. We are acutely aware that taxing an activity discourages it, and wish to structure our tax system in a way that does not discourage such beneficial activities as work, saving, and investment. At the same time, as economist David Ricardo made clear nearly two centuries ago, the effort can be only to create a tax that is *relatively* neutral, because we can never fully succeed in removing the undesired disincentives of taxation:

> There are no taxes which have not a tendency to lessen the power to accumulate. All taxes must either fall on capital or revenue. If they encroach on capital, they must proportionably diminish that fund by whose extent the extent of the productive industry of the country must always be regulated; and if they fall on revenue, they must either lessen accumulation, or force the contributors to save the amount of the tax, by making a corresponding diminution of their former unproductive consumption of the necessaries and luxuries of life. Some taxes will produce these effects in a much greater degree than others; but the great evil of taxation is to be found, not so much in any selection of its objects, as in the general amount of its effects taken collectively.[f]

More recently, Professor Jeffrey Kwall made much the same point in recognizing that the need for revenue is the paramount purpose of taxation, and that equity and efficiency—traditionally, the major concerns of tax policy—are actually relegated to a subsidiary position:

---

e. Wilbur Mills, *Foreword, in* HOUSE COMM. ON WAYS AND MEANS, 86th Cong., 1st Sess., 1 TAX REVISION COMPENDIUM ix (1959).

f. DAVID RICARDO, THE PRINCIPLES OF POLITICAL ECONOMY AND TAXATION 95 (Everyman's Library ed. 1992) (1817).

If a need for revenue did not constrain tax reform, efforts to further equity and efficiency logically would lead to the elimination of all taxes. The realistic reform goal, therefore, is to minimize on a system-wide basis the adverse impact on equity and efficiency of a tax system required to generate a given amount of revenue.[g]

Finally, the student of tax policy must remember that consideration of change to an existing tax provision entails somewhat different considerations from those presented at the time of enactment. At a time in which every election seems to be a referendum on sweeping tax change, Professor Walter Blum's admonition is pertinent: "In respect to taxation there is, generally speaking, considerable gain in merely preserving ancient rules intact and avoiding change."[h] Dr. Herbert Stein explained why this is so:

In general, there is a tendency for the market to adjust to different tax treatments of incomes from different sources in such a way as to reduce the net effects on income after tax. * * *

This is one aspect of the more general and very important proposition: Old taxes are good taxes. The economic system has adjusted to them so as to reduce discriminatory effects they might have had when first introduced. Moreover old taxes often, although not always, have a degree of acceptance they did not have when first imposed. Therefore the considerations relevant to the removal of some tax provision that has been in effect for some time are very different from the considerations that would be relevant to its initial adoption.[i]

At the same time, the maxim that "old taxes are good taxes" cannot be taken to an extreme, or it would forever lock in any existing tax provision, however unjust or unwise.

With these very general guidelines and admonitions in mind, we approach the study of tax policy.

---

g. Jeffrey L. Kwall, *The Uncertain Case Against the Double Taxation of Corporate Income*, 68 N.C. L. REV. 613, 616 (1990).

h. Walter J. Blum, *Tax Policy and Preferential Provisions in the Income Tax Base, in* HOUSE COMM. ON WAYS AND MEANS, 86th Cong., 1st Sess., 1 TAX REVISION COMPENDIUM 77, 78 (1959).

i. Stein, *supra* note b, at 112.

PART I

INTRODUCTION TO THE INCOME TAX

The federal tax system is overwhelmingly based on income. The individual income tax accounts for nearly half of all federal revenues.[a] When combined with the corporate income tax and with the Social Security tax and related social insurance taxes, which are also income-based, the total rises to over ninety percent.[b] Moreover, it is fair to say that the popular perception of "federal taxes" is that of income taxes, as opposed to tariffs, estate and gift taxes, or any of a number of other levies that account for relatively small amounts.

Most of Parts III, IV, and V of this book deal with particular income tax issues. The first five chapters, however, deal with fundamental issues relevant to the income tax as a whole.

Chapter One deals with the role of the income tax in implementing fiscal policy. This involves understanding the role of balanced budgets, the impact of budget surpluses and deficits on the economy, and the extent to which fiscal policy should (and can) be used to control the direction of the economy. The conventional government budget is contrasted with a capital budget, under which capital expenditures would be accounted for over a number of years.

Chapter Two discusses when income should be measured and subjected to tax. The discussion revolves around the Haig-Simons definition of income, which has become the standard used by most academics in judging the income tax system. Both the practical shortcomings of the Haig-Simons definition and its merits and flaws at a theoretical level are described. The Haig-Simons approach is contrasted with the present generally applicable requirement of realization in determining income subject to tax.

Chapter Three deals with the outer limit of income subject to tax, addressing the benefits received from ownership of property and from the performance of services for one's self or family. Although it is not practical to tax such "imputed income," not doing so has important consequences affecting the equity of the income tax. Indirectly, the failure to tax imputed income

---

a. Preliminary figures indicate that in 2002, the individual income was estimated to generate $949 billion, or 48.8% of total federal revenues of $1.946 trillion. U.S. BUREAU OF THE CENSUS, STATISTICAL ABSTRACT OF THE UNITED STATES, tbl. 454, at 308 (122d ed. 2002).

b. Payroll taxes generated an estimated $708 billion in 2002, and corporate income taxes an additional $201 billion. These taxes, when combined with the individual income tax, generated more than 95% of federal revenues. *Id.*

affects society quite broadly, influencing the type of housing we live in, the choice between work and leisure, and the decision of wives (principally) to enter the paid labor force.

Chapter Four discusses how the national income tax burden should be divided among taxpayers with different incomes. This involves arguments for and against progressivity in the tax rate structure. The issues include equity between taxpayers with different levels of income, whether generalized conclusions as to the marginal utility of additional income are valid, the practical problems caused by differing tax rates, and the problem of arriving at a cap for top rates.

Chapter Five deals with the choice of the taxable unit: the individual; married couples; families extended to include children; or other, less conventional, arrangements. This chapter brings together issues discussed in Chapter Three, dealing with imputed income (important in the family context); and in Chapter Four, covering progressivity (the primary reason that the choice of taxable unit is important). The issues raised in Chapter Five involve equity between differently situated taxpayers, whether sociological considerations should be taken into account, the extent to which common law or community property law in the various states should impact the federal choice of taxpaying unit, and the relevance of family arrangements outside the standard husband-wife-children relationships. Rules providing relief from the joint liability assumed in filing a joint return are considered. Finally, special provisions relating to children and to elderly taxpayers are examined.

CHAPTER ONE

THE PURPOSES OF TAXATION

The central public finance question facing any country is the appropriate size of its government.[a]

A. TAXATION TO FINANCE GOVERNMENT EXPENDITURES

The obvious objective of taxes is to raise revenue. The first question is: How much revenue? Intuitively, the answer is "enough to cover the government's expenditures," but this answer perhaps is simplistic on two counts. First, it is not necessarily true that the level of taxation should be controlled by the level of expenditures any more than that the level of expenditures should be determined by the amount of revenue the government receives. (Individuals, for example, are more likely to adjust their spending to match income than vice versa.) Even more basically, the intuitive answer assumes that revenues and expenditures should balance, but that assumption may be unwarranted. Most public discussion of the budget is premised on the implicit assumption that an annual balance between total receipts and total expenditures is desirable, even as the government routinely spends more money than it receives. But should a balanced budget, even over the long term, necessarily be viewed as a goal of government policy?

Assuming a balanced budget to be desirable, a possible alternative to a crude test of gross receipts versus gross expenditures would be a budget modeled on business practice. Businesses do not attempt to cover capital improvements by current receipts. Instead, they capitalize purchases of assets that have useful lives of more than one year, and account for these expenditures over a period of years rather than entirely in the year of acquisition. By similar reasoning, perhaps the federal government should spread an expenditure for a new highway, or courthouse, or aircraft carrier, over a period of years. Such a budget is termed a *capital budget*. Discussing these and other issues in the first excerpt, Professor Robert Eisner suggests that we need not be unduly worried about annual cash-flow deficits as he argues against a proposed balanced budget Constitutional amendment.

On the other hand, the business model can be utilized to argue that our annual cash-flow government accounting method substantially *under*states our long-term problems. In the second excerpt, Professor Daniel Shaviro warns that the annual budget approach fails to account for long-term government

---

a. Martin Feldstein, How Big Should Government Be?, 50 NAT'L TAX J. 197, 197 (1997).

obligations. Just as a business that has promised pension benefits must budget for future pension expenses before the workers retire, so should the federal government take account of its long-term promises. By this reasoning, particularly as the Baby Boom generation approaches retirement, with attendant Social Security and Medicare outlays, the federal government's fiscal house is in substantially worse shape than annual deficits reveal.

WE DON'T NEED BALANCED BUDGETS
Robert Eisner[*]
Wall Street Journal, January 11, 1995, at A14

It has been suggested that we combine two of the currently proposed amendments to the U.S. Constitution: Put into the supreme law of the land a requirement that the public schools have prayers for a balanced budget. Since ordering a balanced budget is like commanding the tides to retreat, we may, after all, require some kind of divine intervention.

The "balance" apparently contemplated is an equality between federal government outlays (expenditures) and revenues (tax receipts). But both of these are variable and quite beyond the short-run control of the government. Tax receipts, of course, go up and down with the state of the economy. And some outlays—for unemployment insurance, for example—go down and up with the economy, too.

Each additional percentage point of unemployment is associated with at least $50 billion of additional deficit, as revenues shrink and outlays grow. If unemployment were to rise from the current 5.4% to, say, the 7.6% of June 1992, the deficit could be expected to rise by more than $110 billion. What would the law then tell us to do? Tell taxpayers to try harder? Stop some "entitlement" checks (for unemployment insurance, Social Security, Medicare and Medicaid)? Or pray?

Balancing Checkbooks

It is widely asserted: "I balance my checkbook. Why can't the government balance its?" But we would not dream of keeping our checkbooks balanced the way a balanced budget would require the government to. We borrow to buy houses and automobiles and to send our kids to college. If we lose our job or suffer a financial reversal, we may well borrow to tide ourselves over to a better time. In 1993, net borrowing of the U.S. government was $256 billion; that of private households was $294 billion. * * *

And how many businesses could get along without borrowing? Borrowing to invest and expand is the hallmark of business success. U.S. Treasury debt

---

[*]. At time of original publication, Professor Emeritus, Northwestern University and a past president of the American Economic Association.

is now some $3.5 trillion. U.S. nonfinancial business owes more than $3.8 trillion. And private households owe about $4.5 trillion.

But government debt is somehow viewed as different. We are told that state governments balance their budgets and are widely required to do so in their constitutions. The great majority of state governments, though, have separate capital budgets. They balance only their operating or current budgets and borrow—that is, run deficits—for capital expenditures.

To require the federal government, which keeps no separate capital budget, to keep revenues equal to outlays would mean that all public investment would have to be financed out of current taxes. But capital investment is intended to offer benefits in the future. To ask current taxpayers to meet all of that burden is unfair, and most are likely to refuse—with the result that public investment in infrastructure, research, education and crime-fighting is likely to be starved.

Government debt is indeed different from private debt. In fact, it is its opposite! For every borrower there must be a lender. The federal debt of savings bonds and Treasury bills, notes and bonds is overwhelmingly owned by the private sector and our state and local governments. Eliminate or reduce the federal debt and we eliminate or reduce our own assets. It is widely asserted that we are currently leaving a debt of $3.5 trillion for our children and grandchildren to pay. But we are leaving the bulk of that amount (minus the minor portion owned by foreigners) to our children and grandchildren as their assets of Treasury securities.

The real question about government deficits should be: What would be the effect on the economy of the drastic deficit reduction necessary to get to "balance"? Government bonds are wealth to their holders and if the government spends more than it is taking in, it adds to their wealth. With government deficits, the rest of us are getting more from the government than we are giving. As this increases our purchasing power, the deficits and debt are fueling private spending and thus keeping American business prosperous. Eliminating the deficits and debt may well cut that prosperity short.

It is argued that deficit-induced private spending and private lending to government hold down private investment. The facts, though, appear otherwise. Bigger structural federal deficits have indeed encouraged consumption, but my own work with data of the past 40 years has shown that the deficits and increased consumption have in fact also increased gross private domestic investment. It should not be hard to understand why. If the government, by running a deficit, leaves our after-tax income higher and we go out and buy Buicks, Fords and Chryslers, the auto companies invest more, not less. And if government belt-tightening and/or tax increases to balance the budget leave us with less, so that we don't buy those new cars, the companies will surely invest less.

This is not an argument for unlimited deficits. They can be too large, and induce too much spending. A good rule of thumb would be similar to that for any household or business. Run deficits—borrow—to the extent that your debt stays in line with your income, and except when pressed by temporary hard times, use your borrowing not for current expenses but for investment.

For our federal government, with the national income growing at 6% per year on average (and more at the moment), that means that the debt can grow at 6% per year and keep the roughly 50% debt-to-GDP ratio from growing. (That ratio, while twice what it was before the 1980s, is less than half of what it was just after World War II.) But this implies a permanent deficit equal to 3% of GDP. * * *

Repeated assertions to the contrary notwithstanding, it is hardly clear, then, that a balanced budget—as opposed, for example, to merely keeping the debt from outrunning our income—is desirable. But suppose the balanced budget amendment became the law of the land. How would it be enforced? What would we do if a downturn in the economy created a deficit? Would we put the tax-collectors or Congress in jail for violating the Constitution?

Or should we, in a time of recession, cut government payments to people or raise taxes? Almost everyone recognizes that this would be exactly the wrong thing to do. Would three-fifths of Congress vote then to waive the balanced budget requirement, or would a politically minded minority refuse to do so?

Given the economic hardship and political difficulty in reaching and maintaining a balanced budget, we can look for all kinds of evasive tricks. A major one, already anticipated by most of our governors, would be to foist federal outlays off on the states. The federal government currently gives grants-in-aid of $200 billion a year to state and local governments. We could eliminate the deficit by canceling them.

The federal government could also substitute regulations and mandates for its own outlays, requiring private business and individuals or state and local governments to make expenditures and thus save the federal budget. * * *

Creative Accounting

Or we could go in for all kinds of creative accounting. My own preference, as suggested above, would be to set up a separate capital budget and include only depreciation, not new capital outlays, in the current budget, which would be what we would balance. Will the new constitutional amendment not only require a balanced budget but prescribe the accounting rules by which it should be measured?

* * *

Economists and politicians have varying views on these matters. But surely it is improper to sanctify any economic philosophy or ideology and put it into our long-lasting and very difficult-to-change Constitution. * * *

THE GROWING US FISCAL GAP
Daniel N. Shaviro*

World Economics, vol. 3, no. 4, Oct-Dec. 2002, at 1, 1-7

In January 2001, when the second Bush Administration took office, United States policymakers were entirely unaware of what the immediate future held. No leading public figure foresaw the events of 9/11. * * *

United States policymakers in early 2001 were equally out of touch with what the more distant future holds. An unexpected run of annual federal budget surpluses led to a mistaken consensus that the long-term fiscal picture underlying a decade of bipartisan deficit reduction efforts had fundamentally changed. The switch from deficit to surplus emboldened then-Governor Bush to propose enormous federal tax cuts, which his Administration successfully pushed through Congress in the first half of 2001. The Democrats, despite accusing Bush of fiscal imprudence, actually differed but little in their assessment of what the budget surpluses meant. They proposed significant through smaller tax cuts, along with greater spending increases such as an unfunded expansion of Medicare * * * to offer costly new prescription drug benefits.

* * * US policymakers' misreading of the long-term fiscal picture * * * clearly could have been avoided. Economists who were talking to the leaders of both parties thoroughly understood the inadequacy of the annual budget surplus or deficit as a measure of the government's fiscal posture. They realized, moreover, that the long-term picture had improved only slightly (in retrospect, largely due to tax revenues resulting from the stock market bubble). America's fiscal policy remained on an unsustainable long-term course, with implications for current workers' retirement and for future generations that politicians and voters evidently were not ready to discuss. The 2001 tax cuts have now made the long-term picture significantly worse.

The core problem with the annual budget measure is its looking only at current-year cash flows. If the government has a surplus but is failing to finance its future obligations, its position resembles that of a parent who is paying this year's bills but failing to save for his children's college education. A more long-term measure, extending indefinitely into the future because so many of the government's commitments are expected to do so, is therefore

---

*. At time of original publication, Professor of Law, New York University.

needed. To be sure, such a measure must rest on forecasts (such as of future economic and demographic trends) that are uncertain, changeable, and controversial. The difficulty of making long-range forecasts does not, however, counsel looking only at the short term picture. * * * Indeed, the risk implied by facing a broad range of plausible future scenarios calls, if anything, for greater prudence rather than less.

Economists have recently developed a measure called the fiscal gap, estimating "the size of the long-run increase in taxes or reductions in non-interest expenditures (as a constant share of [gross domestic product, or] GDP) that would be required immediately" in order to keep current government debt constant as a percentage of GDP.[1] Using official US government data and projections, adjusted in certain respects to make them more realistic, the long-term US fiscal gap was recently estimated at 11.07 percent of GDP.[2] Since US GDP currently stands at around $10 trillion, this suggests that an immediate tax increase of more than $1 trillion annually would be needed to place the US budget in long-term balance, and thus to pay for everything that Washington either has promised or seems likely (under current policy) to spend.

In the above formulation, the fiscal gap is stated as a flow, like the annual budget deficit or the amount you must pay each year on a bank loan. The fiscal gap can also be stated as a stock, like the national debt or the principal you owe on a bank loan. To state the fiscal gap as a stock rather than as a flow, one must determine the present value, under an appropriate interest or discount rate, of the annual tax increase amounts that the flow measure implies. Using R to denominate the real interest rate and G to denominate the real growth rate of GDP, the stock fiscal gap can be stated as the flow fiscal gap divided by (R - G). Suppose we assume that R is 3 percent, as in the US government's official long-term Medicare forecasts, and that G is 1.5 percent, its average in the US since the end of World War II. Under these assumptions, the stock fiscal gap now stands at about $74 trillion. By contrast, the explicit US public debt, as of mid-2002, was barely over $6 trillion.

Lest one misconstrue this as purely an American problem, it should be noted that such countries as France, Germany, Italy, the Netherlands, and Japan have recently been estimated to face even greater long-term fiscal imbalances relative to their economies. The United Kingdom's fiscal gap, on the other hand, is less than 10 percent as great relative to GDP. An important difference between the US and UK lies in their currently expected policies. Most UK social benefits, including * * * pensions, are expected only to be price-

---

1. Auerbach, Alan J., Gale, William G., and Orszag, Peter R., "The Budget Outlook and Options for Fiscal Policy" at 12 (2002). Available on-line at http://emlab.berkeley.edu/users/auerbach/index.html. [The footnotes in this excerpt were unnumbered in original (Ed.)]

2. *Id.*, Table 4.

indexed rather than wage-indexed like Social Security. In addition, the growth rate of UK healthcare spending after 2005 is supposed to be held to that of per capita GDP, in sharp contrast to US expectations under Medicare. The US and UK pictures would move much closer together if we assumed either that the US will adopt these restraints or that the UK will not maintain them.

How does a US stock fiscal gap of $74 trillion compare to having an explicit public debt of that amount? The main difference, leaving aside uncertainty, is that the fiscal gap, as merely an implicit debt under an assumed set of policies, can be renounced through policy change without an act of explicit default. This difference is reduced, however, by the fact that some of the possible policy changes, such as reducing Social Security or Medicare benefits, would be viewed by many people, including influential political actors, as almost on a par with explicit default. Others such as reducing "discretionary" government spending (i.e., all that other than on entitlements programs such as Social Security and interest payments on the national debt) relative to GDP may be politically unlikely whether or not one believes they would be desirable.

The 2001 Tax Act contributed about 1.9 percent to the US fiscal gap in "flow" terms or nearly $13 trillion in "stock" terms. However, the main reason for the long-term US revenue shortfall—and for similar shortfalls in most other economically advanced nations—is the twin "disasters," from a budgetary standpoint, of increased life expectancy and rising healthcare expenditure, the latter of which mainly reflects the development of costly yet valuable new medical treatments.

Needless to say, these are not really disasters. Almost everyone would be glad to live longer and have better medical treatment options than those existing in the past. However, these changes substantially raise the cost of government programs that provide seniors with life annuities and subsidized healthcare. A rational individual if required to pay for his own retirement, would respond to an increase in life expectancy and medical treatment options by saving more during his working years. Retirement saving is more valuable if you will need to draw on it for longer and can use it to a greater effect than previously to improve your quality of life.

A country that collectivizes retirement financial risk by enacting social insurance programs for retirees ought similarly respond to rising life expectancies and costly healthcare improvements by collectively saving more, whether through private or government saving. However, Americans (like people in many other countries) have resisted this course both in their personal lives and in the policies they select through the political process.

To be sure, any estimate of the US fiscal gap is extremely sensitive to one's economic and demographic assumptions, and extremely subject to change from year to year. The prediction of a huge fiscal gap, however, is quite resilient. This reflects that its principal cause, population aging due to increasing life expectancy, has been an ongoing process and is expected to continue. Moreover, even conservative extrapolations suggest that US healthcare expenditure on the elderly will continue to rise significantly relative to GDP.

What about economic growth? History provides various examples of countries, such as England after the Napoleonic Wars and the US after the Civil War, that simply outgrew explicit public debts that contemporary commentators had feared would prove ruinous.

Over the long term, however, the US fiscal gap is surprisingly growth-proof. Not only taxes but various expenditure programs are roughly pegged to GDP over the long run. For example, Social Security benefits rise with career earnings and productivity growth. Thus, they should rise and fall with the rate of GDP growth over time, although they do not fluctuate annually with the business cycle. Similarly, Medicare expenditures follow changes in GDP to the extent that the healthcare sector has a constant relative size (and in fact its relative size has been growing). Discretionary government spending is a harder case to predict, but there is no shortage of wish-list items that Congress might be expected to enact promptly if the available resources were greater.

Thus, an economic expansion that made future Americans far wealthier than expected might fail to "help" very much, if at all, in narrowing the fiscal gap. This should alert us, however, to the fact that something is missing from the analysis thus far. How could it possibly *not* help to grow richer, when the underlying question has something to do with what expenditures the US can afford?

Also counseling against undue panic is the fact that the fiscal gap is merely a projection of current policy. * * * Yet statements of expected policy are just words, and surely will be changed in due course.

Why, then, does the existence of a fiscal gap matter? An analogy may help to sharpen the issue. Suppose a high-earning corporate executive and his non-working wife get divorced. Having incompetent lawyers, they reach the following alimony agreement: Each year he will pay her 30 percent of his salary, and she will get 50 percent of his salary. Thus, if he earns a million dollars next year, he is supposed to pay $300,000, and she is supposed to get $500,000.

Much like the currently stated US fiscal policy, this does not add up. She cannot get from him more than he pays her. Moreover, the financial gap in their agreement is growth-proof, since both sides of the ledger are pegged to his salary. Even if he earns a billion dollars rather than a million, there will still be a twenty percent difference between what he is supposed to pay and what she is supposed to get. Growth in his salary, therefore, does not "help."

In truth, however, it plainly does help. Each spouse would be far better off losing the dispute over how to split a salary of a billion dollars than winning it as to a salary of a million dollars. So what really is the problem, whether here or in the US budgetary case? For example, wouldn't retirees be better off if Social Security reneged on the higher (because growth-indexed) obligations that it would owe them in a wealthier future society, than if it fulfilled the lower obligations it would owe them in a poorer future society?

The answer is surely yes. Still, there are a number of reasons why the fiscal gap is nonetheless genuinely problematic. To illustrate this, we can start by returning to the alimony example. Suppose the husband, having looked only at the clause concerning his own payments, spends 70 percent of his after-tax salary, while the wife, having only looked at the clause concerning her receipts, uses credit to spend 50 percent. * * *

The problems potentially resulting from the fiscal gap are similar, and include the following:

1) *Systematic error*—People who are alive today must make long-term plans, such as for their own retirements, that reflect, among other factors, their expectations concerning future government policy. Those who expect the retirement benefits that current policy seems to promise may learn too late that they have saved too little if the benefits are significantly reduced.

2) *Needless uncertainty*—Even to the extent that people today understand the risk that their retirement benefits will be reduced, the absence of an agreed long-term policy path may hamper their long-term planning. Some, for example, might end up tightening their belts too much. * * *

3) *Harmful resolution of the policy mis-specification*—Ignoring the fiscal gap until a crisis is at hand may prompt panicky last-minute responses by the political system that could have been avoided by planning further in advance. An example might be printing money, at the risk of hyperinflation, in order to keep things going a bit longer. Or the government might engage in some sort of default or confiscation that needlessly harms people's confidence in its commitments.

4) *Loss of policy options over time*—Since time moves relentlessly forward, not back, delay in eliminating the fiscal gap continually reduces the available means of eliminating it. In effect, not to decide is gradually to decide. * * *

With respect to generational distribution, once the members of a given age cohort have died, they can no longer be asked to share in the pain of tax increases or benefit reductions. Even while they are alive, with each year the opportunity to make them share the burden through general income and payroll tax increases (or benefit reductions after they retire) grows less. So does the opportunity to increase their share of the burden without leaving them with too little saving for their own retirements.

Ineluctably, therefore, perpetuation of the fiscal gap tends to transfer consumption opportunities from younger to older generations. Whether this is a problem depends upon what one thinks about inter-generational justice. Is there anything wrong with our leaving behind large unfunded obligations that our descendants will have to pay (whether through tax increases or reductions in their own benefits)?

One argument against objecting to this transfer would start by noting that the US, like most other economically advanced countries, has for many decades been growing ever wealthier. * * * Worker productivity and real per capita GDP have been steadily on the rise. If this technology-driven trend continues, each succeeding generation will continue to be wealthier on a lifetime basis than the one before. The fiscal gap's generational distribution therefore is progressive, transferring money to groups that have less and thus might be thought likely to value an extra dollar more.

Now, however, suppose we enrich our comparison of the circumstances faced by different generations. A narrowly monetary measure such as GDP is misleading, not just because money isn't everything, but because (standing alone) it isn't anything. It is only worth what it can be used to buy, which has changed over time for technological and other reasons.

Given the pace of technological advance in recent decades, the increase in real per capita GDP may actually understate the real improvement in material conditions. * * *

Consider electrification and the spread of car and air travel in the first half of the twentieth century, followed more recently by gadgets ranging from personal computers to cellular phones to DVD players to microwave ovens. Or consider that millions of people still live who were born at a time when penicillin had not yet been introduced, and pneumonia was known as the "old person's friend." Life expectancy has been increasing for decades and is expected to continue doing so. The amount that we would be willing to pay for antibiotics to cure pneumonia, and that people for centuries would have been willing to pay, surely is far greater than its present costs.

From an egalitarian perspective, if GDP understates the real improvement over time in material conditions, the generational transfers that result from the fiscal gap may look better still. There is also an opposing consideration, however. If money can buy even better things as time passes, then people who live later might value an extra dollar more than their precursors, even though they are better off. Suppose that you could give a million dollars to either of two individuals who suffer from advanced colon cancer: one living in 2005 who cannot be helped, or one living in 2045 who can actually, at great expense, be cured. It is hard to argue against giving the money to the latter individual, even if he is better-off in absolute terms.

This is as good a way as any to dramatize the main ground for hoping that the US and other similarly situated countries will take action sooner rather than later to narrow their fiscal gaps and thus reduce the now-expected transfer through government policy from future to current generations. In the US, greater healthcare rationing and belt-tightening for the elderly are likely at some point in any event, but they will have to be stricter if less advance provision is made for them. And the stricter they are, the greater the extent to which retirees (or workers if their taxes are increased to support retirees) will find that their opportunities to live well and get the best healthcare are deficient relative to what they know is possible, even if in some ways better than what anyone enjoys today.

Notes and Questions

1.   Professor Eisner says that if the government spends more than it is taking in, it is adding to the wealth of its bondholders. In fact, of course, the bondholders' wealth would not have disappeared had the government not needed to borrow it; they simply would have invested it differently. Eisner probably is making the point that Americans are the primary lenders to the government so that, as it is sometimes stated, "we owe the national debt to ourselves."

2.   Professor Eisner suggests that the government deficit appears larger than it actually is, because the conventional budget requires current accounting of capital expenditures. Should the government have a separate capital budget?

3.   Professor Eisner was particularly disdainful of attempting to mandate a balanced budget by constitutional amendment. (He referred to one proposal that would require three-fifths-majority votes in Congress to allow a deficit.) Do you agree with Eisner?

4.   Automatic counter-cyclical adjustments, such as higher income taxes during economic upturns and increased unemployment compensation payments during downturns, clearly have failed to prevent booms and recessions in the economy. Does this mean that John Maynard Keynes and Keynesian successors were mistaken as to the ability of government to use fiscal policy successfully?

5.   Professor Eisner discounted concern about borrowing by the federal government by noting that households and private businesses each borrow comparable amounts. Does this show that federal borrowing is not a matter of serious concern, or that borrowing on all levels, and not just by the federal government, is excessive?

6.   While Professor Eisner argues that the annual budget deficit overstates the problem, Professor Shaviro's analysis may lead to the opposite conclusion. Shaviro refers to the "fiscal gap," a new economic measure that attempts to quantify the present value of the government's unfunded future "promises." The amounts suggested by this analysis—the equivalent of either an annual revenue shortfall of more than $1 trillion or of increasing the national debt by $74 trillion—dwarf the conventional computations of budgetary deficit and national debt. Voters and politicians are no doubt more concerned with the conventional deficit than with the fiscal gap. Which do you view as more important?

7.   What are the "disasters"—only in budgetary terms—to which Professor Shaviro attributes the fiscal gap?

8.   Why do increases in life expectancy and medical advances mean that we should save more as a society?

9.   It is unsurprising that other Western countries, with politics and policies similar to ours, face similar fiscal gaps. A significant exception is Britain, whose fiscal gap is less than ten percent of ours, as a percentage of GDP. Shaviro attributes much of this difference to a seemingly small difference in how the two governments adjust government pensions and other entitlements programs for inflation. What is this difference, and why does it have such an enormous impact on the fiscal gap?

10. What is the difference between a national debt of $74 trillion and a fiscal gap of $74 trillion?

11. Professor Shaviro states that our fiscal gap is "growth-proof." Why?

12. As Shaviro points out with the example of the divorcing couple with the unbalanced divorce decree, they will still be out of balance if the husband's income increases from $1 million to $1 billion. (Indeed the imbalance will have grown a thousand-fold—from 20 percent of $1 million to 20 percent of $1 billion.) At the same time, the increased income will improve the position of

both. The wife, for example, would be better off receiving 30 percent of $1 billion than 50 percent of $1 million.

13. Are today's elderly and middle-aged generations unfairly passing on debt to future generations? Or, if we assume that technological growth will keep living standards advancing, are the older (and, on this assumption, poorer) generations merely borrowing against some of this future growth?

14. Consider Professor Shaviro's example of the sufferers from colon cancer in 2005 and 2045. Do you agree that this is a reason to curtail the present fiscal imbalance? Or, might this example be turned around, and used to justify increased current spending (for colon cancer research, in this case) in order to effect an earlier cure?

15. Most discussions of government budgets focus on deficits, with a balanced budget usually the assumed ideal. What would be the consequences of a budget surplus?

B. TAXATION TO CONTROL THE ECONOMY

The present conventional budget has practical uses; for one, the conventional deficit or surplus provides a measure of the federal government's impact on the economy. Planned manipulation of revenues, expenditures, and the gaps between them (surplus or deficit) are the major tools in *fiscal policy*. The government is committed to some form of fiscal policy management, a commitment enshrined in the Full Employment Act of 1946. At a political level, presidents and their parties win or lose elections depending upon whether the country is prosperous or in recession.

Fiscal policy means the use of taxes and the overall level of government expenditures to manage the economy. Fiscal policy is not consistent with consistently balanced annual budgets. Routinely, political leaders propose tax policies for the stated purpose of improving the economy. For example, the Treasury Department, in forwarding President Bush's 2003 tax proposals to Congress, argued that the Administration's "economic growth package * * * is designed to invigorate the economic recovery, create jobs, and enhance long-term economic growth."[b] Even at the cost of increasing deficit, the Administration argued that tax cuts were warranted because, especially following the terrorist attacks of September 11, 2001, "the recovery is slow. Businesses are expanding production only slowly and too few jobs are being

---

b. DEPT. OF TREASURY, GENERAL EXPLANATION OF THE ADMINISTRATION'S FISCAL YEAR 2004 REVENUE PROPOSALS 1 (2003).

created. Many employers lack the confidence to invest and hire additional workers."[c]

Use of fiscal policy is consistent with Keynesian thinking, which was the dominant view of macroeconomics for decades after the Great Depression of the 1930s. In recent years, however, economists have become less certain of their ability to manage the economy through use of the tools of fiscal policy. The article by Donald W. Kiefer summarizes changes in attitudes toward fiscal policy management. He discusses various reasons that have led many economists to discard the Keynesian economic models, and now to think that it is very difficult to use fiscal policy in a constructive manner.

WHATEVER HAPPENED TO COUNTER-CYCLICAL ECONOMIC STIMULUS

Donald W. Kiefer[*]

National Tax Association Forum, Winter 1993, at 1-5

In the 1960s and 1970s several tax cuts were implemented to boost the economy out of periods of slow growth or recession, and a tax increase was adopted to restrain inflation. In the 1980s and 1990s fiscal policy has not been used for counter-cyclical purposes. What has changed?

In short, Murphy's Law struck with a vengeance; everything that could go wrong did. Four important factors are highlighted in this article (not necessarily in order of importance): 1) collapse of the theoretical underpinnings of counter-cyclical fiscal policy, 2) structural changes in the economy, 3) policy disappointments, and 4) the current policy setting.

Collapse of the Theoretical Underpinnings of Counter-Cyclical Fiscal Policy

The high confidence in counter-cyclical fiscal policy in the 1960s and early 1970s was based on Keynesian macroeconomics, the theoretical structure built on the writings of John Maynard Keynes. Two elements were crucial. The first was the notion that fiscal policy—primarily increases or decreases in the government deficit—could stimulate or restrain short-term economic growth. The second element was not actually derived from the writings of Keynes, but was appended later and became a key underpinning of both "Keynesian" fiscal policy and counter-cyclical monetary policy theory. This was the Phillips Curve, the notion that there was a stable tradeoff between inflation and unemployment.

The Phillips Curve implied that lower unemployment would result in higher inflation and vice versa. According to this relationship, for example, if

---

c. *Id.* at 3.

*. At time of original publication, Senior Specialist in Economic Policy, Congressional Research Service, Library of Congress.

unemployment were maintained at a low level, inflation would be higher than at higher unemployment rates but would remain at a relatively constant rate. The implication of this relationship was that policy makers could choose a point along the inflation/unemployment tradeoff that they believed to be optimal and adjust policy to achieve it. In the early 1960s, policy makers chose to strive for "full employment," which was typically defined as an unemployment rate of 4 percent. This was thought to be the level at which most unemployment would be frictional or structural.

In 1967, in his presidential address to the American Economic Association, Milton Friedman argued that the Phillips Curve relationship is incorrect. He posited a "natural unemployment rate" that would exist if the economy were in equilibrium. This natural rate is determined by real factors in the economy—the composition of the labor force, the nature of the unemployment compensation system, and the pace of technological change, for example—but not by the rate of inflation.

Friedman argued that any tradeoff between unemployment and inflation is strictly a short-term phenomenon. If policy attempted to keep unemployment below the natural rate, the inflation rate would rise. But soon the expected rate of inflation would rise to match the actual inflation rate, and as that happened equilibrium would be restored in the economy and unemployment would return to the natural rate. At the new equilibrium, unemployment would again be at the natural rate, but it would be paired with a higher rate of inflation. Attempting to keep unemployment permanently below the natural rate would require continuously increasing inflation. The implications were that macroeconomic policy actually could do rather little to affect the unemployment rate, at least in the long term, and that the inflationary effects of reducing unemployment were much greater than previously believed.

Friedman's interpretation and conclusions were not immediately accepted by the mainstream of the economics profession. During the 1970s, however, the advent of "stagflation" (simultaneous increases in unemployment and inflation) forced a broad re-examination of the unemployment/inflation relationship. Stagflation is inconsistent with the Phillips Curve, but it is not inconsistent with the natural rate of unemployment hypothesis. Today the natural rate hypothesis is the most widely held view, although there are significant competing theories. In general, the theory serves relatively well in providing an explanation of the observed relationship between unemployment and inflation over the post-war period. * * *

Friedman's theoretical contribution was notable not only because it introduced the concept of the natural rate of unemployment, but also because of its attention to expectations, how they are formed, and how they affect behavior. Prior to this time, most economic theory ignored expectations or relied on a simplistic view of how expectations are formed. Typically, expectations were assumed to be based on simple extrapolations of past trends; any new information—such as a policy change—that should affect the course of the economy was assumed to be ignored until its effects appeared in the trends of economic data. But during the last two decades a new branch of economic theory has been developed, based on the assumption that economic agents form their expectations rationally, that is, incorporate all relevant information. Some of the early contributions to this rational expectations school of thought did serious damage to the first element of Keynesian economics that provided the basis for counter-cyclical fiscal policy: the notion that such policy could stimulate or restrain short-term economic growth.

In one of the most provocative papers, Sargent and Wallace in 1975 developed the argument that in a world of rational expectations, systematic counter-cyclical policy has no real effects on the economy. In such a world, events that are known beforehand have no economic effect because they are already factored into expectations. Only events that come as complete surprises (or the aspects of events that are surprises) can have economic effects. This implies that systematic counter-cyclical policy can have no effect because it will be fully anticipated; people will adjust their behavior to offset the policy and still achieve their objectives.

Shortly thereafter, the empirical foundations of counter-cyclical policy were attacked, using a rational expectations framework. In what became known as the "Lucas Critique," Robert Lucas argued that the econometric evidence supporting the effectiveness of counter-cyclical policy was flawed because the models used to estimate the policy effects were misspecified. * * *

These papers and others—together with applied research finding disappointing effects of the counter-cyclical fiscal policies enacted in the 1960s and 1970s * * * destroyed essential elements of Keynesian economics as understood in the 1960s. * * * An effort ensued to reexamine and rebuild macroeconomic theory from the ground up. * * * The process is still underway, but it is unlikely to yield a single general model of the economy that enjoys the support of a substantial majority of the economics profession, as the Keynesian model once did. Instead, several different paradigms are being developed.

While space does not permit reviewing these paradigms, their implications for the points developed here can be summarized. The natural rate of unemployment hypothesis, or some variant thereof, is consistent with most of the new models. While only one of the new paradigms fully incorporates rational expectations, virtually all serious economic modeling in the last two decades has incorporated expectations—how they are formed and how they affect behavior—in one form or another.   (The rational expectationists got their comeuppance in the early 1980s when the recessions were far more severe than they predicted would result from a pre-announced tightening of monetary policy to squeeze the inflation out of the economy.) And while early in the process new models were developed within which counter-cyclical policy could affect short-term economic growth even with rational expectations, in none of the current models is counter-cyclical policy as strong or as efficacious as it was believed to be in the Keynesian models of the 1960s.

Structural Changes in the Economy

Important structural changes in the economy have occurred since the 1960s, some of which have weakened the effectiveness of counter-cyclical fiscal policy.   More specifically, in 1971 flexible exchange rates replaced the earlier system of fixed rates of exchange between currencies.   The international capital market also has developed very rapidly in the last few decades as a result of advances in telecommunications and computerization. These changes have resulted in more efficient capital markets, but they also have weakened the ability of fiscal policy to affect domestic economic activity.

A tax cut to stimulate the economy, for example, will increase the budget deficit and result in higher interest rates.   The higher interest rates will attract capital in the international capital markets as investors in other countries shift assets to earn the higher rate of return. With flexible exchange rates, the greater inflow of foreign capital will drive up the value of the dollar in relation to other currencies.   This will make foreign goods and services cheaper to Americans and U.S. goods and services more expensive to foreigners. Hence, U.S. net exports will decline, offsetting the initial effects of the fiscal stimulus. This effect is sometimes characterized as "exporting the stimulus" because the decrease in net exports (increase in imports) will create jobs in other countries. (Under fixed exchange rates, the greater demand for dollars in the foreign exchange markets would force an expansion of the money supply; this monetary expansion would reinforce the fiscal stimulus.)

* * *

Another important structural change affecting fiscal policy is the indexation of the Federal individual income tax. Until the mid-1980s, the individual income tax burden increased automatically each year as a result of inflation—the so-called "bracket creep" phenomenon. Periodic counter-cyclical tax cuts enacted during recessions or stagnant periods offset the bracket creep that occurred during the growth years. Unless inflation got really out of hand, tax increases to restrain the economy were not needed; in a politically convenient fashion they occurred automatically due to bracket creep.

Now, however, the income tax is indexed for inflation; bracket creep is largely a phenomenon of the past (though real income growth still results in bracket creep). In this setting, a counter-cyclical tax cut has to be followed by a counter-cyclical tax increase to avoid a long-term reduction in government revenues. Given the difficulty with which our political structure confronts a tax increase (or spending cut), counter-cyclical fiscal policy implies pro-cyclical legislative gridlock.

Policy Disappointments

The third factor affecting the use (or nonuse) of counter-cyclical fiscal policy is that we tried it and it didn't work, or at least it didn't work as well as expected. The three major counter-cyclical fiscal policies implemented during the 1960s and 1970s—the 1964 tax cut, the 1968 surtax, and the 1975 tax cut—were the subject of much economic research. While this research cannot be reviewed here in detail, three general conclusions from the research can be summarized.

First, the magnitude of the peak effect of a tax increase or decrease, in terms of the change in real GDP, is only about equal to or somewhat smaller than the size of the tax change itself. This contrasts to earlier beliefs that the tax change multiplier could be as high as 2 or 3.

Second, the effectiveness lags for tax changes are longer than had been expected. Tax cuts or increases had been expected to have rather immediate effects. Instead, the effects grow slowly, peaking in the second or third year after implementation when economic stimulus or restraint may no longer be needed (or appropriate).

Third, in the short-run period when the effect of a tax increase or decrease is desired, a permanent tax change has more effect than a temporary tax change (both the 1968 surtax and the 1975 tax cut were temporary). In the first year, a temporary tax change probably has no more than half the effect of a permanent tax change. This finding is consistent with the theoretical developments in the 1970s and 1980s concerning the role of expectations. * * *

Another lesson was learned from the enactment of the 1975 tax cut: it is frequently impossible to know the stage of the business cycle early enough, and to design and implement legislation quickly enough, to offset an economic fluctuation.

The state of the economy was debated throughout 1974 during the first episode of stagflation in the aftermath of the 1973 OPEC oil price increase. Some people maintained the economy was overheating and that policy should aim to slow it down. Others believed it was slipping into recession. In October 1974 President Ford, siding with the first group (which was probably the majority of observers at that point), proposed a surtax to curb inflationary pressures. * * * It soon became clear, however, that the economy was, in fact, sliding into deep recession. In January 1975, the President recommended a tax cut to stimulate the economy out of the recession. It was enacted with uncharacteristic speed; the President signed the tax cut legislation on March 29, 1975, only 10 weeks after recommending it.

Despite the speed with which the 1975 tax cut was enacted, its implementation came after the recession had ended. With the advantage of hindsight and data that were unavailable concurrently, the recession was eventually dated as lasting from November 1973 to March 1975. The initial implementation of the tax cuts under the legislation did not occur until May 1975. Hence, the recession ended before the tax cut was put into effect. (It is possible, however, that the tax cut contributed to the end of the recession by giving a boost to expectations.)

The Current Policy Setting

Because of the factors summarized above—revisions in economic theory, structural changes in the economy, and disappointing policy experiences—views about the efficacy of counter-cyclical fiscal policy have changed substantially since the 1960s. One way to discern this change is to contrast statements of the Council of Economic [Advisers] (CEA) in the 1960s and 1980s.

In the 1962 *Economic Report of the President*, the CEA—comprised of Walter Heller, Kermit Gordon, and James Tobin—made the following statements:

> To capitalize on the potential gains of stabilization requires skillful use of all economic policy, particularly budget and monetary policy. (p. 70)

> To be effective, discretionary budget policy should be flexible. In order to promote economic stability, the government should be able to change quickly tax rates or expenditure programs, and equally able to reverse its actions as circumstances change. (p. 72)

In the report, the President proposed that he be given stand-by authority to temporarily reduce individual income tax rates by as much as five percentage points and to initiate temporary capital improvement projects as counter-cyclical measures.

The views of the 1982 CEA—comprised of Murray Weidenbaum, Jerry Jordan, and William Niskanen—also expressed in the *Economic Report of the President*, are in sharp contrast:

> Although the Federal Government is the appropriate agent for stabilizing the economy, the limits of such action must be understood. This Administration believes that "fine tuning" of the economy—attempting to offset every fluctuation—is not possible. The information needed to do so is often simply not available, and when it becomes available it is quite likely that underlying conditions will already have changed. As a result, a policy of fine

tuning the economy is as likely to be counterproductive as it is to be helpful. Though it is necessary for the government to have macro-economic policies, including both monetary and fiscal policies designed to achieve some desired growth of income, such policies are not suitable for correcting small fluctuations in economic activity. (p. 36)

While these statements were written by different economists working for different Administrations representing different political parties, the most important reason for their differences is probably the broadly changed views regarding counter-cyclical policy. Despite their differences, the statements in the two reports probably reflected the mainstream view of economists at the time they were written.

* * *

It should be noted, however, that even though *discretionary* counter-cyclical fiscal policy is no longer in vogue, the Federal budget still contains a number of *automatic* stabilizers. The progressive income tax, for example, automatically claims a larger portion of income as incomes rise and a smaller portion as incomes fall. Welfare programs and unemployment compensation automatically increase payments to individuals as the economy slows down and reduce the payments as the economy speeds up. These programs result in significant automatic increases or decreases in the size of the deficit at different points in the business cycle. Hence, fiscal policy does not remain neutral with regard to the business cycle even though new fiscal policy legislation may not be enacted specifically to counter a given economic turn.

Notes and Questions

16. Dr. Kiefer argued that economists are much less sanguine than earlier about fiscal policy playing an effective role. First, he pointed to "the collapse of the theoretical underpinnings of counter-cyclical fiscal policy," most particularly with regard to the government's power effectively to combat unemployment through fiscal policy. What are the older theories and what theories have replaced them?

17. Why do floating foreign exchange rates (in effect since 1971), and more efficient capital markets, make fiscal policy less effective?

18. While the heyday of Keynesian macroeconomics may be past, not all economists are as pessimistic about fiscal policy as Dr. Kiefer's article might suggest. For example, Dr. Kiefer quoted the 1962 *Economic Report of the President*, which was highly supportive of fiscal policy, and contrasted the 1982 report, whose authors thought that "fine tuning" the economy was impossible.

But at least one member of the 1962 Council of Economic Advisors, Professor James Tobin, continued to advocate economic fine-tuning thirty years later, when addressing President-Elect Clinton's 1992 Economic Conference:

> [I]n virtually every previous cyclical recovery since World War II, monetary policy has had active fiscal help.
>
> * * *
>
> Fiscal policy for recovery is bound to raise the budget deficit temporarily.   * * *   I recommend stimulus of $60 billion a year for the two years 1993 and 1994, about 1 percent of GDP, capable thanks to secondary "multiplier" effects of adding 1.5 percent to GDP demand, a modest amount relative to the 6% shortfall of GDP from its potential.[d]

19. Consider whether political leaders have an incentive to voice the merits of Keynesian economics even if they do not believe them. If a politician wants to cut taxes or increase expenditures (rarely the opposite measures) for policy or political reasons unrelated to stimulating the economy, economic stimulation may nonetheless provide a convenient rationale. For example, it may be argued that economic stimulus was not really President Bush's primary motivation in proposing tax cuts in 2003; certainly, however, the Administration attempted to "sell" the tax cut proposals in those terms.

C. TAXATION TO CHANGE BEHAVIOR

The broadest and least controversial fiscal policy goals (at least in terms of desirability) are to achieve something approaching full employment coupled with relative price stability. In addition, other, more specific goals have been proposed. Some have been implemented, at least in part. Some of these objectives are quite broad, such as increasing savings and/or investment; encouraging home ownership; and redistributing wealth or, at least, reducing differences in income levels. Other objectives are much narrower. These include targeting depressed geographic areas, supporting a domestic maritime industry, and encouraging the development of oil and gas reserves. (Favorable tax provisions designed to induce behavior are termed "tax expenditures," and are discussed in greater detail in Chapter Eleven.) Any tax provision designed to encourage particular actions by taxpayers raises issues of fairness between taxpayers in the favored categories and those left out.

The articles excerpted in this subchapter deal with a broad goal of fiscal policy that has gotten increasing attention in recent years, the encouragement of savings. This is in response to a widespread understanding that the savings

---

d. James Tobin, *Policy for Recovery and Growth*, Statement to President-Elect Clinton's Economic Conference (December 16, 1992).

rate has sharply declined in the United States. This objective is used to justify more liberal tax treatment for Individual Retirement Accounts (IRAs) and, in a broader context, to justify proposals to shift an increased share of the tax burden from income to consumption. (Consumption taxes are the subject of Chapters Six and Seven.)

SAVINGS, INVESTMENT, AND THE TAX REFORM ACT OF 1986

Edward M. Gramlich[*]

National Tax Association-Tax Institute of America

79th Annual Conference 13-19 (1986)

One of the oldest questions in public economics is whether to tax income or consumption. The difference is saving, which at least until recently equaled investment. This implies that the question of whether consumption or income is the appropriate tax base gets very close to the question of whether inducements for saving or investment should be provided in an income tax.

* * *

Should Saving/Investment Be Promoted?

The saving/investment issue is one of the most basic in economics, yet one of the most difficult to discuss objectively. Beginning with definitions, the standard national income accounts identity shows that private plus government savings equals the sum of capital investment plus the export surplus. When a country has an export surplus, it is by definition increasing its claim on foreigners, or lending abroad. These new international assets should be added to its domestic capital formation in deriving the impact of its saving on national net worth. Conversely, when a country has an import surplus, as does the U.S. right now, it is borrowing from abroad to put its domestic capital in place, and this borrowed capital should be deducted from total capital formation to determine the change in national net worth.

Either way, the newfound importance of trade and capital flows with other countries requires that physical capital formation be distinguished from wealth accumulation, or domestically-owned capital formation. In either case, wealth accumulation, not capital formation, is the best measure of how much of the nation's output is being diverted from present-day consumption to the provision of the future.[2] In either case incentives that promote saving must

---

*. At time of original publication, Congressional Budget Office and The University of Michigan.

2. The statement is not meant to downgrade the usefulness of other measures. If one were interested in labor income or labor productivity, one should focus on capital put in place in the United States. And, the fact that borrowed capital has less impact on long term living standards than does domestically-owned capital does not obviously mean that it has no impact. Given that lack of saving, the fact that the U.S. *is able to* borrow from foreigners does keep U.S. living standards now

also be distinguished from incentives that promote investment. Since the two are no longer the same, incentive effects will not be either.

The more difficult question is the normative one of how much a country *should* save, or devote to wealth accumulation. At least four types of answers have been provided in the economics literature, none with absolutely compelling logic.

The market answer

The first impulse of American economists and politicians these days is to ask what "the market" would do. By this standard, the tax system should be neutral with respect to saving and investment and fiscal policy should be too. National saving rates would equal private saving rates, and each generation would pay for its public goods.

While the standard has superficial plausibility, there are many problems with it. First off, how can a country with both an income and a corporate tax ever attain neutrality, given the well-known double taxation of both dividend and interest income? Second, one can think of many other actions taken by government, such as in its public provision for retirement or its own investment portfolio, that have non-neutral effects on saving and investment. * * *

[S]omething that might be called "pragmatic neutrality" can be achieved by setting the long run governmental budget deficit equal to zero. But even this standard remains surprisingly amorphous as a pragmatic guide to policy. Does this government deficit that is set to zero include state and local deficits or not, their trust fund surpluses or not, is it a capital or a current operating deficit, correcting for the cycle or not, corrected for inflation-induced capital gains on debt or not, corrected for capital gains in assets or not? These questions are not answered by the underlying logic, but each one turns out to matter enormously in practice. We are left with as many questions as we started with.

The time series answer

According to this standard, society might be thought of as an intergenerational compact where the generations cannot determine their proper saving rate, but they can agree to do whatever their parents did. If their parents devoted ten percent of national output to wealth accumulation, they should too. Under this standard, whatever exists is right, and changes in saving, particularly declines, are inappropriate.

As with the market standard, the problems with a time series standard are obvious. Should a generation forced to defend its homeland be held to the same standards as its parents, who may have lived in more peaceful times?

---

and in the future above what they should be otherwise.

More relevant to today's problems, what about a generation that finds itself with a costly strategic deterrence burden? What if there are new resource discoveries that promise to shift living standards up in the future? Or depletion that promises to shift down living standards? There may be some horizontal equity argument for the time series standard, but it is only if many important factors are held constant, factors that cannot possibly be held constant in real life.

The cross section answer

According to this standard, the U.S. is in a competitive rat-race for international markets, and should save as much as its neighbors. Which neighbors? And in a world of fluctuating market exchange rates, why keep up? If for some reason the U.S. gradually loses competitiveness, or has creeping inflation, its currency will slowly decline so as to maintain purchasing power parity. This implies a slow increase in relative prices for foreign goods, but so what? Relative prices change all the time. The cross section answer also leaves much unanswered.

The theoretical answer

Growth theorists have long recognized the existence of a "golden rule" of capital accumulation.[5] That yields a savings rate that, if maintained, maximizes the path of consumption per capita over time. * * *

In addition to the bizarre spectacle of having basic political questions being decided by assumptions from abstract growth models, one can raise the same problems as with the time series standard—why should society save at the same rate over time?

So none of these answers is fully, or perhaps even partially, convincing. A true skeptic will come out of this discussion believing that there is no proper savings rate policy, and by implication no limit from these considerations on government budget deficits.[6] But for those with any inclination at all to make subjective normative judgements about fiscal policy, it is interesting to note that at least for the early 1980s, all four standards clearly point to the fact that the U.S. should raise its national saving (wealth accumulation) rate. For the market standard, since 1980 deficits by any measure have risen sharply, and overall fiscal policy is definitely nonneutral—[the data] strongly suggest that these deficits have reduced the national wealth accumulation rate well below the private rate. The same numbers show a sharp drop in the national wealth

---

5. Edmund S. Phelps, "The Golden Rule of Capital Accumulation: A Fable for Growthmen," *American Economic Review*, September, 1961, vol. 51, pp. 638-642.

6. There could be other limits. If, for example, the interest burden grew steadily as a share of GNP, the government could be put in a position of having either to repudiate its debt, or to monetize it (and repudiate it through inflation). At present this interest burden growth in the United States has been contained, and we are now in the position of deciding whether there are other, more subjective, reasons for reducing deficits.

accumulation rate, which argues for a higher saving by the time series standard. And even before the drop occurred, the U.S. was under-saving by both cross section and theoretical standard. Something as subjective as the proper saving rate can never be conclusively determined, but there does seem to be very strong evidence that the U.S. should try to save more than it now is, at least as much as the country did back in the 1960s.

> * * *

Implications

The clearest message here is that national saving is important, there are many reasons to believe that the U.S. is not doing enough of it lately, and that this is a good reason why the country should continue its difficult fight against government budget deficits.

> * * * [T]here seems to be no substitute for honest-to-goodness deficit reduction, however painful that may be, as a way to increase national saving rates.

ACCOUNTING FOR SAVING AND CAPITAL FORMATION IN THE UNITED STATES, 1947-1991
Richard Ruggles*

7 Journal of Economic Perspectives 3, 3, 12-16 (1993)

This paper is concerned with accounting for the saving and capital formation taking place in different sectors of the U.S. economy. In brief, where does saving arise and where is it used? Do some sectors save more than they spend for capital formation and thus are net lenders? Do other sectors save less than is required for their capital formation and thus are net borrowers? The U.S. national income accounts contain the basic data relating to these questions. However, at several points, these data must be recast in order to yield analytically useful results. When such a reformulation is made, the conclusions that can be drawn differ strikingly from much of the currently received conventional wisdom.

> * * *

Summary and Conclusions

The reformulation of the household sector account to take into account their ownership of houses and their actual receipts of pension benefits, indicates that, on balance, households have not been net providers of saving to other sectors in the economy. Although the gross saving of both the enterprise and household sectors approximate their capital formation, it does not mean that there is no inter-sectoral financing. Many households may be the source of finance for small business or venture capital. Conversely, many

---

*. At time of original publication, Professor Emeritus of Economics, Yale University.

enterprises may extend consumer credit to households or finance owner-occupied housing mortgages.

Given the observed patterns of sector saving and capital formation three sets of questions need to be examined. First, how robust are the empirical findings about sector saving and capital formation? Are the observations relating to sector net borrowing and net lending valid even if more restrictive or broader concepts of saving and capital formation are used? Second, how relevant are the data on sectoral saving and capital formation to questions of the determinants of saving and capital formation in the economy? Are increased saving and capital formation both necessary and sufficient for productivity and economic growth? Finally, what are the implications of the cyclical changes in sectoral saving and capital formation for economic policy? What policies should be followed to ensure a high level of economic activity without inflation?

Robustness of the Empirical Findings

The absolute differences observed between saving and capital formation—that is, net lending and net borrowing—for the different sectors * * * are unaffected by differing definitions of saving and capital formation. * * *

Even if the concept of enterprise capital formation were to be expanded to include intangible capital such as research and development, worker training, environmental improvements and repair and maintenance, enterprise sector net lending and net borrowing would not be affected. * * * Indeed, even employing net saving and net capital formation concepts would not alter the empirical findings relating to sector net lending and sector net borrowing.

Relevance of Sector
Saving and Capital Formation

These findings are directly relevant to understanding the process of saving and capital formation in the economy. The conventional view that saving by individuals provides the basis for enterprise capital formation is contradicted by the evidence. On balance, households are not net lenders to enterprises or government. For many enterprises, capital consumption allowances and retained earnings are the major source of funds for capital formation. The role of reserves held by employer pension and insurance funds against future liabilities also should be recognized as having a central role in the behavior of financial markets as a source of funds. Finally, from the volatile behavior of capital formation, it appears that the willingness of enterprises to undertake capital formation is, in most periods, a more important determinant than the availability of funds provided by saving in the economy. The balance sheets of many enterprises indicate that they have financial resources available to undertake capital formation in periods when nevertheless they are contracting their capital outlays.

Economic theory generally views capital as tangible goods yielding a flow of future services and representing a factor of production. However, many tangible goods, such as shopping malls, housing, consumer durables, public facilities and some highways, may primarily yield a flow of consumption services. Such consumption services are useful and important, but they may not have significant impact on increasing productivity and sustained growth in the economy. On the other hand, many other kinds of current expenditures for such things as research and development, employee training, education, [and] improvement of the environment may make major contribution to future increases in productivity.

Thus, the emphasis on the importance of saving and capital formation for economic growth and productivity may be misplaced. The production of some tangible producer and consumer goods, while important for economic growth, are not the sole determinants of productivity and development of the economy. More emphasis needs to be directed to encouraging and developing those economic and social activities that are recognized as having a significant impact on the productivity of the economic system.

The Cyclical Implications of Sectoral Saving and Capital Formation

The cyclical patterns of saving and capital formation of households, enterprises and government have important implications for economic policy directed at maintaining full employment and price stability. In periods of recession, households reduce their expenditures on consumer durables and their purchases of new owner-occupied housing. One consequence is that their borrowing for such expenditures decline, while at the same time their previous level of repayment on consumer debt and mortgages continues. Enterprises selling to consumers face a slackening in their sales and rising excess capacity, and as a consequence their profits and retained earnings decline and at the same time they also reduce their capital expenditures and their employment. The government in this situation is faced with declining tax revenues and rising needs of recession-related expenditures, with the consequence that government deficits increase.

It is apparent in this situation that although there has been a decline in saving in each sector, it has not been the cause of the decline in capital formation, income and employment. Efforts to stimulate saving in the expectation that it will induce more capital formation are misguided. Policies that raise income and profits and encourage spending and capital formation are needed. Thus, in recession, tax reductions and expansion of government expenditures on infrastructure are appropriate.

Because state and local governments are not permitted to indulge in fiscal policy, they are required to have balanced budgets. This means that in periods of economic decline, they must raise taxes and reduce their expenditures. This has the perverse effect of accentuating the decline in the economy. During this last recession, many economists and business leaders have urged that such balanced budget policies also be adopted by the federal government—thus prohibiting it also from engaging in fiscal policy. The extent to which fiscal policy should be used to stimulate the economy can be questioned, but unenlightened contractionary policies should not be taken by governments in periods of recession.

Finally, the analysis also has implications for saving and capital formation policies in periods of economic boom. During periods of economic expansion, both households and enterprises expand their capital formation. The increases in tax revenues and imports act as automatic stabilizers to some extent, but speculative expansions of capital expenditures (especially in the area of building construction) may result in rising prices and unsustainable levels of capital formation. The consequence may be overexpansion and economic collapse, such as occurred during the saving and loan crisis. Again, the major policy effort should not be directed to encouraging sectoral saving by offering incentives such as reductions in capital gains taxation, but rather at curbing investment in speculative capital that result in unwarranted and/or undesirable capital formation.

The major lesson from the analysis of sectoral saving and capital formation is that in peacetime and in periods of recession, the major focus should be on stimulating useful capital formation rather than encouraging saving. The encouragement of saving is appropriate in periods when large expenditures for such things as national defense are unavoidable and they generate income that exceeds the availability of consumable goods in the economy. During World War II, the restriction of spending and encouragement of saving was appropriate, but in today's economic climate, new policies are required.

Concluding Thoughts

Both economic theory and national accounting have failed to provide an adequate understanding of the process of saving and capital formation. To a major extent, this failure has been due to the simplistic formulations of saving and capital formation by both neoclassical and Keynesian economic theory. Reformulations of economic theory are needed so that the institutional aspects of modern economic systems can be taken into account.

The viability of capitalist market economies depends on their achieving levels of saving and capital formation that are compatible with economic growth and full employment equilibrium without inflation. The primary tools for achieving and maintaining such an equilibrium have been monetary and fiscal policy. However, past experience suggests that simple guidelines relating to regulation of the money supply or control of the federal budget are not sufficient for this task. * * *

Notes and Questions

20. Dean Gramlich discussed four theories for deciding how much the United States "should" save, but found flaws with each theory. How, then, was he able to arrive at the conclusion that the level of saving should be increased?

21. Dean Gramlich noted that the seemingly simple principle of balancing the budget "remains surprisingly amorphous as a pragmatic guide to policy." Why?

22. Both Gramlich and Ruggles make the frequently ignored point that the budgets of state and local governments are relevant to carrying out fiscal policy, as well as to the measurement of savings. For example, if fiscal policy calls for a governmental deficit while states and localities are operating at a surplus, an expansionary federal fiscal policy must more than offset the state and local surplus before it can become an effective stimulus.

23. In measuring the fiscal impact of states and localities, current cash flow is all important. For purposes of determining proper fiscal policy, state and local expenditures for capital projects count toward a deficit, while taxes imposed to amortize the debt over a period of years count toward a surplus. This is true even if the state or locality regards its budget as balanced in each year. Because many states use a capital budget, both expenditure on a capital project and repayment over a period of years may be consistent with a state constitutional requirement that the state's budget be "in balance."

24. Recalling the discussion from Subchapter B, observe that Professor Ruggles appears to favor an active fiscal policy, rejecting the view that the federal government, like the states, should follow a balanced budget policy that would prevent an expansionary fiscal policy in time of recession.

25. Professor Ruggles contends that we should be interested in capital formation rather than saving. Moreover, government policy should be directed to encourage specific types of capital formation. Which types of capital formation are less important, and which more important, according to Ruggles?

26. Monetary policy, such as relaxing or restricting credit and lowering or raising interest rates, appears to be more effective in restricting the economy than in stimulating it, at least over the short run. Monetary policy has been compared to a string, which can be used to hold back the economy, but cannot be used successfully to push the economy.

While fiscal policy may in theory be effective in both expansion and contraction, politically it is much easier to cut taxes or raise expenditures than the contrary.

The political insulation of the Federal Reserve means that monetary policy is the primary tool for restraining an overheated economy. While Governors of the Federal Reserve System do not enjoy the life tenure of federal judges, they are much less sensitive to short-term public pressure than are politicians who expect to stand for reelection.

27. If the rate of savings is of concern, would it be better to tackle it by cutting the federal deficit rather than attempting to increase private savings by offering tax benefits (such as more liberal treatment of IRAs)—which themselves will increase the deficit?

28. Professor Ruggles concluded that households have not been net providers of savings to other sectors of the economy. What are the more important financial sources of capital formation, according to Ruggles? Would Ruggles focus tax benefits on sectors of the economy other than households to achieve more capital formation?

D. THE MIX OF REVENUE SOURCES

Federal government revenues come from a variety of sources. These shift over time in response to changes both in tax law and in the economy. In 2001, the Congressional Budget Office reviewed changes over the preceding two decades (through 1997, the most recent year for which comprehensive data were available). The CBO report examines a period in which Congress was able to tax a growing economy more lightly, and yet, due to the real (inflation-adjusted) growth, still obtain an increase in real revenue. The report disaggregates federal tax receipts in two quite distinct ways: by income strata of taxpayers and by type of tax. The report also includes brief discussion of the six most important tax statutes enacted during the period, including the monumental Tax Reform Act of 1986 (to which the present Internal Revenue Code owes its name).[e] Because the report was issued in the first year of

---

e. The present code is termed the Internal Revenue Code of 1986, having been so christened by Congress at the time of the most massive tax statute in history. Many people (including your editor) think the code should still be named the Internal Revenue Code of 1954, because the 1986

President George W. Bush's administration, it does not take account of the important statutes enacted in 2001 and 2003.

EFFECTIVE FEDERAL TAX RATES, 1979-1997
Congressional Budget Office Report — October 2001
pages xv-xix, xxii-xxiv, 1-2, 4-5, 9-10,12-13

Summary and Introduction

The past two decades have witnessed the passage of 15 federal tax bills, the longest peacetime economic expansion in U.S. history, and major demographic and labor-market shifts. A backward look at the period also reveals substantial growth of real (inflation-adjusted) pretax household income, distributed unevenly among income groups. That higher income, although accompanied by lower effective tax rates (total taxes as a percentage of total income) throughout the income distribution, led to record federal revenues that claimed the largest share of gross domestic product since World War II. Six major observations stand out in the analysis of taxes and incomes reported in this study:

- Between 1979 and 1997, the effective federal tax rate fell for every quintile, or fifth, of the income distribution. Had 2000 tax law been in effect in 1997, the declines in effective rates would have been even greater (see Summary Figure 1).

- Over the same period, however, the income of households with the highest income (which therefore face the highest tax rates) grew substantially faster than the income of other households. As a result, the effective federal tax rate for all households as a group increased by one-half of a percentage point, or from 22.3 percent to 22.8 percent.

Act—important as it was—did not replace or fundamentally reorganize the 1954 code.

Summary Figure 1.

Reduction in Total Effective Federal Tax Rates Between 1979 and 1997, by Income Quintile

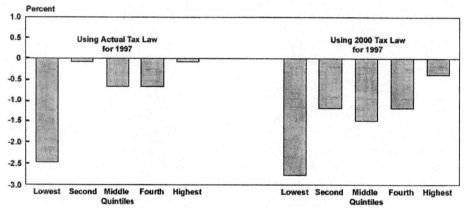

SOURCE: Congressional Budget Office.

NOTES: The effective tax rate equals total tax liabilities (individual income, corporate income, payroll, and excise) as a percentage of total income. Quintiles, or fifths, of the income distribution contain equal numbers of people.

- Trends in effective tax rates varied widely among the major sources of federal revenues. Social insurance, or payroll, taxes (which finance Social Security, Medicare, and federal unemployment insurance) claimed a larger share of income in 1997 than in 1979, and corporate income taxes accounted for a smaller share. Effective individual income tax rates changed little overall, but they dropped for the 80 percent of households with the lowest income and rose for the 20 percent with the highest income (see Summary Figure 2).

Summary Figure 2.

Effective Federal Tax Rates, by Revenue Source and Income Quintile, 1979 and 1997

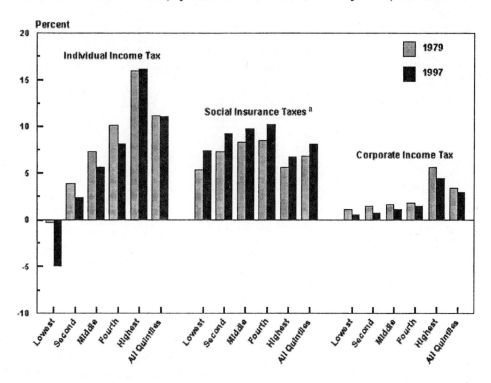

SOURCE: Congressional Budget Office.

NOTES: The effective tax rate equals tax liabilities as a percentage of total income. Quintiles,
          or fifths, of the income distribution contain equal numbers of people.

a.   Payroll taxes financing Social Security, Medicare, and federal unemployment insurance.

- Although revenues from individual income taxes are nearly 50 percent greater than revenues from social insurance taxes, households in the bottom 80 percent of the income distribution on average pay nearly twice as much in payroll tax as in income tax. In 1997, 9.6 percent of that group's income went to payroll taxes, compared with 5.2 percent going to income taxes (see Summary Figure 3).

Summary Figure 3.
Effective Federal Individual Income and Social Insurance Tax Rates, by Income
Quintile, 1997

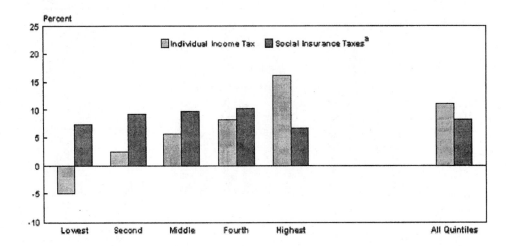

SOURCE: Congressional Budget Office.

NOTES: The effective tax rate equals tax liabilities as a percentage of total income. Quintiles,
          or fifths, of the income distribution contain equal numbers of people.

a.   Payroll taxes financing Social Security, Medicare, and federal unemployment insurance.

- Average real household income before taxes rose by nearly 30 percent
  over the 1979-1997 period, but that growth was highly unequal
  among quintiles (see Summary Figure 4). The average income of
  households in the highest quintile was more than 50 percent higher
  in 1997 than in 1979, while that of the bottom fifth of households was
  nearly 4 percent lower. Because of substantial movement of
  households among quintiles, however, those changes do not indicate
  whether particular households became better or worse off over the
  period.

Summary Figure 4.

Percentage Change in Real Pretax Comprehensive Household Income, by Income Quintile, 1979-1997

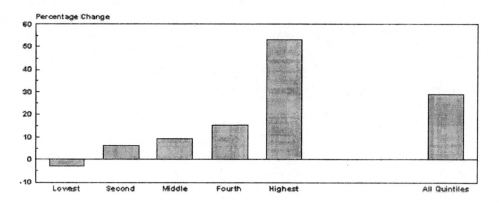

SOURCE: Congressional Budget Office.

NOTES: Households are people who share a single housing unit, regardless of the relationships among them. Real pretax comprehensive household income (which is measured in 1997 dollars) equals cash income plus income from other sources. Cash income is the sum of wages, salaries, self-employment income, rents, taxable and nontaxable interest, dividends, realized capital gains, cash transfer payments, and retirement benefits. Other sources of income include the corporate income tax and the employer's share of Social Security, Medicare, and federal unemployment insurance payroll taxes as well as all in-kind benefits (Medicare, Medicaid, employer-paid health insurance premiums, food stamps, school lunches and breakfasts, housing assistance, and energy assistance). Households with negative income are excluded from the lowest income category but are included in totals.

Payroll taxes are distributed to households paying those taxes directly or paying them indirectly through their employers. Corporate income taxes are distributed to households according to their share of capital income.

Quintiles, or fifths, of the income distribution contain equal numbers of people.

●   The rapid growth of income at the top of the distribution sharply increased the highest quintile's shares of pretax and after-tax income as well as federal tax liabilities for that group (the taxes people in the

quintile owe). In 1997, the fifth of households with the highest
income earned 53 percent of total pretax income and paid 65 percent
of federal taxes, up from 46 percent and 57 percent, respectively, in
1979 (see Summary Figure 5). Again, however, households in the
highest quintile in 1997 were not the same households in that
quintile in 1979.

This study examines in detail the effective federal tax rates faced by
households in different parts of the income distribution from 1979 through
1997. The analysis considers the four largest sources of federal revenues:
individual income taxes, social insurance taxes, corporate income taxes, and
excise taxes. * * *

Summary Figure 5.

**Shares of Real Pretax Comprehensive Household Income and Total Federal Tax
Liabilities, by Income Quintile, 1979 and 1997**

Shares of Real Pretax Comprehensive Household Income

Shares of Total Federal Tax Liabilities

SOURCE: Congressional Budget Office.

Trends in Effective Federal Tax Rates
* * *

Shares of Income and Taxes

The distribution of income among households grew substantially more
unequal during the 1979-1997 period. The share of pretax income going to the
highest quintile of households climbed from 46 percent in 1979 to 53 percent in

1997, while the share going to the lowest three quintiles dropped from 32 percent to 27 percent. At the very top of the distribution, the highest 1 percent of households took home 16 percent of total pretax income in 1997, up from 9 percent in 1979. It is important to note, however, that substantial movement of households among quintiles occurred over the period, so the households in a given quintile in 1997 were not the same households that had been in that quintile in 1979. (One study, for example, showed that nearly one-third of individuals moved into a higher quintile over a 10-year period while a similar number moved to a lower one.) Furthermore, the increasing inequality shown in the declining share of income going to the lowest quintiles does not imply greater poverty. Average income can grow throughout the distribution even if relatively greater gains at the top lead to increased inequality.

The increasing inequality within the income distribution led to similar shifts in the distribution of tax liabilities. Households in the highest income quintile paid 65 percent of the four largest federal taxes in 1997, up from 57 percent 18 years earlier. In contrast, households in the bottom three quintiles paid roughly 17 percent of those taxes. The shares paid by the different quintiles varied widely among revenue sources. In 1997, households in the highest quintile bore 78 percent of individual income taxes, 82 percent of corporate income taxes, 44 percent of social insurance taxes, and 32 percent of federal excise taxes. In the same year, households in the lowest three quintiles paid 7 percent, 9 percent, 31 percent, and 47 percent of those taxes, respectively.

The Nature of the Analysis
* * *

Quintiles contain equal numbers of people. Because households vary in size, quintiles generally contain unequal numbers of households. * * *

Cautionary Notes
* * * [A]ny choice of a period over which to assess changes in effective tax rates or incomes is arbitrary. This study frequently reports the changes that occurred between 1979 and 1997, the first and last years for which the data needed for the analysis are available. Changes over other periods may show markedly different patterns. For example, between 1979 and 1997, average real pretax comprehensive income for households in the lowest quintile fell slightly. In contrast, between 1983 and 1997, that measure rose by 12 percent. In fact, however, comparing values for 1979 and 1997 may provide a more valid comparison, since those years were both high points in the business cycle whereas 1983 was the low point of a deep recession. * * *

Limitations

* * *

The study's focus on effective tax rates means that it is not a comprehensive analysis of the federal tax system. * * * Nor does the study look at the benefits households receive—in the form of goods, services, and transfer payments—that are funded by the taxes they pay. For example, the analysis considers the burden of the Social Security payroll tax but does not take into account the benefits that workers who are currently paying the tax will receive during retirement. * * *

The Distribution of Effective Tax Rates and Income

Over the past two decades, rising real incomes—incomes adjusted for the effects of inflation—have driven federal tax revenues upward while a series of changes in tax laws has first lowered and then raised effective tax rates (tax liabilities as a percentage of income). Federal taxes claimed 22.3 percent of household income in 1979; that rate fell to 20.2 percent in 1983 before climbing to nearly 23 percent in 1997. * * *

Federal taxes overall and federal income taxes in particular are progressive: the effective rate rises with income. Households in the top quintile face an effective tax rate that is more than five times that of households in the lowest quintile. Furthermore, progressivity has increased over the past two decades, primarily because the rate faced by households with the lowest incomes fell by nearly a third with the expansion in the 1990s of the earned income tax credit (EITC). * * *

Factors Contributing to Changes in Effective Tax Rates

The fall and subsequent rise in the effective rates of federal taxes over the past 20 years stem from a number of factors. The Congress has enacted multiple laws that have changed both the bases of the various federal taxes and the rates applied to them, raising or lowering revenues and shifting the relative importance of different tax sources.   The composition of income—the percentages ascribable to wages, nonwage income, and capital gains—has changed, as has the distribution of income among households facing different tax rates. And demographic shifts have increased the number of elderly, single-parent, and childless households, all of which face effective tax rates that differ from those for the shrinking population of married couples with children.

Changes in Tax Law

The Congress has enacted 15 tax bills since 1979, 11 of which boosted revenues. Those laws shifted the relative amounts of revenue raised by different taxes as well as the distribution of each tax among households. Some of the legislation focused on corporate and excise taxes; six of the laws made major changes in individual income and social insurance taxes, which together account for about five-sixths of all federal revenues. Those six laws and their important features include the following:

- The Economic Recovery Tax Act of 1981 (ERTA) cut individual income tax rates by a cumulative 25 percent over three years, dropping the top rate from 70 percent to 50 percent.[5] ERTA also indexed tax brackets for inflation, reducing the bracket "creep" that subjected taxpayers to ever higher rates as their income rose to keep pace with higher prices. * * *

- The Social Security Amendments of 1983 sped up scheduled social insurance tax increases, thus raising revenues in 1984, 1988, and 1989. The amendments also set those tax rates for self-employed people equal to the combined employer-employee taxes for other workers. The law made some Social Security benefits subject to income tax for the first time, assigning all revenues from that tax to the Social Security trust funds.

- The Tax Reform Act of 1986 (TRA-86) made major changes in the tax base and tax rates for the individual income tax. Under the law, many deductions and exclusions were limited or eliminated. In addition, the number of rate brackets was collapsed from 14 to two, and prior statutory rates that had ranged as high as 50 percent were cut to 15 percent and 28 percent. (Some taxpayers were subject to a marginal rate of 33 percent as the benefits of the 15 percent rate and exemptions were phased out.) TRA-86 also increased the levels of the personal exemption and the standard deduction. The act further changed the taxation of capital gains: it removed the 60 percent deduction and made all gains subject to ordinary tax rates, thus making the maximum rate on long-term gains for top income earners 28 percent. The law increased the amount of the EITC and indexed the credit for inflation. * * *

- The Omnibus Budget Reconciliation Act of 1990 expanded the EITC and raised the top individual income tax rate to 31 percent. The maximum statutory rate on long-term capital gains remained at 28 percent. The law also instituted a phaseout of exemptions and limited itemized deductions for upper-income taxpayers. * * *

- The Omnibus Budget Reconciliation Act of 1993 added two new tax brackets—36 percent and 39.6 percent—for high-income taxpayers. In addition, it raised the EITC further for families with children and extended the credit to childless taxpayers. The cap on wage income subject to the health insurance payroll tax was removed, thus

---

5. A maximum rate of 50 percent already applied to earnings; ERTA extended it to other sources of income.

increasing payroll taxes on high-income workers. The law also increased to 85 percent the percentage of Social Security benefits subject to income taxes for high-income taxpayers.

- The Taxpayer Relief Act of 1997 (TRA-97) established a tax credit of $500 for each dependent child under age 17, created education tax credits for postsecondary school costs, made interest on student loans deductible, and reduced the tax rate on long-term capital gains.

* * *

Changes in tax law influence the effective rate in two ways. Most directly and most obviously, they affect the taxes people pay. But they also affect the behavior of households and corporations, influencing both how much income taxpayers receive and the form in which they receive it. * * *

In combination, changes in tax law since 1979 have first lowered effective individual income tax rates and then, for high-income taxpayers, moved them back up. Expansions of the EITC sharply lowered income tax rates for low-income working households, but higher social insurance taxes offset some of those gains. In addition, removing the cap on wages subject to health insurance taxes increased payroll taxes for high-income taxpayers.

* * *

Changing Sources of Federal Revenues

The distribution of federal taxes among taxpayers depends in part on the relative importance of the four major sources of federal revenues: individual and corporate income taxes, social insurance taxes, and excise taxes. Corporate taxes fall more heavily on taxpayers at the top of the income distribution, social insurance taxes claim a larger share of middle-class income, and excise levies disproportionately affect low-income households. Over the past 20 years, the shares of federal revenues coming from those sources have varied widely. (See Figure 1-7).

The share of revenues from individual income taxes trended downward during the late 1980s, partly as a result of the cuts in rates and indexation of brackets and other parameters enacted in the Economic Recovery Tax Act of 1981 and partly because of rising payroll tax rates. Only with the steep climb in incomes since 1995 and rate increases in 1990 and 1993 has the fraction of revenues from that source returned to the levels of the early 1980s. In fiscal year 2001, individual income taxes will provide fully half of all federal revenues.

Corporate income taxes fell sharply as a share of federal revenues in the early 1980s as the economy dipped into a deep recession. Between 1983 and 1997, the trend reversed: corporate profits rebounded, and the corporate income tax share of revenues nearly doubled. * * * In fiscal year 2001, corporate taxes will make up about one-tenth of federal revenues.

Figure 1-7.

Shares of Total Federal Revenues, by Source, 1979-1997

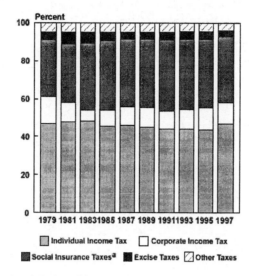

SOURCE: Congressional Budget Office.

a.   Payroll taxes financing Social Security, Medicare, and federal unemployment insurance.

Social insurance levies will provide roughly a third of all federal revenues in fiscal year 2001. The legislated increases in tax rates during the early 1980s raised the share of revenues from that source by more than a fifth, to nearly 38 percent in 1992. That share has drifted downward since then as a result of the extraordinary climb in income taxes.

The share of revenues coming from excise taxes declined steadily over the 18-year period, dropping from its high of nearly 7 percent in 1981 to less than half that level in fiscal year 2001. Much of the drop results from levies that are set not as a percentage of the price of a good but rather as a fixed dollar amount per unit sold.

Effective Tax Rates

* * *

Individual Income Taxes

The effective rate of the individual income tax for all households dipped during the 1980s before returning to essentially the same level in 1997 as it had reached in 1979 (see Figure 1-8). That lack of change over the period reflected a drop of nearly 5 percentage points (to -5.0 percent) for the lowest fifth of households, a decline of at least 1.5 percentage points for each of the middle three quintiles, and a slight rise for households with the highest incomes. Trends in effective rates during the 1990s that moved downward for low-income households and upward for those with high incomes stemmed in part from expansion of the EITC, in part from new tax brackets with higher rates, and in part from the rapid growth of income at the top of the distribution that pushed more income into the highest tax brackets. * * *

Figure 1-8.

Effective Individual Income Tax Rates, by Income Group, 1979-1997

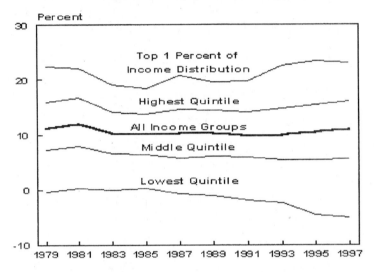

SOURCE: Congressional Budget Office.

NOTES: The effective tax rate equals individual income tax liabilities as a percentage of total income. Quintiles, or fifths, of the income distribution contain equal numbers of people.

The dramatic shift of pretax income toward the top quintile—its share increased from 46 percent to 53 percent over the period—joined with reductions in rates to shift the burden of individual income taxes onto the highest-income households. The top quintile of households paid 78 percent of total individual income taxes in 1997, up from 66 percent 18 years earlier. * * * The top 1 percent of households bore the bulk of that change: their share rose from 19 percent to 33 percent over the interval.

Social Insurance Taxes

The effective social insurance tax rate climbed steadily over most of the past two decades, rising from 6.8 percent in 1979 to 8.6 percent in 1995, as the Congress pushed up levies to improve the long-run stability of Social Security and Medicare. The rate settled slightly lower in 1997 only because more income went to the highest-income households, for whom the cap on Social Security taxes limited their exposure.[10] Over the entire period, the effective tax rate rose for every quintile, with the largest rate of increase affecting households with the lowest incomes.

Corporate Income Taxes

Between 1979 and 1997, the effective rate for the corporate income tax first declined by nearly half and then rose to a level that was half a percentage point below its level in 1979. The principal cause of that trend was the fall and subsequent rise of corporate profits. * * *

Excise Taxes

Over the past two decades, despite legislated increases in statutory rates, excise taxes have claimed a nearly constant share of income—at or just under 1 percent. That virtual lack of change in effective rates, however, obscures markedly different effects within different income categories. The lowest quintile first saw excise taxes dip from 2.1 percent of their income in 1979 to 1.6 percent in 1981 and then climb to 2.8 percent in 1997. In contrast, the quintile with the highest incomes experienced a drop in the effective rate from 0.7 percent to 0.5 percent over the same period. The overall effect was to make a regressive tax even more regressive: excise taxes claimed five times the share of income from the lowest-income households that they claimed from the highest-income households. However, to the extent that one intent of imposing excise taxes is to reduce the consumption of particular goods, that regressivity may be viewed as less onerous.

* * *

Notes and Questions

29. Over the 1979-97 period, federal tax receipts fell slightly as a percentage of gross domestic product (GDP), but rose more rapidly than the rate of inflation. Which comparison is more important in measuring whether the government's tax bite is growing?

30. A significant economic development during 1979-97 was an increase in inequality, particularly because real incomes at the top of the spectrum increased significantly. Federal revenues benefitted from this development, because an increasing share of national income was taxed at the higher rates applicable to high-income taxpayers.

---

10. Taxes for Old-Age, Survivors, and Disability Insurance are levied on earnings up to a maximum amount, which is set at $80,400 in 2001. Earnings above that limit are subject only to the Medicare payroll tax.

This led to the counterintuitive result that although tax rates fell for each income quintile, overall tax rates increased. How can this be so? If the income of high-income taxpayers is increasing more rapidly than that of taxpayers in general, a larger percentage of national income will be taxed at the higher rates applicable to high-income taxpayers. And, even after the statutory reductions, those rates were still higher than the rates applicable to lower-income taxpayers at the start of the period.

31. Observe that for the bottom quintile, the income tax rate is negative. During the 1979-97 period, the rate has dropped from approximately zero to negative five percent. This development is primarily attributable to increases in the Earned Income Tax Credit (EITC), which was further liberalized in 2001. The EITC is discussed in Chapter Eleven.

Incidence of taxation

32. In order to compile distributional tables, it is necessary to determine who bears the tax, and in some instances economists and other experts disagree. In some instances, the tax may be regarded as being borne by a party other than the taxpayer. Consider the Social Security and Medicare taxes levied on employers and employees—a total of 7.65 percent each. If the taxpayer were viewed as bearing the burden of the tax, equal amounts of tax would be borne by employees (lower income taxpayers, as a group) and half by employers (higher income taxpayers, as a group).[f] On the other hand, it might be argued that the employers' half of the tax is "really" borne by employees, because employers would pay the extra amount in higher wages if the tax did not exist. CBO, makes "[t]hat assumption, which is shared by virtually all economists."[g] This significantly affects the distribution of tax burden, because employees will tend to fall in lower quintiles than will employers.

33. CBO acknowledges that "[l]ess agreement exists on the incidence of corporate income taxes,"[h] but concludes that the tax should be allocated to owners of capital–"to households in proportion to their income from interest, dividends, rents, and capital gains"[i]—generally higher-income taxpayers. The

---

f. Because of the earnings ceiling applicable to Social Security taxes, employers pay slightly more than employees. Suppose an individual was employed by two employers during the year, and earned $100,000 from each. Of the $200,000 of total earnings, the employee would have to pay tax on only $87,000 (in 2003), but *each* of the employers would have to pay tax on the first $87,000 paid to the employee by that employer.

g. Congressional Budget Office, Effective Federal Tax Rates, 1979-1997, October 2001.

h. *Id.*

i. *Id.*

problem of the incidence of the corporate tax is discussed in Subchapter B of Chapter Fourteen.

Elimination of "bracket creep."

34. Every tax statute has political effect in appealing to, or antagonizing, certain segments of the electorate. For example, the elder President Bush's agreement to the Omnibus Budget Reconciliation Act of 1990 was widely viewed as violating his "Read my lips—no new taxes" pledge, and contributing to his defeat in 1992.

The Economic Recovery Tax Act of 1981, enacted in the first year of President Reagan's administration, made a seemingly minor change in tax law that has had lasting and growing significance, politically and economically. The income tax is progressive, which means that as incomes rise the tax increases as a percentage. If a taxpayer's income rises by twenty percent, for example, it is likely that the taxpayer's income tax will increase by somewhat more than twenty percent. Suppose that the increase in income represented no increase in buying power, because inflation increased by twenty percent during the same period. In that case, the taxpayer's *nominal* income would have increased, but his *real* income would not. With no increase in real income, the taxpayer nevertheless would find himself in a higher bracket. This phenomenon is referred to as *bracket creep*. Bracket creep enabled the Government to enjoy "automatic" tax increases without Congress being forced to vote for increases. Indeed, Congress was able to enjoy the political benefit of voting for regular tax cuts, which might return only a portion of the increase attributable to bracket creep. The 1981 Act indexed several important figures–notably tax brackets, personal and dependency exemptions, and standard deductions–so that they automatically increased with inflation. The result was that the automatic tax increases attributable to bracket creep disappeared. To avoid the political pain of voting for tax increases, Congress would have to forego additional revenue; to enjoy the political benefit of voting for tax cuts, Congress would have to make real tax cuts, and perhaps cuts in spending programs.

35. Many excise taxes are *specific*: the tax is expressed as a stated amount per unit (a specified number of cents per package of cigarettes or gallon of gasoline). Other excise taxes are *ad valorem*—for example, a tax expressed in terms of a percentage of the charge for long distance telephone calls. Why do revenues from specific excise taxes tend to lag both the rate of growth of the economy and the rate of inflation?

36. Why are excise taxes generally regressive with respect to income—that is, take a larger proportion of the income of lower-income

taxpayers than of higher-income taxpayers? What does the CBO mean in the last sentence of the excerpt, when it observes that this is "less onerous" if the tax is intended to reduce the consumption of particular goods. What is an example of such a tax?

37. Why does the increased reliance of corporations on debt adversely affect corporate income tax receipts?

Social Security taxes and Social Security benefits
38. Payroll taxes are somewhat regressive. First, unlike the income tax, payroll taxes generally do not feature a graduated rate structure. Second, the taxes are levied on earned income, which may constituted almost all the income of "working class" taxpayers, but be a much smaller proportion of income for the "moneyed class." Finally, even considering earned income alone, the biggest payroll tax, the Social Security tax, is levied only on the first $87,000 of earned income (in 2003). This means that the tax applies to all the earned income of most, but only a portion of the earned income of the highest earners.

39. While the Social Security *tax* is regressive, the Social Security *system*—taxes and benefits, taken as a whole—is markedly progressive. The CBO report does not consider the uses of Social Security taxes (or of any other taxes).

40. Consider the political arguments that could be made, legitimately, from the preceding two notes.
Similar analysis explains many of the seemingly inconsistent statements made by politicians and others speaking with political goals. Given the importance of these statements in changing tax policy, it is well for the student to observe how a single, coherent document, such as the CBO report, can be interpreted to support a range of seemingly inconsistent propositions.
For example, the top quintile and the top one percent are paying a significantly higher proportion of the federal tax burden than they were paying in 1979; at the same time, their tax rates have been cut, and they have a significantly higher share of after-tax income than in 1979.
Given that the poor pay a negative income tax at present, it might be argued that they should not share in the benefit from any cut in the income tax. On the other hand, if total tax burden is considered—and if the progressive benefit structure of the Social Security system is ignored—the lowest quintile is paying a positive tax.
What arguments currently being made in the political debate about taxes could be supported by data in the CBO report?

CHAPTER TWO

WHEN SHOULD INCOME BE TAXED?

Under the definition of "income" most widely accepted by economists, an increase in the taxpayer's net worth during the relevant accounting period constitutes income, and a decline in net worth is an offset against income. * * *

Other than by negative inference, the Code does not expressly require realization as a prerequisite for taxing income, but realization is nevertheless so basic to the taxing structure of existing law that the general principle is simply not challenged.[a]

A. INTRODUCTION: THE TIME VALUE OF MONEY

During the past quarter century, the world has changed, and tax law has not kept pace. Technological changes, and related changes in the securities markets—on-line trading, lowered brokerage commissions, the rise of no-load mutual funds, and the development of derivatives and other new financial products—have facilitated cheap and easy realization when desired for tax purposes. Taxpayers and their advisers have become much more sophisticated regarding the time value of money. In the late 1970s, at the same time computers were making computations easier, extremely high inflation and interest rates increased the stakes of tax accounting issues. One result of these developments is that the realization rule and related issues of tax accounting have been the subject of intense academic scrutiny, which we shall examine in this chapter.

The rules for measuring income for tax purposes are derived from the rules that evolved as generally accepted accounting principles. The objectives of the accounting principles, however, differ from the objective of measuring income to be subjected to tax. For accounting purposes, profit or loss is computed so owners of a business and prospective lenders or investors can know how well, or how poorly, the business is doing. Similarly, accounting defines the assets and liabilities of a business to serve the needs of its owners and creditors, and of prospective investors.

For tax purposes, the objective is to measure profit to determine the portion to be paid as income tax. Timing is extremely important for this purpose. If a taxpayer enjoys an accession to wealth but can postpone the associated tax liability, the taxpayer then can earn subsequent profits on what

---

a. BORIS I. BITTKER & MARTIN J. MCMAHON, JR., FEDERAL INCOME TAXATION OF INDIVIDUALS ¶3.2 (2d ed. 1995).

is, in essence, the Government's share. How important this is depends on the length of deferral, and on the current levels of tax rates and interest rates.

Taxpayers can postpone tax liability if they can speed up business expense deductions so that the deductions precede actual cash outlays—for example, by setting up a reserve for anticipated expenses. On the receipts side, tax liability can be postponed if the benefits from appreciation in the value of assets can be converted into additional earning potential before the appreciation in value has been taken into account.

An appreciation of the importance of the time value of money is extremely important in the study of tax law and policy. As indicated above, three variables are involved. First is the amount deferred, which, in the case of a deferred tax obligation, is usually dependent on the marginal rate of tax. The value of deferring an obligation to pay a given amount depends upon the length of the deferral, and the assumed rate at which money can be invested over the deferral period. Consider the value to a taxpayer of postponing payment of a $1,000 tax versus paying the $1,000 currently. If one assumes a five percent rate of interest and a five-year deferral, the present value of the obligation shrinks to $784; if the deferral is for 10 years, the present value is $614; and a 30-year deferral reduces the present value to only $231. If the rate of interest is assumed to be 10 percent, the five-year deferral reduces the present value of the obligation to $621, the 10-year deferral to $386, and the 30-year deferral to a mere $57. Observe that a very lengthy deferral—for example, the purchase of a deductible IRA by a young person, who pays tax many years later during retirement—removes the bulk of the tax burden if a modest rate of interest is assumed, and virtually eliminates the tax if a higher rate is assumed. But even a one-year deferral has noticeable value; if 10 percent interest is assumed, the present value of the deferred $1,000 obligation is reduced to $909.[b]

An important application of the time value of money is growing recognition among policymakers that immediate expensing of capital expenditures is the equivalent of *eliminating* (and not merely reducing) tax on the income ultimately generated by the capital. In the following brief excerpt, Professors Alan Gunn and Larry Ward explain this counterintuitive phenomenon:[c]

---

b. All figures in this note are derived from MICHAEL J. GRAETZ & DEBORAH H. SCHENK, FEDERAL INCOME TAXATION: PRINCIPLES AND POLICIES 853 (Appendix A, Table 1) (1995).

c. Professors Gunn and Ward state that "[t]he equivalence between current deductibility and exemption of return was first noted in Brown, Business-Income Taxation and Investment Incentives; in L. Metzler et al., Income, Employment and Public Policy; reprinted in R. MUSGRAVE & C. SHOUP, Readings in the Economics of Taxation (1959)." ALAN GUNN & LARRY D. WARD, FEDERAL INCOME TAXATION 288-89 (5th ed. 2002).

FEDERAL INCOME TAXATION
Alan Gunn[*] & Larry D. Ward[**]

Pages 287-88 (5th ed., 2002)

[A]llowing an immediate deduction for the cost of a long-lived income-producing asset produces the same effect as capitalizing the cost and exempting the income the asset earns from taxation, providing certain conditions are met.[b] Consider a taxpayer who pays $100,000 for a machine with a ten-year life and no salvage value. The machine will generate $20,000 in revenue each year (a 20-percent pre-tax return on the $100,000 cost), all of which (except for income taxes) the taxpayer will spend on consumption. Assume that the taxpayer has a large amount of other income, and that the taxpayer is subject to a flat-rate 40-percent income tax. If the taxpayer capitalizes the cost of the machine and takes straight-line depreciation, the taxpayer's decision to purchase the asset rather than to spend its purchase price on consumption amounts to a decision to give up $100,000 of consumption in the year the machine was bought in exchange for $16,000 annual consumption[c] over a ten-year period.

Now suppose the taxpayer is offered a tax exemption for the earnings from the machine. Because the machine produces no taxable income, no depreciation is allowed. The taxpayer will be able to spend $20,000 a year for ten years.

If, instead of an exemption for the machine's earnings, an immediate deduction for the purchase price of the machine (and of similar machines) were allowed, the taxpayer would still be able to spend $20,000 a year for ten years. We have assumed that the taxpayer was willing to give up $100,000 of current consumption to buy a non-deductible machine. If the cost of machines is deductible, the taxpayer can buy $166,666.67 worth of machines by giving up $100,000 of consumption (because the out-of-pocket cost of an immediately deductible $166,666.67 investment to a 40-percent taxpayer is $100,000). The gross return on this investment will be $33,333.33 (20-percent of $166,666.67) a year. This amount will be fully taxable (no depreciation being allowed because the cost of the machine was deducted at the time of purchase). Therefore, the taxpayer will be able to spend 60-percent of this sum, or $20,000, each year.

---

*. At time of original publication, John N. Matthews Professor of Law, University of Notre Dame.

**. At time of original publication, Dykstra Professor of Law, University of Iowa.

b. The conditions are that rates of return on investments and tax rates are constant, and that the taxpayer has enough income so that deductions are not wasted. [Footnotes b and c in this excerpt are the authors' footnotes, as designated in the original source. (Ed.)]

c. The machine will generate a $20,000 annual cash return, but only $10,000 in taxable income (because of the $10,000 annual depreciation deduction). Each year's income tax will be $4000, leaving the taxpayer $16,000 to spend.

The equivalence between an immediate deduction and an exemption for return on investment holds for any constant rate of return and tax rate. * * *

Notes and Questions

1.   Application of the principle demonstrated by Professors Gunn and Ward is not limited to capital equipment. For example, compare a traditional individual retirement account and a Roth IRA.   Under the traditional arrangement, qualifying taxpayers can deduct the amount of the contribution, compound the investment tax-free until distribution (typically in retirement), then include the entire amount of the distributions in income. Every dollar of investment income is taxed; the tax benefit is "merely" deferral. With a Roth IRA, no deduction is allowed on the initial contribution, but upon distribution, the entire amount is received free of taxation. Unlike the traditional IRA, the taxpayer investing in a Roth IRA is never taxed on the investment income. As Gunn and Ward explain, economically—though not obviously, and for that reason, not politically—the taxpayer's advantage of immediate deduction (traditional IRA) is equivalent to the advantage of investing with after-tax dollars and receiving the investment return tax-free (Roth IRA).

2.   The "equivalence" of immediate expensing and forgiveness of income—or of a traditional IRA and a Roth IRA—is subject to qualifications.

First, equality holds only if the amounts involved are in fact equivalent. For example, if we assume a 25 percent tax rate, a taxpayer who invests $1,000 in a traditional IRA is economically in the same position as a taxpayer who invests $750 in a Roth IRA. (In the year that the two IRAs are established, the after-tax cost of either will be $750.) By contrast, if the Roth IRA investor actually invests $1,000 (at a greater initial cost, because in after-tax dollars), that taxpayer will ultimately have more after-tax dollars in retirement.

3.   And are the two tax approaches "equivalent" from the Government's perspective? Yes, in that the expected revenue costs of allowing traditional IRAs and Roth IRAs are equivalent in present value terms. But they are completely different regarding when the revenue costs hit. The traditional IRA reduces government revenues immediately; the Roth IRA does not. At the other end, when the taxpayers receive distributions from the IRAs, the situation is reversed: the Government receives full revenue from distributions from the traditional IRA, but no revenue from the Roth IRA.

Especially when one considers the budgetary rules under which Congress operates (a topic considered in detail in Chapter Seventeen, Subchapter C), the political differences are enormous. The revenue cost of a traditional IRA will show up immediately. But if Congress is focusing on a five- or ten-year budget window, implementing generous Roth IRA deductions may appear to cost the Government very little.

4.   The preceding note suggests that the political effect of the equivalence of immediate deduction and later deferral will lead Congress to opt, as with the Roth IRA, for later deferral. At least one political effect points the other way, however. When Congress allows an immediate deduction, as with expensing under section 179, it appears that Congress is "simply" allowing an appropriate deduction early—a "mere" timing matter. It may look more like a "giveaway to special interests" if Congress permanently exempts income from taxation.

5.   For business accounting purposes it is useful to match receipts and expenses in order to measure profit or loss on a particular segment of business operations, either for an operating division or for a time segment. Should such matching be the standard for measuring taxable income?

B. THE HAIG-SIMONS DEFINITION OF INCOME

Subject to very limited exceptions,[d] the present tax system does not take appreciation in value into account until the appreciation has been realized—typically by sale of the appreciated asset.

Professor Henry Simons, an economist, challenged the conventional accounting definition of income. Departing from the constraints of realization, he wrote: "Personal income may be defined as the algebraic sum of (1) the market value of rights exercised in consumption and (2) the change in the value of the store of property rights between the beginning and end of the period in question."[e] In recognition of earlier work, this is sometimes referred to as the Schanz-Haig-Simons definition or, more frequently, the Haig-Simons definition. In the first excerpt, written in 1938, Professor Simons strongly criticized use of accountants' conservative definition of income for tax purposes. In the second excerpt, published posthumously in 1950, he presented a set of examples that he thought demonstrated the unfairness of postponing until realization the treatment of appreciation in value as income.

Even if one assumes the theoretical validity of the Haig-Simons definition, significant practical problems limit its utility. Mr. Louie's note focuses on marketable securities, an area in which the Haig-Simons definition could realistically be implemented because market prices are known and valuation problems would be minimized. The excerpt, however, summarizes practical advantages and disadvantages of taxing unrealized appreciation in general.

Application of a pure form of the Haig-Simons definition is impractical because it would require annual appraisal of assets. There is also the possibility that it would be unconstitutional, a topic addressed by Marvin

---

d. The mark-to-market method, which taxes unrealized appreciation, can be applicable to securities dealers and with respect to commodity contracts. See sections 475 and 1256.

e. HENRY C. SIMONS, PERSONAL INCOME TAXATION 50 (1938).

Chirelstein in the final excerpt of this subchapter. In *Eisner v. Macomber*,[f] the Supreme Court endorsed realization as a constitutional requirement for taxing income. Is this 1920 decision still binding? Professor Chirelstein thinks the answer is clearly "no," but he does not assume that Congress should tax unrealized appreciation even if the Constitution permits it to do so.

PERSONAL INCOME TAXATION
Henry C. Simons[*]
Pages 80-83 (1938)

We turn now to brief consideration of the familiar criterion of realization. A standard manual on our federal income tax quotes Professor Haig's definition of income and then remarks: "It should include the word realized"[53]—as though the omission were only a careless oversight! This view is widely held by accountants, by the courts, and even by some economists. It derives clearly enough from the conventional practices of financial accounting. The accountant, faced with problems of valuation for which data are often meager, has developed and followed religiously a rule-of-thumb procedure which sacrifices relevance to "accuracy." Instead of attempting the best estimates which can be made, he is usually content to employ figures already available in his accounts and thus to minimize demands upon mere judgment.[54]

His methods appear to be founded upon profound mistrust of both his professional colleagues and his employers. The reputable accountant never loses sight of the fact that his income statements are influential in matters of dividend policy. Income, for him, is perhaps only what may be reported safely to unsophisticated directors as income. He aims, it would seem, never to ascertain what income is, in any really definable sense, but rather to devise rules of calculation which will make the result a minimum or at least give large answers only in the future. Conventional accounting, moreover, not only employs a procedure with a markedly conservative bias but promptly repudiates this procedure whenever it shows signs of working the other way. When prices drawn from actual transactions on his books afford excessive estimates, the accountant promptly appeals to the market for his valuations.

That such worship of conservatism—and professional conspiracy against truth—is an unmixed evil, in a world of corruptible accountants and optimistic

---

f. 252 U.S. 189 (1920).

*. At time of original publication, Professor of Economics, University of Chicago.

53. Montgomery, *Income Tax Procedure* (New York, 1926), p. 590. One wonders how Haig may react to his colleague's proposal to destroy his definition by introducing an innocent little participle. Likewise, one might wish to know with what feeling Schanz may have read Max Lion's essay in the volume dedicated to Schanz (*Beitrage zur Finanzwissenschaft*) [Tubingen 1928], II, 273-300). Lion * * * finds that Schanz is not clearly free from the careless error which Montgomery has noted in Haig!

54. One might say that he often eschews valuation entirely. At least, one finds difficulty in the idea that an inventory is being "valued" when different parts of an inventory of identical goods are priced differently—as is approved practice.

directors, one may hesitate to assert. Where such rule-of-thumb procedure is so universal, however, there is undue resistance to departure from it where different methods are clearly desirable. Furthermore, there is in many quarters a disposition to maintain that methods of calculation deemed expedient in business indicate exhaustively the real meaning of income. It is easy for most people to elevate rules-of-thumb into logical necessities; and persons do seriously maintain, with more than verbal paradox, that income not realized is not income. Our comments need imply no criticism of the accountant's practical wisdom; yet one may lament the effects of his practice and preaching upon unwary minds, especially in a world where courts insist upon investing somewhat technical terms with their connotations in everyday usage.

Advocates of the recurrence criterion have undertaken to construct a concept of personal income from that of productivity or yield from things. Those who emphasize realization are attempting to define personal income in terms of transaction profit. In either case, it simply cannot be done. If all business ventures were initiated and completed within the fiscal period, the realization criterion would lead to no serious confusion. But, in a world where ventures often have neither beginning nor end within the lives of interested parties, it is hard to argue that one may grow richer indefinitely without increasing one's income. Furthermore, since transaction income implies no imputation to preassigned periods of time, how may one develop from it a conception wherein such imputation is fundamental?

The emphasis of accounting upon the transaction of sale would be fairly appropriate for merely merchandising enterprises, if only prices were extremely stable. It is always more appropriate to merchandising than to manufacture and, in general, is least expedient for enterprises where the selling function is least important. But surely no adequate conception of annual, personal income can be built around the notion of transaction profit. To be sure, one never knows the final result of a business venture until it is completed. But the whole notion of accrual must be abandoned if one adheres rigorously to the test of realization. The argument that recognition of appreciation involves "anticipation of profit" which may never be obtained, fails to recognize the fundamental continuity of economic relations and ignores the essential value implications of income.

* * *

FEDERAL TAX REFORM
Henry C. Simons[*]
Pages 61-65, 67 (1950)

At risk of laboring the obvious, let us now indicate, in terms of some extreme possible cases, how existing procedure actually works. For this

---

[*]. At time of original publication, Late Professor of Economics, University of Chicago.

purpose, it seems best to proceed in terms of the law as it stood before 1920, since the "realization procedure" with which we are mainly concerned was simpler under earlier legislation and, while becoming more complicated, has persisted throughout the years substantially unaltered in its essential features. In some of the cases, incidentally, it may be useful to think of "the corporation" as an investment-trust, widely diversified, with many large shareholders subject to high surtaxes and with a numerous minority interest as well.

Case I.—A very wealthy diversifying "operator" might, through a most profitable life, show little or no taxable income at all, while living like a king and steadily increasing his net worth. The trick, of course, is simply to "realize" all of one's losses on investments and none of one's gains; or—in an irresistible phrasing—to have and to hold all faithful (appreciated) investments till death (do us part) and to divorce opportunely all unfaithful (depreciated) shares. The appreciation, as potentially taxable gain accrued, vanishes completely at the moment of parting of body and soul.[g] Save for death duties (which of course depend on current value, not at all on the decedent's unrealized gains or losses) the next generation can start all over, and with greatly elevated "bases" for future loss realizations.

Case II.—Saving through unrealized appreciation (undistributed corporate earnings) *vs.* other savings: the income tax as spending tax on some, as income tax on others.

Jones and Smith are born on the same day, inherit estates of $2.5 millions simultaneously, hold common stocks in companies which each year earn exactly 4 per cent, and die simultaneously. Each maintains the same consumption outlay or living scale throughout life—"spending," say, $50,000 per year—and reinvests any residual income each year.

Jones invests entirely in companies which (irregularities aside) pay out all their earnings in dividends. Thus, at 4 per cent, his income is exactly $100,000 every year. He pays his income tax each year on that amount (say, a tax of $35,000, or an average rate of 35 per cent) and reinvests what's left ($100,000 - $50,000 - $35,000 = $15,000) in additional stock of the same companies.

Smith, on the other hand, puts his $2.5 millions all in a big investment-trust corporation—which, as it happens, owns the same stocks as Jones and in the same proportions. The corporation earns exactly 4 per cent, of course, but invariably pays out only two-thirds of its earnings in dividends, reinvesting the other one-third. Smith thus has a "real income" each year of $100,000 but a taxable income of only $66,667. Letting the corporation do his saving for him, he is able to exclude his savings from income tax, confining his taxable income (i.e., dividends) to the amount he needs to meet his taxes and his consumption

---

g. Simons is referring to the generous tax treatment of giving heirs a basis equal to fair market value at death, thereby exempting decedent, estate, and heirs from income tax on any appreciation. *See* section 1014. This is the subject of Chapter Ten. (Ed.)

outlays. Thus the taxes (at an average rate of 25 per cent) might amount to $16,667.

Thus, Smith with the same initial wealth and real income as Jones, and the same "spendings," has much more left ($33,333 *vs.* $15,000!) for reinvestment the first year, consequently more income each year thereafter and, so, still more to reinvest than Jones. When they die, Smith will be enormously wealthier than Jones; and the little Smiths and little Joneses will thereafter be regarded as belonging to families at different social and economic levels.

Now Jones may, in the circumstances, be called either stupidly scrupulous about eschewing avoidance opportunities or just plain stupid. Consider, however, what he could have done to keep up with Smith (Smith's wealth-headstart apart) if his income had been a salary income; if it had come from a partnership (say, a law firm); or how he could have exploited the avoidance opportunity if his wealth and income had initially been smaller, and his income not such as to permit much saving. "The richer you are, the faster you should be allowed to get richer," says our realization procedure, while the bracket-rates raucously dissent.

Case III.—Capital-gain income versus other income: taxable income excluding saving and much of "spendings," i.e., excluding even much income realized and consumed.

Brown and Gray each inherit $2.5 million simultaneously at age 21. Both consume their whole real incomes throughout life, saving nothing but preserving their estates intact, and then die simultaneously. They are equally successful in their investments, getting yields, including imputed earnings undistributed, of 4 per cent annually. (We may conveniently assume that changing market values of their shares reflect, at least at death, merely changes of book-values, i.e., undistributed corporate earnings.)

Brown invests exclusively in businesses which pay out regularly their full (and stable) earnings. Thus, his taxable income is $100,000. After paying his income tax (say $35,000), he spends all the rest ($65,000).

Gray puts his estate entirely in shares of an investment company, whose portfolio has, it happens, the same composition as Brown's. By tacit understanding among executives and the numerous shareholders, this company pays no dividends at all but maintains the market price of its shares at the current break-up value. * * * Gray's share in earnings is, of course, $100,000 per year; the market price of his shares rises by 4 per cent (compounded) annually. To meet his living expenses, i.e., to "realize" his full annual income, *he sells each year 4 per cent of his (then remaining) shares.*

The arithmetic here gets a bit complicated as the years pass. The crucial point, however, should be apparent, Gray's taxable income will never even approximate his stable real income of $100,000. Maintaining his capital at the same level as Brown's, he can spend far more than Brown and leave him far behind in the social game of invidious consumption. Thus, in the first year,

Gray sells (almost) 4 per cent of his shares for $100,000. His gain *on these shares* is 4 per cent or only $4,000, which *is* his total *taxable* income for the first year. Compound interest makes for arithmetic complexity from here on. However, his taxable income for the second year will be only a bit over $8,000; for the third year, $12,000 plus; and so on, until, in the seventeenth year, it reaches about $50,000, or half of Brown's! Taking account of family exemptions and progressive rates, one sees that while Brown pays tax of, say, $35,000 every year, Gray pays a few *hundred* dollars at first, pays more each year until, in the seventeenth year, he is paying perhaps $12,000, and would get up to, say, $20,000 (taxable income of $75,000) only after his shares had quadrupled in price (35 years, at 4 per cent compounded). Remember that the two taxpayers started with the same wealth, got the same return on their investments, and kept at the same wealth level. Brown has $65,000 left to live on each year after taxes. Gray has over $99,000 left to "spend" the first year, $88,000 in the seventeenth year, and still $80,000 in the thirty-fourth year!

Adding insult to injury, present law says that only half of Gray's realized capital gains shall be treated as income![h] Thus, he pays *on* only $2,000 the first year; *on* $25,000 in the seventeenth year; *on* $37,500 in the thirty-fourth year * * *—while Brown pays on $100,000 every year! * * *

The cases considered above are symptomatic, not merely descriptive. They should suffice to persuade people that something is rather fundamentally wrong with our income tax, present and past, to support our diagnosis, and to establish a *prima facie* case for the surgical or remedial measures here prescribed. Surely there is something radically wrong with a law under which such flagrant avoidance is legal and feasible—under which the cases described *could* occur frequently or at all.

* * *

NOTE, REALIZING APPRECIATION WITHOUT SALE: ACCRUAL TAXATION OF CAPITAL GAINS ON MARKETABLE SECURITIES

Mark L. Louie[*]

34 Stanford Law Review 857, 861-71 (1982)

The realization requirement is a significant administrative rule in any income tax system; it determines what increments of wealth will be presently taxed and what increments will be taxed in the future. The realization requirement enables taxpayers to strategically target gains and losses for particular tax years. This Part discusses the advantages and disadvantages of requiring the taxpayer to recognize all income in the year it accrues.

The Advantages of Annually Taxing Appreciation

The federal tax system relies primarily on the personal income tax to

---

h. Under present law, all capital gain is subject to tax, but generally at rates lower than those applicable to ordinary income. Section 1(h).

*. Student author.

generate governmental revenues, and generally favors taxing the appreciation of capital assets in the year the appreciation occurs.[19] Taxing without regard to realization has three principal advantages: It broadens the tax base, it improves the equity of the tax system, and it encourages efficient asset sales.

Broadening the income tax base

Under an income tax, income is taxed unless substantial policy reasons justify excluding it from the tax base. The annual appreciation in the value of capital assets is part of the tax base and should be taxed unless doing so can be shown to be substantially disadvantageous. Eliminating the realization requirement for capital assets would result in unrealized capital gains being included in the tax base; exclusion reduces the size of the tax base and forces the remaining items to bear a higher tax rate.

Improving the equity of the income tax

A second advantage of eliminating the realization requirement is that it would improve the equity of the tax system. Wealth in the United States is generally more concentrated than income.[22] Because of the realization requirement, the wealthiest members of society can defer the payment of taxes on substantial amounts of unrealized capital gains income. This ability to defer taxes amounts to an interest-free loan from the government to the taxpayer; consequently, the realization requirement allows the wealthy to keep more funds invested, increases the return on their initial investment, and allows them to defer even more taxes. Furthermore, when they eventually sell their capital assets, the deferral means that fewer real dollars are paid in taxes. The result is that the effective rate of tax on the appreciation of capital assets is much lower than the nominal rate.

The principle of vertical equity requires that individuals be taxed according to their ability to pay. Well-to-do taxpayers have a greater ability to pay than low-income taxpayers, and therefore should bear relatively larger tax burdens. The realization requirement allows well-to-do taxpayers to defer payment of taxes on unrealized capital gains income and, in some cases, to escape payment of taxes entirely through section 1014's stepped-up basis at death. * * * Eliminating the realization requirement would improve the general equity of the income tax by increasing its progressivity.

The "lock-in" phenomenon

The realization requirement and the stepped-up basis at death combine to lock investors into their investment portfolios. Because taxpayers do not have to pay taxes on the increase in value of an asset until they sell or exchange it, taxpayers will resist selling appreciated property even though

---

19. R. MUSGRAVE & P. MUSGRAVE, PUBLIC FINANCE IN THEORY AND PRACTICE (2d ed. 1980), at 231.

22. The wealthiest 20% of American households hold roughly 76% of all net wealth, and the wealthiest 1% hold 20% of all net wealth. By contrast, the 20% of the population with the highest money incomes received only 41% of all money income. R. MUSGRAVE & P. MUSGRAVE, *supra* note 19, at 348.

they may have better available investments, or are in need of cash. The investors are said to be "locked in" because of the tax penalty that they would incur if they were to sell their property and realize the gains. If the investor is well-to-do and elderly, the lock-in problem becomes even more acute: The incentives to hold an asset until death so that the basis can be increased to market value—allowing the unrealized gain to escape taxation entirely—become even greater.

The lock-in problem not only inconveniences investors who would prefer to sell their appreciated assets, but also impedes the flow of capital from one investment to another. Older investments that are no longer as profitable as newer ones tend to be kept longer, and new investments have more difficulty attracting capital than would be optimal. Eliminating the realization requirement would mean that capital gains income would be taxed regardless of whether the asset had been sold. Taxpayers would therefore have no incentive to retain less profitable investments to avoid paying taxes, and the lock-in phenomenon would be eliminated.

Problems With Taxing Appreciation

Although eliminating the realization requirement will increase the theoretical accuracy of the tax system, in application it could encounter significant problems. These problems relate to the valuation of capital assets, the "paper" nature of unrealized capital gains, the effect on the capital markets, and the economic responses of private parties to the change in the tax rules.

Valuation and liquidity

One argument against taxing unrealized capital appreciation is that capital assets cannot be accurately valued until they are sold. Some assets are easier to value than others. Closing stock prices appear in the financial sections of major newspapers and are accurate indicators of value. Valuing real estate or partnership interests, on the other hand, requires an appraisal and involves significant administrative costs. Silver and art collections are still harder to value, the results even more uncertain, and the attempt to value even more expensive.

The difficulty of valuation is linked to the liquidity of the asset: The less liquid an asset, the harder it is to value and the less reliable is the result.

* * * [S]tocks, bonds, and other marketable securities are very easy to value and can readily be converted into cash; therefore, valuation and liquidity problems do not pose a barrier to including their appreciation in the tax base.

Paper gains and cash flow problems

Even if valuation could be performed accurately, the gain is only a "paper gain"—one that accrues even though the taxpayer receives no cash. This paper gain can be lost at any time until the taxpayer sells the underlying asset. Shareholders with substantial paper gains in one year are at risk until they liquidate their investment; they can easily lose the profit if the market falls in subsequent years. If the asset is illiquid and the investor is unable easily to convert the asset to cash, or if he can do so only at a substantial cost, taxing the unrealized capital gains income may create inequity.

Because a paper gain does not generate cash, taxing such a gain can create cash squeezes. Taxpayers may have tax liabilities, but not the cash necessary to pay them. To pay their taxes, they will be forced to sell some of their assets. If the taxpayers cannot borrow against their unrealized gains, they will have to sell assets they otherwise would have retained.

Effect on equity markets

Annually taxing stock appreciation would drive down stock prices, or at least cause them to increase less rapidly, because it would reduce a stockholder's after-tax return. Corporations that raise capital in the equity markets would therefore find equity capital to be relatively more expensive; they would have to sell more shares at a lower price to raise the same amount of capital.

For most large corporations, increasing the cost of equity capital would not be troublesome because capital requirements can be met by borrowing funds and using retained earnings. But some sectors of the economy must frequently go to the equity markets and would be particularly hurt by an appreciations tax. Public utilities, for example, have an enormous need for capital and frequently go to the equity and debt markets. Similarly, high-growth companies must frequently raise additional equity capital and could be adversely affected by an appreciations tax. Because of their rapid expansion, high-growth companies may not be able to generate enough capital through retained earnings and debt to finance optimal or efficient rates of growth. These firms are forced to go to the equity markets. And in the case of smaller high-technology firms and start-up companies, debt capacity is limited and equity capital may be the only viable alternative.

The higher cost of equity capital can be expected to cause some corporations to decide not to issue equity and to delay or curtail expansion plans and purchases of capital equipment. Investors who were willing to take a certain amount of risk for a given return may be unwilling to take as much risk when an appreciations tax reduces the after-tax rate of return. As a result, less growth will occur in some of the most dynamic and productive sectors of the economy.

Corporations currently in need of capital have a number of incentives to borrow rather than to sell equity: Interest is deductible, investment bankers charge substantially smaller underwriting fees, and debt does not dilute equity ownership interests. Taxing the appreciation of corporate stock would give corporations yet another reason to prefer debt. Although dividends are now taxed twice—once at the corporate level and once at the individual level—retained earnings are exempt from the individual tax. Stock appreciation reflects, in part, the increased value of a company due to retention and investment of earnings. Taxing the annual appreciation of corporate stock would eliminate a portion of the present favorable tax treatment of retained earnings, but interest payments would still be deductible. A corporation would prefer a higher debt/equity ratio.

A primary reason that corporations are interested in obtaining debt financing is that the leverage provided by borrowed funds increases return on equity so long as the firm's before-tax rate of return is greater than the interest rate it must pay on the funds that it borrows. But lenders require borrowers to make interest payments regardless of the borrower's financial condition. Interest payments are fixed costs, whereas dividend payments are not. * * * [T]he presence of fixed interest costs and the smaller equity base cause a leveraged firm's return on equity to fluctuate much more than its earnings before interest and taxes. Increasing a firm's debt levels thus leads to a more volatile after-tax earnings record, which means the investment is riskier.

* * * This suggests that corporations will not be willing to raise large amounts of capital by borrowing. But an appreciations tax will make raising equity capital seem relatively expensive, and the corporations may be reluctant to pay the returns that the equity markets demand. With less new capital raised through debt and less new capital raised through equity, there could be less investment and slower economic growth, particularly in the sectors most dependent on equity.

An appreciations tax also seems likely to increase the pressures for higher dividend payments, further reducing a corporation's available cash. Under current tax law, dividends are taxed twice, while retained earnings are taxed only at the corporate level. With an appreciations tax, both retained earnings and dividends would be taxed twice, and the bias against paying dividends would be reduced. In addition, shareholders, especially those with substantial holdings, could be expected to demand higher dividends to provide cash to pay the appreciations tax. * * *

Private responses to changed rule

Since some assets are more liquid and more easily valued than others, most proposals to eliminate the realization requirement target specific groups of assets. To avoid thorny valuation and liquidity problems, these proposals would tax only the appreciation of those capital assets that are easily valued and relatively liquid. Other capital assets would continue to be taxed as they are under the current tax law. Unfortunately, the decision to tax only some assets' capital appreciation probably would cause private investors to shift their funds from assets subject to the appreciations tax into assets not subject to the tax, thereby distorting optimal investment behavior.

In tax law, the problem of drawing lines between taxed and untaxed behavior is troublesome because there are powerful financial incentives to be on the untaxed side of the line, and large amounts of capital tend to flow from more heavily taxed investments into those less heavily taxed. If only stocks traded on major exchanges were taxed, there would be a tremendous incentive not to be listed on the exchanges. If shares of all publicly held corporations were taxed, there would be a drive to "go private" or stay private. If

commercial real estate is taxed and residential real estate is not, capital will flee the commercial real estate market into the residential market. Arbitrary line-drawing in the tax area creates substantial economic distortion; any division between those assets made subject to the appreciations tax and those assets not made so should seek to minimize this distortion.
* * *

FEDERAL INCOME TAXATION
Marvin A. Chirelstein[*]
Pages 71-73 (7th ed. 1994)

It is important to remind oneself at the outset that realization is strictly an administrative rule and not a constitutional, much less an economic, requirement of "income." Early cases, like *Macomber*[i], do give support to the idea that the Constitution limits "income" to realized gains, but at present most tax commentators would be likely to feel that the Congressional taxing power is not seriously restricted by such an implied requirement, and that Congress is free to treat gains and losses as "realized" pretty much whenever it chooses. Congress could surely tax property appreciation at gift or at death if it desired to do so, and while a gift or bequest can be regarded as a realization event through semantic manipulation, it is difficult to suppose at this late date that the constitutionality of taxing such appreciation would depend on whether gifts and bequests could be forced into the mold of "realization."

Assuming, moreover, that "income" refers to the annual increase in one's disposable wealth, then, from an economic standpoint, a stock owner whose unsold shares have appreciated in value by $1,000 over the course of a year has just as much "income" as a stock owner who receives $1,000 in dividends or a speculator who sells his shares and realizes $1,000 of trading profits. The latter two, of course, are taxed currently, while the former, owing to the realization requirement, is permitted to treat his gain as exempt from tax until he disposes of his appreciated shares. Yet the increase in disposable wealth is identical for each, though reflected in cash in the latter cases and in kind in the former. To be sure, stock that has gone up one year may go down the next and finally be sold for no more than the original purchase price. But the same is true for the trader who sells his stock at year-end and reinvests the gain in other shares which subsequently decline, or of the dividend-recipient whose company sustains an operating loss in the period following. We may indeed wish to do something about fluctuating income through the adoption of an averaging device of some sort but the possibility that income will fluctuate from year to year, or that gains *may* be succeeded by losses, can hardly be taken to show that the taxpayer has not been enriched when the value of his property appreciates. * * *

---

[*]. At time of original publication, Professor of Law, Columbia University.

i. Eisner v. Macomber, 252 U.S. 189 (1920). (Ed.)

Yet all this argumentation should not be taken to mean that an overall change in the realization requirement is contemplated or even desirable. Our tax system does not reach mere changes in property value, and apart from recurring proposals to treat gifts and bequests as realization events, few commentators would suggest that the realization requirement should be materially altered. The difficulty of making annual property appraisals may be the chief reason for this attitude of acceptance; the absence of ready cash to pay the tax on property appreciation and the consequent "forced liquidation" of assets to meet tax obligations is another. To be sure, neither reason is especially compelling where readily marketable property (*e.g.*, listed securities) is concerned; nor * * * does the law shrink from taxing compensation even when received in kind. Still, the justifications for a realization requirement seem reasonably strong to most observers, and as stated, no overall change is imminent. My main purpose here, in any case, is not to question realization as a policy matter; rather, my object is to stress that because the realization requirement exists, the income tax is a tax on *transactions* instead of being a tax on income in the economic sense. Dividends, interest and rents, gains on sales of property, salaries, wages and fees—all these are taxable because they occur through the medium of an "exchange." Property appreciation, though undoubtedly an enrichment to the property owner, is exempt from tax precisely because the transactional aspect is thought to be lacking.

[The application of the realization requirement] in close cases is fairly arbitrary. In that respect, as in others, realization bears a resemblance to the problem of cost-recovery. Once again, what is chiefly at stake from the taxpayer's standpoint is the anticipation or deferral of tax payments—that is, the timing of taxable income. An investor who sells appreciated property for cash pays a tax on the appreciation currently and can reinvest only the after-tax proceeds. An investor who retains his appreciated property—or who can somehow dispose of it without triggering off a "realization"—pays no tax and therefore has more available for reinvestment. Although unrealized appreciation may be taxed in the future if the property is sold, the postponement can be of considerable value to the property-owner, * * * and it is often worth his while to litigate when the application of the realization rule is in doubt.

* * *

Notes and Questions

6.   In the excerpt from his 1938 book, Professor Simons harshly criticizes the approach of accountants in failing to use market value of assets when it is higher than cost. If viewed as criticism of the accounting profession rather than of the tax system, is this criticism deserved?

7.   Simons was concerned that accountants' traditional conservative assumptions would lead to understatement of income for tax purposes.

However, he did not necessarily condemn this "worship of conservatism" in the non-tax setting. After all, this is "a world of corruptible accountants and optimistic directors," an observation no less true today than in 1938. Recent experience indicates that while accountants and management are likely to work together to show the lowest possible income for tax purposes, accountants sometimes fail to assure that management does not overstate income for non-tax purposes. Recent scandals, such as those brought to light in the collapse of Enron and WorldCom, remind us that failure to adhere to accepted accounting practices can have serious consequences for a company's creditors, shareholders, and employees.

8. Modern writers also emphasize the differences of tax accounting and financial accounting. Professor Deborah Geier takes aim at the accounting principle of matching income and related expenses: "While the matching principle is a highly valued one in the financial accounting profession, for quite understandable reasons, it is not one that should be considered a value at all in a system that seeks to collect revenue."[j] Geier argues that "time value of money is critically important in a system that measures tax liabilities periodically. The matching principle, as developed by financial accounting, is often antithetical to time-value-of-money principles."[k]

9. Simons argues that adherence to the realization rule leads to "defin[ing] personal income in terms of transaction profit." Similarly, Professor Chirelstein states that "because the realization requirement exists, the income tax is a tax on *transactions* instead of being a tax on income in the economic sense." Are these observations accurate? If so, is a transactional tax objectionable?

10. Professor Simons is amused (see footnote 54 from Simons' 1938 book) at the results of traditional procedures of inventory valuation during periods of inflation. Does business accounting, using the Last In, First Out (LIFO) method, accurately measure merchandising profit in periods of inflation?

11. In assessing Simons' 1950 condemnation of the realization principle, it should be remembered that he is condemning the more-or-less "pure" form of the realization principle that existed in the years immediately following 1913, and not always actual law as it existed even in 1950 (and even less today). Thus, it might be argued that it has been possible to close off many of the worst abuses of the "pure" realization system without abandoning its relative simplicity.

---

j. Deborah A. Geier, *The Myth of the Matching Principle as a Tax Value*, 15 AM. J. TAX POL. 17, 22 (1998).

k. *Id.* at 25.

12. Is Professor Simons' Case I still an accurate criticism of the law?

13. Although Simons uses examples of income earned by corporations, the examples do not acknowledge the potential for double taxation at the corporate and shareholder level. This issue is discussed in Chapter Fourteen.

14.   Treatment of long term capital gain is not as lenient now as it was when Professor Simons wrote his Case III, though present section 1(h) taxes long term capital gains more gently than ordinary income. If "Gray" desires to sell part of his stock each year he may find it advantageous to invest in corporations that reinvest all their earnings instead of paying out dividends. One might think such corporations would be vulnerable to the section 531 tax on unreasonable accumulations, particularly since section 532(c) now makes the tax applicable to widely owned corporations. In fact, however, the Revenue Service does not attempt to apply the tax to widely held corporations. (Professor Simons referred to the tax on unreasonable accumulations as a "lightening hazard," equating the slight risk of the tax being imposed to the risk of being struck by lightening.[1])

15.   What does Simons mean by the observation, at the end of Case II: "'The richer you are, the faster you should be allowed to get richer,' says our realization procedure, while the bracket-rates raucously dissent."?

16.   Mr. Louie states at the outset that there is a prima facie case for taxing unrealized appreciation because unrealized appreciation "is part of the tax base." Obviously, unrealized appreciation is, in fact, not part of the tax base; Louie's statement is an assertion of his view that it should be. Most scholars would probably agree with Louie *if* practical problems of taxing unrealized gain could be overcome. Defenders of the realization rule, however, might argue that Louie simply assumes his conclusion.

17.   Stated differently, it seems clear that deferral of income tax on realized income amounts to an interest-free loan from the Government in the amount of the deferred tax.   Is Louie correct in asserting that the Government's failure to currently tax unrealized appreciation also amounts to an interest-free loan?

18.   The lock-in phenomenon discussed by Mr. Louie is discussed generally in Chapter Fifteen and, with particular reference to stepped-up basis at death, in Chapter Ten. Treating death as a realization event would solve a major part of the lock-in problem more easily than would abandoning the realization requirement.

---

1. HENRY C. SIMONS, FEDERAL TAX REFORM 66 (1950).

19.   Both the Louie and Chirelstein excerpts describe the "paper gain" argument in favor of the realization rule: that prior to realization the taxpayer has only a paper profit that remains at risk in the market. Is Professor Chirelstein correct in arguing that this is not basically different from the situation where a taxpayer sells an asset at a profit, reinvests the proceeds, and then risks losing the reinvested profit?

20.   *Eisner v. Macomber* held that a statute which clearly attempted to tax stock dividends was unconstitutional because stock dividends did not constitute "income" under the Sixteenth Amendment. Most legal scholars agree with Professor Chirelstein that the case was wrongly decided. Even if the realization requirement is accepted, taxing stock dividends might be considered valid now on the grounds that there is no constitutional objection to looking through the corporate shell and taxing shareholders on corporate earnings, whether or not distributed. This approach, however, would leave unanswered the question of the constitutionality of taxing unrealized appreciation in general.

21.   Professor Chirelstein observes that "because the realization requirement exists, the income tax is a tax on *transactions* instead of being a tax on income in the economic sense." For example, a taxpayer with a portfolio of securities, some of which have increased in value while other have decreased, can realize only the losses. In such a system, the barrier of transaction costs looms large as a practical limitation on tax-motivated sales—a barrier that may be falling. Professor David Bradford argues that "it is transactions costs that protect the income tax from much more extensive tax arbitrage than currently occurs. * * * One of the most striking developments in financial markets in recent years has been a steady decline in transactions costs."[m]

The effect of near-frictionless transactions, especially when coupled with taxpayers' increasingly sophisticated appreciation of the time value of money, is to make issues of tax accounting more important than in past decades.

C. CRITIQUES OF THE HAIG-SIMONS APPROACH

All agree that taxation of unrealized appreciation, in accord with the Haig-Simons definition of income, poses daunting questions of practicality. In this subchapter, several writers challenge such a tax in principle.

The Haig-Simons definition is, in part, a visceral reaction to the perceived unfairness of a situation in which two persons with equal amounts of income (excluding unrealized appreciation) are taxed the same even though the assets of one of the two have appreciated in value. This is, however, only one aspect

---

m. David F. Bradford, *Fixing Realization Accounting: Symmetry, Consistency and Correctness in the Taxation of Financial Instruments*, 50 TAX L. REV. 731, 736 (1995).

of the failure of an income tax to take into account differences in wealth that affect the burden of the tax. For example, the burden of a 40 percent income tax on income of $100,000 is greater on a taxpayer worth only $200,000 than on a taxpayer worth $1 million. This difference exists whether the assets represent unrealized appreciation, savings from previously taxed earnings, or an inheritance.

In the first excerpt below, Professor Fred Peel argues that an unrealized "paper profit" does not warrant the current imposition of tax. Currently taxing the asset's yield—which does not violate the realization rule—is sufficient.

Most scholars have embraced the Haig-Simons definition of income as the ideal for tax policy, even while acknowledging that thorough implementation would not be feasible. Professor Victor Thuronyi challenges the Hiag-Simons definition on another front, arguing that the Haig-Simons formulation leaves considerable ambiguity in its definition of income.

Even though application of the pure Haig-Simons definition is generally considered administratively impractical, its status in tax theory frequently leads scholars to test tax systems and proposed changes against it. A tax revision proposal may be accepted or rejected (at least among academics, if not in Congress) depending upon whether or not it brings the tax system closer to the Haig-Simons ideal. In the final excerpt, J. Gregory Ballantine, despite accepting Haig-Simons as "[t]he first best income tax rule," argues that the theory of second best does not support this approach.

CAPITAL LOSSES: FALLING SHORT ON FAIRNESS AND SIMPLICITY
Fred W. Peel, Jr.[*]

17 Baltimore Law Review 418, 423-24 (1988)

Some opposition toward allowing the taxpayer to time his realization of capital losses to offset other income probably stems from a belief that unrealized gains and losses should be taken into account annually. Such belief is part of the Haig-Simons definition of the ideal income tax base. This definition has been accepted as the ideal with a surprising lack of critical analysis. * * *

Market value of property is determined by either current yield or anticipated demand or a combination of these two factors. The current yield itself is taxed presently. To the extent that the value of property is determined by current yield, taxation of both current yield and accretion in value of the underlying asset that is a reflection of the yield would be unfair. Except in the case of collectors' items, to the extent that an asset's appreciation in value has not been accompanied by a commensurate current yield, the owner of the asset has received no benefit beyond a feeling of satisfaction at having made a shrewd investment.

---

[*]. At time of original publication, Ben J. Altheimer Professor of Law Emeritus, University of Arkansas at Little Rock.

An unrealized gain unaccompanied by current benefit is, in common terminology, a "paper profit." Entirely aside from the administrative problems of annual valuation involved in applying the Haig-Simons definition, the principal problem with such definition is the absence of any benefit to the owner that justifies the imposition of an income tax on an unrealized accretion in value. Thus, the theoretical basis for this component of the Haig-Simons definition of income is at least questionable.

* * *

THE CONCEPT OF INCOME
Victor Thuronyi[*]
46 Tax Law Review 45, 45-47, 61-62 (1990)

The concept of income serves as a touchstone against which the rules of the current income tax can be evaluated and is, therefore, of critical importance in the debate over what those rules should be. The meaning of income is also of interest to those charting the distribution of income, so as to have a quantitative measure of the degree of economic inequality in a society.
* * *

Given the importance of these uses of the income concept, the manner in which income is defined can make a difference. For example, if it is considered desirable for the income tax to approximate the ideal concept of income as closely as possible, it becomes important whether that ideal treats gifts and bequests as income. Moreover, the pattern of income distribution and the effects of a change in tax or other policy on that distribution can vary significantly depending on how income is defined.

The income concept that is now widely accepted by analysts was formulated by Henry Simons in the 1930's, and is commonly referred to as Haig-Simons income, to acknowledge the prior contribution of Robert Haig.[5] It holds that an individual's income is the sum of his consumption plus accumulation during the taxable period. Despite its wide acceptance, Haig-Simons income remains elusive and ambiguous, since the terms "consumption" and "accumulation" are open-ended. In light of the slipperiness of these terms, some writers have questioned whether the Haig-Simons formulation is, at base, a coherent one and is really helpful in deciding what is income.[6] Indeed, one noted economist has concluded that "the problem of *defining* individual income, quite apart from any problem of practical

---

[*]. At time of original publication, Associate Professor of Law, State University of New York at Buffalo (on leave; temporarily serving as Counsel (Taxation), International Monetary Fund).

5. See, e.g., Pechman, Comprehensive Income Taxation: A Comment, 81 Harv. L. Rev. 63, 64-65 (1967). Some writers have referred to the "Schanz-Haig-Simons" definition of income to acknowledge the contribution of George von Schanz. E.g., S. Surrey & P. McDaniel, Tax Expenditures 4 (1985).

6. See, e.g., Bittker, A "Comprehensive Tax Base" As a Goal of Income Tax Reform, 80 Harv. L. Rev. 925 (1967).

measurement, appears in principle insoluble."[7] Despite these theoretical objections, the term "economic income," or Haig-Simons income, is commonly employed as if it were a relatively well-defined or well-understood concept. The fact that some use economic income as a workable concept while others question its validity suggests that the nature of the concept is not well understood and has not been fully explored, despite the inordinate volume of literature on the subject. This article begins with an inquiry into the nature of the income concept appropriate for tax policy. A selective survey of the extensive literature on the definition of income suggests that there is confusion about the philosophical groundwork supporting the Haig-Simons concept, largely because the concept was borrowed from economics to be used in law. While the language used to define income has meaning in economic theory, that meaning collapses when it is applied in the real world.

* * *

Income is not an "elegant" concept. It is by its nature highly practical, flexible and ad hoc. If it is determined, for example, that medical expenses should not be deducted in determining income, it is not because the concept of a deduction for medical expenses is completely antithetical to a comprehensive income tax, but rather because, on balance, it is considered more equitable to determine income without such a deduction. The definition of income must take into account the fact that many criteria that might be used in determining taxable capacity are not measurable and, accordingly, cannot be incorporated into the income concept, or are measurable, but deficient for one reason or another. The Simons definition of income is misleading in this respect, since it looks fairly elegant. Indeed, Simons defended his definition on the basis that it was elegant.[64] Any hope of elegance should, however, be dispelled quickly when consideration is given to exactly what the terms "consumption" and "wealth" in his definition mean.

Not only are these terms inherently vague, but also the very notion of capital maintenance on which the Simons definition of income rests is arbitrary. If income is defined as the amount that an individual could have consumed while leaving his capital intact, this at first seems a straightforward idea. But now consider what is meant by maintaining capital intact. What it ultimately might mean is that income is the amount that an individual could spend during a period while still being as well off (in a financial sense) at the end of the period as at the beginning. But if the fair market value of an individual's capital is maintained, is he necessarily as well off at the end as at the beginning? If interest rates have declined, the individual's initial capital may have gone up in value. But if this increase in value is consumed, the remaining capital will produce an income stream lower than the income stream that would have been produced if the rate of interest had not declined. The individual is less well off in the sense that his capital can now provide a

---

7. N. Kaldor, An Expenditure Tax 70 (1955).
64. H. Simons, Personal Income Taxation 125 (1938).

smaller amount of annual consumption in the future. He is as well off only in the sense that if he liquidated his capital, he could buy the same amount of present consumption as he could have at the beginning of the period. While income can be defined in terms of the amount that could be consumed while maintaining the fair market value of the individual's capital intact, this means that two individuals with the same income may, in a certain sense, not be equally well off (even in purely financial terms).

    * * *

THREE FAILURES IN ECONOMIC ANALYSIS OF TAX REFORM

J. Gregory Ballentine[*]

National Tax Association-Tax Institute of America

79th Annual Conference 3, 4-5 (1986)

Income Tax Reform and the Theory of Second Best

The third failure that I will discuss is different. It applies to the principles used to design good income tax policy, and it arises from ignoring an existing, well understood economic principle: the theory of second best. Early on in the practical discussion of tax reform it was agreed—wisely, in my view—that income taxation, rather than consumption taxation, would form the basis for designing tax reform. The first best income tax rule is essentially given by the Haig-Simons definition of income. That is, first best income tax policy implies measuring Haig-Simons income for all individuals and taxing that income.

In my experience at Treasury, the "right" practical tax policy—as opposed to the political compromise that might be required—was always defined as an application of the Haig-Simons first best rule, with little or no thought given to second best issues. Treasury I demonstrated that same approach: it essentially proposed applying the first best, Haig-Simons rule everywhere it was deemed feasible, with no regard for the fact that major deviations from the first best rule are inevitable.

While optimal tax formulas derived from sophisticated second best modeling are often quite arcane and not practical, there is a clear general lesson from the theory of second best that has not permeated most practical discussions of income tax reform and that is inconsistent with the Treasury approach. That lesson is that, if constraints prevent application of the first best rule in major areas, then, in general, the second best policy will require deviations from the first best rule in many other areas where the constraints do not apply.[2]

---

   *. At time of original publication, principal, KPMG Peat Marwick, Washington, D.C.

   2. While this general point has not been influential in most tax policy discussions, it has not been entirely ignored. In my view, the clearest and most compelling explanation of it is given by Boris Bittker in "A Comprehensive Tax Base as a Goal of Income Tax Reform," 80 HARV L. REV. 925 (1967).

Owner occupied housing and other non-business capital is a salient example of the need for a second best approach to income tax reform. A practical constraint of income tax reform is that the imputed income on owner occupied housing will remain tax exempt. This is no minor constraint: approximately 30-35 percent of the depreciable capital stock of the U.S. is owner occupied housing. Given this major tax exemption for non-business capital, at the minimum there should be no presumption that the practical goal for income tax reform involves applying the Haig-Simons rule to the taxation of business capital income. Nonetheless, that is precisely the presumption inherent in Treasury I. Further, suggestions that the taxation of business capital should be reduced to offset the inevitable business/non-business tax distortion are usually treated as proposals to shift the basic system to *consumption* taxation, rather than as proposals to improve the practical design of an *income* tax in a second best world. Yet it is in the latter context that proposals for tax incentives for business investment have their most compelling practical justification.

Second best analysis is not only needed for major issues such as the treatment of business capital income; many smaller issues can benefit from such analysis. An excellent example comes from Bittker's article and Treasury I. Following Haig-Simons definition of income, Treasury I proposed taxing scholarship and fellowship income in excess of the amount used for tuition.[3]

The rationale given for this proposal was essentially that scholarship and fellowship payments are part of Haig-Simons income and, therefore, should be taxable.

In dealing with this same case, Bittker pointed out that most state universities, in effect, provide scholarships and fellowships to in-state students through reduced charges for tuition, room, and board. For example, room, board, and tuition of the University of Virginia for a Virginia resident is approximately $4000 per school year. At many comparable private institutions, room, board, and tuition may be $16,000 or more. Surely, one of the practical constraints of our tax system is that we will not impute scholarship income to in-state students attending the University of Virginia and tax that income. Once that fact is recognized, it is not so clear that taxing explicit scholarships and fellowships is good income tax policy. Of course, one may still conclude that taxing a portion of explicit scholarship or fellowship income is good tax policy, but that conclusion cannot be based on the simple assertion that scholarships fit the Haig-Simons definition of income just like wages. A more sophisticated rationale weighing different, but inevitable, distortions from the Haig-Simons rule is needed.

* * *

---

3. Indeed, Treasury I argued that "[i]n theory" *all* scholarship and fellowship income should be taxed. The continued exclusion for scholarships used to pay tuition was, apparently, a concession to concerns about public acceptance. See *Tax Reform For Fairness, Simplicity, and Economic Growth*, U.S. Treasury, Vol. 2, p. 58.

Notes and Questions

22.   Professor Peel argues that unrealized appreciation is attributable to some combination of two factors—increased yield and anticipated demand. Why does he contend that this means that unrealized appreciation should not be taxed?

23.   Do you agree with Peel that the owner of an investment asset that appreciates in value but not in current yield "has received no benefit beyond a feeling of satisfaction at having made a shrewd investment?"

24.   Professor Thuronyi asserts that the Haig-Simons approach "collapses when it is applied in the real world," and not just because of such practical problems as valuation. More basically, he regards the terms "consumption" and "wealth," upon which the Haig-Simons definition depends, as "inherently vague." Do you agree with his critique?

25.   Thuronyi posits the case of a bondholder whose bonds rise in value due to a decline in interest rates. In what sense is the bondholder not better off as a result of the increased value?

26.   Mr. Ballentine regards the Haig-Simons definition as the theoretical ideal, but unattainable in the real world. Does this mean that the tax system should tax income according to the Haig-Simons definition whenever practical? If the Haig-Simons definition of income is ideal, and that definition would include scholarships, does this mean that scholarships should be taxed?

D. RECENT PROPOSALS FOR AVOIDING THE REALIZATION RULE

There is general—though clearly not universal—agreement that taxation of unrealized appreciation along Haig-Simons lines is theoretically desirable. Certainly the authors represented in this subchapter find the realization rule to be a source of inefficiency and inequity. Nevertheless, as Professor David Shakow has observed, taxation of unrealized appreciation "has never attracted a large group of adherents because its twin problems of valuation (How can all assets be valued every year?) and liquidity (How can taxpayers pay taxes if they do not sell their assets?) have never been solved."[n] (Shakow himself regarded taxation of unrealized appreciation as feasible in many instances; his detailed proposal is briefly presented in Note #34 below (page 97).)

The two excerpts in this subchapter are representative of recent attempts to devise structures that would tax unrealized appreciation comparably to other capital income, while minimizing valuation and liquidity problems. Professor Weisbach suggests that we consider parallel structures, imposing

---

n. David J. Shakow, *Taxation Without Realization: A Proposal for Accrual Taxation*, 134 U. PA. L. REV. 1111, 1113 (1986).

mark-to-market taxation where feasible, while retaining the realization rule for "illiquid or hard-to-value assets, such as real estate or small businesses."[o] Rough economic equivalence for the two systems would be obtained by imposing a higher nominal rate on gains still taxed under the realization regime.

Mr. Land's proposal derives from a view of the Government as a silent partner in every profit-oriented investment. The Government's share should reduce the investor's rate of return by a constant percentage, regardless of when a realization event may occur. He suggests imposing the tax at a convenient time (as the realization rule provides at present), but calculated to make the after-tax rate of return the same as that imposed on capital income taxed currently. Mr. Land argues that, in theory, this could lead to a tax system under which the economic burden of tax on all transactions could be made to exactly equal the burden that would be imposed under the Haig-Simons ideal.

A PARTIAL MARK-TO-MARKET TAX SYSTEM
David A. Weisbach[*]

53 Tax Law Review 95, 95-105, 121-24,
128-29, 131-32, 135 (1999)

Introduction

Haig-Simons taxation generally is viewed as the ideal form of income taxation. It is simple, fair, and efficient. All income within the Haig-Simons system would be taxed at a uniform rate under a single, simple set of rules. Taxpayers with equal accessions to wealth would be taxed equally. Avoiding tax by manipulating the form of a transaction would be almost impossible. Haig-Simons taxation (which, following current convention, I refer to as mark-to-market taxation), however, would require taxpayers to value assets prior to and to pay tax prior to the receipt of cash. These requirements, valuation and liquidity, are thought to be unreasonable for many assets. Thus, current law generally does not require tax to be paid until income is "realized," which is generally when the asset producing the income is sold.

The valuation and liquidity concerns, however, do not apply to many assets subject to the realization system. In particular, many financial assets and many commodities are easily valued and highly liquid. Furthermore, realization taxation has been particularly troublesome for many of these assets. It is hard to see why these assets are not subject to mark-to-market taxation, other than as a historical accident. This Article examines whether it is feasible to expand mark-to-market taxation to cover most liquid assets such as financial products and commodities, while leaving illiquid or hard-to-value assets, such as real estate or small businesses, on the realization system.

---

o. David A. Weisbach, *A Partial Mark-to-Market Tax System*, 53 TAX L. REV. 95, 96 (1999).

*. At time of initial publication, Associate Professor, University of Chicago Law School.

It is not clear that a mixed system (one that imposes both mark-to-market and realization taxation) would be an improvement over current law. It may solve some problems posed by the realization system, particularly as applied to evolving financial markets, and it may produce a simpler, more efficient tax system. Nevertheless, in a mixed system, income would be taxed under two very different regimes, mark-to-market and realization. The system will require line drawing and precise definitions to separate the regimes. Wherever the line is drawn, similar transactions on either side of the line will be taxed differently, causing taxpayers to distort their behavior and requiring the complexity and anti-avoidance rules of current law. The problem of the second-best may mean that a partial move toward the ideal may not be an improvement.

One of the problems with studying a mixed system is that there are a vast number of interrelated design choices, many of them subject to significant policy and political uncertainty. For example, integration of the corporate and individual taxes substantially affects the design of a partial mark-to-market system. International considerations affect integration. There are literally dozens of interdependent choices, and an article of reasonable length cannot explore each possible branch of the decision tree.

Given this constraint, this Article has two goals. First, the Article explores how the decisions regarding the details of a mixed system should be made in light of second-best considerations. In particular, the Article explores the considerations in setting the relative rates and bases. Second, it evaluates whether some version of a substantial expansion of mark-to-market taxation has the potential to improve the tax system. Thus, it considers plausible design decisions and evaluates whether they would produce an improvement.

The normative standard I use for the design and evaluation of the system is efficiency (with administrability considered a subset of efficiency). The obvious question is why fairness is not a relevant consideration, particularly because equitable apportionment of tax burdens was one of the primary motivations behind the Haig-Simons notion of income used here. The reason is that generally the change to a mixed system can be made distributionally neutral by adjusting overall rates. For example, setting the tax rate for assets subject to mark-to-market taxation to approximate the current burden of these assets under the realization system would have few effects on distribution but may increase efficiency. Thus, the question considered is whether one can improve efficiency while holding distribution constant.

* * * Whether it is desirable to give up some of the efficiency gains for distributional goals is left for another day.

* * * As the details of implementation could fill hundreds of pages, the goal of this Article is to give a sense of the simplification possibilities of a partial mark-to-market regime rather than provide a detailed blueprint.[10]

The Relative Tax Rates on the Mark-to-market and Realization Bases

Perhaps the most important decision in designing a partial mark-to-market tax regime is setting the relative tax rates on the mark-to-market and realization tax bases. For reasons explained below, mark-to-market assets and realization assets should be taxed at different nominal rates. The nominal rate on mark-to-market assets should equal the average effective rate on realization assets.

This conclusion follows from the basic proposition that the most efficient method of taxing capital income is to impose the same effective rate on all such income. By imposing the same effective rate on all capital income, behavioral distortions are minimized because there will be no tax advantage from choosing one asset or activity over another.

Rates are set efficiently by making *effective* rather than *nominal* rates equal. By definition, the effective tax rate on mark-to-market assets equals the nominal rate on such assets and is uniform for all such assets. The effective tax rate on realization assets, however, is always less than the nominal rate because taxpayers can defer taxation until gain is realized. Therefore, to have the same effective rates, the mark-to-market base must have a lower nominal rate than the realization base.

Unfortunately, the effective realization rate varies from asset to asset. The effective realization rate on an asset is determined by the period of deferral (and the interest rate), which, in turn, is determined by the period the taxpayer held the asset and the timing of any changes in value. Assets in the realization system have different periods of deferral and, therefore, different effective tax rates.

To minimize differences in effective tax rates across assets, the statutory rate on mark-to-market income should be set equal to the average effective rate on realization assets.[13] That is, if effective tax rates are equal on average,

---

10. This Article does not consider the effects of inflation on the mark-to-market base. The current system does not have specific adjustments to prevent the taxation of inflationary gains but the deferral allowed by realization is a rough proxy. The longer an asset is held, the greater the absolute amount of inflationary gains and the greater the deferral. In a mark-to-market system, the effects of inflation are not offset by deferral and, therefore, are more severe. Reed Shuldiner, Indexing the Tax Code, 48 Tax L. Rev. 537 (1993), includes a discussion of indexing in a mark-to-market system. Shuldiner suggests that if gains are not indexed for inflation, it may be inappropriate to impose mark-to-market taxation. Id. at 557. Indexing in a full mark-to-market system may not be that difficult. Indexing in a partial mark-to-market system, however, presents different problems and should be evaluated further before a partial mark-to-market system is adopted. A discussion of this issue is beyond the scope of this Article.

13. Until the scope of the mark-to-market base is determined, the rates on the mark-to-market and realization bases cannot be set. Rough estimates based on overall numbers are possible. Given deferral, selective realization, forgiveness of gains at death, and the variety of special preferences, the average rate on noncorporate capital income was estimated in 1994 to be about 20%. * * *

taxpayers faced with a choice of investing in an asset in the realization base and an asset in the mark-to-market base will face tax rates that are as similar as possible and, therefore, taxes will have the least influence on behavior. Thus, the nominal rate on mark-to-market assets should be equal to the average effective rate on realization assets.

This conclusion is based purely on efficiency. Setting the rates this way (which I refer to as setting the rates neutrally) has administrative benefits as well. Minimizing the difference between the rates on mark-to-market assets and the effective rates on realization assets reduces the incentive to structure investments to fall on the better side of the line. (This is the efficiency result.) This, in turn, reduces the need for complex rules preventing this type of behavior, simplifying the tax system. Similarly, determining whether a particular asset is in the realization base or the mark-to-market base will be less important, which will reduce tax administration costs for both taxpayers and the government.[15] In effect, the efficiency gains and the administrability gains come from the same source: They both stem from the fact that setting equal average effective rates will reduce tax-induced changes in behavior.

A source of confusion on the rates is that mark-to-market taxation eliminates deferral and deferral lowers effective tax rates. Thus, a common assumption is that adoption of a mark-to-market regime necessarily raises effective tax rates. Mark-to-market taxation, however, implies nothing about appropriate tax rates. It merely eliminates deferral, which is important not because the current rates are too low but because deferral causes economic distortions. Deferral causes income to be taxed at different rates and creates an incentive to hold assets longer than economically appropriate. Thus, the argument for neutral rates implies nothing about the appropriate overall level of taxation of capital income. The argument only concerns the relative statutory and effective rates for the mark-to-market and realization bases. For example, if, given the current realization rate and a neutral mark-to-market rate, the resulting tax on capital is too high, overall rates on capital income should be lowered, retaining the relative relationship between the mark-to-market rates and the realization rates.

* * *

The 20% figure is an average rate, not a marginal rate. To keep current progressivity, the highest mark-to-market marginal rates would be higher than 20% and the lowest would be lower.

Note also that rates may have to be adjusted on a regular basis to take into account significant changes in interest rates. The effective tax rate on realization assets depends on deferral, the value of which is determined by interest rates. As interest rates change, the effective tax rate changes and keeping the effective rates the same will require periodic adjustments.

15. As noted in text accompanying note 13, using neutral rates will not eliminate problems with taxing different assets differently because the rates can be set equally only on average and only for a given interest rate (which determines the value of deferral and, hence, the effective realization rate). Nevertheless, neutral rates significantly reduce the administrative problems with a partial mark-to-market system.

The Scope of the Mark-to-Market Tax Base
* * *
Criteria for Setting the Mark-to-Market Base

The decision whether a particular asset (or liability) should be in the mark-to-market base is, of course, a cost-benefit analysis. The benefits of mark-to-market taxation are that it is simple and efficient. It eliminates the problems of lock-in, deferral (that is, the differential rates caused by deferral), the avoidance potential of the realization requirement, and the complex rules necessary to implement the realization requirement. The costs of mark-to-market taxation are the need to value assets before sale and the need to pay tax before cash is received.

For many assets, this straightforward list of costs and benefits will be sufficient. For example, publicly traded assets are liquid and easy to value. They generally should be in the mark-to-market base. Small businesses and real estate are illiquid and difficult to value. They should be in the realization base. A wide variety of assets (or liabilities) can be categorized on this basis.

What this simple analysis omits, however, is the problem created by imposing different tax regimes on similar assets. That is, deciding which assets should be in the mark-to-market base and which should remain in the realization base means drawing a line. Wherever the line is drawn, similar items on either side of the line will be taxed differently. Taxpayers will shift their portfolios or adjust their behavior along the border to minimize taxes, creating tax-induced inefficiencies. In addition, taxpayers will engage in arbitrage, buying one asset and selling another, to create tax benefits, reducing tax revenues. Setting the rates neutrally minimizes the differences between the two bases, but because the realization rates vary from asset to asset, the differences would not be eliminated.

To minimize inefficiencies along the border, assets should be taxed the same as their closest substitutes. If close substitutes are taxed identically, there is less incentive to shift behavior to reduce taxes. In addition, if close substitutes are taxed alike, the cost of shifting behavior or portfolios to reduce taxes increases because taxpayers must shift further from their desired behavior to obtain the desired tax benefit. Less incentive to shift behavior and higher costs of doing so means tax-induced changes in behavior will decrease. And if close substitutes are taxed alike, arbitrages will be less available. Taxing substitutes the same also helps administrability because drawing and enforcing lines between similar items is generally more difficult than drawing and enforcing lines between dissimilar items. Keeping substitutes together is a key feature in designing the tax base.[20]

Of course, most investments are, to some degree, substitutes for other investments, and a prescription to keep substitutes together would require all investments to be taxed the same (contrary to the basic assumption in this

---

20. See David A. Weisbach, Line Drawing, Doctrine, and Efficiency in the Tax Law, 87 Cornell L. Rev. (forthcoming 1999), for a more general analysis of line drawing problems in the tax law.

Article that there would be two regimes). The benefit of keeping substitutes together must be weighed against the costs and benefits of putting each particular asset, considered by itself, under either the mark-to-market system or the realization system. If, for example, valuation and liquidity are serious problems for an asset, they may outweigh the need to keep substitutes together, but where an asset is a very close substitute for a mark-to-market asset, the need to keep substitutes together may outweigh valuation and liquidity problems.

* * * The key is to find an appropriate dividing line that puts only assets that are liquid and that can be easily valued in the mark-to-market base and that taxes close substitutes alike.

The process is complex, and the appropriate boundaries of the mark-to-market base may change over time. Policymakers will need to study each type of transaction in detail before decisions are made. * * *

Evaluation

This Section evaluates a partial mark-to-market system that follows the basic structure suggested above. Roughly, the mark-to-market base would have a nominal rate equal to the average effective rate on realization assets. Publicly traded assets, positions in traded assets, and most debt instruments would be marked to market. Other assets would be left in the realization base (although many assets on the border are left unspecified at this point). * * *

There are two major sources of potential gains from a partial mark-to-market system The first is simplification. Many of the complex, realization-based rules might be eliminated. The second is efficiency. Mark-to-market taxation makes tax rates more uniform, eliminates lock-in, and limits tax avoidance behavior engendered by gaps in the realization system. I consider each in turn.

Simplification
* * *

The Potential to Eliminate Realization-Based Rules

Much of the complexity of current law stems from the realization requirement. Pure mark-to-market taxation potentially offers dramatic simplification because all of the realization rules could be repealed. The potential for simplification in a partial mark-to-market system is much lower than it is in a pure system because of the need to keep the realization rules in place for the retained realization system. The benefits of simplification, however, are still positive both because the complex realization rules apply to a smaller universe and because some can be repealed altogether. As a sample of these types of issues, this Subsection considers (1) the capital gains rules, (2) the loss restriction rules * * *.

Capital Gains

The capital gains regime is the quintessential realization rule. It is defined by a sale or exchange and exists largely because of flaws in the realization system. In a pure mark-to-market system, the reasons for the capital gains preference would be eliminated and the preference presumably, also would be eliminated.[79]

In a partial mark-to-market regime, however, portions of the realization base would remain. Absent an independent move to eliminate the capital gains structure for realization-based assets, most of the capital gains rules would remain. Thus, the simplification benefit of the partial mark-to-market system is that it reduces the universe of assets subject to the complex capital gains rules.[80]

Loss Restrictions

* * *

[T]he limitation on the use of capital losses could be eliminated altogether. The limitation on capital losses is designed to prevent selective realization of losses. Mark-to-market taxation eliminates selective realization and, therefore, the capital loss regime would not be necessary for assets (or liabilities) in the mark-to-market base. Moreover, if the mark-to-market base includes all liquid capital assets, there is no reason to retain the capital loss rules for the realization base either because selective realization would be difficult for illiquid assets. Therefore, the capital loss rules could be repealed.

* * *

New Rules Needed to Implement a Partial Mark-to-Market System

To implement the partial mark-to-market system, several sets of new rules would be needed. Most importantly, a set of rules would be needed to define the mark-to-market base with precision. The number of assets and liabilities at the border would be large and the basic definitional set of rules might very well be complex. In addition, the valuation requirement would impose complexity and create disputes.

Moreover, in a partial mark-to-market system, there would be incentives for taxpayers to shift assets between these regimes. * * *

For example, suppose publicly traded stock were marked to market at a 20% tax rate, and closely held partnership interests were in the realization base and were taxed at a nominal rate of 40%. If a taxpayer had substantial

---

79. The most plausible reason for a special capital gains rate is the so-called "lock-in" effect. Because taxation of capital gains is deferred until realization, taxpayers have an incentive to hold assets to increase the value of deferral. The incentive is increased because there is no tax on gains at death. IRC § 1014(a). Arguably, to reduce the lock-in effect, the tax on the sale of capital assets should be reduced so that the decision to hold or sell is more neutral. Thus, the logic is that because Congress gives taxpayers deferral or forgives their tax altogether, it must further reduce their tax. Under mark-to-market taxation, the lock-in effect is largely eliminated because tax would be due on gains regardless of whether there is a sale.

80. Note that eliminating the capital gains preference for mark-to-market income does not mean that the tax rate on this income would be higher than for realization income. If neutral rates were adopted, the mark-to-market rate would incorporate any benefit of a capital gains preference for the realization assets, so the effective rates would be the same. Eliminating the capital gains preference for mark-to-market income only means that all such income would be taxed at the same rate rather than having different rates apply to different portions of the income.

loss in a stock and the current nonrecognition rules were retained, the taxpayer could contribute the stock to a partnership without recognizing gain[106] and then sell the partnership interest. The taxpayer, thereby converts the loss from a mark-to-market loss taxed at 20% to a realization loss taxed at 40%. Similarly, if real estate were in the realization base, a taxpayer with gain in real estate could contribute it to a publicly traded entity before resale, converting the gain from 40% realization to 20% mark-to-market gain. And if it was uncertain whether an asset is in the mark-to-market base, taxpayers could wait until year end to make the most advantageous determination. Many base-shifting transactions would be costly, but if the gain or loss was sufficiently large, the incentive to attempt to shift assets between the bases will be high. This means that the tax law would need rules to prevent shifting of assets between the bases. These rules might be complex.

* * *

Efficiency

The other potential benefit of a partial mark-to-market regime is that it might be more efficient than current law. There are three major efficiency benefits. First, a partial mark-to-market regime with neutral rates would reduce the disparity in tax rates on capital income. Second, it would eliminate the lock-in effect for assets subject to the mark-to-market regime. Third, it would reduce behavior designed to avoid or reduce taxes.

A partial mark-to-market regime would reduce the disparity in effective rates from that of current law. Under current law, income is taxed at different rates both because of the large number of special regimes and because of deferral and selective realization. Deferral and selective realization would be eliminated for assets in the mark-to-market base, and all income within the mark-to-market base would be taxed at a uniform rate. With neutral rates, the uniform mark-to-market tax rate would approximate the effective realization tax rate. These factors would reduce the disparity in tax rates found under current law. * * * By imposing a more uniform rate on capital income, a partial mark-to-market system improves efficiency.

A partial mark-to-market regime also would eliminate the lock-in effect of assets subject to mark-to-market taxation: The lock-in effect is the incentive under current law to retain assets to defer taxes even if selling an asset would be efficient or desirable. A similar result, known as the lock-out effect, occurs when taxpayers are induced to sell assets to accelerate losses. Both effects are thought to cause significant misallocations of resources. Within the mark-to-market regime, both the lock-in effect and the lock-out effect would be eliminated.

Finally, a partial mark-to-market regime would reduce tax planning opportunities and the resulting distortions of behavior and revenue loss. * * *

---

106. IRC § 721

Conclusion

Whether the United States should expand mark-to-market slowly with the goal of achieving the better system in the long run is primarily a political strategy question. Small changes do not necessarily improve the system. Taking a quarter step is risky unless it is certain it will help in going all the way because the quarter step may make things worse. This Article demonstrates, however, that something well short of a move to pure mark-to-market taxation can be a substantial improvement over current law.

DEFEATING DEFERRAL: A PROPOSAL FOR RETROSPECTIVE TAXATION (1996)
Stephen B. Land[*]

52 Tax Law Review 45, 46-51, 53-56, 58-59, 61,

65-67, 71, 73-74, 78-79, 82-83, 86-87, 110-12 (1996)

Introduction

The next best thing to not paying tax is putting it off. This principle, more than any other, has motivated tax planning over the years. In the quest for tax deferral, a taxpayer's best friend is the realization requirement: Gain from an appreciated asset typically is not taxed until a sale or other realization event. Too much deferral, however, threatens the federal revenue. Indeed, much of the complexity in the tax law comes from provisions designed to restrict deferral.

How much is tax deferral worth? Deferral sometimes is described as an interest-free loan from the government. Is it worth the taxpayer's borrowing cost? The taxpayer's overall cost of capital, including equity? The government's borrowing cost? At short-term or long-term rates? Commentators have bruited about all of these possibilities.

This Article proposes a different way to look at tax deferral. Under this view, the tax deferred represents less of a loan from the government than an equity investment by the government in the appreciated asset. Such an investment should participate on a pro rata basis in any future earnings from the asset. Not having to pay this share of earnings to the government is the value of deferring the tax.

Two surprising propositions flow from this view of tax deferral. First, *the value of tax deferral is independent of the length of the holding period.* If you double your money in two years or twenty, the value of being able to defer tax until sale is the same. Second, *the value of tax deferral is independent of whether the appreciation occurred early or late in the holding period.* This second proposition can be made even stronger, because the value of tax deferral is the same even if the asset value fluctuates wildly over the holding period, and in portions of the holding period, the value goes down as well as up. The value of deferral depends on how much is earned, not on when it is

---

*. At time of original publication, Partner, Linklaters & Paines.

earned. These conclusions are sufficiently counter-intuitive that some form of formal proofs are called for. These I provide, but how to measure the value of deferral is a question of tax policy as much as mathematics.

The propositions are of more than academic interest. They point the way to eliminate the tax benefits of deferral. The proposed solution is a form of "retrospective taxation," which preserves the realization requirement but adjusts the tax to offset the benefit of deferral. The tax is adjusted so that the after-tax sale proceeds provide a yield on the investment that is equal to its pretax yield reduced by the tax rate.[4] Such a tax is immune to strategic trading; that is, a taxpayer cannot alter the tax burden by trading in and out of the investment. Moreover, the tax as computed in this fashion is the *only* form of retrospective taxation of gains and losses that has this property.

* * *

The Realization Requirement
The Dilemma

Economically, income is earned as an asset appreciates, not when it is sold. There is a wide consensus that a theoretically ideal income tax would be imposed on the Haig-Simons conception of income, which is the value of the taxpayer's consumption during the relevant accounting period plus any increase (or minus any decrease) in the fair market value of the taxpayer's wealth.[5] Such a tax would have no realization requirement: Asset appreciation is income, whether the asset is sold or not. Viewed against this standard, the realization requirement mismeasures income every time it applies. Yet, the realization requirement is widely considered to be essential to make the tax system administrable. What can be done?

---

4. This particular method of retrospective taxation has been considered before, by me and others. See, e.g., Cynthia Blum, New Role for Treasury: Charging Interest on Tax Deferral Loans, 25 Harv. J. on Legis. 1, 13-15 (1988); Mary Louise Fellows, A Comprehensive Attack on Tax Deferral, 88 Mich. L. Rev. 722, 748-51 (1990); Mark P. Gergen, The Effects of Price Volatility and Strategic Trading Under Realization, Expected Return and Retrospective Taxation, 49 Tax L. Rev. 209, 234-35 (1994); Stephen B. Land, Contingent Payments and the Time Value of Money, 40 Tax Law. 237, 283-88 (1987); Alvin C. Warren, Jr., Financial Contract Innovation and Income Tax Policy, 107 Harv. L. Rev. 460, 477-78 (1993). What does not appear to have been noticed before is that this method is free of the flaws commonly attributed to retrospective taxation based on charging interest on the tax deferred.

5. Henry C. Simons, Personal Income Taxation 50 (1938); Robert M. Haig, The Concept of Income—Economics and Legal Aspects, in The Federal Income Tax 1, 7 (Robert M. Haig ed., 1921), reprinted in American Econ. Ass'n, Readings in the Economics of Taxation 54 (Richard A. Musgrave & Carl Shoup eds.,1959). Although the Haig-Simons norm is a widely accepted ideal for an income tax, some have argued that it would be better to replace the income tax with a tax on consumption, allowing wealth to accumulate tax-free. E.g., William D. Andrews, A Consumption-Type or Cash Flow Personal Income Tax, 87 Harv. L. Rev. 1113 (1974). This Article steers clear of that debate, but is nonetheless relevant to it. Much of the motivation for a consumption tax is to avoid the problems associated with the realization requirement. See William D. Andrews, The Achilles' Heel of the Comprehensive Income Tax, in New Directions in Federal Tax Policy for the 1980's, at 278, 280-85 (Charls E. Walker & Mark A. Bloomfield eds., 1983). To the extent that retrospective taxation can alleviate these problems, the case for a consumption tax becomes less compelling. Moreover, retrospective taxation can be implemented in a manner that achieves an income tax result on a consumption tax base.

Why We Can't Live With It

A host of evils can be attributed to the realization requirement. It is unfair and inefficient; it makes investing riskier; and it increases the complexity of the tax law. These problems have been extensively catalogued by others; the most prominent problems are summarized here.

Horizontal Inequity

Horizontal equity is the principle that taxpayers with equal incomes should pay equal amounts of income tax. Suppose *Andrea* and *Bob* each own shares of GM stock that have gone up $30,000 in value; *Andrea* sells her shares and buys Ford stock instead. *Andrea* pays tax on her gain, but *Bob* does not, even though both have made the same amount of money on their investments.

Moreover, the realization requirement favors income from capital over income from labor. *Charlotte,* who has no investments but earns $30,000 in salary, lacks the choices available to *Andrea* and *Bob;* she must pay tax on her income, come what may.

Vertical Inequity

Vertical equity is the principle that taxpayers with more income should pay more tax than those with less income. Under progressive taxation, the effective rate of tax on the rich should be higher than on the poor.

The realization requirement undermines progressive taxation. Bill Gates, arguably the richest man in the world, has paid no tax on the appreciation in his retained Microsoft stock. * * *

Lock-In Effect

The realization requirement creates a lock-in effect that discourages taxpayers from selling assets in circumstances where, absent tax considerations, it would make sense to do so. * * *

Loss Limitations

Although the realization requirement applies to losses as well as gains, the failure to derive any tax benefit from unrealized losses is mitigated by the fact that investors can choose to sell at any time, claim the tax loss, and reinvest in something similar. While the wash sale rules disallow tax losses from sales of stock or securities where the proceeds are reinvested in substantially identical stock or securities, they do not preclude reinvestment in other stocks or securities that offer a similar profile of risk and reward. Because investors can choose when to sell, there is nothing symmetric about applying the realization requirement to both gains and losses. For this reason, the tax law limits the deductibility of realized losses that exceed realized gains.[13]

* * *

---

13. Individuals can deduct only $3,000 of net capital losses annually, but can carry forward the excess as a loss deduction in future years, subject to the same restriction. Corporations cannot deduct any net capital losses, but can carry these losses back for up to three years and forward for up to five years. IRC §§ 1211, 1212.

Although the loss limitations lack teeth in most circumstances, they impose a serious burden on unfortunate investors who suffer losses on their portfolios as a whole. These investors have suffered a real economic loss, but are not entitled to apply any resulting tax losses against ordinary income. As a result, they may end up paying substantial amounts of tax on their ordinary income, even though, taking the capital losses into account, they have only broken even or worse.

Forcing taxpayers with zero or negative net income to pay an income tax is not merely offensive to notions of horizontal and vertical equity; it also makes investing riskier. The tax law promises deferral and a favorable rate to investment winners, but denies a tax benefit to the losers. This magnification of risk should be a serious concern to those who want the tax law to promote investment.

There would be no need for these loss limitations if there were no realization requirement. Taxpayers would be required to report both unrealized gains and losses; actual trading would be irrelevant. There would be no opportunity for taxpayers to realize losses selectively while deferring the realization of gains, so special limitations on loss deductibility would be unnecessary.

* * *

Revenue Effects

The realization requirement costs the government money; the lost revenue has to come from someplace. To the extent that the revenue comes through higher income tax rates, the realization requirement intensifies the adverse effects that higher rates are thought to have: reduced incentives to work and invest, and a focus on tax factors rather than economic factors in business planning.

Complexity

Several developments over the past two decades increased the importance of the realization requirement. First, a period of high inflation, followed by persisting high real interest rates, made the benefits of tax deferral more valuable. This expanded the market for tax shelters. * * * Second, governments allowed interest and currency rates to fluctuate more freely in response to market conditions, increasing the demand for hedging arrangements such as interest rate and currency swaps, options, and futures contracts, and these financial instruments evolved rapidly to cover other types of risks. These derivative instruments (so-called because the payoff is "derived" from the performance of something else) act as a universal solvent on the barriers that the tax law erects to classify income into various categories with differing tax treatment. Finally, the tax law struggled to deal with the new financial instruments in an intelligent way, and to curtail the proliferation of tax shelters. While great progress was made towards these goals, a serious side effect was a level of complexity undreamt of 20 years ago.

Even back then, denouncing the complexity of the tax law was a campaign platitude.

* * *

Why We Can't Live Without It

Academics dream of an "accretion" tax, under which appreciation is taxed annually regardless of whether the asset is sold. Doing away with the realization requirement is tempting. Yet, except in limited circumstances, an accretion tax generally is thought to be a pipe dream. The two biggest obstacles are liquidity and valuation.

Liquidity

* * *

The income tax appears to be politically acceptable largely because it is based on ability to pay. This ability to pay depends on liquidity as well as net worth. A system that taxes increases in net worth without regard to liquidity will disrupt the affairs of taxpayers far more than a system that simply scoops up some of the cash when it appears at the time of sale.

Valuation

The bigger bugaboo is valuation. An accretion tax would require all assets to be valued at the end of each accounting period. The resulting administrative burden is thought to be prohibitive.

* * *

Valuation generally is viewed as a practical problem. Under this view, each asset has its worth; it is just sometimes hard to know what it is. With enough information, and sufficiently sophisticated analysis, one could zero in on the "true" value of any asset. Yet, there is a deeper problem with valuation. The very idea assumes that for each asset there is some objective number that represents its value. It may be hard to find out; it might even be unknowable; but it is there.

This objective concept of value is hard to sustain in light of how value conventionally is defined: the amount that a willing buyer would pay a willing seller, each being under no compulsion to buy or sell and each having knowledge of all relevant facts. This definition is a counterfactual: It is based on what hypothetical people would do, not on what actual people are actually doing. Except for assets that are publicly traded or can be readily converted to cash (which are the only easy cases), valuation is an exercise in make believe. * * *

These considerations weaken one's faith in the Haig-Simons definition of income. Defining income by references to changes in value, when the values are not well defined *even in theory*, yields a definition of income that is not well defined *even in theory*. Yet, the very purpose of the Haig-Simons definition is to serve a theoretical benchmark, against which actual schemes of computing income can be assessed.

Thus, the problem with accretion taxation is not simply that it is hard to figure out the proper amount of taxable income. There simply is, at bottom, no proper amount of taxable income to figure out.

What We Can Do about it

The tax law uses three methods to cut back the scope of the realization requirements. The first method is to require unrealized gains and losses to be reported annually. While this method is the most straightforward, it currently is used only in contexts where the liquidity and valuation problems are thought to be manageable. The second method is to use concepts of accrual accounting to redefine when realization takes place. This method avoids valuation problems because income is determined under these accounting concepts rather than by asset valuation. The third method is to charge interest on the tax liability that is deferred by reason of the realization requirement. This last method avoids liquidity problems because the tax is not due until a realization event occurs.

Mark to Market

Under a mark-to-market system, gains and losses are taken into account each year whether realized or not. On the last day of the year, each asset that has not been sold is marked to market by treating it as if it had been sold on that day at a price equal to its fair market value, and then reacquired at the same price. The tax law uses mark-to-market sparingly, because of the liquidity and valuation problems that such a wholesale abandonment of the realization requirement entails.

    * * *

Accrual of Income

In a sense, the entire accrual method of accounting is an affront to the realization requirement. Semantically, the issue is suppressed by redefining the realization event to be something other than the receipt of cash or other property. An accrual basis seller recognizes income at the time of sale, rather than the time of payment. Periodic items such as rent and interest are reported as earned, rather than when paid.

Liquidity problems arising from the erosion (or redefinition) of the realization requirement are accepted without complaint. * * *

Valuation problems under accrual accounting are dealt with by a set of formal rules that substitute for actual valuations. * * *

Interest on Deferred Tax

Mark-to-market is confined to limited spheres in which liquidity and valuation concerns are absent. Accrual accounting works well for predictable types of income, but is much more problematic when applied to contingent returns. A third approach respects the realization requirement but seeks to compensate for the effects of deferral. Under this approach, the income ultimately realized is allocated over the years in the holding period according to a formula. The additional tax that would have been due in each such year on that year's income is determined, and is payable in the year of realization together with interest over the interval between the year to which the income was allocated and the year in which the tax is paid. The interest charge approach meshes perfectly with the idea of tax deferral as an interest-free loan from the government. If the problem is the interest-free nature of the loan, the solution is to charge interest.[85]

The tax law has only occasionally used this interest charge approach. The most noteworthy example is the treatment of private foreign investment companies (PFICs). A PFIC is a foreign corporation with a significant portion of its assets of a type that generate passive income such as dividends, interest, and royalties.[86] PFICs generally are permitted to accumulate income tax-free, but upon a realization event (such as a sale of stock or an extraordinary dividend), the realized income is allocated over the shareholder's holding period on a ratable basis.[87] The amount of income allocated to each prior year is subject to tax at the highest marginal rate then in effect for that year, and an interest charge is computed from the prior year to the year the income is realized.[88] The interest charge is based on a rate equal to three percentage points over the average market yield on U.S. Treasury securities for each calendar quarter, and is compounded daily.[89]

* * *

The problems with the interest charge approach flow from its view of tax deferral as an interest-free loan from the government. Under this view, the tax that would have been paid under an accrual system, but which was not paid because of the realization requirement, is considered to have been loaned by the government to the taxpayer, and repaid at the time of the realization event. Current law, of course, does not charge interest on this deemed loan; the taxpayer gets the use of the government's money for free. Any proposal to charge interest on the deferred tax must address two questions. First, what is the principal amount of the deemed loan? Second, what should be the interest rate?

* * *

Principal on the Deemed Loan

* * *

The PFIC rules could be refined. Straight line accrual is more rapid than accrual at a constant rate, because of the effects of compounding. Simply

---

85. Many have advocated this approach. See, e.g., Blum, note 4, at 7-12; Roger Brinner, Inflation, Deferral and the Neutral Taxation of Capital Gains, 26 Nat'l Tax J. 565, 570-71 (1973); Roger Brinner & Alicia Munnell, Taxation of Capital Gains: Inflation and Other Problems, New Eng. Econ. Rev. Sept.-Oct. 1974, at 3, 12-21; Congressional Budget Office, Revising the Individual Income Tax 78-81 (1983); Fellows, note 4, at 810; John Helliwell, The Taxation of Capital Gains, 2 Can. J. of Econ. 314, 315 (1969); Institute for Fisc. Stud., The Structure and Reform of Direct Taxation 132-35, 148-49 (1978) (Meade Report); James W. Wetzler, Capital Gains and Losses, in Comprehensive Income Taxation 115, 152-53 (Joseph A. Pechman ed., 1977).

86. IRC § 1297(a).

87. IRC § 1291(a).

88. IRC § 1291 (c).

89. IRC § 6621.

stated, over the term of the investment, any undistributed earnings generate income after they are reinvested, so one would expect, if the rate of return were constant, that larger amounts of income would be earned towards the end of the holding period than towards the beginning. The straight line approach is biased in that it assumes more tax deferral than would occur if income had been earned at a constant rate. Investors recognize this bias, and the PFIC rules are widely believed to over-compensate for the benefits of deferral.

     * * *

Problems With the Interest-Charge Approach

An interest-charge approach would be a vast improvement over the current system. In a crude way, it would offset the benefits of deferral, without the liquidity and valuation problems that an accretion tax would create. Yet, the approach is not without its own significant problems, which can be illustrated by the use of this approach in the PFIC context. As noted above, PFIC investors regard this method as somewhat punitive in its effects. * * * Even if the formula were adjusted to reflect accrual of income at a constant rate, the formula will undercorrect for the benefits of deferral income in cases where most of the gains occur early in the holding period, and will overcorrect for these benefits where the gains occur late in the period.

These under- and overcorrections will prompt tax-motivated behavior. * * *

The Yield-based Method

There is a way to offset the benefits from tax deferral without the drawbacks of the interest charge approach. The key is to focus on the yield earned by the investment. The discussion in this Section assumes an investment that generates no interim cash flows, only a single contingent payment upon sale or maturity, such as a growth stock that does not pay dividends. A constant tax rate also is assumed. If there were no benefits from tax deferral, investments with the same pretax yields would have the same after-tax yields. In each case, the after-tax yield would be equal to the pretax yield times 100% minus the tax rate. For example, if the pretax yield were 10% and the tax rate were 35%, the after-tax yield would be 6.5%.

This focus on yield points the way to what the tax on sale should be. The government should take away just enough so that what the taxpayer has left is precisely what the taxpayer would have had if the return on the investment had been equal to the after-tax yield. If the taxpayer invests $1,000 at a 10% pretax yield, the investment will grow to $2,718 in 10 years. If the investment were sold then, the tax should be an amount that would leave the taxpayer with $1,916, which is the proceeds of $1,000 invested for 10 years at 6.5%. The difference of $802 is the proper amount of tax to compensate for the effects of deferral. This tax should be compared with the tax of $601 that would be imposed under the current system, which is obtained by applying the 35% tax rate to the nominal gain of $1,718. The extra $201 compensates for the privilege of deferring the tax until sale.

An Aside on Compounding

A reader who tries to verify the numbers in the preceding section with a pocket calculator probably will get different answers. The difference has to do with the compounding of the investment return over time.   If annual compounding is used, an investment of $1,000 at a 10% yield grows to $2,594,108 rather than $2,718, as stated above. The $2,718 figure is the result of continuous rather than annual compounding. * * *

Effect on Trading Decisions

An ideal income tax would have no effect on the choice of investments or on decisions when to buy or sell. The realization requirement causes the current income tax to fall well short of that ideal. Investments that offer tax deferral are favored over investments that do not, and tax considerations favor the retention of appreciated investments and the sale of depreciated investments.

The yield-based method of retrospective taxation eliminates these biases. The formula was derived so that the after-tax yield on each investment is exactly proportional to its pretax yield.   To the extent that investment decisions are based on expected yield, the yield-based method does not disturb the relative attractiveness of alternative investments. Volatility of yield is also a factor: Investors tend to prefer safer investments over riskier ones. The yield-based method also preserves relative volatility: If one investment has a more volatile pretax yield than another, it also will have a more volatile after-tax yield.

In general, the yield-based method has an overall effect of reducing risk, because the government is in effect a partner, sharing in profits and losses. This sharing may cause some investors to become more tolerant of risk, and a safer investment that might have been chosen in the absence of tax considerations might be rejected in favor of a riskier one. This bias, however, is endemic to any form of taxing net income, and indeed might be considered a benign way to promote riskier ventures that otherwise might have difficulty obtaining capital.

The yield-based method is "path independent" in that the amount of the tax does not depend on the path of the asset's fair market value over the holding period. The appreciation could have occurred early or late; the tax is the same. A consequence of this property is that the tax is immune to strategic trading: The taxpayer cannot improve his or her position by a wash sale, in which the asset is sold and the after-tax proceeds are invested in an identical asset.

* * *

Philosophical Underpinning
Irrelevance of Periodic Valuations

Path independence liberates the yield-based method from any concern over fair market value other than when the asset is bought and when it is sold. In contrast to accretion and interest-charge systems, the yield-based method requires neither periodic valuations nor accounting conventions that substitute for valuations. By making intermediate values irrelevant, the yield-based system preserves an aspect of the realization requirement that is very much worth preserving.

Unrealized gains are in some sense unreal. Academics scoff at this idea, noting that a mere sale, itself not a wealth-creating event, can turn unrealized gains into very real cash. Yet, since the taxpayer has decided not to sell, the unrealized gain is based on a contrary-to-fact hypothesis. If the owner of a closely held business realizes $x upon a sale of the business at time t_1, the fact that she could have realized $y upon a sale at some earlier time t_2 is of only academic interest to her, since, in fact, she did not sell at that time. The same is true even if the asset is not a closely held business but is a portfolio of publicly traded securities, and the amount obtainable at time t_2 can be ascertained with a fair degree of accuracy. Of course, the fact that investors regard unrealized gains as "paper profits" is no justification for giving investors the deferral benefits offered by the realization requirement. But a tax formula that eliminates this deferral benefit without relying on interim valuations is a promising way out of this dilemma.

* * *

Investments with Multiple Cash Flows

The yield-based method seems almost too good to be true, and in a sense it is. The basic case discussed so far involves a single investment with a single payoff at maturity. Real investments typically provide intermediate as well as final payments, and sometimes additional investments in an asset must be made subsequent to the initial purchase. These more realistic types of investments present serious conceptual difficulties as well as more complicated calculations, all of which raise formidable obstacles to any practical implementation of the yield-based approach. * * *

Life Under the Yield-Based Tax
* * *

Evaluating the Yield-Based Tax
* * *

Behavioral Effects

The yield-based method would have some salutary effects on investor behavior. The most prominent would be the elimination of the lock-in effect that discourages investors from selling appreciated assets under current law. By eliminating the tax disincentive to sell, the yield-based method would allow capital to flow more freely to its most productive uses.

An accretion system of taxation also would eliminate the lock-in effect. But accretion would substitute a different evil: forced sales to pay taxes. A yield-based system approaches the ideal of neutrality, in which investors sell no sooner, and no later, than they would in a world without taxes.

* * *

Could it Really Happen?

* * *

Translating a concept into legislation requires attention to detail on a scale far beyond the scope of this Article. It also requires political support. Correcting for the effects of the realization requirement is a favorite concern of the tax law academic community, but it lacks a political constituency. * * *

Even if it never happens, the yield-based tax is worth studying. Deferral remains a concern in particular areas of the tax law, such as offshore investments and long-term debt and leases. The effectiveness of any particular proposals to address the realization requirement is best judged against the standard that the yield-based method can provide. * * * Finally, the yield-based method offers insights into the dynamics of the time value of money. Many of these insights are surprising and counterintuitive. Even if the yield-based method does not usher in a new tax system, it sheds light on the current system.

Notes and Questions

27. Why is taxation of unrealized appreciation, as the Haig-Simons model suggests, referred to as "mark-to-market" taxation?

28. What does Mr. Land mean by the statement: "In a sense, the entire accrual method of accounting is an affront to the realization requirement?"

29. Professor Weisbach proposes a *partial* mark-to-market system—applicable to some assets, but not to others. Why not utilize a single system applicable to all assets?

30. A given rate of taxation is always less onerous under the realization regime than under mark-to-market, because the delay in paying tax on unrealized appreciation gives the taxpayer the benefit of the time value of money. (The effect on losses is just the opposite; see below.) Yet Professor Weisbach suggests that effective rates can be made comparable for assets in each of the two regimes. How would he set rates in order to achieve this outcome?

31. Professor Weisbach suggests marking to market many assets now taxed under the realization rule. Given that realization taxation defers tax, on its surface his proposal would appear to increase the overall tax burden on capital. Why does Weisbach assert that this is not so?

32. Weisbach proposes two tax rates. Assets taxed under the mark-to-market regime would be taxed at a given nominal rate, which would also be the effective rate. Assets taxed under the realization regime would be taxed at a higher nominal rate, which, on average, would offset the deferral advantage afforded by the realization rule and, on average, impose an effective rate equivalent to the rate imposed under the mark-to-market regime. Observe, however, that the equivalence is only achieved on average. Because the same tax rate would be imposed on all realization assets—whether held for three years or thirty—the effective tax rate for some realization assets would be higher than the mark-to-market rate, while the effective tax on realization assets held for a very long period of time would be lower.

33. For any given asset, therefore, the taxpayer's tax burden will be either lower or higher under the realization regime than under mark-to-market, but equal only in the rare case in which the deferral is exactly equal to the average deferral for all assets under the realization regime. With this problem in mind, Professor Weisbach states: "To minimize inefficiencies along the border, assets should be taxed the same as their closest substitutes." What does he mean by this?

34. Weisbach is not the first to suggest applying mark-to-market taxation much more widely than at present, but still without applying it to all assets. In an excellent earlier contribution, Professor David Shakow concluded that for many types of assets, current taxation of unrealized appreciation was not only theoretically correct, but also administratively feasible. Shakow summarized the scope of his proposal as follows:

> Some assets—notably owner-occupied residences and inexpensive consumer items—would be excluded from the system completely. Items that are particularly difficult to value—notably closely held stock and collectibles—would be taxed only on realization, but with an adjustment to the final gain or loss that is intended to compensate for the fact that interim gains and losses were not taxed annually. The realization rules for such assets, however, would not include all the special nonrecognition rules of current law. Certain business assets—notably inventories, accounts receivable, and depreciable personal property—could be included in the system through modified versions of current law already applied to them that approximate accrual taxation. Other intangible assets—good will and going concern value—would not be treated on an accrual basis. Business and investment liabilities would generally be incorporated in the system.[p]

---

p. Shakow, *supra* note n, at 1183.

35.   While most recent scholarship has focused on how to move the tax system closer to Haig-Simons principles, realization still finds scholarly support. Professor Edward Zelinsky observes that realization has fallen in the courts from its pinnacle as a constitutional requirement (*Eisner v. Macomber*), and that "[a]mong academics and tax policy experts, the doctrine of realization has fallen even lower."[q] Nonetheless, Zelinsky argues that realization is the better system because its "virtues * * * are attainable," while accretionism is attractive only in theory:

> Even the most ambitious plans to tax unrealized gains and losses could not reach major sectors of the economy: real estate, closely held businesses, pension interests, human capital, investment-grade art, and intellectual property; these important portions of the economy would either be left to realization-based taxation or would be subject to substitute forms of accretionism such as a deferral charge regime or an imputation system which assumes appreciation pursuant to a formula. There is no reason to believe that such sectoral accretionism would in practice be fairer and less distortionate than realization-based taxation. Hence, the realistic choice is not between the virtues of realization and the benefits of universal accretionism but between the attainable benefits of realization, on the one hand, and, on the other, sectoral accretionism which shares many of the shortcomings of realization-based taxation without also entailing those virtues.[r]

36.   Present law tends to "lock in" investors, who must pay tax immediately if they realize gains, but can postpone the tax indefinitely by postponing realization. (The postponement can be permanent if the asset is held to death; see section 1014 and Chapter Ten.) Pure Haig-Simons taxation would end the lock-in, by ending the opportunity for postponement. What would be the effect of Professor Weisbach's proposal on the lock-in problem with respect to assets moved to the mark-to-market system? With respect to assets left under the realization regime?

37.   Present law contains many imperfections, some of which tend to offset each other. For example, the realization rule (and its resulting undertaxation) tends to be a rough offset for the tax system's failure to index assets for inflation (which results in overtaxation, because nominal gains attributable to inflation are taxed). It is arguable that ending or restricting the

---

q. Edward A. Zelinsky, *For Realization: Income Taxation, Sectoral Accretionism, and the Virtue of Attainable Virtues*, 19 CARDOZO L. REV. 861, 861 (1997).

r. *Id.* at 864-65.

realization rule without also adopting some system of indexing would make the overall system less fair and efficient than present law. This is one aspect of Professor Weisbach's observation that "[t]he problem of the second-best may mean that a partial move toward the ideal may not be an improvement."

38.   On the other hand, the fact that present imperfections in the law result in overtaxation as well as undertaxation, could mean that change is more attainable in political terms than might be expected. As Professor Daniel Halperin observes, "elimination of the separate corporate tax on public corporations, indexation for inflation, and full allowance of losses should make mark-to-market more palatable."[s]

39.   Section 1211 severely limits the degree to which capital losses can offset ordinary income. What is the reason for these limitations? Would adoption of rules largely ending the deferral benefit of the realization rule end the justification for these limitations?

40.   Mr. Land asserts that his proposal would tend to make investments less risky. Why might this be so?

41.   Mr. Land indicts the realization rule on many familiar fronts, including horizontal and vertical inequity, and inefficiencies in investment decisions, notably as a result of the lock-in effect. He notes one effect that is frequently overlooked in the debate—the effect of the realization rule on overall tax rates, including taxes on labor income: "The realization requirement costs the government money; the lost revenue has to come from someplace."

42.   Haig-Simons taxation would require annual valuation of all assets, which is universally conceded to be impractical. Mr. Land, however, questions whether the Haig-Simons valuation requirement is correct even in theory, and thus to some extent joins ranks with Peel and Thuronyi, whose views are discussed in subchapter C. Does every asset have a "true value," however difficult it may be to ascertain?

43.   Professor Weisbach's proposal offers relief from the lock-in problem for those assets that would be taxed under the mark-to-market regime, but not those still taxed according to the realization rule. Would Mr. Land's proposal provide a more satisfactory solution to the lock-in problem?

---

s. Daniel Halperin, *Saving the Income Tax: An Agenda for Research*, 24 OHIO N.U. L. REV. 493, 494 (1998).

44. Mr. Land states that broad application of the interest-charge approach under which private foreign investment companies (PFICs) are currently taxed "would be a vast improvement over the current system." Why? What objections does Land have to current PFIC tax rules?

45. The Land article has been excerpted to present only the simplest situation—such as purchase of an asset followed by sale in a later year, without the asset producing any other income along the way. The heading "Investments with Multiple Cash Flows" has been edited to a single paragraph that offers the reader the smallest tip of a large and complex iceberg. Also edited out is the counterintuitive result that a loss would give the taxpayer a smaller tax benefit under Land's proposal than under present law. While Land's proposal is interesting and valuable, a reading of the full article suggests that we must put aside any hope that his proposal can be implemented without considerable complexity.

46. First-year law students learn that "property" is "a bundle of rights," not all of which are necessarily owned by the same person. For example, one individual may own a life estate in Blackacre, while another owns the remainder interest. Professors Noël Cunningham and Deborah Schenk suggest that "the rules with respect to the concept of realization are needlessly flawed,"[t] because of the tax law's insistence "that there is a single 'owner' of 'the property' at any given time."[u] Instead, Cunningham and Schenk suggest that the tax law treat all taxpayers with a financial interest in property as the current owner of that interest. Moreover, if the interest is one that predictably grows in value merely through the passage of time—such as a future interest—"a minimum rate of return would be imposed. The effect would be to narrow the scope of the realization requirement so that all income due solely to the passage of time would be taxed as it accrues."[v]

47. Haig-Simons income is usually discussed in terms of individuals. After all, for most individuals the primary component of Haig-Simons income is consumption, with a (usually) relatively minor adjustment for the increase or decrease in net worth. Corporations do not consume.

Professor Michael Knoll has recently proposed an interesting method of measuring corporate income in accord with Haig-Simons principles—by

---

t. Noël B. Cunningham & Deborah H. Schenk, *Taxation Without Realization: A "Revolutionary" Approach to Ownership*, 47 TAX L. REV. 725, 726 (1992).

u. *Id.*

v. *Id.* at 727.

reference to the current market value of the corporation's outstanding securities.[w] Because the corporation does not consume, the increase or decrease in the corporation's net worth, plus any distributions to investors, is the proper Haig-Simons measurement. Assuming an efficient securities market, the value of a corporation's outstanding securities should equal the present value of the corporation's expected future income. Does this seem a reasonable measure of corporate income? Why must distributions to investors be included in the measurement?

E. SHOULD THE TAX REPORTING PERIOD BE ONE YEAR?

Income tax in the United States and elsewhere has utilized the annual approach. This is not essential. Income could be accounted for more or less frequently than once per year. In the excerpt below, Professor Soled proposes that this country's income tax system utilize returns—and more importantly, an accounting period—of two years rather than one.

A PROPOSAL TO LENGTHEN THE TAX ACCOUNTING PERIOD
Jay A. Soled[*]

14 American Journal of Tax Policy 35, 35-55, 63-68 (1997)

New York City is separated from New Jersey by the Hudson River. Several years ago, bridge and tunnel commuters had to pay a toll when traveling into the City and another traveling out of the City. To alleviate congestion in the City and to reduce the costs of administration, officials at local New York and New Jersey transit authorities conceived the simple, revenue-neutral plan of having commuters pay a single toll, at double the fare, upon entry into the City. Implementing this plan has proven to be a boon to commuters and the local transit authorities alike: commuters are able to streamline their daily commute and the local New York and New Jersey transit authorities save millions of dollars annually of administrative expenses.

What does toll collection in New York City have in common with federal tax collection? The Internal Revenue Code requires tax returns to be filed annually on the basis of an annual accounting period. These requirements were introduced in the original version of the Code and have never been changed. The success of the New York City toll collection plan provides an opportunity to consider whether the administrative, revenue, and equity goals of the annual tax accounting period can be achieved by extending this period

---

w. Michael S. Knoll, *An Accretion Corporate Income Tax,* 49 STAN. L. REV. 1 (1996).

*. At time of original publication, Associate Professor, Rutgers University.

(and the related tax filing requirement) to two years (the biennial approach). If the biennial approach is feasible, tremendous benefits can flow to taxpayers, information return providers, *e.g.*, brokerage houses and banks, and the government. Among the many immediate benefits, taxpayers would have to spend less time and expend fewer resources gathering tax information, preparing tax returns, and filing these returns with the Internal Revenue Service. Information return providers would only have to meet their obligations biennially, rather than being burdened with supplying information returns on an annual basis. The government, too, would be a major benefactor of this proposal, as it would only have to process (and possibly audit) half the number of tax returns it currently receives under existing Code requirements.

The idea of establishing a biennial accounting and return period is radical; it attempts to transform a long and uninterrupted history of contrary practice. But the annual filing period was a product of yesterday's concerns regarding administrative needs, revenue collection, oversight, and automation. Now, in an age of withholding, estimated taxes, information returns, and the Service's sophisticated monitoring abilities and computers, stretching the annual accounting period to two years is technically feasible and fiscally responsible. Furthermore, because the potential advantages stemming from a biennial approach greatly outweigh its potential disadvantages, politicians and the general public alike would probably be receptive towards adopting this proposal.

* * *

Rationale Underlying the Annual Tax Accounting Period

Prior Rationale

To be operational, the government requires a regular flow of revenue. * * * [T]o ensure regularity in the case of an income tax, something more is needed: A method of tax accounting that ascertains a taxpayer's income over a particular period of time. There is nothing, however, sacred or immutable about using a twelve month period as a measuring rod. As long as the government's regular flow of revenue is not disrupted or jeopardized, any definite period of time would suffice.

Why, then, did Congress originally choose a twelve month tax accounting period? Although there is no legislative history on this issue, Congress probably chose a twelve month accounting period on the basis that it was successfully used as a measuring rod in other countries with an income tax, *e.g.*, Great Britain, the federal government was on the verge of determining its budget annually, and accountants had long used a twelve month period as the financial accounting cycle. * * *

Obsolescence of Prior Rationale

The Code has evolved from its humble origins as a simple tool to raise revenue into a sophisticated legislative device that goes well beyond revenue raising and attempts to set social and economic policy. The purpose of financial accounting is to inform management and investors of the financial means of a business and the purpose of income tax accounting is to measure income for purposes of raising revenue, setting social policy, and regulating the economy. Because of this fact, the determination of income differs immensely between the tax and accounting disciplines.

* * *

In addition, revenue needs no longer represent a legitimate reason to maintain a twelve month accounting period. The institution of estimated tax payments combined with stringent withholding requirements has made the issue of annual revenue collection moot. The government now typically refunds more taxes than it collects at the time tax returns are filed.

Taxpayers no longer have to manually maintain voluminous tax records. The advent and the growth of information return requirements, coupled with the computer revolution, have made this responsibility unnecessary. * * * Whether numeric entries encompass a one or a two-year accounting period would be a matter of indifference to most computer users.

* * *

Analysis of the Biennial Approach

Prior to evaluating the merits of the biennial approach, the salient features of this proposal require elaboration. First, this proposal goes well beyond having taxpayers staple two years of tax returns together, or requiring a single tax return with two columns, each column representing a separate tax year. Although having some merit, adoption of either of these more limited proposals would defeat one of the fundamental goals of the biennial approach, which is to alleviate the time consuming burdens that confront taxpayers, information return preparers, and the government on an annual basis.

Second, the biennial approach would have to extend to all taxpayers. Certainly, there is a superficial appeal to limiting this proposal on an initial basis to special categories of taxpayers, such as salaried workers earning less than $100,000. These workers have a steady stream of income that is easily measurable and their income tax returns are, in general, relatively simple. Amalgamating two of their tax years into one seems straightforward and using this category of taxpayers, at least on a trial basis, appears inviting. Upon closer examination, however, limiting this proposal to a particular category of taxpayers (in this case, salaried workers) could prove nettlesome because (i) classifying taxpayers is not as easy as it sounds and (ii) application of the law in this fashion could prove inequitable.

In terms of the classification issue, a worker, for example, could be salaried during that worker's day job and be an independent contractor on a night job; alternatively, a worker could be salaried during part of the tax period and an independent contractor during another part of the tax period. * * * Employers and financial institutions, too, would have the perplexing task of ascertaining whether a worker was subject to a one year or two year accounting cycle. * * *

Similarly, it would probably not be advisable that this proposal apply to some taxpayers in one year and to others in the next year, *e.g.*, taxpayers whose social security numbers end in an even number filing in even numbered years and taxpayers whose social security numbers end in an odd number file in the odd numbered years. A "rolling" filing system might generate certain administrative efficiencies, *e.g.*, staff at the Service and at tax accounting firms could be maintained at a fairly constant level. But a rolling system would be certain to generate issues of fairness, *e.g.*, to which group of taxpayers would a new set of tax laws first be applied.[37] To limit the confusion that would be attendant to implementation of the biennial approach, it should be applied universally to all taxpayers.[38]

　　　* * *

Finally, because many states, in one fashion or another, use the federal government's definitions of income as the benchmark for their own taxpayers, it would be important that state legislatures acquiesce to the biennial approach.[42] State governments adopting the biennial approach, like the federal government, would reap the benefits of this proposal. Maintenance of the annual accounting period by certain states could jeopardize many of the advantages of this proposal, *e.g.*, information returns would again have to be

---

37. If a rolling filing system were adopted, a number of novel, but not insurmountable challenges would arise. For example, what would be the proper accounting period for a joint return filed by an odd year taxpayer who married an even year taxpayer?

38. One possible way to test the biennial approach would be to institute it experimentally with respect to certain tax-exempt entities, such as charities and pension plans. If the biennial approach is successful in the tax-exempt contest, consideration should be given to expanding the proposal to all taxpayers.

42. Aside from state legislatures, banks and foreign nations might object to the implementation of this proposal. Before extending credit, banks usually like to review a debtor's most recent tax returns to gauge the financial health of a potential debtor. It may be difficult for some banks to assess creditworthiness on the basis of tax returns that may be close to two years old under the biennial approach. Because adoption of the biennial approach might have a disruptive effect on the tax collections of other nations, they, too, might object to its implementation. Even in the absence of objections, a number of existing income and estate tax treaties would have to be renegotiated and amended if the biennial approach were adopted. The Treasury Department has been in this position before. For example, in recently proposed regulations regarding the taxation of computer software, the Treasury Department was placed in the position of having "to encourage international tax authorities to conform to the US benchmark." *Computer Software Regs Kick Off Treasury Focus on Internet Taxes*, 73 TAX NOTES 777, 777 (Nov. 18, 1996).

prepared on an annual basis for taxpayers of a nonadopting state. And although the failure of a particular state or states to adopt the biennial approach would not necessarily be catastrophic to the success of this proposal at the federal level, it might present some practical problems for taxpayers who have multistate operations.

Having described some of the salient features of the biennial approach, the analysis next turns to a closer examination of the potential advantages and disadvantages resulting from this proposal. * * *

The Pragmatic Criteria

Efficiency

* * * The annual accounting and filing requirements entail compliance costs that consist of two elements. The first element includes out-of-pocket expenditures for professional advice, books and manuals, and computer software. The second element includes opportunity costs incurred by taxpayers who must spend time on tasks related to the filing of returns, *e.g.*, maintaining and organizing records, learning the law, and working with tax professionals.

These compliance costs are not small. About half of all individual taxpayers turn to an accountant or other professional advisor at the time of filing. And this advice does not come cheaply: tax return data indicates that individual taxpayers on average spend over two billion dollars annually for the services of tax professionals.[48] The price for such advice per taxpayer currently averages about $158 annually.[49]

In addition to the actual cash outlays made by taxpayers, there are enormous opportunity costs incurred by taxpayers. * * * [O]ne study conducted in 1989 concluded that individuals annually spent about three billion hours, or an average of about 27 hours per year per taxpayer, dealing with federal and state personal income taxes.[52] * * * [T]he compliance costs in the business context are just as staggering, *e.g.*, a 1985 study estimates that

---

48. INTERNAL REVENUE SERVICE, STATISTICS OF INCOME — 1988 (Publication 1304), Individual Income Tax Returns (1991) at 50.

49. JOEL SLEMROD & JON BAKIJA, TAXING OURSELVES 131 (1996).

52. Marsha Blumenthal & Joel Slemrod, *The Compliance Cost of the U.S. Individual Income Tax System: A Second Look After Tax Reform*, 45 NAT'L TAX J. 185 (1992). A recent Service report indicates that individual and business taxpayers spend approximately 5.3 billion hours annually keeping records, learning the laws, and preparing and sending their tax returns. 75 TAX NOTES 463, 467 (Apr. 28, 1997). This report estimates federal income tax compliance cost taxpayers $122.7 billion in 1997. *Id.* at 468.

businesses and their paid advisors spent an annual total of 3.6 billion hours dealing with issues relating to income taxation.[54] * * *

Combining the two elements of compliance costs, cash out-lays and opportunity costs, researchers have recently made a strong argument that the national cost for personal income tax compliance alone ran $50 billion in 1995.[56] * * *

Furthermore, over a trillion information returns are prepared and filed every year. * * * Each information return results in a de minimis expenditure on the part of the preparer or responsible party, but when these expenditures are aggregated, the overall costs are substantial.

     * * *

Extending the annual tax accounting period and requiring tax returns to be filed biennially concededly would not reduce by half the time taxpayers spend in the return preparation and filing process. There would, however, be tremendous savings of time and money from biennial filing. * * *

Administrability

Direct Costs

In addition to receiving over a trillion information returns, the Internal Revenue Service received 116,147,596 individual income tax returns in 1994 (the latest tax year for which data are available). Even the size of this daunting figure, however, fails to convey the entire picture. Every year the Service mails millions of blank income tax returns to taxpayers for completion, staffs a toll-free information and advice line with tax professionals to aid taxpayers, and advertises in various media regarding the need to file tax returns in a timely fashion. The costs of completing these tasks and offering these services are not adequately broken down in the Service's budget, but the annual cost must be measured in millions of dollars.

The Service's main responsibility is to process and audit the returns. Expenditures for this activity exceeded five billion dollars in 1995 (the latest tax year for which data are available). Yet, in 1994 (the latest tax year for which data are available), the Service could audit only 1.36 percent of the returns it received due to its limited resources.[65]

* * * In particular, the savings achieved by the biennial proposal could be redirected by the Service to conduct more audits or to enhance the quality of its other monitoring procedures.

---

54. INTERNAL REVENUE SERVICE, DEVELOPMENT OF METHODOLOGY FOR ESTIMATING THE TAXPAYER PAPERWORK BURDEN, FINAL REPORT TO THE DEPARTMENT OF THE TREASURY (1988). A more recent study draws a similar conclusion. *See* Joel B. Slemrod & Marsha Blumenthal, *The Income Tax Compliance Cost of Big Business*, 24 PUB. FIN. Q. 411 (1996).

56. SLEMEOD & BARIJA, *supra* note 49, at 131.

65. *Id.* at Table 11. The fact that so few tax returns are audited causes many taxpayers to consider playing what is known in tax parlance as the audit roulette game.

Indirect Costs
* * *

[I]f Congress were to adopt the biennial approach, it seems * * * likely that the taxpayers would have no difficulty mastering the requirements of biennial filing and adapting to it. Indeed, taxpayers would only have to educate themselves biennially rather than annually regarding changes to the tax law.
* * *

Macroeconomic Effects
Stabilization and Growth
* * *

It might seem that extending the accounting period and filing requirement to two years would make it more difficult for Congress to adjust the economy's health using the income tax system. A sick patient hardly wants to be told that a cure is on the way—in two years. The proposal, however, will not reduce the ability of Congress to intervene in the economy quickly because most of the tax will be—as it is now—collected by withholding and estimated tax payments. Revised withholding tables can take effect almost immediately. Most taxpayers will adjust their estimated payments to the revised tax rules quite promptly. Further, the use of retroactive provisions is no secret to Congress. If Congress can achieve these results in the context of an annual accounting period, there is no inherent reason why the outcome would differ under a biennial approach.

Revenue

In theory, adoption of the biennial approach should have a minimal effect on revenue flow to the government because the vast majority of tax is collected by means of withholding and estimated tax payments. But, as often is the case, theory may not comport with reality. More specifically, under the biennial approach, tax compliance would probably suffer a small decline. A tax return serves a notice function to the Service that something in the taxpayer's financial life may be askew. Delaying that notice for an extra twelve months may leave the government in repose when it should be taking action against the noncompliant taxpayer. The more expeditiously the government can ascertain a noncompliance problem and protect its interests by filing an assessment, lien, or levy, the more likely it will recover on a potential deficiency.
* * *

Another potential deficiency of the biennial approach stems from the fact that, like any debtor, the more a taxpayer owes, the harder it may be for that taxpayer to pay. A taxpayer owing $5,000 of taxes after one year may be in a much better position to pay the tax due than another taxpayer owing $10,000 of taxes after two years.

Congress could allay these concerns by instituting a series of compliance measures and a deferred tax installment payment method. * * * In addition, because fewer returns would be filed, the government should have additional resources at its disposal to step-up enforcement and monitoring efforts. * * *

Requisite Changes to the Code to Effect the Proposal

* * * This section of the analysis discusses in detail the more important Code amendments that adoption of the biennial approach would require.

Adjustment to Rate Schedules and Other Thresholds

To achieve revenue neutrality, adoption of the biennial approach would require that Congress adjust various income tax rate schedules. Failure to make a rate adjustment would result in a tax increase for most taxpayers by subjecting more of their income to the higher rates. To illustrate, a married couple [who file] jointly and have taxable income [of] $100,000 annually would be subject to a tax of $22,656 under 1997 income tax rates and thus $45,312 during a two-year period. Applying the present rate schedule to their $200,000 income under the biennial approach would result in a tax of $56,068.50.

Simply doubling the brackets would solve this problem. The inflation adjustment factors, however, would have to be computed on a biennial basis in order to adjust the brackets correctly.

A related change would have to be made with respect to specific dollar thresholds prevalent throughout the Code. * * * It seems in general that doubling the present amounts would produce the right result.

A somewhat different question arises with percentage limitations, such as the 7.5 percent threshold for the deduction of medical expenses. This is a substantial barrier to the deduction of medical expenses for most taxpayers in its present form. If the 7.5 percent threshold were applied to twice as much income in a biennial filing system, the absolute dollar amount would make it even more unlikely that taxpayers who do not have a very high level of recurring medical expenses could deduct any medical expenses.
* * *

Enhancement of Taxpayer Compliance

The American Bar Association Section of Taxation (Tax Section) has periodically voiced a series of recommendations to enhance taxpayer compliance, primarily focusing on the expanded use of information returns and withholding requirements.[113] To compensate the Service for what will likely

---

113. *See generally*, INCOME TAX COMPLIANCE: A REPORT OF THE ABA SECTION OF TAXATION INVITATIONAL CONFERENCE ON INCOME TAX COMPLIANCE (1983).

be a more challenging task of ensuring taxpayer compliance under a biennial approach, Congress should give renewed consideration to instituting these recommendations.

Information returns have proven to be a tremendous stimulant of voluntary compliance. In light of this fact, the Tax Section has consistently recommended that the use of information returns be expanded in the area of self-employment and most capital gain transactions. * * *

The Tax Section has also voiced strong support to expand withholding requirements, particularly with respect to interest and dividend payments. * * *

Summary

Although this survey of suggested Code amendments is not exhaustive, it permits certain general observations to be made. First, the changes under review are not sweeping; most Code sections would remain wholly intact were Congress to adopt the biennial approach. Second, the changes associated with the biennial approach are not novel; in one fashion or another, changes regarding rates, income deferral, and compliance have all been made in the past for other reasons. Third, most of the proposed Code changes address one of the central concerns likely to be voiced by the critics of this proposal, namely issues of tax compliance. Finally, Congressional adoption of these recommended Code amendments and others would alleviate the apprehension of skeptics of the biennial approach.

Conclusion

* * *

If neither the Egyptians nor anyone else had discovered the length of time it takes the Earth to make one full rotation around the Sun, our conception and measurement of time would probably be quite different. Under those circumstances, the determination of income could have been made over a hundred or perhaps a thousand day period. The length of time so chosen would not be significant as long as the taxpayers' and government's respective needs could be satisfied. In the end, what this analysis reveals is that although there is nothing inherently or logically wrong with a twelve-month accounting period, there is nothing inherently or logically right about it either. Because the biennial approach offers significant advantages over the annual tax accounting convention, Congress should strongly consider adopting this proposal.

Notes and Questions

48. Professor Soled never mentions the dominant role of agriculture in the economy of the world throughout history. The fact that the calendar year begins and ends in winter accords with the agricultural cycle of the northern

hemisphere. For millennia, farmers have made payments in kind, by surrendering a share of the crop—not just to government, but to other creditors, such as landlords. Even where payment was made in cash, it was likely to be determined with reference to the cash that was received upon sale of the harvest.

Agriculture is frequently an annual undertaking. The farmer expends money and labor for much of the year in order to achieve a harvest late in the same calendar year. For these reasons, the annual basis for the income tax made eminent sense when agriculture dominated the economy and the lives of most people—which was still the case in the United States when the Sixteenth Amendment was ratified in 1913. The decline of the relative importance of agriculture may be a more convincing reason to consider Soled's proposal than technical factors such as the use of computers and tax withholding.

49. Why does Soled reject implementing the biennial approach, at least initially, only for taxpayers with relatively simple returns, such as low-income wage earners?

50. Professor Soled proposes that all taxpayers file at substantially the same time, every two years (for example, in the spring following every even-numbered year). It might seem that the administrative advantages of biennial filing, especially for the Internal Revenue Service, would be greatest if half the population filed each year (for example, taxpayers whose Social Security numbers ended in an odd digit would file following odd-numbered years, and even-digit taxpayers following even-numbered years). Would such a "rolling" system be more or less workable than the approach Soled prefers? What of the joint return problem Soled mentions in footnote 37?

51. Would it be important that states go along with the change to biennial taxation, or could the change be implemented for federal taxes while some states retained annual taxation?

52. How would adoption of biennial filing lead to increased compliance problems? In what ways might biennial filing improve compliance?

53. Professor Soled discounts the possibility that his proposal "would make it more difficult for Congress to adjust the economy's health using the income tax system." Do you think Congress would be less likely to make frequent changes? If so, would you view this as an advantage or a disadvantage of the biennial approach?

54.   If medical expenses were deductible only to the extent they exceeded 7.5 percent of the taxpayer's biennial income, would this greatly affect the value of the medical deduction?

55.   The primary theme of this chapter has been the tension between the theoretical appeal of the Haig-Simons definition of income and the practical limitations of a real-world tax system. The proposal to move to a biennial system seems far removed from this debate, but might have some impact.

The longer the accounting period, the less likely that realization will fall in a different period than the period during which the associated Haig-Simons income arose. At the extreme, a tax levied over an accounting period spanning an entire lifetime would raise relatively few such problems. Biennial returns would leave fewer such problems than do annual returns. On the other hand, biennial returns could lead to even more tax maneuvering at the margin. For example, postponing a sale of appreciated property from December to January might be meaningless in some years, but provide a two-year deferral in others.

56.   Some proposals addressing the problem of realization contemplate shortening the tax period. For example, as discussed in Note #47 (page 100), Professor Michael Knoll has suggested that the appropriate way to measure Haig-Simons income for corporations is by reference to the current market value of the corporation's outstanding securities. One practical problem might be that corporations would have an incentive to release unfavorable information at the end of the year, thereby reducing share prices and the corporation's tax bill. The tax period need not be so long as a year, however. Professor Knoll suggests that "the tax period can be made very short, approximating that of continuous accretion, without substantially complicating administration."[x]

---

x. Knoll, *supra* note w, at 16.

CHAPTER THREE

IMPUTED INCOME

*Imputed income may be defined * * * as a flow of satisfactions from durable goods owned and used by the taxpayer, or from goods and services arising out of the personal exertions of the taxpayer on his own behalf.*

*Imputed income is non-cash income or income in kind. But all non-cash income, or income in kind, is not included in the category of imputed income. * * ***

*Imputed income is * * * a species of the genus income in kind, and its distinguishing characteristic is that it arises outside the ordinary processes of the market.*[a]

A. INTRODUCTION

Neither of the two broad categories of imputed income—that arising from property and that arising from services—is included in the base of the federal income tax. The classic example of *imputed income from property* is the economic benefit arising from the taxpayer's ownership of his residence. The taxpayer who purchases a home for $100,000 receives as a return on her investment the right to live rent-free, and tax-free, in a $100,000-home. By contrast, if the taxpayer had invested the money in securities, using the income generated to rent a residence, she would have been taxed on the income but have received no offsetting deduction for the expenditure. While housing is the most important example, imputed income from property arises from the ownership of any tangible asset of long life, such as an automobile or refrigerator, or even a tennis racket or ash tray.

Imputed income from services is the economic value of services rendered by the taxpayer for the benefit of himself or his family, or of others whom the taxpayer wishes to benefit. For example, the taxpayer who mows his own lawn or waxes his own car confers an economic benefit upon himself, without the burden of taxation. By contrast, if the taxpayer works in the market, then uses his earnings to pay someone to mow the lawn or wax the car, he will be taxed on his income and receive no deduction for his payment. The classic example of imputed income from services is the household and child care services rendered by a housewife to her family.

It is important to keep in mind the distinction between imputed income and other types of *income in kind*. While imputed income arises from the

---

a. Donald B. Marsh, *The Taxation of Imputed Income*, 58 POL. SCI. Q. 514 (1943).

113

taxpayer's use of his own property or services to benefit himself (and members of his family or household), income in kind can be a method of payment for a transaction with another. For example, if an employee is allowed to live rent-free in a house owned by his employer, this in-kind benefit is not imputed income and, unless it fits within an exception to the general rule,[b] is included in the employee's gross income.

B. IMPUTED INCOME FROM PROPERTY

Serious proposals have been made to include in the tax base major categories of imputed income from property, particularly housing. As discussed in the following excerpts, this has been done in some jurisdictions and proposed for the United States. (Note that since Dr. Goode wrote, the United Kingdom has ceased including such imputed income in its tax base.)

Assuming it is decided that the failure to tax imputed income is a problem (and there is no unanimity on this question), it remains uncertain what, if anything, should be done about the problem. Although taxing the imputed income may be the most obvious remedy, others have been proposed, notably allowing renters some form of benefit to offset the perceived advantage of owner-occupiers. Doing nothing may emerge as not only the most likely course of action, but the best.

IMPUTED RENT OF OWNER-OCCUPIED DWELLINGS UNDER THE INCOME TAX
Richard Goode[*]
15 Journal of Finance 504, 504-07, 512-14, 518-25 (1960)

Most economists agree that the rental value of a dwelling is part of the income of an owner-occupant. The services of the dwelling give the owner power to satisfy his wants, and that power is susceptible of valuation in terms of money.[1] In support of the view that the imputed rent of owner-occupied houses is income, the British Royal Commission on the Taxation of Profits and Income advanced two arguments: (1) the owner could rent his house if he wished, and his failure to do so indicates that the value of the occupancy to him must be at least equal to the rent foregone; and (2) an owner-occupant is better off than a tenant with the same money income.[2] The commission might have added that the homeowner has the alternative of investing his capital in other

---

b. Section 119 excludes from income the value of lodging under certain circumstances. Note that even when this exclusion applies, the value of the lodging is obtained in a market transaction and therefore is *not* imputed income.

*. At time of original publication, Brookings Institution.

1. In his classic definition, Haig said: ". . . Income becomes the increase or accretion in one's power to satisfy his wants in a given period in so far as that power consists of (*a*) money itself, or, (*b*) anything susceptible of valuation in terms of money" (see Robert Murray Haig, "The concept of Income—Economic and Legal Aspects," in *The Federal Income Tax*, ed. Haig [New York: Columbia University Press, 1921], p.7).

2. *Final Report* (Cmd. 9474 [June, 1955]), pp. 249-50.

assets, and the choice of a house shows that he considers the return from it superior to the yield of other income-producing investments.

The imputed rent of owner-occupied houses is taxable income in the United Kingdom and many other countries. In the United States, however, imputed rent has never been included in the base of the federal income tax. The state of Wisconsin taxed the estimated rental value of owner-occupied residential property under its original income tax law of 1911 but discontinued this practice in 1917. Many economists have favored the inclusion of imputed rent in taxable income for purposes of the federal tax. In 1921 Haig concluded that this income should be taxed "if it is practicable to evaluate it."[3] Taxation of imputed rent has been recommended by Simons, Vickrey, Pechman, and others.[4]

The usual proposal is for the taxation of net rent, defined as imputed gross rent minus necessary expenses of ownership. The expenses consist of interest on mortgage debt, property taxes, depreciation, repairs and maintenance, and casualty insurance. * * *

Discriminatory Effects of the Exclusion of Imputed Rent and of Deductions for Interest and Taxes

The omission of imputed net rent from taxable income and the deductions for mortgage interest and property taxes on owner-occupied dwellings impair the uniformity of the income tax by producing differences in the taxation of persons with equal real incomes and by altering the usual relation between the tax liabilities of persons at different income levels. First and most obviously, the exclusion and deductions favor homeowners and discriminate against renters. The part of the owner's income which takes the form of imputed net rent and his expenditures for mortgage interest and property taxes are free of tax. The renter must use taxable income to pay his full housing costs. Second, the investor in an owner-occupied house is favored in comparison with other investors. * * *

Among owner-occupants, the exclusion and personal deductions favor those with high incomes compared with those in lower brackets. This is true because the value of an exclusion or deduction from taxable income varies directly with the marginal tax rate. * * *

The present arrangement also favors persons with a high preference for housing as against those who care less for this form of consumption. It favors those who like accommodations of a kind that are easily owner-occupied compared with those who have other tastes. For example, families who prefer

---

3. *Op. cit.*, p. 24.
4. Henry C. Simons, *Personal Income Taxation* (Chicago: University of Chicago Press, 1938), p. 211, and *Federal Tax Reform* (Chicago: University of Chicago Press, 1950), p. 36; William Vickrey, *Agenda for Progressive Taxation* (New York: Ronald Press, 1947), pp. 18-24; Joseph A. Pechman, "Erosion of the Individual Income Tax," *National Tax Journal*, X (March, 1957), 14-15, and "What Would a Comprehensive Individual Income Tax Yield?" in House Ways and Means Committee, *Tax Revision Compendium* (1959), 1, 261-62.

to live in the suburbs are favored compared with others who prefer a residential hotel in the central city. The benefits of the exclusion and deductions are more easily available to persons who lead settled lives than to those whose occupation requires them to move frequently.

Ownership of consumer durable goods resembles homeownership, in that the investment in the durables yields a real return which is not subject to income tax. The same general argument can be made for taxing the imputed service value of consumer durables as for including imputed net rent of owner-occupied houses in taxable income. * * * [C]onsumers' investment in durables is large, although smaller than their investment in dwellings. Nevertheless, an attempt to tax the service value of consumer durables is seldom recommended because of administrative difficulties. The renting of consumer durables is less prevalent than the renting of dwellings, and the problem of discrimination between renters and owners is less acute for durables than for houses. In addition to renters of equipment, however, there are many consumers who obtain through the market services similar to those provided by durables. The patrons of commercial laundries and public transportation, for example, suffer a discrimination compared with owners of home laundry equipment and automobiles which is similar to that experienced by tenants compared with homeowners. It seems likely that ownership of durables is positively correlated with homeownership and that the effects of omitting imputed returns on the two kinds of investment are generally cumulative rather than offsetting.

* * *

The Effect on Housing Consumption and Homeownership of the Exclusion and Deductions

* * *

The tax saving due to the exclusion and deductions may be viewed as a reduction in the price of housing services for owner-occupiers who are subject to income tax or who would be subject to tax if imputed rent were included in the tax base. Inasmuch as the prices of rental housing and other goods and services are not directly affected by the exclusion, the price of housing services from owner-occupied dwellings is reduced relative to the prices of rental housing and all other goods and services. * * *

The presumption is that the changes in relative prices cause a shift from renting to owning one's dwelling and an increase in the total amount of housing services consumed relative to other goods and services. For these shifts to occur it is not necessary that consumers calculate the effect on relative prices of the income tax advantages of homeownership and adjust their budgets accordingly. Many may be conscious of the tax value of the deductions for interest and taxes, but probably only a sophisticated few recognize the significance of the exclusion. * * *

As an influence on decisions to buy houses, the deductions for interest and taxes seem to be more important than the exclusion of imputed net rent. One reason is that, in the aggregate, the deductible items are substantially larger than net rent. A second reason is that net rent is likely to be especially small, relative to interest and property taxes, for new buyers. Most new buyers have smaller equities in their houses than the average for all owner-occupiers. * * *

Policy Implications

In appraising the economic significance of the omission of imputed rent from taxable income it is necessary to ask whether the stimulation of housing consumption and the promotion of homeownership are recognized objectives of public policy. If these are policy objectives, a further question is whether the present tax treatment is an appropriate and effective means of achieving them. If they are not specifically intended, the changes in consumption and ownership patterns impair the efficiency of resource allocation, and the question is whether the loss is great or small.

Much support can be found for the view that the improvement of housing standards is highly desirable, and there are some indications that public opinion and government policy accord a special status to housing. The emphasis, however, has usually been on slum clearance and the provision of minimum facilities for low-income groups and the elderly rather than on a general increase in housing consumption. At times, the promotion of housing construction has been favored as a means of stimulating general economic activity. The encouragement of homeownership appears to attract wide social approval. Homeownership is often thought to be associated with active interest and participation in community affairs and thus to have important intangible values. * * *

On the assumption that promotion of homeownership is a policy objective, the present income tax provisions work in the right direction but may be inefficient. The strongest stimulus to homeownership is given where least needed—to those with high incomes and high marginal rates of tax. * * * It seems entirely possible that the federal government could give broader and more effective encouragement to homeownership and housing by increasing expenditures for housing programs in an amount equal to the revenue loss attributable to the failure to tax imputed rent.

Implications of Revising the Income Tax Treatment of Owners and Renters

The present discrimination between homeowners and renters could be eliminated by broadening the income tax base to include imputed rent or could be reduced by allowing tenants to deduct rental payments from taxable income. Another approach would be to eliminate the personal deductions that owners are now allowed for payments of interest and property taxes, without requiring net imputed rent to be included in taxable income. These revisions would differ considerably in revenue implications, administrative complexity, and effectiveness in equalizing taxation of different groups.

Taxation of Imputed Rent

The only exact method of eliminating the discriminations between homeowners and renters would be to include in taxable income the net rental value of owner-occupied dwellings. * * *

Administrative problems would be involved. * * * The unique problem would be the estimation of gross rental value. Estimates have always been important in the allocation, between activities and over time, of contractual outlays or receipts. Depreciation allowances are an outstanding example. The items, however, can nearly always be traced back, if necessary, to transactions involving the payment or receipt of money or the exchange of property. The estimation of the gross rent which an owner-occupied dwelling would command could not be referred so directly to a market transaction. It would not be especially difficult to make fairly accurate estimates. They are prepared, as a matter of course, by FHA appraisers and others. But a higher standard of accuracy is demanded for income tax assessments than for mortgage appraisals and many other valuations. The estimation of imputed rent would involve the federal income tax authorities in a new kind of problem, and it would be necessary to deal with a large number of cases.

* * *

It has been suggested that, in order to minimize the administrative difficulties involved in determination of imputed net rent, the figure be approximated by taking a standard rate of return on the owner's equity in the property, while allowing no deduction for interest, depreciation, and other costs. * * * The simplicity of this approach, however, is deceptive. In most cases the determination of capital value and owner's equity would not be much easier than the direct estimation of gross rental value. The difficulty of keeping assessments up to date would be the same under the modified computations as if an exact computation of imputed rent were required. In view of the rapid changes in property values that often occur and the experience of depreciation and obsolescence, it would be seriously objectionable to take as the owner's equity original cost minus current mortgage debt. * * *

The experience of the United Kingdom in taxing imputed rent does not shed much light on the practicability of doing so in the United States. In the United Kingdom, rent of owner-occupied dwellings has been included in * * * income from the beginning of the income tax, and its taxation is in accord with tradition rather than an innovation. The British custom of referring to the value of a house as its annual rent rather than its capital value may also contribute to popular acceptance of the inclusion of imputed rent in taxable income. Property taxes (local rates) are assessed against rental value rather than capital value. * * *

The administrative problems that would be presented by the measurement of imputed net rent with reasonable accuracy do not appear to be insuperable or even intrinsically very difficult. These problems, however, would be novel for the federal tax authorities. The staff that would be required for satisfactory administration of this provision would probably be large relative to the total administrative force for the income tax. The public would no doubt find the new provisions complicated and distasteful. With due regard for institutional and political considerations, the taxation of imputed rent must be considered difficult but not impossible.

Deduction of Rent

Under the Civil War income tax, tenants were allowed to deduct annual rental payments on their residences, beginning with the act of 1863. All taxpayers were allowed to deduct all federal, state, and local taxes and interest payments. Imputed rent was not taxable. The deduction for rent was intended to place tenants and homeowners in the same position, but it actually favored tenants, since the deduction of gross rent exceeded the sum of the deductions and exclusion allowed owner-occupants. Gross rent covers depreciation and repairs and maintenance, which were not deductible by owner-occupants, as well as taxes and interest, which were deductible. The Civil War tax, nevertheless, appears to have resulted in much more nearly equal treatment of renters and owner-occupants than has been achieved in the modern income tax law. Although allowance of a deduction for rent would reduce present inequalities and would involve no special administrative difficulties, it cannot be recommended in view of its revenue cost and the favoritism it would show to housing compared with other forms of consumption. *It might be feasible to modify the approach by allowing tenants to deduct only adjusted net rent, defined as gross rent minus an allowance for depreciation and other costs not deductible by owner-occupants. This would approximately equalize the taxation of renters and owners but would not avoid discrimination in favor of housing. * * *

Disallowance of Personal Deductions for Interest Payments and Taxes

Another approach would be to discontinue the personal deductions for payments of interest and property taxes with respect to owner-occupied dwellings without requiring imputed rent to be reported for tax purposes. Although it would be quite appropriate to allow deductions for interest and taxes if imputed rent were included in taxable income, it is illogical to allow the deduction (from other income) of costs associated with the realization of non-taxable income. Congress has explicitly denied deductions for interest on "indebtedness incurred or continued to purchase or carry" tax-exempt securities (*Internal Revenue Code*, Sec. 265). * * *

Quantitatively, the elimination of personal deductions for mortgage interest and property taxes on owner-occupied houses would achieve much of the results that could be obtained by taxation of imputed net rent. * * * There would, nevertheless, be significant difference between the two approaches.

The disallowance of the interest deduction would lessen the discrimination between renters and those who own their dwellings subject to heavy mortgages. * * * On the other hand, the elimination of the interest deduction would not affect the tax liability of persons owning their houses free of mortgage debt and hence would do nothing to reduce the present discrimination between this group and renters. Among homeowners, the interest deduction has the merit of recognizing that owners with mortgages are less favorably situated than those without mortgages. Denial of the deduction would remove a difference in taxable income of the two classes of owners which corresponds to a difference in their real income. * * *

IMPUTED INCOME AND THE IDEAL INCOME TAX
Thomas Chancellor[*]

67 Oregon Law Review 561, 605-09 (1988)

Can the failure to tax net imputed rent be properly viewed as a violation of horizontal equity, discrimination against renters, or a distortion in the efficient allocation of resources?

The difference in tax treatment between home ownership and renting a home is illustrated by the following example which assumes that imputed rent is not taxed. At the beginning of the year George and Mary each have $100,000 (after taxes) to invest. Mary spends $40,000 to purchase a home for her own use and she invests the rest in a bond paying eight percent, the going pretax rate on safe investments. George invests his entire $100,000 in bonds, paying eight percent. To simplify the example, assume that there is no inflation and that net income is taxed at a flat rate of fifty percent. George's interest of $8000 per annum is subject to tax and he therefore has $4000 available to pay rent (a net after-tax return of four percent on his investment). As for Mary, she has no taxable income from her home ownership but she would be responsible for paying property taxes and insurance, maintaining the house, and establishing a reserve for depreciation to rebuild the house at the end of its forty-year useful life. Assume these expenses total $2400 per year: property taxes, $700; insurance and maintenance, $700; and depreciation (2.5% per year), $1000. George desires to rent a house, identical to Mary's, owned by Charles (the landlord) who recently purchased it for $40,000. Assume that the landlord's expenses will be the same as those incurred by Mary on her home. Since the established after-tax rate of return is four percent, Charles will expect the same return. Therefore, he will demand a gross rent of $5600 to achieve a net after-tax return of $1600 (four percent on his investment).[156] George will not be able to rent the house if his only source

---

[*]. At time of original publication, Professor of Law, University of Utah.

156.	Gross rent	$5600
	Property taxes	(700)
	Insurance and maintenances	(700)
	Depreciation (2.5% per year)	(1,000)
	Taxable income	$3200
	After-tax income	$1600 (4% on 40,000)

of payments is his after-tax return from the $100,000 investment because he will have only $4000. By contrast, Mary will be able to pay for the $2400 of owner expenses from the $2400 after-tax return she receives from her remaining $60,000 investment.[157]

The foregoing example demonstrates that for an annual rent of $4000, Charles, as an investor, would be unwilling to pay $40,000 for the house as rental property because it would not yield the established after-tax return of four percent. How much would Charles pay for the house if the maximum obtainable rent was $4000 per annum? With the assumption that expenditures for property taxes, maintenance, and insurance remain constant regardless of price, an investor requiring a four percent after-tax return would pay no more than $24,762 for the house as a rental property.[158] If owner-occupied housing could be completely isolated from the owner-landlord market there would be no tax disadvantage to renters. The purchase price of owner-occupied housing would exceed the price of identical rental housing. George could use the after-tax income ($4000) from his $100,000 to rent a house from Charles which the latter had purchased for $24,762. Mary would use her $100,000 to buy an identical house for $40,000 and pay the taxes, maintenance, and insurance with the after-tax income on her remaining $60,000. Under these circumstances, therefore, there would be no tax advantage to home ownership.[159]

The difficulty is that the two markets cannot be isolated. Because imputed rent from home ownership is not taxed, an owner-occupier will pay more for a given house than a taxpayer who will be an owner-landlord. Owner-occupiers will bid up the price of new and existing single-family housing well beyond the level that could be justified as an investment. Over time, single-family residences would be owned by owner-occupiers rather than owner-landlords.

The failure to tax imputed rent changes the equilibrium that would otherwise exist between consumer assets and investment assets in a nontax world. Does this justify taxing imputed rent? A desire to remove allocative

---

In this and the following examples assume the entire cost basis is allowable to the depreciable improvements. This avoids the necessity of allocating the purchase price between land and improvements.

157. Mary's gross income is $4800 (.08 x 60,000); after-tax net income is $2400. It is here assumed that, contrary to current law, property taxes are not deductible by an owner-occupier such as Mary. Thus the nondeductible expenses for taxes, maintenance, insurance and the reserve for depreciation total $2400.

158. This value was calculated as follows: X is the price Charles would pay for the house as rental property; .08X (required pretax return) equals $4000 (gross rent) minus .025X (annual depreciation) and less $1400 (real property taxes, insurance, and maintenance). Solving for X: $24,762.

159. Home ownership offers a variety of important psychic benefits (e.g., long-term security; freedom to make improvements) that may enhance the value of a house to an owner-occupier. * * * This suggests that in a world with no taxes the rent paid by a long-term tenant should be somewhat less than the owner-occupier's amortized cost for the same house because a rental arrangement may be less attractive than owner occupancy.

inefficiencies may be a reason to reject income as the tax base, but once we have accepted income as the tax base, allocative efficiency should not be a criterion in the definition of income. An acknowledged feature of an income tax is that it encourages consumption over investment. The favorable treatment of home ownership and other consumer asset ownership (as compared to ownership for investment) is merely a manifestation of this difference.

It is frequently asserted that the difference in treatment between homeowners and renters constitutes horizontal inequity. As described above, a system that does not tax imputed rent results in an incentive to own rather than rent housing. Is that fact alone enough to justify including imputed rent in an ideal tax base? I think not. The principle of horizontal equity demands that people with equal income be taxed the same. Proponents of taxing imputed income argue that imputed rent must be treated as income so that renters and owner-occupiers have the same income. The existence of horizontal equity depends on the fundamental threshold issue: is the benefit of using an owned asset to be treated as income? Only if the answer to that question is "yes" must the imputed benefit be taxed to achieve horizontal equity. It is circular to argue that the answer to that question must be "yes" in order to justify equalizing the incomes of renters and owner-occupiers. In the end, horizontal equity is a question of subjective judgment which should not be allowed to trump the definition of income.

Only if one views owner-occupied housing as an investment is taxing imputed rent mandated. In that case, the tax law would be making one form of investment more favorable than another. Since an investment, if successful, produces new purchasing power, the purchase of a consumer asset is the antithesis of investment; housing and other consumer assets are a form of consumption, not a form of investment. The owner-occupier and the owner-landlord are not similarly situated.

       * * *

Notes and Questions

1.   Through most of its history, the British income tax system included the rental basis of owner-occupied housing in the tax base. The imputed rental values were not updated after 1939, and, on account of inflation, "became increasingly ludicrous."[c] By 1963, adjustment to current rental values would have resulted in significantly increased taxes; the government instead opted to drop imputed rent from the tax base altogether.[d]

---

c. J.A. KAY & M.A. KING, THE BRITISH TAX SYSTEM 55 (1986).

d. *Id.*

2. Do you agree with Dr. Goode that "[t]he omission of imputed rent from taxable income * * * favor[s] homeowners and discriminates against renters"? Contrast the reasoning of British commentators Kay and King:

What the tax system favours is owner-occupation, not owner-occupiers, and this distinction is not always made clear. * * *

[New purchasers of housing are] faced with buying houses at prices which have been forced up by the tax-stimulated demand for them: prices which reflect the capitalized value of the tax concessions. * * * Thus current house-buyers obtain relatively little benefit from the concessions. Indeed they may be worse off, since young married couples are forced to save for deposits towards house purchases at a time in their lives when incomes are low, outgoings high, and large compulsory savings of this kind inappropriate. * * *

[T]his account demonstrates why tax capitalization is such a dangerous trap: although we believe it would be better if the system had never incorporated these concessions, it does not seem that it would now be either equitable or desirable to withdraw them. The losses from doing so would be principally borne by those who are currently struggling to meet the initial mortgage repayments on a house—people who have derived little benefit from the concessions and who may have actually suffered from them.[e]

3. Would the objection to taxation of imputed income from housing raised by Kay and King be met if the change were phased in over a period of many years?

4. Professor Chancellor demonstrates rather convincingly that a rational taxpayer should be willing to pay more for a house to live in than for the same house to rent out in a market transaction. Given the impossibility of isolating the two markets, this suggests a constant pressure in favor of housing becoming owner-occupied. What tax treatment seems to lead to this result?

5. Keep in mind that economic models can never be sufficiently nuanced to tell the whole story. For example, Professor Chancellor's figures assumed that his hypothetical house would encounter real economic depreciation of 2.5 percent per year regardless of ownership, and that this accurately-computed cost would be deductible by the landlord. But what if the tax system allows landlords depreciation deductions greatly in excess of economic depreciation? For example, many buyers appear to think that no depreciation at all is to be expected—that housing is more likely to increase in value than to

---

e. *Id.* at 56-57.

decrease—yet the tax system allows depreciation, currently over 27.5 years,[f] and recently over as little as 15 years.[g] Tax deductions for depreciation are not allowed to owner-occupiers. Generous tax treatment for depreciation, taken alone, should result in landlords being willing to pay more for housing than would owner-occupiers. This factor would appear to partially counter the favorable treatment afforded the imputed income of owner-occupiers.

The most constant influence of the tax system may be not so much discrimination favoring owner-occupiers vis-à-vis landlords and renters, but a bias in favor of housing as compared to other assets.

6.   In principle, there seems to be little or no difference between imputed income from housing and from consumer durables. Administrative difficulties in comparison to revenue generated appear to be much greater with regard to consumer durables, however. If it were conceded that imputed income from consumer durables is not to be taxed, would considerations of fairness and consistency require that imputed income from housing also be exempt?

7.   Does the failure to tax imputed income from housing result in a misallocation of resources to housing? To a particular type of housing?

8.   Professor Chancellor concludes that the failure to tax imputed income from owner-occupied housing is problematic if we view such housing as an investment, but not if it is viewed as consumption. What is his argument?

9.   Is political and social stability improved if a significant portion of the population lives in owner-occupied housing? If so, does this justify the current favorable treatment of housing, including the exclusion of imputed income from the tax base? Or do you agree with Dr. Goode that these tax provisions are inefficient, and that the "government could give broader and more effective encouragement to homeownership and housing by increasing expenditures for housing programs in an amount equal to the revenue loss attributable to the failure to tax imputed rent"?

10.   Elderly taxpayers are more likely than others to have lived in a house long enough to have accumulated significant equity, and thus may benefit disproportionately from the exclusion of imputed rent from income. Does this justify the exclusion?

---

f. Section 168(c)(1).

g. A 15-year depreciation period for real property was adopted in the Economic Recovery Tax Act of 1981, and remained in force until enactment of the Tax Reform Act of 1984. The 1984 Act extended the recovery period to 18 years, and subsequent statutes have extended the recovery period to its present 27.5 years for residential real estate, and 39 years for nonresidential real estate. Section 168(c).

11. The national saving rate of the United States is among the lowest of industrialized nations. Home mortgage payments, each of which includes a payment of principal, can be viewed as a form of forced savings. Is favorable treatment of housing justified in order to encourage saving? Is Dr. Goode correct in asserting that the exclusion of imputed income from the tax base is not important to the decision to purchase a house?

12. If the United States decided to include imputed income from owner-occupied housing in the tax base, how should the program be structured? Are the administrative problems overwhelming?

13. Suppose we conclude that imputed rent should be taxed in theory, but that such a tax is impracticable. Should we then consider a more workable "proxy"? Dr. Goode mentions two possibilities—allowance of some deduction for rent paid, and removal of deductions for mortgage interest and real estate taxes on personal residences. Does either of these appear attractive?

14. As Dr. Goode observed at the conclusion of his excerpt, "the interest deduction has the merit of recognizing that owners with mortgages are less favorably situated than those without mortgages. Denial of the deduction would remove a difference in taxable income of the two classes of owners which corresponds to a difference in their real income." For a more extensive statement of this argument, see the Oliver excerpt at page 731.

15. In Canada, imputed income is not taxed, but no deduction is allowed for mortgage interest and property taxes on the taxpayer's home. At least with respect to owner-occupied housing, the Royal Commission on Taxation recognized the theoretical correctness of taxing imputed income and the severe discrimination that resulted from not doing so, but concluded that "the determination of this net income for owner-occupied dwellings, even if arbitrary rules were adopted, would be fraught with uncertainly and would entail detailed administrative examination."[h] The Royal Commission asserted that the inequity of not taxing this imputed income was less severe in Canada than in the United States, because Canada allows no deduction for interest and property taxes on the taxpayer's residence.[i] Is this assertion always correct?

16. In theory, should the concept of imputed income extend to a taxpayer's share of public goods? Charles Hulten and Robert Schwab have argued:
> [T]here are no essential economic differences between publicly owned capital (e.g. streets, parks, schools) and privately owned capital (e.g.

---

h. 3 REPORT OF THE ROYAL COMMISSION ON TAXATION 48 (1966).
i. *Id.* at 49.

owner-occupied housing). * * * It therefore follows that some portion of the imputed income from the street in front of a family's home must be included in the base of a comprehensive income tax, just as the income from the home itself must be included.[j]

Hulten and Schwab make clear that their argument is purely theoretical: "If it is politically impossible to tax the imputed income from owner-occupied housing, it would be political suicide for Congress to propose taxing imputed income associated with public streets, schools, police cars, etc."[k]

17. Many bank depositors receive low or no interest on their demand deposits, but are rewarded by receiving free or discounted check printing, checking account services, safety deposit boxes, and the like. Are these services properly viewed as imputed interest income?[l]

18. Apart from issues of policy, the Constitution may restrict possible choices. A strained argument might be made that failure to include imputed income in the tax base constitutes impermissible discrimination. That argument was rejected by the Supreme Court shortly after ratification of the Sixteenth Amendment, in *Brushaber v. Union Pacific R.R.*[m] The United States Supreme Court upheld the 1913 income tax, rejecting the plaintiff's argument that "[i]f the renter cannot deduct as an expense what he pays as rent, the owner, who has no such expense, should be charged with the rental value of his home . . ."[n] "[S]ince the *Brushaber* case there can be no serious constitutional objection to the *ex*clusion of imputed income, but the question remains as to the constitutionality of its *in*clusion."[o]

While Congress is thus free not to tax imputed income—and there are now nine decades of practice to build on the *Brushaber* decision—there is a more serious possibility that Congress is barred from including at least some forms of imputed income from property because it does not constitute "income" under the Sixteenth Amendment. Almost certainly, Congress could not tax imputed income from services. The constitutionality of taxing imputed income from owner-occupied housing is placed in question by the Supreme Court's seventy-year-old dicta in *Helvering v. Independent Life Ins. Co.*: "If the statute lays taxes on the part of the building occupied by the owner or upon the rental value of that space, it cannot be sustained, for that would be a direct tax

---

j. Charles R. Hulten and Robert M. Schwab, *A Haig-Simons-Tiebout Comprehensive Income Tax*, 44 NAT'L TAX J. 67, 67 (1991).

k. *Id.*

l. For further discussion, *see* Melvin I. White, *Consistent Treatment of Items Excluded and Omitted from the Individual Income Tax Base, in* HOUSE COMM. ON WAYS AND MEANS, 86TH CONG., 1ST SESS., 1 TAX REVISION COMPENDIUM 317, 323-25 (1959).

m. 240 U.S. 1 (1916).

n. Transcript of Record at 21, Brushaber v. Union Pacific R.R., 240 U.S. 1 (1916) (No. 140).

o. Bruce L. Balch, *Individual Income Taxes and Housing*, 11 NAT'L TAX J. 168, 170 (1958).

requiring apportionment."[p] The Court concluded that Congress had intended no such tax, and thus its holding did not reach the constitutional issue.

C. IMPUTED INCOME FROM SERVICES

Unlike the situation regarding imputed income from property, there is no realistic thought of imposing a tax on any form of imputed income from services. If nothing else—and there is much else—while the constitutionality of taxing imputed income from property may be questionable, it almost certainly would be unconstitutional to tax imputed income from services.

Nonetheless, the inquiry into the theoretical correctness of regarding these benefits as income informs our understanding of the nature of income and, more concretely, may lead us to conclude that certain "second best" approaches, which *are* workable and constitutional, are appropriate. With respect to imputed income from home ownership, for example, a possible "proxy" would be to allow a deduction for rent. Similarly, while there is no realistic consideration of taxing a family for the benefit conferred by a housewife and mother, should that failure to tax be offset by allowing a deduction for the expense of a maid and nanny employed by a working mother?[q] Such a provision might be thought of as a "proxy" for taxing the imputed income generated by "nonworking" wives and mothers. That is, assume that we would prefer to tax the imputed income generated by a housewife, but we cannot for administrative, political and constitutional reasons. On this assumption, we think families with housewives are being given unfairly favorable treatment. Can we end the perceived unfairness indirectly, by proxy, by giving the family that does not have a housewife a deduction for purchasing the services that many housewives perform?

Present law (section 21) allows a credit for a portion of a taxpayer's expenses for child care or care of an adult unable to care for himself. If the taxpayer pays for care of such a "qualifying individual," the credit also covers payments for household services. The credit is limited to expenses that enable the taxpayer to work, and, in furtherance of that limitation, the amount of expenditure qualifying for the credit cannot exceed the earned income of the taxpayer or, if married, the earned income of the lower-earning spouse. In no event can qualifying expenditures exceed $6,000 ($3,000 where only one qualifying individual is present). Of the qualifying expenditures, the taxpayer's credit ranges from a maximum of 35 percent for taxpayers with

---

p. 292 U.S. 371, 378 (1934).

q. This text and the articles excerpted generally discuss the issue in terms of a working mother rather than a working father. In most couples, if one spouse is considering not working in the market, that spouse will be the wife. Similarly, where small children requiring custodial care are in a home headed by a single parent, it is usually the mother. Fathers are much more likely to occupy either of these roles than in decades past, but still less frequently than mothers. The analysis is identical if "father" and "husband" are substituted for "mother" and "wife."

adjusted gross income of $15,000 or less, decreasing to 20 percent when AGI exceeds $43,000.

The first three excerpts speak in terms of deductions rather than credits for child care and household services, in part because they were written when predecessors to section 21 were in effect.[r] The policy discussion remains almost unchanged, and therefore these articles continue to be relevant.

TAXATION OF THE FAMILY IN A COMPREHENSIVE AND SIMPLIFIED INCOME TAX
Michael J. McIntyre[*] & Oliver Oldman[**]
90 Harvard Law Review 1573, 1607-15, 1617-20 (1977)

A direct corollary of our conclusion [earlier in the article] that one-half of the consolidated marital income of a couple should be attributed to each of the spouses is that equal-income couples should pay equal taxes. * * *

In this Part, we reexamine the proposition that couples with equal monetary income should pay equal taxes in light of the arguments made for adjusting the burdens on one- and two-job couples on account of perceived differences in the imputed income typically available to each. If imputed income should be taxed under the CTB [comprehensive tax base] ideal, and if two-job couples have less imputed income than one-job couples, then our decision to tax equally couples with equal monetary income discriminates against two-job couples.[117] Hence, consideration of the issue of imputed income, although principally a problem of defining the appropriate tax base, has implications for the attribution of income within the family.

The case for including at least some self-performed services in income is illustrated by the following example: A_1 and B_1 are married and each has a forty-hour-a-week job with an annual salary of $10,000. At the end of a work day, A_1 and B_1 are seldom in the mood to cook; instead they either eat out at a restaurant or heat up in the oven a frozen convenience dinner purchased at the supermarket. They also hire a maid to clean the house and handle other domestic chores and they send their dirty clothes to the laundry. A_2 and B_2 are

---

r. Congress initially allowed a tax concession for such expenses by enactment of section 214 in 1954, which allowed a sharply limited deduction. The provision was liberalized in 1963, 1964 and, most importantly, in 1971. By 1971, the limitations on deductibility were similar to the present limitations on expenditures qualifying for the credit. The use of a deduction made a qualifying dollar of expenditure of greater value to a high-bracket taxpayer; the present provision reverses this preference. On the other hand, high-income taxpayers could claim no deduction at all; present law allows even the millionaire a credit of 20 percent of qualifying expenses. For further discussion of the development and details of section 214, *see* William A. Klein, *Tax Deductions for Family Care Expenses*, 14 B.C. INDUS. & COM. L. REV. 917, 917-32 (1973) and Alan L. Feld, *Deductibility of Expenses for Child Care and Household Expenses: New Section 214*, 27 TAX L. REV. 415 (1972).

*. At time of original publication, Professor of Law, Wayne State University.

**. At time of original publication, Learned Hand Professor of Law and Director of the International Tax Program, Harvard Law School.

117. Although the discussion is framed in terms of the possible disparity in treatment of one-job and two-job couples in the failure to tax imputed income, similar considerations have been raised as to the comparative treatment of single individuals and one-job couples.

married. A_2 has a full-time job paying \$20,000 a year and B_2 has no employment outside the home. B_2 spends a good bit of time, however, baking bread, cooking fancy meals, canning fruits and vegetables, cleaning the house, sewing, and doing laundry.

If the services performed by B_2 in the above example produce taxable income as a matter of definition under the CTB ideal, then the value of the services should in principle be included in the pool of income attributed to A_2 and B_2. * * * We conclude that the pattern of distribution of imputed income from self-performed services is so complex that the failure to take imputed income into account in determining relative tax burdens leads to no particular disadvantage for two-job couples.

        * * *

According to Simons, the definition of income (1) should be objective rather than subjective; (2) should be quantitative and measurable; and (3) should have a minimum number of implicit arbitrary distinctions. These three minimum tests for an acceptable definition of income provide a convenient framework for an analysis of the case for taxing the imputed income from self-performed services.

The variety of self-performed services which in some sense constitute income range from the sublime to the ridiculous, from the priceless private poetry of an Emily Dickinson to the thumb-sucking of a small child. Putting a handle on the self-performed service concept is something like defining a capital gain: we think we know what we mean, but if we articulate a definition, we end up with either nothing fitting the description or everything fitting it. For example, which if any of the following services should be taxable: Getting up in the morning? Doing exercises? Singing in the shower? Grooming oneself? Fixing breakfast? Chewing food? Processing it within the stomach? Walking to work? Baking bread? Growing roses? Fixing the car? Driving in the country? Watching T.V.? Reading a novel? Reading bedtime stories to one's children? Playing backgammon?

As these examples illustrate, almost every activity we undertake is in some sense a self-performed service, since the possibility of imposing a market model on nonmarket activity has no logical limits. A general inclusion of all imputed income from personal services in the definition of taxable income would cause the definition to fail all three of Simons' tests, since it would present hopeless problems of subjectivity and measurement and would require entirely ad hoc decisionmaking. At a minimum, therefore, some categories of imputed income ought to be excluded from the tax base.

        * * *

Take an apparently minor item such as shaving. At the minimum market price of \$2 per shave, imputed income from shaving would exceed \$700 per year for a person who shaves daily. Similarly the imputed income from dressing oneself each day, measured by the market price for a valet, would be in the thousands of dollars. In fact, potential income from even a narrow definition of self-performed services would be likely to exceed salary income for a majority of taxpayers. * * *

The practical policy choice is between ignoring imputed income from self-performed services entirely or employing some indirect method of taxation. All indirect methods require a discernible pattern, since they cannot operate unless there is some factor other than the imputed income item itself for identifying who is being disadvantaged. That factor would be used as a proxy for the presence or absence of the benefits of a particular type of self-performed service.

* * *

A challenge to our tentative conclusion that couples with equal monetary income should pay equal tax is dependent, therefore, on a showing that the exclusion of certain items of imputed income from the tax base results in a definite pattern of discrimination against two-job couples.[127]

Estimating the Patterns of Imputed Income from Self-Performed Services of One-Job and Two-Job Married Couples

Our analysis of imputed income was prompted by the concern that equal tax treatment of couples with equal monetary income might discriminate against two-job couples. As discussed above, a claim of discrimination depends

---

127. Whether or not a pattern of discrimination exists must be judged according to fairness criteria, not efficiency criteria. Much of the support for tax measures in favor of two-job couples nevertheless rests on considerations of efficiency. In analyzing the economic component of the choice between working in and working outside the market, economists find it useful to include income from self-performed services within the concept of income, since the optimum choice for efficiency purposes is the one which maximizes the total of market and nonmarket income. The failure to tax certain types of self-performed services probably creates a distortion in the labor market in favor, for example, of a woman working in the home rather than working at a job which pays a taxable salary. The utility of including self-performed services in the income concept for purposes of eliminating this distortion, however, has no bearing on the merits of including it in income for purposes of determining fairness. Arguments addressed to the social and economic consequences of a particular mode of taxing self-performed services have usually sidestepped the issue of fairness and instead have focused on considerations of efficiency or social engineering. Proposals for accomplishing these nontax goals should be subjected to a tax expenditure analysis and must be justified, if at all, under budget criteria, not tax criteria. A discussion of the merits of proposals for adjusting the burden of one-job and two-job couples on efficiency grounds is beyond the scope of this Article.

If we did reach the merits, we would begin by examining the implicit assumption of all efficiency arguments—that the maximization of economic goods is a desirable social goal. We would want to see what the arguments are for encouraging market activity at the expense of leisure and self-performed services. Our suspicion is that giving money rewards for some kinds of activities but not for others already distorts the choice among activities in favor of paying jobs. There are a number of possible gains in a tax system which counteract this distortion. We think, for example, that citizen participation in the political processes of the country is desirable and is inhibited by the economic incentives which pull people away from volunteer political work. On the other hand, we can appreciate arguments for encouraging market behavior in other situations. None of the efficiency literature we have seen addresses itself, however, to this fundamental point. For a discussion of efficiency arguments, see H. Rosen, Application of Optimal Tax Theory to Problems in Taxing Families and Individuals (U.S. Dep't of Treasury, OTA Paper 21, November 1976) (also referring to much of the literature on the subject).

on the existence of identifiable patterns in the distribution of imputed income which disadvantage two-job couples. A stereotyped view of the activities of working and nonworking wives might suggest that a clear pattern exists. In this Section, we attempt to go behind the stereotype. * * *

To avoid some of the definitional ambiguities discussed above, we will be concerned exclusively with a limited group of self-performed services which many taxpayers commonly purchase in the market—"household services," such as cooking, cleaning, sewing, and caring for children; and "handy-person services," such as shoveling snow, fixing the television, and repairing the roof. In examining the widely held perception that one-job couples have more imputed income from these services than two-job couples have, we are unable to refer to existing empirical studies. * * *

First, we can find no predictable difference between one- and two-job couples in the consumption of self-performed child-care services. Obviously, and most importantly, such services are rarely performed by couples without children, in which case disparity between one- and two-job couples is nonexistent. In addition, when there are children a substantial amount of child-care services are performed by both two-job couples and one-job couples.[128] It is true that some one-job couples and even more two-job couples purchase child-care services in the market. Those who purchase probably have less self-performed child-care services than those couples with children who do not purchase. But the ratio of purchased as opposed to self-performed child-care services may be more closely related to inclination than to whether both spouses work, especially if child-care services are defined more meaningfully than as one parent's mere physical presence for long stretches of time.
* * *

The one advantage which a one-job couple consistently has over a two-job couple is the extra time available for nonemployment activity. Although it cannot be assumed that this time is in fact used to perform services the couple would otherwise have to purchase in the market, some advocates of a tax allowance for two-job couples assert that leisure itself constitutes "consumption," and thus should be taxable. Treating leisure as consumption for tax purposes raises most of the problems of treating self-performed services as income. First of all, what is the policy reason for wanting small children, retired persons, students, and the unemployed—those most likely to have

---

128. Some studies have been made on the patterns of child-care arrangements of working mothers with small children. The most common arrangement is for the child-care to be provided by either the father or another relative. According to a 1973 survey, 49% of working mothers paid nothing for child-care, and in a large number of other cases, the out-of-pocket expenses were "very small," because the services were provided by relatives. In 26% of white two-job families and 14% of black two-job families surveyed, the mother and father arranged working hours [so] that they could handle their child-care requirements themselves. Child-care in the home is also apparently preferred by the majority of two-job and one-parent families. *See* Woolsey, *Pied Piper Politics and the Child-Care Debate*, DAEDALUS, Spring 1977, at 127, 130-32.

substantial amounts of leisure "income"—to pay an increased share of the tax burden? * * *

Indirect Methods for Taxing Imputed Income from Self-Performed Services

Despite the preceding analysis, some may still feel that an ideal income tax somehow must take self-performed services into account. In this Section, we assume the validity of that perception and consider practical proposals for taking it into account. Since direct taxation of imputed income is universally acknowledged to be unfeasible, the objective is to find some indirect method of approximating the distribution of tax burdens which would result from direct taxation. We will discuss the merits of three possible indirect methods of taxing imputed income: a deduction for cash outlays for the purchase of personal services, an earned income allowance, and adjustments in the rate schedule. Given the conceptual problems with any definition of imputed income and the complex patterns of distribution of self-performed services among the groups of taxpayers, any indirect method of adjusting burdens will be crude indeed. The most that can be hoped for is a system which reduces the perceived disproportionate burden arguably imposed currently on two-job couples without creating greater unfairness for other taxpayers. We conclude that none of these proposals achieves even that limited goal.

Deductions for Purchases of Personal Services

Amounts spent on personal services—to hire a maid or gardener, for example—normally constitute consumption, and the income which finances the consumption is taxable. If many taxpayers receive these same benefits tax-free by performing the services themselves, a deduction for cash outlays for services may be in some circumstances a satisfactory indirect method of taxing self-performed services. The function of the deduction would be to equalize the tax treatment of purchased services and self-performed services by in effect making both kinds of services exempt from tax.

A deduction for cash outlays for personal services is defensible in an ideal income tax only if the amount spent to purchase services is a good proxy for differences in the distribution of self-performed services. For example, if all taxpayers either mow their own lawn or hire someone to do it, and if the amount of mowing which must be done is about the same for all taxpayers, then a deduction for the costs of hiring someone else to mow has about the same effect on relative tax burdens as including imputed income from mowing in taxable income. On the other hand, if a significant number of taxpayers do not have a lawn to mow, or mow it very infrequently, then a deduction for the purchase of mowing services is not an acceptable indirect method for taxing self-performed mowing services. The higher tax rates necessitated by the deduction unfairly increase the tax burden on persons who do not mow.[136]

---

136. Assume a universe with only three taxpayers, M, H, and N, each with pecuniary income of 100. The required revenue yield of the tax system is 30. Assume M mows his lawn, H hires someone to mow, and N has no lawn and never purchases lawn mowing services or performs them

This example illustrates that while a deduction for purchases of any type of services is fair as between persons who typically perform the services themselves and those who purchase, a deduction is unfair as between those who purchase and those who neither purchase nor perform the services themselves. A deduction for mowing is unfair to most renters; a deduction for shoveling snow is unfair to taxpayers in the South.

Of greater practical significance, a deduction for child-care expenditures is unfair to those without children, assuming that the purpose of the deduction is to make allowance for the failure of the tax system to tax imputed income from child-care services. If self-performed child-care services are to be treated as income, the proper adjustment is a large deduction for taxpayers without children, with a more modest deduction for those with children who purchase child-care services.

This analysis suggests that a minimum requirement for permitting a deduction for cash outlays for services must be that the service in question is one which virtually all taxpayers either perform themselves or purchase in the market. This requirement, although a necessary one, is not, however, a sufficient one to identify the purchases for which a deduction is an acceptable "second best" adjustment for the failure to tax self-performed services directly. Cooking may be the most pervasive example of a service which is either performed or purchased. A deduction for amounts spent at restaurants is, however, a poor index of the value of the self-performed services of those who eat at home. Amounts spent at restaurants vary considerably even among persons who frequently eat out; those who eat at expensive restaurants should not be allowed a tax benefit which is only vaguely related to the value of the self-performed cooking services of persons who eat at home. Cleaning house is another chore which is widely purchased or performed for oneself. The allowable deduction would have to be small, however, to avoid unfairness to people with small houses, people without children, and people with a high tolerance for untidiness.[137]

---

himself. If mowing for oneself should be taxable in an ideal income tax system, then M should pay more tax than H or N, and H and N should pay the same tax. If only H is allowed a deduction for mowing, then the tax on M and N will be increased to make up for the revenue loss. This is fair to M, who has more "income" than H, but unfair to N, who has the same income as H. The only fair solution is to give the deduction to both H and N. Assume further that H purchases some mowing services and also performs some for himself. The only way to approximate the "ideal" solution of taxing mowing services would be to give a big deduction to N (perhaps 30), a smaller deduction to H (say 10) and no deduction to M.

137. A maid service deduction, if regarded as an indirect method of taxing self-performed housecleaning services, should of course be available to all taxpayers, not simply those with a qualifying dependent for whom the expense is somehow job-related. *See* I.R.C. § 44A [and present section 21]. We suspect, however, that a deduction for maid services, if divorced from the business expense rationale which in part explained the political acceptability of the present household services credit, would be perceived by the public as a subsidy to the rich, who are more likely to pay for the performance of housework than are poorer people regardless of whether both spouses work. The problem of an apparent lack of equivalence between self-performed and purchased services may be particularly blatant here even though theoretically the two groups are being treated alike. It is

TAX DEDUCTIONS FOR FAMILY CARE EXPENSES
William A. Klein[*]

14 Boston College Industrial & Commercial Law Review 917,

917-19, 932-35, 937-40 (1973)

Prior to 1954 the only Code section under which a deduction for dependent-care expenses might plausibly have been allowed was the general provision, the predecessor of section 162, allowing a deduction for the "ordinary and necessary expenses [of] carrying on any trade or business."[2] The leading case denying the deduction under that language was *Henry C. Smith*.[3] While the opinion is not enlightening, it is sufficiently provocative to warrant careful examination. The facts are simply stated. Mr. and Mrs. Smith were both employed and filed a joint return[4] in which they claimed a deduction for the expense of hiring someone to care for their young child. According to the opinion of the Board of Tax Appeals, the Smiths' argument was simply that "but for" the fact that Mrs. Smith was working the child care expense need not have been incurred.[5] Since there was no suggestion that the Smiths would have hired a caretaker for the child even if one of them had been unemployed, the "but for" argument seemed to have considerable force, and the Board's rebuttal to this argument missed the point. Adopting a *reductio ad absurdum* approach, the Board stated that if the Smiths' argument were accepted, then a deduction for food and shelter should also be allowed as a business expense since without food and shelter a person would be physically unable to work. The obvious irrelevance of that observation lies in the fact that the cost of food and shelter is unavoidable for nonworkers as well as workers, whereas child care expenses are unavoidable only for workers.

The Board's attack on the "but for" argument would have been more persuasive if it had been launched from another angle. The Board neglected the fact that child care expenses are not incurred by all workers, but only by those who have children. The expense, therefore, is attributable not only to the decision to work—taking children as given—but also to the decision to have children—taking work as given. In other words, the expense at issue can be looked upon in part as a cost of working and in part as a cost of having children—that is, as a trade or business expense and a personal expense—but not as either one alone. Such an observation scarcely resolves the question of

---

unclear how a system of deductions could deal with this problem.

    *. At time of original publication, Professor of Law, University of California, Los Angeles.

    2. Int. Rev. Code of 1939, § 23(a)(1). In one case, in a rather unique set of circumstances, a deduction for child care expenses was claimed as a medical expense under the predecessor of § 213, on the theory that the taxpayer's health was imperiled by the necessity of caring for the children. The deduction was denied. Ochs v. Commissioner, 195 F.2d 692 (2d Cir. 1952).

    3. 40 B.T.A. 1038 (1939), aff'd per curiam, 113 F.2d 114 (2d Cir. 1940).

    4. The case arose before the era of split income, but even then married couples were permitted to file a joint return and in certain circumstances could gain a modest advantage by doing so.

    5. It was no doubt a sign of the times that the possibility was not even considered that Mr. Smith, rather than Mrs. Smith, could have been the child's caretaker.

deductibility, but at least it avoids spurious causative analysis and brings into sharper focus the central issue of the case.

Passing from its discussion of the "but for" or causative argument, the Board referred to the notion of the wife (not, it may be noted, the husband) as a provider of "services as custodian of the home and protector of its children," and pointed out that ordinarily these services are provided without financial reward. To use the jargon of the present-day economist, the nonworking spouse, husband or wife, provides imputed income in the form of services to the household or family. What is curious about the Board's observation is that it may be used to support rather than undercut the allowance of a deduction for child care expense. Because the cash income of the working wife is taxed while the imputed income of the nonworking wife is not, a deduction for child care can be defended as a means of mitigating the inequality in tax results. This argument seems to have escaped the Board.

* * *

As suggested earlier, child care expenses are not strictly comparable to business expenses such as wages, costs of goods sold, and so forth, because the former are incurred only by a certain class of earners—those with children—and that class is defined by a nonbusiness phenomenon. Such a characterization, however, does not require disallowance of the deduction for dependent care expenses in the interests of economic neutrality. In other words, the admitted distinction between dependent-care and other business-related expenses does not necessarily require that any deduction for the latter be characterized as a "subsidy" to child-bearing any more than a deduction of wages by a manufacturer is a "subsidy" to manufacturing.[85] To reach general conclusions regarding the proper characterization or treatment of the dependent care deduction, in relation to the goal of economic neutrality, would require an economic analysis far more detailed and sophisticated than seems justified for the purposes of this article.[86] I offer the suggestion, however, that anyone who attempts such an analysis will quickly discover that the issues cannot be resolved easily or in simple terms, but that if one makes certain assumptions[87] it is plainly the case that the dependent care deduction is not a

---

85. No one would bother to observe that a deduction for wages means more to a high-bracket manufacturer than to a low-bracket manufacturer, but the same kind of observation about the dependent care deduction has been made (indeed, belabored) by some sophisticated tax experts.

86. The kind of analysis I refer to would require examination of the kinds of decisions that would be made—in all types of individual circumstances, with and without a tax system and with and without a deduction—as to whether or not to work, and for how many hours, and whether or not to have children. The variety of types of individual circumstances (including, for example, different states of mind about work and child bearing, and different family circumstances) is large, and the analysis is complicated by the fact that our interest is in a deduction, but the deduction can be examined only in the context of a tax system and that tax system itself has significant effects on the work decision and, possibly, on the childbearing decision.

87. One such assumption would be that the decision whether or not to work arises after a decision to have children has already been made and carried out (as where a widow with young children seriously contemplates working only after the death of her husband); another, that the child

"subsidy." Even if it were feasible to engage here in a complete inquiry into what would be an economically neutral tax rule for the dependent care expenses there is reason to doubt the value of such an effort, since other provisions of the tax law[89] as well as other social and economic pressures are blatantly non-neutral as they relate to the work and childbearing decisions.

One can, nonetheless, make certain limited but valuable observations about the effect of the deduction on decisions to work and decisions to have children. We can begin by asking what effects a deduction for dependent care expenses will have on a person's decision to work, given the fact that the family has a dependent requiring care during working hours. Once we take such a dependent as given, and once we assume that the dependent care services provide the taxpayer with no significant personal benefit,[91] the financial reward from working, the amount that provides the incentive to work, is the net figure arrived at by subtracting the dependent care expenses from earnings (net of other expenses). If the deduction were disallowed, a person would be taxed on more than his or her net income, and for such persons the financial reward of working would be reduced to a net figure below that of other persons with similar net incomes but with no dependents needing care. This observation by itself implies an economic distortion. Moreover, if the deduction is allowed the financial reward for working will be increased for those people who hire others to perform dependent care services, but, disregarding the possibility of a personal return from the purchase of such services,[92] the effect of allowing the deduction will certainly not be to increase the financial reward of working above what it would be in the absence of any tax system. On certain assumptions, then, the tax rule permitting the deduction is economically neutral.

* * *

Fairness

One's views on whether fairness requires that the income tax system include a provision for deduction of the expenses of caring for dependents can be significantly affected by the kind of comparison one makes in examining the issue. In most economic analyses it seems to be assumed that all adults are married and have children and that the only relevant variable is whether or

---

care services provide no personal gratification.

89. For example, the provisions that make it advantageous for married couples to file joint returns (Int. Rev. Code of 1954, § 1) have the effect of imposing on the secondary worker (in our society, usually the childbearing wife) a marginal tax rate determined with reference not to his or her own income but rather with reference to that income plus the income of the primary worker.

91. For purposes of the present analysis I will assume away the possibility of personal benefit. To the extent that the dependent care services provide personal gratification, the offset for the cost of those services should be reduced by the value of that personal benefit. * * * [T]he assumption of no personal benefit worth worrying about does not seem highly unrealistic, particularly since many people enjoy caring for children. Still, that assumption is weakened if we also assume that a significant amount of housework will be provided by the provider of dependent care: such provision must be classified as personally gratifying.

92. See note 91 supra.

not the wife works. The children are taken as given, but the wife's job is not.[107] The comparison is then drawn between two families with dependent children and with equal total earnings; in one of the families the wife does not work while in the other she does. Unfairness results from the fact that the nonworking wife performs child care services for the family unit. That family is therefore said to have imputed income from those services—income that should be taxed in the interests of fairness but cannot be taxed because of other considerations. On the other hand, the family with the working wife must pay for child care services with after-tax dollars. To reduce the unfairness resulting from the nontaxation of imputed income to the first family, the deduction for child care expenses is offered to the second family.

A similar conclusion can be reached more directly simply by observing that the family with a working wife must of necessity incur an expense that the other family does not incur and that the purchase of the service, by hypothesis,[110] does not provide the family purchasing the service with any personal benefit. However, stating the comparison in this manner should give us pause. In one sense it is true that the expense is one that "must of necessity" be incurred, but in another sense it is not. The correctness of the conclusion may be thought to depend on one's time perspective. The expense is necessary at a given point in time only because the couple had previously made a decision to have children.

To pursue this last point from a different perspective, consider a comparison between two families, one consisting of husband and wife, without children, and the other of husband, wife and child. Assume also that in both families the wife is working. Obviously the childless couple avoids an expense that the couple with a child must incur. But what is the significance of that observation? One approach is to conclude that the couple with the child has an added expense stemming in part from their decision to have children. Another approach is to take the perspective of the childless couple and conclude that one consequence of their decision to remain childless is that they save money on child care. It seems perfectly reasonable and just that their saving should be available to them for other pleasures. From this perspective, fairness does not seem to require a deduction for child care expenses.

With this perspective in mind we can profitably return to the original comparison of the two couples, both with children, only one of which has a working wife. Assume that the couple with the working wife made a

---

107. See, e.g., W. Vickrey, Agenda for Progressive Taxation 32-33 (1947); M. White, Proper Income Tax Treatment of Deductions for Personal Expense, 1 Tax Revision Compendium, House Comm. on Ways and Means, 86th Cong., 1st Sess. 365, 371-72 (1959).

110. See note 91 supra. There appears to be no disagreement over the proposition that the expense should not be deductible to the extent that the service relieves that family of an expense that it would have incurred regardless of the job, or to the extent that it provides the family with a personal benefit. Obviously it will be difficult to draw the distinctions suggested by this statement and arbitrary rules will be required. The phase-out of the deduction as income rises above $18,000 is such a rule and seems to me to be a sensible one, though perhaps a bit generous.

deliberate, conscious decision to have a child, knowing that one of the costs of that decision would be the expense of hiring baby sitters while both the husband and wife were working. In this situation it would appear that the child care expense is more properly regarded as a cost of having children—a cost of personal consumption—and not a cost of working. On this assumption, then, it would be difficult to argue that fairness requires a deduction of the child care expense for such a couple, except for the troublesome fact that their counterpart family with the wife not working has the benefit of the wife's untaxed services in kind.[116] However, this result is part of a much broader problem, which is that many taxpayers or taxpaying couples with identical earnings have different amounts of free time available either for leisure or for the performance of services for themselves; this is a general problem of tax policy, not limited to the area of child care. It creates a dilemma for which there is no entirely satisfactory solution.

The preceding analysis should suggest that the question of fairness is subject to the same complexities and uncertainties as is the question of economic effects. Consequently I will venture only this tentative generality: if we assume that childbearing will increasingly be seen as a conscious, volitional phenomenon, and if we assume that people as time goes by will increase their leisure time in proportion to their working time, the "fairness" argument for allowing the deduction for child care expenses will weaken.[118]

The deduction for household expenses again requires only brief comment. In the first place, whatever may be the justification for a deduction for such expenses on grounds of fairness, there is no defense whatever for conditioning the deduction on having a qualifying dependent in the household. Second, it may be true that the allowance of the deduction improves the fairness of the system by offsetting the advantage a couple can achieve where one spouse stays home and performs untaxed services for the family. At the same time, however, household chores, unlike dependent care duties, can be accomplished after working hours and on the weekends. Thus the major effect of allowing the deduction may be simply to allow people to purchase more leisure time. The potential invidious effects of this phenomenon are aptly described by the economist Richard Goode:

> Even if certain expenses could be identified as costs, a deduction for
> them would be unfair to families—usually those with low and low-
> middle incomes—in which the household work is done by the

---

116. Suppose that all women worked and that the only variable was whether they bore children and retained responsibility for them. In such circumstances, I can think of no sound basis for allowing a deduction for child care expenses unless there were some good reason for wanting to increase the population.

118. My analysis implicitly dismissed two theories of childbearing that might have required more attention in an earlier time or in other countries. Both theories would deny that children are produced for the personal gratification of the parents. One would assert that children are produced as economic assets with future returns to the parents and the other would claim that children are produced out of a sense of obligation to God or society.

working wife or other family members in the evenings or on weekends compared with families which hire household help and enjoy more leisure. The practical effect of an allowance for expenses for household help would be discrimination in favor of upper-middle income groups.[120]

* * *

TWO CHEERS FOR THE CHILD CARE DEDUCTION
Daniel C. Schaffer & Donald H. Berman[*]
28 Tax Law Review 535, 536-40, 542-45 (1973)

There is certainly no principle in our tax law that every expense combining business and pleasure is nondeductible. The cost of a meal taken while traveling away from home in the pursuit of a trade or business, the expense of a drink over which business discussions take place, the premium paid for first class air travel—all have a personal element and all are deductible. * * *

The truth is that we have no one guiding principle with which to determine whether expenses which are for personal and business purposes at the same time are deductible. To the extent that the problem is resolvable at all, each such deduction must be viewed ad hoc, and the advantages and disadvantages of allowing it considered.

We suggest that the deduction for child care can be defended as promoting the efficient allocation of labor. We take it as a postulate that taxpayers should be allowed to choose among available jobs according to the interplay of their personal preferences and the wage offered for each job, and that the tax system should distort this choice as little as is practically possible. * * *

[M]others are given the choice between work in the labor force, the income from which is taxable, and child care, the imputed income from which is not taxed. This is hardly a neutral system of taxation. It may induce a mother whose productivity in the labor force is higher than her productivity as a mother (measured by the fair market value of her services as a mother) to stay out of the labor force, even if she prefers paying work to caring for her children. This would be an irrational allocation of labor. Normally, the price system would attract such a woman into the labor force but may be frustrated when the income from one kind of work is taxed, and that from another is not. This observation is by no means original. Vickrey made it in 1947,[17] and he may not have been the first.

A misallocation may exist even if the value of the mother's services in the home and in the labor force are the same, or the former is higher than the latter. There are two reasons: (1) The mother may prefer a job in the labor

---

120. R. Goode, The Individual Income Tax 81 (1964).

*. At time of original publication, both authors were professors at Northeastern University School of Law.

17. VICKREY, AGENDA FOR PROGRESSIVE TAXATION 44-45 (1947).

force to homemaking. Quite apart from productivity there is something wrong with a tax system that for no particular purpose diverts people into work they would otherwise choose not to do; (2) Even if a mother likes housework as much as labor force work and renders services in the home which the market would value as highly as her work in the labor force, she might prefer a cash wage to a return in the form of housework accomplished. A housewife both renders and (with her family) consumes her services. As a consumer, she may prefer the goods and services she can buy with a cash wage to her achievements in her home, even though the market would place the same value on each. This is no more than to say that given the same incomes, we might each spend them differently. An educated woman may be worth $15,000 per annum in the market both as a nanny and as, say, a computer programmer; she may like both jobs equally; but she may prefer to earn $15,000 in cash, spend $5,000 to hire child care inferior (in the market's view, and perhaps her own) to what she could provide to her children herself, and spend the remaining $10,000 on other pleasures. The income tax ought not to impede this choice.

A way to make the tax system more neutral as to a mother's choice of work would be to tax the imputed income which she generates. The difficulty of valuation of her services, the fact that we would be increasing a family's tax at just the moment when current policy calls for the tax to decrease—upon the birth of a child—and, if the tax is large enough, the family's problem of finding cash to pay tax on income which is neither in cash or in kind, all make this impractical. The only other solution is a child care deduction or credit of some kind. Those who see the deduction as one for a personal expense would say that it reduces the rate of income tax imposed on a mother's earned income below that imposed on other taxpayers. The justification is that the usual rates of income tax would have an unusually deterring effect on the entrance into the labor force of one who could work (as a mother) without being taxed at all.

We do not know if the theoretical disincentive which arises from taxing the labor force income, but not the imputed child care services income of a mother, really results in a large misallocation of labor. We can calculate the income tax penalty for entering the labor force in the case of any given mother, if we value her child care services and know her income tax bracket, but we do not know whether the income tax penalty influences a mother's choice of work often, sometimes, rarely or never. * * * What is important is to understand what questions we should be asking in evaluating [the child care deduction]. This is not to revert to the question of whether the deduction is really "personal." If every mother in the United States were in the labor force full-time, it would be clear that the unneutrality of the income tax was not misallocating labor, but the problem of whether child care was a personal or business expense to these mothers would remain.

    * * *

We have been assuming that a mother's decision to stay at home or go out to work will be an efficient decision if she simply takes into account her own preferences, the value of her services in the home and the wage she can earn in the labor market. But suppose that her decision hurts or helps the rest of us (including her children), because children raised by surrogate parents tend to be juvenile delinquents (or, in the alternative, model citizens). Then the wages and costs which the wife faces will not reflect the costs and benefits of her decision to society. Because the costs and benefits of her decision are "externalized," that is, borne by others, including perhaps her children, rather than herself, her decision cannot be expected to maximize welfare. It is common in such cases to resolve the conflict with a tax subsidy or penalty. Parents may choose not to pay for their children's education. The rest of us feel so strongly affected by this decision that we [both pay for] the child's education and compel it. There is nothing wrong with asking whether a mother's entering the labor force has so great an effect, for good or for ill, on the rest of us that we would prefer to pay her to stay in her home or to get out of it. But this is hardly an issue for tax lawyers to resolve. [The child care deduction] should indeed be discussed in terms of its effects on children and on the rest of us, but as tax lawyers we bring very little expertise to the discussion. The question is important, but it is for someone else to answer. We *would*, however, ask those who favor a subsidy to keep mothers in the home why they think that the tax rates found in section 1(a) of the Internal Revenue Code are a proper measure of that subsidy.

* * *

Conclusion

Perhaps the most vulnerable point in our defense of [the child care deduction] is that our argument may imply something that no tax lawyer (including ourselves) would agree to for a moment: All personal expenses for services should be deductible. If the failure to tax the imputed income of a mother who stays home and cares for her children while taxing her income if she enters the labor force may result in a misallocation of labor, why is that not equally true of every other service which a taxpayer renders to himself and his family, the imputed income from which is not taxed? If a deduction for a mother's cost of employing others to care for her children is a defensible device to correct the possible misallocation of her labor, why should not, on the same grounds, every taxpayer who is in the labor force be able to deduct the cost of employing another to perform personal services for him?

To be more specific, a taxpayer may have to choose between spending a Saturday cleaning his house, mowing his lawn, washing his car, shopping and washing his laundry, on the one hand, and working overtime at his job, on the other. That his imputed income from performing chores goes untaxed while his overtime pay is taxed, may lead him to perform chores himself even though he is both more efficient and happier on his job, in which case his labor is misallocated. * * *

When a taxpayer employs another to wash his car or mow his lawn, he cannot argue that the expenditure is even partly a business one in the sense of the tax law. It is purely personal, not partly personal and partly business. This is because the taxpayer cannot argue that "but for" hiring someone to do his personal chores, he could not work overtime. The taxpayer cannot make the but for argument because he is free to work overtime and leave his personal chores undone. He may not enjoy driving a dirty car or having an unmowed lawn, but that is his personal choice. He is not forced to choose between doing his chores and working at his job. A mother's position is quite different; where her husband holds a job, she could not possibly be expected to leave her child unattended in order to enter the labor force, if only because to do so would in most cases violate state law. In the child care case (but not in the case of mowing the lawn or washing the car), the taxpayer could not work but for her expenditure. Of course, a but for relationship between expense and income is not *sufficient* to make the expenditure deductible (if it were we could all deduct the cost of our food and clothing), but it is *necessary*. Thus the child care deduction fits into a different legal category—that of mixed business and personal expenses —than do deductions for other services.

　　　* * *

TAXATION AND THE FAMILY: A FRESH LOOK AT BEHAVIORAL GENDER BIASES IN THE CODE
Edward J. McCaffery[*]

40 University of California at Los Angeles Law Review 983, 1001-05, 1055-58 (1993)

The failure to tax imputed income contributes to a bias against labor force participation by secondary earners. This failure has long been noted as a theoretical shortcoming of the tax system, although it is widely believed that its existence is of practical necessity. "Imputed income" is the value that flows from owner-supplied resources or labor.

Consider the basic accounting identity that sets income equal to the sum of consumption plus savings: all income must be either spent or saved. The present income tax may be viewed as an attempt to capture all items of savings and consumption measured over a set period of time, typically the taxable year. Imputed income, however, constitutes an entire class of items that never materialize into a visible cash stream, because the individual supplies her own consumption. Imagine a taxpayer who is handy around the home—perhaps she paints the house. Were she not so talented, she would have to earn the money to pay the painters—assume a fee of $1000. That $1000, however, would be taxable, as consumption, so that the taxpayer would have to earn $1000 *after* taxes in order to pay the painters. By painting her house on her own, she has performed services worth $1000, and she has the equivalent

---

*. At time of original publication, Associate Professor of Law, University of Southern California Law Center.

amount of consumption value, but she has been able to do so with *before* tax value.

The relevance of imputed income to married couples is clear, although the precise effects are highly contextual and complex. Virtually all of the services that the spouse who stays at home performs constitute untaxed imputed income. The demand for such services increases, first with marriage, and later, dramatically, with children. Consider a scenario where a secondary earner in a family with young children leaves the home to go to work. The family would then have to pay for a variety of services—child care and housekeeping among them—with after-tax dollars. By performing these services herself, the wife obtains a tax benefit for the family: it is precisely as though she were receiving a discount of her marginal tax rate. Thus, at a 33% tax rate, a wife would have to earn $15,000 merely to replace $10,000 worth of services that she had been supplying to the home. It is therefore not surprising that economists have now been studying the elasticity of nonmarket, as well as market, work to tax rates, and have found distinct gender-based patterns. Indeed, this distinction between market and nonmarket work reveals the normative biases of the more traditional variants of the "labor-leisure" distinction, which quite often divided time into market work and all else.

Calibrating the effects of a bias in favor of imputed income is a difficult undertaking. These effects are, as demonstrated above, a function of the tax rates facing the worker. But they also depend on the actual amount of imputed income generated by a potential worker; the costs of alternatives to the imputed income—such as child care provided by other family members, for example; and the utilities of money income and leisure. What is important is to set the imputed income phenomenon in a *behavioral* context, as opposed to the distributive setting where traditional tax policy discussions have located it for years. Measuring levels of imputed income for purposes of making static distributive comparisons is difficult. One could attempt to make crude *a priori* guesses about the levels, or try to devise some technique to measure exact amounts, or develop some proxy for getting at imputed income. Alternatively, one could realize that imputed income is one of the factors that makes the classical ability-to-pay income taxation model impossible of attainment.

What are less difficult to measure, and perhaps more important to see, are the behavioral effects flowing from the fact that the marginal-earner spouse must compare after-tax labor market income with before-tax imputed earnings. This is especially important for the current problem, because it will be comparatively easy to ascertain the steps necessary to put single- and dual-earning families on nominally equal footing: reforming social security, the treatment of mixed business-personal costs, and the like. But even once those steps are taken that will move the law toward its stated ideal of equal taxation for equal-earning couples, the largely invisible imputed income effect, tilting towards single-earner households, will remain.

Some may argue that the imputed income effects benefit families by encouraging personal care of children and other dependents. But when the effects are examined from the perspective of the behavioral impact on familial structure, what is disturbing is the push towards a gender division of labor. In the traditional single-earner household, the wife's imputed income effect will be measured relative to her *husband's* income. Given that the wife is apt to have less market power, and perhaps be socialized into the role of care-provider, it becomes more likely that it will be she who takes advantage of the imputed income bonus. Note the irony: The more the husband is taxed, the more we "pay" the wife to stay home and, perhaps, the more the man works to compensate for the loss due to taxes.

One solution to the behavioral aspects of the imputed income problem clarifies these points. A *subsidy* to secondary earners, financed by a higher rate on primary earners, would move the law in a new direction. This change would not entirely remove the imputed income effect—no traditional income tax will—but it shifts its incidence and degrees. If the wife stays home full time, she will effectively be taxed by forgoing the subsidy available to her if she works. On the other hand, if the husband cuts back on his labor market hours to help with the children and the housework, he will receive a full imputed income bonus—possibly higher than exists under current law, given the need to raise rates on primary earners. Details and magnitudes aside, this type of solution could begin unraveling centuries of gendered patterns. * * *

Choice of Family Structure

The problem of taxation and the family may be approached as one of an individual's freedom of choice regarding family structure. Current institutions push for traditional single-earner families, and away from more modern conceptions. * * *

In a first-best world or from the vantage point of the hypothetical original position, the concern with freedom to choose family structure might indeed lead to taxing equal-earning couples equally, or ignoring marriage altogether in the allocation of tax burdens. But in the present tense, the ideal would require greater sensitivity to impediments to married women's participation in the labor market, and to the deeply entrenched sexual division of familial labor. At a minimum, it would purge the law of those biases where two-earner families are treated worse than single-earner ones —changing social security, the child care credit, fringe benefit rules, and so forth. But full implementation of the notion would undoubtedly go beyond these preliminary steps, to move to correct and reverse deep-seated patterns of gender discrimination, and to look closely at the questions of ex ante incentives. * * *

One problem that the ideal of freedom to choose family structure encounters is that there are many types of family, defined functionally. It is not enough to talk just of literal marriage *vel non*, or to ask whether a household has one or two earners. At the most fundamental level, we are concerned with the human bonds that familial structures foster and nurture.

As a practical proxy for these types, simple one- and two-earner marriages have been used throughout most of this Article. Indeed, much could be gained by acknowledging the factual prevalence and normative appeal of the two-earner model, and, in the face of laws and reality slanted against it, taking steps to place it on a genuinely equal footing with the traditional single-earner model. These steps may not be enough, however. * * *

Gender Bias and Inequality

A second general nonwelfarist approach, suggested by the above discussions, is to finesse the particular questions of family structure altogether, and instead look directly to the issue of women's rights. A good deal of the problems with present familial arrangements can be seen as a direct or indirect function of the pervasive gender bias in society. Women are the marginal workers; women are put to the hardest choices between parenting and working; women bear the greatest burden of juggling the two realms; and women suffer most when marriages break up, or fail to come about in the first place. All three of the dominant incentive effects discussed affect women especially painfully. Women are hurt by the failure of marriage, especially among the lower classes. Women are the stay-at-home spouse in traditional single-earner families. And women pay the greatest price for being on the cuff of an all-or-nothing labor decision that discourages part-time labor. Both symptomatic and causative of these problems and patterns is the fact that the dominant images of family, and the basic structure of our laws, have arisen out of a highly gendered, patriarchic world. If we take steps to alleviate these problems by empowering women, we will create the conditions under which a nongendered family model or models can arise, *whatever* they happen to be. In this manner, we can remain "neutral" regarding choice of family structure, without ignoring the gendered nature of society that makes the static neutrality of tax policy such a misguided idea.

Equality between the genders, although it is of course sadly far from the norm in either theory or practice, is an idea with obvious normative appeal. But even if we aim for equality between the genders, and not a neutrality between family types directly, we still want to look closely at the particular tax rules regarding family. As shown throughout this Article, the problems of married women are not the same as the problems of women generally; the family is not an institution we can simply ignore. Unmarried women suffer much less labor market discrimination. The situation of married mothers may lie at the center of the self-perpetuating cycle of socialized gender roles. Marriage neutrality alone is not enough. If our goal were to eliminate gender biases in the workplace and the gendered structure of the sexual division of labor, a perfectly good idea to study, for example, is an earned income credit targeted to secondary earners.

* * *

Notes and Questions

19. In a portion of their article not excerpted above, Professors McIntyre and Oldman favor imposing an equal tax burden on all married couples of a given income level. How might untaxed imputed income be viewed as making such an approach unfairly favor one-earner couples vis-à-vis two-earner couples? One-earner couples vis-à-vis singles? Do you agree with McIntyre and Oldman that no "pattern" of unfairness would result?

20. Should a credit or deduction be available for the expenses of child care? Should the deduction or credit be available even if a healthy parent is neither working nor studying (*e.g.*, is a housewife)? Is your answer to either question influenced by whether you think the value of a nonworking parent's services to the family should, in theory, be taxed?

21. If untaxed imputed income of nonworking parents justifies (as a proxy for taxing the imputed income) a child care deduction for working parents, what about childless taxpayers who generate absolutely no untaxed imputed income from child care? Do you agree with the argument of Professors McIntyre and Oldman that "[i]f self-performed child-care services are to be treated as income, the proper adjustment is a large deduction for taxpayers without children, with a more modest deduction for those with children who purchase child-care services"? (This argument is put forward, of course, only in an attempt to refute the idea that imputed income from child care justifies a deduction for those who purchase child care services.)

22.   Professor Klein's article emphasizes that our societal expectations of the norm may strongly influence choices made in the tax laws and, in turn, the tax laws may influence decisions about having children and about working. Clearly, our society is not now typified by the so-called "traditional" family, consisting of a working husband and a nonworking wife who cares for their children. Is today's norm one in which virtually all adults work, some having children and others remaining childless? Or would a more correct description be that virtually all adults become parents, some continuing to work and others staying home to care for their children? What tax policies are suggested by each paradigm?

23. Even if a norm existed, it would not necessarily provide an answer. Professors Schaffer and Berman argue that "[i]f every mother in the United States were in the labor force * * * the problem of whether child care was a personal or business expense to these mothers would remain." Do you agree?

24. Is the proper approach to child care expenses to allow a partial deduction (or the substantial equivalent, in the form of a credit), in recognition that the expense has both business and personal components? Consider the

business meal, which Schaffer and Berman offer in the first paragraph of their 1973 excerpt as an example of a fully deductible expense despite "a personal element." Currently, in recognition of this personal element, Congress allows a deduction for only half the cost of most business meals. Section 274(n).

25. Are present tax policies, including the failure to tax imputed income generated by housewives, consistent with the view that "a woman's place is in the home"? Or, by contrast, does the child care credit subsidize mothers who prefer to work outside the home? Or both? Should the tax laws be neutral, as Professors Schaffer and Berman "postulate," or should they subsidize the decision either to stay home or to work?

26. Professor McCaffery argues that the tax law tends to influence married women, in particular, toward work in the home, and that the influence increases as their husband's taxable income rises. Why is this so?

27. Professor McCaffery acknowledges that any system of income taxation cannot entirely remove incentives in favor of imputed income. (All agree that direct taxation of imputed income from services is not under serious consideration.) Nevertheless, he directly challenges the neutrality postulate of Professors Schaffer and Berman (see Note #25 above), and calls for acknowledgment of the "normative appeal of the two-earner model." What effect would his proposed tax subsidy for secondary workers (usually wives) have? Would the proposed tax subsidy mean higher tax rates for taxpayers who cannot, or do not, qualify for the subsidy (one-earner couples, for example)? Is his proposed subsidy system fair? Is Professor McCaffery correct that "disturbing is the push toward a gender division of labor," or, by contrast, is his proposal objectionable precisely because it would inefficiently lead to reduced specialization of husbands and wives? Would it lead to better child care or worse? Again, this proposal raises the issue of whether the tax system should be neutral toward the wife's decision to enter the labor force, or encourage or discourage that decision, and makes clear the impact of tax law on the structure of society.

28. Professor Anne Alstott observes that "[l]ike other feminist tax policy proposals, [Professor McCaffery's proposals] are open to feminist objections."[s] For example:

> [F]eminists who see the devaluation of women's family labor as
> the central obstacle to women's autonomy, power, or happiness could
> oppose market work tax incentives. Although tax incentives would
> not force any woman to go to work if she prefers not to, they would

---

s. Anne L. Alstott, *Tax Policy and Feminism: Competing Goals and Institutional Choices*, 96 COLUM. L. REV. 2001, 2034 (1996).

increase the rewards of market work relative to those of family labor. To the extent that married women's market work decisions are made jointly with other family members who will benefit from the extra family income, wives may face pressure to take advantage of the incentive regime. * * * Although McCaffery frames his proposal as a tax cut for "women" paid for by higher taxes on "men," that overstates the case. * * * [T]he aggregate tax burden on the couple is likely to affect both the husband's and the wife's income and consumption. Thus, McCaffery's proposal is more accurately described as a tax cut for two-earner couples and a tax increase on single-earner couples.[t]

29. What of allowing a deduction for household care? Given that all families, with or without children, must either perform or pay for some amount of household care, should we account for the difference between performing (and generating untaxed imputed income) and paying for (with after-tax dollars) by allowing a deduction for payments? If we are concerned that this would unfairly benefit high-income taxpayers, can this objection be met by allowing the deduction but increasing the progressivity of the tax rates? Does this provide a perfect example of imputed income, which might be accounted for by allowing a deduction to those who hire others to perform the work?

30. At present, section 21 allows, under certain circumstances, a credit for household expenses as well as dependent care, but only if the taxpayer maintains a household with a child or other "qualifying individual." Focusing only on household expenses, is there any justification for tying the credit to whether the taxpayer supports a qualifying individual? If the expense of maids should give rise to a tax benefit (perhaps as a proxy to the untaxed imputed income of those who care for their own houses), should it be available to all taxpayers, regardless of family status?

31. At present, many persons who provide services in the home are paid in cash, with payors and payees colluding to evade income taxes and Social Security taxes. To the degree that such payments are deductible or creditable by the payor, the payor has a strong incentive not to allow the fraud to take place. (For example, taxpayers claiming the credit under section 21 must report the Social Security number of the recipient of their payments; this, in turn, greatly increases the chance that the recipient will report and pay tax on the payment.) Does this anti-fraud effect justify some form of deduction or credit?

---

t. *Id.* at 2035-36.

32. In a 113-page article, Professor Norman Lane argues that his "exchange model" of income is useful "both as a precis of our existing tax law and as a normative ideal."[u] Under this model, "[o]nly transactions which derive from the production and exchange process ought to increase the aggregate tax base."[v] This result is justified by the enormous increase in productivity and wealth occasioned by use of markets and specialization. With regard to imputed income from services,[w] Professor Lane argues that not only does it lie outside the proper scope of taxable income, but that no serious misallocation of resources results from this demarcation:

> [T]he exchange model sharply distinguishes between satisfying present wants through direct effort to that end, and satisfying them by participating in markets. The individual who grows his own vegetables in his home garden and cooks them on his own range is not taxed on the value of his output, while the individual who works for wages and purchases vegetables at the store must confront a tax wedge between the two activities. The exchange model assumes, quite reasonably, that technological conditions are such that the latter route provides far more vegetables per unit of time expended than the former even after the tax is paid.[x]

Is this persuasive in the case of vegetables grown in the back yard? In the case of a housewife's services to her family?

Leisure as imputed income

33. It is difficult to describe the outer limit of imputed income from services. McIntyre and Oldman argue that "almost every activity we undertake is in some sense a self-performed service," and provide a list including several such "services" that are generally regarded as leisure, including watching television, reading a novel, and playing backgammon.

In theory, the tax base might pick up all imputed income and leisure by levying a tax on earning *capacity* rather than actual income earned, as Professor Daniel Halperin explains:

> It might be said that ideally an income tax should be based upon earning capacity. This method would best reflect the individual's potential to acquire resources and thus may "best assess the sacrifice a particular taxpayer is making when he is asked to give a certain sum of money to the state."[y]

---

u. Norman H. Lane, *A Theory of the Tax Base: The Exchange Model*, 3 AMER. J. TAX POL'Y 1, 18 (1984).

v. *Id.*

w. Professor Lane's treatment of imputed income from housing and other consumer durables is somewhat more complex. *See id.* at 34-41.

x. *Id.* at 23.

y. Professor Halperin is quoting from Mark G. Kelman, *Personal Deductions Revisited: Why They Fit Poorly in an "Ideal" Income Tax and Why They Fit Worse in a Far from Ideal World*, 31 STAN. L. REV. 831, 841 (1979).

Implementation of this concept raises a number of questions. Would actual earning in excess of the amount expected from an individual of a particular ability also be taken into account? While individuals who spend their time beachcombing or who leave their money in a mattress would have some income imputed to them, it is more difficult to determine the correct treatment of a taxpayer who tries but is unsuccessful, either in investment or in exploiting the value of her personal services. * * *

These questions have not been explored because no one argues that the tax base should actually be based upon capacity. * * * [A] law school professor might be forced to practice law in order to pay the tax.[z]

34. While no one suggests that leisure can or should be subjected to tax, perhaps it should be taken into account in setting the rate schedule for the income that is taxed. Don Fullerton and Diane Lim Rogers have argued that "leisure is important for distributional issues."[aa] Under a model assuming that "high income groups take relatively more leisure, a good that is excluded from any tax on labor, on capital, or on consumption * * * all U.S. taxes look more regressive."[bb] Is the underlying assumption—that high-income taxpayers generally enjoy more leisure than others—valid?

---

z. Daniel Halperin, *Valuing Personal Consumption: Cost Versus Value and the Impact of Insurance*, 1 FLA. TAX R. 1, 9-10 (1992).

aa. Don Fullerton and Diane Lim Rogers, *Lifetime Versus Annual Perspectives on Tax Incidence*, 44 NAT'L TAX J. 277, 285 (1991).

bb. *Id.* at 281.

CHAPTER FOUR

PROGRESSIVE TAX RATES

Unlike proportionality, progression provides no principle which tells us what the relative burden of different persons ought to be. * * * [T]he argument based on the presumed justice of progression provides no limitation, as has often been admitted by its supporters, before all incomes above a certain figure are confiscated, and those below left untaxed.[a]

A. INTRODUCTION

The choice of appropriate tax levels involves a variety of often contradictory considerations. Public acceptance is of prime importance.

The primary concept underlying progressive taxation is ability to pay. At the lowest income levels, this may imply a goal of imposing no tax liability whatever—or perhaps a negative tax. At higher income levels, ability to pay has provided the rationale for progressive tax rates.

Revenue needs underlie the choice of tax levels. Revenue needs were of overwhelming importance in setting high tax rates during World War I and World War II. When the factors of ability to pay and public acceptability were factored in, it was predictable that the wartime rates also would be sharply progressive.

In wartime and peacetime, a variety of other considerations are taken into account. Federal tax decisions must take into account the revenue needs of state and local governments. Consideration must be given to the tendency of high tax rates to encourage tax evasion, or, at the least, to lead to elaborate and economically wasteful tax avoidance. Efforts must be made to minimize distortion of market choices. In a market-driven economy, taxes that distort market choices result in investment decisions that fail to maximize the economy's potential. Taxes also affect incentives to work, though here it is more difficult to determine their impact. There is the obvious effect of discouraging more work when the alternative is tax-free leisure (the "substitution effect"), but in a society with highly developed consumer demand there is an alternative pressure to work harder to earn enough after-tax income to achieve a desired standard of living (the "income effect"). The best example of the latter is the increase in the number of two-earner families.[b]

---

a. Friedrich A. Hayek, quoted in 69 TAX NOTES 1674 (1995).

b. The two-earner phenomenon has bloomed in the face of a tax system that imposes its highest rates on marginal earnings. If one spouse (typically the wife) is a marginal earner, who may or may not be in the labor force, it is plausible to view that spouse's earnings as being taxed at a rate

The Tax Reform Act of 1986 revised the size and pattern of the tax rate schedules, and in so doing it changed drastically the frame of reference for debate on progressivity. Under the impetus of a drive for a broad-based flat rate tax, but also under the constraint to produce a revenue-neutral bill, in 1986 Congress enacted a three-bracket system (zero tax, 15 percent, and 28 percent), dropping the top rate from 50 percent. The top rate has since been increased, but it is difficult to imagine a top rate as high as the 91 percent in effect as recently as 1964. In the present political climate, it is hard to foresee an income tax (at least in peacetime) that will tax personal income at an explicit rate higher than 50 percent.

B. PROGRESSIVITY: PROS AND CONS

This subchapter surveys the arguments for and against the desirability of a progressive income tax. For the most part, the arguments are wide-ranging, not limited by the frame of reference set by recent statutes.

The principle of tax rates keyed, at least to some degree, to ability to pay is not seriously challenged. Even a flat rate tax with a liberal exemption provides significant progressivity.[c] Consequently, the discussion revolves around the appropriate formula establishing the degree of progression and, equally important, the search for a rationale for a cap on the top rate.

Professor JB McCombs' article reviews the theoretical arguments on progressivity. The excerpt focuses on *The Uneasy Case for Progressive Taxation*, an influential book written by Professors Walter J. Blum and Harry Kalven, Jr. in 1953, which had questioned the theoretical basis for progressivity.

The selection by Professor Dan Throop Smith, an economist and at one time the principal expert on tax policy in the Treasury, challenges progression in principle. His discussion, however, is directed primarily at the problem of setting rational limits on the degree of progressivity.

The selection by Professor Boris Bittker defends the fairness of a progressive federal income tax. Notably, he contends that proportionality is no more logical than progressivity, so there is no reason to put the burden of proof on proponents of progressivity. He also argues that the progressivity of the federal income tax is offset, at least in part, by other federal, state, and local taxes that are regressive.

---

effectively higher than that imposed on the other spouse. This problem is a central issue of Chapter Five.

    c. See the discussion of flat tax proposals in Chapter Seven. (As Professor McCombs indicates in the first excerpt below, this form of progression is sometimes referred to as "degression.")

AN HISTORICAL REVIEW AND ANALYSIS OF EARLY UNITED STATES TAX POLICY SCHOLARSHIP: DEFINITION OF INCOME AND PROGRESSIVE RATES

JB McCombs*

64 Saint John's Law Review 471, 512-25 (1990)

Blum and Kalven: The Critical View

In 1953, Professors Walter J. Blum and Harry Kalven, Jr., wrote a short book critiquing progressive taxation. They did not quickly convert the nation to proportionate taxation, but perhaps they demonstrated that Henry Simons was right in his contention that progressivity is an issue more concerned with ethics than rationality.

Blum and Kalven seemed to prefer Simons' approach. In 1963, when the book was reprinted, they recorded some additional thoughts on the view of progressivity as an ethical issue.

> Ten years ago we were puzzled as to why Henry Simons' bluntness had not had more impact on the tone of discussions in the United States. Writing in the late thirties, he exasperatedly asserted that the whole superstructure of sacrifice and ability-to-pay theorizing was simply nonsense and that the case for progression was no more and no less than the case for mitigating "unlovely" economic inequality.[157]

The authors claimed to have approached their topic with a bias favoring progressivity. Appropriately, Blum and Kalven's *The Uneasy Case for Progressive Taxation* begins with a careful definition of the central issue, particularly with reference to the difference between progression arising from a constant rate tax with a personal exemption, and the type of progression (relative to both total and taxable incomes) obtained from actually graduating the statutory marginal rates. The former is defined as degression. Based upon their conclusion that "[i]t is almost unanimously agreed that some exemption keyed to at least a minimum subsistence standard of living is desirable,"[160] the authors put aside the issue of degression and focused their attention on the latter form of progression.

The authors discussed three general objections often lodged against progressivity. First, they pointed to the additional complication progressivity adds to an income tax and its administration. Income splitting and other problems related to identifying the proper taxpayer fit into this category.

---

*. At time of original publication, Assistant Professor of Law, University of Nebraska College of Law.

157. W. BLUM & H. KALVEN, JR., THE UNEASY CASE FOR PROGRESSIVE TAXATION xiv (1953).

160. *Id.*, at 4.

Progressivity also creates the problem of identifying or defining the appropriate taxable unit in family matters. With a flat tax, husbands, wives, and children can be taxed together or separately with no difference in impact or tax liability. The difference between married, single, and head-of-household taxpayers would disappear (except with respect to the appropriate size of the exemption). Splitting income among different years is the temporal equivalent of splitting income among different individuals, and it is aggravated (though not created) by a progressive rate structure. Under a flat tax, the seemingly inescapable year-end ritual of deciding whether to accelerate deductions into the expiring year and delay income into the coming year, or vice versa, becomes purely a matter of the time value of money. The question of the year in which the individual will be in a higher tax bracket drops out of the equation.

> And one of the few plausible arguments, if not the only one, for special treatment of capital gains stems from this characteristic of progression. Because a capital gain may have been in the making for many years, it seems unfair to tax all of it as the income of a single year.[163]

The authors also implied that the reduced importance of timing, which would result from elimination of progressive rates, would allow repeal of the rules for the net operating loss carry back and carry forward, installment sale method, last-in first-out ("LIFO") inventory method, and carryover of capital losses. Such an implication is not sound, however, for several reasons: the installment sale method is motivated in large part by a sympathy for the taxpayer who has a realized gain that is much greater than his cash from the transaction; the LIFO method is driven by desire to reduce the effective tax rate on inflationary gain by delaying the tax as long as possible; and net operating loss and capital loss carryover provisions are primarily based on the government's reluctance to give immediate refunds for such losses.

The second general objection to progressivity is that it is "politically irresponsible." This is the "tyranny of the majority" argument, which questions the right of the majority to impose such a burden on the higher-income minority. The response to this, which the authors acknowledged, is that such an objection applied to every decision made by a democratic government. The authors made reference to constitutional limitations on the power of the majority in certain areas, such as free speech, which merely highlights the fact that those who framed and adopted our Constitution never deemed the upper end of a highly paid person's income to rank with the fundamental individual freedoms protected by the Bill of Rights.

---

163. *Id.* at 16-17.

The third general objection to progressivity is that it reduces total national output. Blum and Kalven noted that a progressive tax is not the only type that can reduce the productivity of our economy:

> It is worth a reminder that the disadvantages of progression, as well as its advantages, in this connection and in all others, are to be assessed only by contrasting a progressive system which raises a given amount of revenue to a proportionate one which raises an identical amount of revenue.[170]

Nevertheless, the comparable progressive tax will subject the most highly paid (and therefore, arguably, most productive) citizens to a higher marginal tax rate than would the revenue-equivalent proportionate system.

One fundamental assumption that the authors made regarding productivity deserved more thought than it received. They asserted that "[i]t is not difficult to concede that money is the dominant stimulus to work in our society."[171] Others would disagree with this assumption, however, especially with respect to high income individuals. It ignored the large number of "workaholics" in higher income strata. It also gave inadequate attention to the nonmonetary rewards that often flow from highly paid positions. Simons, whom the authors quote only briefly on this point, saw money as only one stimulus at work in our society.

It also can reasonably be argued that much of the interest of the rich in money is in having *relatively* more than their peers. This is a corollary to Simons' assertion that "[p]overty, want, and privation are in large measure merely relative."[173] Because a rational, progressive income tax will not upset the relative pre-tax order (of rich, richer, richest), this kind of egotistical stimulus to working will not be impaired by progressive taxation.

Another element in the productivity debate is the possible discouragement of saving and investing. There is widespread agreement that progressive taxation has a negative effect on capital accumulation and that such accumulation is an important element in economic growth. Simons wrote that "[w]ith respect to capital accumulation, however, the consequences are certain to be significantly adverse;"[174] but that, in his opinion, the incremental loss of productivity is probably justified by the reduction of inequality. Blum and Kalven agreed with him on the first conclusion but parted company with him on the second. They identified two phases in the formation of "real capital": the decision of an individual with discretionary income to save, rather than

---

170. *Id.* at 21.

171. *Id.* at 22.

173. H. SIMONS, PERSONAL INCOME TAXATION: THE DEFINITION OF INCOME AS A PROBLEM OF FISCAL POLICY 25 (1938).

174. *Id.* at 21.

consume, a part of it; and the decision by that same, or another, person to invest those savings in a business or other venture. The authors recognized that the effect of progressive taxation on the decision to save is unclear. Some people save in response to the rate of interest their savings can earn. For high income people who save for this reason, the incentive to save is reduced by the higher tax rates that accompany a progressive system (as opposed to a proportionate system that generates equal revenue). On the other hand, other people save to accumulate a specific amount of money for retirement. For them, reduction in rate of return due to the tax burden will actually force them to save more to achieve the same retirement goal. The authors recognized that, since the magnitudes of these two savings incentives are unknown, the net effect on saving of a particular tax rate is also unknown.

Blum and Kalven's analysis of the effects of progressivity on investment (*i.e.*, risk-taking) is not applicable under the current United States tax system with its extremely wide rate brackets. If one thinks back (or forward) to a rate structure containing a large number of relatively narrow brackets, however, the discussion is valuable. Under such a system, if an investment is successful, the profit will push the investor into a higher tax bracket and such profit will be taxed at a rate higher than the investor normally experiences. If the investment is unsuccessful, the loss will pull the investor down to a bracket lower than normal. As a result, the government takes a higher than normal percentage of investment profits, while it absorbs through loss deductions a lower than normal percentage of investment losses (assuming full deductibility of losses). Again, Blum and Kalven distinguished between high tax rates in general and high tax rates generated by progressivity. While a high tax rate itself may discourage investment, its impact is enlarged by a progressive system. Ultimately, the "relatively wealthy," a significant source of investment funds, are taxed under progression at rates higher than the single rate prevalent under a proportionate tax rate.

Blum and Kalven identified the effect of progressivity on levels of saving and investment as central to the debate over progressivity, and referenced Simons' idea of government capitalism. Thus, it may be in order to consider the capital formation issue more broadly, and in a modern context. Simons did not go into much detail in his discussion of government capital formation, but he did suggest that the government might appropriately purchase all regulated utilities. This, he believed, could be accomplished without a major overthrow of our economic system. If inadequate capital formation is a valid concern, however, perhaps we should be searching for possible ways to implement Professor Simons' concept of government capitalism, structured in ways and within limits that impose acceptably small costs in terms of greater government control over the private economy.

It is not at all clear that changing from progressive to proportionate taxation will increase private capital formation sufficiently to satisfy those who are concerned about it. Indeed, progressivity of federal taxes was reduced by the several tax reform acts of the 1980s, yet Congress is still grappling for ways to increase the United States saving rate. One point remains clear—taxes are not the only significant variable in capital formation. Cultural attitudes toward consumption and saving are also important ingredients.

Desire to retain progressive taxation, therefore, might not be the only force leading to endorsement of government capitalism. For example, in the United States, gradual changes in cultural attitudes could, over a span of multiple generations, produce a situation in which people save a lower percentage of their incomes than did their grandparents under otherwise identical circumstances. Furthermore, despair over the chances of economic development in the third world outstripping population growth could convince industrialized nations to assume the role of capitalists for less developed countries.

On the subject of a reduction in production caused by a progressive tax, the parallel between the Blum and Kalven team and Henry Simons continues, despite their inapposite conclusions on progression. The continuation of these diametric conclusions gives some validity to Simons' claim that progressivity ultimately rests upon an ethical judgment rather than logical reasoning.

In contrast, a number of theories have been advanced in support of a progressive income tax. One is the suggestion that a progressive tax is highly sensitive to contraction and expansion of the overall economy, and that it reacts to each in an appropriate manner. During a recession, for example, revenues produced by a progressive tax will fall faster than those from a proportionate tax, leaving more money in the private economy at a time when it is especially needed. During an expansion, revenues produced by a progressive tax grow faster than the economy, and faster than revenues from a proportionate tax, reducing the likelihood that the economy will become "overheated" and inflationary. During recession and expansion, these effects occur more quickly than federal spending changes could be made, and also reduce the amount of spending and monetary adjustments necessary to stabilize the economy.

The sacrifice theory is another supportive theory. According to Blum and Kalven, "[i]t ignores the benefits received from government and treats taxes as though they were a confiscation of property. The problem then becomes one of confiscating in an equitable manner."[182]

---

182. W. BLUM & H. KALVEN, JR., *supra* note 157, at 39.

Although the term "equality of sacrifice" is often used in this context, it is used generally to describe a condition under which each person suffers a proportionate, rather than truly equal, sacrifice. If "sacrifice" is taken to mean the number of dollars surrendered, then proportionate sacrifice theory simply leads to proportionate taxation. If, however, sacrifice is to be measured in terms of potential satisfaction surrendered to the government, and if that meaning is combined with the theory of declining marginal utility of money, then proportionate sacrifice in terms of potential satisfaction will require progressive surrender in terms of dollars.

Blum and Kalven separated the truly equal sacrifice idea from that of proportionate sacrifice, although the distinction is difficult to discern. They demonstrated that the truly equal sacrifice approach does not necessarily lead to progressive rates. Simons has already stated that if the utility curve for money slopes downward only gradually, a goal of equal sacrifice will produce regressive tax rates. Blum and Kalven added that:

> This is an important step since it is one thing to assume that the utility of money declines but quite another to assume the rate at which it declines. Clearly, the fewer the demands the argument makes on knowledge of the slope of the curve, the stronger the argument will be.[185]

Both of these sacrifice theories involve a two-step process. First, each must establish a normative proposition of how the sacrifice of paying taxes should be shared. Second, a tax rate structure that achieves the proposed sharing must be shown. The equal sacrifice theory is strong on the first step and weak on the second. The proposal that a sacrifice for the good of the group should be borne equally by all its members is, superficially, very appealing. As discussed above, however, under this theory, support for progression depends upon the idea that the marginal utility of money decreases faster than income increases, and this supposition is subject to serious challenge.

Conversely, the proportional sacrifice theory as an argument for progression is strong on the second step, but at first glance seems weak on the first. Assuming for a moment the normative proposition that each person should suffer a proportionate sacrifice to pay for government expenditures, progressive taxation with respect to income is necessary and appropriate to

---

185. *Id.* at 41. In my opinion, the equal sacrifice approach must be abandoned, because, as stated by British economist A.C. Pigou, "[i]n order to prove that the principle of equal sacrifice necessarily involves progression we should need to know that the last £10 of a £1000 income carry less satisfaction than the last £1 of a £100 income; and this the law of diminishing utility does not assert." A.C. PIGOU, A STUDY OF PUBLIC FINANCE 86 (3d rev. ed. 1962). Personal reflection leads to the intuitive conclusion that the utility curve for money does not decline that steeply. At least, many reasonable people could so conclude, which takes the strength out of this theory's support for progression.

achieve that goal. Any normal, declining marginal utility curve for money will support the claim for progression.   Under any normal, downward sloping utility curve, even a gentle slope, a tax that takes twenty percent of income from both high income and low income taxpayers will be proportionate with respect to dollars but regressive with respect to satisfaction sacrificed. Because the high income individual will pay the tax with less valuable (*i.e.*, less satisfying) dollars, that person will sacrifice a lower percentage of his satisfaction. It is very clear that progressive tax rates are necessary to achieve proportionate sacrifice.

The more difficult part of the analysis is to make a compelling argument for the first step, *i.e.*, the proposition that taxpayers should suffer a proportionate, rather than equal, sacrifice of the potential satisfactions represented by their incomes.   Surprisingly, Blum and Kalven presented a convincing argument that proportionate sacrifice is the superior choice.

> Any theory of equalizing the sacrifice of taxpayers implicitly assumes that the taxes are a necessary evil falling upon a distribution of money, and therefore upon a distribution of satisfactions, which [distributional pattern] is otherwise acceptable.   With this assumption the problem is not to use the tax system to adjust existing inequalities in that distribution but simply to leave all taxpayers equally "worse off" after taxes.   The vice of the equal sacrifice formula is that it is regressive when measured by satisfactions and this becomes compellingly clear if large enough sacrifices are exacted equally from each taxpayer. The corresponding virtue of the proportionate sacrifice formula is that it remains neutral as to the relative distribution of satisfactions among taxpayers.   Under it they are all equally "worse off" [in terms of satisfaction, not dollars] after taxes.[188]

In *The Uneasy Case for Progressive Taxation*, one can discern strength in each of the two steps that are required to support progressive taxation with the proportionate sacrifice theory.   Although Blum and Kalven were not fully convinced by their own arguments, upon close analysis their arguments on behalf of the proportionate sacrifice theory are compelling.   They summarize them as follows:

> [The proportionate sacrifice theory] makes relatively few demands on knowledge about the utility curve for money, other than that it declines; and it narrows considerably the issue between progressive and proportionate taxation. As between one who favors proportional taxation on grounds of its neutrality and one who favors the

---

188. W. BLUM & H. KALVEN, JR., *supra* note 157, at 43-44.

proportionate sacrifice standard on grounds of its neutrality there is only the issue of whether there is a meaningful and sufficiently ascertainable money utility curve for all taxpayers.[189]

The only remaining difficulty is how to devise a specific rate schedule that implements the proportionate sacrifice theory. To remain true to the reasoning behind the theory, some estimated utility curve for money must be constructed. It seems likely that there have been many years in which the United States statutory rates have been much more progressive than could be justified under this theory, with any reasonably estimated money utility curve.

Furthermore, even if it could be proven that the actual shape of the utility curve for money justifies rates above fifty percent, it is still possible to reject such high rates under this theory by following Carver's lead.[d] He began with the minimum sacrifice theory, which endorses the most extreme form of progressivity, and then superimposed a rate-limiting theory that considered the burden on others from the overall productivity loss caused by the extremely high rates. His second step could be added to the proportionate sacrifice theory in the same manner. In this way, with some estimates of productivity losses caused by various rates, one could construct a declining marginal utility curve for money that maps the "boundary," below which one is not willing to follow the proportionate sacrifice theory. If the utility curve for money declines so steeply that the proportionate sacrifice theory prescribes unacceptably high rates at some income levels, Carver's theory of productivity losses can be used to constrain the rates ultimately selected to more reasonable levels.

One objection to progressivity raised by Blum and Kalven was that even if these various theories have some validity as general arguments in favor of progression, none gives any hint of what the theoretically justifiable rate structure should be. Properly conceived, their objection should not be used as a general argument against progressive taxes, but is valid only against highly progressive taxes. If it is agreed that the proportionate sacrifice theory demonstrates only that the ideal rate structure is progressive and nothing about the proper degree of progressivity, then it is highly likely that a moderately progressive set of rates will be closer than a strictly proportionate tax to the unknown theoretical ideal. As the proposed rate structure becomes more progressive, this likelihood is reduced. Seligman made an argument of this nature, without identifying the fact that the likelihood of being near the

---

189. *Id.* at 44-45.

d. The reference to Carver is to a Nineteenth Century writer cited by Blum and Kalven: Carver, *The Ethical Basis of Distribution and Its Application to Taxation*, 6 ANNALS 95 et seq. (July, 1895). (Ed.)

ideal varies when the proposed progressivity is changed.[194] As long as the argument is restricted to the defense of moderately progressive rates, it provides the better response to this issue. With this in mind, Blum and Kalven seem almost disingenuous in their complaint that the perfect proportionate sacrifice rate package cannot be determined.

* * *

HIGH PROGRESSIVE TAX RATES: INEQUITY AND IMMORALITY?
Dan Throop Smith[*]

20 University of Florida Law Review 451, 452-63 (1968)

As on all issues of tax policy, progressivity must be appraised from the standpoint of equity, economic effects, revenue, and administrative complications. The equity and economic issues were stated in a condensed form by three children in a one-room school in Montana where the author had the challenge of discussing tax policy at the invitation of his daughter, the teacher. In response to the question: What would be a fair tax on a family with an income of 5,000 dollars if a family with 2,000 dollars income paid 200 dollars? The first child said, "500 dollars," thereby showing a predisposition for proportional burdens and perhaps a desire to make use of a newly-acquired familiarity with percentages. A second child immediately disagreed, with the comment that the payment should be more than 500 dollars because "each dollar isn't so important" to the family with the larger income. A third child agreed but with the reservation that the additional tax over 500 dollars shouldn't be "too much more or they won't work so hard." Elaborate theoretical structures concerning diminishing utility and incentives and

---

194. *See* E.R.A. SELIGMAN, PROGRESSIVE TAXATION IN THEORY AND PRACTICE 293-94 (2d ed. 1908). Seligman wrote:

> It may, indeed, frankly be conceded that the theory of faculty cannot determine any definite rate of progression as the ideally just rate. To this extent there seems to be some degree of truth in Mill's contention that progressive taxation cannot give that "degree of certainty" on which a legislator should act; as well as in McCulloch's assertion that when we abandon proportion we "are at sea without rudder or compass." It is true that proportion is in one sense certain, and that progression is uncertain. The argument, however, proves too much. An uncertain rate, if it be in the general direction of justice, may nevertheless be preferable to a rate which, like that of proportion, may be more certain without being so equitable. . . . In truth, a strict proportional tax, if we accept the point of view mentioned above, is really more arbitrary as over against the individual taxpayers, than a *moderately* progressive tax. The ostensible "certainty" hence involves a really greater arbitrariness.

Id. (emphasis added [by Professor McCombs]).

      *. At time of original publication, Professor of Finance, Harvard Graduate School of Business Administration.

disincentives are all really refinements of the quasi-intuitive opinions of those children and may not lead to any greater certainty.

The diminishing marginal utility of successive units of any single product is a familiar fact and has been an integral part of economic theory for about a century. But extension of this concept from a single commodity to income in general, which represents a claim on all commodities present and future and gives a choice between consumption and savings, is questionable in principle and quite unsatisfactory in practice if one hopes to measure the *rate* of decrease in marginal utility. The concept becomes even less suitable as a basis for public policy when one attempts to extend it to interpersonal comparisons. Though there is probably agreement that there is some decline in marginal utility for an individual's income, as well as for specific items of consumption, and that a decline also exists when one considers a total amount of income distributed among many people, there is no agreement on or even basis for determination of the extent of decrease. Though some progression would generally be regarded as more equitable than a proportionate tax, it is quite possible that under political pressure and confusion about the extent of changes in tax rates as well as the absolute level of rates, progressivity may be carried to such excesses that it is more inequitable than proportionality.

Quite apart from uncertainty about the degree of decline in the marginal utility of income, there is no agreement concerning whether it would be more equitable to strive for minimum aggregate sacrifice or equal proportionate sacrifice among taxpayers. The former sounds plausible and has in fact been advocated by some writers, but a strict application of it would mean that taxes would equalize incomes down to the point where the required revenue was secured. There would be a 100 per cent tax on all incomes (or other tax base) above that point, with no tax on lesser amounts. This follows logically from the proposition that any dollar of a larger income represents less want-satisfying power than any dollar of a small income. Until the largest income is brought down to the level of the next largest income, any taxation of the next largest involves greater sacrifice than additional taxation of the remaining balance of the largest.[5]

---

5. In a simplified example, if an income distribution consisted of one income of $150,000, two of $100,000 each, ten of $50,000 each, and eighty-seven of $20,000 each, and only $50,000 revenue was required, it should all come from the income of $150,000 under the theory of minimum aggregate sacrifice, since even the 50,000th dollar from it presumably represents less satisfaction than any one of the dollars of the person with an income of $100,000. If total revenue requirements do not exceed $200,000, all revenue should come from the three incomes above $50,000 and reduce them to that level. Only if total revenue required exceeded $590,000 would there be any tax on incomes of $20,000; equalization down to that level would produce $590,000. If $690,000 were required, incomes would be equalized down to $19,000. Alternatively, one might try to attain equal marginal sacrifice, recognizing that a small payment by someone with the smaller income may represent no more *relative* sacrifice than some part of the large payment by the person with the larger

The idea of equalization of net incomes through taxation to the point where adequate revenue is secured is for many a valid *reductio ad absurdum* of the whole idea of progression. If one contemplates a so-called negative income tax at the bottom end of the scale, taxation under this concept would become a device for complete equalization of after-tax net incomes. Even the most ardent equalizers, or the most rigorous logicians, usually stop short of 100 per cent marginal tax rates, if only on pragmatic grounds.

The alternative standard of equal proportional sacrifice throws one back to the confusion about the rate of decrease in marginal utility. No basis of psychological measure has yet been found to remove the uncertainty that impelled McCulloch to make his much quoted statement about progression almost a century and a quarter ago that "the moment you abandon . . . the cardinal principle of exacting from all individuals the same proportion of their income or their property, you are at sea without rudder or compass, and there is no amount of injustice or folly you may not commit."[6]

A precise analysis in terms of equity is made even more difficult by the need to relate tax burdens to benefits from government services. Though taxation is the means to pay for government services, which, hopefully, are confined to the activities providing general benefit which can only, or most effectively, be provided collectively, government services in fact give direct benefits in varying degrees to individuals. In many respects the services are intended to help those who can least afford to help themselves and hence any attempt to match taxes against benefits would contravene the very purpose of the government program. But enough of the services are quasi-commercial, or yield benefits that do not have to involve a redistribution of income to be effective, to make a comparison of taxes to benefits not wholly irrelevant. Though theoretically valid, an attempt to carve out and value a segment of individual benefits from the body of general benefits is as frustrating as an attempt to establish the shape of a curve representing the declining utility of income. The existence of this two-fold problem further weakens any confidence one might have in any scientific establishment of equity in a tax system.

Quite apart from equity, one may argue that progressive taxation is justified by the need to reduce inequality and thereby establish a more attractive society (some refer to a more aesthetically satisfying society), the need to reduce social and political tensions, and the need to create greater equality of opportunity. All these are valid and appealing objectives, but some are purely subjective, and the role of taxation in others is quite indeterminate.

---

income. In the example above, a $10,000 tax on the incomes of $100,000 might involve the same relative sacrifice as a $30,000 tax on an income of $150,000, to produce $50,000 of revenue. But marginal utilities and sacrifices are elusive, if not nebulous.

6. J. MCCULLOCH, TAXATION AND THE FUNDING SYSTEM 142 (1845).

They cannot, however, be brushed aside as irrelevant. Blum and Kalven conclude that an extensive analysis simply:[7]

> [S]uggests the tantalizing combination of plausible, ingenious and improbable ideas which make up the case for progression in terms of sacrifice and ability to pay. It likewise suggests why these notions have such a stubborn appeal. But it tends to demonstrate that the hold of these notions on the general public must derive from the fallacies that have frequented the theories and not from their truths which are difficult to drive to and once found would not support any firm conviction about the validity of the progressive principle.

When one turns to the economic significance of progression, the analysis must be made from several standpoints, only two of which are simple and straightforward. The revenue from a progressive income tax invariably fluctuates more with changes in national income than does a proportional tax. It thus exerts a counter-cyclical effect and is referred to as an automatic stabilizer.[8] On this point, the facts and conclusions seem incontrovertible, though opinions differ on their importance. Many other counter-cyclical forces are available, including timely changes in tax rates and structures by legislation.

A second fairly certain economic result of progression in taxation is that it favors consumption over saving because of a somewhat higher marginal propensity to save from larger and from increasing incomes. In the 1930's with the prevalence of the fallacy of the mature economy and the presumption that savings would always outrun investment opportunities, progressive taxation was regarded as especially suitable to reduce those incomes that were most likely to be saved. With the more recent emphasis on the need for investment to increase productivity and minimize inflationary effects of large annual increases in wage rates, a tax factor that discriminates against potential savings is more likely to be regarded as undesirable. From this standpoint, the very high degree of progression seems particularly unfortunate when it exists in some of the underdeveloped countries that so desperately need both capital and enterprise even to maintain their present low per capita incomes.

---

7. W. BLUM & H. KALVEN, THE UNEASY CASE FOR PROGRESSIVE TAXATION 68 (1953).

8. In economic terms, a "counter-cyclical factor" is one that operates in the opposite direction from the familiar cyclical forces. An increase in welfare payments during a recession is counter-cyclical to the decrease in private income from employment and investment. An automatic stabilizer is one that arises without the need for new legislation or administrative action. Progressivity in income taxation has an automatic stabilizing effect in that revenues fall off more sharply than total personal income in a recession because it is the highest segments of income that are subject to the highest tax rates; government expenditures are thus likely to be covered by deficit financing, which in turn is likely to have an expansionary effect.

The effects of progression on incentives for work and investment are more important and less clear than the effects on fluctuations in revenue and on the availability of net incomes most likely to be saved. Extreme critics are disposed to say that high progression will so destroy incentives that an economic system will grind to a halt. This is manifestly absurd, but the fact of continued growth in countries with high marginal tax rates is no reason to ignore their possible adverse influence on the amount and direction of human effort and investment. With a better tax structure, the growth might be greater.

Personal activity is stimulated by many incentives, among which pecuniary reward is only one. The old presumption of the "economic man," concerned only with maximizing the material gains from his efforts, has long been superseded. An entire field of study has been developed around human behavior in large and small organizations, with much of the analysis devoted to the nonpecuniary satisfactions and dissatisfactions in job situations. Perhaps surprisingly, more attention has been given to people employed in routine work than to those in higher levels of management and entrepreneurship. It is the latter who have the greater opportunities for such nonpecuniary rewards as power, prestige, and the satisfaction of one's various desires and talents for creative and socially constructive activity and whose motivations therefore are presumably the more complex. But it is now so clear that material rewards are by no means so dominant that any analysis of the effects of taxation which is based on the assumption that it operates on a simple "economic man" is woefully inadequate. Since taxation operates primarily to modify the pecuniary rewards of work, the effects of taxation should be appraised with full appreciation of the fact that pecuniary rewards are not necessarily dominant. Subject to this broad and important reservation, the direction of the effects of progressive taxation are quite clear.

By progressively reducing the net return from any given increment of gross income or gain, progressive taxation discourages additional efforts or activities, or a change in the direction of efforts or activities, which might be prompted by greater material rewards. It is always important to note the marginal rate of tax. Too often, defenders of the existing pattern of progression brush aside criticism by noting that the average rate of tax is lower than the marginal rate of tax. This is, of course, true by definition. The average rate gives a quick indication of the fractions of a total income taken by taxation and left for consumption or saving. But it gives virtually no indication about the effects of taxation on incentives.

A moment's reflection will indicate the difference, for example, of the effects on incentives if one compares two people each with taxable income of 20,000 dollars and each subject to an average tax rate of 50 per cent. In one case the tax is a flat 50 per cent; in the other the tax is 20 per cent on the first 10,000 dollars and 80 per cent on the second 10,000 dollars. They each pay a total tax of 10,000 dollars and have a net income of 10,000 dollars, but the first man can keep 50 cents of each extra dollar earned while the second man can keep only 20 cents on each dollar. In virtually all respects regarding incentives, it is the marginal rate of tax on increments of income that is significant.

On a transitory basis, an increase in taxation, through greater progression or a general increase in rates, may stimulate greater effort to maintain an existing standard of living. Two people may react quite differently to a tax structure depending, among other things, on their status under an earlier tax structure. The standards of living of executives and professional people with similar incomes differ on the basis of the scale of expenditure to which they became accustomed under lower taxes. * * *

The possibility of extra income for extra effort varies greatly with the line of activity. An executive does not have the chance for increments of income from overtime or secondary employment. Even independent professional men may have commitments to established clients or patients that require full-time availability and hence activity. But the author recalls having heard, at the end of World War I, the phrase "income-tax golfer" used to describe those who opted for more recreation in preference to full activity in business or professional work. And it is not uncommon for even academic people to remark in casual conversations that they have declined an invitation to speak or prepare a paper because the honorarium was so reduced by income taxation. It would be interesting and useful to know whether it is the reduced absolute level of the net honorarium or the fact that a major fraction of a given amount had to be paid in taxes that was the principal disincentive. For most people, both aspects probably have some importance.

* * *

Investments, in contrast to personal activity, do not typically yield non-pecuniary rewards that offset or compensate for lack of material gain. To be sure, ownership of land may provide prestige and emotional satisfaction, as well as an inflation hedge. * * * [T]here is no general nonpecuniary pressure of capital to become active. Idle capital does not get bored or develop a sense of frustration because of its wasted talents. In brief, investment is much more susceptible to purely pecuniary calculations and hence to tax influences than personal activity.

The higher the marginal tax rate the greater the inducement to move away from investments that yield regular taxable income toward either tax-exempt bonds or equity investments that have prospects for capital appreciation. The supply of tax-exempt bonds is so large that it exceeds the demand by high-bracket investors and for many years the yield has had to be high enough to attract medium-bracket investors, with a resulting large tax advantage to the intra-marginal holders. (With top-grade municipals selling to yield about 70 per cent of that on AAA corporate bond yields, the two types give an equivalent yield of an investor subject to a 30 per cent marginal tax, assuming that the securities are equally attractive except for the different tax status. But an investor taxed at a 70 per cent marginal rate would secure a net income 2.33 times higher than that on taxable bonds.) The reduction in the top bracket rate from 91 to 70 per cent between 1964 and 1966 had little effect on the yield differential.

* * *

The fact of the lower tax on capital gains profoundly influences both the direction and the total amount of investment. The reason for the effect on the direction of investment is self-evident. The higher the spread between the marginal rate on income and the capital gains rate, the greater the influence in favor of the capital gains. The effect on total investment is less obvious, but it arises from the fact that taxation at full rates would require liquidation of more capital to pay the tax when investment is shifted from one asset to another. Also, if the rates are very high, it might force some capital funds into idleness because net yields would be inadequate to compensate for the risk and effort of investment.

The greater attraction of capital gains would appear to increase the supply of funds for equity-type and higher-risk investments which, in turn, permits the financing of innovation and new ventures. From this standpoint, the shift in direction of investment because of high marginal rates on regular income may actually foster economic development, so long as the capital gains rate is not unduly repressive. But against the favorable influence on the direction of investment must be set the unfavorable impact on the supply of savings. Thus, though the direction of investment may be improved, the total amount of investment may be reduced, with the net effect indeterminate. With a somewhat higher marginal propensity to save from higher and growing incomes, progressive taxation hits disproportionately the segments of income most likely to be saved.

Each country has its own set of tax-sheltered investments, depending on the details of its tax laws. Real estate investments receive especially favorable treatment in this country, as do many aspects of agriculture. Tax-exempt mergers are favored over taxable sales of companies to new owners who would continue them as independent entities. Particular forms of capital structures are encouraged and others discouraged, especially in closely controlled corporations. Even a company with no growth can be made attractive if an older generation in a family takes senior securities that are retired with retained earnings, thereby increasing the value of a highly-leveraged common stock held by a younger generation.

Religious institutions, by an unjustified exemption from the tax on unrelated business income applicable to other tax-exempt organizations, are put in a position to pay higher prices than other potential purchasers of business concerns and to do so in a manner that is least likely to build up the enterprise after purchase. Cooperatives are favored over fully-taxable businesses. Extractive industries receive differential tax treatment with consequent lower prices to consumers or higher returns to investors. The list could be extended almost indefinitely. Some of the differential effects are intended and others arise from general provisions of the law. But they are all made more significant by high and progressive tax rates.

Among the economic effects of high and progressive rates, one must include the diversion of intelligence and effort into attempts to minimize taxes. Whenever a tax rate exceeds 50 per cent, it becomes more important to save a dollar of taxes than to earn a dollar of income, and this fact cannot fail to divert attention from truly productive activities. Though the incomes of those concerned with tax minimization enter the gross national product as fully as do those of all other producers of goods and services, their contribution to the general welfare seems at best ambiguous.

Progression typically contributes a very minor fraction of total revenue. When government expenditures amounted to 10 per cent of the gross national product or less, it would have been possible to construct a tax system that would have received most of the revenue from the higher brackets in a generally low-rate tax structure. But when expenditures absorb 25 or 30 per cent of the gross national product, the bulk of the revenue must come from the great mass of taxpayers. The higher income rates contribute only a very minor fraction of the total yield. * * * One can say categorically that progression, with all its distorting effects, is not required to provided adequate revenue. It must be justified on other grounds.

Nor can progressive rates be said to facilitate tax administration, either for tax collectors or taxpayers. The result is quite clearly the contrary. Not only do differences in rates complicate calculations, they make impossible a really effective system of withholding and, by encouraging shifts to tax-sheltered activities and investments, require loophole-closing amendments to the laws, which further complicate it. Or conversely, Congress is moved to adopt special relief provisions because the full burden of high-bracket rates is recognized as intolerable for certain types of incomes, and the special relief provisions are likely to be as complicated as those that close loopholes; in fact, adoption of a relief provision is likely to be followed by or itself be complicated by the need to prevent abuse of it. Progressive rates clearly and markedly complicate the tax law and its administration.

The existence of personal exemptions in the individual income tax provides a very real form of progression in average effective rates toward the bottom of the income scale since those whose incomes are just above the exemption pay only a very small tax. Progression from this source is quite pronounced until the taxable income is several times the personal exemption. And this sort of progression does simplify tax administration by making unnecessary the filing of many returns. One thus must distinguish between progression that arises automatically from the existence of a basic exemption and progression arising from a progressive rate structure. The former, a sort of built-in progression, is usually simplifying; the latter is almost inevitably complicating.

Probably the most serious burden that high progressive rates place on the tax administration comes from the strain on taxpayer morale. Our whole system relies heavily on self-assessment and tax evasion is generally still regarded as socially reprehensible in our country. But when marginal tax rates are made quasi-confiscatory for long periods, as distinct from short periods of war or other national emergency, tax evasion may come to be condoned by both the private and public conscience. And once a part of a tax is flouted with impunity, the rest of the tax system is in peril. * * *

As one appraises the present status of progressivity in tax rates, the principal problems seem to arise from what may be referred to as the "each and every" fallacy. Progression has been so vociferously advocated and so indiscriminately accepted that it has become a virtual fetish in political life, with two unfortunate results. There is, first, a presumption that each and every tax should be in and of itself progressive. Sales and property taxes are criticized and at times rejected because they are not progressive. Surely it is the distribution of the local tax burden that must be judged in the light of equity and consistency with social policy. It seems as ridiculous to insist that every tax be progressive as it would be to insist that everything in a meal be salted because salt is a necessary item in a diet. The result of the obsession about progression is a very real political difficulty in developing a balanced tax structure.

Total revenue requirements are so large that no one tax, not even a "least bad" income tax, should be relied on as a sole or even dominant source of funds. With a combination of taxes, rates on each one can be kept from becoming excessive, and the inevitable defects of each may hopefully balance out the defects of the others. The rates of those taxes most suitable for progression can be set to give whatever degree of progression is deemed appropriate in the composite burden.

The author favors a maximum marginal income tax rate of 50 per cent on grounds of equity and social policy. This rate also seems to have merit on economic grounds for reasons already enumerated. A limitation to this figure in no sense suggests approval of all aspects of conspicuous consumption by the very rich, which after all may seem no more foolish or offensive than the forms of conspicuous consumption of those with modest or even small incomes. But taste in consumption is an individual matter, and the income tax is both an inefficient and an inappropriate device for regulation.

When there is a happy coincidence of large potential revenue and a consensus on the need for regulation, selective excises may be used advantageously, as has been done in the liquor and tobacco taxes. But it is doubtful whether the tax system should be regarded as a principal instrument for solving social problems. Fines and penalties directly imposed are preferable to special taxes and tax credits in the control of pollution of the environment. * * * An attempt to find ways to modify tax systems to make them help at least in a small way in dealing with the population explosion—the greatest social problem of all—without adding to the individual problems of the disadvantaged, should be regarded by tax theorists and technicians as a major challenge. * * *

The second manifestation of the "each and every" fallacy appears when tax rates are changed. Very high marginal rates have developed because of confusion over the form of a tax increase. In 1932, when the range of rates was from 1.5 to 25 per cent, the bottom rate was raised to 4 per cent to secure more revenue. The percentage increase in the rate was applied to the top rate, pushing it to 63 per cent, an increase that from one point of view might be considered merely proportionate. But in terms of the impact on net income it was almost fantastically progressive. At the bottom, net income was reduced from 98.5 cents to 96 cents, or by a little over 2.5 per cent, while at the top it was reduced from 75 cents to 37 cents or by more than half. A continued application of this "proportionate" form of tax increase would have pushed the top rate to 315 per cent when the bottom rate rose to 20 per cent.

In fact, even an increase of an equal number of percentage points is highly progressive when added to an existing progressive rate structure. One percentage point added to a 14 per cent rate reduces net income from 86 to 85 or by 1.16+ per cent, while the same one percentage point addition to a 70 per cent rate reduces the net income from 30 to 29 or by 3.33 per cent.

The proposal to increase tax liabilities by a uniform percentage has the effect of greatly increasing the progressivity of the tax system. A 10 per cent increase in liabilities would push the bottom rate from 14 to 15.4 per cent the top rate from 70 to 77 per cent. A 40 per cent increase in liabilities would leave the bottom rate at 19.6 per cent, below the 20 per cent level at which it recently stood, while pushing the top rate to 98 per cent![e]

* * *

On reductions of rates the reverse analysis can be applied. A reduction from 90 to 70 per cent increases marginal net income three-fold while a complete abolition of a bottom rate of 20 per cent could no more than increase income by 25 per cent. To a considerable extent, the very high marginal tax rates have arisen from confusion about the arithmetic and definitions regarding equal, proportionate, and progressive changes in rates when the changes are made in a rate structure that is already highly progressive. Protagonists of each position make the calculations to fit their program, but the fetish of progressivity too often obliterates reasoned analysis and comparisons.

Progressivity in income and inheritance taxation, though universally adopted and almost universally supported in theoretical literature, lacks a solid base for a rational determination of the appropriate degree of progression. A succession of standards has been advanced in attempts to give precision to the concept of ability to pay, which is generally presumed to support progressive taxation. But none of these standards has received general acceptance even by those who intuitively favor progression on grounds of equity and support it as a matter of social policy. The economic effects of progression are more likely to be harmful than beneficial. Its revenue importance is negligible. It complicates tax administration and, when pushed to excess, strains taxpayer morale.

Some element of progression appeals to an almost intuitive sense of fairness, which is widely held. It is also consistent with a social policy of preventing indefinitely large accumulations of wealth. But progression as it exists is the result of the play of political forces in an area that has lacked clear definitions and analysis. In its excesses it may indeed approach inequity and immorality.

---

e. The effects of across-the-board percentage changes are less striking with our current, flatter, rate structure than when Professor Smith wrote. In 2003, rates on ordinary income range from 10% to 35%. Section 1(i). A 10% increase in tax liabilities applied to 2003 tax rates would raise the bottom rate from 10% to 11%, and the top rate from 35% to 38.5%. A 40% increase in tax liabilities applied to 2003 tax rates would raise the bottom rate to 14% and the top rate to 49%. (Ed.)

THE INCOME TAX:
HOW PROGRESSIVE SHOULD IT BE?*
Charles O. Galvin & Boris I. Bittker
Second Lecture, by Boris I. Bittker
Pages 25-43 (1969)

As a lawyer and teacher of law, my professional focus on federal income taxation has given me an understanding of the impact of progression on the tax structure; but when this brings me up against the moral and economic foundations of progression, I am a layman—at most, an educated layman—with no expertise or professional discipline to guide me in choosing among the conflicting claims with which this area abounds.

* * * I believe that in the choice of an income tax rate schedule, one cannot avoid, in the end, a decision that rests more on faith, personal preference, or fiat than on logic. I will pursue the road of rationality as far as I can trace its tracks; but for me, the final destination is not attained without wandering in the wilderness with only one's soul for guidance.

* * * [T]he concept of progression has evoked an immense body of literature, characterized by a wealth of ingenious theories and a paucity of consensus among the theoreticians. In the time allotted to me, I cannot review, let alone analyze, these efforts to support or undermine progression. Fortunately, however, this task was undertaken only 17 years ago [in 1952] by Professors Walter J. Blum and Harry Kalven, of the University of Chicago Law School, in their painstaking examination of the intellectual history of progression, *The Uneasy Case For Progressive Taxation.*[2] Like them, I find the economic arguments, whether based on theoretical models or empirical evidence and whether concerned with stability, growth, productivity, or incentives, to be rather inconclusive; and I have no special competence for resolving the conflicting assertions of economic experts. I would like, therefore, to devote myself primarily to the question of fairness, which all commentators, even those who hold strong views about the economic impact of progression, agree is of major importance.

In this emphasis on the moral issues, I follow Blum and Kalven, who set the stage for their analysis with these introductory remarks:

> Like most people today we found the notion of progression immediately congenial. Upon early analysis the notion retained its

---

*. This book provides the text of a debate, sponsored by the American Enterprise Institute, between Dean Galvin (who favored a flat-rate income tax) and Professor Bittker (who spoke in favor of progressivity). The excerpted material is from Professor Bittker's presentation. At the time of the debate, Professor Bittker was Southmayd Professor of Law at Yale University.

2. Walter J. Blum and Harry Kalven, Jr., *The Uneasy Case for Progressive Taxation* (Chicago: University of Chicago Press, 1953), reprinted from 19 U. CHI. L. REV. 417 (1952).

attractiveness, but our curiosity as to the source of its appeal increased. The somewhat paradoxical character we detected in the topic is suggested by certain aspects of its literature. A surprising number of serious writers note that progression seems to be instinctively correct, although they then go on to explore it on rational grounds. More striking is the fact that the most devastating critics of the defenses for progression are almost invariably its friends. It is close to the truth to say that only those who ultimately favor progression on some ground have been its effective critics on other grounds. It is as though those who have most clearly detected the weaknesses of various lines of analysis previously offered to support progression were under a compulsion to find some new way to justify it rather than give it up. The hunch that there must be some basis on which an idea as initially attractive as progression can be justified is stubborn indeed.[3]

By way of conclusion, they sum up their quest in these words:

The case for progression, after a long critical look, thus turns out to be stubborn but uneasy. The most distinctive and technical arguments advanced in its behalf are the weakest. It is hard to gain much comfort from the special arguments, however intricate their formulations, constructed on notions of benefit, sacrifice, ability to pay, or economic stability. The case has stronger appeal when progressive taxation is viewed as a means of reducing economic inequalities. But the case for more economic equality, when examined directly, is itself perplexing. And the perplexity is greatly magnified for those who in the quest for greater equality are unwilling to argue for radical changes in the fundamental institutions of society.[4]

The strength of conviction in this area is amply demonstrated by the reviews of the Blum-Kalven study. John Chamberlain, in whose eyes the Sixteenth Amendment "legalizes a theft," welcomed the book for conferring "academic recognition" on "the intellectual sapping operation against the progressive principle."[5] Randolph Paul, on the other hand, asserted that the book "has confirmed rather than shaken my belief that there should be more, rather than less, progression in the American tax system."[6]

In addition to commentators like Chamberlain and Paul, both of whom found support for their contradictory conclusions in the Blum-Kalven book,

---

3. *Ibid.*, pp. 2-3.
4. *Ibid.*, pp. 103-04.
5. Book review, 21 U. CHI L. REV., 1954, p. 502.
6. Book review, 67 HARV. L. REV., 1954, pp. 725, 730.

there was a third group, who felt that instinct, not reason, is bound to be controlling in choosing one rate structure rather than another. * * *

I would like to make three principal points in support of my own predilection for a progressive federal income tax rate structure.

My first point is that there is no magic in the idea of proportionality, as distinguished from progression: put another way, if the case for progression is "uneasy," so is the case for a proportional rate schedule. In Dan Smith's anecdote [concerning the Montana school children; see first paragraph of Smith excerpt], the first child favored a proportional tax, *viz.*, a $500 tax on the $5,000 family, given that the $2,000 family was to pay $200. As Mr. Smith suggests, this conclusion may have reflected no more than the child's fascination with percentages or fractions, leading to a result that was arithmetically "correct," without regard to any other considerations. Perhaps, however, the use of a precise rule rather than a discretionary judgment stemmed from the same desire for certainty that led J. R. McCulloch, a century ago, to insist, in a much-quoted remark, that a departure from proportionality would be disastrous:

> The moment you abandon . . . the cardinal principle of exacting from all individuals the same proportion of their income or their property, you are at sea without rudder or compass, and there is no amount of injustice or folly you may not commit.

Whether or not this conviction that proportionality is an indispensable navigational instrument was endorsed by Dan Smith's Montana schoolchild, it has found much favor among theoreticians.

I think it is fair to say that all, or nearly all, commentators on the principle of progression have assumed that it must meet the burden of proof. Conversely, they have accepted the fairness of proportionality as self-evident, needing no affirmative justification; so that proportionality is to be qualified or rejected as the governing principle only if a convincing case can be made for adopting a progressive rate structure. (Regression, however, is ordinarily rejected out-of-hand.) This acceptance of proportionality may be explicit, as in McCulloch's case, or implicit, as where persuasive objections to progression are thought to end the matter, on the unarticulated premise that proportionality needs no defense. Sometimes this bias in favor of proportionality is buttressed by the argument that progression, lacking an internal limiting principle, invites the majority to oppress the minority, and hence must be resisted at all cost as an irretrievable step on the road to tyranny. This argument, applicable to all exercises of governmental power, seems quite inconclusive to me, especially since the abuse that is feared could be accomplished, even with proportional taxation, by an unfettered use of the expenditure power to redistribute wealth.

It is also argued that progression is responsible for many complications in the income tax law and difficulties in its administration, creating a prima facie case for proportionality. * * * [P]roportionality would not contribute very much to simplicity. Timing questions, if they involve postponement or acceleration of tax for more than a year or two, would continue to perplex us; and income-splitting issues are inevitable once we decide to allow personal exemptions and a standard deduction. They are also inevitable if progression in the income tax rate schedule is accepted as a counterweight to regressive tendencies in other taxes, an aspect of progression that is tolerated, even favored, by some of the most vigorous opponents of progression per se.[8]

In my view, therefore, the premise that a proportional tax rate is presumptively fair, with its corollary that a progressive rate is ipso facto suspect, has been an important obstacle to the process of judgment in this area, at least among theoreticians. I do not quarrel with the Blum-Kalven conclusion that the case for progression is "uneasy," in the sense that the arguments for progression are not wholly conclusive and sometimes carry implications that the advocates of progression are not willing to press to their logical extremes. An equally painstaking examination of the case for a proportional rate structure, however, would in my opinion have ended with the same inconclusive verdict, *viz.*, that the case for proportionality is "uneasy." * * *

Let me expand on my heresy, *viz.*, that proportionality is no more entitled to a presumption of fairness than progression; and, conversely, that the case for proportionality must be tested by the same canons of criticism as the case for progression. What could be more clearly "proportional" than a per capita tax: one man, one dollar? Let us suppose that the amount to be raised by taxation in the United States is $200 billion, averaging out to $1,000 per person. If we pursued the principle of proportionality with sufficient enthusiasm we could raise the amount required by imposing a tax of $1,000 on every man, woman, and child, collecting this amount by levying on his or her property or wages and compelling those who could not pay to perform services to the value of $1,000. A more refined system, still adhering to the principle of proportionality, would be to exempt all persons who could not pay either in cash or in services, and divide the aggregate burden per capita among the others.

Is it not clear that such a head tax, whether crude or refined, would be instinctively rejected by almost everyone—despite its faithful adherence to the principle of proportionality? And is it not almost as clear that today's rationale

---

8. Friedrich A. Hayek, "Progressive Taxation Reconsidered," in Sennholz, ed., *On Freedom and Free Enterprise* (Princeton: Van Nostrand, 1956), pp. 265, 269-70.

for rejecting this proportional allocation of the tax burden would be that it disregarded ability to pay? And that an earlier generation of theorists would have argued that the hypothetical tax was unfair because it was not geared to the unequal benefits received from government by the taxpayers? And that a third group of commentators would argue that equality of sacrifice is the only fair principle of tax allocation, and that the head tax, though ostensibly the same for every taxpayer, actually calls for unequal sacrifices because $1,000 means more to a poor man than to a rich man? And that a fourth group would criticize the proposed head tax because it does nothing to reduce economic inequality?

Those who are familiar with the intellectual history of progression will recall that "ability to pay," "payments in accord with benefits received," "equality of sacrifice," and "reduction of inequality" are the principles that, with various refinements and in various combinations, are regularly used to support progressive tax rates. As Blum and Kalven have pointed out, if these ideas are relentlessly subjected to rigorous analysis, they have shortcomings. For example, if a progressive income tax with rates ranging from 10 to 70 percent requires a taxpayer with $10,000 of income to pay $1,000 of tax and a millionaire taxpayer to pay $700,000, we cannot know—other than by intuition—whether their "sacrifices" are equal.[9] And "ability to pay," taken as a normative standard rather than as a credit manager's assessment of collectibility, is merely another label for "sacrifice." Finally, "benefit" theory (which I will refer to again later) is similar to "sacrifice" theory in calling for interpersonal comparisons that are in the end intuitive rather than logical: who *really* knows whether the millionaire taxpayer is getting benefits from the government that are worth 700 times as much as the benefits received by the $10,000 taxpayer? As for distributive justice, if a progressive rate structure is favored as a means of reducing inequalities of income or wealth, Blum and Kalven properly point out that this indicates a dissatisfaction with the market's allocation of rewards; and they ask the advocates of progression * * * why they do not follow the logic of this approach to the point of demanding more "radical changes in the fundamental institutions of the society."[10]

While this summary does complete justice neither to the traditional arguments in favor of progression nor to the Blum-Kalven replies, my point is

---

9. See the conclusion of Henry Simons, in *Personal Income Taxation* (Chicago: University Press, 1938), p. 7:

> One derives practical implications from the criterion of equality, or proportionality, of sacrifice precisely in proportion to one's own knowledge of something which no one ever has known, or ever will know, anything about. Perhaps this goes far toward explaining the popularity of these doctrines among academic writers.

10. *Supra*, note 2, p. 104.

that the same arguments and same criticisms are applicable to the decision to employ an income tax rather than a head tax—or, for that matter, a tax on sales, luxuries, real property, capital gains, or inheritances—to distribute the burden of government expenditures. In short, the case for *every* tax base and *every* rate schedule is "uneasy," since interpersonal comparisons cannot be avoided.

* * * [A] presumption of fairness is no more appropriate in deciding whether to tax income at progressive rather than proportionate rates than in deciding whether to levy an income tax rather than a head tax. One cannot avoid interpersonal comparisons in deciding whether to levy a head tax, an income tax, a sales tax, or a property tax; and, once *that* nettle has been grasped, there is no justification for employing a presumption rather than discretion in fixing the rate schedule for whatever tax base is adopted. If, having candidly acknowledged the difficulties in making interpersonal comparisons, we prefer an income tax to a head tax on "ability to pay" or "equal sacrifice" grounds, the use of a proportional rate in no way purges our decision of any of its uncertainties.

* * * [T]he maxim, "When in doubt, stick with proportionality," is no better guide than "When in doubt, divide the tax burden on a per capita basis." The policy maker *must* exercise judgment in deciding which tax base and which tax rate is best. * * *

In the hope that I have dismantled an obstacle to a fair assessment of graduated income tax rates, I would like now to offer several independent grounds for favoring a substantial degree of progression.

First, progression in the federal income tax serves to counterbalance regressive tendencies in other federal, state, and local taxes. Even those who favor an allocation of the nationwide tax burden that is proportionate to the taxpayer's income are ordinarily prepared to accept progression in one tax structure if it serves only to counterbalance regression elsewhere.

In applying this limited principle, of course, one encounters both conceptual and computational difficulties. If local property taxes are treated as though paid solely by homeowners, tenants, and consumers, this type of tax will seem more regressive than if one assumes that its burden falls partly on the owners of real estate. Conversely, if the corporate income tax is allocated wholly to shareholders, its impact will be more progressive than if it is thought to fall partly on employees and consumers.

Conclusions about the degree of actual progression in the tax system are also heavily affected by the way one defines the base against which the aggregate tax burden is calculated. It is of course familiar learning that the progressive rates of existing law apply to a less-than-comprehensive income tax base, producing the tax result that Henry Simons described as "digging deep with a sieve."[13] * * *

When the aggregate burden of federal, state, and local taxes is computed as a fraction of this expanded income tax base, our tax structure looks a lot less progressive than if the burden is computed against "taxable income" as defined by existing law. Moreover, if one expands the tax base still more, by adding undistributed trust and corporate income (especially if a broad concept of a corporate income is substituted for corporate income as now defined), or by taking into account unrealized increases in the taxpayer's wealth (e.g., growth in the value of marketable securities, real estate, etc.), the "effective rate" of the federal income tax on wealthy taxpayers falls even more.

It seems reasonable, therefore, to conclude that the aggregate tax burden is pushed in a regressive direction by local property taxes, state and local sales taxes, federal excise and employment taxes, and the corporate income tax to the extent that it falls on consumers and employees. The only counterbalancing elements, then, are the federal personal income tax and the corporate income tax to the extent that it falls on shareholders; and the broader the income tax benchmark used for this calculation, the less impressive is their contribution to progression. * * *

[P]rogression in the federal personal income tax is entirely consonant with the achievement of a national tax burden that is proportional to income. Indeed, given this goal, a significant degree of progression is probably indispensable. To be sure, the broader the income tax base, the less progressive a rate structure will be necessary to achieve proportionality; but if we take account of political realities, * * * the advocates of overall proportionality ought to support progressive income tax rates for some years to come.

A second reason for supporting, or at least acquiescing in, progression is that it is an inevitable consequence of allowing a personal exemption in computing income tax liability. Even if we exempt no more than bare subsistence in computing taxable income, and apply a uniform rate to all income above the survival level, the effective rate on total income will start at zero and rise until it is just short of the nominal rate. Thus, a 10 percent rate on all income above the first $1,000 translates into an effective rate of zero for a taxpayer with $1,000 of total income, 5 percent for the taxpayer with $2,000 of total income, 9 percent for the taxpayer with $10,000 of total income, 9.9 percent for the taxpayer with $100,000 of total income, and so on. This type of progression, resulting solely from the allowance of a personal exemption, has special characteristics, of which the most notable is that it calls for—and

---

13. *Supra*, note 9, p. 219.

permits—only two judgments: the amount to be exempted, and the total amount of revenue to be raised. Once these elements are specified, the tax rate follows automatically; there is no room in the system for comparing the $2,000 taxpayer's ability to pay or his "sacrifice" with the $100,000 taxpayer's ability to pay or his sacrifice. For McCulloch, who did not want to go to sea without a rudder or compass, this form of progression should be quite tolerable, and it would also be comforting to Dan Smith's Montana schoolchild, who could display his skill in arithmetic by deriving the proper tax rate, given the distribution of income, the amount of the exemption, and the total revenue to be raised. * * *

TAX FAIRNESS OR UNFAIRNESS? A CONSIDERATION OF THE PHILOSOPHICAL BASES FOR UNEQUAL TAXATION OF INDIVIDUALS
Jeffrey A. Schoenblum[*]
12 American Journal of Tax Policy 221, 223, 257-71 (1995)

The purpose of this Article is to challenge directly the notion that fairness requires that the burden of certain taxpayers be greater than that of other taxpayers, relatively or even absolutely. This Article confronts the widespread acceptance of progressive taxation as fair and as being compelled by fundamental considerations of justice. It also questions the justice of proportional taxation.
        * * *

John Rawls' Theory of Justice and Redistribution
        * * *

Certainly, we would not consider it fair, in the sense of just, to single out a racial, ethnic, or religious group, or a particular gender, for harsher treatment under our laws. We would not deny them liberties or benefits accorded others. * * * Why, then, ought we feel comfortable in depriving one individual of more of what he has earned than another individual? Why is it fair to criticize a class of society publicly for not doing their fair share when they have paid more than others?

The Dictates of Fairness

Fairness, in the sense of a just result, is not an easy concept to define. * * * [P]eople simply cannot agree on its meaning. Those commentators who *assume* a shared concept of fairness are manipulating the argument and should not be permitted to bypass this primary analytical step. "Fairness" connotes in day-to-day parlance what is "just," "good," and "right." But these terms do not further the issue any more than does "fairness." However, by

---

[*]. At time of original publication, Professor, Vanderbilt University School of Law.

claiming fairness or justice, a party obtains a powerful weapon in the political debate. * * * With the hope of influencing the widespread perception of the term, but with no pretension that this author's view is any more correct than another, an argument is presented below that fairness in taxation consists of absolute equal treatment by government based on the equal status of all persons before the government. The consideration of several examples illuminates why fairness dictates not using income taxation to exact more from certain members of society than from others.

Suppose you are sitting in your home and a stranger breaks in and removes, under threat, valuable assets belonging to you or your family. The police come, return your property, and arrest the intruder. He argues at his trial that he was a member of the lower middle class, you were upper middle class, and he wanted to even things up. In addition to the destabilizing political implications of his defense, many persons would be deeply troubled by the unfairness of his being able to take what he had not earned from someone else who had earned it.

If there are many such persons in the community and they band together to authorize democratically elected officials to take the same property, under color of law, this is described as high income earners paying their fair share. * * * In effect, the majority of the society, through democratic, majoritarian processes, approves a system where some are required to work more for the common good than others.

It is fair for a group of persons who have less to take from others who have more? Perhaps this question must be answered in the affirmative if the ultimate values are the community and the equalization of the incomes or property of its members. There is some support for this proposition in communitarian, feminist, and civic republicanism writings, as well as the more extreme examples of communalism represented by socialism and communism. On the other hand, if the overriding value is the preservation of a sizable zone of autonomy for the individual, so that he can freely exercise his energies and thereby contribute to a largely noncoercive community of autonomous beings, the answer is a negative one.

Another example illustrates the point. Suppose one individual works overtime and does work of such quality that he typically receives bonuses as well. Another individual employed in the same job works only the prescribed number of hours and does so at the minimum tolerable level of quality. From a traditional liberal standpoint, there seems no principle of fairness that would justify punishing the competent, hard-working contributor to the community by imposing a lesser burden on the slothful, sloppy employee. Yet that is precisely what is done by differentiated rates of taxation.

As another example, suppose an individual works her way up from poverty and, after attending medical school and completing various fellowships, enters practice at age 33. She saves a lot of lives, works long and irregular hours, but also earns a great deal. Society values her contribution immensely, but the elected government chastises her for not paying her fair share.   No such canard is laid at the feet of her old buddies from the neighborhood. While our doctor was studying and suffering considerable self-denial, they were out partying. The result of their lack of willpower and determination is that they barely get by now. There is unfairness, not fairness, in a system that requires our doctor to compensate for her former friends' shortsightedness.

The examples just given, while mirroring reality, are stacked in that they portray hard-working, productive members of society and contrast them with individuals who are far less productive and socially appealing. Suppose the example is changed in that the doctor's friends were simply not born as smart as she was.   Or suppose they belong to a minority that has suffered discrimination in the past, affording them little tradition of learning or belief in the possibility of social or economic advancement.

In these instances, while we may have more sympathy for the lower income earners, this ought not to justify taking more from our accomplished doctor. We do not alter the tax rates based, for example, on race. After all, the doctor may come from the same disadvantaged background or may be able to point to handicaps in her own life that would qualify her for lower taxation.
* * *

Consistent with the prevalent Zeitgeist, individuals are deemed to exercise little control over their destinies. Life is a random walk, with some receiving less along the way. The fair course under this vision of reality, then, is to attend to the needs of those who, purportedly, beyond their control, have been given less.

But what if lack of achievement is largely ascribable to choice? Under a pure imputed income theory, a person who chooses leisure should also have income. He has effectively paid himself in kind, by way of psychic benefit. Having foregone compensation, the value of his in-kind payment is, presumably, at least equal to what he could have earned. Likewise, if a person fails to earn as much as he might otherwise have, had he persevered, he should be deemed to have income of a nonmonetary sort. The point is not to urge taxation of that income. Rather, it is to emphasize the unjust treatment of the productive. * * *

It is submitted that no convincing case in support of randomness can be made out. First, there is no persuasive evidence that success at earning income is primarily random. Until that assertion is clearly established, the state should not be so intrusive as to take a person's property unequally, because in doing so it may unnecessarily favor certain citizens over others without adequate justification. It may well be penalizing those who are most deserving. Second, even if the attributes that enable high income earning are largely distributed randomly, individuals also are randomly assigned disadvantages. It is simplistic to assume that those who succeed have gotten all the breaks, rather than having had to surmount other, severe obstacles. Third, random beneficial attributes may not persist. There is no way to know whether a person's fortune will reverse. The conception of a class of persons forever blessed, with the rest of society doomed forever to immobile misery, is completely without basis. The argument that justifies tax differentials on the basis of randomness makes a fatal error in overlooking the dynamic, contingent character of life, assuming instead that this year's success is an accurate portrayal of stable, unalterable economic circumstances.

At the heart of the redistributionist's attack is distrust of the free market. Former Assistant Secretary for Tax Policy and Yale Law Professor Michael Graetz has attacked the ethical or moral character of the market, contending that it is subject to fickle and superficial consumer demand. He argues that, even at its best, the market often reacts to matters outside an individual's control. The assumption that each person is entitled to keep what he earns is cast in doubt.[210]

Graetz and other redistributionists err in a variety of important respects. His critique of the market is misplaced to the extent that he believes it places too high a value on the wrong products and services. The individual choices in the market made by autonomous individuals and not state *diktat* are precisely what make it function with overall efficiency, and what assures maximum individual equality of opportunity. If one adopts Graetz's position that imperfections in the market or the fecklessness of its participants justifies deprivation and redistribution of property by the state, there is no plausible barrier to total state control.

Contrary to Graetz, individuals are, in fact, justified in their claims to property derived from their labor or risk-taking. Certainly each such person has a greater claim than any other individual. The fact that external forces may have also added to value is beside the point. Part of the reward is precisely for taking the risks as to whether external forces would add value and how much. Why should the bad risk takers or those who do not take risks at all be entitled to the rewards of the skilled risk taker? They have no standing to make a morally based claim. Even if earnings are not exclusively the result of a single individual's efforts, they are certainly not due to the

---

210. Michael J. Graetz, *To Praise the Estate Tax, Not to Bury It*, 93 YALE L.J. 259 (1983).

efforts of persons who are likely to benefit from a government-devised scheme of redistribution.

A view far more consistent with reality, is that regardless of obstacles in life numerous persons surmount them and achieve success. Millions of persons move up the economic ladder as well as down, often several times in a lifetime. The ultimate income position for an individual is largely one of his own responsibility, though undoubtedly influenced to a lesser or greater degree by random circumstances largely beyond anyone's control. Under this view, there is no justice in taking from a person who devotes his life to maximum productivity, for the purported benefit of others who have utterly no connection to the individual or to the transactions that gave rise to the income.

Apart from randomness, it has been contended that the production of wealth in a modern society is a result of a host of interrelated activities. At its extreme, this has led commentators to conclude that when the state taxes, it is not taking, but only receiving a return on its contribution to the success of the activity. The state earns this return by providing the minimal conditions in which profit can be earned.

Even if all income were inextricably associated with more than one person's efforts, this would only justify claims *inter se* between the parties, which is precisely what contract law regulates. Recognition of more tangential claims simply cannot be proven, and government fiat should not be a substitute for the lack of persuasive evidence. Moreover, since much income-producing activity involves worldwide interactions, the argument made by egalitarians could support the view that our government is not entitled to tax unilaterally or, alternatively, that it can also tax other nations' citizens. Presumably, the relatively impoverished populations of other countries would have a significant claim on the wealth of even the lower income earners in this country, just as, it is argued, the less well-off in this country have against higher income earners under the egalitarian viewpoint. Most significantly, the ideal that persons have no claim to their income because others facilitate its being earned essentially denudes persons of all protection for property. The income earner is effectively nationalized and his assets become part of a pool of assets to promote the common, perhaps even universal, good. It is now the ultimate communalist view.

Another redistributionist rationalization is based on the notion that the original allocation of property was achieved in an unjust manner. * * * While this may be a defensible, theoretical position, it is of no practical significance. * * * The burden should be on the state to so prove and it should act with great caution. Redress cannot fairly be accomplished through an unequal tax, one that does not make any pretense of distributing the tax burden most heavily on those who have garnered the most from oppression. * * *

Ethical Baseline: Fairness as Equal Taxation

* * * The prevailing orthodoxy has led too many outstanding scholars to take for granted the shaky ethical foundation on which any system of unequal taxation rests.

Every attempt to rationalize unequal taxation of income earners has failed. Other than certain egalitarians, who are simply prepared to overlook the centrality of individual liberty, theorists have been terribly troubled by how to justify the disparate price that particular individuals have been compelled to pay to the government for public goods. This unequal treatment runs directly counter to the liberal values and norms undergirding our society.

The theme of this Article is that the discomfort and difficulty that have been experienced are due to the fact that the analysis itself has been flawed. The starting point for determining a person's fair share must be the proposition that, as equals before the state, each of us ought to be required to pay the same absolute amount of tax to it. To date, the notion of an absolutely equal tax, whether in the form of an income tax, a sales tax, or any other variant, has been cavalierly dismissed without analysis or simply ignored. Admittedly, there are immense difficulties with these taxes. There would have to be a degressive rate structure to account for those at a subsistence or lower level. The rate would have to be phased in so as not to penalize persons lifting themselves beyond subsistence levels. Care would also have to be taken to assure that legislative policies did not lead to an expansive definition of subsistence, thereby converting an equal tax into something more akin to a dual-bracket income tax. Fundamental issues as to the role of government and the amount of revenue that it could raise would be implicated.

The important point is that, despite certain difficulties in implementation, the philosophical premise is the correct one. All constituents are to be treated the same by the government; all are equal, largely autonomous members of the community. Nor should moral weight be given to decisions merely because they are reached by a transitory majority. Instead, it is necessary to have an ethical baseline grounded in equality. Even if equal taxation is unattainable, it should serve as a standard by which tax models are evaluated for their fairness. At present the designers of these models are failing to check the very foundation on which their elaborate structures are erected.

* * * [N]o persuasive theory has been developed to date to justify substantially unequal taxation among persons in a liberal society. Taxation is a necessary, but coercive, act by the state. In a liberal state, coercion should be indulged in as little as feasible, and meted out in equal degree to its autonomous, individual constituents. If coercion is differentiated, there ought to be compelling justification. Ordinarily, penalties are imposed by society for conduct that threatens others' autonomy. The labor of highly productive,

valued members of the society, in fact, represents a net, positive contribution to the community. It should not be the basis for penalty. Differentials in taxation may serve the expedient needs of shifting majorities, politicians, bureaucrats, and egalitarians. That does not make them fair.

Notes and Questions

1. Is the principle of ability to pay helpful in setting maximum rates? Can it be applied in combination with other considerations?

2. If the range of the highest tax bracket is widened to apply to lower incomes, does this make the tax more progressive or less progressive?

3. Are multiple tax brackets necessary to a progressive income tax system? How many tax brackets are desirable? Over the years the number of brackets has varied from one to 50.

4. Can a three-bracket tax rate schedule be as progressive as a 15-bracket tax rate schedule?

5. Is an income tax more progressive the larger the group of people who have no income tax liability? Is the degree of progressivity of a tax determined by the number of taxpayers subject to its top rate, by the severity of the top rate, by the difference between the top rate and the next lower rate, by the difference between the top rate and the bottom rate, or by some other measure?

6. Can the ability to pay rationale be defended when it focuses exclusively on income without reference to wealth? Consider two individuals with incomes of $1 million. One has received income at this level for 20 years and the other, a college graduate drafted by a National Football League team, has never earned an appreciable amount of income before.

7. As applied to an income tax, what is meant by the terms (a) proportional, (b) degressive, (c) progressive, and (d) regressive?

8. Due to the realization rule, capital gains that have arisen over a period of years will be taxed in the year of realization. Though most defenders of preferential rates for capital gains would not agree, Blum and Kalven viewed this "bunching" effect as the most plausible argument for such preferential treatment. Why might this be so, assuming a progressive rate

structure? Do you agree that the bunching effect warrants special treatment for capital gains?

9. Professor McCombs argued that Blum and Kalven focused too exclusively on the importance of money in work decisions. Do you agree with Blum and Kalven that in our society money is the dominant stimulus to work?

10. There is probably a high correlation between jobs that pay well and jobs that offer significant nonmonetary satisfactions. If this is true, what implications does it have for progressive taxation?

11. Blum and Kalven asserted that a progressive system discourages risky investments, because such investments are taxed at a high rate if successful, while a losing investment will be deducted from lower-bracket income. Why might this be so? Is this concern equally valid under a system characterized by a few wide tax brackets (as under present law) and a system characterized by many narrow tax brackets?

12. The McCombs excerpt discussed Professor Simons' idea of government capitalism, such as government purchase of public utilities. Would government capitalism be a practical solution to inadequate private saving and investment?

13. McCombs observes that the term "equality of sacrifice" is not ordinarily used to mean the same dollar amount of sacrifice (which would support regressive taxation), or even proportional sacrifice of dollars (which would support proportional taxation), but, instead, to mean proportional sacrifice of utility. If all dollars were of equal satisfaction value, this theory would suggest that proportional taxation is appropriate. Only when proportional sacrifice is determined in the context of the theory of declining marginal utility of dollars—rather than in simple dollar amounts—can it support progressive tax rates.

14. McCombs makes a strong argument that a progressive rate structure logically follows from the proportionate sacrifice theory. He then adds that the "only remaining difficulty is how to devise a specific rate schedule that implements the proportional sacrifice theory." The word "only" is perhaps misleading, because a primary objection to progressivity is that there is no standard to determine how progressive the tax system should be.[f]

---

f. Compare tort law's allowance of damages for pain and suffering, based on a jury decision that is subjective almost to the point of arbitrariness. Would ignoring such damages—in effect,

15. The principle of marginal utility, which is used throughout the study of economics, when applied to the receipt of money, holds that the last dollar received has less utility to the recipient than the next-to-the-last dollar received.

Professor Smith points out problems in applying the theory in a useful manner. First, while it seems reasonable to assume that the marginal utility from money does in fact decrease, the entire concept is more problematic when applied to money than to any good or service. Though an individual will have sharply diminishing utility from marginal bananas, or sports cars, or massages, it is much less clear that additional money loses its attraction. Money is more versatile than any good or service—it can be used for any form of current consumption, and it can be stored for later use or passed on to others.

Second, while the theory of declining utility of money is entirely reasonable, it gives no guidance concerning how sharply the marginal utility curve for money drops. We have little idea of how much utility declines from the first dollar to the last. Without this knowledge, we are reduced to using intuition to determine how steep the progressive tax rate structure should be to achieve proportional sacrifice among taxpayers with different incomes.

Finally, it is obvious that the marginal utility curve varies from one person to another. The tax system, however, cannot take such differences into account; the same tax structure must be applied to the miser and the spendthrift.

16. *Consumer Surplus.* The concept of "consumer surplus" is likely related, in some degree, to the declining marginal of money. The difference between the market price that a consumer pays for a given good or service, and the amount that that particular consumer would be willing to pay, constitutes "consumer surplus." Consider a movie ticket priced at $6. Every patron who attends the movie must subjectively value the experience at a minimum of $6, but almost all (everyone except the marginal purchaser) will value it at more than $6. Clearly, the amount of consumer surplus will vary from person to person. But may it not be reasonable to assume, as a general rule, that a lower-income patron is closer to the breakeven point—perhaps that person would not have attended had the movie cost $7—while a higher-income person would be less sensitive to price? Professor Daniel Halperin suggests "that those with large amounts of income would willingly pay much more than market price for such items as ordinary entertainment and travel. This income

---

allowing zero for pain and suffering—be more acceptable?

effect would create larger consumer surplus for each dollar spent by the well-to-do."[g]

There is absolutely no possibility of directly including consumer surplus in the tax base. Nevertheless, if, theoretically, we were to regard consumer surplus as additional income, this reasoning suggests that there is greater discrepancy between the income of high- and low-income taxpayers than the dollars indicate.   If one accepts this reasoning, Professor Halperin suggests—still speaking in a theoretical vein only—that there would no need to adjust the tax base, because the additional consumer surplus of higher-income taxpayers, as a group, could be addressed by additional progressivity in the existing tax base: "[A]t least in theory, vertical inequities can be eliminated without correcting the tax base."[h]

17.   What is meant by the theory of "minimum sacrifice" (or "minimum aggregate sacrifice")? Why is this theory rejected as the basis for determining the appropriate degree of tax progressivity?

18.   Professor Smith points up the importance, as well as the difficulty, of considering government benefits in evaluating the progressivity of the tax structure. Social Security may offer the clearest illustration of the issue. Taken alone, the Social Security tax is regressive, because it takes the same percentage of income from all earners, up to the maximum taxable amount ($87,000 in 2003), while exempting income in excess of the ceiling from the tax. On the other hand, the Social Security system—taxes and benefits taken together—is markedly progressive, in that low earners can expect a far greater return on their taxes than can high earners.

19.   The automatic counter-cyclical effect of the income tax, discussed in both the McCombs and Smith excerpts, is also touched on in Chapter One. As the economy contracts and income of taxpayers falls, a progressive income tax takes a smaller share of national income, thus providing stimulus when most economists would regard stimulus as appropriate. By the same token, an overheating economy is automatically cooled by a progressive income tax, which then takes a larger share of income. Whether this counter-cyclical effect is large enough to rescue the economy from either recession or high inflation is debatable.

---

g. Daniel Halperin, *Valuing Personal Consumption: Cost Versus Value and the Impact of Insurance*, 1 FLA. TAX REV. 1, 13 (1992).
 h. *Id.* at 14.

20. Professor Michael Graetz repeated Professor Smith's schoolroom experience with his daughter's fifth-grade classroom, "and, remarkably, the first three students to speak gave answers identical to the Montana children. . . . The intuitions about progressive taxation of the children of the 1990s in a New Haven, Connecticut school mirrored precisely those of Montana children in the 1960s."[i]

21. Professor Smith argued that progression in taxation disadvantaged savings vis-à-vis consumption "because of a somewhat higher marginal propensity to save from larger and from increasing incomes"—both of which are targeted by progressivity. Note that Smith was writing in 1968, when income tax rates (if not the overall impact of the income tax on different income levels) were more steeply progressive than at present.

22. We might associate Third World countries with great variations in wealth and income, and expect that progressive rates would be particularly defensible in such countries on grounds of equity. Smith, however, suggests that a steeply progressive tax system in such countries is "particularly unfortunate," due to its effect on saving and investment. Do you agree?

23. What is the significance of Smith's observation that "[i]dle capital does not get bored or develop a sense of frustration because of its wasted talents"?

24. Why is the marginal tax rate—not the average tax rate—the determinant in the work/leisure choice?

25. Are special tax breaks "made more significant by high and progressive tax rates," as Professor Smith asserts?

26. Lower tax rates on higher incomes since the Smith excerpt was written have reduced the overall revenue loss from tax-exempt bonds. The revenue loss arises from the failure to tax the interest received by the bondholders. Consequently, if tax rates drop, the revenue loss from tax exempts declines.

More important, the yield from tax-exempt bonds is compared, in the marketplace, to the after-tax yield of comparable taxable securities. When tax rates are reduced, the after-tax yield on taxable securities increases, so tax-

---

i. Michael J. Graetz, *The U.S. Income Tax: Should It Survive the Millenium?*, 85 TAX NOTES 1197, 1200 (1999).

exempt bonds become relatively less attractive and their price must fall to restore their yield as a percent of cost to a level where they will remain competitive.

27. Smith said that an over-50-percent tax makes tax-saving more important than income-earning. Is this a good reason to place a 50 percent ceiling on tax rates?

28. Professor Smith reverses the usual way percentage increases and decreases in tax rates are viewed. Is it better to compare percentage changes in tax or percentage changes in after-tax income?

29. Most supporters of "flat" rates would provide some degree of progressivity, by providing exemptions (taxed at a zero rate, compared to the single positive rate for income above the exempt level). Why does Smith say that progression arising from exemptions, sometimes referred to as "degression," is simplifying, while progression arising from a progressive rate structure is complicating?

30. Smith suggests that the effect on "taxpayer morale"—the willingness of taxpayers to pay voluntarily the tax owed under the law—is the most serious problem posed by "high progressive rates." Is it high taxes or progressive taxes that undermine taxpayer morale? Does the present tax structure—lower and flatter than when Smith wrote—undermine taxpayer morale?

31. What is Smith's antidote to the "each and every" fallacy—the contention that each and every tax should be progressive?

32. Professor Bittker concedes that the case for progression is "uneasy," but he nevertheless supports it. Why?

33. Do you agree with Professor Bittker that the "burden of proof" should not be placed on the proponents of progression any more than on the proponents of proportionality?

34. Bittker compares a $1,000 tax levied on a taxpayer with income of $10,000 (10 percent) to a $700,000 tax levied on a taxpayer with income of one million dollars (70 percent), and asserts that it is impossible to "know—other than by intuition" which taxpayer is making the greater sacrifice, and also impossible to know whether the richer taxpayer is getting 700 times as much

benefit from the Government. What is Bittker's point? Do you find equal indeterminancy in the relative sacrifice borne by the rich and poor taxpayers, and in the relationship of the tax burden to benefits received by each?

35. Professor Bittker uses the head tax as a "straw man," a proposal that virtually no one would support today. Yet, when exactions are in the form of services rather than money, most governments tend toward levying an equal tax upon all. In medieval times, many taxes were in the form of services owed to the king or to nobles.

In modern times, the primary example of a "tax" in the form of services is military conscription during wartime. This very large service to the government tends to be meted out fairly equally to all within the relevant group (normally, able-bodied young men). In peacetime, jury duty represents a service required of all, regardless of income.

36. While Professor Bittker posits the equal "head tax" as a straw man, Professor Schoenblum asks that we consider it seriously.

Schoenblum's analysis requires that we focus on what is frequently taken for granted. Does fundamental fairness require that the state take the same dollar amount from each individual (head tax), or the same proportion of income from each individual (flat tax), or an increasing share from higher-income taxpayers (progressive tax)? If nothing else, Schoenblum is persuasive in arguing that the answer is not self evident.

37. Do you accept Professor Schoenblum's comparison of unequal tax burdens to legalized theft?

38. Schoenblum acknowledges that his examples are skewed to make the point that higher income may correlate to greater personal effort and merit. It would be easy to construct equally convincing examples of undeserved income differentials—perhaps contrasting professional athletes who earn millions while engaging in abuse of drugs and women, with industrious disabled persons who have difficulty securing minimum wage employment.

39. For almost every individual, economic success is attributable to a combination of personal effort and to factors beyond the individual's control. Whichever factor we regard as most important generally, it must be recognized that literally millions of cases will be exceptions to this general rule. Assuming the correctness of Schoenblum's assertion that "no convincing case in support of randomness can be made out," does it follow that taxes should be apportioned as if randomness played no role at all?

40. Professor Schoenblum asserts that even where income is, in part, attributable to "external forces," this factor should be ignored because part of the successful risk taker's success lies in predicting the nature of such external forces. Might a critic argue that the tax system itself is such an "external force," and that a successful risk taker should take into account that the tax system is likely to be somewhat progressive?

41. Schoenblum acknowledges that there are practical limitations to the ideal of an equal tax contribution from every citizen. If taxes are truly equal for all, those at the very bottom will have income that is less than their tax liability. How would Schoenblum deal with this problem?

42. How does income volatility throughout life affect the progressivity debate? As a practical matter, taxes must be collected throughout a taxpayer's life—annually, for an income tax. As a theoretical matter, however, perhaps the tax system should pursue an equitable distribution of the tax burden on a lifetime, and not merely annual, basis. Empirically, Professors Don Fullerton and Diane Lim Rogers conclude that there may be no significant difference: "The lifetime incidence of personal income taxes is less progressive, and that of consumption taxes is less regressive, but the combined pattern is similar to annual incidence."[j]

C. THE TAX RATE STRUCTURE: PRAGMATISM AND EQUITY

For a generation before enactment of the Tax Reform Act of 1986, writers argued that a broader tax base would permit tax rates to be cut drastically without a loss of revenue. Politically, the 1986 Act provided tax rate cuts in exchange for giving up tax shelters and other favored tax treatment. The maximum rate had already been cut from 91 percent to 50 percent over the preceding 22 years. It is doubtful that it ever would have been possible to impose marginal rates in the 90-percent range to a broad base with no opportunity to escape the top rates. Some observers assert that political equilibrium had been maintained before 1986 by imposing high rates to satisfy populist sentiment while simultaneously providing generous opportunities to avoid imposition of high taxes on large segments of income.

Charles McLure, an economist, is credited with being the principal author of the 1984 Treasury Study (frequently termed "Treasury I") that was modified and recommended to Congress by President Reagan in 1985 ("Treasury II")

---

j. Don Fullerton & Diane Lim Rogers, *Lifetime Versus Annual Perspectives on Tax Incidence*, 44 NAT'L TAX J. 277, 286 (1991).

and eventually led to the comprehensive changes made by the Tax Reform Act of 1986. In the first selection below, Dr. McLure urges that attention be paid to incentives for profit maximization as well as to incentives to stimulate initial investment.

The Shoup Report (so called because it was prepared by a commission headed by Carl Shoup, a public finance professor) was prepared during the American occupation of Japan to assist Japan's post-war recovery. This report includes an explicit analysis of problems caused by extremely high marginal tax rates. Emphasis is more on practical problems of compliance and administration than on theoretical limitations on high rates.

The brief selection from the Treasury I recommendations is a reminder that virtually none of the justifications for progression apply to the corporate income tax. This topic is discussed further in Chapter Fourteen.

COMMENTS ON FUNDAMENTAL TAX REFORM
Charles E. McLure, Jr.[*]
National Tax Association-Tax Institute of America
78th Annual Conference 97, 97 (1985)

It is important to reduce marginal tax rates. The advantages of lower marginal rates are easily understood. At lower rates the disincentive effects of taxation are reduced, and whatever inequities and distortions remain are less important.

It seems that the general pattern of rates proposed in Treasury-I would be a reasonable target. Though the number of marginal rate brackets is not important, except as a cosmetic matter, I do not see any reason to have more than four or five rates. From an aesthetic point of view it might be useful tothink of rates divisible by five. A top rate as high as 40 percent might not be out of the question from an economic point of view, if restricted only to those with very high taxable incomes, say $200,000 or more. But one must realize that if state and local taxes are not deductible,[k] with a top marginal rate that high the aggregate state and federal marginal rate would not be much lower than under current law.

Thinking about the incentive effects of taxation has undergone a transformation in recent years that may not be entirely beneficial. At one time public finance economists focused on the tendency of high tax rates on business income to distort economic decision making, if only by reducing the pay-off from optimization. * * *

---

[*]. At time of original publication, Senior Fellow, Hoover Institution, Stanford University.

k. As discussed in Chapter Thirteen, Treasury I proposed ending the federal deduction for all state and local taxes. In the 1986 Act, Congress ended the deduction for sales taxes, but continued the deduction for state and local income and property taxes. (Ed.)

The focus of policy analysis has recently shifted almost entirely to the effects of taxation on investment decisions. Most commonly, such analysis is conducted by calculating the ex ante effective rate of taxation on income from various investments. Such calculations usually take account of the effects of such provisions as accelerated depreciation, the investment tax credit, and marginal tax rates. (The inclusion of interest indexing and the deduction for dividends paid in Treasury-I[1] forced analysts also to consider their effects on effective tax rates.) A common conclusion is that investment tax credits and accelerated depreciation are to be espoused because they reduce the cost of capital. At the very least, these policies are more effective than rate reduction in stimulating investment. * * *

This focus on investment decisions, while generally appropriate, has almost totally diverted attention from issues of incentives for profit maximization and efficient operation, once investments have been made. I believe that more attention should be paid to these traditional questions, along with issues of incentives for investment. Otherwise we will be too sanguine about high marginal rates.

* * *

REPORT ON JAPANESE TAXATION
Shoup Mission
Vol. 1, at 77-81 (1949)

Taxation of High Incomes

The present Japanese income tax system is superficially a very progressive one. The actual result, however, is somewhat different. There are many ways in which the wealthy taxpayer may legally avoid much of the income tax, through the so-called "loopholes." Also, we have the impression that the administration of the law in the top ranges of income has been relatively ineffective, or at least uneven. Hence many, perhaps most, of the individuals with large incomes are taxed at only a fraction of what the progressive rate schedule seems to indicate. On the other hand, occasional instances arise where seriously excessive burdens have been imposed through overassessment of taxpayers, or even at times merely through the strict application of the law to cases not contemplated when it was enacted.

Among the more serious loopholes in the present law are the exclusion of 50 per cent of capital gains from taxable income, the lack of adequate restraints on the accumulation of earnings in corporations, the flat rates applicable to distributions in liquidation, and the flat rates applicable to certain types of interest, as well as to other forms of income. These loopholes

---

1. Neither of these proposals was adopted by Congress. (Ed.)

have been adequately closed in the various recommendations made elsewhere in this report. But securing adequate progression is more than a matter of having an adequate law; it requires also that law be administered effectively. Otherwise, beyond a certain point further increases in rates or the closing of loopholes add little or nothing to the progressivity of the tax. The result is merely more evasion and a progressive deterioration of taxpayer morale. Moreover, some of the methods used to evade taxes may be wasteful and hence seriously interfere with the attainment of maximum levels of production. Consequently, in an overzealous attempt to shift the tax burden away from the lower classes, the resources available to them are actually diminished.

We conclude that the present top income tax rates in Japan are now much too high in relation to current standards of compliance and enforcement. It is possible that a reduction in these rates, through securing better compliance, would of itself secure a larger revenue from these income classes.

The result would then be an increase rather than a decrease in the real degree of progression, even without any change in methods of administration. In any case, such a reduction of rates is an essential step in securing the greater vigor of administration that is required if substantial improvement in the degree of progression is to be attained. The baneful effects of the various devices resorted to for tax evasion purposes outweigh the slight amount of increased progression that is at present attained by the top rates in practice.
        * * *

A decision as to whether a given rate is too high or not will always require the exercise of judgment. However, there are two specific considerations that help in forming such a judgment.

The first is the average amount of error in the assessment of income. For example, if we can be reasonably sure that in practically all cases the error in estimating the income for tax purposes is less than 5 per cent, then top rates of 80 per cent or perhaps even 90 per cent may be tolerable. However, it is our impression that at present errors of 10 per cent or 20 per cent in assessing the largest income are almost the rule, and errors of 50 per cent or more are not uncommon. Given these degrees of underassessment, a rate of 80 per cent rather than, say 60 per cent produces only a minor improvement in progressivity compared with the evasion and the increased difficulty of administration. For example, if a certain taxpayer's actual income of 20 million yen is assessed at only 10 million yen, an increase in the tax rate from 60 per cent to 80 per cent decreases the income left to this taxpayer by only one seventh. But it cuts in half the income after tax of the honest taxpayer.

On the other hand, suppose that, in the attempt to achieve a higher average progression, arbitrary overassessments are sometimes made, so that an occasional taxpayer with seven million yen income is overassessed at ten million yen. For such a taxpayer, raising the rates on the assessed income from 60 per cent to 80 per cent means moving from a situation where this taxpayer has at least one million yen left after the tax to one where his tax exceeds his income by one million yen. Under these conditions the administration of the tax tends to deteriorate, so that in the long run higher rates may mean less real progression.

The second consideration is the incentive afforded for avoidance or evasion of the tax. A 50 per cent tax rate on income is equal to a 100 per cent rate on the amount retained by the taxpayer, while a 67 per cent rate on income is 200 per cent on the amount retained, and 75 per cent on income is 300 per cent on the amount retained. This means, for example, that if a corporation is to give an official a net increase in salary of 10,000 yen it will cost only 20,000 yen if the rate is 50 per cent, but 30,000 yen or 40,000 yen if the rate is 67 per cent, or 75 per cent. Under a 75 per cent on individual incomes, the corporate official may much prefer that the corporation spend 40,000 yen on entertainments and other perquisites for him, rather than pay him the same amount in salary. Aside from the tax element, the salary would of course be preferred, since it has the advantage that it can be spent in whatever way the recipient pleases. The company official may consider these perquisites to be worth only a third of what they cost the corporation. Still, receiving the 40,000 yen perquisite is better than getting the 40,000-yen salary, paying the income tax, and retaining only 10,000 yen. If the tax rate is reduced to 67 per cent, the corporate official may consider it to be about an even choice between receiving a certain amount of additional compensation in the form of outright salary or in the form of entertainment and other perquisites, and if the tax rate is only 50 per cent, the corporate official may well prefer the salary increment, even though, after tax, he will have only half the money that it would cost the corporation to give him the alternative, tax-free perquisites.

In cases like this, pushing up the rate of income tax not only loses revenue, but induces wasteful expenditure that does not give as much satisfaction to anyone as would a smaller amount of resources put at the free disposal of the taxpayer. It will always be difficult to check this type of evasion or avoidance, since the line between proper business expenses and personal expenses is impossible to fix with precision.

Other means of avoidance develop under the pressure of high rates. For example, a taxpayer may arrange to take a part of his salary in the form of a loan, with the tacit understanding that it need never be repaid. But if the tax rate is as low as 50 per cent, he may prefer to pay the tax rather than risk liability to repay the loan if the corporation gets into difficulties, or risk investigation by tax officials.

In short, we are of the opinion that under present conditions in Japan it is unwise to push the income tax rate much, if any, above 50 per cent. At least, if the rates do rise substantially higher, they should do so only over ranges of income where the number of taxpayers is small enough to permit of a very thorough investigation and assessment of each taxpayer subject to these higher rates.

Nevertheless, we cannot be satisfied with the degree of high-level progression in the tax system that is reflected by nothing much more than an income tax that is limited to a 50 or 60 per cent top rate. Every progressive tax system worthy of the name must provide a substantial obstacle to the accumulation of huge fortunes that threaten to concentrate the control of the economic system in the hands of a few wealthy individuals. This is a danger of particular significance to Japan. Unless such accumulations are prevented by the tax system, they are almost certain to arise, sooner or later.

An improved form of succession tax will be helpful, but is scarcely enough by itself. Its effect is felt only over a long period of time.

The most satisfactory solution to the problem posed here involves the imposition of an annual, low-rate tax on the net worth of well-to-do individuals.[m]

* * *

TAX REFORM FOR FAIRNESS, SIMPLICITY, AND ECONOMIC GROWTH ("TREASURY I")
United States Department of the Treasury
Vol. 2, at 127-28 (1984)

[T]he current progressive rate structure for corporate income serves no affirmative purpose and encourages the use of corporations to gain the advantage of low marginal tax rates. The progressive rate structure for individuals is premised on the ability-to-pay concept, which in turn reflects an assumption that additional amounts of income are increasingly available for discretionary, nonessential consumption. These concepts have no relevance to corporate income, all of which is either distributed or used to produce additional income. Moreover, under current law a small corporation can escape high marginal tax rates on corporate income by electing pass-through treatment as an S corporation. Finally, the Treasury Department proposals include partial dividend relief, which would mitigate the impact of corporate tax rates on all corporations.[n]

---

m. Wealth taxes are discussed in Chapter Nine. (Ed.)

n. The dividend relief proposals were not included in the Tax Reform Act of 1986, though a different form of partial relief was adopted in 2003. This issue is discussed in Chapter Fourteen. (Ed.)

The current low rates of tax for certain amounts of corporate income permit the use of corporations as tax shelters for individuals. Thus, an individual may attempt to accumulate investment income within a corporation in order to defer tax on the income at the individual's rate. Where the corporate rate is significantly below the individual's marginal rate, the deferral advantage can more than offset the extra burden of the corporate tax. Current law attempts to limit this use of the corporate form through a surtax on the undistributed income of "personal holding companies." The personal holding company rules are complex and not uniformly effective.

The progressive tax structure for corporate income also encourages multiple corporations in order to maximize income taxed at the lowest rates. The current rules limiting this use of the corporate form are again complex and not consistently effective.

Proposal

The present corporate rate structure would be replaced by a flat tax rate for corporations of 33 percent.

* * *

Notes and Questions

43. In addition to the formal rate structure, there are a variety of back-door techniques for introducing additional progressivity. For example, the floor on miscellaneous itemized deductions (including most employee business expenses) is two percent of adjusted gross income, so expenses that are largely deductible by low-income taxpayers cannot be deducted to any extent by taxpayers with high adjusted gross incomes. Section 68. The treatment of Social Security benefits is another example. While most recipients are not taxed on Social Security benefits, higher-income recipients are taxed on up to 85% of benefits. Section 86. Similarly, section 151(d)(3) phases out personal and dependency exemptions for high-income taxpayers.

44. Even for lower-income taxpayers, the statutory rates of section 1 do not tell the entire story of progressivity. For example, additional income for a low-income person may entail the loss of earned income credit in addition to the officially-stated income tax.[o] See Section 32, and discussion in Chapter Eleven. Similarly, a taxpayer who deducts medical expenses will find that additional income causes a decrease in the medical deduction. The staff of the Joint Committee on Taxation estimates that "in 1998, 33.2 million tax returns, or approximately one-quarter of the all filing units, will have an effective marginal rate different from their statutory marginal rate."[p] Of these, over

---

o. At very low incomes, additional earned income *increases* the amount of this credit.

p. Thomas A. Barthold *et al., Effective Marginal Tax Rates Under the Federal Income Tax:*

forty percent "face effective marginal rates that differ by 10 percent or more from their statutory marginal rate."[q]

45. Why does Dr. McLure believe more attention should be paid to the effects of taxes on profit maximization and efficient operation once investments have been made, rather than to stimulating new investment?

46. McLure argues that one of the simplest reforms—reduction of rates—is also among the most effective. Lower rates provide incentive; at the same time, "whatever inequities and distortions remain are less important." Why?

47. Credits also have an incentive effect, though somewhat different from that of lower rates:

> By "grossing up" the tax offset by the credit, it is possible to estimate an equivalent amount of income which is made nontaxable. Credits essentially offset taxable income in the lowest brackets first. For example, if a taxpayer has $160 of credits, and if the bracket width is $1,000 for the first two positive rates of 14 percent and 15 percent, then the taxpayer's credits offset $1,000 of income at 14 percent and $133.33 (= $20/.15) at the 15 percent rate.[r]

48. The Shoup Report holds out the possibility that lower tax rates in the upper income brackets, by securing better compliance, might result in more revenue from those with high incomes. Is this relevant for the contemporary United States, with current top rates of 35%, as compared to more than 90% when the Shoup Report was issued?

49. High statutory rates undermine not only compliance among taxpayers, but also congressional support for uniform application of the tax system. Professor Stanley Surrey held positions of high governmental authority during periods in which the top statutory rate exceeded 90 percent—Tax Legislative Counsel in the Truman Administration, and Assistant Secretary for Tax Policy under Presidents Kennedy and Johnson. As he explained, such high statutory rates undermined themselves, in a sense, because they encouraged members of Congress to grant exemptions:

Death by One Thousand Pin Pricks?, 51 NAT'L TAX J. 553, 559 (1998).
    q. *Id.*
      r. Eugene Steuerle & Michael Hartzmark, *Individual Income Taxation, 1947-79*, 34 NAT'L TAX J. 145,151(1981).

The high rates of the individual income tax, and of the estate and gift taxes, are probably the major factor in producing special tax legislation. * * * [T]he average congressman does not basically believe in the present rates of income tax in the upper brackets. When he sees them applied to individual cases, he thinks them too high and therefore unfair. Any argument for relief which starts off by stating that these high rates are working a "special hardship" in a particular case or are "penalizing" a particular taxpayer—to use some words from the tax lobbyist's approved list of effective phrases—has the initial advantage of having a sympathetic listener. Put the other way around, an advocate of the "Louis B. Mayer amendment"[s] would simply make no headway with a congressman who firmly believed in a ninety-one-per-cent top tax rate. But most congressmen apparently do not believe in such a rate—certainly not in the concrete and perhaps not even in the abstract. Since they are not, however, willing to reduce those rates directly, the natural outcome is indirect reduction through special provisions.[t]

50. Why did the authors of the Shoup Report think an increase in the tax rate would be especially unfair to the honest taxpayer?

51. The Shoup Report makes the point that the higher an employee's tax rate, the more advantageous it is to the employee (and to the employer) to substitute nontaxable fringe benefits. The employee receives larger after-tax benefits, and the cost to the employer is less than it would be to provide the employee with the same after-tax amount in the form of taxed salary.

---

s. Professor Surrey described the "Louis B. Mayer amendment" as follows:
Under this provision, amounts received from the assignment or release by an employee of over twenty-years employment of his rights to receive, after termination of his employment and for a period of not less than five years, a percentage of future profits or receipts of his employer are taxed at capital-gains rates if the employee's contract providing for those rights had been in effect at least twelve years. Clearly the blueprint for compliance with this section is quite detailed. It is generally assumed that the amendment at the time covered only two persons, Louis B. Mayer, retired vice-president of Loew's, Inc., and one other executive in the company, and that the amendment saved Mayer about $2,000,000 in taxes.
Stanley S. Surrey, *The Congress and the Tax Lobbyist—How Special Tax Provisions Get Enacted*, 70 HARV. L. REV. 1145, 1147, n.4 (1957).
t. *Id.* at 1149-50.

While structuring executive compensation in this manner is a rational response to high tax rates, such compensation packages not only deprive the government of revenue, but also include dead-weight efficiency losses. Why?[u]

52. The Shoup Report addresses the difficulty of simultaneously pursuing two goals its drafters deemed desirable—reducing income tax rates and hindering the accumulation of large fortunes. To accomplish these dual goals, the Shoup Report proposed to supplement the income tax with an annual, low-rate tax on the net wealth of well-to-do individuals. The Report stated: "Every progressive tax system worthy of its name must provide a substantial obstacle to the accumulation of huge fortunes that threaten to concentrate the control of the economic system in the hands of a few wealthy individuals." Do you agree with this goal for the contemporary United States?

53. The authors of the Shoup Report clearly assumed the theoretical desirability of higher marginal rates than we have seen in the United States for a generation, noting that "we cannot be satisfied" with progression "limited to a 50 or 60 per cent top rate." The Report, however, emphasizes the problems of achieving a high degree of progressivity in practice.

54. Individual income tax rates and corporate income tax rates should be related. In the past they seldom have been. A complicating factor is that corporate earnings are taxed again when paid out as dividends to individuals and any increase in value of corporate stock due to retained earnings is taxed to a selling stockholder. The double tax issue is discussed in Chapter Fourteen.

55. Is ability to pay relevant in setting corporate tax rates? What view is expressed in Treasury I?

56. In determining the appropriate degree of progressivity of the federal income tax, should other federal taxes be taken into account? Should state and local taxes be included? Should adjustments be made for directly related benefits, such as Social Security pensions?

57. Is redistribution of wealth an appropriate objective for the individual income tax? Does it matter whether the gap between high incomes and low incomes occurs in a society where income is largely based on ownership of

---

u. For further discussion of this point, *see* Calvin H. Johnson, *The Case for Taxing Fringe Benefits*, 9 TAX NOTES 43 (1979).

landed estates or in a society where income is keyed largely to entrepreneurial success?

58. When the overall tax burden is changed because of extrinsic circumstances—*e.g.*, higher taxes in wartime or lower taxes in periods of economic recession—should the relationship between tax brackets remain the same? Be widened? Be narrowed?

59. An income tax that taxes different types of income at different rates is called a *schedular tax*. Should income tax rates vary depending on the source of income, such as earned income versus investment income?

60. What is the role of tax simplification in deciding on tax rates?

61. Suppose society were convinced that progressive taxes are fairer than proportional taxes, but also that at some point of progression they would be less fair—and that we had no way of knowing the crossover point. What should we do?

D. PROGRESSIVITY AND OPTIMAL TAX ANALYSIS

The case for progressivity seems intuitively appealing. Certainly, political practice in the past ninety years suggests it enjoys broad support. As we have seen, however, the case for progressivity is weakened when one moves beyond the broad issue of *whether* the tax system should be progressive to the more difficult question of the appropriate *degree* of progressivity. Critics of progressivity assert that when we abandon proportionality we are "at sea without rudder or compass" (in McCulloch's memorable phrase), and even defenders of progressivity, such as Professor Bittker, can defend no particular progressive structure except by "intuition."

Economists, following the lead of Nobel laureate James Mirrlees, have addressed this problem. Two types of assumptions underlie their work. First, as with any model, simplifying assumptions are required in order to render the work feasible and understandable. More important, optimal tax analysis requires normative assumptions about the goals of tax policy; most optimal tax theorists have assumed that utilitarianism, or something akin to it, should be the tax system's holy grail.

Professors Bankman and Griffith take issue with the famous assertion of Blum and Kalven, half a century ago, that the case for progressivity is "uneasy." Bankman and Griffith use optimal tax analysis to argue that while *marginal* rates should not be progressive (indeed, should be regressive), *average* tax rates can and should be markedly progressive. This seeming paradox is achieved by use of a substantial "demogrant"—a cash payment (or "refundable" tax credit) available in equal amount to everyone. The benefit of the demogrant significantly improves the welfare of low-income persons; at the same time, the income tax does not cause a great reduction in work effort because marginal rates fall with increasing income.

Professors Zelenak and Moreland do not contest the theories advanced by Bankman and Griffith and other optimal tax writers. They assert, however, that the demogrant is completely unfeasible politically in the United States. If there is to be no demogrant, significantly progressive average rates can be achieved only by the use of progressive marginal rates—the opposite of the falling marginal rates that optimal tax theory suggests. Zelenak and Moreland argue that in a world without demogrants, the logic of optimal tax theory should lead us to a progressive rate structure not unlike that of present law.

SOCIAL WELFARE AND THE RATE STRUCTURE: A NEW LOOK AT PROGRESSIVE TAXATION
Joseph Bankman[*] & Thomas Griffith[**]

75 California Law Review 1906, 1907-08, 1910-17, 1945-59, 1962-67 (1987)

Introduction

* * * A progressive rate structure has been part of the federal income tax system since its inception in 1913. Notwithstanding its lineage, the progressive rate structure has always been controversial, and the degree of progressivity has been subject to constant, and occasionally radical, change. * * *

The importance and persistence of the tax rate controversy might be expected to have generated a rich legal literature. In fact, although tax lawyers and academics have at various times spoken out in favor of or in opposition to the progressive tax, serious legal scholarship in the field is scarce. The complex issues raised by the progressive rate structure are comprehensively analyzed in only one article, *The Uneasy Case for Progressive Taxation*, written by Professors Walter J. Blum and Harry Kalven, Jr. in 1952.[4] Blum and Kalven's analysis is erudite and thoughtful and has shaped the opinions of two generations of tax scholars. However, Blum and Kalven

---

[*]. At time of original publication, Associate Professor of Law, University of Southern California.

[**]. At time of original publication, Associate Professor of Law, University of Southern California.

4. Blum & Kalven, *The Uneasy Case for Progressive Taxation*, 19 U. CHI. L. REV. 417 (1952). The article was published in book form in 1953.

did not and could not discuss the implications of recent developments in economics and moral theory for the structure of the progressive income tax.

This Article explores the moral, economic, and administrative effects of a progressive rate structure with reference to the insights of modern political theory and economics. * * *

Definitions and Assumptions

The progressivity of a tax rate structure is defined by the effective tax burden on differing income classes. Under a progressive tax, the percentage of income paid to the government, or average tax rate, rises as income rises.

A progressive tax may be implemented through graduated marginal rates: The first $10,000 of income might be taxed at 10%, while all subsequent income might be taxed at 30%. A progressive tax may also be implemented by a combination of constant or declining marginal rates and cash transfers or "demogrants." For example, all income might be taxed at a 30% rate, and all taxpayers might receive a $2,000 demogrant from the government. Under either approach, an individual with an income of $10,000 would pay a net tax of $1,000 for an average tax of 10%; an individual with an income of $20,000 would pay a net tax of $4,000 for an average tax rate of 20%. Each tax structure would be progressive because the percentage of income paid to the government would increase with income.

Under a regressive tax, the percentage of income paid to the government falls as income rises, although the absolute amount paid to the government may rise, fall, or remain constant. Proportionate and regressive taxes, like progressive taxes, may be implemented solely through the marginal rate structure, or through a combination of the marginal rate structure and cash payments.

Under a proportionate, or "flat," tax, the percentage of income paid to the government remains constant as income rises. High income individuals pay a greater absolute amount of tax to the government than low income individuals, but the ratio of tax to income is identical.

> * * *

A Normative Framework

Past Literature: The Default Assumption in Favor of a Proportionate Tax

> * * *

A number of legal scholars have discussed the consequences and desirability of progressivity. Very few, however, have identified the normative theory that supports and drives their conclusions. Key assumptions upon which those conclusions are based are left unstated or unexamined.

Perhaps the most significant and pervasive assumption is that the burden of proof lies on supporters of progressivity. A proportionate tax is often seen as "natural" or "neutral," and therefore is thought to require no justificatory theory. In contrast, arguments in favor of a progressive tax are considered successful only if accompanied by a convincing theory of distributive justice. The theoretical case for a regressive tax, such as one that requires equal contributions from each taxpayer, is thought so weak that it is rarely discussed. * * *

The assumption that a progressive tax must meet an affirmative burden while a proportionate tax need not is perhaps the core premise of Blum and Kalven's influential article, *The Uneasy Case for Progressive Taxation*. * * *

Blum and Kalven then discuss and reject various ethical theories said to support a progressive tax structure. In particular, they reject the argument that welfare would be improved by redistributing wealth from rich to poor. The connection between wealth and welfare, Blum and Kalven state, is too tenuous to serve as the cornerstone of tax policy.

Blum and Kalven's critique of the progressive tax, although in our opinion unconvincing, is detailed and considered. Its impact is dulled, however, by the authors' failure to subject the proportionate tax structure to an equally rigorous critique. While Blum and Kalven closely examine and reject certain theories of distributive justice that might justify progressive taxation, they fail even to articulate what a normative basis of a proportionate tax might look like.

Since the publication of *The Uneasy Case*, academic and popular support for a flat tax has grown. But few tax scholars have identified a theory of distributive justice upon which that tax could be predicated. In fact, while there are a number of plausible theories of distributive justice that support a progressive tax or even certain regressive taxes, it is surprisingly difficult to derive a theory of distributive justice that supports a proportionate tax. * * *

In *The Uneasy Case*, Blum and Kalven claim that a graduated rate structure "greatly complicates the positive law of taxation" and "dampens incentives."

Efficiency fails to justify a proportionate tax for two reasons. First, as noted below, the same efficiency-based reasoning that rejects a progressive tax in favor of a proportionate tax would, if applied consistently, reject a proportionate tax in favor of a lump-sum head tax. A head tax is "efficient" because it is unavoidable and does not change the behavior of any taxpayer. * * *

A proportionate tax might be supported more plausibly as a compromise between the perceived efficiency costs of a progressive tax and the perceived inequalities of a lump sum tax. * * * The difficulty with this position is that it does not explain what conceptions of fairness and justice are strong enough to rule out a regressive tax but are not strong enough to justify a progressive tax. It would appear mere chance that the opposing goals of efficiency and justice should reach equipoise at a proportionate tax.

       * * *

       Perhaps the most realistic, but least satisfying, explanation for the appeal of a proportionate tax lies in the concept of "prominence."[42] This concept is grounded in the tendency of individuals seeking to solve a problem in concert with others to settle on the most prominent, or conspicuous, solution. Because it is so simple, a tax structure that imposes the same rate on all individuals is more "prominent" than any of the countless rate structures that impose different rates on individuals of different rate classes. Faced with a requirement to select a tax structure, an individual might choose a proportionate rate structure simply because no other rate structure comes immediately to mind. It is as if in choosing a tax structure, the polity were a lost traveller faced with a selection of equally well trodden paths. Lacking any convincing rationale to turn right or left, the traveller continues on the path that leads straight ahead.

       Perhaps we can do no better than the lost traveller and are condemned to raise and redistribute a substantial portion of the world's wealth on a formula selected through intuition. But before resigning ourselves to that fate, it would be worthwhile to examine theories of distributive justice that might shape the tax structure.

Entitlement and Welfarist Theories of Distributive Justice

       There are many theories of distributive justice. A detailed discussion of all such theories is beyond the scope of this Article; for our purposes, it is sufficient to explore the differences between entitlement and welfarist theories of distributive justice.

       Under entitlement theories, a person deserves goods becomes of some action the person has taken or some trait the person possesses. One entitlement theory is the notion, sometimes associated with John Locke, that a person has a right to what he produces. A modern variant, offered by Robert Nozick in *Anarchy, State and Utopia,* states that a person is entitled to those goods acquired in uncoerced exchanges with others.[47]

       Welfarist theories of distributive justice, on the other hand, judge the goodness of social states solely by the welfare or utility enjoyed by the individuals in those states. Perhaps the two best known welfarist theories are

---

       42. *See* T. SCHELLING, THE STRATEGY OF CONFLICT 53-80 (1960). One test of the prominence concept involved a game played by isolated individuals, who were asked to respond to the following question: "Name 'head' or 'tails.' If you and your partner name the same, you both win a prize." Respondents overwhelmingly answered "heads." *Id.* at 55 n.1.

       47. R. NOZICK, ANARCHY, STATE, AND UTOPIA (1974).

utilitarianism, which judges the welfare of a society according to the unweighted sum of the utilities of its individual members, and the "leximin," based loosely upon the philosophy of John Rawls, which judges the welfare of a society according to the well-being of its least well off member. Lying between utilitarianism and the leximin with respect to preference for equality are weighted utility theories that, like utilitarianism, consider the welfare of each individual in determining social welfare, but that give greater weight to the well-being of the less well-off members of society.[51]

Although concern for incentive and demoralization effects may lead some welfarist theories to consider how individuals acquired goods in determining distribution, the fundamental focus of welfarist theories is often thought to be at odds with that of entitlement theories. Under entitlement theories and certain other nonwelfarist theories, an individual has a *right* to a good regardless of whether her ownership of the good is consistent with the welfare of others or even with her own welfare. For example, according to Nozick a person who acquires a good in a just manner would have a right to the good even if it were of little or no value to her and of enormous value to others.

In contrast, welfarist theories consider the fact that a person has created a good only to the extent that allocating goods to their creators improves social welfare by encouraging production or stability. The creator would not, however, have a claim to the good derived solely from the act of creation. Thus, welfarist theories of distributive justice permit taxation either to finance public goods or to redistribute income, if the well-being of individuals in the society is thereby improved.

A Welfarist Theory of Distributive Justice

In the following sections we discuss the implications of welfarist theories of distributive justice for the tax structure. We focus on welfarist rather than entitlement theories, in part because we believe that such ethics, while not without problems, have more to commend them. It seems plausible, at least, to judge government policies by the impact those policies have on the welfare of the individuals in the society.

One particularly attractive feature of a welfarist analysis of taxation is its responsiveness to the efficiency effects of various tax structures—effects that nearly everyone finds relevant. Another virtue of welfarist theories is their consistency with the Pareto principle: They view as desirable any change that makes some member of society better off without making any other member worse off. Entitlement theories, on the other hand, may not endorse a tax that

---

51. Welfarist theories that weight the welfare of the better off members of society more heavily than the welfare of the less well-off are logically possible but appear to have no adherents. The least egalitarian of the plausible welfarist theories is utilitarianism.

increases the welfare of an "undeserving" individual even if that change does not reduce the welfare of any other person. * * *

A final reason for our focus on welfarist theories is that entitlement theories do not clearly justify any rate structure. Any tax imposed on an unwilling taxpayer may be inconsistent with a system based on the view that a person has a right to what he produces. * * *

The tax implications of welfarist ethics have been explored in the important economics literature on "optimal taxation." Mathematical models derived from that literature can be used to determine the optimal rate structure under a wide variety of economic assumptions and welfarist ethics. * * *

The Costs and Benefits of Progressivity: a Welfarist Evaluation

A progressive income tax imposes certain efficiency costs and redistributes wealth from high-income to low-income individuals. Under a welfarist approach, the changes brought about by a tax structure are judged according to their effect on the welfare of individuals. To make this judgment, it is necessary to clarify the relationship between income, leisure, and individual utility. It is also necessary to specify the way in which the welfare of individuals determines social welfare.

In the past, scholars have not had a reliable method for assessing the level of social welfare associated with any particular rate structure. Moreover, the dependence of any such calculation upon speculative and unverifiable assumptions as to the relationship between income and individual welfare has cast a large shadow over the welfarist enterprise.

The development of a branch of public economics known as optimal taxation resolves the first difficulty and reduces the significance of the second. Optimal tax models can be used to evaluate tax structures under varying assumptions regarding individual and social welfare. These models also account for the impact of the income tax on the labor supply. The capacity of the models to calculate optimal rates under a wide range of assumptions makes it possible to search for robust results—that is, results that remain constant over such a wide range of assumptions.

The optimal tax model described below produces two results of particular interest. First, under a broad spectrum of assumptions, the optimal tax structure is progressive, although not confiscatory. Second, a progressive tax is best implemented through demogrants combined with constant or even declining marginal rates, rather than through constantly rising marginal rates.

The Mirrlees Optimal Taxation Model

Much of the recent work in optimal income taxation can be traced to James Mirrlees' seminal 1971 article, *An Exploration in the Theory of Optimum*

Income Taxation.[178] In that article, Mirrlees considers the following question: If all income is derived from labor, what income tax rate structure maximizes social welfare, given plausible assumptions regarding the utility of income and leisure to individuals?

Answering that question requires the construction of a complex mathematical model. Mirrlees' specific results and analysis have been criticized in the economic literature and are subject to independent criticism here. However, the basic model he uses to calculate the optimal rate structure, referred to here as the "Mirrlees model," has been adopted by optimal tax scholars.

The Mirrlees model requires the specification of both an individual utility function and a social welfare function. An individual utility function specifies the factors that determine an individual's utility or welfare. A social welfare function specifies the factors that determine the welfare of society. Under the Mirrlees model, the goal of the government is to choose a tax rate that maximizes the welfare of society as defined by a social welfare function.

Assessing Individual Welfare

The factors that determine a person's welfare are complex and many such factors—good looks, a sunny disposition, or a satisfying family life—could not feasibly be incorporated into a tax structure. Mirrlees therefore assumes a simple utility function in which an individual's welfare depends only on the amounts of consumption and leisure she enjoys. While the measurement of these factors is not without difficulty, income can be used as a rough measure of consumption, and hours worked can provide an estimate of the amount of time a person has remaining for leisure. The individual utility function adopted by Mirrlees may be written as $U = C + L$, where U is utility, C is consumption, and L is leisure.

Optimal tax models make two important additional assumptions regarding individual utility. First, they assume that consumption and leisure have declining marginal utility. Second they assume that individuals have identical utility functions.

The assumption that the value of an additional dollar to an individual declines as the number of dollars he owns increases ("declining marginal utility") is common in economic analysis. The assumption of identical utility functions is more problematic because individuals obviously do not have the same tastes. * * * Nevertheless, for purposes of determining tax policy, recommendations based on an assumption of identical utility functions may be unavoidable. * * *

---

178. 38 REV. ECON. STUD. 175 (1971).

Under a utilitarian ethic and in the absence of incentive effects, the assumption that consumption has declining marginal utility and that people have identical utility functions would lead to complete equality of consumption. All incomes above the mean would be taxed at a 100% rate, and all individuals with incomes below the mean would receive grants to bring their income to that level. Put differently, the optimal utilitarian tax structure would consist of a 100% marginal rate on all income and a uniform cash grant, thus ensuring equal consumption for all individuals.

* * * The problem, of course, is that the 100% marginal rates needed to equalize incomes would destroy incentives to produce and thus lower utility for everyone.

Choosing a Measure of Social Welfare

Just as an individual utility function identifies the factors that determine the welfare of an individual, a social welfare function specifies the factors that determine the welfare of a society. The concept of "welfare," however, has a different meaning for a society than for an individual. An individual utility function attempts to measure *objectively* the well-being of each individual. While it is impossible to make a precise assessment of the way in which consumption and leisure affect individual welfare, an individual utility function is value-free in the sense that it attempts to measure what does increase an individual's utility rather than what should increase utility. A social welfare function, on the other hand, reflects an explicit normative theory of the nature of a good society.

* * * Under one ethic, social welfare might be determined by the degree to which its members follow a particular set of religious beliefs, while under another ethic social welfare might be determined by the size of the gross national product. The components of social welfare are varied and may include such factors as the amount of individual liberty, the level of democracy, and the way society's rewards are allocated. * * * Mixed ethics may require a social welfare function whose arguments include all these factors.

Optimal tax models focus on welfarist theories of distributive justice—that is, ethics under which the welfare of a society is determined solely by the well-being of its members. Under welfarist social welfare functions, social well-being always is positively correlated with improvements in the well-being of any individual in the society. Other features of a society, such as individual liberty and democracy, may be valued under welfarist ethics because of the impact they have on the well-being of individuals, but they are not accorded independent value.

Welfarist theories of distributive justice are of three types: utilitarian theories, weighted utility theories, and leximin theories. Utilitarianism is the least egalitarian of these theories. It accords the utility of each person equal weight, so that social welfare is measured by the unweighted sum of the welfare of the individuals in the society. Proponents of utilitarianism desire to maximize welfare, but do not focus on its distribution.

Weighted utility theories are more egalitarian, weighting the welfare of less well of individuals more heavily than the welfare of those who are better off. One common weighting system assumes that social welfare varies with the *product* of the utilities of the individuals in the society. Adherents of weighted utility theories would accept a reduction in the total amount of welfare in a society in exchange for improving the welfare of society's less well off members.

The most extreme weighting of individual utilities occurs under the "Rawlsian" leximin. Under the leximin, the well-being of the least well off person in society determines that society's social welfare. * * *

Integrating Individual Utility and Social Welfare

The mathematical techniques used to derive an optimal rate structure in light of particular social welfare and individual utility functions are complex and of little interest to the nonspecialist. A simplified explanation of the methodology is useful, however, in evaluating the findings of optimal tax models.

Imagine a society of individuals whose well-being depends only on the amount of consumption and leisure they enjoy. Each individual wants to maximize her well-being and so works until the utility of the additional consumption she could enjoy from more earnings is exceeded by the loss in utility from the reduction in leisure that would be necessary to enable her to work more. Thus, the amount an individual works depends on the relative value of consumption and leisure to that individual and on the amount of consumption the individual can enjoy by working an additional hour.

The tax structure influences an individual's work effort by reducing the amount of consumption an individual is able to earn by sacrificing an hour of leisure. If the tax structure provides for lump-sum payments or demogrants to individuals, it will also reduce work effort by increasing the individual's nonlabor income, thus reducing her need for the income that could be earned by working. These influences are the substitution and income effects. * * *

The government will find it difficult to select the combination of taxes and transfers that maximizes welfare because individuals may change their work effort as the government changes the rate structure. Suppose, for example, that the government decides to tax individuals with high incomes at steep rates in order to fund grants to the poor. The government might discover that the tax so reduces work effort that the grants are not feasible. While trial-and-error might eventually lead to a tax structure in which revenues balance expenditures, the results would probably not be optimal.

Optimal tax models provide a means of calculating a tax structure in which revenues equal expenditures and in which social welfare is maximized under the chosen theory of distributive justice. * * *

The methodology of optimal taxation can be illustrated by a simple model that calculates the optimal rate structure under two different welfarist ethics in a society of three individuals. For purposes of this model, we will restrict the government's choice to a linear progressive tax structure consisting of a constant marginal tax coupled with a demogrant. We will not, however, alter the core assumptions and methodology of the Mirrlees model.

Imagine a society of three individuals named Alice, Betty, and Cindy. Assume each individual has an identical utility function in which her utility is determined solely by the level of consumption and leisure she enjoys. Further assume that the marginal utility of an additional unit of either income or leisure is inversely proportional to the amount already owned.[201] This can be represented by letting the utility that an individual enjoys from an amount of consumption or leisure be equal to the logarithm of that amount. * * *

Suppose that Alice, Betty, and Cindy have pre-tax hourly wages of $10, $20, and $40 respectively. Each will choose to work the number of hours that maximizes the sum of the value of her consumption plus the value of her leisure. * * *

It turns out that for Alice, Betty, and Cindy the utility-maximizing choice is to work twelve hours. Indeed, for any wage level greater than zero, the utility maximizing choice is to work this amount. Table 1 illustrates the situation that would exist in a no-tax world.

TABLE 1
NO-TAX WORLD

Name	Wage	Hours Worked	Pre-Tax Income	Net Tax	Consumption	Leisure	Utility*
Alice	$10	12	$120	$0	$120	12	7.272
Betty	$20	12	$240	$0	$240	12	7.966
Cindy	$40	12	$480	$0	$480	12	8.659
Totals		36	$840	$0	$840	36	23.897

* Utility equals the sum of the logarithms of consumption and leisure.

---

201. Under such a utility function, the utility gained from an additional dollar of income is ten times as great to a person who has $10,000 than to a person who has $100,000. Similarly, additional leisure to a person who currently enjoys 10 hours of leisure is worth twice as much as additional leisure to a person who already enjoys 20 hours.

Now consider the role of the government in setting a rate structure. In our model, the government is able to redistribute income through a linear progressive tax consisting of a uniform payment, or demogrant, financed by a constant marginal tax rate. Such a structure effects redistribution because the demogrant will be greater than the amount of tax collected for a low-income individual and less than the amount of tax collected for a high-income individual. If, for example, a rate structure were adopted with a 20% marginal rate and demogrant of $5,000, an individual with an income of $10,000 would pay a $2,000 tax and receive a $5,000 demogrant for a net gain of $3,000. An individual with an income of $100,000, on the other hand, would pay a tax of $20,000 and receive a demogrant of $5,000 for a net reduction in income of $15,000.

After application of the linear progressive tax, each individual's consumption will equal her earned income minus the tax on that income and plus the demogrant. * * *

In the present example, aggregate income in the no-tax world is $840 and the government might expect that a 20% tax on earned income would raise $168 and finance a demogrant of $56 per person. The government will discover, however, that because of the reduction in work effort caused by the tax, such a rate structure would raise only $147 of revenue, $21 short of the amount needed to finance the demogrant.

In order to enact a tax structure that is both feasible and utility-maximizing, the government must determine the unique revenue-neutral demogrant associated with each tax rate and then calculate the marginal rate and demogrant combination that maximizes aggregate utility. In the case of the 20% marginal rate discussed in the last paragraph, for example, the revenue-neutral demogrant is $49.78, which produces an aggregate utility of 24.058. This represents an increase in total utility compared to the no-tax world; it is not, however, the utility maximizing tax rate. Instead, utility is maximized by a tax rate of approximately 31% and a demogrant of $70.88. Table 2 illustrates the effects of such a tax structure.

TABLE 2

UTILITARIAN TAX STRUCTURE

Tax Rate: 31 %. Demogrant $70.88.

Name	Wage	Hours Worked	Pre-Tax Income	Net Tax	Consumption	Leisure	Utility*
Alice	$10	6.86	$68.64	− $49.60	$118.24	17.14	7.614
Betty	$20	9.43	$188.64	− $12.40	$201.04	14.57	7.982
Cindy	$40	10.72	$428.64	$62.00	$366.64	13.28	8.491
Totals		27.01	$685.92	$0	$685.92	44.99	24.087

* Utility equals the sum of the logarithms of consumption and leisure.

As compared to the no-tax world, the utility-maximizing tax reduces total work effor by about 25% and total production by about 18%. The utility of the best paid individual declines, but total utility is higher because the utility of the two less well paid individuals increases. Note that better paid individuals still enjoy a higher level of welfare and work longer hours than those who are less well paid.

The method of determining the optimal tax rate would be essentially the same if the government were to adopt a leximin rather than a utilitarian theory of distributive justice. However, under the leximin the government would enact the tax rate and demogrant that maximizes the utility of the least well-off individual, rather than the tax rate that maximizes total welfare. This turns out to be a marginal tax rate of 58% and a demogrant of $96.67. * * *

What can we conclude from our analysis of the optimal linear tax in a three-person world? First, a progressive rate structure is optimal under both utilitarianism, the least egalitarian welfarist theory, and under the leximin, the most egalitarian theory. Second, the level of progressivity depends on which welfarist ethic is adopted. A leximin dictates a much higher marginal rate and a larger demogrant than does a utilitarian ethic. Third, a progressive rate structure decreases total work effort. Fourth, under both utilitarian and leximin ethics, higher-paid individuals work more hours and enjoy a higher level of welfare than do lower-paid individuals. As we will see, these conclusions are consistent with the more complex model developed by Mirrlees.

The Results of the Mirrlees Optimal Tax Model

The Mirrlees model differs from the simple model described in the preceding section in two important respects. First, it examines a society with a continuous distribution of taxpayers of differing wage levels rather than with just three taxpayers. Second, it permits the government to adopt a tax structure with variable marginal rates rather than limiting the government to a linear structure. Under the Mirrlees model, the government can adopt a tax structure with a demogrant and continuously variable marginal rates rather than a demogrant coupled with a flat rate.

The Mirrlees model calculates the optimal tax structure under both a utilitarian theory of distributive justice like that examined in our simple model, and under a more egalitarian ethic that requires the government to maximize the product of individual utilities. The model also calculates the optimal income tax structure under different assumptions regarding the amount of revenue required by the government for purposes other than redistribution. Finally, the model considers two assumptions regarding the distribution of earning ability.

Like our three-taxpayer model, the Mirrlees model adopts a logarithmic utility function under which the value of an additional unit of consumption is inversely related to the amount already enjoyed. Given this fairly rapid decline in the marginal utility of consumption, Mirrlees expected high rates on the wealthy to be optimal. In fact, his model finds the optimal level of progressivity to be modest. In the utilitarian case, assuming 7% of gross income is required for government purposes other than redistribution, the top marginal rate is 26%. The demogrant is also fairly small, about one-sixth of the median income.

Even more surprising, the highest marginal rate falls on individuals with incomes in the bottom 10% of the population and the marginal tax rate thereafter declines. As a result, an individual with an income in the top 1% pays a marginal rate of approximately 17%—about 40% less than the top rate. The falling marginal rates do not, however, prevent the tax structure calculated by the Mirrlees model from being progressive. As Table 4 shows, because of the demogrant the rich pay a higher average tax than do the poor, so that the after-tax distribution of income is more equal than the pre-tax distribution. Nevertheless, the level of redistribution is not high.

TABLE 4

MIRRLEES MODEL

OPTIMAL TAX STRUCTURE: UTILITARIAN

Elasticity of Substitution = 1.0

Government Expenditures = 7% of goods produced.

Demogrant = 0.03 units. Mean income = 0.17 units.

Income Level	Consumption		Average Tax Rate	Marginal Tax Rate	Income as % of Mean	
	Pre-Tax	Post-Tax			Pre-Tax	Post-Tax
10%	0.09	0.10	—	24%	50%	59%
50%	0.17	0.16	6%	22%	94%	94%
90%	0.29	0.25	14%	19%	161%	147%
99%	0.45	0.38	16%	17%	250%	224%

Mirrlees also finds relatively modest levels of redistribution where the government attempts to maximize the product of individual utility levels. This result is surprising because the government's goal is quite egalitarian. If utility from consumption alone is considered under such a weighted social welfare function * * * the social value of an additional dollar to an individual with an income of $20,000 is 100 times as great as the social value of an additional dollar to a person with an income of $200,000. A transfer of a dollar from the richer individual to the poorer would improve social welfare so long as the poorer individual gains more than a penny for each dollar lost by the richer individual. When utility from leisure is considered, the additional weight given to increases in the consumption of the poor is less. Nevertheless, the social value of additional income to a poor person will be many times greater than the social value of that income to a wealthy person.[214]

Even when the government wishes to maximize the product of individual utilities, the Mirrlees model produces an optimal top marginal rate of 34% and a demogrant of just 30% of the median income. These represent only modest increases from the levels produced under a utilitarian ethic. Again, the top marginal rate falls on individuals with incomes in the bottom 10% of the population and declines steadily thereafter, so that a person in the top 1% of the population again faces a marginal rate about 40% lower than the highest marginal rate.

---

214. The inclusion of utility derived from leisure makes the overall distribution of utility more equal because individuals enjoying disproportionately large amounts of consumption are unlikely also to enjoy disproportionately large amounts of leisure.

The optimal tax literature provides little explanation for these striking results. Our analysis suggests that the relatively moderate level of progressivity is caused by a confluence of two opposing forces. The assumption of rapidly declining utility of money drives the tax toward steep progressivity. On the other hand, the efficiency costs of progressivity become extremely great at high tax rates. As discussed below, the efficiency costs are exaggerated by the Mirrlees model's unrealistic assumptions regarding the willingness of individuals to substitute leisure for consumption.

The shape of the optimal rate structure—a demogrant plus slowly falling marginal rates—can be explained if we assume that for a given level of redistribution, the marginal rates taxpayers face generally will be lower and the efficiency loss will be smaller under a tax structure with a larger demogrant and declining marginal rates * * * than under a structure with a smaller demogrant and rising marginal rates. Moreover, under a tax structure with falling marginal rates, some individuals may work additional hours in order to reach tax brackets with lower marginal rates.

Modifying the Mirrlees Model

The development of a method of determining the optimal rate structure in light of a social welfare function and an individual utility function is a remarkable achievement in public economics. Mirrlees also asks the right question: What tax structure is best, given certain normative values and certain assumptions regarding the effect of taxes on behavior? His focus on this issue may be as important a contribution as his model.

The finding that the optimal tax structure consists of a fairly modest guaranteed consumption level plus relatively low marginal rates that peak in the bottom 10% of the population has led Mirrlees to conclude that the income tax alone is a much less effective method of mitigating inequality than is generally believed, and that the optimal rate structure may consist of a demogrant plus a constant marginal rate.

The merit of these conclusions depends, of course, on the validity of the optimal tax model. Mirrlees' model requires numerous simplifying assumptions with respect to individual and social welfare and with respect to the structure of the economy. We will examine four of those assumptions. * * * [W]e conclude that a more realistic assumption as to the trade-off between consumption and leisure substantially changes Mirrlees' results regarding the appropriate level of redistribution (greatly increasing the optimal marginal rates and demogrant) while leaving his findings about the optimal shape of the tax structure essentially unchanged.

* * *

The Overestimation of the
Substitutability of Consumption and Leisure

The capacity of an income tax to redistribute income effectively depends on whether the imposition of the tax causes people to reduce their work effort significantly. If high-income individuals respond to an income tax by sharply curtailing the number of hours they work, the tax will not only reduce the welfare of those individuals, it will also raise little money for redistribution. In extreme cases, more revenue for redistribution may be raised by a lower rate than by a higher rate. In contrast, if the amount of labor individuals provide is only modestly responsive to taxation, steep marginal rates can provide substantial tax revenues for redistribution without significantly reducing work output.

The imposition of an income tax reduces the amount of additional consumption an individual will earn from an extra hour of work. If other variables remain constant, an individual will respond by working less and enjoying more leisure. The key question is: How much less will the individual choose to work?

The answer depends in large part on the substitutability of leisure and consumption. If an individual is almost as well off with a bit more leisure and a bit less consumption, then the individual will work less and enjoy more free time when his effective wage rate is reduced by an income tax. On the other hand, if an individual finds additional leisure a poor replacement for reduced consumption, then his work effort will not be reduced significantly by the tax.

The ability of an individual to maintain the same level of well-being with a different mix of consumption and leisure will depend on the elasticity of substitution between consumption and leisure. A low elasticity of substitution indicates that an individual maintains a uniform ratio of consumption to leisure even if a high tax rate on labor income makes consumption much more expensive. Conversely, a high elasticity indicates that an increase in the price of consumption relative to the price of leisure causes an individual to reduce significantly his work hours in favor of leisure time.

The original Mirrlees model and most other optimal tax models, including our own three-taxpayer model, adopt a utility function that defines individual well-being as the product of individual consumption and leisure or, equivalently, the sum of their logarithms. Thus, a person enjoying 6 units of consumption and 6 units of leisure would have the same level of well-being as a person enjoying 3 units of consumption and 12 units of leisure. This multiplicative utility function implies a constant elasticity of substitution of 1.0 between leisure and consumption; for small changes, an individual's well-being is unchanged if her enjoyment of one good is decreased so long as her enjoyment of the other good is increased by the same percentage. Thus an individual's well-being is unchanged if her consumption is decreased by one percent so long as her leisure is increased by one percent.

The fact that most optimal tax models adopt a utility function with a constant elasticity of substitution of 1.0 is due to the computational advantages of such a function rather than any evidence that it accurately reflects the way in which consumption and leisure shape individual utility. Indeed, Mirrlees makes no attempt to justify his choice of a unitary elasticity of substitution between consumption and leisure. An examination of econometric estimates of labor supply responsiveness suggest that an elasticity of 1.0 does not reflect accurately the tradeoffs individuals make between consumption and leisure.

Econometric models of the labor supply focus on the impact that changes in the wage rate have on work effort. * * * These results imply an elasticity of substitution between consumption and leisure of approximately 0.5. Looking at the whole range of econometric studies of the labor supply, the most plausible conclusion is that the elasticity of substitution between consumption and leisure lies between 0.3 and 0.8 and almost certainly is less than the elasticity of 1.0 used in the Mirrlees model.

Using an elasticity of substitution of 0.5 in optimal tax models results in optimal marginal rates and a demogrant that are much higher than those calculated by Mirrlees. In the utilitarian case, with government revenues set at 10% of gross income, the adoption of an elasticity of 0.5 almost doubles the optimal marginal rates throughout the income range and almost triples the size of demogrant. The level of redistribution also becomes large in an absolute sense, with the guaranteed consumption level equaling about 40% of mean income and with a negative net tax burden for individuals with gross incomes less than 80% of the mean. Since the current mean income for a family of four is approximately $31,000, this redistribution corresponds to a tax structure with a guaranteed income of about $12,400 and a negative net tax for families with incomes under about $24,000.
     * * *

Although the assumption of a lower elasticity of substitution significantly changes the optimal level of redistribution, it does not alter the shape of the optimal rate structure. As in the unitary elasticity case, the top marginal rate is levied on individuals in the bottom 10% of the population in income and the rate declines slowly as income increases. Mirrlees' findings with respect to the shape of the rate structure appear quite robust.

In sum, adopting a realistic value for the tradeoff between consumption and leisure leads to the conclusion that even under an ethical theory like utilitarianism, which assigns no additional weight to the welfare of less well off individuals, a substantial degree of redistribution is justified. However, the optimal shape of the tax structure—a substantial demogrant followed by flat or even slightly declining marginal rates—is very different from the steadily rising marginal rates associated with traditional progressive taxation.

Conclusion

* * *

Much additional work needs to be done on the ramifications of the optimal tax model.   * * *   Based on what we know now, however, the case for progressive taxation appears to be far less uneasy than has been claimed.

CAN THE GRADUATED INCOME TAX SURVIVE OPTIMAL TAX ANALYSIS?
Lawrence Zelenak[*] & Kemper Moreland[**]
53 Tax Law Review51, 51-69 (1999)

Introduction

It would be easy for a utilitarian to design the ideal tax-and-transfer system—if taxation of earnings did not discourage work. Assuming everyone derives the same utility from any given amount of money, and that money has declining marginal utility, the ideal system would tax all earnings at 100% and then distribute an equal share of the tax revenue to every person. Until incomes are completely equalized, the sum of individual utilities always can be increased by transfers from those with more to those with less. The problem, of course, is that taxation does affect work effort. Faced with a 100% tax, people would decide not to earn any taxable income, and the otherwise ideal system would be a complete disaster.

What, then, is the ideal tax-and-transfer system, retaining the goal of maximizing the sum of the utilities of individuals with identical preferences, but taking into account the work disincentive effect of an income tax? That is the question James Mirrlees addressed in his classic 1971 article, which invented optimal income tax analysis.[2] As originated by him, and developed by him and others, optimal income tax analysis provides sophisticated mathematical techniques for finding the tax-and-transfer system that best balances the utility gains from income redistribution against the efficiency losses from the disincentive effect of taxation.

If the tax administrator could observe individuals' ability levels (that is, wage rates), a tax could be imposed directly on ability. Under such an endowment tax, tax liability would depend only on ability, without regard to an

---

*. At time of original publication, Reef C. Ivey Professor of Law, University of North Carolina.

**. At time of original publication, Professor of Economics, Eastern Michigan University.

2. James Mirrlees, An Exploration in the Theory of Optimum Income Taxation, 38 Rev. Econ. Stud. 175 (1971). Mirrlees received the 1996 Nobel Prize in Economic Science in recognition of his optimal income tax work.

individual's chosen mix of work and leisure. Because tax liability would be unaffected by labor effort, an endowment tax would not discourage market work relative to leisure. Optimal tax analysis, however is based on the realistic assumption that the tax administrator can observe taxpayers' incomes, but not their wage rates.

Optimal tax analysis depends critically on a few assumptions about the state of the world: the distribution of income-earning ability in society, the rate at which the marginal utility of income declines, and how much the imposition of an income tax causes individuals to curtail their work efforts.[5] For any set of assumptions, an optimal tax analyst can derive the utility-maximizing tax-transfer system, in the form of a tax rate schedule and a universal cash grant ("demogrant") of some specified amount per person. The model may or may not also provide for taxation to fund government activities other than redistribution.

In the utilitarian version of optimal tax analysis, the optimal tax-transfer system is the one that maximizes the sum of individuals' utilities. Each individual's utility is a function of her leisure[6] and her consumption (with consumption equaling after-tax income). Both leisure and consumption are assumed to have declining marginal utility.

The sharper the decline in the marginal utility of consumption, the greater the potential utility gains from redistribution. But the more taxation causes individuals to replace taxed labor income with untaxed leisure (including imputed income), the greater the efficiency cost of taxation. The interaction of these two forces, pushing in opposite directions, determines the optimal tax rate schedule and the optimal demogrant.

Optimal tax analysis also can incorporate distributive philosophies more egalitarian than simple utilitarianism. For example, one might believe that any individual's marginal utility of income is inversely proportional to the amount

---

5. More precisely, the key question in terms of work effort is the extent of the substitution effect (as reflected in the elasticity of substitution between consumption and leisure). Taxation of earned income has two effects on work effort, operating in opposite directions. The substitution effect decreases work effort. Confronted with a tax on earned income, people tend to replace it with untaxed imputed income or leisure. But the income effect increases work effort. * * * Knowing that taxes reduce their pay, people work harder to replace the lost income. The net result of the two effects may be an increase, a decrease, or no change in labor supply. The efficiency loss from taxation, however, depends solely on the substitution effect—on the wedge that taxation drives between the value of one's labor and the amount one receives for it. Joseph Bankman & Thomas Griffith, Social Welfare and the Rate Structure: A New Look at Progressive Taxation 75 Cal. L. Rev.1905, 1920 (1987). * * * Although it is counterintuitive, taxation creates an efficiency loss from the substitution effect even if the net result of the substitution and labor effects leaves the amount of labor unchanged.

6. Leisure is any time not devoted to market labor. Unpaid work one does for oneself and one's family—in tax policy jargon, work that produces imputed income—is leisure in this specialized usage.

of income she already has,[9] but have a social preference for equality that values the utility of the poor more than that of the rich. * * *

There are, of course, infinite possible variations on this theme of weighted utilitarianism. At the extreme, an analyst can determine the optimal tax-transfer system under a leximin or maximin social welfare function, commonly associated with John Rawls,[11] under which the goal is to maximize the utility of the least well-off member of society.[12]

The level of optimal tax rates and the size of the optimal demogrant are very sensitive to the factual assumptions and to the choice of social welfare function, but one important finding is quite robust. Unlike the actual tax rate structures in the United States and most other advanced economies, optimal marginal tax rates do not rise steadily with income. As Matti Tuomala has noted, "One of the main conclusions to be drawn from the Mirrleesian optimal non-linear income tax model is that it is difficult (if at all possible) to find a convincing argument for a progressive marginal tax rate structure throughout."[14] For a wide range of factual assumptions and social welfare functions, the shape of the optimal tax curve is surprisingly robust: The marginal tax rate rises through the bottom decile of the societal wage distribution, and falls as income increases thereafter. If the model permits only two rate brackets, instead of unlimited variation in marginal rates, the optimal result is again marginal rate regressivity—that is, the rate that applies at higher income levels should be lower than the rate that applies at lower income levels. Marginal rate regressivity remains optimal even under a maximum social welfare function. Increasing social aversion to inequality increases the size of the demogrant and the level of tax rates, but it does not significantly affect the shape of the optimal marginal tax rate schedules.

At first glance, the optimal tax rejection of progressive marginal rates is surprising. It is easy to see how the utility gains from redistribution push the optimal tax in the direction of progressive marginal rates. But there is a powerful countervailing force, the influence of which is less obvious. High tax rates impose an efficiency cost only when they apply at the margin—that is, at the point where a taxpayer actually is choosing between paid work and leisure. When a high tax rate applies to a taxpayers' submarginal earnings, it raises revenue for utility-enhancing redistribution without substitution effect

---

9. In that case, an additional dollar to a person with $10,000 would have 10 times the utility of an additional dollar to a person with $100,000.

11. John Rawls, A Theory of Justice 75-83, 152-56 (1971).

12. * * *

At first glance, it may seem that the leximin leads to * * * 100% tax and complete income equalization. * * * In fact, it does not. Income the rich choose not to earn because of high tax rates cannot be redistributed to the least advantaged.

14. Matti Tuomala, Optimal Income Tax and Redistribution 14 (1990).

distortion. To that taxpayer, the high rate on submarginal income functions as a nondistorting lump sum tax.

From an efficiency standpoint, then, an attractive income range at which to apply a high marginal rate will be a range where there are many taxpayers for whom that range is submarginal, relative to the number of taxpayers at the margin within that range. Most of the revenue raised by a high tax rate in that range will come without any substitution effect distortion. Conversely, efficiency concerns suggest the tax rate should be low in any income range where the ratio of submarginal taxpayers to marginal taxpayers is low. Because the range is marginal for a high percentage of the taxpayers to whom it applies, a high rate tax at that range will impose a high efficiency cost per tax dollar collected. * * * Although the declining marginal utility of money pushes the optimal tax toward progressive marginal rates, the decreasing submarginality of rates at high income levels pushes strongly in the opposite direction.

In fact, one of the few general results of optimal tax analysis is that the tax rate on the last dollar earned by the most able (that is, highest wage) member of society should be zero. That rate is marginal for one taxpayer, and is not submarginal for anyone. If there were any tax at the margin, the most able worker would choose untaxed leisure over the taxed marginal dollars of income. Eliminating the tax at the margin improves her welfare[20] and harms no one else because the tax would have raised no revenue in any event.

Optimal tax analysis appears to be a death sentence for the graduated (progressive marginal rate) income-tax. What is so devastating about this analysis to the case for graduated rates is that it concedes all philosophical issues to the proponents of the graduated tax. If you are a utilitarian who has no rights-based philosophical objection to redistribution, that is fine with optimal tax analysts. If you are a weighted utilitarian who values the utility of the poor above the utility of the rich, that is also fine. It is even fine if you are a Rawlsian who cares about nothing but the welfare of the poorest. Optimal tax analysis grants your philosophical premise, and merely asks you to consider the impact of the efficiency cost of taxation on your ability to achieve your goals through progressive marginal rates. Once those effects are considered, it seems that *no one* should support a graduated income tax

There is an irony here. The only detailed discussion of optimal tax analysis in the legal (as opposed to economic) literature is a superb article by Joseph Bankman and Thomas Griffith, in which they use optimal tax analysis to *defend* progressive income taxation.[21] Their article is a response to the

---

20. At the margin, she values the leisure alternative more than the after-tax labor income (if there is any tax), but less than tax-free labor income.

21. Bankman & Griffith, note 5.

skepticism about progressivity reflected in a classic, decades-old article by Walter Blum and Harry Kalven.[22] How can Bankman and Griffith think that optimal tax analysis supports progressivity? Simply enough, they focus on *average* rate progressivity rather than *marginal* rate progressivity. They explain that the effect of the demogrant is to make optimal average tax rates rise with income, even as marginal rates fall. If it seems impossible that average rates can be progressive when marginal rates are regressive, consider a simple example. Suppose the demogrant is $10,000, and there are only two tax rates. The first rate is 30%, the second rate is 20%, and the breakpoint between the rates is $50,000. At the breakpoint, the $15,000 tax resulting from the 30% rate is reduced to $5,000 net tax by the demogrant, giving an average tax rate of 10%. Since any income above $50,000 is taxed at a rate higher than 10%, the average rate increases as income increases above $50,000.

Whether standard optimal tax analysis supports a progressive income tax thus becomes a matter of what is meant by progressivity—average rate or marginal rate progressivity. Contrary to Bankman and Griffith, we believe that the more important issue is marginal rate progressivity, at least in the current U.S. political context.

This Article examines whether graduated marginal rates can survive the apparently devastating results of optimal tax analysis. It begins with an explanation of why marginal rate progressivity is an important issue. It then considers six situations that have received little or no attention in the optimal tax literature, in which progressive marginal rates may be optimal, and discusses the significance of each.

The first is that progressive marginal rates may be optimal if demogrants are ruled out on political grounds, so that the only purpose of the income tax is to finance nonredistributive government functions. * * * Other optimal tax studies, with their use of demogrants have an air of political unreality. This study recognizes the political implausibility of demogrants, and modifies the optimal tax analysis in response. It turns out that, in a world without demogrants, the reports of the death of the graduated income tax are greatly exaggerated.

The next four situations in which progressive marginal rates may be optimal are reported in the existing literature, but are not widely known. Progressive rates may be optimal if envy figures into the social welfare function, if taxation serves as a form of insurance against wage uncertainty, if high income taxpayers are especially nonresponsive to the work disincentive effect of taxation, or if the of ability (wage rates) in the population is different

---

22. Walter J. Blum & Harry Kalven, Jr., The Uneasy Case for Progressive Taxation, 19 U. CHI. L. REV. 417 (1952).

than usually is assumed. The final situation is that progressive marginal rates might be optimal in a labor market consisting in large part of winner-take-all competitions. Such a labor market has yet to be modeled in an optimal tax study.

If Average Rates Are Progressive, Why Care About Progressive Marginal Rates?

There is a ships-passing-in-the-night quality to the progressivity debate between Blum and Kalven, and Bankman and Griffith. Blum and Kalven explain—at considerable length—that their interest is in whether a graduated rate structure can be justified; they do not find the average rate progressivity of a flat tax-plus-subsistence exemption of great interest or importance.[24] But Bankman and Griffith believe they have adequately dealt with Blum and Kalven's objections to progressivity, by demonstrating that optimal tax analysis supports a flat tax-plus-demogrant, which has average rate progressivity without graduated rates. Blum and Kalven could object that Bankman and Griffith have done nothing to dispel their skepticism about graduated rates; instead, they have shifted the terms of the debate from marginal rate progressivity to average rate progressivity, without explaining why that shift is appropriate.

Although Bankman and Griffith do not supply an explanation for the shift, it is easy enough to do it for them. Start with the idea that what ultimately matters in determining whether the tax burden is fairly distributed among income classes, is *average* rates[26]—what percentage of income individuals pay in tax at different income levels. If *Dives* is paying an appropriately higher percentage of his income in taxes than is *Lazarus*, it is irrelevant on fairness grounds how much each pays at the margin.[28] In the world of Blum and Kalven, there are no demogrants,[29] so significant average rate progressivity[30] can be achieved only with graduated rates. Without demogrants, the question of graduated rates and the question of meaningful average rate progressivity are the same. But with the introduction of demogrants, it is possible to have

---

24. Blum & Kalven, note 22, at 420, 506-11. A tax system with a zero rate on subsistence income and a single rate above that level will have modest average rate progressivity. As income increases, the average tax rate approaches, but never quite reaches, the single flat tax rate. This sometimes is called a degressive tax.

26. When the question is the behavioral effects of taxation, rather than fairness of the distribution of tax burdens, the focus is on marginal rates.

28. But see A.B. Atkinson, Public Economics in Action: the Basic Income/Flat Tax Proposal 79 (1995) (decrying the unfairness of the "poverty trap" created by high marginal rates at low income levels).

29. This appears to be because the possibility of demogrants never occurred to them, and not because they considered and rejected demogrants.

30. Significant average rate progressivity requires more than the minor progression created by a subsistence exemption combined with a flat tax.

significant average rate progressivity—and significant redistribution—without graduated rates. Hence the belief of Bankman and Griffith that they have answered the objections to progressivity without having answered the objections to graduated rates.

Although we agree with Bankman and Griffith that the ultimate fairness question is about average rates, we disagree with their implication that those who favor progressivity need not be concerned about marginal rates, for two reasons. First, as a technical matter, there is a close relationship between average and marginal rates; some arguably desirable distributions of average rates simply cannot be achieved with a demogrant and a flat tax. Second, and even more important, the political reality in the United States is that there are not going to be any universal cash transfers; once demogrants are politically ruled out, significant average rate progressivity means marginal rate progressivity.

The Technical Relationship
Between Average and Marginal Rates

In a tax system with a demogrant—or even with merely an exemption—there will be average rate progressivity without graduated rates. What, then, do graduated rates add? One way of explaining the effect of graduated rates is that they increase the rate of increase in average rates. Another explanation is that graduation permits an increase in the average rate of those making more than a given amount, without also affecting those making the given amount or less. In a flat rate system—with a demogrant or exemption—the average rate can never exceed or even quite equal the flat rate. Suppose the tax system was a $10,000 demogrant and a 30% flat tax. Then Bill Gates' average rate would be just below 30%. If we decided that his average rate was too low, what could we do about it if we were committed to a flat tax? We could increase his average rate to just below the level to which we increased the flat rate, but that would also increase the marginal rate on everyone else. With a flat tax, to increase Gates' average rate, we must increase everyone's marginal rate and affect nearly everyone's average rate.[32] By contrast, the use of graduated rates would allow an increase in Gates' average rate without affecting the rates of any lower income taxpayers.

The point, most simply, is that graduated rates permit much greater flexibility in average rate distributions than does a flat tax with a demogrant

---

32. Although the increase in the flat rate would increase everyone's marginal rate and affect nearly everyone's average rate, it would not necessarily increase everyone's average rate. If increasing the flat tax rate increased revenue—which depends on the labor supply response—the higher rate could finance a larger demogrant. In that case, there would be some break-even income level, below which the benefit of the increase in the demogrant would outweigh the detriment of the higher tax rate, and above which the demogrant would not be enough to compensate for the rate increase.

or an exemption. For example, suppose lawmakers decide that the average rate at $10,000 income should be zero, at $30,000 should be 20%, and at $100,000 should be 30%. They then ask their staff technicians to devise rules to accomplish this. With graduated rates, there are any number of ways to do so, with or without demogrants. But with a flat tax and a demogrant, it simply cannot be done. * * *

The significance of this loss of flexibility in setting average rates is debatable. Are we really so committed to the average rates of zero, 20%, and 30%, that we would not be satisfied with average rates of zero, 24%, and 27%, which a flat tax of 30% and a demogrant of $3,000 could produce? Maybe the flat tax approximation is good enough. But suppose we have a fourth average rate criterion: The average rate on $1 million income should be 60%. With graduated rates, that easily can be accomplished, but the flat tax-demogrant scheme that was a reasonable approximation for the first three criteria is a disaster for the fourth.[35]

U.S. Politics

On the one hand, there is a real difference in flexibility in setting average rates between a flat tax with a demogrant and a graduated income tax. On the other hand, if the demogrant is substantial and the flat rate is high, the flat tax and demogrant might be sufficiently progressive and redistributive to satisfy even the most liberal Americans today. Bankman and Griffith may be right that, in a world that permits large demogrants and high flat tax rates, the extra flexibility of graduated rates is not worth fighting about. But Blum and Kalven thought graduation was worth fighting about because the possibility of demogrants never occurred to them.[36] Perhaps this was a failure of imagination on their part, but it also may have been a bow to political reality. If the political reality precludes demogrants (and exemptions above subsistence), then the fight over progressive marginal rates is the fight over progressive average rates.

George McGovern proposed a demogrant of $1,000 per person during the 1972 presidential campaign. It proved to be a political disaster, and he quickly disavowed it. Since then, demogrants have become one of the third rails of U.S. politics—touch them and you die. They have received no serious public discussion in the succeeding quarter century. * * * In a political climate in which even need-based welfare-as-we-know-it has been drastically curtailed, a system of universal non-need based transfers has no chance. * * * [T]here are no demogrants in the U.S. future.

---

35. The average tax rate on $1 million would be only 29.7%.

36. They did consider the possibility of exemptions well above the subsistence level. The difference is that high exemptions, unlike demogrants, never result in net transfers from the government to individuals.

By contrast with the political impossibility of demogrants, progressive marginal rates are politically possible—as a glance at § 1 of the Code confirms. If the tax is to have meaningfully progressive average rates, it will be because of a graduated rate structure, not because of demogrants. But graduated rates are under serious political attack. * * * Optimal tax analysis provides intellectual support for the flat tax movement. The irony is that flat tax proponents embrace optimal tax findings concerning rate structure, but reject optimal tax findings in support of large demogrants. It may be that optimal tax analysis does *not* support a flat tax, if the flat tax is not accompanied by demogrants.

A Two-bracket Simulation with Subsistence Exemption and No Demogrant

This Section describes the structure and the results of a model we developed that was intended to determine whether optimal tax analysis supports progressive marginal rates under real world political constraints.

The Structure of the Study

With demogrants nowhere to be found on the political scene, the real world debate about tax progressivity is between a flat tax with a subsistence exemption and the current system of graduated rates above a subsistence exemption. With that in mind, we made the following assumptions: (1) there is no demogrant, (2) there is a subsistence-level exemption (fixed at $12,000), and (3) there may be (at most) two brackets above the exemption. The first two assumptions reflect political reality; the third makes the simulation more manageable. We also assumed the government needed to raise $5,000 per person to fund the government's nonredistributive expenditures. The study grouped wage earners into five hourly wage levels, based on 1994 U.S. wage distribution data. The wage rates ranged from $4.16 for the lowest group to $32.83 for the highest. In the model, each person decides how many hours of labor (from an assumed annual supply of 3,120 hours) to provide at her wage rate, in order to maximize her utility from consumption and leisure combined. * * *

We then determined the optimal tax structure, subject to these constraints, under several social welfare functions (ranging from unweighted utilitarian to a Rawlsian leximin). For each social welfare function, we determined the first rate (above the zero bracket subsistence exemption), the second rate, and the breakpoint between the first and second brackets.[50]

---

50. Although the model did not permit negative tax rates, it did permit either the first or second bracket rate to be zero. It also permitted the first and second bracket rates to be identical.

Relation to Previous Studies

Our investigation bears some similarity to two earlier studies. A 1992 simulation by one of the authors is the only previous optimal income tax study (of which we are aware) to have ruled out the use of demogrants. Moreland assumed the tax system was to consist of a zero bracket and a single tax rate above the zero bracket. He then calculated the optimal breakpoint between the brackets and the optimal rate for the flat tax. The results favored a higher exemption level and a higher tax rate than those featured in most flat tax proposals.[54] The Moreland study ruled out demogrants for the same reason we do so here. The questions investigated by the two studies, however, are quite different. Moreland *assumed* the structure of an exemption (not fixed at subsistence) and one positive tax rate. The study thus ruled out progressive marginal rates.

Nevertheless, the Moreland results are suggestive in terms of rate graduation.   * * *   [T]he study indicated exemption levels well above subsistence were optimal, thus creating significant average rate progressivity. With the exemption level fixed at subsistence in our model, comparable average rate progressivity would require that the second bracket rate be higher than the first.

The second study, by Joel Slemrod, Shlomo Yitzhaki, Joram Maysher, and Michael Lundhelm,[56] was like ours in that it searched for the optimal two-bracket income tax. Unlike our model, however, theirs followed the normal optimal tax approach of including a demogrant. They determined the optimal level of demogrant, the two bracket rates, and the breakpoint, under several sets of assumptions. In all the cases they studied, they found that marginal rate progressivity was not optimal; in every case, the second bracket rate was lower than the first bracket rate. They explained the intuition behind their results: "The additional instrument of a second tax bracket allows the lower marginal tax rate on high-wage people to coax out enough additional labor supply so that the optimal demogrant is increased," to the benefit of lower-wage people.

Despite regressive marginal rates, they also found that in every case the optimal tax system featured average rate progressivity. The average tax rate for a taxpayer with income at the breakpoint is a function of the demogrant and the first bracket rate. As long as the demogrant pulls the average rate at the

---

54. Kemper W. Moreland, The Optimal Exemption, 45 Nat'l Tax J. 421, 429 (1992) ("Even under welfare functions only mildly averse to inequality, optimal tax rates and exemptions were near 45 percent and 16 thousand dollars respectively.").

56. *The Optimal Two-Bracket Linear Income Tax Model*, 53 J. PUB. ECON. 269, 270 (1994).

breakpoint below the second bracket rate, the average rate increases as income increases above the breakpoint.

These results are suggestive in terms of our study. The results reflect both regressive marginal rates and progressive average rates. In our model, by contrast, progressive average rates are possible (beyond the small amount of progression introduced by a subsistence exemption) only with progressive marginal rates. In moving from their model to ours, something has to give, and it is not clear whether it will be regressive marginal rates or progressive average rates. Intuition suggests, however, that the change in models might lead to progressive marginal rates. In their model, lowering the rate on high-wage individuals benefits low-wage individuals by increasing tax revenue, and thus increasing the demogrant. In our model, by contrast, the only way decreasing the tax on high-wage individuals can benefit low-wage individuals is if it raises additional revenue to finance a reduction in the marginal rate on low-wage earners. Thus, the justification for lowering the rate on high earners implies lowering the rate on low earners as well, suggesting that regressive marginal rates would not survive the elimination of the demogrant.

Do the Constraints of the Model Make Sense?

The difference in principle between the full utilitarianism of the standard optimal tax model and the limited utilitarianism of our model can be appreciated best by considering the tax system each model would produce if taxation had no labor disincentive effects. As explained earlier, the standard optimal tax model would result in a tax and transfer system that equalized all incomes—a 100% tax, with the resulting revenue distributed evenly throughout the population. Our model by contrast, assumes that there is to be no redistribution, but that taxation for nontransfer purposes should be based on utilitarian (or weighted utilitarian) principles. In the absence of labor disincentives, the result would be a zero bracket and a 100% bracket above it, with the breakpoint set at \$X, so that there was just enough income above the \$X level to finance government operations. A utilitarian would find the constraints of our model inconsistent. If we are willing to fund government operations on a utilitarian basis, by confiscating income with the lowest marginal utility, then why are we not also willing to redistribute income on a utilitarian basis?

Our answer is based more in experience than in logic. The resounding political rejection of demogrants, the longstanding political triumph of at least moderate marginal rate progressivity, and opinion polling rejecting demogrants but accepting graduated rates, all suggest that our model captures prevailing U.S. attitudes and beliefs. Americans reject pure (let alone weighted) utilitarianism. The concept that one has a right to the fruits of one's labors is strong enough to lead to rejection of the utilitarian idea that it is permissible to transfer income from *Richer* to *Poorer,* just because *Poorer's* utility gain will exceed *Richer's* utility loss. Redistributive transfers to those *below* the poverty level have some political support, but universal redistribution to those *above* poverty has almost none. Since demogrants result in redistribution to many above the poverty level, they are unacceptable.[65] On the other hand, most Americans accept a limited version of utilitarian taxation. It is considered reasonable to require *Richer* to contribute a higher percentage of his income than *Poorer* to fund nonredistributive costs of government, simply because *Richer* will feel the loss of a dollar less than *Poorer.* Thus, progressive marginal rates are acceptable.

        * * *

Sympathetically interpreted, U.S. beliefs and practices reflect a principled compromise between a rights-based ethic and utilitarianism. Redistribution (at least above poverty) is rejected because there is a distribution of earned income, *prior to taxation*, which has sufficient claim to legitimacy to override utilitarian claims for rearrangement of that distribution. My rights-based claim to my own earnings is stronger than any utilitarian claim of lower earners to my earnings. By contrast, there is no "natural" distribution among taxpayers of the cost of government. Redistribution disturbs a presumptively legitimate pre-existing state of nature, but there is no preexisting state of nature with respect to taxation to finance the nonredistributive costs of government. Since the nontransfer costs of government must be financed somehow, and since no allocation of those costs stands out as the natural (rights-based) allocation, we are free to allocate that burden according to utilitarian concerns (taking into account, of course, the disincentive effects of taxation). Absent a rights-based allocation of the burden, we might as well choose the allocation that causes the least total pain.

        * * *

We recognize that the political rejection of universal cash transfers does not mean the rejection of all forms of redistribution. Welfare, the earned income tax credit, Social Security, and the recently enacted "Hope Scholarship" tuition tax credit, are important examples of politically acceptable redistribution. Each is far from universal, however. Each program either is phased out as income increases, or is targeted to specific approved behavior and status, or both. * * *

---

65. * * * [E]ven a demogrant well below the poverty level can result in redistribution to those above the poverty level. Suppose, for example, that the poverty level was $10,000, the demogrant was $5,000, and the tax rate was 25%. Although the demogrant would be only one-half of subsistence, anyone earning less than $20,000 (twice subsistence) would be the beneficiary of redistribution. Until income reached $20,000, a person would receive more in demogrant than she paid in tax.

No existing redistributive program is based on the sort of purely utilitarian redistribution presumed acceptable by standard optimal tax models—taking from *Richer* to give to *Poorer* simply because *Poorer* will enjoy it more.

Our model is admittedly unrealistic in its assumption that no redistribution of any kind is politically acceptable. We believe, however, that it is closer to reality than the standard optimal tax assumption that there are no political constraints on universal transfers. * * *

The Results of the Simulation

The results of the simulation are summarized below. * * * Under the unweighted utilitarian social welfare function, the first tax rate above the $12,000 zero bracket is 11.8%, the second rate is 39%, and the breakpoint between the rates is at $18,240.[81] The effect of weighting the social welfare function (in favor of the welfare of lower ability workers) is to decrease the rate of tax on the lower income bracket and to increase the rate on the higher bracket. In fact, the lower rate drops to zero with even moderate weighting of the social welfare function. * * *

The results are not everything defenders of the current rate structure might hope for. The results do show that progressive marginal rates—with the second rate much higher than the first—may be optimal in the absence of demogrants. * * * On the other hand, the result of the unweighted utilitarian simulation bears a notable resemblance to the two-bracket structure of the Tax Reform Act of 1986, in terms of both rates and breakpoint. For a single taxpayer, the break between the 15% and 28% brackets was at $17,850 taxable income—or, taking into account the standard deduction ($3,000) and one personal exemption ($1,900 in 1987), $22,750 gross income.
* * *

Envy, or the Relative Income Hypothesis
Optimal Tax Studies of Utility Interdependence

The standard assumption in the optimal tax literature is that each person's utility depends only on her own levels of consumption and leisure; her well-being is unaffected by how her consumption compares with that of others in the society. As convenient as that assumption may be, it seems unrealistic. For most people, the utility of their own consumption is probably reduced by the knowledge that it compares unfavorably with the higher consumption of others. This response commonly is called envy. The term is concise and memorable, but its inevitable pejorative aspect—envy is, after all, one of the seven deadly

---

81. The rates are close to the bottom and top rates under the current income tax (15% and 39.6%), although the breakpoint is much lower. For single taxpayers whose taxable year begins in 1998, the 15% bracket ends at $25,350 taxable income and the 39.6% bracket begins at $278,450 taxable income.

sins—suggests the need for a more neutral label, such as utility interdependence or the relative income hypothesis.

How utility is affected by knowledge of the lower consumption of others is more ambiguous.   Bankman and Griffith suggest the response is sympathy—disutility from the knowledge of other's low consumption. That may be right, especially with respect to those near the bottom of the income distribution, but there may also be gloating (to use another loaded term)—utility from knowing one is better off than others.

* * *   Intuitively, the direction of the effect of including relative consumption in the analysis seems clear.   Since relative consumption has declining marginal utility, its inclusion should increase the tendency to pull everyone toward the middle of the income distribution. * * *

The Policy Significance of the Results
* * *

Should Envy "Count"?

To the limited extent envy supports graduated rates, the question arises whether the social welfare function should give any weight to envy, or whether it should be ignored as an anti-social preference. * * *

We are not convinced that "envy" should be excluded from the social welfare function.   Relabelled as "concern for relative well-being," or as a "positional externality," it is not clearly an anti-social preference. * * * Society creates expectations of affluence levels—for example, through advertising—and then, for many people, disappoints those expectations.   Those disappointed expectations sometimes are called envy, but they are not based on hostility, and they are not obviously anti-social. It often has been suggested that the poverty level should be defined partly or entirely in relative terms, but it does not follow that such a definition of poverty implicitly accuses the poor of harboring anti-social feelings. * * *

The Implications of the U.S.
Politics of Taxation for "Counting" Envy

* * * [T]ax policy based on envy is rejected even if envy is not considered anti-social. * * * [T]axation to ameliorate envy violates the rights of those taxed, even assuming envy is not anti-social.

Taxation as Insurance

The standard optimal tax analysis assumes people have perfect knowledge of their wage rate at the time they decide how much labor to supply. But suppose people do not have perfect information. * * *

One effect of wage uncertainty is to provide a new rationale for redistributive taxation. If all individuals face wage uncertainty, and all are risk-averse, they would favor redistributive taxation as insurance against low wages.   * * *   Unlike utilitarian redistribution, wage insurance is not antithetical to rights-based philosophies. * * * [T]he insurance rationale assumes risk-averse individuals would agree to taxation as wage insurance, while their wages were still uncertain. * * *

Implications of the Literature: Uncertainty About Uncertainty

* * * In order for tax as insurance to make sense, it is not necessary that there be wage uncertainty at the time the labor is performed; it is sufficient that there be wage uncertainty at the time the labor supply decision is made. In some cases, that may be long before the labor is performed. One may decide to become a lawyer, for example, on the basis of very limited knowledge—both of one's own ability, and of the market for legal services years or decades hence (and with even less knowledge, perhaps, of future wage rates in potential alternative careers). If entering law school committed one to working as a lawyer for 2,000 hours a year for 40 years, there would be only one labor supply decision for a lawyer, and it would be made in the face of massive uncertainty. Year by year, during her professional career, the lawyer might know her wage with precision, but at those times, there would be no labor supply decision to be made. This story is most persuasive with respect to careers requiring heavy early investments in education, and even for such careers, the story is an overstatement. Nevertheless, it contains a kernel of truth. Important long-term labor supply decisions are made at the education stage, when wage uncertainty is high. * * *

At this point, the case for graduated rates based on an insurance rationale is certainly not proven. * * * Still, based on what we do know, it is fair to say that consideration of wage uncertainty makes the optimality of graduated rates much more plausible than usually is supposed.

　　　* * *

If the Elasticity of Substitution Between Consumption and Leisure Declines as Income Increases

Optimal tax studies almost invariably assume the elasticity of substitution between consumption and leisure is the same for everyone. There is, of course, no reason to think that every person, or every demographic group, really views the trade-off between consumption and leisure in the same way. In fact, it is well-established that the elasticity of substitution for married women is significantly higher than for other groups.

Similarly, elasticities might vary systematically across the population by wage rates. If it could be established that low-wage individuals have high elasticities, and high-wage individuals have low elasticities, progressive marginal rates might well be optimal, even in a standard tax-and-transfer (demogrant) analysis. Low rates on low-wage individuals then would be attractive on both efficiency and distributional grounds. High marginal rates on high earners would be attractive—as always—on distributional grounds, and the usual efficiency objection would be muted if high earners responded little to high tax rates. * * *

There is simply not enough evidence that elasticity decreases as the wage rate increases, to serve as a foundation for tax policy. Until that evidence appears, this case for progression resembles the case based on insurance for wage uncertainty—theoretically interesting, but insufficiently based on established fact.
    * * *

Progressive Taxation in a Winner-Take-All Society

* * * Frank and Cook offer an unorthodox description of the modern American labor market as consisting largely of winner-take-all competitions, in which a few entrants win huge rewards, while most win little or nothing. [196] These competitions attract an inefficiently large number of entrants because each person decides whether to enter based solely on the expected payoff to herself, without taking into account the negative externality her entrance imposes on all other entrants (by reducing their chances of winning).[197] A progressive income tax could help correct this misallocation of effort. If winners in the winner-take-all competitions were taxed at higher average rates than those who work in other fields, relative expected payoffs would decrease, and the number of entrants would decline to a more efficient level.[198] * * *

[I]t is not clear how large a role winner-take-all competitions play in the overall U.S. labor market. Frank and Cook are convincing when they claim that winner-take-all accurately describes a few fields, such as sports and entertainment. They also make a strong case that in recent years, the markets for professional services, such as law and medicine, have developed more winner-take-all features. They do not prove, however, that the winner-take-all

---

196. Robert H. Frank & Philip J. Cook, The Winner-Take-All Society (1995).

197. Id. at 106-09. Frank and Cook note that this is a variation on the "tragedy of the commons." Id. at 108. As a highly stylized example, they describe a society in which there are only two career choices: being a potter for a certain income of $10,000, or entering a one-winner singing contest, in which the winner's reward increases with the number of entrants. Id. at 106-08. With 99 entrants, the winner's payoff is $1,999,000, and the addition of a 100th entrant would raise the payoff by $1,000, to $2 million. Id. at 108. A 100th person will enter (if she is risk-neutral) since her expected payoff of $20,000 (1/100 X $2 million) is twice a potter's wage, but that entry is inefficient. Id. It increases societal income by only $1,000, compared with the $10,000 she would have produced as a potter. Id.

198. Id. at 121-22. Consider the example described in note 197. A flat tax would not change the decision of the 100th entrant. If the tax rate was 20%, the expected after-tax reward to a singer ($16,000) still would be twice a potter's after-tax wages ($8,000). But if the potter was taxed at an average rate of 10%, while the winning singer was taxed at an average rate of 60%, the potter's $9,000 would exceed the singer's expected $8,000.

phenomenon is as pervasive as they claim. On the other hand, the entire economy need not be based on the winner-take-all model for the Frank and Cook analysis to lend support for progressive marginal rates near the top of the income distribution. Even if few earners are in winner-take-all fields, it may be that most extremely high earned incomes are in such fields. If so, high marginal rates on seven-figure incomes might prevent an inefficiently large number of entrants into winner-take-all competitions.

     * * *

Conclusion

     * * * This Article has shown that the implications of optimal tax theory for graduated rates are not so dire, after all. The standard version is based on several unrealistic assumptions—most importantly, that the political system is open to demogrants, that people do not care about relative levels of consumption, and that there is no wage uncertainty. Once those assumptions are corrected, the optimal income tax probably does have progressive marginal rates. The reports of the intellectual death of the graduated income tax are indeed exaggerated.

Notes and Questions

    62. Bankman and Griffith note that progressivity can be achieved by the use of a progressive rate structure, but can also be achieved even if the rate structure is flat or regressive. Indeed, they note that optimal tax models usually have the highest marginal rates at low income levels. How can a generally progressive tax system be achieved by a tax system with a regressive rate structure?

    63. Bankman and Griffith assert that the case for proportionality may depends less on logic than on "the concept of 'prominence'." What is meant by "prominence" in this context?

    64. Bankman and Griffith briefly consider entitlement theories—income presumptively belongs to the person who earns it—but ultimately prefer "welfarist" theories. The best known welfarist theory is utilitarianism, traditionally described as "the greatest good for the greatest number," or, in drier academic language, "the unweighted sum of the utilities of its individual members." Why do Bankman and Griffith prefer welfarist theories over entitlement theories?

    65. Bankman and Griffith seek welfarism, but emphasize that efficiency is a part of welfare. If we ignore efficiency, welfare would be maximized by "a 100% marginal rate on all income and a uniform cash grant, thus ensuring

equal consumption for all." The problem, of course, is that complete egalitarianism would make even the bottom members of society worse off, because the destruction of incentive would cripple the society's overall output. The pie would be equally divided, but the pie would be very small. The former Soviet Union, though it never implemented pure Communism, demonstrated the economic problems that accompany the substantial destruction of personal economic incentive.

66. Bankman and Griffith describe three forms of welfarism—utilitarianism, weighted utility theories, and Rawls' leximin.
   Utilitarianism seeks to maximize total utility. An ideal tax system would maximize the *sum* of utility for all individuals.
   Weighted utility theories value the utility of some—typically, those at the bottom—more than the utility of others. Thus, we might try to maximize the *product* of the utilities of the individual members. In such a system, doubling John Doe's utility would justify halving the utility of Bill Gates—and think how many poor people's utility could be doubled by halving that of Gates.
   The leximin takes account of the welfare of only the person at the bottom. An improvement in that person's welfare justifies any negative impact on the welfare of those above.
   Which is most attractive? Which is most likely to guide tax policy?

67. Under optimal tax analysis, the optimum tax system couples some form of demogrant with marginal rates that *decline* with income. What accounts for this counterintuitive result?

68. A key assumption in optimal tax analysis is the trade-off between income (or consumption) and leisure. Mirrlees assumed "elasticity of substitution" of 1.0, meaning that an individual would be equally satisfied by doubling leisure and halving income. Bankman and Griffith argue that people are less inclined to substitute, suggesting an elasticity of substitution of 0.5, and conclude that this supports higher marginal rates and a larger demongrant. Why might this be so?

69. While Bankman and Griffith argue for higher rates than Mirrlees, they agree that the optimal marginal rate structure should decline as income increase. Yet they argue that their analysis supports a much greater degree of income redistribution than the proportional income tax system favored by Blum and Kalven. How are these positions reconciled?

70. Professors Zelenak and Moreland explore whether optimal tax analysis can support progressive marginal rates. This is a tall order, given that they acknowledge the theoretical correctness of the conclusion (shared by both Mirrlees and Bankman and Griffith) that *marginal* rates should fall with income (even as *average* rates increase). They even acknowledge that the marginal rate of tax on the highest earner should be zero. (Why?)

71. Zelenak and Moreland note that progressive marginal rates allow for much greater flexibility in implementing policy choices than does the combination of flat (or declining) rates with a demogrant. Why?

72. The key observation of Zelenak and Moreland is not theoretical but practical—namely, that demogrants are not politically feasible in the United States. Do you agree, given the political feasibility of non-tax welfare programs as well as tax provisions such as the earned income credit?

73. Once they rule out demogrants on political grounds, Zelenak and Moreland observe that significant progressivity in average rates will require significant progressivity in marginal rates. They argue that while demogrants are not politically feasible because they violate the rights-based notion that the earner is presumptively entitled to his earnings, progressive rates are politically feasible because "there is no preexisting state of nature with respect to taxation to finance the nonredistributive costs of government."

74. Remarkably, Zelenak and Moreland conclude that optimal tax analysis supports a progressive rate structure that fairly closely resembles the tax structure adopted in the Tax Reform Act of 1986.

75. The importance of optimal tax theory is not limited to the progressivity debate. For example, Professor Eric Zolt takes issue with the notion that efficiency means that all Haig-Simons income should be subjected to equal, or neutral, taxation. Optimal tax theory may suggest that capital gains and income from second earners (notably, married women) should be taxed at lower rates than those applied to other types of income.[v]

With respect to affording favorable tax treatment to married women, recall Professor McCaffery's article from Chapter Three (page 142).

76. What effect would taking account of "envy" have on the tax structure?

---

v. Eric M. Zolt, *The Uneasy Case for Uniform Taxation*, 16 VA. TAX REV. 39 (1996).

77. In what sense do progressive tax rates perform an "insurance" function?

The "winner-take-all" economy

78. The term "winner-take-all" has emerged as descriptive of economic pursuits in which very small differences in talent or luck are likely to result in enormous differences in income.

Clearly, winner-take-all does not describe the entire economy. If *A* and *B* each devotes the same level of labor and other resources to potato farming, but *A* is a somewhat more efficient farmer than *B*, perhaps *A*'s income will be ten percent higher. Similarly, if *C* and *D* are both insurance salesmen who work the same amount, but *C* is a bit better salesman, *C*'s income will be somewhat higher.

Contrast two football players, each of whom hopes to play in the National Football League. Both are large, strong, skilled, and healthy—but *E* can run five percent faster than *F*. It is not unlikely that *E* will earn $5 million per year playing football, while *F* is unable to play football professionally at all.

Similarly, consider the entertainment industry. *G* and *H* are both excellent actresses, but *G* a bit better—or perhaps just luckier in getting the famous "break." It is entirely possible that *G* will make $10 million per movie, while *H* will act in dinner theaters and wait tables to supplement her income.

79. How does winner-take-all analysis interplay with optimal tax theory? As all writers agree, optimal tax theory suggests that efficiency is improved by regressive *marginal* tax rates—work will be little deterred, because more income will place the taxpayer in a *lower* tax bracket. Most models applying this theory would couple the regressive rate structure with a demogrant, which, as Bankman and Griffith argue, will assure progressive *average* rates.

Zelenak and Moreland do not examine this issue in detail, but suggest (see footnote 197 and accompanying text of their excerpt) that a progressive rate structure is more likely to be efficient in those parts of the economy that are characterized by a winner-take-all market.

80. In a detailed and excellent presentation of the argument, Professors Martin McMahon and Alice Abreu argue that winner-take-all is very descriptive of those at the very top of the income pile—not just entertainers and sports figures, but the top figures in business (whose annual income may exceed $100 million). The important thing, Martin and Abreu assert, is to win—to get the massive pay check, and the glory and recognition that accompany it, rather than being left out in the cold. Thus, "winning" is much more important than just how big the big pay check is, or—for our purposes—whether the marginal

rate structure at the very top is flat or sharply progressive.   (Does anyone really think that a professional athlete will slacken his efforts, and risk being "cut," because of high marginal tax rates?)

It follows that we should have a very different tax structure, and a very different tax analysis, for those at the very top:

Tax policy has failed to consider the ways in which the distribution of income within the top quintile should affect the distribution of the tax burden. Congress, like most policy analysts, apparently has assumed that those within the top quintile are just slightly different from one another, or that they differ from one another only incrementally. But the data show that families in the top quintile but below the 95th percentile have a lot more in common with one another and with families in the third and fourth quintiles than with families in the top 5th percentile, and especially with families in the top 1%. Families in the top 1% are truly in a class of their own. These data, and the winner-take-all distribution it reveals, have significant implications for tax policy and tax system design.

Acknowledging the existence, expansion and unique operation of winner-take-all markets can serve to illuminate various aspects of tax policy. For instance, if people play to win, then taxing the second half of the winnings more steeply than the first half should not decrease the incentive to play the game. Put another way, the existence of winner-take-all markets presents a serious challenge to the classical argument that progressive taxation is inefficient because it distorts the decision to create additional income or to consume at the margin, and so entails trading efficiency for equity. In a winner-take-all market, progressive taxation may be not only efficient, it may be nearly optimal; it may raise revenue from people whose incentive to make more money is nearly unaffected by the existence of the tax.

The absence of a linear relationship between effort, ability, and compensation in winner-take-all markets lends special force to arguments that rest on the diminishing marginal utility of money. Even a model that makes conservative assumptions about the rate at which the marginal utility of money declines shows that in winner-take-all markets progressive taxation results in greater total private utility after taxes than proportional taxation.   In a society dominated by winner-take-all markets, then, we do not need to trade equity for efficiency. Progressive income taxation can provide both.[w]

81. Professors McMahon and Abreu emphasize the growing importance of this segment of the economy: "The winner-take-all phenomenon, long the hallmark of the sports and entertainment markets, has spread throughout the U.S. economy over the last two decades."[x]

The Congressional Budget Office report excerpted in Chapter One (page 37) provides data consistent with the spread of winner-take-all markets. The CBO notes the rapid increase of income of top earners in both absolute and relative terms:

> Average household income before taxes grew in real terms by nearly one-third between 1979 and 1997, but that growth was shared unevenly across the income distribution. * * * [A]verage income in 1997 dollars for the top 1 percent of households more than doubled, rising from $420,000 in 1979 to more than $1 million in 1997.
>
> The uneven gains in income generated sharp changes in the shares of pretax income. * * * Households in the top 1 percent saw their share of income rise by more than two-thirds, growing from 9 percent [in 1979] to nearly 16 percent [in 1997].[y]

82. Do you agree that the winner-take-all phenomenon is important and growing? If so, do you think it justifies sharply progressive rates at the very top end of the income range (for example, annual income in excess of $1 million)?

---

w. Martin J. McMahon, Jr. & Alice G. Abreu, *Winner-Take-All Markets: Easing the Case for Progressive Taxation,* 4 FLA. TAX REV. 1, 9-11 (1998).

x. *Id.* at 3.

y. CONGRESSIONAL BUDGET OFFICE, EFFECTIVE FEDERAL TAX RATES, 1979-1997, at 6-7 (2001).

CHAPTER FIVE

TAXING FAMILIES

We expect all persons to make all important decisions in life in light of their tax effect. For the tax-minded young man or woman, with a substantial income, the Code adds to the attractiveness of a prospective spouse without taxable income, and detracts from one with it. Thus the provisions may have an income-leveling effect. But we have no data showing that as yet they operate in that manner. Love and marriage defy economic analysis.[a]

A. HISTORY OF THE TAXING UNIT

This subchapter tells the story of how we got to the present system, which imposes a tax penalty on some marriages and gives a tax reward to others.

The initial tax policy choice is whether the taxpaying unit should consist of an individual or of a family (however defined). At the outset, the federal income tax was based on the individual as the taxpaying unit, with some recognition of the family unit through allowance of dependency exemptions. In the 1930 *Lucas v. Earl* decision, the Supreme Court, speaking through Justice Holmes, refused to give income tax effect to a contract between husband and wife, valid under state law, providing for income splitting between them:

> [T]his case is not to be decided by attenuated subtleties. It turns on the import and reasonable construction of the taxing act. There is no doubt that the statute could tax salaries to those who earned them and provide that the tax could not be escaped by anticipatory arrangements and contracts however skillfully devised to prevent the salary when paid from vesting even for a second in the man who earned it.[b]

It was not immediately clear, however, how the tax applied in states that had some form of community property for married couples, and thus provided for income splitting between spouses by operation of law, rather than by private contract. The answer came later in the same year, with the Supreme Court's decision in *Poe v. Seaborn*. As is evident from the first excerpt below, the *Poe* Court seemed to base its decision on one of the "attenuated subtleties" rejected in *Lucas v. Earl*. Anticipatory arrangements devised by state legislators would be honored when they prevented a salary from vesting in the

---

a. Judge Philip Nichols, Jr. *in* Mapes v. United States, 576 F.2d 896, 898 (Ct. Cl. 1978).

b. Lucas v. Earl, 281 U.S. 111, 114-15 (1930).

spouse who earned it.

The combination of *Lucas v. Earl* and *Poe v. Seaborn* thus disallowed income splitting in the large majority of states following common law property rules, while automatically allowing it in community property states. This distinction was problematic in policy terms, and ultimately proved untenable politically. The issue is important because of the progressive rate structure: As a general rule, $100,000 of income is taxed more heavily than are two incomes of $50,000 each. The excerpt from the Joint Tax Committee Staff Report summarizes the evolution of the taxation of individuals and couples since *Poe v. Seaborn*. The Report then discusses the impossibility of reconciling three basic policy preferences.

Congress addressed the problem of "marriage penalties" in 2001 (and to a lesser degree in 2003), making the law more marriage-friendly. It is not clear that married couples as a whole deserved help. As the brief excerpt from Messrs. Feenberg and Rosen indicates, before 2001 the average tax penalty was modest and nearly as many married couples were benefitted by marriage as were penalized. What is clear is not that married couples were systematically penalized, but that marriage was anything but tax neutral—almost all married couples paid a different amount than the same people would have paid if living together without marriage. The final excerpt, from the House Ways and Means Committee report leading up to the 2001 legislation, explains the reasoning behind that legislation.

POE v. SEABORN

282 U.S. 101, 108-11, 113, 116-17 (1930)

MR. JUSTICE ROBERTS delivered the opinion of the Court.

Seaborn and his wife, citizens and residents of the State of Washington, made for the year 1927 separate income tax returns as permitted by the Revenue Act of 1926.

During and prior to 1927 they accumulated property comprising real estate, stocks, bonds and other personal property. While the real estate stood in his name alone, it is undisputed that all of the property real and personal constituted community property and that neither owned any separate property or had any separate income.

The income comprised Seaborn's salary, interest on bank deposits and on bonds, dividends, and profits on sales of real and personal property. He and his wife each returned one-half the total community income as gross income and each deducted one-half of the community expenses to arrive at the net income returned.

The Commissioner of Internal Revenue determined that all of the income should have been reported in the husband's return, and made an additional assessment against him. Seaborn paid under protest, claimed a refund, and on its rejection, brought this suit.

    * * *

The case requires us to construe sections 210(a) and 211(a) of the Revenue Act of 1926, and apply them, as construed, to the interests of husband and wife in community property under the law of Washington. These sections lay a tax upon the net income of every individual.[1] The Act goes no farther, and furnishes no other standard or definition of what constitutes an individual's income. The use of the word "of" denotes ownership. It would be a strained construction, which, in the absence of further definition by Congress, should impute a broader significance to the phrase.

The Commissioner concedes that the answer to the question involved in the cause must be found in the provisions of the law of the State, as to a wife's ownership of or interest in community property. What, then, is the law of Washington as to the ownership of community property and of community income, including the earnings of the husband's and wife's labor?

The answer is found in the statutes of the State, and the decisions interpreting them.

* * *

Without further extending this opinion it must suffice to say that it is clear the wife has, in Washington, a vested property right in the community property, equal with that of her husband; and in the income of the community, including salaries or wages of either husband or wife, or both. * * *

The taxpayer contends that if the test of taxability under Sections 210 and 211 is ownership, it is clear that income of community property is owned by the community and that husband and wife have each a present vested one-half interest therein.

The Commissioner contends, however, that we are here concerned not with mere names, nor even with mere technical legal titles; that calling the wife's interest vested is nothing to the purpose, because the husband has such broad powers of control and alienation, that while the community lasts, he is essentially the owner of the whole community property, and ought so to be considered for the purposes of Sections 210 and 211. * * *

We are of opinion that under the law of Washington the entire property and income of the community can no more be said to be that of the husband, than it could rightly be termed that of the wife.

We should be content to rest our decision on these considerations. Both parties have, however, relied on executive construction and the history of the income tax legislation as supporting their respective views. We shall, therefore, deal with these matters.

* * *

The Commissioner urges that we have, in [principle], decided the instant question in favor of the Government. He relies on *United States v. Robbins*, 269 U.S. 315; *Corliss v. Bowers*, 281 U.S. 376, and *Lucas v. Earl*, 281 U.S. 111.

---

1. The language has been the same in each act since that of February 24, 1919, 40 Stat. 1057.

In the *Robbins* case, we found that the law of California, as construed by her own courts, gave the wife a mere expectancy and that the property rights of the husband during the life of the community were so complete that he was in fact the owner. * * *

The *Corliss* case raised no issue as to the intent of Congress, but as to its power. We held that where a donor retains the power at any time to revest himself with the principal of the gift, Congress may declare that he still owns the income. While he has technically parted with title, yet he in fact retains ownership, and all its incidents. But here the husband never has ownership. That is in the community at the moment of acquisition.

In the *Earl* case a husband and wife contracted that any property they had or might thereafter acquire in any way, either by earnings (including salaries, fees, etc.), or any rights by contract or otherwise, "shall be treated and considered and hereby is declared to be received, held, taken, and owned by us as joint tenants . . ." We held that, assuming the validity of the contract under local law, it still remained true that the husband's professional fees, earned in years subsequent to the date of the contract, were his individual income, "derived from salaries, wages, or compensation for personal service," under * * * the Revenue Act of 1918. The very assignment in that case was bottomed on the fact that the earnings would be the husband's property, else there would have been nothing on which it could operate. That case presents quite a different question from this, because here, by law, the earnings are never the property of the husband, but that of the community.

* * *

INCOME TAX TREATMENT
OF MARRIED COUPLES AND SINGLE PERSONS
Staff of the Joint Committee on Taxation
Pages J6-J8 (1980)

After *Lucas v. Earl* and *Poe v. Seaborn* were decided, Congress and the Department of the Treasury made several attempts to change the taxation of married couples. The provisions considered and rejected during the 1930s and early 1940s included (1) mandatory joint returns for all married couples; (2) the taxation of community income to the spouse exercising management and control of such income; and (3) mandatory joint returns with a special allowance for the earned income of the husband or wife.

Through 1947, community property spouses continued to benefit from the splitting of income on separate returns. In the early years, however, this advantage over common law spouses was minimized by the relatively low tax rates. For those subject to tax during the years 1913 to 1915, the lowest tax rate was one percent, and it applied to the first $20,000 of taxable income. From 1919 until 1939, the lowest rate ranged from 1.5 to 4 percent and was applicable to the first $4,000 of income. In addition, only a small portion of the population was required to file tax returns because of the relatively high levels of exempt income.[20]

As the tax rates increased, particularly during World War II, the income tax advantage enjoyed by community property spouses increased. Not surprisingly, common law States began to adopt community property laws so that the benefits of income-splitting could be realized by their married residents.[21]

1948–1969

The debate on the taxation of married persons culminated with the enactment of the Revenue Act of 1948. Under the 1948 Act, married couples who filed jointly were in effect taxed as two single persons each reporting one-half the couple's aggregate income. This was achieved by taking half of the taxable income shown on the joint return, determining the tax thereon, and multiplying the result by two. The splitting of all taxable income between a husband and wife was available for all married persons filing jointly. In effect, all married couples were given the benefit which previously had been restricted to community property States.

The Finance Committee Report summarized the intended effects of the income-splitting provisions as follows:

> Adoption of these income-splitting provisions will produce substantial geographical equalization in the impact of the tax on individual incomes. The impetuous enactment of community-property legislation by States that have long used the common law will be forestalled. The incentive for married couples in common-law States to attempt the reduction of their taxes by the division of their income through such devices as trusts, joint tenancies, and family partnerships will be reduced materially. Administrative difficulties stemming from the use of such devices will be diminished, and there

---

20. The pre-World War II portion of the civilian labor force filing Federal income tax returns was as follows:

Year	Total Federal income tax returns as percentage of civilian labor force
1915	0.9
1920	17.6
1925	9.2
1930	7.9
1935	8.9
1940	26.4

Source: *1941 Statistics of Income*, Table 14, p. 208; *Historical Statistics of the U.S.*, Series D 1-10, p. 126.

21. By 1948, Oregon, Nebraska, Michigan, and Oklahoma had adopted community property laws. Pennsylvania's attempt to adopt community property laws was held unconstitutional by that State's highest court.

will be less need for meticulous legislation on the income-tax treatment of trusts and family partnerships.[22] * * *

The 1948 Act was successful in stopping the adoption of community property laws by the common law States. In fact, Nebraska, Michigan, Oklahoma, and Oregon repealed their recently adopted community property laws. To this day, however, community property laws are in effect in Arizona, California, Idaho, Louisiana, Nevada, New Mexico, Texas, and Washington.

The 1948 Act in effect created two rates of income taxation, one applicable to married couples filing jointly and one applicable to all other individual taxpayers. As a result of income-splitting, one-earner married couples paid a much smaller tax than a single taxpayer with the same amount of taxable income.

In 1951, a third set of tax rates was enacted for "heads of households," single taxpayers who maintain households for certain relatives. The new rates applicable to heads of households were calculated to give heads of households approximately one-half of the benefits of income-splitting accorded married couples.

The head of household provisions were extended in the Internal Revenue Code of 1954 to include taxpayers who met certain support requirements with respect to their mother or father, even though the parents did not live in the taxpayer's house. The 1954 Code also extended the full income-splitting benefits enjoyed by married couples to a surviving spouse for 2 years after the death of the other spouse.

1969–present

The last major revision in the comparative income tax treatment of married and single individuals occurred in 1969. Since the enactment of income splitting for married couples in 1948, single persons generally had paid significantly higher taxes than married couples at the same income levels. For example, in 1969, at some income levels a single person's income tax liability was as much as 42.1 percent higher than the income tax liability of a married couple filing a joint return with the same amount of taxable income. In 1969, Congress concluded that, while some difference between the rate of tax paid by single persons and married couples filing jointly was appropriate to reflect the additional living expenses of married taxpayers, the then current differential of as much as 42 percent could not be justified on that basis.

Accordingly, the Tax Reform Act of 1969 included a new rate schedule for single persons effective in 1971. The new rate schedule was designed to impose on middle-income single persons tax liabilities no more than 20 percent above those for married couples.

Another new rate schedule, halfway between the new rate schedule for single persons and the rate schedule for married couples, was enacted in 1969 for heads-of-households. The former rate schedule for single persons was

---

22. S. Rep. No. 1013, 80th Cong., 2d Sess. 25 (1948).

retained for married persons filing separate returns because, if each spouse were permitted to use the new tax rate schedule for single persons, many couples, especially those in community property States, could arrange their affairs and income in such a way that their combined tax would be less than that on a joint return.

With the new rate schedule for single persons, many married couples filing a joint return paid more tax than two single persons with the same total income. This was a necessary result of changing the income-splitting relationship between single and joint returns. At the time, the marriage penalty was justified on the grounds that, although a married couple has greater living expenses than a single person and hence should pay less tax, the couple's living expenses are likely to be less than those of two single persons and, therefore, the couple's tax should be higher than that of two single persons.

* * *

Marriage neutrality versus equal taxation of couples with equal incomes

Any system of taxing married couples requires making a choice among three different ideas of tax equity. One principle is that the tax system should be "marriage neutral"; that is, the tax burden of a married couple should be exactly equal to the combined tax burden of two single persons one of whom has the same income as the husband and the other of whom has the same income as the wife. A second principle of equity is that, because married couples frequently consume as a unit, couples with the same income should pay the same amount of tax regardless of how the income is divided between them. (This second concept of equity should apply equally well to other tax units which may consume jointly, such as the extended family or the household, defined as all people living together under one roof.) A third concept of equity is that the tax should be progressive; that is, as income rises, the tax burden should rise as a percentage of income.

Unhappily, these three concepts of equity are mutually inconsistent. A tax system can generally have any two of them, but not all three. The current tax system specifies the married couple as the tax unit so that couples with the same income pay the same tax, but it thereby foregoes marriage neutrality. A system of mandatory separate filing for married couples would sacrifice the concept of "equal taxation of couples with equal incomes" for the principle of "marriage neutrality" unless it were to forego progressivity. It should be noted, however, that there is an exception to this rule if refundable credits are permissible. A system with a flat tax rate and a per taxpayer refundable credit would have marriage neutrality, equal taxation of couples with equal incomes and some limited progressivity.

There is no right or wrong answer to the question of whether "equal taxation of couples with equal incomes" is a better principle than "marriage neutrality." (This discussion assumes that the dilemma cannot be resolved by moving to a proportional or flat-rate tax system.)

Those who hold "marriage neutrality" to be more important argue that tax policy discourages marriage and encourages "living in sin," lowering society's standard of morality. Also, they argue that it is simply unfair to impose a "marriage tax" even if the tax does not actually deter anyone from marrying.

Those who favor the principle of equal taxation of couples with equal incomes argue that, as long as most couples pool their income and consume as a unit, two couples with $20,000 of income are equally well off regardless of whether their income is divided $10,000-$10,000 or $15,000-$5,000. Thus, it is argued, they should pay the same tax, as they do under present law. A marriage-neutral system with progressive rates would involve a larger combined tax on the couple with the unequal income division.

An advocate of marriage neutrality could respond that the relevant comparison is not between a two-earner couple where the spouses have equal incomes and a two-earner couple with an unequal income division, but rather between a two-earner couple and a one-earner couple with the same total income. Here, the case for equal taxation of the two couples may be weaker, because the non-earner in the one-earner couple benefits from more time which may be used for leisure, unpaid work inside the home, child care, and other activities. It could, of course, be argued in response that the "leisure" of the non-earner may in fact consist of necessary jobhunting or child care, in which case the one-earner couple may not have more ability to pay income tax than the two-earner couple with the same income.

The attractiveness of the principle of equal taxation of couples with equal incomes depends on the extent to which married couples actually pool their incomes and single persons do not. In a society where many marriages last no longer than the typical single person's romance, or where married couples frequently live apart and single persons frequently live together, marriage neutrality would clearly be the better principle. However, as long as differences in lifestyle between married couples and single persons are pronounced, the issue is less clear.

Census data show that 1.3 million households in 1979 were shared by two unrelated adults of the opposite sex. Three-fourths of these "unmarried couples" had no children. Half had never been married before, nearly a third had been divorced, and the remainder were either widowed or married to someone else. The number of "unmarried couples" has grown 157 percent since 1970. The Census report, however, concludes:

> Despite the spectacular nature of the recent increase in this unmarried-couple living arrangement, the 2.7 million "partners" in these 1.3 million households represent a very small portion of all persons in "couple" situations. In 1979, there were an estimated 96.5 million men and women who were married and living with a spouse. Thus, the partners in unmarried couples represented only about 3 percent of all persons among couples living together in 1979.

The continuing predominance of marriage among couples suggests that "equal taxation of married couples with equal incomes" is still an important concept for many people.

The actual size of the marriage bonus or penalty depends on the combined effect of all the provisions of the tax law which treat the married couple as something other than two distinct individuals. However, the most important factors are the tax rate schedules and the zero bracket amount.[c] * * *

RECENT DEVELOPMENTS IN THE MARRIAGE TAX
Daniel R. Feenberg[*] & Harvey S. Rosen[**]
48 National Tax Journal 91, 91-95, 99-101 (1995)

Introduction

President Clinton's changes in the personal income tax, embodied in the Omnibus Budget Reconciliation Act of 1993 (OBRA 93), will affect the tax liabilities of many Americans. The changes at the two extremes of the income distribution are particularly important. At the high end, marginal tax rates have been increased substantially. At the low end, there has been a major expansion of the earned income tax credit. * * * One issue that has received relatively little analysis is the impact of the new law on the tax consequences of marriage. * * *

We predict that 52 percent of American couples will pay an annual average marriage tax of about $1,244, and 38 percent will receive an average subsidy of about $1,399. Relative to the old law, there is not much of a change in the aggregate marriage tax. But the aggregate figures mask important differences for certain income groups. Specifically, some low-income families will face much higher marriage taxes than before. In this way, they are similar to their counter-parts at the opposite end of the income scale, for some of whom the tax on being married will increase by thousands of dollars. * * *

Background

* * *

Earned Income Tax Credit

The * * * earned income tax credit (EITC) * * * is a percentage of household earnings that depends on the number of children in the family. It ranges from 7.65 percent if there are no children to 30.0 percent if there are two or more. The credit is applied to each dollar of earnings in a phase-in range, reaching a maximum at the end of this range. Then it is implicitly taxed away over a phase-out range. Importantly, if the individual's tax

---

c. The "zero bracket amount," or ZEBRA, was abandoned in the Tax Reform Act of 1986, when Congress returned to the terminology "standard deduction." The present form of the standard deduction has the same effect as the ZEBRA, in that it exempts from taxation the same amount of income for every taxpayer of a given status (principally marital or family status) who does not itemize deductions. See section 63. (Ed.)

*. At the time of original publication, National Bureau of Economic Research.

**. At time of original publication, Department of Economics, Princeton University.

liability is less than the EITC, the difference is refunded.

The key point in the marriage tax context is that on a joint return, eligibility for the EITC is based on the couple's joint earnings. Hence, an unmarried individual with a child may lose part or all of the credit upon marriage.[d]

Standard Deduction

The standard deduction allowed on each type of return is recorded in the bottom of Table 1. Note that the standard deduction associated with two single returns or two head-of-household returns exceeds the standard deduction on a joint return. These differences tend to create a penalty for marrying, *ceteris paribus*.

* * *

Conclusion

The changes in the rate schedules and EITC embodied in the new tax law have implications for the tax consequences of marriage. On average, the income tax now imposes a mild tax on marriage of $124, while under the previous law there was a small subsidy of $143. However, the small average figure conceals the fact that some families will be paying substantial taxes or receiving substantial subsidies for being married. In 1994, about 52 percent of U.S. families will pay an average marriage tax of $1,244. This corresponds to a total of about $33 billion. At the same time, about 38 percent of the families will receive a marriage subsidy averaging $1,399 per family; the aggregate amount will be about $27 billion.

Our results lead naturally to the question of whether the new marriage tax will affect people's behavior. As we showed earlier, at least for some low-income couples, the size of the marriage tax is now quite extraordinary, amounting to over 18 percent of total income. An interesting topic for future research will be to see if the incidence of joint filing diminishes in this group. In this context, it is important to note that a reduction in joint filing is not the same thing as a reduction in marriage. It is costly and difficult for the Internal Revenue Service to learn about taxpayers' family situations. One possible response to huge marriage taxes may be that taxpayers will simply not reveal to the IRS that they are married.

---

d. While it continues to be true that marriage can reduce or eliminate the EITC, this form of "marriage tax penalty" was reduced by Congress in 2001. The EITC is discussed in more detail in Chapter Eleven, Subchapter E.

MARRIAGE PENALTY AND FAMILY
TAX RELIEF ACT OF 2001
House Report No. 107-29
Pages 6-7 (2001)

Standard Deduction Marriage Tax
Penalty Relief

Present Law

Marriage tax penalty

A married couple generally is treated as one tax unit that must pay tax on the couple's total taxable income. Although married couples may elect to file separate returns, the rate schedules and other provisions of the Federal tax laws are structured so that filing separate returns usually results in a higher tax than filing a joint return. Other rate schedules apply to single persons and to single heads of households.

A "marriage penalty" exists when the combined tax liability of a married couple filing a joint return is greater than the sum of the tax liabilities of each individual computed as if they were not married. A "marriage bonus" exists when the combined tax liability of a married couple filing a joint return is less than the sum of the tax liabilities of each individual computed as if they were not married.

Basic standard deduction

Taxpayers who do not itemize deductions may choose the basic standard deduction, which is subtracted from adjusted gross income ("AGI") in arriving at taxable income. The size of the basic standard deduction varies according to filing status and is indexed for inflation. * * *

For 2001, the basic standard deduction amount for single filers is 60 percent of the basic standard deduction amount for married couples filing joint returns. Thus, two unmarried individuals have standard deductions whose sum exceeds the standard deduction for a married couple filing a joint return.

Reasons for Change

The Committee is concerned about the inequity that arises when two working single individuals marry and experience a tax increase solely by reason of their marriage. Any attempt to address the marriage tax penalty involves the balancing of several competing principles, including equal tax treatment of married couples with equal incomes, the determination of equitable relative tax burdens of single individuals and married couples with equal incomes, and the goal of simplicity in compliance and administration. The Committee believes that an increase in the standard deduction for married couples filing a joint return in conjunction with the other provisions of the bill is a responsible reduction of a marriage tax penalty. The increase in the standard deduction provides tax relief to approximately 23 million married couples filing joint returns in 2002. Further, approximately 2 million couples who currently itemize their deductions will realize the simplification benefits of using the larger basic standard deduction in 2002.

Explanation of Provision

The provision increases the basic standard deduction for a married couple filing a joint return to twice the basic standard deduction for an unmarried individual filing a single return. The basic standard deduction for a married taxpayer filing separately continues to equal one-half of the basic standard deduction for a married couple filing jointly; thus, the basic standard deduction for unmarried individuals filing a single return and for married [individuals] filing separately is the same.

* * *

Expansion of the 15-Percent Rate Bracket for Married Couples Filing Joint Returns

Present Law

In general

Under the Federal individual income tax system, an individual who is a citizen or resident of the United States generally is subject to tax on worldwide taxable income. Taxable income is total gross income less certain exclusions, exemptions, and deductions. An individual may claim either a standard deduction or itemized deductions.

* * *

Regular income tax liability

Regular income tax liability is determined by applying the regular income tax rate schedules (or tax tables) to the individual's taxable income and then is reduced by any applicable tax credits. The regular income tax rate schedules are divided into several ranges of income, known as income brackets, and the marginal tax rate increases as the individual's income increases. The income bracket amounts are adjusted annually for inflation. Separate rate schedules apply based on filing status: single individuals (other than heads of households and surviving spouses), heads of households, married individuals filing joint returns (including surviving spouses), married individuals filing separate returns, and estates and trusts. Lower rates may apply to capital gains.

For 2001, the regular income tax rate * * * bracket breakpoints for single individuals are approximately 60 percent of the rate bracket breakpoints for married couples filing joint returns.[2] The rate bracket breakpoints for married individuals filing separate returns are exactly one-half of the rate brackets for married individuals filing joint returns. * * *

Explanation of Provision

Increase in 15-percent regular income tax bracket

The provision increases the size of the 15-percent regular income tax rate bracket for a married couple filing a joint return to twice the size of the

---

2. The rate bracket breakpoint for the 39.6 percent marginal rate is the same for single individuals and married couples filing joint returns. [Beginning in 2003, the highest marginal rate under section 1 is 35%. The breakpoint for entry to this bracket continues to be the same for singles and for married couples filing jointly. (Ed.)]

corresponding rate bracket for an unmarried individual filing a single return. This increase is phased * * * in over six years. * * *

Notes and Questions

1. Taxpayers have the option of itemizing deductions or claiming the standard deduction. When first implemented, the standard deduction was a simplification measure, which offered taxpayers the choice of keeping records to itemize deductions, or claiming a "standard" figure that was a rough approximation of a low range of itemized deductions that might be expected for such a taxpayer. Use of the standardized deduction simplified life for both taxpayers and the Internal Revenue Service, while leaving taxpayers the option of keeping detailed records and itemizing deductions (or of keeping the detailed records, and deciding at the time of preparing the return whether to itemize). As a realistic approximation of itemized deductions that might have been expected, the standard deduction increased with income.

The philosophy behind the standard deduction has changed radically, and the most important indication of this changed philosophy is that, under the Tax Reform Act of 1986, standard deductions became flat amounts, regardless of income. For large numbers of taxpayers, particularly lower-income taxpayers, the standard deduction significantly exceeds the itemized deductions that the taxpayers would have been entitled to claim. Rather than offering a realistic alternative to itemized deductions, the standard deduction has become an integral part of the progressive rate structure. When combined with personal and dependency exemptions, the standard deduction results in protecting individuals and families near the poverty line from any income tax liability. The standard deduction for singles was set at approximately 60 percent of the standard deduction for a married couple filing a joint return. Singles who qualified as heads of household were allowed a standard deduction about 88 percent as large as that allowed married couples filing jointly; married individuals filing separately were allowed half the deduction allowed a couple filing jointly.

The amount of standard deductions are adjusted each year to account for inflation. By 2002, the standard deduction amounts were as follows:

Married couples filing jointly and qualified surviving spouses (section 1(a))	$7,850
Heads of households (section 1(b))	$6,900
Singles (section 1(c)	$4,700
Married persons filing separately (section 1(d))	$3,295

Pro-marriage legislation in 2001 and 2003

2. One of the primary goals of the significant tax cuts enacted in 2001 and 2003 was relief for married taxpayers. For 2003 and several other years (but

not all) prior to 2010, the standard deduction for married couples filing a joint return will be 200 percent of the standard deduction for singles. (In those years, the standard deduction for married persons filing separately will equal the standard deduction for a single person.) Under the sunset provisions, the deductions will revert to prior law in 2011.

3. Congress also moved in 2001 and 2003 to shield married couples from some of the "penalty" that the graduated rate structure can impose. Under the graduated schedules of sections 1(a) and (c) in effect before 2003, a single person's 15 percent bracket extended approximately 60 percent as high as a married couple's; stated differently, a married couple's breakpoint was about 167 percent as high as that of singles. (As we have seen, this could result in marriage penalties. To use simplified figures, suppose the first $24,000 of taxable income for a single person, and the first $40,000 of taxable income for a couple, were taxed at 15 percent, and the excess at higher rates. Two single persons with $24,000 of taxable income each would find upon marriage that a portion of their joint income was pushed into a higher bracket.) Congress provided, for 2003 and some (but not all) other years prior to "sunsetting" in 2011, that the breakpoint for married couples filing jointly would be 200 percent of the breakpoint for singles.

4. Were the 2001 and 2003 changes fair?

5. It is difficult to criticize the recent changes insofar as they remove aspects of the marriage penalty from married couples who were in fact being penalized. Millions of married couples, especially those in which husband and wife had roughly equal amounts of income, paid a substantial marriage penalty. As to those couples, the 2001 and 2003 legislation removed a tax penalty hard to justify in policy terms.

6. As Feenberg and Rosen indicate, a substantial minority of married couples were receiving a marriage bonus even before the 2001 and 2003 legislation. Nevertheless, Congress chose in 2001 and 2003 to make things better for all married couples, including those already benefitting from their marital status.

7. The Democrats offered an unsuccessful alternative, which would have allowed married taxpayers the option of filing as singles. One of the benefits asserted for this approach is that it "would not expand marriage bonuses."[e] Note that even the Democratic alternative would not have been marriage neutral—married taxpayers would have been able to file jointly if they enjoyed a marriage bonus, or to file as singles to avoid a marriage penalty.

---

e. S. REP. NO. 106-253, at 20 (2000).

8. The 2001 and 2003 legislation did little for high-income married taxpayers—the changes in both the standard deduction and the 15 percent tax bracket were of little importance at the top.[f] Yet married couples with two high earners face large marriage penalties, because the highest bracket takes effect at the same income level for both singles and married couples filing jointly. Using 2002 figures, two single persons, each with $307,050 of taxable income (the breakpoint to the highest tax bracket, then 38.6 percent), would each have $94,720 of tax liability, a total of $189,440. If they married, their combined taxable income of $614,100 would result in a joint liability of $207,802, an increase of $18,362.

9. The marriage penalty has also been significant in very low-income married couples, due to the structure of the earned income tax credit (EITC). The credit phases out as income increases, and prior to 2001 the phase-out began at the same income level, whether for a married couple or a single taxpayer. Thus, two single individuals with $15,000 of income would have been entitled to EITC; if married, their combined $30,000 income would disallow the EITC. The 2001 Act provided some relief. The EITC is discussed more extensively in Chapter Eleven.

10. Note the radical difference in lifestyles of the two tax-favored groups of couples: traditional one-earner married couples, and unmarried two-career couples (both heterosexual and homosexual).

11. The Staff of the Joint Committee pointed to census data indicating that "partners in unmarried couples represented only about 3 percent of all persons among couples living together in 1979." Obviously, the prevalence of unmarried couples is growing rapidly. Census figures for 2000 indicate that the number of such households has more than quadrupled since 1979.[g]

What is the relevance for tax policy of the increased number of unmarried couples?

12. Do higher tax rates make the marriage tax penalty greater?

13. What income levels are least affected by the differences in income tax rates between married couples and single persons?

---

f. The 2001 and 2003 legislation also provided relief to married taxpayers with respect to the alternative minimum tax, a change of greater importance to high-income couples.

g. Compared to the 1979 figure of 1.3 million unmarried couples cited by the Staff of the Joint Committee, the Census Bureau reported 5,475,768 "unmarried-partner households" in 2000. U.S. BUREAU OF THE CENSUS, STATISTICAL ABSTRACT OF THE UNITED STATES, tbl. 49, at 48 (122nd ed. 2002).

14. What tax consequences are there for marriage by persons with incomes so low that they do not exceed the bottom tax bracket whether they marry or remain single?

15. *Poe v. Seaborn* did not impose a constitutional barrier to taxing earned income of a taxpayer in a community property state to the earner rather than to the community. The Supreme Court was construing a statute, not the Constitution. Under present law, employment taxes are imposed on the individual earner even in community property states, not half to each spouse. Section 1402(a)(5).

16. What would be the result if *Poe v. Seaborn* were to be repealed by Congress, joint returns were made optional, and the special rate schedules for marrieds were to be repealed?

17. As the Staff of the Joint Committee discusses, and as elucidated further in Subchapter B, the principal conundrum is that desirable tax policy with regard to marriage is thought to have three elements—(1) marriage neutrality and (2) equal taxation of equal-income couples, while (3) maintaining a progressive rate structure. Tax systems cannot achieve all three.

18. Would a flat tax resolve all the issues of marriage penalties and marriage bonuses?

19. Pursuant to sections 215 and 61(a)(8), alimony is deductible by the payor and included in gross income of the recipient. Does this treatment fit the concept of the family as the taxpaying unit or the individual as the taxpaying unit? Alimony is usually thought of as a division of the income of the payor ex-spouse, but it is included in the gross income of the recipient even if the payor has no income. In that respect, alimony treats the individual as the taxpaying unit. Insofar as alimony is a division of income (the usual case), it is consistent with the family as the taxpaying unit, albeit a family that has split.

Similarly, transfers of property between spouses incident to divorce are treated, under section 1041, as gifts with carryover basis. Section 1041 legislatively reversed *United States v. Davis*,[h] which had treated transfers of property incident to divorce in at least some common law states as taxable transactions of property in exchange for relinquishment of marital rights. Although the spouse receiving property under the rule of the *Davis* case got a fair market value basis—as befits a taxable transaction—the Revenue Service never had the courage to be consistent and treat the recipient as having

---

h. 370 U.S. 65 (1962).

taxable gain equal to the excess of the fair market value of the property received over the zero basis of the marital rights relinquished.

20. Under section 2(b)(1), a person can qualify for head of household filing status if his home also is the place of abode of a son, daughter, or other descendant, even though (so long as the son, daughter, or other descendant is not married) the head of household does not furnish over half of the support of the descendant. Should maintenance of the household be sufficient, without regard to a dependency test?

B. CONFLICTING THEORIES OF THE PROPER TAXPAYING UNIT

With the exception of married couples, the federal income tax system generally treats each individual as a separate economic unit. This concept has generated a great deal of debate among commentators. The following excerpts from articles by Professors Boris Bittker, Lawrence Zelenak, Marjorie Kornhauser, and Fred Peel present conflicting theories on the proper unit for imposition of the individual income tax.

The articles by Professors Bittker and Zelenak deal with the intersection of tax theory with social, economic, and political realities. The post-World War II legal shift to allow joint returns for married couples was essentially pragmatic—a response to the differing treatment of taxpayers in common law and community property states brought about by the Supreme Court's decisions in *Lucas v. Earl* and *Poe v. Seaborn*. (The problem keyed on earned income; even under *Lucas v. Earl* it had always been possible for married couples in common law states to transfer their income-producing property to joint ownership. Moreover, under present law, such interspousal gifts are exempt from gift tax.) Both Bittker and Zelenak consider how the joint return rule, fashioned to meet a pragmatic political problem in an earlier generation, will and should fare in the future.

Bittker emphasizes the importance of real or perceived social norms in shaping tax rules. Zelanak's article centers on guiding the choice among the three inconsistent tax policy goals regarding the taxation of married couples, and on design problems inherent in separating income and deductions between husband and wife.

Professor Kornhauser discusses changing societal definitions of family, and questions the appropriateness of treating married couples differently from people in many other living arrangements.

Professor Peel argues that instead of overcoming *Lucas v. Earl* by allowing joint returns, Congress should legislatively reverse *Poe v. Seaborn* and tax married residents of community property states on their separately earned income.

FEDERAL INCOME TAXATION AND THE FAMILY
Boris I. Bittker[*]

27 Stanford Law Review 1389, 1391-99, 1416-20, 1425-26 (1975)

A persistent problem in the theory of income taxation is whether natural persons should be taxed as isolated individuals, or as social beings whose family ties to other taxpayers affect their taxpaying capacity. From its inception, the federal income tax law has permitted every taxpayer to file a personal return, embracing his or her own income but excluding the income of the taxpayer's spouse, children, and other relatives. On the other hand, married couples may elect to consolidate their income on a joint return, many exemptions and deductions take account of family links and responsibilities, and the income or property of one member of a family is sometimes attributed to another member for a variety of tax purposes. The Internal Revenue Code, in brief, is a patchwork, its history being a myriad of compromises fashioned to meet particular problems.

While this tension between rugged individualism and family solidarity permeates the entire Code, four broad questions capture the major themes:

— Should family members—husbands, wives, children, or others—be required, allowed, or forbidden to amalgamate their separate incomes in order to compute a joint tax liability?

— If amalgamation is either permitted or required, what should be the relationship between the tax liability of a family on its amalgamated income and that of a person living outside any family unit on his or her individual income?

— Should the taxpayer—whether an individual or a family entity—receive a tax allowance for supporting children, parents, or other relatives?

— How should the tax law treat transfers, sales, and other financial and property arrangements between family members, and for what tax purposes (if any) should the law attribute the income or property of one family member to another?

The responses of today's law to these questions are, of course, influenced by the need for revenue, by the Internal Revenue Service's capacity to audit returns and enforce the rules, by legislative and administrative efforts to minimize inconsistencies within the statute and regulations, and by other objectives, constraints, and values that are "internal" to the tax system. But the impact of these factors on Congress, the Treasury, and the public has always depended on a much more influential context—society's assumptions about the role of marriage and the family.

* * *

The goal of this Essay is to examine the theories and pressures that shaped today's Internal Revenue Code and to suggest how its provisions may fare in the maelstrom of changing social attitudes toward marriage, women's

---

[*]. At time of original publication, Sterling Professor of Law, Yale University.

rights, the two-job couple, communal living patterns, birth control, population growth, and intrafamily rights and liabilities. * * *

Consolidation of Family Income
Theoretical Considerations
The case for consolidation

By and large, tax theorists have espoused the doctrine "that taxpaying ability is determined by total family income regardless of the distribution of such income among the members of the family," rather than the contrary theory "that family as a unit has no combined taxpaying ability per se; that its taxpaying ability is composed of the separate taxpaying abilities of its individual members; and that the taxpaying ability of each of these is determined by the amount of income of which he or she is the owner without reference to the income of the other members of the family."[2] The philosophy of consolidation was recently championed in an influential report by the Canadian Royal Commission on Taxation. Its legislative proposals in this area were not enacted, but the Commission's statement in favor of consolidating family income is an excellent exposition of the social premises that underlie this position:

> We conclude that the present [Canadian tax] system is lacking in essential fairness between families in similar circumstances and that attempts to prevent abuses of the system have produced serious anomalies and rigidities. Most of these results are inherent in the concept that each individual is a separate taxable entity. Taxation of the individual in almost total disregard for his inevitably close financial and economic ties with the other members of the basic social unit of which he is ordinarily a member, the family, is in our view [a] striking instance of the lack of a comprehensive and rational pattern in the present tax system. In keeping with our general theme that the scope of our tax concepts should be broadened and made more consistent in order to achieve equity, we recommend that the family be treated as a tax unit and taxed on a rate schedule applicable to family units. Individuals who are not members of a family unit would continue to be treated as separate tax units and would be taxed on a schedule applicable to individuals. . . .

> We believe firmly that the family is today, as it has been for many centuries, the basic economic unit in society. Although few marriages are entered into for purely financial reasons, as soon as a marriage is contracted it is the continued income and financial position of the family which is ordinarily of primary concern, not the income and financial position of the individual members. * * *

> Where the family grows by the addition of children, further

---

2. Treasury Department, *The Tax Treatment of Family Income, reprinted in Hearings on Revenue Revision Before the House Comm. on Ways & Means*, 80th Cong., 1st Sess., pt. 2, at 851 (1947).

important financial and economic decisions are made in the family as a unit. Questions of the extent of education, time of entrance into the labor force and, frequently, choices of a career are decided on a family basis, although of course there are many exceptions to this statement. In some circumstances the income of the child is added to the family income, and, even where this is not done directly, the fact that a child has income of his own will have some bearing on the main family expenditure decisions. Certainly when the child becomes self-supporting he is normally expected to relieve the family of further expenditure on his behalf. * * * [4]

This rationale implies that the tax on a family with a given amount of consolidated income should be the same regardless of the proportion of each spouse's contribution to their total income, and it also suggests, though less clearly, that the ratio of parent-child contributions should be irrelevant. A corollary of this emphasis on the family's consolidated income is that legal ownership of property and income within the family should be disregarded in judging its taxpaying capacity. For at least 50 years, a major theme in the taxation of income from property transferred within the family has been that bedchamber transactions are suspect because the allocation of legal rights within the family is a trivial matter.

But the persons concerned may have a less cavalier attitude toward their legal rights. Taxpayers pass up many opportunities to reduce their taxes by intrafamily gifts, possibly from ignorance or inertia, but perhaps because they attach more significance to their legal rights than academicians assert. The contemporary women's rights movement is a reminder of the long struggle for married women's property laws, whose underlying premise was that the division of legal rights between husband and wife is a significant matter, not a trivial one. * * * Moreover, at least among upper-income taxpayers, it is not uncommon for separate accounts to be maintained for property owned by each spouse at the time of the marriage, inherited thereafter, or accumulated from earnings or household allowances, especially if the household includes children of a prior marriage. It may be, therefore, that tax theorists have excessively downgraded the importance of legal rights within the family, and that a swing of the pendulum is in the offing.

Since 1948, however, the Internal Revenue Code has imposed the same liability on all equal-income married couples, whether the combined income is generated by the earnings or investments of one spouse or both and without regard to the division of ownership between them. So long as family harmony prevails, equal-income married couples can purchase equal quantities of goods and services and probably make their economic decisions in a substantially identical fashion. These common characteristics have been regarded by most theorists as more important in fixing the tax liability of equal-income married

---

4. 3 REPORT OF THE ROYAL COMMISSION ON TAXATION (Carter Commission) 122-24 (1966).

couples than differences in their ownership of property, even though technical ownership may become crucial if the marriage is dissolved. For this reason, the 1948 statutory principle of equal taxes for equal-income married couples has been "almost universally accepted" by tax theorists, except for suggestions that a two-job married couple should not pay as much as a one-job married couple with the same joint income.

Tax-equality or marriage neutrality?

There is, however, a cloud on the horizon. It is increasingly argued that the income tax on two persons who get married should be neither more nor less than they paid on the same income before marriage. This call for a marriage-neutral tax system stems sometimes from the conviction that the state should neither encourage nor discourage marriage by a tax incentive or penalty, and sometimes from a belief that ceremonial marriages in today's society are not sufficiently different from informal alliances to warrant a difference in tax liability. * * * Proponents of this reform, however, often overlook the fact that, given a progressive rate schedule, a marriage-neutral tax system cannot be reconciled with a regime of equal taxes for equal-income married couples.

This collision of objectives is easily illustrated. If we assume a rate schedule taxing single persons at the rate of 10 percent on the first $10,000 of income and 25 percent on amounts above $10,000, the taxes paid by four unmarried persons on the amount of taxable income set out in Table I would be as shown therein.

If Alpha marries Beta and Theta marries Zeta, and all four continue to earn the same amount of income as before marriage, the consolidated income of each married couple will be $20,000. If their marriage is to have no effect on their tax liabilities, Alpha-Beta should continue to pay a total of $2,000 and Theta-Zeta a total of $2,900 in taxes. But if this difference in their tax burdens is deemed to be unwarranted, and a new rate schedule is prescribed for married couples that will cause Alpha-Beta and Theta-Zeta to pay the same tax since they have the same joint income ($20,000), marriage will either (1) decrease the tax burden for both couples, (2) decrease it for one and leave the other's unchanged, (3) decrease it for one and increase it for the other, (4) increase it for one and leave the other unchanged, or (5) increase it for both—depending on the rate schedule applicable to married couples. * * *

In short, we cannot simultaneously have (a) progression, (b) equal taxes on equal-income married couples, and (c) a marriage-neutral tax burden. A corollary of this conclusion is that a tax system with a progressive rate schedule can be marriage-neutral if individual legal rights over income and property are controlling even after marriage and each spouse reports his or her own income, but not if the tax is based on the couples' consolidated income.

For these reasons, advocacy of a marriage-neutral tax system collides directly and irretrievably with a dominant theme of tax theory for at least 50 years—the irrelevance of ownership within intimate family groups. * * *

TABLE 1

HYPOTHETICAL INCOME AND TAXES BEFORE MARRIAGE

	Taxable Income	Tax
Alpha	$10,000	$1,000
Beta	10000	1000
Theta	4000	400
Zeta	16000	2500

The income of children

Returning to the Canadian Royal Commission's rational for taxing families on their consolidated income, it will be recalled that the Commission advocated consolidation of the income of children as well as the income of spouses. In a society whose children are expected to work and to contribute their earnings to the family pool without voicing any opinions on the way funds are used, the case for consolidation is strongest. But even in a society that accords more financial independence to children, their earnings affect the economic behavior of the parents; as the children's income grows, the parents are relieved of pressure to support the children currently and to pass on an inheritance to them. The larger the *aggregate* pool of resources, it is argued, the greater the group's capacity to pay taxes.

The theory is not without appeal. But the justification for consolidating family income is not "tax logic," or any other factors peculiar to the tax system, but rather a social phenomenon—more precisely, the observer's perception of social realities. The Canadian Royal Commission itself implicitly acknowledged this by proposing a series of limits to the inclusion of children's income in the family's consolidated tax base. First, consolidation was to be compulsory only if the children were minors or disabled. Other children, whether living with their parents or not, were excluded, except that students between 21 and 25 years of age could elect to have their income included in the family tax base. Moreover, minors over the school-leaving age could elect to be excluded if employed and living apart from their parents. Finally, regardless of a child's age, gifts and bequests received by him (which were to be included in taxable income under another Commission proposal) could be deposited in an "Income Adjustment Account," a quasi-trust device for holding the property intact until the child's departure from the family unit (usually at 21) and taxing the accumulated income to him at that time. This exception to consolidation was evidently confined by the Commission to property acquired by gift or bequest in the belief that such property is more likely to be treated as sacrosanct by the parents than would be the child's personal earnings. If so, we have one more illustration of the pervasive influence of social customs—actual or perceived—on the tax system.

These exceptions to the principle of consolidation acknowledge that children should eventually be regarded as autonomous persons whose tax paying capacity is independent of their parents. * * *

Defining the group whose income is to be consolidated

If income is to be consolidated, the entity subject to this treatment must be defined, *e.g.*, "married couple," "family," "household," etc. Sociologists may find it useful to study groups that engage in joint decisionmaking or that manifest a common interest in the economic well-being of their members, but it would be difficult if not impossible to administer a law that employed such squishy phrases. Any more precise definition, however, will inevitably exclude groups that are only marginally different, so far as relevant economic or social relationships are concerned, from those within the magic circle. If married couples are taxed on their consolidated income, for example, should the same principle extend to a child who supports an aged parent, two sisters who share an apartment, or a divorced parent who lives with an adolescent child? Should a relationship established by blood or marriage be demanded, to the exclusion, for example, of unmarried persons who live together, homosexual companions, and communes?

The most objective boundary lines are those based on legal characteristics such as marital status, obligation to support, or right to inherit. Under existing law, the principal determinant of the tax burden is marriage, a status that is usually unambiguous. In a society that increasingly questions the legitimacy of traditional legal distinctions, however, one is tempted to substitute social "realities" in defining the boundaries of the group whose income is to be consolidated. But every departure from readily established definitional lines increases the problem of enforcement. If the tax on two unmarried persons depends on whether they live together, for example, how is their status to be verified by the Internal Revenue Service without an intolerable intrusion into their private lives?[16] * * *

Relative Tax Burdens of Married Couples and Other Taxpayers

The Problem Emerges

The congressional committee reports recommending enactment of the 1948 joint return argued at length that all equal-income married couples should pay the same amount of income taxes, but said nothing about the relationship of that burden to the tax burden on other taxpayers. It is easy to account for this silence. An unspoken premise of the 1948 legislative debate was that married couples in the community property states were not to be subjected to a tax increase; the bruising political fight of 1941, ending in the defeat of two proposals that would have produced such an increase, was still fresh in mind. Given this constraint, Congress was led almost irresistibly to extend the tax advantages of the community property system to married taxpayers in other states. If these taxpayers were to be equalized with

---

16. In Sweden, we are told, the social and legal lines between marriage and informal cohabitation have become quite hazy, but unmarried persons who live together are treated as a tax unit only if they were previously married (in which event the dissolution of their marriage is a suspect "tax divorce") or have borne children. *See* Sundberg, *Marriage or No Marriage: The Directives for the Revision of Swedish Family Law*, 20 INT'L & COMP. L.J. 223 (1971). To aid the enforcement of these provisions, Swedish taxpayers must state annually in their tax returns whether they are living with another person. *See id.* at 223.

community property couples, and the latter were not to be stripped of their historic privilege of paying the same tax as two unmarried taxpayers each with one-half their combined income, the relationship between the tax liability of married couples and that of unmarried taxpayers was predetermined; no discussion seemed necessary.

Once enacted, however, income splitting for married couples came to be seen as a tax allowance for family responsibilities. So viewed, it was assailed as unfair by taxpayers with similar family responsibilities, such as unmarried persons with dependent children or parents, who argued that their taxpaying capacity was no greater than that of a married couple with the same amount of income. To be sure, anyone supporting a dependent was entitled to an exemption, but this allowance ($600 per dependent, under 1948 law) was far less generous than the special rate schedule applicable to married couples filing joint returns.

Acknowledging merit in this complaint, in 1951 Congress prescribed a special head of household ("HOH") rate schedule for an unmarried person maintaining his home as the principal place of abode for a dependent or for a child (or other descendent) even if not a dependent. The new schedule for HOH returns produced a tax liability for a given amount that was midway between the liability of a single person and that of a married couple filing a joint return.

Thus, the rate concession to heads of households was only half a loaf, when compared with the tax advantage of the joint return. But the Code does not require HOH taxpayers to amalgamate their income with the income of their fellow householders, and this sometimes enables a two-person household to pay less than a married couple with the same aggregate income. But if the head of household is the only breadwinner, the HOH tax liability is heavier than the tax on a married couple, even if their income and family expenses are identical.

The 1951 reform was reexamined by Congress only 3 years after its enactment. In 1954, the House proposed to extend the full benefit of income splitting to any "head of family," a new concept that was broader in some respect and narrower in others than the term "head of household" as defined by the 1951 legislation. * * *

The Senate Finance Committee recommended a rejection of the House proposal, because it "did not treat all income groups equally and benefits primarily the middle- and upper-income groups."[88] When the bill went to conference, the dispute between the House and the Senate was compromised by expanding the existing HOH provisions to embrace a dependent parent, even if that parent were living separately from the taxpayer, and by according full benefits of income splitting to a "surviving spouse" (defined as a widow or widower whose home is the principal place of abode for a dependent child) for two taxable years after the spouse's death.

The HOH and surviving spouse provisions of 1951 and 1954 responded to the complaint of unmarried taxpayers with dependents that their family

---

88. S. REP. No. 1622, 83d Cong., 2d Sess. 5 (1954).

responsibilities were comparable to those of married couples. But the provisions did not question—indeed, they implicitly ratified—the tax differential established in 1948 between a married couple and a single person with the same income. * * *

The Insoluble Dilemmas

Some tax theorists have been unable to locate a justification for these differentials. They see income splitting of the 1948 variety as a "subsidy" for getting married and, since the benefits rise with the couple's income, as an "erosion" of the progressive rate structure—even as a "loophole." These pejorative labels imply that the separate rate schedule for married couples is an unjustified departure from a generally accepted standard. What, then, is the "proper" relationship between the tax rates on joint and individual income?

In offering answers to this question, tax theorists have customarily pointed to the following differences between the economic status of single persons without family responsibilities and married couples with the same amount of income, but without agreeing on the weight or even on the relevance of all of these characteristics:

1. The income of a married couple must support two persons, not one.

2. As compared with two single persons, a married couple benefits from economies of scale—a single kitchen will suffice, for example, and their food can be purchased in larger quantities.

3. If only one spouse is employed, the married couple enjoys the untaxed housework performed by the other spouse.[i]

This summary of differences compares single persons who live alone and have no dependents with one-job married couples. As will be seen there is ample room for disagreement about the relative tax burdens that should be borne by these two polar cases. But, alas, these are neither the only, nor necessarily the most significant, actual living patterns of American taxpayers. Attention must also be given to single persons who support children or other dependents, whether in their own homes or elsewhere, unmarried persons who share the expenses of a single household, two-job married couples, and taxpayers with still other arrangements. Unfortunately, when the debate is enriched by these complexities, the already divergent pathways to reform dissolve into a skein of competing trails.

* * *

MARRIAGE AND THE INCOME TAX
Lawrence Zelenak[*]
67 Southern California Law Review 339, 339, 342-48, 353-66, 368-69, 380-84, 390-93, 404-05 (1994)

Introduction

The federal income tax treats a married couple as a single economic unit. Spouses report their combined income on a joint return, and calculate their tax

---

i. The tax treatment of imputed income of housewives is discussed in Chapter Three. (Ed.)

*. At time of original publication, Reef C. Ivey Research Professor of Law, University of North Carolina.

liability based on that combined income.[1] Married couples will often have a tax liability different from the combined tax liabilities the spouses would have if single. These differences are called marriage penalties and marriage bonuses.
* * *

The only way to avoid both marriage bonuses and penalties is to abandon marital status as a tax determinant and to require that spouses file separate returns. However, this would mean that different couples with the same combined incomes, but different income distributions between husband and wife, would be taxed differently. * * *

The Uneasy Case for Joint Returns
* * *

A Historical Review

From its inception in 1913 until 1948, the income tax treated spouses as two separate taxpayers. * * *

In the years following [*Lucas v. Earl* and *Poe v. Seaborn*], a number of separate property states rejected centuries of tradition and adopted community property systems, thus entitling their inhabitants to the benefit of *Poe v. Seaborn*. * * * Husbands in separate property states attempted self-help income splitting, through both gifts of property and by making their wives business partners. This led to controversy and confusion regarding when a husband had given up sufficient control over property to make his wife the tax owner and when family partnerships would be respected for tax purposes. Eventually, in 1948 Congress provided for automatic income splitting between spouses as a matter of federal income tax law. Under the new system, a married couple would have the same tax liability as two single persons, each with half of the couple's income. This automatic perfect income splitting made state marital property law irrelevant, and all the states which had adopted community property after 1930 quickly recanted.
* * *

Rather than being based on bedrock beliefs about the nature of marital sharing, the 1948 legislation was essentially a historical accident—a response to the geographic discrimination and legal confusion resulting from the combination of *Lucas v. Earl* and *Poe v. Seaborn*. If *Seaborn* had not permitted income splitting in community property states, there is no indication that Congress would ever have decided to treat a married couple as a taxable unit.
* * *

After 1948, tax scholars sought a more compelling justification for joint

---

1. Spouses do have the option of filing separate returns, under I.R.C. § 1(d), but the tax rates are designed so that the combined separate-return tax liabilities will be at least as great as their joint-return liability. Separate returns may result in lower total tax liability, however, in the unusual situation where the use of separate returns reduces total taxable income reportable by the couple. This occurs when an expense is incurred by one spouse, and the expense is deductible only to the extent that it exceeds some specified percentage of adjusted gross income. Examples include miscellaneous itemized deductions, I.R.C. § 67(a); casualty losses, I.R.C. § 165(h)(2); and medical expenses, I.R.C. § 213(a). Separate returns can reduce the percentage floor, thus increasing the amount of the deduction and decreasing taxable income. Even then, however, the separate-return advantage of reducing taxable income may be more than offset by the disadvantage of higher rates.

returns than the accident of *Poe v. Seaborn*, and developed theories based on pooling. At best, however, these are after-the-fact justifications for what Congress had done, not explanations for why Congress had done it.

* * *

It is possible, of course, that the joint spousal return is a lovely child, despite its accidental conception. * * * It is still necessary to consider the evidence concerning marital pooling and its relevance to tax policy.

Do Spouses Pool Their Income?

There has been remarkably little empirical research into the income-sharing patterns of married couples. Indeed, a leading scholarly defense of joint returns took it as self-evident that "married couples should be assumed to share their income equally,"[35] and cited no supporting research. * * *

It might be nice if there were more studies of marital pooling beliefs and practices, but whether the focus is on attitudes, reported behavior, or income and expenditure patterns, the evidence of pooled marital income consumption is quite strong. * * *

Shared Consumption or Shared Control?

Given the need for a workable bright-line test, joint returns for married couples (and only for married couples) is the right answer—if the existence of shared consumption is the right question. But *is* that the right question? Proponents of joint returns say it is. * * *

Except for joint returns, the federal income tax *does* determine tax liability according to who controls income, by earning it or by owning the income-producing property. This is the lesson of *Lucas v. Earl* itself, which remains fundamental law outside of the joint-return context.[75] An important application of this rule is the income tax treatment of gifts and bequests as neither taxable to the donee nor deductible by the donor. This treatment separates the income tax liability on the income used to acquire the gifted property (which was imposed on the donor, and which is not shifted by the gift) from the ability to consume (which was transferred to the donee).

Even within the nuclear family, consumption is not treated as the test for taxability *except for married couples*. If shared consumption and a shared standard of living were the key, the taxable unit would be the entire family, including minor children. Except for substantial amounts of unearned income of children under age fourteen, however, the income of children is not aggregated with parental income by the income tax.[77] In keeping with this

---

35. Michael J. McIntyre & Oliver Oldman, *Taxation of the Family in a Comprehensive and Simplified Income Tax*, 90 HARV. L. REV. 1573 (1977), note 13, at 1578.

75. 281 U.S. 111 (1930). The analogous case with respect to income from property is Helvering v. Horst, 311 U.S. 112 (1940).

77. I.R.C. § 1(g) (West Supp.1993), the "kiddie tax," taxes the unearned income of a child under 14, in excess of $1,000 (adjusted for inflation), at the parents' marginal tax rate. For a proposal to treat the family as the taxable unit, see Martin J. McMahon, Jr., *Expanding the Taxable Unit: The Aggregation of the Income of Children and Parents*, 56 N.Y.U. L. REV. 60 (1981). Family unit taxation has long been used in France. The French system is described in Louise Dulude, *Taxation of the Spouses: A Comparison of Canadian, American, British, French and Swedish Law*, 23 OSGOODE HALL L.J. 67, 71-73 (1985).

focus on control rather than consumption, amounts spent to support a child are not deductible by the parent and not taxable to the child.

There is considerable evidence that control over marital income—the power to decide how the income shall be used—is much less shared than the consumption of the income. The spouse who earns the income tends to retain control over how the money is used, even if that spouse's decision results in shared consumption. The higher-earning spouse typically decides whether the couple will live frugally or extravagantly, and what its extravagances will be.
      * * *

Despite the evidence that consumption decisions are much less shared than the consumption itself, the point may be too controversial with the general public to serve as a basis for tax policy. * * * It is not necessary, however, to reach any decision about * * * the distribution of marital decision-making power * * * in order to apply basic income tax principles to the taxation of spouses. The basic principles are very simple. Earned income is taxed to the earner, and property income is taxed to the owner. The law normally looks no further into questions of power than that, and reasonably so.
* * *

If, then, the focus is on consumption of income, a joint-return system is appropriate. If the focus is on control, separate returns are called for. The choice of focus depends on whether consumption or control is a better measure of ability to pay. Ability to pay is crucial because the choice of a taxable unit matters only under a progressive tax system, and progressivity is based on the premise that ability to pay increases more than proportionately with income.
      * * *

Refereeing the Battle of the Neutralities
      * * *

It might be objected that since we do not have a separate-return system, we cannot know how strong the popular objections would be to such a system. That is not entirely true, however, for three reasons. First, there is the pre-1948 experience with an income tax based on separate returns. The only equity-based complaints with that system concerned the geographic discrimination created by *Poe v. Seaborn* in the taxation of the earnings of *husbands*. There is no indication of any objection to the unequal taxation of one-earner and two-earner couples with equal combined incomes. Second, there is the more recent experience with the two-earner deduction. From 1981 to 1986 the law allowed a deduction of 10% of the earned income of the lower earning spouse (with the deduction not to exceed $3,000). The deduction alleviated, but did not eliminate, the marriage penalty. In so doing, the deduction violated the principle of equal tax on equal income couples. A two-earner couple with two $30,000 earned incomes would have $3,000 less taxable income than a $60,000 one-earner couple.[99] There was no resulting outcry from angry single-earner couples. When the deduction was repealed in 1986, the official explanation was that the reduced progressivity of the rate

---

99. Because taxes were still determined on a joint-return basis, from 1981 to 1986 the tax system violated both couples neutrality *and* marriage neutrality.

schedules reduced marriage penalties to the point where additional relief was not needed. Discrimination against one-earner couples was *not* cited as a reason for change.

Finally, and most significantly, there has been no public outcry against the separate taxation of spouses under the social security wage tax. Under this tax each person, regardless of marital status, pays tax at a flat rate of 7.65% on the first $57,000 of earnings. This means that a two-earner couple may pay much more social security tax than an equal-income one-earner couple. * * * This separate-taxpayer system is not an administrative necessity. Nor is it explicable on the grounds that the social security tax has some features of a retirement savings plan, rather than a pure tax, because marital status *is* relevant in determining eligibility for retirement benefits. Thus, the relationship to benefits suggests the couple *should* be the taxable unit.

* * *

I can only speculate why the non-neutrality inherent in joint returns (marriage penalties and bonuses) bothers people so much more than the non-neutrality inherent in separate returns (different taxes on equal-income couples), but I do have some ideas. First, I suspect that people find marriage neutrality the more compelling of the two principles. They simply believe that it is more important for the tax system not to encourage or discourage marriage (especially the latter) than it is for equal-income couples to pay equal taxes. Second, I think people are more aware of marriage penalties and bonuses than they are of whether equal-income couples are paying equal taxes. Marriage penalties and bonuses can be determined without reference to any other taxpayers. When you get married (or contemplate marriage), you see the penalty (or bonus) without the need to compare yourself to anyone else; so too when you get divorced or contemplate divorce. * * *

There may be another reason why victims of the marriage penalty do not accept the explanation of the need to impose equal tax on equal-income couples (couples neutrality). They may realize that the couples neutrality justification fails even on its own terms, because one- and two-earner couples with equal taxable income are generally not equal in taxpaying ability. The one-earner couple is significantly better off because of its greater imputed income from self-performed services and its lesser nondeductible work-related expenses (such as for clothing and commuting). * * *

The Behavioral Effects of Joint Returns

The discussion thus far has concentrated on equity concerns— whether separate returns would be fairer than joint returns. It turns now to behavioral concerns—whether the joint-return system inappropriately encourages or discourages certain behaviors. If, for example, the system taxes a two-earner married couple more heavily than two single persons with the same incomes, the issue is fairness. If the greater tax burden causes a two-earner couple not to marry (or to obtain a divorce), the issue is behavioral effects. McCaffery criticizes most of the literature on the taxation of spouses for its "focus on static, distributive concerns of what groups pay how much tax," rather than on the behavioral incentives created by the tax rules.[112] The two major behavioral effects are on decisions whether to marry and on wives' decisions whether to work.

The Decision to Marry

Since a man and woman who both work full time will usually pay more tax as a married couple than as singles, the tax laws could discourage such people from marrying (or encourage them to divorce).[113] * * * In the absence of good evidence, it seems likely that the behavioral effect is significant in only two situations.

First, since marital filing status for an entire year depends on whether the marriage exists as of December 31, some couples may delay a marriage from December to January for tax purposes. Even if this effect exists, it is not particularly troubling.

Second, McCaffery suggests that the behavioral effect may be significant on lower income couples, because the marriage penalty at lower income levels is especially severe, and because "legally-sanctioned marriages might be most sensitive to economic conditions" at lower income levels.[117] The special severity is due to the phaseout of the earned income credit, which has the effect of increasing the marginal tax rate over the phaseout range. The marriage penalty created by the credit phaseout is worse than the penalty created by the basic rate structure, because the phaseout range and rate are identical for married and single persons. It is thus the equivalent of a joint filing system with the same rate schedules for marrieds and singles, which creates severe marriage penalties and no marriage bonuses. * * *

Despite these two special situations, widespread effects of the tax laws on decisions to marry are unproven. * * * Equity is, of course, an important tax policy consideration. A two-earner couple that says, "We're not going to get divorced because of the marriage penalty, but we're mad as hell," has a serious complaint, but the complaint is not behaviorally based.

Wives' Decisions to Work
Work Disincentives Caused by Joint Returns

The more serious behavioral concern is the effect of the joint-return system on wives' decisions whether to enter the labor force. If a couple views the wife as the marginal wage earner (in the sense that the husband's job is a given, and the decision to be made is whether the wife should also take a job), then the effect of joint returns is to stack the wife's income on top of the husband's. This means that the first dollar of the wife's earnings will be taxed at a high marginal rate—possibly as high as 39.6% under current law, and frequently 28% or higher.[123] This contrasts sharply with the initial tax rates the wife would face under a separate-return system: 0% on the income

---

112. Edward J. McCaffery, *Taxation and the Family: A Fresh Look at Behavioral Gender Biases*, 40 UCLA L. REV. 983, 992 (1993). [This article is excerpted in Chapter Three. (Ed.)]

113. It is also possible that in situations where marriage would reduce tax liability, because one person has high income and the other little or no income, the tax system may induce some marriages which would not otherwise occur.

117. McCaffery, *supra* note 112, at 1016.

123. Even if the I.R.C. § 1(a) rate schedule indicates the marginal rate is 15%, the true rate will be much higher if the phaseout of the earned income credit is in effect.

sheltered by her personal exemption and the standard deduction, and 15% after that.

Many commentators have argued that this stacking effect of joint returns inappropriately discourages women from working. McCaffery's statement of this position is the most recent, and is especially powerful. He notes the strong evidence for the high labor-supply elasticity of married women.[125] That is, wives' decisions whether to work are highly sensitive to their after-tax wages—much more so than the work decisions of husbands and unmarried men and women. Thus the decrease in after-tax wages caused by joint return income-stacking is a significant work deterrent for married women. McCaffery criticizes this result from two perspectives.

The first perspective is that of optimal tax theory. Any tax will discourage the activity subject to tax. If the taxed activity is economically beneficial, the disincentive effect of the tax is inefficient. Optimal tax theory considers how best to limit this inefficiency—how to raise a given amount of revenue with the least possible disincentive effect. The answer is that activities should be taxed in inverse relation to their elasticities. The heaviest taxes should be imposed on activities least sensitive to tax. To an optimal tax theorist, the joint-return system gets things exactly backwards—the first dollars earned by hard-to-discourage husbands are taxed at low rates, and the first dollars earned by easy-to-discourage wives are taxed at high rates.

* * *

Separate returns, although not the optimal optimal tax solution, would be a great improvement over current law in optimal tax terms, and a great improvement over favoritism for wives on fairness grounds. Separate returns would present a married woman with low marginal rates in making the initial decision to participate in the labor force; higher rates would apply when the question is whether to work more or less (rather than whether to work at all) and elasticity decreases. If this is not perfect in optimal tax terms, it is at least good. On the equity side, separate returns are not merely acceptable in terms of fairness; if my earlier analysis is right separate returns will be perceived as much fairer than current law (let alone a tax designed by an optimal tax proponent).

* * *

Designing a Separate-Return System

If spouses are required to file separate returns there must be rules for determining how income (especially property income), deductions, and credits are allocated between the spouses. For the most part, advocates of separate returns have given scant consideration to these design issues. These issues deserve more consideration than they have received, for two reasons. First, however strong the theoretical case for a separate-return system, the system will be accepted only if fair and workable solutions to the allocation problems can be developed. Second, thinking through the allocation problems affords a good test of the theoretical arguments for separate returns. The allocation problems are not merely practical; they are difficult precisely because there *is*

---

125. McCaffery, *supra* note 112, at 1039 n.211 (citing studies).

a great deal of marital pooling. Problems of abuse of and disrespect for the tax system arise when behavior of little or no non-tax significance is accorded tax significance. If couples that pool resources consider who owns property or who incurs expenses of no non-tax significance, but the tax system treats those factors as determinative, there will be problems: There will be opportunities for some to manipulate the system and pitfalls for others.

These allocation problems are, in fact, the strongest argument in favor of retaining the joint-return system. * * * [T]his one advantage of joint returns is not enough to overcome the superiority of separate returns in other respects. In addition, a separate-return system avoids one practical problem inherent in joint returns: the need to determine marital status for federal income tax purposes. This determination can be surprisingly difficult in some situations. * * *

Allocation of Earned Income

Taxing earned income to the earner is at the core of the justification for separate returns—both in terms of imposing the tax on the person in control of the income source and in terms of removing the second-earner disincentive of current law. Thus a separate-return system should retain *Earl* and reject *Seaborn*.

In the vast majority of cases there is no question as to which spouse earned a particular item of income, so taxation to the earner will involve neither complexity nor opportunity for abuse. In family businesses, however, there will be some incentive for artificial allocations of earned income to spouses (typically wives). This was also an issue under pre-1948 law, which was addressed by family partnership litigation. It remains an issue today because of the potential for splitting income with family members other than spouses.[208] It does not appear to be a major problem, however. Stanley Surrey opined in 1948 that the courts were "doing a respectable job in separating the wheat from the chaff in this field,"[209] and the area has not been heavily litigated in recent years.
    * * *

Allocation of Income from Property

The allocation of property income is less important than the allocation of earned income, because there is much less of it and because the most important behavioral effect is on earned income. It is a more difficult problem, however, because there is more opportunity to manipulate a rule that taxes property income to the owner than there is to abuse a rule that taxes earned income to the owner.

There are five important options for the treatment of property income. (1) Tax the income to the owner of the property. This is the general income tax rule. (2) Tax the income according to ownership, except do not give tax effect to interspousal transfers of property. Under this approach, if a husband gave

---

208. In 1951 Congress entered this area by enacting the predecessor of current I.R.C. § 704(e), concerning family partnerships. The focus of the provision, however, is on the taxation of income generated by capital, rather than by services.

209. Stanley S. Surrey, *Federal Taxation of the Family—The Revenue Act of 1948*, 61 HARV. L. REV. 1097, 1111 (1948).

property to his wife, he would continue to be taxed on the income from the property (or any replacement property). (3) Allocate all property income to the higher-earning spouse. (4) Allocate property income between the spouses in proportion to their earned incomes. (5) Allocate property income equally between the spouses.

    * * *

    On balance, I find the first option most attractive. It is the only option that achieves true marriage neutrality and thus is fully consistent with the underlying premise of separate returns. The control that goes with ownership has sufficient economic reality to justify respecting ownership for tax purposes, even as between spouses. Although I would not adopt a rule for the purpose of encouraging gifts to non-earning wives, I am happy to accept that encouragement as a side effect. On the other hand, the first option does have a few drawbacks. It places a heavy premium on careful tax planning, it is more complicated to administer than an automatic allocation rule, and it reintroduces a significant work disincentive when the husband has made major gifts to the wife.

    I think these drawbacks are tolerable, but someone more troubled by these drawbacks would select the third option (all property income taxed to the higher-earning spouse). It eliminates tax planning concerning property ownership, it is simple to administer, and it creates no work disincentive for the wife. * * *

Allocations of Deductions and Credits

    The obvious rule for deductions and credits associated with the production of income (either earned or from property) is to allocate those items to the spouse reporting the related income. It is not obvious, however, how personal deductions and credits (not associated with taxable income) should be allocated between spouses. The possible rules for allocating deductions and credits between spouses are similar to the choices for allocating property income. The important options are: (1) Allocate items to the spouse who incurred the deductible or creditable expense. Thus, for example, medical expenses would be deductible by the treated spouse, state and local taxes would be deductible by the spouse (or spouses) liable for the taxes, and home mortgage interest would be deductible by the debtor spouse (or spouses). Charitable contributions, which do not ordinarily involve the incurring of a liability, would be deductible by the spouse making the payment. (2) Allocate all items to the spouse making the payment, regardless of who incurred the liability. (3) Allocate items according to some formula, without regard to either liability or payment. Possible formulas include allocating items 100% to the higher income spouse, allocating items evenly between spouses, or allocating items in proportion to income.

    Only the first option is truly marriage neutral. * * *

    There is a serious practical problem, however, with the first option: the possibility that deductions will be lost because the spouse incurring the expense does not have enough income to use the deduction. * * *

    Congress may decide that the occasional lost deduction is a price worth paying for marriage neutrality and adopt the first option in its pure form. But consider the likely behavioral effect of that rule, as applied to the home mortgage interest deduction and the property tax deduction. In order to ensure that the deductions were not wasted, one-earner couples would hold their homes (and other assets subject to property tax) solely in the name of the earner spouse. Just as marriage neutral treatment of income-producing property works to the benefit of traditional wives, marriage neutral treatment of deduction-producing property works to the detriment of traditional wives. For the many couples whose most important asset is their home, the detrimental effect on the deduction side is more significant than the beneficial effect on the income side. Although I do not think it is the duty of the federal income tax to encourage transfers of property to non-earning spouses, a rule that actively discourages home (and other asset) ownership by married women is unacceptable.

What, then, of the other options? The second option (allocation of deductions based on payment) would put a tremendous premium on tax planning, and would be almost impossible to enforce. A formula allocation rule is clearly preferable. Among the possible formulas, I would reject a fifty-fifty rule, because it has one of the same problems as the first option: It creates the possibility that one spouse will not have enough income to use the allocated deductions. This problem could be avoided by allocating deductions between spouses in proportion to their incomes. It could also be avoided by the most taxpayer-favorable of all possible rules: Allocate deductions entirely to the higher income spouse until the deductions have equalized taxable incomes, and after that allocate deductions evenly between the spouses.

Either allocation in proportion to income or taxpayer-favorable allocation is a reasonable choice for deductions not associated with the production of income. I would combine one of these rules with allocation of income-related expenses to the spouse taxable on the income.

* * *

Conclusion

There is no absolutely right or wrong way to tax married couples. A system that is right for one time and place may be wrong for another. Whatever the merits of joint returns may have been for mid-twentieth century America, the joint-return system fits poorly with American attitudes and living patterns at the close of the century. The difficult question is when the dissatisfaction will become so great as to overcome the inertia of present law. The answer will depend partly on developments external to the tax system—the evolution of social attitudes and behaviors. It may also depend, however, on the degree of progressivity of the income tax: The more progressive the tax, the larger the marriage penalties and the greater the discouragement of working wives. Increases in the progressivity of the tax will hasten the demise of joint returns. But assuming an income tax with any significant amount of progressivity, the joint return will eventually disappear—the only question is when.

LOVE, MONEY, AND THE IRS: FAMILY, INCOME-SHARING, AND THE JOINT INCOME TAX RETURN

Marjorie E. Kornhauser[*]

45 Hastings Law Journal 63, 63-77, 92-105 (1993)

While tax theorists have debated the appropriateness of the joint return, they have not examined the premise behind the joint return: that married people—and only married people—share not only their hopes and dreams, but also their money.

* * *

Many people believe that the joint return is necessary because it promotes family values. To the extent that the return does so, it does so poorly. The joint return discriminates against many groups that provide their members with the same values of responsibility, caring, sharing, and support that traditional families provide. Moreover, contrary to popular myth, the joint return harms many traditional families. * * * By "penalizing" the second worker, the joint return discourages married couples from having a second earner (usually the wife), putting both psychological and economic stress on these families, on the wife in particular.

* * *

What is a Family?

* * *

The major demographic changes of the past thirty years—declining fertility, rising divorce rates, increasing rates of out-of-wedlock births, aging population—have caused the decline of the traditional nuclear family and an increase in the number of divorces, single-parent families, nonmarried cohabitation, and two-earner families. Nonmarital households in the United States increased nearly 400 percent from 1970 to March 1991.[12] The rapid rise in nontraditional living arrangements calls into question assumptions about patterns of sharing resources, as well as the concept of family itself.

* * *

The household concept encompasses people who physically live together, but who may not be an economic unit because they do not pool resources. Thus, roommates may count as one household for census purposes, but may only share the rent on the apartment. In contrast, two or more people may live together and share all expenses. People may live together either in a platonic or intimate sexual relationship, or they may live in a religious community or a hippie commune. In each situation people can and do share resources. These people functioning as one economic unit must be examined in discussing the taxable unit. However, people may function as an economic unit even if they do not live in the same house. Children may support their parents and vice versa. Nonrelated men and women also can support each other.

Flawed as they are, the statistics indicate the decline of the traditional,

---

[*]. At time of original publication, Professor of Law, Tulane School of Law.

12. U.S. BUREAU OF THE CENSUS, STATISTICAL ABSTRACT OF THE UNITED STATES tbl. 56 (112th ed. 1992). There were 1,094,000 nonfamily households in 1970 and 4,440,000 in March 1991. In 1988, nonfamily households comprised 4.4% of total households, but only 1.7% in 1970.

one-earner nuclear family on which both the joint return and the married couple as taxable unit are based. * * *

If commitment is key, then sexual cohabitation and gender of partners is irrelevant. For instance, two same-sex adults, one adult and her children, or three adult siblings can comprise a family unit.
    * * *

The main problem with such a functional approach is uncertainty. * * * Moreover, as Martha Minow suggests, a functional approach may lead to abuse of the system by those who wish to be treated as a married couple for some but not all purposes. Finally, basing tax liability on a functional approach invites administrative complexity. * * *

Although documentation of pooling involves some administrative complexity, the expanding existence of alternative relationships underscores the growing under-inclusiveness of allowing only marital units to file joint returns.
    * * *

Different theories underlie the two basic types of taxable units. If the tax unit is the individual, then tax-paying ability is based solely on each individual's earnings and on income produced by property titled in her name. This position holds that only individuals, not groups, have tax-paying capacity. The contrasting theory holds that the family is the taxable unit since the family, not the individual, is the basic economic unit within which financial resources are shared, regardless of the source of the wage or investment income.
    * * *

The justifications for treating the marital unit as the appropriate tax unit are economic unity, marital obligations, and economies of scale.

Economic Unity

The first and most important justification is economic unity. Traditionally, society views a marriage as an economic unit in which the members share the economic resources. * * * There are several criticisms of this justification. First, people other than married couples pool income. This criticism accepts the economic unit theory, but holds that the marital unit is only one type of economic unit. To single it out for special tax treatment is unjust. A fairer approach would be to treat all households or families as economic units, although such an approach has its own problems, such as defining "household" and "family."

Second, some critics attack the underlying assumption of pooling that couples always share income. For example, taxpayers ignore many opportunities to lower their taxes by means of intra-family gifts, not simply because of ignorance or inertia, but possibly because they attach significance to legal title.

Third, the women's rights movement undermines the pooling justification by emphasizing women's increasing access to economic independence as yet another indication that title is significant. More importantly, feminist theory undercuts the very premise that the family is an economic unit. * * *

Finally, the pooling rationale is criticized because it focuses on income consumption, which is more appropriate for a consumption-based tax than an income tax that measures accessions to wealth. * * *

Marital Obligations

Another justification for treating a married couple as a taxable unit is that marriage alters an individual's rights and obligations, thereby justifying treating a married couple as one taxable unit. Critics note, however, that individuals other than spouses have a legal obligation of support, and question why these people are treated differently than spouses. * * *

Economies of Scale

A final justification for treating the married couple as a taxable unit is that economies of scale that result from living together need to be taken into account. * * * Again, the critics reply that people other than two married people live together and share resources. It is inequitable to treat them differently. Moreover, economies of scale are too varied and difficult to measure.

The Dilemma of the Current Situation

* * *

Not only is our present treatment of the taxable unit inconsistent and inaccurate, but it is based on outdated, unexamined premises. In 1948, when the joint return was established, certain assumptions prompted creation of the joint return as a response to perceived inadequacies in the system. First was the assumption that spouses pooled all their resources regardless of who earned or owned them. The second assumption was that sharing of income automatically meant that control of the income was also shared. Finally, the joint return, in order to be helpful to married couples, assumed a "traditional" marriage in which there was only one earner in each family. In today's world, these assumptions are no longer tenable.

Even in 1948 these assumptions were not entirely accurate. If all income were jointly shared, then why had all states not switched to a community property system? Carolyn Jones presents evidence that many states rejected community property laws precisely because they gave rights to spouses who had not earned the income. Nevertheless, pooling of income, at least at the lower levels of income, was generally assumed despite a general absence of empirical evidence to support it. The second assumption concerning equal control, a prerequisite to taxability under general tax principles, lacked universality. The final assumption of one-earner couples also was not uniformly true: In April 1948, 23.1% of all married women participated in the labor force.

These discrepancies are even greater today than they were in 1948. First, many more nonlegal families exist. To the extent that these families are treated differently from married couples, such treatment is inequitable. Furthermore, while the partnership model of marriage may be more true today from a legal standpoint than it was in 1948, pooling, which is a concomitant of the partnership model, is far from universal. Legally, even the community property system still does not require complete joint management and control.

* * *

AN APPROACH TO INCOME TAX SIMPLIFICATION
Fred W. Peel, Jr.[*]
1 University of Arkansas at Little Rock Law Journal 1, 17 (1978)

Further simplification could be achieved if Congress would be willing to impose the tax without regard to the assignment of income imposed by statute in the community property states.[104] This would have the additional advantage of solving the nagging problems of tax rate discrimination against unmarried individuals and against married couples when both husband and wife have substantial income. In other words, earned income could be taxed to the spouse who earns it in community property states as well as in common law states (as is already done in the case of the tax on self-employment income)[105] and the spouse who owns an investment could be taxed on the investment income. Married couples in community property states would have some advantage over those in common law states under such a system because of the splitting of investment income from community property, but couples in common law states could be permitted to redress the balance by equalizing their ownership of investment assets by interspousal gifts. Joint returns still could be permitted as a convenience to married taxpayers, but they would be practical only in cases where combining the incomes would not result in a higher marginal tax rate.

* * *

Notes and Questions

21. The central problem in taxation of married couples is the inconsistency of three goals—marriage neutrality, taxing equal-income married couples equally, and progressivity. Why can our tax system not achieve all three goals simultaneously?

22. In Subchapter A, the Staff of the Joint Committee asserts that "a flat tax rate and a per taxpayer refundable credit would have marriage neutrality, equal taxation of couples with equal incomes and some limited progressivity." Is this the way to resolve the three "incompatible" goals? Is the resulting degree of progressivity—similar to that resulting from a "degressive" tax (as described in Chapter Four)—adequate? Why is it essential that the credit be "refundable" (i.e., result in a negative tax to those with low incomes)?

23. Do you agree with the principle that the income tax should be marriage neutral, or should the tax system be designed to encourage marriage? (No one appears to argue that marriage should be discouraged.)

---

[*]. At time of original publication, Professor of Law, University of Arkansas at Little Rock.

104. Poe v. Seaborn, 282 U.S. 101 (1930), holding that the Revenue Act of 1926 did not tax all income to the spouse who earned it in a community property state, involved a question of statutory construction. The Court did not hold that it would be unconstitutional to tax income to the earner before it became property of the marital community. *Cf.* Lucas v. Earl, 281 U.S. 111 (1930).

105. I.R.C. § 1402(a)(5).

24. The actions of the Republican majority in Congress in recent years may be viewed more accurately as favoring marriage, rather than as reducing or ending the marriage penalty. In 2000, in reporting a tax bill ultimately vetoed by President Clinton, the Ways and Means Committee opined that "the marriage tax penalty may undermine respect for the family and may discourage family formation."[j] As note Note #6 of Subchapter A (page 256) observes, the 2001 and 2003 Acts provided "relief" to all married taxpayers, including those already enjoying a "marriage bonus."

25. From 1981 to 1986, a deduction was allowed to two-earner couples for 10 percent of the earned income of the lower-earning spouse (to a maximum deduction of $3,000). Similarly, in the proposed (but not enacted) Contract with America tax bill put forward by the new Republican House majority in 1995, a credit of up to $145 was allowed to married couples whose joint liability exceeded "the hypothetical tax liabilities that would result if the individual income tax rates applicable to single filers were applied to each spouse's earned income, allowing for one personal exemption and the standard deduction allowed for single filers."[k] Are either of these approaches preferable to the provisions enacted in 2001 and 2003?

Interestingly, *Poe v. Seaborn* was not deemed a problem. Both the 1981-86 deduction and the 1995 proposed credit were "computed without regard to any community property laws."[l]

26. How do present tax provisions affect the choice by spouses between working and staying at home?

Assertions of discriminatory sexual and racial effects of joint returns

27. As we have seen, the largest marriage penalties tend to be suffered by couples whose income is split equally, and the largest marriage bonuses enjoyed by those where all income is earned by one spouse. Professor Amy Christian asserts that "joint return tax rates have a substantially biased effect against women in their application. * * * While the Code may not have been *intended* to discriminate against women, it has that effect because of its application to larger, preexisting social patterns.[m] With respect to the effect of the tax law on the employment patterns of married women, Professor Christian argues that "By benefiting disparate-income couples, the income-splitting feature of the joint return rewards working patterns that conform to sexist stereotypes while failing to reward taxpayers who challenge the stereotype."[n]

---

j. H.R. REP. NO. 106-493, at 6 (2000).

k. H.R. REP. NO. 104-84, at 13 (1995).

l. *Id.* at 14.

m. Amy C. Christian, *The Joint Return Rate Structure: Identifying and Addressing the Gendered Nature of the Tax Law*, 13 J. LAW & POLITICS 241, 245 (1997).

n. *Id.* at 279-80.

28. Professor Christian sees the tax law as forcing lower-earning wives to economically subsidize their higher-earning husbands: "[T]he 'poorer' wife essentially pays part of her 'richer' husband's tax burden by letting him shift part of his tax liability into her lowest bracket and then by having her own income taxed in a higher tax bracket."[o]

Is Professor Christian correct to focus on the impact of the tax laws within the marriage—between husband and wife—or should the focus be on whether the couple comes out ahead or behind? How do most married taxpayers consider the matter (if at all)?

29. Whether or not we accept Professor Christian's arguments, it is clear that the joint return has implications tied to sex, and to traditional and new sex roles. Less obvious is Professor Dorothy Brown's assertion that the scholarly literature assessing taxation of married couples overlooks a racial dimension. She argues that observations such as "as the husband's income increases, the participation rate [in the labor force] of the [wife] decreases * * * [describe] primarily the experiences of upper-income white households."[p]

Professor Brown argues that black wives are more likely than white wives to be in the labor force. For that reason, black couples are less likely than white couples to present cases in which almost all the couple's income is earned by one spouse—the situation providing the biggest marriage bonus. Professor Brown presents unpublished Census Bureau data from 1990 indicating that in every income strata considered, more white couples than black couples derive at least 90 percent of their income from one spouse.[q]

30. The tax law is likely to affect not only decisions about earned income, but also the form in which married persons own property. Why did Professor Zelenak express concern that, in moving to a system of separate returns, allowing deductions only to the spouse who made payment might lead couples to transfer ownership of the family home to the higher-earning spouse (usually the husband)? What might be the likely effect of a separate taxing system on the ownership of income-producing property (as distinct from the home, which produces only tax deductions)? Should the tax system be concerned about these effects?

31. Many states employ a system that allows married persons to file a single return in which the spouses are taxed separately—thus allowing the first dollar of each spouse's income to be taxed at the lowest rate, but without sacrificing the simplicity of the joint return. Typically, spouses filing in this manner jointly report itemized deductions not attributable to the income of either spouse, then allocate these deductions in a manner prescribed by the state, which usually tracks one of the allocation formulas suggested by Professor Zelenak.

---

o. *Id.* at 348.
p. Dorothy A. Brown, *Race, Class, and Gender Essentialism in Tax Literature: The Joint Return*, 54 WASH. & LEE L. REV. 1469, 1499 (1997).
q. *Id.* at 1500.

32. The Canadian Carter Commission determined that married couples view the family, and not the individual, as the basic economic unit. Do you agree?

33. If the Carter Commission's read on the attitude of married couples is correct, does this resolve the issue of whether the family or the individual should be the taxpaying unit?

34. A recurring issue in the scholarly literature, including that represented in the articles excerpted, is the degree to which a married couple shares *consumption* regardless of which spouse earns income, and the degree to which a married couple shares *control* of consumption decisions. Obviously, no set of answers will hold for all couples, but our views of the norm may influence our views of appropriate tax policy. To the degree that consumption and control are shared, the case for taxing equal-income couples equally is strengthened, because it suggests that it matters little whether income is split between husband and wife 100-0, or 70-30, or 50-50. But if the spouse who generates the income disproportionately consumes it, or at least controls consumption decisions, the case for taxing married taxpayers as individuals seems more persuasive.

In your experience, what pattern is most descriptive? Is it possible that different answers may be typical regarding shared consumption and shared decision-making about consumption? If so, which of the two should be more important in shaping tax policy?

35. Is ability to pay affected by family circumstances?

36. As a matter of political history, is Professor Kornhauser correct in stating that the joint return was established in 1948 as a response to certain social assumptions, now outdated, including the assumption that spouses pooled all their resources and that sharing of income automatically meant that control of the income was also shared?

37. How does the old saying, "Two can live as cheaply as one," affect the choice between the family and the individual as the proper taxing unit? Does the widespread acceptance of unmarried couples living together diminish the relevance of this point for tax purposes?

38. If the present differences between separate returns for single persons and joint returns are retained, should joint returns be made available to other joint living arrangements as well as to married couples, as Professor Kornhauser may be implying? What other joint arrangements should be included? How would they be defined?

Do you agree with Professor Bittker's suggestion that structuring the tax law around "squishy" phrases describing living patterns, rather than upon legal relationships, would lead to a tax law "difficult if not impossible to administer"?

39. As the excerpts of this chapter make clear, the weight of modern scholarship agrees with Professor Peel's proposal that *Poe v. Seaborn* be repealed, so that earned income would be taxed to the earner, and property income to the owner. Ownership of property could be transferred to take advantage of lower rates, *if* the owner (typically, the higher-earning husband) were willing to part with legal title.

While agreeing with this approach, Professor Christian argues that the lot of married women could be improved by a reform that seems to move in the opposite direction—legislative repeal of *Lucas v. Earl*:

> [A] completely different approach to solving these problems would be for Congress to eliminate joint returns and simultaneously to override *Lucas v. Earl*, allowing assignment of income by contract, regardless of state marital property laws. If this avenue were pursued, geographic disparity need not return upon the institution of mandatory separate filing because couples in all jurisdictions would be permitted to contract to split the ownership of their incomes. To obtain the benefits of income splitting under the contract approach, actual ownership in the income would have to be transferred. In this regard, the last approach is superior for women to the automatic income splitting currently available where actual ownership of earnings is not transferred.[r]

Is Professor Christian's proposal desirable? If so, should *Lucas v. Earl* be repealed only with respect to married couples, or for any situation in which an earner entered into a binding contract to split income with another?

40. Apart from questions of filing status and rate structure, Congress must repeatedly decide whether to treat married couples as one taxpayer or two, and it acts inconsistently. Many provisions, such as the cap on depreciable business assets that can be currently expensed under section 179, allow the same deduction to single taxpayers and married couples. Many others, such as section 1244 limiting the annual amount of losses on small business stock that can offset ordinary income, give a double benefit to married couples filing joint returns.

C. INNOCENT SPOUSES AND FORMER SPOUSES

Taxpayers are required to file returns (assuming they have the requisite minimum of income).[s] They are not required to file joint returns, even if married. The overwhelming majority of married taxpayers, however, do in fact file jointly—for some combination of tax saving, convenience, tradition, spousal pressure, or from a mistaken belief that joint returns are required of married taxpayers. After filing a joint return, married taxpayers are not allowed to file

---

r. Christian, supra note m, at 362.
s. Generally, filing is required when income exceeds the amount of the personal exemption plus the standard deduction. Section 6012(a).

amended returns changing their filing status to married individual filing separately, though they are allowed to change from separate to joint.[t]

By filing a joint return, husbands and wives become jointly and severally liable for the tax due for the year—even as to or income not disclosed on the return. The policy question arises as to what relief and under what circumstances, if any, a married taxpayer should be relieved of liability attributable to the income of the spouse. Congress first allowed relief to "innocent spouses" in 1971, and has since broadened the scope of relief and the circumstances under which it is available. A notable loosening of the rules was enacted in 1998, as the conference report excerpted below explains.

Writing shortly before the 1998 legislation, Professor Martha Jordan described proposed limitations on joint liability arising from joint returns. While not defending the traditional rule of joint liability, Professor Jordan displayed more concern than most writers, and, arguably, more concern than Congress in 1998, about the Internal Revenue Service's legitimate needs in collecting tax from married taxpayers.

INTERNAL REVENUE SERVICE
RESTRUCTURING AND REFORM ACT OF 1998
H.R. Report No. 105-599 (Conference Report)
1998-3 Internal Revenue Cumulative Bulletin 747, 1003-09

Relief for Innocent Spouses and for Taxpayers Unable to Manage Their Financial Affairs Due to Disabilities
Relief for innocent spouses
Present Law

Under present law, relief from liability for tax, interest and penalties is available for "innocent spouses" in certain circumstances. To qualify for such relief, the innocent spouse must establish: (1) that a joint return was made; * * * (3) that in signing the return, the innocent spouse did not know, and had no reason to know, that there was an understatement of tax; and (4) that taking into account all the facts and circumstances, it is inequitable to hold the innocent spouse liable for the deficiency in tax. * * *

House Bill

The House bill generally makes innocent spouse status easier to obtain. The bill eliminates all of the understatement thresholds and requires only that the understatement of tax be attributable to an erroneous (and not just a grossly erroneous) item of the other spouse.

The House bill provides that innocent spouse relief may be provided on an apportioned basis. A spouse may be relieved of liability for the portion of an understatement of tax even if the spouse knew or had reason to know of other understatements of tax on the same return.

* * *

Senate Amendment
In general

The Senate amendment modifies the innocent spouse provisions to permit

---

t. Section 6013(b).

a spouse to elect to limit his or her liability for unpaid taxes on a joint return to the spouse's separate liability amount. In the case of a deficiency arising from a joint return, a spouse could elect to be liable only to the extent that items giving rise to the deficiency are allocable to the spouse. The separate liability election also applies in situations where the tax shown on a joint return is not paid with the return. In this case, the amount determined under the separate liability election equals the amount that would have been reported by the electing spouse on a separate return. However, if any item of credit or deduction would be disallowed solely because a separate return is filed, the item of credit or deduction will be computed without regard to such prohibition. Special rules apply to prevent the inappropriate use of the election. The separate liability election may not be used to create a refund, or to direct a refund to a particular spouse.

Items are generally allocated between spouses in the same manner as they would have been allocated had the spouses filed separate returns. The Secretary may prescribe other methods of allocation by regulation. The allocation of items is to be accomplished without regard to community property laws.

The election applies to all unpaid taxes under subtitle A of the Internal Revenue Code, including the income tax and the self-employment tax. The election may be made at any time not later than 2 years after collection activities begin with respect to the electing spouse. It is intended that the 2 year period not begin until collection activities have been undertaken against the electing spouse that have the effect of giving the spouse notice of the IRS' intention to collect the joint liability from such spouse. For example, garnishment of wages or a notice of intent to levy against the property of the electing spouse would constitute collection activity against the electing spouse. The mailing of a notice of deficiency and demand for payment to the last known address of the electing spouse, addressed to both spouses, would not.
* * *

The Internal Revenue Service is required to notify all taxpayers who have filed joint returns of their rights to elect to limit their joint and several liability under this provision. * * *

Conference Agreement
In general

The conference agreement follows the Senate amendment with respect to deficiencies of a taxpayer who is no longer married to, is legally separated from, or has been living apart for at least 12 months from the person with whom the taxpayer originally filed the joint return. The conference agreement also includes the provision in the House bill expanding the circumstances in which innocent spouse relief is available. Taxpayers, whether or not eligible to make the separate liability election, may be granted innocent spouse relief where appropriate. In addition, the conference agreement authorizes the Secretary to provide equitable relief in appropriate situations. * * *

Deficiencies of certain taxpayers

The conference agreement follows the Senate amendment with respect to deficiencies of a taxpayer who, at the time of election, is no longer married[16] to, is legally separated from, or has been living apart for at least 12 months from the person with whom the taxpayer originally filed the joint return. Such taxpayers may elect to limit their liability for any deficiency limited to the portion of the deficiency that is attributable to items allocable to the taxpayer.

For example, a deficiency is assessed after IRS audit of a joint return. The deficiency relates to income earned by the husband that was not reported on the return. If the spouses who joined in the return are no longer married, are legally separated, or have lived apart for at least 12 months, either may elect limited liability under this provision. If the wife elects, she would owe none of the deficiency. The deficiency would be the sole responsibility of the husband whose income gave rise to the deficiency.

If the deficiency relates to the items of both spouses, the separate liability for the deficiency is allocated between the spouses in the same proportion as the net items taken into account in determining the deficiency. For example, a deficiency is assessed that is attributable to $70,000 of unreported income allocable to the husband and the disallowance of a $30,000 miscellaneous itemized deduction allocable to the wife. * * * [T]he husband's liability would be limited to 70 percent of the deficiency (if he elects) and the wife's liability limited to 30 percent (if she elects). * * * If either spouse fails to elect, that spouse would be liable for the full amount of the deficiency, unless reduced by innocent spouse relief or pursuant to the grant of authority to the Secretary to provide equitable relief.

If the deficiency arises as a result of the denial of an item of deduction or credit, the amount of the deficiency allocated to the spouse to whom the item of deduction or credit is allocated is limited to the amount of income or tax allocated to such spouse that was offset by the deduction or credit. The remainder of the liability is allocated to the other spouse to reflect the fact that income or tax allocated to that spouse was originally offset by a portion of the disallowed deduction or credit.

For example, a married couple files a joint return with wage income of $100,000 allocable to the wife and $30,000 of self employment income allocable to the husband. On examination, a $20,000 deduction allocated to the husband is disallowed, resulting in a deficiency of $5,600. Under the provision, the liability is allocated in proportion to the items giving rise to the deficiency. Since the only item giving rise to the deficiency is allocable to the husband, and because he reported sufficient income to offset the item of deduction, the entire deficiency is allocated to the husband and the wife has no liability with regard to the deficiency, regardless of the ability of the IRS to collect the deficiency from the husband.

If the joint return had shown only $15,000 (instead of $30,000) of self employment income for the husband, the income offset limitation rule discussed above would apply. In this case, the disallowed $20,000 deduction entirely offsets the $15,000 of income of the husband, and $5,000 remains. This remaining $5,000 of the disallowed deduction offsets income of the wife.

---

16. For the purpose of this rule, a taxpayer is no longer married if he or she is widowed.

The liability for the deficiency is therefore divided in proportion to the amount of income offset for each spouse. In this example, the husband is liable for 3/4 of the deficiency ($4,200), and the wife is liable for the remaining 1/4 ($1,400).

    * * *

The special rules included in the Senate bill to prevent the inappropriate use of the election are included in the conference agreement.

First, if the IRS demonstrates that assets were transferred between the spouses in a fraudulent scheme joined in by both spouses, neither spouse is eligible to make the election under the provision (and consequently joint and several liability applies to both spouses).

Second, if the IRS proves that the electing spouse had actual knowledge that an item on a return is incorrect, the election will not apply to the extent any deficiency is attributable to such item. Such actual knowledge must be established by the evidence and shall not be inferred based on indications that the electing spouse had a reason to know.

The rule that the election will not apply to the extent any deficiency is attributable to an item the electing spouse had actual knowledge of is expected to be applied by treating the item as fully allocable to both spouses. For example a married couple files a joint return with wage income of $150,000 allocable to the wife and $30,000 of self employment income allocable to the husband. On examination, an additional $20,000 of the husband's self-employment income is discovered, resulting in a deficiency of $9,000. The IRS proves that the wife had actual knowledge that $5,000 of this additional self-employment income, but had no knowledge of the remaining $15,000. In this case, the husband would be liable for the full amount of the deficiency, since the item giving rise to the deficiency is fully allocable to him. In addition, the wife would be liable for the amount that would have been calculated as the deficiency based on the $5,000 of unreported income of which she had actual knowledge. The IRS would be allowed to collect that amount from either spouse, while the remainder of the deficiency could be collected from only the husband.

Third, the portion of the deficiency for which the electing spouse is liable is increased by the value of any disqualified assets received from the other spouse. Disqualified assets include any property or right to property that was transferred to an electing spouse if the principal purpose of the transfer is the avoidance of tax (including the avoidance of payment of tax). A rebuttable presumption exists that a transfer is made for tax avoidance purposes if the transfer was made less than one year before the earlier of the payment due date or the date of the notice of proposed deficiency. The rebuttable presumption does not apply to transfers pursuant to a decree of divorce or separate maintenance. The presumption may be rebutted by a showing that the principal purpose of the transfer was not the avoidance of tax or the payment of tax.

Other deficiencies

The conference agreement also includes the provision in the House bill modifying innocent spouse relief. Taxpayers who do not make the separate liability election may be eligible for innocent spouse relief. For example, a taxpayer may be ineligible to make the separate liability election for a deficiency because he or she is not widowed, divorced, legally separated, or living apart (for at least 12 months) from the person with whom the taxpayer originally joined in filing the joint return. Such a taxpayer may apply for relief of any deficiency that is attributable to an erroneous item of the other spouse, provided he or she did not know or have reason to know of the understatement of tax and it would be inequitable to hold the taxpayer responsible for the deficiency. * * * The rule in the House bill allowing innocent spouse relief to be provided on an apportioned basis is included in the conference agreement.

Other circumstances, including tax shown on a return but not paid

The conference agreement does not include the portion of the Senate amendment that could provide relief in situations where tax was shown on a joint return, but not paid with the return. The conferees intend that the Secretary will consider using the grant of authority to provide equitable relief in appropriate situations to avoid the inequitable treatment of spouses in such situations. For example, the conferees intend that equitable relief be available to a spouse that does not know, and had no reason to know, that funds intended for the payment of tax were instead taken by the other spouse for such other spouse's benefit.

The conferees do not intend to limit the use of the Secretary's authority to provide equitable relief to situations where tax is shown on a return but not paid. The conferees intend that such authority be used where, taking into account all the facts and circumstances, it is inequitable to hold an individual liable for all or part of any unpaid tax or deficiency arising from a joint return.
* * *

THE INNOCENT SPOUSE PROBLEM: DEFINING A PROPORTIONATE SOLUTION

Martha W. Jordan[*]

24 Ohio Northern University Law Review 517, 517-18, 526-29, 532-33, 543-46, 548-50 (1998)

Introduction

Under current law, when a joint return is filed, both spouses are jointly liable for the tax. The only way that a spouse may be relieved of liability for an underpayment of tax is for that spouse to meet the criteria for innocent spouse relief, an imprecise standard requiring, inter alia, proof that the putative innocent spouse has no knowledge of the understatement of tax and that it would be inequitable to hold the spouse liable for the understatement. For years, critics have deplored the severity of joint and several liability and the inadequacy of the relief granted by the innocent spouse rule. Recently, the focus of much of that criticism has been on the inappropriateness of joint and several liability as a means of allocating the tax burden between spouses who file jointly. * * *

[T]his article starts with the premise that joint and several liability will be replaced by a proportionate liability standard. * * * Finally, this article

---

*. At time of original publication, Associate Professor, Duquesne University School of Law.

suggests various ways to make a proportionate liability standard more acceptable to the Internal Revenue Service.

Proportionate Liability

* * *

Proposed Alternatives to Joint and Several Liability

* * *

Proportional Liability

Proportional liability allocates a couple's joint tax liability between the spouses based on the tax each spouse would have paid if they had filed separate returns instead of a joint return. Under proportional liability, each spouse's share of the joint tax liability equals an amount that bears the same ratio to the joint tax liability as that spouse's separate tax liability bears to the spouses' aggregate separate tax liability. Whenever there is an underpayment of tax, each spouse's share of the joint liability is recomputed, and each spouse is liable for the underpayment to the extent that the spouse's prior tax payments are insufficient to cover the spouse's proportional share of the joint tax.

Under proportional liability, the starting point for determining a spouse's share of the joint liability is the spouses' separate tax liabilities. Determination of the spouses' separate tax liabilities requires that the income and deductions claimed on the joint return be divided between the spouses in the same manner as such income and deductions would have been apportioned for separate returns.

As a general rule, when spouses file separate returns, income and deductions are allocated between them based on property ownership. Earned income is reported by the spouse who performed the personal services. Income generated by separate property is reported by the spouse who owns the property. Income from property that is held jointly or as community property is allocated equally between the spouses.   Deductions attributable to a spouse's separate property or income producing enterprise are allocable to that spouse. Other deductions are generally allocated based on the origin of the funds used to pay the expense. If joint funds or community funds are used to pay the expense, each spouse is generally entitled to deduct one-half of the expense. If the funds used to pay the expense are the separate property of one spouse, that spouse is entitled to claim the entire deduction. Certain deductions, however, may only be claimed by the spouse who is liable for the underlying expense. Taxes may be deducted only by the spouse on whom they are imposed. Similarly, interest is deductible only by a spouse who is liable for the underlying indebtedness.   Losses and deductions for charitable contributions are allocated in the same manner as deductions; only the spouse who owned the property may claim the loss. Personal exemptions for the couple's children may, as a general rule, be claimed by either spouse, but cannot be prorated.

* * *

Evaluating the Proposed
Alternatives to Current Law

Proportionate liability would limit each spouse's primary liability with respect to the joint return to that spouse's proportionate share of the joint tax liability. Adopting a proportionate liability system, however, does not mean that the government will never be able to pursue the wife when it is unable to collect in full from the husband. The wife may be secondarily liable for the husband's unpaid tax under the theory of transferee liability. The existence and extent of transferee liability is determined by state law. Although the requirements may vary from state to state, generally, the requirements for transferee liability parallel the requirements for setting aside a fraudulent conveyance. The following distillation has been given of the most common elements. The government must show that the husband transferred property to the wife for inadequate consideration. The government must prove that the transfer occurred after the husband's tax liability had accrued. The government must show that the husband was either insolvent at the time of the transfer or was rendered insolvent as a result. If the government establishes that transferee liability exists, the government may recover from the wife an amount equal to the value of the property received from the husband. Even though the government establishes the existence of transferee liability, the government must exhaust its remedies against the husband before it may proceed against the wife, which means, generally speaking, that the government will only be able to proceed against the wife when the husband is insolvent.

* * *

Making Proportionate Liability
More Acceptable to the Government

* * * A proportionate liability standard should be acceptable to the government provided it does not unduly limit the government's ability to collect tax.

As a general rule, filing jointly reduces a couple's aggregate tax liability. A proportionate liability standard, however, may reduce not only the couple's aggregate tax liability but also each spouse's individual tax liability. Furthermore, a proportionate liability standard may reduce a spouse's individual tax liability even though the government has not collected the total, albeit reduced, tax liability. This preferential treatment of the taxpayer at the expense of the government raises three legitimate objections the government should make. First, a proportionate liability system may limit a wife's primary liability to such an extent that, even though the joint tax is not paid in full, the wife pays less tax than the wife would have paid if separate returns had been filed. Second, under a proportionate liability system whenever filing jointly, reduces a couple's combined tax liability the wife may benefit from this reduction without a corresponding increase in the wife's primary liability for the joint tax. And, finally, because the marital relationship offers unique opportunities for the husband to transfer property to the wife and still receive the benefit of that property, transferee liability may overly restrict the government's ability to collect the husband's unpaid share from the wife.

Although eliminating these possible objections would make the law more complicated, such modifications should make a proportionate liability standard more acceptable to the government.

Modifying Proportionate Liability

The first two objections can be resolved by modifying the proportionate liability standard so that it no longer favors the taxpayer over the government. Two modifications are possible. The first would define a spouse's minimum share of responsibility by reference to the spouse's separate tax liability. The second modification requires each spouse to be responsible for any tax savings created by filing jointly.

Defining Responsibility by Reference to a Spouse's Separate Tax Liability

One possible solution is to modify proportionate liability so that each spouse's share of the joint tax equals the greater of the spouse's proportionate share of the tax or the spouse's separate tax liability.   Under such a modification, whenever one spouse's separate tax liability exceeds that spouse's proportionate share of joint tax, both spouses would be jointly liable for a portion of the tax. Consequently, the government could proceed against either spouse to the extent of the overlap.   Although this would enable the government to proceed against the wife without exhausting its remedies against the husband, this should not be objectionable because the wife would not be required to pay more than the wife would have paid if separate returns had been filed.

This approach can be easily demonstrated by returning to the example in which $30,000 of income is omitted from the return. In that example, husband and wife have joint income of $140,000 and a joint tax liability of $35,929. The husband pays $33,909 and the wife pays $2,020 with the return. If separate returns had been filed, the husband would have reported taxable income of $125,000 and would have owed tax of $37,764 and the wife would have reported taxable income of $15,000 and would have owed tax of $2,250. The Internal Revenue Service assesses a $10,800 deficiency resulting from the omission of $30,000 of gross income attributable to the husband.

The first step is to determine each spouse's proportionate share of the joint tax. Assuming proportional liability is adopted, the husband's separate taxable income would be $155,000, including the $30,000 of omitted income, and his separate tax liability would be $49,644.   The wife's separate tax liability would remain $2,250. Therefore, the husband's proportionate share of the $46,729 joint tax liability would be $44,703, and the wife's proportionate share would be $2,026. The next step is to determine each spouse's share of the joint tax. The husband's share of the joint tax equals the greater of his proportionate share of $46,729 or his separate tax liability of $49,644. The wife's share of the joint tax equals the greater of her proportionate share of $2,026 or her separate tax liability of $2,250. Taking into account the prior tax payments made by the spouses, the Internal Revenue Service would have the option of collecting the entire $10,800 deficiency from the husband or collecting up to $230 from the wife and the balance from the husband.

Defining Each Spouse's Share of Liability to Include the Tax Savings

Another possible way to make a proportionate liability standard more palatable to the government is to assume that both spouses benefit from any reduction in the spouses' collective tax liability and, therefore, to require the spouses to be jointly liable for the joint tax up to the extent of that reduction. Under this approach, both spouses would be individually liable for their proportionate share of the tax and jointly liable for any deficiency to the extent of the tax savings.

* * *

Conclusions

* * *

Of these two possible modifications the first, defining the spouse's share of liability by reference to their separate tax liabilities, is the more appropriate. The first modification, although it may increase a spouse's share of liability for the joint tax, never requires a spouse to pay more tax than is warranted based on the spouse's income. The second modification is more likely to have the effect of increasing the liability of the lower-income spouse in an amount that is disproportionate to the spouse's income, a result which is inequitable if the lower-income spouse did not, in fact, benefit from the tax savings. Additionally, the first approach is less complicated than the second and easier for the average taxpayer to understand.

Revising Transferee Liability to Expand the Government's Collection Ability with Respect to Spouses

Under a proportionate liability system, transferee liability will frequently leave the government unable to collect the deficiency from the husband and unable to proceed against the wife. If the husband transfered property to the wife prior to the year in which the tax deficiency accrues, the government may not recover that property. In addition, if the husband was solvent at the time of the transfer, the government may not recover the property, even though the husband subsequently became insolvent. Furthermore, not all property that passes from the husband to the wife would be recoverable through transferee liability.

If a proportionate liability standard is adopted, transferee liability should be expanded and these hurdles removed so that the government's collection interests are adequately protected. If a proportionate liability standard is adopted, transferee liability should be amended to provide that with respect to deficiencies pertaining to joint returns the government is permitted to recover, to the extent necessary to satisfy the deficiency, all property transferred from one spouse to the other without adequate consideration, if the government has exhausted its collection activities against the spouse primarily liable for the tax and is still unable to collect the tax. It should be immaterial whether the transfer occurs before or after the tax deficiency accrues, so long as the spouses are married at both the time of the transfer and the time the tax deficiency accrues. Furthermore, it should be immaterial whether the husband is insolvent at the time of the transfer. If the government is unable to collect from the husband, it should be able to recover any property gratuitously transferred from the husband to the wife. In addition, the government should be able to pursue the wife for all property that passes to the wife by operation of law to the extent that the husband provided the original consideration for the property.

     * * *

Notes and Questions

41. The oldest and least controversial relief has been granted in the most extreme cases—the husband forged the wife's signature, or obtained her signature without her even realizing that she was signing a tax return, or obtained her signature through the use or threat of force. (The law is equally applicable to innocent husbands, of course. However, it is almost always the wife who claims to be an "innocent spouse." For simplicity, the notes use "wife" to refer to the taxpayer claiming the status of "innocent spouse.")

42. Beyond the extreme cases described in the preceding note, should the wife be allowed any relief? After all, if the Government is unable to collect from either spouse, other taxpayers must make up the balance. Suppose society, in effect, says to the wife: "You married him. You signed the return. If he is a bum and a liar, you were in a better position than anyone to know that."

43. Frequently, lenders to married people will ask that both spouses agree to be liable for repayment. Would a creditor in such a case be foreclosed from collecting from the wife because she did not fully understand her husband's financial situation, or because she divorced her husband before the creditor commenced collection activity? If not, should the Government be in a worse position regarding the collection of tax liability?

44. Suppose the wife did not know about a portion of the husband's income, which the husband had fraudulently omitted from the joint tax return. But further suppose that the husband spent the income on the support of the family, at a time when the taxpayers were living together as husband and wife. Should the wife still be entitled to avoid liability?

45. Should nonpayment be treated the same as nondisclosure? Suppose a joint tax return accurately discloses liability of $10,000, but the couple does not pay the amount due. Should the wife later be able to avoid liability if the joint income were attributable to the husband?

46. Should the termination of the marriage, without more, terminate joint liability at the option of either spouse? Would you be concerned about tax-motivated divorces?

47.   Should relief from joint liability be limited to those cases in which the marriage has dissolved by separation or divorce? After all, any couple could avoid joint liability by initially filing separate returns. Similarly, under bankruptcy laws, a husband may file for bankruptcy and his wife not do so, without any requirement that the couple separate. Why do you think that Congress limited the relief to spouses no longer living together (except where the wife can claim to be "innocent")? Does Professor Jordan agree with this limitation? Do you?

48.   Suppose a couple files a joint return, claiming deductions or making elections that are not available to married taxpayers filing separately. (For example, married taxpayers may claim the child care credit only if they file a joint return.[u]) Subsequently, the now-divorced wife seeks protection from joint liability. Should she still be able to obtain the benefits available from the joint return? What is the approach taken by Congress? The approach proposed by Professor Jordan? Which is preferable?

49.   Do you agree with Professor Jordan that the Government is unduly limited in pursuing assets transferred to the wife by the husband?

50.   Does the problem of the innocent spouse, coupled with the prevalence of divorce, offer an additional argument for ending the joint return?

D. CHILDREN AND THE INCOME TAX

People are taxed either as individuals or, if they elect to file a joint return, as married couples. There is no "family" category. Children are taxed as individuals (if they have sufficient income to be taxed), but they also affect their parents' income tax liabilities in several ways. Tax benefits from children are described in the excerpt from Professor Zelenak's article. (While some of the statutory details have changed, the basic policy issues have not.)

Professor Samansky's article considers how the tax obligations of parents should be affected by their obligation to support children. It may be important to consider the benefit of children to their parents and to society, and also to consider whether having children should be viewed as optional or as a more-or-less automatic consequence of marriage.

A family's cost of living does not go up proportionately as the number of children in the family increases. The Internal Revenue Code, however, allows the same dependency exemption for the second, or subsequent, child as for the first. The interplay of personal and dependency exemptions, standard deductions, and the poverty line for singles and families of various sizes is discussed by Dr. Pechman.

---

u. Section 21(e)(2).

CHILDREN AND THE INCOME TAX
Lawrence Zelenak[*]
49 Tax Law Review 349, 350-53 (1994)

All children are not equal under the federal income tax. Under different circumstances, the addition of a dependent child to a taxpayer's household may save the taxpayer in excess of $2,000 to absolutely nothing. At one extreme, the first child of a low income single parent produces a tax benefit of more than $2,700. The first child of an unmarried middle income taxpayer is almost as valuable, resulting in tax savings of almost $2,000. At the other extreme, there is no tax benefit from any child of very high income parents or from third and later children of low income parents. Between these extremes, the typical child of middle income parents produces tax savings ranging from about $400 to $700. A dependent child can trigger four tax benefits: the dependency exemption, head of household status, the earned income tax credit ("EITC") and the child care credit. There are different rules concerning the effect of the number of children and of the taxpayers's income level on each benefit.

The enormous variation in the tax consequences attributable to children suggests a need to evaluate how the income tax adjusts for family responsibilities. * * * Although the focus has been more on increasing tax benefits to families with children than on rationalizing the distribution of benefits among families, the legislative interest in the subject presents an opportunity to reconsider both the level and the distribution of these benefits.

This Article * * * begins with a description of current tax benefits for families. * * *

The Four Child Tax Benefits for Children

The most widely available of the four benefits is the dependency exemption. The exemption functions as a deduction of a flat $2,500 for each dependent child,[8] regardless of how many children the taxpayer may have. The tax savings from the exemption depend on the taxpayer's marginal rate. For example, one exemption saves $375 for a taxpayer in the 15% bracket and $700 for a taxpayer in the 28% bracket. Although the size of the exemption for a child does not depend on the number of other dependents, it is sensitive to the taxpayer's income. Phaseout of the exemption begins at parental adjusted gross income ("AGI") of $172,050.[9] Eventually, the exemption is phased out entirely, so that dependents entitle very high income parents to no exemptions.

Unlike the dependency exemption, the benefits of which increase proportionately with the number of children, head of household status produces a large benefit for the first child of an unmarried taxpayer, and no

---

[*]. At time of original publication, Reef C. Ivey Research Professor of Law, University of North Carolina.

8. IRC § 151(d)(1), (4). The amount of the exemption is indexed for inflation, and is $2,500 for 1995. [Throughout Professor Zelensak's excerpt, all figures are for 1995. With the exception of the child care credit, which was increased in 2001, all amounts specified in this excerpt are indexed for inflation. (Ed.)]

9. IRC § 151(d)(3). The $172,050 figure is for a married couple filing a joint return. Phaseout begins at $143,350 for a head of household. A taxpayer loses 2% of all exemptions for each $2,500 (or fraction thereof) by which AGI exceeds $172,050 (or $143,350). The phaseout is complete at $294,550 for a joint return and $265,850 for a head of household.

additional benefit for more children. A single person with no dependents is entitled to a standard deduction of $3,900 and is subject to an unfavorable tax rate schedule.[10] A single person living with at least one dependent is entitled to a standard deduction of $5,750 and is subject to a more favorable tax rate schedule.[11] In contrast to the dependency exemption, the benefit of head of household status continues regardless of the taxpayer's income level.[12]

The refundable EITC functions as a wage supplement of low income workers.[v] Until the 1993 amendments, the credit was available only to a worker living with a "qualifying child." A childless worker is now eligible for a maximum credit of $314.[15] A dependent child makes a dramatic difference, increasing the maximum credit to $2,094.[16] A second child makes a smaller, but still significant difference: The maximum credit rises to $3,100.[17] There is no benefit for additional children. Thus, sensitivity of the credit to the number of children differs from both the dependency exemption, which is equally sensitive to all children, and from head of household status, which is sensitive only to the first child. Like the exemption and unlike head of household status, the credit is tied expressly to the taxpayer's income level. The one child credit is fully phased out at $24,396 AGI, and the two child credit at $26,673.

The child care credit is the only one of the four child-related tax provisions that depends on amounts actually spent on children. The credit is a percentage—20% for most taxpayers[19]—of the amount spent by a taxpayer on child care "to enable the taxpayer to be gainfully employed."[20] The ceiling on expenses eligible for the credit is $2,400 if there is one eligible child, and $4,800[w] if there are two or more.[21]

* * *

---

10. IRC § 63(c)(2)(C) (standard deduction); § 1(c) (rate schedule).

11. IRC § 63(c)(2)(B) (standard deduction); § 1(b) (rate schedule). The existence of one or more dependents does not affect the standard deduction or tax rate schedule of a married couple.

12. The benefit of the more favorable rate schedule remains at all income levels. The benefit of the larger standard deduction also continues, but it becomes less important at high income levels because most high income taxpayers itemize.

v. The EITC is discussed in Chapter Eleven, Subchapter E.

15. The credit is 7.65% of the first $4,100 of earned income, with the credit phased out at 7.65% as AGI exceeds $5,130. See IRC § 32(b)(1) (credit percentages and phaseout percentages), § 32(b)(2) (earned income amounts and the phaseout amounts).

16. The credit is 34% of the first $6,160 of earned income. A 15.98% phaseout begins at $11,290 AGI. IRC § 32(b).

17. The credit is 36% (40% for years beginning after 1995) of the first $8,640 of earned income. A 20.22% (21.06% for years beginning after 1995) phaseout begins at $11,290 AGI. IRC § 32(b).

19. The credit rate is 30% for taxpayers with AGI of $10,000 or less, declining gradually until it becomes 20% for taxpayers with AGI of more than $28,000. IRC § 21(a)(2).

20. IRC § 21(b)(2)(A).

w. Congress has increased these amounts to $3,000 for one child and $6,000 for two or more. (Ed.)

21. IRC § 21(c). A different tax benefit for child care is provided by § 129, which excludes from income (the equivalent of inclusion and deduction) child care provided by an employer pursuant to a dependent care assistance program. This provision is even less sensitive to family size than the child care credit. The maximum amount excludable is $5,000, without regard to the number of children. IRC § 129(a)(2)(A).

TAX POLICY AND THE OBLIGATION
TO SUPPORT CHILDREN

Allan J. Samansky[*]

57 Ohio State Law Journal 329, 329-31, 362-363, 365-380 (1996)

This Article explores how the tax liability of parents should be affected by the obligation to support their children. Children are certainly an economic burden; family resources that otherwise could be used to purchase goods satisfying the parents' needs must be used for support of the children. But, of course, children are much more than a burden. Parents hope and expect that their children will be a source of happiness and fulfillment. They want their values to be transmitted to their children, and perhaps their yearning for immortality can be realized, in part, through their children. Because children have a profound and multifaceted impact on their parents, issues involving tax consequences of children are complex and controversial.

* * *

The primary objective of this Article is to explore how children affect parents' ability to pay tax. It can, of course, be argued that parents should be encouraged to make expenditures benefiting children and that therefore tax benefits with respect to children should exceed their effect on ability to pay. One problem with this argument is that there is no assurance that most of a family's reduction in tax liability will be spent in a way that benefits the children. In addition, policy makers should know what a neutral tax policy is before enacting provisions designed to benefit families with children. Otherwise, they cannot intelligently evaluate whether proposed benefits are too great or too small. Therefore, this Article concentrates on determining what a neutral tax policy with respect to children should be. Not surprisingly, there is no simple answer.

Review of Current Law

Current law provides a variety of benefits with respect to children. As the discussion in this section illustrates, however, the results are frequently anomalous, and Congress has usually not provided a satisfactory rationale for its decisions. The inescapable conclusion is that there is no underlying theory and that many of the decisions have been made on an ad hoc basis.

* * *

Children and Ability
to Pay--General Considerations
Horizontal and Vertical Equity

As is usually recognized, appropriate tax allowances for children involve horizontal equity, which is the principle that taxpayers with equal ability to pay tax should be making equal sacrifices. A comparison of two unmarried adults (A and B) illustrates this principle. Each has income of $75,000, but A is childless and B is the parent of two young children. The first issue is whether there should be any tax allowances for children at all in this situation. If A and B have equal ability to pay, they should have equal tax liability. If, on the other hand, we conclude that B's ability to pay is lower than A's, we

---

[*]. At time of original publication, Professor of Law, The Ohio State University College of Law.

need to determine what income a childless person should have for her tax capacity to be the same as B's. If that income is $65,000, then an equal sacrifice should be required of B and a childless person with income of $65,000 in determining their respective tax liabilities.[111]

It may appear that the appropriate tax allowances for children can be determined without concern for vertical equity, which is the principle that a person with greater ability to pay than another should be bearing an appropriately higher tax burden. The issue of how much more tax a person with $ 60,000 income should pay than a similarly situated person with $20,000 income is conceptually separate from whether a tax allowance for children is appropriate and what amount it should be. After any tax allowances for children have been established, tax rates and other aspects of the tax structure can, at least theoretically, be set to produce desired tax revenues and the appropriate degree of vertical equity. This reasoning, however, ignores a basic problem—the effect of generous exemptions on tax rates.

Generous exemptions result in a smaller tax base; consequently, marginal and average rates must then be higher to produce a given amount of revenue. There is, however, a benefit to keeping tax rates as low as possible. High rates, particularly high marginal rates, make the tax system more intrusive and encourage persons to change their behavior. For example, a person subject to a 50% marginal rate may choose not to work overtime since the government will claim 50% of her additional earnings; a 20% marginal rate would be less likely to have this effect. High marginal rates also increase the value and importance of tax planning by increasing the value of tax losses. * * * Of course, one may still favor generous allowances for children if it is concluded that they are necessary to distinguish among households of different sizes. * * *

Low and Moderate Income Families

Few will disagree with the conclusion that there needs to be some type of tax allowance for children in low income families. For these families children unambiguously reduce the ability to pay. When most or all resources are being used for subsistence, each member of the family is making an economic sacrifice if there is an additional person to support and no additional income. * * *

The issue then becomes how much of a deduction to allow a low income family for each child. A sensible starting point is that families at or below the poverty threshold should not have to pay any income taxes. Although the poverty threshold is inherently subjective, it represents a societal judgment that persons below it do not have an acceptable standard of living and thus

---

111. B and the single person making $65,000 (whom we can call "C") should probably not pay equal amounts of tax. An equal sacrifice, which is appropriate, would mean that B and C would have the same economic well-being after-tax since they had equal capacity before tax. This would probably require a greater tax payment by B. For example, B and C might be equally well off after-tax if B has after-tax income of $52,000, and C has after-tax income of $45,000. B should then have tax liability of $23,000, and C should have tax liability of $ 20,000. See Eugene Steuerle, *The Tax Treatment of Households of Different Sizes, in* TAXING THE FAMILY 73, 81 (Rudolph Penner, ed. 1983).

represents a reasonable level of income at which tax liability should begin. Congress has apparently accepted this reasoning. Consequently, a deduction for the subsistence cost of raising a child, which is the increase in the poverty threshold on account of the child, should be allowed low income families. This deduction will keep those below the poverty threshold off the tax rolls.

A deduction for the subsistence cost of a child should also be available for middle income families. If the effect of children on ability to pay is recognized for parents who are at or close to subsistence, then the tax allowance should not be suddenly revoked when the parents' income is modestly above subsistence. For such families as well, paying for necessities consumes a major portion of available resources and supporting a child reduces what is available for others. * * *

Current law allows a deduction for each child that approximates the amount needed to support that child at subsistence according to official definitions of poverty. The 1995 Poverty Guidelines published by the Department of Health and Human Services provide that each additional child in a household adds an additional $2560 to the poverty threshold, and the 1995 personal exemption for a child is $2500. Each amount is indexed to the Consumer Price Index and increases annually. Therefore, it is important to evaluate the sufficiency of the poverty guidelines.

The official poverty guidelines used in the United States are based on a series of studies undertaken in the 1960s for the Social Security Administration by Millie Orshansky.[131] The poverty threshold was determined by first estimating the cost of a nutritionally adequate diet for various types of families. This amount was then multiplied by three on the assumption (supported by some evidence from surveys) that low income families spent approximately one third of their income for food. The original design of the poverty index could, of course, be criticized. However, the index was widely accepted, and its widespread use was an indication that it conformed with public opinion on the determination of what constitutes poverty.

Possibly the most serious shortcoming in the current poverty guidelines is the lack of any adjustment since 1969 except for general indexing by the Consumer Price Index. Three types of problems can be identified. First, society may revise its standards for what is a minimally necessary standard of living. For example, prices tend to rise more slowly than incomes, and thus the gap widens between what is needed to emerge from poverty and what the average person is consuming. We should expect that, as our general standard of living increases, our determination of what is needed for a minimally adequate lifestyle should also increase. Second, there has been a change in consumption patterns over the last twenty-five years. For example, the increased prevalence of women working and two wage earners per household has changed the importance of expenses like commuting costs and taxes. Also, new products have appeared that were not available in earlier years. At one

---

131. See Millie Orshansky, *Counting the Poor: Another Look at the Poverty Profile*, 28 SOCIAL SECURITY BULL. 3 (January 1965); Millie Orshansky, *Children of the Poor*, 26 SOCIAL SECURITY BULL. 3 (July 1963).

time telephones and televisions were not considered "necessities"; now they probably should be. Videocassette recorders, microwaves, and even computers may be considered necessities in the near future. Third, to the extent that low income persons have different consumption patterns than middle and high income persons, changes in the overall consumer price index will not reflect changes in the cost of living of low income persons. For example, if low income persons spend a disproportionate amount on shelter compared to the population at large, they will be more severely impacted by an increase in the cost of housing.

Many different methods have been used to estimate poverty thresholds, and the results, not surprisingly, differ significantly. In a study authorized by the Joint Economic Committee of Congress, a panel for the National Research Council listed eleven published estimates for two-adult, two-children families. The official poverty guideline was the lowest, with the highest estimate being 50% larger than the official guideline. Currently, the official poverty guidelines calculate that the subsistence cost of an additional child is $2560. A 50% increase would result in a subsistence cost of $3840.

To the extent there is any uncertainty about the appropriate size of a deduction for a child, it should be resolved in favor of a larger deduction. Certainly, it is better to undertax, rather than overtax, low and moderate income families with children. Any lost revenue should be relatively small, especially if the benefit is not fully extended to affluent families. Consequently, a deduction of at least $4000 per child for low and middle income families seems appropriate.

There are three additional issues concerning tax allowances for low and moderate income families. The first is whether the deduction allowed for each child should vary according to the number of children. * * * Studies confirm that, although total expenditures on children generally increase when the number of children increases, the amount spent per child decreases. One reason for this is economies of scale. For example, children can share a room and hand-me-down clothes, and food can be purchased more economically in larger quantities. * * * Making these distinctions would add some complexity to the tax laws, but tables listing the total exemptions based on number of children per family should make the task manageable.

A second and similar issue is whether the deductions should vary according to the age of the children. Amounts spent on children increase significantly as they become older. The study by the Department of Agriculture shows that, for low income families with two adults and two children, the annual amount spent on a child is estimated to be $4960 for a child less than two years old and $6260 for a child between fifteen and seventeen years old, a 26% increase. As with the number of children, there is a strong theoretical argument for taking account of the effect of age on subsistence cost in determining the personal exemptions. The problem is that exemption amounts depending on ages of children may increase complexity of the tax forms substantially. An additional reason for not taking account of age is that the deductions will balance out over the childhood years. The issue is "only" one of timing.

The third issue is the most complex: whether there should be a greater deduction for children of single-parent families than two-parent families. A larger deduction might be appropriate because, with only a single parent, there is less adult time to be devoted to the children and correspondingly cash expenditures may have to be increased to compensate for the lack of time. For example, convenience foods and frozen dinners, which are more expensive than basic food products, might have to be purchased more often by single parents because they have less time to prepare meals.

Single parents spend a greater proportion of their income on children than two-parent families with the same total number of children, but this result is not surprising. With less people to share the income, one would expect each person in a family to receive a greater share. * * *

* * * I would support larger tax allowances for children in households with single parents, if more detailed data confirm that the economic burden is greater for low income single parents and provide some basis for estimating the magnitude of the difference.

Affluent Parents

Although the income level where middle income status ends and affluence begins is inherently arbitrary, the fact that there are both middle income and affluent persons should be noncontroversial. * * * In my opinion, determining the appropriate tax benefits for affluent parents is a much more complex undertaking than for low and middle income parents. I believe that the merits of any proposal with respect to affluent parents will not be based on immutable principles, but rather on the weighing of alternatives and possibly the acceptability of simplifying assumptions.

Certainly, a cogent argument can be made that children should reduce the tax liability of affluent parents. Children have economic needs that must be met, and the parents (no matter how affluent) must redirect some of their resources to meet those needs. An affluent family with a new baby must purchase items such as baby formula and diapers, while an otherwise identical family with no children can spend that money on a luxury car. * * *

Members of the second family may disagree with this reasoning, however. Presumably the first family chose to have the child and decided that the benefits outweighed any lost consumption. * * *

This analysis could, of course, be made for low and middle income families as well as for affluent families. We can choose to treat consumption by the child as adding to the parents' economic well-being in either case. Nevertheless, it seems reasonable to conclude that a person who spends money on her child rather than purchasing a custom-made suit or a piece of jewelry has not diminished her economic well-being. The consumption by the child can be considered a substitute for the suit or jewelry. It seems less reasonable to conclude that consumption by a child is a substitute for a needed car repair.

The contention that the ability to pay of affluent parents is not reduced by children can be based on three propositions. Although all three might not be logically necessary, realistically the reader probably must accept all three to accept the conclusion. They are as follows: (1) most persons plan the number of children that they have and are generally successful in this planning; (2) those who have children do not regret their choice, especially when the children are still young (and thus qualify for a tax allowance); and (3) parents obtain happiness and fulfillment from their children. The first and second propositions are quite straightforward, and require relatively little discussion.

* * *

The third proposition is more complex. It is not merely that there should be no tax allowance for children since parents have made a voluntary decision and are happier as a result. The argument is also that much, if not all, that is spent on a child also benefits the parent directly or indirectly. Distinguishing between amounts spent for the benefit of the child and those spent for the benefit of the parents is inherently arbitrary.

Parents obtain satisfaction from consumption by their children in two ways. The first is simply altruism; parents are happy when their children are happy. * * * In addition, the parent might obtain pleasure directly from a child's use of resources regardless of any pleasure obtained by the child. One example might be a cute outfit purchased for a little child. Another might be piano lessons that the child dislikes, but the parent gains satisfaction from having a child trained in music. In both cases, the parent's pleasure is independent of the child's feelings. Finally, some events, such as a family dinner, may contribute to a parent's satisfaction in both ways. * * *

I am not contending that there is only one correct method of taxing affluent families with children. Rather, the claim is only that not providing tax allowances to affluent families is a reasonable approach. Whether or not deductions, credits, or other tax benefits for a child should be allowed depends on practical decisions and the weighing of alternatives.

Evaluation of Current Law and Some Tentative Proposals

Replacement of Personal Exemption by Credit

In the previous section I have contended that low and moderate income parents should be allowed a tax benefit that is substantially greater than the current $2500 deduction for each child. There is no conceptually correct number, but a $4000 deduction (or equivalent benefit) can be easily justified. I have also suggested that the benefit should probably vary according to the number of children although I did not provide a specific schedule or formula.[155]

* * *

I have also contended that there is not a compelling need to provide any tax benefits to affluent parents. The phaseout of the personal exemption, which starts at $172,050 for married persons filing jointly and $143,350 for those filing as heads of households, is consistent with this position, although it might be argued that it should begin at lower income levels. * * *

The problem with deductions (or credits) that are phased out at higher incomes is that they are equivalent to increases in the marginal rate for

---

155. If this proposal were accepted, the recommended $4000 deduction (or equivalent benefit) would be the average amount allowed for children. The deduction for the first child might be larger than $4000, and the deduction for the second child might be smaller than $4000.

affected taxpayers. The existing phaseout of personal exemptions is quivalent to an increase in the marginal rate of almost three-quarters of a percentage point for each exemption for a married couple who is in the 36% nominal bracket and has adjusted gross income between $172,500 and $294,550. Consequently, with four personal exemptions, there is an increase in the marginal rate of almost three percentage points. One result is that the marginal rate goes down as soon as adjusted gross income exceeds $294,500. A decline in the marginal rate when income increases does seem perverse.

A fixed tax credit for each child may be an appropriate compromise. Affluent parents would obtain some tax benefit, but a limited benefit can be justified since they too must support their children. Unlike a deduction, however, a credit is not worth more to high income taxpayers than to those with low incomes; it provides a fixed benefit varying only according to number of children. A credit also avoids the need for drawing a line between moderate income and affluent taxpayers. The credit would be fully available to the affluent, but obviously a fixed benefit becomes relatively less important as one's income and tax liability increases. For a moderate income family the proposed credit should provide a tax benefit that is equivalent to the deduction that was recommended above. The recommended deduction was $4000, and the equivalent credit would be $600 since moderate income persons are in the 15% tax bracket. It might be noted that a $600 credit, although much more valuable to moderate income persons than the current $2500 deduction (which for them is equivalent to a $375 credit), is less valuable to those high income taxpayers who are still obtaining the full benefit of the deduction; a taxpayer in the 36% bracket saves $900 from the $2500 deduction.

* * *

A phaseout of the recommended credit would also be a possibility. The small temporary increase in effective marginal rates as the credit is phased out may be warranted if it is accepted (as argued in this Article) that a tax benefit for children is not necessarily appropriate for affluent families. There is no scientific method to determine where the phaseout should begin; determination of who is affluent is a matter of judgment and politics.

Head of Household Status

The separate tax schedules for those filing as heads of households should be repealed because they primarily help affluent unmarried persons. There is no reason that a child should reduce the tax liability of an unmarried person with adjusted gross income over $150,000 by $2395, in addition to any saving from the personal exemption.

On the other hand, the increase in the standard deduction for heads of households can be defended. As argued in the previous section, children may be more of an economic burden for unmarried persons than for those who are married, and a tax allowance might appropriately reflect this disparity. Because the standard deduction primarily helps low and moderate income persons, the increased standard deduction can be justified as appropriately taking account of the reduced ability to pay of these persons. * * *

If further analysis confirms that children place more of an economic burden on unmarried than on married persons, my preference would be that an increased credit or deduction (whichever is the basic tax allowance for moderate income parents) be substituted for the increase in the standard deduction. Whether a person will benefit from an increase in the standard deduction depends on factors that have nothing to do with the effect of a child on ability to pay. For example, the increase in the standard deduction would be less useful to taxpayers in states with high income taxes than in states with no income taxes since the former are more likely to itemize their deductions and thus not utilize the standard deduction.

A higher per child benefit for unmarried than for married persons is troubling in one respect. Some might assert that the tax laws would be "rewarding" unmarried parents more than married couples for having children. This contention is not valid, however, if the unmarried parent is raising the child herself. When the extra benefit only reflects the additional cost of being an unmarried parent, the tax code is neutral with respect to married and unmarried parents. On the other hand, if the two parents were unmarried, but living together and raising the child, a higher benefit than that available to married parents would be unwarranted. This result is similar to the marriage penalty under current law.

* * *

Conclusion

The Article has * * * attempted to establish three principles. First, there is no theoretical approach that should be systematically used for all taxpayers in determining the effect of children on appropriate tax liability. Second, low and middle income parents should be allowed a deduction (or equivalent benefit) for each child that at least equals the subsistence cost of raising a child. Third, any benefits provided to low and middle income parents need not be extended to affluent parents. * * * The major recommendation was that the $2500 deduction for each child be replaced by a $600 credit.

FEDERAL TAX POLICY
Joseph Pechman[*]
Pages 83-86 (5th ed. 1987)
Relative Exemptions for Different Family Size

If a family of two must spend x dollars to achieve a certain scale of living, what proportion of x would a single person spend, and how much more than x would families of three, four, five, or more people spend to maintain an equivalent standard? Clearly, the answer depends on the criteria used for measuring equivalence. The standard criteria used by the federal government, which are included in the official poverty-line estimates published annually by the Census Bureau, are based on the amount of income needed to maintain an adequate diet.

As shown in table 4-3, the financial needs of a household do not increase in direct proportion to the number of people in the household. The relative incomes that would provide roughly equivalent standards of living appear to be in the ratio of 80:100:25 for single persons, married couples, and

---

[*]. At time of original publication, Senior Fellow, The Brookings Institution.

dependents, respectively. Income tax exemptions plus the standard deduction give a ratio of approximately 55:100:20 for 1989. Although the per capita exemption is too liberal for dependents and too small for single persons, the addition of the standard deduction adjusts the ratio more nearly in line with the relative needs of families of different sizes except for single persons who maintain a separate household.

Table 4-3. *Indexes of the Minimum Taxable Level under the Federal Individual Income Tax and Estimated Poverty-Level Budgets for Families of Various Sizes, 1989*
Two-person family = 100

	Index	
Size of Family	Minimum Taxable Level	Poverty-level budget
1	56	78
2	100	100
3	122	123
4	143	157
5	165	186
6	187	210

Level of Exemptions

The adequacy of the *level* of exemptions may be judged by comparing the official poverty-level incomes with the minimum taxable thresholds for families of different sizes (see table 4-4). The minimum taxable levels equal the statutory per capita exemptions plus the standard deduction. As a result of the passage of the 1986 tax reform, these two elements will be sufficient to raise the minimum taxable levels above the poverty lines for all family sizes except for single persons in 1989, when the increase in exemptions becomes fully effective.

It is clear from table 4-4 that the standard deduction plays an important role in correcting the inadequacy of the per capita exemption. The purpose of the standard deduction is to augment the regular exemptions at the bottom of the income scale without incurring the heavy cost of raising the exemptions for all taxpayers.

Tax Credits in Lieu of Exemptions

Before 1975 income tax allowances for taxpayers and dependents were generally given in the form of exemptions deducted from income in computing taxable incomes. An alternative method, now used in several states, is to convert the allowance to a credit computed by multiplying the value of the exemption by the first-bracket tax rate or some higher rate. With a 15 percent first-bracket rate, the $2,000 exemption would be converted to a credit of $300; at a 20 percent rate, the credit would amount to $400; and so on. The credit limits the tax value of the exemption to the same dollar amount for all taxpayers. It would increase the tax liabilities for those with taxable incomes above the bracket chosen to calculate the value of the credit and reduce them for those with taxable incomes below that level. * * *

Table 4-4. *Minimum Taxable Level under the Federal Individual Income Tax and Estimated Poverty-Level Budgets for Families of Various Sizes, 1989 Dollars*

Size of family	Exemptions	Standard deduction[a]	Minimum taxable level[b]	Poverty-level budget[c]	Difference
1	2000	3120	5120	6235	-1115
2	4000	5200	9200	7978	1222
3	6000	5200	11200	9773	1427
4	8000	5200	13200	12527	673
5	10000	5200	15200	14828	372
6	12000	5200	17200	16753	447

Sources: Minimum taxable levels are based on the personal exemptions and standard deductions for single and married persons under the Tax Reform Act of 1986. Poverty levels are 1985 data from U.S. Department of Commerce, Bureau of the Census, *Current Population Reports*, series P-60, no. 154, "Money Income and Poverty Status of Families and Persons in the United States: 1985," p. 33, projected to 1989.

    a. Adjusted for the estimated increase in the consumer price index from 1988 to 1989.

    b. Sum of the first two columns.

    c. Poverty-level budgets for 1985 were adjusted for an estimated increase in the consumer price index of 14 percent from 1985 to 1989. [Footnotes a-c are in the original. (Ed.)]

Complete replacement of the exemption by a credit would be generous for large families in the lowest income classes and would reduce the tax differences by size of family in the higher classes. To avoid this effect, it has been proposed that a tax credit be allowed as an alternative to the exemption rather than as a substitute for it. Low-income taxpayers would use the credit, and those in the higher classes would continue to use the exemptions. But an optional credit would complicate the tax return and be confusing to many taxpayers. Moreover, roughly the same effect among income classes could be obtained without narrowing tax differences based on family size by retaining the exemption and adjusting the tax rates in the higher income classes. But proponents of the credit are not persuaded that the rate adjustments would actually be made.

Between 1975 and 1978, Congress departed from previous practice and provided a relatively small per capita credit ($30 in 1975 and $35 in 1976-78) instead of increasing the personal exemptions. The adoption of a small credit was a compromise between those who wanted to replace the entire exemption with a credit and those who preferred to increase the exemption. The credit was eliminated when it became clear that it added to the complexity of the tax return without accomplishing very much.

A Vanishing Exemption

Carried to the extreme, the logic of a tax credit would lead to an exemption that vanished at some point on the income scale. A vanishing exemption is supported on the ground that exemptions are not justified for persons with very large incomes, since at these levels they are not needed to meet essential consumption requirements for the taxpayers and their children.

For the first time in U.S. tax history, the 1986 tax reform bill adopted a variant of the vanishing exemption. The particular device chosen was to phase out the personal exemption at the rate of 5 percent of taxable income beginning when the benefit of the first-bracket tax rate phases out (in 1988, taxable income of $89,560 for single persons, $123,790 for heads of households, and $149,250 for married couples). There is no rationale for phasing out the exemption in this particular way, except to save revenue. A more gradual phaseout that did not raise the marginal tax rate by as much as 5 percentage points would be more appropriate. But, as in the case of the credit, it would be better to retain the personal exemption throughout the income scale and adjust the top tax rate to make up the revenue loss.

* * *

Notes and Questions

51. Arguably, a logical extension of the joint return would be to include children as well as spouses. Although Congress has never taken this step, the "kiddie tax" of section 1(g), which was adopted in 1986, approximates this result with respect to the child's unearned income. The kiddie tax was adopted as a response to the practice of parents giving income-producing assets to their children to achieve an income-splitting benefit. The kiddie tax cannot be characterized as reflecting any deeper consideration of the whole family as a taxing unit—otherwise the child's earned income would have been included as well.

52. Professor Zelenak discusses four tax advantages that flow to parents. What are these?

53. A significant new child-related tax benefit was added to the Internal Revenue Code in 1997, and expanded in 2001 and 2003. The child tax credit of section 24 allows a credit of up to $1,000 per child. The credit is partially refundable,[x] and is phased out as the parents' income increases.[y]

---

x. Section 24(d).

y. Section 24(b). The phase-out is $50 of credit per thousand dollars (or fraction thereof) of adjusted gross income in excess of the threshold amount—$110,000 joint or $75,000 for unmarried taxpayers (usually, in this case, heads of household).

54. Zelenak's analysis suggests that no unifying vision informed Congress as it enacted these provisions over the years. Three of the four advantages (as well as the child tax credit discussed in the preceding note) end as the parent's increases to some (varying) point—but head of household status does not.

How many children justify congressional concern? One child kicks in the maximum tax advantage for HOH status, while the child tax credit and dependency exemptions provide constant per-child amounts regardless of the number of children. The child care credit and earned income tax credit are both more for two children than for one, but after two, additional children do not matter.

Should these inconsistencies bother us?

55. The earned income tax credit, which provides an important tax benefit to low-income taxpayers, particularly if they have children, is discussed more fully in Chapter Eleven, Subchapter E.

56. Professor Samansky suggests the tax allowance for dependent children is, and should be, related to poverty guidelines. Do you agree? If the tax benefit should be related to subsistence living standards for poor families, why would Samansky continue it for middle-income taxpayers?

57. Professor Samansky criticizes the official poverty guideline as setting too low a figure for the poverty threshold. Why?

58. Samansky asserts that "[c]ertainly, it is better to undertax, rather than overtax, low and moderate income families with children." Most people would agree in the abstract—the problem arises when we attempt to put flesh on the terms "undertax" and "overtax." But most people would also agree in the abstract that it would be better to undertax than to overtax low and moderate income persons who were childless. Should we err on the side of protecting lower-income *parents*, through generous child tax advantages, or err on the side of protecting all lower-income taxpayers, likely through the rate structure?

59. All of the child-related tax benefits are reduced as income rises, and most are eliminated entirely at some maximum level of income. Is such an approach defensible? Congress recognizes, for example, that a childless couple with $30,000 income has more ability to pay taxes than an otherwise similarly situated couple with children. Is it not similarly true that a childless couple with $500,000 income has more ability to pay than an otherwise similarly situated couple with children? Would equity be improved if the tax burden among high-income persons were reallocated by allowing high-income taxpayers the child-related tax benefits available to taxpayers of more modest

income, and paying for these benefits through higher tax rates on all high-income taxpayers?

60. What problem of economic inefficiency does Samansky see from the approach suggested in the preceding note—allowing tax advantages to affluent parents, and making that up by raising marginal rates for all affluent taxpayers?

61. Samansky asserts that money spent by affluent parents on their children benefits the parents as well. Is this more true of the affluent than of lower-income parents, assuming that almost all parents love their children, and are gladdened by anything that makes the child better off or happier?

62. Using 1995 figures, Professor Samansky suggested substituting a $600 credit for the $2,500 dependency exemption. What was his rationale for using a credit rather than a deduction (a more accurate term for the dependency exemption)? What was his rationale for the $900 figure?

63. Note that at present, Congress provides both an exemption and a child tax credit. The credit is of equal-dollar value to all taxpayers who receive it; the deduction is worth more to taxpayers according to their tax bracket. Both, however, phase out with income, at different levels.

The overall treatment of parents under present law is more favorable than Samansky suggested for low-income taxpayers, and less favorable for high-income taxpayers. (Samansky would have allowed all taxpayers his proposed credit, while current law completely phases out both the exemption and credit at high income levels.)

64. Like Professor Samansky, Dr. Pechman suggests that a per-child (or per-person) personal and dependency exemption is flawed. Should each child give rise to the same benefit, or should the tax code reflect the idea that children are "cheaper by the dozen"?

65. Interestingly, Dr. Pechman's analysis suggests that the taxpayers most in need of relief may be single taxpayers. Should personal and dependency exemptions be restructured to reflect the fact that children, while expensive, are cheaper to maintain than adults?

66. Of importance in our analysis is whether society wishes to give benefits to parents not just as a matter of equity, but in order to influence people in their decisions about having children.

Some, pointing to worldwide population growth and ecological concerns, think that governments should be attempting to restrain population growth.

On the other hand, while population growth remains strong in the Third

World, this is not so for much of the developed world. In Japan and much of Western Europe, childbearing rates are not sufficient to maintain current population. In Western Europe, and perhaps in the United States, future workers may come from immigration as much as from birth.

Should tax policies be structured in order to increase or decrease population growth?

67. For taxpayers who are members of a family, what should the proper taxing unit be—the individual, the husband and wife, or the parents and minor children? Why?

E. TAX TREATMENT OF THE ELDERLY

While not to the extent of children, elderly taxpayers are the beneficiaries of a number of special tax provisions. In the following excerpt, Professor Forman argues that most of these special provisions are unjustified, and should be repealed or curtailed:

RECONSIDERING THE INCOME TAX TREATMENT OF THE ELDERLY: IT'S TIME FOR THE ELDERLY TO PAY THEIR FAIR SHARE

Jonathan Barry Forman[*]

56 University of Pittsburgh Law Review 589, 593, 595-96, 613-19 (1995)

Economic Resources of the Elderly

Income and Poverty

* * *

While the elderly generally have lower cash incomes than the nonelderly, family units with unit heads in their 60's tend to be fairly well off. Indeed, the median incomes of families age 60-64 and 65-69 are greater than the median family incomes of families age 20-24 and 25-29. All and all, there can be little doubt that many elderly families have incomes greater than a significant portion of younger families.

The elderly are also less likely to be poor than are other demographic groups. For example, in 1992, when the overall poverty rate was 14.5 percent, only 12.9 percent of the elderly were poor. In contrast, almost 22 percent of children were poor that year. It is worth noting, however, that among the elderly, the poverty rate goes up as people get older. For example, while just 10.7 percent of those age 65 to 74 were poor in 1992[,] 15.3 percent of those age 75 to 84 were poor, and 19.8 percent of those age 85 and over were poor.

* * *

Wealth

Moreover, the elderly tend to be wealthier than the nonelderly. * * * [O]n average, the elderly are twice as wealthy as the nonelderly. Indeed, * * *

---

*. At time of original publication, Professor of Law, University of Oklahoma.

families with a household head aged 70-74 are the wealthiest of all families.
* * *

It's Time for the Elderly to
Pay Their Fair Share of Taxes
The Elderly Are Undertaxed

* * * [T]he elderly are generally better off than we think. Many of the elderly have higher incomes and more wealth than their nonelderly counterparts. In particular, the elderly often have higher incomes and more wealth than young couples starting families. Moreover, many of the elderly, are able to work, and if they did work they could often earn relatively higher pay than their younger counterparts. All in all, there would appear to be little justification for government policies which lump those age 65 and over together into a single homogenous group for special treatment. Their federal tax liabilities should comport with their actual abilities-to-pay tax, not with some archaic, 19th century notion that demands reverence and special treatment for the elderly. In particular, the special tax provisions for the elderly seem to be gratuitous and misplaced. True, some elderly Americans are poor and perhaps in need of a special tax preference. On the other hand, it just does not make sense to let wealthy, high-income retired individuals get special tax preferences. The special tax preferences for the elderly appear to be more a response to the political power of elderly voters than a rational response to the needs of the elderly.[93]

Of course, the special tax preferences for the elderly might be appropriate if we believed that the elderly have paid too much tax earlier in their lives. Many economists believe that the proper tax base of an income tax is lifetime income. On that view, an annual income tax is, at best, a practical compromise that enables governments to collect revenues without having to wait until the death of the taxpayer to determine the theoretically proper amount to collect.

Nevertheless, it seems unlikely that anyone could conclude that the current generation of elderly have paid more than their fair share of income taxes before reaching age 65 so that they should somehow be entitled to tax preferences merely because they have made it to the golden years.[95] The country is facing annual budget deficits of almost $200 billion a year for the rest of the century, and the public debt is more than $4 trillion. This suggests that the current elderly have not paid for anywhere close to all of their

---

93. For example, in the 1992 election, more than 70% of the elderly voted, while just 45.7% of 21 to 24 year-olds voted. U.S. DEPT. OF COMMERCE, STATISTICAL ABSTRACT OF THE U.S. 287, tbl. 448 (114th ed. 1994).

95. In fairness, it should be noted that simply comparing the taxes paid by various generations ignores the value of other important contributions made by the generational cohort. For example, shouldn't a generational comparison take into account the lost earnings of those who fought World War II? And what of those who were killed or disabled in the war? *See generally* LAURENCE J. KOTLIKOFF, GENERATIONAL ACCOUNTING: KNOWING WHO PAYS, AND WHEN, FOR WHAT WE SPEND (1992). *See also* Lawrence A. Frolik & Alison P. Barnes, *An Aging Population: A Challenge to the Law*, 42 HASTINGS L.J. 683, 707-10 (1991).

consumption in government-provided goods to date. Moreover, according to virtually all analyses of current federal spending, more than half of the domestic spending goes to pay for programs that primarily benefit the elderly, such as Social Security and Medicare.

Nor should anyone believe that today's elderly have anted up their fair share of Social Security taxes before reaching their golden years. Table 10 shows the payroll tax rates and applicable wage base since the Social Security tax system started. From Table 10 it is clear that earlier generations of workers historically paid less Social Security taxes than the current generation of workers.[98] Not surprisingly, most analysts agree that early generations of retirees have received disproportionately more Social Security and Medicare benefits than their meager tax contributions would justify.

All in all, it seems that the elderly are undertaxed. The elderly have a greater ability to pay tax than the nonelderly, yet the income and Social Security tax laws favor the elderly. * * *

Some Initial Steps: Repeal the Special Tax Provisions for the Elderly

At the outset, this Subpart suggests repealing the special tax expenditures that favor the elderly. Alternatively, it might be appropriate to limit these special tax breaks to a portion of the elderly, such as the old old (age 75 and over). There just doesn't seem to be much reason for across the board special tax breaks for the near old and the young old.

Repeal the Additional Standard Deduction for the Elderly

Congress should repeal the additional standard deduction for the elderly. The basic standard deductions generally insure that low-income taxpayers are protected from income taxation. There is simply no reason to believe that all elderly taxpayers need more tax relief than nonelderly taxpayers.

For example, reconsider the tax treatment of married couples without children. * * * [T]he poverty level for a married couple without children was $9,840 in 1994 and * * * the tax threshold for a nonelderly couple was $11,250. On the other hand, because it could claim two additional $750 standard deductions, an elderly married couple benefited from a tax threshold of $12,750 in 1994. Yet there is no reason to believe that an elderly married couple without children has a lesser ability to pay income taxes than a comparable nonelderly couple. Indeed, it is more likely that the elderly couple owns its own home, has paid off its mortgage, collects tax-free Social

---

98. Dep't of Health & Human Serv., 1995 Cost-of-Living Increase and Other Determinations, 59 Fed. Reg. 54, 464 (1994). Of course, a proper comparison should index the Social Security taxes paid in the past for inflation. In nominal dollars, the maximum wage base in 1954 was just $3,600. *Id.* Nevertheless, even in real 1992 dollars, the 1954 maximum wage base translates into just $26,165, *id.* at 11, still far less than the $55,500 maximum wage base actually imposed on workers in 1992, *id.* at 76, and the 2% tax rate of 1954 was far less than the 7.65% rate actually applicable in 1992, *id.*

Security and Medicare benefits, and has no employment-related business or child care expenses. Hence, fairness mandates repealing the additional standard deduction for the elderly.

   * * *

  Alternatively, the eligibility age for the additional standard deduction should be raised to age 70 or age 75. * * *

  [T]he empirical evidence suggests that 65 is not old. Most 65 year olds are healthy, have long life expectancies, and can continue to work. Raising the age at which individuals could receive the additional standard deduction for the elderly would help communicate the idea that 65 year olds can and should work and be active.

Tax Social Security Benefits Like Private Pensions and Repeal the Tax Credit for the Elderly

  Social Security benefits are as spendable as other forms of cash income. Nevertheless, the income tax provides a partial exclusion from taxation for Social Security benefits. Instead, the income portion of Social Security benefits should be taxed.

  Taxing Social Security benefits like private pensions would be the fairest way to tax Social Security benefits. Under current law, an individual receiving benefits under a private pension plan usually excludes just a small fraction of those benefits from income. That fraction (the so-called exclusion ratio) is based on the amount of after-tax contributions to the pension by the individual when she was an employee. The exclusion ratio enables the employee to recover her own after-tax contributions tax free and to pay tax only on the remaining portion of pension benefits which represents income.

  If Social Security benefits were taxed like private pensions, beneficiaries would be allowed to exclude only a small fraction of their benefits from income. That fraction would be based on the amount of Social Security taxes they actually paid over their working careers. Social Security beneficiaries could recover their contributions tax-free, but they would have to include the remaining portion of Social Security benefits in income.

  Taxing Social Security benefits like private pensions would make the tax system fairer. For example, an elderly couple with, say, $20,000 of Social Security benefits and $12,000 of interest income would pay almost the same amount of income tax as a nonelderly couple with $32,000 of income. On the other hand, standard deductions and personal exemptions would generally protect low-income elderly individuals from any increased income tax liability. Moreover, if Social Security benefits were taxed like private pensions, there would be no reason to retain the credit for the elderly (and disabled), and it, too, could be repealed.

**TABLE 10. PAYROLL TAX RATES FOR EMPLOYEES
AND EMPLOYERS AND WAGE BASE LEVELS**

Calendar Years	OASDI wage base	Tax rates (percent)
1937-49	$3,000	1.000
1950	3,000	1.500
1951-53	3,600	1.500
1954	3,600	2.000
1955-56	4,200	2.000
1957-58	4,200	2.250
1959	4,800	2.500
1960-61	4,800	3.000
1962	4,800	3.130
1963-65	4,800	3.630
1966	6,600	4.200
1967	6,600	4.400
1968	7,800	4.400
1969	7,800	4.800
1970	7,800	4.800
1971	7,800	5.200
1972	9,000	5.200
1973	10,800	5.850
1974	13,200	5.850
1975	14,100	5.850
1976	15,300	5.850
1977	16,500	5.850
1978	17,700	6.050
1979	22,900	6.130
1980	25,900	6.130
1981	29,700	6.650
1982	32,400	6.700
1983	35,700	6.700
1984	37,800	7.000
1985	39,600	7.050
1986	42,000	7.150
1987	43,800	7.150
1988	45,000	7.510
1989	48,000	7.510
1990	51,300	7.650
1991	53,400	7.650
1992	55,500	7.650
1993	57,600	7.650
1994	60,600	7.650
1995	61,200	7.650
1996-99	(²)	7.650
2000+	(²)	7.650

2. Increases automatically with increases in the average wage index.

Taxing Social Security benefits like private pensions would also make the current elderly appreciate how little of their Social Security benefits are earned and how much represents transfers from the current generation of workers. Also, taxing Social Security benefits like annuities * * * could be used for other purposes. It has been estimated that this change could raise more than $98 billion over the next five years.[102]

Tax the Insurance Value of Medicare Benefits

It would also make sense to tax the insurance value of Medicare benefits. In particular, as Medicare is not means-tested, many Medicare beneficiaries are relatively well-off. In effect, Medicare payroll taxes collected from low-income working taxpayers are being used to pay for health care benefits for well-off retirees. That hardly seems fair.[104] Taxing the insurance value of Medicare benefits could raise more than $83 billion over the next five years.[105]

Other Changes

Along the same lines, it would make sense to repeal the general exclusion from gross income for welfare benefits. Taxing welfare benefits would improve the equity of the federal income tax and raise some revenue. Standard deductions and personal exemptions would continue to protect almost all low-income elderly individuals from any increased income tax liability.

Notes and Questions

68. If the special provisions affecting the elderly are not justified, why do you think Congress enacted them?

69. At present, Social Security benefits are tax-free to most recipients, while higher-income recipients can be taxed on a maximum of 85 percent of benefits. Is this exclusion justified? Is it relevant that a large proportion of Social Security beneficiaries cannot work?

70. What would be the effect of taxing Social Security benefits like private pensions? Would this improve the law? Would this violate broad societal understandings regarding Social Security?

---

102. U.S. CONGRESSIONAL BUDGET OFFICE, REDUCING THE DEFICIT: SPENDING AND REVENUE OPTIONS 304-05 (1994) [hereinafter REDUCING THE DEFICIT]. The Congressional Budget Office estimate is based on making taxpayers include 85% of their Social Security benefits in income. Over the next few years, at least, taxing Social Security benefits like annuities would result in taxpayers including even more than 85% of their benefits in income and so would raise even more revenues. Robert J. Myers, *Is the 85-Percent Factor for Taxing Social Security Benefits Perpetually Correct?*, 50 TAX NOTES 1545-46 (1993).

104. Admittedly, the health care costs of the elderly tend to be higher than those of the nonelderly. Consequently, rather than requiring the elderly to include the full insurance value of their Medicare benefits in gross income, it might be appropriate for the elderly to include a lesser amount.

105. REDUCING THE DEFICIT, *supra* note 102, at 313-14.

71. Many elderly persons are almost wholly dependent on their Social Security benefits. Would adoption of Professor Forman's proposals increase their tax burdens?

72. Professor Forman asserts that Medicare benefits should be subjected to tax, noting that Medicare benefits are not means tested, and therefore that "many Medicare beneficiaries are relatively well-off." At the same time, millions of well-off younger taxpayers also enjoy tax-free health benefits. Does the logic of Professor Forman's argument suggest that employer-provided health benefits, now excluded from income by section 106, should be taxed?

73. Consider footnote 95 of Professor Forman's article. What intergenerational effect should be given to the contributions of the elderly in overcoming the Great Depression and fighting World War II? The sacrifices of the current generation of elderly Americans, unmatched by the relatively pampered generations that followed them, arguably established the foundations for our security and for the unprecedented prosperity of the past 60 years.

74. Many considerations can be brought to bear on the complex issue of intergenerational tax justice. For example, if today's 25-year-olds and 45-year-olds are significantly better off than today's elderly were at age 25 or age 45—likely, given overall economic growth—does this comparison provide a justification for taxing today's elderly more gently?

PART II

CONSUMPTION TAXES

Reliance on income as the base for taxation is so well established in this country as to seem almost in harmony with natural law. Indeed, taxes not based on income are frequently evaluated with reference to income. For example, state sales taxes are often criticized as "regressive," a characterization accurate only if the tax is evaluated with reference to income and not to its own tax base.[a] In a sense, the federal government's reliance on consumption taxes long predates the first income tax statute. From the earliest days of the republic, the federal government has levied *excise taxes*, which are consumption taxes imposed only on selected goods and services. At present, for example, the federal government taxes such varied items as alcoholic beverages, tobacco products, gasoline and other fuels, telephone services, automobiles deemed "gas guzzlers," firearms, and even bows and arrows. (This list is by no means exhaustive.) In the first 150 years or so of this country's existence, excise taxes yielded an impressive share of the government's total revenue. Given the massive revenue requirements since the Second World War, however, such narrow-based taxes cannot be viewed as realistic alternatives to the income tax as the foundation of federal revenues.[b]

Although the income tax has long been sharply criticized, its dominance makes it the appropriate focus of federal tax policy analysis, and of this book. Nevertheless, rational taxing systems can be based on criteria other than income, and calls for movement away from the income tax are heard with increasing frequency from members of Congress and others who influence federal tax policy. The principal purpose of Chapters Six and Seven is to examine some form of broad-based federal consumption tax as a possible replacement of, or significant addition to, existing federal taxes. Chapter Six focuses on the value added tax, a generally "flat" rate tax, which would be collected and remitted by businesses. Chapter Seven examines a wholly different type of consumption tax, which could be at flat rates or progressive, and which would be paid by individuals on an annual basis in much the same way the income tax now is. Chapter Seven also considers the degree to which

---

a. The term "regressive" is usually used to mean "regressive with respect to income." Sales taxes normally use uniform rates, so it is technically correct to describe these taxes as "proportional," with respect to their base. Because lower-income persons spend a higher proportion of their income on goods and services subject to sales taxes than do higher-income persons, however, the sales tax is regressive with respect to income.

b. Preliminary figures indicate that in 2002, federal excise taxes amounted to some $67 billion, only 3.4% of federal receipts. U.S. BUREAU OF THE CENSUS, STATISTICAL ABSTRACT OF THE UNITED STATES, tbl. 454, at 308 (122d ed. 2002).

our present "income" tax incorporates principles of consumption taxation. The division of the material into two chapters is artificial to some degree, because many policy issues are common to any consumption tax system.

CHAPTER SIX

VALUE ADDED TAXES

As recently as 25 years ago, the VAT existed only in France, and even there in only a very rudimentary form. Since then, adoption of the VAT has been made a prerequisite for membership in the European Community (EC), several European countries that are not members of the EC have adopted the VAT and the tax has spread throughout the Third World.[a]

A. INTRODUCTION

Foreign experience alone suggests that the value added tax, or VAT, merits serious consideration. In 1999, Professor Alan Schenk reported that approximately 100 nations employed VAT[b] and that soon "the United States will have the distinction of being the only country of the large industrialized nations that form the Organization for Economic Cooperation and Development (OECD) that does not levy a VAT at the national level."[c] Is it possible that the rest of the world is on to something? Or does foreign dependence on VATs simply reflect an inability to achieve a level of income tax compliance comparable to ours?

As will be developed in the excerpts and notes, several systems of taxation can be properly described as VATs. While these variations are not unimportant, the economic impact of each major form of the tax is similar. (The primary variations from country to country derive not from employing different VAT systems, but rather the particular country's deviations from that system, such as allowing certain entities and transactions to be exempted from the tax, or taxed at preferential rates.)

The VAT is not well understood in this country. Many Americans describe it as a national sales tax, which is somewhat misleading. While it is true that the economic effect of a comprehensive VAT should closely approximate that of a comprehensive retail sales tax, the structures of the taxes are quite different. Moreover, in the United States, reference to a "national sales tax" leads one to think of state sales taxes, which are much less comprehensive than most VATs, especially with respect to the taxation of services.

---

a. George R. Zodrow & Charles E. McLure, Jr., *Implementing Direct Consumption Taxes in Developing Countries*, 46 TAX L. REV. 405, 407 (1991).

b. Alan Schenk, *Radical Tax Reform for the 21st Century: The Role for a Consumption Tax*, 2 CHAPMAN L. REV 133, 138 (1999). This article is excerpted in Subchapter B.

c. *Id.*

Thus, it may be well to begin with a very simple illustration of the world's most common form of VAT, the European-style credit-invoice destination-principle VAT. Suppose that the United States imposed such a VAT, at a rate of ten percent; and that a farmer milked a cow and sold a gallon of milk to a dairy for fifty cents, the dairy processed the milk and sold it to a grocery store for eighty cents, and the grocery store sold the milk to a consumer for one dollar. The farmer would collect from the dairy, and remit to the government, five cents VAT (ten percent of fifty cents).[d] The farmer's invoice would reflect a selling price of fifty cents plus five cents VAT. The dairy would collect eight cents VAT from the grocery store (ten percent of eighty cents), but would remit only three cents to the government, because it would receive a credit for the five cents it had paid to the farmer.[e] (Its claim to a credit would be supported by the VAT shown on the invoice for its purchase of milk from the farmer; hence, the terminology "credit-invoice" form of VAT.) The remitted tax, three cents, would be ten percent of the value added by the dairy, which, by its processing and transportation, increased the value of the milk from fifty cents to eighty cents. Finally, the grocery store would collect ten cents from the consumer (ten percent of one dollar), and would remit two cents to the government, because it would receive a credit for the eight cents it paid when it bought the milk. Again, the tax remitted equals ten percent of the value added by the grocery store (twenty cents, the increase from eighty cents to one dollar). Thus, the total tax, ten cents (5¢ + 3¢ + 2¢), equals ten percent of the final sales price. It is reasonable to assume that this tax is passed on by each seller, and is the economic equivalent of a single ten-percent tax paid by the final consumer.[f]

Most American states employ *retail sales taxes (RSTs)*, which are flat-rate taxes on most goods.[g] (Although there is considerable variation from state to state, services are not subjected to RSTs to the same extent as goods, and in some states are wholly exempt from sales taxes.) Intermediate steps in the production chain are normally not subject to RST. To use the example in the

---

d. In the real world, it is impossible to start at the beginning of a chain of production. In this example, the farmer would have various costs that would reduce the value added at this stage of production. For example, the farmer's purchases of feed, or of milking machines, would generate a VAT credit comparable to the VAT credits described in the text for the dairy and grocery store. This credit would not affect the amount of VAT the farmer would collect from the dairy, but it would reduce the amount of VAT that the farmer would remit to the government.

e. The credit for VAT paid at purchase and the remission of VAT collected at sale might be reported on the same or on different VAT returns; either way, the net effect would be as described in the text.

f. If the milk were sold by the grocery store to a restaurant, which re-sold it, glass by glass, for a total of five dollars, the restaurant would continue the process. It would charge its customers fifty cents VAT, claim a credit for ten cents VAT paid, and remit forty cents. Thus, the government would receive a total of fifty cents—ten cents from the three earlier businesses and forty cents from the restaurant—which amounts to ten percent of the final sales price to the consumer.

g. Many states exempt some items, such as food and prescription drugs, that are deemed necessities. The resulting tax is less regressive with respect to income than would be a uniform sales tax applicable to all goods.

preceding paragraph, a typical RST would not reach the farmer's sale to the dairy or the dairy's sale to the grocery store, but the consumer would pay, and the grocery store collect and remit, RST on the full final price of one dollar.[h] The ultimate economic effect under either tax should be substantially identical—a total tax of ten cents would be collected, all of which would be borne by the consumer.

Almost all VATs and state RSTs rely on the destination principle. Particularly in the case of a substantial national VAT, this is generally (although not universally) thought to have important consequences with respect to the treatment of exports and imports. The theory of the destination principle is that a VAT is a consumption tax, and that the place of consumption—not the place in which the value was added—should determine whether the tax applies. Thus, to continue with the simple example above, if the retailer (the grocery) exported the milk to Canada, the foreign sale would be "zero-rated." This means that the sale abroad would generate no American VAT to be collected and remitted to the American government by the exporter (the retailer), but that the retailer would still be allowed its credit for eight cents of VAT it had paid. Thus, the entire series of sales, reflecting considerable addition of value in the United States, would generate no net American VAT, because the consumption occurred abroad. By the same reasoning, an imported product would bear the full American VAT, even though most of the value was added abroad, because the consumption took place here. Whether this treatment of exports and imports is a reason to adopt a VAT is a matter of some debate.

Compared to an income tax, VATs and RSTs are relatively simple to administer (as are excise taxes), if for no other reason because fewer entities are responsible for filing returns and remitting tax. Although under both of these taxes the consumer bears the tax (VATs paid earlier in the production/distribution chain are recouped upon resale), no return need be filed by the consumer, because all the tax has been collected by the seller at the point of sale. Thus, the government needs deal only with sellers, which means that a far smaller number of returns are necessary than with an income tax, which reaches virtually every household.

Subchapter B briefly recounts the origin and spread of VAT. Subchapter C, the heart of the chapter, examines the central policy issues related to the consideration of an American VAT. Finally, Subchapter D provides two alternatives to "routine" VAT proposals, one calling for a VAT coupled with

---

h. RSTs do not in operation always allow tax-free purchases before the sale to the final consumer. To the degree RSTs are imposed earlier in the production or distribution chain, they are built into the final price, and included in the RST tax base at final sale. This results in a "cascading," or tax-on-a-tax, effect. Professor Schenk cites sources suggesting that "at least fifteen to twenty-five percent of state sales tax revenue is derived from RST's paid on business inputs," and that the comparable figure for Canadian provincial RSTs is even higher. Alan Schenk, *Choosing the Form of a Federal Value-Added Tax: Implications for State and Local Retail Sales Taxes*, 22 CAP. U. L. REV. 291, 316 (1993).

measures to achieve progressivity, the other for targeted excise taxes rather than the broad-based VAT.

B. HISTORY OF THE VALUE ADDED TAX

Dean Lindholm's article explains the surprising country of origin of this "foreign" tax, and traces its development from theory to practice. Professor Alan Schenk, who was reporter for the ABA Committee's Model Act and is the most prolific American writer on VAT, recaps the status of VAT, in the U.S. and abroad, at the end of the Twentieth Century.

THE ORIGIN OF THE VALUE-ADDED TAX
Richard W. Lindholm[*]
6 Journal of Corporation Law 11, 11-14 (1980)

The value-added tax is not a new idea. Many European countries have utilized the tax for many years. The European experience with the VAT and the hesitancy of the United States to adopt such a tax often obscures the fact that the value-added approach to taxation was first examined, explained and advocated by American fiscal experts. * * *

The early American interest in the value-added tax is at least partially explained by the early embrace by American economists of statistical economic and business analysis. Prior to the development of statistical methods of analysis the study of economics was confined primarily to armchair philosophy and unconfirmed or unverifiable theory. Mathematical formulae enabled economists to put old theories to the test and to measure with relative precision economic trends.

Data based economics was particularly important to the origin of the VAT. At the turn of the century proponents of economic realism, armed with the new mathematical tools of economics, developed the formula for calculating gross national product (GNP). The gross national product is determined by adding the market values of effort expended at each level of the production process. Because GNP represents an increment in value to raw materials as finished products it was all but inevitable that economists and fiscal experts would devise a method of utilizing GNP as a tax base. The method devised was a tax on total production that becomes a part of the cost of consumption of goods and services purchased in the marketplace. In addition to providing the tools to calculate a tax base, data oriented economics made it possible for economists to more accurately predict the various effects that implementation of the value-added tax would have on the economy. This, in turn, provided both proponents and opponents ammunition with which to support or oppose adoption of the tax.

---

[*]. At time of original publication, Emeritus Dean & Professor of Finance, College of Business Administration, University of Oregon.

While the value-added tax has yet to be enacted in the United States, its proponents have been vocal and at times influential. One of the most important early advocates of the VAT was T.S. Adams. Adams supported the value-added approach to taxation as early as 1911. It was in 1921, however, that Adams published a paper in which he set forth his reasons for supporting the VAT. Adams claimed that the value-added tax was the most efficient and desirable method of taxing the business sector of the economy.[5] Later, Dr. Gerhard Colm, a German-trained fiscal expert who became a leading tax specialist for the federal government, published an article in which he discusses the operative aspects of the VAT and then urges that it be adopted on the federal level.[6] In 1940, Paul Studensky, one of the most distinguished tax scholars in the United States, published an article discussing his ethical and philosophical basis for supporting the VAT.[7] * * *

Adams, Colm and Studensky were important vocal advocates of the value-added tax. Despite their urgings, however, Congress failed to enact the VAT. The response of the VAT proponents was two-fold. First, many proponents began to urge the states to adopt value-added taxes. During the 1930's, for example, the Brookings Institut[ion] urged adoption of the VAT in Alabama and Iowa. With the exception of Michigan, which adopted the VAT in 1953 and again in 1975, the state campaigns met the same fate as the campaign to have a federal VAT adopted. The second approach taken by VAT enthusiasts was to "export" the VAT concept to other countries. For example, shortly after World War II the United States sent a team of tax experts to Japan to assist in the reconstruction of the Japanese economy. The American Taxation Mission[12] strongly urged Japan to adopt a value-added tax. The Japanese Diet did adopt a value-added tax for raising revenue for local governments. A variety of circumstances, however, prevented implementation of the tax and it was later repealed.

Partially in response to the "exportation" efforts of American economists and partially as a result of independent experimentation and initiative, the value-added tax found much greater acceptance in Europe than in the United States. * * *

The French VAT, entitled *taxe sur la valeur adjoutee* (TVA), was implemented to remedy a serious post-World War II fiscal crisis. The roots of the TVA, however, begin much earlier. In 1917 France enacted a general consumption or gross turnover tax which evolved quickly from a luxury tax into a form of sale stamp tax. This, in turn, became part of a larger well-organized stamp duty system. * * * As with the rest of Europe, the end of

---

5. Adams, *Fundamental Problems of Federal Income Taxation*, 35 J. ECONOMICS 527 (1921).

6. BROOKINGS INSTITUTION, REPORT ON A SURVEY OF THE ORGANIZATION AND ADMINISTRATION OF STATE AND COUNTY GOVERNMENTS OF ALABAMA 319-42 (1932).

7. Studensky, *Toward a Theory of Business Taxation*, 48 J. POLITICAL ECON. 621 (1940).

12. The American Taxation Mission has also been known as The Shoup Mission after its leader, Carl A. Shoup of Columbia University.

World War II found France both devastated and at the threshold of economic opportunity. As reconstruction advanced the French economic system took on a new vitality. At the same time, the government had a growing need for revenues to meet the increasing demands being placed upon it by the reconstruction process. In this atmosphere proponents of the TVA urged the French government to adopt the TVA as a part of a broad economic development philosophy. They argued that the TVA was an ideal way to raise the revenue needed by the government without stifling continued economic growth. Moreover, proponents argued that the TVA would provide a more stable source of revenue than the earlier tax system provided. The French government was convinced and adopted the TVA in 1954.

     * * *

The skepticism of the value-added tax demonstrated in the United States is difficult to explain. It has been demonstrated that the value-added approach to taxation grew out of the American economic and business environment. Calculation of the value-added base is made relatively simple since essentially the same formula for calculating GNP is used to calculate the VAT base. Moreover, the value-added approach to taxation would appear to be consistent with the principles underlying the American free market economy. For example, the VAT avoids, to a large extent, dictating to taxpayers where they should save or invest their resources. Moreover, the VAT does not treat the profits of successful business ventures more harshly than wages or interest income. Lastly, the value-added tax does not favor one method of organizing a business over another. * * *

RADICAL TAX REFORM FOR THE 21ST CENTURY: THE ROLE FOR A CONSUMPTION TAX
Alan Schenk[*]

2 Chapman Law Review 133, 137-39 (1999)

Introduction

The end of the millennium is a time to reflect on the past and make proposals for the future. Politicians and commentators have been active in proposing ways in which Congress can radically change the federal tax system. Members of Congress * * * coupled taxpayer discontent over the existing system with proposals to replace some or all of the income taxes, and maybe some other federal taxes as well. A variety of federal taxes on consumption have been proposed to raise the lost revenue. If the United States were to completely replace the federal income taxes with a tax on consumption, indeed, the United States might become the most attractive tax haven in the world.

---

[*]. At time of original publication, Professor of Law, Wayne State University Law School

* * *

United States Watches World Tax
Systems Shift to Value Added Taxes
Introduction

During the last several decades of the twentieth century, the most dramatic change in tax systems around the world has been the conversion of turnover and other national sales taxes to value added taxes (VATs). The movement began with the adoption of a limited form of a VAT in France in 1954. France eventually extended the tax down to the retail stage.

The Treaty of Rome, which created the European Economic Community, requires all member states to adopt a VAT as a condition of membership. The expansion of the European Union thus increased the number of nations with a VAT. In addition, the International Monetary Fund has assisted many developing countries in drafting VATs to provide the revenue needed to place themselves on a sounder financial footing. The emerging countries of the former Soviet Union followed this trend and adopted VATs. New Zealand, Canada, and Japan enacted VATs to replace other forms of sales tax. The Australian government is committed to replacing its single stage sales tax with a VAT. Once Australia enacts a VAT, the United States will have the distinction of being the only country of the large industrialized nations that form the Organization for Economic Cooperation and Development (OECD) that does not levy a VAT at the national level. There are now about 100 countries with VATs.

Consistent with their obligations under the World Trade Organization (formerly the General Agreement on Tariffs and Trade), WTO member nations can impose border tax adjustments (BTAs) for indirect taxes. Nations with VATs impose the VAT on imports and rebate the tax on exports. Countries like the U.S., which rely on direct taxes like income taxes, cannot rebate those taxes on exports.

Congressional Proposals to
Board the Global VAT Rocket

In 1970, the Nixon administration considered, but did not propose, a value added tax to fund a revenue-sharing program aimed at forcing states to reduce reliance on property taxes to fund education. House Ways & Means Committee chair Al Ullman proposed a value added tax in 1979 and 1980 to finance reductions in federal income and payroll taxes. Nevertheless, it was not until the 1990s that politicians from both major parties made proposals for radical tax reform that attracted significant public attention.

Recent congressional proposals to radically change the federal tax system are marked by the use of the revenue from a new broad-based tax on consumption, either to close down the Internal Revenue Service and have the states administer the new tax, or to abolish federal income taxes (and reduce or abolish payroll taxes). These proposals create revenue-neutral shifts in taxes. * * * [Other proposals] use a new VAT as a source for additional federal revenue.

* * *

Notes and Questions

1.   When and where was the modern VAT conceptualized? How is VAT related to the computation of gross national product (GNP)? What were the first jurisdictions to enact a VAT?

2.   *The Japanese experience.*   War—particularly war ending in unconditional surrender and occupation—makes possible political breakthroughs. In 1949, the Shoup Mission, acting under the authority of General Douglas MacArthur, proposed sweeping changes in Japanese tax structure, including a VAT.   "The value-added tax became the most controversial single proposal of the *Shoup Report*. It represented a first attempt to put into practice a proposal which had become well known because of a long history in public finance literature."[i] The Japanese Diet initially enacted the VAT in 1950, but, perhaps because Japan shortly thereafter regained full control of its domestic tax system, "[t]he enactment date of the value-added tax was postponed twice, and finally the tax was repealed without ever having gone into effect."[j]

The failure of Japan's post-war VAT effort may be attributable to its novelty (in actual practice, though not in academic literature) and to the taint of its being imposed by foreign conquerors, in addition to the usual substantive arguments that can be made against the tax. Nearly forty years passed before, in 1989, Japan enacted a VAT at the modest rate of three percent.[k]

3.   Professor Schenk's article makes clear that the VAT continues to gain momentum abroad.   Is the fact that the U.S. is virtually alone in the industrialized world, in itself, reason for the U.S. to adopt a VAT?

---

i. M. Bronfenbrenner & Kiichiro Kogiku, *The Aftermath of the Shoup Tax Reforms*, 10 NAT'L TAX J. 236, 241 (1959).

A contemporary reader of the *Shoup Report* might not have suspected that the VAT proposals were particularly important. The report's table of contents makes no reference to VAT, which is modestly included in Chapter 13, "Other Local Taxes." The proposed VAT was not to be a national tax, but an improved method of computing the prefectural (provincial) "enterprise tax." The VAT discussion covered only three pages of a four-volume report.

j. *Id.* at 245.

k. Alan Schenk, *Japanese Consumption Tax: The Japanese Brand VAT*, 42 TAX NOTES 1625 (1989); Barry M. Freiman, *The Japanese Consumption Tax: Value-Added Model or Administrative Nightmare?*, 40 AMER. U. L. REV. 1265, 1265 (1991).

4.   The last paragraph of the Schenk excerpt indicates that current VAT proposals fall into two broad groups with respect to the uses of revenue from the VAT. What are these two groups? What political interests would be likely to support each vision of VAT?

C. THE ULLMAN PROPOSAL AND ITS AFTERMATH

As Dean Lindholm's article explains, serious American interest in the VAT at the academic level dates to the start of the Twentieth Century. The landmark event that moved VAT to prominence on the national political stage, however, was the strong support given VAT by the most important tax-writing member of Congress—Al Ullman, then Chairman of the Ways and Means Committee. The 1979 Ways and Means Hearing Announcement explains his VAT proposal. Five years later, the drafters of Treasury I examined VAT in some detail—devoting one of its three volumes to VAT—before rejecting the concept. The ABA Committee drafted a model statute and explanation, from which the Ullman bill was the point of departure, without taking any position on whether the United States should enact a VAT. Dr. McLure, on the other hand, unabashedly argued in favor of VAT as a revenue measure. Professor Due examined whether VAT would be a means of taxation friendlier than existing federal taxes to saving and capital formation. Professor Schenk's article examines both economic and equity issues.

COMMITTEE ON WAYS & MEANS, HEARING ANNOUNCEMENT ON THE TAX RESTRUCTURING ACT OF 1979
Statement By Representative Al Ullman (D., Oregon)
H.R. 5665, 96th Cong., 1st Sess., WMCP 96-38, at 6-12 (1979)

What is a value added tax?

A value added tax is a tax on consumer goods and services. It is a flat tax—a 10 per cent tax—that falls every time the item passes from one firm to another on the way to the final market place. At every step, the tax is collected and sent to the government. Using a system of rebates on taxes paid along the line, the cumulative tax at the retail level cannot exceed 10 per cent.

The VAT is not a new tax concept. It is used by most of our competitors in the free world—countries that are surpassing us in economic growth.

Many attack VAT as a "national sales tax." A sales tax is imposed only once—at the retail level. If the final seller does not collect the tax, the revenue is lost. A VAT, by contrast, is collected all along the way. It is more efficient than a sales tax, and, consequently, minimizes economic distortion. But, like all taxes on business, the value added tax is ultimately paid by the consumer.

A tax on consumption would give us an even flow of tax revenue. Today's boom and bust cycles have turned tax receipts into a guessing game. Every time we sink into recession, tax revenues fall off because more workers are out of jobs—and, at the same time, federal spending increases to pay for higher insurance protection. A value added tax would be paid all the time—by all the people. And the effect on economic certainty and stability would be dramatic.

The VAT in my bill is virtually a tax without loopholes. Everyone would pay—including those engaged in the "underground" economy. Those who spend more would pay more. Although those with limited budgets typically would pay proportionally more than those with large incomes, a VAT can be shaped into a fair tax—certainly less regressive than the payroll tax which nearly everyone now pays.

   * * *

A VAT would also help improve our trade posture by putting American workers and manufacturers on a more equal footing with our trading partners. Unlike payroll and income taxes the VAT could be rebated to manufacturers when products are exported and could be imposed on imported goods. Such border taxes are now levied in most other free world countries, [which] helps to explain our current unfavorable trade balance.

   * * *

The choices are few. An American value added tax is not the easiest answer—but it is the most realistic.

   * * *

Brief summary of the Tax Restructuring Act of 1979

The bill would restructure our tax system to promote investment and productivity growth. Total tax reductions would equal $130 billion on a calendar year 1981 basis. Net proceeds from the value added tax imposed by the bill would also equal $130 billion.

Tax Reductions

Social Security—$52 billion
- A 2.15-percentage point reduction on the employee and employer rates, with comparable reductions for the self-employed.

Individual Income—$50 billion
- Rate reductions.
- Earned income credit increased.
- Increased AFDC payments.
- Special savings accounts.

Business Income—$28 billion
- Corporate rate cuts.
- Liberalize depreciation.
- Liberalize the investment tax credit.

Value Added Tax

The bill would impose the VAT at each stage of the production and distribution process, including the retail stage. The tax would generally be 10 percent of the value of property or services and would be included in the price which a business charges its customers. Each business in the production and distribution chain would receive a credit for the VAT previously paid on its purchases of property and services from other businesses (including purchases of plant and equipment). Thus, each business would pay a net tax equal to 10 percent of the value it adds to the product, and the total tax paid with respect to sales to consumers would be 10 percent of the retail value of the product.

To avoid narrowing the VAT base, special rules or special tax rates have been limited except where considered absolutely essential. Food, medical care, and residential housing would be taxed at only a five-percent rate at the retail level. Transactions of charities, public and private nonprofit educational institutions, mass transit, and nonretail sales by farmers and fishermen have been given a zero tax rate, which means there would be no tax but the taxpayer would receive applicable VAT credits. Governments and nonprofit organizations other than charities have been exempted from the VAT; they would pay no tax and get no credit. The bill provides special rules for real property, interest transactions, and insurance companies. Also, businesses which have sales of property and services below $10,000 per year could elect to be exempt from the VAT.

The VAT would be imposed on imports. Exports have been zero rated to permit a rebate of VAT previously paid for goods and services associated with the export. This "border tax adjustment" will permit American exporters to compete more effectively with foreign businesses.

* * *

TAX REFORM FOR FAIRNESS, SIMPLICITY, AND ECONOMIC GROWTH ["TREASURY I"]
United States Department of the Treasury
Vol. 3, at 5-13, 16-23, 26, 39-42 (1984)

The Nature of the Value-Added Tax
Alternative Forms of Tax

There are three separate types of value-added tax: gross product, income, and consumption. They differ in their treatment of capital equipment that has been purchased from other firms. This difference may be illustrated by assuming that a firm calculates its value added by subtracting its purchases from other firms from its sales and then applying the tax rate to the resulting value added to determine its tax liability, even though this is not the method normally used to calculate tax liability under a value-added tax. For the sake of simplicity and clarity of explanation, this illustration will also not consider the question of whether exports or government purchases would be subject to the tax.

Gross Product Type

In determining its tax liability under a gross product value-added tax, a firm would be allowed to deduct its purchases of raw materials from its sales, but it would not be allowed to deduct the cost of its purchases of capital equipment, or even the depreciation on that capital equipment. Since gross investment purchases (including depreciation) are subject to taxation, the economic base of a gross product value-added tax is similar to gross national product. Capital investment is, in effect, taxed twice under the gross product tax. Capital goods are taxed at the time they are purchased and also when the products they produce are sold to consumers. * * *

A gross [product] type of value-added tax would create significant administrative difficulties in those borderline cases where it is difficult to distinguish expenditures for capital goods from those for items that are exhausted currently in production or for repair and maintenance purposes. * * *

Of the three different types of value-added tax, the gross product version places the heaviest tax burden on capital goods. It would discourage saving, discriminate against capital intensive methods of production, and cause firms to delay modernization and upgrading of plant and equipment by minimizing expenditures on capital assets. The gross product tax is best relegated to the realm of conceptual curiosities and should not receive serious consideration in public policy discussions.

Income Type

Under the income variant of the value-added tax, both purchases of raw materials and depreciation on capital goods would be deducted from sales in computing a firm's value added. Since net investment purchases (gross investment less depreciation) are subject to taxation, the economic base of this tax is similar to net national income. By taxing net investment, this tax would impose a tax burden on net purchases of capital goods. Because this type of value-added tax requires the calculation of depreciation allowances, it would have some of the same administrative problems that arise under an income tax. * * * As long as the United States has an income tax there is no reason to adopt an income-type value-added tax.

Consumption Type

Under the consumption-type value-added tax, all business purchases, including those for capital assets, would be deductible in calculating a firm's value added. Since a full deduction is allowed for gross investment, this alternative would result in a tax base equivalent to total private consumption.

A consumption value-added tax avoids the need to distinguish between capital and current expenditures or to specify asset lives and depreciation allowances for capital assets. As noted above, both the gross product and income versions of the value-added tax would penalize capital investment by placing an additional tax burden on capital equipment purchases; the tax would be imposed on the capital good itself and on the output produced by the capital good. In contrast, a consumption-type value-added tax would be neutral between methods of production since substituting capital for labor (or vice versa) would not affect a firm's total taxes; it also would be neutral between the decision to save or consume. Because of these characteristics, the consumption version is the type of value-added tax used in Europe and the only type that should receive consideration in the United States.

Alternative Methods of Calculation: Subtraction, Addition, Credit

Though value added is often thought of as the difference between a firm's sales and its purchases, value-added tax liability may be calculated by three different methods: by subtraction, credit, or addition. These three alternatives are illustrated by the example in Table 2-1. That example assumes an economy with only three firms (one each in manufacturing, wholesaling, and retailing) and in which the manufacturing sector sells all of its output to the wholesale sector; the wholesale sector buys only from the manufacturing sector and sells all of its output to the retail sector. The rate of tax is 10 percent.

Subtraction Method

Under this method, illustrated in the top part of Table 2-1, a firm calculates its value-added tax liability by subtracting its purchases from other firms from its sales and applying the tax rate to the difference. With a consumption value-added tax, the deduction for purchases would include any capital equipment bought during the period. * * *

Credit Method

The credit, or invoice, method is used by all of the member countries in the European Economic Community (EEC) [now the European Community (EC)] and by most other countries that have a value-added tax. Under the credit method, a firm's tax liability is determined by allowing the firm to subtract value-added tax paid on purchases from tax due on its sales. This method is illustrated in the middle panel of Table 2-1. The amount of deductible tax paid on purchases would include the full amount of tax paid on any capital equipment purchases in the case of a consumption-type value-added tax. * * *

An important characteristic of the credit method is that except in the case of outright exemption of intermediate stages of production the tax on a product depends on the tax rate that prevails at the final taxable stage; this would be

Table 2-1
Comparison of Three Methods of Calculating
Value-Added Tax Liability
(10 percent value-added tax)
STAGE OF PRODUCTION

	Firm A Manufacturer:	Firm B Wholesaler:	Firm C Retailer:	Total Economy:
1. SUBTRACTION METHOD:				
Sales	$350	$850	$1,100	$2,300
Purchases	100	350	850	1,300
Value added	250	500	250	1,000
(sales minus purchases)				
Value-added tax	25	50	25	100
2. CREDIT METHOD:				
Sales	350	850	1,100	2,300
Tax on sales	35	85	110	230
Purchases	100	350	850	1,300
Tax on purchases	10	35	85	130
Value-added tax	25	50	25	100
(tax on sales less tax on purchases)				
3. ADDITION METHOD:				
Factor payments plus net profit				
Wages	150	300	200	650
Rent	50	100	20	170
Interest	25	75	20	120
Profit	25	25	10	60
Total	250	500	250	1,000
Value-added tax	25	50	25	100

the rate levied at the retail stage in the case of a value-added tax that extends through the retail level. Thus, any value-added tax evaded by firms prior to the retail level would result in higher taxes at the retail level; lower tax rates at pre-retail stages would be offset by full collection of the tax at the retail level. * * *

Addition Method

Though value added is equal to the difference between a firm's sales and its purchases, it also is equal to the payments for the labor and capital that generate the value added. Under the addition method, a firm's value-added tax liability is calculated by adding together the components of value added, wages, rent, interest, and net profit, and then applying the tax rate to that sum. It is illustrated in the lower panel of Table 2-1. Since net profit normally reflects a capital depreciation allowance, the addition method is usually associated with an income type of value-added tax. * * * If the objective is a consumption value-added tax, this can be achieved more easily under the credit method than by calculating net profit (with capital expensing) and adding it to the other factor payments. The calculation of net profit involves all of the problems that plague the current income tax.

Analysis and Summary

The subtraction, credit, and addition methods should be viewed as equivalent only in the case of a single rate of tax applying to nearly all goods and services. In such a situation, the three methods would work equally well and would generate the same amount of total tax revenue. A more realistic situation is one in which policy makers may prefer a single-rate value-added tax for administrative and efficiency reasons, but in which it will be necessary to tax some goods and services at special rates. In a world in which all goods and services are not taxed at the same rate, the credit method is superior to either the subtraction or addition alternatives.

Under the subtraction approach, virtually every sector of the economy would exert political pressure for special treatment. This is because ultimate tax liability on a given product would depend on two factors: value added in each sector or industry and the tax rate applied to that value added. Assuming that firms do not incorrectly overstate purchases or understate sales, they would have relatively little control over their value added subject to tax. But they would try to minimize their value-added tax liability by seeking preferential, or perhaps even zero, rates of value-added tax on their own sector or industry.

With the credit method, in contrast, since tax liability on final consumption depends on the tax rate imposed at the final or retail stage, the mining, agricultural, manufacturing, and other non-retail sectors would have less incentive to seek special treatment and be less likely to do so. Because any tax charged on their sales may be credited by their (non-retail) customers, it should (record keeping considerations aside) be a matter of indifference to firms making non-retail sales as to whether or not they are subject to the tax. Indeed, as shown below, exemption from tax would actually be adverse to the exempt firm's non-retail customers.

Special rates, which would be more likely under the subtraction or addition method than under the credit alternative, would have a number of adverse economic consequences. They would unfairly favor those consumers with strong preferences for lightly-taxed goods and penalize those preferring to buy more heavily-taxed items. To the extent that the nonuniform rates induced changes in buying habits, consumer satisfaction would decline and the government would collect less revenue. As explained below, a so-called indirect tax, such as a value-added tax, may be rebated on exports under international trading rules. With differential rates for various sectors or products, it would be virtually impossible under the subtraction method to calculate the correct amount of tax that would be permitted as a rebate on exports and collected on imports. Differential rates would make the tax more complex, both for taxpayers and tax administrators, thus increasing compliance and administration costs.

Though multiple rates are far less satisfactory than a single rate value-added tax, the experience of other countries demonstrates that it may not be possible to avoid them. The credit method is attractive not only because it makes the tax base less vulnerable to erosion from pleas of special interest groups for tax relief, but because it is superior to the subtraction method in accommodating the demands that will be made for tax relief for some goods or services. Under the credit method, goods and services can be freed of tax by simply applying a rate of "zero" at the retail stage and allowing a full credit for pre-retail taxes. In similar fashion, the accurate rebate of tax on exports occurs automatically. The same result could only be achieved under the subtraction method by applying a rate of zero at each and every stage of production or distribution through which the tax favored good or service passes.

* * *

Border Tax Adjustments

In 1983, U.S. exports of goods and services were equal to about 10 percent of the economy's output. In the United States, as in other countries, the design of a value-added tax must take into account the fact that the movement of goods and services across national borders is commonplace.

* * *

[A] value-added tax may be implemented on a destination basis. In this case, value-added tax is imposed only where the good is consumed, not where it is produced. This necessitates a rebate of any tax imposed in the exporting country and a compensatory tax in the importing country to equalize the tax burden with a good that is domestically produced and consumed. The export rebate and import tax, designed to place traded [imported] and domestically-produced goods on an equal tax footing in the country where they are consumed, are known as border tax adjustments. State retail sales taxes are levied under the destination principle. A state retail sales tax is not imposed on goods destined for export out of the taxing state, but is levied on any imports sold to consumers in the taxing state.

The credit method of determining value-added tax liability is superior to either the addition or subtraction approaches for implementing the destination principle. The rebate of tax on exports is accomplished by simply applying a tax rate of zero at the export stage and giving the exporter full credit for any tax paid on inputs purchased to produce the export good. * * *

Unless the import good is purchased directly by the final consumer, rather than from a taxable firm, it is not even necessary for the importing country to explicitly levy the value-added tax at the import stage to implement the destination principle. Under the credit method, the tax on a product depends on the rate applied on the final sale to the consumer. * * * [P]rovided there is at least one taxable firm between the import stage and final consumer, the credit method will insure that consumption of imports and domestically-produced goods takes place on an equal tax footing, as required by the destination principle.

In contrast to a credit method value-added tax, there are substantial complexities to implementing the destination principle under either the subtraction or addition methods. * * *

If the policy debate in the United States ever focuses on choosing a form of value-added tax, it should concentrate on a value-added tax with the following characteristics:

      1. consumption type;

      2. credit method of determining tax liability; and

      3. destination principle of border tax adjustments.

[T]he tax should also have a broad base, with only minimal and well justified exclusions, and it should be imposed at a single, uniform rate.

Evaluation of a Value-Added Tax

This chapter evaluates a consumption-type value-added tax with tax liability calculated under the credit method from an economic and political perspective. This is the form of tax that has been adopted by the member countries in the European Economic Community (EEC) and would be the most likely candidate for the United States, if a policy decision were made to adopt a value-added tax.

Some of this discussion necessarily involves comparing a value-added tax with other taxes, such as the personal and corporate income taxes and the social security or payroll tax. This is because revenue generated by a value-added tax could also be raised by one of these other levies, or could permit these other taxes to be reduced. * * *

Economic Effects

Neutrality

A neutral tax is one that does not interfere with the economic behavior of individuals or firms. Compared to the situation that would exist if no tax is imposed, a neutral tax would not interfere with the decisions of individuals to work or not work, to save or consume, or to consume one good or another; or with the decisions of firms on what to produce and what production methods to use. A cigarette tax, for example, is not neutral because it may discourage consumers from buying cigarettes. While some taxes are intended to change consumer behavior, neutrality is generally viewed as a desirable objective of tax policy because it is assumed that both the value of economic production and consumer satisfaction will decline if a tax forces either firms or individuals to change their behavior.

Production neutrality

In a market-oriented economy, business firms are motivated by competitive forces to use the most efficient production techniques. In this way, the goods and services demanded by consumers are produced, and at the lowest possible cost. If a tax interferes with these production decisions, resources are used less efficiently and less output is available to satisfy consumer demand.

A consumption-type value-added tax would score high in production neutrality. By allowing a full deduction for the tax paid on purchases of capital equipment it would not distort production or investment decisions. Compared to a no-tax situation, the tax would not encourage firms to favor the use of either labor or capital in the production process. The total tax liability incurred by a firm, consisting of both the tax on its purchases and the tax on its sales (after allowing for the tax on purchases) would be the same regardless of the precise capital-labor mix. The corporate income tax has many distortions, it favors debt over equity finance, noncorporate over corporate products, labor over capital, and consumption over saving. As explained in the next section, a value-added tax would be neutral between consumption and saving. Since purchased consumption goods are subject to taxation, a value-added tax may discourage work effort by those who have the alternative of using leisure time to produce goods and services that would be taxed if purchased. An example of this result would be an individual using leisure time to paint a house or tend a garden. In contrast to a value-added tax, the individual income tax, because it is progressive and applies to both income that is saved as well as the return on saving, may discourage saving and risk taking, as well as work effort. Even though the payroll tax applies to most forms of labor, it probably is not neutral. It may discourage work effort, and the pay-as-you-go financing of social security may reduce saving.

Consumption neutrality

In a market-oriented economy, individuals "vote" for the goods and services they want to buy by signaling the prices they are willing to pay. These price signals are received by business firms, who produce those goods and services valued most highly by consumers. If a tax changes the structure of net relative prices determined in the market place, consumers respond by buying more of some goods and less of others. The end result is reduced consumer satisfaction and a less efficient use of the economy's resources. A broad-based value-added tax, imposed at a single rate, would constitute a relatively uniform percentage of all consumer expenditures. Thus, it would be a reasonably neutral tax. * * *

[I]t is unlikely that a Federal value-added tax would apply to all forms of consumption. Either for social, distributional, or administrative reasons, the tax would probably not apply in full to housing, medical care, insurance and finance, education, and religious and welfare activities. At most, the tax would apply to about 77 percent of total personal consumption expenditures. Exclusions from the tax base would make the tax less neutral and distort consumption and production decisions in favor of the preferentially-taxed items. The experience of other countries indicates that nonuniform coverage and rate differentiation are the prime sources of nonneutrality in the value-added tax. It is for this reason, as well as to avoid administrative complexity, that departures from a broad base should be minimized and that rate differentiation reduction should be avoided, particularly if alternatives exist for alleviating the burden of the tax on lower income groups.

Saving

Unlike an income tax, a value-added tax would be neutral toward the saving-consumption choice. Suppose that in an economy without taxes the interest rate is 10 percent. An individual with $100 of income could either purchase $100 of consumption goods this year or could save the $100 and purchase $110 of consumption goods next year. This individual could consume 10 percent more next year by not consuming (by saving) the $100 now. A value-added tax would not alter the basis for this choice between consumption and saving. Consider a value-added tax rate of 20 percent, levied on the tax-inclusive value of goods and services. Now the choice is between consuming $80 this year and paying $20 in tax or saving the $100 this year, allowing it to grow to $110, and consuming $88 next year and paying the remaining $22 in tax. Note that the net rate of return on saving is not affected by the value-added tax; it is still 10 percent. By postponing $80 of consumption this year, the individual can consume $88 or 10 percent more next year.

In contrast, a tax on income from capital, such as the corporate income tax or the individual income tax on interest or dividends, is not neutral between consumption and saving. * * * Continuing the same example, an individual subject to a 20 percent income tax could, after paying the tax, purchase $80 of consumption goods this year or save the $80 in order to consume $86.40 next year, after paying a 20 percent tax on the $8 in interest earned on the $80 in savings. In the income tax case, the net return to saving is now only 8, rather than 10, percent. * * *

This example demonstrates that a value-added tax is neutral with regard to the choice of whether to consume now or save for future consumption; the value-added tax does not discourage saving the way an income tax does. Assuming any increased saving is absorbed by higher real investment spending, a value-added tax may be superior to an income tax in fostering capital formation and economic growth. The amount of the increase in saving would depend on the responsiveness of saving to higher after-tax rates of return.

Equity

Consumption expenditures, as a percentage of income, fall as income rises. * * * Thus, a broad-based value-added tax imposed at a uniform rate would absorb a larger percentage of the income of those at the lower income levels than those at the middle and upper income levels. In other words, a value-added tax would be regressive, assuming no exemptions or differential rates for "necessities" or "luxuries." The individual income tax, in contrast, is progressive, since it allows for personal exemptions and a zero bracket amount and because tax rates rise with income. * * *

[R]egressivity has two facets: the absolute burden of the tax on those below the poverty level and the regressive effect on those above the poverty level. For those with income above the poverty level and subject to the income tax, the regressivity of the value-added tax can be offset by adjusting the income tax rates. But for those who are below the poverty level and not subject to the income tax, this approach is not helpful; the value-added tax could, however, be offset by a refundable tax credit administered through the income tax system or by increased transfer payments.

Generally speaking, reduced rates for purchases of certain commodities and exemptions from the tax base are not a desirable means of alleviating regressivity. * * *

Prices

A value-added tax accompanied by an accommodating monetary policy and no offsetting reduction in other taxes would probably lead to a one-time increase in consumer prices in direct relation to the coverage and rate of tax. * * *

The experience of those countries which have adopted a value-added tax confirms the view that it may generate a one-shot increase in the price level, but not an annual inflationary spiral. * * *

Balance of Trade

It is frequently argued that a value-added tax would improve the U.S. trade balance by making U.S. goods more competitive in world markets. This argument is based primarily on the realization that the value-added tax can be rebated on exports and levied on imports. Though there may be some validity to the argument, it is important to specify clearly the circumstances under which it would prevail.

The General Agreement on Tariffs and Trade (GATT) permits destination principle border tax adjustments for indirect taxes such as sales or value-added taxes, but not for direct taxes such as the corporate or individual income tax or social security taxes. That is, indirect taxes, like the value-added tax, can be rebated on exports and imposed on imports, but no corresponding adjustments can be made for direct taxes.

Imposing a value-added tax without any reduction in the income tax, or some other direct tax, would not directly improve the U.S. balance of trade. Export subsidies and import taxes could, in a system of fixed exchange rates, increase a country's exports and reduce its imports. But, the export rebate and import tax allowed for the value-added tax are merely border tax adjustments required to put the value-added tax on a destination basis. The export rebate merely allows exports to enter world markets free of value-added tax, not at a subsidized price below the pre-tax price. Similarly, imposing a value-added tax on imports merely places imports on an equal footing with domestically produced goods; it does not penalize imports. * * *

The analysis is somewhat different if a value-added tax is part of a revenue-neutral substitution for an existing direct tax, such as the corporate income tax or payroll tax. As noted above, under GATT neither the corporate income nor payroll tax may be rebated on exports and imposed on imports. Under traditional assumptions that these taxes are borne by share-holders or by labor, respectively, reducing them would have no effect on prices, and partially replacing them with a value-added tax would have no effect on the competitiveness of U.S. industry. The substitution of a value-added tax for either of these direct taxes could improve the U.S. trade balance only if the domestic price level remains unchanged, or at least increases by less than the full amount of the value-added tax. This would occur if one of these taxes is shifted to consumers and would be "unshifted" if reduced. Under these circumstances, the export rebate would reduce the price of U.S. exports, and the import tax would increase the price of imports relative to those of domestically-produced goods. In this instance, there would be a tendency for the U.S. trade balance to improve. Even this conclusion, however, requires some important qualifications.

First, it assumes that exchange rates are fixed, or at least are not allowed to adjust fully over time. Exchange rates, of course, have been allowed to adjust since 1971. Thus, any expansion in net exports resulting from the substitution of the value-added tax for the corporate income tax would be dampened by an appreciation of the dollar relative to other currencies. Second, other countries also have payroll and social security taxes. Thus, they could act to offset any expected improvement in the United States trade balance by substituting increases in their (already existing) value-added taxes for these other taxes. Third, even if the partial replacement of the corporate income or payroll tax would improve the U.S. trade balance, the choice of whether to adopt a value-added tax is much too important to be driven by this consideration.

A value-added tax may be associated with an improved U.S. trade balance in a different way. To the extent that it allowed the corporate income tax to be reduced, U.S. industry may become more vigorous and better able to compete in world markets.

* * *

Political Concerns
State-Local Tax Base

A Federal value-added tax or retail sales tax might be viewed as an unwarranted intrusion by the Federal government into the fiscal domain of state and local governments. Forty-five states and the District of Columbia, as well as many local jurisdictions, impose general sales and use taxes, a revenue source which they may view as exclusively their own. Sales and gross receipts taxes account for about 35 percent of overall state and local tax revenue. * * *

While the Federal government should be sensitive to the impact a national sales or value-added tax would have on state and local governments, it is not clear that this should preclude Federal adoption of such a tax. Experience with the income tax, of course, demonstrates that there can be Federal, state, and local government taxation of the same tax base. * * *

Major Design Issues
Zero Rating versus Exemption

Under a value-added tax, commodities, transactions, or firms can receive preferential treatment in two ways, by zero rating or exemption. Under zero rating, all value-added tax is removed from the zero rated good, activity, or firm. In contrast, exemption only removes the value-added tax at the exempt stage, and it will actually increase, rather than reduce, the total taxes paid by the exempt firm's business or non-retail customers. It is for this reason that a sharp distinction must be made between zero rating and exemption in designing a value-added tax.

If a commodity or service is zero rated, no tax applies to its sale and the seller of the zero-rated item receives a credit for the tax paid on the purchase of materials and other inputs used to produce it. By this procedure, the zero-rated commodity is freed of all value-added tax; the user bears no tax with respect to a zero-rated good or service. By contrast, if a commodity is exempted, the sale is not subject to tax, but the seller receives no credit for tax paid on the purchase of materials and other inputs used to produce the exempt item. Users of the exempt item will thus bear some tax.

If a commodity, for example, is exempt only at the retail level, then only the retail level is freed of value-added tax. Although the retailer would not charge value-added tax on its sale, the retailer would not be entitled to a credit for tax paid on the purchase of an exempt item. Thus, exemption of a commodity through all of its production and distribution channels would be necessary to free it of its entire value-added tax burden. But, with zero rating, unlike exemption, only the final sale of the commodity needs to be zero rated, since any tax previously paid would be credited on the last sale.

* * *

The choice between zero rating and exemption should be made on the basis of two principal considerations: (1) Is it desirable to free the users of the good or service completely from value-added tax, or only partially? (2) Is it desirable to exclude certain firms from the requirement to register and file returns? Even from the standpoint of the firms themselves, there are conflicting considerations. Zero rating frees a firm and its customers completely from value-added tax, but the zero-rated firm must register and file a tax return. If a firm is exempt, it is not required to register and file a return, but the customers of an exempt firm bear the tax incurred by the exempt firm on its purchases. This may be particularly objectionable to the exempt firm's business customers who cannot receive credit for this tax. In this instance, exemption would place the exempt firm at a competitive disadvantage.

One further advantage of zero rating is that it avoids the complications that would arise if a firm handles both taxable and exempt commodities. With zero rating, such a firm receives credit for tax paid on all its purchases, whether for production or distribution of zero rated or of taxable goods. But if some goods are exempted, then the firm selling the exempt items is entitled to a credit only for the tax on those purchases of materials and other inputs that are used to produce taxable (or zero-rated) goods. It does not receive a credit for tax paid on purchases related to the exempt transactions.

     * * *

Thus, in general, zero rating is superior to exemption of commodities and services and of transactions, such as exports. Exemption is desirable only for those firms which the government does not wish to register, for administrative or other reasons, and/or does not seek to remove all the value-added tax from their customers. Farmers, small service establishments, sidewalk vendors, and charitable and religious organizations are possible examples of firms for whom exemption may be appropriate.

     * * *

VALUE ADDED TAX: A MODEL STATUTE AND COMMENTARY
American Bar Association, Committee on Value Added Tax of the Section of Taxation
Pages 4-9, 11-15, 38-39, 41, 59-62, 64-65, 68-71 (1989)

Introduction
    * * *

Comparison of invoice VAT and BTT

Compared to an invoice method VAT [also referred to as credit-invoice method or credit method VAT], a BTT-type sales-subtractive VAT has some disadvantages. The BTT [business transfer tax, also referred to as subtraction method VAT], because it is a period tax, does not provide the audit trail available with the transactional invoice method VAT. Under the invoice method, with sales from business-to-business, the sales invoice can be used to verify the seller's output tax liability on sales and the buyer's input tax credits on purchases. It is difficult to rebate the VAT component in export sales under a BTT with the precision that is possible under an invoice method tax. The BTT, as a period tax, is buried in export prices. Unless the BTT is broad-based and levied at a single rate, the BTT component can only be estimated. The invoice method VAT is a transactions tax, with tax on sales listed on tax invoices and tax on purchases eligible for input credit. The precise invoice VAT component in exports therefore can be removed with the zero rating procedure.

If, for administrative reasons, some midstream sales[10] are removed from an invoice VAT base, revenue lost on these sales will be recouped when sales are made at a subsequent stage of production or distribution. On the other hand, if midstream sales are removed from the BTT or other sales-subtractive VAT base, the tax base is reduced permanently, unless the statute contains an administratively complicated rule that would disallow deductions for purchases that were not subject to VAT earlier in the production-distribution chain. The BTT poses a significant transition problem because it does not provide a mechanism (and cannot do so without unduly complicating the law) upon the introduction of VAT or change in tax rate to tax the full value of goods sold after the effective date at the introductory or new rate. Under an invoice method VAT, sales to consumers after the effective date of a rate change are taxed at the new rate. Because the BTT is buried in the price of goods and services, sales to consumers shortly after the effective date of a rate change will be taxed in part at the old rate and in part at the new rate. The BTT base can be calculated by adjusting accounts maintained for income tax purposes. For some sellers, the cost to comply with a BTT therefore may be less than with an invoice VAT. The principal reason the Model Act adopts the tax invoice method rather than the cost-subtractive method VAT is that the invoice method is a transactions tax rather than a period tax. As such, the invoice VAT avoids many of the negative features of the BTT noted above.

* * *

Comparison of invoice VAT and retail sales tax

The invoice method VAT also has advantages over a single-stage retail sales tax (RST), especially if the combined federal, state and local sales tax rate is high enough to tempt evasion. The Canadian Royal Commission on Taxation estimated this point at 14 percent.[15] A retail sales tax can be designed with the same tax base and the same revenue potential as an invoice VAT.[16] For political reasons, however, the tax bases may differ. Also, the invoice VAT may operate and may have to be administered differently. This report does not thoroughly analyze the differences between a retail sales tax

---

10. The term "midstream sales" is used to refer to sales between taxable businesses at various stages of production and distribution, but it does not include retail sales to consumers.

15. *See* 5 Report of the Royal Commission on Taxation, Sales Taxes and General Tax Administration 50 (1966) (the report is commonly known as the Report of the Carter Commission).

16. For an in-depth comparison of VAT and RST, see, Cnossen, *VAT and RST: A Comparison*, 35 CAN. TAX. J. 559 (1987). For other detailed discussions of the differences between VAT and RST, *see* Due, *The Case for the Use of the Retail Form of Sales Tax in Preference to the Value-Added Tax*, in BROAD-BASED TAXES: NEW OPTIONS AND SOURCES 205 (R. Musgrave ed., 1973); Shoup, *Factors Bearing on an Assumed Choice Between A Federal Retail Sales Tax and a Federal Value-Added Tax*, in BROAD-BASED TAXES: NEW OPTIONS AND SOURCES 215 (R. Musgrave ed., 1973).

and an invoice VAT. The following material summarizes some of the major differences between these two forms of sales tax.

Under an invoice VAT, most sellers are not required to distinguish between sales to businesses and sales to final consumers. The requirement that the seller charge VAT on sales regardless of the buyer's use of the item purchased simplifies compliance for the seller and administration for the Service. Under a RST, a mechanism such as a resale exclusion certificate is required in order effectively to identify buyers who purchase for resale and therefore are not subject to the tax.

An invoice VAT provides an incentive for the seller to report sales. To obtain an input credit for tax on purchases, the buyer must obtain a tax invoice from the seller. Pressure from buyers will tend to encourage the seller to report all of his sales, at least to other businesses. There is no comparable incentive under a RST.

If a federal RST or invoice VAT is a consumption-style tax, the tax should be removed from capital goods purchased by taxable businesses. A RST can achieve this result by requiring the seller to monitor the exempt status of sales of capital goods to businesses. Capital goods are more easily eliminated from an invoice VAT base by granting business purchasers input credits for the VAT charged on such purchases. * * *

An invoice VAT base probably will include sales of more services than a retail sales tax base, especially if the RST follows the state model. An invoice VAT generally does not distinguish between sales of goods and of services, and therefore taxes all but the services statutorily removed from the base. Theoretically, the same base could be constructed for a RST; but this is less likely to occur.
* * *

Jurisdictional Reach of the Tax

The jurisdictional rules governing international transactions dictate whether a VAT is an origin or destination principle tax. An origin principle VAT imposes tax on value added within the taxing nation, regardless of where the goods or services are consumed. Imports are not taxed, and exports bear tax. A destination principle VAT imposes tax in the nation where the goods and services are consumed, regardless of where the goods are produced or the services are rendered. Under the destination principle, imports are taxed and exports are free of tax. Foreign VATs typically employ the destination principle. The Model Act also is a destination principle tax.
* * *

Inclusion of Capital Goods in the Tax Base

* * * An advantage of a VAT over other forms of consumption tax is that a VAT provides a convenient mechanism (the input credit) to eliminate tax on

capital goods. By eliminating tax on capital goods purchased by businesses making taxable sales, a C-VAT imposes tax only once on the goods and services produced with the capital goods. If it is desirable to enact a federal tax on personal consumption, it would be inappropriate for Congress to tax capital goods under a GNP- or NI-variant VAT. Foreign VATs invariably are consumption-style taxes, and the Model Act is a C-VAT.

Guidelines for VAT Project

The VAT committee deliberately refrained from taking a position favoring or opposing the adoption of a VAT. It believes that this is a political issue to be resolved by Congress. Nevertheless, if Congress decides to adopt a VAT, the committee recommends a European-style invoice method VAT with a base of personal consumption.

Former Ways and Means Committee Chairman Al Ullman's proposed VAT served as the springboard for the Model VAT Act, but the Model Act departs from the Ullman bill on many policy issues. * * *

Four general principles have influenced the development of the Model Act. First, the tax should be imposed on a broad tax base to permit the adoption of the lowest possible rate. Congress should accommodate social or economic concerns, such as the regressive effects of a VAT, outside the VAT regime.

Second, the VAT should provide horizontal equity among consumers and should be neutral with respect to consumer choices. Consumers are expected to bear the tax, and the Model Act attempts to tax alike sales of identical goods and services, even if the consumers acquire the goods or services from different sources.

Third, the VAT should not be levied on the same value added to products or services more than once. The Model Act attempts to minimize the grant of VAT exemptions, especially before the retail stage, in order to avoid multiple tax.

Fourth, the Model Act should include only basic VAT rules. Countries outside the European Economic Community generally pattern their VATs on the Common Market-style VAT, a detailed statute that combines features of both our Internal Revenue Code and Treasury Regulations. The Model Act adopts the American tradition of providing basic rules in the statute and leaving many of the details to regulations.

Summary of Model Act

The Model Act is a consumption-style, destination principle, invoice method VAT imposed on the seller's sale of taxable property and services. The Model Act adheres closely to the economic concept of a destination principle tax, taxing imports and zero rating exports of property and services. This report discusses most of the broad policy issues pertaining to a VAT, but it does not attempt to cover all issues that may arise under an American VAT.

The tax is imposed at a single rate on imports by anyone and on taxable sales of property and services in the United States by a taxable person in connection with a business. For example, the lease of property is a taxable service. On the other hand services provided by an employee to his employer are not taxable. Exports are treated as taxable transactions in order to remove all VAT from the price of exports. A casual sale for modest consideration, such as a sale of a used refrigerator to a neighbor, is not taxed; a casual sale of a high-priced item is taxed. * * *

The Model Act zero rates exports and exempts from tax the supply of property and services by income tax-exempt organizations and government entities for which the supplier does not receive consideration other than contributions or general taxes. [T]he Model Act does not provide special treatment for most other sales that were zero rated under the Ullman Bill. The Model Act departs from most foreign VATs by not providing a small business exemption for taxable persons with low quarterly or annual turnover; however, a rule is proposed if Congress decides to grant a small business exemption.
* * *

Treasury regulations can authorize related businesses to elect to be treated as a single taxable person and can authorize a single business to elect to treat divisions or branches as separate taxable persons. * * *

Imposition of Tax on Taxable Transactions
* * *

Transfers to employees

An employer may transfer property or services to an employee as compensation for services. A neutral and comprehensive VAT should tax these fringe benefits the same as the employer's payment of compensation in cash and the employee's purchase of these benefits with his cash salary. Indeed, economic distortions may result if some fringe benefits are removed from the VAT base. * * *

Under our individual income tax, compensation paid in kind generally is taxable, but, for administrative and other reasons, certain no-additional-cost services, qualified employee discounts, working condition fringes, and de minimis fringe benefits are not taxed. Fringes that are taxable under the income tax should be taxable under the VAT, and the tax should be imposed on their fair market value.

The problem in distinguishing between taxable benefits and working condition fringes under the income tax carries over to a VAT. For administrative convenience or other reasons, Congress may apply the income tax rules to identify transfers treated as nontaxable working condition fringes under the VAT. For administrative or political reasons, Congress also may treat as nontaxable other fringes excludable under section 132. To retain part of the value of these consumption items within the VAT base, Congress could deny employers any input credit for VAT on purchases attributable to these fringe benefits, or it could require employers to charge output tax on these transfers, based on the employer's cost instead of fair market value.

The Model Act taxes compensatory transfers of property or services to employees, except when such transfers are excludable from the employee's gross income for income tax purposes. * * *

Employee services for employer

The cost of labor is part of an employer's value added tax base. An employee's services rendered for his employer therefore does not constitute the sale of services subject to VAT. * * *

Tax Base Issues–Zero Rated Exports and Zero Rating Or Exemption for Certain Sales and Sellers

The Model Act * * * removes a small group of transactions from the tax base by designating them as nontaxable transactions. As a destination principle VAT, the Model Act also zero rates exports and taxes imports.

In addition to defining taxable and nontaxable transactions and adopting the jurisdictional rule governing international transactions, the legislature must decide if the tax will be used strictly as a revenue raising measure or will be used also to achieve social, economic, or other nonrevenue goals. If the VAT will serve only the revenue raising function, and regressivity or other economic and social concerns will be addressed through adjustments to the individual income tax or through direct grant programs, VAT should be imposed on all taxable transactions. Foreign VATs typically provide special treatment for some sales to achieve nonrevenue goals. The nature and extent of these exceptions vary from country to country. Some zero rate or exempt a broad range of goods and services. * * * These exceptions add considerably to the complexity of a VAT.

Kinds of exceptions

The exceptions from the rules taxing sales at the standard rate may take three basic forms—sales taxable at a higher or reduced rate, sales taxable at a zero rate, and sales exempt from tax. * * *

Sales of necessities to consumers may be taxable at a lower than standard rate in order to reduce the impact of the VAT on low-income households. Sales of luxuries to consumers may be taxable at a higher rate in order to increase the VAT burden on high income households. The Model Act, except for zero rating exports as required by a destination principle tax, does not impose VAT at a higher or lower than standard rate on any taxable sales. * * *

Zero-rated sales

Sales subject to a zero tax rate are taxable sales. If sales are zero rated at the retail stage only, the final purchaser will buy the article free of VAT. For example, if a retailer makes $1,200,000 of zero-rated sales and has $1,000,000 of purchases on which it pays $100,000 VAT, the retailer does not charge VAT on sales and is entitled to input credits (refunds) for $100,000 VAT on purchases.

    * * *

Exempt sales

If a sale is exempt from tax, the seller does not charge tax on the sale and is not entitled to an input credit for tax on purchases attributable to the exempt sale. * * *

De minimis exemption; sales by government and income tax-exempt organizations

Congress, for administrative or other reasons, could provide special VAT treatment for some sellers. For example, to remove small traders from the tax rolls, Congress could add a de minimis exemption for businesses making sales less than a quarterly or annual threshold. The Model Act does not include a de minimis rule. * * *

Taxation of international transactions-in general

A VAT must include jurisdictional rules governing international transactions. The jurisdictional rules may be based on the origin or the destination principle. Under the origin principle, tax is imposed on value added from business activity within the taxing jurisdiction, regardless of where the goods are consumed. VAT is not imposed on imports (value added outside the United States) nor is it rebated on exports (value was added in the United States). Under the destination principle, VAT is imposed on goods and services consumed in the taxing jurisdiction, regardless of where they are produced. VAT is imposed on imports for consumption in the United States, and VAT is rebated on exports to be consumed elsewhere. The Model Act is a destination principle VAT.

Treasury authority to zero rate other sales deliberately omitted

The Ullman Bill authorized the Secretary to issue regulations that zero rated de minimis sales or sales that would not raise sufficient revenue to justify the tax administration and compliance costs. * * *

There may be some taxable transactions that present appealing facts for the administrative grant of zero rate relief; but, if the Ullman proposal were enacted, the Treasury would be deluged with requests to zero rate a wide range of transactions. Without statutory guidance on the kinds of transactions eligible for zero rating on revenue and administrative grounds, it would be difficult for the Secretary to decide which preferences to grant. It is more appropriate for Congress to make these mixed political-administrative judgments. * * *

The Ullman Bill would have zero rated certain food, housing, and medical care, mass transit, interest, and sales by farmers or fishermen.

Food

In 1985, food accounted for approximately 16 percent of all personal consumption expenditures. * * *

The Model Act adopts a broad tax base and does not provide special treatment for necessities to reduce the regressive effects of the VAT. The Act therefore does not exempt or zero rate food. If it is desirable to remove the VAT burden on food purchased by low income households, Congress should use direct grant programs targeted to these consumers, such as increases in food stamp allotments, refundable income tax credits, or reductions in income taxes. * * *

THE VALUE-ADDED TAX: KEY TO DEFICIT REDUCTION?
Charles E. McLure, Jr.[*]
Pages 10-12 (1987)

Many Americans concerned about fiscal affairs seem to be increasingly convinced that a new source of federal revenue must be found. Although this perception appears to be shared across the political spectrum, a variety of very different reasons probably underlie the common perception.

Many observers, of all political persuasions, believe that the federal budget deficit must be substantially reduced, if not eliminated. Again, concern about the budget deficit has a variety of roots. At one level is the simple intuitive belief that the federal government must pay its own way over the long haul, just as households must, and that continued deficit finance will eventually become inflationary and lead to a need for difficult adjustments to eliminate inflation.

A more sophisticated version of this view is based on the realization that the federal government is not merely borrowing from its own citizens. Rather, * * * the nation (on combined public and private account) has been borrowing substantial amounts abroad. During 1985 the United States resumed the status of a net debtor—a position more appropriate to a developing country. Thus it can no longer be said sanguinely of the national debt that "we owe it to ourselves." The reduction in net international balances of the United States

---

*. At time of original publication, Senior Fellow at the Hoover Institution, Stanford University.

seems anomalous to many observers. Why, they ask, should the richest nation in the world not be able to pay its own way? Some observers find it unconscionable that the United States should be absorbing so much of the world's scarce supply of net saving, when countries of the third world need capital so badly.

A somewhat different concern has focused on the implications of budget deficits for international trade. The higher real interest rates resulting from the budget deficit have stimulated capital inflows. Borrowing abroad has led to an overvalued dollar, which has made it extremely difficult for American business, whether in farming, mining, or manufacturing, to compete in world markets. A substantial reduction of the deficit has been seen as essential to permanent success in the effort to bring the value of the dollar to a more realistic level.

Of course, there is no reason that the present federal taxes could not be used to raise additional revenue. But following that course would necessitate one of two things: income tax rates substantially above those in the recently enacted tax reform; or further base broadening, such as taxation of fringe benefits and repeal or substantial limitation of the itemized deductions for state and local income and property taxes and for mortgage interest.

Many analysts believe that the reduction of the top marginal tax rate to below 30 percent is important for incentive reasons and that a top marginal rate below 30 percent is essential if capital gains are to be taxed as ordinary income. Not only do lower marginal tax rates entail fewer disincentives; they also provide less reward for the uneconomical behavior that has caused so much concern about the tax system and spurred interest in tax reform. * * *

Concern that excessive reliance on the income tax creates too great a bias against saving and in favor of present consumption provides further impetus for interest in a value-added tax. Many observers, including many prominent economists, would like to see a shift from income taxation toward greater reliance on taxes on consumption. Consumption-based taxation could be levied on the personal expenditures of households—for example, through a cash-flow-based tax on consumption[1]—or it could be implemented through indirect taxes on transactions, such as a VAT or other form of general sales tax.

The more liberal members of Congress would use revenues from an alternative source for yet another reason. They would avoid budget cuts. * * * In their more optimistic dreams they would use additional revenues to expand government provision of goods and services.

[I argue in this book] that if a substantial amount of additional revenue is to be raised, it should be through the VAT or some other form of broad-based

---

1. This type of consumption tax is the subject of Chapter Seven. (Ed.)

federal sales tax, rather than through one of the more narrowly based taxes on consumption recently being discussed. The possibility of a broad-based federal sales tax poses a dilemma for both liberals and conservatives. Although many liberals would like to see an important new source of federal revenue introduced to reduce the deficit without sacrificing federal programs, they are concerned about the potential distributional effects of the VAT: because the base of the tax is consumption, the VAT is regressive unless explicit steps are taken to avoid regressivity. Many conservatives would welcome a reduction of the deficit and a shift in the relative emphasis of taxation from income to saving, but they are worried about handing the Congress a new and, they fear, relatively painless source of federal revenue that could be used to expand the scope of government.

　　* * * According to this line of reasoning, Congress will exercise fiscal responsibility by reducing expenditures rather than by raising taxes only if no new source of revenue is available. Moreover, if further growth of government is to be avoided, a "money machine" such as a VAT must be kept out of the hands of Congress.

　　I believe that the federal budget deficit is a major problem and that the American people do not want to see the deficit reduced entirely by cutting federal spending. While I share the concern that revenues from a federal sales tax might lead to greater federal spending than is optimal, I have come to view the continuation of large deficits as a greater threat than the money machine. The regressivity of the VAT or other form of sales tax can probably be dealt with satisfactorily. Problems of intergovernmental relations strike me as being somewhat more serious. Thus I believe that it is time to start seriously discussing the VAT, one type of federal sales tax that might be employed to reduce the deficit to an acceptable level.

　　* * *

ECONOMICS OF THE VALUE ADDED TAX
John F. Due[*]

6 Journal of Corporation Law 61, 65-70 (1980)

The argument for a federal value added tax centers around economic considerations. Thus, an analysis of economic effects is necessary to properly assess the desirability of the tax. Such an analysis, however, requires assumptions about revenue utilization. There are three principal use alternatives, which can be accepted individually or in combination: (a) substitution of the tax for the corporation income tax; (b) replacement of a major portion of the personal income tax; and (c) replacement of the payroll tax

---

[*]. At time of original publication, Professor of Economics, University of Illinois, Urbana.

for social security financing. The Ullman bill provides for substitution of a value added tax for portions of the revenues from all three of these taxes. Another alternative is increased federal revenue, absent any further tax reductions. * * * If the tax is to be used to increase federal spending, however, the tax would be an alternative to raising some combination of the other three levies. The analysis of economic effects is thus essentially the same as if the revenue were used to allow reduction in the existing levies.
        * * *

The Relative Effects of a Value Added Tax on avings and Real Capital Formation

Currently, the argument for a value added tax centers on the capital formation issue. The effects of the VAT, however, must be compared to the consequences of the tax or taxes for which the value added tax is substituted.

Personal Income Tax

The personal income tax is based on income received (assuming no shifting); the value added tax is related to consumption. The relative effects, therefore, are those of income versus consumption related taxes generally. The change would reduce the relative tax on persons whose consumption-income ratio (C/Y) was relatively low and increase the relative burden on those with high C/Y ratios. Liability for the income tax is increased by earning additional income and reduced by earning less; the value added tax liability is not affected by changes in income alone, but instead varies with consumption expenditures. These differences should result in a higher overall savings-income ratio (S/Y), that is, a higher percentage of national income would be saved, for two reasons.

The first reason is that the redistribution of burden from persons with low C/Y ratios to those with high C/Y ratios would force many of the latter to curtail consumption as they have little or no margin between income and consumption. * * *

The second reason is that the change could have some effect upon incentives to save and consume. The income tax not only provides no incentive to save rather than consume, but in a sense it makes savings less attractive by taxing the return earned from such savings. By contrast, the value added tax would give some incentive to save instead of consume. Tax liability could be reduced by so doing, and the interest from the savings would not be directly subject to tax. The interest returns would be taxed only indirectly when they were ultimately spent on consumption. * * *

The only offsetting influence is the possible "income" effect of the income tax. By reducing the return from savings, the income tax may encourage some persons to attempt to save more (rather than less) to have a certain after tax annual return from savings for retirement or other purposes.

* * *

The significance of the argument that a switch to a value added tax will increase incentive to save is based upon the assumption that the S/Y ratio—persons [sic] preferences for savings—is highly responsive to the rate of return on savings. This conclusion is still open to question. Traditionally, it was argued that the return to be obtained from savings had only a minor influence on savings. Instead, the motives (such as old age, etc.) are not directly related to the return. A widely quoted study by Boskin at Stanford found the rate of return[10] did have substantial influence on a person's decision to save. Other studies have questioned his econometric analysis, however. The question, therefore, remains unanswered. But quite apart from the incentives, the shifting of relative burden in the direction of persons with high C/Y ratios undoubtedly would result in a somewhat higher percentage of national income saved with the value added tax even if incentives are not affected.

* * *

Substitution of the Value Added Tax for the Corporation Income Tax

A 10% value added tax would allow complete elimination of the corporate income tax, or, with partial use of the revenue to replace other taxes, a reduction in the corporate rate. A major problem encountered in comparing the effects of the corporate and value added taxes is that the incidence of the corporate tax is unknown.[m] Many studies, econometric and otherwise, have investigated the question, with widely differing results, ranging from complete forward shifting (into the prices of goods and thus distribution on the basis of consumption), to no forward shifting at all, the burden resting on the owners of the corporation.

To the extent that the corporate income tax is not shifted, replacement by a value added tax should result in an increase in the percentage of national income saved. A lower corporate tax (assuming that the tax is not shifted forward) permits either an increase in dividends or an increase in undistributed profits held in the firm. Dividend receivers are concentrated heavily in the higher income group, and have a high propensity to save, relative to the average of the taxpayers whose real incomes are reduced by the value added tax. Corporate undistributed profits are, of course, automatically saved, and thus the ratio of national income saved is increased by replacement of the corporate tax by value added taxation, to the extent that profits are not distributed.

---

10. M. Boskin, *Taxation, Saving and the Rate of Interest*, 86 J. POL. ECON. S3, S16 (1978).

m. The incidence of the corporate tax is discussed in Chapter Fourteen, Subchapter B. (Ed.)

The major problem, however, with complete elimination of the tax on corporate profits is that a major segment of current income would go completely untaxed. The result would be serious distortions in the economy, including a great incentive to incorporate when other circumstances did not dictate this form of organization, and to increase the percentage of profits held in the company. These effects would increase even further the percentage of national income saved, but at the expense of economic distortions and, by usual standards, serious loss of equity. * * * [A]llowing undistributed profits to go completely untaxed, with the relatively light taxation of capital gains, * * * would be politically intolerable.

To the extent that the corporate income tax is shifted forward into prices paid by consumers, it resembles a value added tax in burden distribution, except that the burden will vary widely among different commodities according to the ratio of profits to sales and the ability of the firms to shift. As a consequence, the effects of the two levies on savings are very similar, except that the S/Y ratios of the various groups of consumers are affected differently by the two taxes.

Effects Upon Real Investment

In summary, a shift from either form of income tax (or to some extent, both, as proposed in the Ullman bill), to a value added tax will almost certainly increase the percentage of national income saved. This, in turn, would allow a higher rate of real capital formation, which would then permit a higher rate of growth of labor productivity. But an increase in the S/Y ratio does not automatically increase real investment and the rate of capital formation; it merely makes such increase possible. * * *

[A]n increase in savings should lower the interest costs of borrowing and make more funds available for real investment.

Numerous other factors affect the return from real investment. It is charged that both corporate and personal income taxes, by reducing the rate of return (assuming no or incomplete forward shifting of tax to consumers), diminish the incentive to undertake real investment. Thus, a shift to the value added tax, by lessening the tax on the return from new investment, would lead to increased real investment in the same manner it encourages additional savings. It is argued that reduction in corporate income tax would be particularly effective since this removal would immediately and directly increase the returns from additional capital investment.
        * * *

The critics, however, are not as certain that the change will in fact have much effect on the overall savings ratio. Moreover, they fear that if there is a substantial change, the result will be more unemployment and an even lower rate of capital formation. The evidence is not adequate at this time to determine which view is correct. * * *

It should be noted that there obviously are other factors leading to the declining rate of savings in the United States besides income taxes. One is the social security program, which makes savings for old age less essential. The other factor is the fear of continuing inflation, which leads persons to buy now instead of saving for the future. The transition to a value added tax will not alter either of these influences, unless the productivity increase from additional capital formation would be so significant as to slow inflation by increasing supply of goods. Some proponents of the value added tax argue this will occur, but whether this effect will be sufficient to offset the immediate inflationary effect is questionable.

Furthermore, if there is a serious capital shortage, there are other forms of tax adjustments that can increase the percentage of national income saved. A relatively simple step is to exclude from taxable income certain types of interest on savings—for example, a greater portion of dividends than is now allowed, and/or portions of bond interest. At the same time, real investment can be further stimulated by additional investment tax credits and changes in depreciation allowances. There are objections to all such exclusions in terms of overall equity of the income tax system, but they may be preferable to the drastic change involved in the establishment of a value added tax.
        * * *

A Value Added Tax to Replace the Social Security Payroll Taxes

Use of value added tax revenue to replace the payroll taxes, or a portion of the payroll tax revenue, would have less clear cut effects upon the savings/income ratio. A basic problem with this analysis, however, is that the incidence of the payroll taxes is subject to great dispute. A number of studies on this issue have been done, producing results all the way from complete shifting of the entire burden to workers to no shifting of the employer part at all.

If the payroll tax is directed entirely, or primarily at the workers, the change to a value added tax would transfer a portion of the tax burden to nonworkers. The burden would thus be borne, in part, by higher income capital owners, with higher savings ratios on the whole than workers, and partially by lower income persons with low nonfactor incomes. The net result of these transitions is difficult to determine. If the burden rests in part on the employers, it will either reduce profits and thus have a relatively greater effect by reducing savings, or it will be shifted to consumers in the form of higher prices. In the former case, shift to a value added tax will increase the overall S/Y ratio; in the latter, it will have minimal general effect as this portion of the payroll tax is distributed in the same overall pattern (but differently on different consumer expenditures) as the value added tax. * * *

VALUE ADDED TAX: DOES THIS CONSUMPTION TAX HAVE A PLACE IN THE FEDERAL TAX SYSTEM?
Alan Schenk*

7 Virginia Tax Review 207, 260, 263-64, 267-77 (1987)

VAT advocates frequently claim that there are economic advantages of adding this national sales tax to our federal tax system. The analysis in this subsection covers the impact of taxes on inflation, capital formation and savings, equity or fairness, and economic efficiency. For purposes of this discussion, it is assumed that federal revenue must be increased. Thus, for each economic issue, the impact of a new VAT will be compared with increases in existing federal taxes. * * *

Inflation and Price Stability

Enactment of a broad-based VAT can be expected to cause a one-time increase in product prices for the taxed items by the rate of the new tax. * * *

[I]f Congress decides to increase revenue and wants the tax increase to serve to stabilize prices and control inflation (or at least not create an inflationary effect), then it should not increase revenue with a new VAT. Quite the contrary, a new VAT likely will increase product prices more than increases in income or payroll taxes, especially a progressive income tax.

Capital Formation and Savings (Economic Growth)
* * *

A VAT ultimately is borne by consumers of taxed items. For individuals choosing between current consumption and saving, the enactment (or increase in rate) of a tax on consumption should provide an incentive to defer consumption—in other words, it should encourage savings.
* * *

A VAT is preferable to existing federal taxes as a fiscal device to encourage savings. Income taxes withdraw funds individuals would otherwise use for consumption or savings. An income tax increase therefore does not encourage savings. Since payroll taxes do not directly burden income from savings or the use of savings for consumption, they do not encourage either. On the other hand, if Congress increased the cost to consume with a VAT (or to a lesser extent selective excise taxes), in effect, it may encourage taxpayers to save rather than consume.

---

*. At time of original publication, Professor of Law, Wayne State University Law School.

Equity or Fairness

One significant criterion used to measure the quality of a tax system or a particular tax within the system is tax equity or fairness. Explaining the mission's recommended changes in the Japanese tax system following World War II, Carl Shoup, head of the American Tax Mission, noted that a nation's "tax system must satisfy the deep, widespread feelings of the people as to what is fair."[191] He added that "no one remains in the tax field for long without realizing that nothing he recommends will stand up unless it meets the test of fairness in the distribution of the tax burden."[192]

Two economic concepts traditionally have influenced our view of distributive justice—the "benefit" and the "ability to pay" principles. Based on the benefit principle, each taxpayer should contribute to the revenue "in line with the benefits which he receives from public services." A tax based on the benefit principle may link revenue to government expenditure policy; for example, highway user taxes and tolls to fund the maintenance of roads, and to some extent social security taxes to fund retirement and disability programs are taxes levied on the benefit principle. Taxes that fund general government services such as defense cannot be explained under the benefit principle. Congress could levy a VAT to finance specific programs. For example, Congress considered the possible adoption of a form of VAT to finance the Superfund to clean up hazardous waste. However this article assumes that a broad-based VAT will be enacted only if substantial revenue is needed either to reduce the budget deficit or to finance general government services. It therefore is more appropriate to judge VAT by the ability to pay principle.

Three broad gauges may be used to measure individual ability to pay taxes—income, consumption, or wealth of a taxpayer or a taxable unit. Since economic income equals the sum of consumption, savings, and taxes, the basic difference between a tax based on income and a tax based in consumption is that under the latter, income not used for consumption is not taxed. Wealth taxes have been viewed as a possible supplementary index of ability to pay, since income does not adequately take account of the fact that wealth represents command over resources. This article does not compare VAT with a possible annual wealth tax.

In the United States, where the economic system distributes income unequally and family responsibilities may affect ability to pay taxes, the income tax tailored to individual differences may effectively distribute the tax burden in accordance with ability to pay concepts. A graduated consumption

---

191. See Gen. Headquarters, Supreme Commander for Allied Powers, Tokyo, 1 Report on Japanese Taxation 17 (1949).

192. *Id.* at 16.

tax like an annual expenditure tax also may distribute tax burdens in accordance with taxpayers' ability to pay tax.[n]

The "ability to pay" principle is subdivided into two elements of distributive justice—horizontal and vertical equity. To achieve horizontal equity, taxpayers situated equally should be taxed equally. If income (what a taxpayer adds to community resources) is viewed as an appropriate measure of ability to pay tax, then taxpayers with equal incomes should be taxed equally. If consumption (what the taxpayer withdraws from community resources for personal use) is deemed an appropriate measure of ability to pay, then taxpayers with equal levels of consumption should be taxed equally. For this purpose, equity may be measured by individuals' lifetime or annual consumption. In this section, however it is assumed that annual income is a better yardstick of ability to pay taxes.[204]

Vertical equity assumes that the tax burden should be progressive as to income. For many years, the federal tax system relied on steeply progressive individual income tax rates to implement our concept of vertical equity. However, since the early 1960s, Congress has cut the top individual tax rate from ninety-one percent to twenty-eight percent. Judged by traditional support for a progressive federal tax system, the VAT is not as equitable as progressive income taxes. However, consider (1) the recent dramatic reduction both in the number of brackets and the top rate for the individual income tax, resulting in mildly progressive rates for taxpayers remaining in the tax system; (2) the reduced rate corporate income taxes; and (3) the flat-rate payroll taxes. In light of this new federal tax structure, it is no longer clear that Congress and the taxpaying population would view a single rate, broad-based VAT as providing an "inequitable" distribution of the tax burden.

Broad-based sales taxes are considered regressive because they impose a higher tax burden, as a percentage of income, on lower income groups (especially those below the poverty level) than on higher income groups. But there are two points worth noting. First, there is some evidence that a VAT burden is proportional to income, rather than regressive.[206] Second, the regressivity of one tax may be accommodated by making adjustments in the

---

n. See Chapter Seven. (Ed.)

204. Typically, a tax period of one year is used to judge equity in the distribution of the tax burden of a particular tax. See Bradford & Toder, Consumption vs. Income Base Taxes: The Argument on Grounds of Equity and Simplicity, 1976 Proc. of 69th Ann. Conf. on Tax'n of Nat'l Tax Ass'n 25, 30-31. But see J. Pechman & B. Okner, Who Bears the Tax Burden 52 (1974) (arguing that family economic decisions, such as housing and other consumption choices, tend to [be] made on the basis of expected income over a period of years, and thus "effective rates of tax based on income for a single year may not be representative of the tax burdens of families with unusually low (or high) incomes").

206. Pohmer, Germany, in The Value Added Tax: Lessons from Europe 96-97 (H. Aaron ed. 1981).

progressive taxes if, as a result, the overall federal system possesses an acceptable degree of progressivity.

The Treasury Department, in its 1984 report on tax reform, discussed the concept of progressive and regressive taxes. It suggested that there are two equity issues that affect taxes like sales tax or VAT—the regressivity of the tax and the absolute burden of the tax on the poor. Congress can reduce the regressivity of a VAT by granting tax preferences on necessities that account for most or all of the consumption by lower income taxpayers. However, it would be more difficult for Congress to offset the absolute burden of a VAT on the poor, unless Congress grants a refundable tax credit or reduces other taxes that they now pay. With the movement to reduce the number of return-filing taxpayers (individual income tax returns), it is less likely that Congress would offset the burden of a VAT on the poor through refundable credits obtained by filing returns.

Based on principles of horizontal and vertical equity and using income as the standard by which equity principles are measured, VAT does not fare as well as income and payroll taxes. Testing for horizontal equity, the individual income tax scores well. By tailoring the tax to individual circumstances, Congress can tax those with equal taxable incomes equally. Assuming that the corporate tax is borne by shareholders, the corporate tax does not meet the standards of horizontal equity. At various levels of individual income, stock ownership, as well as dividend policy among corporations, vary widely. Assuming that the employer's and employee's share of social security taxes are borne by labor, the payroll taxes deviate somewhat from the standard of horizontal equity. Since they are imposed only on taxable wages, a retired person earning $25,000 income exclusively from social security benefits and from savings is not subject to the social security taxes, while a worker with $25,000 income earned exclusively from wages would be subject to this tax. Testing for horizontal equity, VAT ranks quite low. At the low and middle income ranges, because taxpayers spend most or all of their disposable income on consumption, there is a significant correlation between income and consumption. This is not true at higher income levels, and even within other ranges, taxpayers have different kinds and amounts of consumption expenditures. Selective excise taxes are worse than a broad-based VAT. There are wide variations in the excise tax burden for individuals at any given level of income because it is totally dependent upon their level of consumption of the taxed items.

A progressive individual income tax can be designed to achieve vertical equity. * * *

Selective federal excise taxes and VAT do not fare well when tested by a traditional view of vertical equity, at least when measured annually rather than over a lifetime. Excises on items like alcohol and tobacco tend to be regressive as to income because consumption of these items represents a decreasing proportion of income as annual income increases. If a consumption tax like a VAT has a broad base, it may, at best, be proportional as to consumption. However, the proportion of income used for consumption tends to decline as individual or household income increases. Thus, even if basic necessities are exempt from tax, a VAT or other general consumption tax likely will not become progressive as to income.

Some commentators have suggested that an analysis of equity in the distribution of the tax burden must consider not only the incidence of the tax imposed, but also the distribution of benefits financed by the tax. However, this approach conflicts with the focus of an ability to pay analysis. If (1) it is desirable that lower income families receive benefits that outweigh their tax burden and (2) ability to pay taxes is the appropriate standard, then a VAT is less desirable as a funding source for social welfare programs than income taxes.

Based on traditional views about horizontal and vertical equity, a progressive rate individual income tax permits the most equitable distribution of tax burden, with corporate income and payroll taxes less desirable but better than selective excise taxes. A VAT would rank higher than selective excises, would be difficult to compare with social security taxes, and would be decidedly worse than corporate and individual income taxes. However, while it is too early to make a definitive judgment, in light of the 1986 reforms that dramatically reduced the top corporate and individual income tax rates, and reduced to two the number of individual tax rate brackets, it is possible that taxpayers collectively have changed our concept of vertical equity and no longer consider highly progressive taxes essential to achieve an equitable distribution of the federal tax burden. If so, then a VAT may not rank so poorly, based on ability to pay principles.

Neutrality or Economic Efficiency

A common tax policy goal is to develop a tax system that fosters economic efficiency or neutrality. A tax is economically efficient if it does not distort economic behavior; that is, the tax is neutral as to: (1) a business' choice among various forms of operation; (2) a consumer's choice among possible consumption expenditures; (3) an individual's choice between consuming now or saving for future consumption; and (4) an individual's choice between working or preferring leisure.

If Congress considered increasing the existing income-based individual income tax or enacting a broad-based C-style VAT and neither choice would change relative prices of goods or services, then these alternatives would be neutral as to consumers' choices among consumer items. However, if the VAT were riddled with exemptions or other preferences, it would not foster economic efficiency. Such a VAT would distort choices consumers must make between taxable and tax-preferred consumption items. Similar inefficiency would occur if Congress increased the income tax that incorporated preferences for the consumption of certain goods or services.[219]

Whether or not increases in individual income tax or VAT change relative prices, these tax increases may create other distortions. Compared with a new broad-based VAT, an increase in a progressive individual income tax may distort choices individuals make between current and future consumption or between work and leisure. With the 1986 base broadening and rate reducing reforms, these distortions under the individual income tax have been reduced substantially. However, if the new VAT included a substantial number of "item" preferences, the resulting VAT may distort an individual's decision to consume now or save to consume in the future (the incentive to consume exempt items currently may distort this choice), but to the extent of the preferences, it may be neutral as to an individual's decision to work or prefer leisure, since neither labor income used to consume exempt goods nor the value of leisure would be subject to a VAT.

The corporate income tax is not a neutral tax because it distorts a business' choice of form of operation. * * *

It has been asserted that the corporate tax may serve as an umbrella to protect inefficient corporations that otherwise could not compete with profitable taxpaying corporations. To the extent that industry leaders are able to shift part of the corporate tax forward into product prices, this price increase permits the more inefficient corporations to compete with the price setting leaders and thereby remain in business despite their inefficiency. For example, assume the price setting (PS) Corporation shifts its corporate tax (amounting to about $.50 per widget) into the $10.50 price for widgets. An inefficient, competing (IC) Corporation has higher production costs, but still can obtain customers for its widgets if it sells them for not more than $10.50 per unit. At this price, the IC Corporation earns no profit and therefore pays no corporate tax. If the corporate tax were replaced with a VAT, PS Corporation could sell at a pre-VAT ten dollar price and add a VAT on the sale. At this ten dollar pre-tax price, the IC Corporation would sustain losses of $.50 per unit and ultimately may close. Over time, if the corporate tax is shifted, the replacement of the corporate tax with a VAT can be expected to drive the inefficient corporations out of business. However, it is not clear that Congress supports a national goal of promoting economic efficiency in business, if it

---

219. For example, the existing individual income tax exempts health and accident insurance provided by employers from taxation, thus encouraging workers to take part of their wages in this tax-free form.

occurs at the cost of insolvency for marginal businesses. Indeed, new businesses typically are not very efficient during their formative years and national policy promotes capital formation for new enterprises to hire additional workers. The replacement of most or all of the corporate tax with a VAT could produce a federal tax structure that distorts economic decisions on the form of business operation if corporations could become tax shelters for owners to accumulate earnings and avoid the shareholder level tax. However, if Congress coupled the adoption of a VAT with the integration of the individual and corporate income taxes, the tax shelter phenomenon could be avoided.

Payroll taxes are imposed on wages up to a statutory ceiling for covered employees and self-employed individuals and, as taxes withheld from wages, are neutral as to individuals' choices among consumer items and as to individuals' choices between current consumption and savings for future consumption. Since they are imposed on wages up to a statutory ceiling, payroll taxes may create individual preferences for leisure over work until the ceiling is reached; they then do not distort this choice, since they then do not tax either work or leisure. A broad-based VAT does not have any significant efficiency or neutrality advantages over existing payroll taxes, except as to the latter's preference for leisure over work at payroll levels below the statutory cap.

VAT as a Fiscal Tool to Promote Economic Goals

The focus of the 1986 tax reforms was to broaden the base and reduce the top rates for the individual and corporate income taxes. In the process, Congress reduced the role of income taxes in affecting economic or industrial policy. For example, Congress reversed prior tax policy that encouraged the modernization of plants and equipment with the investment tax credit and rapid depreciation, and that had encouraged the investment in research and development and in certain kinds of real estate. It would be ironic if Congress now found VAT attractive as a fiscal tool to promote economic or industrial policy goals. Yet, a VAT can be used as a fiscal tool to affect the economy in very discreet ways.

If Congress enacted a VAT and granted the President the power to alter the VAT rates within a prescribed range (to alter a ten percent VAT rate by twenty percent—up to twelve percent or down to eight percent), then the government may be able to increase the VAT rate to reduce consumption and thereby slow down an overheated economy or may reduce the VAT rate to stimulate a stagnant economy. If Congress retained the power to make these modest short term rate changes, they may be less effective as a fiscal tool. While Congress debated a bill to increase the rate to stifle consumption, consumers could accelerate their purchases to avoid the proposed increase.

Likewise, if Congress wanted to cut the VAT rate temporarily to stimulate consumer spending, the normal tax legislative process might delay enactment of the tax cut until it was no longer needed.

Congress could alter VAT rates on selected consumer items to stimulate or dampen demand in particular industries or particular segments of the economy. For example, to reverse a recession in the auto industry, Congress or the President (if the latter is granted power to adjust rates) could stimulate car buying by cutting the VAT rate on automobiles for a limited period of time.

Notwithstanding the attractiveness of a VAT as a fiscal tool to achieve economic, social, or other national policy goals, it would be undesirable to enact a new VAT to serve these functions rather than to serve basically as a revenue raising measure. If the federal government wants to stimulate or dampen the economy, it may find that it would be more effective to rely on monetary than fiscal policy. Congress cannot justify adoption of a broad-based federal tax on consumption just to obtain this potential fiscal tool.

On balance, the economic considerations discussed do not favor the use of a VAT as a fiscal tool. Instead, reliance on existing federal income and payroll taxes is a better course, and a VAT should be considered only as a revenue raising measure.

Notes and Questions

The Ullman proposal

5. Although Congressman Ullman's proposed Tax Restructuring Act of 1979 was never enacted,[o] its introduction marked a political milestone in this country's consideration of the VAT. What form of VAT would it have imposed? For what transactions and entities did it propose preferential treatment, what form did the preferential treatment take, and what justification could be offered for such preferential treatment? What use would have been made of the revenue generated by the VAT?[p]

6. Ullman asserted as an advantage of VAT that the flow of revenue would be more constant than under the income tax, where "boom and bust cycles have turned tax receipts into a guessing game," with the uncertainty compounded by expanded federal payments in time of recession. Do you agree with Ullman, or with those who see tax revenues falling and expenditures

---

o. Congressman Ullman re-introduced his proposal in 1980, again unsuccessfully. H.R. 7015, 96th Cong., 2d Sess., 126 Cong. Rec. 7481.

p. It should be noted that the 1979 estimates significantly understate the revenue that a VAT would generate today. In the final excerpt of this chapter, Professor Graetz cites a Congressional Budget Office estimate that in 1996 a five percent VAT (half the level proposed by Congressman Ullman) could have raised between $70 billion and $140 billion, depending on exemptions.

rising in time of recession, and the opposite forces at work in boom times, as a salutary "automatic stabilizer"?

7.   Congressman Ullman held the most important tax-writing position in the country—Chairman of the Ways and Means Committee—at the time he proposed the Tax Restructuring Act of 1979. In two important political senses, VAT was dealt a serious setback by Mr. Ullman's defeat in the 1980 general election. First, the new committee chairman did not choose to pick up the VAT flag after Mr. Ullman was felled. Second, other potential supporters of VAT may have been deterred by noting that Mr. Ullman's support of VAT was used against him in the campaign.[q]

8.   Perhaps thinking of Mr. Ullman's fate, Professor Michael Graetz, in advocating a VAT, cautions: "Because a VAT has long been considered dangerous to politicians who advocate it, another name will be necessary; call it a goods and services tax, a business sales tax, or simply a consumption tax."[r]

9.   *Types of VAT: national tax base.* VATs can be categorized in various ways. Treasury I identifies two ways in which VATs might be differentiated from each other. First, we might consider the theoretical national tax base—gross national product, national income, or total private consumption. The difference among the three depends on the treatment of capital equipment. What is the basic difference in the treatment of capital equipment necessary to meet each of these three tax bases? Which does Treasury I find most supportable? Why?

10.   *Types of VAT: method of calculation.* Whatever the tax base (let us assume that a consumption-base VAT is chosen), VATs can also be categorized by the method of calculation—addition, credit, or subtraction. As the Treasury I excerpt explains, the addition method assumes that the value added by a given taxpayer, at a given stage of production, can be thought of as the contribution by each of various factors of production. The tax base for each taxpayer thus consists of the sum of the return to the four classic factors of production—land (rent), labor (wages and salaries), capital (interest) and

---

q. Mr. Ullman's support of VAT was criticized particularly by his opponent in the Democratic primary, which Ullman won. However, those attacks may have softened his support in the general election, which he lost. Professors Oldman and Schenk opine that it is inaccurate to attribute Ullman's loss to his VAT proposal. Oliver Oldman & Alan Schenk, *The Business Activities Tax: Have Senators Danforth & Boren Created a Better Value Added Tax?*, 65 TAX NOTES 1547, 1548 (1994).

r. Michael J. Graetz, *The U.S. Income Tax: Should It Survive the Millennium?*, 85 TAX NOTES 1197, 1200 (1999).

entrepreneurship (profit). The addition method finishes last on most lists. It seems that the addition method is presented more out of a sense of academic tidiness than because it merits serious consideration. Twenty-five years ago, the method was rejected by an ABA Committee in a report focusing on the addition method,[s] and there appears to be no more enthusiasm in recent times, either in this country or abroad.

The two remaining methods of computation—the European credit-invoice method and the subtraction method—are serious contenders.[t] The credit-invoice method VAT is a *transactional* tax. The seller in any taxable transaction collects the stated purchase price plus a separately stated VAT, which is computed with reference to the stated purchase price. The invoice for each individual sale should reflect the VAT paid.[u] If the payor is not the ultimate consumer, the payor is entitled to claim a credit for the VAT paid, and can do so in its next return (even before resale). Thus, the *full* VAT is paid on *each* sale, at whatever stage of production. Because any payor other than the final consumer receives a credit for the VAT paid, however, the net tax remitted is based upon the difference between purchase price and sales price—that is, upon value added. The invoice makes the proper amount of the credit definite. In addition, the credit-invoice method should produce a paper trail (now, perhaps, an electronic trail) to simplify audit. To use the simple example from the introduction, the dairy, which purchased the milk for fifty cents and sold it for eighty cents would (with a ten percent tax) pay five cents to the farmer, but promptly claim a credit for that amount, then collect and remit eight cents. (When the credit and the tax payment are netted, the dairy should have paid a net tax of three cents—ten percent of its value added—and the entire tax has been passed on to its customer.) Observe that the tax to be collected by the dairy from the grocery store does not directly depend on the amount of value added by the dairy—the computation of which might be difficult for any single item, especially in a business other than purchasing and reselling—but upon the more-readily-determined selling price.

Under the sales-subtractive VAT, which the ABA committee referred to as the business transfer tax, or BTT, the tax base is not the price paid in each

---

s. American Bar Association, Special Committee on the Value-Added Tax of the Section of Taxation, *Evaluation of an Additive-Method Value-Added Tax for Use in the United States*, 30 TAX LAW. 565 (1977).

t. The credit-invoice method has been more popular throughout the world and is the preferred form of VAT according to Congressman Ullman, Treasury I and the ABA Committee (all excerpted above). However, serious BTT proposals have been advanced in this country—former Senator Roth, and former Senators Danforth and Boren, have proposed BTTs, and the USA Tax discussed in Chapter Seven includes a VAT component that utilizes the sales subtractive method.

u. Japan has adopted a credit form of VAT that does not depend on an invoice for credit to be allowed. *See* Oldman & Schenk, *supra* note q, at 1550-51.

transaction. Instead, each taxpayer in the chain of production pays a tax based upon its value added, as computed by its sales minus its purchases. The taxpayer is not entitled to a credit, because, unlike the invoice method, the tax at each level is not based on total value (*i.e.*, sales price) but on the value added. Again using the dairy from the introduction, the dairy would compute its value added—the tax base—as eighty cents minus fifty cents—and would remit the tax on the resulting thirty-cent base (three cents, undiminished by any credit). Unlike the credit method, this tax cannot readily be stated separately upon sale, because the tax cannot easily be known by, or demonstrated to, the buyer. The tax depends upon the seller's costs and profit, rather than the selling price. Instead of a separately stated VAT, the seller would simply absorb VAT and pass it along not as a separately stated tax, but rather in the form of a higher price.

Comparison of credit-invoice method and
subtraction method/business transfer tax.

11. Both Treasury I and the ABA Committee prefer the credit-invoice method to the subtraction method/business transfer tax, for a number of reasons. Why is a BTT more likely to lead to political pressure for exemptions? Why are exemptions under the credit-invoice method, even if granted, less likely to cost the government revenue?

12. Why is rebating VAT—such as rebating VAT paid on goods that are exported after some value has been added—easier under the credit method than under the BTT?

13. Under a credit-invoice system, the VAT is clearly stated in every sale, all the way through to the final sale to the consumer. Under the sales-subtractive BTT, the VAT is buried in prices, which are raised by each member of the chain of production and distribution to reflect this additional cost. Assuming the economic effects of the two forms of tax to be substantially identical—*i.e.*, that either tax is ultimately borne by the consumer—what political effect would you expect from the form of the tax, given that the tax is more obvious under the credit-invoice method than under the BTT? Would you regard this effect as an advantage of the credit-invoice method or of the BTT?

14. The fact that the BTT is buried in the price of goods rather than being separately stated might make it easier to coordinate that form of federal VAT with existing state RSTs; see Note #45 below (page 378).

Compliance and fraud

15. The credit-invoice method is said to facilitate compliance. Auditors can follow a paper trail of invoices. Perhaps more important, "downstream" taxpayers other than the ultimate consumer have an incentive to make certain that invoices generated by their purchases properly reflect VAT paid, so that they can claim the VAT credit. Consider the dairy in the example from the introduction. If it failed to obtain an invoice showing VAT paid to the farmer, it could not claim its credit when it re-sold to the grocery; that accurate invoice, in turn, makes the farmer more likely to remit the VAT due upon his sale to the dairy.

By contrast, a taxpayer's BTT depends not upon VAT paid to each supplier, but upon its total costs of inventory and supplies of goods and services from all suppliers. The tax paid is not reflected on invoices, which may make it easier for upstream suppliers to understate their liability. In his article comparing three forms of consumption taxes—the credit-invoice VAT, the BTT, and the retail sales tax (RST)—Professor Sijbren Cnossen gives the nod to credit-invoice VAT with regard to fraud-related problems:

> [F]ictitious claims for refunds through counterfeit invoices, particularly at the export stage,[v] do provide an opportunity for fraud under [the invoice-credit form of] VAT that is not available under RST. On balance, however, VAT's self-enforcement mechanism and broader control of evasion, lead me to conclude that dishonesty commands a higher price under VAT than it does under RST (or, for that matter, BTT). * * *
>
> Retailers are perhaps the most troublesome sector under VAT. Since consumers are not eligible for tax credits or refunds, neither they nor the retailer have any compelling inducement to ensure that the latter's sales are reported accurately. In other words, VAT's self-enforcement mechanism does not operate at this stage. Still, VAT seems to have an advantage over RST here, since the tax auditor has a presumptively accurate record of the retailer's purchases and therefore can estimate sales on the basis of an average industry mark-up. Moreover, the fact that retailers do have to pay the tax on their purchases makes evasion less likely to succeed for the full amount of the tax. To be sure, they can take credit for the tax on purchases and may file false refund claims, but unless taxable goods

---

v. Because exports are zero-rated, a firm that exports a product not only pays no additional tax but is entitled to a refund of VAT it paid when acquiring the product. This gives an incentive to creation of a fraudulent invoice, which supports an undeserved credit for VAT that was not in fact paid.

are zero rated refund claims should result in a detailed scrutiny of the return.[w]

Observe that even in defending VAT, Professor Cnossen does not fall into the error of some naive VAT supporters, who seem to believe that a VAT would be almost self-enforcing. Moreover, not all commentators share his view that credit-invoice VAT, while imperfect, is better than its rivals. Professor Mario Leccisotti and Dr. Mauro Mare argue that "VAT, far from emerging as the best way of taxing consumption, appears as a form of taxation with very considerable administrative and compliance costs."[x] They refute Cnossen's arguments concerning "the self-policing mechanism and the ease of cross-checks":

> The argument is correct, but it overlooks an essential fact. Although the buyer gains from a high purchase price in the invoice, he or she has a much greater interest in paying a lower tax, but the buyer must pay a higher tax in order to benefit from a higher tax credit. Since the alternatives are a higher tax and a higher credit versus a lower tax and a lower credit, under normal conditions no reasonable person would prefer to pay a higher tax now, in order to be entitled to a higher credit in a more or less remote future.

> Moreover, the buyer has very important reasons for desiring to keep the invoice price low, since by reducing costs and turnover for the treasury, the income tax may be evaded more easily.

> Given this situation, contrary to the opinion of VAT's supporters, both sellers and buyers have an interest in showing in the invoice a price as low [as] possible. Thus, in all stages the price will tend to be below the true one. * * * [T]he possibility of tax evasion is greatly reinforced by the fact that the final consumer has no interest in paying a higher tax for which he is not entitled to any refund, and asks for a low invoice price.[y]

The student should keep in mind that the realistic goal can never be to create a tax that cannot be evaded. No tax can meet such standards. We seek taxes that are relatively difficult to evade, and that offer relatively low incentives to evasion. How does the credit-invoice VAT compare to more familiar American taxes, such as state RSTs and the federal income tax?

---

w. Sijbren Cnossen, *Broad-based Consumption Taxes: VAT, RST, or BTT?*, 6 AUSTL. TAX R. 391, 418 (1989).

x. Mario Leccisotti & Mauro Mare, *On the Presumed Technical Superiority of VAT*, 9 AUSTL. TAX R. 259, 259-60 (1992).

y. *Id.* at 265.

16. VAT offers one attractive opportunity to cheat not matched by the RST. The zero-rated export gives a seller not only an opportunity to evade a tax, but to create phony invoices and thereby obtain a refund for a tax never paid. (The seller is normally entitled to a credit for VAT paid by it to upstream sellers. In the usual case, the credit merely reduces VAT liability. In the case of a zero-rated export, however, the credit results in an actual refund.)

17. The ABA committee suggests that the VAT may be both simpler and less prone to fraud than the RST with respect to sales not to final consumers ("midstream" sales). Under the credit-invoice VAT, such sales are taxable, although the purchaser will later be entitled to a credit. The purchaser has a strong incentive to make the invoice reflect the full selling price and correct VAT, because the invoice will support the purchaser's claim for VAT credit. Under the RST, the business purchaser will simply be allowed, generally by recording the purchaser's resale exclusion certificate number on the invoice, to purchase without payment of sales tax. Fraud at this stage—by disguising a sale to a consumer as a sale to a business, for example—avoids the entire RST, permanently. In the case of a purchaser claiming RST exemption for a purchase actually intended for the purchaser's personal consumption, it is likely that the purchaser's fraud alone, without participation by the seller, could defeat the RST. False invoices designed to defeat VAT will usually require complicity of both buyer and seller, making this form of fraud less likely.

18. If a retail seller goes bankrupt or simply disappears before remitting taxes, the loss of RST is complete. By contrast, a considerable portion of VAT will have already been collected through sales prior to the retail stage.

19. Perhaps the key to controlling fraud is to keep tax rates low. Higher rates naturally increase the incentive to any form of tax evasion. A significant federal VAT coupled with state RSTs could push the combined rate to a level that would tempt considerably more fraud than would either tax alone. The ABA committee cites Canada's Carter Commission to the effect that a rate of fourteen percent tempts significant evasion,[z] although this obviously will vary widely from taxpayer to taxpayer. Does this argue that there should be many types of taxes, each relatively low? For example, would we expect lower evasion with an income tax of ten percent and a VAT of ten percent than with either tax at twenty percent? But would the imposition of multiple taxes not

---

z. American Bar Association, Committee on Value Added Tax of the Section of Taxation, VALUE ADDED TAX: A MODEL STATUTE AND COMMENTARY 6 (1989), *citing* 5 REPORT OF THE ROYAL COMMISSION ON TAXATION, SALES TAXES AND GENERAL TAX ADMINISTRATION 50 (1966).

increase compliance costs for taxpayers and administrative costs for government?

International trade

20. What is the theoretically different tax base under the "destination principle" and its alternative, the "origin principle"? How does the theory chosen affect the taxation of imports and exports?

21. In practice, the destination principle is invariably chosen "[f]or competitive reasons or because international trade is a significant element in the nation's economy."[aa] Why might it be expected that a nation's producers—a group with obvious political clout in any country—would prefer that the national VAT embody the destination principle?

22. It seems obvious that exporting firms would be attracted to a destination-principle VAT, because exports are "zero rated." Not only can the exporter sell without having to collect a VAT from its purchaser, but it obtains a rebate for VAT it has paid to its suppliers.

It is perhaps less obvious that the destination-principle VAT is also attractive to producers that do not export, but compete in the domestic market with foreign producers. Why is this the case?

23. The European Community (EC) is moving to implement an origin-principle VAT for trade within the EC, while maintaining the destination principle for trade with the rest of the world.[bb] What considerations might prompt this dual approach?

24. The key trade advantage of VAT vis-à-vis other taxes derives from the rules of the General Agreement on Tariffs and Trade (GATT) (which first came into effect in 1947 and since 1994 has been administered by the World Trade Organization (WTO)). What effect do WTO rules have on the ability of adhering nations (most nations of the world, including the United States and its major trading partners) to support exports? How are these rules applicable to VAT as compared to alternative taxes, such as payroll taxes and corporate income taxes?

---

aa. Alan Schenk, *Value Added Tax: Does This Consumption Tax Have a Place in the Federal Tax System?*, 7 VA. TAX REV. 207, 231 (1987).

bb. *See* Craig A. Hart, *The European Community's Value-Added Tax System: Analysis of the New Transitional Regime and Prospects for Further Harmonization*, 12 INT'L TAX & BUS. LAW. 1 (1994).

25. The favorable effects of an American VAT on this country's international trade are extremely important in the eyes of some VAT supporters, and virtually nil in the view of detractors. Mr. Ullman, for example, claimed that the United States would derive substantial trade advantages from utilizing the VAT. On the other hand, the drafters of Treasury I were considerably more cautious concerning the contributions to the balance of trade to be expected from implementation of a VAT. They not only conclude their discussion of the issue by noting that the decision to implement VAT is too important to be driven by the possible trade benefits, but list two factors that cast doubt on whether the trade benefits would in fact materialize. What are these factors that might rain on VAT's trade-advantage parade?

26. Some VAT supporters question its supposed trade advantages. Gerald Brannon maintains that "[t]here are good arguments for VAT[cc] but balance of trade is not one of them."[dd] In addition to noting the problems identified in Treasury I, Professor Brannon argues that the trade advantages accrue only if VAT, which increases prices but is "border-adjusted" (*i.e.*, rebated on exports), takes the place of another tax that increases prices but is not border-adjusted. FICA may or may not increase prices; it depends on the uncertain question of who—laborer, employer or consumer—bears the tax. With respect to the corporate income tax, Professor Brannon argues that the tax is not shifted to the price of the good:

> Why don't firms * * * simply raise the price * * * even without a tax?
> The answer must be that the firm figured the higher price would
> lose enough sales to reduce profit. Now introduce CIT [corporate
> income tax]. It is no more sensible to raise the price after CIT than
> it was before.[ee]

Finally, Mr. Brannon reminds us that even if we are successful in improving the lot of domestic producers, their benefit may come at the expense of domestic consumers:

> [T]he higher exports and lower imports will help exporters and firms
> that compete with imports. It doesn't raise the living standard of
> Americans. * * *

---

cc. Brannon cites his earlier article, *The Value Added Tax is a Good Utility Infielder*, 37 NAT'L TAX J. 303 (1984).

dd. Gerald M. Brannon, *Does VAT Provide a Balance of Trade Advantage?*, 30 TAX NOTES 1387, 1387 (1986).

ee. *Id.* at 1388. The incidence of the corporate tax is discussed in Chapter Fourteen, Subchapter B.

The basic policy here, assuming it works, is not much different from the protective tariff. * * *

On the export industry side, this switch of VAT for CIT or FICA is a pot of pure honey because the VAT is refunded on exports.[ff] Does the "trade advantage" claimed for VAT amount to favoring American producers over American consumers? Assuming the answer to be "yes," can a principled defense of VAT nonetheless be maintained?

27.   Because WTO rules allow rebate of indirect taxes such as VAT but not direct taxes such as the corporate income tax, the choice between credit method VAT and BTT may be important in obtaining whatever advantages derive from the right to rebate VAT to exporters. Commentators have observed that the BTT "looks more like a tax on a business than on a product. * * * Thus, other countries may object to applying the destination principle to permit rebate of the business transfer tax on exports from the United States and its imposition on imports."[gg]

28.   WTO rules, of course, are not holy writ. Stanley Surrey, who was sharply critical of VAT, suggested that the quest for desirable trade effects should lead us not to adopt a VAT, but to seek amendments to trade rules:

> One aspect of the reexamination [of international trade rules] could well be to permit countries not having a high indirect tax system permanently to adopt within limits border adjustments independent of their domestic tax structures if they so desire. It could result also in imposing some upper limits on the total border adjustments countries with indirect tax systems could make. This approach would provide an appropriate international accommodation to the basic question we are considering, that of freedom for domestic tax action without prejudicing a country's trade position.[hh]

To date, however, WTO rules remain unchanged, and American economic influence may be less than in 1969, when Professor Surrey wrote.

29.   *Zero rating vs. exemption.* If a transaction is zero rated, it is a sale within the VAT system. The sale is taxed at a rate of zero percent, but the seller is entitled to claim credit for VAT paid. Exports are zero rated, with the result that the foreign purchaser bears no VAT imposed by the country of

---

ff. *Id.* at 1389.

gg. George N. Carlson & Richard A. Gordon, *VAT or Business Transfer Tax: A Tax on Consumers or on Business?*, 41 TAX NOTES 329, 332 (1988).

hh. Stanley S. Surrey, *A Value-Added Tax for the United States—A Negative View*, 21 TAX EXEC. 151, 171 (1969).

production. The same approach could be used to allow any product, such as food, to be sold free from VAT.

If a seller is VAT-exempt, however, the sale is outside the VAT system. For example, small businesses or nonprofit organizations might be exempted. As in the case of zero rating, no VAT liability results from an exempt sale, but the seller is not entitled to a credit for VAT paid. Thus, it may be expected that the selling price reflects VAT paid by the seller.

What are the economic effects on the purchaser and seller of zero rated items? On the purchaser and seller where the seller is VAT-exempt? Why does exemption of midstream sales actually increase VAT liability? What policy advantages accrue to exemption?

Additional tax or replacement for existing taxes?

30. Professor Due, writing in 1980, viewed VAT as a tax that would replace or reduce existing federal taxes, while Dr. McLure, seven years later, argued in favor of VAT as an additional source of revenue. This difference is probably attributable, at least in part, to the changed situation. The deficit was much larger in 1987 than in 1980; moreover, much of the tax reduction that Due might have envisioned in 1980 had been obtained in the Economic Recovery Tax Act of 1981.

31. Professor Michael Graetz, author of the 1997 book *The Decline (and Fall?) of the Income Tax*, recommends a VAT to replace the income tax for most taxpayers:

> [W]e should return the income tax to its pre-World War II status–a relatively low-rate tax on a thin slice of the wealthiest Americans. Enacting a value added tax (VAT) of 10 to 15 percent would finance an income tax exemption of up to $100,000 and would allow a vastly simpler income tax at a 20 to 25 percent rate to be applied to incomes over $100,000. * * *
>
> Such a change would eliminate more than 100 million of the 115 million tax returns that are filed each year."[ii]

32. What political risk do conservatives see in VAT, according to Dr. McLure? Why is McLure undeterred by this risk?

33. The danger of VAT encouraging unwise government expansion may be unfounded. One commentator presented data which led him to conclude that "there is essentially no difference between the behavior of the size of the

---

ii. Graetz, *supra* note r, at 1200.

government sector in VAT and non-VAT countries. This suggests that other political and economic factors are determining the relative size of government."[jj]

Effect on national savings

34. Professor Due contended that the argument for VAT "centers on the capital formation issue." Would you expect enactment of VAT, accompanied by equivalent reductions in other taxes, to increase national rates of saving, investment, and capital formation?

35. Professor Due's evaluation of VAT generally assumes that federal revenues will be x dollars. Thus, the question is whether the best way to raise x dollars is by use of existing taxes at whatever level is necessary to produce x dollars, or by using a lower level of existing taxes coupled with a VAT. In terms of increasing national savings, how does Professor Due compare VAT to the personal income tax? To the corporate income tax? To payroll taxes? Does it matter whether one assumes that payroll taxes are passed through to a company's customers?

36. VAT proponents contend that saving would increase, not so much because VAT encourages saving but merely because VAT would provide tax neutrality to the saving-consumption choice, as contrasted to the income tax, which encourages consumption.

37. One empirical study of twenty-three nations casts doubt on whether adoption of a VAT would in fact lead to increased national saving: "Although it seems theoretically sound to contend that placing greater reliance on a VAT or consumption taxes to raise government revenue would result in increased saving, we have been unable to find any empirical evidence that that happens in practice."[kk]

38. Similarly, some observers suggest that VAT's supposed neutrality should be accepted only with a grain of salt:
> While the VAT is less inherently nonneutral than some taxes, its flexibility makes it possible to mold it into a highly nonneutral tax. The VAT could attain its high potential degree of neutrality only if the Congress made a conscious effort * * * to avoid a major VAT

---

jj. J.A. Stockfish, *Value-Added Taxes and the Size of Government: Some Evidence*, 38 NAT'L TAX J. 547, 549 (1985).

kk. Ken Militzer, *VAT: Evidence from the OECD*, 47 TAX NOTES 207, 207 (1990).

impact on business decisions. Such a conscious effort has not generally characterized the behavior of legislative bodies.[ll]

Equity

39.   Unquestionably, the most potent argument of VAT opponents is that the tax flunks the test of vertical equity. At first blush, at least, this argument has considerable force. Why?

40.   How did the Ullman bill address such concerns?

41.   Is granting of favorable tax rates to food and other necessities a good method of addressing equity concerns? Why do you think this approach was rejected in the ABA committee's Model Act?

42.   European countries traditionally have attempted to increase progressivity in their VATs both through low rates on necessities and high rates on luxuries. Common as these provisions are, almost all commentators agree with the ABA committee that they are unwise. Gerald Brannon, in typically irreverent language, observes:

> The most common anti-regressivity "fix" within a VAT or a sales tax is to exempt things like food. This has two very severe drawbacks and one advantage.
>
> The first drawback is that it doesn't do a decent job of reducing regressivity. * * *
>
> A more important problem is that a food exemption greatly complicates the system. * * *
>
> The big advantage of the food exemption in a VAT is that it gives the legislator something that he can tell his middle-class constituents he did for them. This is valuable but it is also hokum since a 4 percent tax without a food exemption is practically indistinguishable for most people from a 5 percent tax with the food exemption.[mm]

The EC is moving toward a single uniform rate with most preferences being phased out.

43.   We might couple VAT with changes in the income tax that favored low-income taxpayers, such as an increased standard deduction and personal exemption, or a credit for low-income persons. Why would the credit have to

---

ll. L.L. Bravenec & Kerry Cooper, *The Flexibility of the Value-Added Tax*, 55 TEX. L. REV. 453, 469 (1977).

mm. Brannon, *supra* note cc, at 306-07.

be "refundable" (available to taxpayers with no income tax liability to offset)? Are such techniques a good method of addressing equity concerns raised by VAT?

44.   Is the key in proper analysis of the equity of a VAT to evaluate what the VAT proceeds will be used for? In the words of Professor Arthur Laffer:

[I]t is imperative to know the second entry or balancing transaction. If a value-added tax were introduced to eliminate a poll tax or to increase the pay of conscripted soldiers, it would be hard to argue that the VAT package was anything other than a progressive package. * * * Similarly, it would be difficult to argue that a VAT package was progressive if, in fact, the second entry was a reduction in capital gains taxes or a nationwide reduction in the upper-income bracket tax rates.[nn]

Federal-State relations

45.   In considering a federal VAT, serious consideration must be given to the fact that approximately 45 states have retail sales taxes (RSTs). This could lead to political opposition to a VAT, especially a credit-invoice type of VAT, as opposed to the BTT form that buries the tax in the price of the product. Professor Schenk suggests that both political and efficiency concerns could point toward the BTT form of VAT, rather than the credit-invoice form, if a federal VAT were to be adopted.

A state with a high-rate RST may feel that its tax base will be threatened more by a European Community-style invoice VAT than a BTT because consumers may resist an increase in the combined rate of the separately stated RST and European Community-style invoice VAT more than the adoption of a federal BTT that is buried in the prices of goods and services.

* * *

If the states were inclined to harmonize their RST's with a federal VAT, it may be more likely to occur with a European Community-style invoice VAT than a BTT because the invoice VAT looks more like a sales tax. It may not be very realistic, however, to assume that states will harmonize their RST's with any form of federal VAT. * * *

State and local governments' support or opposition to a federal VAT ultimately will depend not only on the proposed form of VAT, but on such factors as the state's RST rate and the kind of federal

---

nn. Arthur B. Laffer, *The International Impact of a Value-Added Tax*, 6 J. CORP. LAW 119, 119 (1980).

programs that will be financed with the VAT revenue. * * * [I]f the VAT is a hidden BTT that is not added to the consumer's cost at the check-out counter, the BTT may not affect the state and local governments' ability to raise revenue from [their RSTs].

Finally, assuming state and local RST's continue to operate basically in their existing form, a BTT would be more compatible and less costly to administer and compliance costs would be lower than a European Community-style invoice BTT. The reason is that a BTT is hidden and therefore does not clash with the separately stated RST's. Is it, however, good public policy to choose a particular form of VAT because it does the best job of masking its identity as a tax on consumption?[oo]

Professor Schenk points out that a federal BTT buried in prices, because it would increase the prices on which state RSTs are based, would actually increase state revenues. Does coordination with state RSTs constitute a significant argument for the BTT form of VAT?

46. Might VAT provide opportunities for federal-state cooperation, rather than rivalry? Dr. McLure has suggested that upon federal enactment of VAT, states should also move from RST to VAT, with the incentive that the federal government would "collect state taxes piggybacked on the federal VAT, as many states currently collect local supplements to their retail sales tax."[pp] Professor John Miller, on the other hand, suggests that the simpler approach would be for the federal government to adopt RST, and turn collection over to state sales tax authorities.[qq] Federal-state cooperation could lower not only administrative costs for both levels of government, but compliance costs for businesses.[rr]

47. *The underground economy.* VAT proponents, such as Mr. Ullman, claim that VAT will reach the "underground economy," and thus bring in revenue from taxpayers who evade the income tax. Surely drug dealers and prostitutes would not be more likely to collect and remit VAT on their illegal sales of goods and services than to pay income tax on such illegally derived income. In what sense would VAT be successful in reaching the underground economy?

---

oo. Schenk, *supra* note h, at 319-20.

pp. Charles E. McLure, Jr., *State and Federal Relations in the Taxation of Value Added*, 6 J. CORP. LAW 127, 136 (1980).

qq. John A. Miller, *State Administration of a National Sales Tax: A New Opportunity for Cooperative Federalism*, 9 VA. TAX REV. 243 (1989).

rr. See generally Schenk, *supra* note h.

48.   Professor Schenk raised but rejected the idea of using VAT as a fiscal tool—that is, increasing rates of VAT taxation to cool an overstimulated economy, and reducing rates to stimulate the economy.   Particularly interesting was the observation that Congress acted so slowly in enacting tax law that it might grant to the President the power to vary VAT tax rates, within a specified range. Is this a desirable approach? Might the President be too willing to reap the political benefit of reducing the tax? Is it realistic to think that a President would *ever* raise the rate? If Congress were willing to cede this power, should it be to the President or to a body not so intensely involved in the political process, akin to the Federal Reserve System?

D. RELATED PROPOSALS

This subchapter contains excerpts of two articles that embrace only certain aspects of the argument favoring a generalized VAT.   Professor Isenbergh argues that shifting the primary basis of taxation to consumption is desirable and important due to inadequate saving and capital formation. For that reason, he advocates a VAT, but with significant additional measures designed to achieve progressivity at both the high and low ends of the income spectrum.   Professor Graetz also sees virtue in increased reliance on consumption taxes. Rather than a broad-based VAT, however, he argues for significantly higher federal excise taxes levied only on specified products. In both articles, the dollar amounts used by the authors are outdated; the ideas expressed remain current, however.

THE END OF INCOME TAXATION
Joseph Isenbergh[*]
45 Tax Law Review 283, 283-84, 349-56, 360-61 (1990)

[T]he last decade has brought the lowest rates of saving by Americans in our peacetime history. * * *

[C]oncern over our fiscal habits is warranted. The justification for this concern is neither the absolute level of deficits nor the apparent dearth of saving—although these are hardly reassuring—but the specific influence of our indigenous system of income taxation on capital formation. Income taxation, particularly as practiced in the United States, systematically favors current consumption over saving. There is a resulting distortion of individual choices that is not, and cannot readily be, offset by other fiscal actions of government. In short, capital formation in the United States is weaker than it would be with a different tax system.

* * *

---

*. At time of original publication, Professor of Law, University of Chicago.

A VAT and Progressivity

If a uniform across-the-board VAT were the sole federal tax, it would be open to the immediate objection that it was not progressive with respect to wealth and economic income. Whatever the ultimate merit of this objection, the premise on which it rests is correct. A pure consumption tax does not tend, by its nature, to be progressive. A flat VAT will weigh more heavily on those whose incomes are low, because the lower the income, the greater the percentage that is likely to be consumed currently, if only as a matter of survival. Other forms of tax on consumption can be given a degree of progressivity, but it is not easy to do so across the full range of economic incomes. A tax on consumed income (i.e., an income tax with an unlimited deduction for saving) could, for example, be made progressive on its own base simply by adopting graduated rates, and this would approximate progressivity with respect to income in the ranges of income where the propensity to consume is high.[ss] A tax on consumed income, no matter how steeply graduated, does not reach the unconsumed portion, however. The larger the income, the larger the portion that may remain beyond the current reach of the tax.

Progressive taxation has been viewed as everything from the cornerstone of a civilized society to theft. Progressivity can be understood broadly as a measure of the economic redistribution resulting from a tax. It is only a partial measure, however, of the redistributive effect of a fiscal system overall, which depends also on how transfers made *by* government are directed. Because there is no decisive economic argument for or against progressivity (or redistribution generally, for that matter), it remains at bottom an aesthetic question. That does not make progressivity any less important or legitimate a concern. It does mean, however, that the degree of progressivity of a tax system is more likely to reflect the respective success of different constituencies than any irresistible calculus of efficiency. The real constituency for progressive taxation is quite large; the rhetorical constituency larger still.

It is, therefore a reasonable working hypothesis that a reformed system of taxation based primarily on consumption could not itself find a constituency unless it preserved a measure of progressivity. To be sure, there are some who question or oppose the value of progressive taxation, for whom the regressivity of taxes on consumption would be a virtue. But their support for a change would be far weaker than the opposition of those who favor progressivity, because those most opposed to progressive taxation are very nearly the same

---

ss. This form of tax is discussed in Chapter Seven. (Ed.)

as those opposed to taxation period, which makes them a reluctant constituency for *any* new tax.

That poses a problem for a proposed tax system built around a uniform VAT. An unalloyed VAT-as-single-tax regime will not sweep the country if it is not modified in some way to the end of greater progressivity. There are different approaches to this end, some that modify the VAT from within, and others that add other taxes and transfers with offsetting effect. The latter, in my view, is the better way. On the low end of the income spectrum, I propose a refund system to offset the amount of VAT paid; on the high end, I propose a flat tax on increases in individual net worth. The next section discusses these proposals.

A Universal Refund

The most obvious way to offset the weight of the VAT on lower incomes, without complicating the tax itself, is to refund the amounts paid by people with low incomes (on the plausible assumption that they spend virtually their entire incomes on consumption). Among the possibilities is a negative income tax: a payment, inversely proportional to income, in an amount designed to reimburse the entire VAT paid in the lowest income bracket, then declining and disappearing as income increases. The idea would be a full refund of the VAT paid by those who are below or at the poverty level, a partial refund for those who are somewhat better off, and none for the middle-middle class and beyond. The amount of the payment would be a function of the rate of the VAT.

Such a system, while by no means impossible, would have its problems. First, people at all levels of income would have to file some sort of return containing a reckoning of their income, although it could be a relatively simple one. Almost inevitably, some people would conceal some of their income to claim a larger refund. Second, this type of negative income tax would reduce the incentive of those in the lower range of income to pursue more.

Therefore, I propose instead what could be called an "exemption system," that is, a universal refund of the amount of VAT paid on consumption up to a basic level, and perhaps a partial refund of additional amounts. The effect would be to leave a minimum amount of consumption wholly or partly exempt from VAT. If, for example, the exempt amount were to be consumption up to the recognized poverty level of income (now roughly $12,000 for a family of four) and the VAT were 25%, a family of four would receive a payment of $3,000. A schedule of refund payments that would fit these numbers would be $1,000 for each adult and $500 for each child. Both to simplify the administration of the refund and to blunt adverse incentives, every man, woman, and child in the United States (if a U.S. citizen or a legal permanent resident) would receive a payment. The payment to adults would be roughly twice the payment to children under 16 which would be paid over to their parents. (And since you ask, yes, Sam Walton, Oprah Winfrey, Carl Icahn, and Gordon Getty would all get a refund payment.) There are roughly 250 million Americans, of whom about 190 million are 16 or over. The cost of the refunds at the levels just indicated would therefore be $220 billion. The cost of these payments would have to be reflected in the rate of the VAT itself (higher, obviously, than if the exemption were smaller or less widespread) and in some measure in the additional tax on increases in net worth discussed below. This system would preserve some incentive to save at all levels of income, because the marginal rate of tax on consumption would be the same for all, while the effective rate would be graduated.

A Net Worth Tax

A universal exemption would make a VAT progressive at the lower end of the income spectrum, but not at the higher end. To reintroduce an element of progressivity at the upper end of the scale of income and wealth one possibility would be to couple the VAT with a tax on annual increases in net worth above a threshold level. The floor of the tax would establish an exempt level of wealth that can be accumulated tax-free in a lifetime. Beyond that, all increases would attract the tax. Every individual who had crossed the threshold of the tax would have a cumulative amount of previously taxed net worth. The total at the end of each year (unless there had been a decline in the year) would be used as the starting point to determine the following year's increase.[291] In order to reach *real* increases in wealth, the annual base of the net worth tax should be adjusted for inflation. That is, the nominal increase would be reduced by a percentage of the taxpayer's total assets tied to some broad-gauged measure of inflation such as the GNP deflator.

Both the level of wealth at which the tax applies and its rate should reflect its main function, which is not to raise large revenues, but to add a measure of progressivity to a system of taxation that nonetheless burdens saving less than the present system. Given this objective, the rate of tax on increases of wealth should be no more than half that imposed on current consumption (12%, for example, if the VAT were 25%). The reason for the rate difference is that even at high levels of income, the immediate tax cost of saving should be less than the tax cost of consuming. Similarly, to remove any tax penalty, even relative, on saving in the middle range of incomes and wealth where the propensity to consume remains fairly high, the threshold of net worth that triggers the net worth tax should be set above a basic middle-class

---

291. To keep the mechanics of the tax simple, it is probably best not to grant refunds on account of net *declines* of wealth in a given year. Gains that merely retrace previous declines in net worth should be shielded from the tax, however, which would in effect create a system of loss carryovers.

accumulation of wealth. The threshold should not be much lower than $250,000.

* * * The rate of the net worth tax should be half that of the VAT, while the total revenue raised by it should be at the most one-tenth of that brought in by the VAT. Those boundaries would permit, by extrapolation from known data about the amount and distribution of individual wealth in the United States seasoned with a little trial and error, the determination of an exempt level of lifetime wealth.

To set the revenues derived from the net worth tax as no more than one-tenth of those derived from the VAT will doubtless strike some as too little and others as too much. The latter will observe, correctly, that a net worth tax does nothing to advance the cause of capital formation. The former might rejoin that, within appropriate bounds, it would not be fatal to that end either. The merits aside, however, it would be difficult to create a consensus around taxation based solely on consumption.

The tax on net worth just sketched is an *income* tax, despite the vocabulary in which I have clothed it. As such, it imposes a toll charge on deferred consumption through a double tax on saving. This is why the rate of the net worth tax should not exceed half that of the VAT. A rate difference of this degree would at least keep the immediate tax cost of saving below that of consumption, although the ultimate tax cost of saving will be greater. In the range of economic incomes in which it applies, the net worth tax at half the VAT rate would be similar in its effect to the allowance of a tax preference for saving under an income tax. If a flat rate tax on income were moved in the direction of a tax on consumed income by allowing a deduction for *half* of amounts committed to saving, the result would be similar to the combination of a VAT and net worth tax I have proposed here. To allow every individual taxpayer a fixed lifetime allowance of fully deductible saving before the half-level deduction for saving would parallel fairly closely the exemption feature of my net worth tax. If the difficulty of framing the tax base of such a system were not considerably greater than in the system I propose here (largely because of problems of realization), it would be an eminently plausible way to shift the base of our present tax system toward consumption.

There is a possible argument of an entirely different order for retaining a component of income taxation in a regime predominantly based on consumption. It is that accumulation (the part of an income tax base that escapes immediate taxation under a VAT) may bring with it some value *as consumption* before it is explicitly converted to consumption. There is, I think, a common suspicion (especially widespread among those not dynastically rich) that simply *having* wealth brings with it consumption value long before that value is realized through exchange. This possibility is obvious, inevitable in fact, when the wealth takes the form of ancestral manors and old master paintings that produce a stream of imputed income, but cannot be dismissed even where the wealth is intangible, to the extent that known wealth may be the catalyst of others' attention, kind regard, even love, as well as an enhanced sense of self. In this light, the net worth tax I have sketched could be conceived as a surtax on the deferred material consumption of those whose wealth brings intangible value in consumption currently. * * *

An obvious difficulty in designing a tax to reach annual changes in net worth is the valuation of property. Except for widely-traded financial assets, the value of property is not self-revealing. * * *

One possibility is to impute some sort of rate of appreciation to assets not readily amenable to specific annual valuation, while using realization events and occasional valuations as a check against large deviations from reality. Another, better to my mind, is to allow, at the election of taxpayers, the deferral of the valuation and taxation of accrued gains in certain classes of assets until a triggering event of realization, such as sale, transfer by gift, or death. The net worth tax attributable to their value would then be paid with an interest factor reflecting the length of the period of deferral of taxation. The amount and vintage of the tax giving rise to interest payments would be determined under the assumption that increases in the value of assets accrued ratably during the period they were owned by the taxpayer.[300]

* * *

If stated public positions are any guide, my proposal will go nowhere. Conservatives oppose taxes on consumption, basically because they are taxes, and liberals oppose them because they are efficient.

* * *

One point that gets lost in the current debate over whether and how to change the tax system is that the real level of taxation is not a function of the transfers called "taxes." Real taxation occurs when public claims are asserted against resources. The claims of those who have financed our submarines and bombers, while supplying us with VCRs and BMWs, will not disappear. The debate over what we call "taxation" is ultimately about who will bear those claims and when. Assuming that the claims are to be paid —and neither default nor its cousin, runaway inflation, is a serious option— someone out there will have to be taxed explicitly.[315] How much tax will be paid overall is by now largely determined. What is at stake in the unfolding political contest

---

300. There is a thorough description and analysis of such a system of taxation in Fellows, A Comprehensive Attack on Tax Deferral, 88 MICH. L. REV. 722 (1990).

315. Even if defaults and inflation are used to depreciate the value of the claims against the public, the losses to the holders of the claims can be regarded as a tax, in the form of a reduction of private wealth representing the cost of public outlays.

over taxation is how consumers and suppliers of capital will fare vis-a-vis each other as the United States lurches toward the millennium. It is not yet 1789 (when one of the world's great economic powers came apart after losing its hold on its fiscal destiny), but it is later than you think.

REVISITING THE INCOME TAX VS. CONSUMPTION TAX DEBATE
Michael J. Graetz[*]
57 Tax Notes 1437, 1439-42 (1992)

As has been true throughout the more than two decades that the prospect of value-added taxation has been rising and falling on the national political agenda, its most impressive attribute is its prodigious revenue-raising capacity. The Congressional Budget Office, for example, estimates that a five-percent value-added tax could raise anywhere from $70 billion to $140 billion annually by 1996, depending on whether such things as food, housing, and medical expenses were included or excluded from the value-added tax base.[13]

* * * On the other hand, substantial deficit reduction seems unlikely to occur without a significant revenue-raising component, and such taxes should be levied in the manner most conducive to long-term economic growth: by taxing consumption rather than increasing the tax burden on savings and investment. The question then becomes: Assuming that we are going to tax consumption, how should we do it?

There are, I think, three major broad-based consumption tax contenders. First, we might adopt a federal retail sales tax. * * *

Alternatively, the United States could adopt a federal value-added tax of the credit-invoice method commonly used in Europe. * * *

It might well be easier politically to enact a subtraction-method value-added tax—also called a business transfer tax (BTT). * * *

In my view, any of these flat rate, broad-based consumption taxes— with the retention of some relatively low-rate (integrated one would hope) corporate income tax and individual income tax at upper-income levels— would be preferable to a progressive, individualized tax on consumption,[tt] which would probably require sharply progressive and high top rates to satisfy distribution concerns.

---

[*]. At time of original publication, Justus S. Hotchkiss Professor of Law, Yale University.

13. Congressional Budget Office, Reducing the Deficit: Spending and Revenue Options 335-337 (1992).

tt. Professor Graetz is referring to the consumption-type personal income tax discussed in Chapter Seven. (Ed.)

Let me, however, echo here the sentiments expressed by Treasury Secretary Andrew Mellon in the 1921 hearings. Secretary Mellon then urged Congress not to replace a long list of federal excise taxes with a broad-based sales tax. Even at that time, this position was contrary to the prevailing economic wisdom. Certainly, at least since the Excise Tax Reduction Act of 1965 (until very recently), it has been quite unfashionable to urge selected federal excise taxes, in either the Academy or to Congress.

Current circumstances, however, make this conventional wisdom wrong. In the 1990 budget negotiations, a broad-based tax on energy consumption was examined in detail but ultimately was not adopted. I will not rehearse here the reasons for increasing the price of energy relative to other commodities and for reducing energy consumption, but instead will simply note that an energy tax is supported by concern both for the environment and reducing our dependence on foreign sources of oil.

The base of a broad energy tax is just over one-quarter the size of a likely value-added tax base (one that has exclusions for housing, food, medical expenses, and the like, or provides a similar measure of low-income relief). This means that a 10-percent energy tax, for example, could raise approximately half the revenue of a five-percent value-added tax, although low-income offsets would be required here as well. The narrower base and higher rates create something of a natural ceiling on the potential revenue raising capacity of an energy tax in contrast to a VAT. A broad-based energy tax, either based on heat (BTU) content or on an ad valorem basis, would distribute more neutrally across the regions of the country than either of its two major competitors: increased gasoline taxes or a carbon tax. * * * If more revenue were required, the combination of, say, a 10-percent broad-based energy tax and additional gasoline taxes would be possible. Unlike gasoline tax increases, however, where there is great pressure to finance additional spending for highway construction, broad-based energy taxes could be used for deficit reduction or earmarked to finance extension of health insurance to the uninsured.

There also remains considerable potential for increasing federal taxes on alcohol and tobacco, and well-known good reasons for reducing the consumption of each. For example, the Yale Health Plan recently informed us that cigarette smoking is responsible for 21 percent of all mortality from heart disease and that smoking doubles the incidence of coronary artery disease and increases mortality by about 70 percent.

These taxes are low, both by our own historical standards and in comparison to alcohol and tobacco taxes in Europe or Japan, either as a percentage of revenues or a percentage of price. An additional $5 billion or so a year could be raised by increasing all alcoholic beverage taxes from their current levels to $16 per proof gallon and equalizing the taxes on beer and wine. * * *

Likewise, the tobacco tax could readily be doubled, from the 24-cents-per-pack level (which it is scheduled to reach in 1993) to 48 cents per pack, and another $4 billion of revenue a year would be collected. Indexing both of these taxes for inflation (or converting them to an ad valorem basis) would produce another $1 billion to $2 billion annually, for a total of about $10 billion.

There are a variety of other candidates for specific excise taxes if these three prove inadequate in terms of revenue, although the implementation problems of many of the other environmentally motivated excise taxes signal caution. * * * The federal government could probably raise $1 billion to $2 billion a year by taxing newsprint and the lead in automobile batteries, for example, but to take a contrary example, it seems a practical impossibility to tax virgin materials generally to encourage recycling, as some have proposed.

A 10-percent broad-based energy tax, in combination with the suggested increases in the alcohol and tobacco taxes, would produce about $50 billion of additional tax revenues annually. The major distributional complaint about broad-based consumption taxes, however, applies here as well; these taxes fall more heavily on lower- and middle-income taxpayers than on high-income taxpayers.

This context, however, where taxes are being increased on specific items of consumption that the nation wants to reduce, may create an opportunity for Congress to begin looking at tax distributional issues on a new basis. In contrast to a broad-based consumption tax, people could reduce substantially their tax burdens by shifting to less harmful consumption patterns. If we were to regulate, rather than tax, these items to reduce consumption, Congress would demonstrate little concern for distributional burdens. * * *

Notes and Questions

49. Professor Isenbergh's VAT proposal attempts to help low-income taxpayers by providing *all* families or individuals a payment roughly equal to the VAT that would be paid by a family or individual at the poverty line. Why would he give the payments to millionaires?

50. Without discussion of the point, Professor Isenbergh notes that his proposed universal refund would be limited to U.S. citizens and legal permanent residents. This would give no refund to nonresident aliens, some of whom (students, primarily) lawfully spend years in this country. More important, what of the millions of illegal permanent residents? Would you

view the exclusion of these groups from the universal refund as an advantage or as a disadvantage of Isenbergh's proposal? Why?

51. In the final excerpt of Chapter Four, in addressing optimal tax concepts, Professors Zelenak and Moreland dismiss as politically unrealistic any income tax proposal that is coupled with a "demogrant," or universal payment. Is Professor Isenbergh's proposal equally subject to this criticism?

52. What role does Professor Isenbergh's proposed net worth tax, which he concedes is really an income tax, play? Why would he include as a feature of this tax a fifty-percent deduction for savings?

53. Professor Isenbergh briefly addresses the problem of valuation in connection with his proposed net worth tax (or income tax). This issue is discussed at length in Chapter Two.

54. Professor Graetz argues for sharply increased consumption taxes on specified goods rather than a broad-based consumption tax such as VAT. What goods are singled out for heavy taxation, and why? Do you agree that excise taxes on specific products are better than a VAT? Do you agree that it is proper and desirable for the government to influence consumption patterns through excise taxes? Are you concerned about the regressive impact of the taxes he proposes?

55. Many states have sharply increased cigarette taxes in recent years. Do you think these increases have significantly contributed to the reduction in smoking?

56. Some medical evidence now suggests that drinking in moderation may be more beneficial to the drinker's health than total abstinence. Would such evidence lead us to reject Professor Graetz's call for increased taxes on alcoholic beverages?

57. Would the logic of Professor Graetz's proposal suggest that other products harmful to health (bacon cheeseburgers, for example) should be subjected to special excise taxes?

CHAPTER SEVEN

A CONSUMPTION-TYPE INCOME TAX

[T]he equality of imposition consists rather in the equality of that which is consumed than of the riches of the persons that consume the same. For what reason is there that he which labors much and, sparing the fruits of his labor, consumes little should be more charged than he that, living idly, gets little and spends all he gets, seeing the one has no more protection from the commonwealth than the other? But when the impositions are laid upon those things which men consume, every man pays equally for what he uses; nor is the commonwealth defrauded by the luxurious waste of private men.[a]

A. INTRODUCTION

This is the longest chapter of the book, and with reason. An appreciation of the issues discussed here is essential to an understanding of a major strain of tax scholarship—perhaps *the* major strain—over the past thirty years. Moreover, this chapter illuminates the existence and growing importance of consumption tax principles as an integral part of our present "income" tax law.

The materials in this chapter examine two related issues. First, should the principal basis for taxation, and particularly for national taxation in this country, be consumption or income? This issue was raised in Chapter Six, but the discussion will be broadened here.

Second, what form should a broad-based consumption tax take? In comparison to the income tax, and to the forms of consumption tax discussed in this chapter, value added taxes (VATs) and retail sales taxes (RSTs) are relatively simple to administer. What, then, is the objection to VAT and similar forms of consumption taxes? *Fairness.* A hallmark of the federal income tax is progressivity. It is impossible to operate VATs and RSTs that are progressive with respect to final consumers without giving up the administrative simplicity of point-of-sale collection. If the taxpayer buys a lawn mower from a retailer, for example, the seller has no way of knowing whether the taxpayer will spend $10,000 or $250,000 during the year;[b] for that reason, the seller could not be expected to charge the correct tax unless the tax rate were the same for all purchasers of a given product.

Is it possible to levy *progressive* consumption taxes? In theory, each

---

a. THOMAS HOBBES, LEVIATHAN 271 (Liberal Arts Press, 1958) (1651).

b. It thus would be impossible to structure the tax so that it would be progressive with respect to its base, consumption; for similar reasons, it would also be impossible to structure a VAT or sales tax so that it would be progressive with respect to income.

taxpayer could be required to keep careful records of all expenditures at the grocery store, day-care provider, barber shop, restaurant, candy vending machine, etc. At the end of the year, the taxpayer would pay a tax based on the total of the year's consumption, at progressive rates. It is obvious that such a tax would be unworkable, and by comparison would make the present income tax seem a model of administrative simplicity. While most individuals receive income from only a few sources—frequently only one—many of those same individuals make thousands of purchases during the year. A progressive consumption tax on this model would be extremely burdensome on law-abiding taxpayers who would have to keep records of every expenditure, and it would be impossible for the Internal Revenue Service to police.

Thus, if one is persuaded of the desirability of moving to a system of consumption taxation but without sacrificing progressivity, the challenge is to envision a consumption tax that is both progressive and administratively feasible, and that includes a system for withholding taxes. This has been done.

Most proponents of a progressive consumption tax envision a calculation that would start with income, as at present—indeed, the systems are frequently described as consumption-type income taxes. Withholding by employers and other payors of income would continue. However, certain items would be treated differently—items relating to savings and investment and/or return on savings and investment—to convert the tax base to one more closely approximating consumption than income. The resulting tax base could be taxed at progressive rates, or, even if a flat rate were employed, a considerable element of progressivity could be achieved through personal and dependency exemptions and standard deductions. (Some consumption-type proposals envision a "family allowance" sufficiently generous that many lower-middle-class individuals who are taxpayers under present law would have no liability.) Itemized deductions could be provided as desired under such a system.

In this form, the consumption tax has generated considerable academic interest. More surprising and more important, a number of proposals by political "heavy hitters" mean that there is a real chance that some form of consumption tax could actually replace the present income tax.

Outright repeal of the income tax still seems unlikely. However, the principles underlying consumption taxation can exert powerful influence on the law without the necessity of a formal change. Indeed, those principles have already proved sufficiently powerful that some scholars assert that consumption tax principles already provide a more realistic description of present law than does the Haig-Simons "ideal."

B. ACADEMIC EXPOSITION

As this chapter's opening quotation illustrates, utilizing the taxpayer's overall level of consumption as the principal tax base has been discussed for centuries. John Stuart Mill proposed a tax base of income minus savings—essentially the tax base of current proposals—in the Nineteenth Century. In response to the persuasive writing of Nicholas Kaldor in the middle of this century, India and Sri Lanka briefly adopted expenditure taxes.[c]

Nonetheless, Professor Andrews' 1974 article, excerpted below, is frequently and accurately described as "seminal." It has been the catalyst of extensive academic examination of the proper tax base—the Haig-Simons definition of income ("accretion"); consumption; or, as at present, some hybrid of the two.

A CONSUMPTION-TYPE OR CASH FLOW PERSONAL INCOME TAX
William D. Andrews[*]

87 Harvard Law Review 1113, 1113-25, 1140, 1148-54, 1156-59, 1167-69 (1974)

Serious thought about personal income tax policy has come to be dominated by an ideal in which taxable income is set equal to total personal gain or accretion, without distinctions as to source or use.[1] It will be convenient to call this ideal an accretion-type personal income tax.

Accretion is the sum of personal consumption plus accumulation.[2] This relation is the real counterpart of the accounting identity by which income equals spending plus saving, income being the source of funds whose uses are spending and saving. Computation of money income, however, does not require analysis of its spending and savings components, because income can be independently determined by reference to sources of funds, without regard

---

c. Richard Goode, *The Superiority of the Income Tax, in* WHAT SHOULD BE TAXED: INCOME OR EXPENDITURE? 49, 50 (Joseph A. Pechman ed., 1980) (citing Indian and Sri Lankan government reports attributed to Kaldor's writing). *See also* NICHOLAS KALDOR, AN EXPENDITURE TAX (1955).

*. At time of original publication, Professor of Law, Harvard Law School.

1. H. SIMONS, PERSONAL INCOME TAXATION (1938), is the classic statement. For different views about the usefulness of any general prescriptive model, see B. BITTKER, C. GALVIN, R. MUSGRAVE & J. PECHMAN, A COMPREHENSIVE INCOME TAX BASE? A DEBATE (1968) (mostly reprinted from 80 HARV. L. REV. 925 (1967) and 81 HARV. L. REV. 44, 63, 1016, 1032 (1967-68)). For an argument that even the accretion ideal, properly understood, will admit some distinctions among current uses of funds but none among sources as such, see Andrews, *Personal Deductions in an Ideal Income Tax*, 86 HARV. L. REV. 309, 375 (1972). This Article is in some respects an extension of the argument there.

2. H. SIMONS, *supra* note 1, at 50. Arguably accretion should be defined to equal consumption plus accumulation plus the tax itself, since taxable income is computed without any deduction for the income tax itself. * * * But the failure to deduct the tax itself may be viewed as just a computational shortcut, since any particular rate of tax on taxable income is the equivalent of a tax at a higher rate on disposable income—that is, taxable income minus the tax.

to uses. Insofar as economic activity is adequately represented by monetary measures and transactions, therefore, it may seem that accretion need not be analyzed or measured in terms of its consumption and accumulation components.

But economic activity is not wholly reflected in monetary transactions. Taxable income in a true accretion-type tax would include money income (as a proxy for purchased consumption and accumulation in the form of investment purchases and money savings) plus unpurchased consumption and unpurchased accumulation. Consumption and accumulation thus serve to identify two categories of adjustments that are needed to get from money income to total real accretion. The tax falls short of the ideal in relation to consumption insofar as it fails to reflect consumption income in kind, whether enjoyed as an incident of employment or as imputed income from services or property, or even the direct enjoyment of leisure time and activities. Similarly, the tax falls short of the ideal in relation to accumulation insofar as it fails to reflect accumulation in kind in such forms as unrealized capital appreciation and the accrual of pension rights. As we think about the tax in real terms, consumption and accumulation emerge as two distinct components of the underlying subject matter in terms of which the tax should ultimately be understood and evaluated.

Consumption and accumulation adjustments are analytically different in several ways. For one thing, failure to tax an item of unpurchased consumption is a matter of permanent exemption; if it is not taxed now it will not be picked up later on. Accumulation, on the other hand, is essentially a matter of timing; if pension rights are not taxed as they accrue, for example, pension income will be fully taxed if and when it is paid. Moreover, accumulation may be either positive or negative. Consumption, on the other hand, is always positive. Consumption is not always less than accretion; it will be more during any period of net disaccumulation. Indeed even accretion may be negative if disaccumulation exceeds consumption.

If we think about the personal income tax in real terms, as a tax on accretion, and of accretion as consumption plus accumulation (or minus disaccumulation), reflection will show that its worst inequity, distortion, and complexity arise out of inconsistency in the treatment of accumulation. Under existing law, as we shall see, the effect is often to impair the integrity of the tax in relation to consumption as well as accumulation, so that some taxpayers with high standards of living pay limited taxes. But the underlying source of difficulty is with the accumulation component of accretion. Savings out of ordinary income are fully taxed, while accumulation of wealth in kind through appreciation in value of property already owned is not reflected in current taxable income. Further complications arise from this disparity. Some gains, though realized, are unrecognized by reason of special statutory provisions like those governing corporate reorganizations. These are among the most complex provisions in the statute, and have a substantial effect upon the structuring of financial transactions. Recognized long-term capital gains are taxed at not more than half the regular rate. This discrepancy in rates means that realized capital gain income is partially permanently exempted from tax, even if and when devoted to consumption instead of accumulation. Wealth whose accumulation has already been taxed or permanently exempted is not to be taxed again, and so the statute has complex and imperfect provisions for computing and subtracting basis on sales, and for amortizing basis against ordinary income in the case of depreciable property. Distortions in the computation of depreciation and other items are sometimes grossly magnified by the way borrowing is treated in the case of leveraged investments, so that a limited passive investment may produce an artificial loss which shelters other income from tax even though that other income remains freely available for current consumption or other investments.[d]

The way out of these difficulties, according to the accretion ideal, is to make taxable income provide a more comprehensive reflection of real accumulation, and therefore accretion, by including unrealized changes in the value of property in taxable income. Literal achievement of that goal would require that all assets be taken into account at current fair market value at the end of each accounting period. Although practical exigencies may prevent comprehensive inclusion of unrealized appreciation, improvement is thought to lie in that direction.

Another remedy for present difficulties lies in just the other direction. It involves putting the income tax treatment of business and investment transactions more completely on a simple cash flow basis. Investment expenditures would be deductible when made; on the other hand, all receipts from business and investment activities, including loan proceeds, would be immediately and fully includable in taxable income. This would have the effect of treating accumulation consistently by excluding it from taxable income even when it is represented by investment of realized gains or of ordinary income.

On its face this possibility may seem to be a step in the wrong direction, a step further away from fairness and equity as represented by the prevailing accretion ideal. But a cash flow income tax would correspond very closely to another ideal, that of a tax whose burdens are apportioned to current personal consumption expenditures rather than to total accretion. Net cash flow from business and investment activities is a simple and practical measure of cash flow devoted to consumption expenditure. It will be convenient to call this

---

d. This article was written before enactment of sections 465 (generally limiting deductible losses to amounts at risk) and 469 (limiting passive activity losses and credits). (Ed.)

kind of tax a consumption-type personal income tax. Such a tax has been discussed and advocated in the economic literature,[7] and even tried, briefly, in Sri Lanka (formerly Ceylon) and India. But it has been discussed as an alternative or supplement to an income tax, not as an ideal implicit in or appropriate for the personal income tax itself.

Insofar as one thinks of economic activity as adequately represented by money transactions and historical costs, the existing personal income tax is largely an accretion-type tax. Money income is generally taxed whether spent or saved. But in real rather than monetary terms, the existing tax is a hybrid, closer in many respects to a consumption-type than an accretion-type tax. Unrealized capital appreciation and accruals under qualified pension and profit-sharing plans are a large portion of total real accumulation, yet are not taxed. For many persons they represent most real accumulation, and for such persons the existing tax may be well represented by the model of a consumption-type tax.

A person with a moderate amount of income-producing property, for example, may live on the yield without either drawing down or adding to principal. He may take care of the future by investing in securities that will show some appreciation in value as well as current yield. Money income for him provides a close measure of consumption expenditure. Real accretion, however, would also include unrealized changes in the value of his property.

Or an employee may spend his whole salary, without saving or dissaving, if his employer is making adequate provision for his retirement and other emergencies through pension plan contributions and the like. Again, current money income will provide a measure of current consumption expenditure, not of total real accretion which would also have to include the increase in value of accrued pension rights each year.

The question whether our existing personal income tax is better represented by the accretion model or by a consumption model can be restated by asking who to take as typical, an individual whose accumulation is represented by savings bank deposits and interest or one whose accumulation takes the form of unrealized capital appreciation or pension accruals. And the question of whether to prefer the consumption model or the accretion model as an ideal can be restated by asking whose tax treatment to take as a prototype. There is clearly a discrepancy in our present treatment, which ought to be

---

7. The best and most comprehensive discussion is N. KALDOR, AN EXPENDITURE TAX (1955). Earlier advocates Include I. FISHER & H. FISHER, CONSTRUCTIVE INCOME TAXATION (1942); T. HOBBES, LEVIATHAN ch. 30 (1651); J. S. MILL, PRINCIPLES OF POLITICAL ECONOMY bk V, ch. 1, § 4 (Laughlin ed. 1884); A. PIGOU, A STUDY IN PUBLIC FINANCE, 102-133 (3d rev. ed. 1949); W. [VICKREY], AGENDA FOR PROGRESSIVE TAXATION 329-66 (1947); Marshall, *The Equitable Distribution of Taxation* (1917), *in* MEMORIALS OF ALFRED MARSHALL 340, 350-51 (A. Pigou ed. 1925).

removed, but there is no a priori reason to think the way to remove the discrepancy is by taxing unrealized appreciation and pension accruals. It may well be simpler, fairer, and more efficient to provide generally for tax deferral on savings accounts and other forms of saving out of realized income, while taxing eventual disinvestment from savings accounts and capital assets alike at full, ordinary income rates.

This conclusion may be resisted by one who looks to the income tax as a device for curtailing the accumulation of wealth as well as consumption. But the existing income tax has not been fair or effective in relation to accumulation of wealth, and it would not be easy to make it so. Even if it were practical, it is not clear that we should want to tax the accumulation of fresh wealth without some corresponding imposition on existing stocks of wealth. If we are serious about reaching wealth, therefore, it would be better to strengthen and rely on estate and gift taxes for that purpose, focusing the income tax on the consumption component of accretion where it can be made to be most fair and effective.

Prevailing patterns of thought are reflected in common vocabulary. An accretion-type personal income tax is usually simply called an ideal or comprehensive income tax, personal income being defined to mean accretion.[9] No distinction is thus maintained between practical and ideal bases (money income and real accretion); or at least no name is saved for the former. A consumption-type personal income tax, on the other hand, has been called an expenditure tax, suggesting that it is something quite different from an income tax, indeed somehow its opposite, income and expenditure being contrary notions. This terminology obscures the fact that in practice such a tax would be based on a simple cash flow computation of net yield from business and investment activities, with no more effort to keep direct track of particular consumption expenditures than under the existing income tax.[10]

---

9. The most familiar instance is in H. SIMONS, *supra* note 1, at 50:
> Personal income may be defined as the algebraic sum of (1) the market value of rights exercised in consumption and (2) the change in the value of the store of property rights between the beginning and the end of the period in question.

10. There is some tendency to think an expenditure tax base would have to be defined net of tax, since whatever is paid in tax is unavailable for expenditure. Then, to get the equivalent of income tax rates over 50% one would have to have expenditure tax rates in excess of 100%. But there is no more to that point in relation to a consumption-type tax than an accretion-type tax; if tax payments are not part of consumption, they are not part of accretion either. * * * [A]s a matter of computational convenience, it may well be better to define the practical base on a gross basis, as consumption expenditures plus the tax itself. * * * Statutory rates can then be kept on a scale of less than 100%, a scale with which we are familiar, though the effective rate in relation to what is left after tax will sometimes exceed 100% just as it does under present law. *See* note 2 *supra*.
* * *

Throughout this Article it is assumed that in both the accretion and consumption models, as under existing law, taxable income is determined without any deduction for the tax itself.

In this Article, *personal income tax* means any tax whose practical computation is based on personal income transactions. *Income* thus refers primarily to the money transactions that make such a tax a practical possibility. *Consumption, accumulation,* and *accretion* refer to real values, accretion being the sum of consumption plus accumulation. The monetary counterparts of consumption and accumulation, which add up to money income, are called *spending* and *saving.* The prevailing prescriptive model of a personal income tax is called an *accretion-type personal income tax,* and a model in which accumulation is comprehensively excluded is called a *consumption-type personal income tax.* The latter is also called a *cash flow personal income tax* because that describes its practical computation. For shorthand it will be convenient often to refer simply to the accretion model or ideal on the one hand, and the consumption or cash flow model on the other. The existing tax is a *hybrid personal income tax* since it conforms to the accretion ideal in some respects and the consumption ideal in others, but neither with any consistency.

The difference between an accretion-type and a consumption-type personal income tax involves only accumulation, and it is in an important sense only a difference of timing. If an item of accumulation is not reflected in taxable income, the tax is not waived but only deferred. Under either kind of ideal, what is ultimately subject to tax is the same—funds or wealth available for private consumption.

This difference in timing corresponds to a difference in methods of accounting for business and investment activities. For a consumption-type tax, accounting should be on a pure and simple cash flow basis.[12] For an accretion-type tax, accounting must be put on something approximating fair-market-value accounting for business and investment assets. Our existing hybrid tax can then be defined in relation to these ideals by reference to its method of accounting, in which the cost of business and investment assets is required to be capitalized but subsequent increases in value are not generally taken into account until realization.

The difference in timing between a consumption-type and an accretion-type tax is, however, immensely important in defining the real burden of the tax. Under the accretion ideal capital accumulation and its subsequent yield are both to be taxed as they occur, and such a tax would cast a heavier burden on some taxpayers than if the tax on capital accumulation is deferred until subsequent disinvestment. Consider a farmer who plants and grows 100 fruit trees. A 30% tax on his fruit, if and when it appears for harvest, with no tax on the growth of the trees unless and until they are disposed of, would leave

---

12. Cash receipts and disbursements accounting as authorized under the existing income tax corresponds to cash flow accounting with respect to accounts receivable and payable.

him with the fruit of 70 trees. But if the Government took 30% of the trees themselves as they mature, and 30% of the fruit of the remaining 70 trees, the farmer would be left with the fruit of only 49. Or, similarly, consider an individual setting aside funds for retirement. A 30% tax deferred until retirement will leave him with 70% as much to spend as he would have had in the absence of tax. A 30% accretion-type tax imposed on the funds as earned and also on the yield from investing what is left, will leave substantially less.

Nevertheless, the consumption and accretion ideals reinforce one another in important ways. Consumption is the major component of accretion for most taxpayers most of the time, and therefore under either ideal, the tax is in the long run mostly a tax on household consumption. The principal purpose of the tax, in terms of real goods and services, is to curtail private consumption so that resources will be released for public uses. What makes a personal income tax the fairest tax we have is that its burdens are generally cast in sensible relation to standards of living.

More particularly, the consumption ideal reinforces the main lesson of the accretion ideal: that distinctions should not be drawn, for personal income tax purposes, because items of income accrue from different sources. * * *

I believe, for reasons to be developed, that the consumption model offers better solutions to the question of how to treat accumulation than does the prevailing accretion model. But even if one is not prepared to abandon the accretion model as a goal, the consumption model can help achieve a better understanding of the existing tax by providing another frame of reference for critical evaluation. Indeed, the two models together may provide a kind of binocular or stereoscopic view that will give a better sense of depth and perspective than does either model alone. Studying the model of a consumption-type personal income tax will help us to be more analytic about accretion, separating the problems and implications of taxing its consumption component from those of also including accumulation. That may enable us to see better what can and must be done to preserve the integrity of the tax in relation to the consumption component of accretion, whatever one may further decide to do about accumulation.

The main purpose of this Article is to set forth the model of a consumption-type personal income tax as an alternative for understanding the practical potential of the existing tax. * * *

This Article is only about personal taxes. It is almost entirely about the personal income tax, with some limited reference to estate and gift taxes. * * *

The Value of Deferral

It has sometimes been thought that mere deferral of income taxes was not of great importance so long as every element of accretion was eventually accounted for. Sophisticated taxpayers and their counsel, however, have realized that deferral is often of immense importance, and recent writing on matters of tax policy has come to reflect that realization. Some appreciation of the value of deferral is essential for an understanding of the argument in this Article because the difference between accretion and consumption ideals is essentially one of deferral, and because the defects in present law that make it an unacceptable hybrid arise from inconsistencies in matters of timing.

Deferral may be valuable under existing law partly because it leads to ultimate outright exemption or taxation at lower rates. Unrealized appreciation is completely exempted in the case of property held until death, because no income tax will have been imposed on such appreciation and the succeeding owner is given a stepped-up basis equal to value at or shortly after date of death.[e] Income whose recognition is deferred until after retirement is often taxed at lower rates then than if it had been taxed during higher-income, active employment years, and not infrequently the corollary of deferral is taxation at capital gain instead of ordinary income rates.

But the important, underlying fact is that even if rates do not change and nothing is ever permanently exempted, mere deferral can be immensely important. Deferral reduces the burden of a tax because of the time value of money; it requires less than a dollar put aside today to meet a dollar of tax liability in the future. The magnitude of the effect, which is a function of interest rates, tax rates, and length of deferral, can be illustrated by several examples.

Productive Investment

The fruit farmer in the introduction is one example. A 30% tax on the growth of his 100 trees when they reach maturity would leave 70 trees, and an annual 30% tax on the fruit thereafter would leave the taxpayer each year with the fruit from 49. On the other hand, if all tax on the trees could be deferred until the trees were disposed of, with a current tax being imposed only on the fruit harvested, the taxpayer would keep 70% of the fruit of 100 trees, which is 42.9% more than the fruit from 49.

     * * *

Retirement Income

Consider a dollar of earnings put aside for retirement. Assume this sum is invested at 9% compound interest, and that it is to be utilized 24 years later. In the absence of tax the one dollar set aside would support eight dollars of retirement consumption 24 years later.

Now consider the effect of a 33% accretion-type tax. This would take away one-third of the original dollar when earned, leaving only 67 cents to invest;

---

e. *See* Chapter Ten. (Ed.)

and it would cut the rate of growth from 9% per annum to 6%. At 6% per annum for 24 years, 67 cents will produce a retirement fund of only $2.67, as compared with $8.00 in the absence of tax. On the other hand, if the tax were deferred until retirement, the taxpayer would pay only $2.67 tax out of $8.00, leaving $5.33 to spend. Deferral of the tax, without any change in rate, would double what the taxpayer has left to spend.

The effect is greater for higher interest rates, higher tax rates, and longer periods. A dollar held at 12% for 36 years, for example, would produce a fund of $64. A 70% true accretion-type tax would reduce the original dollar to 30 cents, and the rate of growth from 12% to 3.6%. At 3.6%, 30 cents will grow to about $1.07 in 36 years, which represents a reduction from $64.00 of about 98.3%. A 70% tax deferred until retirement would take only $44.80 out of $64.00, leaving $19.80 to spend. This is more than eighteen times the amount left by a 70% tax imposed on a true accretion basis.

* * *

The Existing Hybrid Treatment of Accumulation
* * *

[M]any of the most intractable problems in the personal income tax arise directly out of the hybrid character of our treatment of accumulation. The complexities of corporate distributions and reorganizations, for example, at the individual taxpayer level, all have to do with matters discussed here: realization and nonrecognition, basis determination and recovery, capital gain or ordinary income treatment, and treatment of debt. Other seemingly, simpler provisions like that governing installment sales, have essentially to do with deferral or nonrecognition. The trust and partnership provisions involve complex problems of defining when gain will be recognized by individuals and whether it will be capital gain or ordinary income. The partnership provisions, in particular, have very complex provisions concerning the determination and recovery of basis, and the treatment of partnership borrowing. The whole matter of qualified pension and profit-sharing plans is primarily one of deferral, and other compensation schemes, like stock option plans, are designed to defer recognition of gain and to secure capital gain treatment when recognition occurs. Most of the problems that occupy most of the time of tax practitioners and administrators (not to speak of teachers, students, legislators, and taxpayers themselves) arise immediately out of our failure to take a consistent and comprehensive position with respect to inclusion or exclusion of real accumulation in taxable income.

* * *

True Accretion Treatment of Accumulation
* * *

A true accretion-type personal income tax would be free of many of the complexities and inequities of the existing tax. But a true accretion-type tax is hardly attainable in practice. Even a rough approximation of an accretion-type tax would require an utter transformation of the practical administration and computation of the tax from one depending mostly on cash transactions to one in which current, comprehensive property valuation would play a central role. In practical operation the tax would become largely an incremental net wealth tax as well as a tax on income transactions.

Any partial step in the direction of fuller reflection of total accretion remains a compromise in which inconsistencies are inevitable. Some compromises are undoubtedly better than others, and some of our existing problems could probably be ameliorated by fuller reflection of real accretion, but no practical solution in this direction offers anything approaching the simple practicality of a consumption-type or cash flow personal income tax.

A Consumption-Type Personal Income Tax

A consumption-type personal income tax is often assumed to involve all the practical difficulties of the existing personal income tax plus whatever new ones are involved in getting from income to consumption expenditure. The tax would, of course, be computed on personal income plus or minus net dissavings or savings, and discussion has focused on how much additional difficulty the adjustments for saving or dissaving would produce.

This discussion overlooks the fact that a consumption-type tax would avoid all the difficulties that arise from the failure of money income to provide a satisfactory reflection of real accumulation. Income, to be sure, includes savings, and savings are a partial, imperfect, monetary measure of accumulation. A consumption-type tax requires deductions and additions to eliminate savings and dissavings. But these, being based solely on money transactions, are incomparably simpler than either making adjustments to include unrealized appreciation under a true accretion-type tax or living with the complexity and distortion that result from the existing hybrid treatment of accumulation.

Under a consumption-type personal income tax, capital transactions are treated on a simple cash flow basis. Investments are simply deducted when made and proceeds of sales and other capital transactions are added to income when received. All that is required is to separate business and investment activities on the one hand from personal consumption activities on the other, as under present law, and then to keep track of the former on a cash flow basis. Cash flow accounting for business and investment activities automatically provides a measure of cash spent on consumption activities, which is what we are after.

Precise measurement of current consumption spending would require exact accounting for cash and loan balances which might be something of a nuisance. But in practice there is no need for precision because only short term tax deferral or acceleration and relatively small amounts are involved. Ordinary cash balances, including checking accounts and consumer loans, can therefore be left wholly out of account. In effect, both ordinary cash balances and consumer loans can be treated as falling in the consumption sector of an individual's activity rather than the business or investment sector, without any significant distortion of tax burdens.

A precise measure of current consumption would also seem to require separation of consumption from the investment element in the purchase of consumer durables. Strictly speaking it is the current use value rather than the purchase price of an automobile, for example, that constitutes consumption. But again strict precision is unnecessary. The purchase price for a durable item represents the discounted value of its future usefulness, and the tax burden will tend to be the same in the end whether one is taxed or the other. Therefore, it would be acceptable to deal with the consumer durable problem on a simple cash flow basis, although it may be desirable in some cases to give taxpayers the option of deferring taxation on part of the purchase price with interest. Because purchase price can be taken as a proxy for use value, the consumer durable problem is much more manageable under a consumption-type tax than under a true accretion-type tax. Under the latter, the money invested should be taxed when earned, and the imputed return received in the form of use value should also be taxed.

One of the general advantages of a consumption-type tax is that short-term deferral in the interest of simpler administration can be more readily tolerated than in the case of an accretion-type tax. Under a consumption-type tax the benefit of deferral is offset by a corresponding increase in the amount subject to tax at a rate equal to whatever interest rate the market charges the taxpayer for extensions of credit. No such offset occurs under an accretion-type tax where postponement has the effect of reducing the effective rate of taxation on income. Reverting to the example of the fruit farmer, it makes no difference whether we tax the growth of trees or the fruit under a consumption-type tax, because the ultimate burden is the same either way. Under an accretion-type tax it makes a substantial difference whether we tax the trees because we are supposed to tax the fruit, too, in any event, and a tax on both is substantially more burdensome.

These general observations are elaborated in the following discussion of how particular items would enter into the practical computation of a consumption-type personal income tax.

Ordinary Income

Ordinary income—wages, salaries, fees, dividends, interest, rent, and so on—would be treated exactly the same way under a consumption-type personal income tax as under any other personal income tax. They would be fully includable in taxable income for the period in which received and would continue to form the backbone of the tax. Withholding from salaries and wages could be continued as under the existing tax, and it could just as readily be extended to dividends and interest. Most people spend most of their ordinary income for current consumption, and to that extent a consumption-type personal income tax would be no different from the existing tax. Deductions and additions to reflect savings and dissavings would for most taxpayers be in the nature of relatively minor adjustments that would not impair the general relationship between the tax and ordinary income as its chief determinant and as the source of funds with which to pay it.

Similarly, ordinary, current deductions, business and personal, would be essentially unaffected by the shift to a pure consumption-type tax because they are addressed to the consumption rather than the accumulation component of accretion. Ordinary personal deductions for medical expenses, charitable contributions, and alimony, for example, would have the same justifications and problems as under existing law. Furthermore, personal exemptions and a standard deduction could readily be continued under a consumption-type tax.

Ordinary Investments

The most obvious difference about a consumption-type income tax would be that ordinary investments would be accounted for on a pure cash flow basis. The cost of investment assets would be deductible in the year paid, while the proceeds of sale would be fully included in taxable income in the year received. This does not necessarily mean there would be a large tax in a year when substantial sales are made, since it is likely that taxable proceeds would be largely offset by deductions for reinvestment in that year, or for extraordinary, yearend cash balances.

There is a tendency to think of this treatment of investment assets as involving at least some complication over and above the existing income tax treatment, because in a year when part of a taxpayer's income is invested a deduction must be claimed. But this is viewing the matter in too narrow a time frame. Under the existing income tax the cost of an investment cannot be ignored; it must be recorded for future use as a basis either for amortization or in computing gain or loss on sale or other disposition. Surely it is simpler in the long run, for taxpayer and Government alike, to have deductions based on investment costs paid during the current year rather than on costs incurred in several past periods, some quite long ago. * * * [J]ust as a matter of accurate accounting and reporting, cash flow treatment of ordinary investments would represent a vast simplification.[89]

---

89. Immediate deductibility of capital expenditures, partly for the sake of accounting simplification, is familiar under present law.

Moreover, this treatment of ordinary investments would eliminate a whole host of complications in the existing income tax beyond the mere ascertainment of historical costs. Individual taxpayers would no longer compute depreciation or use other forms of cost amortization, since business and investment costs would be simply deducted forthwith. Furthermore, there would be no problems concerning realization and nonrecognition of gain or loss when an individual changes investments. If a taxpayer receives new investment property in exchange for old, or as an increment to old property in the case of a stock dividend or other dividend in kind, it would make no difference whether the transaction is one on which gain is realized and recognized under present law, since any gain recognized would in effect be offset by a deduction for the fresh investment. Thus, in the case of an exchange of securities there would be no need to determine whether it is pursuant to a plan of reorganization, since the deduction for reinvestment would offset any gain recognized. The whole law of corporate reorganizations as it bears on individual investors would be rendered obsolete.

Cash flow treatment of ordinary investments would also resolve present problems about when to account for compensation for services in the form of investment property such as stock bonuses or restricted property.[91] Again, cash compensation that the recipient invests would incur no tax; therefore no tax need be imposed on compensation paid in kind in investment property. Tax would properly await sale of the investment property and devotion of the proceeds to consumption expenditure in either case.

Finally, and above all, this treatment of ordinary investments would eliminate any need for special rates of tax on capital gains. The best justification for capital gain rates is to mitigate the disparity in treatment between unrealized gains and realized but reinvested gains. A cash flow treatment of ordinary investments would eliminate that disparity entirely. Proceeds from the sale of investment property would be taxed only if devoted to personal consumption, in which event there would be no reason to distinguish them from ordinary earned income also directed to consumption.

Less persuasive justifications for capital gain rates would also be inapplicable. The argument based on inflation would be met by the fact that no tax on the accumulation represented by the initial investment would have been paid in uninflated dollars, as it would have been under an accretion-type tax. * * * Even the notion that capital gain rates are justified to offset the hardship, given progressive tax rates, of realizing in one year a gain accrued over many would be met, since only proceeds devoted to current consumption would be subject to tax.

---

91. *See* CODE §83 (dealing with compensation in the form of property to which restrictions are attached).

Business and Investment Loans

Business and investment loans would be treated, just like ordinary investments, on a simple cash flow basis. Loan proceeds would be reported as income in the year received, and repayments of interest and principal would be deductible when paid. This treatment is unfamiliar, but would represent a clear net simplification for reasons similar to those favoring a cash flow accounting for ordinary investments.

Cash flow accounting for loans, as for investments, is only a matter of reporting currently events that would have to be recorded for future reference under the present tax or an accretion-type tax. While we do not tax loan proceeds as such under present law, we do tax forgiveness of indebtedness, or satisfaction of indebtedness by the conveyance of appreciated property, even when the result is a substantial tax liability in a year in which there are no cash receipts with which to pay the tax.[95] A record of money received and repaid on account of loans must be accurately kept in order to compute such gains. Cash flow accounting is only a matter of taking each receipt and payment into account in the year when it occurs.

Inclusion of loan proceeds in income would not ordinarily require large tax payments in the year of a loan, because normally such loans are to pay for capital investment that would be immediately deductible under a consumption-type tax. * * *

Consumer Credit

A strict computation of current consumption would seem to require that consumer loans and credit, like business and investment loans, be treated as income when incurred and deductible when repaid. But it is much simpler and quite acceptable just to leave ordinary consumer loans and credit arrangements out of account. The effect of that is to treat payments on account of consumer loans, rather than the use of the loan proceeds, as taxable consumption expenditures. * * *

Consumer Durables

* * *

Theoretically, under a consumption-type tax, the purchase price should be deductible like any other investment, and rental value should be imputed to the owner over the useful life. But in practice imputed rental value is adequately reflected, on a discounted basis, by the purchase price. * * * The practical thing to do, therefore, is to treat the purchase of [a consumer durable such as] a personal automobile like any other consumption expenditure, ignoring its investment aspect. This is accomplished by simply leaving such a purchase out of account in computing taxable income, thus making the

---

95. *See* Crane v. Commissioner, 331 U.S. 1 (1947); United States v. Kirby Lumber Co., 284 U.S. 1 (1931); Parker v. Delaney, 186 F.2d 455 (1st Cir. 1950), *cert. denied*, 341 U.S. 926 (1951).

expenditure subject to tax. * * *

When an automobile is purchased on credit, the loan should be treated as a consumer loan. In practice, therefore, neither the purchase of the automobile nor the loan would enter into the computation of taxable income, and the result would be that consumption use of the automobile would be reflected in taxable income each year in the amount of payments of principal and interest on the loan.

If consumer durable purchases in a particular year were substantial in amount, it might be appropriate to permit a taxpayer to defer them over a limited period, even if they were not financed by borrowing. The procedure would be to claim a deduction in the year of purchase but then to return the deducted amount to income with interest. * * *

Owner-Occupied Housing

Similar general conclusions apply to owner-occupied housing, which undoubtedly represents the most substantial item of consumer durable investment made by most taxpayers. Purchase price, however, is a less acceptable proxy for use value in the case of very longlife items like housing, because tax rates may change and property may go up or down in value for reasons not anticipated at the time of purchase. Nevertheless, it is still the case that the existing treatment of owner-occupied housing is more nearly consonant with a consumption-type model than with a true accretion-type model. Furthermore, whatever accommodations may be made to ease practical computation represent less of a distortion or departure from a consumption ideal than from a true accretion ideal.

A strictly correct treatment of housing would be to allow a deduction for purchase price and capital expenditures, but then to impute full rental value, with periodic changes in imputed rental to reflect market changes. This would involve the difficulties of real estate assessment and valuation on a national scale. It would also involve a duplication of the hardship that is now perceived by some to result from increasing real estate taxes in the case of elderly homeowners who do not have any corresponding increase in money income with which to pay those taxes. The fact is that home ownership during a period of rising real estate prices operates to allow older people to live in houses that are more expensive than they could afford to move into now, and that effect may be judged to be generally desirable. Furthermore, we may feel we do not want our income tax to impair that aspect of homeownership by creating a tax liability that increases over time and that can only be met by having an increasing cash income. The economics of homeownership allow a person to buy a home for a lifetime out of the earnings of his relatively early productive years at price levels prevailing when he makes his initial purchase. It may well be enough for the income tax law to take this economic situation as it is and be satisfied with taxing a person on the cash expenditure it takes to provide lifetime housing, as the expenditure is made.

The treatment of owner-occupied housing then would be virtually the same as under present law, except that there would be no deduction for mortgage interest, and there might be an option to deduct an initial downpayment, returning it to income over a short period of years with interest added annually to the deferred balance at a specified rate.

Proceeds on the sale of a house would present some new problems. The present rule permitting a homeowner to sell at a profit without tax if proceeds are reinvested in another principal residence should be continued.[103] This rule, for example, enables a person to move and purchase comparable housing in another location, without making the additional investment that would be required if he had to pay a tax on the heretofore unrealized appreciation on his first home. Profit on the sale of a house not reinvested in another residence would be included in taxable income, though no tax would be paid if proceeds were invested in any ordinary investment assets. The new question would be whether that part of sale proceeds that represents a return of basis or costs and is not reinvested in housing should be able to be spent for other consumption on a taxfree basis on the ground that it represents a refund of money on which consumption tax has already been paid. The answer to that question should probably be yes, and again that answer is in accord with present law under which the sale proceeds from a house, to the extent they represent return of basis rather than profit, are freely available for consumption spending.[105]

Finally, it should be reemphasized that any practical solution to the problem of owner-occupied housing is more consonant with the consumption model than with the accretion model. The accretion ideal requires that the purchase price of a home come out of after-tax income because it is an item of accumulation, and then it requires that there be further additions to taxable income to reflect both imputed rental income and unrealized appreciation. The existing treatment of housing falls short of the accretion ideal immediately upon purchase and occupation of a home, without any change in value, by

---

103. CODE § 1034. [Section 1034 has been repealed. In most cases, however, present section 121 enables taxpayers to avoid tax upon sale of their principal residences, without the requirement of reinvestment. (Ed.)]

105. The law might provide that proceeds from the sale of a house, to the extent that they represent a return of cost or basis, would not be included in taxable income. In addition, if the funds representing a return of cost were invested, the taxpayer would get a deduction for the investment itself, but would be taxed on subsequent disinvestment and consumption. Alternatively, one could grant no deduction for the investment of such funds, but instead give the taxpayer a cost basis in the assets purchased. When the investments were then later liquidated and spent for consumption, the proceeds would be excluded from income to the extent of that basis.

reason of failure to include imputed rental income. As a house increases in value, existing treatment falls doubly short by failing to include both an increase in imputed rental income and the appreciation in value as such. By contrast, existing treatment (except for deductibility of mortgage interest) is initially consistent with the consumption ideal since taxation of the purchase price serves as a proxy for taxing imputed rental value. * * *

Fairness and Efficiency

* * *

It may nevertheless be objected that a saver is not to be viewed as a philanthropist contributing more to society than he withdraws. Accumulation is not consumption foregone; it is consumption deferred. Since a saver has not given up the claim against future output represented by his accumulated income, what reason can there be to exempt him from tax upon it?

But the issue as between an accretion-type and a consumption-type tax is not one of exemption; it, too, is only one of deferral. Under a consumption-type tax, deferred consumption is subject to deferred tax. Of course, deferral makes a difference, and in general the burden of a deferred tax is less than that of an immediate tax at the same rate. * * * But to say the burden of a deferred tax is less does not indicate which kind of tax is fairer. The most sophisticated argument in favor of a consumption-type tax is that the lesser burden of a deferred tax is more appropriate because it ultimately imposes a more uniform burden on consumption, whenever it may occur, than does an accretion-type tax. Put the other way around, a consumption-type tax is preferable because an accretion-type tax imposes an excessive burden on deferred consumption.[119] Neutrality with respect to consumption is important not only because it promotes efficiency in the allocation of income, but because it keeps the tax from bearing more heavily on one person than another on account of differences in need or taste for particular goods or services, now or in the future.

---

119. An accretion-type tax is sometimes defended by reference to neutrality, treating saving as just one more thing a person may do with his income. A consumption-type tax, it is said, would impose a penalty on spending as compared with saving. *See* Musgrave, *In Defense of an Income Concept*, 81 HARV. L. REV. 44, 46 (1967). Or, more elaborately, it is said that saving must involve some combination of satisfactions equal to what could have been derived from a little more spending at the margin; otherwise the person would have spent more and saved less. *See, e.g.*, Aaron, *What Is a Comprehensive Tax Base Anyway?*, 22 NAT'L TAX J. 543, 544 (1969).

But this line of reasoning is essentially like an argument against the deductibility of business expenses—one must get as much pleasure from a business expenditure as from a personal consumption expenditure, at the margin, or else he would make more of the latter and less of the former. What we recognize immediately, of course, with respect to a business expense is that satisfactions to be derived from it may be at least one step removed. * * * Saving, similarly, can be viewed as an instrumental expenditure, made as a means of supporting future consumption. The way to achieve neutrality between ultimate ends—future and present consumption—is, as we have seen, to exempt savings, not to tax them.

Consider again the case of a working person who puts $100 aside for retirement. At 9% compound interest, in 24 years it will grow to $800. A tax of 33% imposed on a consumption basis would take 33% of $800 leaving $533 to spend. A 33% accretion-type tax would cut the $100 to $67 at the outset, and cut its rate of growth from 9% per annum to 6%. At 6%, the $67 would double only twice making $267, or just half what is left under a consumption-type tax. The effective rate of tax in relation to consumption ultimately supported by the earnings in question is thus not 33% but 67%. All this is without even taking account of graduated rates, which are likely to make the relative burden of an accretion-type tax even heavier by subjecting earnings to high-income rates even when put aside to support consumption in low-income retirement years.

The logic of a consumption-type tax is that a 33% taxpayer who would have had $800 to spend in the absence of tax should have $533 after tax whatever combination of earnings and savings may have gone to produce the $800. An accretion-type tax is discriminatory because it will leave much less for the retiree whose potential $800 is the product of work and saving than for another taxpayer with $800 of current income.

Mill called the discrimination of an accretion-type tax against deferred consumption a double tax on savings, once as they accumulate and again as they produce their own return.[121] Unfortunately, ensuing discussion has sometimes focused more on definitional than on substantive issues; the accumulation of savings and earnings of a return on the accumulation represent separate items of income or accretion, it is said, and therefore taxing both does not represent double taxation of a single item. For all the argument, no careful writer seems to have denied that an accretion-type tax imposes a heavier ultimate burden in relation to deferred consumption than to current consumption.

This discussion of neutrality has only to do with neutrality as to expenditures. A personal income tax is not neutral by any means, unfortunately, with respect to questions of productivity—how hard to work and how much, what risks to take with capital, and so on. Either a consumption-type or an accretion-type personal income tax will have substitution effects in favor of leisure over work, and, less clearly, in favor of conservative over risky investment. While both types of taxes are biased with respect to these things, a consumption-type tax is apparently less so.[123] This is an important advantage, though collateral, as it seems to me, to preserving expenditure neutrality between present and deferred consumption.

Insofar as accumulation is viewed as deferred consumption, a

---

121. J.S. MILL, *supra* note 7, at 545-46.
123. *See* N. KALDOR, *supra* note 7, at 102-14.

consumption-type tax seems fairer and economically more efficient than an accretion-type tax. If an accretion type tax is to be preferred over a consumption-type tax it must be because accumulation somehow represents something more than deferred consumption, something that would not be adequately captured or reflected or burdened by the deferred imposition of a consumption-type tax if and when consumption ultimately occurs.

  * * *

Notes and Questions

 1. Why does Professor Andrews term the measurement of income by the Haig-Simons definition an "accretion" measurement?

 2. The assertion that the accretion measurement overtaxes savings is central to the proponents of consumption-type taxes. (Professors Gunn (in Subchapter C) and McNulty (in Subchapter F) challenge this assertion.) What examples of asserted overtaxation of savings does Professor Andrews offer?

 3. Accretion and consumption are not the only possible models of the ideal tax base. The realization model—which present law tracks to a considerable degree—could be viewed as an ideal. See Chapter Two. See also, for example, Professor Gunn's defense of present law (and not of the accretion ideal) in Subchapter C. Most scholars, however, regard present law as a hybrid of the accretion and consumption ideals.

Mechanics of Professor Andrews' proposal
 4. The ultimate tax base of the consumption-type income tax is consumption, not income (or accretion). Yet the first step in computing the tax base is quite similar to that of present law—initially including all income in the tax base, without regard to whether the income was consumed or saved. If the tax base is consumption, why start with income?

 5. Most taxpayers consume the great bulk of their after-tax incomes. For such taxpayers, the tax base under either an income tax or under the proposed consumption-type tax would be almost the same. "[U]nder either ideal," Andrews observes, "the tax in the long run is mostly a tax on household consumption."

 6. Does "consumption" include money paid in taxes? Consider a taxpayer who earned $50,000, but whose employer withheld $10,000 for taxes and paid only the remaining $40,000 to the employee. If the employee spent the $40,000 on consumption, should the taxpayer's consumption-tax base be

$40,000 or, as under Professor Andrews' proposal, $50,000?

7.   A tax-exclusive base could lead to extremely high nominal tax rates. Suppose the consumption tax base did not include taxes. What rate of consumption taxation would be necessary to equal the effect of an income tax rate of 50 percent for a taxpayer who spent all after-tax income on consumption? What rate would be necessary to equal an income tax rate of 75 percent?

8.   Professor Andrews argues that failure to tax consumption (*e.g.*, nontaxation of imputed income) results in permanent tax avoidance, while failure to tax appreciation (or "accumulation") generally results only in moving the tax burden to a different year. Why is this generally true? Will accretion ultimately be taxed if the taxpayer holds the appreciated property until death?

9.   It might be argued that an income base is to be preferred to a consumption base, because tax liability should take account of wealth as well as current living standards. Professor Jeff Strnad argues that two of the principal "norms that have motivated scholars and policymakers to favor accretion taxation" are wealth-based: "The first norm is that intangible benefits from holding wealth should be taxed. The second norm is that the tax system should address disparities in wealth as well as disparities in consumption."[f]
On what grounds does Professor Andrews reject the argument that an income tax effectively and appropriately addresses differences in wealth?

10.   Do transfer taxes (estate and gift taxes) have any role to play in Andrews' proposed system?

11.   Many advocates of consumption taxation, including Andrews, support transfer taxes. One reason is that the consumption-type tax will not reach income at any time during life, or at death, if the income is not consumed but is passed on to heirs. (Even then, the consumption tax is merely delayed—until consumption occurs by the heir. This delay, however, could extend indefinitely—for generations.)

The Simplification Claim
12.   Why does Professor Andrews contend that his consumption tax would be less complex than either current law or the accretion ideal? (Reserve

---

f. Jeff Strnad, *Periodicity and Accretion Taxation: Norms and Implementation*, 99 YALE L.J. 1817, 1820 (1990).

judgment on the simplification issue until you have studied Subchapter E, which presents actual proposals for implementation of consumption-type taxation.)

13. Why might such disparate provisions of current law as payments of compensation in the form of stock of the employer, corporate reorganizations, and exchanges of like-kind business or investment property be simplified under a consumption-type income tax?

14. For simplicity, Professor Andrews would count items such as cash balances and checking account balances—amounts clearly not consumed in fact—as consumption. How would you expect taxpayers to react to such a legal rule?

15. A taxpayer's expenditures for plant and equipment are usually deducted over a period of years (*i.e.*, depreciated) under present law. How would such costs be recovered under a consumption-type tax? Why the different treatment?

16. Under present law, one source of controversy is whether a given expenditure should be viewed as an ordinary business expense, such as a repair (which is "expensed," or immediately deducted), or treated as a capital expenditure (which is capitalized and deducted over time). Under the consumption-type taxing method, the expenditure would be immediately deducted either way, ending this source of controversy.

17. Under present law, neither loans nor repayments of loan principal have tax effect. Under Professor Andrews' proposal, the proceeds of many loans would be taken into the tax base, while the repayment of those loans would give rise to a deduction. What is the justification for this treatment? What would happen in the case of cancellation of indebtedness, which is generally taxable under current law?

18. Professor Andrews suggests treating consumer loans differently, giving no tax effect either to the loan or to its repayment. Why?

19. Consider Andrews' suggested treatment of consumer durables. In theory, the purchase of a consumer durable should be an investment, which yields a flow of consumption in the form of imputed use value. However, the purchase price "represents the discounted value of its future usefulness," so the much simpler approach of treating the purchase price of the consumer durable

as consumption in the year of purchase works reasonably well.

If the durable is purchased on credit, Professor Andrews says that we can still look simply to the cash payments over time. This treats the principal plus the interest as consumption, and thus automatically increases the tax to offset the benefit to the taxpayer of having deferred the tax.

For example, consider two taxpayers, Carl Cash and Bill Borrower, with identical incomes of $200,000 and identical consumption patterns. In year one, each taxpayer buys a new $50,000 automobile, and each spends $150,000 on other consumption items. (Remember that under Andrews' proposal, the payment of tax gives rise to no deduction, and thus, in effect, counts as consumption.) Carl pays cash for the car, and saves nothing during the year. Carl is thus immediately taxed on $200,000 consumption. Bill finances his car, and pays it off at a rate of $11,000 per year for five years, thus paying a total of $55,000, including $5,000 interest. In the first year, Bill spends a total of $161,000, saves $39,000 for which he receives a deduction, and is taxed on only $161,000, deferring tax on the balance of the automobile purchase price. In subsequent years, Bill's nondeductible car payments mean that he must pay the consumption tax on consumption from a prior year, but he has enjoyed the benefit of deferral.

The benefit of Bill's deferral, however, is offset by the fact that he is taxed on more total from the car purchase. While Carl is taxed on consumption of $50,000 in Year One, Bill is taxed on $55,000 spread over Years One through Five. Because the interest in effect counts as consumption (because payment of interest gives rise to no deduction), there is an automatic tax cost from deferring payment for consumption items. The tax cost roughly balances the benefit of the tax deferral.

20. What is the theoretically correct treatment of housing under Professor Andrews' proposal? What, instead, does he advocate? Why?

21. What should happen under Andrews' proposal when a taxpayer sells a house?

Capital gains

22   How would capital gains taxation work under the consumption-type tax? What problems of current law would be reduced or eliminated?

23. One of the major justifications of favorable capital gains treatment is that the gain may be illusory, the result of inflation rather than real gain. Traditionally, capital gains have been taxed much more gently than ordinary income, in part due to the inflation factor. Another suggestion is to index the

basis of capital assets to adjust for inflation, but complexity, among other problems, would result. (See Chapters Fifteen and Sixteen.)

If the consumption-type tax were in place, the taxation of capital assets would seem devoid of the inflation problem. There would be no basis; at the time of purchase, a full deduction of the amount of the purchase price would be granted, so no inflation adjustment would be justified. Upon disposition, the total amount realized would be taken into account and taxed in that year, and again no inflation adjustment would be necessary.

Suppose this system had been in place for many years, and that a taxpayer who purchased stock in 1970 for $7,000 sold the stock in 2004 for $10,000, thus realizing a nominal gain of $3,000. Obviously, the "gain" would be illusory, because $7,000 in 1970 would be much more valuable than $10,000 in 2004. Assuming a tax rate of ten percent, the taxpayer's "losing" investment would generate $300 tax in 2004. This is troubling under the present income tax; the nominal gain is taxed despite the fact that the transaction resulted in a "real" loss.

Under the consumption-type tax, the problem is automatically cured. Still assuming a 10 percent tax rate, the deduction of $7,000 in 1970 is worth $700 *in 1970 dollars*; when the $10,000 amount realized is taxed in 2004, it results in $1,000 tax *in 2004 dollars*. If, in fact, inflation means that the "real" value of the sales proceeds are worth less than the "real" value of the initial investment, so will the "real" tax on the proceeds be worth less than the "real" value of the deduction granted when the investment was made.

Asserted consistency of consumption-type income tax

24. Why do proponents of consumption taxation contend that unrealized appreciation is more troubling to the income tax system than to a consumption-type system?

25. Is our present federal income tax a consumption tax, or an accretion tax? In what ways does it resemble each?

26. To say that a tax system is entirely coherent and follows its "ideal" pattern at all times is not to say that it is a good system. For example, if our basic system were a head tax, requiring exactly $1,000 in annual tax from each person, there would be no inconsistency about how to handle capital gains or unrealized appreciation or any other of the thousands of perplexing questions under our tax law—the head tax would call for the same amount of tax regardless of any of these events. It does not follow that we should adopt a head tax in place of the income tax.

27.   Would a tax in the form proposed by Professor Andrews more closely resemble a point-of-sale consumption tax, such as a comprehensive sales tax or European-style value added tax, or our present income tax? Consider factors such as tax base, vertical and horizontal comparisons of tax incidence, and administration.

C. THE INCOME TAX DEFENDED

While the consumption-type income tax has created considerable academic and political interest, many experts defend income as the more appropriate tax base. The excerpts in this subchapter provide a sampling of three very different types of defenses.

Professor Warren analyzes the issue from an extremely academic, and arguably socialistic, perspective. He argues that each member of society who generates income does so as part of a social system; accordingly, society should have first claim on the income produced, and society should decide what portion of that income the individual producer is to retain.

Professor Gunn counters what is perhaps the central justification for consumption taxation—the assertion that an income tax overtaxes saving vis-à-vis consumption. Addressing examples of Professor Andrews and other advocates of consumption taxation, Professor Gunn argues that saving is taxed fairly by the income tax.

Finally, we consider Treasury I, whose drafters found considerable merit in a consumption-type income tax. Ultimately, however, they rejected it for a number of theoretical and practical reasons.

WOULD A CONSUMPTION TAX BE FAIRER THAN AN INCOME TAX?
Alvin Warren[*]

89 Yale Law Journal 1081, 1090-93 (1980)

Using the Haig-Simons concept of income in order to compute each taxpayer's share of the annual social product, an income tax serves to deflect to the government a progressive portion of each citizen's share of the product otherwise allocated to him by transfers and the marketplace. Whether the tax proceeds are used for public goods and services or for redistribution to some persons, either in cash or in kind, those uses are funded by the output of labor and private capital during the current period. Levying the tax on income is on this view simply a logical concomitant of the proposition that society in general has a claim on its annual product that is prior to the claims of its individual citizens.

---

[*]. At time of original publication, Professor of Law, University of Pennsylvania Law School.

The existence of a collective claim on privately produced resources is so well-established as part of our polity that justification may seem superfluous. Nevertheless, economic theorists have formally shown that certain goods and services are best produced in the public sector,[31] while political theorists have argued for centuries over the nature and extent of the collective claim for redistributive purposes, a subject that has commanded renewed attention in recent years.[32] But neither the theories of public goods nor those of distributive justice have depended on the source of revenues used for the two analytically distinct governmental purposes. Discussions of redistribution generally either have considered the appropriate distribution of economic resources without identifying the best measure of such resources or have assumed that it is income (as product) that is or is not subject to a collective claim. As a result, existing theories of distributive justice and public goods have little to add to the case for the income tax beyond establishing a social claim on private resources.

Specifying that claim as on social product can be justified on the theory that a producer does not have a controlling moral claim over the product of his capital and labor, given the role of fortuity in income distribution and the dependence of producers on consumers and other producers to create value in our society—factors that create a general moral claim on all private product on behalf of the entire society.[33] This rationale would apply *a fortiori* to other increments in Haig-Simons income, such as gifts and windfalls, which come to the recipient without even the claim due to production. Such a proposition is, of course, no more demonstrable than the proposition that society has a prior moral claim on wealth or consumption rather than on product. As Professor William Andrews has stated, the ultimate choice among these alternatives is not a matter of logical proof but of exposing the assumptions and identifying the consequences of each.[34]

Given that limitation, the case for taxing income can be stated by identifying as a plausible assumption the view that, for the reasons suggested above, the distribution of social product is a matter for collective decision. The collective decisionmaking apparatus of the society is conceived of as deciding

---

31. *See, e.g.*, Samuelson, *The Pure Theory of Public Expenditure*, 36 REV. ECON. & STATISTICS 387, 387-89 (1954); Samuelson, *Diagrammatic Exposition of a Theory of Public Expenditure*, 37 REV. ECON. & STATISTICS 350 (1955).

32. The seminal work in rekindling interest in distributive justice is J. RAWLS, A THEORY OF JUSTICE (1971).

33. *See id.* at 72-74, 100-08, 310-15. For a recent argument that treatment of an individual's genetic endowment as an accident devoid of moral significance is inconsistent with basic concepts of individuality, see Posner, *Utilitarianism, Economics, and Legal Theory*, 8 J. LEGAL STUD. 103, 128 (1979).

34. Andrews, *Fairness and the Choice Between a Consumption-Type and an Accretion-Type Personal Income Tax: A Reply to Professor Warren*, 88 HARV. L. REV. 947, 950 (1975).

both the amount and type of public goods to be produced and the distribution of that portion of private social product that remains after diversion of resources into the public sector to produce those public goods that are not financed by service charges. Whatever after-tax distribution is decided upon, that decision is implemented by the income tax, which is levied on the amount of social product otherwise distributed to each taxable unit.[35]

As anticipated, this argument for the income tax does not appeal to some independently demonstrable principle but is tautological in the sense that it follows simply from the premise of the tax: given a legitimate social concern with the distribution of society's product, the income tax is justified as a means of effecting the desired after-tax distribution. The nature of the desired distribution goes to the content of the tax, rather than to its justification. Extreme egalitarianism would presumably argue for a tax characterized by progressivity, culminating in a confiscatory rate on positive income with corresponding provisions specifying a minimum after-tax income. A social decision to reduce inequality in the distribution of product, but not to the extent of eliminating incentives to work and invest, might lead to less progressivity with rates always under one hundred percent. It is a judgment of this latter type that seems to underlie much current discussion of distributive justice.[36]

Unlike the foregoing argument, the traditional case for the income tax in terms of fairness has appealed to some external standard to establish that income is an appropriate basis for taxation. Generally it has been argued that income is a superior index of an "ability to pay," and that the tax should be structured to result in "equal sacrifice" by taxpayers, the latter being especially relevant to the rate structure. Unfortunately, centuries of elucidation have failed to provide sufficient content to these concepts. For example, ability to pay has been defined as "the capacity of paying without undue hardship on the part of the person paying or an unacceptable degree of interference with objectives that are considered socially important by other members of the community."[37] Such definitions reduce to statements that society should appropriately tax what it should appropriately tax. This approach is no less tautological than the one taken here; it just appears so in that apparently, but not really, independently verifiable grounds, such as ability to pay, are said to

---

35. This view includes the possibility of negative taxes and assumes that the desired after-tax distribution of income is a function of no personal characteristic other than pretax income. For example, if after-tax income were to be allocated on the basis of weight, intelligence, merit, or whatever, the Haig-Simons definition could be used for collection of revenue, but not for the simultaneous achievement of a given after-tax distribution.

36. *See, e.g.,* A. Okun, Equality and Efficiency—The Big Tradeoff (1975); J. Rawls, *supra* note 32, at 150-61.

37. R. Goode, The Individual Income Tax 18 (1964).

justify the tax.

To summarize, the personal income tax follows from, and is justified by, a societal judgment as to the appropriate distribution of social product or personal income. Society's interest in the distribution of income, in turn, depends on the view that the importance of fortuity and the interrelationships of contemporary society deprive producers of a controlling moral claim to what would be distributed to them in the absence of a tax system.

* * *

THE CASE FOR AN INCOME TAX
Alan Gunn[*]
46 University of Chicago Law Review 370, 370-78 (1979)

Recent studies by the United States Treasury Department[1] and the Meade Committee[2] in England recommend a progressive tax on personal consumption as an alternative to an income tax. Neither adds anything fundamental to the expenditure-tax controversy, but each contains one intriguing feature: a discussion of the practical problems of substituting consumption for income as the tax base.[3] This development may mean that the replacement of the income tax by an expenditure tax should be taken as a serious practical possibility. And even if the possibility of so radical a change in our tax structure is remote, the arguments of the expenditure-tax theorists may encourage changes in the income tax in the form of additional relief for savers or a supplemental tax on expenditure. The time when the expenditure tax could be dismissed as lacking practical significance has long passed.

Arguments based on considerations of equity, administrative convenience, and economic efficiency play an important role in the case for an expenditure tax. I will not address the question of "efficiency" directly, although some of my "equity" arguments may bear on efficiency as well as equity. I will focus on the most important noneconomic issues in the debate between expenditure and income taxation: whether an income tax imposes "double taxation" on savings, [and] how income compares with other bases for taxation in terms of fairness.[5] * * *

---

[*]. At time of original publication, Professor of Law, Cornell University

1. DEPARTMENT OF THE TREASURY, BLUEPRINTS FOR BASIC TAX REFORM (1977) [hereinafter cited as BLUEPRINTS]. This report presents two alternative "model tax systems"—an expenditure tax and a comprehensive income tax with rates much less progressive than the existing rates—without choosing between them.

2. INSTITUTE FOR FISCAL STUDIES, THE STRUCTURE AND REFORM OF DIRECT TAXATION (1978) [hereinafter cited as MEADE COMMITTEE REPORT].

3. BLUEPRINTS, *supra* note 1, at 204-12; MEADE COMMITTEE REPORT, *supra* note 2, at 187-92.

5. The tax base defended here resembles that of the existing federal income tax, tidied up somewhat, perhaps, but not fundamentally altered. I have no desire to defend an "ideal" tax based on the Haig-Simons definition.

The Expenditure Tax, the Income Tax, and the Double Taxation of Savings
The Basis of Expenditure-Tax Theory

The earliest proposal for an expenditure tax that is still cited today was made by Thomas Hobbes. Hobbes thought consumption to be the best tax base because it measures the benefits taxpayers receive from society; an expenditure tax would charge individuals equally in proportion to the goods they withdraw from the common stock. Hobbes's ideas are recognizable in the position of some modern expenditure-tax theorists that the income tax is unfair to investors and wage earners because it taxes them while not taxing rich people who chose to be economically idle and live off their principal. Few people today accept Hobbes's principle that taxes should be levied in proportion to benefits received, and the idea that only those who spend receive benefits from society seems bizarre.

Modern expenditure-tax theory is closer to the position of John Stuart Mill. Mill viewed an income tax without an exemption for income saved as discriminating against savers because taxpayers would be "taxed twice on what they save, and only once on what they spend."[9] He argued that an income tax taxes savers both upon principal (the money originally earned) and the earnings from investing that principal. This, Mill argued, is unfair to the saver, because "if he has the interest, it is because he abstains from using the principal; if he spends the principal, he does not receive the interest. Yet because he can do either of the two, he is taxed as if he could do both...."[10] Mill's fundamental idea, that the income tax is unfair to savers, is common today, as is the picturesque language with which he expressed this conclusion: the saver is "taxed twice" under an income tax.[11]

Some influential proponents of the expenditure tax have gone beyond Mill in important respects. Mill thought a consumption tax impractical because measuring annual personal consumption directly was impossible. Modern writers have shown, however, that consumption can be measured, perhaps even more easily than income. Irving Fisher pointed the way by demonstrating that modern accounting techniques make it no harder to compute personal savings or dissavings than business savings. He argued for an "income" tax (really an expenditure tax) under which all receipts—including gifts, inheritances, and withdrawals from savings—would enter into the definition of taxable income, but savings would be deductible, thus adding only

---

9. 2 J.S. MILL, PRINCIPLES OF POLITICAL ECONOMY 407 (1874)

10. *Id.*

11. *E.g.*, M. CHIRELSTEIN, FEDERAL INCOME TAXATION 260-61 (1977) (presenting the notion that savings are doubly taxed under an income tax as fact, with no suggestion that the conclusion is open to doubt).

two steps to present computations.[14] William Andrews has argued, more recently, that a spending tax would actually be easier to administer than an income tax, because the underlying computations would be simpler.[15] His claim is that an expenditure tax would not require the resolution of such troublesome problems of present law as distinguishing capital gains from ordinary income, computing depreciation, and drawing a line between business expenses and capital expenditures.

Mill's "double taxation" argument, in the form in which he made it, is circular. To say, as he does, that one who invests money "abstains from using" it is to say, at least implicitly, that consumption is the only "use" of money that should be considered in devising a tax. But modern writers have rescued the "double taxation of savings" argument from circularity. They argue that an income tax discriminates against savers because it makes saving less attractive relative to spending than would be the case in a world without taxes. I will use Andrews's figures to illustrate the argument.[16]

In a world without taxes or with an expenditure tax, a person who decides to save $1.00 of income and invest it at nine percent will have eight times as much to spend after 24 years as he could have spent initially; but with an equivalent income tax he will have only four times as much to spend under the same conditions.

Tax	(1) Available after Taxes if Spent Immediately	(2) Available after Taxes if Spent In 24 Years	Ratio 2:1
No Tax	$1.00	$8.00	8:1
33 1/3 % Income Tax	0.67	2.67	4:1
Equivalent Expenditure Tax	0.67	5.33	8:1

Even in this illustration, the expenditure tax does not reproduce the no-tax world in all respects, because any tax, by reducing the total amount a taxpayer has available for saving and spending, will normally affect the proportion he decides to allocate to each use. But to the extent that an individual is influenced by what a dollar saved at the margin can earn, the incentive to save appears the same under an expenditure tax as in a no-tax

---

14. I. FISHER, THE INCOME CONCEPT IN THE LIGHT OF EXPERIENCE (n.d.) (pamphlet) 14-17, which appears to be Fisher's own translation of a paper originally published in German [in 1927] [hereinafter cited as THE INCOME CONCEPT].

15. Andrews, *A Consumption-Type or Cash Flow Personal Income Tax*, 87 HARV. L. REV. 1113, 1148-65 (1974).

16. *Id*. at 1125.

world and different under an income tax that contains no exemptions for saving.

This argument is convincing only if one accepts a no-tax world as a standard for judging the desirability of a tax. Economists use the model of a no-tax world as a heuristic device to measure the likely effect of different taxes on the economy and as a standard of comparison in measuring "efficiency." As a starting point in making rough guesses about the effects of changes in existing arrangements, the "tax-free society" device may serve a useful purpose. But the model rests on so many assumptions about behavior under hypothetical conditions that any conclusions based on it must be problematic and tentative. As Coase has asked in another context:

> In a state of laissez faire, is there a monetary, a legal, or a political system, and if so, what are they? . . . Whatever we may have in mind as our ideal world, it is clear that we have not yet discovered how we get to it from where we are. A better approach would seem to be to start our analysis with a situation which naturally exists, to examine a proposed policy change, and to attempt to decide whether the new situation would be, in total, better or worse than the original one.[19]

Reduction to Present Value and Fairness

Even if we assume, for purposes of argument, that "no-tax society" comparisons are useful in determining economically efficient solutions to complex practical problems, it does not follow that "discrimination" against savings under an income tax (when both income and expenditure taxes are compared to a no-tax society) is unfair. The unfairness argument seems to rest on the notion that people generally prefer to consume as they earn and so must be induced by interest to defer consumption. Interest income is thus merely compensation for delaying consumption. It does not represent a true increase in value to the saver, and a tax on that interest—like a tax on a nominal profit that reflects only monetary inflation—is in reality a levy on capital, a second tax on the earnings whose consumption was delayed. The following example illustrates the thrust of this argument.[21] Two people earn $10,000 in one year.

---

19. Coase, *The Problem of Social Cost*, 3 J.L. & ECON. 1, 43 (1960).

21. The example in the text is inspired by Fisher's famous three brothers example. THE INCOME CONCEPT, *supra* note 14, at 12-13. Three brothers inherit $100,000 each. The first chooses to spend only the interest; the second allows his interest to accumulate until his money has doubled, and then spends the interest on this sum; the third buys a $20,000 a year annuity for six years, after which he has nothing left. Fisher assumes a 5 percent rate of return and a 10 percent tax. Under a conventional income tax, the first brother could take care of his future tax burden by setting aside $10,000 in the year of the inheritance, the second would have to set aside $17,140, while the third, "improvident," brother would need only $1,577,30. Under a consumption tax, each brother would have to set aside $10,000.

One spends all his after-tax income, while the other saves half his after-tax income the first year and spends it the second. With a flat 30 percent income tax and a 10 percent interest rate, net return after taxes is 7 percent. Ignoring their second-year salaries, we get the following results:

	Spender	Saver
(1) Spends year 1	7,000	3,500
(2) Tax	3,000	3,000
(3) Saves	–	3,500
(4) Interest pre-tax	–	350
(5) Tax on int.	–	105
(6) Spends Year 2	–	3,745
Present Value:		
of (5) at 10%	–	95
of (6) at 7%	–	3,500
of (1) + (6)	7,000	7,000

Although the "present value" of what the saver and the spender eventually spend is the same, the saver must set aside more for taxes—not only does the saver pay more taxes in total dollars ($3,105 vs. $3,000), the present value of his taxes is greater ($3,095 vs. $3,000). Under an expenditure tax, the present value of their taxes would be the same, no matter how much or how long one saves. The argument that the net interest rate should be used to reduce future consumption and future taxes to their present value, and that, as a consequence, the saver and the spender in the illustration above "really" consumed the same amount but were taxed unequally, is the essence of the modern justification for the view that the income tax is a "double tax" on savings.

Reduction to present value is often an essential step in comparing people's well-being. If two people receive $10,000 each in a taxable transaction, the one who is allowed to pay the tax later needs to set aside less for that purpose than the one who must pay the tax immediately, because money set aside to pay a fixed sum in the future earns interest until the sum is paid. But this type of analysis, so useful for comparing the burden of taxes, cannot be used in a straightforward way as a technique for determining the present value of future consumption to a saver. If a taxpayer can obtain a secure after-tax return of ten percent, he is indifferent whether he pays $1.00 in tax now or $1.10 a year later, and this is true whether the total tax deferred is $1.00 or $1 million. But this does not mean that if a person lends $10,000 at minimum risk for one year at ten percent, he values $11,000 of consumption a year from now no more than $10,000 now.[24]

The interest rate reflects the "time value of consumption," if at all, only at the margin. The interest rate at which a person lends his money measures the value to him of the last dollar he saves. If the interest rate were lower, he would probably still save, although he would probably save a different amount—less or more.[26] The money he would save with a lower rate of interest produces benefits, if invested at the higher going rate, greater than those of current consumption. Use of the after-tax rate of interest to reduce future spending to present value, when applied to measure the present value of savings, ignores that part of a person's interest income that inures to him when he is able to invest part of his savings at a higher rate than he was in fact ready to accept.

Reduction to present value is essential to the argument that the income tax involves "double taxation of savings" and is therefore unfair to savers. Fisher said that it is "unjust" to impose taxes that are different, when reduced to present value, on people whose consumption, also reduced to present value, is the same.[27] This judgment rests on at least two assumptions: first, that a tax is just only if it taxes equal benefits or enjoyments equally;[28] second, that the

---

24. The differences between straightforward time-value calculations as applied to the receipt of cash and the same calculations as applied to consumption can be easily shown by a simple if somewhat extreme comparison. Suppose a taxpayer who could expect to receive a secure income of $10,000 a year for the next ten years were offered, as an alternative, a present lump-sum payment of $100,000. Ignoring any possible effects of a progressive income tax, any rational person would accept the offer, since the opportunity for an investment return makes $100,000 now worth more than $10,000 a year for ten years to anyone. But it is surely not the case that any rational person who expected to consume $10,000 a year for the next ten years and who could give up that opportunity in exchange for $100,000 consumption this year, on condition he consume nothing for nine years, would accept the offer.

26. If consumption had a declining marginal utility for everyone, people would save more as the interest rate went up, and would save less as it went down. This analysis, however, leaves many factors out of account. For example, someone who is saving for a particular goal, such as a college education for his children or a particular level of retirement income, may reduce the proportion of his earnings that he saves as the interest rate goes up. Just as the income tax tends to encourage some people to substitute nontaxable leisure for taxable work (the "substitution effect") and encourage others to work harder to replace money taken in taxes (the "income effect"), a tax with an exemption for income saved would encourage some people to save more while encouraging others, such as those trying to accumulate a fixed sum, to save a smaller proportion of their earnings than they would under an income tax.

27. THE INCOME CONCEPT, *supra* note 14, at 12-13.

28. * * * It should be pointed out here that Fisher's view that it is fair to tax equally—and fair only to tax equally—people whose future consumption reduced to present value is the same assumes, among other things, that the only benefit people get from saving is increased future consumption. But as Guillebaud has pointed out,

interest rate measures the benefits forgone by delaying consumption. If the interest rate measures these benefits only at the margin, this second assumption is undermined and the argument loses much of its force. And a case can be made against reducing postponed consumption to present value, even at the margin, for the purpose of assessing the justice of a tax. As is indicated by the title of the revised (1930) edition of Irving Fisher's famous work on the rate of interest, *The Theory of Interest as Determined by Impatience to Spend Income and Opportunity to Invest It*, interest can be viewed as payment for the cost of postponing consumption—resisting impatience to spend—rather than for the supposedly lesser value of future consumption. To an economist, a forgone benefit is a cost, but not all costs are equivalent for judging the fairness of a tax.

If we view the interest rate as paying the saver for the cost to him of resisting the impulse to spend immediately, the "double taxation" argument becomes an argument for allowing taxpayers who incur the "resisting impatience" cost a tax benefit to put them on a par with current spenders, who do not incur such a cost. But to allow this cost to be taken into account in devising a tax is inconsistent with accepted principles not only of income taxation but of expenditure taxation as well. The psychological cost of deferring consumption is like any other cost of giving up lost opportunities; such costs are not, and could not be, taken into account generally under either an income or an expenditure tax. We do not say that a worker's cost in boredom, or in giving up leisure, or in physical effort should be deducted in computing either his taxable income or, under an expenditure tax, his expenditures from current earnings, even though these things are regarded as costs by economists concerned with predicting behavior. In effect, the "double taxation of savings" argument for expenditure taxation is an argument for allowing a very common kind of cost to be deducted when incurred by savers, but not by those who earn and spend, even though we know that they also incur such costs.

The foregoing discussion does not mean that an expenditure tax is

---

the saver has immediately a new asset in the shape of his savings as a capital sum, in terms of its present exchange value, which is valuable to him not merely, and often not principally, as a source of future income, but as a protection and reserve against emergencies which may at any time befall him. There also comes into the question the prestige value of accumulated wealth, the desire to bequeath large sums at death, the knowledge of the power that derives from the possession of wealth . . . .

Guillebaud, *Income Tax and the "Double Taxation" of Saving*, 45 ECON. J. 484, 490-91 (1935).
* * *

A person who values accumulation for its own sake will save and, under an expenditure tax, never pay tax on his accumulation, because his enjoyment comes from the possession itself. It is hard to see, on Fisher's own "benefits" approach to taxation, why it is "fair" to tax him less than a person whose benefit comes from consumption, present or future.

necessarily less desirable than an income tax, but the case for an expenditure tax cannot rest upon the argument that the income tax subjects savings to "double taxation." The justification for abandoning income as a tax base—if indeed there be one—must derive from other considerations of tax policy.

　　　* * *

TAX REFORM FOR FAIRNESS, SIMPLICITY, AND ECONOMIC GROWTH ["TREASURY I"]
United States Department of the Treasury
Vol. 1, at 30-33 (1984)

　　　Consumption provides an alternative to income as the basis for personal taxation. A personal tax on consumption, or consumed income, would be levied by exempting all saving from tax, allowing a deduction for repayment of debt, *and* taxing all borrowing and withdrawals from savings. Consumed income would be reported on a form much like the present form 1040. Deductions would be allowed for deposits in "qualified accounts" similar to existing individual retirement accounts (IRAs); withdrawals from such accounts would be subject to tax.

　　　Though a flat rate could be applied to the consumption base calculated in this way, most proposals for a consumed income tax postulate personal exemptions and graduated rate schedules. Thus, a consumed income tax could be progressive, if that were desired. Itemized deductions could also be allowed, as under the existing tax.

Administrative Advantages

　　　The current income tax is based on the principle that income should be taxed annually as it is realized. It represents a practical compromise between administrative feasibility and the objective of taxing income as it accrues. Conceptually, accrued income can be defined as the amount a taxpayer could consume without reducing his or her net wealth, that is, as the total of what the taxpayer actually consumes plus the change in his or her net wealth. Many practical difficulties plague application of this conceptual ideal as the basis of an income tax. Compromise between achieving the ideal, on the one hand, and avoiding complexity, on the other, produces a system that departs significantly from the conceptual ideal. Examples of compromise include taxation of capital gains only when they are realized, commonly by sale of an asset, rather than as they accrue. Compromises such as this can allow tax on large amounts of income to be postponed indefinitely, or even avoided altogether, as when appreciated property is transferred at death. On the other hand, efforts to administer the tax on an accrual basis, by levying tax before realization occurs, can introduce significant complexity and hardship. For example, if tax were levied on unrealized gains on closely-held business, valuation would be difficult; payment of tax, moreover, could frequently be required even though there is no cash flow with which to pay the tax.

Because it avoids the problems inherent in accrual taxation, a tax on personal consumption is simpler in many respects than an income tax. The consumed income tax is simpler because all costs of investment are deducted immediately ("expensed"), rather than depreciated over the life of assets; because all costs of creating inventories are expensed, rather than being recognized only as goods are sold; and because capital gains are not taxed, as such. A corporate income tax is not an essential part of an ideal tax system based on consumption; if retained, it would serve only as a withholding device.

The consumed income tax has another major administrative advantage over the income tax. Under the present income tax, the measurement of income is commonly distorted by inflation. Because consumption inherently occurs in dollars of the current year, the measurement of the base of the consumed income tax cannot be distorted by inflation. Since depreciable assets and inventory investments are expensed, inflation cannot erode the value of future deductions because there are none. Interest is not taxed, unless spent on consumption, and thus the inflation premium is not taxed. Purely inflationary capital gains are not taxed, because there is no tax on capital gains, per se.

Economic Advantages

Advocates of a consumed income tax argue that it is preferable to the ordinary income tax on conceptual and economic grounds, as well as on administrative grounds. First, an income tax penalizes saving by inducing taxpayers to consume rather than save for future consumption. By comparison, under certain circumstances, a tax on consumption does not distort the choice between consuming now and saving for future consumption. This is a major attraction of any tax on consumption.

Second, seen from a lifetime perspective, a tax on consumed income is said to be more equitable than an income tax. A taxpayer's total tax burden on consumed income does not depend on when income is earned or spent, at least under fairly restrictive simplifying assumptions. By comparison, an income tax imposes a heavier burden on those who earn income relatively early in life or spend it relatively late.

Despite the manifest attractions of the tax on consumed income, the Treasury Department does not propose it as either a replacement for, or a supplement to, the income tax. Several defects and difficulties of a consumed income tax lead to this conclusion.

Transition Problems

First, the current existence of substantial wealth, much of which has been accumulated from after-tax income, poses difficult transition problems. Taxing all consumption financed from such wealth would constitute a cruel trick on those who did not expect it—especially those who have saved after-tax dollars for retirement. Nor would complete exemption of consumption financed from existing wealth be satisfactory. Such an exemption would either be enormously expensive in terms of lost revenue or entail extremely high tax rates during the transition period. Worse, it would allow wealthy taxpayers to escape taxation for many generations if they consumed only old wealth and saved all current income.

On equity grounds, a compromise between complete exemption and full taxation of consumption from existing wealth would be necessary. Such a compromise might allow each taxpayer above a given age to enjoy a given amount of tax-free consumption during his or her lifetime. But phasing in a consumed income tax in this way would involve transition rules that could complicate the tax system for ordinary taxpayers for a generation.

A different type of transition problem would result from the possibility of avoiding taxes by hoarding money before the effective date of the new tax. After the effective date the taxpayer could either deposit the hoarded funds in a qualified account in order to get a tax deduction for saving or use them to meet living expenses without paying tax. Alternatively, pre-effective date investments in foreign banks could be liquidated after the effective date and reinvested as tax-deductible saving. Even though this would be a temporary problem of transition, it would undermine both the revenue yield and fairness of the tax during that period.

Perception Problems

Even though a taxpayer's standard of living, as reflected by his level of consumption, may be considered by many to be an appropriate base for taxation, the consumed income tax suffers from an important perception problem. Taxpayers presumably would welcome the opportunity to postpone taxes on amounts saved, paying tax only when dissaving and consumption occurs; such is the tax treatment currently accorded saving in qualified pension accounts. But to be consistent, it would also be necessary to tax amounts borrowed and allow a deduction for repayment of loans. This treatment of saving and dissaving would create a pattern of tax liabilities over the lifetime of the taxpayer that might be perceived to be unfair. Relative to experience under current law, tax liability would be greater during early adulthood and during retirement—periods when financial resources are commonly strained. Tax would be relatively lower during middle age, the time when many taxpayers receive most of their income. The fairness of including amounts borrowed in taxable consumption might be questioned, and this tax treatment might even require a constitutional amendment.

Complexity for Individuals

A consumed income tax would be more complicated than the existing income tax for many individual taxpayers. Under the present income tax, amounts withheld on wages and salaries roughly offset tax liabilities for many taxpayers who have only modest amounts of income from capital. Relatively few taxpayers must worry about estimating liabilities and paying significant amounts of tax in addition to amounts withheld. Under the consumed income tax the situation could be quite different. Withholding might be required on borrowing and withdrawals from savings; if so, "reverse withholding" would be appropriate when a loan is paid off. Even then, far more taxpayers might need to file estimated returns than now, because it would be difficult to adjust withholding rates on financial transactions to the personal circumstances of taxpayers. Moreover, many young adults and retired individuals are not required to file or pay tax under an income tax, but would be required to file and pay tax under a consumed income tax.

Owner-occupied housing would not be treated as an item of consumption, to be taxed in full in the year of purchase. Rather, inclusion of the purchase price in taxable consumption would be spread over the lifetime of the home, in effect, by requiring taxpayers to pay tax as their mortgages were paid off. This could be accomplished through special treatment of mortgages outside of qualified accounts. But purchases of homes from amounts saved in qualified accounts could require special averaging features that would complicate compliance for taxpayers. Ironically, individual taxpayers would, in a sense, be asked to keep accounts resembling depreciation accounts at the same time that such accounts were eliminated for businesses.

The Dilemma of Gifts and Bequests

The proper treatment of gifts and bequests under a tax on consumed income is a fundamental issue. Under one view such transfers would not be taxed to the person making the gift or bequest; they would only be taxed when consumed by the recipient. Under a very different view, transfers would be taxed to the donor, as well as when consumed by the recipient. Advocates of this second approach argue that taxing gifts and bequests is necessary in order to realize fully the beneficial equity and efficiency effects of a consumption-based tax. They refer to this type of tax as a tax on lifetime income, to distinguish it from the conventional tax on annual income. The distributional differences in the two ways of treating gifts and bequests are, of course, substantial. The first approach would allow great fortunes to be passed from generation to generation without tax, whereas the second would subject transfers to tax.

International Aspects

No country has a tax on consumed income, although Sweden and the United Kingdom have considered it, and India and Sri Lanka (then Ceylon) attempted to impose the tax for a brief period following World War II. Any country imposing a consumed income tax would be very much out of step with its trading partners, all of which employ income taxes, and would face the task of renegotiating its foreign tax treaties.

* * *

Notes and Questions

Fairness

28. Professor Warren's analysis relies on conceptions of societal structure that are not universally shared. Do you agree with "the proposition that society in general has a claim on its annual product that is prior to the claims of its individual citizens"? Should annual production in the United States be viewed as societal production ("*its* annual product"), or as the individual production of its millions of citizens (and aliens)?

29. Do you accept "the theory that a producer does not have a controlling moral claim over the product of his capital and labor, given the role of fortuity in income distribution and the dependence of producers on consumers and other producers"?

Fortuity and interdependence are important determinants of income. Professional athletes provide a dramatic example of the dependence of producers on both consumers and other producers. How much would it be worth to throw a ball into a hoop if no one wanted to watch? Or if television had not been invented?

The same analysis holds for all market-based economic activity (*i.e.*, all economic activity above the level of hunting and gathering or subsistence agriculture). What is the value of a baker's ability to make a cake if no one else wants cake? And could the baker make the cake had not others produced flour and sugar?

30. Professor Warren asserts that society has a legitimate interest in achieving a desired after-tax distribution of society's product. Social and legal structures are, in effect, means of allocation. An income tax "is levied on the amount of social product otherwise distributed to each taxable unit."

Note that an income tax of general application, regardless of its degree of progressivity (so long as it is less than 100 percent), will leave all taxpayers in the same rank order of after-tax income that they had with respect to pre-tax income.

31. Whether we agree with Professor Warren's position concerning the extent of society's claim against individuals, the legitimacy of any taxing system depends upon the validity of some degree of societal claim. Does Professor Warren demonstrate that this claim should be asserted against income, rather than against consumption or wealth?

32. Professor Charles O'Kelley argues that there can be debate about the relative merits of a consumption tax and an accretion tax only if we assume that the pre-tax division of income is just. If the initial distribution of income is unjust, Professor O'Kelley views the accretion tax as the clear choice:

> Consider * * * individual A who in year one earns and spends $20,000 and individual B who in year one earns $1,000,000, but spends only $20,000. Under a consumption-type income tax A and B would each have taxable incomes of $20,000, which taxable incomes would not reflect the relative unjustness of B's pre-tax income. Therefore, a consumption-type income tax would be unable to correct an initially unjust distribution of income.[g]

33. Is ability to pay best measured by income, or by consumption? What arguments can be made for each proposition?

"Double tax" on saving

34. John Stuart Mill argued that an income tax taxes savings twice, because "if he has the interest, it is because he abstains from using the principal; if he spends the principal, he does not receive the interest. Yet because he can do either of the two, he is taxed as if he could do both." Professor Gunn labels Mill's argument as circular. What is Gunn's reasoning?

35. Professor Gunn states that modern advocates of consumption taxation rescue the "double taxation of saving" argument from circularity by comparing the effects of an income tax and a consumption tax to a "no-tax world." While any tax leaves a taxpayer worse off in comparison to a no-tax world, a consumption tax does not change the relative attraction of immediate consumption versus saving. Gunn illustrates this point through Professor Andrews' example of an investor whose 24-year investment (at nine percent) in a no-tax world would allow eight times as much deferred consumption as would have been available in immediate consumption. A consumption tax would reduce the absolute amount of consumption that would be possible immediately or in 24 years, but would leave the relative attractiveness of

---

g. Charles R. O'Kelley, Jr., *Rawls, Justice, and the Income Tax*, 16 GA. L. REV. 1, 4 (1981).

saving unchanged—eight times as much consumption would be made possible by saving and waiting. A 33 percent income tax, however, would reduce not only the absolute return on saving but the benefit of saving vis-à-vis immediate consumption—the saver could consume only four times as much after 24 years.

36. Does Professor Gunn agree that the best way to evaluate the impact of a tax is by comparison to a no-tax world?

37. Gunn also acknowledges the argument of consumption-type tax advocates that the excessive tax burden on saving is demonstrated by reducing the tax to present value. Under a consumption tax, the present value of the tax is the same, whether the taxpayer consumes immediately or saves and later consumes both the original principal and the earnings generated by the saving. (See footnote 21 of Gunn excerpt and accompanying text.) Under an income tax, the present value of the tax is less if the taxpayer consumes immediately than if the taxpayer saves in order to consume more later.

38. In addressing the reduction of tax burdens to present value, Professor Gunn argues that such a reduction would be appropriate only if the saver actually values future consumption less than present consumption at a rate measured by prevailing interest rates—that is, only if the interest at prevailing rates does not really make the saver better off, but merely makes the future consumption equal in value to present consumption.

But, Gunn argues, the saver is actually made better off, and reduction to present value is of little relevance in this context. Indeed, sometimes future consumption is more valued than the same amount of additional present consumption. What argument is Gunn advancing in footnote 24 of his article?

39. Even if reducing future consumption to present value were appropriate, Professor Gunn argues that discounting at prevailing market interest rates would be inappropriate. Why, according to Gunn, do market interest rates overstate the amount that the saver loses by deferring consumption?

40. Professor Gunn argues, in sum, that additional tax on investment income is appropriate because the saver ultimately has *more* than the nonsaver. It is not the same amount reduced to present value, it is more.

41. Assuming real interest rates are positive (*i.e.*, that interest rates exceed inflation), an individual can choose between consuming x now, or x plus real interest at a future time. Professor Gunn argues that this return to

investment might be viewed as a payment to the saver for resisting the impatience to consume immediately. Gunn compares the interest payment to a wage paid a worker for resisting the temptation toward leisure. Viewed in this manner, would taxing the interest be overtaxing the saver?

Treasury I

42. Although they ultimately recommended against moving to a consumption-type tax, the drafters of Treasury I acknowledged that it would create a lower, and arguably fairer, tax on saving, and, in theory, that it could be simpler than the income tax. (Simplicity is easier to achieve in theoretical discussions than in concrete proposals. See Subchapter E.)

43. A major consideration in adopting a consumption-type tax would be the transition from the present system. Perhaps the most important aspect of the problem concerns accumulated wealth that has already been subjected to the income tax: Would such wealth also be subjected to the new consumption-type tax? Note that either system consistently applied would lead to only one tax—the time of wealth creation under the income tax, or the time of expenditure under the consumption-type tax. Without complicated transition rules, changing forms of tax could result in tax at both occasions. (A corresponding problem is that funds borrowed under the income tax system would have given rise to no income tax, but repayment under the new consumption regime would, absent special provision, give rise to a deduction.) Transition problems are further explored in Subchapter E.

44. Treasury I also raises what might be termed the life-cycle objection to the consumption-type tax. A typical life pattern is to consume more than is earned during young adulthood (for example, students have been known to take out loans); save during middle age; then consume savings during retirement. Does such a pattern suggest problems in the consumption tax system? Can these problems be met by making the consumption tax system sufficiently progressive?

Gifts under a consumption-type tax

45. As Treasury I points out, gifts present a conceptual challenge under a consumption tax. First, the theoretical problem is whether the donor has "consumed" the money (or money's worth) given. Presenting the "utility" view, which would treat making a gift as an act of consumption, Professor Carolyn Jones observes that "[t]he utility [a donor] derives from making the gift equals or exceeds the satisfaction to be derived from any other use" of the money

given.[h] (Else why would the donor have made the gift?)

The competing "preclusive use" approach favored by Professor Andrews holds that the donor has not made use of society's resources in a way that would prevent another from using them, and thus should not be regarded as having "consumed" by making a gift. Satisfaction, Andrews argues, is irrelevant for tax purposes: "Taxing income in the end does not and cannot provide an accurate reflection of either power or pleasure. It is, rather, simply the accumulation or utilization of economic resources, measured at market value, for private consumption."[i]

Which theory is to be preferred? Would the utility approach lead to double taxation?

46. If the preclusive-use theory were adopted, a high-bracket taxpayer could "give" money to a low-bracket family member or friend as part of a fraudulent arrangement (fraudulent if the money were to be spent for the benefit of the high-bracket "donor"). A similar problem exists under present law. Gifts of appreciated property give rise to no tax to the donor, and the donee takes a carryover basis. Upon sale, all gain is taxed to the donee, who may be in a lower bracket than the donor.

Is the fraudulent gift problem any greater under a consumption-type tax than under present law?

D. ANALYZING DIFFERENT TYPES OF SAVING

As Professor Andrews first observed, our income tax is a hybrid, with elements of both consumption and accretion taxation, and the difference between the two lies in the treatment of savings. As we have seen, the proper tax treatment of savings is debated on grounds of fairness and efficiency by advocates of consumption taxation and defenders of income taxation.

In the excerpt below, Professor McCaffery argues that in analyzing income and consumption tax bases we should recognize significant advantages and drawbacks to both ideals. Because the choice between the two ideals turns on the taxation of savings, it is important to realize that we need not automatically assume that all savings must be given equal tax treatment. Instead, each category of savings should be analyzed, to see whether economic and equity goals point toward giving relatively favorable or relatively unfavorable tax treatment to the particular type of savings. It follows that we should be open to the possibility that the ideal tax base may be some hybrid

---

h. Carolyn Jones, *Treatment of Gratuitous Transfers: Unraveling the Case for a Consumption Tax*, 29 ST. LOUIS L.J. 1155, 1171-72 (1985).

i. William D. Andrews, *Personal Deductions in an Ideal Income Tax*, 86 HARV. L. REV. 309, 356 (1972).

structure that offers more favorable tax treatment to some types of savings than to others.

Professor McCaffery's article should be read not as a proposal for any particular tax structure so much as for a method of analysis. To the degree that his article points toward a particular policy, it may be less important in the income-versus-consumption debate than in the suggestion that estate taxes may undercut important societal goals.

TAX POLICY UNDER A HYBRID INCOME-CONSUMPTION TAX
Edward J. McCaffery[*]

70 Texas Law Review 1145, 1147-48, 1165-67, 1169-73, 1175-79,

1181-92, 1194, 1196, 1198-1213, 1216 (1992)

This Article * * * has several central themes. First, we have a hybrid income-consumption tax, the precise nature of which turns on the treatment of savings. Primarily as an illustration and following the economics literature, this Article divides savings into three categories based on the positive uses of the savings: life cycle, precautionary, and bequest savings. Second, because of the different values we place on the different types of savings, some form of a hybrid may in fact be ideal and not merely a practical necessity. These values come into relatively clear focus when we break analysis down into three broad normative categories: individual welfare, aggregate or macroeconomic welfare, and general equity concerns. Finally, this Article uses these categories to show that we may indeed support a hybrid as an ideal tax scheme. * * *

[T]his Article indicates the types of questions we ought to be asking about tax policy. * * * At the end of this undertaking, much of the work on the road to concrete policy formulation will lie ahead. * * *

The Case Against the Extremes
  * * *

The Income Tax

The traditional case for an income tax rests perhaps most strongly on equitable notions of ability to pay. * * *

[A] tax based solely on income may not be ideal.

The individual efficiency concern is that the income tax distorts the choice between consumption and savings by doubly taxing the latter, thus causing taxpayers to consume more and to save less than they otherwise would. * * *

A second and logically distinct argument against the income tax is that its double tax discourages saving and leads to too little capital formation.

---

*. At time of original publication, Associate Professor of Law, University of Southern California.

* * * Indeed, a very broad consensus among political economists is that, in the long run, the world would be a better place under a consumption tax. * * *

Finally, there are also fairness arguments against an income tax and for a consumption tax. * * *

Consider the example of retirement savings. * * * Americans would be hard-pressed to understand that, while they certainly ought to save for their own retirement, those who do will be left with half as much, in present value terms, as those who do not![115] But this is exactly what an income tax does to savers. * * * It may be fairer—not just more efficient—to levy a tax based on the resources that taxpayers devote to their own needs, when and as they do so.

The Consumption Tax

* * *

In a partial equilibrium setting that considers only the consumption-savings decision, a consumption tax reduces the consumption-savings distortion and thus leads to a welfare gain and individual efficiency. Yet the partial equilibrium assumption is unrealistic; we must look beyond the consumption-savings choice alone. Given a need for constant revenue, tax rates will almost certainly go up under a consumption tax, at least in the short term. This rate increase will cause a decrease in the after-tax benefit that taxpayers receive from working, thus distorting the tradeoff between labor and leisure and producing an offsetting welfare loss. There is no a priori way of calibrating which set of distortions will be worse. * * *

Like the individual efficiency argument, the macroeconomic argument for a pure consumption tax is not completely persuasive. The inevitable rub with the argument—assuming the validity of all features leading to its basic soundness—lies in the short run, where mere mortals dwell. The argument for greater welfare in the long run is, on its own terms, predicated on reduced consumption in the present. Economists concede that there would be an instantaneous welfare loss under an immediate transition to a consumption tax. To understand what is normally presented as a graph, imagine that we are travelling along at eighty percent of our optimal capacity relative to a pure consumption tax. A change to a consumption tax promises the ultimate attainment of full capacity, but, before getting there, we will have to drop down to some lesser welfare state, perhaps sixty percent of the optimum, for a while. The problem for economists is to answer what "for a while" means—that is, to ascertain the precise period during which we would all be worse off under a

---

115. The example is based on that used by Professors Andrews, Bradford, and Warren. *See* William D. Andrews, *A Consumption-Type or Cash Flow Personal Income Tax*, 87 HARV. L. REV. 1113, 1125 (1974). * * * It compares two workers in the 33% tax bracket with the saver saving for 24 years at 9% interest rates.

transitional regime. Here, the happy consensus of economists breaks down, and the estimates vary from a low of four or five years to a high of one hundred years.

* * *

Finally, although its advocates make some strong equity arguments for the consumption tax, the income tax proponents are far from defenseless in this debate. * * * A persistent thought in our society and among income tax advocates is that wealth per se matters and ought to be taxed. * * *

Framing Discussion: The Uses of Savings

The hybrid tax system turns on the treatment of savings. * * * There are also different *types* of savings, and no a priori reason why we should treat them all the same way. * * *

Life Cycle Savings

Life cycle savings are those designed solely for the saver's future, selfish needs. The standard economic models discuss this category of use mostly in terms of the young earner's savings to fund future consumption (*e.g.*, retirement savings). Life cycle savings can be generalized, however, to include any future consumption. Saving to buy a car or a house is different only in degree from saving to fund one's retirement: in all cases, one is foregoing consumption now in order to consume later. * * *

Precautionary Savings

Whereas life cycle savings are aimed at smoothing out a consumption path throughout the taxpayer's life for normal consumption purposes, precautionary savings are built up to provide for extraordinary circumstances (*i.e.*, to hedge against risk). The most commonly thought-of risk may be sickness: a taxpayer saves to have money for medical care in the event of future illness. But any risk can lead to precautionary savings, such as risks of interrupted or lessened future earnings, of general economic troubles, or of the early death of someone on whom the taxpayer depends for support.
* * *   [A] financial vehicle—here, insurance—can perfectly match the precautionary savings need under ideal conditions. Indeed, Medicare and Medicaid are forms of paternalistically provided precautionary savings, analogous to social security's paternalistic life cycle savings. As would be expected with precautionary savings, the economics literature indicates that government-sponsored insurance programs have tended to decrease private savings.

Bequest Savings

Bequest savings represent capital built up to be given away. * * *

Residual Uses

Life cycle, precautionary, and bequest savings may not exhaust all savings motives. Some taxpayers may attempt to accumulate capital for private or public power, for peace of mind, or for lack of other things to do with their money. But ultimately money will be spent in the ordinary course of events, or it will be spent under extraordinary circumstances, or it will be given away. Our mortality assures this. Sooner or later, one of the basic labels will come to fit all savings.

It may appear that a greater problem is the overlap among the uses of savings. For example, taxpayers may save for life cycle reasons while intending that any leftovers be used for bequests. Even so, it may be quite possible, depending on the outcome of our normative exploration, to tailor a system that remains agnostic regarding the classification of savings until the moment of conversion to final use. At that moment, the distinction will necessarily become apparent, and we can tax or not tax accordingly. * * *

The Case Against Identical Treatment of Savings
* * *

Neutrality Among Different Forms of Savings

Another argument for treating all savings alike is that tax laws should be neutral across different types of savings. For reasons of equity or efficiency or both, we should not relatively encourage or discourage any one type of savings. Whatever playing field the tax law creates, it should at least be level.

This argument confuses and exalts the role of neutrality as an efficiency condition. *Ceteris paribus,* tax laws ought to be as neutral as possible to avoid distortions between choices such as savings versus consumption. But all things are rarely equal, and almost never so in the byzantine world of tax. In a no-tax setting, for example, people might appear to be indifferent between apples and oranges, consuming equal amounts of each. But it does not follow that, in a taxed world, it is efficient or even "neutral" to levy the same tax rate on apples and oranges. Consumer demand for apples at the pre-tax level might be rather inelastic—perhaps because consumers place a premium on consuming enough apples to keep doctors away. At a tax rate of fifty percent on both apples and oranges, consumers might react by continuing to purchase apples and altogether eliminating oranges, for which they have a less strong preference. * * * [A] better, more efficient—and probably even more neutral—approach would have been to tax apples alone, leaving consumers to allocate their reduced after-tax dollars among all goods, including oranges, as they deemed fit.

* * * [E]fficiency does not necessarily dictate taxing all things equally. Rather, a long-standing tenet of optimal taxation has been that when lump sum (nondistortionary) taxation is unavailable, efficiency dictates taxing commodities based on their relative elasticities: the higher the elasticity, the lower the tax. We may call this technique "Ramsey pricing," after its originator. This technique would lead to a high tax on apples, which have a

low elasticity, and a low (or no) tax on oranges, which have a high elasticity. It is Ramsey pricing and not a blind adherence to the principle of neutrality that will maximize efficiency. Neutrality becomes a mere rule of thumb to be followed when no information about the relative elasticities of different goods is available.

Of course, the efficiency norm of Ramsey pricing may yield to equity concerns. Taken to its limit, for example, Ramsey pricing would mean exorbitant excise taxes on necessities. * * *

Life Cycle Savings

This and the next two Parts examine the arguments for and against favoring each type of savings. For the most part, "favoring" will mean taxing the savings under the single, consumption tax model, and "disfavoring" will refer to the double tax, income model. * * *

The Case for Favoring
* * *

Beginning with efficiency arguments, perhaps the easiest and strongest argument for favoring life cycle savings is that the income tax distorts the choice of present versus deferred consumption by double taxing the latter. If we assume that much savings is life cycle—and the economics literature for years has supported this assumption—then the distortion of life cycle savings is particularly important. As mentioned above, a change to a consumption tax on savings leads to an unambiguous welfare gain when the savings-consumption choice alone is considered.

The second efficiency argument for life cycle savings looks to market failure. * * * [A] classic externality may be involved—a failure to provide for one's own future needs may impose costs on society as a whole in the form of increased social-welfare spending. * * *

Finally, there are at least two major equity arguments for favorable tax treatment of life cycle savings. The first is that it is fair, for one reason or another, to tax individuals on their standard of living, or what they appropriate from the common pool for their personal use. * * * The central idea is that only a consumption-type tax preserves the equality of the saver and the spender in an after-tax setting relative to their equality in a no-tax setting. * * *

The second equity argument for favoring life cycle savings is based on the belief that we should tolerate lifetime disparities in wealth because they are earned. This belief leads to a hybrid that favors life cycle and precautionary savings but not bequest savings. We can refer to this hybrid as a "consumption-*cum*-transfer tax" model. * * *

The positions of Mill, Kaldor, Rawls, Andrews, and others are rather interesting in that each favors some form of bequest or inheritance tax in addition to a personal consumption tax. Philosophically, this result is not surprising if we focus on life cycle savings. The equity notion underlying the consumption model becomes a lifetime, individualistic one. The core concept is that it is presumptively fair to allow taxpayers to decide when they should spend their own money. Yet any transfer tax is a tax on accumulation because what is transferred away as a gift or bequest is not consumed by the donor. Mill saw this clearly enough, but he defended a tax on inheritance because he viewed some tax on capital as acceptable and because he considered a tax on bequests as raising no adverse incentive effects: an heir who receives a 1000-pound bequest subject to a ten percent inheritance tax "considers the legacy as only 900 pounds."[200] This latter point, however, reflects an important misconception regarding the incentives for savings. Modern economic scholarship has shown that savers are motivated by a desire to leave bequests.[201] Thus, the adverse incentive effect is at the donor's level, not the beneficiary's. * * * If taxpayers are saving for intergenerational transfers, * * * hindering their ability to make such transfers may indeed reduce savings. We will return to this point when we consider bequest savings more directly.

Bequest saving accumulates income for the purpose of making gratuitous transfers. Gift and estate taxes impose a tax on the accumulated income upon transfer. To the extent that other types of saving are taxed only once under a consumption model, while bequest savings are taxed twice—both initially and on transfer—a hybrid system results. In describing a system of lifetime consumption taxes plus some form of tax on gratuitous transfers, Mill, Kaldor, Rawls, Andrews, and others advocate what is essentially a hybrid system that favors life cycle (and precautionary) savings but not bequest savings—that is, a consumption-*cum*-transfer tax system. * * *

The Case for Disfavoring

Recall that the first efficiency argument supporting consumption tax treatment of life cycle savings rests on the distorting effects of the income tax on the savings-consumption decision. This argument is very persuasive. But it is undermined somewhat by the fact that before-tax interest rates are likely to rise under an income tax, minimizing the welfare loss to individuals. There are two more significant problems with the argument. First, given a constant need for revenue, a move to a consumption tax will result in increased wage taxes in the short term, compounding the labor-leisure distortion. Second, unless we are prepared to go all the way to a pure consumption tax, the questions raised by the hybrid are relative ones—that is, do life cycle savings

200. JOHN S. MILL, PRINCIPLES OF POLITICAL ECONOMY, bk. V, ch. II, §7, at 822 (W.J. Ashley ed., Logmans, Green & Co. 1909) (1848).

201. *See* Laurence J. Kotlikoff, *Intergenerational Transfers and Savings*, J. ECON. PERSP., Spring 1988, at 41 [and other sources].

stand out as an efficient form of savings to tax compared to other forms of savings? Again, this depends on the compensated elasticity, or substitution effect, of the tax. There are some very good intuitive reasons to conclude that life cycle savings have a relatively low elasticity and are therefore a relatively efficient type of savings to tax. Life cycle savers may be motivated to amass a given nest egg regardless of cost. Put another way, life cycle savings may be more in the nature of necessities than luxuries.

* * * [A]n expanded social security system might be a more efficient form of favoring life cycle savings than a consumption-style tax. We might even be better able to advance equity concerns through such a public system by better apportioning life cycle savings according to need.

* * *

[F]avoring life cycle savings, especially if we do not also favor bequests, may generate perverse incentives. * * * By definition, a consumption-*cum*-transfer tax hybrid would place an added burden on accumulated capital gratuitously transferred. The flip side of this effect is that such a hybrid will favor consumption during a taxpayer's lifetime over gifts and bequests. The model would create an economic incentive to "spend down" one's resources late in life—exactly the opposite effect desired. * * * Not only would such consumption undermine the macroeconomic argument, it might even be the type of excessive, conspicuous consumption that leads to inequities, both real and perceived.

This analysis brings us to the first of the two equitable arguments against favorable tax treatment of life cycle savings: that the existence of private wealth is somehow inimical to social norms. This raises the central question of what bothers us about wealth. * * *

Instead of possession, however, it may be the private use of wealth that troubles us. This concern leads us to the second set of equitable arguments against consumption tax treatment of life cycle savings. We might share with Thorstein Veblen and others a concern with conspicuous consumption and its attendant problems for the allocation of resources and public morale.[234] Or we might agree with Kaldor that spending power is what matters, or with Andrews that standard of living is somehow the appropriate thing to be taxing. All of this discussion relates to Hobbes's argument and the general cultural case for saving, which favors (or at least does not disfavor) the hard-working saver over the idle consumer. If these were our concerns with wealth, we might logically be heading in quite a different direction than the consumption-*cum*-transfer tax ideal. If we were concerned mainly with the conspicuous

---

234. *See* THORSTEIN VEBLEN, THE THEORY OF THE LEISURE CLASS 68-101 (B.W. Huebsch ed., 1918) (1899) (discussing extensively the role an individual's consumption plays in identifying and maintaining his social class, thereby perpetuating the existence of a social hierarchy).

consumption aspect of the private use of savings, we would want a persistently progressive lifetime consumption tax and a lower tax or even no tax on transfers by gift or bequest. This combination would directly and indirectly discourage excessive consumption: directly by the progressive tax and indirectly by not discouraging bequests. I will call such a system a consumption-*sans*-transfer tax hybrid.

* * *

This extended discussion of the possible effects of the consumption-*cum*-transfer tax hybrid has illustrated * * * equity arguments against favoring life cycle savings. * * * [P]articularly if we also had a steep bequest tax, a life cycle consumption model might lead to conspicuous consumption and other real and perceived inequities without creating the optimal incentives for long-term, private savings that might truly alleviate the long-run condition of the worst off. * * *

Precautionary Savings

Precautionary savings are a form of self-insurance. Unlike life cycle savings, which are designed to meet needs in the ordinary course of life and hence to smooth out consumption paths, precautionary savings are designed to meet extraordinary needs. * * *

The Case for Favoring

A good deal of what I have said about life cycle savings applies to precautionary savings. Indeed, the traditional tax policy literature does not separate out the two uses: both fit under what Andrews would call "consumption deferred." * * * [M]any of the equity and efficiency arguments explored above apply with equal force to precautionary savings. * * *

[F]avoring precautionary savings with consumption tax treatment might correct for market failure. Taxpayers may be likely to mis-save for their own future insurance needs either because they wrongly estimate future contingencies or because they fail to consider the social benefits that such savings generate, such as lessened welfare and emergency-care spending. * * *

Finally, the equity case for favorable tax treatment is apparent. In fact, precautionary savings is the category of uses that the law is most likely to put on the favorable no-tax model. * * * [T]axpayers suffering under a hardship may lack the relative ability to pay or the capacity of unaffected taxpayers. Professor Andrews, for example, has made clear that he does not feel that medical expenditures form part of a taxpayer's material well-being.[265]

---

265. *See* William D. Andrews, *Personal Deductions in an Ideal Income Tax*, 86 HARV. L. REV. 335-37 (1972).

The Case for Disfavoring

It may at first seem hard to imagine why we would not want to favor precautionary savings, given the strong equity and efficiency appeals of this use. Upon further consideration, however, we can see that there are reasons to stop short of a full-scale consumption model for precautionary accumulation.

Precautionary savings may very well be seen by taxpayers as a type of necessity and thus be a relatively efficient type of savings to tax. This application derives from the Ramsey pricing idea. * * *

[I]t may very well be that precautionary savers are driven by a desire to obtain a certain quantum of insurance. Tax laws that help savers attain their precautionary goals sooner rather than later might ironically free up resources for consumption. * * *

Perhaps the problems with favoring precautionary savings come into focus most clearly when we look at the choice between government-sponsored and private care. If we prefer private care, then we should encourage private precautionary savings, either through institutional or self-insurance, with consumption tax treatment. But there is no a priori reason to believe that privately funded care is better than government-sponsored care. Indeed, public care may actually be more efficient and more equitable than private care. * * *

The Once and Future Hybrid

We do generally favor precautionary savings with consumption tax treatment. Life, medical, and disability insurance are all taxed essentially under the prepayment model. In the case of life insurance, the tax laws do not allow a deduction for premium payments, but the inside build-up of cash value or whole life policies is not subject to current taxation, and the proceeds or death benefits are not usually taxed. Similarly, for medical insurance, the premium payments are not generally deductible, but the proceeds are tax free. Public care programs like Medicare are also funded with after-tax dollars and the benefits, when received, are not taxed. In certain cases, the Internal Revenue Code even allows deductions for insurance premiums (or exclusions for certain employer-paid premiums), in which case the insurance receives the most favorable, no-tax treatment.
* * *

Bequest Savings

* * * [T]his Part looks first at the case for disfavoring [bequest] savings because that side of the debate has dominated the literature. * * *

To clarify one technical matter in advance, favoring bequest savings means not imposing a tax on the transfer itself, either at the beneficiary or the donor level. The beneficiary would take the bequest with a zero basis and would be subject to the consumption tax upon consuming the wealth. We can think of this model as consumption tax treatment of bequests—we are in effect allowing the beneficiary a deduction for saving (i.e., for not spending) the inheritance. I go into this matter here because the literature itself is not consistent on how it uses the term "consumption" in the context of wealth transfers, and it is necessary to make clear a meaning from the start.

The Case for Disfavoring

As seen in Mill, among others, there is a very old case made against gifts and bequests. * * *

The principal equity theme is highly egalitarian: large inheritances create an unlevel playing field. * * *

Consumption tax advocates similarly support gift and estate taxes to assure that wealth is taxed at least once each generation. * * *

The equitable case for favoring some type of bequest taxation is not typically thought to be undercut by economic considerations. If savings are actually motivated largely by precautionary and life cycle uses, taxing bequest savings ought to be relatively efficient. Again, this is an empirical matter of looking at the relative elasticity of bequest savings. Advocates of bequest taxation often seem to believe that such savings are mere leftovers, such that taxing them will not interfere with any important nontax incentives. * * *

In sum, wealth transfer taxes are a favorite in the literature. The most frequently articulated hybrid proposal is the consumption-*cum*-transfer tax model. * * *

The Case for Favoring

The case for disfavoring bequests is appealing and has dominated scholarly debate for centuries. It may nonetheless be wrong. The whole tenor of discussion begins to change when we consider some facts from the economics literature. A good deal, if not most, of savings may be motivated by a bequest motive,[307] and relatedly, bequest savings may be rather elastic to tax law changes.[308] Taxing bequests may indeed interfere with saving incentives at the donor's level. Bequest savings may be the best form of savings to favor * * * as the type of savings having the most elasticity to tax rules and by its nature having the longest, most beneficial time profile. One study has shown that prohibiting all bequests could reduce aggregate United States wealth by as much as fifty percent.[309] * * * Even though taxing bequests is not as onerous as prohibiting them, such a significant effect should give the transfer tax

---

307. *See supra* note 201 and accompanying text.

308. The actual elasticity of bequest savings is an empirical matter that requires further study. However, compared to life cycle and precautionary savings, there are strong intuitive reasons to believe that bequest savings are relatively elastic because of their "leftover" status.

309. *See* Laurence J. Kotlikoff, *Introduction to Part I: Saving Motives, in* WHAT DETERMINES SAVINGS? 39, 41 (1989).

advocates pause. * * *

[Bequest] savings may be a stable source of capital. The marginal propensity to consume out of income appears to be greater than out of wealth, which means that people are more likely to spend their wages than reach into savings or a bequest. * * *

In any event, the various studies and statistics begin to cast considerable doubt on the tendency of the literature to advocate a lifetime consumption-*cum*-transfer tax. This tendency may rest on the naive assumption, evident in Mill, that because bequests represent leftover savings, taxing them would not create adverse incentives and would have little effect on capital accumulation. If people save for the purpose of transferring wealth, however, and if such savings are responsive to the effective tax rate on bequests, then quite a different story emerges. At least to the extent that we are concerned with the macroeconomic and efficiency gains promised by the consumption model, we should be reluctant to impose too high a toll on bequests.
        * * *

If we are going to settle for a hybrid, a certain logic argues for choosing the consumption features most likely to achieve long-run benefits. Of all forms of savings, bequest savings may have the greatest payoff in this sense. Indeed, this logic continues to advocate a persistently progressive lifetime consumption tax combined with a reduced or eliminated transfer tax *(i.e.,* a consumption-*sans*-transfer tax hybrid)—precisely the opposite of the balance struck by Mill, Rawls, and others. This may not be simply a matter of preferring efficiency to equity. Instead, it may well be a principled view that, across generations, the best way to advance the cause of the least advantaged may be to allow and even encourage bequest savings.
        * * *

The progressive lifetime consumption-*sans*-transfer tax hybrid would allow wealth to stay in private hands, but the public would effectively have a lien on the wealth: if and when savers attempted to consume their savings—that is, to appropriate their wealth for private use—the government would step in to claim its share. In the case of large amounts of savings, under the steep and persistent progressivity that would be an integral feature of this hybrid, the government's share would be generous. This solution would thus allow wealth to be private for the purposes of investment decision, but in an important sense, the law would convert much of the capital into public form.

        * * * If the concern is with the private use of wealth rather than with its possession—a position arguably inherent in the logic of the consumption tax theory—then exempting bequests may lessen the offensive excess consumption at the donors' level. Once again, the point comes into sharper focus when we consider the common consumption-*cum*-transfer tax model: by disfavoring

bequests relative to consumption, this model encourages private consumption. If we are concerned about accumulating and maintaining a common pool of funds, however, we should do precisely the opposite—steeply taxing conspicuous private consumption and exempting bequests. * * *

Indeed, if it is the possession of wealth and not its use that concerns us, we should confront the possibility that this concern is motivated by envy. Once we have shown that private capital is a form of public good and taken steps to hinder its private appropriation, what further reason do we have to disparage its presence? * * *

If we continue to oppose all bequests, we might have to live with a lower standard of living for all. * * *

Notes and Questions

47. Professor McCaffery states that both efficiency and fairness arguments can be levied against the income tax. What are these?

48. The income tax is said to distort the choice between saving and consumption, but a consumption tax would, at least initially, be expected to have higher rates than an income tax. Why? These higher rates would carry their own distortion—taxpayers would inefficiently substitute leisure for labor.

49. Professor McCaffery notes that economists are in agreement that our economy would be benefitted in the long run by the change to a consumption tax. But we would be worse off "for a while." For how long would we be worse off, according to the economists?

50. Professor McCaffery's article focuses on savings, because the essential difference between the consumption tax and the accretion tax turns on how we treat savings; consumption is part of either tax base. For purposes of analysis, he then divides savings into three components. What are these? How is each described?

51. As Professor McCaffery acknowledges, people frequently save for mixed motives. "For example, taxpayers may save for life cycle reasons while intending that any leftovers be used for bequests." In such cases, which may well account for a large fraction of total savings, does McCaffery successfully explain how we can treat savings differently based upon the motivation for the saving?

52. Professor McCaffery argues that we should not necessarily tax all savings the same. We should, generally, tax more heavily forms of saving that

are relatively inelastic (*i.e.*, saving that will tend to occur even in the face of relatively heavy taxation). (Similarly, he states, we should tax apples and not oranges if the demand for apples is relatively inelastic and the demand for oranges is relatively elastic.) Why should we do this? What is meant by Ramsey pricing?

53. Professor McCaffery suggests that "life cycle savers may be motivated to amass a given nest egg regardless of cost." What is the relevance of this observation for tax policy?

54. In discussing life cycle and precautionary savings, Professor McCaffery refers to an "externality" that may lead to undersaving in preparation for old age or disability. What is this externality? In what direction does it point with respect to treating these forms of savings favorably in the tax system?

55. What are other arguments that suggest the tax system should favor life cycle savings?

56. Consider McCaffery's suggestion that expanding the Social Security system might be more efficient than adopting consumption taxation in fostering life cycle savings. Social Security taxes can be regarded as forcing saving for retirement (life cycle saving), while consumption taxation might only encourage such saving. McCaffery might reasonably argue that, given the spending habits of most Americans, mere encouragement would be insufficient for most.

The political problem of government-forced saving is that a government program will do more than merely require saving for the benefit of the saver—it is likely to redistribute as well. McCaffery views this as an advantage ("We might even be better able to advance equity concerns"), but not all will agree.

57. Professor McCaffery points to several indications in present law that precautionary saving is favorably taxed. What are these present-law provisions?

58. Professor McCaffery suggests that the issue of whether the taxing system should treat precautionary saving favorably may come down to "the choice between government-sponsored and private care." Why might this be the case? Which should the tax system encourage?

59. The consumption tax model as applied to bequest saving would levy no tax at all on the testator who accumulated the wealth, because the testator did not consume; the heir would take a zero basis and therefore pay consumption tax when consumption occurred—which could be a long time.

Professor McCaffery notes that most supporters of consumption taxation also favor transfer taxes. Their "consumption-*cum*-transfer" model is less favorable to bequest savings than the consumption tax alone (the "consumption-*sans*-transfer" model). On the other hand, the combination of consumption and transfer taxes is more favorable to bequest savings than an accretion tax plus transfer taxes—arguably, a three-level tax.

If we imposed a consumption tax plus transfer taxes, which forms of savings—life cycle, precautionary, and bequest—would be favored and disfavored relative to the others?

60. Professor McCaffery views the imposition of estate taxes in addition to the general tax base (income or consumption) as disfavoring bequest savings. What are the traditional arguments supporting such a policy?

61. As noted above, most advocates of consumption-type taxation also favor transfer taxes. Why might the arguments favoring transfer taxes be viewed as stronger under a consumption tax regime than under an income tax system? Do you think the case for transfer taxation would be stronger under a consumption tax than under the income tax?

62. Professor McCaffery argues that policy should take account of the likelihood that much saving is motivated by the desire to leave a bequest, and that "bequest savings may be relatively elastic to tax law changes." Do you think these propositions are correct? If they are correct, what would be the impact on national savings of taxing bequest savings heavily?

63. The last sentence excerpted from Professor McCaffery's article argues that opposition to bequest savings could result in "a lower standard of living for all." Why might "all" suffer if only the estates of the wealthiest one or two percent of decedents are subject to estate taxes?

64. Why might discouraging bequest savings—through high transfer taxes, for example—encourage conspicuous consumption? Would that be bad?

65. Adoption of a consumption-type tax rather than an income tax would tend tend to favor saving in general.

But what practical use, if any, can we make of analysis of different types of savings? Obviously, the tax system cannot attempt to determine individual motivation in saving, so we cannot tailor a tax provision based on why an individual taxpayer engaged in a particular form of saving. If we concluded that tax law should favor life cycle savings, or precautionary savings, or bequest savings, how might those conclusions be reflected in actual tax provisions?

66.   After praising the hybrid, in the end Professor McCaffery exhibits considerable sympathy for a progressive consumption tax coupled with abolition of transfer taxes. He argues that savings are good for society as a whole, and that we should encourage elderly taxpayers to pass along their savings to the next generation rather than engage in conspicuous consumption. If the heirs continue the investment, society is benefitted; if, instead, they liquidate and consume the savings, they will be subjected to a consumption tax "of steep and persistent progressivity."

Readers of the article excerpted above will not be surprised that two years after its publication, Professor McCaffery set forth a detailed proposal for a "progressive consumption-without-estate tax."[j]

67.   Keep the issues raised in this subchapter in mind when studying transfer taxes in Chapter Nine.

E. PROPOSALS IN THE POLITICAL ARENA

Thus far, this chapter has focused on the academic debate about a consumption-type tax. We turn now to a sampling of the same debate cast in a form directed at Congress and the broader public.

Professor Hall and Dr. Rabushka advocate what they describe as a single consumption tax comprised of two components—an individual tax on wages, salaries, and (when received) pensions; and a business tax. The business tax base allows for deduction of inputs from other businesses and for labor costs, but, notably, no deduction for interest. Both taxes would be imposed at the same flat rate (the authors suggest 19 percent). Considerable progressivity (more technically, degressivity) would be introduced into the individual tax by allowance of a large, untaxed "personal allowance."

The second excerpt is from an extensive and detailed "prototype" prepared by Alliance USA, a nonprofit corporation urging adoption of the Universal Savings Allowance, or USA, tax proposal. Businesses would be subjected to a flat-rate tax of about 10 percent (a subtraction-type VAT). The USA business tax would have a broader base than the Hall & Rabushka business tax,

---

j. Edward J. McCaffery, *The Uneasy Case for Wealth Transfer Taxation*, 104 YALE L.J. 283 (1994).

because USA would allow no deduction for employee compensation. Individuals would pay a progressive tax on income, including not only wages and salaries but income from property, but would be allowed an unlimited deduction for net savings.

Former Representative Richard Armey (R-TX), then House Majority Leader, introduced a bill based on the Hall & Rabushka proposal. Former Senators Nunn (D-GA) and Domenici (R-NM) offered a bill quite similar to the Alliance USA prototype. References (in the Penner and Nolan excerpts) to "the Armey bill" or to "Nunn-Domenici" can generally be understood as also referring, respectively, to the Hall & Rabushka and Alliance USA proposals.

The third excerpt is from an article written by Dr. Rudolph Penner, an economist who consulted in the crafting of the Alliance USA and Nunn-Domenici proposals. In addition to explaining the proposals, Dr. Penner's article discusses the enormous difficulty—both technical and political—involved in moving beyond the model of a new tax system to deal with the multitude of issues that must be addressed in constructing an actual new system. Among the most difficult of the practical problems is the transition from present law to the proposed new system; this topic will be further explored in the Notes and Questions.

Finally, a distinguished member of the tax bar, John Nolan, compares proposed consumption-type taxes to present law. While Mr. Nolan finds favorable features in the proposals, he is generally skeptical.

THE FLAT TAX
Robert E. Hall[*] & Alvin Rabushka[**]
Pages 52-64, 71-73, 78-80, 99-100 (2d ed. 1995)

Tax forms really can fit on postcards. A cleanly designed tax system takes only a few elementary calculations, in contrast to the hopeless complexity of today's income taxes. In this chapter, we present a complete plan for a whole new tax system that puts a low tax rate on a comprehensive definition of income. Because its base is broad, the astonishingly low 19 percent tax rate raises the same revenue as does the current tax system. The tax on families is fair and progressive: the poor pay no tax at all, and the fraction of income that a family pays rises with income. The system is simple and easy to understand. And the tax operates on the consumption tax principle—families are taxed on what they take out of the economy, not what they put into it.

Our system rests on a basic administrative principle: income should be

---

[*]. At time of original publication, Professor of Economics and Senior Fellow at the Hoover Institution, Stanford University.

[**]. At time of original publication, Senior Fellow at the Hoover Institution, Stanford University.

taxed exactly once as close as possible to its source. * * *

Under our plan, all income is taxed at the same rate. Equality of tax rates is a basic concept of the flat tax. Its logic is much more profound than just the simplicity of calculation with a single tax rate. Whenever different forms of income are taxed at different rates or different taxpayers face different rates, the public figures out how to take advantage of the differential.

Progressivity, Efficiency, and Simplicity

Limiting the burden of taxes on the poor is a central principle of tax reform. * * * We reject sales and value-added taxes for this reason. The current federal tax system avoids taxing the poor, and we think it should stay that way.

Exempting the poor from taxes does not require graduated tax rates rising to high levels for upper-income families. A flat rate, applied to all income above a generous personal allowance, provides progressivity without creating important differences in tax rates. * * *

Our proposal is based squarely on the principle of consumption taxation. Saving is untaxed, thus solving the problem that has perplexed the designers of the current tax system, which contains an incredible hodgepodge of savings and investment incentives. As a general matter, the current system puts substantial taxes on the earnings from savings. On that account, the economy is biased toward too little saving and too much consumption. * * * In our system, there is a single, coherent provision for taxing the return to saving. All income is taxed, but the earnings from saved income are not taxed further. * * *

An Integrated Flat Tax

Our flat tax applies to both businesses and individuals. Although our system has two separate tax forms—one for business income and the other for wages and salaries—it is an integrated system. When we speak of its virtues, such as its equal taxation of all types of income, we mean the system, not one of its two parts. As we will explain, the business tax is not just a replacement for the existing corporate income tax. It covers all businesses, not just corporations. And it covers interest income, which is currently taxed under the personal income tax.

In our system, all income is classified as either business income or wages (including salaries and retirement benefits). The system is airtight. Taxes on both types of income are equal. The wage tax has features to make the overall system progressive. Both taxes have postcard forms. The low tax rate of 19 percent is enough to match the revenue of the federal tax system as it existed in 1993, the last full year of data available as we write.

Here is the logic of our system, stripped to basics: We want to tax consumption. The public does one of two things with its income—spends it or invests it. We can measure consumption as income minus investment. A really simple tax would just have each firm pay tax on the total amount of income generated by the firm less that firm's investment in plant and equipment. The value-added tax works just that way. But a value-added tax is unfair because it is not progressive. That's why we break the tax in two. The firm pays tax on all the income generated at the firm except the income paid to its workers. The workers pay tax on what they earn, and the tax they pay is progressive.

To measure the total amount of income generated at a business, the best approach is to take the total receipts of the firm over the year and subtract the payments the firm has made to its workers and suppliers. This approach guarantees a comprehensive tax base. The successful value-added taxes in Europe work this way. The base for the business tax is the following:

Total revenue from sales of goods and services

less

purchases of inputs from other firms

less

wages, salaries, and pensions paid to workers

less

purchases of plant and equipment

The other piece is the wage tax. Each family pays 19 percent of its wage, salary, and pension income over a family allowance (the allowance makes the system progressive). The base for the compensation tax is total wages, salaries, and retirement benefits less the total amount of family allowances.

Table 3.1 is a calculation of flat-tax revenue based on the U.S. National Income and Product Accounts for 1993. The first line shows gross domestic product, the most comprehensive measure of income throughout the economy. The next line is indirect business taxes that are included in GDP but that would not be taxed under the flat tax, such as sales and excise taxes. Line 3, income included in GDP but not in the tax base, is mostly the value of houses owned and lived in by families; this income does not go through the market. Wages, salaries, and pensions, line 4, would be reported on the first line of the wage-tax form and would be deducted by businesses. Investment, line 5, is the amount spent by businesses purchasing new plant and equipment (each business could also deduct its purchases of used plant and equipment, but these would be included in the taxable income of the selling business and would net out in the aggregate). Line 6 shows the taxable income of all businesses after they have deducted their wages and investment. The revenue from the business tax, line 7, is 19 percent of the tax base on line 6. Line 8 shows the amount of family allowances that would be deducted. The wage-tax base on line 9 shows the amount of wages, salaries, and pensions left after deducting all family allowances from the amount on line 4. The wage-tax revenue on line 10 is 19 percent of the base. Total flat-tax revenue on line 11 is $627 billion. Lines 12 and 13 show the actual revenue from the personal and corporate income taxes. The total actual revenue on line 14 is also $627 billion. The flat-tax revenue and the actual revenue are the same, by design. We propose to reproduce the revenue of the actual income tax system, not to raise or lower it.

TABLE 3.1

FLAT-TAX REVENUES COMPARED WITH CURRENT REVENUES

Line	Income or Revenue	Billions of Dollars
1	Gross domestic product	$6,374
2	Indirect business tax	431
3	Income included in GDP but not in tax base	217
4	Wages, salaries, and pensions	3,100
5	Investment	723
6	Business-tax base (line 1 minus lines 2 through 5)	1,903
7	Business-tax revenue (19 percent of line 6)	362
8	Family allowances	1,705
9	Wage-tax base (line 4 less line 8)	1,395
10	Wage-tax revenue (19 percent of line 9)	265
11	Total flat-tax revenue (line 7 plus line 10)	627
12	Actual personal income tax	510
13	Actual corporate income tax	118
14	Total actual revenue (line 12 plus line 13)	627

These computations show that in 1993 the revenue from the corporate income tax, with a tax rate of 35 percent, was $118 billion. The revenue from our business tax at a rate of 19 percent would have been $362 billion, just over three times as much, even though the tax rate is not much more than half the current corporate rate.[k] There are three main reasons that the flat business tax yields more revenue than does the existing corporate tax. First, slightly more than half of business income is from noncorporate businesses—professional partnerships, proprietorships, and the like. Second, our business tax does not permit the deduction of interest paid by businesses, whereas the corporate income tax does. Third, the business tax puts a tax on fringe benefits, which escape any taxation in the current system.

    * * *

Another limitation on our calculations is that we do not consider the way the economy would respond to tax reform. In [a portion of the book not excerpted], we discuss why the flat tax would increase national income and tax revenue. But part of that process might involve a burst of investment, which would temporarily depress flat-tax revenue because of the expensing of investment. Only a detailed analysis using data not available to us would determine whether we have over- or underestimated the revenue from the flat tax. We do not think we are far off, however.

The Individual Wage Tax

The individual wage tax has a single purpose—to tax the large fraction of income that employers pay as cash to their workers. It is not a tax system by itself but is one of the two major parts of the complete system. The base of the tax is defined narrowly and precisely as actual payments of wages, salaries, and pensions. Pension contributions and other fringe benefits paid by employers are not counted as part of wages. In other words, the tax on pension income is paid when the retired worker actually receives the pension, not when the employer sets aside the money to pay the future pension. This principle applies even if the employer pays into a completely separate pension fund, if the worker makes a voluntary contribution to a 401(k) program, or if the worker contributes to a Keogh, IRA, or SEP fund.

    * * * To make the tax system progressive, only earnings over a personal or family allowance are taxed. The allowance is $25,500 for a family of four in 1995 but would rise with the cost of living in later years. All the taxpayer has to do is report total wages, salaries, and pensions at the top, compute the family allowance based on marital status and number of dependents, subtract the allowance, multiply by 19 percent to compute the tax, take account of withholding, and pay the difference or apply for a refund. For about 80 percent of the population, filling out this postcard once a year would be the only effort needed to satisfy the Internal Revenue Service. What a change from the many pages of schedules the frustrated taxpayer fills out today!

For the 80 percent of taxpayers who don't run businesses, the individual

---

k. Present law taxes corporations under a progressive rate structure, which begins at 15%, for corporations earning less than $50,000, and rises to 35%. Section 11. (Ed.)

wage tax would be the only tax to worry about. Many features of current taxes would disappear, including charitable deductions, mortgage interest deductions, capital gains taxes, dividend taxes, and interest taxes. * * *

Anyone who is self-employed or pays expenses directly in connection with making a living will need to file the business tax to get the proper deduction for expenses. Fortunately, the business-tax form is even simpler than the wage-tax form.

Again, we stress that the wage tax is not a complete income tax on individuals; it taxes only wages, salaries, and pensions. The companion business tax picks up all other components of income. Together they form an airtight tax system.

The Business Tax

It is not the purpose of the business tax to tax businesses. Fundamentally, people pay taxes, not businesses. The idea of the business tax is to collect the tax that the owners of a business owe on the income produced by the business. Collecting business income tax at the source of the income avoids one of the biggest causes of leakage in the tax system today: Interest can pass through many layers where it is invariably deducted when it is paid out but frequently not reported as income.

Airtight taxation of individual business income at the source is possible because we already know the tax rate of all of the owners of the business—it is the common flat rate paid by all taxpayers. If the tax system has graduated rates, taxation at the source becomes a problem. If each owner is to be taxed at that owner's rate, the business would have to find out the tax rate applicable to each owner and apply that rate to the income produced in the business for that owner. * * * Source taxation is only practical when a single rate is applied to all owners. Because source taxation is reliable and inexpensive, it is a powerful practical argument for using a single rate for all business income.

The business tax is a giant, comprehensive withholding tax on all types of income other than wages, salaries, and pensions. It is carefully designed to tax every bit of income outside of wages but to tax it only once. The business tax does not have deductions for interest payments, dividends, or any other type of payment to the owners of the business. As a result, all income that people receive from business activity has already been taxed. Because the tax has already been paid, the tax system does not need to worry about what happens to interest, dividends, or capital gains after these types of income leave the firm, resulting in an enormously simplified and improved tax system. Today, the IRS receives more than a billion Form 1099s, which keep track of interest and dividends, and must make an overwhelming effort to match these forms to the 1040s filed by the recipients. The only reason for a Form 1099 is to track income as it makes its way from the business where it originates to the ultimate recipient. Not a single Form 1099 would be needed under a flat tax with business income taxed at the source.

The way that we have set up the business tax is not arbitrary—on the contrary, it is dictated by the principles we set forth at the beginning of this chapter. The tax would be assessed on all the income originating in a business but not on any income that originates in other businesses or on the wages, salaries, and pensions paid to employees. The types of income taxed by the business tax would include:

* Profits from the use of plant and equipment
* Profits from ideas embodied in copyrights, patents, trade secrets, and the like
* Profits from past organization-building, marketing, and advertising efforts
* Earnings of key executives and others who are owners as well as employees and who are paid less than they contribute to the business
* Earnings of doctors, lawyers, and other professionals who have businesses organized as proprietorships or partnerships
* Rent earned from apartments and other real estate
* Fringe benefits provided to workers

All a business's income derives from the sale of its products and services. On the top line of the business-tax form goes the gross sales of the business—its proceeds from the sale of all its products. But some of the proceeds come from the resale of inputs and parts the firm purchased; the tax has already been paid on those items because the seller also has to pay the business tax. Thus, the firm can deduct the cost of all the goods, materials, and services it purchases to make the product it sells. In addition, it can deduct its wages, salaries, and pensions, for, under our wage tax, the taxes on those will be paid by the workers receiving them. Finally, the business can deduct all its outlays for plant, equipment, and land. * * *

Everything left from this calculation is the income originating in the firm and is taxed at the flat rate of 19 percent. In most businesses, there is enough left that the prospective revenue from the business tax is the $362 billion we computed earlier. Many deductions allowed to businesses under current laws are eliminated in our plan, including interest payments and fringe benefits. But our excluding these deductions is not an arbitrary move to increase the tax base. In all cases, eliminating deductions, when combined with the other features of our system, moves toward the goal of taxing all income once at a common, low rate and achieving a broad consumption tax.

Eliminating the deduction for interest paid by businesses is a central part of our general plan to tax business income at the source. It makes sense because we propose not to tax interest received by individuals. The tax that the government now hopes (sometimes in vain) that individuals will pay will assuredly be paid by the business itself.

We sweep away the whole complicated apparatus of depreciation deductions, but we replace it with something more favorable for capital formation, an immediate 100 percent first-year tax write-off of all investment spending. Sometimes this approach is called expensing of investment; it is standard in the value-added approach to consumption taxation. In other words, we don't deny depreciation deductions; we enhance them. More on this shortly.

Fringe benefits are outside the current tax system entirely, which makes no sense. The cost of fringes is deductible by businesses, but workers are not taxed on the value of the fringes. Consequently, fringes have a big advantage over cash wages. As taxation has become heavier and heavier, fringes have become more and more important in the total package offered by employers to workers—fringes were only 1.2 percent of total compensation in 1929, when income taxes were unimportant, but reached almost 18 percent in 1993. The explosion of fringes is strictly an artifact of taxation and thus an economically inefficient way to pay workers. Were the tax system neutral, with equal taxes on fringes and cash, workers would rather take their income in cash and make their own decisions about health and life insurance, parking, exercise facilities, and all the other things they now get from their employers without much choice. Further, failing to tax fringes means that taxes on other types of income are all the higher. Bringing all types of income under the tax system is essential for low rates.

Under our system, each business would file a simple form. Even the largest business (General Motors Corporation in 1993, with $138 billion in sales) would fill out our simple postcard form. Every line on the form is a well defined number obtained directly from the business's accounting records. * * *

The taxable income computed bears little resemblance to anyone's notion of profit. The business tax is not a profit tax. When a company is having an outstanding year in sales and profits but is building new factories to handle rapid growth, it may well have a low or even negative taxable income. That's fine—later, when expansion slows but sales are at a high level, the income generated will be taxed at 19 percent.

Because the business tax treats investment in plant, equipment, and land as an expense, companies in the start-up period will have negative taxable income. But the government will not write a check for the negative tax on the negative income. Whenever the government has a policy of writing checks, clever people abuse the opportunity. Instead, the negative tax would be carried forward to future years, when the business should have a positive taxable income. There is no limit to the number of years of carry forward.

Moreover, balances carried forward will earn the market rate of interest (6 percent in 1995). * * *

Investment Incentives

Expensing investment eliminates the double taxation of saving, another way to express the most economically significant feature of expensing. Under an income tax, people pay tax once when they earn and save and again when the savings earn a return. With expensing, the first tax is abolished. Saving is, in effect, deducted in computing the tax. Later, the return to the saving is taxed through the business tax.

The easiest way to show that expensing investment is a consumption tax arises when someone invests directly in a personally owned business. Suppose a taxpayer receives $1,000 in earnings and turns around and buys a piece of business equipment for $1,000. Under the flat tax, there is a tax of $190 on the earnings but also a deduction worth $190 in reduced taxes for the equipment purchase. On net, there is no tax. The taxpayer has not consumed any of the original $1,000. Later the taxpayer will receive business income representing the earnings of the machine, which will be taxed at 19 percent. If the taxpayer chooses to consume rather than invest again, there will be a 19 percent tax on the consumption. So the overall effect is a 19 percent consumption tax.

Most people, however, don't invest by directly purchasing machines. The U.S. economy has wonderfully developed financial markets for channeling savings from individual savers to businesses who have good investment opportunities. Individuals invest by purchasing shares or bonds, and the firms then purchase plant and equipment. The tax system we propose taxes the consumption of individuals in this environment as well. Suppose the same taxpayer pays the $190 tax on the same $1,000 and puts the remaining $810 into the stock market. For simplicity, suppose that the share pays out to its owner all the after-tax earnings on equipment costing $1,000. (That assumption makes sense because the firm could buy $1,000 worth of equipment with the $810 from our taxpayer plus the tax write-off worth $190 that would come with the equipment purchase.) Our taxpayer gets the advantage of the investment write-off even though there is no deduction for purchasing the share. The market passes the incentive from the firm on to the individual investor.

Another possibility for the taxpayer is to buy a bond for $810. Again, the firm issuing the bond can buy a $1,000 machine with the $810, after taking advantage of the tax deduction. To compete with the returns available in the stock market, however, the bond must pay the same returns as a stock selling for the same price, which in turn is equal to the after-tax earnings of the machine, so it won't matter how the taxpayer invests the $810. In all cases, there is effectively no tax for saved income; the tax is payable only when the income is consumed.

In our system, any investment, in effect, would have the same economic advantage that a 401(k), IRA, or Keogh account has in the current tax system. And we achieve this desirable goal by reducing the amount of record keeping and reporting. Today, taxpayers have to deduct their Keogh-IRA contributions on their Form 1040s and then report the distributions from the funds as income when they retire. Moreover, proponents of the cash-flow consumption tax would extend these requirements to all forms of saving. Our system would accomplish the same goal without any forms or record keeping.

Capital Gains

* * *

Capital gains would be taxed exclusively at the business level, not at the personal level. In other words, our system would eliminate the double taxation of capital gains inherent in the current tax system. To see how this works, consider the common stock of a corporation. The market value of the stock is the capitalization of its future earnings. Because the owners of the stock will receive their earnings after the corporation has paid the business tax, the market capitalizes after-tax earnings. A capital gain occurs when the market perceives that prospective after-tax earnings have risen. When the higher earnings materialize in the future, they will be correspondingly taxed. In a tax system like the current one, with both an income tax and a capital gains tax, there is double taxation. * * *

Capital gains on owner-occupied houses are not taxed under our proposal. Few capital gains on houses are taxed under the current system—gains can be rolled over, there is an exclusion for older home sellers, and gains are never taxed at death. Excluding capital gains on houses makes sense because state and local governments put substantial property taxes on houses in relation to their values. Adding a capital gains tax on top of property taxes is double taxation in the same way that adding a capital gains tax on top of an income tax is double taxation of business income.

The Transition

* * *

Depreciation Deductions

Existing law lets businesses deduct the cost of an investment on a declining schedule over many years. From the point of view of the business, multiyear depreciation deductions are not as attractive as the first-year write-off prescribed in the flat tax. No business will complain about the flat tax as far as future investment is concerned. But businesses may well protest the unexpected elimination of the unused depreciation they thought they would be able to take on the plant and equipment they installed before the tax reform. Without special transition provisions, these deductions would simply be lost.

How much is at stake? In 1992, total depreciation deductions under the personal and corporate income taxes came to $597 billion. * * *

If Congress chose to honor all unused depreciation from investment predating tax reform, it would take about $597 billion out of the tax base for 1995. To raise the same amount of revenue as our 19 percent rate, the tax rate would have to rise to about 20.1 percent.

* * *

If Congress did opt to honor past depreciation, it should recognize that the higher tax rate needed to make up for the lost revenue is temporary. Within five years, the bulk of the existing capital would be depreciated and the tax rate should be brought back to 19 percent. From the outset, the tax rate should be committed to drop to 19 percent as soon as the transition depreciation is paid off.

Interest Deductions

* * *

Our tax reform calls for the parallel removal of interest deduction and interest taxation. If a transitional measure allows deductions for interest on outstanding debt, it should also require taxation of that interest as income of the lender. If all deductions are completely matched with taxation on the other side, then a transition provision to protect existing interest deductions would have no effect on revenue. In that respect, interest deductions are easier to handle in the transition than depreciation deductions.

If Congress decides that a transitional measure to protect interest deductions is needed, we suggest the following. Any borrower may choose to treat interest payments as a tax deduction. If the borrower so chooses, the lender must treat the interest as taxable income. But the borrower's deduction should be only 90 percent of the actual interest payment, while the lender's taxable income should include 100 percent of the interest receipts.

Under this transitional plan, borrowers would be protected for almost all their existing deductions. Someone whose personal finances would become untenable if the mortgage-interest deduction were suddenly eliminated can surely get through with 90 percent of the earlier deduction. But the plan builds in an incentive for renegotiating the interest payments. Suppose a family is paying $10,000 in annual mortgage interest. It could stick with this payment and deduct $9,000 per year. Its net cost, after subtracting the value of its deduction with the 19 percent tax rate, would be $8,290. The net income to the bank, after subtracting the 19 percent tax it pays on the whole $10,000, would be $8,100. Alternatively, the family could accept a deal proposed by the bank: The interest payment would be lowered to $8,200 by rewriting the mortgage. * * * The deal will be beneficial to both.

* * *

As far as revenue is concerned, this plan would actually add a bit to federal revenue in comparison to the pure flat tax. Whenever a borrower exercised the right to deduct interest, the government would collect more revenue from the lender than it would lose from the borrower. As more and more deals were rewritten to eliminate deductions and lower interest, the excess revenue would disappear and we would be left with the pure flat tax.

Charitable Contributions

Deducting contributions to worthy causes would be a thing of the past under our tax reform. Will the nation stop supporting its churches, hospitals, museums, and opera companies when the tax deduction disappears? We think not. But we should also be clear that incentives matter—the current tax system with high marginal rates and tax deductions provides inappropriately high incentives for some contributions. The immediate effect of tax reform may be a small decline in giving. Later, as the economy surges forward under the impetus of improved incentives for productive activity, giving will recover and likely exceed its current levels.

In 1991, total cash contributions to charitable causes were about $117 billion. Of this, only $61 billion was deducted on personal tax returns. Almost half of all contributions were not affected by the law permitting deduction. We confidently expect that the $56 billion in contributions being made today without any special tax benefits will continue. Further, the bulk of contributions are from people in modest tax brackets—only $28 billion in contributions were deducted in 1991 by families with taxable incomes of more than $75,000. In this connection, it is important to understand that well more than half of all cash contributions go to churches and that these gifts are generally from the middle of the income distribution.

Churches have nothing to fear from tax reform and, like most people and institutions, would have much to gain from better economic conditions brought about by reform. Despite their dominant position in gifts, churches are not the leaders in fighting a tax reform that denies deductions. Instead, institutions serving the absolute economic and social elite—universities, symphonies, opera companies, ballets, and museums—are protesting the loudest. No compelling case has ever been made that these worthy undertakings should be financed by anyone but their customers. * * *

Major tax cuts in 1981 and 1986 cut the top marginal tax rate from 70 percent to 50 percent and then to 28 percent. As a result, major donors shifted from spending thirty-cent dollars to spending fifty-cent and then seventy-two-cent dollars for tax-deductible gifts. Despite these major reductions in incentives for the rich to give, donations to charity grew robustly. * * *

UNLIMITED SAVINGS ALLOWANCE (USA) TAX SYSTEM
Alliance USA*

66 Tax Notes 1482, 1487-94, 1514-15 (1995)

The USA Tax System is designed to replace on a revenue-neutral basis the present corporate and individual income taxes in Subtitle A of the IRC of 1986. The proposed new tax system consists of two parts.

A [10%][1] flat-rate Business Tax that applies to all organizational forms of businesses, corporate and noncorporate, and that allows a deduction for business capital investment.

A graduated-rate Individual Tax that applies to individuals and that allows a deduction for personal savings.

The centerpiece of the USA Tax System is the Unlimited Savings Allowance from which the new tax system for America's future derives its name. The concept is a simple but powerful one that views Americans not as payers of taxes but as the producers of the income and the providers of the savings on which a growing economy and higher living standards depend. Everyone has a stake, a large one, in fact, in the national stock of savings whether or not they personally own any of that savings at the present time.

Under the USA Tax System, when people earn income, save part of it and add to the national stock of savings, they get a tax deduction. When they take their income out of savings and reduce the national stock, they pay tax on that income. For so long as people have their income invested for everyone's benefit, including their own, they do not have to pay tax on that income.

Putting aside a part of earnings in a savings account, a stock or bond or in their own small business is not the only way that Americans can invest in the future and create even more income for themselves and everyone else. They can and should also invest in human capital. Investment in their own education and training and in the education of their children will produce a large, long lasting return on investment in which everyone will share.

The USA Tax System provides a limited deduction for education expenses. This deduction works in tandem with the Unlimited Savings Allowance. Parents will be able to set aside tax-deferred income for their children's education. When they withdraw the income in the future to pay

---

*. The paper was prepared for Alliance USA by two legal consultants, Ernest S. Christian and George J. Schutzer, with advice from two economic consultants, Rudolph G. Penner and Barry K. Rogstad, at the request of the Alliance's co-chairmen, Paul H. O'Neill and Robert K. Lutz, and under the administrative supervision of its Executive Director, Barbara W. North.

1. Throughout this document, the drafters placed tax rates in brackets, apparently contemplating that their concept might be used with different tax rates. (Ed.)

qualified tuition, the income will not be taxed to the extent offset by the deduction for education expenses.

For lower and middle-income Americans who work for salaries and wages, the existing FICA payroll tax withheld from their paychecks is a heavy burden. The USA Tax System provides a payroll tax credit that phases out as income rises and the payroll tax becomes less of a burden in proportion to income.

The USA Tax System contains important new rules related to imports and exports, and for American companies directly competing in the global marketplace. These innovations are intended to level the international playing field and let American goods, skill and know-how, including emerging new technologies and services, be more competitive.

* * *

The core principles of the USA Tax System are of overriding importance.

In order for there to be income, there must be savings but in order for there to be savings, there must be income.

Human labor and skill is the ultimate source of all income but the amount of income that people produce and enjoy will be less without sufficient savings and investment.

The existing tax system is biased against saving and, therefore, against earning income and the human dignity and well-being that go with it. By allowing people a fair opportunity to save, the USA Tax System removes the bias against earning greater incomes from human effort and skill.

* * *

Understanding the Business Tax in the Context of the Individual Tax and Vice Versa

The Business Tax and the Individual Tax are merely two interrelated parts of a tax applied to a single tax base that happens to appear at two different points in the process by which income is created and received.

The tax base first emerges when businesses create income by producing and selling goods and services. That is when the Business Tax applies. Next, the tax base reappears when individuals actually receive that income, net of the Business Tax, in the form of wages, salaries, interest, dividends and similar distributions to the owners of a business. It is at that point where the Individual Tax applies.

Because the basic operating rules of both parts of the new two-tier tax system are largely interactive, it can best be understood by looking at both the Business Tax and the Individual Tax, separately and in relation to one another, and then by looking at detailed examples where both taxes are applied to illustrative sets of facts.

Basic Operating Rules and Principles of the Business Tax

Rules

Although supplemental rules are needed to make the Business Tax work properly and consistently in all situations, the basic operating rules are few and simple.

1. Every business, incorporated or unincorporated, that is producing and selling goods and services, and, therefore, creating income for its employees, owners and lenders, must file an annual business tax return and pay a [10%] tax on its annual "gross profit" which is a defined term under the Business Tax.

2. In calculating its gross profit tax base to which the [10%] tax is applied, the business adds only the amount it actually received from sales of goods and services and subtracts only the amount it actually paid out to other businesses for the goods and services it had to buy from them (plant, equipment, inventory, supplies, rent, utilities, telephones, fuel, legal and accounting fees, etc.). Excluded from the gross profit calculation are financial receipts and payments. For example, the business neither includes interest and dividends received nor deducts interest and dividends paid. Also excluded are compensation payments to employees. * * *

3. Amounts received from export sales of goods to a purchaser outside the United States and for services rendered outside the United States are excluded from the calculation of gross profit. Correspondingly, a [10%] import tax is imposed on the sale of goods into the United States from abroad. E.g., a foreign business that manufactures outside the United States but sells its products in the U.S. market will pay the import tax.

4. A tax credit is allowed for the 7.65% employer payroll tax (commonly called FICA or Social Security Tax) that businesses must pay on wages paid to employees.

5. The Business Tax is territorial. U.S. businesses will not include in gross profit the proceeds from sales made or services provided outside the United States and they will not subtract amounts paid for the purchase of goods or the provision of services outside the United States. U.S. businesses will not be taxed on dividends paid by foreign subsidiaries. Foreign businesses will include in gross profit amounts received for goods sold or services provided in the United States and will subtract amounts paid for goods acquired and services provided in the United States.

Discussion of General Principles

Because of the special definition of gross profit under the Business Tax, it makes no distinction between that portion of a business's income that is produced and received by its owners and that portion produced and received by its employees. The business calculates its gross profit tax base before paying employees their share, before paying owners their share, before paying creditors their share, and before paying taxes owed by the business.

* * *

The often-drawn line between capital income and work income is, however, indistinct at best. In the case of smaller corporations and partnerships, all or most of the owners also themselves work in the business and receive their shares of the gross profit in part as salary (or "guaranteed payments" or draws) and in part as "dividends" in proportion to their investments of time and effort, as well as capital. Even in the case of large privately held corporations, many of the founders who own all or most of the stock may also work in the business. The key executives of large publicly held corporations nearly always own stock. They too will receive both salaries and dividends out of gross profit.

In the case of the many unincorporated businesses operating as "proprietorships," the owner of the business is almost by definition also the operator of the business. Proprietorships are usually small businesses, such as a farm, retail shop, pharmacy, small-town plumber or electrician, or a doctor or dentist operating as a sole practitioner. The owner-employee is usually the only one who has capital invested in the business (mostly reinvested earnings) and is sometimes the only "employee," although family members may also work full or part time in the business. Here, even for bookkeeping purposes, the distinction between a dollar of gross profit produced and received from working in the business like other employees, and a dollar produced and received for having provided the capital necessary for anyone to earn any income from the business, is as blurred and irrelevant as it is in reality.

The present income tax system makes huge distinctions in the foregoing cases depending on the form of business organization, on the size of the business, on whether income is said to be produced by labor or by capital, and on whether income is said to be received as an employee or as an owner of capital. In the process of making all these fine-spun distinctions, present law imposes vastly different tax liabilities on different parts of what is in fact a single tax base.

In contrast, the Business Tax is even-handed in the amount of tax it imposes on the labor and capital incomes produced by a business. After all, no one, including the Commissioner of Internal Revenue or the President or Congress of the United States, actually knows exactly how much of any business' gross profit is produced by labor instead of by capital, or vice versa, or even has a particularly realistic way of defining either one. We do know that gross profit exists, do know how to measure it in the case of any business and in total for all businesses, and do know that it is ultimately the source of everyone's income. We also know that gross profit is the result of some combination of labor and capital. * * *

The Business Tax responds to the reality of these knowns and unknowns simply by collecting [10%] of gross profit when it is produced at the business level, without distinctions as to who or what contributed more or less to its creation, and leaving to the business' owners and employees, operating within the inexorably accurate forces of the marketplace, to determine who gets and, therefore, who produced, how much of the total.

Applied in this way, the Business Tax serves as a step-one pre-collection of tax even before the respective shares of gross profit are determined, and before people actually receive their respective shares, net of the pre-collection, as wages, salaries, dividends, interest, and mixtures thereof. When people receive their income, the Individual Tax will be collected directly from them. The Business Tax plus the Individual Tax will be the total tax on their shares of what is in reality a single tax base flowing from production (business) to producers (people).

Not only does the Business Tax make no arbitrary distinctions among different dollars of income—based on presumed origins or otherwise—it proceeds from a correct definition of "income" in the first place. All businesses have some capital invested in machinery, inventories, etc. Under the gross profit calculation used in the Business Tax, that cost is subtracted so that the business is first allowed to recover capital. It is only income (not the capital itself) that is included in the business' gross profit tax base and that is ultimately, net of Business Tax, reflected in any person's share of gross profit.

Under the Individual Tax, the counterpart of the business' ability to recover capital before having taxable gross profit, is the ability of a person who receives wages, salaries, dividends, interest, etc. to defer tax on that portion which he or she saves and converts into capital. * * *

Basic Operating Rules and Principles of the Individual Tax

Rules

Although, here again, some supplementary rules are necessary, the basic operating rules of the Individual Tax are few and simple.

1. All individuals must file an annual return and pay tax at graduated rates ranging from [X to Z%] on their taxable income for the year.

2. In calculating taxable income, the individual generally includes in gross income all amounts received from all sources other than gifts, bequests, the proceeds of loans, and certain income transfers or substitutes received from governments. Thus, gross income would generally include wages, salaries, interest, pensions, annuities, the proceeds of a life insurance contract, dividends, equivalent distributions from a partnership or other unincorporated

business, and most amounts received from the sale of assets.

3. If an individual defers receipt of gross income by saving it, i.e., by investing it in a savings asset such as a stock or a bank deposit, the individual is allowed a deduction for that savings. This is called the Unlimited Savings Allowance. This deduction serves to defer tax on income the actual receipt of which the individual has deferred by recontributing it to the national stock of savings. When, later, the individual withdraws savings from the national savings pool, the amount withdrawn is at that time included in the individual's gross income.

4. The individual also deducts from gross income (i) personal and family exemptions, (ii) a Family Living Allowance deduction, and (iii) a few personal deductions generally related to home ownership, charitable contributions and education.

5. Individuals do not deduct on their personal tax returns any "trade or business" expenses such as are now reported on Schedule C of Form 1040. If an individual is self-employed and does incur such expenses, they are reported on a self-employed business tax return along with the gross sales revenues associated with that business entity. Only the net results of that self-employed business, minus the Business Tax, are reported on the individual's personal tax return and, then, only to the extent actually withdrawn from the business.

6. In general, individuals are allowed a credit for the 7.65% employee payroll tax (commonly called FICA or Social Security Tax) that their employers are required to withhold from their wages. Because this credit is phased-out as income rises, some individuals will get only a partial credit and high-income individuals will get no credit. A similar phased-out credit is allowed for self-employed individuals. In addition, employees are allowed a credit for any Individual Tax that is explicitly withheld from their wages or salaries, the same as in the case of present Form W-2 withholding of income tax. In general, W-2 type withholding will operate the same way as under present law.

Discussion of General Principles

The deduction allowed an individual for the purchase of "savings assets" illustrates the interactive combination of the Individual Tax and the Business Tax. That deduction also illustrates the goal of correctly defining income and thereby eliminating the bias under present law against an individual's choice and need to save income and against a business' choice and need to invest in order to create income for its owners and employees. These choices are two parts of the same thing because unless people save, businesses cannot invest and unless businesses invest, people cannot earn income.

Under the Individual Tax, "savings assets" are generally defined as financial assets such as stocks of corporations (and equivalent investments in an unincorporated business by an owner-partner or an owner-proprietor), bonds and notes, both commercial and governmental, annuity contracts, life insurance contracts, and deposits in banks and similar depository institutions.

As defined under the Individual Tax, savings assets do not include properties such as art objects, antiques, classic cars, owner-occupied housing, and land even though such properties may have long-term value in that they may frequently be sold at a later date for as much as or more than the price paid for them. Even though their purchase may be savings in a broader economic definition, there are several reasons why the Individual Tax distinguishes these admittedly valuable properties from such obvious savings assets as stock in a corporation and a bank deposit.

An art object, for example, inherently involves personal enjoyment and pleasure, and derives its value solely therefrom. The more aesthetic enjoyment a painting produces, the "better" it is, and the more valuable it is. Otherwise, it is merely $10 of canvas and paint. Except by price, and the degree and longevity of personal consumption enjoyment and service provided (which is reflected in price), it is difficult to draw the line between a 50 [cent] soft drink, a $50 bottle of wine, and a $5,000 art object. By defining a "savings asset" to include only financial assets such as stocks, bonds and deposits, the Individual Tax eliminates the need to make such distinctions.

This definition of savings assets also serves to allow people who produce and earn otherwise taxable income to defer that tax when they purchase an asset such as a stock that derives its value solely from the fact that it will in the future result in the production of additional income that will also be taxable to the owner-saver. If a person earns a $100X salary and uses current taxable income to purchase a stock that presently has a value of $100X only because it will in the future produce dividends (or the combination of dividends and liquidation or resale proceeds) that have a present value of $100X, and if that person will have to pay tax on the dividends when received (which will be the case), that person must be allowed to deduct the cost of the stock. Otherwise, the $100X of current salary will be taxed twice. In contrast, if the person uses the $100X of currently taxable salary income to purchase an asset (such as an art object, a personal automobile, or a personal residence) that will produce nontaxable income in the form of the personal service or enjoyment it provides, the person should not be allowed to deduct the cost of the asset. Otherwise, the $100X of salary income would not be taxed at all; not even once.

By allowing a savings deduction for the purchase of assets that will produce taxable income in the future, the Individual Tax assures that income is taxed once. If a person buys a savings bond for $25 that will mature in 10 years and pay back $50 ($25 being $50 discounted for 10 years at 7.18%), the Individual Tax allows a deduction for $25 in the year the bond is bought but includes $50 in taxable income in the year the bond matures. * * * Thus, tax is deferred, not forgiven, and all the income is taxed.

* * *

Deferring tax on deferred income is exactly the concept of the IRA (Individual Retirement Account). Prior to 1987, all individuals could defer tax on up to $2,000 of income per year by depositing it in a special IRA Account at a bank. In general, the funds in the IRA Account can only be invested in financial assets such as stocks, bonds and so forth.

The Unlimited Savings Allowance is the same in concept, although structurally different, more flexible and more efficient. In the case of the IRA, withdrawal had to occur at or during retirement. When withdrawn, the original deposit plus accumulated earnings, such as interest and dividends, were taxed. If withdrawn before retirement age, an additional penalty tax was imposed. Under the Individual Tax, there is no $2,000 limit, no special account is necessary, and the use of saved and deferred income is not restricted to retirement. Income and the earnings thereon can be withdrawn from savings at any time.

* * *

Basic Example Illustrating the Business Tax and the Individual Tax Operating in Combination—Domestic Business

* * *

[W]hat might be called "consequential rules" * * * are actually results that inevitably arise from the previously stated basic rules, although these results may not be immediately obvious. Among these, for starters, are the following.

Compensatory stock awards (or options) to employees will not immediately result in taxable income to the employee even though they are the equivalent of cash and under present law are taxable. Reason: Stock is a deductible savings asset and receiving stock in lieu of cash salary is the same as receiving cash and then buying deductible stock.

All corporations and their shareholders can have a fully flexible "dividend reinvestment" system where, when the corporation declares a common stock dividend, one common shareholder can receive taxable cash and another can elect to receive either nontaxable stock or nontaxable debt. Reason: Same as above. Even though under state corporate law the electing shareholder had the "right" to receive cash (which right is taxable under present law), the election to receive stock or debt provides an equal and offsetting deduction for savings.

* * *

Basic Rules That Are Illustrated

In the case of the Business Tax:

> The tax rate applies only to the gross profit tax base, which is the net positive result of sales minus purchases from other businesses of goods and services.

> Only cash (or the equivalent) actually received or actually paid is taken into account, i.e., the cash method of accounting is uniformly applied.

> Positive or negative net cash flow from financial transactions is, however, not taken into account.

> Although gross profit is computed without regard to employee payroll cost (or the employer payroll tax paid thereon), a tax credit against the Business Tax is allowed for the 7.65% employer payroll tax.

In the case of the Individual Tax:

> An individual's gross income includes wages, salaries, interest and dividends.

> Deductions are allowed for the costs of savings assets purchased. * * *

Why [allow deduction for] goods and services purchased from other businesses? The Business Tax is intended to be the first in a two-step process of collecting a tax on income. Therefore, the Business Tax begins with the source—Gross Domestic Product (GDP), which can for this purpose be viewed as the sum of all goods and services produced and sold by all businesses together minus, in order to avoid duplication, those that they bought from one another. * * *

Why Not Also Deduct Employee Payroll? * * *

Answer: Employees, as such, are not a business required to file a business tax return and to pay the [10%] Business Tax. If Widget Corporation deducted its payments to them against its business tax base, there would be no corresponding inclusion of that amount in any other business' tax base, and no [10%] Business Tax would be pre-collected on that portion of income.

* * * It is appropriate to deduct [a payment for] accounting "services" where [the payee's] CPA firm is an outside independent contractor that is itself a business subject to the [10%] Business Tax, but it is not appropriate to deduct the salary paid for similar accounting services to an inside employee-accountant who is not a business subject to the [10%] Business Tax. * * *

It is true that the employee's salary will be *included*, when received, in the employee's personal tax return under the Individual Tax but the tax rates under the Individual Tax are lower than they otherwise would be, precisely because of the pre-collection of the [10%] tax. * * *

It is, however, also the case that in addition to the [10%] Business Tax, Widget Corporation must, as under present law, pay a 7.65% payroll tax on wages up to $60,000[m] per year per employee; whereas in the case of the share of gross profit that goes to interest and dividends, there is only the [10%] tax. It is for this reason that the Business Tax also gives Widget Corporation a full tax credit for the 7.65% employer payroll tax.

It is by a combination of all these means—including splitting the overall tax rate between businesses and individuals—that the Business Tax and the Individual Tax achieve the intended result of correctly measuring income and being even-handed among all forms of income and the recipients thereof.

Why are financial receipts and payments excluded from the gross profit calculation? Part of the answer, at least in terms of the accounting procedure of matching deductions with income and vice versa, has already been stated in explaining that allowing no "deduction" for dividend and interest payments is the same as allowing no "deduction" for wages and salaries to employees.

There are other reasons for excluding all financial receipts and, correspondingly, all financial payments. The heart of the matter goes back to the concept of GDP which fundamentally arises from the production and sale of goods and services. GDP is not increased to a still higher number because of financial flows such as interest and dividends back and forth between businesses or between businesses and individuals. * * *

Therefore, the GDP-based Business Tax for regular, nonfinancial businesses excludes all interest, dividends and similar financial flows among businesses, except to the extent that they may be treated as implicit payments for services. * * *

Under the Business Tax, neither the lender nor the borrower takes into account the transfer or receipt of funds in loan transactions. Loans made are not deducted, repayments received are not included, loan proceeds received are not included, and loan repayments made are not deducted.

* * *

---

m. The OASDI tax (6.2%) and Medicare tax (1.45%) was levied on approximately $60,000 of an employee's earnings when this proposal was published. The tax rates have remained unchanged, but the earnings ceiling has not. The earnings ceiling for the OASDI tax is adjusted annually, and is $87,000 in 2003; the earnings ceiling for the Medicare tax has been removed.

Basic Rules of the Individual Tax

* * *

Deduction for Net Amount Saved

Individuals may deduct, without any dollar limit, their additions to the national stock of savings. * * *

[A] netting calculation will be made. If the netting results in more withdrawals and sales than deposits and purchases of savings assets, the net amount will be included in the gross income line. If the netting results in a net savings deduction, it will be subtracted in the deduction line.

Determining the Net Amount Saved in the Simple Case

Most taxpayers will be able by very simple calculations to determine the net amount saved. * * *

a. When income is earned and deferred by saving, the tax on the income for that year is deferred, generally, by including the amount earned and deducting the amount saved.

b. When in a later year, the income is withdrawn from savings, the amount is included in gross income for that later year.

c. If, however, the withdrawal from savings was merely to shift the same amount of savings from one savings asset to another, the person should not be taxed on the income which, after the shift, is still in the national savings pool.

* * *

Rules to Keep the Calculations Simple

Borrowing

* * * The USA Tax System should not encourage borrowing to save, because that is not really savings. On the other hand, the Individual Tax should be as simple as possible. To balance these competing concerns, the Individual Tax contains special rules for the certain kinds of debt ordinarily incurred by individuals:

i. Mortgage debt on a person's personal residence is not taken into account in determining the net savings deduction.

ii. Debt of up to $25,000 directly related to the purchase of personal property such as furniture, appliances or a family automobile is disregarded.

iii. An additional $10,000 of debt incurred for any purpose is also disregarded in determining the net savings deduction.

* * *

Tax Basis

The simple case calculations will not work properly in cases in which an individual sells a savings asset with a tax basis. If the individual were to then save all of the proceeds, the individual would have no new savings, but if he included in gross income the excess of the proceeds of the sale of the savings asset over the basis of the asset, and deducted the full amount of the proceeds saved, he would have a net savings deduction.

* * *

To minimize the problems caused by tax basis, the Individual Tax rules permit taxpayers who have total tax bases in savings assets of less than $50,000 to elect to assign a zero tax basis to each savings asset and to amortize and deduct their total basis in savings assets ratably over three years. * * *

The tax-basis complication cannot be fairly solved by simply disregarding tax basis in savings assets. Tax basis generally reflects the cost of the assets. Since these assets were purchased with after-tax dollars, the basis reflects amounts of gross income that were previously taxed. To avoid double taxation of income, the basis would have to be taken into account on the sale of assets. By eliminating the basis of most assets and allowing amortization deductions to offset the previously recognized income, the amortization election makes the new tax system simpler.

The amortization election is limited because taxpayers now have substantial bases in savings assets. If all taxpayers were permitted to amortize their tax bases over a short period, there would be a substantial revenue shortfall during the early years of the USA Tax System. * * *

IS RADICAL TAX REFORM IN OUR FUTURE?
Rudolph G. Penner[*]

21 National Tax Association Forum, Spring 1995, at 1, 2-5

At about the same time [1993], Senators Nunn and Domenici were developing a much more radical reform proposal. * * * In it, a subtraction-type VAT replaces the corporate tax and taxes on non-corporate business reflected on Schedule C, and provides a 100 percent credit for payment of employer payroll taxes. The payroll tax structure is maintained to avoid disturbing current social security arrangements.

Businesses total their sales and subtract purchases from other businesses, including investment goods, to arrive at the tax base. In the aggregate, it approximately equals consumption as defined in the national income accounts. Payroll tax payments are then credited against the tax liability. To be revenue neutral in the long run would require a tax rate of slightly less than 10 percent.

The tax is border adjustable. That is to say, it does not apply to exports, but it does apply to imports. Border adjustability has a strong appeal to many businessmen who believe that they are at a disadvantage relative to competitors producing in countries with border adjustable VATS. * * *

---

[*]. At time of original publication, Managing Director of the Barents Group, a subsidiary of KPMG Peat Marwick. Dr. Penner was a consultant to the authors of the substantially identical Nunn-Domenici and Alliance USA proposals.

The business tax is territorial. That is to say, it only applies to value added generated in the United States. Foreign investments cannot be deducted and the return to them is not taxed. * * *

The proposed business tax is extremely simple compared to the current system. * * *

The individual tax reform is less simple. In the ideal, it would operate on a cash flow basis. Income from wages, rent, interest and dividends would be computed much as it is today. The proceeds from asset sales and borrowing would be added to purchases and asset acquisitions and the repayment of debt and interest would be subtracted. Note that the calculation is equivalent to computing income and deducting saving. It is similar to having a completely unlimited IRA.

The system can be made progressive by increasing the earned income credit and by providing generous exemptions and a large zero-tax bracket. A progressive rate structure can be applied to the remaining tax base. The Nunn-Domenici proposal allows a full credit for the payment of employee payroll taxes.

* * *

Practical and political considerations prevented Nunn and Domenici from adopting the pure cash flow system. In a pure system, the taxpayer would need to keep track of numerous credit card and accounts payable transactions and of changes in currency balances. This would involve a major effort. Some tax-free borrowing had to be allowed to reduce record keeping and for the purchase of lumpy consumer durables such as cars. The repayment of such loans is not deductible.

Owner-occupied housing represents an immense political and practical challenge to any tax reformer. It escaped the net of [the Tax Reform Act of 1986] and it largely escapes the Nunn-Domenici reform, which retains the current law treatment of the in-kind return and the mortgage and real estate tax deduction. Capital gains on housing sales, however, would be fully taxed to the extent that they are converted into consumption. * * *

Subsequent to the Nunn-Domenici proposal, House Majority Leader Armey proposed a "flat tax" that has gained a great deal of attention. The proposal is based on a design by Robert Hall and Alvin Rabushka, and David Bradford has designed what he calls an "X tax" that has a similar base, but with a tax rate structure that makes it considerably more progressive.

The Armey business tax base is similar to that used by Nunn and Domenici with the important difference that wages are deductible. That means that the tax would not be border adjustable under current GATT rules. Wages are taxed at the individual level. In the Armey proposal, generous exemptions and deductions are combined with a flat rate on what remains. The Bradford proposal would add a progressive rate structure.

These proposals have not been worked out in the same excruciating detail as has Nunn-Domenici. That gives them the appearance of being much simpler. Conceptually, the base of the Armey/Bradford tax is very similar to that used by Nunn and Domenici. It approximately equals value added in the production of consumption goods. It is only a slight oversimplification to say that Armey and Bradford tax income when it is earned; Nunn-Domenici taxes it when it is spent. If all income is spent over a lifetime and tax rates remain constant, the present value of the lifetime tax burden is the same.

Inherently, it may be simpler to tax earnings rather than cash flow, but it is not quite as simple as it seems in the Armey proposal. Because capital income is explicitly exempt at the individual level under the Armey proposal, there is a huge temptation to convey compensation using capital assets. For example, some technique must be designed to handle stock options which can be ignored until converted into cash under Nunn-Domenici.

Nunn and Domenici have elected to try to keep their tax reform distributionally neutral whereas the Armey proposal would result in a large redistribution of the tax burden away from the most affluent.

The rates required for distributional neutrality, however, are extremely difficult to estimate. * * *

An equally disturbing problem is that distributional neutrality cannot be defined without specifying an elaborate theory of tax incidence. Is the current corporate tax largely paid by capital owners or by wage earners because it drives investment abroad? Will the Nunn-Domenici business tax be shifted forward into prices or backward to factors? Who really knows? It is clear that the distributional tables that play such a huge role in political debates over tax policy rest on a foundation of quicksand.

Effect on Saving

Economists are generally skeptical about the use of tax policy to increase private saving and investment. After all, the decline in the saving rate continued in the 1980s in the face of increased saving and investment incentives early in the period and lower marginal rates later. * * *

The effects of a revenue neutral tax reform should, however, be very different from that of a cut in marginal rates. The average taxpayer will be no better off. The same tax will be squeezed out [of] the average person and the only impact will be a greater reward for saving. Moreover, the redistribution of the tax burden within each income class should also increase saving substantially. Those with a high inherent propensity to save will get a tax cut. They should save a relatively high share of it. Those with a high propensity to spend will face a tax increase. They will have to finance it largely by cutting spending. * * *

International Implications

[B]order adjustability is an important issue in the business community. Economists tend to argue that, all else equal, its effects will be washed out by countervailing exchange rate movements. I have never met a businessman who believes this argument.

     * * *

Transition and Other Problems

     * * * Transition issues have taken more time for the designers of Nunn-Domenici to resolve than any other issues. To my knowledge, transition issues have not been confronted by the proponents of the Armey proposal and proponents of value added taxation generally manage to ignore them.

In the Nunn-Domenici proposal, the most important transition issue involving individuals concerns the treatment of savings accumulated out of after-tax income under the current tax regime. The cost basis of those old savings has already been taxed once. Should it be taxed yet again when it is consumed under the new regime? That would be particularly unfair to retirees.

Ideally, it would be nice to allow the use of old cost basis tax free, both for consuming and for investing in new deductible assets. However, there are trillions of dollars of old cost basis out there and its tax free use might deprive the government of all revenues for several years. Therefore the use of old basis must be limited. But how? * * *

People with less than $50,000 compute their old cost basis on the effective date of the new tax and simply deduct it from their tax base over a limited period, say, three years. The advantage of this approach is that it cannot be gamed. The records underlying it are the same as those now used to compute capital gains taxes.

For those who are wealthy and have complicated investments, * * * the revenue implications of allowing them to write it all off over a limited time period would be very significant since the very wealthy hold most of the nation's wealth.

The designers of Nunn-Domenici have created a fairly simple tax form that allows people to use old basis only to finance consumption in excess of income. Assets acquired by selling old basis are not deductible and the tax form tracks this old basis much as today's tax form tracks accumulated loss carryovers.

The problem with this approach is that many will never consume in excess of their income (e.g. Ross Perot), and will never be able to use old basis tax free. Others with less saving will have an incentive to concentrate the purchase of consumer durables into one year in order to facilitate the use of old basis. This is one of the few distortions in the proposed system, but any system for limiting the use of old basis is likely to inspire intense tax planning.

* * *

THE MERIT OF AN INCOME TAX
VERSUS A CONSUMPTION TAX
John S. Nolan[*]

12 American Journal of Tax Policy 207, 207-19 (1995)

The current political debate focuses heavily on the idea of a simple "flat tax"—accompanied by the foolish notion that it could be so simple and at such a low rate that we might even disband the IRS! The real issue lying behind the two major proposals on the table—the Armey flat tax and the Nunn-Domenici USA Tax—is, however, whether we should substitute a consumption form of taxation for our present income tax system. * * *

The most obvious forms of consumption tax are the retail sales tax and the credit-invoice type of value added tax used in Europe. The VAT has exactly the same effect as a retail sales tax; it simply is collected differently. Both forms of tax end up taxing the value of goods and services added by labor, plus "profits" or "rents" in the sense that economists use those terms, which exclude all the normal return on capital investment. Thus capital investment is clearly favored as compared to the impact of an income tax.

The business level USA Tax, and the combined business level/individual level elements of the Armey flat tax, are, in substance, simply subtraction method VAT taxes. As such, they have the same effect as a retail sales tax or a traditional credit-invoice VAT. To illustrate this equivalence, the USA business level tax allows an immediate deduction for all purchases, including the cost of plant and equipment. It allows, however, no deduction for salaries, wages, or fringe benefits. The result is that the tax base, as in a retail sales tax or traditional VAT, is the value added by labor plus profit.

The USA individual level tax then includes wages, salaries, and fringe benefits, as well as dividends, interest, capital gains, and all other forms of income in gross income for tax purposes. The resulting taxable income can, however, be completely offset by contributions to an unlimited IRA account. As a result, the combined USA business and individual taxes are levied on consumption only—that is, they tax income consumed but not income saved.

The Armey flat tax achieves exactly the same effect in a somewhat different way. Unlike the USA business level tax, the Armey business level tax

---

*. At time of original publication, partner, Miller & Chevalier, Washington, D.C. This paper was presented as the Erwin N. Griswold Lecture to the annual meeting of the American College of Tax Counsel, in New Orleans, on January 19, 1996.

allows a deduction for wages, salaries, and qualified retirement plan contributions, though not for fringe benefits. Like the USA business level tax, it also allows an immediate deduction for all purchases, including the cost of plant and equipment. The Armey individual level tax is then imposed on salaries, wages, and qualified retirement plan distributions, but not on interest, dividends, capital gains, or other investment income. The net result is to tax all forms of income only once, at either the business level or the individual level, just like the USA Tax, except that, in Armey's case, the tax is a single flat rate.

The result in both cases is, as previously stated, to achieve the same effect as a retail sales tax or traditional VAT. The USA Tax taxes salaries and wages at the business level, while the Armey flat tax taxes salaries and wages at the individual level. While the USA Tax includes salaries and wages in the tax base for the individual tax, that tax can be avoided by saving that income, or any other form of income, by use of the unlimited IRA deduction. While the Armey flat tax taxes salaries and wages at the individual level, it does not tax investment income either at the business tax level or the individual tax level.

The key to understanding the basic equivalence of these two systems as being solely taxes on consumption is that the economic effect of not taxing an amount received, but taxing the investment returns on that amount, as in the USA Tax, is exactly the same as taxing the amount received but not taxing the investment returns, as in the Armey flat tax. As a result, both the USA Tax and the Armey flat tax end up being imposed only on income consumed. Each effectively exempts from tax income that is saved.

The political rhetoric focuses upon the flatness of the rate of tax, but that is a red herring. We could obviously achieve that result with our present income tax system, taxing all income, whether saved or consumed, at a single rate. * * *

The tax base would, however, be very considerably narrower under the USA Tax because of the unlimited IRA deduction feature, or, under the Armey flat tax, because of the exclusion of all forms of investment income from the tax base. We will be taking one huge fiscal gamble that the sought-after greater inducements to savings will produce an increase in investment capital sufficient to yield larger or even equal revenues from a narrower tax base.

It is against this background that we should assess the relative merits of our income tax and these proposed forms of consumption tax.

The United States Income Tax

The U.S. income tax is not, of course, a "pure" income tax. Income set aside in qualified retirement plans, or under the limited IRA provisions of existing law, is not taxed to the employee until withdrawn. The investment returns on such savings also are not taxed until withdrawn. These provisions of existing law require a disciplined program for these savings— probably more complex and intrusive than necessary—but nonetheless valuable in a broad sense. For the most part, such savings cannot be withdrawn without penalty until the worker reaches retirement age. These provisions could be substantially simplified and improved. Even so, these provisions have resulted in a substantial volume of savings in the U.S.

Similarly, life insurance, also by its nature a disciplined pattern of saving, is favored; the investment earnings reflected in cash surrender value are not taxed, and the policy proceeds on death are not income. Individuals make regular premium payments every year, and there is effectively a built-in penalty for failing to continue to do so.

Owner-occupied housing, the single most important investment asset held by most Americans, is clearly favored. * * *

Our existing U.S. income tax has also been carefully crafted to serve other valuable economic goals. Employer-provided health insurance, group-term life insurance, disability insurance, and other benefits also represent, in effect, disciplined forms of savings to meet vital needs— burdens which might otherwise fall upon government.

Similarly, our existing income tax serves important social goals. The charitable contributions deduction supports an enormous range of activity that reduces the costs and burdens of government. The refundable earned income tax credit provides welfare-type benefits to low income persons who work to provide for their own needs, but for whom the economy does not provide sufficient support.

All of these other economic and social policy elements of our existing U.S. tax system could, of course, be included in a consumption tax system, but their efficacy might be drastically affected. Thus, for example, the USA Tax allows a charitable contribution deduction. But even under the USA Tax, will the same incentive to give exist in light of the unlimited IRA deduction opportunity? The wealthy can avoid tax completely by saving; the charitable contribution deduction to them loses much of its force.
　　　* * *

The Armey flat tax allows no mortgage interest deduction and no charitable contribution deduction. The absence of a mortgage interest deduction has an important practical result. The wealthy, who can finance their own home ownership, can still acquire a home but middle class homeowners and prospective middle class homeowners would clearly be disadvantaged.

Both the USA Tax and the Armey flat tax would substantially increase the tax burdens on the middle class. Would this increased tax burden in and of itself adversely affect home ownership?

This is all untested ground.

The Armey flat tax also would repeal the earned income tax credit. Further, nonpension fringe benefits would not be deductible in determining the business level tax and would be includible in income under the individual level tax.

What would be the effect of these Armey flat tax changes? I do not find it sufficiently reassuring to hear that the economy will grow rapidly so that interest rates will fall enough to more than compensate for denying the home mortgage interest deduction. * * * Or to hear that people will give as much to charity without a deduction; major givers, induced by such tax saving opportunities as charitable remainder trusts, are very important to the support of many major charities. Even smaller givers take the tax deduction into account in making charitable contributions. Will employers still provide health, life, and disability insurance with no deduction for such costs? Can we really be sure that wage levels will rise sufficiently that the low income working poor will not need the help that the earned income tax credit presently provides?

* * *

The Advantage Of A Consumption Tax

The consumption tax advantage, to the extent one exists, rests on the proposition that our existing income tax system discourages savings, at least without regard to the retirement income provisions. There has been a substantial decline in U.S. household savings over the past forty years, and this has been correlated to some degree to declining U.S. business investment in real terms in plant and equipment. * * * [I]t is arguable that the decline in savings in the U.S. is caused in some substantial part by the burden of our income tax system on savings.

* * *

A consumption tax, on the other hand, while still reducing the amount available for consumption either today or in the future, eliminates this bias against current saving. Under a consumption tax, either the income saved is not taxed when saved, until it is later consumed, as in the USA Tax, or the returns on the savings are not taxed, as in the Armey flat tax. The result under either type of consumption tax is exactly the same—the present value of the future fund accumulated by saving for later consumption will be exactly the same as the income available for consumption immediately. That being so, there is no bias against saving, as there is in an income tax. As a result, the amount saved, which is available for future consumption, is substantially higher than it would be under an income tax system.

This analysis, however, overlooks an important consideration. Since the income tax is imposed on a broader base, in a perfect world the income tax

would be imposed at lower rates to produce the same level of revenue for the government. But tax rates under our income tax system have not been low in modern memory, except for the brief period when the 1986 Act rates remained in effect. * * * [T]he rates under either the USA Tax or the Armey flat tax would very likely be increased after an initial period of euphoria.
    * * *

Comparative Advantage

Against this background, we may evaluate the relative merit of an income tax structure versus a consumption tax structure. For this purpose, we apply the four customary criteria—economic efficiency, equity or fairness, simplicity, and administrability.

Economic Efficiency. In a theoretical world, the greatest advantage of a consumption tax is that it will increase savings as compared to an income tax. In the real world in which we live, however, this advantage is greatly moderated by the provisions of the U.S. tax system as to qualified retirement plans, limited IRAs, life insurance, home ownership, and income exclusions and deferrals (fringe benefits, gain on sale of a residence, and others).

A true flat rate tax would have the advantage of eliminating some bracket arbitrage—both between or among years by timing the recognition of income and deductions, and between or among taxpayers. * * * But the USA Tax has progressive rates, and in any event, tax lawyers like us will still find ways under a consumption tax to defer income and accelerate deductions.

Both of the proposed forms of consumption tax would largely eliminate the double taxation of corporate earnings, though by different means. The Armey flat tax simply exempts dividends from the individual tax base. The USA Tax would allow a shareholder to defer the tax on dividends until such income is consumed pursuant to the unlimited IRA deduction.

My greatest concern in this area is that both the USA Tax and the Armey flat tax tend to remove any incentive for employer-sponsored qualified retirement plans and the comparative advantage of permanent plan life insurance versus other forms of savings. While I believe generally in a free market, my enthusiasm for free markets is tempered by some degree of paternalism, at least to the extent of providing a tax incentive for these disciplined forms of saving. * * *

Without employer retirement plans, it is far from clear whether individual workers will maintain the same disciplined pattern of savings throughout their working years. There would be no constraints on using savings for consumption at any time prior to retirement except good judgment, which is not always uniformly exercised in making consumption versus savings decisions. Similarly, by eliminating the comparative advantage of life insurance, largely a form of retirement saving, we would eliminate or reduce the attraction of that form of disciplined saving. In all, we would be embarking upon a wholly untried experiment in free market economics. By abandoning the comparative advantages of these incentives, savings could actually decrease.

Equity. Equity or fairness, like beauty, is largely in the eyes of the beholder. Even so, most Americans instinctively consider it fairer to tax all income, including interest, dividends, and capital gains. * * * Most Americans also feel, despite the political rhetoric being now spewed out, that it is fairer to tax persons with higher incomes at somewhat higher rates pursuant to the ability to pay rationale of our existing system.

In any event, consumption taxes tend to be regressive, as compared to income taxes. Higher income individuals spend a smaller percentage of their income on consumption. Higher income individuals have a higher percentage of their income from savings. To achieve the same distribution of burden by income class, the rate structure of a consumption tax must be more progressive than that of an income tax.

The Armey flat tax attempts to address this concern by a generous personal allowance—$21,400 for a married couple filing jointly, for example —and by a generous personal allowance—$5,000 per dependent. Even so, burden tables recently released by Treasury show disturbing effects by income class of the combined Armey business level and individual level flat taxes. Whether the 17 percent proposed flat tax rate for the business tax and for the individual tax is used, or the 20.8 percent flat tax rate Treasury says is necessary to achieve revenue neutrality, which is a must, the Treasury numbers show an extraordinary pattern of increases in tax burden compared to present law except for high income taxpayers. Persons with incomes over $200,000 would enjoy a significant decrease in tax burden. The heaviest increases in tax burden fall squarely on the middle class.

The USA Tax also addresses the regressivity concern by a substantial standard deduction-type family living allowance and personal exemptions. For a family of four, these would provide a threshold for taxation of $17,600. Unfortunately, however, the lowest nominal rate is 19 percent, rising fairly quickly to 27 percent, and then again fairly quickly to 40 percent. These rates are effectively reduced by the credit for the employee share of payroll taxes—7.65 percent—but even so the net tax rates are very substantial in the middle income range. A family of four will pay an effective rate of 32.35 percent on wage and salary income over $41,600. This 32.35 percent USA Tax tax rate is considerably higher than the 28 percent marginal rate on such income under present law. Just as in the case of the Armey flat tax, middle income families who need their income for basic consumption will pay substantially higher taxes under the USA Tax.

The Armey flat tax has been severely criticized on the ground that middle class working families save mostly by buying a home and then use much of their excess savings to assist their children in obtaining a college education. These investments in "human capital" are ignored under the Armey flat tax. The USA Tax addresses them by its home mortgage interest deduction and a token deduction for higher education expenses up to $2,000 per child per year, with a maximum of $8,000 for all children. God help the Irish and those large families like mine in the younger generation!

Finally, there is also a fundamental fairness issue in changing from an income tax-based system to a consumption tax-based system. Existing U.S. taxpayers have a massive investment in tax-paid savings even apart from qualified retirement plan savings, life insurance savings, and owner-occupied housing. There is a severe degree of unfairness in moving to a system that taxes these savings again in later life when they are consumed.

The USA Tax attempts to address this issue with exceedingly complex transition rules. Unfortunately, in their present form, they would not work and could result in manipulation by the wealthy to their advantage. Al Warren and Marty Ginsburg have demonstrated this all too well in recent papers they have written.[n] The Armey flat tax so far makes no effort to address this problem. It is far from clear that any workable solution can be devised to resolve this transitional unfairness.

Simplicity. The existing U.S. income tax system is inordinately complex for business taxpayers and for individual taxpayers with special circumstances. * * * For the average middle income U.S. taxpayer whose principal source of income is wages or salaries, however, the existing U.S. system is not complicated and in most respects has not fundamentally changed in the last fifty years. * * *

Although the theoretical model of a consumption tax might be simpler in some respects than an income tax, this does not mean, however, that any consumption tax actually enacted will necessarily be simpler than our current income tax system. While any income tax system presents some problems of income measurement, perhaps a greater source of the complexity of the current system is the large body of rules providing preferential treatment for certain types of income or transactions. The same political considerations that prompted Congress to adopt these rules under the income tax may lead to the adoption of similar rules under a consumption tax regime. Therefore, any consumption tax that emerges from the political process may be no simpler

---

n. Mr. Nolan is probably referring to Alvin C. Warren, Jr., *The Proposal for an "Unlimited Savings Allowance,* 68 TAX NOTES 1103 (1995), and Martin D. Ginsburg, *Life Under a Personal Consumption Tax: Some Thoughts on Working, Saving, and Consuming in Nunn-Domenici's Tax World,* 48 NAT'L TAX J. 585 (1995). (Ed.)

than the current income tax system.

In addition, knowing the abilities of this group, I am sure we will have the same arguments as to the definition of consumption, and the timing of consumption that we presently have as to the definition and timing of income.

In my view, the goal of simplification could be achieved through reform of the income tax system without replacing the current system with a consumption tax. In short, the choice between an income and consumption tax should probably be made on the basis of fairness or efficiency rather than simplicity.

Administrability. Administrability depends upon the relative underlying complexity of the system as enacted by, and frequently changed by, Congress. There is no basis for claiming that either the USA Tax or the Flat Tax—as they are likely to be enacted by Congress to serve various interstitial economic and social objectives—will be any simpler to administer than the existing U.S. income tax system.

In several respects, a consumption tax would be more difficult to administer. Withholding the appropriate amount from wages would be more challenging, because the taxpayer's ultimate tax liability would depend on whether the taxpayer uses the wages for consumption or investment. Increased information reporting might be required for transactions involving loans and investment assets, because the taxability of these amounts would depend on the use of the proceeds. It might even become necessary to withhold on the proceeds of these transactions, if not reinvested.

    * * *

We know what we have. It works reasonably well. We should not embark on such a massive experiment without much more assurance that it will be economically more efficient, and at least as fair, simple, and administrable as the present system.

Notes and Questions

Simplification

68. An issue of importance is whether, and to what extent, adoption of a consumption-type proposal would simplify tax law and administration. As we have seen, beginning with Professor Andrews' vision in Subchapter B of taxing on "a simple cash flow basis," proponents of consumption-type tax proposals speak of simplification as a major advantage. Even many opponents of consumption-type taxation, such as the drafters of Treasury I (excerpted in Subchapter C), concede that, once fully implemented, "a tax on personal consumption is simpler in many respects than an income tax."

Hall & Rabushka make perhaps the most expansive claims of simplification, asserting that every taxpayer, including General Motors, could file a postcard-sized return. Do you think this is possible?

69. Is the primary problem in achieving considerable improvements in simplicity that even an ideal system would have to be fairly complicated? For example, are you confident in the assertions of Hall & Rabushka that their system is "airtight," and that their business tax returns could be postcard-sized because "[e]very line on the form is a well-defined number obtained directly from the business's accounting records"? Or is Mr. Nolan correct that "we will have the same arguments as to the definition of consumption, and the timing of consumption that we presently have as to the definition and timing of income"?

70. Examination of the full presentation of Hall & Rabushka reveals some complications that are not apparent in the excerpted portions of their book. For example, they advise that "[b]usiness meals in restaurants would be fully deductible."[o] We have learned from decades of experience with the income tax law that "business meal" is not a self-defining term. The same complex statutory and regulatory provisions drawing the line between business and personal meals would be necessary under the consumption-type tax.

Similarly, simplicity is missing in the advice Hall & Rabushka give to a travelling saleswoman:

> All self-employed individuals will file Form 2, the business tax form, where they can deduct travel and other business expenses. To take advantage of the personal allowance, you will want to pay yourself a salary of at least $16,500 if you are married. Report this amount along with your husband's earnings on Form 1, the individual wage tax. In this way you will be able to deduct your legitimate business expenses and receive the personal allowance. You will need to keep records to document your income and expenses.[p]

The proposed tax treatment entails the artificiality—generally limited to closely held C corporations under present law—of this saleswoman paying herself a salary. She is advised that she can deduct her "legitimate" expenses—but much complexity is entailed in establishing which expenses of a traveling saleswoman are deemed "legitimate," even if there were no concern about fraud. And, of course, Hall & Rabushka recognize the danger of fraud—and thus advise the taxpayer that she is to keep complete records, even though they would not have her reveal the details of those records in her postcard tax return.

---

o. ROBERT E. HALL & ALVIN RABUSHKA, THE FLAT TAX 106 (2d ed. 1995).
p. *Id.* at 116-17.

Indeed, many of the most difficult questions of current law involve distinguishing business expenses from consumption. In addition to meals and travelling expenses, this issue is raised by expenditures for entertainment, gifts, uniforms, "hobby farms," personal computers, automobile expense, education, "home offices," and club memberships, among others. The complexity of classifying these expenditures would remain. As Professor Andrews observed, "ordinary, current deductions, business and personal, would be essentially unaffected by the shift to a pure consumption-type tax."

71. It is always simpler to describe an idea in generalities than to work out all the concrete details. Dr. Penner argues that the proposals of Armey/Hall & Rabushka and others "have not been worked out in the same excruciating detail as has Nunn-Domenici. That gives them the appearance of being much simpler." The same observation could be made of academic discussion of consumption taxation.

72. Another aspect of the simplification problem is that no proposal—even one worked out in "excruciating detail"—will be enacted intact. It is almost inconceivable that sweeping tax changes of the type discussed in this chapter could be adopted without complications reflecting the input of many affected taxpayers, the political and policy judgments of many members of Congress and the Administration, and the conflicting views of many experts. Mr. Nolan and others caution against comparing the present income tax law to an idealized consumption-type proposal.

The income tax could also be made much simpler if a professor were allowed to put together a single, coherent revision. As one example, both the Hall & Rabushka and USA proposals would end the double-tax discrimination against doing business in the corporate form. This discrimination is not inherent to an income tax, however; many proposals have been advanced that would address the problem by revision of the income tax. See Chapter Fourteen.

73. The important issue of simplicity versus complexity can be viewed from different angles. Professor Boyd Kimball Dyer reminds us of the importance of administrative costs, which are not limited to the budget of the Internal Revenue Service: "By far the greater part of administrative costs is what the private sector spends to keep records, file reports, and get answers to questions about taxes. Part of these costs is the cost of keeping transactions from incurring taxes."[q] Professor Dyer concludes that "on the criterion of

---

q. Boyd Kimball Dyer, *The Relative Fairness of the Consumption and Accretion Tax Bases*, 1978 UTAH L. REV. 457, 483.

transaction costs, the consumption base is best because it alone treats each taxable year as sufficient to itself. There is no need for depreciation, keeping track of basis, adjustments for inflation or other concepts that tie one year to another."[r]

Mr. Nolan argues that present law "is inordinately complex for business taxpayers and for individual taxpayers with special circumstances," but is "not complicated" for most middle-income taxpayers. Is that a sufficient goal for simplicity, even if the Internal Revenue Code remains difficult to comprehend?

74. Professor Clifton Fleming devoted a 1995 article to evaluating leading consumption-type proposals in terms of simplicity, coming to the conclusion that "the devil is in the details."[s] He concluded his article with the following paragraphs, which draw an ominous parallel to the adoption of the income tax in 1913:

> A persistent theme of this article has been that the political process is quite likely to deliver a much more complicated consumption tax package than initially seems possible when one reads textbook descriptions of the VAT and the consumed income tax. Consumption tax advocates will probably view this as unduly pessimistic, and they may be correct. However, it is useful to recall that in 1913, when America stood optimistically poised to adopt a new tax system, the House Ways and Means Committee said:
>
> > In view of the many valuable Governmental purposes to be subserved, those citizens required to do so can well afford to devote a brief time during some one day in each year to the making out of a personal return of income for purposes of taxation. This is done without complaint under the operation of all the general property tax laws of the States. All good citizens, it is therefore believed, will willingly and cheerfully support and sustain this, the fairest and cheapest of all taxes, in order to secure to the largest extent equality of tax burdens, an adjustable system of revenue, and in all respects a modernized fiscal system.[271]
>
> These confident predictions of compliance burdens that would involve no more than a brief period of time on a single day and of warm public support for the income tax now seem laughable. The

---

r. *Id.*

s. J. Clifton Fleming, Jr., *Scoping Out the Uncertain Simplification (Complexification?) Effects of VATs, BATs and Consumed Income Taxes*, 2 FLA. TAX REV. 390, 441 (1995).

271. H.R. Rep. No. 5, 63d Cong., 1st Sess. (1913), reprinted in 1939-1 C.B. (Part 2) 1, 3.

1913 income tax proponents, being merely human, could not begin to foresee the complexities that would emerge over time from a system that appeared so promising at the outset. Likewise, unimagined and extensive complications may be lurking in the VAT and the consumed income tax, particularly in the latter, that will make this article's complexity speculations seem naively understated. As our experience with the income tax shows, U.S. tax systems have a way of coming to reflect thoroughly the intricacy of our society and its economy.[t]

Transition problems

75. As we have seen, there are many arguments for and against the adoption of a consumption-type tax. If we concluded that the consumption-type system were superior, we then would face the difficult question of how to get there from here.

The preceding notes have considered the issue of simplification assuming a consumption-type tax had been fully implemented. But there are many transition issues to be considered in a change so massive as moving from present law to a consumption-type system. Even if a consumption-type system might be simpler than present law once in operation, the transition problems are of daunting complexity.[u] Dr. Penner noted that the drafters of Nunn-Domenici/USA had spent more time on transition issues than on any others.

76. Perhaps the most important transition issue affecting individuals is the treatment of previously-taxed assets. Consider the simple case of a taxpayer, Alex Bell, purchasing 100 shares of AT&T for $5,000, then selling in a future year for $6,000 (and using the sales proceeds for consumption).

The rules of present law or of any of the consumption-type proposals applied separately are straightforward, and give internally consistent results. Present law would give Alex no deduction and a $5,000 basis at purchase; at sale, he would have $1,000 income. The USA proposal would give Alex a $5,000 deduction and no basis at the time of purchase; when Alex sold, the USA system would tax the entire $6,000.

But suppose Alex purchased under present law—and thus got no deduction for the purchase price—and sold after adoption of the USA system—which, absent some sort of transition rule, would require tax on the

---

t. Fleming, *supra* note s, at 442-43.

u. In this connection, recall Professor McCaffery's observation in Subchapter D that while economists agree we would ultimately be better off under a consumption tax, we would suffer a detriment "for a while"—which various economists estimated could last from four or five years to 100 years.

entire $6,000 received. This would result in an unfair double tax—a extra tax from changing the tax system that neither system alone would have imposed.

77. The most obvious transition rule would allow taxpayers to keep their basis in assets purchased pre-transition. On post-transition sale of such assets, taxpayers would not be taxed on the entire sales proceeds, but only to the extent the sales proceeds exceeded basis. What is the problem with this approach, according to Dr. Penner?

78. Dr. Penner explains that Nunn-Domenici allows people of modest wealth ($50,000 or less) to deduct their basis in pre-transition assets over a short period, perhaps three years. Having been allowed to deduct their basis, they then would have a zero basis, and have been effectively (and fairly) converted to the new system.

79. For those with more assets, however, the revenue costs to the government of allowing an automatic write-off were deemed too great. So these taxpayers will keep their basis in pre-transition assets.

Without more, this would give the wealthy a great incentive to "churn" their assets. A wealthy taxpayer could sell old assets (with income recognized only to the extent that amount realized exceeded basis), and purchase new assets (with a full deduction under the new USA system). This would cost the government enormous revenue in the early post-transition years.

Thus, Dr. Penner explained, the USA solution was to allow use of old basis, but not to taxpayers making new investments in the same year; the basis could be used "only to finance consumption in excess of income."

80. Unfortunately, the Nunn-Domenici/USA solution to the pre-transition basis problem may provide the wrong incentive. The proponents of consumption-type taxes want to give incentives to invest, but the most favorable tax treatment for wealthy owners of pre-transition property would go to taxpayers who liquidated investments in order to engage in large-scale consumption.

Another problem is that the system could be manipulated, according to Professor Martin Ginsburg: "[E]veryone decently wealthy will be a net saver in some (perhaps odd-numbered) years and a net dissaver in other years."[v] The reason for this, Professor Ginsburg explained, is that if the wealthy taxpayers show net savings in every year, they can never recoup their pre-transition basis. But by arranging their affairs to show net dissavings in some years,

---

v. Ginsburg, *supra* note n, at 588.

they will be allowed to deduct their pre-transition basis.

81.   The drafters (led by Deputy Assistant Secretary David Bradford) of *Blueprints for Basic Tax Reform*, an influential 1977 Treasury study, discussed various solutions to the transition problem should a consumption-type tax be adopted. Their recommended approach would have required, among other things, that some taxpayers compute their taxes both ways—under the income tax and the new consumption-type tax—for a 10-year period, paying the higher liability each year.[w] For these taxpayers, the promised simplicity of consumption-type taxation would be absent for at least 10 years.

82.   The complexity involved in providing comprehensive transition relief to owners of pre-transition property led Professor Michael Graetz to propose very limited transitional relief only for elderly taxpayers who would be promptly using pre-transition assets during retirement.[x] As is frequently the case, there seems to be a trade-off between simplicity and fairness.

83.   Although less obviously, the same transition issues are presented by substituting any form of consumption tax, including a VAT, for the present income tax. Dr. Penner observed that "proponents of value added taxation generally manage to ignore" transition problems.

Limiting the tax base to consumption

84.   The proposals of both Hall & Rabushka and Alliance USA are designed to tax consumption, and thus to avoid the "double tax on savings." Alliance USA follows the route suggested by Professor Andrews in Subchapter B—individuals are allowed a deduction for savings in "savings assets," and are taxed on sales proceeds of savings assets (unless the proceeds are reinvested). Interest, dividends and other returns on investment are included in the tax base. The USA approach is comparable to a fully-deductible IRA with no penalty for early withdrawal—making the IRA-like investment gives rise to a deduction, and withdrawals are taxed.

Hall & Rabushka, on the other hand, allow no deduction for investments by individuals not engaged in business, but do not tax their investment returns. The individual tax base is limited to compensation—cash wages, salaries, and pensions (when received).

Both Nolan and Penner describe these forms of taxation as economically equivalent (as explained in Chapter Two, Subchapter A). The form, however,

---

w. U.S. DEP'T OF THE TREASURY, BLUEPRINTS FOR BASIC TAX REFORM 209-11 (1977).

x. Michael J. Graetz, *Implementing a Progressive Consumption Tax*, 92 HARV. L. REV. 1575, 1653-58 (1979).

is radically different. Dr. Penner states that, generally, the Armey/Hall & Rabushka proposal taxes income when earned, while the Nunn-Domenici/USA proposal taxes income when spent.

85. The economic equivalence of the two proposals is in terms of present value. This can be demonstrated by the two systems' methods of taxing capital gain. Assume that a taxpayer purchases a stock for $100 in Year One, and sells the stock in Year Two for $110 (and uses the sales proceeds for consumption). Further assume that this 10 percent annual appreciation exactly equals the prevailing rate of return in financial markets.

Hall & Rabushka use a very simple approach. They allow no deduction for the purchase; they levy no tax upon sale. Individuals are not taxed on income from property under the Hall & Rabushka system.

Under the USA approach, the taxpayer would be allowed a deduction of $100 in Year One, and would be taxed on the entire $110 sales proceeds in Year Two. Observe that when we apply a 10 percent discount rate, 110 Year Two dollars have a present value equal to 100 Year One dollars. Assuming a constant tax rate—say 20 percent—the $22 tax in Year Two dollars would have a discounted value equal to the $20 tax saving in Year One dollars.

Thus, in this example, the two tax systems would levy a tax that is equal in terms of present value. The USA system taxes an extra $10, but this is offset by the fact that it delays for one year taxing $100.

86. The equivalence would also be present if, in the preceding example, we substituted income produced by the property for income resulting from appreciation in value. Suppose the taxpayer purchased a $100 one-year bond in Year One, which paid the prevailing market rate of 10 percent. One year later, the taxpayer received $10 interest plus $100 principal, all of which was spent on consumption.

Hall & Rabushka would grant no deduction, and levy no tax.

USA would grant a $100 deduction in Year One, resulting in a $20 tax saving (assuming a 20 percent tax rate). In Year Two, USA would tax $110—the interest plus the "dissaving" of using the bond redemption proceeds for consumption. Discounted at 10 percent, the resulting tax, $22, would be equal in present value to the $20 of tax savings one year earlier.

87. In the preceding two notes, it may initially appear that the taxpayer avoids any tax at all, in present value terms, despite ultimately consuming $110. When and how is the tax paid under the USA tax? Under the Hall & Rabushka proposal? (Hint: Assume the taxpayer earned $50,000 in Year One, but consumed only $49,900, and invested the remaining $100.)

88. Hall & Rabushka claim that their approach to avoiding double taxation of saving—the yield-exemption approach—is simpler than allowing a taxpayer a deduction for saving, then taxing the return. The deduction/inclusion approach is envisioned by the proposals of Andrews and of Alliance USA, and is the traditional approach taken by the law in favoring retirement saving. The recent trend, however, has been toward yield exemption, as in the Roth IRA.

The simplicity claim is persuasive, because instead of two tax entries—deduction or exclusion in the year of contribution, inclusion years later upon receipt—Hall & Rebushka require neither deduction/exclusion nor later inclusion. Arguably, however, the simplicity comes at the cost of equity, as explained in the next note.

89. The approaches are equivalent in an *ex ante* sense, as we saw in Chapter Two, Subchapter A. However, in an *ex post* sense, the equivalence no longer holds. Compare two taxpayers, Gladstone Gander and Donald Duck, each of whom earns the same amount, and each of whom, on the same day, invests $10,000 to purchase common stock. At the time of purchase, the equivalence of market value of the two stocks means that the future expected (by the market) returns of both investments, discounted to present value, equals $10,000. The two investments do not in fact provide the same returns, of course. Gladstone is more skilled, or luckier, in his stock selection. Gladstone's stock, the next Wal-Mart or Microsoft, earns ongoing returns greatly in excess of the expected return, and Gladstone uses these handsome dividends, and ultimately a large capital gain, to increase his standard of living. The company in which Donald invests goes bankrupt; Donald loses the principal amount of his investment, and gets no return whatever.

Hall & Rebushka, like the present Roth IRA, would treat Gladstone and Donald the same. Andrews, Alliance USA, and the traditional IRA would tax Gladstone on his unexpectedly large return, and would take account of Donald's loss by never recouping the original deduction allowed him. Which approach is more appropriate? (Assume that from all investors taken as a group the government gets the same overall revenue, discounted to present value, from either approach.)

The difference between these two approaches is considered further in Subchapter F.

Capital gains and owner-occupied housing

90. The USA proposal indirectly taxes capital gain on "savings assets"—such as stock—by allowing a deduction in the year of purchase, then taxing the entire selling price in the year of sale (unless the sales proceeds are

reinvested).

But if a taxpayer "invests" in a painting, the USA proposal allows no deduction in the year of purchase, and would tax any gain as under present law. In effect, this treats the purchase as an item of consumption—which it may be. This approach allows the tax system to avoid difficult problems of classifying a purchase as either personal or for investment. Suppose the taxpayer is purchasing a painting because he likes it, and does not really expect economic gain. While the taxpayer owns the painting, the taxpayer obtains the personal, untaxed satisfactions that come from ownership, which may justify in the taxpayer's mind a low or even negative return on investment.

91. Consistent with its approach on taxing the gain on sale of the painting, the USA tax would continue present law by taxing capital gain on owner-occupied housing (assuming the proceeds were not reinvested, either in a replacement residence or in "savings assets").

Hall & Rabushka would not tax an owner-occupier's gain. What is the justification offered by Hall & Rabushka for not taxing the gain on owner-occupied housing?

Which approach do you find more justifiable?

Progressivity and vertical equity

92. A major concern about any form of consumption tax is that it will be unfair to lower-income taxpayers, by comparison to our present income tax. Perceived unfairness arises from the fact that lower-income people spend a larger portion of their income on consumption. How does Nunn-Domenici/USA address these concerns? Is Dr. Penner convinced that the plan achieves vertical equity?

93. The USA proposal envisions a progressive rate structure, and the system is made more progressive by its treatment of Social Security taxes. Employers are granted a full credit for Social Security taxes, and employees a credit that is phased out as income rises. In effect, Social Security taxes are folded into the proposed USA tax, except for high-income employees. Merely ending Social Security taxes would increase progressivity, because Social Security taxes, disregarding benefits, are somewhat regressive. USA goes even further, by maintaining the tax only for high-income employees. (Looking at Social Security taxes in isolation takes a narrow view; the present Social Security *system* of taxes and benefits combined is markedly progressive.)

A simpler approach might have been simply to eliminate the separate Social Security taxes altogether, and address the desired degree of progressivity in the primary tax. Why was this approach not taken?

94.   Hall & Rabushka acknowledge that a VAT would tax consumption more simply than their proposal, but they term a VAT "unfair because it is not progressive." Assuming progressivity to be necessary to a fair tax (an issue considered in Chapter Four), how do Hall & Rabushka address equity concerns while employing a flat rate tax?

Effect on businesses

95.   The general approach of both Armey/Hall & Rabushka and Nunn-Domenici/USA is that a business can claim a deduction for purchases from other businesses, on the assumption that the other business will be paying the business-level tax. (Under both systems, the business tax is not limited to corporations, as it is under present law.)

The two proposals take differing approaches with respect to payments of wages and salaries, with Hall & Rabushka, but not USA, allowing a deduction. (USA would allow a deduction for the services of an outside accounting firm, for example, but not for the services of an employee accountant.) What is the theory of each approach?

96.   Perhaps the most striking change in business taxation is that neither proposal would allow a deduction for interest, even if paid to another business. Interest and dividends would be treated identically.

97.   Consider first the Hall & Rabushka proposal with respect to interest. What is the justification for reversing present law, which generally allows a deduction for interest paid and taxes the recipient, and moving to a no-deduction/no-inclusion model? Business interest, after all, is a business expense. Hall & Rabushka recognize that they may be taxing businesses that are not profitable, but argue that their "business tax is not a profit tax." Would businesses that borrow be hurt? How would Hall & Rabushka deal with existing debt?

98.   The USA proposal does not allow the business any deduction for interest (or dividends) paid. Businesses that receive interest need not take it into income, but individual recipients of interest are taxed. In the case of a payment of interest by a business to an individual, what is the justification for denying the business an interest deduction if the individual creditor is taxed?

99.   Dr. Penner points out that the USA business tax is designed to be border adjusted, but that under current WTO (or GATT) rules, the Armey/Hall

& Rabushka business tax could not be border adjusted because it allows deduction of wages. As Dr. Penner notes, the economic importance of border adjustment is debatable, but it is desired by American business. The issues involved in border adjustment are the same under a consumption-type tax as under a European-style VAT, and are discussed in Chapter Six, especially Notes #20-28.

Effect on saving and borrowing

100. A major objective of all consumption-type tax proposals is to stimulate saving and investment, by removing the "double tax on savings." Yet Mr. Nolan expresses concern that abandoning present law might actually undercut saving incentives. Why? Do you share his concern?

101. Alternatively, the problem might be a revenue shortfall attributable to too much saving, at least initially. Hall & Rabushka base their conclusion of revenue neutrality on figures from a past year (1993). Yet a major purpose of moving to a consumption tax is to encourage a change in taxpayer behavior, leading to increased saving and investment. Hall & Rabushka state that they anticipate "a burst of investment, which might temporarily depress flat-rate revenue because of the expensing of investment." They argue that the adverse effect on revenues would be temporary, because increased investment would result in economic growth and thus increased revenues.

Mr. Nolan, on the other hand, fears that under any consumption-type tax, "[w]e will be taking one huge fiscal gamble that the sought-after greater inducements to saving will produce an increase in investment capital sufficient to yield larger or even equal revenues from a narrower tax base."

Would you expect higher or lower revenues?

102. The theory of the USA tax should require borrowed funds to be taxed in the year of borrowing. Why? Why does Nunn-Domenici/USA not fully follow this theoretically correct approach? What approach is taken instead? What problems arise from the approach taken?

103. *Charitable contributions.* Hall & Rabushka would end the charitable contribution deduction, but suggest that any drop in contributions are unlikely to be significant in amount or permanent. They note that of $117 billion contributed in 1991, only $61 billion was deducted "on personal tax returns." (The size of corporate deductions, which also would be ended, is not mentioned.) Nunn-Domenici/USA allows a deduction, but Mr. Nolan questions the attraction of the deduction under a tax system that would allow a potential donor the same deduction for simply calling a broker (or clicking keys on a

computer) and buying stock.

Do you think adoption of a consumption-type tax would undermine charitable giving? Would that be a reason to oppose adoption of a consumption-type tax?

104. After reviewing these proposals, do you think the United States should adopt some form of consumption-type tax to replace the income tax? Why or why not? If so, what form? Why?

F. THE NEW CENTURY DAWNS: CONSUMPTION TAXATION BY EVOLUTION?

In the thirty years since Professor Andrews' groundbreaking article appeared, tax scholars have generally accepted his observation that our present "income tax" is in fact a hybrid, containing elements of both income and consumption taxation. This means that the intellectual debate concerns not two but three contenders—an income tax in the accretion, Haig-Simons sense; a consumption tax; and our present hybrid. (In Subchapter C, for example, Professor Gunn advises us at the outset (see footnote 5) that "[t]he tax here defended here resembles that of the existing federal income tax. * * * I have no desire to defend an "ideal" tax based on the Haig-Simons definition.") The two recent articles excerpted in this subchapter reveal yet another side of the debate—that of an evolving hybrid.

The portion of Professor McNulty's article excerpted here focuses on the fairness of consumption and income tax models, disputing the assertion that a consumption tax more fairly taxes savings. He also rejects a radical shift to consumption taxation as a leap from a known system that works to an unknown system that may not deliver the benefits claimed by its supporters. At the same time, Professor McNulty clearly recognizes that our present system may be moving toward a consumption model, and in his conclusion may even endorse such changes at the margin.

Professor Goldberg carries this argument further. He demonstrates that our present system has many components that more closely resemble a consumption tax system than an income tax system, and, moreover, that the recent trend is moving us decisively in that direction. He challenges the typical view of the present hybrid as an income tax with consumption tax features, arguing that a more accurate conception may be that of a consumption tax with income tax features. If we "really" have a consumption tax, this significantly affects such important analytical devises as the tax expenditure budget. For example, perhaps retirement saving is not really tax-advantaged, but, instead, the deviation from the normal (consumption tax) baseline is the disadvantageous (accretion model) taxation of some investment income.

FLAT TAX, CONSUMPTION TAX, CONSUMPTION-TYPE INCOME TAX PROPOSALS IN THE UNITED STATES: A TAX POLICY DISCUSSION OF FUNDAMENTAL TAX REFORM

John K. McNulty[*]

88 California Law Review 2095, 2143-48, 2150-63, 2169, 2171-75, 2177-82 (2000)

The Question of Fairness

Of all of the issues surrounding taxation and tax reform, issues of fairness are perhaps the most important and yet the hardest to analyze and evaluate. * * *

The Fairness Arguments

A consumption-type or cash-flow income tax is alleged to be fairer than an accretion model income tax, simply because it taxes consumption, not production (or receipt or realization of income or gain). Thereby, it removes the alleged over-taxation of saved income, and it supposedly taxes people equally, according to their ability or obligation to pay, regardless of time preferences, or as viewed from a lifetime perspective.

Typically, consumption tax advocates invite us to consider two individuals who have equal education, motivation, and skills, and who work at the same jobs all their adult lives, earning exactly the same annual compensation for their labor. Hence they have identical power to consume, if viewed ex ante. They differ, however, in that Taxpayer A, the "spendthrift," spends nearly every dollar he earns at once, while Taxpayer B, the "saver," defers some consumption and saves significant amounts to provide for a comfortable retirement. * * *

The key question is whether these two taxpayers, viewed over their lifetimes, have or should be treated as having equal taxpaying ability or obligation. They earned the same wages or salaries (paid at the same times) and had the same capacity or opportunity to consume immediately out of earned income. But, in fact, Taxpayer B consumed more (though later) during her lifetime (working years and retirement) because she saved some of her wage income and thereby earned capital income in addition. If their actual streams of consumption are discounted to the same starting point, however, they each enjoyed an equal present value of lifetime consumption.

Some thoughtful observers may say that the two have equal consumption in present value terms and hence have identical ability to pay tax, and favor

---

*. At time of original publication, Roger J. Traynor Professor of Law, School of Law, University of California, Berkeley (Boalt Hall).

a consumption-type tax because it would tax them "equally." Others, looking at the different totals of income and spending on consumption, determined by adding up annual amounts without discounting to present value, would say they had different taxpaying abilities and that an accretion-type income tax would more correctly determine their relative tax burdens. A consumption-type income tax would either allow the saver to deduct amounts saved or, similarly, would exempt income from savings from further tax.

However, one important view is that a tax that includes capital income actually is preferable to a tax that measures only rights actually exercised in consumption. * * * Wealth, for example from accumulated income, as well as consumption, arguably gives rise to taxable capacity. In this view, an income tax, in measuring "changes in wealth" as well as consumption, comes closer to measuring lifetime wealth or capacity to consume and to pay tax.

Consumption tax advocates also criticize the income tax for its failure to tax equally two taxpayers who have equal earnings, regardless of when they choose to consume. They assert that a consumption tax, even though applied and collected annually, would do a better job of taxing lifetime wealth, or ability to pay tax. * * * An income tax is likely to mismeasure "lifetime wealth" by imposing an overall lighter tax burden on an individual who earns and consumes early in life and a heavier one on the individual who postpones consumption, or earns more income but later, even though both had equal consumption power measured (at birth) in present value terms. A consumed-income or consumption tax is argued to be fairer than an income tax. Hence saved income should be deductible, or the yield excluded from an income-tax base.

Whether it would be wise to substitute a consumption-type tax system for our income-type system depends partly on public (taxpayer) perceptions of its fairness and acceptability. Whether it appears to be fair to the layperson can be as important a question as whether, under sophisticated economic or legal analysis, the proposed system is fair. There are serious appearance or transparency fairness considerations in moving in this direction toward fundamental tax reform.

Viewed through an annual snapshot, a consumption-based tax appears to be much more regressive than does an income tax, even if the income tax has the same rate structure, because in any particular year low-income people generally consume a much higher fraction of their income, while high-income people save more (in proportion), and saving would exempt them to a greater extent from a consumption-type tax. But viewed over a life cycle, during which people consume rather consistently even though their annual incomes vary, things may look different. Apart from gifts and bequests and transfer payments, we generally consume what we earn, so that the base of a tax on consumption will add up to much the same total over a lifetime as that of a broad-based income tax. But graduated rates applied to annual income may impose quite different tax burdens. However, an annual income tax can be constructed to minimize the differences between it and a longer-term or lifetime income tax.

Several academics who write about taxation issues have incorporated philosophical arguments about fairness into their work. For example, Professor Alvin Warren took up six fairness arguments in favor of a consumption tax in his insightful 1980 *Yale Law Journal* article.[189] In particular, Warren evaluated fairness issues from an ex ante and ex post perspective, and concluded that fairness in taxation "should depend on outcomes, not expectations."[190] Warren found the accretion-type income tax to be fair from an ex post perspective and the various consumption-type taxes to be fair only in an ex ante sense.

* * *

Evaluating the Fairness Arguments

Arguing for the greater fairness of a consumption tax over an income tax, proponents seem to invoke three closely-related "entitlement" propositions, as indicated in the foregoing text, that should be examined in more detail. The first seems to be an argument that a consumption tax is fairer than an income tax because it taxes equally consumption that is equal in present value terms. The second similar thought is that the consumption tax does not "discriminate" between equal income taxpayers with different tastes for present and future consumption ("spenders" and "savers"), while an income tax does do so. The third proposition, also similar, is that the consumption tax retains the same ratio of after-tax consumption power between present and future consumption as that existing in a world without tax. * * *

One question is whether any or all of these propositions is "true." Even assuming all three descriptive propositions to be true, the further question arises whether it therefore follows that the consumption tax is "fairer"?

The merits of a consumption tax seem to be argued based on the proposition that the time of consumption, rather than the time of income, is the relevant fairness criterion for judging the "horizontal equity" of each tax base.

One intervention might be "let's tax ourselves only when we spend and consume income (and wealth or borrowings?)" because that is when each of us takes a share out of the common wealth and resources of the world. * * * Is that somehow clearly the time when we should be taxed and on the amount that we then withdraw (perhaps under graduated rates)? In what sense do we

---

189. *See* Alvin Warren, *Would A Consumption Tax Be Fairer Than an Income Tax?*, 89 YALE L. J. 1081, at 1098-99 (1980).

190. *Id*. at 1100, 1152.

withdraw from a common pool when we consume? Is my corn, growing on my property, part of the common pool, until I eat it? Or allow it to rot? Or give it away? Or use it to seed my farm? Maybe so in some way. If the resource consists of a longer-lived plant, a tree for example, and I didn't consume it, it will be there for my heirs or will escheat to the state, and somebody else will get to "consume" it. And maybe my crop in part can be attributed to the science, safety, know-how and respect of others of the population who contributed to the product.

But if I am paid the corn or the tree for the work I do, and I become thereby richer and could eat the corn or cut up the tree to make a log cabin, may not that receipt be the time when my capacity to pay is best determined, based on what compensation I received for my labor, properly valued, and the time when human intuition makes me most agreeable to pay the tax, even if I have to sell some of the corn to get the cash to pay tax on the receipt of all the corn? * * *

So, one form of response to the fairness and "discrimination" argument against an accretion-type income tax is that the argument seems circular. If the criterion for taxation of equal taxpayers equally is "consumption" or "equality of consumption" or "time-value of consumption," then an income tax that includes the yield on savings can be said to treat high-level consumers, who spend most of their income as soon as it is earned, differently from equal-income high-level savers, who spend more later in life, and hence to "discriminate" against the savers. But the conclusory label of "discrimination" depends on adoption of consumption as the fairness standard. The conclusion simply depends on the predicate.

The fairness argument against accretion-type income taxation should stand independent of a prior presupposition that consumption is the fairer tax base. So far, it hasn't done so.

The argument in favor of the income tax can be asserted in a parallel way. That is, one can assert that income rather than consumption simply is the better gauge for determining the fair distribution of tax burdens. * * *

So it is sometimes conceded that the income tax changes the relative positions of the two taxpayers. But again there arises the question, what is the significance of the stipulated "no-tax world" ratio? Why is it "unfair" (or "discriminatory") to disturb the relationship between spenders and savers that supposedly would exist in a world without tax? * * *

Yet there is nothing absolutely necessary or compelling about the present-value analysis. * * * Earning or receiving the income is the time when the taxpayer has effective choice and control over the increased economic resources. The income tax then does not unfairly "discriminate" at all between consumers and savers, if the reference point is not base Year 1 but the year of earning or receipt.

Earlier earning would seem to give a taxpayer such as the youthful basketball star more choices (in some sense) than the late-earning concert pianist, or more security. * * *

One way of formulating much the same issue is to ask for argumentation as to why the tax burdens of two taxpayers such as the (early earning) basketball pro and the (later earning) concert pianist should be geared to expectations rather than outcomes. Most dramatically this question applies to "winners and losers" in a yield-exemption consumption tax world (which treats equal expectations alike regardless of differences in outcome) compared to those in a cash-flow income tax (consumption tax) world (which taxes the two differently, according to outcomes and actual resources available for consumption). * * *

The Use of a Tax-Free Frame of Reference

The consumption tax advocates' argument is that it is unjust for any tax to discriminate between the current consumer of $100 earned now and the counterpart who earns $100 now but saves it for a year to consume $110 a year hence. A consumption tax or consumption-type income tax imposed on both taxpayers when they each earned $100 would not differentiate between the two, and so it is said to be fairer than an income tax that would tax the yield (at, say, 33%) and leave only $106.70 for consumption a year later. * * *

Granted, in a 10% risk-free yield world the choice would be between $100 now and $110 a year later. But arguably that does not matter. Contemporary taxpayers live in a world with tax, an accretion-type income tax. Admittedly the tax affects the ratio of the values of present and future consumption. * * * Does that make the income tax "unfair" or "discriminatory"? Or just something that may discourage deferral of consumption?

* * *

[D]oes the difference between treatment of taxpayers when compared to a no-tax world make the income tax unfair or less desirable? This is so only if one assumes that interest rates do not adjust to compensate for this difference, and if one accepts that the relationships between present values or costs of immediate or deferred consumption are optimal and form the only or best standard against which post-tax relationships are to be judged.

Temporal Choices and Present Valuation

The present value of income received in the future to fund later consumption is lower than that of income received in the present and used for immediate consumption. The burden of a deferred tax on income amounts to less than that of an immediate tax (at the same rate) on income, and a consumption-type tax either defers both payment of the tax and determination of the taxable amount until actual consumption (as with a retail sales tax), or imposes no tax on the yield from saving and investing income (deferred consumption). Moreover, the lower burden of that deferred tax is said to be "correct" because in the end it imposes a more uniform burden (in time-value-of-money terms) on consumption, whenever it occurs, than does an accretion-type income tax, which is said to place an excessive burden on deferred consumption.

The same neutrality, vis-à-vis consumption of a consumption-type tax, means that the tax does not fall more heavily on one taxpayer or another solely because of inter-temporal differences in need or taste for goods or services, now or later. This is put forward as a great virtue.

    * * *

But it seems valid to argue that if the cumulative amount and present value[228] of the saver's income are greater than the cumulative amount and present value of the consumer's income, and if ability or obligation to pay tax is measured by gain, command over resources, or power to consume, it seems entirely fair to tax (as income) the enhanced power to consume more heavily than the lesser income and power. Even if the yield be partly or wholly compensation for the pain of deferring consumption, psychic deprivation, risk or some other cost or loss borne by the taxpayer, taxing the added income resembles the accepted practice of taxing the person more if he had worked longer hours, sacrificed leisure, or endured more fatigue to generate more labor income during the year. It does not seem attractive to say that the rewards of work should be taxed but not the return from capital that has been saved and invested. * * *

The advocates for consumption taxation over income taxation assert the greater fairness (and neutrality) of a tax that applies when a person consumes (his income) rather than when he earns or receives income that will fund present or future consumption. But this argument in a way depends on its own premise, that is, the assertion that the time of receiving income (which contributes to the ability or capacity to consume) is not the appropriate point of reference and that the time of consumption is the better reference point.

There may be arguments in favor of this predicate but one may assert the contrary, and argue it, as well. Perhaps the time a taxpayer earns or receives economic resources and becomes able to consume or save or donate (or waste) them as he chooses is the better reference point. At this point of production or receipt, society may properly assert its prior claim, prior to that of the individual recipient. Economic power, the choices it offers, and the benefits it

---

228. *See* Richard Goode, *The Superiority of the Income Tax*, *in* WHAT SHOULD BE TAXED: INCOME OR EXPENDITURE? 55 (Joseph Pechman ed., 1980). * * * The saver pays more tax than the consumer not merely because he postpones consumption, but because he is compensated for doing so and obtains interest income, which enhances his power to consume.

provides perhaps do not consist solely of explicit "consumption"; and the fairness comparison of "equals" may tend to beg the question.

Interest, Renting Money and Yield

In a world without tax, borrowers with different resources, needs, time preferences (for consumption) and productive capacities will negotiate with borrowers or lenders to "rent" their money at some interest rate. This capital market will presumably reach an equilibrium and a positive interest rate that is determined by the time preferences, at the margin, of the various actors. Suppose that rate would be 10%, compounded annually. If an income tax distorts that rate, because the interest is taxable (and maybe not always deductible by borrowers, or is deductible at different tax rates, and so forth), then the tax may be said to have interfered with an efficient market solution. Perhaps now the rate has to be, and becomes, 12%. Less borrowing and lending (saving) will probably follow.

That distorted result will not be the efficient or optimal one, but it is not necessarily an unfair one. If the before-tax 12% rate amounts to an 8% after-tax rate for a 33 1/3% bracket lender, rather than the 10% after-tax rate we think would prevail in a world without income tax, the fact that the 8% rate differs from the 10% rate is not necessarily a fairness matter, it is an efficiency or non-neutrality issue, a distortion and a difference introduced between before and after-tax interest rates, with the probable result of less saving and investment than would be optimal. Future generations may not be as well off. But as to fairness between living taxpayers with equal initial incomes, a saver or spender can make decisions in this world about how much present consumption to defer, given the prevailing after-tax costs and rewards and his needs or preferences. An income tax that applies to the capital income of the saver is not discriminating against him in the sense of violating some horizontal equity criterion.   Rather, it is constituting the world and the conditions he faces.

    * * *

Conclusions about the Time-Value of Consumption

To summarize, my position is first that there is no demonstrated inherent preference in all individuals for early consumption rather than deferred consumption. * * *

Since receipt of $100 now, rather than a year hence, often has value to an investor equal to or even over and above the $10 yield that it can obtain in the capital market, the early earner (or late consumer) often has more utility or benefit or gain from receiving his $100 at Time 1 rather than a year later, at Time 2, more even than the 10% interest yield. Hence it is, or may be, a relevant difference for purposes of tax equity that one taxpayer is an earlier receiver or a later consumer than the other. A tax differential, particularly a heavier burden in present value on the early earner or late consumer, is not necessarily unfair or discriminatory in an unjust way. An income tax may be as fair as, or fairer than, a consumption tax.

The relevant differences partly involve the untaxed consumption or benefit, of a psychic or of a tangible form, that saving or early receipt of income provide. Having income early and saving at least some of it often provides not just more tangible consumption later, $110 worth in a year rather than $100 worth now (always assuming constant prices), but real benefits that a consumption tax does not reach, such as imputed or hidden consumption or utility. There may be a "consumer's surplus." The early earner (who then saves) can enjoy more leisure or economic security, partly at least in the form of mental relief from anxiety about an impoverished old age, than the late earner or the early consumer. He may also enjoy prestige in the community, admiration or ingratiating behavior from family or friends, more choices in forms of (taxable) consumption, pride in his actions or in his ability to provide security for himself and his dependents, freedom from guilt, more enduring, happy and nostalgic memories derived from his or her consumption or more happy and confident anticipation of future, enhanced, consumption. Above all, he has the easy freedom of choice. He or she need not depend on borrowing in an uncertain capital market to fund consumption, subsistence or luxury; the taxpayer can choose more readily, in economic and social, personal or even political ways than can the starving early consumer or later earner. These benefits are not reached by a consumption model tax; they are potentially (or crudely) reached by the existing income tax when it taxes the explicit financial yield or market gain represented in the simple example by the 10% interest earned on each $1.00 saved. Hence the higher tax burden imposed by an income tax is, or at least may be, fair enough and even fairer than a consumption tax, if such values are thought to be relevant to the measure of appropriate tax burdens, or taxpaying capacity.

Admittedly, others may find the morality of the saver's behavior, or the socially and economically beneficial consequences of the saver's actions to be relevant to the fairness of tax burdens. That argument should be evaluated, but it differs from an argument that any tax that distorts the time-value-of-money proportions that would exist in a no-tax world is therefore, automatically, in that way, unfair or unjustifiably discriminatory. Such an argument circularly depends on, and merely reasserts, its own premise—that the time value of expenditure or consumption in a no-tax world sets the standard. * * *

Nothing suggests that savers in a taxed world are "entitled" to the same ratio of present and future consumption power that they would have in an untaxed world. This remains true even if it is assumed that interest rates would be the same in both worlds.

To be sure, there would seem to be unfair "discrimination" between savers in a taxed world if some wage earners were taxed by an income tax on receipt of wages and others were not taxed until they expended their wages. The first group would bear heavier tax burdens than the second group, and if no difference between the groups justified the disparate treatment, if it were random or according to the whimsy of the law-giver, the result would be unjustified, and unfairly discriminatory. Each group would appear equally entitled to enjoy the same after-tax consumption power.

But as between savers and consumers in a taxed world, or as between savers in a taxed world and savers in a (postulated) untaxed world, no such equal entitlement appears. So to tax them differently is not to violate some evident principle of equal justice and distributive equity. It can be a wise or unwise tax policy for purposes of encouraging or discouraging saving, but that is a dimension separate from a horizontal equity or other fairness dimension.

* * *

Appearance of Fairness

Appearance of fairness concerns also figure in considering which of the particular consumption tax models to use. Do people prefer an ex ante or an ex post approach to defining ability to pay? For example, either a cash-flow approach, which allows deduction of investment and imposes taxation on yield, or a yield-exemption tax prepayment approach, which has no deduction for investment but exempts yield from tax, could be chosen and viewed as theoretically or financially equal. But they differ in that a yield-exemption approach fails to tax big winners more heavily than small winners or losers.[260]

---

260. To illustrate this point, consider a real world, one in which returns to investment vary and there are "winners" and "losers." Consider two taxpayers, C and D, under a cash-flow system. Each saves $10,000 out of a $100,000 salary. Taxpayer C, makes a saving or investment choice that in one year earns her a yield of 30% ($3,000), three times what was expected and three times what the other and less lucky taxpayer, Taxpayer D, earned at 10% ($1,000). Since each one got a deduction of $10,000 when he or she saved or made the investment, the yield is taxable, at the assumed uniform rate of 33%. So Taxpayer C has to pay $1,000 in tax ($3,000 yield times 33% tax) and Taxpayer D has to pay $330 in tax ($1,000 yield times 33% tax). Each has paid a tax proportional to his or her earnings. Since Taxpayer C earned three times as much as did Taxpayer D, C must pay three times the tax, after paying which she has three times the spending power ($2,400) of Taxpayer D ($670). Fair enough to many people, especially given the flat rate of tax, which takes a proportional approach at the margin.

Now compare the treatment of identical winner-loser events in a yield-exemption world. Neither gets a deduction for saving $10,000, so each one pays $3,300 in "income" tax on the $10,000 of income he or she actually saved in Year 1. In Year 2, the yield is exempt to each: Taxpayer C has $3,000 yield and $13,000 to spend; Taxpayer D had $1,000 yield and $11,000 to spend. But, earlier, each paid the same total tax, $3,300 ($10,000 x 33%) at the same time. So D paid tax of $3,300 on income of $11,000 ($10,000 in Year 1 and $1,000 earned on saving), for an effective rate of $3,300/$11,000 or 30%. In contrast, Taxpayer C paid tax of $3,300 on income of $13,000 ($10,000 earned in year one and $3,000 earned on her saving or investment), for an effective rate of $3,300/$13,000 or only 20%.

The tax treatment was not flat, single, uniform, or, in the view of some, fair. The yield-exemption

An important question is whether that result is acceptable.

* * *

Thoughts for the Future of Tax Reform
Overall Strengths and
Weaknesses of Reform Proposals

The most serious weaknesses of substituting a consumption-based tax for an income tax seem to be potential, actual, or perceived regressivity or lack of progressivity; equally and thus unfairly taxing winners and losers, at least if the tax-prepayment or yield-exemption method is employed; and transition issues. Also a consumption tax alone does not limit accumulation of wealth the way an income tax probably does, even though wealth provides, it should be repeated, power, prestige, security, command over resources, and untaxable consumption. * * *

The suggested strengths of a consumption-type tax include an improved lifetime perspective (lifetime consumption generally equals lifetime income, although the timing may be different); the base is argued to be fairer if emphasizing consumption; the timing may be thought by some to be right as to present and future consumption; and the changes could induce increased savings. In addition, there might be greater long-term simplicity. The dimensions of simplification could appear in the areas of cost recovery: cash-accrual accounting methods; similar tax treatment of all businesses, regardless of form; diminishing income-shifting advantages; abolition of the Alternative Minimum (Income) Tax; removal of the entire system of taxing long-term capital gains at special rates; and restricting the allowance of capital losses, and the attached or implicated rules and sub-systems. Inflation would probably raise fewer tax base problems.

But a host of implementation problems would remain or arise. Among the problems remaining are those of definition, such as what is "business" versus "personal," what is "consumption," what is "saving," or "investment"? There would be significant problems of valuation of fringe benefits, barter, and compensation "in kind." Issues of imputed consumption would also pose particularly serious problems. So would loss carryovers, mixed-motive (personal and business) expenditures, treatment of non-profit institutions and government entities, financial intermediation services, and treatment of U.S. citizens living and consuming abroad. Lawyers and economists have

---

method ignored (or could not take into account) the $2,000 difference in consumption power between the big winner and the loser or ordinary winner. The cash-flow or immediate deduction method took the difference into account in determining their tax burdens, because the tax was imposed upon withdrawal, ex post, when the amount actually available for consumption was known. * * *

Consequently, the method chosen may prove to be very significant, even though they are generally regarded as equivalents.

previewed some of the avenues for evading a cash-flow or yield-exempt direct consumption tax, sometimes through the use of cross-border transactions. And tax relief for poor individuals might be desired, but it, or its form, could be controversial.

Some of the most significant considerations have to do with a consumption tax's supposed economic effects. * * *

What can be expected in the way of macroeconomic effects? Would a shift from a hybrid income tax to a tax mainly on consumption actually curtail consumption? Would it increase private saving? Even if a consumption tax increases the incentive to save or, compared to an income tax, reduces the income tax disincentive to save, the change in incentive may not produce a big change in behavior: saving. Evidence from the United States suggests that private saving and work are not very responsive to the after-tax rate of return. * * *

Also, new distortions may be added. Investment and effort that produces or enhances exempt capital income would be favored. Lower-taxed foreign consumption might be favored. Disguising consumption as saving would save taxes as would, in some systems, disguising retail purchases as business inputs. Physical capital might benefit at the expense of investment in human capital, yet with fewer positive externalities.

What about investments in human capital, such as through education, training, health care, and other such things? Our present income tax may be seen as favoring investment in physical or financial capital over investment in ourselves and our capacity to earn income by rendering useful services. A cash-flow type income tax or a consumption tax would do so even more, because the costs of all material investments could be deducted currently, and consequently more compensating allowances for human capital investments might be needed for neutrality and for desirable social development.

Finally, if one regards a tax on a base of income—command over resources, ability to save or consume—to be the fairest measure of ability to pay, shifting to a consumption tax would reduce the equity of the main tax system.

Some Observations on Preferable Tax Reform

When all is said and done, it would seem better to retain the tried-and-true income tax in the United States and somehow manage to integrate the corporate and individual taxes. Probably the income tax base should be broadened, for example, to include fringe benefits, perhaps by denying deductibility of their costs by employers. In addition, some exclusions should be repealed, such as (possibly) those for gifts and bequests, municipal bond interest, gain on sale of one's principal residence, and other such exclusions (or deductions).

Improving the income tax should also involve adding better inflation-indexing or price-level adjustments, taxing capital gains at ordinary income rates or increasing the mark-to-market (pre-realization) coverage, trying to make more uniform the taxation of income from capital, rationalizing the system (if any) of savings incentives, simplifying the law at the compliance level (repealing the A.M.T., phase-outs of exemptions and deductions) and at the "incentive/strategic" level (capital-gains relief, § 1014 stepped-up basis, marriage tax bonus/penalty, I.T.C., R.&D. credit, and so forth), even at the expense of some equity losses. And the income tax could be improved by minimizing consumption and investment distortions (tax-free fringe benefits, various personal credits, muni-bond interest exclusion, percentage depletion, exclusion of life insurance build-up, and maybe even allowances for home mortgage interest, charitable contributions and medical expenses).

If the United States wanted to, it could expand savings allowances such as IRAs, Keoghs, and §403(b) or §401(k) plans still further, and thereby the income tax would shift further toward a consumed-income tax base, with encouragement for higher savings rates, but without the economic and legal shock, transition costs and great uncertainties that would come from substituting a whole new consumption or cash-flow tax regime.

Perhaps the United States should repeal the estate and gift taxes and repeal the § 102 exclusion for gifts and bequests, so as to tax the donees on receiving such economic income. Or donors could be given constructive realization treatment of gains and losses at the time of transfer.

As to excise taxes, one certainly could argue that we should tax gasoline much more heavily, at least to bring the after-tax prices closer to those prevailing in most other industrialized countries in Europe and Asia. Also the United States might tax more heavily certain behaviors or de-merit goods, such as consumption of cigarettes, alcohol, and activities that generate high levels of pollution.

Another approach draws from the experience of our major allies and industrialized trading partners, but it is so obvious that it may escape our attention. Perhaps the United States should add a national VAT or consumption-type tax or premium to our existing tax base as a long-term policy and reduce or reform the income and other taxes in order to spread and reduce the distortions, revenue-raising capacity, and marginal rate incentives to avoid tax. The revenues might also be used to reduce the national debt and to support desirable public programs.

Given the uncertainties, transitional unfairness, transaction and legislative, administrative and compliance and other costs of substituting a relatively high rate, new consumption-type tax for our income taxes, with which we have great experience and know-how, the add-on rather than the replacement approach seems the much sounder policy path to follow. Even Nicholas Kaldor supported proposals to use the expenditure tax as a supplement to, rather than as a replacement for, the income tax.[280] Or as recommended by S.O. Lodin, Congress might retain but flatten the income tax and place a new graduated expenditure tax on top. Alternatively, or in addition, it might adopt a periodic wealth tax, as the Meade Report also recommended.[281] Or, some would say, wealth, or wealth transfers (and hence "wealth" itself), could be taxed more heavily.

* * *

THE U.S. CONSUMPTION TAX: EVOLUTION NOT REVOLUTION
Daniel S. Goldberg[*]
57 Tax Lawyer 1, ___ (2003)[y]

Introduction

Much of the recent discussion in the literature regarding fundamental tax reform has centered around the abandonment of the income tax in favor of a consumption tax. Not as well publicized is that there has been significant movement toward a consumption tax already, through evolution. And, the income tax is likely to move even further in that direction in the coming years. This article focuses on these thoughts and observations and considers their implications for fundamental tax reform.

* * *

A Consumption Tax: The Alternative Methods

One way to measure personal consumption is to begin with a taxpayer's income and then subtract savings or increase in wealth. Income is generally defined for economic purposes as a taxpayer's (1) personal consumption during the year plus (2) increase in wealth during the year. As such, the tax base in an income tax would generally encompass both of those elements. By subtracting savings from income, the resulting tax base would capture only a taxpayer's personal consumption. This model of the consumption tax is sometimes referred to as the "cash flow consumed income tax" or simply the "consumed income tax." It was originally proposed by William Andrews, a

---

280. Joseph J. Minarik, *Conference Discussion*, in WHAT SHOULD BE TAXED: INCOME OR EXPENDITURE 303.

281. *See* J.E. MEADE, INSTITUTE FOR FISCAL STUDIES, THE STRUCTURE AND REFORM OF DIRECT TAXATION (1978).

*. At time of original publication, Professor of Law, University of Maryland School of Law.

y. This article is being excerpted prior to publication in Tax Lawyer. For that reason, no citation is given to precise pages. It is possible that in the final editing process before publication in Tax Lawyer, changes may be made, so that this excerpt may be slightly inconsistent with the article as published. It is anticipated that such changes, if any, will be minor. (Ed.)

Professor of Law at the Harvard Law School, in a 1974 Law Review article published in the Harvard Law Review. That article is generally regarded as the genesis for serious thinking about the consumption tax as a replacement for the income tax.

Another way to tax consumption is to tax all income from labor and business, regardless of whether it is saved or spent, but exclude income earned on investment assets. This model of the consumption tax is referred to as "yield exemption." Under certain assumptions, this method of achieving a consumption tax is the economic equivalent of the consumed income version. This equivalence and its implications are discussed below.

Finally, a third way to tax consumption is to impose a tax on the consumption expenditures at the point of sale. This model of the consumption tax is referred to as "point of sale taxation." A retail sales tax and its cousin the value added tax use this method.

* * *

Consumption Tax Provisions of the Internal Revenue Code

The current Internal Revenue Code already contains many consumption tax provisions. As discussed below, it seems likely that more are on the way.

* * *

Retirement Plans

Retirement plans represent the largest statutory inroad of a consumption tax feature into the income tax regime. Corporate defined contribution retirement plans including those that permit employees to indirectly fund their own accounts by voluntarily reducing their wages to provide a source for employer funding, referred to generally as section 401(k) plans, Keogh Plans for self employed and Individual Retirement Accounts ("IRA"s), both traditional and Roth, are the principal types of retirement plans. Section 401(k) plans, Keogh plans and traditional IRAs provide tax deferral. They permit deductions or exclusions for amounts contributed to the plan by or for the benefit of the taxpayer and tax-free build-up of interest, dividends or appreciation as long as the funds remain in the plan, but require income inclusion when funds are withdrawn. In this sense, the plans operate in the same manner as a cash flow consumed income consumption tax would, but are limited to amounts contributed to the designated retirement accounts. In addition, amounts that may be contributed to the plans and therefore deferred as income are subject to annual limitations. The highest of these limitations is $40,000 for Keogh Plans and defined contribution corporate sponsored plans with employer contributions. Employee elective contributions to section 401(k) plans are limited to $12,000 in 2003, increasing to $15,000 per year when the changes under the 2001 Act are fully phased in for 2005 (subject to the overall

$40,000 contribution limit mentioned above) and traditional IRAs currently have even lower contribution limits of $3,000 increasing to $5,000 in 2008.

The aggregate amounts involved in retirement plans are by anyone's measure quite large. * * *

As of November, 2002, it is estimated that there were 432,403 section 401(k) plans, involving 47,210,000 participants, with estimated total assets in these plans of $1.81 trillion.

Retirement plans differ from a consumption tax, however, in their treatment of distributions from the plan. Distributions are taxable to the recipient when received, whether or not consumed. Moreover, retirement plans (other than Roth IRAs) require that distributions begin no later than when the beneficiary attains the age of 70½, and that they continue during the periods following commencement of distributions based upon an actuarial measure of the beneficiary's remaining life (and the life of the surviving spouse, if elected). Further, even upon the death of the plan beneficiary, the amounts in the plan (other than a Roth IRA) will be subject to tax upon distribution as income in respect of a decedent, although with significant additional deferral, particularly for a surviving spouse, who can roll it over into her own IRA.

Nevertheless, because of the rules requiring distributions, retirement plans approach but do not quite reach the cash flow consumed income consumption tax model.

Both contribution limitations and distribution requirements are being reviewed by Treasury, and it is likely that allowable contribution amounts will be expanded and distribution requirements will be eased in future years in order to encourage savings and not force dissaving. During the past few years, in fact, the contribution limits have increased for all types of plans.

Roth IRAs contain their consumption tax feature by means of exemption of the earnings from taxation rather than by allowing a deduction or exemption for the contribution itself. As long as funds remain in the plan, earnings on those funds will enjoy permanent exemption from tax. The future earnings on funds once distributed are no longer free of tax. In contrast to the traditional IRA, however, the Roth IRA, as currently in effect, does not provide for mandatory distributions during the owner's lifetime. As such, they represent a means of accumulating wealth to be transmitted at death. Further, it is contemplated by Treasury and likely that section 401(k) and Keogh plan participants in the future will be able to choose the Roth yield exemption regime for these plans rather than contribution deduction or exemption.

Curiously, both traditional and Roth IRAs permit penalty-free distributions for various specified purposes other than upon death, disability or attaining age 59½, referred to as a "qualified special purpose distribution." These include traditional IRA distributions for certain medical expenses, those made during periods of the owner's unemployment, subject to requirements and limitations, those made for an owner's "qualified higher education expenses, and "qualified first-time homebuyer distributions."

Roth IRA penalty free distributions are more limited, but include distributions up to $10,000 lifetime maximum used to purchase a principal residence by or for a first time homebuyer who is the owner of the IRA, her spouse, a child, grandchild or ancestor of the owner or spouse.

These flexible distribution rules, which allow distributions for reasons other than retirement, belie the original purpose of creation of the accounts as individual retirement accounts. This flexibility, which post-dates the original enactment of the traditional IRA legislation, evidences the more general consumption tax nature of the arrangements.

If one were to posit the simplifying assumptions that retired people spend all of the amounts that they saved previously in their lives, because for example, they purchase an annuity with the balance in their retirement accounts for their lives (including spouses), or a distribution schedule can be selected to reflect their consumption pattern, then the equivalence to a consumption tax pattern is complete, at least with regard to retirement plans. Thus, if legislation under the income tax would better permit taking distributions only when consumption was desired, a consumption tax pattern would be approached.

But what about savings outside of retirement plan? These savings are not treated preferentially. But, unrestricted savings of most wage earners (apart from their home) pale in comparison to the savings built into retirement plans and anticipated future social security benefits.

The Bush Treasury proposal would have both simplified and expanded individual retirement arrangements by replacing traditional, Roth and nondeductible IRAs with Retirement Savings Accounts (RSAs) and permitted other kinds of tax advantaged savings through Lifetime Savings Accounts (LSAs).

The proposal, in general, would have permitted a taxpayer to contribute up to $7,500 per year to each type of account. Both are yield exemption accounts, so that after-tax money is contributed (no deduction is allowed for the contribution), but the amount earned in the accounts would not be subject to tax and could be withdrawn tax-free. The Lifetime Savings Accounts, for which there would be no income limitations, would allow withdrawals freely regardless of the age of the owner or the use of the distributions and there would be no minimum distribution requirement during the owner's life. The Retirement Savings Accounts, as proposed, would require for withdrawal that the taxpayer be at least 58 years old, disabled or deceased. Importantly, both yield exemption provisions would likely soak up a taxpayer's available money, leaving little other money that would earn a currently taxable yield. The Lifetime Saving Accounts, in particular, could have this effect because the $7,500 limit on contributions applies per account holder, so that an individual can make separate contributions in that amount to accounts for other individuals. Neither the retirement nor savings proposals were enacted in the 2003 Jobs and Growth Act, but may very well be proposed again in the future.

Section 529 Education Plans

Section 529 authorizes states to create "qualified tuition programs" under which income from funds invested in the program is exempt from Federal income tax as it accumulates and, further, is exempt from Federal income tax if it is distributed and used to pay for qualified higher education expenses of the beneficiary. These include tuition, fees, books, supplies and equipment required for enrollment at an eligible educational institution.

Section 529 Plans, as they are sometimes called, allow a great deal of flexibility to the creator to choose when distributions will be made, change beneficiaries, and generally use the funds at her own discretion as long as they are segregated into designated accounts and remain there until paid for the tuition expense of the designated beneficiary, who may but need not be some member of the creator's family. In addition, the designation can be shifted from the original designated beneficiary to a member of the designated beneficiary's extended family (up to first cousin, but as a practical matter more likely to be siblings, children or grandchildren).

No Federal income tax deduction is allowed for contributions to the plan (although some states allow a minimal deduction for state income tax purposes), but the earnings on the invested funds, if ultimately used for qualified higher educational expenses, are completely exempt from tax. As such, these plans represent a yield exemption form of consumption tax feature, like a Roth IRA.

Home Ownership

The income tax benefits associated with home ownership are (1) non-taxability of imputed income from the use of the home—a benefit similar to the periodic return on the investment in the home, (2) excludability from income of all or most of the gain (for most taxpayers) on the sale of the home, and (3) deductibility of home mortgage interest, subject to statutory limits and real property taxes. The first two of these benefits accorded a home would accomplish a yield exemption model of a consumption tax for a home purchased with after-tax money. But, the treatment of a home is even better than pure consumption tax treatment, because the interest expense from the home mortgage, fairly regarded as either part of the cost of the home, or an expense of earning tax exempt income, is allowed a deduction.

To explain, if the treatment of the home followed the consumed income model, then the home would be regarded as a rental property rented to the owner herself. Under that treatment, the purchase price net of borrowed funds would be deductible as the net investment in the home and the interest charges for the mortgage would be deductible as a rental activity expense. On the other hand, imputed income from the use of the house and any proceeds from sale, if not reinvested, would be included in the tax base.

Under the yield exemption consumption tax model, in contrast, the cost of the investment would not be deductible, but the yield on the investment would not be includible. The imputed income, net of mortgage interest, plus unrealized appreciation represents the net return on invested equity, which should be exempt from tax in this model. The current income tax does even more than that. It exempts the entire imputed rental income and appreciation (for most homeowners) and further has the effect of exempting otherwise taxable earnings that are used to pay interest on the mortgage, the effect of allowing a deduction for the interest. Thus, the current tax treatment of a home reflects a yield exemption consumption tax regime, to the extent that gains are within the statutory exclusion limits. But, even analyzed under a consumption tax regime, home ownership enjoys special status, because it benefits from the tax incentive provision allowing for the deduction of home mortgage interest, within the statutory deduction limits of section 163(h), as well as the favorable tax deduction treatment of real estate taxes on the home.

The amount of forgone revenue attributable to home ownership as measured in the tax expenditure budget is huge.[90] Moreover, more than two thirds of families own their primary residence.

Business Tax Incentives

As discussed earlier, the distinguishing feature of a consumption tax at the business level in the form of an annually collected subtraction style VAT (and therefore its economically equivalent point of sale counterparts, the retail sales tax and credit style VAT) from an income tax is the complete deductibility of business expenditures, free of the capitalization requirement.

---

90. Tax Expenditures for 2003 attributable to home ownership are as follows:
(In millions of dollars)

Deductibility of mortgage interest on owner-occupied homes	66,110
Deductibility of State and local property tax on owner-occupied homes	23,580
Capital gains exclusion on home sales	20,260

Tax Expenditure Budget (2003) at 99. Imputed income of the rental value of owner occupied housing is not regarded as a tax expenditure, technically, because it is not a deviation from the reference tax baseline, even though it is a departure from a pure comprehensive income tax. Id. at 112.

* * *   In contrast, an income tax requires capitalization of long-term expenditures coupled with depreciation where appropriate.

Business tax incentives currently in the income tax take the form of either an immediate deduction of the cost of an item that would generally have to be capitalized, as under section 179, extra or accelerated depreciation, or a tax credit for all or a portion of the expenditure. Of late, immediate expensing or accelerated deductions have been the elixirs of choice.[96] For example, section 179 allows immediate expensing for tangible personal property, like equipment, used by the taxpayer in his trade or business, up to $100,000 (reduced to $25,000 in 2006 and thereafter) purchased in a taxable year for businesses that purchase no more than $400,000 (reduced to $200,000 in 2006 and thereafter) of qualifying property during the year, above which the $100,000 is reduced. In addition, section 174 allows an immediate deduction for research and experimental expenses incurred in connection with the taxpayer's trade or business, which would otherwise have to be capitalized.

MACRS depreciation allows depreciation deductions on equipment more quickly than the item is likely to get used up economically. New bonus depreciation, as it is called, accelerates the depreciation into the first year of 50 percent of the purchase price (adjusted basis) of "qualified property" as it is defined in the section, with the remaining adjusted basis depreciable under the older statutory method.

Tax credit incentives allow tax credits for a portion of the expenditures that the government desires to encourage. Tax credits include the business tax credits as well as energy tax credits, research and development tax credits and others.

Absent from this list is the investment tax credit (ITC), originally enacted in 1962 as a tax credit of seven percent of the cost of depreciable personal property, *i.e.* equipment, purchased or constructed by the taxpayer for use in the taxpayer's trade or business, later increased to ten percent and ultimately repealed in the Tax Reform Act of 1986. The ITC, however, is reproposed perennially as a stimulus to business investment.

A tax credit is a more precise and easily understood subsidy in the income tax that is not dependent on the recipient's tax rate. As such, it is sometimes

---

96. Tax expenditures for 2003 attributed to business tax incentives are as follows:
(In millions of dollars)

Accelerated depreciation of buildings other than rental housing	4,240
Accelerated depreciation of machinery and equipment	36,480
Expensing of certain small investments	1,420
Exclusion of reimbursed employee parking expenses	2,190
Exclusion of employer-provided transit passes	360

Tax Expenditure Budget (2003) at 99-100.

viewed as a separate class of business tax incentive. However, it can be readily converted to its deduction equivalent for any particular taxpayer by reference to the tax rate applicable to that taxpayer. * * *

Each new business tax incentive in the form of immediate expensing, faster write-off or tax credit brings the income tax closer to the subtraction method VAT form of consumption tax model described earlier for business entities. * * *

Observation

It appears that the current Federal income tax really presents a hybrid system, containing several important consumption tax features and trending even more in that direction with every enactment of and proposal for additional savings incentives. To the extent that the current system can be characterized as a hybrid consumption tax, then certain income tax features could be viewed as penalties on certain behavior or disincentives. For example, one might view the current income tax system as something close to a consumption tax in which some savings (those outside of retirement accounts or section 529 plans) are penalized. Taxable interest and dividends from bonds and stock owned in non-tax advantaged accounts, for example, represent the principal area of disadvantaged savings. That is particularly true of stocks, because dividends yield no corporate tax deduction to the paying corporation, unlike interest on bonds, which is deductible. In contrast, savings that are in tax-advantaged retirement accounts, newly enacted education accounts, medical saving accounts and even home ownership all can be interpreted as elements of a disguised consumption tax system.

As such, it would be a mistake to view the provisions enacted under the 2003 Jobs and Growth Act or the Bush Treasury proposals as radical departures from an income tax model currently in effect, because it would be incorrect to view the current system as such an income tax. Arguably, the recently enacted provisions and the Bush Treasury proposal could be viewed as eliminating penalty provisions in an essentially consumption tax system. At the very least, the current tax system is an income tax-consumption tax hybrid, with the trend toward the consumption tax side in an evolutionary process.

* * *

Reflections on the Evolution to the Current Hybrid System

The Hybrid System in General

If one were to design a consumption tax with components, as opposed to adopting one of the three primary models, one could treat individual items in accordance with one of the three. For example, one could employ a value added tax for businesses and a cash flow consumed income or yield exemption method for individuals. Indeed, that was the approach taken in the USA ("Unlimited Savings Account") Tax proposed by Senators Nunn and Domenici several years ago.

Even more eclectically, one could vary the approach among individual items. For example, ownership of corporate stock could be treated under a yield exemption approach, excluding dividends and capital gains on sale from income, but allowing no deduction for purchase price. At the same time, ownership of real estate or other business assets could be treated under a cash flow method, allowing a deduction for its purchase price. Such an approach makes it more difficult to understand any unifying theory of the tax, but may be more feasible politically, easier to administer or more amenable to transition. For example, adopting yield exemption for current stockholders would be a welcome improvement, whereas adopting a cash flow approach to stock may be viewed as a day late and a dollar short by the stockholder who had paid for his shares previously with after-tax dollars. Change is much easier to accomplish politically by bestowing benefits on everybody, both current stock owners and future stock owners, as under a yield exemption enactment, than on only some people, *i.e.*, new purchasers, as under a cash flow model. But even under the cash flow model, it is possible to construct transition rules that would allow a stock seller to offset sales proceeds by historical basis in determining gain, but deduct completely the reinvestment of the sales proceeds. And, in all cases, owners should expect the value of their holdings to be greater than it would have been absent the legislative tax change, resulting from the tax favored position that would be accorded stocks, although the market may not exhibit an immediate upward movement because of a myriad of other, unrelated factors.

The current tax system represents at least in theory a system grounded in the income tax but replete with tax incentives in the form of special deductions, yield exemptions and special rates, to encourage expenditures and savings deemed worthy by Congress. In effect, these incentive provisions, each an element of a consumption tax when evaluated separately, hybridize the current system. As such, it has become difficult to characterize the current system as an income tax because for many high income people, it functions much more like a consumption tax system. And, for low income taxpayers, who do not save significant amounts, there is not much difference between an income tax and a consumption tax.

For example, a high bracket taxpayer whose wealth consists largely of assets in tax deferred retirement plans (corporate pension plans, Keogh plans, IRAs, 401(k)s), a personal residence and, to a lesser extent, investment assets the sale of which would give rise to long-term capital gain (or be subject to step up under section 1014 in the event of the death of the taxpayer), it is essentially earnings from personal services (and some interest and dividends) that would be subject to tax. Most of the taxpayer's capital is subject, in effect, to a consumption tax regime.

Recent tax legislation has shown a marked trend to shift the system even further toward a consumption base. Education savings accounts, and the other special provisions discussed earlier in this paper, all aimed at high income taxpayers, who have discretionary income and savings, clearly demonstrate this trend. Yet, we still refer to our system as an income tax.

Finally, current tax proposals for dividend exclusion and preferred savings accounts may take us the rest of the way to a consumption tax at the individual level. If enacted, they could complete the evolution.

Critique of the Hybrid System

* * *

Limitation of Tax Expenditure Analysis

* * *

On the other hand, if we acknowledge that the system is not an income tax system but rather is a hybrid system, combining both income tax and consumption tax features, each being regarded as standard or structural in the system, then the battleground of the foregoing disagreement shifts. All special provisions that we now regard as tax expenditures that stimulate business activities such as the cash flow model provisions of the deduction for contributions to retirement accounts, fast depreciation and an exception from the requirement of capitalization, as well as yield exemption provisions that exempt earnings from current tax, would not be viewed as tax expenditures because they are structural in at least some form of consumption tax. Admittedly, some provisions could still be viewed under the tax expenditure lens, such as those that distinguish between profit-seeking expenditures regardless of timing, and personal consumption (e.g. charitable contributions, deductions from medical expenses and the like). Yet, under an acknowledged hybrid system, many of the tax expenditures contained in the tax expenditure budget would be eliminated and much of the accountability under the current form of the tax expenditure budget would be lost.

Notes and Questions

105.   Do you agree with Professor McNulty that consumption *plus* wealth (or changes to wealth) provides a better measure of a taxpayer's ability to pay than does consumption alone?

106.   Consumption taxation is open to the charge that it unfairly shifts the tax burden toward lower-income taxpayers, because they consume virtually all of their after-tax income, while taxpayers with higher incomes also

have a higher propensity to save. Consumption tax advocates, of course, dispute this. Professor McNulty argues the point in theory, but also asserts the importance of appearances: "[W]hether [a tax system] appears to be fair to the layperson can be as important a question as whether, under sophisticated economic or legal argument, the proposed system is fair."

Do you agree with Professor McNulty's observation as a matter of politics? Do you think that policy makers *should* pay more attention to actual fairness, or to what appears fair to the man in the street, where those two measures diverge? (In this regard, compare the views of Professor Daniel Shaviro. In a article excerpted in Chapter Fifteen, at page 973, he criticizes the notion of "perceptional equity," concluding: "Perhaps, after all is said and done, the best way to seem fair is simply to try as best one can to be fair."[z])

107. McNulty accuses consumption tax advocates of circular reasoning in arguing that a consumption tax is fairer, because "this argument in a way depends on its own premise; that is, that the time of receiving income * * * is not the appropriate point of reference and that the time of consumption is the better reference point." Do you agree with McNulty that fairness arguments in favor of consumption taxation "may tend to beg the question"?

108. Even if an income tax depresses the level of saving and investment as compared to that which would obtain in a no-tax world or under a consumption tax, Professor McNulty asserts that the problem is one of efficiency, not fairness. Taxpayers, after all, know the tax rules when they make decisions about saving, spending, and investment. Do you agree with McNulty? Or do you view his argument as an extreme form of the "Old taxes are good taxes" argument that we first encountered on page 4 of the Prologue?

109. While McNulty sees only inefficiency, not unfairness, in possibly overtaxing savers, he contrasts the unfairness that would result "if some wage eaarners were taxed by an income tax on receipt and others were not taxed until they expended their wages," at least "if no difference justified the disparate treatment." This distinction may amount to little as a guide for policy. Given that no two situations are identical, it may almost always be possible to point to plausible bases for special treatment. (Consider the arguments that might be advanced to support special treatment for each of the following: entrepreneurs, teachers, soldiers, medical workers, low-income workers.)

---

z. Daniel N. Shaviro, *Uneasiness and Capital Gains*, 48 TAX L. REV. 393, 416 (1993).

110. Should the tax system take into account the intangible benefits enjoyed by the saver/investor over the spendthrift? Among others, McNulty lists economic security, relief from mental anxiety about old age, prestige, pride, and freedom from guilt.

111. Professor McNulty appears to be particularly opposed to the yield-exemption form of consumption taxation (*e.g.*, Roth IRA, in which no deduction is allowed, but the yield is never taxed). As we have seen (*e.g.*, in Chapter Two, Subchapter A, and in Note #89 of this chapter (page 492)), this approach is equivalent in present-value terms to the more traditional approach of allowing a deduction or exclusion at the front end and taxing the full amount received at distribution (which is the form of consumption tax proposed by Professor Andrews). McNulty correctly observes that the equivalence is present only ex ante, and approvingly quotes Professor Warren's statement that fairness in taxation "should depend on outcomes, not expectations." For better or for worse, Professor Goldberg's article suggests that yield-exemption is the wave of the future.

112. Professor McNulty expresses concern that a consumption tax might skew investment toward physical capital and away from human capital, absent special allowances supporting the latter. Why might this occur?

113. While McNulty opposes substituting the consumption tax for present law wholesale, his map for possible reforms of present law includes at least two components consistent with the drift toward consumption taxation. What special justification does he offer for expansion of savings allowances for IRAs, Keoghs, and the like? For adoption of a VAT as a supplement to (not replacement of) the present income tax?

114. Professor Deborah Geier sees considerable political risk in adding a VAT to an income tax applicable only to upper-income taxpayers. (She was commenting specifically on Professor Michael Graetz's proposal in his 1997 book, *The Decline (and Fall?) of the Income Tax*, that a VAT be coupled with an income tax applicable above the level of $75,000 or $100,000 annual income, indexed for inflation.) She envisions two future political outcomes, either of which would frustrate the vertical distribution of tax burden that Graetz proposes.

First, a future Congress might lower the large exemption to the income tax, or fail to exempt it for inflation. This would follow the path of the income tax in the Twentieth Century, which began as a tax on the rich, and, as the budget expanded to finance wars and the modern welfare state, was expanded to cover most of the population.

Alternatively, "one could even envision it going the other way." In this scenario, the income tax would be attacked much as the estate tax is currently attacked, as an unfair tax on success. A future Congress might then end the income tax, and depend entirely on a flat-rate, regressive, VAT.[aa]

115. As we have seen throughout this chapter, the key difference between a consumption tax and an income tax lies in the treatment of savings. Professor Goldberg gives several examples that evidence an increasing tilt toward the employment of consumption tax principles in taxing savings.

The tax treatment of retirement saving represents perhaps the most important example of the use of consumption tax principles in present law. Most retirement savings cannot be withdrawn before retirement age without additional penalty (in addition to being taxed on the distribution itself, as would be the case for a distribution at retirement age). Professor Goldberg notes that Congress has liberalized the rules allowing penalty-free early distributions, and observes that such liberalization undermines the original purpose of encouraging taxpayers to prepare for their retirements. He makes the less obvious assertion that such liberalization "evidences the more general consumption tax nature of the arrangements." In what sense is this true?

116. Preparing for the higher education of children is one of most significant motivations for saving for millions of taxpayers. How do the relatively new educational saving plans, such as Section 529 Plans, demonstrate the growing strength of consumption tax principles in the income tax?

117. Professor Goldberg asserts that saving in the form of home ownership is taxed is some respects in accord with consumption tax principles, and in some respects even more favorably than consumption tax principles would suggest. What feature of present law is even better than consumption tax treatment?

118. Goldberg states that nontaxation of imputed income from owner occupied housing—the primary return on the investment—is consistent with consumption tax principles. For purposes of the tax expenditure budget, adoption of consumption tax principles is regarded as a deviation from income tax principles, and therefore normally results in the item's classification as a tax expenditure. In footnote 90, Goldberg he points out that nontaxation of

---

aa. Deborah A. Geier, *Incremental Versus Fundamental Tax Reform and the Top One Percent*, 56 SMU L. REV. 99, 166 (2003).

imputed income from owner occupied housing is *not* listed as a tax expenditure. Why not?

119. Professor Goldberg suggests that instead of an income tax with elements taxed according to consumption tax principles, we have the opposite—a consumption tax with elements taxed according to income tax principles. Professor Andrews suggested this possibility thirty years ago, and Goldberg demonstrates that we have moved closer to the consumption model in recent years.

Acceptance of this reasoning would affect our baseline for analysis. For example, instead of viewing retirement savings as preferentially taxed, perhaps we should view this treatment as the norm, and view the current taxation of investment return as a penalty tax provision.

120. How might such analysis affect our view of the more favorable treatment of dividend income (taxing such income at capital gains rates, rather than as ordinary income) enacted by Congress in 2003?

121. Professor Goldberg anticipates that consumption tax principles will hold even greater sway in the future. He suggests that Congress may choose to implement such principles in different ways, sometimes employing the yield exemption approach, and sometimes an Andrews-style cash flow approach. Why not use a consistent pattern?

122. Professor Geier views the coming trend toward consumption taxation with unease, if not alarm. She contrasts the allocation of present tax burdens (particularly when one takes account of payroll taxes) as a marked contrast to the original vision of the income tax. She argues that in the early days of the Sixteenth Amendment, the income tax was intentionally structured as a tax not on labor income but on income from capital:

> The income tax that was eventually enacted in 1913 was thus specifically aimed at income from capital by establishing personal exemption amounts that were high enough to free most labor income earned by most workers from taxation. So, although it was denominated a tax on "income," it's not too far-fetched to say that it acted primarily as a tax on the capital income of the wealthy.[bb]

123. Professor Geier's reservations about consumption tax principles are primarily focused on their effect at the very top—the upper one percent in

---

bb. *Id.* at 102.

terms of income and wealth. She emphasizes the importance of this top tier: "Focusing on the top 1% might seem myopic * * * but that small segment of the population pays more than 33% of the tax collected under our hybrid income/consumption tax, and it owns nearly 40% of the private wealth in this country."[cc]

It is easy to see a basis for Professor Geier's concern. For most taxpayers, a tax on income is not markedly different from a tax on consumption. (At the bottom, little saving occurs. For the middle class, the difference may be primarily one of timing—dissavings in early adult life and retirement roughly balance savings in the middle years.) But at the very top, vast wealth is accumulated that will not be needed for consumption at any foreseeable point, either by the accumulator or even the accumulator's heirs.

124. The continued availability of the interest deduction casts in question whether tax law is trending toward a true consumption tax model, or is, instead, moving toward a system that simply favors those who can obtain capital for tax-favored investment. The argument that the interest deduction is inconsistent with (properly understood) principles of consumption taxation can be illustrated by the following examples, for individual and business taxpayers.

On the individual level, consider a taxpayer who earns and consumes $60,000 (counting the payment of taxes as consumption). During the same year, the individual borrows $2,000, and invests $2,000 in an IRA. (For simplicity, assume that the money is borrowed at six percent interest, and is invested at six percent interest in the IRA.) Thus, in economic substance the taxpayer has saved nothing, and has made a "wash" transaction of borrowing and investing. Nonetheless, in the case of a traditional IRA, the taxpayer is rewarded with an immediate $2,000 deduction for the supposed retirement "savings." Or, if the investment takes the form of a Roth IRA, the taxpayer claims a current deduction for the six percent interest expense, while permanently excluding the six percent yield within the IRA. (It is crucial to the argument that the interest expense be deductible. While there are important limitations on the interest deduction—personal interest (section 163(h)(1)), investment interest (section 163(d)), interest on indebtedness to purchase or carry tax-exempt obligations (section 265(a)(2))—it is entirely possible that the transaction can be structured so that the interest expense is deductible. A likely avenue will be a home equity loan, under section 163(h)(3)(C).)

At the business level, consumption tax principles are reflected in allowing

---

cc. *Id.* at 109.

taxpayers to expense, rather than depreciate, purchases of capital equipment. As we have seen (in Chapter Two, Subchapter A), immediate expensing of capital equipment is the equivalent of exempting the yield on the equipment—consistent with consumption tax principles. But if the taxpayer is borrowing money to purchase the equipment, and currently deducting the interest paid, then the tax treatment is, at least arguably, even more favorable than principles of consumption taxation would suggest.

125. Our present system is clearly a hybrid, with elements of both income and consumption tax principles. Which do you think predominates? Do you agree that the trend is toward consumption tax principles? If so, do you think this trend desirable?

PART III

DEATH AND TAXES

It is said that "nothing is certain but death and taxes," but tax professionals know that this proverb is only half true. Whatever the certainty of taxation during life, Congress taxes wealth passing at death rather gently—excluding from taxable income the proceeds of life insurance policies, providing permanent forgiveness of income tax on unrealized appreciation through stepped-up basis, and imposing estate taxes on the estates of only about one percent of decedents. The issues discussed in this Part—particularly the future of the estate tax—are part of a huge political battle likely to continue at least through this decade.

Chapter Eight evaluates the tax treatment of the owners and beneficiaries of life insurance policies. The propriety of the rules that deny a deduction for premiums and that exclude proceeds payable at death are considered. The primary focus of the chapter is the proper treatment of "inside buildup"—earnings credited on the cash value of permanent life insurance.

Chapter Nine considers transfer taxes—primarily, the estate tax. The estate tax is a source of unending controversy, among academics and in Congress. The proper role of the estate tax—breaking up large concentrations of wealth, serving as a "backstop" to a porous income tax, increasing the progressivity of the overall federal tax system, or simple generation of revenue—has never been decided. The status of the estate tax is uncertain, with Congress enacting legislation in 2001 that will repeal it in 2010—after which it will return in 2011. Proposals considered in Chapter Nine range from outright repeal of the tax to strengthening it to provide for confiscation of most estates in excess of $250,000. Other proposals in the chapter would convert present transfer taxes, which are levied on the transferor, to taxes levied on the transferee. The continuing role, if any, for the gift tax after possible repeal of the estate tax is evaluated. The final subchapter considers the imposition of a broad-based tax on wealth, a form of tax never used by the United States Government but common in Europe.

Chapter Ten addresses the income tax treatment of property passing at death and by gift. The focus is on the treatment of property conveyed at death. Almost no one attempts to defend present law—stepped-up basis, which permanently forgives tax on unrealized appreciation—but there is no consensus on what should replace it. Several alternatives are discussed in the chapter. Carryover basis—a solution adopted in the Tax Reform Act of 1976 and retroactively repealed, and again adopted in 2001 to accompany repeal of the estate tax—would utilize the technique currently used for taxing gain on property transferred by *inter vivos* gift. Constructive realization would treat death (and perhaps the making of a gift) as a realization event, thus taxing all unrealized appreciation at the time of death (or gift). A more radical approach would tax the recipient of gifts and bequests on the full value of receipts, not merely the appreciation component.

CHAPTER EIGHT

LIFE INSURANCE

Life insurance policies usually combine pure insurance and saving features. * * *

Inasmuch as most forms of investment income are taxable, the present law discriminates in favor of saving through life insurance compared with other forms of saving and financial investment. This discrimination prompts questions of equity and economic policy.[a]

A. INTRODUCTION

This chapter examines the tax treatment of the owners and beneficiaries[b] of individual[c] life insurance policies. Life insurance is designed to reduce the financial risk of death by spreading that loss among a wide number of individuals facing the same risk. The probability of death within the coming year for a healthy 34-year-old man is approximately two in one thousand (2/1000).[d] For any individual, however, death within the coming year is not a partial event; it either will or will not occur. Thus, if a company agreed with *one* such person to pay his family $500,000 in the event of his death during the coming year, in exchange for a payment of $1,000, the "insurer" would be engaging in a transaction best described as gambling. It would either gain $1,000 or lose $499,000, depending upon an unpredictable result. Insurance companies are not in the business of gambling. Like casinos, insurance companies rely on the "law of large numbers." This mathematical principle holds that a large number of events of given probability, each unpredictable taken alone, becomes eminently predictable as a statistical matter—if a sufficiently large number of insurance policies are issued, or roulette wheels turned. The essence of insurance is the spreading of risk among many exposed

---

a. Richard Goode, *Policyholders' Interest Income From Life Insurance Under the Income Tax*, 16 VAND. L. REV. 33, 33 (1962).

b. In the main, this chapter ignores the interesting, but extremely complex, treatment of life insurance companies. Life insurance companies may be divided into two groups: stock and mutual. Stock companies are corporations owned by their shareholders, and policyholders are their customers. Policyholders are both the customers and the owners of mutual companies, which are regarded as corporations without shareholders. Both types of companies are generally taxed as C corporations, with a bewildering set of special rules found in Subchapter L (sections 801 et seq.). See additional discussion in Note #20 (page 544).

c. Most of what is said in this chapter is equally applicable to group life insurance. While the premiums on individual policies are not deductible, an employer can deduct premiums on group life insurance provided as a tax-free fringe benefit. Section 79.

d. Commissioners' 1980 Standard Ordinary Table of Mortality, cited in KENNETH BLACK, JR. & HAROLD D. SKIPPER, JR., LIFE INSURANCE 518 (12th ed. 1994).

to a risk—of death at age 34, for example—so that the many who avoid the slight risk of loss pay a small amount in order to create a substantial sum for the benefit of the few who sustain the loss. The insurance company does not so much bear risk as facilitate the creation of a pool of risk bearers.

Life insurance policies are issued in thousands of variations by hundreds of companies. An understanding of the principal tax policy issues requires some understanding of two basic models—term insurance and cash-value insurance.[e]

Term life insurance is "pure" insurance comparable to fire insurance or automobile liability insurance. For example, using the figures discussed above, an insurance company might insure a healthy 34-year-old man for $500,000 for one year for a premium of $1,000 (the *mortality charge*), plus an amount to cover the company's expenses and profits (the *loading charge*). If the insured lived through the year, his $1,000 would be lost, just as his fire insurance premium would be lost if his home suffered no fire damage. He would then have the option of insuring his life, or his house, by payment of another year's premium.[f]

The tax treatment of term life insurance is simple and relatively noncontroversial. No deduction is allowed to those who live and "lose" their premiums, and the beneficiaries of those who die do not take the policy proceeds into income.[g]

Term life insurance is significantly different from other forms of pure insurance in that the premium must rise each year, because the risk of death increases with age in a statistically predicable manner. At advanced ages, the premium can become burdensome, prompting many policyholders to forego continued coverage. The policyholders most likely to drop their coverage are those in good health, which tends to increase mortality costs even more for those who continue coverage. (The phenomenon of poorer risks being more inclined than good risks to enter an insurance risk pool, or to remain in the pool, is termed "adverse selection.") In response to this problem, and independent of tax considerations, the life insurance industry developed *cash-value life insurance*. The classic model is the level-premium, whole-life policy. The initial premium is considerably higher than for term insurance, but it is

---

e. The explanation provided here is kept as simple as possible, in some cases artificially so, in order to move as quickly as possible from the intricacies of life insurance to a consideration of related tax policy matters. For a fuller explanation of the mathematics of life insurance, and of types of life insurance policies not discussed here, see Tommy Thompson, *The Tax Advantaged Treatment of Life Insurance*, 4 TAX L.J. 27, 29-53 (1989).

f. For simplicity, this discussion assumes that the insured is the owner of the policy and pays the premiums. In many cases, the policy is purchased by someone other than the insured, frequently the beneficiary. Income tax treatment is generally the same, assuming the original purchaser owns the policy until the insured's death.

Ownership is important for estate tax purposes, however. If the owner of the policy is the insured, policy proceeds paid at death are included in the estate.

g. Section 101(a)(1). Section 101(a)(2), which provides an exception to this general rule, is discussed in Note #5 (page 532).

never increased. An insurance company issuing a whole-life policy to a healthy 34-year-old man might charge a premium of perhaps $4,000, as compared to the term policy's $1,000 first-year premium (plus loading charges for either policy). From the point of view of the insured, the extra expense would be justified by the knowledge that the premium would never increase; the term policy's premium would increase each year, ultimately to an annual cost greatly in excess of $4,000. From the point of view of the insurance company, the higher initial premium would be necessary to compensate it for providing insurance at the same premium later in the insured's life, when mortality charges would be much higher. Or, stated differently, the insurance company would need to charge a larger premium early in life in order to establish a fund which, together with interest earned by investment of the fund, will cover the face amount of the policy at the inevitable death of the insured.

This extra amount—the difference between the cost of term insurance and whole-life insurance—is placed into the insurance company's "reserves," to provide the fund to meet its future, and ever more likely, obligation to pay the face amount of the policy at the death of the insured. Thus, the premium for a cash-value life insurance policy has two components—the cost of pure insurance for the current year, and a saving element to fund the higher costs of protection in future years.[h] The insurance company, of course, invests this savings element during the life of the insured. Although the investment income is received directly by the insurance company, it inures to the benefit of the insured, at least in part, because the insurance company sets its whole-life premiums taking into account the fact that it will be able to invest the extra premiums, probably for many years. Here, as elsewhere, the magic of compound interest is of supreme importance. The earnings attributable to each cash-value policy are referred to as *inside buildup*. The policyholder can borrow the *cash value* of the policy—the portion of premiums not needed for current protection or loading charges plus the inside buildup—with no security other than the policy. Or, the policyholder can simply surrender the policy, stop paying premiums, and pocket the cash value.

The tax treatment of cash-value life insurance is substantially the same as for term insurance—the premiums are not deductible, and section 101(a)(1)

---

h. Although the cost per $1,000 of insurance increases throughout life (after approximately age 10), the amount of pure insurance provided decreases as cash value builds in the policy. Thus, if an insurance company agrees to pay $500,000 in the case of the insured's death, but the policy has $50,000 in cash value, the insurance company will actually lose only $450,000 by the insured's immediate death because the insured would have been entitled to $50,000 anyway. The mortality charge will be figured on only $450,000, rather than $500,000. Under a normal whole-life policy, the cash value increases throughout life, and, under the usual industry practice, reaches the face amount of the policy at age 100. (If the insured survives to that age, the company pays him the face value of the policy as if he had died at that time. For tax purposes, however, the transaction is treated as if he had surrendered the policy; see below.) Late in life, the cash value grows so close to the face amount of the policy that the insurance company's amount at risk is relatively small, and, even though the mortality charge per $1,000 at risk is very high, the total mortality charge may be lower than earlier in life.

allows the beneficiary to exclude the death benefit from income. If policy proceeds are received other than by reason of the death of the insured—if, for example, the policyholder surrenders the policy in exchange for its accumulated cash value—the protection of section 101(a)(1) is not available. In that case, the policyholder has income, but only to the extent, if any, that the amount received exceeds the total premiums paid.[i] Because a substantial portion of the premiums will have been absorbed by mortality charges and loading charges, the taxable element will be much less than the amount of the inside buildup, and in most cases will be zero.

Some insurance policies generate considerably more inside buildup than a whole-life policy. An extreme example is the "single-premium" policy, under which the insured makes a single lump-sum payment for the policy, which the insurance company can then invest—tax-free to the insured—for the remainder of his life.[j]

B. IS LIFE INSURANCE A "SPECIAL" INVESTMENT?

THE INCOME TAX TREATMENT OF INTEREST EARNED ON SAVINGS IN LIFE INSURANCE
Charles E. McLure, Jr.[*]

in THE ECONOMICS OF FEDERAL SUBSIDY PROGRAMS:
A COMPENDIUM OF PAPERS SUBMITTED TO THE
JOINT ECONOMIC COMMITTEE OF THE
CONGRESS OF THE UNITED STATES
Part 3, at 370, 393-94 (1972)

[T]he conceptually most satisfactory way of treating life insurance for tax purposes would be to allow full deduction of all premiums (and interest on loans to pay premiums) and full inclusion of all benefits—whether received by reason of the death of the insured or during his lifetime—in computing income for tax purposes.[71]

---

i. Section 72(e)(5).

j. To prevent life insurance companies from selling tax-advantaged investments with only a nominal insurance element, Congress has defined life insurance for tax purposes in section 7702. As part of the complex definition, section 7702 provides that if the policy's investment component exceeds that of a single-premium policy, the contract is not regarded as life insurance for tax purposes. See Note #9 (page 541).

*. At time of original publication, Professor of Economics, Rice University.

71. Theoretically the deduction for premiums could be allowed in the year in which paid and the proceeds could be included in income when received. This would accord saving in life insurance tax treatment similar to that for qualified pension plans, by allowing postponement of taxation. A more conventional approach would be to allow deduction of total costs in calculating taxable gain at death, surrender, or maturity. This would mitigate both the possibility that premium deductions might exceed income in a given year and the problems caused by bunching of income in the year of the insured's death.

Under this approach the Federal Government would automatically participate in both the pure insurance gains and the interest income components of death benefits, as well as the interest income received on surrender or maturity of policies during the life of the insured. There would be no necessity to allocate premiums between savings, pure insurance protection, and loading, since the entire premium would be deductible. Conversely, there would be no question of distinguishing between pure insurance proceeds, return of principal, and interest income so far as death proceeds are concerned, and no reason to try to identify the interest income component of benefits received during life. All net proceeds would be taxed, regardless of when realized.

It might be argued that this approach would not alter the present tax advantage of being able to offset costs of insurance (including loading) against interest income. This is true, but only half of the story. The present offset is, and would be, of advantage only to taxpayers who had been "unsuccessful" in their bet against the mortality tables and therefore remained alive to surrender their policies before death. There would, of course, be a corresponding group who had died and been taxed upon their insurance gain. Actuarially the two should balance out, with the Federal Government sharing in both mortality gains and losses, as well as interest income.

The problem with this approach is obvious: it would involve levying an income tax on death benefits. That the tax would be levied at progressive rates on interest income earned over a period of years and bunched with the pure insurance proceeds in the year of death of the insured need not be a controlling factor; averaging provisions could be modified to relieve that inequity. Nor is it that a large tax liability would be incurred even on averaged income, since allowance could be made for payments spread over a number of years.[73]

Rather, the problem is simply that there seems to be a decided reluctance to apply income taxation to insurance proceeds realized by reason of death, per se. This reluctance would probably apply almost equally strongly whether the insured were a man of 25 just starting out on a program of cash value life insurance (or covered by term insurance), whose beneficiaries would receive almost entirely pure insurance gain and virtually no interest income and return of [principal], or a man of 95 with a whole life policy, whose beneficiaries would receive virtually no pure insurance gain, the total death benefit representing return of savings and compound interest on it.

* * *

---

73. And one of the usual roadblocks to efforts to tax unrealized capital gains at death—the lack of liquidity—would presumably be less crucial in the case of life insurance, except where a lump sum settlement option had not been elected.

Notes and Questions

1. Most criticism of present law has been leveled at the tax treatment of inside buildup. But what of the basic provision in section 101(a)(1), applicable to both term and cash-value insurance, that allows exclusion of death benefits? Suppose 500 people each paid $1,000 for a lottery ticket, and the winner received $500,000. The losers would receive no deduction for their loss, but the winner would be taxed on $499,000.[k] Should the life insurance "winner" be treated more favorably than the lottery winner, given that the "losers" are treated the same?

2. Professor McLure argued that "conceptually" the gain element—policy proceeds less amounts paid for the insurance—should be included in income. This could be accomplished by either of two methods. First, the United States could follow the practice of some other countries by allowing a deduction for premiums paid, then tax the full amount of the death benefit. Or, instead of allowing a current deduction for premiums paid, the deduction might be deferred until the insured died or the policy was surrendered; at that time, the deduction and inclusion would partially offset.[l] Which of the two approaches would be preferable? Would either be preferable to present law, which allows no deduction for premiums and requires no inclusion of death benefits?

3. X wishes to provide $500,000 for his family in case he dies during the next year. He can purchase a one-year term policy for $1,000. Under present law, he would receive no deduction if he lived, and his beneficiaries would exclude the $500,000 if he died. Assume a constant tax rate of 33-1/3 percent. If the law were changed as Professor McLure suggested, X would be forced to purchase $750,000 in order to provide an after-tax benefit of $500,000. The premium for the larger policy would be $1,500, but his after-tax cost would be the same $1,000. Does this demonstrate that present law is superior to the deduction/inclusion model with regard to term insurance? With regard to cash-value insurance?

4. The preceding question assumed a constant tax rate. If insurance proceeds were included in income in the year of death, however, there would be a problem of "bunching." For example, a middle-income person might receive a lump-sum payment of $500,000, and face very high marginal rates. Is this a major objection to taxing death benefits?

Policies transferred for value during the life of the insured

5. The original purchaser of a life insurance policy can re-sell the policy to a third party. Congress denies the exemption of section 101(a)(1) if the

---

k. Section 165(d) allows losers a deduction for gambling losses during the year, to the extent of gambling gains. This is a miscellaneous itemized deduction. Sections 62, 67.

l. See footnote 71 of Professor McLure's article.

policy was purchased after issuance, with the result that the purchaser (and new beneficiary) has income to the extent the policy proceeds exceed the amount paid for the policy, including premiums subsequently paid by the purchaser.[m] Section 101(a)(2). Such transfers of policies have considerably expanded since the outbreak of the AIDS epidemic in the 1980s, with the emergence of companies that make a business of purchasing life insurance policies from persons with short life expectancies.

Is section 101(a)(2)'s denial of an exclusion to a purchaser of a policy appropriate? The reason for this limitation is sometimes said to be a desire to discourage speculation in the deaths of unrelated parties. An alternative view is that Congress is not penalizing a disfavored transaction, but simply refusing to confer an unjustified tax benefit. There may be little justification for the exclusion of policy proceeds if the new beneficiary is sufficiently at arms' length from the original owner (frequently the insured) that consideration is paid for the transfer of the policy.

6. Consider the same transaction from the viewpoint of the terminally ill policyholder who sells the policy. From the seller's viewpoint, the policy is sold at a "profit," because the sales price approximates the face value (less a substantial discount to compensate the purchaser for its (usually brief) wait for the insured's death, for the uncertainty that death will in fact occur as quickly as expected, and to cover the purchaser's expenses and profit margin). The general rule of section 101(a)(1) would not protect the seller's gain from taxation, because the purchase price was not paid "by reason of the death of the insured." Note, however, that the terminally ill taxpayer would be likely to have substantial taxable gain, because, *due to his impending death*, the purchaser will be willing to pay far more than the policy's cash value. Does this mean that the same tax policy justifications that support the section 101(a)(1) exclusion are applicable? Section 101(g)(1)(A) now treats an amount received under a life insurance policy by a "terminally ill individual"[n] as having been paid by reason of the death of the insured, and thus eligible for the exclusion of section 101(a)(1).

Section 101(g)(1)(B) extends the favorable treatment to sales of policies by "chronically ill" individuals.[o] Do the same tax policy justifications apply as in the case of sales by policyholders who are terminally ill?

---

m. If the policy is transferred by gift—typically within the family—the exclusion of section 101(a)(1) still applies. Even if the transfer is for value, the exclusion applies if the policy is sold to the insured, or to a partnership or corporation in which the insured has an interest.

n. A "terminally ill individual" can "reasonably be expected" to die within 24 months, in the opinion of a physician. Section 101(g)(4)(A).

o. A "chronically ill individual" is someone who requires substantial assistance in carrying out basic "activities of daily living" (bathing, dressing, toileting, etc.) or who suffers from a similar level of disability; the term explicitly excludes persons who are" terminally ill." Sections 101(g)(4)(B) and 7702B(c).

7. *"Key-Man Insurance" and "Janitors' Insurance."* The insurance industry has long recognized that businesses may have an insurable interest in certain employees. "Key-man" insurance policies protect the employer against the business' economic loss occasioned by the death of a top executive or similar key employee.[p] Assuming the business is the original purchaser of the policy, section 101(a)(1) excludes the death proceeds from the business' income.

In recent years, a number of companies have taken out policies on a large number of rank-and-file employees, sometimes without their knowledge, and, upon their death, have claimed the benefit of the section 101(a)(1) exclusion. Economically, the outcome to the fisc is the same as usual: While technically, perhaps the premium should be deductible and the death proceeds taxable, the no-deduction/exclusion model seems a reasonable approximation. However, businesses that have purchased such policies have been criticized for purchasing what the critics term "janitors' insurance" or "peasants' insurance" (terms emphasizing that the insureds are not "key" employees). Indeed, the economic loss to the business from the death of a rank-and-file employee—or former employee—is not obvious, and in the wake of public criticism companies appear to be pulling back from the practice. Should employers be allowed to purchase policies on rank-and-file employees for the benefit of the employer? Should the section 101(a)(1) exclusion apply?

C. THE PROBLEM OF "INSIDE BUILDUP"

While the present tax treatment of pure term insurance is rarely questioned (notwithstanding the McLure excerpt in Subchapter B), the treatment of cash value insurance has been the subject of considerable criticism. This criticism has intensified in the past thirty years, as insurance companies have developed "universal life" policies. Purchasers of these policies can vary their premium payments from year to year, or pay a substantial amount and then stop paying for years. This flexibility makes the policy appear more like a term policy coupled with an optional investment component, and provides ammunition to critics who argue that the investment component of cash-value insurance should be currently taxed to the owner of the policy.

---

p. This is entirely separate from the issue of whether the employer pays for insurance to protect the key employee's family in the event of the employee's death.

REFLECTIONS ON THE MEANING OF LIFE: AN ANALYSIS OF SECTION 7702 AND THE TAXATION OF CASH VALUE LIFE INSURANCE

Andrew D. Pike[*]

42 Tax Law Review 491, 524-30, 533-34 (1988)

It is impossible to reconcile the tax treatment of investments made in the form of cash value life insurance with the treatment of other financial investments. The interest or other investment income[171] credited to life insurance contracts is not taxed until (and unless) cash or other property is distributed to the policyholder prior to the death of the insured. For this purpose, a loan from the life insurance company secured by a contract's cash value generally is not treated as a distribution. Moreover, no limitations are imposed on the amount that a policyholder can invest in a life insurance contract.

Interest income generally is included in income currently. The most significant exceptions to this general rule involve interest on state and local bonds and interest income credited to qualified pension plans, individual retirement accounts (IRAs), and deferred annuities. Although qualified pension plans and IRAs receive extremely favorable treatment under the Code, restrictions limit the amount that an individual can invest in these tax favored savings vehicles. In addition, loans from pension plans, individual retirement accounts, or annuities (or loans secured by these assets) are generally treated as taxable distributions and result in the immediate taxation of tax deferred amounts.

Many commentators question the justification for treating interest credited under a life insurance contract differently from other forms of income from savings. Several arguments have been advanced, however, in defense of this favorable treatment. These arguments are discussed and evaluated below.

Would Current Taxation of Interest Credited Under a Life Insurance Contract Constitute a Tax on Unrealized Appreciation?

The first argument raised in support of the existing tax treatment of life insurance is that an increase in the cash value of a life insurance contract represents unrealized appreciation: "taxing a policyholder currently on the increase in the cash value of a life insurance policy would be like taxing a homeowner each year on the appreciation in value of the home even though

---

*. At time of original publication, Professor of Law, American University.

171. The same tax treatment applies to owners of both variable life insurance contracts and nonvariable life insurance contracts. See H.R. Rep. No. 432, 98th Cong., 1st Sess., Vol. 1, at 145 (1983); S. Rep. No. 169, 98th Cong., 2d Sess., vol. 1, at 572 (1984). In effect, the owner of a variable life insurance contract invests the contract's cash value in assets such as money market funds, bond funds, common stock funds, or real estate funds. K. Black & H. Skipper, Life Insurance 68 (11th ed. 1987).

the home has not been sold."[182]   Consequently, it is argued, the interest credited should not be subject to tax until the gain is realized.

    * * *

[A]ssuming retention of the general realization requirement, it is questionable whether an increase in a life insurance contract's cash value represents the type of appreciation taxed only upon realization. Treating an increase in cash value as unrealized appreciation ignores the distinction between changes in the value of an asset caused by market forces, which are not taxed until realized through disposition, and those reflecting current compensation for the use of the asset which are currently realized and taxed in accordance with the taxpayer's method of accounting. In many situations, property owners are taxed on investment income that is not received. Partners in a partnership and shareholders of S corporations are taxed currently on their shares of income earned and retained by the business entity. Interest accruing on debt instruments having original issue discount, including a certificate of deposit issued by a bank, is included in income despite the absence of a sale of the instrument.

In each of these examples, the property values reflect income earned but not received by property owners. Current taxation of the property owners in these instances, however, is not premised on the doctrine of constructive receipt. The income is includable irrespective of the taxpayer's ability to command the receipt of cash. For example, limited partners and owners of minority interests in corporations and partnerships often lack either the legal power or the effective ability to convert the income into cash without selling the property.

The cash value of a life insurance contract, like the properties discussed above, is an asset that generates income. A life insurance company's crediting of interest constitutes compensation for its use of the policy's cash value. The cash value reflects the interest credited, just as the values of the partnership interest, the S corporation stock, and the debt instrument with original issue discount also reflect income that has not been severed from the underlying asset. Because income derived from these other forms of property is taxed despite the lack of receipt, actual or constructive, the realization doctrine, standing alone, does not justify treating the owners of cash value life insurance contracts in a different manner.

    * * *

Is the Current Tax Treatment of Life Insurance Necessary to Encourage Financial Security?

A second argument in support of the current tax treatment of cash value life insurance is that an incentive is needed to encourage taxpayers to provide for their families' financial security. Though laudable, the objective of

---

182. Tax Reform Proposals-XXII, Hearings Before the Senate Committee on Finance, 99th Cong., 1st Sess. 394 (1985) (statement of the American Council of Life Insurance).

protecting one's family against financial adversity does not, of itself, justify preferential tax treatment. Beyond laudability, two further criteria must be satisfied: (1) Favorable tax treatment must induce changes in taxpayer behavior that significantly advance the perceived social goal; and (2) the behavior likely to be changed must be sufficiently important to justify the revenue loss. The goal of promoting financial security satisfies neither of these requirements.

The preferential tax treatment of investment income earned under a cash value life insurance contract is likely to induce taxpayers to invest more resources in this financial product. How does the purchase of cash value life insurance protect an individual against financial adversity? Cash value life insurance can enhance an individual's financial security by protecting against the loss of two distinct income streams. First, the contractual death benefit provides funds to replace the insured's salary in case of death before retirement. Second, the cash value provides funds that can replace a taxpayer's salary following retirement. The analysis of the current taxation of cash value life insurance requires separate consideration of each function.

Life Insurance as a Source of Post-death Income Replacement

The unique risk shifting function of life insurance relates primarily to the post-death replacement of the insured's income. A parent, for example, may be concerned that the loss of her income would leave her dependents without adequate means of support.

An individual often earns both investment income and income from personal efforts. Because the insured's investment assets remain in existence following her death, cash value life insurance is not needed to replace the insured's investment income. Admittedly, the buildup of the contract's cash value increases the individual's wealth which may generate post-death investment income for an insured's dependents. Saving in the form of a life insurance contract's cash value, however, does not differ from other forms of savings in this regard. Consequently preferential values is not justified.

The portion of the death benefit that consists of term insurance protection provides a fund that can generate investment income to replace the insured's income from personal efforts. The existence of this type of fund undeniably enhances the financial security of the insured's family. Unfortunately, existing tax incentives, perversely, are likely to induce undesirable changes in taxpayer behavior. To the extent that the tax law induces a switch from term insurance to cash value life insurance, the taxpayer is likely to obtain less insurance protection. The premium charged for a level-premium cash value life insurance contract is much larger than the initial premium for a term contract with an identical death benefit. Unless the taxpayer greatly increases the portion of her budget allocated to life insurance, the amount of insurance protection will decline.

Paradoxically, the current tax treatment also provides the greatest tax benefit to taxpayers whose insurance needs are modest: those who can most easily afford to obtain their current insurance protection in conjunction with a savings program. Taxpayers with substantial wealth, who can afford to purchase large amounts of single premium insurance, enjoy the largest tax benefits. Yet, the accumulated wealth of these taxpayers makes it more likely that their families could maintain their standard of living without life insurance protection.

Less, if any, incentive is provided, however, for taxpayers with little wealth. For those taxpayers for whom single-premium policies are too expensive, but who can afford to purchase a level-premium cash value contract, the tax benefits are less generous, but are still substantial. For taxpayers who cannot afford to pay the higher premiums charged under a cash value contract, financial protection is available only in the form of term life insurance, the cost of which, however, is not generally deductible. Because of the irrational inverse relationship between the need for insurance protection and the distribution of tax benefits, existing tax incentives to provide financial security should receive a low national budgetary priority.

Life Insurance as a Source of Retirement Income

Cash value life insurance purportedly enhances an individual's financial security by providing a source of post-retirement income. The same is true, however, of a savings account, taxable bonds, or any other savings vehicle. The income from these alternative savings vehicles generally is fully taxable on a current basis, and the savings feature of cash value life insurance provides no distinguishing characteristic that justifies more favorable tax treatment.

* * *

Would Current Taxation Create Excessive Administrative Burdens?

A third argument raised in defense of the existing tax treatment accorded life insurance is that taxing the interest as earned would create unmanageable administrative burdens. * * * Although these concerns may have been valid in the past, they have significantly less legitimacy today. * * * The industry's existing computerized record keeping and reporting systems indicate that compliance with a current taxation regime is feasible.

* * *

Does the Existing Tax Treatment of Cash Value Life Insurance Improve Vertical Equity?

The defenders of preferential tax treatment of cash value life insurance argue, fourthly, that the benefits accrue to the middle class, thereby providing a degree of vertical equity for these taxpayers compared to the wealthy. Even if the current life insurance tax regime primarily benefits the middle class, it is not clear, following the enactment of the Tax Reform Act of 1986, that vertical equity is enhanced by retaining this tax treatment. Enactment of provisions that limit the benefits of most tax sheltered investments, as well as the expanded scope of the alternative minimum tax, limit the extent to which (or at least the ease with which) the wealthy can substantially reduce their tax liabilities. Indeed, investments in cash value life insurance are currently promoted as one of the last remaining tax favored investments.

      * * *

TAX REFORM FOR FAIRNESS, SIMPLICITY, AND ECONOMIC GROWTH ("TREASURY I")
United States Department of the Treasury
Vol. 2, at 246-47 (1984)

[T]he favorable tax treatment of inside interest build-up on life insurance policies can be obtained through a contract that provides a relatively small amount of pure insurance coverage.

Interest income on comparable investment vehicles generally is not tax free or tax deferred. Instead, interest income credited on such investments generally is subject to tax whether or not the interest is currently received by the taxpayer. For example, taxpayers generally are subject to current tax on interest credited on certificates of deposit although the interest is not received until the certificate of deposit matures.

Moreover, life insurance is not subject to the significant limitations on the timing and amount of contributions, withdrawals, and loans that apply to other tax-favored investments, such as qualified pension plans and individual retirement accounts (IRAs).

The benefit of deferring or avoiding tax on the inside interest build-up on life insurance policies goes only to individuals with excess disposable income that enables them to save, and particularly to individuals in high tax brackets. This benefit is not available to lower income taxpayers and other individuals buying term insurance since it derives solely from the investment component of a policy (which is not present in a term insurance policy).

The tax-favored treatment of inside interest build-up encourages individuals to save through life insurance companies rather than other financial institutions and perhaps to purchase life insurance that they would not buy except to gain access to the favorable tax treatment of the investment income. This distorts the flow of savings and investment in the economy.

Proposal

Owners of life insurance policies would be treated as being in constructive receipt of the cash surrender value (taking into account any surrender charge or penalty) of their policies. Thus, a policyholder would include in interest income for a taxable year any increase during the taxable year in the amount by which the policy's cash surrender value exceeds the policyholder's investment in the contract. A policyholder's investment in the contract would be equal to the aggregate of his gross premiums, reduced by the aggregate policyholder dividends and other distributions under the policy and by the aggregate cost of renewable term insurance under the policy.

The investment component of a long-term life insurance contract would be eligible for any general savings incentive available to comparable investments. For example, the otherwise-taxable interest income produced by an increase in the cash surrender value of a life insurance contract during a taxable year could be designated as a contribution to an IRA.

Effective Date

The proposal would be effective for all interest build-up credited to policies sold on or after January 1, 1986: In the case of policies outstanding on December 31, 1985, inside interest build-up would continue to be free from tax until December 31, 1990. Beginning in 1991, this proposal would be phased in over a five-year period, so that future inside interest build-up on policies sold before January 1, 1986 would be fully subject to tax starting in 1995. Deferral of untaxed inside interest build-up would continue until withdrawal of funds from the policy. The policyholder's investment in the contract would not be reduced by the cost of term insurance for any period prior to January 1, 1986.

Analysis

Taxing the inside interest build-up on life insurance policies would eliminate the largest tax distortion in the financial services area and would place competing financial products and institutions on more equal footing. This would promote the efficient flow of long-term savings.

Current taxation of inside interest build-up also would eliminate the need for complex rules and restrictions in several areas, including the determination of tax liability when a policy matures or is surrendered and the definition of contracts that qualify as life insurance. * * *

Notes and Questions

8.   Advocates of current taxation of inside buildup argue that this form of saving should not enjoy a tax advantage over other forms of saving, such as certificates of deposit. Some commentators, notably William Andrews, question the assertion that the earnings generated by saving are, in fact, generally subjected to current taxation. Professor Andrews points to broad exceptions to this supposed general rule. Note that this issue would disappear under his proposed "consumption-type or cash flow personal income tax" discussed in Chapter Seven. Under the Andrews proposal, current taxation of inside buildup clearly would be incorrect.[q]

---

[q]. One commentator argues that "life insurance policies are correctly taxed, or even overtaxed, from a consumption tax point of view." C. David Anderson, *Conventional Tax Theory and "Tax Expenditures:" A Critical Analysis of the Life Insurance Example*, 57 TAX NOTES 1417, 1418 (1992). Mr. Anderson goes on to argue that even under an accretion model, life insurance is not undertaxed "when the effects of inflation and policy cancellations are considered." *Id.*

9.   A significant set of tax policy issues revolves around the definition of life insurance. It is possible to envision an arrangement of pure investment, with a tiny amount of insurance thrown in as a "fig leaf" to provide favorable tax treatment. For example, suppose a taxpayer placed thousands of dollars in a "life insurance policy," which provided for a death benefit of an amount $100 more than the cash value. Realistically, this transaction would be designed to provide not insurance, but a place for tax-free compounding of the taxpayer's investment. As Professor Thompson observes, "some definition is required to insure that the tax benefits of life insurance are properly targeted to products with sufficient insurance elements and properly limited savings or investment elements."[r]

Achieving a successful definition of life insurance for tax purposes has proven difficult. Congress has defined life insurance in section 7702, using language so abstruse that one commentator observes that the statute "sometimes appears to have been co-authored by James Joyce and Casey Stengel."[s] The drafters of Treasury I (in a statement not excerpted above) commented on the limited success of the then-existing statutory definition:

> Although the definition of life insurance places some broad limits on the use of life insurance as a tax-favored investment vehicle, it is still possible to design an insurance policy meeting this definition under which the cumulative investment earnings at currently prevailing interest rates are projected to be eight times as large as the cumulative insurance costs.[t]

Even after changes in the 1980s designed to limit favorable tax treatment to "true" life insurance, continued concern led Congress in 1988 to mandate reports, by both the Treasury and the General Accounting Office, of the policy issues involved in the tax treatment of life insurance products, including "the effectiveness of the revised tax treatment of life insurance products in preventing the sale of life insurance primarily for investment purposes."[u] To date, however, section 7702 has not been further amended.

10. Assume that life insurance is defined in a reasonable manner that limits favorable tax treatment to traditional life insurance products. After a thorough analysis, Professor Thompson concludes that "the investment potential of the inside buildup simply is not attractive. The investment potential of even a single premium policy is not great enough that a

---

r. Thompson, *supra* note e, at 53.

s. Theodore Paul Manno, *The Federal Income Taxation of Life Insurance, Annuities and Individual Retirement Accounts After the Tax Reform Act of 1986*, 60 ST. JOHN'S L. REV. 674, 674 (1986).

t. UNITED STATES DEP'T OF TREASURY, 2 TAX REFORM FOR FAIRNESS, SIMPLICITY, AND ECONOMIC GROWTH 246 (1984).

u. UNITED STATES GENERAL ACCOUNTING OFFICE, TAX TREATMENT OF LIFE INSURANCE AND ANNUITY INTEREST 1 (1990). Substantially identical language is found in UNITED STATES DEP'T OF TREASURY, REPORT TO THE CONGRESS ON THE TAXATION OF LIFE INSURANCE PRODUCTS 1 (1990).

policyholder would purchase the policy for investment purposes."[v] In other words, the mortality charges and loading charges more than offset the tax advantage given inside buildup. Does it follow that present law is correct in not taxing inside buildup?

11. Does neutral application of the realization rule require that inside buildup not be taxed until the owner or beneficiary receives money? In other words, does inside buildup more closely resemble unrealized appreciation of a capital asset, or interest credited on a long-term certificate of deposit (which is taxed currently)?

12. Tax academics sometimes seem to think that everyone considers the tax consequences of investments with the same care they would. In fact, most purchasers of life insurance are probably unaware of the tax treatment of inside buildup, and salesmen do not mention it to any but their most sophisticated clients. Nevertheless, the favorable treatment causes more money to be invested in cash-value life insurance, simply because the favorable tax treatment means that the insurance company can provide the same coverage at a lower premium. Are the principal beneficiaries of the tax benefit the purchasers of policies, or the insurance companies that enjoy a competitive advantage over other entities attempting to attract investors?

13. Professor Thompson argues that Congress has never decided on the policy bases for its taxation of insurance, and that rational taxation cannot be attained without them. For example, different tax treatment is appropriate if Congress seeks to encourage maintenance of permanent insurance protection for beneficiaries than if it seeks to foster saving for retirement."[w]

14. Favorable treatment of inside buildup favors permanent cash-value insurance, but offers virtually nothing in support of term insurance. Is favorable tax treatment of inside buildup justified because it encourages individuals to maintain *permanent* insurance, even later in life when premiums on term insurance might seem prohibitively expensive?

15. Does Professor Pike agree with the proposition that Congress should encourage permanent rather than term insurance? He argues that the tax treatment of inside buildup induces taxpayers to purchase smaller cash-value policies rather than larger term policies. Why might this be so? Assuming this to be correct, is it bad?

---

v. Thompson, *supra* note e, at 157.

w. *Id.*

16.   Is favorable tax treatment of cash-value insurance justified because it encourages saving? Is it sufficient to answer that saving in many other forms is not so encouraged?

17.   Is it important that the tax saving associated with inside buildup will be significant only if the policy is maintained for many years? Congress encourages long-term saving in other areas, such as qualified pensions and individual retirement accounts ("IRAs"). On the other hand, the amounts that can be contributed to those investment vehicles are limited, while taxpayers can purchase life insurance in unlimited amounts.

18.   Treasury I would have taxed inside buildup, but allowed it to be regarded as a contribution to an IRA. At the time of the proposal, everyone with $2,000 of earned income could contribute that amount to a deductible IRA. The drafters of Treasury I proposed a system under which very few working taxpayers would actually be required to pay tax on inside buildup, if they were willing to reduce their contributions to other IRA investments.[x] Would the Treasury I approach be equally appealing with the present restrictions on deductible IRAs?[y]

19.   If Congress were to change its approach to the taxation of insurance, what should it do about insurance policies that are outstanding at the time of the change? Whole-life insurance policies are extremely long-term contracts, so a grandfather provision would mean different treatment for holders of insurance policies throughout the Twenty-First century. Treasury I would not have taxed inside buildup on existing policies for five years, and would have phased in the tax for five years after that.

---

x. In a portion of Treasury I not excerpted, the drafters estimated that in 1983 families holding cash-value policies had average annual inside build-up of $355. Even among families with economic income in excess of $200,000, average annual inside buildup amounted to only $3,050, an amount less than the $4,000 that then could be contributed to deductible IRAs if both husband and wife had earned income. UNITED STATES DEP'T OF TREASURY, 2 TAX REFORM FOR FAIRNESS, SIMPLICITY, AND ECONOMIC GROWTH 249, Table 1 (1984).

y. Under present law, section 219(g) allows a full deduction of contributions to an IRA only if neither the taxpayer nor his spouse is covered by a tax-favored pension plan, or if adjusted gross income is less than the "applicable dollar amount" specified in section 219(g)(3)(B).

On the other hand, other recent statutory changes in IRA rules have been quite favorable to taxpayers. The amounts that can be contributed to IRAs were sharply increased by the 2001 Act. Section 219(b)(5). Taxpayers whose adjusted gross income is too high to allow for a deductible IRA may qualify for a Roth IRA, subject to more liberal income limitations. Section 408A(c)(3)(C)(ii). While contributions to a Roth IRA are not deductible, taxation of the earnings is not merely postponed, but permanently avoided. Section 408A(c)(1), (d)(1).

Even if the taxpayer's income is too high for either a deductible IRA or a Roth IRA, a working taxpayer can still make an after-tax contribution to a traditional IRA, and defer taxation on the earnings until distribution during retirement.

20. Some commentators suggest that the goal of taxing individual policyholders on inside buildup can be reached indirectly, by taxing the insurance companies more heavily, a cost that would be passed along in higher premiums. This should not be regarded as a panacea; many complexities would be entailed.[z]

This chapter does not cover in detail the distinctions between nonparticipating and participating policies and between stock and mutual companies, but limited discussion of these distinctions may be helpful at this point. Stock companies are owned by shareholders, and policyholders are their customers. Traditionally, they have sold primarily nonparticipating policies, which means that the policyholder is entitled to a fixed return, and any profits benefit the shareholders. Mutual companies are corporations without shareholders; in theory, they are owned by their policyholders. Because the policyholders double as owners, mutual companies have traditionally sold only participating policies, which means that the policyholders share in the profits of the company, usually through a premium reduction. Stock companies can also sell participating policies, and many now do so.

With regard to the issue of increasing taxes on companies as a proxy for taxing policyholders on inside buildup, the problems are wholly different depending on whether we are dealing with participating or nonparticipating policies. If Congress levied a tax on inside buildup against the insurance company, owners of nonparticipating policies would not be affected—they still would be entitled to their contractual rate of return. Such a tax might threaten the solvency of an insurance company that sold only nonparticipating policies, because its expected investment income would be reduced, but its obligations would not be.

The proxy tax would work much better in the case of participating policies. The owners of participating policies would immediately and directly bear the economic cost of the additional tax, because their policy dividends would be reduced.

21. In Canada, the Carter Commission in 1966 recommended taxing policyholders annually on investment income, and taking into account

---

z. If the tax were made applicable to reserves covering existing policies, the companies would have to pay the tax and would not have the investment income assumed when the policies were sold; the solvency of some insurers would be imperiled. *See* Goode, *supra* note a, at 54.

A tax on insurance companies as a proxy for taxing policyholders does not take into account different tax rates. All policyholders would bear the tax at the rate imposed on the insurance company. *See* Charles McLure, *The Income Tax Treatment of Interest Earned on Savings in Life Insurance*, in The Economics of Federal Subsidy Programs, A Compendium of Papers Submitted to Joint Economic Committee 370, 398 (1972).

Whatever its drawbacks, the proposal has been used in Canada. *See* Note #21, final paragraph.

mortality gains and losses at death (or when the policy matured or was surrendered).[aa] These proposals were not adopted.

Three years later, however, Canada adopted "a 15 percent tax on the investment income of life insurance companies in lieu of taxation of policyholders on this income."[bb]

22. The problems discussed in this chapter are in part unique to life insurance, and are in part common to other investments. For example, critics of the present treatment of inside buildup in life insurance policies also propose change in section 72, which generally provides the same favorable tax treatment of inside buildup in annuities.

aa. 3 REPORT OF THE ROYAL COMMISSION ON TAXATION 441-55 (1966).
bb. RICHARD GOODE, THE INDIVIDUAL INCOME TAX 133 (Rev. ed. 1976).

CHAPTER NINE

TRANSFER TAXES AND WEALTH TAXES

[A]part from its limited base, it is hard to devise a better tax than a death tax. Estates represent ability to pay. And as they are mere windfalls to the beneficiaries, they should be taxed more heavily than any other kind of acquisition.[a]

A. INTRODUCTION AND HISTORICAL ORIGINS

The subject matter of this chapter could hardly be more topical. In political terms, the estate tax has become *the* tax policy issue in the first decade of the new century. President Bush and Republicans in general have advocated abolition of the "death tax." The principal achievement of the first major tax legislation of the Bush presidency, in 2001, was a reduction of the estate tax in the years 2002-09 and outright repeal in 2010—followed, one year later, by a restoration of the tax pursuant to the "sunset" provision under which the 2001 Act was passed. This statutory posture, coupled with the fact that both parties seem to regard the estate tax as a line in the sand, suggest that throughout the remainder of this decade an ongoing political fight will determine the future of the estate tax after 2010.

Transfer taxes are imposed on the gratuitous *transfer* of wealth, at death or by *inter vivos* gift. Wealth taxes, which are less familiar in this country, are imposed on the *possession* of wealth. The income tax, which is principally concerned with the *creation* of wealth, is not a principal focus of this chapter (although, as discussed in Chapter Ten, some scholars would include inheritances and gifts in the income tax base).

Transfer taxes. *Death taxes*, which were used by the ancient Egyptians, Romans, and Greeks, are the most common form of transfer taxes, and have been used by the federal government intermittently since the Eighteenth Century.[b] Since 1916, the federal government has imposed one of the classic death taxes, the *estate tax*. An estate tax is a tax, typically progressive, imposed on an estate and based upon the amount of property passed from the decedent by reason of, or in contemplation of, death. The estate tax is the basic federal transfer tax, but it is bolstered by two other transfer taxes, both of which have traditionally been regarded as attempts by Congress to protect its policy decision to impose an estate tax.[c] Because it is possible to avoid death

---

a. Louis Eisenstein, *The Rise and Decline of the Estate Tax*, 11 Tax L. Rev. 223, 256 (1955-56).

b. *Id.* at 223, 225-26.

c. Note, however, that the 2001 Act does *not* repeal the gift tax in 2010. See Subchapter D.

* * * taxes by giving property *inter vivos* rather than holding it until death, Congress in 1932[d] added the *gift tax*. The estate and gift taxes, taken in concert, were designed to tax substantial transfers of property from one generation to the next, whether accomplished by gift or at death. Significant avoidance of the death/gift tax system could be achieved, however, if, for example, a wealthy individual transferred property in a trust to his children for life, then to his grandchildren for life, with remainder to his great-grandchildren.[e] Such a transfer would result in imposition of estate or gift taxes, but only once. By contrast, if the property were transferred by the more normal route, outright to children, then by the children to their children, etc., transfer taxes would be due on each transfer, from generation to generation. In response to this avoidance technique, Congress in 1976 enacted the *generation-skipping tax*.[f]

Although the details of the substantive law governing the estate and gift taxes, not to mention the extraordinarily complex generation-skipping tax,[g] are beyond the scope of this book, a few comments are in order. The transfer taxes have never been broad-based taxes; these taxes are borne only by taxpayers who are considerably wealthier than the average. Since 1976, the estate and gift taxes have been unified, and, in effect, progressive rates are applied based upon the current taxable transfer on top of all previous taxable transfers made by the donor or decedent. To ensure that the tax is borne only by the well-to-do, Congress provides that no tax at all is due until the "applicable credit" is exhausted. Under the 2001 Act, the applicable credit protects otherwise taxable gifts of $1 million, cumulative for the donor's lifetime.[h] In a break with prior law, the credit under the 2001 Act is more protective of property passing at death—in the years 2004-09, the credit continues to protect only $1 million of gifts, but for estates the credit is increased until it protects up to $3.5 million of otherwise taxable estates in 2009.[i] After the estate tax is repealed for the single year 2010, the sunset provision in the 2001 Act takes effect in 2011, restoring the estate tax and the pre-law level of credits.

Once the applicable credit is exhausted, the tax rate on taxable gifts and estates is high and relatively flat. In 2003, when the applicable credit protects $1 million of either gift or estate, the effective tax rate begins at 41 percent[j]

---

d. A gift tax was temporarily in effect from 1924 to 1926.

e. This assumes that the transfer could be structured so as not to violate the rule against perpetuities.

f. Section 2601 et seq. Like the estate tax, the generation-skipping tax is repealed by the 2001 Act for the year 2010, only to be restored in 2011 by the Act's sunset provision.

g. One commentator terms the generation-skipping provisions "one of the most complicated sections of an already barely penetrable tax code." G.P. Verbit, *Do Estate and Gift Taxes Affect Wealth Distribution?*, 117 ESTS. & TRS. 674, 674 (1978).

h. Section 2505.

i. Section 2010.

j. Ostensibly, the tax begins at 18%, and includes brackets of 20, 22, 24, 26, 28, 30, 32, 34, 37, and 39% before reaching the 41% bracket. However, the brackets under 41% cover only the first $1,000,000 of transfers, and are thus protected from tax by the applicable credit. *See* sections 2001, and hits a maximum of 49 percent at $2 million.[k] In subsequent years prior to 2010,[l] the tax rates are reduced at the top, making the rate schedule even flatter.[m]

These high rates, however, are imposed only on taxable transfers. Many devices other than the applicable credit are available to taxpayers and their advisors to transfer property without tax. Three major escape routes are worthy of note here. First, donors can give $11,000 per donee per year (husband and wife donors can combine their exclusion to give $22,000), to each of an unlimited number of donees, without payment of gift tax or utilization of the applicable credit.[n] This exclusion—which was increased to $10,000 from $3,000 in 1981 (and indexed for inflation after 1998)—goes considerably beyond the *de minimis* exclusion universally recognized as necessary in a gift tax system. Second, unlimited amounts can be transferred to spouses tax-free, either by gift or at death.[o] The unlimited "marital deduction" also dates from 1981, although some form of limited marital deduction had been part of the law since 1948. The theory of the current provision appears to be that a transfer from a married couple should be taxed only once, and that the single tax should not be levied until the death of the surviving spouse, when the property finally passes from the married couple.[p] Third, transfers to charity are exempt from transfer taxes, without limit.[q]

Although the federal government has chosen the estate tax, the student of tax policy should be aware of other forms of death taxes. The principal alternatives are the *inheritance tax* and the *accessions tax*. Under both of these, the tax is imposed on the transferee rather than the transferor. (As a matter of administration, state inheritance tax laws may require the executor rather than the individual heirs to make payment, but the tax is computed by reference to each individual heir, not to the estate as a whole.) The difference in technique does more than change the identity of the taxpayer. Under a progressive estate tax, the same tax is imposed whether the decedent leaves his wealth to one heir or fifty, because the tax base is the amount of the taxable estate. Under an inheritance tax, by contrast, the progressive nature of the tax is diminished if the inheritance is divided. Moreover, many state inheritance taxes impose differential rates based on the closeness in kinship

---

2010.

k. Section 2001.

l. For the single year of 2010, the 2001 Act not only repeals the estate tax, but implements a new and lower gift tax with a maximum rate of 35%. Section 2502(a). All these provisions sunset after 2010.

m. The maximum rate in 2007-09, for example, is 45%.

n. Sections 2503(b), 2513. The exclusion is $11,000 in 2003. This amount is indexed for inflation, but changes only in increments of $1,000.

o. Sections 2056, 2523.

p. The concept of treating the couple as a single entity was subsequently adopted in section 1041. This income tax provision provides that no gain or loss shall be recognized on transfers between spouses (or incident to divorce). The transferee takes a carryover basis.

q. Sections 2055, 2522.

of the heir and decedent; the federal estate tax makes no distinction, except for the total exclusion of amounts left to the spouse.

Like the inheritance tax, the accessions tax—which has not gone past the proposal stage in this country—would tax recipients. The progressivity of the tax, however, would be based on taxable gifts and inheritances received throughout life. Thus, if the taxpayer inherits $1 million this year but had inherited (or been given) $1 million ten years before, the new inheritance would bear the higher marginal rate applicable to the second million of accessions.

Wealth taxes. Broad-based wealth taxes are virtually unknown in this country, although taxes on certain forms of wealth—especially real estate—are familiar. Broad-based wealth taxes are used by a number of industrialized countries. Instead of a substantial tax infrequently imposed—the model of transfer taxes is to tax wealth once each generation—wealth taxes are imposed much more frequently, typically annually, but at a correspondingly lower rate.

Transfer taxes receive emphasis that seems completely inappropriate for taxes that generate only slightly over one percent of federal revenues.[r] Virtually every law school offers a separate course in estate and gift taxation. These taxes are central to the practice of many attorneys, and are the object of considerable interest both in academic writing and on Capitol Hill. It is plausible to argue that taxpayers spend more money avoiding the taxes than the Government receives from them.

As we shall see throughout this chapter, the merits of transfer taxation tend to be debated—by both advocates and detractors—in terms that have relatively little to do with the revenue they provide. In light of that fact, it is easy to believe that the taxes were never really motivated by a desire to obtain revenue but instead to achieve nonrevenue goals. In the following excerpt, Mr. Eisenstein discusses not only the nonrevenue goals of early estate tax proponents, but also the revenue considerations that actually led to congressional action.

THE RISE AND DECLINE OF THE ESTATE TAX
Louis Eisenstein[*]

11 Tax Law Review 223, 224-31 (1956)

If we guide ourselves by prevailing notions, the estate tax is animated by a singe purpose—the confiscation of excessive accumulations of wealth. Congressman Kean recently echoed these notions when he approved the tax

---

r. In 2000, estate and gift tax receipts totalled approximately $30 billion, about 1.4% of total federal receipts. U.S. BUREAU OF THE CENSUS, STATISTICAL ABSTRACT OF THE UNITED STATES, tbl. 464, at 314 (122d ed. 2002).

*. At time of original publication, partner in Paul, Weiss, Rifkind, Wharton & Garrison, New York.

"entirely on the basis of the social benefit in preventing the piling up of too big estates."[6]

Evidently the estate tax is not regarded as a levy designed to produce revenue. This view of the tax easily implies certain conclusions. As long as the tax prevents estates from "piling up" too high, it presumably does all that can be expected of it. While the tax produces a modest revenue, the revenue is inevitably incidental to its assault upon aggregates of wealth. The tax can hardly appropriate property without gathering some revenue in the process. But its performance is not to be judged by the size of its fiscal haul. Though its yield may be small, it may still be effective.

This understanding of the tax usually satisfies those who applaud it and those who deplore it. The first group can always argue that it is immaterial whether the tax produces much revenue because revenue is not the purpose of the tax; the crux of the matter is that the tax breaks down hereditary estates, and this vital task is sufficient unto itself. On the other hand, the second group is able to argue that the relatively small yield reinforces its conviction that the tax is a pernicious levy; not only does the tax level wealth, but this evil is not even excusable on the ground of revenue. Both schools are equally loyal to the same error of which neither is aware. It may come as a surprise, but death taxes in the United States were devised to produce revenue. * * *

Though skeptics say that history teaches us nothing, at the very least it may be informative here. Death taxes, no less than other taxes, derived from a desire to obtain revenue. What was true abroad was equally true here. The first federal death tax appeared shortly after the Constitution was adopted. In 1797, amid deteriorating relations with France, Congress levied a stamp duty on legacies and intestate shares of personality. * * *

Federal death duties reappeared during the Civil War. * * * Again Congress was wholly inspired by the revenue required for military exigencies. * * * After the war the death duties were discarded. * * *

Within two decades the scene changed. By the close of the century a death tax movement had emerged [, which] irrevocably identified death duties with the social control of hereditary wealth. "The seething spirit of the times," writes Myers, "was equally concerned with striking hard and deep at plutocracy's wealth as well as its political power." A federal death tax assumed messianic proportions in the minds of those who wished to strike hard and deep. "Steep taxes would tend to shatter great fortunes. They would decrease the number of social drones. Heirs would have less funds to indulge in lavish

---

6. *Hearings before the Committee on Ways and Means on Revenue Revision of 1950*, 81st Cong., 2d Sess. 125 (1950). A year later Congressman Kean was of the same opinion. The estate tax, he said, "was not chiefly for the production of revenue, but rather for a social benefit, in order not to allow these great piles of capital to grow and grow." *Hearings before the Committee on Ways and Means on Revenue Revision of 1951*, 82d Cong., 1st Sess. 68 (1951).

expenditures." And a death tax "could not be shifted so as to become a tax on the laboring or consuming public."[18]

The propaganda for a death tax soon acquired the invaluable virtue of respectability. In 1889 Andrew Carnegie became a traitor to his class by joining the movement. At the time of his treason Carnegie was worth about $30 million, though he "was not one of the richest Americans." "Why," he asked, "should men leave great fortunes to their children? If this is done from affection, is it not misguided affection? Observation teaches that, generally speaking, it is not well for the children that they should be so burdened." The wealthy who are wise, he declared, should hesitate to provide more than "moderate sources of income" for wife and daughters, and "very moderate allowances indeed, if any, for the sons." The "thoughtful man" would just as soon leave to his son "a curse as the almighty dollar," for "the parent who leaves his son enormous wealth generally deadens the talents and energies of the son, and tempts him to lead a less useful and less worthy life than he otherwise would." In the light of his startling analysis Carnegie welcomed the "growing disposition to tax more and more heavily large estates left at death." It was "a cheering indication of the growth of a salutary change in public opinion." "Of all forms of taxation," he wrote, a progressive death duty "seems the wisest." He found it "difficult to set bounds to the share of a rich man's estate" which the government should appropriate. But he was sure that the tax should be graduated; that it should exempt "moderate sums" to dependents; that it should rise "rapidly as the amounts swell"; and that "of the millionaire's hoard" at least 50 per cent should be taken."[21]

* * *

The death tax movement penetrated into the White House. In the spring of 1906 Theodore Roosevelt made a proposal which others found appalling. He recommended "the adoption of some such scheme as that of a progressive tax on all fortunes, beyond a certain amount, either given in life or devised or bequeathed upon death to any individual—a tax so framed as to put it out of the power of the owner of one of these enormous fortunes to hand on more than a certain amount to any one individual."[29] * * *

The tax, he stated, "should increase very heavily with the increase of the amount left to any one individual after a certain point has been reached." The President emphasized that it "is most desirable to encourage thrift and ambition, and a potent source of thrift and ambition is the desire on the part of the bread-winner to leave his children well off." But, he added, this "object can be attained by making the tax very small on moderate amounts of property left; because the prime object should be to put a constantly increasing burden on the inheritance of those swollen fortunes which it is certainly of no benefit

---

18. MYERS, THE ENDING OF HEREDITARY AMERICAN FORTUNES 222-223 (1939).
21. CARNEGIE, THE GOSPEL OF WEALTH [xxii, 8, 9, 10, 49, 50] (1933).
29. 18 WORKS OF THEODORE ROOSEVELT 578 (Memorial Ed. 1925).

to this country to perpetuate." He discreetly refused to say "how far" the tax should, in effect, limit the transmission of "the enormous futures in question."[32]

In 1907 the President saw things more clearly and hence he was more analytical. He focused upon the essential conflict between inheritance of wealth and equality of opportunity. "A heavy progressive tax upon a very large fortune," he declared, "is in no way such a tax upon thrift or industry as a like tax would be on a small fortune. No advantage comes either to the country as a whole or to the individuals inheriting the money by permitting the transmission in their entirety of the enormous fortunes which would be affected by such a tax; and as an incident to its function of revenue raising, such a tax would help to preserve a measurable equality of opportunity for the people of the generations growing to manhood."[33] * * *

Congress, however, refused to be seduced. In 1909 and again in 1913 it disapproved of death taxes.

In three years, as war approached, the picture changed. * * *

The 1916 Act allowed an exemption of $50,000 and fixed rates which ranged from one per cent on the first $50,000 of taxable assets to ten per cent on any amount over $5 million. Within six months the rates were increased by 50 per cent because of "extraordinary appropriations for the Army and Navy and fortifications."[40] * * *

In another seven months the rates rose once more when Congress imposed an additional war estate tax. The rates now climbed from two per cent on the first $50,000 of taxable assets to 25 per cent on sums over $10 million. * * *

At this point I should pause to generalize. Although the estate tax rates pushed upward for a fleeting period, they made no discernible attempt to level inherited wealth. The tax was initially imposed in response to the need for revenue, and the rates increased as the need increased. The purpose of Congress did not embrace the destruction of large fortunes. Under the 1921 Act the effective rate on an estate of $10 million, before allowance of the exemption, was only 16.7 per cent. Of course, many who urged higher rates were very anxious to regulate wealth and the power which it confers. But what they sought and what they got were not the same. * * *

Notes and Questions

1.   The federal estate tax has been in effect since 1916. What were the reasons for its enactment? Which reason predominated at the time?

2.   At present, the merits of transfer taxes are usually debated, by supporters and detractors alike, in terms of nonrevenue effects. The primary reason for this is that transfer taxes no longer contribute a significant portion

---

32. 17 WORKS OF THEODORE ROOSEVELT 432-434 (Memorial Ed. 1925).
33. *Id.* at 504-505.
40. H.R. REP. No. 1366, 64th Cong., 2d Sess. 3-5 (1917).

of the budget, and even their defenders think they are unlikely to do so under any politically possible scenario.

From 1935-40, transfer taxes produced more than six percent of federal revenue, compared to a bit more than one percent today. This is largely due to the fact that the federal budget has grown so rapidly. That is, although the numerator of the fraction (transfer tax revenues) has risen considerably in absolute terms, the denominator (the federal budget) has exploded. At the same time, several statutory changes—in particular, those in 1976, 1981, and 2001—have reduced the yield of transfer taxes.

3.   Do you think that Congress would permanently repeal transfer taxes except for the associated revenue loss?

4.   One of the traditional justifications of inheritance taxes has been the perceived ill effect of inheritances on the recipients. Andrew Carnegie, quoted in the Eisenstein excerpt, opined that undeserved inheritances could constitute a "curse," a view that continues to find support in academic literature. For example, George Gilder, while ultimately concluding that the institution of inheritance should be protected, observed:

> [Inherited wealth] all too often leaves [heirs] broken and debauched. * * * Supine on expensive piles of pillows, they receive injections of more legal drugs from elegant doctor feelgoods or have their Q-spots probed by maritally ambitious nurses and suave trustees of museums, universities, and environmental societies. * * *
>
> Conservatives who decry the corrupting impact of welfare payments of a few hundred dollars a month will have trouble denying the potential damage to be caused by a trust fund yielding tens of thousands. * * *
>
> Whether money is doled out in foodstamps and spent on booze, or assigned in a bequest and poorly invested, the act of giving may well reduce the total level of wealth, employment and wellbeing in the country.[s]

Obviously, the "victims" themselves do not call for relief. The dominant feeling among potential heirs is perhaps best summed up by the character Tevye in *Fiddler on the Roof*: "May the Lord smite me with [the curse of wealth]! And may I never recover!"

Do you think Mr. Gilder's portrait of the heirs of great fortunes is accurate in many cases? Do you agree that the receipt of unearned, undeserved wealth is a curse for the recipient?

---

s. George Gilder, *Wealth, Poverty and Inheritance: The Voice from the Coffin*, 11 PROB. LAW. 1, 2-3, 6 (1985).

B. THE GOAL OF EQUALIZATION OF OPPORTUNITY

As discussed in Subchapter A, one of the primary justifications for the estate tax is the nonrevenue goal of breaking up the largest concentrations of wealth. This is said to serve the egalitarian goal of equality of opportunity. In the following excerpt, Professor Ascher carries the social equality argument to its logical extreme: Our goal should be abolition of inheritance, accomplished through a death tax of one hundred percent (subject to important limitations).

CURTAILING INHERITED WEALTH
Mark L. Ascher[*]

89 Michigan Law Review 69, 70-78, 80-93, 96-104, 106-07, 110, 116-17, 121 (1990)

One of the most dominant themes in American ideology is equality of opportunity. In our society, ability and willingness to work hard are * * * supposed to make all things possible. But we know there are flaws in our ideology. Differences in native ability unquestionably exist. Similarly, some people seem to have distinctly more than their fair share of good luck. Both types of differences are, however, beyond our control. So we try to convince ourselves that education evens out most differences. Still, we know there are immense differences in the values various parents imbue in their children. And we also know there are vast differences in the educations parents can afford for their children. Here too, however, we feel there is little to be done. We respect, if regret, cultural differences that lead some parents to value the education of their children less than others do. And we believe to the bottoms of our souls in the worthiness of the capitalistic game we ask ourselves and our children to play. So we take pride in the fact that some parents can provide their children with the finest educational opportunities imaginable. We have no interest in discouraging excellence in education, even if it is disproportionately available to the children of the fortunate. Instead, we satisfy ourselves with providing an educational safety net for all our children: our taxes support public education and land grant universities, and our charity funds scholarships.

When forced to acknowledge these differences in ability, luck, and educational opportunity, we admit that we do not play on a completely level field. But because each of these differences seems beyond our control, we tend to believe the field is as level as we can make it. It is not. For no particularly good reason, we allow some players, typically those most culturally and educationally advantaged, to inherit huge amounts of wealth, unearned in any sense at all. So long as we continue to tolerate inheritance by healthy, adult children, what we as a nation actually proclaim is, "All men are created equal, except the children of the wealthy."

---

[*]. At time of original publication, Professor of Law, University of Arizona College of Law.

Meanwhile, [t]he continuing failure of the federal government seriously to address the deficit indicates to many * * * that higher taxes are inevitable. * * * The only real issue is what type of tax could help reduce the deficit least painfully while achieving significant social objectives.

About $150 billion pass at death each year. Yet in 1988 the federal wealth transfer taxes raised less than $8 billion.

Obviously, these taxes could raise much more. If, to take the extreme example, we allowed the government to confiscate all property at death, we could almost eliminate the deficit with one stroke of a Presidential pen.[15] This nation, however, rarely has used taxes on the transfer of wealth to raise significant revenue. Our historical hesitancy in this regard strongly suggests that we as a nation are unwilling to abolish inheritance in order to raise revenue. Nonetheless, thinking about using the federal wealth transfer taxes to abolish inheritance may not be entirely futile. It may permit an entirely new type of analysis. Conventional attempts to reform the federal wealth transfer taxes inevitably bog down in the Anglo-American tradition of freedom of testation. As begrudged intruders upon a general rule, these taxes necessarily end up playing an inconsequential role. One willing, for purposes of analysis, to discard freedom of testation could start from the proposition that property rights *should* end at death. Inheritance then would be tolerated only as an exception to that general rule. This article does just that. * * *

My proposal views inheritance as something we should tolerate only when necessary—not something we should always protect. My major premise is that all property owned at death, after payment of debts and administration expenses, should be sold and the proceeds paid to the United States government. There would be six exceptions. A marital exemption, potentially unlimited, would accrue over the life of a marriage. Thus, spouses could continue to provide for each other after death. Decedents would also be allowed to provide for dependent lineal descendants. The amount available to any given descendant would, however, depend on the descendant's age and would drop to zero at an age of presumed independence. A separate exemption would allow generous provision for disabled lineal descendants of any age. Inheritance by lineal ascendants (parents, grandparents, etc.) would be unlimited. A universal exemption would allow a moderate amount of property either to pass outside the exemptions or to augment amounts passing under them. Thus, every decedent would be able to leave something to persons of his or her choice, regardless whether another exemption was available. Up to a fixed fraction of an estate could pass to charity. In addition, to prevent circumvention by lifetime giving, the gift tax would increase substantially.

My proposal strikes directly at inheritance by healthy, adult children. * * * Children lucky enough to have been raised, acculturated, and educated

---

15. I obviously do not share Michael Graetz's opinion that federal taxes on the transfer of wealth have no significant role to play in dealing with the deficit.

by wealthy parents need not be allowed the additional good fortune of inheriting their parents' property. In this respect, we can do much better than we ever have before at equalizing opportunity. This proposal would leave "widows and orphans" essentially untouched. The disabled, grandparents, and charity would probably fare better than ever before. But inheritance by healthy, adult children would cease immediately, except to the extent of the universal exemption.

* * *

Inheritance in Principle

John Locke, in his *Two Treatises of Government*, first published in 1690, argued that inheritance was the natural right of children. He derived that right from the fact that children were "born weak, and unable to provide for themselves." Their right to inheritance rested, in Locke's words, on their "Right to be nourish'd and maintained by their Parents."[36]

Despite Locke's powerful influence on those who founded this nation, his conception of inheritance as a natural right never took firm root here. * * *

According to Blackstone, inheritance was merely a custom turned into positive law. * * *

Blackstone's positivistic theory, rather than Locke's natural rights theory, has always dominated this country's thinking on inheritance. * * * In 1898 the Supreme Court of the United States bluntly stated, "The right to take property by devise or descent is the creature of the law, and not a natural right . . . ."[49] According to one author, the courts of every state except Wisconsin have reached the same conclusion.[50] Thus, when President Theodore Roosevelt addressed Congress in 1907, he was on solid political and theoretical ground in stating that "[t]he Government has the absolute right to decide as to the terms upon which a man shall receive a bequest or devise from another."[51] * * *

In a letter to James Madison dated September 6, 1789, Jefferson asserted that it was "self evident"

> *"that the earth belongs in usufruct to the living"*: that the dead have neither powers nor rights over it. The portion occupied by an individual ceases to be his when himself ceases to be, and reverts to the society. . . . If [the society has] formed rules of appropriation, those rules may give it to the wife and children, or to some one of them, or to the legatee of the deceased. So they may give it to his creditor. But the child, the legatee, or creditor takes it, not by any natural right, but by a law of the society[63] * * *

---

36. J. LOCKE, TWO TREATISES OF GOVERNMENT bk. 1, § 88, at 206-07 (P. Lassett ed. 1988).

49. Magoun v. Illinois Trust & Sav. Bank, 170 U.S. 283, 288 (1898).

50. Kornstein, *Inheritance: A Constitutional Right?*, 36 RUTGERS L. REV. 741, 766-67, 789-91 (1984).

51. T. Roosevelt, *Seventh Annual Message* (Dec. 3, 1907), in 16 MESSAGES AND PAPERS OF THE PRESIDENTS 7070, 7084 n.1.

63. 15 T. JEFFERSON, THE PAPERS OF THOMAS JEFFERSON 392-93 (J. Boyd ed. 1958) (emphasis

Still, the natural rights conception may help to explain Americans' continuing fascination with inheritance. * * *

Inheritance–Property or Garbage?

Locke found an owner's entitlement to property in the labor expended to acquire it:

> The *Labour* of his Body, and the *Work* of his Hands . . . are properly his. Whatsoever then he removes out of the State that Nature hath provided, and left it in, he hath mixed his *Labour* with, and joyned to it something that is his own, and thereby makes it his *Property*. It being by him removed from the common state Nature placed it in, it hath by this *labour* something annexed to it, that excludes the common right of other Men.[65]

Curtailing inheritance in the way I suggest is consistent with Locke's vision of property, because healthy, adult children generally do not participate in the acquisition of the property they inherit. * * *

According to John Stuart Mill, * * * no presumptions in favor of the propriety of inheritance were to be drawn from its antiquity, because Mill believed the feudal family to be fundamentally different from our own. In feudal times, the King dispensed land not to any particular individual, but to a family. The extended family, as a unit, worked on and defended that land. Each family member was in some sense responsible for the productivity of the land. Thus, each had a certain entitlement to the land, regardless of who "owned" it. * * *

In short, in a feudal society, it made sense to think of inheritance as a necessary component of property. But it does not make sense in an industrial society composed of individuals. Instead, according to Mill, inheritance amounts only to the passage of "unearned advantage" to those who "have in no way deserved" it. * * *

Another of the important characteristics of our notion of property is that an owner can give it, during lifetime, to another. Curtailing inheritance would not itself disturb this aspect of property, either. However, if restrictions on inheritance are to be effective, there must also be an ambitious gift tax. Thus, parents could continue to make gifts during their lifetimes to their healthy adult children or anyone else; it would simply become more expensive to do so.

Under current law, property owners also have the right to determine who will own their property after their deaths. Curtailing inheritance obviously would limit this aspect of our notion of property. But allowing those who once owned property to do after death what they were unwilling to do during lifetime has never made sense. When a parent makes a gift to a child, the parent necessarily feels a sentiment something like, "Johnny needs x." Or, "I want Suzy to have y." Curtailing inheritance would not alter parents' ability

---

in original).

65. J. LOCKE, TWO TREATISES OF GOVERNMENT bk. 2, § 27, at 287-88 (P. Lassett ed. 1988) (emphasis in original).

to satisfy either sentiment at any time during life, for any reason or for no reason at all. What it would disallow is waiting until death to do it. Why? Transferring property at death requires of a decedent neither sentiment. Transferring property by intestate succession requires no sentiment whatever. And transferring property by will requires only a very different sentiment. What a testator says is, "Johnny needs x but can have it only if it is left after my death." Or, "I want Suzy to have y, but she cannot have it until I am completely finished using it." Both sentiments are distinctly less emphatic and less worthy of enforcement by society than those underlying lifetime gifts. They are undeniably secondary sentiments. The primary (and often exclusive) sentiment with respect to death-time transfers is always, "I want x." Or, "I need y." * * * What this proposal eliminates is, therefore, garbage-can parental "giving" to healthy, adult children. A parent would not be allowed to use his or her property until it no longer had any usefulness (to the parent) and then expect the government to collect whatever was left over and deliver it, neatly recycled, to his or her healthy, adult children. Instead, when death placed a property owner's garbage at the curb, the government would simply pick it up.

Constitutional Concerns

* * * In 1942, the Supreme Court of the United States * * * wrote, "Nothing in the Federal Constitution forbids the legislature of a state to limit, condition, or even abolish the power of testamentary disposition over property within its jurisdiction."[79] Since no state has ever attempted to abolish inheritance, all such statements are, of course, merely dicta. These statements are, nonetheless, overwhelmingly in favor of such legislative power.

Concluding that a state legislature could abolish inheritance does not, however, also justify concluding that Congress could do so. * * * But Congress' authority to raise revenue from property passing at death appears to extend to anything less than complete abolition of inheritance. As long as Congress continues to allow every decedent the right to transmit a reasonable amount of property, almost any reform of the federal transfer taxes would appear to pass constitutional muster.

Inheritance as a Matter of Policy
Society's Stake in Accumulated Wealth

Individuals never acquire property on their own. Society plays a crucial role in every individual's acquisitive activities. Society determines the rules by which individuals acquire property. Society also educates (to one extent or another) every individual. And society enacts and enforces laws that protect individuals' enjoyment of what they acquire.

* * * Put another way, the wealth they accumulate is "largely the result of the recipient being favorably positioned vis-a-vis the structure of

---

79. Irving Trust Co. v. Day, 314 U.S. 556, 562 (1942).

civilization."[91] Such wealth is, therefore, "in large part produced by society itself."[92] President Theodore Roosevelt put it this way: "The man of great wealth owes a peculiar obligation to the State, because he derives special advantages from the mere existence of government."[93] * * *

Arguments in Favor of Curtailing Inheritance
Leveling the Playing Field

The inequality of accumulation that occurs as the by-product of capitalism is hardly to be despised, as Andrew Carnegie and Theodore Roosevelt well realized. Thus, absolute equality is a goal for which society ought not to strive and that, in any event, society could never even approximate without eugenics and state socialism. Equality of opportunity, however, is at the very core of American values. Philosophers tend to agree that equality of opportunity is a fundamental good. It is hardly open to debate that inherited wealth contradicts equality of opportunity. According to one authority, "inherited wealth account[s] for half or more of the net worth of every wealthy man and for most of the net worth of equally wealthy women."[102] How society reallocates accumulated wealth at death is, therefore, a critical determinant of the degree of equality of opportunity succeeding generations will enjoy. Thus, Thomas Jefferson advocated a steeply progressive death tax as a "means of silently lessening the inequality of property."[104] So did Thomas Paine. President Theodore Roosevelt advocated the predecessor of the current federal estate tax largely on the basis that it would guarantee "at least an approximate equality in the conditions under which each man obtains the chance to show the stuff that is in him when compared to his fellows."[106]

Inheritance nonetheless continues to enjoy widespread support, even from eminent philosophers. F.A. Hayek, for example, writes:

> Egalitarians generally regard differently those differences in individual capacities which are inborn and those which are due to the influences of environment, or those which are the result of "nature" and those which are the result of "nurture. . . ." [N]o more credit belongs to him for having been born with desirable qualities than for having grown up under favorable circumstances. The distinction between the two is important only because the former advantages are due to circumstances clearly beyond human control, while the latter are due to factors which we might be able to alter.
> * * *

---

91. Brannon, *Death Taxes in a Structure of Progressive Taxes*, 26 NAT'L TAX J. 451, 451 (1973).

92. *Id.*

93. T. Roosevelt, *Sixth Annual Message* (Dec. 3, 1906), in 16 MESSAGES AND PAPERS OF THE PRESIDENTS, *supra* note 51, at 7023, 7042.

102. R. MUSGRAVE & P. MUSGRAVE, PUBLIC FINANCE IN THEORY AND PRACTICE 483-84 (4th ed. 1984).

104. T. JEFFERSON, *supra* note 63, at 82.

106. T. ROOSEVELT, *supra* note 51, at 7085.

Once we agree that it is desirable to harness the natural instincts of parents to equip the new generation as well as they can, there seems no sensible ground for limiting this to non-material benefits. The family's function of passing on standards and traditions is closely tied up with the possibility of transmitting material goods.[112]

In my opinion, the benefits of the family Hayek dwells on, acculturation and education, are separable from the purely financial advantage inheritance represents. * * *

In short, my proposal attempts to distinguish those types of inequalities that are inevitable in the family context from those that are distinctly less so. * * *

Deficit Reduction in a Painless and Appropriate Fashion

Another reason to curtail inheritance is the prospect of raising revenue. If $150 billion pass at death each year, curtailing inheritance has the potential to raise a substantial amount of revenue. Unfortunately, my proposal would raise nowhere near $150 billion. It contains so many generous exceptions that its very structure limits its promise. Taking those exceptions into account, my best guess is that it might raise $25-30 billion.[120] Even so, it would raise almost four times as much as the federal wealth transfer taxes currently raise. But the exceptions are not the only limitations on the proposal's promise. Its economic effects are unknown. If it decreased incentives to work or save, its revenue yield might be lower still. All these uncertainties suggest that raising revenue is not the most important reason to implement this proposal. On the other hand, a country with a government that insists on consistently spending

---

112. F. HAYEK, THE CONSTITUTION OF LIBERTY 87, 88-89, 91 (1960).

120. Forty-five-thousand-eight-hundred estates of decedents dying in 1986 filed returns reporting at least $500,000. Combined, they reported assets of $66 billion. Johnson, *Estate Tax Returns, 1986-1988*, STATISTICS OF INCOME BULL., Spring 1990, at 27. If half of all decedents qualified for (and fully utilized) the unlimited material exemption, the tax base would drop to $33 billion. Assuming all other decedents fully utilized the universal exemption, the tax base would drop an additional $6 billion (one half of 45,800 estates times $250,000). Thus $27 billion would remain. The rough nature of this estimate should be obvious. It ignores four of the exceptions my proposal would allow. Three, however, would be relatively inexpensive: the exemption for dependent lineal descendants, because few parents die with children under age 25; the exemption for disabled lineal descendants, because few beneficiaries are totally and permanently disabled; and the exemption for lineal ascendants, because few parents survive their children. The charitable exemption would be more costly, but I see no way to predict its cost. Each omission suggests the $27 billion figure is too high. Other factors, however, suggest the $27 billion figure is too low. First, the 1986 figures used above reflect only estates exceeding $500,000. This proposal would apply to estates above $250,000. Second, fewer than half of all decedents could and would utilize an unlimited marital exemption. (Only 45% of 1986 decedents whose estates filed estate tax returns passed *anything* to a surviving spouse, despite the fact that all who were married at death automatically qualified for an unlimited marital deduction. Johnson, *supra*, at 48-50 (Table 2).) Third, an invigorated gift tax would yield additional revenue. Fourth, if the amount of wealth passing at death increases as much as some expect, the prospects for future growth in revenue are substantial.

substantially more than it takes in ought to consider seriously any proposal with reasonable prospects for raising any significant amount of revenue.

Denying healthy, adult children the property that once belonged to their parents is about as painless a tax as one could imagine. * * *

A tax on inheritance by healthy, adult children falls squarely on those whose only claim is by accident of birth. To them, inheritance is little more than a windfall. They, more than anyone else, truly have the ability to pay. And the extent to which a tax is based on ability to pay is widely accepted as a primary measure of a tax's fairness.

Protecting Elective Representative Government

In America, our covenant that "all men are created equal" secures much more than the legitimacy of the capitalistic game we ask ourselves and our children to play. It also secures the form of elective representative government we cherish. * * *

The existence of billionaires in our country today poses the same dangers the framers sought to avoid by eliminating primogeniture and entail two centuries ago. If we were willing to curtail inheritance, we could simultaneously eliminate one of the most blatant sources of inequality and improve the prospects for another two centuries of elective representative government in America.

Increasing Privatization in the Care of the Disabled and the Elderly

As the extended family vanishes, it leaves behind many victims. Elderly parents and grandparents, as well as the disabled, are often, in effect, homeless. Increasingly, the cost of supporting these individuals has fallen to the government. The government, however, often provides care for such individuals in a poor and insensitive fashion. Moreover, the cost of providing such care is an expense we as a nation seem unable to afford. A system that encourages family members to provide for the care of the elderly and disabled is, therefore, desirable. Increased privatization would ensure not only better and more sensitive care, but also reduction of the costs borne by the government.

My proposal would encourage private expenditure for the care of the elderly and disabled. It would allow a generous exemption for disabled lineal descendants. In addition, it would allow an unlimited exemption for lineal ascendants, most of whom would be elderly. * * *

No doubt the truly wealthy already take care of their elderly and disabled. Thus, curtailing inheritance might produce little privatization at that level. Those at lower wealth levels, however, do not always take care of their own. "Divestment planning," a new type of estate planning, caters to clients desiring to shift the costs of caring for elderly and disabled relatives to the government. By making it much more expensive during lifetime to give large amounts to one's children, and by limiting the amount healthy children could inherit, this proposal would achieve much greater privatization at the "near-rich" level.

* * *

Increasing Lifetime Charitable Giving

* * * Given the incentives for lifetime giving that reallocation at death would create, the allowance of a gift tax charitable deduction would surely result in a marked increase in lifetime charitable giving.

* * *

Arguments Against Curtailing Inheritance
The Effect on the Economy

Several lines of argument suggest that curtailing inheritance might adversely affect the economy. The adverse economic effects most frequently mentioned fall into three categories: decreased incentives to work, increased consumption leading to decreased savings, and decreased privately held capital.

Incentive to work

One of the first retorts to any proposal to curtail inheritance is the assertion that such a proposal would eliminate incentives to work. According to this line of reasoning, one works in large part for the opportunity to pass something to one's children at death. People, however, work for many other reasons. First are the power and prestige that work and accumulation provide. Money makes the world go round. We work primarily to earn it. Money allows us to feed, clothe, and house ourselves. It also provides us with luxuries and amusement for our leisure. Money provides us with security. * * *

Another of the most important reasons we work and accumulate is to "provide" for others, particularly our children. * * * Curtailing inheritance would have *no effect* on parents' ability to satisfy these desires.

Undoubtedly it is important to ask how curtailing inheritance would affect incentives for work. But with so many other, more important incentives, it is hard to believe curtailing inheritance by healthy, adult children would have any measurable impact. * * *

The failure of the federal government to address the deficit suggests that new or higher taxes are inevitable. The only issue is what type of tax could reduce the deficit with the least adverse economic consequences. Whatever the disincentive effects of an increase in taxes at death, the authorities are all but unanimous that such effects are smaller than those of an increase in the income tax,[180] Congress' traditional tax of choice.

---

180. *See, e.g.*, J. PECHMAN, FEDERAL TAX POLICY 234 (5th ed. 1987) ("[E]ven [critics] would concede that death taxes have less adverse effects on incentives than do income taxes of equal yield."); C. SHOUP, FEDERAL ESTATE AND GIFT TAXES 104 (1966) ("[Transfer taxes] tend less than other taxes to check entrepreneurial drive. They have little tendency to push investors either toward or away from risk taking."); M. WEST, THE INHERITANCE TAX 212 (2d ed. 1908) ("The inheritance tax is less a discouragement to industry than an income tax . . . ."); Harris, *Economic Effects of Estate and Gift Taxation (1955)*, in READINGS IN DEATH AND GIFT TAX REFORM 41, 43 (G. Goldstein ed. 1971); Gutman, *A Practitioner's Perspective in Perspective: A Reply to Mr. Aucutt*, 42 TAX LAW. 351, 352 (1989); Graetz, *To Praise the Estate Tax, Not to Bury It*, 93 YALE L.J. 259, 284 (1983) ("[T]axes on bequests are preferable to high tax rates on income."); Brannon, *supra* note 91, at 451-

Increased consumption and decreased savings

The second economic argument against curtailing inheritance focuses on its supposed tendency to encourage consumption. For years, estate planners have teasingly told their clients that the best estate planning was spending. If inheritance were curtailed, that advice would be truer than ever before. Anyone worried about what would happen to his or her wealth after death could consume it prior to death. If property owners generally followed such advice, curtailing inheritance would raise little revenue. More important, consumption would increase, and savings would decrease.

* * * [U]nder the current system, which itself provides strong incentives to transfer wealth during life, parents almost always keep their money. In short, the incentives to retain property dwarf the incentives to give it away.

Would this parental tendency to retain property change if inheritance were curtailed? * * * [T]he demand for the power, prestige, flexibility, and security money provides seems relatively inelastic—even in persons old enough to be worrying about what happens to their property after death. In short, the instinct for self-preservation would continue to limit spending, even if inheritance were curtailed. Curtailing inheritance might, therefore, increase consumption only slightly. * * *

Curtailing inheritance as suggested in this article would affect less than 10% of the population. Its impact would thus be limited to that group of individuals least likely to engage in additional consumption.

Even if curtailing inheritance did have some adverse impact on savings, the forgoing analysis considers only the behavior of the decedent. It ignores those who, under current law, stand to inherit property. If imposition of a more burdensome tax at death is thought an incentive to consumption on the part of those for whom death is near, ought it not also be seen as an incentive to save on the part of those whose inheritances would be adversely affected? * * *

Looking at the issue from a completely different angle, one is tempted to ask whether an increase in spending would necessarily be bad. The answer would surely depend on what form the additional spending took. * * *

52; Westfall, *Revitalizing the Federal Estate and Gift Taxes*, 83 HARV. L. REV. 986, 989 ("[E]state and gift taxes, unlike the income tax, have a minimal impact on risk-taking, entrepreneurial drive, and resource allocation."); Groves, *Retention of Estate and Gift Taxes by the Federal Government*, 38 CALIF. L. REV. 28, 30 (1950) ("Death taxes reduce savings more than income taxes and impede production and investment incentive less.") *But see* Boskin, *An Economist's Perspective on Estate Taxation*, in DEATH, TAXES AND FAMILY PROPERTY 56, 62 (E. Halbach ed. 1977) ("[O]verall, a substantial decrease in 'expenditures' (saving) for bequests can be expected from increasing transfer taxes relative to income Taxes."); B. BITTKER & E. CLARK, FEDERAL ESTATE AND GIFT TAXATION 1, 3 (6th ed. 1990) ("The personal income tax . . . can accomplish infinitely more in the way of checking inflation than even a confiscatory estate tax."). Of course, none of these authors advocated a death tax with a flat rate of 100%.

Were I worried about the government appropriating my wealth at death, I would consider insuring myself and my family against all sorts of risks. First, I would want unlimited, lifelong medical coverage, and only the Mayo Clinic or a close equivalent would do. Second, I would want a super "life care contract" that would guarantee nursing-home care in a degree of privacy and quality rarely, if at all, currently available. And only a reputable, thoroughly financially backed institution would do. Third, I would want lifelong access for my descendants to the finest private education available. Each would be expensive, and together they would amount to a significant portion of my wealth, especially if I also tried to provide such protection to collateral relatives or friends. This spending, however, is hardly bad. To the extent I provide, by private means, for medical, nursing-home, and educational needs, I relieve society of the burden of doing so. * * *

Decrease in capital privately held

By reallocating to the government a larger portion of what is owned at death, and by subjecting lifetime transfers to higher gift taxes, this proposal would remove from the private economy a large amount of capital. This concern is, however, irrelevant to a tax providing deficit financing. * * *

Emigration—of Capital and Citizens

Curtailing inheritance may also encourage emigration of both capital and citizens. Much wealth consists, however, of interests in business enterprises or real property. Such wealth generally is not moveable. * * *

As to the movement of citizens, there should be fewer limitations. Nonetheless, to escape the current federal estate tax one must not only cease residing in the United States but also renounce American citizenship. These are drastic measures few would undertake, even under a system that curtailed inheritance. * * *

"Wiping Out the Dream"

* * *

I suggest *curtailing* inheritance, not abolishing it. A universal exemption would allow *every* decedent to bequeath a substantial amount of property. If set at $250,000, this exemption would exempt approximately 98% of the population. Thus, for the vast bulk of society, all my proposal would do is "wipe out the dream" of inheriting a purely imaginary fortune or passing a purely imaginary fortune to healthy, adult children. For the few truly wealthy, my proposal would, of course, represent a major change in the wealth transmission process. But even the truly wealthy could still pass, in addition to lifetime gifts, and in addition to other exempted amounts, $250,000 to whomever they wished. The psychological needs of 2% of the population to control more than that amount of wealth after death ought not prevail over the benefits my proposal promises.

* * *

Notes and Questions

5.   Professor Ascher advocates an extreme form of estate tax, claiming that it would increase both revenue and social justice. Which of these is more important to Professor Ascher?

6.   Professor Ascher contends that his proposal would generate considerable revenue. (See footnote 120.) But suppose we decided that no additional revenue would be obtained from its implementation. For example, hypothesize that the Government's cost of administering and collecting the tax would exactly equal the tax revenues derived. Can an argument still be advanced that such a tax would be beneficial to society? Such a tax would have the effect of making some taxpayers (the rich, the near-rich, and their heirs) poorer without making the government richer. Would such a tax be simply legislating envy into law? Conceding, *arguendo*, that large inheritances by healthy adults are undeserved accessions to wealth, does it follow that society is improved if the wealth is removed?

7.   Leaving aside the questions usually raised when any tax proposal is considered—revenue, efficiency, equity, etc.—would outright confiscation of a decedent's property be morally wrong?

8.   Certainly taxes that appear to have as their principal purpose punishment of the taxpayer or his activities rather than revenue have been levied. For example, a state might levy a high tax on illegal narcotics. Regardless of whether we think fines a wise way to combat illegal drugs, we can realize that such a tax would be a thinly disguised form of fine,[t] and might not be surprised if administering and collecting the fine cost the Government as much as the money collected. Can transfer taxes, at least in some cases, be justified on a similar theory? Do you find dispositive the fact that accumulating wealth, unlike trafficking in narcotics, is legal?

9.   Professor Ascher acknowledges the inevitability, and in some senses desirability, of inequality arising from differences in important matters such as ability, luck, education, and nurturing. Why would he single out inherited wealth as the area in which to move toward socially mandated equality?

10.   Which is the more economically valuable thing to inherit from a parent—$1 million in cash; or the genes, nurturing, and encouragement that will enable one to play professional sports at a salary of several millions of dollars per year? Do you find persuasive the argument of F.A. Hayek (quoted

---

t.   *See Dept. of Rev. of Montana v. Kurth Ranch*, 114 S. Ct. 1937 (1994). In this case, the Supreme Court held, five-to-four, that imposition of the Montana Dangerous Drug Tax constituted an unconstitutional imposition of double jeopardy, because the taxpayers had already been subjected to criminal punishment for their drug activities.

in the Ascher excerpt) that "there seems to be no sensible ground for limiting [parental efforts to benefit their children] to non-material benefits"?

11. The most important benefits fortunate children receive from their parents—such things as a sense of values; religious faith; self discipline; appreciation of the world, of nature, of people, of art—have little direct economic effect. Why should these major benefits go untaxed, while something as relatively trivial as an inheritance of $1 million is taxed? Does the fact that some children receive these intangible benefits from their parents and others do not doom taxation as a means of achieving equality of opportunity?

12. The income tax treatment of parents who choose either additional nurturing time or additional working time—both, let us hypothesize, with the goal of benefitting their children—differs considerably. The nurturing parent generates untaxed imputed income, while the working parent creates taxable income. What might be made of these facts in the debate concerning transfer taxes?

13. An obvious concern with confiscatory taxation is its effect on incentives. Do you agree with Professor Ascher that adoption of his proposal would not materially undercut the incentive to work of parents who would be unable to bequeath their wealth to their offspring? What effect would it have on the working patterns of the sons and daughters who would lose inheritances they otherwise would have received?

14. A related concern is that high death taxes create an incentive toward too much consumption. Some proponents of high death taxes have suggested coupling transfer tax increases with greater reliance on consumption taxation.[u]

15. Professor Edward McCaffery, by contrast, argues for a steeply progressive consumption tax (steeper still if the consumption is out of inherited wealth), but with no transfer tax at all. He maintains that this approach would create optimal incentives and disincentives. It would not discourage (desirable) creation of wealth, but would discourage (undesirable) conspicuous consumption. Using the example of billionaire H. Ross Perot, he argues:

> We may actively want Mr. Perot * * * to work and save, because we value whatever he does to produce that wealth and we appreciate his accumulation of capital, but we may be afraid of his spending his billions personally and quickly. If we are concerned about curtailing his extravagant consumption, however, then we have to let him pass on his wealth. We cannot concede Mr. Perot his earnings while at

---

u. *See, e.g.,* Gerald M. Brannon, *Death Taxes in a Structure of Progressive Taxes*, 36 NAT'L TAX J. 451, 452-53 (1973).

the same time checking both his consumption and his savings: Something has to give. Under the progressive consumption-without-estate tax with a higher rate schedule on spending out of inheritance, we do not burden Mr. Perot's earnings or savings or wealth transfers *per se*. Instead we monitor the use of the wealth, both at Mr. Perot's and later generation's levels, to make sure that such use is not decadent or offensive, without pushing Mr. Perot to consume it himself.[v]

16. Professor Ascher would protect the right of even the rich to give property, while sharply curtailing their right to transfer property at death. (Gifts would be subject to transfer taxes much higher than under present law, but still considerably more favorable than the 100 percent marginal rate he would impose on certain transfers at death.[w]) He justifies the difference, in part, because transfers at death reflect sentiments "less worthy of enforcement by society," and amount to "garbage-can parental 'giving.'" Do you agree with his characterization of transfers at death?

17. Professor Ascher noted but dismissed the argument that taxpayers would emigrate and renounce American citizenship to avoid a confiscatory estate tax.

State death taxes have raised a somewhat comparable problem. Although the taxes have never approached the 100 percent envisioned by Professor Ascher, considerably less drastic measures were necessary in order to defeat the tax; simply moving to another state sufficed. As a result: "Competition among the states for the aged wealthy was very keen and took the form of outdoing other states in leniency of death taxes."[x] To deal with this perceived problem, Congress enacted a credit against the federal estate tax for state death taxes up to a stated maximum. Section 2011. After enactment of section 2011, no state had any incentive to reduce its death taxes below the amount of the allowable federal credit, because the reduction would benefit not the estate but the federal government.

Interstate rivalry in this arena may soon reemerge, because Congress has fundamentally changed the legal and political landscape. The 2001 Act phases out the credit of section 2011 in the years 2002-04, and ends it in 2005. (Like

---

v. Edward J. McCaffery, *The Uneasy Case for Wealth Transfer Taxation*, 104 YALE L.J. 283, 353 (1994). See also the McCaffery excerpt in Chapter Seven (page 435) .

w. In a portion of his article not excerpted (*see* 89 MICH. L. REV. at 137-48), Professor Ascher proposed gift tax rates that would increase with age (*i.e.*, would increase as the taxpayer approached death and the proposed confiscatory estate tax). The range would be from 100 percent to 300 percent of the amount of the gift. This is still less than a 100 percent estate tax, however. While a 100 percent estate tax is simply confiscatory, a 100 percent gift tax means that a gift can still be made, but that it results in a tax of equal amount.

x. Harold M. Groves, *Retention of Estate and Gift Taxes by the Federal Government*, 38 CAL. L. REV. 28, 32 (1950).

the rest of the 2001 Act, this provision will sunset in 2011 and prior law will return.)

18. In some respects, Professor Ascher would reduce the burden of death taxes. For example, a disabled child or grandchild of any age would be allowed a substantial tax-free bequest (Ascher suggests $5 million). Should this general idea be incorporated into whatever form of death taxation is utilized?

C. THE ROLE OF TRANSFER TAXES IN A PROGRESSIVE TAX SYSTEM

Transfer taxes do not exist in a vacuum, but are one relatively minor element of the tax system. In the pair of excerpts in this subchapter, the authors express sharply different views concerning the appropriate role for these taxes. Professor Graetz argues that Congress should retain and strengthen transfer taxes, not because they either bring in much revenue or break up concentrations of wealth, but because they contribute to the progressivity of the overall tax system. Professor Dobris, by contrast, proposes repeal, pure and simple, arguing that transfer taxes have not and will not fulfill *any* of the roles that supposedly justify their existence, and that they cause myriad problems. (It is interesting to note that each writer expresses pessimism that the change he recommends will be adopted.)

TO PRAISE THE ESTATE TAX, NOT TO BURY IT
Michael J. Graetz[*]

93 Yale Law Journal 259, 259-64, 268-73, 284-86 (1983)

For several decades, total revenues raised by estate and gift taxes have roughly equalled those raised by excise taxes on alcohol and tobacco.[1] Yet no law journal has ever asked me to write on alcohol or tobacco excise taxes. The law firms of America do not routinely have divisions devoted to excise tax planning. We do not hear of the suffering of widows and orphans (or even of farmers and small businesses) because of alcohol and tobacco taxes. Philosophers and economists do not routinely debate the merits of such taxes. Perhaps most significantly, increases in such excise taxes do not arouse fears that we are about to eliminate the concept of private property in this country and embrace socialism, or even communism. The estate tax, however, evokes just such responses.[2]

---

[*]. At time of original publication, Professor of Law, Yale University.

1. U.S. BUREAU OF CENSUS, STATISTICAL ABSTRACT OF THE UNITED STATES: 1981, at 256 (102d ed. 1981). Actually, the alcohol and tobacco excise taxes together have consistently raised several billion more dollars per year than have the estate and gift taxes. A closer comparison is between revenues from the alcohol excise tax alone and from the estate and gift taxes; the latter exceeded the former only in 1977 ($7.4 billion vs. $5.4 billion) and 1980 ($6.5 billion vs. $5.7 billion). *Id.*

2. *See, eg., Federal Estate and Gift Tax: Public Hearings and Panel Discussions Before the House Comm. on Ways and Means*, 94th Cong., 2d Sess. 390 (1976) (statement of Edward

Recent Trends in Estate Taxation

A review of the most recent history of the estate tax suggests special ironies. Just seven years ago, in 1976, after nearly thirty years of neglect, Congress adopted a series of revisions intended to make the estate and gift taxes apply on a more regular and uniform basis * * *. In 1976, Congress enacted a series of provisions unifying estate and gift taxes into a wealth transfer tax with one cumulative rate schedule and one exemption level, expanding the marital deduction, and establishing a new tax on generation-skipping trusts. Through that legislation, Congress endeavored to produce a structurally more coherent tax—to move toward a genuinely progressive estate and gift tax, typically to be imposed once each generation without huge tax disparities due to decedents' patterns of lifetime giving. Not all of the structural problems were solved in the 1976 legislation—for example, the gift tax continues to be imposed on a net base exclusive of tax, while the estate tax applies identical rates to a gross base including the tax—but on the whole, the 1976 changes significantly improved the structure of the estate and gift taxes.

In light of subsequent events, however, it requires emphasis that although the 1976 changes—principally the phased-in increase in the size of tax-exempt estates from $60,000 (or $90,000 if the lifetime gift tax exclusion was fully used) to $175,625 and the expansion of the marital deduction for smaller estates—were predicted to lose revenue in the short run, they were to have no effect on revenue over the longer run. The drop in estate tax revenues in the short term from the increased exemption level and marital deduction was, in the long term, to be offset by additional revenues from the new tax on generation-skipping trusts and by application of the carryover-basis rules applicable to appreciated property transferred at death. In fact, the enactment of the carryover basis was an explicit trade-off for the support of the estate tax revisions by crucial Democrats on the House Ways and Means Committee.

The 1976 revisions, of course, were not free of problems. * * * The complexities and technical difficulties that haunted the carryover-basis provision from the outset prompted a delay in its effective date in 1978 and ultimately were a major cause of its demise in the Crude Oil Windfall Profit Tax Act of 1980. The generation-skipping provisions have met with similar technical objections. * * * Nevertheless, in 1976 Congress enacted major structural revisions to the taxation of gifts and bequests in an effort to have

---

Pendergast) (suggesting that forced sale of small businesses to meet estate tax burdens "encourage[s] people to take the 'safe' route and work for some impersonal monolithic giant"); *id.* at 436-37 (statement of Sen. Gaylord Nelson) (quoting 121 CONG. REC. 22,683 (1975)) (asserting that existing scheme of estate taxation "undermine[s] our values and institutions" and threatens "to change the historic character of our free enterprise system from reliance on independent, imaginative small businesses and family farms to absolute dependence on massive corporations"); *id.* at 548 (statement of Rep. Bill Archer) (equating estate taxation to "the question of the private ownership of property, whether the Government should have the power to confiscate the earnings of a citizen").

these taxes apply in a more even-handed way, *without reducing* the total level of deathtime taxation.

Having moved toward a basically sound and well-structured wealth transfer tax system, Congress then reversed direction a few years later and moved to emasculate it. In 1980, Congress repealed the carryover-basis rules and returned to the unfair and economically distorting step-up of basis to fair market value at death. * * * Then, in 1981, Congress enacted an additional increase in the wealth transfer tax credit to produce immediately a tax-exempt level of $275,625, and phased in further credit increases to produce an exemption for all estates with net worth of $600,000 or less. At the same time, Congress extended an unlimited marital deduction to all estates regardless of size, reduced the top rate of estate tax—applicable only to estates with net worth of ten million dollars or more—from seventy to fifty percent, and increased from $3000 to $10,000 the amount which can annually be transferred to any donee free of gift tax. These changes reduce the deathtime tax base by about seventy percent and reduce the long-term revenue from taxing bequests to at most one-third of that which would have been collected if the 1976 structure had remained unchanged.

When the 1981 changes are fully phased in, the amount of appreciated property transferable at death without being subject to either income or estate taxes will have been increased ten-fold since 1976, from $60,000 to $600,000. With such an exemption level, no more than $3 billion of the more than $20 billion of unrealized appreciation annually passing through estates (at 1979 levels), or only fifteen percent, will be subject to estate tax. The other eighty-five percent will escape both income and estate taxation.

In 1975, the $60,000 estate tax exemption (which had been in effect since 1942) meant that only the wealthiest 6.5 percent of decedents paid estate tax. If the $60,000 exemption had remained unchanged, the estate tax would have applied to about the wealthiest ten percent of decedents in 1982. The 1976 Act's increase to a $175,000 exemption level meant that in 1981 the estate tax applied only to the wealthiest three percent of persons dying that year. The immediate additional $100,000 increase, to a $275,000 exemption level, provided by the 1981 Act resulted in only the top one percent of 1982 decedents being subject to estate tax, and the further phased-in increase to a $600,000 level will exempt all but a small fraction of the wealthiest one percent of decedents from the tax.

In summary, the 1976 legislation, which produced a more rational, more neutral, and fairer tax on gifts and bequests with no long-term reduction in revenues, was followed only five years later by legislation which made the tax all but disappear—not only in terms of the number and percentage of decedents affected, but also in terms of its contribution to federal revenues.

Recent General Trends in Federal Taxation

The schizophrenic attitude of Congress toward the estate tax, manifested by the contrast between the 1976 and 1981 legislation, reflects a fundamental tension in the tax system that has dominated tax policy debates during recent years. Broadly speaking, the tension is one between a desire for structural tax reform, which would move the tax system towards greater horizontal and vertical equity, and a desire for tax provisions designed to stimulate increased savings or capital formation. This tension produces a direct conflict between the need to tax capital or the income from capital in order to achieve a progressive tax burden and the perceived need to exempt capital and capital income from tax in order to induce economic growth.

    * * *

Public-opinion polls invariably reflect a public taste for a fairer tax system, but if that taste reflects concern other than a lowering of each individual's own taxes, it seems politically impotent.

    * * * [T]he dominant economic factor influencing tax policy today is the projection of very large current and future deficits. If spending is—as seems to be the case—not likely to be reduced further in substantial amounts, the deficit can be narrowed only by additional revenues. Economic recovery may partially close the revenue gap, but, as state and local governments are learning, increased and new taxes will undoubtedly prove necessary. This need for revenues, however, is constrained by great reluctance, by both this Administration and important members of Congress, to increase the tax burden on capital or capital income for fear of stifling economic growth. In contrast, fairness in the distribution of the tax burden seems of little political significance since it currently enjoys no meaningful constituency.

The Role of the Estate Tax

These conditions combine to make the estate tax a very minor player indeed. Since it is a tax on savings, proposals to increase the estate tax run headlong into concerns over "capital formation." Moreover, the estate tax has very limited potential as a source of federal revenues. * * *

The limitation on potential estate tax revenues is an inherent one, not merely a product of political obstacles. Decedents annually transfer a total of about $120 billion in net assets. An average effective tax rate of twenty percent would produce total revenues of about $24 billion, approximately three times the current level. With any substantial exemption, plus exclusions for certain amounts of property passing to surviving spouses or charities, a higher average effective rate seems unrealistic. The inherent limitation on bequests as a source of revenue cannot be overcome by even a dramatic structural revision of estate and gift taxes, such as converting to an inheritance or accessions tax, or taxing gifts and bequests as income to the recipient (or, in a consumption tax world, as consumption of the donor). A tax on deathtime transfers of wealth will thus not serve as a major source of federal revenues.

So we must look elsewhere than the production of revenues if we are to justify strengthening, rather than eliminating, the estate tax. That place should be its role in the distribution of the tax burden, in particular, its role in providing an important element of progressivity in the federal tax system.

Other than the dramatic increases in total revenues, the most striking characteristic of changes in the federal revenue sources described above is the diminishing relative significance of progressive tax sources. Viewed as a system of purchasing retirement and disability insurance from the government, the huge rise in employment taxes reflects a dramatic increase in taxes grounded in notions of "benefit" rather than "ability to pay." By contrast, if current employment taxes are considered to be taxes on the current generation of workers to fund the current retirement benefits of predecessor generations, rather than insurance purchased by current workers—a view that may well reflect the views of current workers—a far greater share of federal tax is imposed on labor income than in the past. In addition, employment tax ceilings on taxable labor income exempt a portion of the wages of highly salaried individuals. The employment tax increases, in combination with recent cutbacks in the top rates of individual income taxes and reductions in estate and corporate income and capital gains taxes, pose significant threats to the progressivity of federal taxation.

Moreover, the proposals for significant long-term changes in federal taxation that currently enjoy the greatest favor in both academic and political circles—a flat-rate tax and a consumption tax—pose further threats to progressivity. * * *

To view the estate tax, however, as contributing an important element of progressivity to the federal tax system requires shedding a myth which has come to dominate its political discussion. This myth—repeated most recently in the legislative history of the 1981 Act—is that the proper function of the estate tax (as well as its historical role) is only to "break up large concentrations of wealth." The clear implication—indeed, the principal justification for raising the tax-exempt level of estates to $600,000—is that no estate tax should be imposed on "smaller or moderate-sized estates." In 1981, "smaller and moderate-sized estates" meant those of the wealthiest one to six percent. If the 1976 tax-exempt level of $60,000 had been maintained, the estate tax would now apply to the wealthiest ten percent of decedents. The narrowing of the estate tax base that accompanies political acceptance of this myth necessarily defeats the contribution of this tax to the progressivity of the federal tax system. The tax becomes as narrow in its intended function as it is in its contribution to the government's revenue. A strong case can then be advanced for its elimination altogether.

In fact, however, the estate tax has done very little to dilute the greatest concentrations of wealth. * * *

Looking instead at the contribution of the estate tax to the progressivity of the tax system reveals a quite different picture: It has had a significant progressive effect. In 1970, the average ratio of tax to adjusted gross income on individual income tax returns was 13.7 percent. Those taxpayers who were taxed at an average rate of at least 14 percent paid a total tax of $43 billion. If they had paid their tax at the average rate, the government would have received only $30.5 billion. The total revenue raised through individual income taxes in excess of the average rate was therefore $12.5 billion. By comparison, the fiscal year 1970 estate and gift tax collections from upper-income decedents were just under $3.7 billion. Thus, the estate and gift taxes—despite their low revenue yield—contributed nearly one-third as much to the progressivity of our tax structure as did rates in excess of the average individual income tax even though the estate tax imposed a smaller levy on inheritances than would have been imposed if bequests had been taxed as ordinary income.

* * * Data for the most recent year available, however, reveal a different picture. The average income tax rate had not changed greatly but the revenue raised by the estate tax amounted to only about twelve percent of that raised by income tax rates greater than the average—a far smaller contribution to progressivity than before. With the further increases in the estate tax marital deduction and tax-exemption enacted in 1981, the relative importance of the estate tax will decline even further. Professor Harry Gutman has estimated that if the estate tax changes of the 1981 legislation were fully effective in 1981, "the contribution to progressivity [of the estate tax] would be reduced to approximately 4 percent."[95] Whatever progressivity remains in the federal tax system will be supplied entirely by the income tax.

Reliance on progressive income tax rates as the sole mechanism for ensuring that this nation's tax burden is distributed in accordance with ability to pay poses a number of problems. Realized rates of return apparently tend to fall as wealth increases. Thus, any tax system which relies solely on an income tax to attain progressivity will not sufficiently tax the underlying wealth that generated the income. High income tax rates both create marginal disincentives to productivity and stimulate legal and illegal noncompliance. Moreover, many preference provisions that have long been a part of the income tax exempt certain sources of income from capital. * * *

The principal reason, therefore, to revise the estate tax is to rescue this mechanism for achieving progressivity, and perhaps to rescue progressivity itself, from both short- and long-term threats. Deciding that restoration rather than repeal is the appropriate course requires three steps: (1) a judgment that progressivity in taxation is just and therefore good; (2) a view that the estate tax can and should play an important role in achieving progressivity; and (3) a conclusion that progressivity should not be abandoned because of the adverse impact of progressive taxation in general (and the

---

95. Gutman, *Federal Wealth Transfer Taxes After the Economic Recovery Tax Act of 1981*, 35 NAT'L TAX J. 253, 262 (1982). Professor Gutman contends that the Graetz and Treasury methodologies do not provide "a precise measure of the annual contribution of the transfer taxes to progressivity," *id.* at 262, because annual transfer-tax receipts are only "a proxy for aggregate annual individual accruals to discharge future transfer tax liabilities," *id* at 267 n. 42. He suggests that progressivity would be more accurately measured by comparing income and employment taxes paid by an individual today with the present value of the estate tax to be paid by the same individual tomorrow.

estate tax in particular) on capital formation.   I shall now turn to an examination of these three propositions.

     * * *

What Does This Mean for the Estate Tax?

     * * * It is my view, therefore, that the nation's tax laws should move in the direction of the 1976 legislation, not that of the 1981 law, and that the estate tax should be rejuvenated and returned to its prior status as an important contributor to the progressivity of the tax system. But having urged this as the direction it *should* go, I cannot close without also examining where it will likely go.

     There are two practical barriers to my preferred course of strengthening the role of the estate tax in the federal system. The first I have already described—namely the inherent limitation on the revenue potential of an estate tax. As I have detailed above, there simply is not enough wealth transferred annually to permit a wealth transfer tax (an estate and gift tax) to become a significant source of federal revenue. Given the current and projected levels of federal deficits, only substantial revenue sources seem likely to dominate the political agenda in the near-term. Thus, tax increases grounded predominately on distributional fairness would seem to have little chance of success.

     * * *

     The most puzzling political obstacle to estate tax revision, however, is that the American people do not seem to like heavy taxes on bequests. George McGovern's proposal in 1972 to confiscate inheritances above a certain amount was not well received, and a recent California initiative to repeal the state's inheritance tax garnered a sixty-four percent positive vote. * * * The only convincing explanation that has occurred to me for this phenomenon lies in the optimism of the American people. In California, at least, sixty-four percent of the people must believe that they will be in the wealthiest five to ten percent when they die.

     The combination of these political obstacles to the estate tax's rejuvenation and the tax's inherent limitations as a significant revenue source leads me to conclude that the estate tax seems far more likely to wither than to grow stronger. As I have suggested, this prediction makes me fear the demise of progressive taxation in the United States. * * *

     If my prediction (as opposed to my desire) is fulfilled, and the years ahead complete the demise of the estate tax, the federal tax system will have lost more than an important and useful mechanism for achieving progressivity; it will have lost a source of great humor. * * * [J]ust the other day, I heard today's version of thoughtful estate planning advice in the office of a well-known New York practitioner. A client had asked with great anxiety what he might do to minimize the estate taxes of his ninety-year-old widowed mother who had a large fortune, composed of extremely valuable art and cash. The lawyer thought for a great long while, no doubt running through his bag of estate planning tricks, when all of a sudden, with a gleam in his eye, he looked up and said calmly, "Marry her." It would be a real shame if a tax which produces such creative advice were to disappear.

A BRIEF FOR THE ABOLITION
OF ALL TRANSFER TAXES
Joel C. Dobris[*]

35 Syracuse Law Review 1215, 1217-26 (1984)

There are meaningful arguments in favor of abolishing all transfer taxes in our federal tax system. They include: (1) the gift and estate tax does not raise a meaningful amount of revenue, (2) the current gift and estate tax does not adequately vindicate any of the social policies it is supposed to, and (3) the tax is costly and inefficient in many ways.

First, the gift and estate tax does not raise a meaningful amount of revenue and never will. Not enough property is transferred to use a transfer tax as a source of revenue, especially if the rates are not confiscatory. * * *

Second, the current gift and estate tax arguably does not adequately vindicate any of the social policies it is supposed to. Many people believe a gift and estate tax is supposed to break up concentrations of wealth, achieve a more equitable distribution of resources, or assert the hegemony of the common people or the egalitarian nature of our society. Assuming that it is desirable to do any of this, through the tax system or otherwise, then the current gift and estate tax is not a worthwhile tool. The transfer tax does not break up concentrations of wealth. It does not function in a meaningful way to redistribute wealth in order to enhance the quality of life for persons with less wealth. Indeed, it might be said that no politically acceptable transfer tax system can obtain such a result.[26] The tax would have to be confiscatory in order to accomplish this—a politically unacceptable result at the present time.
* * *

If the current system is not working to eliminate concentrations of wealth, that is certainly an argument for reform of the system now in place. Is it, however, an argument for abolition? I believe that it is legitimate to call for the abolition of something that is not working, and has not worked, to achieve one of its important purposes. Moreover, it is not at all clear that people want these concentrations broken up, or that a just America requires it.[34]

---

[*]. At time of original publication, Professor of Law, University of California, Davis.

26. Indeed, the current transfer tax might be categorized as a cruel hoax. *See generally* Boskin, *An Economist's Perspective on Estate Taxation*, in DEATH, TAXES AND FAMILY PROPERTY: ESSAYS AND AMERICAN ASSEMBLY REPORT (E. Halbach ed. 1977) (economic effects of the estate tax). Another understanding of the current situation is that it allows the middle-income taxpayer the illusion that we are taxing the rich and that we have brought the rich to heel. This appears to be the current state of affairs in Great Britain. *See* Wolman, *The Tax That Didn't . . .*, Financial Times (London) March 24, 1984, at 20, col. 3.

34. As Professor Graetz notes, the McGovern proposal "to confiscate inheritances above a certain amount was not well received" and the people of California, in 1982, cheerfully repealed the

The transfer tax does not accomplish another of its social purposes—the importation of progressive taxation into our tax system. * * *

It is clear that the transfer tax does not strongly contribute to progressivity. Moreover, it is unclear if we as a society are committed to progressivity in our tax system or if progressivity is an obvious social goal.[41] * * * Given the failure to obtain progressivity with the current tax and the meaningful uncertainty about progressivity as a tax goal, it is quite legitimate to consider abolition insofar as progressivity is an important policy underlying the tax.

   * * *

A third argument favoring abolition is that the tax is costly in many ways, both direct and indirect. The direct costs include both the costs of the constant reform of the tax and the cost of complying with the tax.

Constant reform of the tax is costly. As long as the tax is in existence it seems that it will be changed. Formulating proposals for change, seeing them through the Congress, interpreting the new law, and educating the private and the public sectors to enable them to deal with the new law, all involve substantial costs that repeal would save.

Over recent years, the following pattern has developed. Inflation has increased the face value of property in the hands of "middle-class" taxpayers. As a result, it has appeared that these people would be subject to estate taxes. This situation has forced lawyers to master the estate tax structure in order to service their clients. Congress then changed the law to essentially exempt such taxpayers from estate tax. This wastes the work of many lawyers who plan estates for "middle-class" people, not only because the law is changed, but also because their middle-class clients no longer need estate planning and the lawyers do not have access to richer clients. This waste of time is very meaningful.

Second, taxpayer compliance and the enforcement of compliance also generate substantial direct costs. Taxpayers choose, wisely I might add, to devote substantial time and money to obtaining estate planning and tax-oriented estate administration. Thus, the very existence of the tax places an improper premium on obtaining expert advise. The government also spends substantial amounts on compliance. Abolishing the tax would free meaningful numbers of sophisticated Internal Revenue Service personnel for work more likely both to produce revenue and to obtain the goals of the tax system. It is

---

state's death tax by popular initiative. *See* Graetz, *To Praise the Estate Tax, Not to Bury It*, 93 YALE L.J. 259, 285 (1983).

41. Let us assume there is good in progressivity. One is tempted to ask whether progressivity is inherently good or only valuable if the populace perceives its existence. *See generally* Keene, *What Do We Know About the Public's Attitude on Progressivity?*, 36 NAT'L TAX J. 371 (1983) (outlining the public's varying responses to differently worded questions in public opinion polls on progressivity, and the lack of specific knowledge of the public's attitude toward progressivity).

a mistake to allocate substantial resources to an area that does not produce revenue. Abolition would also free large numbers of private sector planners.
* * *

The transfer tax affects, to an unknown degree, the investment decisions of rich people. It can be argued that the planning required to avoid or minimize the tax creates too many intrusions on financial matters and encourages manipulative actions.

It is argued in favor of abolition that an indirect cost of transfer taxation is that death tax discourages savings and encourages consumption, thereby interfering with capital formation via savings. * * * I am not sure I agree that a death tax interferes with capital formation. * * * I believe it requires confiscatory death tax rates, which we obviously do not have, to inspire the kind of unwholesome consumption in lieu of savings that is of social concern.

Repeal might well reduce the amount of money held in trusts. This might well result in more money being invested in riskier investments, which, in turn, might result in economic growth. I am suggesting that many trusts are created only to avoid estate tax, and that trustees invest conservatively. * * *

Another reason favoring abolition is that, arguably, the existence of the current transfer tax is interfering with the efficient functioning of the federal tax system. I believe that legal, proper tax planning will spawn improper tax avoidance schemes if the public fails to see the difference between planning and impropriety. Thus a wise government limits legitimate tax avoidance to limit illegitimate tax avoidance. One way to do this is to limit opportunities for planning. Arguably, repealing transfer taxes wipes out estate planning, thereby reducing the public perception that there is a candy store of tax planning reserved for rich people. The risk is that the repeal of the transfer tax system will be seen as giving a whole other store away.

People, the political system, and the tax system can only accommodate a finite amount of general complexity and, more specifically, complexity in the imposition of tax and complexity occasioned by the imposition of tax. In the face of the growing complexity of our society and of our tax system, perhaps it is a mistake to waste the capacity for accommodation of complexity on a disliked tax that does not raise a great deal of revenue, that does not seem to be accomplishing its social purposes, and that absorbs large amounts of public and private sector effort. Repeal of the costly and complex transfer tax system offers an opportunity to obtain simplification of our tax structure.
* * *

A final argument favoring abolition is that the estate tax creates serious liquidity problems for a small, but economically important, group of decedents—owners of closely held businesses, real estate and farms. * * *

Notes and Questions

Nontraditional justification of transfer taxes:
interplay with the income tax

19. Professor Graetz supports strengthening transfer taxes, despite the "inherent" limitations on the revenue possibilities of those taxes, and notwithstanding the fact that the transfer taxes have done little to break up concentrations of wealth. If the transfer taxes do not fulfill their traditional goals, what policy consideration justifies the transfer taxes to Professor Graetz?

20. Assuming the desirability of greater progressivity in the tax system, why would Professor Graetz prefer to utilize transfer taxes rather than the more obvious route of increasing the progressivity of the income tax?

21. Professor Harry Gutman asserts that the Economic Recovery Tax Act of 1981 "has emasculated the wealth transfer tax as an effective component of our tax system,"[y] a state of affairs he finds particularly distressing given the less-than-comprehensive income tax base:

> That the current tax system excludes large amounts of income from the income tax base provides the most compelling reason for retaining a transfer tax. With a seriously eroded income tax base, a transfer tax is needed to ensure that each taxpayer eventually bears a fair share of the tax burden. The transfer tax serves as a "backstop" to the income tax by taxing the wealth that taxpayers accumulate through tax-preferred income sources."[z]

Do you agree that the transfer tax can and should serve as a "backstop" for the income tax system? Is Professor Gutman adequately answered by the argument that "[t]he flaws of the income tax should be addressed and amended through the income tax laws, not through a dual system of taxation."[aa]

22. Professor Gutman characterizes the transfer tax as a backstop to the income tax as "a second-best solution,"[bb] the preferred approach being to broaden the income tax base. And he concedes that structuring the transfer tax system for a role as backstop to the income tax system would be difficult and imperfect:

> Critics of this proposal may also argue that such a rate schedule sacrifices aggregate horizontal equity to achieve tax progressivity. The decedent whose estate is comprised solely of assets purchased

---

y. Harry L. Gutman, *Reforming Federal Wealth Transfer Taxes After ERTA*, 69 VA. L. REV. 1183, 1271 (1983).

z. *Id.* at 1191.

aa. Edward J. Gac & Sharen K. Brougham, *A Proposal for Restructuring the Taxation of Wealth Transfers: Tax Reform Redux?*, 5 AKRON TAX J. 75, 87 (1988).

bb. Gutman, *supra* note y, at 1212.

with after-tax wage income is subject to the same transfer tax as the decedent whose equivalent estate has been accumulated through inheritance or through the reinvestment of an income-tax-free yield. If the purpose of the transfer tax is principally to recoup unpaid income tax, the former decedent is overtaxed, and the latter remains undertaxed. Aggregate horizontal equity in this regime could be achieved by confining the transfer tax base to assets whose value is traceable to income tax preferences. Alternatively, one could establish a transfer tax credit to compensate for previously paid income tax. Either alternative would require adjustment of the rates. * * * Both alternatives would also create difficult administrative problems. Thus, aggregate horizontal inequity may have to be tolerated.[cc]

23. Professor Gutman also suggests that transfer or wealth taxes have a place even if we attain a well designed income tax:

If one were to design a tax system de novo, one would undoubtedly ask whether an excise on wealth transfers is a necessary component. Commentators have noted that a tax on wealth transfers is indistinguishable from a tax on income because in economic terms wealth is simply the capitalized present value of future income. The argument implies that if economic income were fully taxed, wealth would be fully taxed as well, making a wealth transfer tax unnecessary.

Even if this argument is correct, however, a wealth transfer tax can be justified on a number of other grounds. Suppose, for example, one believed that greater progressivity and higher marginal rates were necessary to accomplish an appropriate redistribution of income and wealth. One alternative for implementing such a goal is simply to tax income at the rates necessary to achieve the desired distribution of the tax burden. An income tax with a high maximum marginal rate, however, might have unacceptable efficiency effects of locking in invested capital and encouraging current consumption rather than saving. Such efficiency concerns have in fact been the basis for recent income tax rate reductions. Many economists also believe that a transfer tax has less allocative impact on investment decisions than an income tax. * * *

Other supporters of the wealth transfer tax have argued that wealth reflects an ability to pay beyond that represented by its future income stream. * * * Still others have contended that a wealth transfer tax should exist to disperse the attributes of

---

cc. *Id.* at 1215-16.

economic power and opportunity that are thought to accompany large accumulations of wealth.[dd]

Are these arguments in favor of transfer taxes persuasive? Assuming an improved transfer tax (Professor Gutman certainly concedes the need for considerable improvement), could his arguments be countered?

24. Do older Americans have a particular stake in the estate tax (or its repeal)? Frequently, political appeals concerning repeal of the estate tax are focused on the concerns of elderly persons who desire to pass on their wealth to younger generations. Professor Richard Kaplan argues that the problem should not be a central political concern of elderly taxpayers. First, and most obviously, the economic impact of the tax will not be borne by the deceased person—"the decedent's lifestyle need never be affected by this levy, however onerous it may seem. Accordingly, it is fundamentally incorrect to characterize estate tax reform as an elder law issue. It is, instead, an issue for one's survivors, and only for survivors of the very well off at that."[ee] Even recognizing the interest that elderly persons frequently have in their children and grandchildren, Kaplan argues that a number of other issues—prescription drugs, long-term care insurance, and federal regulation of pensions, *inter alia*—are of more "genuine consequence" to older Americans at all levels of income and wealth.[ff] Accordingly, elderly Americans should not be distracted by "peripheral concerns * * * that, in reality are relevant only to the wealthiest among them."[gg]

Arguments against transfer taxes

25. Professor Graetz argues that the explanation for popular opposition to death taxes "lies in the optimism of the American people. In California, at least, sixty-four percent of the people must believe that they will be in the wealthiest five to ten percent when they die." Others, including Professor Ascher, similarly appear to attribute popular opposition to death taxes to a combination of unrealistic optimism and ignorance. Do you agree? Is there another explanation for the popular opposition to death taxes? Professor McCaffery argues that "our experience with estate taxation seems to reflect * * * some form of anti-envy. The majority of citizens and our well-evolved practices are opposed to levying a tax exclusively on the wealthiest elite."[hh]

26. While Professor Graetz, who has served in tax policy positions in Republican administrations, wishes to strengthen transfer taxes, Professor

---

dd. *Id.* at 1187-88.

ee. Richard L. Kaplan, *Crowding Out: Estate Tax Reform and the Elder Law Policy Agenda*, 10 ELDER L.J. 15, 18 (2002).

ff. *Id.* at 45.

gg. *Id.* at 46.

hh. McCaffery, *supra* note v, at 287.

Dobris, who describes himself as "a person of modest means [and] a registered Democrat,"[ii] argues for their abolition. Professor Dobris agrees with Professor Graetz that transfer taxes generate little revenue and fail to break up concentrations of wealth. While Professor Graetz argues for the taxes because of their contribution to progressivity, however, Professor Dobris questions both the desirability of progressivity and the contribution of transfer taxes to progressivity.

The heart of Professor Dobris' opposition to transfer taxes appears to arise from his conclusion "that the tax is costly in many ways, both direct and indirect." What are some of these costs, according to Professor Dobris? Do you agree that these costs exist? That they justify repeal of transfer taxes?

27.   Professor Dobris and other critics of transfer taxes argue that the taxes tend to push assets into trusts, which is said to be detrimental because of conservative management. Professor Thomas Robinson, however, observes that trustees are not the worst of possible money managers:

This leads to a discussion of trust management, which the wealth transfer taxes have always encouraged. * * * [W]hile it is clear that the qualifications of some professional trustees are professionally adequate, their motivations to maximize benefits from property under their care may be inhibited both by law and by inclination. And a further price of trustee management is often inefficient dead-hand control by the settlor. But since *someone* must manage property, in many cases trustee management is preferable to management by those who would mismanage or squander it, including an incapacitated settlor, his inexperienced wife, or his worthless children.

Waiting in the wings, of course, is the government, which can be both the best and the worst alternative. * * * [I]f it uses the money so received to displace other revenue sources, particularly those used for income transfer payments, then arguably this is the best of policies, harmonizing both the goal of encouraging good management of the nation's resources and the goal of equally distributing those benefits. * * * Of course, insofar as the government attempts to manage the assets itself, it provides the worst of alternative managers.[jj]

Scope of exemptions from transfer taxation

28.   Assuming that transfer taxes in some form should be continued, do you agree with the present tax policy of allowing an unlimited marital deduction? As noted in the introduction, this provision dates only from 1981.

---

ii. 35 SYRACUSE L. REV. at 1215.

jj. Thomas A. Robinson, *The Federal Wealth Transfer Taxes—A Requiem?*, 1 AM. J. TAX POL'Y 25, 37-38 (1982).

What justifications exist for treating a surviving spouse differently from other relatives?

29. As the last paragraph of Professor Graetz' article whimsically suggests, the marital deduction opens up the possibility of marriage undertaken in form for the purpose of tax avoidance. An extremely tax-motivated taxpayer could marry a younger family member as the taxpayer approached death; this avoidance technique could be repeated as the young spouse aged, without theoretical limit. (Inexplicable as it may appear to tax professors, many people marry without tax concerns uppermost in their minds. The tax strategy described in this note would raise, among other problems, concerns about bigamy, societal disapproval, and the possibility that a young spouse might die unexpectedly or use the property in a manner not contemplated by the elderly taxpayer.)

While Professor Graetz apparently meant only to end his article on a light note, others have taken the problem seriously. In Canada, the Carter Commission recommended that marriage not protect transfers from tax until the marriage had either lasted five years or resulted in the birth of a child.[kk] Professor Ascher's proposal would not allow a full marital exclusion until the couple had been married twenty years.[ll]

Professor Russell Osgood argues that "[p]olicing the genuineness of marriages seems distasteful at best."[mm] Assuming we agree, is this nevertheless a distasteful problem that should be addressed? (Note that Professor Osgood himself *does* address the problem, suggesting that a spouse who is more than twelve-and-one-half years younger be treated as a member of a younger generation for purposes of the generation-skipping tax.)

30. An extremely young surviving spouse may suggest the image of a "gold digger," with the result that imposition of a significant estate tax would cause many people little concern. A spectacular example is the widow of billionaire oilman J. Howard Marshall, who stood to inherit hundreds of millions of dollars following his death in 1995, at age 90. An Associated Press story, reporting on the long-running litigation between the widow and other heirs, gives this background to the one-year marriage: "Smith was working as a stripper at a topless bar in Houston when she met the elder Marshall in 1991. When they married in 1994, she was 26 and he was 89, and she had become *Playboy*'s playmate of the year."[nn]

---

kk. 3 REP. ROYAL COM'N ON TAX'N 146 (1966).

ll. 89 MICH. L. REV. at 123-26.

mm. Russell K. Osgood, *Carryover Basis Repeal and Reform of the Transfer Tax System*, 66 CORNELL L. REV. 297, 322 (1981).

nn. C. Bryson Hull, *Oilman's Widow Gets $450 Million in Ruling*, Ark. Democrat-Gazette, Sept. 29, 2000, at A2.

31. Professor Gutman does not challenge the congressional decision to treat marital partners as a single unit through the unlimited marital deduction. He suggests, however, that the logical extension of this policy should be that when the estates of the spouses are taxed, they should not be treated as separate taxpayers for purposes of the applicable credit and the progressive rate structure.[oo]

32. The annual exclusion shields up to $11,000 per year per donee from tax, or even from counting against the applicable credit. Married couples can give $22,000 per donee. Such gifts can be made to an unlimited number of donees. Consider a married couple with three married children and nine married grandchildren. The couple could give each of the twelve descendents and each of the descendents' spouses $22,000 each—or a total of $528,000 per year—without touching their applicable credits.

All agree that some amount of gift must be allowed tax-free, because Congress has no intention of requiring a gift tax return from a grandmother who sends a $20 birthday check. (Similarly, some *de minimis* exclusion for the recipient would be necessary under an accessions tax.) But is the present exclusion too generous?

Professor Robert Smith argues that Congress allowed the annual exclusion for the purpose of avoiding the necessity of keeping track of numerous small gifts, but that taxpayers routinely use the annual exclusion only with respect to significant transfers of wealth, and simply ignore relatively small birthday and Christmas presents. Such an approach subverts the justification for the annual exclusion, Professor Smith asserts. He would lower the exclusion to $5,000 per donee and $20,000 per donor.[pp]

Professor John Steinkamp, on the other hand, defends present law, particularly with respect to limiting gifts on a per-donee, rather than a per-donor, basis. Discussing a 1990 proposal of the Joint Committee on Taxation to impose a $30,000 per donor limitation, he argued: "If Taxpayer A can give each of his three children $10,000 per year free of tax, Taxpayer B should be allowed to give each of his six children $10,000 per year free of tax."[qq]

How, if at all, should the annual exclusion be changed? Should the per-donee annual exclusion be reduced? Should a per-donor limitation be introduced?

33. As discussed in the preceding note, the annual exclusion for gifts can be used to transfer considerable wealth free of transfer taxation. The annual exclusion, unlike the applicable credit, is a use-it-or-lose-it proposition. This

---

oo. *See* Gutman, *supra* note y, at 1218-39.

pp. Robert B. Smith, *Should We Give Away the Annual Exclusion?*, 1 FLA. TAX REV. 361 (1993).

qq. John G. Steinkamp, *Common Sense and the Gift Tax Annual Exclusion*, 72 NEB. L. REV. 106, 170-71 (1993).

creates an incentive to transfer wealth early and often. (Other aspects of the transfer tax system also encourage early giving; for example, transfer by *inter vivos* gift rather than waiting for transfer at death protects post-gift appreciation from tax.) Professor McCaffery argues that because the transfer tax system encourages giving, and encourages giving early:

> [T]he wealthy young receive their wealth, or become certain of its ultimate receipt, early in life. This wealth may undercut their incentives to work and save. * * * [I]t may be better for them to receive their wealth later in life, say when they are fifty-five years old, than for them to receive it earlier, when their work incentives will be more affected and when their propensity to consume is greater.[rr]

Charitable contributions

34. The charitable exclusion has generated relatively little academic comment. Note that the exclusion from transfer taxation is not the only tax benefit; the same charitable contribution that protects property from transfer taxes, if made *inter vivos*, also gives rise to an income tax deduction.

A key issue is whether one thinks that the goals of transfer taxation are sufficiently met if wealth is transferred to charities, rather than a large portion (but not all) of that wealth going to the government. A charitable contribution or bequest absorbs the entire amount, while the transfer taxes claim only a fraction; does this mean that the charitable contribution is more effective than the tax itself? On the other hand, is a sufficient public purpose effected if the donor can avoid tax by diverting his wealth to a charitable foundation bearing his name, controlled by his friends, and benefitting causes particularly dear to his heart? On policy grounds, how does the charitable deduction under the transfer taxes compare to the charitable contribution deduction allowed under the income tax?

35. Do you think permanent repeal of the estate tax would have a significant effect on charities? If so, is this a justification for retaining the tax?

D. A CONTINUING ROLE FOR THE GIFT TAX AFTER REPEAL OF THE ESTATE TAX?

As discussed in Subchapter A, the 2001 Act calls for repeal of the estate tax, though the repeal will not become effective until 2010 and will sunset the following year. Whether permanent repeal is in our future is uncertain as this book goes to print.

The gift tax has traditionally been regarded as necessary undergirding for the estate tax—a death tax could be avoided too easily if *inter vivos* gifts were untaxed. On this theory, it might have been expected that when it repealed

---

rr. McCaffery, *supra* note v, at 320-21.

the estate tax, Congress would have simultaneously repealed the gift tax. Instead, Congress retained the gift tax, apparently as a support for the income tax. If there were no gift tax, the following abusive arrangement might be hard to prevent: A high-bracket owner of appreciated property gives the property to a lower-bracket trusted friend or relative who sells the property and, in an ostensibly separate transaction, returns the after-tax proceeds to the original owner.

In the excerpt below, Professor Lischer acknowledges the problem, but expresses a preference for addressing problems of income tax avoidance with changes to the income tax law. As Lischer makes clear, however, it will be difficult to draft workable anti-abuse provisions that are narrowly tailored to the problem presented.

INCOMPLETE TRANSFER TAX REPEAL: SHOULD THE GIFT TAX SURVIVE?
Henry J. Lischer, Jr.[*]

56 Southern Methodist University Law Review 601, 609-12, 614-25 (2003)

Congressional Action
Repeal of the "Death Tax"

The Economic Growth and Tax Relief Reconciliation Act of 2001 ("EGTRRA") made profound changes to the structure of the U.S. tax system. * * *

Gift Tax is Retained

Even though Congress decided in EGTRRA to repeal the estate tax and the generation-skipping transfer tax, it decided to retain the gift tax. In other words, the 2001 law effected only partial repeal of the transfer tax system. Interestingly, the Conference Committee Report is silent as to why the gift tax is retained, but (1) retention of the gift tax reduced the revenue loss associated with the legislation and (2) the gift tax apparently was considered to be a device by which to discourage income-shifting abuses. The Joint Committee staff reportedly was prepared to offer some techniques within the income tax, rather than the gift tax, for dealing with income-shifting abuses, but the members were disinclined to deal with such new income tax anti-abuse provisions due, in part, to time pressure to complete work on the legislation by Memorial Day, as desired by the President. Instead, the gift tax was retained.

During the phase-in of EGTRRA, the gift tax unified credit exemption equivalent amount rises to $1,000,000. Lifetime gifts in excess of the exemption equivalent amount (other than qualifying transfers between spouses, which will continue to be tax-free without limitation under § 2523) are discouraged because they would be subject to gift tax if made during life, even though any post-death transfer would not be subject to tax because of the absence of an estate tax.

---

*. At time of original publication, Professor of Law, Southern Methodist University.

Significantly, the gift tax rate ends up eventually (at the end of the EGTRRA phase-in period) at 35%, which is equal to the highest § 1 income tax rate. Thus, the gift tax moves closer to being a surrogate for the income tax. The gift-tax-as-surrogate-for-income-tax rationale is not fully accomplished, however, because (1) the gift tax applies to the entire value of the gift property, not just the gain element, and (2) the gift transfer does not generate a basis step-up to fair market value, which would result if the property were sold and the income tax applied to the gain. Indeed, imposing a gift tax on an income-shifting transfer is a very crude and imprecise substitute for collection of the appropriate income tax on the shifted income.

Although I do not favor repeal of the transfer tax system, it strikes me as logically inconsistent to retain a gift tax while having no estate or generation-skipping transfer tax. It is painfully obvious that the existence of a gift tax, but not an estate tax, creates no end of incentives for structuring imaginative lifetime transfers, which provide immediate economic benefit to the donee, to be deemed incomplete for gift tax purposes so that (1) the lifetime gift tax does not apply and (2) the transfer is complete at death and, thus, not subject to any tax. Accordingly, I am willing to consider income-shifting anti-abuse mechanisms (other than the non-statutory doctrines described above) within the income tax, rather than the gift tax. If adequate income-tax-based mechanisms were available, I would favor repeal of the gift tax as logically congruent with repeal of the estate tax and the generation-skipping transfer tax.

* * *

Post-EGTRRA Viability of Income-shifting Techniques

* * *

Assessment of Income Shifting After EGTRRA

* * *

Is the Transfer-Retransfer Technique Viable?

The proffered techniques assert that income shifting can be accomplished by the transfer of appreciated property to a trusted relative or friend with eventual return to the transferor of the after-tax proceeds of disposition. EGTRRA considered, but did not enact, provisions to deal directly with this technique.

The transfer-retransfer scenario presents troubling issues. To the extent that the two transfers are independent, each transfer should be honored (with the result that any gain from disposition of the transferred property by the transferee would be taxed to the transferee). To the extent that the initial transfer is effective and without restriction, the transferee is the owner of the property and has interests that are adverse to the interests of the transferor. If the initial transfer and the retransfer are interrelated or the rights of the transferee are incomplete, however, the transaction may not be worthy of respect to the extent that any built-in gain should be taxed to the transferor.

Deciding whether the transfers are related and complete would involve an exceedingly difficult factual determination, which would challenge both counsel for taxpayers in planning transactions and the IRS in administering the tax laws.

* * *

I do not address whether present law non-statutory doctrines (agency, some type of informal trust, sham, step transaction, substance over form, business purpose, and lack of economic substance) cannot adequately police the income-shifting techniques that EGTRRA invites. It is far from clear to me that these doctrines will be inadequate to deal with the transfer-retransfer technique, but I do not undertake such an analysis in this brief comment. I do feel compelled to observe, however, that two close-in-time transfers between related persons beg for special scrutiny and might call for imposition of some of the non-statutory doctrines described above that, if applicable, would recharacterize the events so as to treat the transferor as having sold the property. Application of the non-statutory doctrines depends upon the particular facts of each situation, however, so I admit to some uncertainty as to the tax results. Accordingly, for purposes of the following discussion, I am willing to admit that this transfer-retransfer technique may be viable, and I next address income tax statutory provisions that might prevent income-shifting abuses.

Statutory Mechanisms Within the Income Tax to Deal with Income Shifting

Identification of the Income-Shifting Problem

Before considering what mechanisms might be effective with respect to income-shifting abuses, it is necessary to identify the income-shifting problem that needs attention. Three transactions might be considered as producing an income shift for federal income tax purposes: (1) post transfer income shifting (no built-in gain is shifted), (2) built-in gain income shifting in which the transferee realizes and reports all gain (including the built-in gain) and does not make a retransfer to the transferor, and (3) built-in gain income shifting in which the transferee realizes and reports all gain (including the built-in gain) and does make a retransfer to the transferor.

The first-listed transaction involves no income-shifting abuse because the periodic income and gain are taxed to the owner of the property during the period such income and gain accrue. Accordingly, no income-shifting remedy is needed for this transaction.

The second-listed transaction does involve a shift of accrued gain from the transferor to the transferee, but U.S. tax law explicitly permits this transaction. Inter vivos gain shifting has been permitted in the past and will continue after 2009 under §§ 1015 and 1022, so it seems that no remedy is needed for this transaction.

The third-listed transaction seems to generate the most visceral negative reaction, and this transfer (with built-in gain)-retransfer transaction was the poster child for the income-shifting articles. Given the statutory rules generally permitting income shifting, it seems that only this transfer-retransfer transaction merits an anti-abuse rule. I consider below the income tax anti-abuse mechanisms that would apply to the built-in gain transfer-retransfer transaction.

* * *

Technical Solutions
Dealing with Built-in Gain

As discussed above, the sole income-shifting abuse situation seeming to merit an anti-abuse provision is the transfer-retransfer transaction, which occurs if three conditions are satisfied: (1) the transferor transfers property that has built-in gain, (2) the transferee of the property disposes of the transferred property in a taxable transaction, and (3) the transferee makes a transfer to the transferor (or anyone related to or designated by the transferor).[90]

As a preliminary matter, it should be noted that income shifting of built-in gain is worthwhile only if the transfer causes the income or gain to be taxed [at] a lesser effective rate of tax than it would in the hands of the transferor. * * * [A] flat-rate income tax (a politically unlikely outcome) would negate the income-shifting advantage. * * *

I now evaluate various statutory anti-abuse mechanisms to determine whether the mechanism would reach an administrable and appropriate income tax result (and, thus, would permit repeal of the gift tax). Various technical and policy choices are reflected in the following anti-abuse mechanisms: (1) does it apply only to the transfer-retransfer transaction, (2) does it require that all trigger events (e.g., the transfer, disposition, and retransfer) occur [within] a prescribed time period, and (3) does it require built-in gain at the time of the first transfer?

Grant Authority to IRS to Recast Transaction

H.R. 8, a transfer tax repeal bill considered in 2001, contained a proposed new § 7701(n), which would have provided to the IRS an additional statutory anti-abuse rule. If applicable, the proposed § 7701(n) would have authorized the IRS to ignore the original gift transfer and deem the transferor the owner with respect to any gain resulting from the disposition of the property (by someone else). * * *

Enactment of this provision would have raised many immensely difficult factual questions, including (1) did the transferor (or any other identified person) receive anything of value directly or indirectly and (2) was there an understanding or expectation that the transferor (or any other identified person) would receive something of value directly or indirectly? It appears to me that there would have been considerable uncertainty as to the applicability

---

90. Any statutory anti-abuse rule might (1) require the transfer and retransfer to occur within a prescribed period of time and (2) exempt transactions that do not exceed an annual or lifetime exemption amount.

and scope of the provision. * * * Although such a statutory rule might have an *in terrorem* effect on income shifting, I doubt its viability.

Gift as Realization Event

An income shift would not occur as to the built-in gain if the initial transfer of the appreciated property were to be deemed a realization event to the transferor. Such a realization-upon-gift rule would be a big policy change, as well as a big political hurdle, and it could create a liquidity problem to the transferor, who would have to pay an income tax on the built-in gain at the time of the transfer. Given the long-standing rule to the effect that a gift generally is not realizing event, this anti-abuse mechanism strikes me as unlikely to be implemented. The gift-as-realization mechanism * * * would not be applicable only to the transfer-retransfer transaction. * * *

Rate Borrowing

Another method by which to reduce the tax advantage of shifting built-in gain would be to apply the transferor's tax rate to the built-in gain. The taxable event would not be the initial transfer (as would be the case with the gift-as-realization rule discussed above); instead, the tax would be deferred until the subsequent taxable event.

Prior law § 644 (now repealed) provided such a rate-borrowing mechanism with respect to transfers of built-in gain property to a trust. Section 644 prevented any income tax rate advantage with respect to built-in gain by calculating the tax on the trust by reference to the income tax rates of the transferor, even though the gain was reported by the trust. Section 644 applied if (1) the trust (or a transferee trust) sold or exchanged the property within two years of the initial transfer in trust, (2) the property was disposed of at a gain, and (3) the fair market value of the property at the time of the initial transfer in trust exceeded the adjusted basis of the property to the trust immediately after the transfer. * * *

Section 644 was restricted to property transferred to a trust, but the § 644 rate-borrowing concept could be applied more broadly. The rate-borrowing mechanism could apply to any built-in gain property transferred for less than full and adequate money's worth consideration (other than an arm's-length bad bargain). The scope of the provision could be restricted to trusts or defined related persons such as family members, but applying the provision to any such transfer to any person (other than a charitable organization) might discourage use of a non-related person for temporary income shifting and would avoid complexities in defining related persons.

* * *

To avoid over-inclusion of transactions within the rate-borrowing mechanism, its scope might be limited to apply only if all requirements for application of the provision occur within a prescribed time period. For example, § 644 required that the taxable event, the disposition of the property by the trust, occur within two years of the transfer to the trust. * * *

Apply rate-borrowing mechanism
to transfer-retransfer transaction

A technical problem with implementing a time period requirement with respect to the transfer-retransfer transaction is determination of the taxable event; is it (1) the taxable disposition by the transferee or (2) the retransfer to the transferor? Conceptually, the event that should invoke the rate-borrowing mechanism (which is predicated on the occurrence of each of (1) transfer of built-in gain property, (2) disposition by the transferee, and (3) retransfer) should be the last to occur of the required events. If the taxable disposition by the transferee and the retransfer occur in the same taxable year, the rate-borrowing device will work as described. * * *

If the retransfer were to occur in a taxable year after the taxable disposition by the transferee, however, the transferee would be required to report the gain in the year of the taxable disposition without application of the rate-borrowing mechanism. In the subsequent taxable year during which the retransfer occurs, the conditions for application of the rate-borrowing mechanism would be satisfied, but the gain would have been reported previously and taxed according to the circumstances of the transferee. To apply the rate-borrowing mechanism in this situation would require either (1) an amended return for the transferee for the year during which the gain was reported or (2) a device by which to increase the tax of the transferee for the year of the retransfer (to reflect the increase in tax that would have resulted if the rate-borrowing mechanism had applied in the prior year of the disposition). Neither option seems appealing.

Another complication associated with a rate-borrowing mechanism triggered by the transfer-retransfer transaction is that extensive reporting requirements would be necessary for enforcement of the provision. * * *

Apply rate-borrowing mechanism
without requiring a retransfer

Because application of the rate-borrowing mechanism to the transfer-retransfer transaction raises complicating issues, a more restrictive rate-borrowing rule may be appropriate. Application of the rate-borrowing mechanism would be considerably simplified if it were to be applied to any transfer of built-in gain property, regardless of whether a retransfer occurs. This more restricted scope for the rate-borrowing technique would cause it to apply if (1) the transferee (or a further transferee) sold or exchanged the property within a prescribed period of time of the initial transfer and (2) the fair market value of the property at the time of the initial transfer exceeded the adjusted basis of the property to the transferee immediately after the transfer. Such a rate-borrowing device would be very similar in concept to § 644, but it would expand the scope of § 644, which applied only to a transfer in trust, to include any transfer for less than full and adequate money's worth consideration other than (1) an arm's-length bad bargain, (2) a transfer to a charitable organization, and (3) any transfer within prescribed exempt amount/s.

Mandatory high tax rate on built-in gain

Another relatively simple device to negate the income tax advantage of shifting built-in gain would be to tax any built-in gain recognized by the transferee within a prescribed period of time at a mandatory high rate of tax. This would avoid the computational complexities and tax-return-information sharing that § 644 required.

To summarize the foregoing anti-abuse mechanisms, the transfer-retransfer transaction is the most deserving of a special anti-abuse rule, but any mechanism tailored to the transfer-retransfer transaction would require a fairly complex statutory provision, the crafting of which would be a challenge. A less complex rate-borrowing technique would be activated if the transferee were to sell the built-in gain property at a gain within the prescribed period of time, regardless of any retransfer. This less complex solution is not ideal, as it includes within its reach not just the abusive transfer-retransfer transaction; it also would apply to any transfer of built-in gain property, regardless of whether a retransfer occurred. To ameliorate this over-inclusion, annual or lifetime exclusion amounts could remove a significant majority of transactions from the provision. * * *

Conclusions

The logical incongruity of repealing the estate tax and the generation-skipping transfer tax, while retaining a gift tax, suggests to me the Congress should revisit the question of retaining the gift tax. If the concern of Congress with respect to complete repeal of the transfer tax system was income tax abuse, then Congress should (1) enact provisions within the income tax to deal with the abuses and (2) repeal the gift tax. * * *

Notes and Questions

36. Professor Lischer observes that after repeal of the estate tax, the surviving gift tax is scheduled to have the same top rate as the income tax (35 percent). This identity emphasizes that the best defense of the gift tax in a post-estate tax era would probably be that the gift tax protected the income tax from abuse. However, Lischer argues, the gift tax would be an imperfect and overbroad approach. First, while the abuse is limited to unrealized appreciation in gifted property, the gift tax would be levied on the entire amount of the gift—even a gift of cash. Moreover, even in the case of property with unrealized appreciation, income tax treatment would suggest that the donee should have a basis equal to fair market value to assure that the gain would not be taxed twice. The gift tax regime, however, does not achieve this result. While section 1015(d) allows a step-up in basis for a portion of gift tax

paid, even after application of this provision the donee is likely to have a basis significantly lower than fair market value.[ss]

37. Professor Lischer states that it "is far from clear to me" that the abuse problem—gift of appreciated property to lower-bracket donee, sale by donee, retransfer of sale proceeds (net of tax) to donor—cannot be addressed by existing non-statutory law, such as the step transaction doctrine or the principle that substance controls over form. Nevertheless, he is concerned that these doctrines might these prove inadequate, and that the "transfer-retransfer technique may be viable." Why might these doctrines prove inadequate?

38. Why would the abuse problem disappear under a flat-rate income tax?

39. Professor Lischer states that the problem which should be targeted is that in which gifted property with unrealized gain is sold by a donee in a lower income tax bracket, and the after-tax sales proceeds are subsequently transferred back to the donor. Note that even if the retransfer does not occur, it might be argued that tax avoidance has occurred, because the gain attributable to the donor's period of ownership is taxed at the donee's lower rate. Lischer correctly points out that "U.S. tax law explicitly permits this transaction," and will continue to do so in 2010.

Does it follow that "no remedy is needed for this transaction," as Professor Lischer states?

40. Treating a gift as a realization event to the donor is considered in some detail in Chapter Ten, Subchapter C.

41. Former section 644 provided that in the case of transfers of appreciated property to a trust, followed by the trust's sale at a gain within two years, the gain would be taxed to the trust at the transferor's rate, assuming it were higher than the trust's normal rate. Could this approach be adapted to block the transfer-sale-retransfer abuse with which Lischer is most concerned? What if it were applied to cases in which the retransfer did not occur?

---

ss. Section 1015(d) allows a step-up in basis for the amount of gift tax that is attributable to unrealized appreciation. Suppose the property has a basis of $1 million and a fair market value of $10 million. Assume the entire gift is taxed at 35 percent, for a tax of $3.5 million. Ninety percent of the tax, or $3.15 million, will be attributable to appreciation. Accordingly, the donee will have a basis of only $4.15 million (donor's basis of $1 million plus $3.15 million increase in basis under section 1015(d)).

E. THE ACCESSIONS TAX (AND OTHER ALTERNATIVES TO THE ESTATE TAX)

The first two excerpts below, like the Dobris excerpt in the preceding subchapter, advocate abolition of the estate tax. Unlike Professor Dobris, however, Professors Rudick and Donaldson would replace the estate tax with an alternative form of death tax. Professor Rudick's article, published more than half a century ago in the maiden issue of *Tax Law Review*, was the first to advocate the accessions tax, which has found considerable favor among academics. The brief excerpt from his article sets out the basics of his proposal.

The excerpt from Professor Donaldson's article explains what he views as the manifest failings of present law, and suggests either of two alternatives, both of which would shift the focus of tax to the recipient. One of his proposed alternatives, excerpted briefly here, is the accessions tax. (The other, treating the receipt of gifts and bequests as income taxable under the income tax, is examined in Chapter Ten, Subchapter D.)

Finally, an excerpt from a recent article by Professor Dodge compares the estate tax to various alternatives, and argues that the present tax regime "is the hardest kind of tax on gratuitous transfers to defend from the angle of political rhetoric and policy." Professor Dodge's preferred approach—including gifts and bequests in income—is examined in detail in Chapter Ten (page 648).

A PROPOSAL FOR AN ACCESSIONS TAX
Harry J. Rudick[*]
1 Tax Law Review 25, 25, 30-32 (1945)

This is a proposal for the abolition of the present federal estate and gift taxes and the substitution therefor of a progressive tax on each recipient of money or other property by way of inheritance or *inter vivos* gift. The brackets of tax would progress not according to the size of the donor's taxable dispositions but according to the aggregate taxable acquisitions of the donee, no matter from whom. Tax liability for a particular year would be computed in the same way as under the existing gift tax law,[tt] that is, by first computing a tax on the aggregate taxable acquisitions of the taxpayer during the taxable year and prior years, and then deducting from this figure the tax * * *on the taxpayer's aggregate taxable acquisitions in prior years. For want of a better name, we call the suggested new tax an "accessions tax."

    * * *

---

[*]. At time of original publication, Professor of Law at New York University and a partner of Lord, Day & Lord, New York City.

[tt]. Professor Rudick wrote prior to the "integration" of the estate and gift taxes in 1976. Under current law, the language in the text would describe the estate tax as well as the gift tax, because there is a unified credit and a unified rate structure for all transfers from an individual, whether during life or at death. (Ed.)

Alternative Bases for Death Duties and Superiority of Accessions Tax in Attaining Objective

There are, of course, a number of methods by which, through progressive death duties, the tendency of wealth to concentrate can be counteracted. In considering them we should remember that dead men pay no taxes: the tax depletes what is left for the survivors—they are the real taxpayers. The method we now operate under imposes a graduated tax measured solely by the size of the decedent's estate. Hence, if a man died leaving a net estate of one million dollars, the federal estate tax at current rates would be $325,000, regardless of whether he left the entire million (or rather the residue after death taxes) to one person or twenty persons.

Another procedure—adopted by many jurisdictions including a number of our states—ignores the size of the decedent's estate and graduates the rates according to the amount received by the legatee from the particular decedent. Thus, if a decedent divided his million equally among ten persons, the aggregate tax on these ten people would be very much less than the tax on one legatee who received the entire million. Under this system, no regard is given to any amounts a legatee may have inherited from other decedents. Thus, if a husband died leaving a million dollars to his son and later the widow died leaving another million dollars to the son, the tax would be much less than if the son had inherited the entire two million from one of his parents.

* * *

Examined from the viewpoint of whether they attain their object of deconcentrating excessive accumulations of wealth, each of the * * * devices described above has shortcomings. The first does not in any way encourage the wider distribution of wealth: the tax is the same whether the estate is divided among two or fifty beneficiaries. The second does tend to impel an allotment of smaller shares to more people, but by failing to take into account other inheritances, it does not produce optimum distribution. * * *

It is submitted that the proposal herein will attain, more effectively than the other methods which have been tried, the real objective of death duties, *i.e.*, preventing undue concentration of wealth. Under this proposal no tax will be imposed on the donor or his estate. Instead, each beneficiary of an inheritance or gift will be subject to a progressive tax on his cumulative acquisitions by inheritance or gift. Thus, if *A* receives a gift of $100,000 from his father in 1946 and a bequest from his mother of $100,000 1947, the tax on the bequest will be at higher rates than the tax on the gift because of the cumulative feature. Donors and decedents will thus have an inducement to transfer their property to those who have previously received or inherited least.

* * *

THE FUTURE OF TRANSFER TAXATION: REPEAL, RESTRUCTURING AND REFINEMENT, OR REPLACEMENT

John E. Donaldson[*]

50 Washington & Lee Law Review 539, 540-46, 548-52, 559-60 (1993)

Whether accumulated wealth is a proper subject of taxation is a matter over which economists disagree and is essentially a political question. Assuming that wealth transfer or receipt is a proper base for the imposition of tax, the question of how much revenue should be derived from such base is also a political question. However, the question of whether a particular system for taxing accumulated wealth is useful and worthwhile, though not devoid of political significance, is essentially a practical and utilitarian matter. This essay suggests that as a practical and utilitarian matter, the present estate, gift, and generation-skipping tax system should be abandoned. It acknowledges that the present system can be improved. It suggests, however, that the improvements possible are not sufficient to warrant retention of the old system. It suggests that if wealth is to be taxed upon transfer, two models which focus on the transferee rather than the transferor, are likely to offer more acceptable methods of accomplishing that task. One of these models is an accessions tax. * * *

Goals of the Transfer Tax System

Several goals have, from time to time, been ascribed to the transfer tax system. * * *

Reducing Concentrations of Wealth
* * *

The transfer tax system simply has not made a significant contribution to a goal of breaking up wealth concentration. Although in 1992 transfer taxes produced revenues of approximately $12 billion from the wealthiest one percent of the population, that amount is relatively minuscule in relation to the objective. Absent a significant change in the political climate, which appears unlikely in the foreseeable future, it is improbable that the system will be called upon to more effectively address perceived problems of wealth concentration.

Production of Revenue

The second, and perhaps the historically more important goal of the transfer tax system, is that of producing revenue. In the mid to late 1930s, the transfer tax system was a major component of the federal tax system, producing more than six percent of total revenues and in one year, 1936, ten percent. * * * Since World War II, however, transfer tax revenues have rarely exceeded two percent of total federal tax collections and as a result of recent changes, have diminished to approximately 1.1 percent. * * *

---

*. At time of original publication, Ball Professor of Law, College of William and Mary.

Even if there were greater desire to use the transfer tax system as a source of revenue, it is doubtful whether such taxes could be adapted to become a major revenue source. In fact, no country, including those which have more socialistic political values, derives significant revenues from wealth transfer taxation. * * *

Contributing to Progressivity

A third goal, or role, of transfer taxes advanced by some is that of contributing to the progressivity of the federal tax system.[38] However, that role has a more historic than continuing significance. * * * * In the mid to late 1930s, when estate tax revenues on occasion were as high as twenty-seven percent to fifty-six percent of individual income tax revenues, the transfer tax contributions to the goal of progressivity were substantial. * * * However, when the affected population drops to approximately one percent, today's level, the role of transfer taxes in contributing to progressivity of the tax system is minuscule.

* * * [E]ven proponents of the progressivity role of transfer taxation are pessimistic that restoration of such a role is politically possible.[46]

Manifestly, current wealth transfer taxation can not be justified by perceived roles either of breaking up or reducing concentrations of wealth or of contributing to the progressivity of the federal revenue system. If these roles are dismissed, a case can be made for repeal of the estate, [gift,] and generation skipping taxes, notwithstanding that they do produce $12 billion in revenue. This revenue, comparatively insignificant, comes at the expense of a "bad" tax system, one that lacks fairness, efficiency, and neutrality.
* * *

Fairness, Efficiency, and Neutrality

Adherence to generally accepted principles of sound tax policy requires that tax systems be fair, efficient, and neutral. The existing transfer tax system severely violates each of these principles.

Fairness

First, the system is not fair, from considerations of both horizontal equity and vertical equity. Horizontal equity suggests that persons transferring equal wealth within the system be taxed in the same manner. Vertical equity (progressivity) suggests that persons of greater wealth be taxed more heavily on their transfers than persons of lesser wealth. Substantial horizontal inequity has been legislated into the system. For example, * * * life insurance proceeds, where the decedent has an incident of ownership, are included in the estate tax base. However, proceeds of life insurance, even when attributable to investment made by decedents, are excluded from the base where incidents

---

38. Michael J. Graetz, *To Praise the Estate Tax, Not to Bury It*, 93 YALE L.J. 259, 271 (1983). *See also* Harry L. Gutman, *Reforming Federal Wealth Transfer Taxes after ERTA*, 69 VA. L. REV. 1183, 1185 (1983) (arguing transfer taxes have "traditionally played, and should continue to play, an important role in contributing to the progressivity of the tax system as a whole").

46. Graetz, *supra* note 38, at 271.

of ownership are lacking, or if once possessed, have been yielded more than three years prior to death.

More important to considerations of both horizontal and vertical equity is the simple fact that where transfer taxes that would otherwise have been imposed are avoided or postponed without penalty, equity is violated. A major industry, that pursued by estate planning professionals, has evolved to exploit opportunities for avoidance and penalty-free postponement of transfer taxes that would otherwise have been payable. * * *

A discussion of all of the tax avoidance and postponement devices available to avoid or delay imposition of transfer taxes is beyond the scope of this essay. The literature on estate planning directed to tax avoidance and minimization is extensive. To make the point, however, a mention of several techniques is sufficient. For example, persons having the greatest wealth, and thus benefitting most in circumventing vertical equity, are more readily able than those having less wealth to utilize the gift tax system, with its "tax exclusive"[56] base to reduce the cost of donative transfers. For example, a person who has $10,000,000 of wealth can, while living, more readily transfer $600,000 in assets considered likely to appreciate in value, using the unified credit to avoid immediate imposition of tax, than can [a person] who has only $1,500,000 in wealth. Also, and for convenience, disregarding the unified credit, persons who would otherwise be in the fifty-percent bracket for both immediate gift tax purposes and for eventual estate tax purposes can choose to make a gift of $1,000,000, at a gift tax cost of $500,000 for total transfer related cost (gift plus gift tax) of $1,500,000. If the "fund" of $1,500,000 tapped in giving $1,000,000 to the donee had been retained until death and taxed at the fifty-percent bracket, only $750,000 would remain after tax to pass to objects of bounty. In this example, the transfer tax saving obtained by using a gift mechanism rather than a testamentary mechanism to pass wealth is $250,000. Another important device for avoiding imposition of transfer taxes is the utilization of the annual exclusion of $10,000 ($20,000 if husband and wife cooperate by using the split-gift election). * * *

A corollary to the foregoing observations regarding ease of tax avoidance and its effect on horizontal and vertical equity is the resulting consequence that to a significant extent transfer taxes are "voluntary taxes," paid largely by wealthy persons who are uninformed or ill-advised, or who simply die before putting their affairs in order—all too frequent occurrences. To the extent that the tax burdens those who bear it only because of the want of effective avoidance planning, it is especially unfair. * * *

Efficiency

Second, the transfer tax is inefficient. This is perhaps the system's most serious shortcoming. It requires an inordinate amount of attention at the

---

56. Unlike the estate tax, which is "tax inclusive" in its base and allows no deduction for tax in measuring the tax, the gift tax is "tax exclusive" and gift taxes payable on a transfer are not included in the measure of the tax. *Compare* I.R.C. § 2001 *with* §2501 (Supp. 1993).

highest levels of government, especially in relation to the relative insignificance of the revenues generated. * * * The creativity of estate planning professionals imposes a continuing drain on the attention of policy makers and legislators. The tax is comparatively expensive to administer. The system's complexity, coupled with the creative devices employed in estate planning, requires the Internal Revenue Service (IRS) to employ lawyers as estate tax examiners, who are compensated at a higher level than other IRS compliance personnel. While only a small fraction of individual income tax returns are examined, 12,000 of the 56,000 estate tax returns filed in 1989 were examined.

Efficiency is not properly measured by compliance costs to the government alone. The transfer tax system imposes enormous resource and opportunity costs in taxpayer compliance and avoidance endeavors and in the time and energy of lawyers, accountants, trust officers, and financial planners required to understand and apply the system. The magnitude of human resources involved is partially suggested by the American Bar Association's estimate that over 16,000 lawyers consider trust, probate, and estate law as their area of concentration. * * * Lawyers may not cavalierly assume that clients of modest wealth when wills are executed will not have substantial wealth at death. Many clients who will, in fact, not have transfer tax exposure, receive legal services predicated on the possibility that they may face such exposure. * * * Although the transfer tax system is intended to affect only a very small portion of the population, such protective drafting causes the system to affect a substantially larger segment, who prudently, but often unnecessarily, receive and pay for complex estate planning services. * * *

There are important consequential costs as well. Prudent fiduciaries are reluctant to distribute and settle decedents' estates before potential estate tax controversies have been settled. The transfer tax system prolongs the administration of estates. Prudent fiduciaries invest conservatively, and prolonged administration delays access to capital by beneficiaries, who may employ it more effectively within the economy. The system also promotes the "trustification" of assets that might otherwise have been transferred outright.

All of the foregoing energy, resources, and opportunity costs are sacrificed on the alter of a tax system that fails to achieve its supposed goals and yields only $12 billion in revenue. A recent study concluded that resources spent in avoiding transfer taxes are of the same magnitude as the revenue produced.[83] The transfer tax system is manifestly inefficient. The resource and opportunity costs generated in relation to revenues obtained are alone sufficient to make the system unacceptable.

---

83. Henry J. Aaron & Alicia H. Munnell, *Reassessing the Role for Wealth Transfer Taxes*, 45 NAT'L TAX J. 121, 139 (1992).

Neutrality

* * * A good tax system should be neutral in that it ought to be nonintrusive—it should not alter choices and behavior that would have occurred in the absence of the system. The current tax system is decidedly nonneutral and intrusive. The system encourages lifetime gifts and penalizes the failure to make them. Further, the system virtually compels use of the marital deduction in most cases involving wealthy married couples. In those instances, it thus discourages substantial outright bequests to others. * * * Because life insurance is a form of wealth that is fully realized at the death of the insured, and because life insurance arrangements can be structured to avoid imposition of transfer taxes, even when funded by the insured, the system encourages investment in life insurance products. The transfer tax system discourages the acquisition and retention of life insurance where the insured retains ownership incidents over the policy. Further, the system strongly encourages the obtaining of professional estate planning advice. The system discourages and renders difficult the prompt settlement of decedents' estates. On balance, the system contributes heavily to the "trustification" of wealth and thus channels the flow of substantial capital into arrangements where, given the prudence of fiduciaries, capital is conservatively invested. Thus to a substantial degree, the system operates to prevent people from making desired dispositions of their property and encourages undesired dispositions. The transfer tax system forces use of complex dispositive mechanisms when simple arrangements are desired. The system is severely intrusive in affecting human choices, investment decisions, and dispositive arrangements. In penalizing and rewarding different choices and decisions, it restricts investment decisions and donative and testamentary freedom and compromises personal liberty. Consequently, the transfer tax system is decidedly nonneutral.

Summary of Deficiencies

* * *

Congress should repeal the existing estate and gift tax system.

* * *

Transferee Centered Models for Wealth Taxation
The Accessions Tax Model

* * *

The accessions tax, centered and imposed on transferees, is inherently fairer than the existing tax system in that persons whose total gift and bequest receipts are comparable are comparably taxed. Because under any transfer tax system the tax costs are ultimately borne by successors to the transferred wealth, horizontal and vertical equity is best measured in terms of impact on the recipient successors. Under the accessions tax, they are treated equally. Also, being focused on the transferees, there are no fairness issues arising from aggressive use of, or failure to use, exemptions of the transferor, in that there are no such exemptions. No one is penalized, for example, for failure to use a

by-pass trust or other device oriented toward the existing unified credit. * * *
The "premium" under the present system associated with equalizing the
estates of husband and wife, and the attendant penalty for failure to do so
disappears under the accessions tax model. When a child receives accessions
of $2,000,000 upon the combined deaths of both parents, it largely matters not
whether the bulk of the accession comes from the first or second parent to die.
* * *

In addition to its inherent capacity for greater fairness and neutrality
than under the present system, the accessions tax model offers the potential
for simpler compliance procedures and mechanisms. The administration of the
accessions tax can be coordinated with the current income tax system.
Additional reporting would be required, but this can be accomplished through
the device of appropriate schedules or supplements to the annual Form 1040.
* * *

COMPARING A REFORMED ESTATE TAX WITH
AN ACCESSIONS TAX AND AN INCOME-
INCLUSION SYSTEM, AND ABANDONING
THE GENERATION-SKIPPING TAX
Joseph M. Dodge[*]

56 Southern Methodist University Law Review 551, 551-62 (2003)

The administration of George W. Bush in 2001 came close to achieving
complete and permanent repeal of the federal estate and generation-skipping
taxes, if not the gift tax (which remains to back up the income tax). Those
opposing repeal have fallen back to the position of conceding the shortcomings
of the federal transfer taxes and of proposing that they be "reformed," mainly
by increasing the per taxpayer lifetime estate and gift tax exemption to a very
large number somewhere in the $2-10 million range. Alternatives to a
reformed estate and gift tax system are a federal inheritance tax, an accessions
tax, or a repeal of the income tax rule that excludes gratuitous receipts from
gross income.[3] A [principal] purpose of this article is to put these alternatives
on the table and to compare them to each other and to a reformed estate and
gift tax system.
        * * *

The theoretical merits of taxing vs. not taxing wealth transfers will not be
taken up in this contribution, which instead focuses on how alternative tax
systems relating to gratuitous transfers would be structured in order to
implement their basic premises. * * *

---

[*]. At time of original publication, Stearns, Weaver, Miller, Weissler, Alhadeff & Sitterson
Professor of Law, Florida State University College of Law.
    3. I.R.C. §§ 101(a) (life insurance proceeds), 102(a) (other gratuitous receipts), and 1014
(excluding pre-death appreciation from any income tax) (2002).

The Inadequacy of the Estate Tax

This Part argues the hardly-startling proposition that the current transferor-oriented system is the hardest kind of tax on gratuitous transfers to defend from the angle of political rhetoric and policy. * * *

Alternative Ways of Taxing Gratuitous Transfers

The core operating concept of the existing federal transfer taxes is that the cumulative (lifetime and deathtime) gratuitous transfers of an individual constitute a cumulative tax base that is subject to progressive rates. The centerpiece of current federal transfer taxes is the estate tax. Both the gift tax and the generation-skipping tax (GST) are back-ups to the estate tax, and the bulk of revenues from the transfer taxes are produced by the estate tax.[15] The estate tax (re-labeled the "death tax") is the target of the repeal rhetoric.

The estate tax concept can be contrasted with three competing transferee-oriented modes of wealth transfer taxation. One (and the oldest) is the inheritance tax concept, where exemptions and (where applicable) progressive rate schedules apply on a per-legatee basis, and rate schedules typically increase as the degree of relationship to the decedent diminishes. The second and third modes are the accessions tax and the income-inclusion system, already alluded to. On its face, any of the transferee-oriented alternatives to the current federal transfer taxes would be better suited to curb undue accumulations of wealth than the estate tax.

Is a Tax on Gratuitous Transfers Necessary To Curb Undue Accumulations of Wealth?

If the problem is stated to be "undue concentrations of wealth," one can argue that a transfer tax is superfluous. Thus, "concentration" of wealth in a single individual by inheritance, given the abolition of primogeniture in the United States, is "naturally" unlikely since wealth tends to be divided among members of an ever-expanding family. The principal of trusts often is eroded relative to inflation, and large trusts are likely to have multiple current beneficiaries and remainders. Moreover, those who receive substantial legacies outright have little incentive to engage in gainful employment and may regress to the mean. There is evidence that *inherited* wealth tends towards dissipation rather than increased concentration and that most very wealthy individuals (other than surviving spouses of wealthy individuals) are not the beneficiaries of large inheritances.

To the extent that these forces operate, it can be argued that the transfer taxes may be largely irrelevant in terms of curbing undue concentrations of wealth. Nature will take its course. * * *

---

15. Estimated net gift tax collections in 2001 were $3.9 billion, and estimated estate tax collections were $24.4 billion. *See Summary of Internal Revenue Collections, by Type of Tax, Fiscal Years 2000 and 2001*, Internal Revenue Service, *at* http://www.irs.gov/pub/irs-soi/01db01co.xls (last visited Nov. 21, 2002).

Redefining the Aim of Taxing Wealth Transfers

The proponents of the wealth transfer taxes have allowed the opponents to frame the debate. The opponents refer to the transfer taxes variously as a tax on death (conveying the message that the suffering of bereaved widows and orphans is compounded by financial sacrifice), or as a tax on success (and, by implication, a penalty on moral virtue). And a defense of the tax on the basis of curbing undue accumulations of wealth is swatted aside by claiming that wealth accumulation (by entrepreneurs and investors) is a good thing, and (as noted above) that concentrated wealth doesn't stay concentrated anyway. Finally, there is no objective standard (or consensus) on what is an "undue" wealth accumulation; the target tends to recede into the distance.[25]

The message needs to be conveyed that any tax on gratuitous transfers is really a tax on gratuitous transferees. * * * Gratuitous receipts (by persons other than the surviving spouse) are passive "unearned" and "windfall" income. Such income (at a certain point) does the legatees *and us* more harm than good by creating disincentives to engage in productive economic activity. A tax on the receipt of unearned wealth (over a certain level) can directly reduce inequality of opportunity. It may even be worthwhile to link revenues from wealth transfer taxes to programs aimed to alleviate such inequalities. Finally, accumulations of unearned wealth allow a person to exercise unearned and unjustified power over others.

Exemption and Rate Structures

Rates and exemptions are so closely linked that they will be discussed in tandem.

Utility Curves

Justifications of multi-tier progressive rate structures are often couched in terms of the declining marginal utility of money. Applying this concept to an estate tax is hazardous due to various possible motives for the making of bequests. Thus, a person with low bequest motives (who saves for retirement or future emergency but dies prematurely) would be insensitive to estate tax rates, as would a compulsive wealth accumulator. For a person who might be sensitive to estate tax rates, a large exemption (effectively a zero rate) would appear to be excessively generous. In any event, anything like a universal utility curve for bequests seems implausible. It is hard to conceive of any theory that would justify the current rate system that, after exhaustion of a very large exemption, effectively starts at a 41% rate and tops off at only a 50% rate.

The idea of a progressive rate structure is more promising with respect to the transferees, who are the ones whose wealth is increased by gratuitous

---

25. The motto might be: "Tax the very wealthy, that is, the people who are a lot richer than us middle-class folks." Since legal academics, media owners, top journalists, members of Congress, and high-level government officials are themselves likely to be (at least) in the upper middle class (top 85-98th percentile in terms of income or wealth), it is not astonishing that there is now little political support for a meaningful wealth transfer tax.

receipts.   But the idea of declining marginal utility to the transferee presupposes a cumulative tax base that encompasses more than the current gratuitous receipt. Obviously, an inheritance tax does not cumulate gratuitous accessions from a particular decedent with anything else, and an accessions tax cumulates current gratuitous accessions only with gratuitous accessions in prior years. Prior gratuitous accessions may be of special interest, but they are still only a subcategory of total transferee wealth at a given point in time or of total income for a period. A person with a large total of cumulative gratuitous accessions may possess a low stock of current wealth or may currently reside in a low income tax bracket. In any event, the declining marginal utility concept cannot justify a large lifetime exemption.

Only the income-inclusion approach cumulates gratuitous accessions with other income of the taxpayer during the year, without special exemption. This feature of an income-inclusion system renders plausible the idea of progressive rates based on the declining-marginal utility idea.

The Windfall Idea

* * *

The usual notion of "windfall" refers to some unexpected "surplus" relative to one's normal "expectations." But this notion of windfall extends beyond gratuitous accessions to encompass such other gains as found objects, prizes and awards, lottery winnings, and perhaps extraordinary investment gains (at least those attributable to blind luck). No tax system, however, has ever moved in this direction. * * *

Redistribution

* * *

The income-inclusion system, which has no fixed-dollar exemptions, is not explicitly tailored to redistributive goals, although it would, of course, further them. If the income-inclusion system were deemed not to have sufficient "punch" at the level of the super rich, it could be combined with an accessions (or estate) tax having a generous exemption. Even without being combined with a wealth transfer tax, an income-inclusion system would probably extract a much greater amount of tax revenue from relatively well-off families than would alternative systems, because (lacking exemptions) the aggregate tax base would be vastly larger. At the same time, the income-inclusion approach would reach lower down the economic ladder, and that might be its political Achilles heel, unless the potentially huge revenue harvest could be linked to a general income tax rate reduction.

The major accessions tax proposals simply assume the fact of a quite substantial lifetime exemption by analogy to the estate and gift tax, without attempting to independently justify it.[38] The size of the estate tax exemption

---

38. William D. Andrews, *The Accessions Tax Proposal*, 22 TAX L. REV. 589, 592 (1967) ($24,000 exemption, comparable to the then estate tax exemption of $30,000); Edward C. Halbach, Jr., *An Accessions Tax*, 23 REAL PROP. PROB. & TR. J. 211, 232 ($700,000 exemption, comparable to the then estate tax exemption of $600,000).

seems to be linked to a political balancing act of maintaining a meaningful revenue flow while exempting roughly 98% of decedents (which translates into targeting only the super rich). Assuming *arguendo* that there should be *some* meaningful lifetime accessions tax exemption system, its size and structure should be constituted according to its particular redistributive rationales, which are more specific than the vague idea of curbing "undue" accumulations of wealth. Thus, any exemption "at the bottom" should be set according to some notion of "unfair inequality of opportunity." Whatever view one might have as to what constitutes an "unfair" advantage to a person receiving gratuitous accessions, surely it must kick in at a level far below the current estate tax exemption. I would suggest $100,000, roughly the amount that would finance (tax free) a good education. * * *

Two of the justifications for an accessions tax (inequality of opportunity and removing the tax disincentive for gainful employment) wane as the transferee advances in age, but the third (concentrations of unearned wealth) does not. This observation could be accommodated by increasing any first-tier exemption (in stages or all at once) after the taxpayer advances past, say, age 30, and by increasing it again as the transferee's age advances beyond, say, age 60.

Dispersing Wealth

Under current law, the per-transferor exemption * * * provides no incentive to disperse wealth among legatees. Stated differently, an estate tax is "neutral" between dispersion and non-dispersion, but that is not necessarily a good thing. In any case, a given transferee can obtain exempt gratuitous transfers from numerous transferors without limit, and thereby amass a vast amount of untaxed, unearned wealth.

Under an inheritance tax, exemptions (and progressive rate schedules) operate on a per-legatee basis. This system creates an incentive for a decedent to disperse legacies among multiple legatees. Although decedents tend to treat their descendants equally at each generation, an inheritance tax might operate to somewhat increase the total level of dispersal. At the same time, a legatee under an inheritance tax can take advantage of multiple per-transferor exemptions with respect to different decedents, and thereby amass a large stock of unearned wealth.

Both the accessions tax and the income inclusion-system favor dispersal. * * *

Summary of Part

Briefly, an estate tax has little to be said for it either from an internal-to-tax perspective or from an external-to-tax perspective. * * * Any transferee-oriented tax on wealth transfers is preferable to an estate tax in theory and is easier to justify. * * *

Notes and Questions

42. As Professor Rudick observed, "dead men pay no taxes." Living people must bear any tax, regardless of the form in which it is levied. Nevertheless, the different forms of the various types of death taxes have substantive importance.

While the federal government has opted for the estate tax, Professor Rudick (not in the article excerpted above) argues that "if the states had not entered the inheritance tax field before the Federal government did, it is not unlikely that we would today have a Federal inheritance tax rather than a Federal estate tax." Congress in 1916 opted for the estate tax, at least in part, because forty-two states already had an inheritance tax while only one had an estate tax; the Federal estate tax would thus result in "a well-balanced system of taxation as between the Federal Government and the various states." Two years later, in 1918, the Senate Finance Committee suggested, "on grounds of fairness and equity," changing to an inheritance tax, but the Ways and Means Committee refused.[uu]

43. Present federal transfer taxes are levied against the donor or the estate. Inheritance and accessions taxes, by contrast, are, in substance at least, levied against the recipient. (In form, state inheritance taxes are frequently payable by the executor, which is probably easier for the state than attempting to collect from multiple heirs, some of whom who may not reside in the state.)

44. Assuming a progressive tax structure, why would either an inheritance tax or an accessions tax give a testator an incentive to divide his estate that does not exist under present law?

45. How does an accessions tax differ from an inheritance tax?

46. According to Professor Rudick, an accessions tax would encourage broader distribution of wealth compared not only to an estate tax but also to an inheritance tax. Assuming a progressive rate structure, why might this be so?

47. Assuming that an accessions tax would encourage wealthy people to disperse their wealth among more donees and legatees, is that necessarily desirable? Professor McCaffery expresses concern about the perpetuation of "a very wealthy elite," and observes that "[i]t may not be better for society to have one thousand millionaires, many of them very young, than a single billionaire."[vv]

---

uu. Harry J. Rudick, *What Alternative to the Estate and Gift Taxes?*, 38 CAL. L. REV. 150, 160 (1950).

vv. McCaffery, *supra* note v, at 324.

48. Professor Donaldson argues that the form of a transfer tax, as opposed to the decision to impose such a tax, "is essentially a practical and utilitarian matter." The excerpt from his article encapsulates much of the argument against the present transfer taxes. He argues that the present taxes fail their traditional goals of breaking up wealth and generating significant revenue, and also fail their more modern justification of contributing to progressivity. Moreover, he concludes that these taxes are unlikely to improve in performance. Is Professor Donaldson on common ground with Professor Graetz, a defender of transfer taxes?

Professor Donaldson argues that in addition to failing to make positive contributions, the present transfer taxes fail in terms of fairness, efficiency and neutrality. Do you concur with Professor Donaldson's dismal assessment of present law?

49. If we are to retain a transfer tax, Professor Donaldson argues that we should move to the accessions tax model. Which of the problems he identified would an accessions tax address?

50. A generation ago, the American Law Institute undertook a project on federal transfer taxes, including as one alternative the accessions tax. The reporter, Professor William Andrews, discussed the proposal in an article published in *Tax Law Review*.[ww] Under the proposal, events that constitute transfers for purposes of the existing transfer taxes generally would constitute accessions for purposes of the accessions tax. The one major exception—and the subject of much of Professor Andrews' article—was the transfer in trust. Under existing transfer taxation, a transfer to a trust normally makes the decedent or donor immediately liable for a transfer tax. But could it be said that the beneficiary had acceded to wealth by the creation of the trust, before any distribution was made to him? The proposal discussed by Professor Andrews took the position that accession normally occurred when money or property was distributed by the trustee to the beneficiary, a result the ALI "considered to be unacceptable in the case of large estates."[xx] Much of the balance of Professor Andrews' article was devoted to possible solutions to this perceived problem, each of which, of course, would have created its own set of problems.

51. Why does Professor Dodge think the estate tax is not justified as a means of curbing excessive accumulations of dynastic wealth?

52. Professor Dodge vigorously defends the notion of imposing taxes on property passing at death. What justifications does he offer for such taxation?

---

ww. William D. Andrews, *The Accessions Tax Proposal*, 22 TAX L. REV. 589 (1967).
xx. *Id.* at 595.

53. Dodge asserts that death-tax proponents have allowed opponents to set the terms of the debate. He argues that it is important that proponents cast the tax as imposed on heirs and not on decedents. Why might this matter?

54. Consider footnote 25 of Dodge's article. Estate taxes, seemingly never a favorite of the public, tend to lose any popularity for any segment of the population who fear that they may become personally liable for the tax.

55. While preferring the accessions tax (or the inheritance tax) to the estate tax, Professor Dodge finds the exemptions in all proposals (as well as under current law) far too generous, suggesting $100,000 as a possible untaxed exemption.

Dodge's preference is repeal of section 102, thereby including gifts and bequests in the income of the recipient. This idea is explored at greater length in Chapter Ten, Subchapter D.

F. WEALTH TAXES

As we have seen, transfer taxes can be viewed as a form of wealth taxation; indeed, breaking up great concentrations of wealth is one of the traditional goals of transfer tax supporters. These taxes, however, do not tax wealth except on the occasion of its transfer—typically, once each generation, as wealth is passed on either by gift or death.

By contrast, the wealth taxes considered in this subchapter envision taxes on the mere ownership of property, typically annually. The tax could be compared to familiar real estate taxes, but here we are dealing with broad-based taxes levied on the taxpayer's entire wealth.

Professor Cooper's lengthy article, briefly excerpted below, argues that the present system of transfer taxation is deficient, and that some form of wealth tax would be preferable to any likely reform of current law. In the final excerpt, Professor Posin argues for a wealth tax coordinated with the income tax.

A VOLUNTARY TAX? NEW PERSPECTIVES ON SOPHISTICATED ESTATE TAX AVOIDANCE
George Cooper[*]
77 Columbia Law Review 161, 162-63, 221, 223, 244-46 (1977)

When William du Pont, Jr., great-grandson of the founder of E.I. du Pont de Nemours & Company, died in 1965, each of his five children received an inheritance of more than fifty million dollars. Each will receive an additional sum, worth more than forty million dollars at 1966 values, on the death of his

---

[*]. At time of original publication, Professor of Law, Columbia University.

or her aunt, Marion du Pont Scott, who is now 82 years old. Thus these five individuals are the sole inheritors of an aggregate family fortune worth almost a half billion dollars in 1966. Barely a handful of fortunes this large exist in the United States. Yet the total of all estate and gift taxes paid on this aggregation of wealth, from its origins in nineteenth century Du Pont Company profits until its receipt by the present generation, including taxes payable on the aunt's death, will be less than $25 million. This wealth has passed through two generations that died while estate taxes were in effect, meaning that the combined effective tax rate for two generations will be only 5%.

The first purpose of this study is to explain how a phenomenon of this nature has occurred. * * * The second purpose is to explore whether the current generation can continue this pattern of tax avoidance in light of the major estate and gift tax reforms enacted by Congress in 1976. The perhaps surprising conclusion compelled by our findings is that today's multimillionaires, as well as persons of lesser wealth, no more need pay a stiff estate and gift tax than did their predecessors. It may be that the real certainties of this world are death and tax *avoidance*.

* * *

Reform Possibilities

What are we to make of this? Clearly, the estate and gift tax is not striking terror into the hearts of the very wealthy, nor is it even seriously burdening most persons who devote effort to avoidance. Everyone does not fully exploit the tax avoidance opportunities, it is true. But we can gain little reassurance from this failure of action. Those who remain burdened by the tax include those who reject tax avoidance for reasons of principle, those who give low priority to engaging in complicated maneuvers solely for tax purposes, those who have no natural alternative to the government for disposition of their fortunes (presumably because they do not have children, do not trust those that they do have, or do not want to burden them with great wealth), and those who die inopportunely.

* * *

In sum, because estate tax avoidance is such a successful and yet wasteful process, one suspects that the present estate and gift tax serves no purpose other than to give reassurance to the millions of unwealthy that entrenched wealth is being attacked. The attack is, however, more cosmetic than real and the economy is paying the price of fettered capital and distorted property ownership for this tax cosmetology. Unless the system can be significantly reformed, consideration should be given to scrapping it, or at least replacing it with a more effective means of accomplishing perceived goals.

* * *

The historical record indicates that the estate and gift tax was originally intended to serve as a revenue producer. This most likely is at least a part of its purpose today, although some would disagree. In addition, a variety of social goals are stated for the tax: supplementing the income tax, breaking up large fortunes, and preventing the creation of a coupon-clipper class.

All of these purposes or goals might better be served by a periodic wealth tax than by the estate and gift taxes. This wealth tax is a tax on net worth imposed recurrently at fixed times, probably annually.[255]

(1) From a revenue viewpoint, a wealth tax is clearly superior to an estate and gift tax. The wealth tax base is not eroded by post-gift appreciation, since wealth in the hands of transferees would continue to be subject to taxation when the next tax period rolled around, rather than shifted out of the clutches of the tax for a generation. This simple fact means that the significance of estate freezing as an avoidance technique would be sharply diminished. (This is not to say that tax revenues might not continue to be affected by intergenerational transfers. Assuming that the wealth tax had progressive rates and was imposed on individuals, rather than family groupings, a transfer of some wealth to a poorer taxpayer would reduce tax collections by reducing the tax bracket, but it could not completely remove property from the tax base. Moreover, the value of intergenerational transfers as a tax avoidance technique would be inherently self-limiting because the more that was given to a person the closer his tax bracket would move to that of the donor. Assuming that a flat top rate would come into effect at some level, the super-rich would soon hit that level and thereby have exhausted the tax avoidance opportunities in bracket-lowering transfers.)

(2) As a supplement to the income tax, the wealth tax seems preferable. The primary goal in this respect is to take account of the fact that the existing income tax underrates accumulated wealth as a source of ability to pay because it reaches only the net realized returns on capital; all the indirect benefits of wealth—power, security, appreciation—must be reached by some other tax, if at all. Another asserted income tax supplementary goal is adding to the progressivity of the overall tax system. While the estate and gift tax serves both these goals, it does so only erratically; the wealth tax would do it more consistently and more evenhandedly.

(3) The wealth tax is also far superior in attacking large fortunes because it does so regularly and promptly and cannot be evaded through generational shifting of ownership.

   * * *

One other major advantage of the periodic wealth tax should also be mentioned. It has always been difficult for people to accept the idea of having a large chunk of property seized by the government in one fell swoop, particularly when the property is in an illiquid form, and payment of the tax may require disposition of some or all of it. This in large part explains why

---

255. Such a tax, which would be a "property tax" on personal property as well as real property with an offset for indebtedness, is a standard part of European tax systems. *See* C. SANDFORD, J. WILLIS & D. IRONSIDE, AN ANNUAL WEALTH TAX, app. C. (1975) (tabular summary of existing European wealth taxes).

Congress has consistently been sympathetic to mitigating the estate tax payment duty of farmers and small businessmen and why the courts have been so sympathetic to valuation discounts for closely-held stock. The result of this understandable sympathy has been a substantial complication of the estate tax and an erosion of its base.

This problem could be eliminated under a periodic wealth tax. Because such a tax would be imposed much more frequently than an estate tax, it could carry correspondingly lower rates than the existing scale for estate and gift taxes. For example, an annual net wealth tax with a flat rate of 1% imposed only on net wealth in excess of $200,000 (thus limiting the tax to only the richest 1% to 2% of the population and even as to them exempting the first $200,000) would have produced approximately the same revenue in 1972 as did the estate and gift tax in that year. Given the greatly increased exemption levels and consequent lowered revenue estimates for the post-1976 estate and gift tax, it is probable that this hypothetical 1% net wealth tax on top wealth holders would be a better revenue producer than the new estate and gift tax, as well as being superior for the other reasons discussed above. Such a 1% tax would of course be far easier on holders of nonliquid assets than the existing high rate estate and gift tax.

* * *

TOWARD A THEORY OF FEDERAL TAXATION:
A COMMENT
Daniel Q. Posin[*]

50 Journal of Air Law and Commerce 907, 923-28 (1985)

An element that could usefully be hammered onto the federal tax system is a wealth tax. As demonstrated in the preceding discussion [not excerpted], the American income tax is really a combination of income and consumption tax elements. It has thus long since surrendered any claim to theoretical purity and any accompanying advantages of simplicity. Moreover, we are not, as stated previously, likely to develop a theoretically pure tax any time soon. Thus, initiating improvements to the present tax system must involve making *ad hoc* changes to what is already an *ad hoc* system. A wealth tax added to the present system would tap an additional legitimate tax base and add balance to the system. Its contribution to the tax revenues would be substantial. * * *

How a Wealth Tax Works

The wealth tax is levied as a percentage of the taxpayer's net worth. For reasons that I will discuss below, the wealth tax should provide a credit for income taxes paid. The literature on this subject describes two forms of the wealth tax. I believe, however, for reasons set forth below, that the two forms

---

[*]. At time of original publication, Associate Professor of Law, Southern Methodist University School of Law.

are really one and the same. Before setting forth my own critique, I will describe the two forms of the wealth tax, as seen in the traditional literature.

The two forms of the wealth tax have various names. I will call them for convenience the weak form and the strong form. The weak form of the tax is limited to a relatively small percentage of the taxpayer's net worth. It is designed to exact a tax of less than a normal rate of return from the taxpayer's capital. Rates for this weak form of wealth tax generally hover around 1% or less of the taxpayer's capital subject to the tax.

The strong form of the tax is designed, according to the traditional view, to take more in tax from the taxpayer's capital than is produced by a normal rate of return less income taxes paid. The rate for the strong form is therefore significantly higher than the rate for the weak form. The strong form is said to be a tax directly on capital, according to the traditional view.

My position is that there is in fact no strong form of the wealth tax—no wealth tax is imposed on capital. This is because when a high rate of wealth tax is imposed, the value of capital subject to the tax drops. This in turn decreases the amount of tax that can be collected by the wealth tax to an amount that can be paid out of income.

Some numerical examples may serve to illustrate:

Example (1) Let us say T has capital subject to the tax of $100,000. If this $100,000 is invested in high-grade corporate bonds paying 10% interest, T's annual income from this capital will be $10,000. Let us assume further that T is in the 50% marginal income tax bracket. Therefore on T's $10,000 interest income, he must pay income tax of $5,000. Let us say also that T is subject to a "weak" form of the wealth tax, which is imposed at the rate of 1% on his investment. By virtue of this tax, T must pay an additional $1,000 in tax. Thus T's income after the income and the wealth tax is $4000. The tax has been paid out of the income from the bonds. On this set of [facts], a wealth tax has operated like an additional income tax on investment income.

Example (2) The facts are the same as in Example 1, except that T is now subject to a "strong" form of the wealth tax. In this case let us assume that the wealth tax is at a rate of 7% of capital. Once again, T has interest income from his corporate bonds of $10,000. Being in the 50% bracket, he pays income taxes of $5000. However, on account of the strong form of the wealth tax, he now also owes $7000 of wealth tax (7% of $100,000). His total tax is $12,000, which he cannot pay solely out of income. Thus he must dip into capital to come up with the extra $2000. He now has only $98,000 invested. This is the confiscatory aspect of the strong form of the wealth tax, according to the literature.

This analysis, however, is flawed. The day a 7% wealth tax is imposed the value of T's corporate bonds will drop. By how much will they drop? Assume for simplicity that all potential buyers of these bonds are also in the 50% marginal income tax bracket. The bonds continue to pay their fixed amount of $10,000 per year. The income tax on that amount continues to be $5000.

However, no one would pay $100,000 for those bonds if the net after tax return was a negative $2000. Therefore the bonds must drop in value by enough to lower the wealth tax to $5000. The bonds will then drop from $100,000 to a value of $71,428. (7% of $71,428 equals $5000). This is a one-time drop. Thereafter, the bonds will continue to trade at around that price and move up and down according to market factors, such as changes in interest rates. In reality, the price will not drop all the way down to $71,428, because some of the potential purchasers of these bonds are not in the 50% marginal bracket. Thus, a taxpayer in the 30% marginal bracket might find these bonds attractively priced at or near $100,000. This would be so because his income tax would be $3000 and his wealth tax would be $7000, if the bonds had a value of $100,000. The bond would not have to drop very much in value for them to have a net positive return to this taxpayer.

What this discussion demonstrates is that there is no such thing as the "the strong form" of the wealth tax. There is no such thing as the wealth tax actually being a tax on wealth. The wealth tax, no matter what its rate, will always be payable out of income from the taxpayer's capital subject to the tax, because the property will drop in value to reflect the imposition of the tax.

Of course, in the case of a wealth tax with a relatively steep rate, such as the 7% in the example above, taxpayers in the 50% marginal bracket have undergone a relatively stiff "tax" on their capital in the sense that their capital has undergone a one-time drop in value on the occasion of the first imposition of the tax. That is a different matter entirely, however, from saying that a wealth tax of relatively high rate is paid out of capital. It is erroneous and leads to incorrect policy decisions to maintain that a wealth tax of relatively high rate is paid out of capital.

Consider, for example, X, an individual, whose wealth is entirely tied up in $10 million worth of undeveloped forest lands. These lands generally appreciate 10% every year. X has no salary and owns no income producing assets. X occasionally sells off some land to meet his modest living expenses. On these facts X has little income (only what may be realized on his occasional land sales). Therefore X pays an inconsequential amount of income tax (assume for simplicity that he pays no income tax). Assume X is subject to a 7% wealth tax. On these facts X has unrealized appreciation on the value of his land of $1 million (10% of $10 million) and pays a wealth tax of $700,000 (7% of $10 million). Thus where X pays little or no income tax, the wealth tax even at a relatively high rate does not cause the value of his assets to fall (at least not to him or others not paying much in income taxes). Indeed, the wealth tax has led to a relatively reasonable result, that a taxpayer of great wealth who would not have otherwise paid any taxes at all, in fact paid some taxes. Note that X in the example given above is a miser with established wealth. Therefore X in the example above would not be significantly reached either by an income tax or a consumption tax.

This discussion leads to the conclusion that a reasonable way to impose a wealth tax of some significant rate is to allow a credit or a partial credit against the wealth tax for income taxes paid with respect to the capital involved. If that were done, then in our Example 2 above, T, having paid $5000 in income taxes on his investment income, would only pay $2000 more in wealth taxes to reach his 7%. That would still leave him with a $3000 after tax return. However, the taxpayer X, above, who owned the forest land, would derive no benefit from the credit for income taxes paid, since he pays no income taxes. As we have discussed, it is appropriate that the wealth tax reach him more heavily.

This discussion has assumed a wealth tax of 7%, which is very much higher than what I would propose or than is in use in Europe or the Indian sub-continent today. Yet even with this relatively high rate, the tax, when combined with a credit for income taxes, works effectively and in a non-confiscatory manner, not overtaxing those who are already paying substantial taxes on income from their capital and yet reaching those who are not otherwise taxed.

While it is not presently on the horizon, the wealth tax may become a useful complement to other methods of federal taxation, in the era of very high budget deficits.

Notes and Questions

56. Professor Cooper's article was published in 1977, between the legislation of 1976 and 1981. The 1976 legislation, it will be recalled, was described by Professor Graetz (in Subchapter C) as a shift "toward a basically sound and well-structured wealth transfer system," prior to the 1981 move "to emasculate it." Yet, even in what defenders of the transfer taxes might term a congressional "lucid interval," Cooper still found that the transfer taxes could be easily avoided by taxpayers.

Professor Cooper contended that the goals of transfer taxes would be better served by an annual wealth tax. What advantages does he identify for a wealth tax vis-à-vis our present system of transfer taxes?

57. Professor Posin describes what he terms a "weak" and a "strong" form of wealth taxation. What is the difference between the two? Why does he contend that the "strong" form does not actually exist?

58. What form would Professor Posin's proposed wealth tax take? Why?

59. Although the United States has not embraced a broad-based wealth tax, Professor Cooper has observed (not in the article excerpted) that "to be

without a wealth tax could be said to be the exception rather than the rule in Western Europe."[yy]

60. The wealth tax has attracted some slight support in the American political arena. Ramsey Clark, who was Attorney General under President Johnson, sought the Democratic nomination to become United States Senator from New York in 1976. In the course of his unsuccessful campaign, Mr. Clark advocated a wealth tax of approximately three percent on family wealth in excess of one million dollars, a levy that he declared would combat "economic royalism."[zz]

61. Barry Isaacs directed the following critique at Mr. Clark's wealth tax proposal, but Mr. Isaacs' cautions—focusing more on practical concerns than purity of policy—may be relevant to many tax proposals, particularly those considered in this chapter:

> Individuals who advocate a redistribution of wealth in America often are so irresistibly drawn to any proposal which has as its purpose the economic leveling of the wealthiest group of individuals, that they are either unmindful or unconcerned about the inherent problems which will ensue. The wealth tax proposal of Ramsey Clark is no different. It assumes a perfectly designed tax as well as an effectively administered one. It foresees nothing but perfect acquiescence by those affected by the wealth tax. It supposes that the tax can be instituted with modest costs. It dismisses any notion that such a tax could have economically adverse consequences. None of these notions is beyond serious challenge.[aaa]

62. The compliance and administrative problems of a wealth tax should not be underestimated. Unless some sort of formula were utilized, annual taxation would require annual valuation. A comprehensive wealth tax could also result in considerable fraud—unlike the familiar real estate tax, which taxes property that is hard either to hide or to move, taxpayers might be able to conceal many assets from a wealth tax.

63. It seems quite possible that a federal wealth tax could run afoul of the constitutional bar on direct taxes that are not apportioned among the states according to population.[bbb] The meaning of "direct" taxes has been

---

yy. George Cooper, *Taking Wealth Taxation Seriously*, 34 REC. ASS'N BAR CITY N.Y. 24, 24 (1979).

zz. This description is taken from an article criticizing Mr. Clark's proposal, Barry L. Isaacs, *Do We Want a Wealth Tax in America?*, 32 U. MIAMI L. REV. 23, 24-25 (1977-78). Mr. Isaacs referred to "Ramsey Clark/Senate '76, Position Papers 1-2 (1976) (on file with the *University of Miami Law Review*)."

aaa. Isaacs, *supra* note zz, at 49.

bbb. U.S. CONST. art. I, § 9, cl. 4.

unclear from the outset: "James Madison's Journal of the Constitutional Convention contains the following entry for August 20, 1787: 'Mr. King asked what was the precise meaning of *direct* taxation? No one answered.'"[ccc] It is hard to see what might be a more direct tax than a property tax or a wealth tax.

64. *Class warfare?* Professor Ronald Chester argues that "the underlying issue in the inheritance controversy is one of class conflict."[ddd] Do you agree? If so, do you think this is any more the case than with respect to many income tax provisions, such as the progressive rate structure and the treatment of capital gains? Professor Chester maintains that "an annual, or even a triennial wealth tax is more productive of equality than a once-in-a-lifetime estate or inheritance tax."[eee]

Australian and Canadian transfer tax repeals

65. Recent Australian history lends credence to the notion that death taxes are not uniformly popular outside the United States. An ordinary citizen—"Sydney Negus, formerly a skilled carpenter and later a smallish building contractor"—started a movement that culminated in Australia's repeal of death taxes, in the process gaining election to the Senate "as an Independent whose single issue campaign was the abolition of death duties."[fff]

66. Canada also abolished death taxes, in 1972, and simultaneously began imposing income taxation on unrealized appreciation of property passed from the taxpayer at death. (For further discussion of Canada's experience with constructive realization, see Chapter Ten, Subchapter C.)

In an article written with the stated goal of reopening the debate, Professor Maureen Maloney observed that the tradeoff between the constructive realization of capital gain and the abolition of death taxes resulted from the perception of avoiding double taxation, a perception that Professor Maloney roundly criticized: "This was a misconception but a politically powerful one. It illustrates a fundamental misunderstanding of the purpose of the two taxes."[ggg]

Among the more interesting arguments advanced by Professor Maloney is that high levels of wealth taxation—whether collected annually or by death taxes—are required by justice, apart from the matter of healthy adults inheriting wealth that they did not create: "Even if a perfect market did

---

ccc. ALAN GUNN & LARRY D. WARD, FEDERAL INCOME TAXATION 2 (5th ed. 2002).

ddd. C. Ronald Chester, *Inheritance and Wealth Taxation in a Just Society*, 30 RUTGERS L. REV. 62, 100 (1976).

eee. *Id.* at 69.

fff. Willard H. Pedrick, *Oh, To Die Down Under! Abolition of Death and Gift Duties in Australia*, 14 U. W. AUSTL. L. REV. 438, 438, 440 (1982).

ggg. Maureen A. Maloney, *Distributive Justice: That is the Wealth Tax Issue*, 20 OTTOWA L. REV. 601, 606 (1988).

reward individuals according to ability, effort and talent, the notion that such a distribution is morally just is still unsupportable. * * * People are of equal moral worth. Moral claims to rewards, therefore, cannot rest on the natural abilities with which one is born."[hhh]

Do you agree with Professor Maloney that justice requires death taxes? That they are required because market outcomes do not provide morally just outcomes?

---

hhh. *Id.* at 617.

CHAPTER TEN

INCOME TAX TREATMENT OF PROPERTY TRANSFERRED AT DEATH OR BY GIFT

The most serious defect in our federal tax structure * * * is the failure of the income tax to reach the appreciation in value of assets transferred at death.[a]

A. INTRODUCTION

As is the case with the estate tax, considered in Chapter Nine, the income tax treatment of property passing at death is in flux. Most tax scholars would assert that the estate tax is logically separate from the income tax issues considered in this chapter. Politics tells a different story. More than once, high-profile, politically-charged change to the estate tax has been accompanied by little-noticed and less-than-fully-considered, but quite important, changes in the income tax treatment of property passing at death. In the Tax Reform Act of 1976, Congress coupled a substantial increase in estate tax exemptions to the adoption of carryover basis (subsequently repealing carryover basis while keeping the higher estate tax exemptions). More recently, when Congress moved in 2001 to phase out the estate tax (though repealing it only for the year 2010, due to the 2001 Act's sunset provision), Congress tied the repeal to the adoption of carryover basis (again, only for the single year 2010). Clearly, many members of Congress intend that the 2010 changes become permanent, and even those in Congress who favor retention of the estate tax do not expect that the 2001 Act will simply expire in 2011. Under these circumstances, the term "present law" must be used with care. References to "present law" of the issues discussed in this chapter will mean the basic rules traditionally applicable—and which, absent further congressional action, are to remain applicable in every future year except 2010.

While not all tax scholars would agree with this chapter's opening quotation in its characterization of the income tax treatment of property passing at death as the worst failing of tax law, virtually none would defend present law on policy grounds. The law governing the income tax treatment of property transferred by gift and at death is familiar ground to all students who have completed a basic course in taxation. Neither the transferor nor the transferee of either a gift or an inheritance has any gross income or deduction

---

a. Jerome Kurtz & Stanley S. Surrey, *Reform of Death and Gift Taxes: The 1969 Treasury Proposals, The Criticisms, and a Rebuttal*, 70 COLUM. L. REV. 1365, 1381 (1970).

by reason of the transfer.[b] In the case of property that is transferred by gift, the donee usually takes the donor's basis (*"carryover basis"*). Section 1015. (In the case of property worth less than the donor's basis, section 1015 requires the donee to use fair market value for purposes of computing loss.) Even though the gift could constitute a realization event, the theory is that it is appropriate to wait until the donee sells or exchanges the property, then require the donee to take into income the full gain attributable to the donor's period of ownership as well as his own.

In the case of property transferred by death, the general rule is one of *"stepped-up basis"*—the heir normally takes as his basis the fair market value of the property at the date of death.[c] Section 1014. No one ever pays tax on any appreciation unrealized at the date of death. Similarly, no deduction is available in the case of depreciated property, whose basis is "stepped-down" at death. While it is difficult to articulate a principled defense for the rule of section 1014—simplicity (by avoiding any difficulty in ascertaining the decedent's basis) is probably the strongest argument available—it is less certain what form a replacement provision should take. There are three leading candidates for reform. First, the rule of carryover basis already applicable to gifts could be extended to inherited property. As noted above, this is the route chosen by Congress in 2001, but it may not be the best choice. Second, the transfer of property at death, and perhaps by gift as well, could be treated as a realization event, with the result that the excess of fair market value over basis would be subjected to income tax on the decedent's final return, or on the donor's return. Third, section 102, which excludes gifts and bequests from the income of the recipient, could be repealed. Repeal of section 102 would subject heirs, and in some cases donees of *inter vivos* gifts, to income tax on the full amount received. The materials in Subchapters B, C, and D discuss each of these options. First, however, the notes and questions immediately below consider present law.

---

b. Section 102 provides for non-inclusion by the recipient, and, consistently, there is no statutory provision for a deduction by the transferor. Non-taxation of the transferor (on unrealized appreciation accrued to the time of transfer) is not specified by statute, but presumably derives from a traditional and "common-sense" view that transferring property and receiving nothing in return, or at least nothing more tangible than a sense of satisfaction, does not constitute income.

c. The estate tax is based on the value of the decedent's estate at the date of death, or, if the executor elects, at an alternative valuation date generally six months after death (or the date of sale for property sold within the six-month period). Section 2032. In the event of an election under section 2032, the basis for income tax purposes is the alternative valuation. Section 1010(a)(2). The policy behind the alternative valuation approach is probably not controversial. It is to protect the estate from a temporary high value of assets—resulting, perhaps, from a "spike" in the stock market—which the assets do not retain by the time the estate is settled and the estate taxes paid. Throughout this chapter, for simplicity, the term "date of death" is meant to include the alternative valuation date where the election is made.

Notes and Questions

1.   Why is stepped-up basis—the present rule applied to transfers of property at death, under section 1014—thought to be inequitable?[d]

2.   Is it clear that section 1014 is in fact inequitable? From the decedent's point of view, where is the realized gain? The decedent manifestly did *not* realize during life, and claiming that he did so by dying is (arguably) entirely artificial. From the heir's point of view, why should the heir be held accountable for gain that occurred during the period of ownership of another taxpayer (the decedent)? True, it may be argued that the heir realized the principal amount of the inheritance, but that would be equally true regardless of whether the property were appreciated, depreciated, or neither. This suggests that section 102 may be wrong, but says nothing about section 1014.

3.   Most modern tax students will instinctively realize that section 1014 is badly out of step with the rest of tax law, but should recognize that such a view was not necessarily present in the early years of the income tax. Initially, the concept of income was tied, much more than today, to trust and accounting concepts, rather than to the more modern principle that economic gain should be taxed even if the gain occurred in a way not ordinarily thought of as income. Only over a period of years was it established that economic improvements such as cancellation of indebtedness,[e] payment of the taxpayer's income tax obligations by his employer,[f] and illegally obtained income[g] constituted income. The symbol of this evolutionary process is the Supreme Court's 1955 decision in *Glenshaw Glass*.[h]   Keep in mind that this decision, which now seems manifestly correct and which was rendered 42 years after the Sixteenth Amendment was ratified, required reversing the settled position of the Tax Court that punitive damages, even in the business context, were not income.

This history may help us understand how, in the early years of the income tax when many economic gains were not understood to be within the tax concept of "income," the rule that taxed neither the decedent nor the heir might have taken root.

---

d. The danger of abuse is controlled by the requirement that the owner die to take advantage of the favorable treatment. Few taxpayers will go to that extent to avoid paying taxes. The gift situation is completely different; see Note #9 below.

e. United States v. Kirby Lumber Co., 284 U.S. 1 (1931).

f. Old Colony Trust Co. v. Commissioner, 279 U.S. 716 (1929).

g. James v. United States, 366 U.S. 213 (1961). *James* overruled Commissioner v. Wilcox, 327 U.S. 404 (1946), which had taken the contrary view.

h. Commissioner v. Glenshaw Glass Co., 348 U.S. 426 (1955).

4.   Jerome Kurtz and Stanley Surrey, well known tax scholars and Treasury officials during the Johnson administration, emphasized the importance of stepped-up basis in undercutting the progressive tax system. (Keep in mind that the dollar figures are those of 35 years ago, when income of $100,000 represented a much higher relative position than today.)

> For the group of individuals whose annual economic income (including annual appreciation in asset values) exceeds $100,000, the annual appreciation that is untaxed—and in the end escapes income tax at death—is about equal to all other income, both taxable and exempt, combined.   * * *   The consequence in the end of not subjecting these large accumulations of income to the income tax is clearly to provide a broad avenue of escape from that tax for the wealthiest families.   * * *[i]

5.   Clearly, Congress has accepted the argument that the estate tax is closely linked in policy terms to the income tax treatment of property passing at death. Is stepped-up basis justified because the decedent's estate may be subjected to the estate tax?

6.   The stepped-up basis rules of present law are said to result in a "lock-in" effect. A taxpayer who owns appreciated property can sell the property, but must pay a capital gains tax. If he holds the property until death, however, he avoids the tax, as do his heirs. Thus, the taxpayer—especially if he is elderly or in poor health—will have a considerable incentive to hold the property.

This lock-in creates an impediment to the optimal use of resources. A perfectly functioning market tends to direct property ownership to the person who can most efficiently use the property, because the property is worth more to that person. Thus, the current owner of appreciated property, who by hypothesis is using it less efficiently than the potential purchaser, would have an incentive to sell because the purchaser would be willing to pay more for the property than it is worth to the current owner. The capital gain tax creates an impediment to this efficient transaction, but, absent the rule of section 1014, the owner would know that the tax would have to be paid sooner or later. Under the rule of stepped-up basis, however, the property owner would have a greater incentive to hold rather than sell, because the capital gains tax could be permanently defeated rather than merely postponed.

7.   Section 1014 mandates a basis equal to fair market value at death, which can be either more or less than the decedent's basis in the property, and

---

i. Kurtz & Surrey, *supra* note a, at 1383.

thus can result in stepped-*down* basis. Why is so much more concern expressed about stepped-up basis than about stepped-down basis? Why does the fact that section 1014 mandates both stepped-up basis and stepped-down basis not mean that untaxed appreciation forgiven by section 1014 is roughly balanced by disallowed deductions with respect to assets that have fallen in value? If we thought such a rough balance occurred with respect to taxpayers as a whole (which it does not), would this be sufficient to satisfy the demands of policy, or would it be necessary that each taxpayer's untaxed gains and disallowed losses roughly balance?

8.   Real estate and intangible assets, of which corporate stock is the most important, tend to appreciate over time, due to inflation if nothing else.

On the other hand, most tangible personal property owned by taxpayers falls in value as it wears out, so that stepped-down basis occurs more frequently than we usually acknowledge. For example, clothing, automobiles, furniture, etc. normally decline in value after purchase. However, if the assets are personal, no loss would have been deductible anyway (see section 165(c)), so in most cases the stepped-down basis would not adversely affect the heir, and did not represent a loss that could have been deducted by the decedent.

If tangible personal property is used in business or for the production of income, so that losses would be deductible, it is likely that depreciation deductions would have reduced basis below value, so that stepped-up basis, rather than stepped-down, would be the general rule.

9.   Why would the rule of stepped-up basis be much more troublesome if applied to gifts than it is when applied to inheritances?

B. CARRYOVER BASIS OF PROPERTY TRANSFERRED AT DEATH

When Congress repealed the estate tax in 2001, it implemented a system of carryover basis for property passing at death. As noted in Subchapter A, both the estate tax repeal and the implementation of carryover basis are effective only for the year 2010, barring further congressional action.

In the excerpt below, the Bush Administration's legislative proposal explains the provision in substantially the form in which it was enacted. Carryover basis sounds simple, but can raise difficult issues. These issues, and their complexity, will vary with the statutory details, of course. Consider, in particular, the differences between carryover basis long applicable to gifted property (section 1015) and the new version of carryover basis for property passing at death (the new section 1022).

GENERAL EXPLANATIONS OF THE ADMINISTRATION'S FISCAL YEAR 2002 TAX RELIEF PROPOSALS

United States Department of the Treasury

Pages 12-16 (2001)

Phase Out Death Tax

Current Law

The estate, gift and generation-skipping taxes form a unified system of taxes on the transfer of property, directly or in trust, during life and at death.

Estate Tax

The estate tax is levied on property owned by the decedent at the time of death. * * *

An inherited asset receives a new basis equal to the fair market value of the asset on the date of the decedent's death (or, if the alternative valuation date is elected, the earlier of the date that the property is sold or distributed by the estate or six months after the date of death). Although this is commonly referred to as a "stepped-up" basis, market conditions could result in a stepped-down basis. Thus, when an inherited asset is sold, only capital gains (or losses) realized between the time of the transferor's death and the time of sale by the transferee are subject to federal income taxation.

Gift Tax

The gift tax rate schedule and unified credit are the same as the estate tax provisions. * * *

Generation-Skipping Transfer (GST) Tax

Property transferred to individuals two or more generations younger than the transferor is subject to the GST tax, in addition to estate or gift tax. * * *

Reasons for Change

* * * Capital gains income that is not realized before death is not taxed under the current income tax system. However, the basis of the investment (that is, the funds used to purchase the asset) may have been taxed under the income tax system. Thus the estate tax amounts to double taxation on the basis. Income should be taxed once—when it is earned—and not again when it is passed on to the next generation.

* * *

Proposal

* * *

After repeal of the estate tax, the basis of property acquired from or passed from a decedent, in the hands of the person acquiring or receiving it, generally would be the lower of the fair market value on the date of the decedent's death or the adjusted basis of the property immediately before the death of the decedent. For purposes of recapture, the character of the gain on the sale of the inherited assets would remain the same as it was in the hands of the decedent. Thus, real estate that has been depreciated and would be subject to recapture tax if sold by the decedent would be subject to recapture tax if sold by the heir.

For every estate of a U.S. citizen or resident, there would be three potential adjustments to basis, so that taxpayers who are not currently subject to estate tax generally would not be subject to capital gains tax on assets held until death. First, each estate would receive $1.3 million of basis to be added to the carryover basis of any one or more of the assets held at death. Second, an estate generally would receive additional basis equal to the sum of (1) the decedent's unused capital loss carryforwards, (2) the decedent's unused net operating loss carryforwards, and (3) the difference between the decedent's basis and fair market value on assets that are assigned a fair market value basis. Other than with respect to net operating losses, this additional basis could not be assigned to depreciable or ordinary income assets. Third, estates would be allowed an additional $3 million of basis, to be allocated among the assets passing to a surviving spouse. No addition to basis could increase the new basis of any asset beyond its fair market value on the date of death. The allowable amounts of additional basis would be indexed for inflation after 2009.[2]

In addition, the current-law exclusion of gain on the sale of a principal residence would be extended to heirs. Thus, an heir who sells the decedent's principal residence within 3 years of the decedent's death could use the 2-out-of-5-years rule with respect to the decedent's use of the residence while alive, and claim a capital gain exclusion.

* * *

A donor would be required to report to the IRS the basis and character of any gifted property with a value in excess of $25,000, along with the name and social security number of the donee. The donor also would be required to report the basis to the donee. Gifts of cash would be excluded from this requirement, as would gifts to charity (other than split-interest gifts). For transfers at death of non-cash assets in excess of $1.3 million, the executor of the estate would report to the IRS the basis in each property, the character of the property, any additional basis allocated to the property, the fair market value of the property on the decedent's date of death, and the name and social security number of the heir receiving the property. Basis information would also have to be reported to the heir. For estates with non-cash assets of less

---

2. Estates of nonresident aliens would be given additional basis on U.S. property of $60,000 (rather than $1.3 million), corresponding to the exemption amount of nonresident aliens under current law. Surviving spouses of nonresident aliens would be entitled to the additional basis of $3 million only if the spouse is a U.S. citizen.

than $1.3 million, this reporting generally would not be required (unless the decedent had received a noncash gift in excess of $25,000 within 3 years of death). The filing requirements would be indexed for inflation after 2009. The reporting to the IRS would be done in connection with the filing of the decedent's final income tax return, with liberal extensions of time available. Penalties would apply if a donor or executor failed to meet the reporting requirements with respect to the IRS or recipients.

Upon the sale of inherited or gifted property, the taxpayer would be required to substantiate the basis of the property. If the basis is unknown but the date of acquisition by the decedent is known, then the basis would be presumed to be the fair market value at the time of acquisition (with any appropriate adjustments, for example, due to improvements or depreciation).

Notes and Questions

10.   The estate tax is levied on the value of all property passing at death, whether or not the property embodies unrealized appreciation. Under present law, section 1014 forgives the income tax on the appreciation (even for property passing from estates not subject to the estate tax). Thus, present law taxes unrealized appreciation of property held at death through the estate tax, but not through the income tax. Many scholars view the problem of present law as its failure also to subject the unrealized appreciation to the income tax.

The Bush Administration, clearly, sees things differently. In its view, the problem is that the value of all property *other than* unrealized appreciation—cash and the decedent's basis in property—is subjected to both taxes. "Thus, the estate tax amounts to double taxation on the basis." Perhaps the key policy question for this chapter is whether the "double tax" characterization is accurate and appropriate.

11.   Carryover basis is the most familiar reform proposal, because it has always served for gift property. When Congress acted to end stepped-up basis in 1976 and again in 2001, both times it opted for carryover basis. Leaving aside the important political fact that carryover basis represents a lower tax burden than the other reform proposals—as well as a lower burden than the estate tax—carryover basis may not be the preferred choice. Speaking of the 1976 legislation, one commentator observed that "[c]arryover was the classic compromise that pleased no one."[j] (Representative Ullman, who was Chairman of the Ways and Means Committee in 1976, is quoted to similar effect in footnote 43 of the Zelenak excerpt in Subchapter C.)

---

j. Howard J. Hoffman, *The Role of the Bar in the Tax Legislative Process,* 37 TAX L. REV. 411, 442 (1982).

12. Under the 2001 Act, the applicable rule for some 99 percent of decedents and their heirs will continue to be stepped-up basis. The basis adjustments allow almost all estates an increase in basis—but only up to date-of-death value—of $1.3 million. Effectively, carryover basis is to be limited to the same upper crust that previously paid the estate tax.

This basis adjustment raises at least two questions. First, is it appropriate that carryover basis be limited to only the richest one percent or so of the population. (Carryover basis of gifts under section 1015 is applicable to all.)

Second, as to the top one percent—the beneficiaries of estate tax repeal—the $1.3 million adjustment limits the effect of carryover basis. Is this limitation appropriate?

13. Is *any* special exemption from carryover basis for property left to a surviving spouse—not to speak of a $3 million step-up—justified? Is the step-up justified as a simplification measure?

The estate tax, which section 1022 is designed to replace (at least in a political sense), contains an unlimited spousal exemption. Do similar considerations justify a substantial spousal exemption from carryover basis?

14. The 2001 Act provides for a basis step-up equal to the decedent's unused losses. Is this provision justified? Would simply passing the unused losses to the heirs make more sense?

15. A basic concern is that carryover basis in the form enacted in 2001 will simply not yield very much revenue, at least in comparison to the $30 billion that the estate tax yielded in 2002. Where the estate tax of present law claims roughly 50 percent of taxable estates, the yield from carryover basis will be lower for at least three reasons.

First, the rate is much lower—capital gains under the income tax are taxed at only 15 percent. Second, the base subject to the tax is much less. While the base of the estate tax is the entire value of the estate, the income tax levied under the carryover basis rules is applicable only to previously untaxed appreciation, and even that is undercut by the basis step-ups described in the preceding three notes.

Finally, the tax contemplated by carryover basis depends on realization by the heir. If we think of estates of hundreds of millions of dollars, it is quite conceivable that realization may be postponed indefinitely—for generations. Is a present estate tax being replaced by a distant and elusive future capital gains tax?

16. As discussed in Subchapter A (see Note #6, page 622), a traditional concern with the present rule of stepped-up basis is that it creates a "lock-in" effect, inducing owners of appreciated property not to sell and pay a tax on the gain, but rather to hold until death and avoid all income tax—from decedent, estate, or heir—on the appreciation.

Will carryover basis entirely eliminate "lock-in" for an elderly owner of appreciated property?

What will be the effect of carryover basis on the willingness of heirs to sell appreciated property? Will a new form of "lock-in" be created?

17. In 1976, executors objected to carryover basis on the ground that it made the equitable distribution of assets among heirs more difficult. It seems likely that the same objection may be raised as 2010 approaches. Why would carryover basis have this effect?

18. Professor Henry Lischer predicts that carryover basis will become less popular as 2010 approaches, and that it will eventually be repealed:

In my opinion, carryover basis is a time bomb waiting to explode. Compliance with it will be very difficult and immensely unpopular with the public, and executors of estates will face an uncomfortable situation in which they must consider, in making distributions of property in kind, both value and adjusted basis of the property. I expect that Congress eventually will do away with § 1022 (as it did with the carryover basis provision enacted in the Tax Reform Act of 1976 and retroactively repealed). * * * [C]arryover basis will become ever less appealing to Congress as the effective date of § 1022 approaches.[k]

Do you agree with Professor Lischer?

19. If carryover basis is attacked on the grounds of complexity and administrative burden, this will be a reprise of the debate in the late 1970s. The role of the organized bar, and of the Tax Section of the American Bar Association in particular, in the earlier repeal of carryover basis was portrayed in generally unflattering terms by Howard J. Hoffman, an attorney.[l] Mr. Hoffman begins by stating his views of the proper role of the bar:

When an attorney participates in the legislative process on behalf of a client, many believe that he is ethically bound—as he would be in a courtroom—to advance the interests of his client

---

k. Henry J. Lischer, *Incomplete Transfer Tax Repeal: Should the Gift Tax Survive?*, 56 SMU L. REV. 601, 618-19 (2003). (Professor Lischer's article is excerpted in Chapter 9 (page 586)).

l. Hoffman, *supra* note j.

unrestrained by considerations of tax policy. An attorney may also participate in the legislative process, however, as an impartial advisor, and offer his expertise of behalf of the tax system rather than on behalf of a client.[m]

Although acknowledging that the 1976 version of carryover basis was fraught with problems that may have merited repeal, Mr. Hoffman generally gives the organized bar a failing grade for its role in the debate leading to repeal of carryover basis:

> Overall, however, the Tax Section and other tax groups did not fulfill their role as evenhanded tax experts. During the early part of the debate on carryover, they seemed to stress technical and practical considerations, and to understate other policy concerns. Throughout the debate, they appeared to present a one-sided view of carryover's technical problems and not to treat fairly the merits of cleanup.[n] Their discussion of policy concerns and of alternatives to carryover also seemed one-dimensional. Some of the Tax Section's actions gave the appearance of manipulating the legislative process to facilitate repeal. Although there were many different reasons for the tax group's views, they had given the appearance of taxpayer or client orientation.[o]

Mr. Hoffman quoted the tongue-in-cheek observation of Representative Corman, who was suggesting that the tax bar's complaints about complexity were merely an excuse for attempting to protect for their clients (and themselves?) the tax advantages of stepped-up basis:

> We have the wrong people drafting the wrong pieces of the tax code. Whoever drafts tax incentives is very, very good. I have never seen them draft one so complicated you could not live with it, but every time we try to impose taxes, they run in the other team and write it so complex you can't live with it.[p]

What should be the role of the bar in tax legislation?

---

m. *Id.* at 413.

n. "Cleanup" is the term used for the unsuccessful efforts to amend carryover basis in ways to make it more workable and less objectionable than the form in which it was enacted in 1976.

o. Hoffman, *supra* note j, at 492.

p. *Id.* at 490-91, quoting *Estate and Gift Tax Carryover Basis and Generation-Skipping Trust Provisions and Deductibility of Foreign Convention Expenses: Hearings Before the House Comm. on Ways and Means*, 95th Cong., 1st Sess. 107 (1977).

C. CONSTRUCTIVE REALIZATION: TAXING DONORS AND DECEDENTS ON UNREALIZED APPRECIATION

Carryover basis would not result in income taxes being payable at the time of transfer. The tax would await sale (or other realization event) by the recipient. The tax on the appreciation, including the appreciation during the transferor's period of ownership, would ultimately be taxed to the transferee, at the transferee's marginal rate. Another approach would be to treat the transfer of property as a constructive realization event to the transferor—the equivalent for tax purposes of a sale at fair market value.

TAXING GAINS AT DEATH
Lawrence Zelenak[*]

46 Vanderbilt Law Review 361, 363-75, 409, 414-16 (1993)

The President's Budget estimates the annual revenue loss from the failure to tax gains at death at more than $25 billion.[5] Current law is objectionable also for its lock-in effect: elderly taxpayers are discouraged from disposing of appreciated assets, because if they hold the assets until death, the appreciation will escape income taxation permanently.[6]

This tax forgiveness did not originate as a conscious policy decision.[7] Rather it occurred almost accidentally from the combination of two ideas that were accepted instinctively during the early years of the income tax: that the mere transfer of property at death did not constitute a realization of gain or loss on the property,[8] and that fair market value basis for heirs was appropriate to prevent taxation of capital, because "'capital' was thought to

---

[*]. At time of original publication, Professor of Law, University of North Carolina.

5. The Budget of the United States Government for Fiscal Year 1993 estimates the revenue loss at $24.365 billion in 1991, $26.8 billion in 1992, and $28.4 billion in 1993. Office of the President, *Budget of the United States Government for Fiscal Year 1993*, Special Analysis G 2-26 (U.S. Gov. Printing Off., 1992).

6. The lock-in effect discourages gifts as well as sales. A lifetime gift does not trigger tax on the appreciation, but it prevents a step-up in basis upon the donor's death. I.R.C. § 1015.

7. Until 1921, no tax statute specified the basis of property received by gift or bequest. The administrative practice was to give such property a basis equal to its value at the date of transfer. Anita Wells, *Legislative History of Treatment of Capital Gains Under the Federal Income Tax, 1913-1948*, 2 Nat'l Tax J. 12, 16 (1949). In 1921, Congress enacted the predecessors of present I.R.C. §§ 1014 and 1015 (setting a fair market value basis for bequests and a carryover basis for gifts). One commentator has noted that the rationale for the Section 1014-type statute is unclear, and that it appears "to have been merely the legislative adoption of a consistent administrative practice." Louis M. Castruccio, *Becoming More Inevitable? Death and Taxes . . . and Taxes*, 17 UCLA L. Rev. 459, 460-61 (1970).

8. The leading early case on realization, *Eisner v. Macomber*, 252 U.S. 189 (1920), indicated that gain was realized only when it somehow was severed from capital. Death, of course, does not produce any such severance.

refer to some tangible thing, whatever its value, rather than to a monetary account keeping track of what has been taxed."[9]

Defenders of the current system have justified it on the grounds that the step up in basis is "paid for" by the estate tax on the appreciation. It is true that appreciation that escapes income tax may not escape estate tax, and the estate tax rate may even be higher than the income tax rate.[11] Nevertheless, there are two problems with this argument. First, the step up in basis applies even to property that is not subject to estate tax (because of the unified credit or the marital bequest deduction). Second, and more important, the income and estate taxes are distinct, both conceptually and practically. Conceptually, there is no reason why appreciation transferred at death should not be subject to both taxes—to the income tax because it is gain, and to the estate tax because it is a gratuitous transfer. Practically, gratuitously transferred income is generally subject to both taxes. If a taxpayer sells appreciated property during life, the gain is subject to income tax, and if at death he transfers the proceeds of the sale (reduced by the income tax paid) to his beneficiaries, the estate tax will apply as well. The treatment of appreciation at death thus produces inequity between taxpayers who realize income during life, and those who transfer unrealized appreciation at death. The inequity is both horizontal (discriminating between different taxpayers of similar income and wealth) and vertical (favoring wealthy taxpayers because a greater portion of their income tends to be in the form of unrealized appreciation transferred at death).

If Congress desires to eliminate the permanent forgiveness of capital gains tax at death, it could do so either by providing that the basis of property transferred at death carries over to heirs and beneficiaries, or by taxing gains at death. During the process that led to the enactment of the Tax Reform Act of 1986, virtually every base-broadening reform with significant support among tax policy experts was discussed by Congress and the administration. The one glaring exception was the forgiveness of gains tax at death.[16] This omission would be astounding,[17] but for some history.

---

9. Calvin Johnson, *The Undertaxation of Holding Gains*, 55 Tax Notes 807, 813 (1992).

11. Under current law, the highest rate on capital gain is 28%, I.R.C. § 1(h), and the lowest estate tax rate (after application of the unified credit) is 37%, *id.* § 2001(c)(1).

16. The only mention was a sort of nonmention. The Treasury Department included "capital gains on appreciated assets transferred at death or by gift" in a list of "items not included in the tax reform proposal." 1 *Tax Reform for Fairness, Simplicity and Economic Growth* (Dept. of the Treasury, 1984), at 147.

17. It is especially surprising because the 1986 Act repealed the so-called *General Utilities* doctrine, which allowed liquidating corporations permanently to avoid corporate level tax on the distribution (or, in some cases, even the sale) of their appreciated assets. Tax Reform Act of 1986, § 631, Pub.L. No. 99-514, 100 Stat. 2058 (1986). The *General Utilities* doctrine is the corporate analog of the forgiveness of gains at death, so it is strange that tax reform would repeal one and not even consider the other.

As part of the Tax Reform Act of 1976, Congress enacted Section 1023 of the Internal Revenue Code, which generally provided a carryover basis (rather than a Section 1014 fair market value at death basis) for inherited property. Congress added the carryover basis provision to the Act very late in the legislative process, with little opportunity for either input from interest groups or careful technical drafting. Affected taxpayers and their representatives harshly criticized it, on both technical and policy grounds, and in 1980 it was repealed retroactively. Regardless of one's views on the merits of carryover basis, its short unhappy life was one of the greatest legislative fiascoes in the history of the income tax. This was recent history in 1986, and it is understandable that Congress lacked the fortitude to revisit the issue so soon.

In the past few years, interest in this area slowly has reawakened. As memory of Section 1023 recedes, as pressure to raise revenue without raising rates increases, and as the remaining opportunities for significant base-broadening reform diminish, it becomes more likely that Congress eventually will revisit the area. And when Congress does, it seems much more likely (for reasons discussed below) that it will tax gains at death, rather than revive carryover basis. * * *

Choosing Between Carryover Basis and Taxing Gains at Death

Either carryover basis at death or a death gains tax would prevent the permanent avoidance of gains tax that occurs under current law. At the theoretical level, the argument for carryover basis is that postponing tax until an actual sale of the property avoids the need to appraise the property[26] and imposes tax at a time when the taxpayer is likely to have cash available to pay the tax. The arguments for gains tax at death are that it appropriately limits the maximum deferral possibility to a single lifetime; it enforces the principle that income should be taxed to the person who earned it; it imposes tax at an ideal time in terms of ability to pay (because the decedent has no use for the amount due as taxes, and whatever the heirs or beneficiaries receive is a windfall); and, unlike carryover basis, it solves the problem of lock-in.[28] Congress will not choose, however, between the two approaches based on such theoretical considerations. Rather, the key issues will be the complexity of

---

26. If Congress imposes a death gains tax only on estates subject to the estate tax, the gains tax will not involve any additional appraisal requirements. It does increase, however, the tax consequences of an inaccurate appraisal.

28. Carryover basis does lessen the problem of pre-death lock-in because elderly taxpayers know their assets will not receive a stepped-up basis at death. However, carryover basis creates a new problem of post-death lock-in: because the heirs inherit with low carryover basis, they are discouraged from selling the assets. Under either current law or a gains tax at death, the heirs take assets with a fair market value basis, so post-death lock-in does not occur.

administering the two approaches and the relative amounts of revenue they would raise.

The most serious administrative difficulty—proof of basis—would loom equally large under either system. In other respects, however, a death gains tax would be somewhat simpler to apply than carryover basis. Carryover basis would create a new problem for executors, because their fiduciary duties would require them to make not only an equitable distribution of *value* among beneficiaries, but also an equitable distribution of *basis*. A death gains tax does not present this problem, because all assets (other than assets going to a surviving spouse, if the system permits deferral of gains on such assets) receive a fair market value basis following the imposition of the tax at death. In addition, carryover basis requires the maintenance of basis records across unlimited numbers of generations; a death gains tax does not.

A major complication of carryover basis is the death tax basis adjustment. In order to make the consequences of carryover basis consistent with the tax consequences of selling appreciated property before death, it is necessary to increase the basis of appreciated carryover basis property by the death taxes (federal and state estate taxes, and state succession tax) attributable to the appreciation.[29] Although the principle is easy enough to state, applying it can be very complex. Section 1023(c) calculated the adjustment for each asset by multiplying the appreciation in the asset by the average tax rate for the entire estate. Since the average tax rate for an estate is a function of the value of every asset in the estate, the basis of every appreciated asset in the estate was uncertain as long as the value of even one asset was uncertain.

   * * *

Another problem of carryover basis is the need for some method—whether by mechanical rules or executor election—of allocating whatever minimum basis adjustment is allowed. Allocation of the adjustment is necessary under carryover basis because gain on different assets may be recognized at different times and by different taxpayers. By contrast, this is not an issue under a

---

29. Suppose, for example, a 50% flat rate estate tax and a 28% flat rate capital gains tax, and a taxpayer with just two assets: $1,000,000 cash, and stock with a basis of zero and a value of $1,000,000. If the taxpayer sold the stock before his death for $1,000,000, the gains tax would be $280,000, and payment of the tax would reduce his estate to $1,720,000. The 50% estate tax would be $860,000, and the beneficiaries would receive $860,000. In order to replicate this result if the taxpayer dies and the stock is then sold by the estate or by the beneficiaries, a death tax basis adjustment is needed. The estate tax liability is $1,000,000 (50% of $2,000,000), of which $500,000 is attributable to the appreciation in the stock. The $1,000,000 cash is used to pay the estate tax, and the beneficiaries receive the stock. The beneficiaries thus take the stock with a basis of $500,000, after the death tax basis adjustment. The gain on a subsequent sale of the stock for $1,000,000 is $500,000, resulting in a tax of $140,000. Reducing the $1,000,000 proceeds by $140,000 leaves the beneficiaries with $860,000—the same amount they would have received if the decedent had sold the stock before death.

death gains tax because all gain is taxed at the same time to the same taxpayer.

Some commentators have argued that a death gains tax with carryover basis for marital bequests would be just as complicated as general carryover basis. They are right that not having a marital exemption is simpler than having one, but they are wrong in arguing that a marital exemption involves all the difficulties of general carryover basis. A marital exemption would require keeping basis records, not over several generations, but only until the death of the surviving spouse. More important, the carryover basis for marital exemption property would be pure carryover basis, without any of the complicating adjustments. There would be no death tax adjustment because the marital bequest would not have been subject to estate tax. No minimum basis adjustment would be allowed for property passing to a surviving spouse, and no transition rule basis adjustment would be made to such property at that time; there would be no need to make either adjustment until the property is actually subject to tax at the death of the surviving spouse.

More important than the modest simplicity advantage of tax at death over carryover basis is the much greater revenue effect of tax at death. The Congressional Budget Office (CBO), for example, estimated that taxing capital gains at death would raise $17.0 billion over four years (1994 to 1997), while carryover basis would raise only $5.2 billion.[39] Part of the reason that Congress was unable to withstand the pressure to repeal carryover basis was that carryover basis did not raise very much revenue. It is difficult to resist impassioned (and plausible) claims that the statute is too complex when the major argument in favor of the statute is that it closes a loophole offensive to some academics. It should be considerably easier to resist the claims that the statute is too complex when a major argument in favor of the law is that it raises very substantial and badly needed revenue.

Although the revenue impact is by far the biggest advantage of the gains tax, it has two additional political advantages over carryover basis. First, it does not carry the historical baggage of carryover basis. The enactment and repeal of carryover basis was such a long and complete fiasco that carryover basis may never be given serious consideration again as long as anyone in Congress remembers that history. * * * Second, there are those (primarily academicians, but also some politicians and practitioners) who strongly believe

---

39. Congressional Budget Office, *Reducing the Deficit: Spending and Revenue Options, Part 2* at 315 (U.S. G.P.O. 1990) (*"Reducing the Deficit"*). How much revenue is raised by either a death gains tax or carryover basis will depend, of course, on the extent of relief given to smaller estates. At any given level of relief, however, a death gains tax will raise substantially more revenue than carryover basis.

in taxing gains at death. By contrast, almost no one considers carryover basis the best way of dealing with gains at death.[43]

Taxing Gains at Death:
Revenue Implications and Policy Choices

How much revenue would be raised by taxing capital gains at death is unclear, but it is clear that it would be significant. The Budget of the United States for Fiscal Year 1993 lists the failure to tax gain at death as the fourth largest item in the tax expenditure budget, with estimated revenue loss of more than $24 billion in 1991, more than $26 billion in 1992, and more than $28 billion in 1993.[44] By contrast, the CBO has estimated the annual revenue gain from taxing capital gains at death at $5.3 billion by 1997. Much or all of the difference in the estimates derives from the fact that the CBO estimate, unlike the budget estimate, is for a tax with substantial exemptions. The CBO estimate is for a tax with marital and charitable exemptions, with the option of using one-half an asset's date-of-death value as basis, with the availability of the $125,000 exclusion for gain on a primary residence (if not used during life), and with a $75,000 exclusion for any remaining gains. * * *

There are general points worth noting about the revenue effect of taxing gains at death. First, much of the revenue effect would be indirect. That is, without the lock-in effect of forgiveness of gains tax at death, elderly taxpayers would realize much more gain while still alive. Thus, much (perhaps most) of the revenue gain from the death tax would not result from assessing the tax

---

43. Howard Hoffman, *The Role of the Bar in the Tax Legislative Process*, 37 Tax L. Rev. 411, 442 (1982) (describing carryover as "the classic compromise that pleased no one"). He remarks that during consideration of repeal of carryover, many who favored taxing gains at death gave carryover little support. Id. at 442-43 n.121. During hearings held early in 1976 before the enactment of carryover basis, a panel of experts resoundingly rejected carryover basis. Federal Estate and Gift Taxes, Public Hearings and Panel Discussions Before the Comm. on Ways and Means, 94th Cong., 2d Sess. 1211, 1435 (1976) (*"Federal Estate and Gift Taxes"*) (A. James Casner, stating that "the worst thing to do is . . . a carryover basis"); id. at 1444 (Edward C. Halbach, Jr., calling carryover "the worst of the possible alternatives"; Rep. Ullman, summarizing the testimony: "The carryover basis is obviously very difficult. No one seems to favor it very much.").

44. Office of the President, *Budget of the United States Government for Fiscal Year 1993* (cited in note 5). The exact figures are $24.365 billion, $26.8 billion, and $28.14 billion. Id. at 2-26. The larger items in the tax expenditure budget are the expenditures for retirement savings, medical insurance, and home mortgage interest. The exemption of capital gains at death is unlike the three larger items in that it is unclear what Congress intended the exemption to accomplish. Whatever one may think of the other three expenditures, it is easy to understand why Congress might choose to subsidize retirement savings, medical insurance, and homeownership. It is much more difficult to understand the purpose of subsidizing the holding of appreciated property until death.

Jt. Comm. on Taxation, *Estimates of Federal Tax 1993-1997 Expenditures for Fiscal Years 1993-1997*, 102nd Cong., 2nd Sess. 14.0 (U.S. G.P.O. 1992), estimates the revenue loss from not taxing capital gains at death to be much lower (although still very large): $11.6 billion in 1993, $12.7 billion in 1994, $14.0 billion in 1995, $15.4 billion in 1996, and $17.1 billion in 1997. Neither the Committee's report nor the Budget explains the discrepancy between the estimates.

at death, but from tax on dispositions during life which would not have occurred in the absence of a death gains tax. Second, since the income tax liability created by the tax on gains at death logically should be deductible under the estate tax as a claim against the estate, a complete analysis of the revenue impact of the gains tax must consider the partially offsetting reduction in estate tax receipts. Consider, for example, $100 of appreciation held at death, with an applicable capital gains tax rate of twenty-eight percent and an applicable estate tax rate of fifty percent. Compared with no capital gains tax, the gains tax increases income tax revenue by $28, but decreases estate tax revenue by $14 (because the fifty percent estate tax is imposed on $72 instead of $100), for a net revenue gain of $14.

Whatever the amount of revenue raised by the tax, there are three major options for what to do with that revenue: use it to reduce the deficit, use it to offset revenue lost from a decrease in the capital gains tax rate, or use it to reduce or even eliminate the estate tax. Congress also could devote the revenue to various combinations of the three uses.

The deficit reduction option is attractive. As a principled and perhaps politically feasible way of raising substantial additional revenue from the income tax without raising rates, it is a rarity. A death gains tax would result in a top combined income and estate tax burden of sixty-four percent on appreciation held at death, assuming a top capital gains rate of twenty-eight percent and a top estate tax rate of fifty percent. From an historical perspective, that is not a particularly high federal death tax rate—as recently as 1981, the top estate tax rate was seventy percent. Nevertheless, it is questionable whether the current Congress would accept the sixty-four percent combined tax burden that would result if the gains tax were used entirely for deficit reduction.

One economist has estimated that a reduction in the capital gains tax rate to 12.5% and the taxation of gains at death would yield approximately the same revenue as the current twenty-eight percent capital gains rate and forgiveness of tax at death.[52] This proposal is attractive in several ways. Both parts of the proposal would reduce lock-in: the lower rate would decrease resistance to recognizing gains during life, and the death tax would eliminate the incentive to hold assets until death. The proposal also would eliminate the horizontal inequity between taxpayers who sell appreciated assets during life and those who hold assets until death, by moving both groups of taxpayers to the same middle ground. It might fare well as a political compromise between those who feel strongly that there should be a significant reduction in capital gains rates and those offended by the forgiveness of capital gains tax at death.

---

52. Donald W. Kiefer, *Lock-In Effect Within a Simple Model of Corporate Stock Trading*, 43 Nat'l Tax J. 75, 90 (1990).

A closely related possibility would use the revenue raised by a death gains tax to pay for indexing of basis for inflation.

The estate and gift taxes raised approximately $12.1 billion in 1992.[53] [I]t is unclear whether the revenue lost by repealing the transfer taxes could be replaced entirely by taxing capital gains at death. Assuming, however, that the change could be made revenue neutral, would it be a good idea? The change might appeal to an "academic desire for tidiness,"[55] because it rationalizes the income tax by eliminating perhaps its most glaring loophole. In addition, it repeals a transfer tax system always objectionable for the many omissions from its base.

Notice, however, that the potential tax base for a capital gains tax on gratuitous transfers is substantially smaller than the potential tax base for a transfer tax system—smaller by the amount of the cost bases of the assets gratuitously transferred. Moreover, at current rates the capital gains tax (twenty-eight percent top rate) will raise less revenue from a given dollar amount of tax base than will the transfer taxes (rates ranging from thirty-seven to fifty percent). Thus, for the capital gains tax to raise as much revenue as the transfer taxes, with a smaller potential base and lower rates, it must include in its actual base a much higher percentage of its potential base than do the transfer taxes. Although some of this might be done through loophole closing, the vast majority would have to be done by using much lower exemption amounts than the $600,000 transfer tax exemption created by the unified credit. Thus, assuming revenue neutrality, replacement of the transfer taxes with a capital gains tax on transfers would result in a major shift of tax burden away from the wealthy and the upper middle class, and onto the middle class. I would oppose the regressivity inherent in a such a change, and it seems likely Congress would agree.

* * *

Special Avoidance Concerns
Taxation of Gain on Gifts During Life

Most plans to tax capital gains at death have included taxation of gains on gifts made during life. The reason is apparent: the premise of the tax at death is that gains should be taxed at least once a generation, but gains tax can be deferred indefinitely if appreciated property is transferred from one generation to another by gift and gain is not taxed at that time. A rule taxing gain on assets gifted in contemplation of death, or within a specified time before death, is not adequate to prevent avoidance because many wealthy taxpayers will be willing and able to transfer much of their appreciation well

---

53. Office of the President, *Budget of the United States Government for Fiscal Year 1993* at 2-3 (cited in note 5). Actual estate and gift tax receipts for 1991 were $11.1 billion. *Id.*

55. *Commissioner v. Duberstein*, 363 U.S. 278, 290 (1960).

before their deaths. Such avoidance will be most practical for the very wealthy, thus reducing the vertical equity of the death gains tax.

It is clear, then, that gifts generally should trigger the recognition of gain.

* * *

A Small Estate Exemption

It seems clear that there should be an exemption from a capital gains death tax for small estates. At some point, estates are small enough that the revenue gained from taxing their appreciation does not justify imposing the complexities of a capital gains tax (or, for that matter, of carryover basis). The difficult question is finding that point. One obvious and attractive possibility is designing the exemption to track (so far as possible) the estate tax exemption provided by the unified credit, so that estates not subject to the estate tax also would not be subject to the gains tax, and estates subject to the estate tax also would be subject to the gains tax. For estates not subject to the gains tax, current law—no realization of gain or loss at death, and fair market value basis for inherited property—would continue to apply. This would limit the application of the death gains tax to a small portion of the decedent population.[224]

Would it be appropriate to equate the estate tax and death gains tax exemptions? In considering this question, the current $600,000 exemption amount need not be viewed as unalterable. One may favor a higher or lower estate tax exemption amount, quite apart from considerations related to a new death gains tax. Or the revenue gained from the death gains tax could be used to raise the exemption amount for both taxes. Whatever the precise exemption amount, there are strong arguments for using the same amount for both taxes. Perhaps most important, equating the exemptions would mean that the death tax would not impose any additional valuation requirements: death gains tax would be imposed only on property that already had to be valued for the estate tax. Estates large enough to exceed the exemption amount should have the necessary resources to handle the administrative burdens of the gains tax. And despite affecting only a small percentage of all estates, the tax still would reach much of the appreciation passing at death, since that appreciation is concentrated in larger estates. Finally, equating the exemptions may be the only way to make the death gains tax politically feasible. The 1976 carryover basis statute was strongly criticized for applying to many estates not subject to the estate tax, and the proponents of carryover basis agreed that the law should be revised to equate the exemption levels.

---

224. An estimated 45,800 U.S. citizens who died in 1986 had gross estates over $500,000 (the exemption amount for that year). They represented about 2.2% of all U.S. decedents. Slightly fewer than half (about 22,000) of those estates were taxable, after deductions. Barry Johnson, *Estate Tax Returns, 1986-1988*, 9 SOI Bull. 27, 27 (Spring 1990).

There are also arguments against equating the exemptions, all of which are based on the fact that a gains tax exemption tied to the estate tax exemption will mean huge amounts of appreciation escaping the tax. * * *

I find the arguments for equating the estate and death tax exemptions persuasive, and I suspect Congress would as well. * * *

BECOMING MORE INEVITABLE?
DEATH AND TAXES . . . AND TAXES
Louis M. Castruccio[*]

17 University of California at Los Angeles Law Review 459, 483-91 (1970)

The basic concept of constructive realization provides that gains accrued on capital assets transferred by gift or at death would be subject to the normal capital gains tax.

Economic Aspects

There are some salutary economic results that might arise from the imposition of a capital gains tax at gift and death. * * * It would appear that all lock-in effects, to whatever extent they do in fact exist, would be eliminated because the ultimate attraction of a transfer at gift or death free of capital gains taxation would be removed. The only possible residual tax benefit remaining for those holding capital assets until death would be deferral of payment of the capital gains tax. * * *

Imposition of a capital gains tax at gift and death would increase government revenues. * * * [T]he exact amount of such increase is uncertain. However, it seems reasonable to include as part of such increase not only the taxes collected upon actual transfers at gift and death, but also those taxes resulting from inter vivos sales and exchanges of capital assets which would not have occurred but for constructive realization.

Equitable Aspects

The constructive realization system would appear to remedy the violation of horizontal equity experienced under the present method of treating capital gains at gift and death. Under constructive realization two taxpayers with similar investment goals will in the long run be treated alike in that ultimately the taxpayer who holds his capital assets until death will be subject to exactly the same capital gains tax as the individual who sells or exchanges his capital assets during his lifetime.

To the contrary, it can be argued that the taxpayer who holds capital assets until death is still obtaining more favorable treatment because he can defer his capital gains tax payment until death. This argument can be answered on the ground that the underlying policy of the capital gains tax has

---

[*]. At time of original publication, member, California Bar.

always been to leave the timing of the tax creating sale or exchange to the taxpayer's decision and that the purpose of constructive realization is to implement this policy in a meaningful manner. Constructive realization accomplishes this result by defining gifts and transfers at death as very real, and particularly in the case of the latter, final tax creating events. Such an approach will prevent the use of the theory of taxpayer timing of taxable events as a means of completely escaping capital gains tax.

Another criticism of the constructive realization approach is that it would have harsh effects upon closely held corporations and small businesses. It is contended that these concerns, which have often been initiated and built by one or a few individuals, aren't amenable to sale during one's life because of the close relationship between owner and business. On this ground it is argued that a taxpayer who owns a small business is in a completely different position in comparison to those who trade in more readily marketable assets such as securities and real estate. It is further argued that to tax a small business upon the death of its initiator would often force a sacrifice sale.

The contentions that small corporations and businesses are not as amenable to sale as other types of assets and that a sale of such a business to meet tax payments might be disastrous are valid to some extent. * * *

Constructive realization will also bring about some improvement in vertical equity. As previously indicated, the present treatment of capital gains at gift and death results in a lack of vertical equity in that the accrued gains of the wealthy and less wealthy alike completely escape capital gains tax. Imposition of the normal capital gains tax rates upon transfers at gift and death will result in progression between the less wealthy taxed at lower marginal rates and the wealthy presumably taxed at the maximum effective capital gains tax rate. * * *

Major Administrative Problems of Constructive Realization at Gift and Death

There are several major administrative aspects of constructive realization which bear close scrutiny. These items are of such importance that unless Code machinery can be tailored to accommodate them, their negative implications may outweigh all the economic and equity benefits which might otherwise accompany the adoption of constructive realization.

As indicated earlier, there is a danger that imposition of a capital gains tax at death may force the dissolution of closely held businesses. In theory this is not a question of horizontal equity, but unless administrative measures are available to alleviate the problem, it may for all practical purposes become a question of horizontal equity. The same problem was faced in connection with the federal estate tax, and it would seem that the same administrative method used in that instance could be integrated into the constructive realization system. That is, if a closely held business accounts for more than a certain percentage of all the capital gains to be recognized at death, then that portion of the capital gains tax attributable to the gains on such business could be paid in installments over an extended period of time.

    * * *

Another formidable administrative problem presented by constructive realization is the treatment of capital losses at death. There are at least three alternative methods available to solve this problem. First, any net losses in the year of the decedent's death, including those recognized under constructive realization, could be offset in full against the decedent's net income in his final tax year. This approach would be unacceptable for at least two reasons. If the decedent was particularly old, had little income in his declining years, yet realized a large capital loss at death, more than likely a great portion of such loss would go unused. Also, if the decedent has a short final year, i.e., a calendar year taxpayer dying on January 10, there would obviously be little income against which to offset any loss recognized under constructive realization.

A second method would allow the net losses recognized under constructive realization, to the extent they exceeded the decedent's final year income, to be carried forward for use by the decedent's heirs or the beneficiaries under his will. It might be argued that this alternative would most nearly parallel the capital loss carryforward available to living taxpayers. At first blush this attempt at similarity of treatment seems quite valid. On closer analysis, however, can it be said that a treatment under which different individuals make use of a decedent's capital losses is at all parallel to a situation where a living taxpayer himself takes advantage of previous losses on his own subsequent tax returns? Beyond this theoretical problem, loss carryforward might cause certain practical problems.

One method whereby losses could be carried forward to survivors would be to allow each separate recipient of a loss asset to also acquire the use of the loss realized upon the transfer of such asset at death. The value of the use of such loss would of course depend in great part upon the tax status of the recipient—whether he had large amounts of capital gains or small amounts, whether he was in a high ordinary income tax bracket or a low one, etc. Potentially more serious problems might arise if a loss asset had to be sold by an estate in order to meet federal estate tax obligations. Would the purchaser of the asset acquire the use of the loss allocable to such asset? If not, would the loss be considered part of the residue of the estate? If it were considered part of the residue, would it have a value for federal estate tax purposes? If it were to be assigned a value for federal estate tax purposes the valuation thereof might depend in some part upon the tax status of the individual residuary beneficiaries.

As can be seen, this loss carryforward approach might become extremely complex. If there is some effective, less involved method of handling net capital losses under constructive realization, it would probably be preferable.

A loss carryback may be superior to a loss carryforward approach. Under a loss carryback system, net capital losses realized under constructive realization would be first applied against all capital gains and then against all ordinary income in the decedent's final tax year. If unused capital losses remained, these could be applied first against capital gains in a set number of previous years and then against all ordinary income in the same number of previous years. To be sure, this would involve reopening back returns. But, the reopening of back returns occurs in many other areas of the income tax law, and if it will improve the overall neutrality of the tax structure, there should be no hesitancy in the use of such a device.

 * * *

The more difficult valuation problem created by constructive realization is that which requires the determination of the adjusted basis of assets held by a decedent. The amount of difficulty in this area will depend upon the extent to which the decedent kept records of his capital assets. It is in this area that the Internal Revenue Service will probably have to be particularly watchful in order to determine that reported adjusted bases are accurate. However, this will not be an entirely new problem for the Internal Revenue Service, as it is faced with much the same problem in cases where donees sell property after death of the donor. Neither of the above aspects of the increased incidence of valuation at death should constitute a bar to the adoption of constructive realization. Both problems, though with less frequency, have been a part of the federal estate and gift tax for many years.

It has been suggested that any tax due under constructive realization be deducted from the taxable gross estate. This appears justified on theoretical grounds. * * *

Some Unique Problems of Constructive Realization and Transfers by Gift

If constructive realization were adopted for taxpayers at death but the present carryover method were maintained as to gifts, this latter treatment would take on new importance. Its position as a transaction receiving favored tax treatment would be heightened, as it would represent the last remaining method whereby one could postpone the incidence of the capital gains tax beyond one's death.

A combination of a constructive realization approach at death and a carryover approach as to gifts might create a unique economic lock-in. Faced with this structure, taxpayers might decide to hold their capital assets for an added period of years at the end of which they would transfer such assets by gift. The possibility that this lock-in might develop must be discounted somewhat on at least two grounds. First the tax benefit presented by carryover is merely a tax deferral, an advantage which is much less significant than the complete escape from capital gains tax available under the present treatment of capital gains at death. Secondly, individuals who are actually faced with the prospect of relinquishing ownership of assets often become reluctant to part with them. This latter fact might result in many assets originally planned for transfer by gift actually passing upon an owner's death and therefore subject to constructive realization. Nonetheless, it cannot be denied that capital gains tax deferral * * * would present attractive tax benefits.

Application of constructive realization to gifts would remove such transfers from a favored tax position and would prevent the development of any economic lock-in due to the differentiation in tax treatment between the sale or exchange of capital assets and their transfer by gift. Constructive realization at gift would necessarily eliminate the possibility that the thought of an impending future gift might overcome maintenance of a present optimum portfolio. If constructive realization were applied to gifts the neutrality of the capital gains tax would be assured since it would be imposed upon the sale or exchange of capital assets and upon the transfer of capital assets by gift or at death. There would also be an administrative benefit arising from the application of constructive realization to gifts, since such treatment would avoid the possibility that determination of adjusted basis would take place at a time even further removed from when the donor's basis was actually determined.

Finally, it should be recognized that the application of constructive realization to gifts is very much like the application of the general capital gains tax to sales and exchanges. In both cases there is the imposition of a tax upon a transaction, the timing of which is left to the taxpayer's discretion. Therefore, the treatment of losses and reporting procedures upon transfers by gift could be the same as they are for sales and exchanges. Any dissatisfaction with such procedures should be directed not to constructive realization but to the general capital gains tax itself.
            * * *

ON CONSTRUCTIVELY REALIZING
CONSTRUCTIVE REALIZATION:
BUILDING THE CASE FOR DEATH AND TAXES
Dan Subotnik*

38 Kansas Law Review 1, 36-38 (1989)

We come now to our final question: What should be done if, notwithstanding the strong equity case for incorporating CR [constructive realization] into the tax system, our options are limited to choosing between CR and an estate tax? Given our past inability to add a second tax applicable at death, this formulation of the question may be the practical consequence of articles such as this. In an important sense the question is not a real one because our review of CR history has shown that it has attracted only limited interest. Perhaps, however, this is because the estate tax is already in place and none of the proposals that have been advanced has raised the possibility of eliminating the estate tax.

From a revenue standpoint, the choice between CR and an estate tax is a toss-up. The transfer taxes bring in roughly $6.5 billion, while estimates are that CR would bring in about $5 billion.

From a number of other vantage points, however, the Canadian [constructive realization] solution makes more sense. Among the nonrevenue arguments advanced in support of the estate tax, three stand out for our purposes. First, the estate tax is a back-up to the income tax in which (on account of prior practice) there are numerous loopholes. Second, the estate tax helps to break up large estates which, left unchecked, would result in the accumulation of economic and thus political power in the hands of a small number of American families. Finally, the estate tax diminishes the likelihood of formation of an effete "leisure class."

Whatever the persuasiveness of these arguments in the past, it is much diminished now. For one thing, thanks to the Tax Reform Act of 1986 and other recent legislation, the loopholes are fewer and farther between. * * *

At the same time, wealth has spread out so significantly and inflation has had such a profound effect that individuals with asset holdings of over $600,000 can no longer be considered a menace to the republic. Moreover, unlike the apparent situation in Great Britain, far from turning into the idle rich, the sons and daughters of our empire-builders are going to the University of Chicago or Harvard Business Schools so that by working eighty-hour weeks, they can successfully make the family empire "world class."

The matter is clearer yet from the administrative perspective on the estate tax versus CR issue. The estate and gift tax rules are spelled out in

---

*. At time of original publication, Professor of Law, Touro College, Jacob D. Fuchsberg Law Center.

about forty code sections. Relating to these sections are innumerable and technical regulations, as well as judicial opinions that frequently are classifiable only as soaring flights of fancy. Estate planning has become so other-worldly and esoteric that it makes up an entire area of professional specialization. If this entire structure could be collapsed and replaced with a few new code sections (we now know that it *can* be done), Congress would finally be able to boast justifiably that it has simplified the tax system.

    * * *

Notes and Questions

20. Constructive realization would treat death as a realization event, and assume that the decedent sold all his assets for fair market value. Thus, the decedent's final income tax return would take account of all unrealized appreciation. The heirs then would receive the property with a stepped-up basis, because the gain already would have been taxed. Proposals to treat death as a realization event usually treat making a gift as a realization event as well, as in both the Zelenak and Castruccio excerpts. In part, this is due to the difficulty of administering a rule that death constitutes a realization event but transfer by gift does not. However, it also seems that the claimed policy advantages of taxing the transferor of property at death generally apply in the gift situation. Except as noted, the term "constructive realization" in these notes assumes that constructive realization occurs upon either transfer. With respect to gifts in trust, see Note #34 at page 672.

21. Do you agree with Professor Zelenak that constructive realization at death results in levying the tax "at an ideal time in terms of ability to pay"? Is your answer affected by whether an estate tax is also applicable?

22. Any constructive receipt proposal that might be adopted would likely entail an unlimited marital deduction, coupled with carryover basis for the spouse who received the property. This approach seems consistent with the recent drift of tax law, notably the adoption of an unlimited marital exclusion under the estate and gift taxes (added to the law in 1981), and the rule of section 1041 that gain and loss is not recognized on transfers between spouses (added in 1984). In a portion of his article not excerpted above, Professor Zelenak discusses problems of this exclusion that may not be immediately apparent, such as whether the law should be concerned about executors funding marital bequests with low-basis property in order to postpone the deemed realization until the death of the spouse.[q] The tension, as so

---

q. Lawrence Zelenak, *Taxing Gains at Death*, 46 VAND. L. REV. 361, 395-401 (1993).

frequently, is between simplicity on the one hand, and revenue (and equity?) on the other.

23.   Professor Zelenak asserts that constructive realization "appropriately limits the maximum deferral possibility to a single lifetime." Is the propriety of this limitation affected by one's view of the realization rule? By one's view of the family as an economic and social unit?

24.   Writing in 1993, Professor Zelenak predicted that when Congress revisited the issue, it would opt for constructive realization rather than carryover basis. He based this prediction on the "key issues" of "complexity of administering the two approaches and the relative amounts of revenue they would raise." In fact, the next time around, in 2001, Congress again chose carryover basis. Why?

25.   One of the problems of current law is the "lock-in" effect created by stepped-up basis (see Note #6 at page 622). Carryover basis is subject to the criticism that it solves one lock-in problem, only to create a new, and arguably worse, lock-in problem (see Note #16 at page 628). Would constructive realization be better in solving the lock-in problem? Would constructive realization remove all tax incentive to hold appreciated property as long as possible (even to death)?

26.   What about losses? Present law sharply limits the deductibility of capital losses, generally allowing deductibility of losses to offset capital gains plus $3,000 of ordinary income, with unused losses being carried forward for life. Sections 1211 and 1212. If we decide to tax gains at death, does it follow that we should allow losses where basis exceeds value? The Castruccio excerpt lists several ways of allowing for losses at death. Which seems best?

If adopted in the case of death, should a rule allowing losses also apply to property passing by gift? (Note that under present law, section 1015 carves out an exception to carryover basis to block the transfer of losses.)

27.   If we were to adopt constructive realization at death, should we extend the rule to charitable bequests? Present law allows taxpayers who make charitable contributions of appreciated property to deduct the full value of the property, and to permanently avoid taxation on the unrealized appreciation. Professor Zelenak contends that "[i]f the gain is not taxed when the property is donated by a living taxpayer, it also should not be taxed when

the donation is made at death."[r] Do you agree? And, if so, is the best solution to forgive tax on appreciation in both instances, or to tax it in both?

28. Assuming revenue to be roughly equal from constructive realization and transfer taxes, do you agree with Professor Subotnik that constructive realization is to be preferred?

29. Whether constructive realization in fact would bring in as much revenue as the transfer taxes is open to question. Professor Zelenak regarded this proposition as "unclear," in part because the tax base is inherently smaller. While transfer taxes are levied on the entire amount conveyed, only the gain portion of transferred property is taxed under constructive realization. Moreover, Zelenak expressed uncertainty at a time when the tax on constructively realized capital gains would have been subject to a tax rate of 28 percent; today's rate of 15 percent would presumably yield much less.

30. Compared to the transfer taxes, constructive realization has a lower base (because the portion of the transfer representing the transferor's basis is not taxed) and a lower tax rate (because the capital gains rate is lower than the transfer tax rate). Under these circumstances, the only way constructive realization could come close to matching the yield from transfer taxes would be if it were applied to many transfers exempt from transfer taxation. (Suppose, for example, that constructive realization were applied to estates and gifts as small as $100,000.) Would this greater reach of constructive realization doom it politically?

31. Professor Subotnik's article, only a small sample of which is excerpted, deals at some length with the Canadian experience with constructive realization. Canada adopted a system of constructive realization in 1972, and at the same time repealed its estate tax. The assertion at the end of the excerpt that "we now know that it *can* be done" is a reference to the generally successful Canadian experience with constructive realization.

32. Constructive realization has also attracted serious political interest in the United States. Professor Subotnik traces a number of serious proposals, starting with one made by the Kennedy Administration.[s] Professor Zelenak quotes then President-elect Clinton as saying that constructive realization "probably should be looked at."[t]

---

r. *Id.* at 401.

s. 38 KAN. L. REV. at 2-4.

t. Zelenak, *supra* note q, at 367.

D. TREATING GIFTS AND BEQUESTS AS INCOME TO THE RECIPIENT

Thus far, this chapter has dealt with the failings of section 1014, which allows permanent avoidance of income tax on the appreciation component of property passing at death. Carryover basis would ultimately tax the appreciation to the recipient, while constructive realization would immediately tax the transferor of either a bequest or gift on the unrealized appreciation.

But what of the rule of section 102, which excludes gifts and bequests from the income tax base? Should recipients of gifts and bequests—regardless of whether the property appreciated during the transferor's period of ownership—be allowed to avoid income taxation on these "undeniable accessions to wealth?" Professors Dodge and Hudson would tax donees and heirs on the full amount received.

In the final excerpt, Professors Douglas and Jeffrey Kahn defend present law, arguing that the exclusion rule of section 102 is at least as reasonable as including gifts and bequests in the income of the recipient. Competing principles are involved, the Kahns argue, and the policy choice adopted by Congress in section 102 is justified.

BEYOND ESTATE AND GIFT TAX REFORM: INCLUDING GIFTS AND BEQUESTS IN INCOME
Joseph M. Dodge*

91 Harvard Law Review 1177, 1179, 1182-92,
1194-95, 1197, 1199-1200, 1209 (1978)

Legislative Enactment of the Proposal

The enactment of the income tax proposal for gifts and bequests would be accomplished by amending the Internal Revenue Code to repeal the gift, estate, and generation-skipping taxes, and section 102 of the Code, which excludes gifts and bequests from the gross income of the recipient. This would result in gifts' and bequests' being included at some time in the income tax base of the donee or legatee, and thus subject to progressive income tax rates. As under present law, gifts and bequests would not be deductible by the donor or by the decedent's estate.

* * *

---

*. At time of original publication, Associate Professor of Law, University of Detroit.

The Justification for Income Tax Treatment of Gifts and Bequests
The Theoretical Basis for the Proposal
Definitional Models of Tax Base

One or more definitional models of a tax base are necessary to determine whether gifts and bequests should be included by [the] transferee in his tax base, and whether they should be deductible by the transferor. A basic proposition is that the justness of a tax system is related to the *apportionment* of the tax burden among the population, and a widely accepted criterion for proper apportionment is that the tax burden should be allocated according to the taxable unit's "ability to pay."

A second proposition is that ability to pay should be determined neutrally, without regard for whether wealth is consumed (spent) or saved. But taxing wealth per se would not neutrally measure ability to pay, since wealth saved would be taxed frequently while wealth consumed would be taxed only once. Two methods have been advanced to construct a more neutral tax base; elements of each are reflected in the current tax structure.

One widely accepted method seeks to tax wealth once in the aggregate by taxing only additions to wealth as they occur. Ability to pay during a taxable period is measured by adding consumption during that period to the increase (decrease) of the unit's stock of wealth during the period. This measurement is the heart of the comprehensive tax base (CTB) model of net income followed by many commentators.[30]

A second method is the "consumption tax" model, which taxes only consumption and not savings. This model postulates that the accumulation and maintenance of wealth are not ends in themselves, but are merely means of providing for future consumption. Consequently, consumption financed through savings should not be taxed more heavily [than] consumption of current receipts, as it is under the CTB model. The consumption tax model, by exempting savings during the taxable period from the tax base, restores equal treatment, and thus neutrality, for present and future consumption.

Under neither of these tax base models should "entities" such as estates, trusts, and corporations be taxed as such. Under the CTB model, though estates and trusts might as repositories of wealth initially be perceived as possessing "ability to pay," this "ability" cannot usually be currently attributed to individuals, since their shares and interests may be unascertainable. If, in contrast, consumption is viewed as the sole measure of ability to pay, then estates and trusts possess no tax base because they do not engage in consumption. Clearly, entities merely serve the ends of individuals; here they

---

30. The CTB model is sometimes referred to as the "Haig-Simons" definition of income.

serve to facilitate gratuitous transfers. Taxation of entities can therefore be justified only as a means of counteracting the deferral of tax that results naturally from the economic function of these entities.

Source and Nature of Receipt

Under both the CTB and "consumption tax" models, it is axiomatic that receipts should be included in income regardless of source or nature.[34] Thus, both models require full inclusion by the recipient of gifts and bequests.

It has nevertheless been argued that gifts and bequests are not income since they do not represent additions to the existing stock of capital in the economy but rather are mere transfers of capital. This argument, while perhaps partially explaining the historical basis for the exclusion of gifts and bequests, confuses income in the economic sense with income in the tax sense.[37] As previously noted, "income" in the tax sense is the term that has been used to describe the measurement of the taxable unit's capacity to contribute to the public sector relative to other taxable units. It is true that the income tax proposal involves "double taxation" in the economic sense in that the grantor is giving after-tax dollars on which the recipient is again taxed, but whatever hindrance to capital formation may arise from this double taxation can easily be offset in other ways. The area of gifts and bequests is not one where economic considerations should predominate over principles of tax equity.

Deduction to the Donor?

Neither the CTB nor the "consumption tax" model results in a deduction for the donor for gifts and bequests. Those supporting a deduction for the donor indirectly through exclusion by the donee argue that the gift was not

---

34. *But see* Andrews, *Personal Deductions in an Ideal Income Tax Base*, 86 HARV. L. REV. 309, 348-356 (1972).

37. The gifts-as-capital argument has been invoked in an attempt to demonstrate that including gifts in income would raise constitutional problems, since gratuitous transfers are not income. *See* Mullock, *The Constitutional Problem of Taxing Gifts as Income*, 53 MINN. L. REV. 247 (1968). Actually, the use of the term "income tax" to describe the present system is misleading; it is derived from historical circumstances relating to the 16th amendment, which authorizes a tax on "income from whatever source derived." However, for a tax to be constitutional it need not be a tax on incomes only but must simply avoid characterization as being an unapportioned direct tax (which is not an income tax). *See* Surrey, *The Supreme Court and the Federal Income Tax: Some Implications of the Recent Decisions*, 35 ILL. L. REV. 779 (1941). Taxes on transfers have long been upheld as indirect (*i.e.*, excise) taxes. *See, e.g.*, Commissioner v. Glenshaw Glass Co., 348 U.S. 426 (1955); Knowlton v. Moore, 178 U.S. 41 (1900). *See generally* Wright, *The Effect of the Source of Realized Benefits upon the Supreme Court's Concept of Taxable Receipts*, 8 STAN. L. REV. 164, 193-201 (1956). Therefore, Congress undoubtedly has the power to include gifts and bequests in income under I.R.C. § 61. *See* J. SNEED, THE CONFIGURATIONS OF GROSS INCOME 115-31 (1967); Del Cotto, *The Constitutional Problem of Taxing Gifts and Bequests as Income: A Reply to Professor Mullock*, 53 MINN. L. REV. 259 (1968); Del Cotto, *The Trust Annuity as Income: The Constitutional Problem of Taxing Gifts and Bequests as Income*, 23 TAX L. REV. 231 (1968); Klein, *An Enigma in the Federal Income Tax: The Meaning of the Word "Gift,"* 48 MINN. L. REV. 215, 219-24 (1963).

part of the income that the donor had available for consumption. This conclusion ignores the basis of the CTB model, since the making of a gift represents the voluntary exercise of the donor's economic power. In other words, the donor's voluntary transfer of the gift itself indicates the donor's ability to pay.

Similarly, under the "consumption tax" model, the fact that a gift may not be "consumption" in the literal sense is no more persuasive with respect to its proper classification for tax purposes than the statement that a gift is not income to the donee under an "income" tax. To begin with, the giving of a gift is more analogous to consumption than to investment. Moreover, the equity rationale of the "consumption tax" model is that the future consumption of the person who saves or invests should not be taxed more heavily than current consumption. Since a gift of cash or of a personal asset does not finance or otherwise involve future consumption by the donor, it should not yield a deduction. Nor should a gift in kind of business or investment property or savings account balance yield a deduction, since a deduction will already have been obtained when the investment was made. In fact, because these savings are no longer a means of providing for future consumption by the donor, the earlier deduction should be "recaptured" by the donor and included in the donor's income for the year of the gift.

Even if one should accept the theoretical propriety of deducting gifts, practical difficulties arise. If gifts were included by donees but deducted by donors, wealthy donors could shift income to lower bracket relatives at will, thereby diluting progressive tax rates. Hence, it is argued, the existing exclusion for donees is an imperfect but justifiable approximation of a deduction for donors. Nonetheless, the income shifting problem, while militating against a deduction to the donor, does not necessarily justify ignoring the donee's increased ability to pay.

Finally, permitting the donor to deduct gifts makes no sense if one postulates that gifts and bequests should be treated equally. Because a deduction for bequests would more than shelter all of the decedent's income for his last taxable period, a bequest deduction would have to apply retroactively to the decedent's past income years in order to be fully equivalent to a deduction for gifts. Not only would the administrative difficulties of such a retroactive deduction be considerable, but the deduction would amount to a retroactive exclusion for accumulated savings. If savings are indeed to be encouraged by means of a deduction, a current deduction for savings would be preferable. Of course, under the "consumption tax" model any deduction for the transfer of accumulated savings would be redundant, since that model postulates current deductions for savings.

A Comparison of the Income Tax Proposal and Specialized Transfer Taxes: Double Taxation, But in What Form?

Those concerned with double taxation (in the economic sense) under the income tax proposal must acknowledge that double taxation of amounts transferred by gift or bequest has existed since 1916 in the form of the estate tax and its subsequent complements, the gift tax and the generation-skipping tax. Thus the question raised by the adoption of the income tax proposal concerns only the form of "double taxation." Moreover, double taxation is not undesirable if it is consistent with the underlying purposes of the particular tax system.

Under the existing transfer tax system, double taxation is proper because the aim of such taxes is to place a levy on the transfer of wealth. The income tax proposal, on the other hand, has the objective of measuring relative ability to pay, and it therefore considers only the economic position of the individual tax unit when imposing taxes. The method of accession to wealth is irrelevant. Double taxation, that is, taxing the recipient on wealth previously taxed to someone else, is consistent with an attempt to measure each person's ability to pay. While the present system subjects unrealized appreciation both to the transfer taxes and, through the carryover basis mechanism of sections 1015 and 1023,[u] to the income tax of the transferee upon realization, the income proposal taxes it only once because carryover basis would be dropped. The income tax proposal, however, would not preclude additionally taxing the transferor on previously unrealized appreciation, resulting in full double taxation on transfers of appreciated property.

The Objectives of Transfer Taxes

Two primary nonequity objectives of transfer taxes are raising revenue and preventing undue accumulations of wealth. The present transfer taxes focus on the transferor, and constitute a delayed penalty on the accumulation of wealth by the transferor. But it is not clear that undue accumulations are best prevented by a delayed penalty on the accumulating taxpayer. The equally plausible goal of curbing the possibility of reaccumulation of existing wealth by passive means is served by accessions taxes, inheritance taxes, and the income tax proposal. * * *

It might seem that these recipient-oriented taxes would be less effective in raising revenue since the number of transferees is usually greater than the number of transferors. But the effectiveness of any transfer tax scheme in raising revenue—as well as in breaking up accumulations of wealth—depends upon its rates and exemptions. Although the present transfer taxes have

---

u. This article was written after carryover basis for property passing at death—section 1023—had been adopted in 1976, but before its repeal in 1980. (Ed.)

considerable potential for accomplishing these goals, recent experience indicates that the political system is unwilling to tap this potential. The income tax proposal, while still subject to some manipulation through exemptions, at least precludes independent tampering with the rate structure. Finally, if any important objective of a transfer tax cannot be accomplished by the income tax proposal, transfer taxes, reduced in scope to bear only on the extremely wealthy, could be retained to supplement the income tax plan.

Tax Base and Rate Structure

Of the recipient-oriented taxes, only the income tax proposal does not contemplate a separate rate schedule for gifts and bequests. Such a separate schedule would contradict a basic premise of the proposal: that the source of receipts should not affect tax liability. * * *

Simplicity of the Proposal: Exclusions, Deductions, and Credits

Adoption of the income tax proposal for gifts and bequests would contribute greatly to the simplification of the tax code. This simplicity of the proposal is both a consequence of its theoretical foundations and an additional justification for its enactment. The existing estate, gift, and generation-skipping taxes would be removed. The portions of subchapter J dealing with the taxation of trusts and beneficiaries would likewise be excised, although those provisions concerned with "grantor trusts" should probably be retained.[69] In addition, the calculation of the basis of in kind property received as a gift or bequest would be vastly simplified for individuals and eliminated for trusts and estates.[70]

The question of what constitutes a gift, now a question of fact which results in much litigation, would be eliminated. Under the income tax proposal, gratuitous transfer exclusions should be allowed only under a de minimis rule to protect the integrity of the tax system in the public eye.[73] Only gifts that are administratively difficult to discover or which are generally not considered transfers of wealth by the public, such as occasional holiday and

---

69. I.R.C. §§ 671-677 (the so-called "Clifford trust" provisions, after Helvering v. Clifford, 309 U.S. 331 (1940), which tax the grantor of a trust because of his retained control, interests, or powers). These provisions would operate independently of the income tax proposal, resulting in taxation of both the grantor of the trust and the recipient.

70. Under the income tax proposal, assets acquired by gift and bequest would normally acquire a stepped-up fair market value basis. Basis would simply be irrelevant with respect to property held by a trust or estate.

73. See 3 ROYAL COMMISSION ON TAXATION, REPORT 497-98 (1966) (Canada) ($250 per donee per year exclusion). Under the accessions tax proposal, gifts up to $1500 per donor per year are excluded only if used by the donee for current consumption. See Andrews, *The Accessions Tax Proposal*, 22 TAX L. REV. 592 (1967). Consumption items of a modest value are probably not publicly viewed as wealth that should be taxed upon transfer even though they do represent ability of donees to pay under both the CTB and consumption tax models.

anniversary gifts, should be excluded from income. Transfers in trust and payments of life insurance premiums, which often qualify—perhaps unjustifiably—for the gift tax present interest exclusion, would not be taxed currently at all under the income inclusion approach. Small distributions from trusts, however, do not fall within the administrative exclusion rationale for small gifts and would therefore be taxed in full.

    * * *

In sum, the theoretical basis of the income tax proposal is more easily followed than the theory underlying other transfer tax schemes, which require complicated distinctions and exclusions. In addition, the income tax proposal encourages spreading gratuitous transfers among lower income recipients, who are subject to lower tax rates. Finally, the income tax proposal facilitates compliance and enforcement of taxation on gratuitous transfers by simply including them in income, whereas other transfer tax schemes require separate returns and, under an accessions tax, separate recordkeeping for prior accessions.

Moreover, if the theoretical basis of the income tax proposal is applied to other tax provisions, further simplification will result. Most important, section 101, which excludes life insurance proceeds, * * * would be repealed, rendering these amounts taxable to the recipient. Section 117, which exempts scholarship and fellowship grants, should also be eliminated, since it originally was a codification of case law under section 102, the gift exclusion provision.

    * * *

Problems of the Income Proposal
Deferral With Respect to Trusts

As noted above, trusts and estates would not be taxed and beneficiaries would be taxed only upon distribution under the income tax proposal. The loss to the tax base resulting from the deferral of taxation of trust income, however, will be fully offset by the eventual taxation of trust and estate income and appreciation upon distribution. * * *

In the case of very large trusts, however, this natural disincentive to defer distribution may be ineffective because security and control of wealth are indirect forms of predistribution enjoyment. It may therefore be desirable in some cases to tax trusts prior to distribution. Moreover, such predistribution taxation would counteract the hiatus in revenue collection. For these reasons, a withholding tax on large trusts has been proposed. This proposal requires that any trust distribution be increased by the amount of the tax withheld that is attributable to the distribution, and that the distributee be given a corresponding credit against his income tax in the amount of the withheld tax.

    * * *

Gifts and Bequests in Kind

Under a "consumption tax" approach, gifts and bequests of cash are included in income, but the recipient would receive a deduction when the cash is invested in nonpersonal assets. A gift or bequest of business or investment property would not be includible, as these transfers are the equivalent of receipt of cash and full reinvestment. Of course, the asset would have a zero basis, so that the full amount realized upon disposition would be included unless it is reinvested.

Under a CTB approach, gifts and bequests in kind would be included in the income of the recipient as an accession to wealth. Inclusion might, however, create a problem for the recipient of raising the cash to pay the additional tax. This problem of liquidity already poses severe difficulties under the estate tax, and various statutory and estate planning devices exist to deal with it. However, liquidity would be less of a problem under the income tax proposal since legatees could be given more time to pay the tax than an estate, which has a limited duration.

There are, however, additional reasons under the CTB model and income tax proposal for deferral of taxation on gifts in kind by excluding them and assigning them a zero basis. Deferral would avoid the problem of valuing the property upon receipt. Moreover, since income-producing property received by a trust or estate would not be subject to tax until distributed, the same deferral might seem to be equitable where income-producing property is acquired outright by an individual.

Those cases in which deferral is desirable, however, are very limited. Deferral treatment cannot be conferred upon personal assets which represent ongoing consumption. Deferral in the case of depreciable business and investment assets is not particularly compelling since the periodic depreciation deductions would ameliorate the effect of immediate taxation. Marketable securities are not difficult to value or liquidate, so deferral for them would not be necessitated by administrative considerations. What remains is largely real property and small business interests which, as under existing law, plausibly deserve special treatment.

* * *

TAX POLICY AND THE FEDERAL INCOME TAXATION OF THE TRANSFER OF WEALTH

David M. Hudson[*]

19 Willamette Law Review 1, 52-58 (1983)

Proponents of including the receipt of gratuitous transfers in the donee's income tax base are attracted by a number of features which they assert make the approach superior to the present wealth transfer tax system. One of the most appealing advantages is the simplification of the Internal Revenue Code. It would be appropriate to repeal section 102, which excludes the receipt of gifts from gross income, the three chapters of the Code which contain the estate, gift and generation-skipping taxes, and the portions of subchapter J which deal with the income tax treatment of estates, trusts, and beneficiaries. On the other hand, a few words should be added to section 61, specifically enumerating gifts and bequests as items of income. It may be desirable to modify the income averaging provisions or to provide an extended period of time for payment of the tax in order to ameliorate the perceived hardship of having large amounts of taxable income, especially when received by bequest, bunched into a single taxable period.

Second, the improved vertical equity of our tax system is another positive attribute of this income tax proposal. A longstanding fundamental tax policy in this country has been that the ability of the taxpayer to pay should be considered when determining how the tax burden will be allocated; the ability-to-pay concept has been an important criteria in measuring a tax system's overall fairness. Wealth received by gratuitous transfer represents an ability to pay taxes imposed thereon to no different degree than wealth received as compensation for performing services, or as gains from dealings in property, or as prizes or other windfalls. Indeed, the income tax approach is an improvement over the accessions tax in that the income tax is measured by the recipient's *present* ability to pay, rather than on his historical record of receiving gratuitous transfers and the supposition that the greater the cumulative amount, the greater the taxpaying capacity.

The fairness of a tax system refers not only to its vertical equity, but also to the manner in which it operates in practice; whether it is administered and enforced in an evenhanded manner; and whether it is easily avoided or evaded. The present wealth transfer taxes have to a large extent become imposed on the unwary or those who do not wish to arrange their affairs to avoid them. The present system, which the public perceives as unfair, should be replaced by one that is at least less unfair, thereby encouraging public confidence in the system.

---

[*]. At time of original publication, Assistant Professor of Law, University of Florida.

The social policy goal of wealth redistribution of the transfer taxes would be enhanced under this income tax proposal for the same reason the accessions tax has been touted as an improvement: donors and decedents would be induced to have less of their wealth paid in tax by transferring it to friends and relatives who are in lower income tax brackets. * * *

Finally, the goal of generating revenue by the taxation of gratuitous transfers could be better accomplished by this income tax proposal. Obviously the amount of tax revenue produced will be a function of the rate structure and any exemptions or deductions allowed, but it has been estimated that by simply including the value of inheritances in income, more than two and one-half times the revenue currently being generated by the transfer taxes would be produced. More importantly, the administration and enforcement scheme for the transfer taxes, which now stands separate from that of the income tax, would be eliminated along with the need for separate returns, forms, basis record-keeping, and other compliance costs.

Two major areas of concern with this income tax proposal are the proper treatment for property left in trust, and the vexing issue of appropriate exclusions and deductions. To be consistent with the approach that people are ultimately the recipients of gratuitous transfers, and that people are the proper taxpayers when they receive such transfers, trusts and estates are merely devices for facilitating transfers and should not themselves be taxpayers. Transfers to an estate or a trust would be tax free; in contrast, distributions to individual beneficiaries would be taxed. Continuing with the conduit theory, income earned with respect to assets held by a trust or an estate would not be subject to income tax when earned, but only when ultimately distributed to beneficiaries. Obviously, wealth that could accumulate in a trust, and the economic power that could be controlled by the trustees, might become enormous. Because of the relatively short duration of estates, the problem seems most acute with respect to trusts. Therefore, a modification has been proposed to impose a tax on the income of large trusts at a rate of fifty percent. A distribution to a beneficiary would be grossed-up by the amount of tax attributable to the distribution, and the beneficiary would be allowed a credit against his income tax by that same amount. In this fashion, the ability to defer tax on income earned by the trust would disappear.
    * * *

The modern transfer taxes have always had some provision for the exemption or exclusion of a certain portion of what would otherwise be a taxable transfer. Currently, transfers of present interests in property to a single donee, up to $10,000 each year, are excluded from the gift tax. The exclusion was originally justified as "obviat[ing] the necessity of keeping an account of and reporting numerous small gifts . . . to cover in most cases wedding and Christmas gifts and occasional gifts of relatively small amounts."[310] Prior to 1977, both the gift tax and the estate tax permitted taxable transfers to be offset by deductions, most recently to a maximum of $30,000 for lifetime gifts and $60,000 in the gross estate. These deductions have been replaced by the unified credit in computing both the gift and estate tax liabilities, but the effect is the same: to permit a certain amount of wealth to be transferred tax free. Finally, neither the gift tax nor the estate tax will be imposed on most transfers to one's spouse or to a qualified charity.

If the income tax proposal is adopted, careful consideration should be given to the adoption of any sort of de minimis exception. Exempting a flat dollar amount that a person could receive each year, whether applied with respect to each donor, or cumulatively, from all donors during the year, would be neither equitable nor necessary. An individual fortunate enough to receive gifts up to the exclusion amount each year would be in a better position economically to pay income tax than an individual who otherwise had the same amount of taxable income, but who received no gratuitous transfers. Instead, the exclusion should be drafted with an eye toward the difference with which the public perceives a gift upon the occasion of some special event, such as a birthday or anniversary, up to a set dollar amount, and a gift which is perhaps motivated by "detached and disinterested generosity," but which is at its essence a transfer of wealth. The horizontal equity of such a tax system would be an improvement over the current one. Similarly, a lifetime exclusion or unified credit would be antithetical to the vertical equity, ability-to-pay element of this income tax proposal.

On the other hand, the marital deduction should be retained in this income tax proposal, as long as the husband and wife are being treated as a unit for income tax purposes by filing a joint return. Transfers to a charity which are exempt from income tax would also be tax free, thus effectively continuing present law.

Replacing the wealth transfer taxes with an income tax imposed on the receipt of gratuitous transfers would have the advantages of simplifying the tax laws and bringing to the overall system a greater degree of fairness and equity. Problems which would be encountered in enforcement, administration and compliance would not be insurmountable, and, indeed, may well be less burdensome than those encountered under the present wealth transfer tax scheme. The revenue which would be derived from the income tax could be at least as great as that presently derived from the wealth transfer taxes. The goal of encouraging wealth redistribution would be more effectively served by this income tax proposal.

---

310. S. REP. NO. 665, 72d Cong., 1st Sess. 41 (1932).

* * *

"GIFTS, GAFTS, AND GEFTS"[1]—THE INCOME TAX DEFINITION AND TREATMENT OF PRIVATE AND CHARITABLE "GIFTS" AND A PRINCIPLED POLICY JUSTIFICATION FOR THE EXCLUSION OF GIFTS FROM INCOME

Douglas A. Kahn[*] & Jeffrey H. Kahn[**]

78 Notre Dame Law Review 441, 452-55, 457-71, 474-75 (2003)

The Tax Policy Justification for Excluding Gifts from Income

The Reasons Offered for Including Gifts in Income

The earliest and most prominent commentator to dispute the gift exclusion and urge that gifts be included in income was Henry C. Simons. * * * Simons rested his rejection of a gift exclusion on his concept of personal income and on the tax policies that are reflected in that concept. Simons's concept of personal income is commonly referred to as the "Haig-Simons definition." * * *

Simons defined personal income as

> [T]he algebraic sum of (1) the market value of rights exercised in consumption and (2) the change in value of the store of property rights between the beginning and the end of the period in question. In other words, it is merely the result obtained by adding consumption during the period to "wealth" at the end of the period and then subtracting "wealth" at the beginning.[57]

* * *

The term "consumption" is not defined in that formulation. We will discuss the meaning of that term later in this Article. For now, we will adopt the definition that Professor Warren used—namely that "'consumption' means the ultimate use or destruction of economic resources." Warren defined "economic resources" as the goods and services that are generally the subject of market transactions in our society, expressly excluding psychic benefits. We would add to Warren's definition the proviso that the "consumption" to which the Haig-Simons definition refers is personal consumption—i.e., consumption

---

1. Despairing of the confusion engendered by the application of different meanings to the term "gift" as it is used in the income and transfer tax areas, the late Judge Frank suggested in *Commissioner v. Beck's Estate*, 129 F.2d 243, 246 (2d Cir. 1942) that Congress should "use different symbols to describe the taxable conduct in the several statutes, calling it a 'gift' in the gift tax law, a 'gaft' in the income tax law, and a 'geft' in the estate tax law."

*. At time of original publication, Paul G. Kauper Professor of Law, University of Michigan.

**. At time of original publication, Assistant Professor of Law, Santa Clara University.

57. HENRY C. SIMONS, PERSONAL INCOME TAXATION 50 (1938).

for the personal purposes of the consumer as contrasted to the use or destruction of economic resources for business or profit-making purposes. * * *

The effect of including current personal consumption in the equation is that the market value of the consumption itself is taxed. If X earns income which X promptly uses to purchase and consume services, X has none of the income remaining at the end of the accounting period, and yet X is taxed on the full amount of the income. There is no meaningful difference between taxing X's income and taxing the consumption itself. What difference is there then between a consumption tax and an income tax? The difference is that a consumption tax imposes a tax when the taxpayer actually consumes some item or service. The tax on income that is accumulated and invested is deferred until that income is used for consumption. In contrast, while the income tax does tax current consumption, it also taxes income that is accumulated during the accounting period. It is the element of taxing accumulated income that distinguishes the two.

Although nominally aimed at measuring income, the Haig-Simons formulation is integrally associated with personal consumption. Indeed, the "income" of an individual can be viewed as a surrogate for consumption—measuring the value of the individual's current consumption plus the present value of the future consumption that can be obtained by the use of the accumulated wealth. The taxation of income effectively is a tax on current consumption plus a tax on future consumption that will be enjoyed by the taxpayer or by someone else. The income tax subsumes an assumption that accumulated income will be used for consumption at some future date, and that it does not matter whether it is so used by the taxpayer or by someone else.

* * *

When an individual uses an amount of income for consumption purposes in the year in which the income was received, the individual has removed the purchased goods or services from the common pool, and they are no longer available to anyone else in society. Those goods or services are captured by the individual to the exclusion of everyone else. It is an appropriate scheme to tax individuals in accordance with the amount of societal goods they have taken to themselves to the exclusion of others, and the income tax system does that in regard to current consumption. In effect, because the Government cannot conveniently take its share of societal goods at their source, the goods are traced to the individuals who capture them, and each individual is taxed in proportion to the amount of societal goods that individual captured for his preclusive use. The common pool concept, which we will discuss below, has its detractors. But, as to the taxation of current consumption, the justification of preclusive use seems unobjectionable.

In certain circumstances, the tax law does not tax a person for his preclusive consumption, but the reason for such exclusions is that the factual circumstances that are present raise competing tax principles or economic issues that Congress deemed sufficient to warrant an exclusion from income. For example, an employee is not taxed on the receipt of certain fringe benefits that are described in specific Code provisions, such as Code §§ 119 and 132. * * * [T]he tax treatment of such items is sui generis and does not contradict our statement of the fundamental principles on which income taxation is grounded.

But, what is the justification for taxing accumulated income? If one were to adopt the preclusive use basis for the income tax (incorporating the common pool concept), would that mean that accumulated income should not be taxed because no goods have been consumed yet? We make no such contention. To the contrary, our view, as explained above, is that the amount of income that is accumulated is properly taxed at that time because it represents the present value of the consumption that presumably will take place at some future date. In other words, an income tax differs from a consumption tax in that the income tax imposes a tax currently on the present value of future consumption instead of waiting until the future consumption takes place and taxing it then. While a case might be made for substituting a consumption tax for the income tax system currently in use, we do not address in this Article the question of which tax is preferable. It is important, however, to recognize that an income tax system incorporates a tax on the present value of future consumption.
        * * *

The Haig-Simons definition is regarded as an expression of an ideal to which the tax system should aspire. It is an expression of good tax policy to which tax rules should conform unless a competing consideration outweighs the virtues of maintaining that policy. * * * While there are reasons to question whether the income tax law should adhere strictly to that definition, we will accept the definition in this Article, but maintain that, contrary to Simons's assertion, some of the tax policies that are reflected in that definition support the exclusion for gifts.

Let us first examine the reasoning of those who contend that gifts should be included in income. The genesis of that contention lies with Henry Simons himself. Simons contended that the accumulation of wealth should be taxed regardless of how the wealth was obtained. Simons stated, "The income tax is not a tax upon income but a tax upon persons according to their respective incomes; and . . . the objective of policy must be fairness among persons, not fairness among kinds of receipts. . . ."[73] Simons also stated,

---

73. *Id.*at 128.

> Our definition of income perhaps does violence to traditional usage in specifying impliedly a calculation which would include gratuitous receipts. To exclude gifts, . . . would be to introduce additional arbitrary distinctions; it would be necessary to distinguish among an individual's receipts according to the intentions of second parties.[74]

In other words, receipts increase an individual's capacity to consume, and the income tax law should focus on that capacity and not on how the individual obtained it. If taken in isolation, this is a powerful argument. While Simons based his view of how gifts should be treated primarily on his conclusion that the underlying principles of an income tax system provide no basis for excluding gifts from income, he also suggested that an exclusion of gifts requires an inquiry into the subjective motives of transferors, which Simons believed would impose an undue administrative burden on the taxing authorities. Experience with the administration of the gift exclusion has not borne out that fear, especially after Congress resolved the treatment of gifts to employees and their spouses in the 1986 amendment to Code § 102.

Subsequent proponents of including gifts in income have adopted Simons's view. For example, in his 1963 article, Professor Klein wrote,

> * * * Simons' position is simply that for tax purposes there is no reason to distinguish gifts from other receipts: "it is hard to defend exclusion of certain receipts merely because one has done nothing or given nothing in return" . . . . His attitude towards the taxation of gifts was basically determined by his view that taxes must focus on the individual and that the best objective measure of equality of individuals for tax purposes treats all forms of enrichment alike.[76]

Klein pointed out that Simons's view of the proper definition of income, including his view of the taxation of gifts, has been widely accepted by economists.[77]

In his 1978 article, Professor Dodge makes similar arguments for including gifts in income and cites Simons and the Haig-Simons definition in support of that view. Dodge states that "it is axiomatic that receipts should be included in income regardless of source or nature."[79]

Double Income Taxation

As previously noted, under the principles reflected in the Haig-Simons definition of income, the justification for taxing income that is accumulated,

---

74. *Id.* at 56-57 (citations omitted).

76. William Klein, *An Enigma in the Federal Income Tax: The Meaning of the Word "Gift"*, 48 MINN. L. REV. 215, 226 (1963).

77. *Id.* at 227.

79. Joseph M. Dodge, *Beyond Estate and Gift Tax Reform: Including Gifts and Bequests in Income*, 91 HARV. L. REV. 1177, 1184 (1978). [This article is excerpted earlier in this subchapter. (Ed.)]

rather than spent in the year it was earned, subsumes an assumption that the accumulated wealth will be spent on consumption in some future year and that the amount of the income currently accumulated provides a fair approximation of the present value of the future consumption. Of course, there is no means of predicting whether the immediate taxpayer will be the one to use the accumulated funds to purchase services or goods at some future date or whether some other person will use the funds to enjoy the future consumption. Thus, the tax laws are indifferent as to who uses the accumulated wealth for consumption purposes; it is sufficient to assume that the wealth will be so used at a future date by someone, not necessarily by the current taxpayer.

The taxing of an individual's income entitles that individual to an equivalent amount of consumption, either in the year that the income is earned or in a future year, without incurring additional income taxes. * * * If a taxpayer transfers previously taxed income to someone else as a gift, can the taxpayer be deemed to have consumed it by making that gift? If the gift does not constitute consumption by the taxpayer, and if the gift is treated as taxable income to the donee, then there would be two sets of income taxation on a single consumption—i.e., the only consumption that would take place would be the consumption that occurs when the donee uses the donated property. Prior to the 1938 publication of Simons's book, some commentators characterized this treatment as "double taxation" and argued that gifts should be excluded to prevent a duplication of the income tax.[81] Professor Zelenak agrees that it is a double taxation, and that it can be justified only if the transferor can be viewed as consuming the transferred property by making the gift;[82] however, he ultimately concludes that double taxation is appropriate for gifts.[83] Simons expressly rejects the contention that there is double taxation on the basis that the gift itself is a kind of consumption by the transferor. Simons states,

> If it is not more pleasant to give than to receive, one may still hesitate to assert that giving is not a form of consumption for the giver. The proposition that everyone tries to allocate his consumption expenditure among different goods in such manner as to equalize the utility of dollars-worths may not be highly illuminating; but there is no apparent reason for treating gifts as an exception.[84]

---

81. *See* SIMONS, *supra* note 57, at 57; Alvin Warren, *Would a Consumption Tax Be Fairer Than an Income Tax?*, 89 YALE L.J. 1081, 1088 (1980).

82. Lawrence Zelenak, Commentary, *The Reasons for a Consumption Tax and the Tax Treatment of Gifts and Bequests*, 51 TAX L. REV. 601, 602 (1996).

83. *Id.* at 603.

84. SIMONS, *supra* note 57, at 57-58.

Professor Dodge acknowledged that the taxation of gifts "involves 'double taxation' in the economic sense in that the grantor is giving after-tax dollars on which the recipient is again taxed," but Dodge opines that the problems engendered by double taxation can be mitigated by some other means.[85] Dodge states that, "the area of gifts . . . is not one where economic considerations should predominate over principles of tax equity."[86] Dodge distinguishes economic considerations from tax equity because he views the problem of double taxation exclusively as one of hindering capital formation, which could be cured by other means—i.e., he does not view the problem as one that conflicts with the principles of the income tax itself. Dodge believes that double taxation is warranted to preserve the proper measurement of the donee's income. Dodge does state that, "[t]he giving of a gift is more analogous to consumption than to investment."[88] One might counter that statement with the observation that gifts are far from analogous to either one.

An important question then is whether a gift is a kind of consumption or something closely related to consumption. A gift does not exhaust any societal resource, and therefore cannot be considered even akin to a consumption. Consider the contrast between a gift of cash or property to a donee and a payment to a third party for services rendered.   Take the example that Professor Klein set forth in his 1963 article to illustrate why he asserts that the intention of a transferor should not affect the income tax treatment of the transfer:

> [T]he argument attempts to establish a distinction based on the position of the donor rather than the donee. Surely no one would argue that if X pays his gardener 4000 dollars per year, the gardener should not be taxed because doing so interferes with X's "right" to use his property. The argument is equally without merit in the case where X pays 4000 dollars per year to his son, out of pure love and affection. While X probably does not want his son to be taxed, he is not so concerned about the gardener. Tax consequences, however, cannot be permitted to turn on considerations such as this.[89]

The same argument was made by Victor Thuronyi, who wrote:

> it is not accurate to say that *the gift* is taxed twice. What is taxed is, first, the amount [of income] earned by the donor and, second, the amount transferred to the donee. The gift is taxed only once, to the donee. Thus, a gift is no more subject to double taxation than is a

---

85. Dodge, *supra* note 79, at 1183-86.
86. *Id.* at 1186.
88. *Id.*
89. Klein, *supra* note 76, at 259.

payment for personal services, which is also "taxed twice"—once when earned by the payor and again when received by the payee.[90]

This argument is fallacious. Take the facts of Klein's example. X's payment to the gardener is a cost of obtaining the gardener's services which were captured by X and used for his benefit to the exclusion of the rest of society. The gardener's services were a societal resource that X consumed, so the payment is an expense for a consumption by X. Assume that the money that X used to pay the gardener was income that had been taxed to X. Having paid income tax on that income, X is entitled to use it for consumption without incurring an additional income tax. But, X did use it to pay for a consumption, and so X has obtained the consumption for which he was taxed. When the gardener receives the payment, he is taxed on that income because he can use it to purchase goods or services that he will capture for his exclusive benefit to the exclusion of the rest of society. Taxing the gardener on the payment he receives does not constitute a double counting of a single consumption. To the contrary, there are two separate consumptions or future consumptions, and so it is proper that there are two separate income tax impositions.

In contrast, when X makes a gift to his son, X has not consumed any of society's resources by making that transfer. The consumption will take place in the future when the son uses the donated property. * * *

In certain circumstances, a person's use of an economic resource will be treated as a consumption even though the use is not preclusive and does not result in the destruction of that resource. Consider the following example. X creates a software program for computers. A person can purchase the use of that program and have it sent to his computer electronically, after which it can be used indefinitely by the purchaser. The transaction is one in which the purchaser obtains a permanent license to use the software. The purchaser's use of the software does not remove anything from society's common store of resources because the same program can be sent to the rest of the world, and the purchaser's obtaining of the program does not deny anyone else access to it. One might say that the specific electronic transmission that the purchaser received was obtained exclusively by that person, but it would be a stretch to classify that as a preclusive use of a societal resource. Why then should the money paid by the purchaser to obtain a license for the use of the software be treated as a consumption? When the software was created, that was a societal resource, a portion of which, in a simpler economy, could have been taken by the government as a tax. However, even if we had an elementary economy, the government could not easily take a portion of the software at the time of production because the producer would still be free to license it to as many

---

90. Victor Thuronyi, *The Concept of Income*, 46 TAX L. REV. 45, 74 (1990).

persons as the producer chooses. While the government could restrict the number of persons to whom the producer can license the software, and the government could go into the business of licensing its share of the software, that is not a viable solution. Instead, the government can take a dollar amount which equals the value of a portion of the software, whose value can best be determined by waiting to see the extent to which the producer actually sells licenses to use it. In effect, the tax is deferred until licenses are sold, and the tax is imposed on the purchaser of each license by treating that purchase as a consumption of a portion of the software. So, for tax purposes, a portion of the resource can be considered to have been consumed at the time that the license is purchased.   The situation is quite different in the case of personal satisfaction; in that case, no resource has been produced, and so none can be consumed.

If personal satisfaction were characterized as consumption, than a taxpayer who enjoyed personal satisfaction from the receipt of income (i.e., the pure joy of seeing his bank account increase), would be deemed to have consumed that income immediately upon receiving it. * * * A person who was deemed to have enjoyed a consumption because of the personal satisfaction of receiving income nevertheless would not be taxed again when the income is used to purchase the preclusive use of a societal resource. * * * Similarly, the psychic benefit derived from making a gift does not erase the right to use those funds to purchase the preclusive use of a societal resource.

* * * [A] donor may derive benefits from the donee such as the latter's gratitude and appreciation. Not all of those benefits can be described as psychic pleasure because they may be converted into influence over the donee.
* * * [T]hose benefits, and the donor's possible anticipation of them, do not prevent a transfer from qualifying as a gift, and the same reasons explain why they do not preclude the exclusion of such transfers from income. In short, one reason is that the donee's gratitude and appreciation are not limited societal resources, and so the "benefit" does not represent the consumption of a societal resource. But, there is a second reason that applies even if our view that consumption requires the exhaustion of a societal resource were rejected. The obtaining of gratitude and accompanying attitudes from the donee is an insubstantial benefit, and, in most cases, it will be virtually impossible to determine whether that was the motivating force for the transfer. The desire to provide the donee with the means of consuming the income that was transferred to the donee often will be the exclusive purpose of the transfer and will virtually always be the dominant motive. * * *

A person (a "donee") may "gratuitously" perform services for another in the hope that the latter will thereby be induced to make a gift of property. If a gift of property is made subsequently, does the donor's consumption of the donee's services satisfy the one-consumption principle so that the donee should be taxed on the gift? Our answer is no. In virtually all such cases, the value of the donee's services will be vastly less than the amount of the gift (otherwise, it would not be a profitable venture for the donee), and so most of the transfer cannot be matched to a consumption of the donee's services. Thus, only a small portion of the transfer can be matched by a consumption and so taxed to the donee, and the administrative burden of ascertaining the identity and value of those services would be enormous, if indeed it is even feasible. More importantly, a donee may have gratuitously performed the services with no ulterior selfish motives, and that is the most likely scenario in all but a few circumstances. The relationship of the parties makes gratuitous motives highly plausible. Cross giving is a common occurrence, and one gift is not deemed compensation for the other. * * *

What is wrong with having two income tax impositions for a single consumption? The answer is that there is nothing wrong with it if there is a compelling policy goal that is furthered by such double taxation. The difficulty here is that, on balance, income tax policy considerations either weigh in favor of a single income tax imposition or, at least, are in equilibrium on that issue.

Vicarious Enjoyment of Another's Consumption

Let us consider X's gift to his son, and again assume that the gift is of accumulated income on which X has been taxed. As previously noted, having paid tax on that income, X is entitled to expend an equivalent amount on consumption without incurring an additional income tax. But X decides that he does not wish to consume any more for himself. Instead, he wishes to enjoy vicariously a consumption by someone he loves, his son. * * * The question then is whether the income tax system should permit a taxpayer to use the full amount of income on which he has paid income tax to enjoy vicariously a consumption by a loved one, or whether the system should permit a full amount of consumption only by the taxpayer himself. While either solution is possible, to allow the taxpayer to enjoy vicariously another's consumption is consistent with the tax policy of taxing accumulated income on the assumption that someone, not necessarily the taxpayer, will use the accumulated funds to pay for a consumption at some future date. In addition, providing the taxpayer the option of vicarious consumption implements the economic goal of minimizing the extent to which the tax system depresses the incentive to produce goods or services that will be converted into income.

The above analysis is not altered if X had not previously been taxed on the property donated to the son. If X obtained the property through a chain of gifts in which the original donor had been taxed on the property as income, the principle that someone in the chain of gifts should be permitted to consume the donated property without incurring an additional income tax would apply with equal force as when X himself was taxed on the income. If the donated property had appreciated in X's hands (and so the appreciation had not been taxed to X), the donee will be taxed on that appreciation when it is realized and recognized, so there will be only one tax and one consumption. If X had inherited the donated property, which was not income in respect of a decedent, and if the property had been appreciated in the hands of the decedent from whom X inherited it, that appreciation will never be taxed to anyone because § 1014 of the Code provides X with a basis in the property equal to its value, typically determined at the time of the decedent's death. Should the appreciated portion of the property for which X had obtained a stepped-up basis be taxed to the donee since there will be no double taxation of that portion of the donated property? The answer again is no. Section 1014 of the Code incorporates the policy that the appreciated portion of the inherited property would not be taxed to X as income if he sold or consumed the property. * * * If, instead of consuming it himself, X elects to enjoy vicariously the consumption of that property by someone of X's choosing, that should not cause income taxation of the consumption any more than X's personal consumption would have done so. Similarly, if all or a portion of the donated property were the product of tax-exempt income that X received (e.g., income from a state bond that is exempt from tax under § 103 of the Code), X should be permitted to have the income consumed by someone of his choice.

Choice Between Competing Principles

The determination of the correct tax treatment of gifts raises two competing tax principles or goals. One principle is that the individual who has been taxed on income should have a virtually unrestricted range of choices as to how that income will be used to purchase consumption. The other principle is that an individual's taxable income should include all his receipts (other than a return of capital) so as to reflect accurately his ability to share the costs of government. It is not possible in the gift setting to adopt a tax rule that will comply with both principles. One must yield to the other. Congress chose to give priority to the principle of providing the taxpayer with a wider range of choices for consumption. A gift is excluded from a donee's income because of that commitment to the donor; the exclusion has nothing to do with the worthiness of the donee. Several commentators would prefer that priority be given to the principle of maximizing the accuracy of the measurement of a donee's ability to pay. While that is not an irrational choice, it is no more reasonable than the opposite choice that Congress made, and may well be less compelling. As discussed below, the congressional treatment of gifts comports with a concept of treating certain parties as a single tax unit for limited tax purposes.

Even some of the commentators who urge that gifts should be included in income, acknowledge that there are circumstances when they should not be or when some amount of them should not be. One example is that administrative expediency requires that minor items be excluded. * * *

Support Payments

Payments in satisfaction of an obligation to support another are not gifts, but their exclusion from income would seem desirable. * * * Only one consumption took place, and so it is appropriate to impose only one income tax.

The tax law's treatment of alimony does not conflict with our view of how support should be treated. * * * The current tax treatment imposes only a single income tax on income used to pay alimony since the amount included in the payee's income is matched by the nonitemized deduction allowable to the payor. The two provisions together (§§ 71 and 215 of the Code) constitute the means of implementing the income-splitting scheme that Congress has provided for divorced couples, and do not impose double taxation.

Single Tax Unit

Dodge acknowledges that transfers between spouses might be exempted on the ground that the two spouses make a single tax unit. Without deciding the question, Klein notes that an immediate family might be regarded as a single tax unit for tax purposes so that transfers within the unit are of no tax significance. But, there is no good reason to limit the single unit concept to spouses or members of an immediate family. The make-up of what constitutes a family has changed in recent years. Many people who are not married live together in a family-type setting. The delineation of a single tax unit should not depend upon formal relationships, such as marriage and blood kinship. The current tax definition of gifts provides an excellent standard for determining whether two people should be regarded as a single unit for certain tax purposes.

When a transferor makes a transfer to another out of "detached and disinterested generosity," the effect of current tax law is to treat the transferor and the transferee as members of a single tax unit for certain (but not for all) purposes. * * *

Even if a donor barely knows the donee, but chooses to make the gift because the donee's consumption would provide the donor with optimum utility from the use of the property, the donor's choice should not be partially frustrated by taxing the donee. For example, X learns from a newspaper story that Y's parents were killed by a terrorist attack, and that Y has financial needs as a consequence. X, who has never met Y or any of her family, is touched by her plight. X sends Y $2000 as a gift. The absence of a relationship between X and Y does not alter the facts that X desires to have his $2000 used by Y, and that X will derive more satisfaction from Y's consumption than he would from using the $2000 for his own consumption. For a very limited tax purpose, *X* and *Y* should be considered a single tax unit so that only one income tax is imposed.

* * *

A Deduction for the Donor

Even if it is agreed that there should be a single income tax on donated property, that does not prove that the gift should be excluded from the donee's income. By excluding the gift from income, the incidence of the income tax is left with the donor who incurred that tax before making the gift.   An alternative approach would be to shift the incidence of tax to the donee. That could be accomplished by including the gift in the donee's income, but allowing the donor a nonitemized tax deduction for the gift. While only a single income tax would then be imposed, the incidence would be on the donee. The reason for rejecting that approach is that it would greatly impair the goal of progressive taxation. * * * [I]t would permit a high bracket taxpayer to shift income to a lower tax bracket donee. * * *

Although the basis transfer rules that now exist permit a shifting of the tax incidence on appreciation to a lower bracket donee, the extent of the injury to progressivity suffered thereby is of much less consequence than the injury that would be suffered if the tax law were to permit wholesale shifting of the tax incidence on all income, including personal service income.   For administrative reasons, Congress is willing to allow a relatively small inroad into progressivity for the appreciated portion of donated property, but it is not willing to allow an expansive escape route for all earned income.

Gift Tax Imposition as Double Taxation

The making of a gift could cause the imposition of a gift tax. Does the possible imposition of a gift tax refute our contention that a taxpayer who has paid an income tax should be allowed to enjoy vicariously the consumption paid for by that income without incurring additional income tax costs and that Congress has chosen to implement that principle and the single unit concept? We do not believe that it does. * * * The gift tax serves an entirely different set of goals. * * *

Notes and Questions

33. Professors Dodge and Hudson advocate the repeal of section 102, which excludes gifts and bequests from the recipient's gross income. There would be no deduction for the transferor. Carryover basis would be abandoned, for gifts as well as bequests, and recipients, having taking the full amount of their receipt into income, would have a basis equal to that amount. (The basis of both donees and heirs would thus be the same as the stepped-up basis presently available to heirs under section 1014.)

34. The other reform proposals, carryover basis and constructive realization, deal only with income taxes and are generally silent regarding estate and gift taxes. (It is true that transfer taxes are discussed, and Professor Subotnik explicitly advocates constructive realization in lieu of transfer taxes. Nonetheless, even Subotnik does not advocate abolition of the transfer taxes, but merely notes that this may be the political tradeoff of adopting constructive realization, and argues that such a trade would be a good one.) By contrast, those who propose repeal of section 102 generally envision repeal of the transfer taxes, as do Professors Dodge and Hudson.

35. A generation ago, Professor Thomas Waterbury maintained, in effect, that the case for constructive realization bears a much lighter burden of proof than does full repeal of section 102:

> [T]he case * * * for gains tax realization at death is a case against the exemption of gain from the *first* income tax upon it. A case for including gratuitous receipts in the income of the recipient must be a case for imposing a *second* income tax upon such receipts in any case in which such receipts were previously exposed to an initial income tax in the hands of the transferor.[v]

Is this argument persuasive? Stated differently, if *A* accumulates $1 million of after-tax wealth, then gives it to his son, *B*, would taxing *B* be improper double taxation? What is Professor Dodge's response to this objection to his proposal? Which position do you find persuasive?

36. Professor Dodge argues that taxing recipients of gifts and bequests is consistent with both the "ideal" income tax—the comprehensive tax base, or Haig-Simons definition of income—and with the consumption tax base. Clearly, the Professors Kahn would not agree. Dodge also acknowledges that Professor Andrews, the leading proponent of the progressive consumption tax, disagrees. (See footnote 34 of the Dodge excerpt, and Chapter Seven.) Do you agree that these receipts demonstrate ability to pay? What is Dodge's answer to the argument that gifts and bequests are not properly regarded as income because they are transfers of wealth rather than creations or additions to wealth?

37. In evaluating the proposed repeal of section 102, it may be important whether we look at the family or at the individual. For example, while it is true that a lottery winner has not created new wealth, but has only received a transfer from the losers, surely the winner is to be taxed. If, on the other

---

v. Thomas L. Waterbury, *A Case for Realizing Gains at Death in Terms of Family Interests*, 52 MINN. L. REV. 1, 42-43 (1967) (emphasis in original).

hand, we look at the donor and donee (or decedent and heir) as two members of the same group—which frequently may be the way at least the transferor looks at it—it may seem that for the group as a whole there is no increase in ability to pay.

On the other hand, the tax law usually treats adult individuals (other than spouses) as entirely separate tax units. Considering the recipient separately from the transferor, it is certainly true that a dollar received as a gift spends as well as a dollar earned from labor or investment.

38. Suppose one were persuaded that the recipient of a gift or a bequest should be regarded as having income, but that the transferor, who has surrendered dominion over the property and received "nothing" in return (true?), should be entitled to a deduction. The Dodge excerpt refers to "[t]hose supporting a deduction for the donor indirectly through exclusion by the donee." If one supports a deduction for the donor, why not provide the deduction directly, rather than by using the recipient's exclusion as a proxy for the transferor's deduction? Is the reason the same whether we are talking of donors or decedents?

39. Professor Hudson argues that the approach of repealing section 102 would encourage donors and decedents to transfer wealth to a greater number of, and to less wealthy, recipients. Why might this happen? Would this be desirable?

40. Consideration of detailed issues of the taxation of trusts, either under current law or the proposal, is beyond the scope of this book. The issue of transfers in trust requires brief mention here, however, because large transfers of wealth are frequently effected in trust form. As a general rule, the Dodge and Hudson excerpts would exempt the trust from tax, and would tax fully the beneficiary on every dollar received from the trust. That, however, is troubling where a huge trust accumulates income for many years. They propose, in some cases, a withholding tax levied at the trust level.

41. Professor Dodge would carve out a special rule for gifts of property in kind that would largely apply to real estate and closely held business interests. The recipient would have no income and a zero basis (instead of inclusion in income at fair market value, and a basis equal to fair market value). What is his justification for this special treatment? Why is it not extended to consumer goods, such as a new car given to an adult daughter for personal use? To marketable securities? Do you agree with this aspect of the proposal?

42. If you accepted Professor Dodge's treatment of gifts (by including them in income), would you also agree with him that scholarships, whose exclusion grew out of the exclusion of gifts, should be taxed?

43. Professor Dodge explicitly leaves open the possibility of not only taxing the recipient on the entire transfer, but also taxing the transferor on any unrealized appreciation, as through the constructive realization proposal. Assuming section 102 were repealed, would it be appropriate to tax the transferor on the unrealized appreciation as well?

44. Repeal of section 102 would not necessarily entail repeal of transfer taxes. Professor Dodge, while generally coupling his proposal with a repeal of transfer taxes, leaves open the possibility of the retention of transfer taxes, "reduced in scope to bear only on the extremely wealthy." If recipients of gifts and bequests were fully taxed under the income tax, should the transfer taxes be repealed?

45. As a crucial part of their analysis, the Professors Kahn assert that the income tax is essentially a tax on consumption. Income is either consumed currently, or consumed later (by the taxpayer or someone else). From this, it follows that income not consumed immediately can be consumed later—either by the taxpayer or by someone else—without additional taxation.

46. In what sense is making a gift consumption by the donor? In what sense is it not? (Recall the discussion of similar issues in Chapter Seven, especially Notes #45 and #46 (pages 433-34).)

47. The Kahns' understanding of consumption usually, but not always, entails *preclusive* utilization of resources. As an example of consumption that does not limit the use of resources by others, they give the example of licensing software. Such examples may not be rare. Consider many forms of spectator entertainment—watching a movie in a theater that is not full, attending a ball game in a stadium that is not sold out, connecting to a satellite television system. Despite the fact that the utilization of these resources is not preclusive in any meaningful sense, presumably no one would deny that all are examples of consumption.

48. The Professors Kahn take issue with Professor Klein's comparison of the transfers to the transferor's gardener and to the transferor's son. Do you agree with Klein that the transfers are essentially indistinguishable insofar as

both constitute consumption by the transferor? Or do you think that the Kahns demonstrate a difference worthy of differing tax treatment?

49. The Professors Kahn approve of the treatment of alimony as income to the recipient. How is this inclusion accommodated to their general argument that gifts should not be taxed to the recipient?

50. The Kahns assert that any gift in the *Duberstein* sense—that the donor acted from "detached and disinterested generosity"—"provides an excellent standard for determining whether two people should be regarded as a single unit for certain tax purposes." This holds, the Kahns assert, even in the unusual situation where the donor is not acquainted with the donee. Do you agree?

Comparison of the proposals
51. Professor Zelenak observes that theoretical considerations of tax policy will not be of nearly so great concern to Congress as complexity and revenue. These crucial issues always deserve careful consideration.

52. Consider the four options presented in this chapter—present law, carryover basis, constructive realization, and repeal of section 102—with respect to revenue. It is also relevant to consider the revenue of transfer taxes—some $30 billion in 2000[w]—because some of the proposals entail or at least consider repeal of the transfer taxes. Will revenue be the driving force for change in this area? Is this an opportunity for a hidden tax increase? How would you rank order the proposals in terms of revenue potential?

53. Why might the reform proposals generate additional revenue indirectly, through influencing taxpayer behavior?

54. How do you rank the proposals in terms of complexity, or simplicity? Keep in mind that there are at least two ways to look at simplicity—simplification of the tax code; and making life easier for the Internal Revenue Service, taxpayers, and advisors.

55. Revenue and simplicity are both greatly affected by the levels of exemptions that are provided. What levels of exemptions should be employed, if any? Does your answer vary from proposal to proposal?

---

w. U.S. BUREAU OF THE CENSUS, STATISTICAL ABSTRACT OF THE UNITED STATES, tbl.464, at 314 (122d ed. 2002).]

TAX EXPENDITURES, EXCLUSIONS, AND DEDUCTIONS

Part IV covers issues involving deductions and exclusions in defining taxable income, and certain related provisions, such as credits. A large number of individual deductions and exclusions could have been made the subject of a chapter. Three topics have been chosen, for specific reasons.

Chapter Eleven deals with the tax expenditures concept. Conceptually, tax expenditures are special tax benefits—deductions, exemptions, credits, preferential tax rates, and deferrals—that have much the same effect as direct government outlays. A basic and pervasive problem is deciding whether a given provision lies within the baseline tax system, or is a "special" exception to the norm. Challenges to the tax expenditure concept are considered. Attention is given to the distinctions between "one-time" and "periodic" incentive tax expenditures. Finally, detailed consideration is given the earned income tax credit, both because the EITC is of growing importance in its own right, and because the EITC is sometimes regarded as a model for future blending of the tax and transfer systems.

Chapter Twelve addresses a particularly difficult issue: the extent to which personal injury awards should be excluded from taxable income. Section 104(a)(2) is perhaps more intriguing than any other exclusion, because its justification is unclear. If the exclusion arises simply from compassion for the injured, it should be analyzed as a tax expenditure. On the other hand, if the exclusion can be justified on the grounds that personal injury awards do not constitute "income," the exclusion merely clarifies section 61. Evolution of the present treatment is described, and various rationales for present law and proposed alternatives are discussed. Finally, particular problems arising from structured settlements are presented.

Chapter Thirteen deals with the interaction of state and local taxes with the federal income tax. In one sense, the issues are common to those of the other major "personal" deductions—medical expense, interest, and charitable contributions. In addition, however, the deduction of state and local taxes raises unique issues in the context of our federalist system of government. The chapter concludes with brief consideration of substituting a federal credit for the current deduction for state and local income taxes.

CHAPTER ELEVEN

TAX EXPENDITURES

The federal income tax system consists really of two parts: one part comprises the structural provisions necessary to implement the income tax on individual and corporate net income; the second part comprises a system of tax expenditures under which Governmental financial assistance programs are carried out through special tax provisions rather than through direct Government expenditures. This second system is grafted on to the structure of the income tax proper; it has no basic relation to that structure and is not necessary to its operation. Instead, the system of tax expenditures provides a vast subsidy apparatus that uses the mechanics of the income tax as the method of paying the subsidies. The special provisions under which this subsidy apparatus functions take a variety of forms, covering exclusions from income, exemptions, deductions, credits against tax, preferential rates of tax, and deferrals of tax.[a]

A. INTRODUCTION

Tax expenditures are tax benefits used as incentives or rewards in lieu of outright payments by the government. As the opening quotation from Professor Stanley Surrey indicates, tax expenditures include credits; exclusions and exemptions; deductions not justified in computing net profit; lower tax rates on specified types of income; and, increasingly, timing benefits such as accelerated deductions and deferrals in accounting for income.

What we now regard as "tax expenditures" have perhaps always been with us. Tax expenditures have grown enormously in recent decades, however. Their growth reflects not only the increased size and complexity of the income tax, but also the Government's increased willingness to influence economic and social choices by individuals and businesses.

Present terminology ("tax expenditure") and our awareness of the phenomenon are both of relatively recent vintage, and Professor Surrey is largely responsible for both. He served as the first Assistant Secretary of Treasury for Tax Policy under Presidents Kennedy and Johnson, and his work in that capacity led to the compilation of a Tax Expenditure Budget for the Fiscal Year 1968, published in the Treasury Secretary's annual report.

Six years later, the Budget Act of 1974 implemented a requirement, still in effect, that both the Congressional Budget Committee and the President

---

a. STANLEY S. SURREY, PATHWAYS TO TAX REFORM 6 (1973).

present annual estimates of the revenue costs of existing tax expenditures. These annual cost estimates help one appreciate the magnitude of the various tax expenditures.

Surrey's key contention was that direct expenditures and tax expenditures were substantively interchangeable. At the same time, the political approval process and the budgetary oversight of the two forms of expenditure were (and remain) completely different. Not being outlays from the Treasury, tax expenditures are not reflected in government expenditures and are not subject to the annual congressional appropriation process. They are not items listed in the budget and affect the budget only through tax receipts being lower than they otherwise would be.

Tax expenditures have obvious political appeal for members of Congress. In the case of new tax expenditures, or of liberalizing existing tax expenditures, some discipline has been introduced by a requirement Congress has imposed on itself that bills reducing revenues must contain offsetting revenue increases over a five- or ten-year span. As discussed in Chapter Seventeen, this budget process is subject to manipulation. Moreover, the process does not affect existing, ongoing tax expenditures. "Sunset" rules, which would terminate existing tax expenditures unless they were explicitly continued, have been proposed but not adopted.

Perhaps the clearest examples of tax expenditures are the incentive tax credits, which are usually calculated as a specified percentage of the taxpayer's expenditure on the rewarded behavior. The investment tax credit ("ITC") was the major tax credit between its initial enactment in 1962 and its sharp curtailment in 1986. Before 1986, the ITC allowed taxpayers making investments in tangible personal property (and some real property) for business use to offset their income tax liability by ten percent[b] of the cost of their qualifying investments. Investment tax credits were presented as explicit incentives to invest. As initially proposed by President Kennedy, the credit would have been available only for incremental investments over the taxpayer's normal replacements of business assets, but the incremental investment approach had been abandoned by the time the credit was enacted.

The ITC was the precursor of a flood of other tax credits. These included a credit for increasing outlays for research and development, a credit for providing low-income housing, a credit for wages paid to workers considered to be disadvantaged in various specified respects, education credits, a child care credit, an earned income tax credit ("EITC") for low-income taxpayers, a child tax credit, and a credit for elderly and disabled taxpayers. Unlike tax credits designed to be incentives, the last two tax credits—and arguably the

---

b. When first enacted in 1962, the ITC was only seven percent.

EITC as well—are designed merely to provide relief from tax. Traditionally, the EITC has been unique in providing actual cash supplements.

With the exception of the EITC, the credits have generally benefitted only persons who otherwise would owe income tax, and thus have provided no incentive to individuals whose incomes are so low that they have no tax liability or to corporations that are operating at a loss. One response to this perceived problem has been to suggest making the credits "refundable"—*i.e.*, an amount equivalent to the tax credit would be given to persons who qualify for the credit whether or not they have tax liability against which to apply it. Thus, a "refund" would be made of a tax that had not been paid. While the EITC remains, by far, the most important refundable tax credit, there has been some recent expansion of the concept. The credit of section 35 for certain health insurance costs is refundable, and section 24(d) makes the child tax credit partly refundable. (For these purposes, the wage withholding tax credit is not regarded as refundable, because the refund is out of tax previously withheld from the taxpayer's compensation.)

Tax exemptions and deductions from adjusted gross income also can be tax expenditures. As with nonrefundable credits, exemptions and deductions are useful only if the eligible person otherwise would owe tax. Tax deductions and exemptions of specified types of income can also be of benefit by increasing net operating losses that are carried over to offset taxable income in other years.

Unlike tax credits, exemptions and deductions vary in value among taxpayers—the higher the tax bracket, the greater the tax expenditure. For example, a $1,000 percentage depletion deduction is worth $350 to a corporation facing a 35 percent marginal tax rate and only $150 to a corporation facing a 15 percent marginal tax rate. If the taxpayer has exhausted the tax basis of the mineral property giving rise to the percentage depletion deduction, the tax expenditure, whether $350 or $150, is an outright benefit—not merely a postponement of tax—because there is no compensating downward basis adjustment.

It is more difficult to calculate the benefit from tax expenditures that arise from accelerating deductions to which a taxpayer eventually would be entitled under "normal" rules. The value of speeding up such a deduction depends on two factors: how long it would be before the taxpayer would have received the deduction in the absence of the tax expenditure provision, and the time value of the tax deferred by speeding up the deduction. The time value to the taxpayer may be different from the cost to the Government of postponing its receipt of tax, raising the question of what interest rate should be used to calculate the amount of the tax expenditure.

Although the basic idea of tax expenditures seems reasonable, putting the concept into use has proved difficult and controversial. Furthermore, even the basic concept has been challenged. As respects exemptions and deductions, the debate over tax expenditures merges into the debate over broadening the tax base.

Notes and Questions

(In)efficiency of tax expenditures

1.   A significant question in using and structuring tax expenditures is whether they are efficient—does the Government get a sufficient bang for its buck? In many instances, such efficiency is difficult or impossible to measure, because of the nature of the benefit sought. (For example, measuring the benefit conferred on society, and on the individual workers, by an employer hiring disadvantaged workers would necessarily be subjective.) Nonetheless, Professor Calvin Johnson argues forcefully that, at least at present, tax incentives are extremely inefficient.

In large part, Professor Johnson bases his argument on the yields of tax-exempt bonds, because there, we can measure rather accurately the efficiency of the subsidy. Section 103 excludes from federal tax the interest on many state and local bonds. If a taxable bond yields 10 percent and an equivalent (considering such things as risk and liquidity) state bond yields 8 percent, this suggests that the investor is paying an "implicit tax" of 20 percent—the investor is voluntarily forfeiting 20 percent of yield in order to avoid taxation. This is a measure of efficiency because "[t]he implicit tax represents the only public return from the exemption system, in the form of cheaper costs for states and localities. The rest of the cost of the exemption is lost in terms of the purpose of the exemption, a cost without any delivered benefit."[c] Purchasing the state bond under the interest rates described would make sense only for a taxpayer whose marginal tax rate exceeded 20 percent. The governmental benefit (aiding the state) and the cost (foregone revenue) can both be measured accurately. If a taxpayer in the 35 percent bracket purchased a tax-exempt $1,000 bond under the interest rates assumed above, the federal Government would lose $35 in foregone revenue ($100 taxable interest x 35 percent) while the state would benefit to the extent of $20 in saved interest. (Note that the exclusion would be ideally efficient if the market drove the rate of the tax-exempt bond to 6.5 percent—this would mean that taxpayers in the top bracket (35 percent) would be indifferent between the taxable and tax-exempt investment, and that all foregone federal revenue

---

c. Calvin H. Johnson, *A Thermometer for the Tax System: The Overall Health of the Tax System as Measured by Implicit Tax*, 56 SMU L. Rev. 13, 14 (2003).

would have been diverted to the intended beneficiary, the state, in the form of lower interest expense.)

Professor Johnson reports that the implicit tax on tax-exempt bonds "has been dropping in recent years, and is modest under current conditions, lower at times than the lowest statutory tax bracket of 10%."[d] Professor Johnson argues that the significance of this finding goes well beyond tax-exempt bonds. The low implicit rate on tax-exempt bonds indicates that investors find it easy to avoid taxes, and therefore are not willing to forego much income in order to achieve tax exemption. For this reason, Professor Johnson concludes that the use of tax incentives should be sharply curtailed and our generally porous tax system repaired:

> More generally, the modesty of the implicit tax means that there is a need for general repairs of the federal tax base. The demand for tax avoidance that would settle the implicit tax at the top statutory rate is swamped, not just by § 103 bonds, but by other investments that Congress has attempted to subsidize by giving or preserving a tax advantage. Congress, for instance, gives or expands the tax benefits of qualified pension funds or houses, and thousands of other things, by giving tax deductions that do not reflect economic cost or by giving exclusions for economic benefits.

> With implicit tax so low, however, the use of the tax system for incentive or subsidy is no longer responsible. The loss to the system in cost is far higher than the benefit delivered. * * *

> The low implicit taxes indicate that the existing rates are fictive, or at least voluntary, for well-advised taxpayers. If they faced more than a paper tiger from the tax system, generally they would pay higher implicit tax. Reducing the rates and repairing the tax base would reduce the harm inflicted by the tax system.[e]

2. Much earlier, reports Dr. Gerard Brannon (in an article excerpted in Chapter Seventeen, at page 1104), the granddaddy of incentive tax provisions, the investment tax credit, had been condemned as inefficient: "That credit [ITC] operates like a uniform reduction in the price of equipment but in truth the price of equipment hasn't been reduced. Leading investors to think that equipment is cheaper than it is will distort investment. * * * When capital seems very cheap one tends to waste it."[f]

---

d. *Id.* at 13.

e. *Id.* at 51-52.

f. Gerard M. Brannon, *Some Economics of Tax Reform*, 39 NAT'L TAX J. 277, 277 (1986).

3.   Do the preceding notes lead you to think that the best form for incentive tax expenditures to take is that they not be employed at all? Consider this question throughout the chapter, keeping in mind that no government program—whether tax expenditure or direct expenditure—works with perfect efficiency.

B. TAX EXPENDITURES DESCRIBED AND DEFENDED

As noted above, since 1974 Congress has required the annual compilation and quantification of tax expenditures. The first excerpt below is the Office of Management and Budget's Fiscal Year 2004 explanation of the tax expenditures concept in operation. In terms of tax policy, this document is of considerable interest in at least two distinct ways. First, a perusal of the pages of tax expenditures gives a sense of the breadth and magnitude of tax expenditures, each of which could be evaluated in terms of its policy justification. But more broadly, the accompanying document makes clear the complexity and uncertainty of the entire concept of tax expenditures and the tax expenditure budget. The concept of tax expenditures requires a "baseline" from which the "special" provision departs; the baseline is not always clear, however. Of particular interest is the Appendix, in which, for the first time, OMB undertook additional computations of tax expenditures assuming either of two "baselines"—a "comprehensive" (or Haig-Simons) income tax baseline, and a consumption tax baseline—each quite different from the baseline thought to underlie our present tax structure. The Appendix also examines an aspect of the issue ignored in traditional tax *expenditure* analysis—a focus on "negative tax expenditures," those instances in which deviations from the norm increase, rather than reduce, the burden on taxpayers.

A related issue is whether it matters, in the real world, whether a given tax provision is classified as a part of the "normal" tax structure or as a "tax expenditure." In one sense, the classification is only an academic exercise—dollars saved from a lower tax burden spend just as well whether the lower tax burden results from a tax expenditure or not. On the other hand, classification as a tax expenditure raises the political exposure of a tax provision. If the provision is viewed as part of the "normal" system, it is less subject to attack than if it is viewed as an "expenditure," which should have to compete for limited federal dollars in a political environment in which it is never possible to spend as many dollars as Congress might wish.

In the second excerpt, Professor Edward Zelinsky, who has written extensively about tax expenditures, takes on the presumption that tax expenditures are in some sense illegitimate. Professor Surrey (and many others following his lead), while acknowledging that tax provisions *could* be as carefully crafted as direct expenditure measures, clearly thought that the direct expenditure process was generally to be preferred. Obvious arguments support a preference for the use of direct expenditures. After all, direct expenditures are enacted through a legislative process centering on substantive congressional committees rather than the less-expert House Ways and Means Committee and Senate Finance Commitee, and are administered by agencies with subject matter expertise rather than the Internal Revenue Service. Professor Zelinsky argues that appearances can be deceiving, and that the tax expenditure process may offer significant advantages.

ANALYTICAL PERSPECTIVES
BUDGET OF THE UNITED STATES GOVERNMENT
FISCAL YEAR 2004
Office of Management and Budget
Pages 101-05, 110-12, 115-17, 130-35, 138-40 (2003)

Tax Expenditures

The Congressional Budget Act of 1974 (Public Law 93–344) requires that a list of "tax expenditures" be included in the budget. Tax expenditures are defined in the law as "revenue losses attributable to provisions of the Federal tax laws which allow a special exclusion, exemption, or deduction from gross income or which provide a special credit, a preferential rate of tax, or a deferral of liability." These exceptions may be viewed as alternatives to other policy instruments, such as spending or regulatory programs. Identification and measurement of tax expenditures depends importantly on the baseline tax system against which the actual tax system is compared.

* * *

Each tax expenditure estimate in this chapter was calculated assuming other parts of the tax code remained unchanged. The estimates would be different if all tax expenditures or major groups of tax expenditures were changed simultaneously because of potential interactions among provisions. For that reason, this chapter does not present a grand total for the estimated tax expenditures. Moreover, past tax changes entailing broad elimination of tax expenditures were generally accompanied by changes in tax rates or other basic provisions, so that the net effects on Federal revenues were considerably (if not totally) offset.

Tax expenditures relating to the individual and corporate income taxes are estimated for fiscal years 2002–2008 using three methods of accounting: revenue effects, outlay equivalent, and present value. The present value approach provides estimates of the cumulative revenue effects for tax expenditures that involve deferrals of tax payments into the future or have similar long-term effects

* * *

The 2003 Budget included a discussion of important ambiguities in the tax expenditure concept and indicated that the Treasury Department had begun a review of the tax expenditure presentation. Particular attention of this review has focused on defining tax expenditures relative to a comprehensive income baseline, defining tax expenditures relative to a broad-based consumption tax baseline, and defining negative tax expenditures, i.e., provisions of current law that overtax certain items or activities. The Appendix presents the results from the preliminary stage of this review.

Tax Expenditures in the Income Tax

Tax Expenditure Estimates

All tax expenditure estimates presented here are based upon current tax law enacted as of December 31, 2002. Expired or repealed provisions are not listed if their revenue effects result only from taxpayer activity occurring before fiscal year 2002. * * *

The total revenue effects for tax expenditures for fiscal years 2002–2008 are displayed according to the budget's functional categories in Table 6–1[g]. * * * As in prior years, two baseline concepts—the normal tax baseline and the reference tax law baseline—are used to identify tax expenditures. For the most part, the two concepts coincide. However, items treated as tax expenditures under the normal tax baseline, but not the reference tax law baseline, are indicated by the designation "normal tax method" in the tables. The revenue effects for these indicated items are zero using the reference tax rules. The alternative baseline concepts are discussed in detail [below]

* * *

Table 6–3 ranks the major tax expenditures by the size of their 2004–2008 revenue effect.

Interpreting Tax Expenditure Estimates

The estimates shown for individual tax expenditures * * * do not necessarily equal the increase in Federal revenues (or the change in the budget balance) that would result from repealing these special provisions, for the following reasons:

(1) Eliminating a tax expenditure may have incentive effects that alter economic behavior. * * * For example, if capital gains were taxed at ordinary rates, capital gain realizations would be expected to decline, potentially resulting in a decline in tax receipts. Such behavioral effects are not reflected in the estimates.

---

g. For clarity of presentation, Table 6-1 as excerpted below provides data for the years 2004-08. (Ed.)

Table 6-1.   ESTIMATES OF TOTAL INCOME TAX EXPENDITURES

(in millions of dollars)

	Total from corporations and Individuals					
	2004	2005	2006	2007	2008	2004-08
National Defense:						
Exclusion of benefits and allowances to armed forces personnel	2,240	2,260	2,290	2,310	2,330	11,430
International Affairs:						
Exclusion of income earned abroad by U.S. citizens	2,680	2,750	2,810	2,940	3,100	14,280
Exclusion of certain allowances for Federal employees abroad	840	880	930	980	1,030	4,660
Extraterritorial income exclusion	5,510	5,890	6,290	6,730	7,200	31,620
Inventory property sales source rules exception	1,620	1,700	1,790	1,880	1,980	8,970
Deferral of income from controlled foreign corporations (normal tax method)	7,900	8,400	8,930	9,550	10,210	44,990
Deferred taxes for financial firms on certain income earned overseas	2,130	2,190	2,260	960	0	7,540
General Science, Space and Technology:						
Expensing of research and experimentation expenditures (normal tax method)	2,760	3,390	3,990	4,270	4,380	18,790
Credit for increasing research activities	4,990	2,910	1,240	520	170	9,830
Energy:						
Expensing of exploration and development costs, fuels	150	80	60	40	30	360
Excess of percentage over cost depletion, fuels	650	610	620	640	650	3,170
Alternative fuel production credit	520	520	520	520	210	2,290
Exception from passive loss limitation for working interests in oil and gas properties	10	10	10	10	10	50
Capital gains treatment of royalties on coal	110	120	120	130	140	620
Exclusion of interest on energy facility bonds	130	140	140	150	160	720
Enhanced oil recovery credit	350	360	360	370	390	1,830
New technology credit	250	270	270	270	270	1,330
Alcohol fuel credit[1]	30	30	30	30	30	150
Tax credit and deduction for clean-fuel burning	70	40	−10	−70	−70	−40
Exclusion from income of conservation subsidies provided by public utilities	80	80	80	80	80	400
Natural Resources and Environment:						
Expensing of exploration and development costs, nonfuel minerals	30	30	30	40	40	170
Excess of percentage over cost depletion, nonfuel minerals	270	280	290	290	300	1,430
Exclusion of interest on bond for water, sewage, and hazardous waste facilities	540	580	610	650	680	3,060
Capital gains treatment of certain timber income	110	120	120	130	140	620
Expensing of multiperiod timber growing costs .	380	380	400	410	410	1,980
Tax incentives for preservation of historic structures	230	240	250	260	280	1,260
Agriculture:						
Expensing of certain capital outlays	170	170	170	170	190	870
Expensing of certain multiperiod production costs	120	120	120	120	120	600
Treatment of loans forgiven for solvent farmers .	10	10	10	10	10	50
Capital gains treatment of certain income	1,120	1,180	1,250	1,310	1,380	6,240
Income averaging for farmers	80	80	80	90	90	420
Deferral of gain on sale of farm refiners	10	10	10	10	20	60

1. In addition, the partial exemption from the excise tax for alcohol fuels results in a reduction in excise tax receipts (in millions of dollars) as follows: 2002 $1,070; 2003 $1,140; 2004 $1,230; 2005 $1,320; 2006 $1,370; 2007 $1,400; and 2008 $1,430.

	Total from corporations and Individuals					
	2004	2005	2006	2007	2008	2004-08
Commerce and Housing:						
Financial institutions and insurance:						
Exemption of credit union income	1,160	1,240	1,320	1,410	1,510	6,640
Excess bad debt reserves of financial institutions	0	0	0	0	0	0
Exclusion of interest on life insurance savings .	20,740	22,470	24,390	26,350	28,310	122,260
Special alternative tax on small property and casualty insurance companies	10	10	10	10	10	50
Tax exemption of certain insurance companies owned by tax-exempt organizations	240	250	270	280	290	1,330
Small life insurance company deduction	100	100	100	100	100	500
Housing:						
Exclusion of interest on owner-occupied mortgage subsidy bonds	1,050	1,140	1,210	1,270	1,360	6,030
Exclusion of interest on rental housing bonds ..	220	240	250	260	280	1,250
Deductibility of mortgage interest on owner-occupied homes	68,440	71,870	74,790	78,160	82,650	375,910
Deductibility of State and local property tax on owner-occupied homes	22,160	19,750	16,240	14,580	13,580	86,310
Deferral of income from post 1987 installment sales	1,100	1,120	1,140	1,160	1,190	5,710
Capital gains exclusion on home sales	20,860	21,490	22,140	22,800	23,480	110,770
Exception from passive loss rules for $25,000 of rental loss	4,920	4,600	4,290	4,020	3,790	21,620
Credit for low-income housing investments	3,640	3,820	3,990	4,160	4,360	19,970
Accelerated depreciation on rental housing (normal tax method)	310	−520	−1,770	−3,310	−4,570	−9,860
Commerce:						
Cancellation of indebtedness	30	50	60	60	50	250
Exceptions from imputed interest rules	50	50	50	50	50	250
Capital gains (except agriculture, timber, iron ore, and coal) (normal tax method)	53,930	54,550	49,870	49,760	51,450	259,560
Capital gains exclusion of small corporation stock	160	210	250	300	350	1,270
Step-up basis of capital gains at death	28,500	29,630	30,490	31,370	32,390	152,380
Carryover basis of capital gains on gifts	450	540	640	650	630	2,910
Ordinary income treatment of loss from small business corporation stock sale	50	50	50	50	50	250
Accelerated depreciation of buildings other than rental housing (normal tax method)	−1,980	−6,520	−9,200	−12,360	−15,820	−45,880
Accelerated depreciation of machinery and equipment (normal tax method)	16,670	−39,310	−35,260	−33,260	−31,570	−122,730
Expensing of certain small investments (normal tax method)	370	1,570	1,830	1,510	1,380	6,660
Amortization of start-up costs (normal tax method)	150	160	160	170	170	810
Graduated corporation income tax rate (normal tax method)	5,700	5,880	6,100	6,350	6,640	30,670
Exclusion of interest on small issue bonds	400	430	450	470	510	2,260
Transportation:						
Deferral of tax on shipping companies	20	20	20	20	20	100

	Total from corporations and individuals					
	2004	2005	2006	2007	2008	2004-08
Exclusion of reimbursed employee parking expenses	2,290	2,410	2,540	2,680	2,810	12,730
Exclusion for employer-provided transit passes .	380	450	530	600	670	2,630
Community and regional development:						
Investment credit for rehabilitation of structures (other than historic)	30	30	30	30	30	150
Exclusion of interest for airport, dock and similar bonds	830	890	950	1,000	1,060	4,730
Exemption of certain mutuals' and cooperatives' income	60	70	70	70	70	340
Empowerment zones, Enterprise communities, and Renewal communities	1,170	1,280	1,410	1,580	1,750	7,190
New markets tax credit	290	430	610	830	870	3,030
Expensing of environmental remediation costs .	20	–10	–10	–10	–10	–20
Education, Training, Employment, and Social Services:						
Education:						
Exclusion of scholarship and fellowship income (normal tax method)	1,260	1,340	1,400	1,410	1,420	6,830
HOPE tax credit	2,880	2,930	2,730	2,900	2,790	14,230
Lifetime Learning tax credit	2,980	2,840	2,610	2,820	2,860	14,110
Education Individual Retirement Accounts	160	240	330	440	560	1,730
Deductibility of student-loan interest	660	680	700	720	720	3,480
Deduction for higher education expenses	2,880	3,620	2,940	0	0	9,440
State prepaid tuition plans	400	470	560	660	750	2,840
Exclusion of interest on student loan bonds	290	310	340	350	370	1,660
Exclusion of interest on bonds for private nonprofit educational facilities	700	760	810	850	900	4,020
Credit for holders of zone academy bonds	90	100	100	100	100	490
Exclusion of interest on savings bonds redeemed to finance educational expenses	10	10	10	20	20	70
Parental personal exemption for students age 19 or over	3,230	2,690	2,020	1,670	1,470	11,080
Deductibility of charitable contributions (education)	4,350	4,640	4,820	4,970	5,230	24,010
Exclusion of employer provided educational assistance	520	550	580	610	650	2,910
Training, employment, and social services:						
Work opportunity tax credit	430	190	80	40	20	760
Welfare-to-work tax credit	80	60	40	20	10	210
Employer-provided child care exclusion	760	810	850	890	940	4,250
Employer-provided child care credit	130	140	150	160	170	750
Assistance for adopted foster children	290	330	380	430	480	1,910
Adoption credit and exclusion	450	500	540	560	570	2,620
Exclusion of employee meals and lodging (other than military)	810	850	890	930	970	4,450
Child credit[2]	21,310	22,480	24,280	23,940	23,660	115,670

2. The figures in the table indicate the effect of the child tax credit on receipts. The effect of the credit on outlays (in millions of dollars) is as follows: 2002 $5,060; 2003 $5,870; 2004 $5,860; 2005 $5,700; 2006 $7,630; 2007 $7,630; and 2008 $7,500.

	Total from corporations and Individuals					
	2004	2005	2006	2007	2008	2004-08
Credit for child and dependent care expenses	3,230	2,860	2,380	2,190	2,050	12,710
Credit for disabled access expenditures	50	60	60	60	60	290
Deductibility of charitable contributions, other than education and health	33,990	35,710	37,360	38,780	41,160	187,000
Exclusion of certain foster care payments	430	440	450	460	470	2,250
Exclusion of parsonage allowances	400	420	450	480	510	2,260
Health:						
Exclusion of employer contributions for medical insurance premiums and medical care	120,160	132,240	144,710	157,180	170,230	724,520
Self-employed medical insurance premiums	3,690	3,940	4,220	4,520	4,980	21,350
Workers' compensation insurance premiums	6,190	6,630	7,020	7,490	8,000	35,330
Medical Savings Accounts	30	30	30	30	20	140
Deductibility of medical expenses	6,340	6,490	6,610	6,980	7,380	33,800
Exclusion of interest on hospital construction bonds	1,440	1,560	1,660	1,740	1,850	8,250
Deductibility of charitable contributions (health)	4,580	4,900	5,070	5,220	5,490	25,260
Tax credit for orphan drug research	180	200	220	250	280	1,130
Special Blue Cross/Blue Shield deduction	310	300	270	300	250	1,430
Tax credit for health insurance purchased by certain displaced and retired individuals	60	30	40	50	60	240
Income security:						
Exclusion of railroad retirement system benefits	400	400	400	400	400	2,000
Exclusion of workmen's compensation benefits .	6,460	6,850	7,270	7,710	8,190	36,480
Exclusion of public assistance benefits (normal tax method)	410	430	450	470	440	2,200
Exclusion of special benefits for disabled coal miners	60	50	50	50	40	250
Exclusion of military disability pensions	120	120	130	130	140	640
Net exclusion of pension contributions and earnings:	0	0	0	0	0	0
Employer plans	67,870	70,540	73,200	67,500	61,440	340,550
401(k) plans	55,290	57,830	61,490	65,060	68,030	307,700
Individual Retirement Plans	23,130	22,400	22,380	20,540	19,800	108,250
Low and moderate income savers credit	1,860	1,670	1,510	850	0	5,890
Keogh plans	7,616	7,904	8,166	8,402	9,196	41,284
Exclusion of other employee benefits:	0	0	0	0	0	0
Premiums on group term life insurance	1,830	1,860	1,890	1,920	1,950	9,450
Premiums on accident and disability insurance	240	250	260	270	280	1,300
Small business retirement plan credit	40	50	50	60	60	260
Income of trusts to finance supplementary unemployment benefits	30	30	30	30	30	150
Special ESOP rules	1,790	1,890	1,990	2,090	2,200	9,960
Additional deduction for the blind	40	40	40	40	40	200
Additional deduction for the elderly	2,050	2,120	2,180	2,110	2,030	10,490
Tax credit for the elderly and disabled	20	20	10	10	10	70
Deductibility of casualty losses	420	440	460	500	540	2,360

	Total from corporations and individuals					
	2004	2005	2006	2007	2008	2004-08
Earned income credit[3]	5,090	5,280	5,410	5,580	5,790	27,150
Social Security:						
Exclusion of social security benefits:						
Social Security benefits for retired workers	18,930	19,210	20,000	21,100	21,550	100,790
Social Security benefits for disabled	3,570	3,950	4,360	4,870	4,390	21,140
Social Security benefits for dependents and survivors	4,140	4,360	4,590	4,920	4,820	22,830
Veterans benefits and services:						
Exclusion of veterans death benefits and disability compensation	3,400	3,590	3,780	3,980	4,190	18,940
Exclusion of veterans pensions	80	90	90	90	100	450
Exclusion of GI bill benefits	90	100	100	110	110	510
Exclusion of interest on veterans housing bonds	50	50	50	60	60	270
General purpose fiscal assistance:						
Exclusion of interest on public purpose State and local bonds	27,310	27,720	27,810	27,530	28,360	138,730
Deductibility of nonbusiness State and local taxes other than on owner-occupied homes	50,910	47,770	40,480	37,190	36,080	212,430
Tax credit for corporations receiving income from doing business in U.S. possessions	2,240	2,200	1,300	0	0	5,740
Interest:						
Deferral of interest on savings bonds	670	750	840	920	1,050	4,230
Addendum—Aid to State and local governments:						
Deductibility of:						
Property taxes on owner-occupied homes	22,160	19,750	16,240	14,580	13,580	86,310
Nonbusiness State and local taxes other than on owner-occupied homes	50,910	47,770	40,480	37,190	36,080	212,430
Exclusion of interest on State and local bonds for:						
Public purposes	27,310	27,720	27,810	27,530	28,360	138,730
Energy facilities	130	140	140	150	160	720
Water, sewage, and hazardous waste disposal facilities	540	580	610	650	680	3,060
Small issues	400	430	450	470	510	2,260
Owner-occupied mortgage revenue subsidies	1,050	1,140	1,210	1,270	1,360	6,030
Rental housing	220	240	250	260	280	1,250
Airports, docks, and similar facilities	830	890	950	1,000	1,060	4,730
Student loans	290	310	340	350	370	1,660
Private nonprofit educational facilities	700	760	810	850	900	4,020
Hospital construction	1,440	1,560	1,660	1,740	1,850	8,250
Veterans' housing	50	50	50	60	60	270
Credit for holders of zone academy bonds	90	100	100	100	100	490

Note: Provisions with estimates denoted normal tax method have no revenue loss under the reference tax law method. All estimates have been rounded to the nearest $10 million. Provisions with estimates that rounded to zero in each year are not included in the table.

---

3. The figures in the table indicate the effect of the earned income tax credit on receipts. The effect of the credit on outlays (in millions of dollars) is as follows: 2002 $27,830; 2003 $30,610; 2004 $31,380; 2005 $32,090; 2006 $33,450; 2007 $34,480; and 2008 $35,380.

(2) Tax expenditures are interdependent even without incentive effects. Repeal of a tax expenditure provision can increase or decrease the tax revenues associated with other provisions. For example, even if behavior does not change, repeal of an itemized deduction could increase the revenue costs from other deductions because some taxpayers would be moved into higher tax brackets. Alternatively, repeal of an itemized deduction could lower the revenue cost from other deductions if taxpayers are led to claim the standard deduction instead of itemizing. Similarly, if two provisions were repealed simultaneously, the increase in tax liability could be greater or less than the sum of the two separate tax expenditures, because each is estimated assuming that the other remains in force. * * *

The annual value of tax expenditures for tax deferrals is reported on a cash basis in all tables except Table 6–4. Cash-based estimates reflect the difference between taxes deferred in the current year and incoming revenues that are received due to deferrals of taxes from prior years. Although such estimates are useful as a measure of cash flows into the Government, they do not accurately reflect the true economic cost of these provisions. For example, for a provision where activity levels have changed, so that incoming tax receipts from past deferrals are greater than deferred receipts from new activity, the cash-basis tax expenditure estimate can be negative, despite the fact that in present-value terms current deferrals do have a real cost to the Government. Alternatively, in the case of a newly enacted deferral provision, a cash-based estimate can overstate the real effect on receipts to the Government because the newly deferred taxes will ultimately be received. Present-value estimates, which are a useful complement to the cash-basis estimates for provisions involving deferrals, are discussed below.

Present-Value Estimates

Discounted present-value estimates of revenue effects are presented in Table 6–4 for certain provisions that involve tax deferrals or other long-term revenue effects. These estimates complement the cash-based tax expenditure estimates presented in the other tables.

The present-value estimates represent the revenue effects, net of future tax payments, that follow from activities undertaken during calendar year 2002 which cause the deferrals or other long-term revenue effects. For instance, a pension contribution in 2002 would cause a deferral of tax payments on wages in 2002 and on pension earnings on this contribution (e.g., interest) in later years. In some future year, however, the 2002 pension contribution and accrued earnings will be paid out and taxes will be due; these receipts are included in the present-value estimate. * * *

Tax Expenditure Baselines

A tax expenditure is an exception to baseline provisions of the tax structure. The 1974 Congressional Budget Act, which mandated the tax expenditure budget, did not specify the baseline provisions of the tax law. As noted previously, deciding whether provisions are exceptions, therefore, is a

Table 6-3. INCOME TAX EXPENDITURES RANKED BY TOTAL 2004-2008
PROJECTED REVENUE EFFECT
(In millions of dollars)

Provision	2004	2004-08
Exclusion of employer contributions for medical insurance premiums and medical care	120,160	724,520
Deductibility of mortgage interest on owner-occupied homes	68,440	375,910
Net exclusion of pension contributions and earnings: Employer plans	67,870	340,550
Net exclusion of pension contributions and earnings: 401(k) plans	55,290	307,700
Capital gains (except agriculture, timber, iron ore, and coal) (normal tax method)	53,930	259,560
Deductibility of nonbusiness state and local taxes other than on owner-occupied homes	50,910	212,430
Deductibility of charitable contributions, other than education and health	33,990	187,000
Step-up basis of capital gains at death	28,500	152,380
Exclusion of interest on public purpose State and local bonds	27,310	138,730
Exclusion of interest on life insurance savings	20,740	122,260
Child credit	21,310	115,670
Capital gains exclusion on home sales	20,860	110,770
Net exclusion of pension contributions and earnings: individual Retirement Accounts	23,130	108,250
Social Security benefits for retired workers	18,930	100,790
Deductibility of State and local property tax on owner-occupied homes	22,160	86,310
Deferral of income from controlled foreign corporations (normal tax method)	7,900	44,990
Net exclusion of pension contributions and earnings: Keough Plans	7,616	41,284
Exclusion of workers' compensation benefits	6,460	36,480
Workers' compensation insurance premiums	6,190	35,330
Deductibility of medical expenses	6,340	33,800
Extraterritorial income exclusion	5,510	31,620
Graduated corporation income tax rate (normal tax method)	5,700	30,670
Earned income tax credit	5,090	27,150
Deductibility of charitable contributions (health)	4,580	25,260
Deductibility of charitable contributions (education)	4,350	24,010
Social Security benefits for dependents and survivors	4,140	22,830
Exception from passive loss rules for $25,000 of rental loss	4,920	21,620
Self-employed medical insurance premiums	3,690	21,350
Social Security benefits for disabled	3,570	21,140
Credit for low-income housing investments	3,640	19,970
Exclusion of veterans death benefits and disability compensation	3,400	18,940
Expensing of research and experimentation expenditures (normal tax method)	2,760	18,790
Exclusion of income earned abroad by U.S. citizens	2,680	14,280
HOPE tax credit	2,880	14,230
Lifetime Learning tax credit	2,980	14,110
Exclusion of reimbursed employee parking expenses	2,290	12,730
Credit for child and dependent care expenses	3,230	12,710
Exclusion of benefits and allowances to armed forces personnel	2,240	11,430
Parental personal exemption for students age 19 or over	3,230	11,080
Additional deduction for the elderly	2,050	10,490
Special ESOP rules	1,790	9,960
Credit for increasing research activities	4,990	9,830
Premiums on group term life insurance	1,830	9,450
Deduction for higher education expenses	2,880	9,440

Provision	2004	2004-08
Inventory property sales source rules exception	1,620	8,970
Exclusion of interest on hospital construction bonds	1,440	8,250
Deferred taxes for financial firms on certain income earned overseas	2,130	7,540
Empowerment zones, Enterprise communities, and Renewal communities	1,170	7,190
Exclusion of scholarship and fellowship income (normal tax method)	1,260	6,830
Expensing of certain small investments (normal tax method)	370	6,660
Exemption of credit union income	1,160	6,640
Capital gains treatment of certain income	1,120	6,240
Exclusion of interest on owner-occupied mortgage subsidy bonds	1,050	6,030
Low and moderate income savers credit	1,860	5,890
Tax credit for corporations receiving income from doing business in U.S. possessions	2,240	5,740
Deferral of income from post 1987 installment sales	1,100	5,710
Exclusion of interest for airport, dock, and similar bonds	830	4,730
Exclusion of certain allowances for Federal employees abroad	840	4,660
Exclusion of employee meals and lodging (other than military)	810	4,450
Employer provided child care exclusion	760	4,250
Exclusion of interest on bonds for private nonprofit education facilities	700	4,020
Deferral of interest on U.S. savings bonds	670	4,230
Deductibility of student-loan interest	660	3,480
Excess of percentage over cost depletion, fuels	650	3,170
Exclusion of interest on bonds for water, sewage, and hazardous waste facilities	540	3,060
New markets tax credit	290	3,030
Exclusion of employer-provided educational assistance	520	2,910
Carryover basis of capital gains on gifts	450	2,910
State prepaid tuition plans	400	2,840
Exclusion for employer-provided transit passes	380	2,630
Adoption credit and exclusion	450	2,620
Deductibility of casualty losses	420	2,360
Alternative fuel production credit	520	2,290
Exclusion of interest on small issue bonds	400	2,260
Exclusion of parsonage allowances	400	2,260
Exclusion of certain foster care payments	430	2,250
Exclusion of public assistance benefits (normal tax method)	410	2,200
Exclusion of railroad retirement system benefits	400	2,000
Expensing of multiperiod timber growing costs	380	1,980
Assistance for adopted foster children	290	1,910
Enhanced oil recovery credit	350	1,830
Education Individual Retirement Accounts	160	1,730
Exclusion of interest on student-loan bonds	290	1,660
Special Blue Cross/Blue Shield deduction	310	1,430
Excess of percentage over cost depletion, nonfuel minerals	270	1,430
New technology credit	250	1,330
Tax exemption of certain insurance companies owned by tax-exempt organizations	240	1,330
Premiums on accident and disability insurance	240	1,300
Capital gains exclusion of small corporation stock	160	1,270
Tax incentives for preservation of historic structures	230	1,260
Exclusion of interest on rental housing bonds	220	1,250

Provision	2004	2004-08
Tax credit for orphan drug research	180	1,130
Expensing of certain capital outlays	170	870
Amortization of start-up costs (normal tax method)	150	810
Work opportunity tax credit	430	760
Employer-provided child care credit	130	750
Exclusion of interest on energy facility bonds	130	720
Exclusion of military disability pensions	120	640
Capital gains treatment of royalties on coal	110	620
Capital gains treatment of certain timber income	110	620
Expensing of certain multiperiod production costs	120	600
Exclusion of GI bill benefits	90	510
Small life insurance company deduction	100	500
Credit for holders of zone academy bonds	90	490
Exclusion of veterans pensions	80	450
Income averaging for farmers	80	420
Exclusion from income of conservation subsidies provided by public utilities	80	400
Expensing of exploration and development costs, fuels	150	360
Exemption of certain mutuals' and cooperatives' income	60	340
Credit for disabled access expenditures	50	290
Exclusion of interest on veterans housing bonds	50	270
Small business retirement plan credit	40	260
Exclusion of special benefits for disabled coal miners	60	250
Exceptions from imputed interest rules	50	250
Ordinary income treatment of loss from small business corporation stock sale	50	250
Cancellation of indebtedness	30	250
Tax credit for health insurance purchased by certain displaced and retired individuals	60	240
Welfare-to-work tax credit	80	210
Additional deduction for the blind	40	200
Expensing of exploration and development costs, nonfuel minerals	30	170
Alcohol fuel credits	30	150
Income of trusts to finance supplementary unemployment benefits	30	150
Investment credit for rehabilitation of structures (other than historic)	30	150
Medical Savings Accounts	30	140
Deferral of tax on shipping companies	20	100
Tax credit for the elderly and disabled	20	70
Exclusion of interest on savings bonds redeemed to finance educational expenses	10	70
Deferral of gain on sale of farm refiners	10	60
Exception from passive loss limitation for working interests in oil and gas properties	10	50
Treatment of loans forgiven for solvent farmers	10	50
Special alternative tax on small property and casualty insurance companies	10	50
Expensing of environmental remediation costs	20	−20
Tax credit and deduction for clean-fuel burning vehicles	70	−40
Accelerated depreciation on rental housing (normal tax method)	1,080	−4,570
Accelerated depreciation of buildings other than rental housing (normal tax method)	−2,530	−15,820
Accelerated depreciation of machinery and equipment (normal tax method)	31,110	−31,570

matter of judgment. As in prior years, this year's tax expenditure estimates are presented using two baselines: the normal tax baseline and the reference tax law baseline. The normal tax baseline is patterned on a comprehensive income tax, which defines income as the sum of consumption and the change in net wealth in a given period of time. The normal tax baseline allows personal exemptions, a standard deduction, and deductions of the expenses incurred in earning income. It is not limited to a particular structure of tax rates, or by a specific definition of the taxpaying unit. The reference tax law baseline is also patterned on a comprehensive income tax, but it is closer to existing law. Tax expenditures under the reference law baseline are always tax expenditures under the normal tax baseline, but the reverse is not always true. Both the normal and reference tax baselines allow several major departures from a pure comprehensive income tax. For example:

• Income is taxable only when it is realized in exchange. Thus, neither the deferral of tax on unrealized capital gains nor the tax exclusion of imputed income (such as the rental value of owner-occupied housing or farmers' consumption of their own produce) is regarded as a tax expenditure. Imputed income would be taxed under a comprehensive income tax, and all income would be taxed as it accrued.

Table 6-4. PRESENT VALUE OF SELECTED TAX EXPENDITURES FOR ACTIVITY IN CALENDAR YEAR 2002
(In millions of dollars)

Provision	Present Value of Revenue Loss
Deferral of income from controlled foreign corporations (normal tax method)	7,180
Deferred taxes for financial forms on income earned overseas	1,740
Expensing of research and experimentation expenditures (normal tax method)	1,800
Expensing of exploration and development costs—fuels	140
Expensing of exploration and development costs–nonfuels	10
Expensing of multiperiod timber growing costs	210
Expensing of certain multiperiod production costs—agriculture	240
Expensing of certain capital outlays—agriculture	270
Deferral of income on life insurance and annuity contracts	24,210
Expensing of certain small investments (normal tax method)	700
Amortization of start-up costs (normal tax method)	30
Deferral of tax on shipping companies	20
Credit for holders of zone academy bonds	120
Credit for low-income housing investments	3,580
Deferral for state prepaid tuition plans	590
Exclusion of pension contributions—employer plans	90,570
Exclusion of 401(k) contributions	81,000
Exclusion of IRA contributions and earnings	10,650
Exclusion of contributions and earnings for Keogh plans	9,290
Exclusion of interest on public-purpose bond	23,560
Exclusion of interest on non-public purpose bonds	6,070
Deferral of interest on U.S. savings bonds	470

• There is a separate corporation income tax. Under a comprehensive income tax, corporate income would be taxed only once—at the shareholder level, whether or not distributed in the form of dividends. * * *

• Values of assets and debt are not generally adjusted for inflation. A comprehensive income tax would adjust the cost basis of capital assets and debt for changes in the price level during the time the assets or debt are held. Thus, under a comprehensive income tax baseline, the failure to take account of inflation in measuring depreciation, capital gains, and interest income would be regarded as a negative tax expenditure (i.e., a tax penalty), and failure to take account of inflation in measuring interest costs would be regarded as a positive tax expenditure (i.e., a tax subsidy).

Although the reference law and normal tax baselines are generally similar, areas of difference include:

(1) *Tax rates*. The separate schedules applying to the various taxpaying units are included in the reference law baseline. Thus, corporate tax rates below the maximum statutory rate do not give rise to a tax expenditure. The normal tax baseline is similar, except that it specifies the current maximum rate as the baseline for the corporate income tax. The lower tax rates applied to the first $10 million of corporate income are thus regarded as a tax expenditure. Similarly, under the reference law baseline, preferential tax rates for capital gains generally do not yield a tax expenditure; only capital gains treatment of otherwise "ordinary income," such as that from coal and iron ore royalties and the sale of timber and certain agricultural products, is considered a tax expenditure. The alternative minimum tax is treated as part of the baseline rate structure under both the reference and normal tax methods.

(2) *Income subject to the tax*. * * * Under the reference tax rules, * * * gross income does not include gifts defined as receipts of money or property that are not consideration in an exchange—or most transfer payments, which can be thought of as gifts from the Government.[1] The normal tax baseline also excludes gifts between individuals from gross income. Under the normal tax baseline, however, all cash transfer payments from the Government to private individuals are counted in gross income, and exemptions of such transfers from tax are identified as tax expenditures. The costs of earning income are generally deductible in determining taxable income under both the reference and normal tax baselines.

(3) *Capital recovery*. Under the reference tax law baseline no tax expenditures arise from accelerated depreciation. Under the normal tax baseline, the depreciation allowance for property is computed using estimates of economic depreciation. * * *

---

1. Gross income does, however, include transfer payments associated with past employment, such as Social Security benefits

(4) *Treatment of foreign income.* Both the normal and reference tax baselines allow a tax credit for foreign income taxes paid (up to the amount of U.S. income taxes that would otherwise be due), which prevents double taxation of income earned abroad. * * *

Performance Measures and the Economic Effects of Tax Expenditures

* * *

Comparison of tax expenditure, spending, and regulatory policies

Tax expenditures by definition work through the tax system and, particularly, the income tax. Thus, they may be relatively advantageous policy approaches when the benefit or incentive is related to income and is intended to be widely available. Because there is an existing public administrative and private compliance structure for the tax system, the incremental administrative and compliance costs for a tax expenditure may be low in many cases. In addition, some tax expenditures actually simplify the tax system, (for example, the exclusion for up to $500,000 of capital gains on home sales).

Tax expenditures also have important limitations. In many cases they add to the complexity of the tax system, which raises both administrative and compliance costs. For example, targeting personal exemptions and credits can complicate filing and decisionmaking. The income tax system may have little or no contact with persons who have no or very low incomes, and does not require information on certain characteristics of individuals used in some spending programs, such as wealth. Verifying eligibility criteria can be costly. The tax system also operates on the basis of annual income and it may be poorly targeted when taxpayer characteristics change within the course of a year. * * * Tax expenditures also generally do not enable the same degree of agency discretion as an outlay program. * * * Tax expenditures may not receive the same level of scrutiny afforded to other programs.

Outlay programs have advantages where direct government service provision is particularly warranted—such as equipping and providing the armed forces or administering the system of justice. Outlay programs may also be specifically designed to meet the needs of low-income families who would not otherwise be subject to income taxes or need to file a tax return. Outlay programs may also receive more year-to-year oversight and fine tuning, through the legislative and executive budget process. In addition, many different types of spending programs—including direct government provision; credit programs; and payments to State and local governments, the private sector, or individuals in the form of grants or contracts—provide flexibility for policy design. On the other hand, certain outlay programs—such as direct government service provision—may rely less directly on economic incentives and private-market provision than tax incentives, which may reduce the relative efficiency of spending programs for some goals. * * * Finally, spending programs, particularly on the discretionary side, may respond less readily to changing activity levels and economic conditions than tax expenditures.

* * *

Appendix: Treasury Review of the Tax Expenditure Presentation

This appendix provides an initial presentation of the Treasury Department review of the tax expenditure budget first described in the 2003 Budget. As previously described, the review focuses in particular on three issues: (1) using comprehensive income as a baseline tax system, (2) using a consumption tax as a baseline tax system, and (3) defining negative tax expenditures (provisions that cause taxpayers to pay too much tax).

The first section of this appendix compares major tax expenditures in the current budget to those implied by a comprehensive income baseline. This comparison includes a discussion of negative tax expenditures. The second section compares the major tax expenditures in the current budget to those implied by a consumption tax baseline, and also discusses negative tax expenditures. The final section addresses concerns that have been raised over the measurement of some current tax expenditures by describing a new estimate of the tax expenditure caused by accelerated depreciation and an alternative estimate of the tax expenditure resulting from the tax exemption of the return earned on owner-occupied housing. The final section also provides an estimate of the negative tax expenditure caused by the double tax on corporate profits.

Differences Between Official Tax Expenditures and Those Based on Comprehensive Income

As discussed in the main body of this chapter, traditional tax expenditures are measured relative to normal law or reference law baselines that deviate from a comprehensive concept of income. Consequently, tax expenditures identified in the budget can differ from those that would be identified if comprehensive income were chosen as the baseline tax system. This appendix addresses this issue by comparing major tax expenditures listed in the current tax expenditure budget with those implied by a comprehensive income baseline. Most large tax expenditures would continue to be tax expenditures were the baseline taken to be comprehensive income, although some would not. A comprehensive income baseline would also result in a number of additional tax provisions being counted as tax expenditures.

Current budgetary practice excludes from the list of official tax expenditures those provisions that over-tax certain items of income. This exclusion conforms to the view that tax expenditures are substitutes for direct government spending programs. However, it gives a one-sided picture of the ways in which current law deviates from the baseline tax system. Relative to a comprehensive income baseline, a number of current tax provisions would be negative tax expenditures. Some of these might also be negative tax expenditures under the reference law or normal law baselines, expanded to admit negative tax expenditures.

Treatment of Major Tax Expenditures From the Current Budget Under a Comprehensive Income Baseline

Comprehensive income, also called Haig-Simons income, is the real, inflation adjusted, accretion to one's economic power arising between two points in time, e.g., the beginning and ending of the year. It includes all accretions to wealth, whether or not realized, whether or not related to a market transaction, and whether a return to capital or labor. Inflation adjusted capital gains would be included in comprehensive income as they accrue. Business, investment, and casualty losses, including losses caused by depreciation, would be deducted. Implicit returns, such as those accruing to homeowners, also would be included in comprehensive income. * * * [C]omprehensive income can be defined * * * as the sum of consumption during the period plus the change in net worth between the beginning and the end of the period.

Comprehensive income is widely held to be the idealized base for an income tax even though it is not a perfectly defined concept. It suffers from conceptual ambiguities, some of which are discussed below, as well as practical problems in measurement and tax administration, e.g., how to implement a practicable deduction for economic depreciation or include in income the return earned on housing or consumer durable goods, including automobiles and major appliances.

Furthermore, comprehensive income represents an ideal tax base only in the tautological sense that the base of an income tax is, or should be, income. Comprehensive income does not necessarily represent the economically most desirable tax base; efficiency or equity might be improved by deviating from comprehensive income as a tax base, e.g., by reducing the taxation of capital income in order to spur economic growth or by subsidizing certain types of activities in order to correct for market failures or to improve the after-tax distribution of income. In addition, some elements of comprehensive income would be difficult or impossible to include in a tax system that is administrable.

Table 1 shows the thirty largest tax expenditures from the 2004 Budget classified according to whether they would be considered a tax expenditure under a comprehensive income tax. Thirteen of the thirty items would be tax expenditures under a comprehensive tax base (those in panel A). Most of these give preferential tax treatment to the return on certain types of savings or investment. They are a result of the explicitly hybrid nature of the existing tax system. * * *

Panel B deals with items that potentially are tax expenditures, but that raise more difficult conceptual issues or raise inconsistencies. The first of these is the deduction of nonbusiness State and local taxes other than on owner-occupied homes. These taxes include both income taxes and property taxes. The stated justification for this tax expenditure is that "Taxpayers may deduct State and local income taxes and property taxes even though these taxes primarily pay for services that, if purchased directly by taxpayers, would not be deductible." The idea is that these taxes represent consumption expenditures, and so are elements of income.

Appendix Table 1. COMPARISON OF CURRENT TAX EXPENDITURES WITH THOSE IMPLIED BY A COMPREHENSIVE INCOME TAX

Description	Revenue Effect (2004)
A. *Tax Expenditure Under a Comprehensive Income Tax*	
Net exclusion of pension contributions and earnings: Employer plans	68,870
Net exclusion of pension contributions and earnings: 401(k) plans	55,290
Capital gains (except agriculture, timber, iron ore, and coal) (normal tax method)	53,930
Exclusion of interest on public purpose State and local bonds	27,310
Net exclusion of pension contributions and earnings: Individual Retirement Accounts	23,130
Capital gains exclusion on home sales	20,860
Exclusion of interest on life insurance savings	20,740
Accelerated depreciation of machinery and equipment (normal tax method)	16,670
Deferral of income from controlled foreign corporations (normal tax method)	7,900
Net exclusion of pension contributions and earnings: Keogh plans	7,616
Extraterritorial income exclusion	5,510
Credit for increasing research activities	4,990
Exclusions of Social Security benefits of dependents and survivors	4,140
B. *Possibly a Tax Expenditure Under a Comprehensive Income Tax, But With Some Qualifications*	
Deductibility of nonbusiness State and local taxes other than on owner-occupied homes	50,910
Step-up basis of capital gains at death	28,500
Child credit	21,310
Exclusion of Social Security benefits for retired workers	18,930
Exclusion of workers' compensation benefits	6,460
Workers' compensation insurance premiums	6,190
Earned income tax credit	5,090
C. *Uncertain*	
Exclusion of employer contributions for medial insurance premiums and medial care	120,160
Deductibility of charitable contributions, other than education and health	33,990
Deductibility of medical expenses	6,340
Deductibility of charitable contributions (health)	4,580
Deductibility of charitable contributions (education)	4,350
Deductibility of self-employed medical insurance premiums	3,690
D. *Probably Not a Tax Expenditure Under a Comprehensive Income Tax*	
Deductibility of mortgage interest on owner-occupied homes	68,440
Deductibility of State and local property tax on owner-occupied homes	22,160
Graduated corporation income tax rate (normal tax method)	5,700
Exception from passive loss rules for $25,000 of rental loss	4,920

Source: Table 6–2, Tax Expenditure Budget.

In contrast to the view in the budget, the deduction for State and local taxes might not be a tax expenditure if the baseline were comprehensive income. Properly measured comprehensive income would include the imputed value of State and local government benefits received, but would allow a deduction for State and local taxes paid. Thus, in this sense the deductibility of State and local taxes is consistent with comprehensive income principles; it should not be a tax expenditure. However, imputing the value of State and local services may be difficult and, as a rough correction, the tax system might disallow the deduction for State and local taxes.[2] So, if the value of services from State and local governments is excluded from the tax base, as it generally is under current law, a deduction for taxes might be viewed as a tax expenditure relative to a comprehensive income baseline.

Step-up of basis at death lowers the income tax on capital gains for those who inherit assets below what it would be otherwise. From that perspective it would be a tax expenditure under a comprehensive income baseline. Nonetheless, there are ambiguities. Under a comprehensive income baseline, all gains would be taxed as accrued, so there would be no deferred unrealized gains on assets held at death.

The lack of full taxation of Social Security retirement benefits also is listed in panel B. To the extent that Social Security is viewed as a pension, a comprehensive income tax would include in income all contributions to Social Security retirement funds (payroll taxes) and tax accretions to value as they arise (inside build-up). Benefits paid out of prior contributions and the inside build-up, however, would not be included in the tax base because the fall in the value of the individual's Social Security account would be offset by an increase in cash. In contrast, to the extent that Social Security is viewed as a transfer program, all contributions should be deductible from the income tax base and all benefits received should be included in the income tax base.

In contrast to either of these treatments, current law excludes one-half of contributions (employer-paid payroll taxes) from the base of the income tax, makes no attempt to tax accretions, and subjects some, but not all, benefits to taxation. The difference between the current law treatment of Social Security retirement benefits and their treatment under a comprehensive income tax would qualify as a tax expenditure, but such a tax expenditure differs in concept from that included in the current budget.

The tax expenditures in the current budget reflect exemptions for lower income beneficiaries from the tax on 85 percent of Social Security benefits. Historically, payroll taxes paid by the employee represented no more than 15 percent of the expected value of the benefits received by a lower-earnings Social Security beneficiary. * * * Thus, the tax expenditure conceived and

---

2. Home mortgage interest and property taxes on owner-occupied housing raise the same ambiguity. Classifying them as probably not tax expenditures arguably is inconsistent. It reflects the judgment that no comprehensive tax is likely to tax the value of State and local services, while it appears somewhat easier to impute and tax the rental income from owner-occupied housing.

measured in the current budget is not intended to capture the deviation from a comprehensive income baseline, which would additionally account for the deferral of tax on these components (less an inflation adjustment attributable to the employee's payroll tax contributions). Rather, it is intended to approximate the taxation of private pensions with employee contributions made from after-tax income, on the assumption that Social Security is comparable to such pensions. Hence, the official tax expenditure understates the tax advantage accorded Social Security benefits relative to a comprehensive income baseline.

* * *

The next category (panel C) includes items whose treatment under a comprehensive income tax is widely acknowledged to be ambiguous. Consider, for example, the items relating to charitable contributions. Under existing law, charitable contributions are deductible, and this deduction is considered on its face a tax expenditure in the current budget.

The treatment of charitable donations, however, is ambiguous under a comprehensive income tax. If charitable contributions are a consumption item for the giver, then they are properly included in his taxable income; a deduction for contributions would then be a tax expenditure relative to a comprehensive income tax baseline. In contrast, charitable contributions could represent a transfer of purchasing power from the giver to the receiver. As such, they would represent a reduction in the giver's net worth, not an item of consumption, and so properly would be deductible, implying that current law's treatment is not a tax expenditure. * * *

Medical expenditures may or may not be an element of income (or consumption), depending on one's point of view. Some argue that medical expenditures don't represent discretionary spending, and so are not consumption. * * * Others argue that there is no way to logically distinguish medical care from other consumption items. Moreover, clearly there is choice in health care decisions. * * *

The final category (panel D) includes items that probably are not tax expenditures under a comprehensive income tax base. But even these raise some issues. Mortgage interest would be deductible from the base of a comprehensive income tax, because comprehensive income would include implicit rental income on owner-occupied housing. Similarly, property taxes on owner-occupied housing would be deductible, since they represent a reduction in net worth. One could argue, however, that because current law fails to impute rental income, the home mortgage interest deduction and the deduction for property taxes constitute tax expenditures. * * *

Major Tax Expenditures Under a Comprehensive Income Tax That Are Excluded from the Current Budget

While most of the major tax expenditures in the current budget also would be tax expenditures under a comprehensive income base, there also are tax expenditures relative to a comprehensive income base that are not found on the existing tax expenditure list. These additional tax expenditures include the imputed return from consumer durables and owner-occupied housing, the difference between capital gains as they accrue and capital gains as they are realized, private gifts and inheritances received, in-kind benefits from such government programs as food-stamps, Medicaid, and public housing, the value of payouts from insurance policies,[25] and benefits received from private charities. Under some ideas of comprehensive income, the value of leisure and of household production of goods and services also would be included as tax expenditures. The personal exemption and standard deduction also might be considered tax expenditures, although they can be viewed differently, e.g., as elements of the basic tax rate schedule or as necessary expenditures that are not items of voluntary consumption. The foreign tax credit also might be a tax expenditure, since it could be argued that a deduction for foreign taxes, rather than a credit, would seem to measure the income of U.S. residents properly.

Negative Tax Expenditures

Under current budgetary practice, negative tax expenditures, tax provisions that raise rather than lower taxes, are excluded from the official tax expenditure list. This exclusion conforms with the view that tax expenditures are defined to be similar to government spending programs.

If attention is expanded to include any deviation from the baseline tax system, negative tax expenditures would be of interest. Relative to a comprehensive income baseline, there are a number of important negative tax expenditures, some of which also might be viewed as negative tax expenditures under an expanded interpretation of the normal or reference law baseline. Among the more important negative tax expenditures is the corporation income tax, which would be eliminated under a comprehensive income tax applied to individuals as discussed later in the Appendix. The passive loss rules, restrictions on the deductibility of capital losses, and NOL carry-forward requirements each would generate a negative tax expenditure, since a comprehensive income tax would allow full deductibility of losses. If human capital were considered an asset, then its cost (e.g., certain education and training expenses, including perhaps the cost of college and professional school) should be amortizable, but it is not under current law.[26] Some

---

25. To the extent that premiums are deductible.

26. Current law offers favorable treatment to some education costs, thereby creating (positive) tax expenditures. Current law allows expensing of that part of the cost of education and career training that is related to foregone earnings and this would be a tax expenditure under a comprehensive income baseline. In addition, some education has consumption value, and under a comprehensive income definition would be taxable to that extent, but is not taxable under current law.

restricted deductions under the individual AMT might be negative tax expenditures as might the phase-out of personal exemptions and of itemized deductions. * * *

Current tax law fails to index for inflation interest receipts, capital gains, depreciation, and inventories. These provisions are negative tax expenditures because comprehensive income would be indexed for inflation. Current law, however, also fails to index for inflation the deduction for interest payments; this represents a (positive) tax expenditure. * * *

Tax Expenditures and the Tax Rate Structure

Under some views, the graduated personal income tax rate structure might result in a tax expenditure or in a negative tax expenditure. To the extent that one views a single tax rate as most compatible with a comprehensive income base, tax rates above the appropriate single rate would yield a negative tax expenditure. To the extent that one views a graduated tax rate structure as most desirable, then differences between the appropriate graduated tax rate structure and the actual tax rate structure would lead to tax expenditures or negative tax expenditures.

Differences Between Official Tax Expenditures and Tax Expenditures Relative to a Consumption Base

This section compares tax expenditures listed in the official tax expenditure budget with those implied by a comprehensive consumption baseline. * * *

Treatment of Major Tax Expenditures Under a Comprehensive Consumption Baseline

* * * [T]he major difference between a comprehensive consumption tax and a comprehensive income tax is in the treatment of saving, or in the taxation of capital income. Consequently, many current tax expenditures related to preferential taxation of capital income would not be tax expenditures under a consumption tax. However, preferential treatment of items of income unrelated to fairly broad-based saving incentives would remain tax expenditures under a consumption baseline.

* * *

Revised Estimates of Selected Tax Expenditures

* * *

Double Tax on Corporate Profits

A comprehensive income tax would tax all sources of income once at a tax rate appropriate for the particular taxpayer. Taxes would not vary by type or source of income. * * *

Appendix Table 3. POSSIBLE FUTURE ADDITIONS TO TAX EXPENDITURES ESTIMATES

	2004	2005	2006	2007	2008
Imputed Rent On Owner-Occupied Housing	20, 517	24, 064	25, 092	28, 052	31, 002
Double Tax on Corporate Profits	– 25, 373	– 32,723	– 31, 590	– 32, 022	– 33, 096

1. Calculations described in the appendix text.
2. This is a negative tax expenditure, a tax provision that overtaxes income relative to the treatment specified by the baseline tax system.

Table 3 provides an estimate of the negative tax expenditure caused by the multiple levels of tax on corporate profits. This negative tax expenditure includes the shareholder level tax on dividends paid and capital gains realized out of earnings that have been taxed at the corporate level. It also includes the corporate tax paid on inter-corporate dividends and on corporate capital gains attributable to the sale of stock shares. The negative tax expenditure is large in magnitude; it grows from $25 billion in 2004 to $33 billion in 2008. It is comparable in size (but opposite in sign) to all but the largest official tax expenditures.

JAMES MADISON AND PUBLIC CHOICE AT GUCCI GULCH: A PROCEDURAL DEFENSE OF TAX EXPENDITURES AND TAX INSTITUTIONS

Edward A. Zelinsky[*]

102 Yale Law Journal 1165, 1165-79, 1181-82, 1184-87, 1190-92 (1993)

Introduction

Few academic doctrines can claim the intellectual and political success of tax expenditure analysis. In roughly a generation's time,[1] Professor Surrey's procedural and substantive critique of tax subsidies has become entrenched in the law school curriculum and in legal scholarship. More impressively, the tax expenditure concept has been enshrined in federal law[4] and become part of the daily discourse of the national budget process.

In earlier articles, I have revisited the substantive tax expenditure indictment of tax subsidies to suggest that the Surrey school's invariable preference for direct government outlays is misplaced. While the classification of particular features of the Internal Revenue Code as either normative or subsidizing is critical to tax expenditure analysis, that classification cannot

---

*. At time of original publication, Visiting Professor of Law, Yale Law School; Professor of Law, Benjamin N. Cardozo School of Law, Yeshiva University.

1. Professor Surrey developed the fundamental premises of tax expenditure analysis—the classification of tax provisions as normative or subsidizing and the equivalence of the latter to direct spending—during the later years of the Johnson Administration when serving as the Assistant Secretary of the Treasury for Tax Policy.

4. *See* 2 U.S.C. § 640(c)(3) (1988) (adopted as part of Congressional Budget and Impoundment Control Act of 1974, requiring promulgation of annual tax expenditure budget).

always be made with confidence.[6] Moreover, the substantive case against tax subsidies depends upon a comparison of such subsidies with an idealized vision of direct spending. In theory, tax expenditures can be designed as efficiently and progressively as programs using direct governmental outlays. On the other hand, if we compare the messy realities of tax preferences with the equally unattractive realities of direct expenditure programs, tax preferences emerge better than most of the Surrey school would acknowledge. Indeed, in particular cases, a tax subsidy may be more efficient than an equivalent direct spending program because such a subsidy uses the pre-existing tax system to communicate federal policy at relatively low marginal cost. Thus, as a matter of substantive policy, a certain agnosticism is in order: in some instances, direct government outlays will be preferable to comparable tax expenditures; in other cases, a subsidy through the Internal Revenue Code will be the preferred means of implementing federal policy.

In this Article, I revisit the procedural aspects of the tax expenditure critique to argue against that critique insofar as it is premised on the asserted expertise of direct expenditure institutions. The core of my argument is that the institutions formulating and administering tax policy are more competitive and visible than their direct outlay counterparts because tax institutions are subject to more numerous and diverse constituencies than the specialized, limited-clientele organizations that design and implement direct government spending. Tax institutions, because of their greater visibility and more competitive nature, are less susceptible to interest group capture and possess greater legitimacy under pluralist criteria than their direct expenditure equivalents. This perspective leads to a form of agnosticism as well: the congressional committees that design and the administrative agencies that implement tax subsidies may, in particular cases, be preferable to their direct expenditure counterparts.

---

6. In particular, I have argued that the Code's present treatment of qualified plans is consistent with the terms of a normative income tax and is therefore underserving of characterization as a tax expenditure. *See* Edward A. Zelinsky, *The Tax Treatment of Qualified Plans: A Classic Defense of the Status Quo*, 66 N.C. L. REV. 315 (1988). I have also criticized the reflexive classification as a tax subsidy of the deduction for certain state and local taxes. *See* Edward A. Zelinsky, *The Deductibility of State and Local Taxes: Income Measurement, Tax Expenditures and Partial, Functional Deductibility*, 6 AM. J. TAX POL'Y 9 (1987). Professor Kahn has similarly suggested that accelerated depreciation may be consistent with the provisions of a normative income tax. *See* Douglas A. Kahn, *Accelerated Depreciation—Tax Expenditure or Proper Allowance for Measuring Net Income?*, 78 MICH. L. REV. 1 (1979). Professor Stein, on the other hand, has vigorously contested my views, defending the classification as a tax subsidy of the Code's qualified plan provisions. *See* Norman P. Stein, *Qualified Plans and Tax Expenditures: A Reply to Professor Zelinsky*, 9 AM. J. TAX POL'Y 225 (1991); Edward A. Zelinsky, *Qualified Plans and Identifying Tax Expenditures: A Rejoinder to Professor Stein*, 9 AM. J. TAX POL'Y 257 (1991); *see also* Douglas A. Kahn & Jeffery S. Lehman, *Tax Expenditure Budgets: A Critical View*, 54 TAX NOTES 1661, 1664 (1992) ("[V]ery few items fit neatly into" categories of normative and subsidizing); Victor Thuronyi, *Tax Expenditures: A Reassessment*, 1988 DUKE L.J. 1155, 1156 (1988) (introducing "substitutable tax provisions" concept).

To develop my argument, I will initially review the procedural case against tax preferences and will then contrast the expertise-based premise of this perspective with the Madisonian/public choice/pluralist tradition in American political thought, a tradition that focuses, not upon the asserted proficiencies of policymakers, but upon the interplay of competing interest groups in the political process. * * * I will then elaborate my argument about the differences between the administrative agencies and congressional committees that formulate and implement direct expenditure programs and the equivalent tax organizations.

Let me emphasize at the outset, what I am not saying: I am not suggesting that the institutions that design and implement the tax law are immune from capture by interest groups or perfectly implement the pluralist model of democracy. I am not declaring that, in all cases, a tax subsidy is better designed and administered than its direct expenditure counterpart or that the interplay of interest groups mechanically dictates legislative and administrative outcomes: ideology, accident, history, inertia, partisanship, public opinion, cultural norms, bureaucratic aggrandizement, the idiosyncrasies of legislators and the legislative process, and the personalities and proclivities of individual decisionmakers, as well as their concern for the public interest, all affect the outcomes of political and administrative processes. The procedures by which taxes are designed and administered are not ideal or pretty or inhabited exclusively by the pure of heart.

I am suggesting that, in the long term, institutional differences of the sort I explore below do systematically affect legislative and bureaucratic outcomes for better and for worse. A defense of the tax system along these lines constitutes an important counterweight to the widespread, contemporary disillusionment with that system.

The Procedural Case Against Tax Expenditures: the Expertise of Direct Expenditure Institutions

In its original incarnation, the procedural critique of tax subsidies embodied two basic concerns: that such subsidies, undisclosed in the federal budget, were not subject to the same scrutiny as direct monetary expenditures, and that such subsidies, designed and implemented by congressional tax-writers and the Department of the Treasury, were not formed or administered using the specialized subject matter expertise of the other committees of Congress and the nontax executive departments.

The first part of this critique gave rise to the proposal for the tax expenditure budget, the annual identification, as part of the federal government's regular budgetary process, of the subsidies contained in the Internal Revenue Code and of their projected costs. Today, the preparation of such a budget is required by statute. Not surprisingly, much political and academic attention has been devoted to determining the items properly included in the yearly tax expenditure budget and the revenues foregone as a result of such items.

While the tax expenditure school had quick (and, I think, useful) success in persuading Congress of the need for an annual tax expenditure budget, it has had less impact *vis-à-vis* the second element of its procedural critique, i.e., the failure, in the design and implementation of tax preferences, to utilize the subject matter expertise of the nontax congressional committees and executive departments. Professor Yorio expressed the concern in these terms:

> The process by which tax subsidies are enacted and administered also increases the risk that they would fail a cost-benefit test. To begin with, a tax subsidy enters the Code after review primarily by the House Ways and Means Committee and the Senate Finance Committee. Charged principally with matters of tax and finance, both committees are usually less informed about the specifics of the problems justifying government intervention than those Congressional committees that grapple regularly with the problems. Moreover, the duty of administering tax subsidies is left to the Internal Revenue Service (IRS), which generally has no particular expertise with respect to the problem that the preference was enacted to remedy. Although it may be theoretically possible for the relevant tax committees and the IRS to obtain and digest the information required to make a rational cost-benefit decision about a specific tax expenditure, the process of education and learning is likely to be haphazard and incomplete. As a practical matter, it is virtually impossible for two congressional committees and one administrative agency to master the plethora and diversity of proposals for using the Code to accomplish societal goals.[15]

From one vantage point, this critique is easily remedied by making the enactment and implementation of tax preferences a joint undertaking of the relevant tax and nontax institutions. Subsidies implemented through the Code can, before or after passage by the Ways and Means and Finance Committees, be submitted to additional expert review by the proper subject matter committees of Congress. Congress can—and, on occasion, does—provide for the joint administration of particular tax subsidies by the IRS and the appropriate nontax administrative agency.[17] * * *

On the most fundamental level, the expertise critique of tax expenditures invokes the important notion in American political culture that disinterested, "trained, nonpartisan experts [can] best manage the subtle and difficult social questions of the modern world."[20] From this vantage point, Professor Surrey's

---

15. Edward Yorio, *Equity, Efficiency, and the Tax Reform Act of 1986*, 55 FORDHAM L. REV. 395, 425 (1987).

17. For example, under the low-income housing credit established in Section 42, important administrative functions are assigned to the U.S. Department of Housing and Urban Development and the U.S. Department of Agriculture.

20. LEWIS L. GOULD, REFORM AND REGULATION, AMERICAN POLITICS FROM ROOSEVELT TO WILSON 210 (2d ed. 1986).

procedural case for the subject matter proficiency of nontax institutions is an appeal to the managerial and technocratic values underpinning such expert-oriented institutions as civil service systems, independent regulatory agencies, and municipal governments run by city managers. Professor Surrey's perspective is thus firmly rooted in the tradition of Progressive, New Deal, and good government reformers who placed great confidence in the processes and outcomes of professional decisionmaking—a tradition which, in Professor Banfield's apt, but wary, description, seeks "to replace politicians with experts."[21]

Interest Group Theory: Madison, Pluralism, Public Choice, and Monitoring Political Agents

James Madison, in contrast, was skeptical of institutional arrangements that presume "[e]nlightened statesmen will . . . always be at the helm" of government.[22] For Madison, self-government is not a matter of entrusting public authority to experts but, rather, of coping with the inevitable "spirit of party and faction in the necessary and ordinary operations of government."[23] * * *

In much contemporary discussion, Madison's concerns are echoed in the vocabulary of public choice. * * * An important variant of this perspective "conceives regulation as a service supplied to effective political interest groups."[29]

Public choice analysis—emphasizing the rent-seeking nature of interest group activity, the incentives of political entrepreneurs to supply such groups, collective action problems which prevent the effective organization of the public at large, and the capture of legislatures and administrative agencies by organized, concentrated constituencies—reinforces Madison's preference for competitive political processes that pit diverse and conflicting groups against one another. While it is possible in a Madisonian process for interests to respond to their situation collusively rather than competitively, attempting to satisfy their respective needs by combining into broad, mutually useful coalitions, nevertheless, insofar as the legislative or administrative environment approaches Madison's ideal, the presence of more diverse and numerous interest groups discourages such logrolling: more heterogeneous groups will find it more difficult to negotiate mutually acceptable positions for a common front; more numerous groups will find it more costly to bargain with one another and more difficult to detect and prevent defection from and freeloading on the coalition.

* * * [R]elatively closed processes, less visible to some groups or to the general public than to other groups, are more easily captured by the interests

---

21. EDWARD C. BANFIELD, HERE THE PEOPLE RULE 170 (2d ed. 1991).

22. *See* THE FEDERALIST NO. 10, at 80 (James Madison) (Clinton Rossiter ed., 1961).

23. *Id.* at 79.

29. Richard A. Posner, *Theories of Economic Regulation*, 5 BELL J. ECON. MGMT. SCI. 335, 356 (1974).

that can readily monitor those processes and therefore intelligently punish and reward such processes' decisionmakers. Conversely, more visible institutions, subject to effective oversight by numerous and diverse interests and by the public as a whole, are less prone to capture by any particular clientele since competing interests and the general public are all watching.

Madison's view of organized constituencies, some would assert, is overly pessimistic, ignoring the possibility (and the reality) that "factions" can (and do) play a constructive role in the body politic.

* * * [F]rom the perspective I advance, it is not necessary that any (or all) of the interest group theories explain exhaustively all political behavior; it is merely necessary to start with their common teaching that political institutions influenced by more numerous and more diverse groups are preferable to governmental organizations influenced by more limited and more homogeneous constituencies.

* * *

It is thus important to reiterate the asymmetry between the invariable preference of the Surrey school for direct monetary expenditures and my more agnostic perspective. I am not advancing a countermyth that the processes that formulate and administer tax subsidies are invariably superior to their direct expenditure counterparts. In particular cases, the benefits flowing from the expertise of a nontax committee or of a direct expenditure department may reasonably be perceived as outweighing the correlative dangers of capture. There are also cases where susceptibility to capture is a desired quality, ensuring an intended responsiveness of governmental arrangements to a favored clientele: a grateful nation might rationally prefer veterans institutions beholden and therefore responsive to those who served in the armed services rather than veterans programs administered with less partiality by the IRS or evaluated with less solicitude by the tax committees. The larger points of this Article are that the trade-off between expertise and capture exists, that the choices this trade-off presents should not be ignored simply by asserting the superior expertise of direct expenditure institutions and that, in some instances, the greater independence and visibility of tax-writers and administrators will be preferable to the alleged subject matter proficiency of their more specialized, capturable counterparts in the direct expenditure system.

The Madisonian Nature of Tax Institutions

For purposes of the Surrey critique, we can view tax and direct expenditure policy as formulated and administered in four stages. Initially, the congressional committees design and authorize programs within their respective jurisdictions. Next, the full houses of Congress act on the committees' product. Third, the President approves or disapproves the decision of the House and Senate. Finally, the appropriate executive department executes the program agreed upon by Congress and the President.

The tax expenditure procedural critique is aimed at the first and fourth stages of this process. At the first stage, the critique asserts that the nontax committees of Congress possess expertise due to their specialization in particular subject matters. This expertise is utilized in the formulation of direct spending programs but is not used in the formulation of tax subsidies since such subsidies are designed by the Ways and Means and Finance panels, generalist bodies with less opportunity and less inclination to acquire subject matter proficiency than the narrowly focused nontax committees of Congress.

A similar analysis applies at the fourth stage of the policy process. Direct outlay programs are administered by specialized executive departments which, it is argued, develop great understanding of the programs they implement and the problems those programs address. In contrast, the Treasury and the IRS, distracted by the need to run the tax system, do not develop comparable expertise as to the subsidies confided to their administration.

The Madisonian/public choice/pluralist perspective suggests that this critique romanticizes the congressional committees that design, and the executive departments that administer, direct spending programs while ignoring the benefits of the more competitive processes through which taxes are formulated and implemented. The specialized orientation of the nontax committees and departments makes each of these institutions highly susceptible to capture by the limited constituencies affected by its comparatively narrow jurisdiction. In pluralist terms, the outcomes emanating from direct expenditure committees and departments possess less legitimacy than if more numerous and more diverse groups were to participate in the deliberations of these institutions.

Consider, for example, the case of agriculture. Many provisions of the Internal Revenue Code can quite comfortably be classified as subsidies for the farm industry.[45] The tax expenditure procedural critique suggests that, as a matter of process, such subsidies should not be designed in Congress' tax-writing committees because these bodies lack the expertise to formulate farm policy. Instead, the agriculture committees should develop farm programs using direct outlays of government funds.

However, within the farm committees there are generally not significant countervailing pressures from nonagricultural constituencies, while in the Ways and Means and Finance panels agricultural interests are forced to contend with the competing pressures of other groups also seeking largesse from the public fisc. * * *

Similarly, the procedural indictment of tax preferences contends that, in the implementation of agricultural subsidies through the Code, the IRS lacks

---

45. For example, a number of farm assets are singled out statutorily for particularly rapid cost recovery: certain horses, I.R.C. §§ 168(e)(3)(A) (1992), certain agricultural and horticultural structures, I.R.C. §§ 168(e)(3)(D)(i) (1992), and fruit- and nut-bearing trees and vines, I.R.C. §§ 168(e)(3)(D)(ii) (1992). Similarly, qualifying family farms enjoy estate tax benefits. I.R.C. §§ 2032A (1992).

the expertise of the Department of Agriculture. However, in the administration of farm subsidies, the Secretary of the Treasury possesses greater independence from farm interests than the Secretary of Agriculture. The Secretary of Agriculture relies on farm lobbies to support his policy agenda and his department's budget. He and his subordinates may have worked with agricultural interests before appointment and may return to agriculture after government service. When a Secretary of Agriculture proposes to abolish farm subsidies, he strikes at the very rationale for his agency's existence. * * *

In the vocabulary of the economic theory of regulation, the Department of Agriculture and Congress' farm committees supply industry-specific services—agricultural subsidies—to a limited number of buyers—farm interests. In contrast, the Treasury and Congress' tax-writers supply more fungible services—tax subsidies—in a more competitive environment, distinguished by many more possible purchasers and consequent collective action problems.
    * * *

Indeed, contra to the Surrey critique, tax institutions, because of their greater political freedom, are better positioned than direct expenditure organizations to design and implement policies informed by expertise. The theoretical skill of direct spending organizations is of little practical significance when the clienteles of such organizations effectively dominate them and their decisions. In contrast, the counterbalancing pressures on tax writers and tax administrators leave them comparatively freer to make decisions informed by expertise if they are so inclined.

In advancing this analysis, I seek neither to demonize direct expenditure institutions nor to create a countermyth about the organizations that formulate and administer tax subsidies. * * *

On the other hand, my analysis is an antidote to the benign, expertise-oriented argument of the Surrey school for the superiority of direct expenditure institutions, and suggests that tax institutions are better than is popularly thought or academically portrayed. Agricultural interests seem to do well in the tax-writing committees; they probably do better in direct spending contexts. Farm interests can view the Secretary of Agriculture as their natural ally; the same cannot be said of the Commissioner of Internal Revenue.[46]
    * * *

Doernberg and McChesney take direct aim at the "political fairy tale"[53] of Gucci Gulch, the hallways outside the tax-writing committees densely packed with high paid, well-dressed lobbyists. The conventional story is that the

---

46. While I have illustrated my case with the example of agriculture, I could have used the transportation industry, the natural resources lobbies, the real estate business, veterans groups or any of the interests that seek and obtain largesse from the federal fisc.

53. Richard L. Doernberg & Fred S. McChesney, *Doing Good or Doing Well?: Congress and The Tax Reform Act of 1986*, 62 N.Y.U. L. REV. 891 (1987), at 893.

denizens of Gucci Gulch lost in 1986, the general welfare prevailing over special interests in the rewriting of the tax code. In the spirit of public choice theory, Professors Doernberg and McChesney tell us the truth is otherwise: "tax politics as usual, with considerable sums of money changing hands,"[55]—tax benefits supplied and purchased.

    * * *

Some hint of this is to be found in the Doernberg-McChesney analysis. In that analysis, a key piece of evidence is the vast quantum of campaign contributions received from diverse sources by the members of the Finance and Ways and Means panels. Yet, the aggregate size of those donations and the variety of sources suggest that Congress' tax-writers are not dependent upon any particular set of contributors. For those concerned about interest group capture, such a state of affairs is preferable to the alternative: legislators heavily indebted for campaign funds to limited constituencies. The economic theory of regulation suggests that the senators and representatives who serve on nontax committees will find themselves in this unfortunate situation, highly reliant for campaign funds upon the relatively homogeneous interest groups serviced by the committees on which such legislators sit.

    * * *

Objections, Qualifications and Refinements

I now want to anticipate some objections to my analysis and, where appropriate, qualify and refine my argument. First, it can be argued that, if the generalists who write and administer the tax laws are not knowledgeable about particular substantive areas of government, their lack of expertise engenders a form of capture stemming from their consequent dependence on the information provided by interest groups. Bureaucrats in direct expenditure agencies and members of Congress on nontax committees can, the reasoning goes, independently evaluate the data and proposals advanced by constituencies within their respective jurisdictions because such legislators and bureaucrats possess independent, countervailing expertise; tax personnel, in contrast, are more dependent upon importuning constituencies because tax personnel cannot assess the validity of what they are told. When, for example, the farm lobby furnishes data and advice to the Secretary of Agriculture or to members of Congress' agriculture committees, those individuals can evaluate that material for themselves or can turn to professional staff which can evaluate it for them. On the other hand, the argument runs, tax writers and administrators, generalists lacking specialized expertise in agriculture, are effectively captured by the farm lobby on whose information they depend.

By way of rejoinder, I should first make explicit my skepticism towards the claim of expertise for direct expenditure institutions[.] * * *

Finally, even if direct expenditure institutions possess superior expertise in the abstract, such institutions, because of their greater proclivity towards

---

55. *Id.*

political capture, are less likely than tax organizations to make decisions actually informed by such expertise. Paradoxically, tax decisionmakers, even if theoretically less knowledgeable in particular substantive areas, are better able to make decisions informed by the expertise they do possess because their more competitive, visible environment frees them to use what expertise they have.

These observations, in turn, suggest further qualification of my thesis: as individuals and institutions in the tax process specialize to acquire proficiency in particular areas of substantive policy, the tension between capture and expertise reemerges. A Treasury lawyer who specializes in the tax problems of agriculture acquires industry-specific skills and knowledge likely to affect his views and future employment; a senator with a narrowly-focused concern about the tax problems of agriculture will develop a relationship with the farm lobby similar to that of a member of the Senate's agriculture panel. If too much substantive policy is channeled through the tax committees and the Treasury, these institutions will be forced to organize themselves internally by subject matter and thus start to resemble their more capturable direct expenditure counterparts. * * * [T]he tax system does not have infinite capacity in the generalist, multi-constituency form in which it exists today; if overutilized, the tax system will be forced to specialize in a fashion which replicates the expertise and capturability characteristics of direct expenditure institutions.

Another possible rejoinder to my analysis would suggest that the competitive nature of the second and third stages of the process for adopting direct government outlays compensates for capture in the first and fourth stages, thereby redeeming the process as a whole from the effects of special interests. The Surrey school could concede that, while the specialized committees of Congress and the nontax departments of the executive branch are highly vulnerable to capture by their respective constituencies, the problem is corrected in the deliberations of the full houses of Congress and in the President's participation in the process. * * *

While there is an element of truth to this line of thought, there is much overstatement in it as well. Left to their own devices, the Department of Agriculture and Congress' agriculture committees would probably devote most of the federal budget to farm subsidies. The full Congress and the President obviously will not let this happen. However, it overstates the corrective influence of the President and Congress as a whole to conclude that they can completely eradicate the consequences of capture in the direct expenditure committees and executive departments. The consensus among scholars studying Congress is that a particular clientele's domination of a committee leads to a final outcome more favorable to that clientele. It is similarly a commonplace among students of American government that an interest group's control of an administrative agency affects the final outcome of the political process in ways favorable to that group.

In terms of the stylized, four stage process, the decisions of legislative committees set agendas and furnish resources for the debates of the full bodies in the second stage, thereby affecting the results of those second stage deliberations. If we view the floors of both houses as arenas dedicated to logrolling, the interest that loses in committee has no log to roll. Conversely, the interest doing well in committee has more logs to roll and, hence, is likely to emerge at the end with a larger portion of the overall largesse being dispensed. By the same token, the President's options are heavily circumscribed by the actions of the federal bureaucracy, actions which frequently constitute services supplied to clientele interests.

* * *

Implications

What, then, are the implications of my analysis? First, and perhaps most important, are its rhetorical ramifications. Embedded in the tax expenditure literature is an invariable preference, procedural as well as substantive, for direct government outlays. Similarly embedded in popular and academic discourse is a pronounced disillusion with the federal tax system. My analysis suggests a more balanced view of the processes for enacting and administering tax subsidies.

* * *

The organizations that design and implement federal taxes are not ideal or populated by the pure of heart. However, Madison, like his near contemporary Adam Smith, reminds us that perfection is not the criterion against which human institutions ought to be measured and that the utility of such institutions does not depend upon the motives or moral worthiness of those who populate them.

My argument further suggests that tax subsidies ought to be preferred to direct expenditures when there is a need for detached administration and oversight by decisionmakers less susceptible to capture. Because of his competing constituencies and functions, the Secretary of the Treasury is more likely to implement an agricultural program independently of farm lobbyists than the Secretary of Agriculture; the Treasury is also more apt than the Department of Agriculture to disapprove a farm subsidy it administers and propose the subsidy's abolition. An important instance of such detached evaluation is the Treasury's 1984 tax reform study which recommended abolishing a variety of federal tax subsidies for, inter alia, transportation, military and mineral interests.[78] It is hard to conceive of the direct expenditure departments proposing such sweeping repeal of the programs they administer. Similarly, the Ways and Means and Finance panels, because of their greater visibility and offsetting clientele pressures, are better positioned

---

78. U.S. DEP'T OF THE TREASURY, 2 TAX REFORM FOR FAIRNESS, SIMPLICITY, AND ECONOMIC GROWTH 47, 223, 324 (1984) (proposing abolition of military-related exclusions from gross income, repeal of variety of tax preferences relative to energy and natural resources, and abolition of tax benefits for merchant marine capital construction fund).

than the direct expenditure committees to oversee subsidy programs objectively.

* * *

Notes and Questions

4.   The Office of Management and Budget (OMB) presents a compilation of tax expenditures, valuing each separately, but expressly notes that it cannot provide a total of all the listed tax expenditures. Why does the whole not equal the sum of the parts?

5.   In most cases, tax expenditures are designed to bring about changes in the behavior of taxpayers. Thus, to the degree the tax expenditure is successful, we might expect less of the subsidized activity if the subsidy were removed. Nonetheless, the OMB does not reflect such "behavioral effects" in its estimates. Why not?

6.   What is the difference between computing tax expenditures on a cash-flow basis and on a present-value basis? Why is the present-value basis likely to be particularly important for tax expenditures that take the form of deferrals?

7.   The 1974 Congressional Budget Act, which mandated the tax expenditure budget, did not specify the "baseline" to which tax expenditures are to be compared. This omission is significant, because the baseline is probably the most important and most controversial aspect of the process. The officials charged with preparing the tax expenditure budgets thus have some leeway to change their approach over time, which may lead to charges of manipulating the process to serve political goals of the party controlling the Presidency (in the case of the OMB) or Congress (in the case of the Congressional Budget Committee).

8.   The problem in selecting the baseline is dramatically demonstrated by the realization rule. As we have seen throughout this book, myriad problems, both conceptual and practical, arise from the failure to tax unrealized appreciation. Should failure to adhere to the Haig-Simons definition of income with regard to unrealized gain be regarded as a massive tax expenditure, or is the realization rule so basic that it is the "norm"? If so, should instances in which the law requires mark-to-market tax treatment be regarded as negative tax expenditures?

9.   OMB compiles the primary tax expenditure budget using "reference law" and "normal tax" baselines. While the reference law baseline is an attempt to derive a supposed norm from present law, the normal tax baseline deviates from present law toward the Haig-Simons "ideal," at least in some

respects. Because the concept of income is broader under Haig-Simons than under present law, OMB observes that "Tax expenditures under the reference law baseline are always tax expenditures under the normal tax baseline, but the reverse is not always true."

Some of the items classified as tax expenditures under the normal tax baseline, but not under the reference law baseline, are of significance. For example, accelerated depreciation (more rapid than economic depreciation) and corporate tax rates below the top rate (35 percent) are regarded as tax expenditures under the normal tax baseline, but not under the reference law baseline.

10. Note, however, that even the normal tax baseline embodies "several major departures from a pure comprehensive income tax." These include the failure to regard unrealized appreciation as income, failure to take account of inflation, and accepting a two-level tax on corporate income as part of the baseline.

11. The Appendix to the OMB tax expenditure budget for FY 2004, for the first time, undertakes the computation of tax expenditures using a comprehensive, or Haig-Simons, baseline. Is such a baseline to be preferred to that used in the primary tax expenditure budget?

12. While tax expenditures, almost by definition, make the Internal Revenue Code longer and more complex, particular tax expenditures can actually simplify compliance with, and administration of, the law. Simplifying tax expenditures include provisions such as section 121 (effectively exempting from income most capital gains on sales of principal residences) and section 179 (allowing many taxpayers to immediately deduct purchases of equipment, rather than deducting the cost over time through capitalization and depreciation).

On the other hand, many tax expenditures clearly result in significant complication on all levels. An important example is the earned income tax credit, which brings millions of individuals who otherwise would not need to file returns into contact with the Internal Revenue Service. Whatever benefits the EITC may bring, simplifying life for either low-income taxpayers or the Service is not among them.

13. The Appendix of the OMB tax expenditure budget attempts to analyze tax expenditures under a true comprehensive, Haig-Simons, definition of income. Difficulties, some perhaps unexpected, immediately appear. Given the broader sweep of income under the Haig-Simons definition than under the norms of current law, one counterintuitive result is that some items presently classified as tax expenditures might not be regarded as tax expenditures under the comprehensive tax baseline. For example, deduction of nonbusiness state

and local income taxes is regarded as a tax expenditure under the current approach. Under a comprehensive income baseline, perhaps the state and local governmental benefits should be included, but the state and local taxes should be deducted. Thus, viewed in isolation, perhaps allowance of the deduction should not be viewed as a tax expenditure under a comprehensive income baseline. (But perhaps the tax expenditure label fits after all, OMB adds, under the view that denial of the deduction would serve as a "rough corrective" for the failure to include the governmental services in income.)

14. Traditionally, little or no official attention has been given to deviations from the norm that increase taxes (such as various limitations on the deduction of losses). Do you find useful the concept of negative tax expenditures explored in the Appendix of the OMB tax expenditure budget?

15. The double tax on corporate earnings can be viewed as a negative tax expenditure. OMB noted that the Bush Administration proposed to end such double taxation; instead, Congress granted partial relief by lowering the tax rate applicable to dividends. The double-tax issue is explored in Chapter Fourteen.

16. Compare the entries for the earned income tax credit in Table 6-1 with the much larger figures in footnote 3 of that table. Why is most of the cost of the EITC not reflected in reduced governmental receipts? The EITC is considered in more detail in Subchapter E.

17. Tax expenditures are thought of as deviations from the normal income tax system (individual and corporate). Can the same concept be applied to excise taxes? Perhaps so. Dr. Bruce Davie has compiled a list of 244 excise tax expenditure provisions "resulting from special exemptions and preferential rates associated with Federal excise taxes."[h]

18. How does a reduction in income tax rates affect tax expenditures?

19. Is the tax expenditures concept merely a way of framing the issue as to what should be included in the income tax base?

20. If a credit against tax is allowed for purchase of a depreciable asset, should the tax basis of the asset thereafter be the full price paid for it or its cost reduced by the tax credit?

---

h. Bruce F. Davie, *Tax Expenditures in the Federal Excise Tax System*, 47 NAT'L TAX J. 39, 39 (1994).

21. Professor Surrey argued that almost any tax expenditure could be duplicated, in substantive effect, by a direct expenditure program. Is this correct? What difference would it make? Would direct expenditures be more closely scrutinized?   Would direct expenditures exclude as potential beneficiaries those with so little income that they paid no income tax, as tax expenditures routinely do?

22. Would charities be indifferent if Congress ended the tax deduction for charitable contributions and substituted, as Professor Surrey suggested, "a direct expenditure program under which the Government matched with its grants, on a no-questions-asked and no-second-thoughts basis, the gifts of private individuals to the charities they selected"?[i] Would such a direct expenditure be constitutional if the charity were a church?

23. Of course, even a tax expenditure in the form of a charitable contribution deduction could be constitutionally suspect. In a detailed review of this topic, Professor Linda Sugin concludes that though the issue is not entirely free from doubt: "Indirect benefits do not imply government support and approval to the same extent as benefits that emanate straight from the government,"[j] and that "it is clear that the economic equivalence of tax benefits and direct spending is not the most important factor to consider in establishment clause analysis."[k]

24. The structure of a tax expenditure can be important. Prior to the Tax Reform Act of 1986, taxpayers over the age of 65 and blind taxpayers were allowed an additional personal exemption, which had the effect of a deduction for all such taxpayers. The 1986 Act, in addition to reducing the amount of the benefit, changed its structure—rather than a personal exemption available to all aged and blind taxpayers, it was restructured as an increased standard deduction, of value only to those who utilized the standard deduction.[l] What policy choices, or what views of the effects of age or blindness, justify one structure as compared to the other? What different set of decisions would be reflected by converting the tax advantage to a "refundable" credit?

25. Why does Congress give a tax advantage to taxpayers who are elderly or blind, and not to taxpayers with other afflictions, such as quadriplegia? Can such distinctions be defended?

---

i. Surrey, *supra* note a, at 133.

j. Linda Sugin, *Tax Expenditure Analysis and Constitutional Decisions*, 50 HASTINGS L.J. 407, 471 (1999).

k. *Id*. at 472.

l. Section 63(f).

26. Tax expenditures arising from deferral of tax liability have attracted relatively little political opposition, because the advantages of deferral are better understood by the beneficiaries than by the general public. Moreover, such tax expenditures are politically defended on the grounds that the tax is "merely" being postponed.

Tax expenditures arising from deferral are difficult to quantify because the cost to the government depends not only on the amount and length of deferment, but also on the interest rate assumed in computing the time value of money. In measuring these tax expenditures, the Office of Management and Budget uses as a discount rate "the interest rate on comparable maturity Treasury debt." Is this appropriate, or should we look to what the typical taxpayer would have to pay to borrow money?

27. Professor Zelinsky asserts that Surrey and his adherents have unfairly painted tax expenditures, in part due to a failure to "compare the messy realities of tax preferences with the equally unattractive realities of direct expenditure programs."

28. Zelinsky asserts that the choice between tax expenditures and direct expenditures may entail a tradeoff between expertise and "capture." Which way does a desire for expert decisionmakers point? What does Zelinsky mean by "capture," and why does he view capture as a serious concern?

29. Zelinsky uses agriculture to illustrate his argument. Given that all three officials are appointed by the President and serve at his pleasure, why is it more likely that the Secretary of Agriculture will be more responsive to a particular constituency (agricultural interests) than the Secretary of the Treasury and the Commissioner of Internal Revenue?

30. Professor Zelinsky makes a telling point, in noting the broad Treasury proposals in 1984 ("Treasury I," which ultimately led to the Tax Reform Act of 1986), and observing that "[i]t is hard to conceive of the direct expenditure departments proposing such sweeping repeal of the programs they administer."

31. For reasons perhaps more obvious, members of the House and Senate agriculture committees are far more likely to be allied with agriculture interests than are members of the Ways and Means and Finance Committees—or than the membership of the House and Senate as a whole. Who is likely to seek a seat on an agriculture committee—a representative of a rural or urban state or district? From what industry can a member of an agricultural committee look to receive a disproportionate share of her campaign contributions?

Professor Zelinsky's point is not that the tax committees are "inhabited exclusively by the pure of heart," but that they are more likely to serve disparate, competing constituencies.

32. After reading Professor Zelinsky's argument, are you, like he, "agnostic" concerning the choice between tax expenditures and direct expenditure programs, or do you generally prefer one approach or the other?

33. A relatively new statute, the Government Performance and Results Act of 1993, offers the possibility of more effective oversight of government programs, including those administered through tax expenditures. Professor Mary Heen concludes that "[t]he Results Act framework, if comprehensively applied, provides a new opportunity to address the management and oversight problems posed by the use of tax expenditures as alternatives to direct expenditure programs."[m] While promising in theory, however, Professor Heen expresses concern, based on early experience with two employment tax credits (Welfare-to-Work Tax Credit and Work Opportunity Tax Credit), that the information generated by the executive review may not lead to effective legislative oversight:

> The lack of integrated review in these particular cases does not derive from a lack of transparency or a dearth of data; instead, it represents, depending upon your view of the legislative process, either "business as usual" or a structural failure to consider tax system and direct spending alternatives as part of a coordinated program review process.[n]

C. THE TAX EXPENDITURES CONCEPT CHALLENGED

Unless carefully confined, the premise of the tax expenditures concept might be ridiculed by *reductio ad absurdum*: any portion of a taxpayer's income that the Government allows the taxpayer to keep would be a tax expenditure. In a slightly less extreme form, under a progressive income tax rate structure, any revenue lost by failure to tax everyone at the top bracket rate might be considered a tax expenditure.

The more limited view of tax expenditures requires the application of normative standards, but, as the excerpts in this subchapter demonstrate, these standards are open to challenge. Professors Kahn and Lehman argue that the definition of the "norm" in tax law cannot be divorced from broader societal judgments—that the tax law "serves to reaffirm public values that are 'normative' in every sense of the word except the one used by advocates of tax

---

m. Mary L. Heen, *Reinventing Tax Expenditure Reform: Improving Program Oversight Under the Government Performance and Results Act*, 35 WAKE FOREST L. REV. 751, 825 (2000).

n. *Id.* at 826.

expenditure budgets." Professor Bittker, perhaps the leading tax scholar of his generation, criticized the tax expenditure concept in 1969, when the idea was new and prior to the 1974 congressional mandate for an annual tax expenditure budget. Finally, the brief excerpt from Philip Oliver may cast doubt on the concept by suggesting that one deduction generally regarded as a classic tax expenditure—the deduction for home mortgage interest—may be helpful in equitably measuring income, rather than merely furthering the nontax goal of assisting taxpayers in purchasing homes.

EXPENDITURE BUDGETS: A CRITICAL VIEW
Douglas A. Kahn[*] & Jeffrey S. Lehman[**]
54 Tax Notes 1661, 1661-63 (1992)

The various tax expenditure budgets prepared in the legislative and executive branches purport to carry out a straightforward task. They claim to identify those situations in which Congress has departed from the "normative," "normal," or "correct" tax rule in a way that is equivalent to the appropriation of public funds. Or, as it is sometimes put, they expose circumstances in which Congress has chosen to subsidize certain activities indirectly, through the Internal Revenue Code.

Yet, the very statement of the task exposes its Achilles heel. It assumes the existence of one true, "correct," "normative" rule of federal income taxation that should be applied to any given transaction. The collection of all such rules stands as a kind of Platonic Internal Revenue Code, an implicit reprimand to the flawed efforts of our mortal Congress.

We believe that questions of tax policy are more complicated than that. An ideal Internal Revenue Code makes no more sense than an ideal Environmental Protection Act or an ideal Penal Code. An income tax stands inside, not outside, the society that enacts it.

The particular contours of our federal income tax serve to reaffirm public values that are "normative" in every sense of the word except the one used by advocates of tax expenditure budgets. The disallowance of a deduction for illegal bribes confirms that we think they are naughty. Similarly, the limitation on losses from wagering transactions shows that we do not consider them to be an appropriate foundation for a career. Conversely, the exclusion from income of tort recoveries is an expression of public compassion. And our refusal to tax people when their neighbors help them move furniture, or (as some have suggested) when they enjoy a few moments of leisure, suggests a shared sense of a private domain in which even the tax collector will respect people's right to be left alone.

Experts can help to clarify the implications of one tax policy choice over another. They can show how one choice favors one particular set of moral,

---

*. At time of original publication, Paul G. Kauper Professor of Law, University of Michigan.
**. At time of original publication, Assistant Professor of Law, University of Michigan.

political, or economic commitments over another. They can argue for greater
consistency in the way tensions among such commitments are resolved. They
can estimate the differences in the amount and distribution of revenues that
would be collected under different regimes. But, the ultimate choice must rest
with the citizen and not the oracle.

The Choice Among Utopias

Let us describe a series of perspectives that are frequently presented
concerning the ideal nature of an income tax:

(1) For some observers of the tax scene, any tax that alters citizen
behavior is terribly unfortunate. Such observers decry any tax that alters
individuals' economic incentives from what they would have been in a world
with no taxes and a perfect marketplace. They would prefer that the
government raise its revenues exclusively by taxing (a) activities that generate
negative externalities, and (b) goods for which the demand is entirely inelastic.
Since no income tax can pretend to be nondistortional, such observers view all
income taxes as tainted by a kind of "original sin."

(2) Other, more practically minded observers, worry that the taxes that
would satisfy perspective (1) would not generate enough revenues for the
government to finance its current level of operations. They believe that
Nicholas Kaldor had it right almost 40 years ago, when he argued that the
proper income tax system is what we now call a consumption tax. Such
observers are willing to accept the fact that a consumption tax biases
taxpayers' choice between labor and leisure. They console themselves with the
observation that at least a consumption tax avoids biasing the choice between
savings and current consumption.

(3) Another set of commentators objects that a consumption tax that
would satisfy perspective (2) ignores the new economic power reflected in
congealed, unconsumed, newly acquired wealth. They contend that all such
economic power should be reckoned in the tax base, perhaps as a proxy for an
(ideal) wealth tax. For such observers, the touchstone of income taxation must
be the sum of consumption and wealth accumulation—what is commonly
known as Haig-Simons income.

(4) Still other commentators find fault with the pure Haig-Simons
approach endorsed under perspective (3). It would offend such commentators'
notions of privacy to tax citizens on unrealized asset appreciation and on
imputed income from services or durable goods. Or, at least, it would require
a preposterous expenditure of administrative resources in an ultimately futile
quest. These observers would prefer that we tax Haig-Simons income to the
extent it is realized through market interactions.

(5) Yet another set of commentators finds fault with even the
market-delimited, realization-qualified version of the Haig-Simons approach
suggested by perspective (4). They believe that such an approach unacceptably
distorts investor incentives, leading them to overconsume and undersave, to
indulge in too much leisure and not enough work. While they are in sympathy

with the political vision that would allocate the tax burden according to accumulating economic power, they favor qualifications to that vision whenever the cost to productive incentives appears to jeopardize economic growth.

(6) Finally, one finds the United States Congress. It apparently believes that even the approach dictated by perspective (5) would leave the American economy in the wrong place. Not enough research and development, not enough low-income housing, not enough money in the hands of working families with children, not enough money in the hands of churches and museums, too many renters and not enough homeowners, etc., etc., etc.

If one is prone to depression, one can view the foregoing list of perspectives from (1) to (6) as identifying a kind of linear decline. Each is one step further from the Garden of Eden of distortion-free taxation. We view them differently. We prefer to see each perspective as emphasizing different elements in a basket of normative values—efficiency (in the neoclassical economic sense), consumption/savings neutrality, privacy, equity, administrability, charity, pragmatism, etc.

What is disturbing about the language of tax expenditures is its tone of moral absolutism. The tax expenditure budget is said to distinguish "normal" tax practice from that which is deviant. Sometimes it is said to distinguish provisions that are "normative" (?) from those that are (presumably) nonnormative (?!). This language is doubly confusing. First, it suggests that provisions that fit *within* the implicit baseline of the tax expenditure budget are somehow pure, safe, and good. They should not be changed because "neutral" principles have blessed them. Conversely, the language suggests that provisions that fall *outside* the implicit baseline of the tax expenditure budget (tax expenditures) are somehow corrupt, dangerous, and evil. They should be changed as soon as possible to conform with the "neutral" position. To flirt with them is to call one's probity into question.

This is, of course, a bit of an overstatement. But, it captures the rhetorical direction of the tax expenditure budget. And that rhetorical direction is grossly misleading. The tax expenditure budget's conception of an appropriate tax base has no legitimate claim to establishing the terms of political debate.
* * *

The Illusion of Value-Free Precision—An Example

The reference point for construction of the tax expenditure budget is a measure of taxable income that is close to position (4) above, with some variations. That may be some people's Platonic Internal Revenue Code, but it is obviously not everyone's. The choice among perspectives is a contestable, contingent, political decision. Thus, while the several existing tax expenditure budgets give an appearance of being the products of a highly sophisticated, expert, neutral examination of the tax system, they could just as accurately be characterized as exercises in mystification. They create only an illusion of value-free scientific precision in a heavily politicized domain.

Consider two features of our tax system. First, it grants a form of accelerated depreciation. Second, it does not tax unrealized gains. The first feature appears in tax expenditure budgets. Moreover, as the *Tax Notes* discussion over the past few months has made clear, many proponents of tax expenditure budgets view that as a good thing because they believe that accelerated depreciation is not "normative." Yet the second feature—the refusal to tax unrealized gains—does not appear in any tax expenditure budget.

The tax expenditure budget baseline, which distinguishes between these two features, is "normative" in the sense that it advances a particular moral or political claim. It reflects a particular balance among the ideals of efficiency, equity, neutrality, administrability, privacy, charity, and pragmatism. But, each of the six perspectives enumerated in the prior section is "normative" in precisely the same way. And at most two of the six perspectives (perspective (4) and perhaps some versions of perspective (5)) would distinguish between these two features. The others would treat both as good or both as objectionable.

One can advance plausible arguments in favor of taxing unrealized gains. One can advance plausible arguments against granting accelerated depreciation deductions. One could also argue for the status quo with regard to each of these features. But, there is no *a priori* reason to classify one feature differently from the other, or to allocate a heavier burden of persuasion to those who attack realization or defend accelerated depreciation than one allocates to those who defend realization or attack accelerated depreciation.

* * *

ACCOUNTING FOR FEDERAL "TAX SUBSIDIES" IN THE NATIONAL BUDGET

Boris I. Bittker[*]

22 National Tax Journal 244, 246-57 (1969)

Although Mr. Surrey did not address himself to the mode of presentation, his proposal implied that "tax benefit provisions" would be reported in the Budget as hypothetical expenditures, to be "classified along customary budgetary lines: assistance to business, natural resources, agriculture, aid to the elderly, medical assistance, aid to charitable institutions, and so on."[5]

* * *

Fleshing out Mr. Surrey's proposal, the Treasury has estimated the revenue lost by virtue of "the major respects in which the current income tax bases deviate from widely accepted definitions of income and standards of business accounting and from the generally accepted structure of an income

---

[*]. At time of original publication, Southmayd Professor of Law, Yale University.

5. Surrey, Taxes and the Federal Budget (speech to Financial Executives Institute, Dallas Chapter, Feb. 13, 1968), p. 13.

tax." These estimates were published, along with a discussion of the conceptual framework governing the items selected for inclusion, in an exhibit to Secretary Fowler's final report as Secretary of the Treasury, under the title "The Tax Expenditure Budget: A Conceptual Analysis." This study should be regarded as only a first step in achieving the "full accounting" envisioned by Mr. Surrey. * * *

It has been a familiar exercise for many years to compute the "cost" of a proposed tax provision by estimating the amount of revenue that would be lost by its enactment; and at first blush, a "full accounting" seems to require nothing more than an aggregation of such estimates, based on existing tax concessions, rather than on proposed ones. If that were its only prerequisite, an expansion of the Treasury's estimating facilities and staff would bring us close to achieving the promise of a "full accounting." To be fully informative, of course, the estimates would have to take account of the fact that tax concessions influence behavior; since the revenue "lost" by virtue of any tax provision depends in part on its absence, its "cost" cannot be accurately measured by merely recomputing the tax liability on the return as filed. It might turn out that the revenue effects of tax incentive provisions, if they succeed in their objective of altering behavior, are especially difficult to estimate—although these are precisely the provisions that are most in need of cost effectiveness studies. * * *

Even if the Treasury's estimates could be refined to take into account tax-induced changes in behavior, however, a major obstacle in achieving a "full accounting" would remain, viz., the fact that a systematic compilation of revenue losses requires an agreed starting point, departures from which can be identified. What is needed is not an ad hoc list of tax provisions, but a generally acceptable model, or set of principles, enabling us to decide with reasonable assurance which income tax provisions are departures from the model, whose costs are to be reported as "tax expenditures." In this connection, it is important to note that the proposed "full accounting" is evidently intended to embrace every provision that serves as the substitute for an appropriation, including those that are solely or primarily distributive in function (e.g., the extra $600 exemption for the blind and the aged).[o]

In listing the exclusion of social security benefits as a "tax expenditure" that ought to be reflected in the Federal Budget as aid to the elderly, the Treasury analysts very likely had in mind the fact that these receipts constitute income under the Haig-Simons definition. Conversely, their study accepts the deduction of business expenses under §162 as necessary to the accurate determination of net income, with the result that the revenue "lost" by virtue of this provision is not reported as a "tax expenditure" to aid private enterprise. In making this distinction, no value judgment is intended: the

---

o. Present law no longer provides an additional personal exemption for aged and blind taxpayers; they are entitled, however, to an increased standard deduction. Section 63(f). (Ed.)

deduction of business expenses and the exclusion of social security benefits are not treated differently because one provision is "good" and the other "bad," but because one is helpful or necessary in defining net income, while the other distorts the computation of income. Thus, in asking that the revenue losses resulting from "deliberate departures from accepted concepts of net income and through special exemptions, deductions and credits" be reported as "expenditures," Mr. Surrey noted that these "tax benefit provisions" will have to be separated from provisions that serve to define income accurately: "We should not, of course, overlook the difficulties of interpretation or measurement involved here."[9] * * * In the same vein, the Treasury study seeks to identify the provisions of existing law that deviate "from widely accepted definitions of income and standards of business accounting and from the generally accepted structure of an income tax."

To effect a "full accounting," then, we must first construct an ideal or correct income tax structure, departures from which will be reflected as "tax expenditures" in the National Budget. Although Mr. Surrey is not explicit on the point, his proposal has much in common with the call for a comprehensive income tax base, which similarly presupposes an ideal tax structure—based on the Haig-Simons definition of income—any departure from which is to be regarded as a maverick that must shoulder a heavy burden of justification.

The call for a "full accounting" does not by itself imply that repeal of all of these provisions is feasible or desirable, but only that the revenue lost by sticking with existing law should be disclosed in the Budget. At the same time, it is not insignificant that Mr. Surrey doubts the "efficiency" of these provisions and their ability to withstand public scrutiny if viewed as expenditures; after all, the purpose of the "full accounting" is to stimulate a re-examination of "tax expenditures," rather than merely to record them for economic historians or antiquarian statisticians. Unless the "full accounting" is to be limited to those provisions that the incumbent Secretary of the Treasury wants Congress to repeal, however, it will require a formidable list of tax provisions to be reflected as "expenditures" if the Haig-Simons definition is to be the criterion for judging the extent of the current Internal Revenue Code's departure from "a proper measurement of net income."

Such a comprehensive list of "tax expenditures" would include a number of items that Congress has so far shown no interest in repealing, despite the magnitude of the revenue "lost" by their preservation. Thus, the cash receipts and disbursements method of accounting for income—which conflicts with the Haig-Simons definition because it does not currently reflect changes in the taxpayer's net worth—can be described as a "tax subsidy," granted for the double purpose of simplifying the income-reporting process for taxpayers with rudimentary records and of easing the payment problem for taxpayers who

---

9. Surrey, The United Income Tax System—the Need for a Full Accounting (speech to Money Marketeers, Nov. 15, 1967), p. 5.

have rendered services or sold property, but have not yet collected from their customers and clients. Another example of a "tax expenditure" that has hitherto been considered sacrosanct is the exclusion of unrealized appreciation from income, a "preference" that is customarily accepted by even the most confirmed advocates of a comprehensive income tax base on the ground that difficulties in valuing the taxpayer's assets make it administratively impossible to apply the Haig-Simons definition in this area. * * *

A whole-hearted enemy of "backstairs" spending might, I suppose, argue that a disclosure of the cost of the cash receipts and disbursements method of accounting or of the realization concept would be a first step to their elimination. * * *

Favorable legislative action on such proposals is so remote a possibility, however, that one may be inclined to argue for reporting in the National Budget only those "tax expenditures" that Congress is likely to repeal—once they have been brought into the open. But if the "full accounting" is to be limited in this fashion, some of the prime candidates for inclusion on the "expenditure" side might fall by the wayside. I am not at all sure, for example, that percentage depletion and the immunity of state and municipal bond interest are more vulnerable to Congressional hostility than the cash method of accounting. * * *

Assuming a consistent application of the Haig-Simons definition, however, there are many other areas that would generate "tax expenditures" for inclusion in the Budget, including the exclusion from taxable income of gifts, bequests, life insurance proceeds, and recoveries for personal injuries and wrongful death; * * * personal and dependency exemptions; imputed income from assets and housewives' services; the non-recognition provisions (e.g., exchanges of like-kind property, corporate reorganizations, etc.); depreciation deductions that exceed declines in market value * * *; current deductions for expenditures that have value beyond the current year (e.g., research and experimental expenses, institutional advertising, and outlays for industrial know-how); special accounting privileges (e.g., installment sale reporting); the foreign tax credit[15] and other items. The Treasury study—perhaps because it is offered as a "minimum" rather than comprehensive list—makes a number of compromises in applying the Haig-Simons definition in these areas. Thus, it estimates the cost of excluding employers' contributions to pension plans and

---

15. The foreign tax credit protects taxpayers with foreign operations against double income taxation; but of all possible ways of accomplishing this end, it is the most costly for the United States. If its cost were reflected as a "tax expenditure," Congress might decide that relief from double taxation could be procured more "efficiently" by hiring more persuasive ambassadors, speaking softly but carrying a big stick, or threatening to reduce our appropriations for foreign aid. In the alternative, Congress might decide that if a deduction is a sufficient recognition of the added burden of a state or local income tax, it is equally sufficient in the case of a foreign tax. The proper treatment of the foreign tax credit is discussed in the Treasury's Tax Expenditure Budget, Annual Report of the Secretary of the Treasury on the State of the Finances (fiscal year ended June 30, 1968) (1969), p. 331; but no estimate of its cost is made because of the complexity of the issues involved.

the interest component of life insurance savings, but not the revenue cost of excluding increases in the taxpayer's net worth resulting from other transactions. Similarly debatable lines are drawn at other points, in that the study estimates the revenue cost of excluding or deducting: public assistance, but not gifts from charitable agencies, friends, and relatives; sick pay and workmen's compensation, but not recoveries and settlements in personal injury suits; child care expenses of employees, but not their moving expenses; accelerated depreciation on buildings, but not straight-line depreciation (even though it too may exceed the property's decline in market value); the expensing of research and experimental expenditures, but not the rapid amortization of such outlays (even if their long-term value is substantial), nor the expensing of comparable outlays for good will, industrial know-how, etc.; nonbusiness state and local taxes, but not foreign taxes. * * *

The revenue cost of the omitted items may have been too difficult to estimate with the data at hand when the Tax Expenditure Budget was prepared; I mention them not to criticize an admittedly "minimum" list for conforming to its self-description, but to illustrate the scope of the Haig-Simons definition. Because I have recently discussed the ramifications of a consistent adherence to this definition, I will not undertake to list here the many other provisions of existing law that, in my opinion, depart from that definition. Suffice it to say that a "full accounting" for these departures would be a formidable undertaking, comparable to Prof. Charles O. Galvin's challenging proposal for a tax model based on the comprehensive income tax base concept. There is, however, a major difference between the two projects, stemming from the fact that the Haig-Simons definition provides no guidance to many structural issues that must be decided in any income tax law. As to these decisions, the unofficial research model proposed by Prof. Galvin can experiment with alternatives, while the Treasury's "full accounting" will have to select one "correct" model against which to measure existing law. Because I see no way to select such an "official" model for these structural provisions, I am not sanguine about the prospects for a "full accounting."

One such area is the rate structure. In 1964, income tax rates were substantially reduced, for the stated purpose of encouraging economic growth. Since an alternative method of accomplishing this objective was a federal subsidy, should the reduction have been reflected in the Treasury's "Tax Expenditure Budget?" The logic of the "full accounting" approach suggests an affirmative response, so that the cost of this effort to increase economic growth by a rate reduction would be constantly brought to public attention, thus encouraging an annual review of both the merits of its objective and its efficiency as compared with other devices and programs to accomplish the same end. * * *

Once it is decided that a rate reduction may be a form of "back door spending," however, we encounter a troublesome—perhaps an insoluble—problem of measurement. The cost of the 1964 experiment in encouraging economic growth by a rate reduction might, I suppose, be ascertained by computing the difference between (a) the revenue actually collected, and (b) the amount that would have been produced if the old rates had been perpetuated. (Ideally, of course, account should be taken of the effect of the reduced rate on the volume of taxable income; but if this is not done for other "tax expenditures," presumably it would not be done in this instance either.) The aggregate cost of the tax reduction would then be allocated among income classes, to reflect the cost of the tax cut for each such group. This process could be repeated for each tax cut in our history, so that the "tax expenditure" section of the National Budget would report, separately, the "cost" of every such change, classified as an aid to investment, a device to encourage consumer spending, and so on, depending on its purpose. The aggregate to be reported for the current year would thus be the difference between the revenue produced by the rates actually in effect, and the amount that would have been produced if the highest rates in history had been preserved. The benchmark year would vary from one taxable income class to another, of course, since the peak rate applicable to each class would be the standard for determining the "cost" of encouraging that group of taxpayers to engage in investment, consumption, or other tax-favored activity.

      * * *

Another problem—equally unsolved by the Haig-Simons definition, but equally troublesome to the "full accounting" approach—is the taxable unit to be used in computing the "tax expenditures" that are to be reflected in the National Budget. The problem can be illustrated by a question: should the difference between the tax liability of a married man (or a head of a household) and that of a single individual with the same taxable income be reflected on the expenditure side of the National Budget, as a subsidy to family life, in the interest of a "full accounting"? * * *

It would simplify the search for a "full accounting" to accept the Code's existing classification of taxpayers, disregarding the possibility that structural decisions in this area constitute "tax expenditures." If this were to be done, however, it would seem equally appropriate to me to treat taxpayers who are blind, over 65, or otherwise "different" as appropriate taxpaying units whose exemptions or other allowances are simply devices for imposing rates appropriate to their divergent taxpaying abilities; and the same could be said of taxpayers who have minor children, support aged parents, suffer from illness, or are victimized by fire or theft. * * *

A taxonomic problem that creates similar difficulties for a "full accounting" arises from the separate rate schedules that are applicable under current law to individuals and corporations. Does the fact that the individual rate is lower than the corporate rate at the $5,000 income level mean that the difference is a "tax expenditure" to aid low-bracket individuals? Conversely, since the corporate rate is lower than the individual rate at the $200,000 level, does *this* difference constitute a "tax expenditure" to aid corporate business?

Or are the two rate schedules simply not to be compared, on the theory that we have two entirely separate income taxes, each levied on its own self-contained group of taxpayers? * * *

Of course, if the Haig-Simons definition were to be applied to individual taxpayers with rigor, there would be no need to compute the income of legal entities like corporations, since the natural person's net worth computation would have fully taken the corporate activities into account. On this theory, the "tax expenditure" to be reported in the interest of achieving a "full accounting" would take account of the taxes that would be collected from individual shareholders if unrealized appreciation and depreciation on their stock entered into the computation of income.   The Treasury's "Tax Expenditure Budget," however, does not attempt such a rigorous application of the Haig-Simons definition, but instead contains estimates of the revenue cost of existing provisions relating to Western Hemisphere Trade Corporations, the excess bad debt reserves of financial institutions, and the deferral of tax on shipping companies.

The study's working hypothesis, stated without independent discussion, is "[t]he assumption inherent in current law, that corporations are separate entities and subject to income taxation independently from their shareholders." * * * Yet the exemption from corporate tax that is granted to Subchapter S corporations and regulated investment companies is not treated as a "tax expenditure"; evidently it is appropriate to view these corporations as conduits rather than entities. * * * [D]ifficulties in deciding whether corporations are conduits or entities suggest that there simply are no "generally accepted" principles specifying the proper relationship between a corporation's income and its shareholders' tax liability—with the result that it is difficult, if not impossible, to apply the "tax expenditure" concept in this area.

The proper classification of tax-exempt organizations presents another problem for the "full accounting" approach. Should the tax exemptions accorded to educational institutions, churches, charitable organizations, social clubs, and other non-profit institutions be reflected as "tax expenditures" to benefit education, religion, charity, and social intercourse? Or is it more appropriate to view the federal income tax as a device by which the government shares in the profits of activities that are carried on for the personal benefit of individual taxpayers, so that the activities of nonprofit institutions are not a proper subject for income taxation? So regarded, the tax exemption accorded to these institutions is an acknowledgment of, rather than a departure from, the "true nature" of the federal income tax; and hence it is not a "tax expenditure" required for a "full accounting" in the National Budget. * * *

The same question—is tax-exemption an "expenditure" or not?—must be answered with respect to state and municipal governmental agencies, which are not taxed by the federal government on their income, whether derived from taxation, the sale of property or services, investments, or other sources. One might, of course, assert that the immunity from federal taxation that is enjoyed by state and local governments constitutes an "expenditure" because it accomplishes the same result as federal grants to these agencies; and that a failure to acknowledge this infusion of federal assistance understates the federal contribution to their well-being. On the other hand, one is tempted to argue that governmental agencies (even if engaged in activities that compete with private business) do not realize "income" in the Haig-Simons sense, or that, if they do, the federal income tax properly exempts them because it is concerned only with activities carried on for private profit. If this view is accepted, their exemption would not be recorded as a "tax expenditure."

If we conclude that the tax exemption accorded to non-profit organizations and governmental agencies is not a tax expenditure, however, a doubt arises about the proper way to reflect the deductions allowed to individuals for charitable contributions and state and local taxes, as well as the exclusion from taxable income of state and municipal bond interest. To the extent that these tax provisions inure to the benefit of the individual taxpayer, they might be properly classified as tax expenditures. To the extent of the benefit inuring to the non-profit or governmental agency, however, should these exemptions be bracketed with the agency's *own* exemption, and excluded from the list of "tax expenditures"? If the purpose of a "full accounting" is to disclose the cost of all "government expenditures made through the tax system," it would seem desirable to fish or cut bait: either record the tax-exempt organization's tax benefits as "expenditures" whether they derive from its own exemption or from concessions allowed to others that are passed on to it; or disregard these benefits entirely. To pick and choose among these tax provisions, recording some but not others as "tax expenditures," is a way of compromising on a middle ground, but it falls short of a "full accounting."

* * *

SECTION 265(2): A COUNTERPRODUCTIVE SOLUTION TO A NONEXISTENT PROBLEM
Philip D. Oliver[*]
40 Tax Law Review 351, 394-96 (1985)

The taxpayer with ready cash can purchase a house outright. Instead of investing his cash to earn a taxable stream of income and then paying nondeductible rent from after-tax dollars, in effect, he can receive a tax-free flow of imputed income from the personal residence. The interest deduction places the taxpayer purchasing his house with borrowed funds in a similar position. For example, suppose each of three taxpayers, A, B, and C, desires to purchase a personal residence costing $50,000. A and B each has $50,000 of ready cash; thus, they can purchase their residences for cash, or invest the

---

[*]. At time of original publication, Associate Professor of Law, University of Arkansas at Little Rock.

cash and purchase the residences with borrowed funds. *C* has no available assets and therefore must borrow in order to purchase his residence. Assume further, and somewhat artificially, that the taxpayers can lend or borrow money at 10% interest. Ignoring the transactions described below, the three taxpayers have equal taxable income and will itemize deductions.

A uses his $50,000 cash to purchase his house. He receives neither taxable income nor a deduction as a result of the transaction. The imputed income of the rental value of the house, of course, is not included in income.

Unlike *A, B* chooses to invest his $50,000 cash at 10% interest. He borrows $50,000, also at 10%, to purchase his house. *B* receives taxable income of $5,000 from his investment, but the deduction for the $5,000 interest paid by *B* will offset the interest income. *B*'s taxable income therefore is equal to *A*'s.[184] Because these taxpayers have engaged in transactions that are substantially equivalent in economic terms, their taxable income should be affected in the same way.

C, having no choice, also borrows to purchase his residence. Like *B*, he receives a $5,000 interest deduction. Since *C* has no offsetting income item, *C* has $5,000 less taxable income then either *A* or *B*. This result, however, is precisely what we should expect. *A* and *B* each has $50,000 of assets that, given a 10% interest rate of return, will produce $5,000 annually.

* * *

The denial of an interest deduction thus would favor those with liquid excess cash and the ability to divert it to investments producing only untaxed imputed income. It would disfavor those who borrow to purchase assets that produce imputed income. The interest deduction thus effectively allows those not having sufficient wealth and liquidity to purchase personal assets without borrowing to enjoy the benefits of untaxed imputed personal income.

* * *

Notes and Questions

34. In criticizing the tax expenditures concept, Professors Kahn and Lehman did not mean that every provision in the Internal Revenue Code is normal because it exists, thus depriving us of any standard for judgment. They are saying, in effect, that "normal" is not a useful standard. Virtually every tax provision has political or social implications. In their view, all provisions

---

184. *A* and *B* may not have identical taxable incomes since *B*'s offsetting income and deduction may affect other computations. * * *

Of more importance is the assumption that all three taxpayers would itemize deductions even without the interest deduction. If this were not the case, *A* would be in a favored position since a portion of the interest deduction of *B* and *C* would be absorbed by the zero bracket amount, and only the excess would be deductible. *See* I.R.C. § 63.

These refinements, however, do not alter the basic point. The interest deduction, even in the case of interest arising from a purely personal expenditure, assures substantial equity among these three typical taxpayers.

should be reviewed on their merits, without trying for an automatic rule that will distinguish tax expenditures from normal provisions.

35. Is it fair to treat failure to adopt the Haig-Simons definition of income as a tax expenditure?

36. Many items generally regarded as tax expenditures are also identified as items of tax preference under the alternative minimum tax provisions (sections 55-59). The AMT provisions demonstrate congressional ambivalence about these items. Does the existence of the AMT provisions support either the proponents or the detractors of the tax expenditures concept?

37. Does Oliver's argument suggest that the home mortgage interest deduction is justified? That it does not constitute a tax expenditure?

38. Note that defense of the present-law home mortgage interest deduction is necessary only because present law fails to reach the imputed income generated by owner-occupied homes. A more ideal system might tax all owners on the imputed income from housing, in which case the interest deduction, as an expense associated with the generation of taxable income, clearly would be appropriate. In that case, the three taxpayers in Oliver's example would have appropriate differences in taxable income as a matter of course.

39. Are we left with a hopeless standoff between the proponents of the tax expenditures approach and its opponents?

D. WHAT FORM SHOULD TAX EXPENDITURES TAKE?

This subchapter opens with a brief excerpt from an article written by William Bradley and Philip Oliver in 1983, not long before the investment tax credit was virtually repealed in the Tax Reform Act of 1986. While the authors focused on the ambiguity in the ITC statute and the Service's administration of it, the broader point made by the excerpt is the importance of clarity in any tax expenditure.

The primary excerpt in this subchapter is from Professor Goldberg's article on "periodic" tax expenditures. Tax expenditures can take many forms. Some, like the former ITC, are one-time exemptions. Under the ITC immediately prior to the Tax Reform Act of 1986, taxpayers who made qualifying expenditures could reduce their taxes by ten percent of the amount expended. No further subsidy from the ITC was to be expected from that year's expenditures (though taxpayers might expect that the program would continue to be available for the next year's expenditures).

Many tax expenditures, however, give rise to ongoing tax preferences. Professor Goldberg terms these preferences "periodic." Examples include the exclusion of interest on most bonds issued by states and their subdivisions (section 103) and the deduction of interest on home mortgages (section 163(h)(3)). Purchasers of state-issued bonds and homes expect to derive a tax advantage not just in the year of purchase, but in the future as well. And they expect to be able to sell these assets to others, who can themselves benefit from the same favorable tax treatment.

Professor Goldberg discusses the problems that arise when Congress changes its mind and removes a periodic tax expenditure.

INVESTMENT TAX CREDIT: THE ILLUSORY INCENTIVE

William H. Bradley[*] & Philip D. Oliver[**]
2 Virginia Tax Review 267, 269-70 (1983)

If ITC is to provide its intended salutary effect, it is apparent that clarity in application of the provisions is important. In fact, while always desirable, clarity is of significantly greater importance here than in most areas of tax law, because a "tax expenditure" such as ITC can be justified only as a stimulus, as a means of encouraging taxpayers to do things which otherwise have nothing to do with taxation or tax policy (in the case of ITC, making investments in certain capital assets).[11]

* * *

The major thesis of this article is that the failure by Congress and the Internal Revenue Service to provide clear guidance to taxpayers with respect to the question of whether particular items of property qualify for the credit has frustrated, to a significant extent, the incentive to invest intended by Congress when it enacted the ITC provisions. In prescribing property which qualifies for the credit, inconsistent and vacillating interpretations by the Internal Revenue Service have compounded the ambiguity of the statute and the regulations. To the extent that the availability of ITC, where the primary governmental goal is unrelated to the raising of revenue, is governed by an unclear legal framework, the likely result is that taxpayers will tend to make the same investment they otherwise would have made, then seek the maximum ITC available. This phenomenon entirely frustrates the

---

[*]. At time of original publication, partner, Sutherland, Asbill & Brennan, Atlanta, Georgia.

[**]. At time of original publication, Assistant Professor of Law, University of Arkansas at Little Rock.

11. Most tax provisions are directed only at the raising of revenue, and while complexity and ambiguity are never desirable, at least in these instances the complexity and ambiguity are likely to be associated with traditional tax goals, such as the accurate determination of the amount, timing, and character of the income.

governmental policy of encouraging investment and converts a stimulus into a windfall.[16]

TAX SUBSIDIES: ONE-TIME VS. PERIODIC—
AN ECONOMIC ANALYSIS OF THE TAX POLICY
ALTERNATIVES
Daniel S. Goldberg[*]

49 Tax Law Review 305, 305-27, 329, 331-47 (1994)

Introduction

The current tax system integrates structural revenue raising provisions with policy-driven tax incentive, or subsidy, provisions designed to induce taxpayers to engage in activities favored by Congress for extrinsic political or social reasons. The wisdom of this dual mission has been the subject of extensive analysis and criticism. Indeed, the Tax Reform Act of 1986 marked a distinct shift away from the use of tax incentives.

It now has become apparent that this country is likely to reverse much of the 1986 tax reform and to resume using the tax system to provide incentives for business and other socially desirable activities. * * *

At this stage in tax evolution, one either could warn again of the dangers of using the tax system to advance social and economic goals, or accept the inevitable and attempt to insure that tax incentives are structured in the best possible way. Adopting the latter course, this Article offers a new and useful framework for structuring tax policy in the 1990's in order to minimize harmful economic and social side effects of tax incentives. The Article identifies the most pernicious type of tax incentives as periodic subsidies, that is, subsidies that are available to taxpayers over a period of years, rather than on a one-time basis. Periodic subsidies are inefficient and are likely to decrease the horizontal equity of the tax system. Drawing on the jurisprudence of just compensation law and on economic theory, the Article concludes that Congress should refuse to succumb to the temptation to use periodic tax incentives as an instrument of tax and economic policy but, instead, should employ only one-time subsidies. In reaching this conclusion, the Article takes issue with the recent scholarship of Professors Michael Graetz[7] and Louis Kaplow[8] whose advice to eschew transition relief for tax changes apparently has gained substantial currency among tax policymakers.

---

16. Even where the law is unclear, the possible availability of ITC will still provide taxpayers some motivation to make a given investment, despite possible challenge from the Service. This would appear to be an inefficient "tax expenditure," however, since it can reasonably be assumed that a taxpayer will not substantially alter its investment policy when it knows that it may be "buying a lawsuit."

*. At time of original publication, Professor of Law, University of Maryland School of Law.

7. Michael J. Graetz, Legal Transitions: The Case of Retroactivity in Income Tax Revision, 126 U. Pa. L. Rev. 47 (1977-1978) [hereinafter Tax Revision].

8. Louis Kaplow, An Economic Analysis of Legal Transitions, 99 Harv. L. Rev. 509 (1986).

* * *

A New Tax Policy Framework for Tax Incentives
The Traditional Approach: Tax Expenditures

All tax incentive provisions have one thing in common, regardless of their form. They are designed to generate a movement of capital or labor into a particular activity by reducing the effective tax on income from that activity. A tax incentive provision works only when it has the effect of reducing a participant's tax. The resultant reduction in the federal government's revenue collection attributable to the tax incentive provision can be viewed as a subsidy to the tax-favored activity. Stanley Surrey referred to the lost revenue attributable to a tax incentive provision as a "tax expenditure."

Commentators sometimes disagree about which tax provisions represent subsidies and which represent integral parts of the income tax structure because they involve measurement of income. Structural components are the so-called normative elements of a revenue raising system. They include the definition of income, the specification of accounting periods, the determination of entities subject to tax, and the specification of tax rate schedules and exemption levels. Thus, a change in tax rates, for example, does not constitute a subsidy. Rather, tax rates represent a cooperative agreement on burden sharing once the tax base has been established.

In contrast, a tax subsidy is a special preference that represents a departure from the normal tax structure, designed to favor a particular industry, activity or class of people. In that sense, tax subsidies represent an alternative to direct government financing of the recipients of those preferences and should be analyzed as such. Examples of tax subsidies include cost recovery deductions exceeding economic depreciation and various targeted tax benefits ranging from the deduction for research and development expenses to the exclusion for scholarships.

Although tax rates are not tax subsidies, the economic benefit of any tax subsidy through deduction or exemption is influenced significantly by the tax rates. The greater the tax rate, the greater will be the subsidy impact of a special deduction or exclusion.

Long before the 1980's, Stanley Surrey and his adherents argued that activities should be encouraged, if at all, through direct government subsidies instead of tax incentives. They contended that using the tax system to subsidize activities was undesirable, and that if the social policy objectives were desired, direct government grants would be preferable to tax incentive provisions.

Under what now has become accepted as traditional tax policy analysis, based upon Surrey's insight, tax incentive provisions are categorized according to the manner in which they operate: by exclusion, deduction or credit. Traditional analysis focuses on the upside down nature of tax subsidies that operate through exclusions or deductions by comparing them to direct expenditures. Thus, tax policy analysis under the traditional approach would ask whether the tax system is a more efficient means for providing the subsidy than a direct grant and, if so, whether the subsidy should take the form of an exclusion, deduction or credit, bearing in mind the equity of each mechanism.

A New Framework: One-Time vs. Periodic Subsidies

A comparison of tax incentive provisions with direct grants and the trichotomy of alternative forms of subsidy, while important, is typically where analysis of tax incentive provisions ends. Tax policy analysis should take the further, and I believe essential, step of dividing tax incentive provisions into two categories: (1) those that provide one-time subsidies in the year of acquisition of the property or commencement of the activity and (2) those that operate each year the property is owned or the activity is conducted by artificially increasing the after-tax yield from the property or activity. This additional step is even more important than the steps under the traditional approach. Such a distinction becomes particularly important whenever a decision is made to discontinue a tax subsidy.

The investment tax credit and the deduction for research and development expenses represent examples of the first category of incentives. Once received by the taxpayer, the subsidy cannot be removed or altered. The decision to purchase the property or engage in the activity is affected by the one-time payment, which would be considered together with the current and long-term financial projections for the activity. This type of tax incentive can be turned on and off by the government without concern for ignoring the taxpayer's reliance because the taxpayer's subsidy cannot be affected by later government policy. To be sure, the following year Congress could increase the subsidy so that taxpayers who waited a year could obtain a greater benefit than those taxpayers who acted earlier. A taxpayer's reliance argument, however, would be no greater than the consumer who purchased an item of clothing at full price when he could have waited for the item to go on sale. The taxpayer may feel unhappy, but has not suffered a direct subsidy reduction; he has received exactly what he bargained for notwithstanding the post-acquisition price reduction.

The second type of tax incentive operates through subsidies made in periodic (generally annual) installments. Examples include accelerated depreciation and tax-exempt interest on municipal bonds. In enacting the tax incentive provision, the government has promised the taxpayer that if she acquires the property, the federal government each year will subsidize the economic yield. For example, accelerated depreciation promises the owner an annual subsidy in the amount of the reduced tax liability resulting from the accelerated portion of the depreciation (reduced by the present value of the anticipated tax on the extra gain at time of sale).[24] Similarly, municipal bonds

---

24. Periodic deductions, such as nonaccelerated depreciation, do not necessarily represent subsidies. For example, depreciation represents a mechanical means of allocating the cost of property

promise the owner an annual subsidy in the amount of the forgone federal tax on the interest received from the issuer. Thus, in deciding whether to acquire property or engage in the desired activity, the taxpayer makes a present value calculation of an annuity of tax subsidies beginning in the year of acquisition and ending with the year of expected disposition (or full depreciation of the property or maturity of the tax-exempt bond). Thus, the taxpayer has a legitimate reliance interest in expecting the subsidy to continue for the life of the activity, unless the duration of the subsidy otherwise was limited initially.[25]

The economic consequences of periodic subsidies are more variable and unpredictable than those of one-time subsidies. The financial impact of a one-time tax subsidy can be computed in a fairly straightforward manner. A taxpayer can value the subsidy because tax rates will be known for the year of the subsidy. Therefore, policymakers can set the subsidy at the appropriate level to elicit the desired activity.

Periodic subsidies, on the other hand, involve economic benefits extending beyond the year of the taxpayer's expenditure. Accordingly, a subsequent event such as a change in the tax rates affects the subsidy. For example, a reduction in tax rates in subsequent years effectively reduces the amount of a periodic deduction or exemption subsidy. If the after-tax yield to a taxpayer in a tax-subsidized activity declines, property customized for or dedicated on a long-term basis to that activity suffers a reduction in value as well. Thus, although changes in tax rates are not themselves subsidies, changes in tax rates from a long-standing norm will affect the level of a subsidy. Periodic subsidies, therefore, represent something of an unguided missile in tax policy.

Whether a subsidy takes the form of an exclusion, deduction or credit, however, often is not the most relevant feature in analyzing the effect of the subsidy. The most significant feature of a subsidy from an economic viewpoint in many cases is whether it is periodic and, therefore, whether taxpayers act currently with the expectation of obtaining benefits in future years.

This feature may have practical political ramifications as well. A one-time subsidy requires an immediate outlay by the government to fund the subsidy.

---

over the property's life; in that sense, it attempts to mirror, as much as practicable, the property's decline in value. As such, this deduction and other periodic deductions do not represent subsidies, but rather are structural as an inherent part of the measurement of income.

25. The low income housing credit, a technically complex tax subsidy, see IRC § 42, allows a tax credit in annual installments over 10 years for qualified low-income rental housing. It has elements of both a periodic subsidy and a series of one-time subsidies. The credit appears to be in the nature of a periodic subsidy because although qualification to receive the credit is determined at the outset, the credit is available in installments. Yet, it also has elements of a series of one-time subsidies because eligibility to continue receiving the tax credit installments depends upon continued qualification each year the credit is claimed (which entails more than merely refraining from disposing of the property), see IRC § 42(g) (defining "qualified low-income housing project"), and there are provisions for recapture of a portion of previously claimed credits if eligibility is not continued throughout a 15-year compliance period, see IRC § 42(j).

Accordingly, it would have to be accounted for entirely in the year it is availed of by the taxpayer, through purchase or expenditure, in the form of lower tax collections, thereby creating a greater budget deficit in that year. In contrast, a periodic subsidy of equivalent value could be accounted for over its entire life. Therefore, although a one-time subsidy may be a theoretical substitute for a periodic subsidy, it may not be a politically viable one.

A government's choice of a periodic subsidy instead of a one-time subsidy masks its real cost. In effect, it allows the government easy tax subsidy payment terms because it is accounted for through reduced tax collections in years subsequent to the year in which the subsidized taxpayer engaged in the desired activity or made the desired expenditure. It therefore creates the illusion that subsidy payments are to be made in the future, whereas the government has committed itself in the initial year to make those payments. In essence, the government has borrowed money in the initial year to make a subsidy payment in the amount of the present value of the series of periodic tax benefits, and will repay that borrowing, plus interest, in installments. The ability to obfuscate the real cost of the tax subsidy through the use of a periodic subsidy, however, should not dictate its use.

The Fundamental Problems in Removing Periodic Subsidies

Equity

Periodic Subsidies Contrasted with One-Time Subsidies

Repeal of a periodic tax subsidy on which the taxpayer has acted in reliance is inequitable and can have a serious destabilizing effect on the economy. As a result, Congress should not remove a periodic subsidy without either transition relief for or compensation of the recipient.

The inequity created by repeal of a periodic tax subsidy can be understood best by observing the dynamics of a periodic subsidy. Introduction of a subsidy may result in some degree of extraordinary profits for recipients. If a lengthy adjustment period is needed for taxpayers to respond to the subsidy, the subsidy could result in windfalls to those recipients who already engage in, or otherwise would have engaged in, the desired activity, or to those who respond to the subsidy quickly. Those windfall benefits would continue until a sufficient amount of the encouraged activity develops to allow market forces to bid down profits from those activities. Excess profits are created during the adjustment period to encourage the desired behavior. The government cannot attempt to recoup the windfalls because to do so would blunt the incentive effect of the subsidy.

Moreover, during the adjustment period, property particularly suitable for the subsidized activity, if in limited supply, would increase in value because the return that it generates, including the subsidy, would increase. The property's increase in value largely would reflect the present value of the excess profits during the adjustment period.

The removal of the subsidy is precisely the reverse side of the coin. When a periodic tax subsidy is reduced or eliminated before the activity is terminated (or prior to an announced termination date), an owner who already has made the expenditure cannot undo that decision. The owner's profit from the activity reflects and is dependent on the subsidy. The owner's reduced profit (or losses) resulting from elimination of the subsidy will continue until aggregate market output in the activity adjusts and is reduced sufficiently to raise prices. During the adjustment period, the owner will suffer reduced income or operating losses. The longer the adjustment period, the greater the overall economic impact of the subsidy's repeal on the owner. Likewise, the value of the activity or property dedicated to the activity will be reduced, reflecting its reduced return, which then would not include the subsidy that has been removed. That economic loss would not merely offset the previous windfall because those who suffer the loss may or may not have been recipients of the previous windfall.[27]

A periodic subsidy represents a government promise of future benefits or subsidy payments that are intended to cause taxpayers to make current expenditures and changes in their investments. A taxpayer's decision to make that expenditure is based upon the estimated present value of the stream of subsidy payments.[28] Removing the subsidy for those who already have responded represents a breach of promise.

The injury resulting from this breach of promise should be analyzed by reference to two distinct interests that the recipient has in the subsidy and for which the recipient may be entitled to protection: first, the interest in continuing to receive the subsidy itself for the agreed-upon term, and second, the right to retain a capitalized value of the subsidy for disposition. From the perspective of both equity and long-term economic efficiency, the recipient of a subsidy should be entitled to continue receiving the periodic subsidy promised, even if the subsidy results in large gains to the recipient. Moreover, in some cases a transferee of the subsidized property or activity also should be entitled to the continuing benefits of the subsidy. If a periodic subsidy is to be removed, however, the recipient should be compensated by the government for the value of the removed subsidy that has been capitalized into the price of the subsidized property or activity.

---

27. For example, a taxpayer who purchased property for its then fair market value, which already reflected the value of the subsidy, will have paid a premium for the subsidy benefits. Removal of the subsidy will cause a loss to that taxpayer equal to that premium, that is, the portion of that taxpayer's purchase price attributable to the subsidy.

28. Professor Graetz, however, would argue, in effect, that such a present value calculation would have been irrational because the taxpayer would have been unreasonable to expect the subsidy payments to continue for the duration of the defined term—for example, years to maturity of a tax-exempt bond, or the entire recovery period of a depreciable asset. Rather, "[i]n the market context, only behavior that takes into account probabilities of change is treated as reasonable." Graetz, Tax Revision, note 7, at 66. Treasury, at least in 1977, took a contrary view. See Treasury Dep't, Blueprints for Basic Tax Reform 187, 200-01 (1977) (favoring grandfathering and phase-ins).

One-time subsidies, in contrast, generally can be removed without inequity to its recipients. When a tax incentive elicits oversupply and therefore production of an unneeded item, the government should be able to eliminate it prospectively. Otherwise, the economy would be saddled forever with any artificially induced market inefficiency.

Repeal of a one-time subsidy is always prospective. To be sure, even one-time subsidies can elicit changes in behavior that reverberate throughout the economy and can have far-reaching effects. That is true regardless of whether the subsidies are made through the tax system or directly. For example, a one-year investment tax credit, if effective, will cause manufacturers to increase their purchases of productive equipment and machinery because of the reduced cost of the machinery. Those purchases should allow expanded production and reduce end product production costs, as well as end product prices, because of the increased supply of the end product. Thus, purchasers of the end product share the reduction in the cost of machinery resulting from the one-time subsidy. The sharing ratio depends upon the elasticity of demand for the end product (that is, the effect of a price change on the amount demanded) and the length of the adjustment period.

Users of that product may come to depend upon lower prices of the product and adjust their behavior and choices accordingly. For example, they may come to depend upon an adequate supply of the product at its prevailing price, even though that price prevails only because of a government subsidy. If the one-time subsidy is eliminated, the cost structure of new producers increases, thereby reducing the supply of that product and pushing up the price. The product user again shares the cost increase. Does that user now have any argument that he reasonably relied upon the subsidy for the product and is entitled to continue buying that product at the subsidized price?

This example illustrates the destabilizing effect on the economy of all subsidies, whether made through the tax system or otherwise, and whether one-time or periodic. Turning the spigot on and off can significantly impact the economics of the subsidized property or activity. Subsidies, therefore, should be used sparingly and then only when overriding policy justifications dictate.

One-time subsidies, however, do not create an interest to recipients on which they can rely for similar subsidies in the future. The immediate recipient of the one-time subsidy (in the illustration, the producer) makes its economic decisions based upon that knowledge, but should be precluded from claiming reliance on any implied promise or expectation that the subsidy will be repeated in future years.

For the user of the product manufactured by the subsidy recipient and others further down the chain, the introduction and later removal of the subsidy are similar to all other changes in cost or demand structure affecting their products. Although the subsidies can be destabilizing, they do not create reliance interests. The user should not be able to rely on the government's continuation of the subsidy.

* * * [T]he harm resulting from destabilizing effects of one-time subsidies is very different in degree from the harm resulting from the removal of periodic subsidies, on which recipients have relied directly in making long-term business decisions. The first elicits objections from businesses that it is difficult to plan purchases and production and that government subsidization policy has made it more difficult. The second, however, elicits objections rising to the level of breach of promise against the government. That objection in the private law context is the type that gives a remedy of damages to the injured party. Although these differences may seem a matter of degree, they are so large that they become differences in kind.

The Right to Continuation of the Periodic Subsidy for the Duration of the Activity

The clearest example of a periodic subsidy for which recipients should be protected by continuation of the subsidy is the exclusion from gross income of interest from state and local bonds. Because a tax-exempt bondholder is not taxable on the interest from the bond, market forces cause the yield or interest rate on a tax-exempt bond to be significantly lower than an equivalent taxable bond. The relevant financial comparison of the two bonds should be their respective after-tax yields rather than pretax yields. The issue price of these bonds, by virtue of market forces, reflects the value of the tax exemption so that the after-tax yield from such bonds approximately equals the after-tax yield of taxable bonds of equivalent credit quality and term. Viewed another way, a prospective purchaser of a tax-exempt bond pays a premium for the bond compared to the price that would be paid for a taxable bond of equivalent pretax yield. The premium reflects the value of the exemption from income tax of the stream of interest payments to be earned on the bond.

The exclusion from income of the interest appears to be a subsidy to bondholders. In reality, however, a large part of the subsidy is transferred to the issuing state or municipality because the exemption permits the state or municipality to borrow money by issuing the bonds at a lower-than-market interest rate. The allocation of the subsidy between the issuer and the private investor depends on the supply and demand of tax-exempt obligations which, in turn, depends on the investors' marginal income tax rates.

If the tax exemption for existing state and municipal debt obligations were eliminated, the owners of those bonds would have a justifiable complaint that they relied on the government's promise of interest income exclusion in making their investment decisions for the term of the bond. These bonds should be entitled to continued exclusion, regardless of whether new bonds issued by states or municipalities are eligible for similar tax-exempt status. Indeed, those investors paid for the promise of tax exemption by paying a premium for the bond relative to an equivalent taxable bond.

Arguably, the risk of reduction or loss of the subsidy, for example, the removal of the tax exclusion for the interest, is discounted by the market and, therefore, also is capitalized in the bonds' value. If that is the case, the government's subsidy is more of an expectation of likely government action or inaction, for which there is no commitment, than it is a promise. Therefore, the tax exclusion would not be fully capitalized, causing the interest rate on the bonds to include a risk premium reflecting the possibility of the change in the law. But it appears certain, given the longstanding existence of the exclusion, that the tax exemption is regarded by investors as a promise. Accordingly, virtually all of the exclusion is reflected in the bond's value.

Thus, it is no more justifiable for the government to terminate unilaterally a periodic subsidy that has already elicited the desired behavior by recipients, without transition relief (that is, grandfathering or compensation) than it is for the government to coerce repayment of a one-time subsidy. This equivalence leads one to conclude that a periodic subsidy should not be removed for current recipients unless transition relief is provided. To restate the proposition, a periodic subsidy should be continued for the current recipient who reasonably anticipated that the subsidy would continue and acted in reliance on it.

* * *

The Right to Receive or Be Compensated for the Capitalized Value of the Periodic Subsidy Upon its Removal

A second problem with periodic subsidies involves the protection of the recipient's interest in a somewhat more debatable manner: the protection of the capitalization of the subsidy in the value of the subsidized property or activity. * * *

Returning to the illustration involving tax-exempt bonds, it is clear that the periodic subsidy now accorded tax-exempt bonds by means of the exclusion of interest from gross income is capitalized in the value of the bonds. The issue price of the bonds at original issue and the subsequent market price of those bonds reflect the value of the subsidy. If that subsidy were eliminated for future holders of the bonds that already have been issued, the bonds would suffer a significant reduction in value, even if the interest income exclusion remained available to the original holders. Such a policy change would render the bonds illiquid, at least at their pre-policy change value, thereby destroying an important attribute of the financial asset, its ready marketability. In that event, only financially distressed holders or those whose tax rates somehow were reduced to zero would seek to dispose of those bonds at the resale price, which would be substantially below the original issue price (regardless of what happened to market interest rates). Holders with continuing financial stability or taxable income also would experience detriment. Interestingly, loss of liquidity experienced by those holders would not be offset against any government savings because the continued exclusion would permit the interest to escape taxation. The described inequity results because the market value of the bonds at any time, and therefore any holder's purchase price, incorporates the tax exemption. In substance, the periodic subsidy in the form of an income exclusion has attached to the bonds themselves rather than being personal to the holders of those bonds. The bonds should continue to be viewed in that light to reflect the reasonable expectations of the bond purchasers who, in reliance upon the promise of present and future tax exemption of the interest from those bonds, purchased those bonds at the original issue price (or, in the after-market, at a price reflecting the tax exemption for the term of the bond).

To the extent that the subsidized property (such as the equipment in the first illustration) is a depreciating asset with a relatively short limited life or liquidity of the property is not an important attribute because, for example, it has a dedicated use that is not easily changed, the problem, as a practical, although not as a theoretical matter, becomes less significant. As long as the owner can and likely will continue to realize the value of the subsidy through continued use of the property, wealth reduction due to loss in resale value may be sufficiently small relative to the cost of determining and administering compensation to the owner that, arguably, it may be ignored. Where, however, the owner is unable to continue to realize the value of the subsidy through continued use of the property or liquidity of the property is an important component of its value, which will be the case, generally, if the subsidized property is of a long or unlimited economic life (such as the tax-exempt bond), the problem becomes much more significant. The market value of the property and, therefore, its purchase price is tied inextricably to its expected future market value upon resale. Accordingly, even retroactive relief by continuation of the benefits of the periodic subsidy to the original owner will not correct the problem, because the resale value of the property is dependent upon the availability of the subsidy to future owners. A prospective purchaser, to whom the subsidy will not be available, would be unwilling to pay a price equivalent to the fair market value of the property when the subsidy existed. * * * [39]

Even if desirable, it may be impossible to compensate the owner for her loss. Determining the magnitude of the owner's loss would be very difficult if compensation were in the form of an outright payment because the amount of loss is dependent upon secondary and tertiary market consequences. Indeed, Professor Graetz has noted that elimination of the tax benefit could cause a reduction in the supply of formerly subsidized property, resulting in an increase in the economic return from the existing property by virtue of its relative scarcity. Professor Graetz concludes that full compensation would have to take these market adjustments into account.

The size and speed of the adjustment resulting from the elimination of a tax benefit and the impact of the elimination on the owner of property receiving the benefit depend upon many factors. * * * These market adjustments and fluctuations, which are inherent when subsidies   are

---

39. For example, suppose Congress proposed elimination of the home mortgage interest deduction available to owners of owner occupied residential real estate. See IRC § 163(h). Elimination of the deduction would increase the after-tax cost of the mortgage payment and therefore the after-tax cost of owning the residence, a property generally purchased with mortgage financing. One would expect a reduction in home prices to follow.

introduced as a fiscal policy tool, likely make it impossible to quantify the loss accurately. That impossibility, however, should not suggest that no compensation is warranted when a periodic subsidy is removed. Rather, it suggests that determining the compensation amount would require simplifying assumptions and likely would result in some degree of over- or undercompensation.

If transition relief took the form of the continued periodic subsidy attaching to the property, great complexity could result. Not all competing properties on the market would offer the same tax attributes. Administering such a system could be very difficult.

    * * *

In sum, these inequities that would arise on repeal of a periodic subsidy and the complexity of any possible relief raise serious questions regarding the wisdom of their use.

The Need for Transition Relief

The government should have the option to remove uneconomic subsidies, even if they are the periodic type with long-term responses, and even if the subsidy has been capitalized into the value of the property. Forcing the government to continue all subsidies for future purchases would doom the economy to permanent inefficiency by resulting in subsidizing activities that already produce adequate supply of product or oversupply. If the subsidy is removed, however, transition rules should be enacted to prevent inequities, and in some cases, current owners should be entitled to compensation for their resultant wealth reduction. To state the proposition advanced in this Section, (1) a periodic subsidy should not be removed, even prospectively for transferees, if the current recipient of the subsidy reasonably anticipated that the property would be transferable, or, alternatively, (2) if the subsidy is removed, the current recipients should be compensated for the present value of the lost subsidy over an appropriate adjustment period. In many cases, only the second of these alternatives is feasible.

Initially, this proposition may seem objectionable or, at the very least, politically impossible to implement. Indeed, the right of a tax subsidy recipient to enjoy continued benefits from a tax provision, either through grandfathering or compensation, has been the subject of significant scholarship. Professor Graetz contends that policymakers should be free to make at least "nominally prospective" changes in the tax law without grandfathering or compensating those adversely affected by the change. "Nominally prospective" changes are changes that alter the rules only for post-enactment periods, but affect the tax treatment and value of assets acquired before enactment and, therefore, have retroactive impact.[46]

Professor Graetz's view essentially is premised on the proposition that a taxpayer whose tax liability is reduced by a tax subsidy is getting away with something, or, in his parlance, is the beneficiary of horizontal inequity. As the

---

46. Graetz, Tax Revision, note 7, at 49.

goal of tax change is to reduce that horizontal inequity, a change in the law with that objective should not necessitate either compensating the adversely affected taxpayer or grandfathering the tax subsidy as it affects the taxpayer.

This Article takes a different view. The legislative choices regarding burden sharing are found in the structural components of the tax law (for example, tax rates). Burdens are and should be shared as provided by those structural components. Tax incentive provisions, in contrast, are equivalent to direct subsidy payments outside the tax system. As tax savings to a recipient are only the medium for such payment, they should be ignored when evaluating burden sharing. Just as one does not take into account direct subsidies in determining whether the tax system is equitable, one should similarly ignore subsidies made indirectly through the tax system.

Removing a periodic subsidy after a taxpayer has acted upon it imposes an additional burden on that taxpayer unrelated to her income level or ability to pay. Accordingly, it results in a deviation from the burden sharing norm inherent in the structural components and lacks appeal to the distributional fairness on which the tax system as a whole relies.

Viewing tax incentive provisions as part of the burden sharing scheme, as Professor Graetz does, incorrectly leads one to view the elimination of periodic tax subsidies as a means of improving horizontal equity. On the contrary, periodic tax benefits which, in static terms, appear to create horizontal inequity, in dynamic terms, represent simply a collection of an amount promised and due from the government. When the subsidy terminated is a periodic subsidy enacted to encourage taxpayer behavior, it should be viewed analytically as a one-time subsidy, payment of which is made on the installment basis. The recipient of a periodic tax subsidy in the form of reduced tax liability, in reality, enjoys merely a deferred payment of a previous period's subsidy. The recipient already has paid for the subsidy by making what Congress determined to be a socially desirable expenditure in a previous year. The wisdom of the legislative policy choice should be addressed with respect to the year in which taxpayers respond to it, not in subsequent years.

This view does not depend upon whether the periodic tax subsidy represents a wise or even a sensible policy choice from an economic viewpoint, or whether it adds to overall equity in the economic system. Indeed, I would suggest that over the years, most periodic tax subsidies have proven to be mistakes. * * *

Professor Graetz's analysis and justifications for nominally prospective tax changes with retroactive effect underscore the uncertainty and danger of periodic subsidies because, once in place, they can be so easily reinterpreted as causing unjustified horizontal inequity. His analysis, therefore, represents another persuasive argument that periodic subsidies should be avoided.

        * * *

One-Time Subsidies, in Contrast

Problems of unfairness, compensation and transition relief that arise upon removal of periodic tax subsidies do not afflict one-time subsidies. After a one-time subsidy has been received, a taxpayer's return on investment is determined solely by market forces, unaugmented by further subsidy. * * * Accordingly, one-time subsidies could be removed equitably, without compensable harm to one who previously has been the recipient of the subsidy. Moreover, one-time subsidies would seem to avoid the perceived problem that some taxpayers are looting the treasury and continue to do so after the incentive is no longer necessary or desirable.

* * *

Economic Efficiency and the Predictability of Tax Laws

One-time subsidies also are superior to periodic subsidies in terms of economic efficiency. First, economic efficiency is served by predictable tax subsidies (assuming there are to be subsidies at all) so that those affected by subsidies can rely on that predictability. Making periodic subsidies uncertain in duration and subject to removal by legislative whim, is economically inefficient because it requires the government to include a risk premium in the subsidy. A risk premium overpays for desired activities unless the subsidy is removed before its expected term has expired.

In contrast, a one-time subsidy is completely predictable because there is 100% certainty that it will be obtained. A periodic subsidy can never attain that level of predictability so long as there is a risk of an uncompensated termination. Moreover, even if the duration of the periodic subsidy were assured, its value could not be assured because of potential changes in the structural components of the income tax (such as tax rates), income levels and market conditions. As a result, the need for risk premiums for periodic subsidies cannot be avoided.

* * *

In sum, periodic subsidies, even if not subject to removal, are less efficient than one-time subsidies. When risk of repeal is factored in, however, they become substantially less efficient.

Illustration: Commercial Real Estate

Periodic subsidies have represented a major component of the government's fiscal policy, and the Code is replete with them. The economic impact of the creation and removal of a periodic tax subsidy is illustrated most graphically by the accelerated depreciation deductions accorded to owners of real estate in the early 1980's and their effective removal through enactment of the passive activity loss rules in 1986. This Section illustrates shortcomings in the periodic tax subsidies accorded real estate during this period and the devastating consequences of their removal without adequate transition relief.

Periodic Subsidy for Real
Estate During the Early 1980's

In 1981 Congress created significant tax incentives for real estate by means of accelerated depreciation. In substance, owners of real estate were able to recover the cost of their depreciable real estate (buildings and other improvements, but not land) over a 15-year period. Thus, for income tax purposes, a building would be regarded as having been used up and valueless after only 15 years even though, in virtually all likely situations, the building would have retained substantial value and in many cases increased in value during that same period. The recovery period was lengthened by subsequent legislation to 18 years and later to 19 years. But, even after these changes, the tax depreciation in most cases greatly exceeded the actual reduction, if any, in value of those buildings.

The legislative judgment to grant special deductions and, therefore, impose a lighter tax burden on real estate and real estate activities was motivated by a desire to increase the production of depreciable real estate for the good of the entire economy. The supply of commercial buildings increased from 1981 to 1986 as a result of new construction, although it is impossible to prove that the 1981 legislation caused the building boom because of the inherent limitations on statistical analysis in a dynamic economy.

Congress did not limit the special tax relief for real estate to new construction. It extended the provision to any depreciable real estate acquired by a taxpayer after the effective date of the legislation, so long as the new owner did not own a significant interest in it beforehand. The accelerated depreciation allowed new owners to purchase old buildings and write off the cost of the buildings over the generously short recovery period of 15 years. The extension of the tax subsidy to existing property appears to have been pure governmental largesse, significantly increasing the purchases and sales of existing depreciable real estate. * * *

Taxpayers fortunate enough to own income producing real property received windfalls. The tax legislation actually increased the demand for and value of their property by allowing a prospective purchaser to obtain a tax benefit from acquiring the existing property. Since vacancy rates were relatively low at that time, the increased value did not result from increased occupancy. Much of the property already was operated at full capacity. Instead, the increased value of the property reflected the new tax subsidy accorded the property.

After 1981, substantial capital flowed into real estate production and resulted in a building boom. Prospective owners no longer needed to be assured of the same tenant demand, low interest financing and relatively low vacancy rate to project a profit from operating a newly constructed building or purchasing an existing building. Production soared and rental space, particularly office space, increased in supply. Net income from operating property tended to decline as a result. Some economists predicted that this phenomenon would continue until real estate activities earned no more on a net after-tax basis than had been the case prior to 1981. However, during the 1980's, it appears that real estate operating yields may have declined even below the level predictable by the subsidy alone, because an expectation of appreciation may have influenced people to accept less in current yield in anticipation of large gains upon sale.

After 1981, capital flowed into real estate activities from sources other than real estate professionals. One might characterize a real estate investor as participating in or acquiring a "tax shelter." * * *

Congress' Response: The Passive Activity Loss Rules

Public antipathy toward tax shelters may explain why Congress enacted a new set of anti-tax shelter provisions, the passive activity loss rules. * * *

The effect of the passive loss rules has been to preclude taxpayers from offsetting earned income and portfolio income (such as investment income from stocks, bonds and bank and money market accounts) with real estate and other tax shelter losses. By precluding the use of those losses, Congress effectively removed the tax subsidy from those activities. Indeed, because even cash operating losses from real estate and other tax shelter investments and actual reductions in value in the investments through deterioration or obsolescence cannot be used to offset nonpassive income until the investment is sold or discontinued, the antishelter rules not only removed the subsidy but, in many cases, also imposed a penalty on the activity.

Yet, Congress made no attempt to compensate property owners for either the loss of the subsidy or the loss in value of the property, which would not enjoy tax-preferred treatment in the hands of a prospective purchaser. In passing the 1986 Act, Congress appeared to recognize the importance of transition rules in preventing inequity, but failed to provide adequate protection. The passive loss provision contained special effective dates and phase-in provisions. On their face, those rules appeared to exclude current owners of real estate and other passive activities from much of the impact of the new rules.[82] These phase-in rules, however, interacted with two other important changes contained in the 1986 Act: (1) the alternative minimum tax (AMT) and (2) the investment interest expense limitation. Most importantly, passive losses allowable under the phase-in rules constituted tax preference items for AMT purposes. Under appropriate circumstances, the passive losses were rendered without tax benefit and, therefore, unusable to an investor. Moreover, by eliminating the subsidy entirely for prospective purchasers of the

---

82. Generally, the passive activity loss rules were effective for years beginning after 1986. Reg. § 1.469-11. However, the rules were phased in for certain post-effective date losses. Passive losses from a "pre-enactment interest" (an interest held on October 22, 1986, the date of enactment, or acquired thereafter pursuant to a written "binding contract" in effect on such date and at all times thereafter) were disallowed in the transition years to the extent of 35% in 1987, 60% in 1988, 80% in 1989 and 90% in 1990. IRC § 469(m).

property, the 1986 Act did nothing to protect the value of the property that had become dependent on the subsidy.

* * *

The Decline of Real Estate Prices and The Savings and Loan Crisis

The crisis in the savings and loan (S&L) industry had many causes, ranging from unpredictable economic changes to bad business judgment to thievery. One of its most significant causes was the decline in real estate prices that resulted from Congress' shift in tax policy toward real estate.

Many S&Ls invested in mortgages on new real estate projects that promised high yields during the 1980's due to generous depreciation recovery rates. * * * As long as real estate values increased during the early 1980's, those loans that had been made prudently were well-secured and safe. Many S&Ls lent money on outrageous projects with little economic feasibility to obtain front-end fees and what appeared to be high, but risky yields. However, even more conservatively managed institutions lent money on real estate projects at prudent loan-to-value ratios (ratios of the amount of the loan to the fair market value of the project securing the loan). Those loans were well-secured as long as real estate values were maintained or increased, which occurred during the transition period of the early 1980's.

The values of those properties depended on the generous tax benefits accorded real estate. The availability of those tax benefits to prospective owners supported the market prices of the property even though the rental income may not have been sufficient to make them economic.

When the government withdrew the subsidies in 1986 by enacting the passive activity loss rules and lengthening depreciation recovery periods for property acquired after 1986, real estate had to be operated or sold without benefit of the tax subsidies. Investors, who could no longer use losses from real estate to offset other income, were less likely to provide the equity funds for new projects or to purchase existing projects. As a result, a major source of equity for real estate acquisitions evaporated. Moreover, by the time Congress passed the 1986 Act, vacancy rates in many buildings had increased with the added supply of rentable space brought about by the tax subsidies.

An insufficient number of buyers existed for real estate projects that were put on the market for sale. Prices for real estate stopped increasing and in many cases began to fall. Consequently, the S&Ls as well as other banking institutions that had been well-secured when real estate values were high became undersecured. That situation was particularly dangerous for institutions that had made nonrecourse loans. Defaults became more common, prices declined further and the market became flooded with available real estate.

Even falling prices failed to attract new buyers. First, without tax subsidies, the projects were not worth as much as they had been previously. Second, the banking industry's reaction to the falling prices was precisely the opposite of what would be necessary to stop those declines. * * *

Prudent policy for any individual S&L on the brink of insolvency dictated that it collect as much as possible of its outstanding real estate loans and refuse to loan additional amounts in a falling real estate market. What represented prudent policy for any individual institution, however, became an unfortunate overall banking policy for sellers of real estate when all financial institutions adopted it. Thus, the surplus of owners needing to sell and the dearth of buyers with ready funding sources transformed predictable price declines into free falls.

* * * [I]t should be recognized that the real estate boom was spurred by the federal government's creation of significant periodic tax subsidies for the industry in 1981. Congress removed them in 1986, and replaced them with what amounted to tax penalties. * * *

[M]any S&Ls and other banking institutions were locked in. Their loan portfolios were created when the real estate securing the loans had value supported by the government subsidies. Only after the loans were made was the collateral devalued. The existence of federal deposit insurance will, of course, leave the federal taxpayers bearing the ultimate economic cost of many of these losses.

* * *

Illustration of Future Tax Policy Choice: Owner-Occupied Real Estate

The experience of real estate owners during the 1980's could be repeated if the periodic tax subsidies accorded other subsidized activities such as tax-exempt bonds and retirement savings were eliminated, even prospectively. Owner-occupied residential property appears to be a potential candidate in Congress' search for base broadening tactics. Economic destabilization could result if these periodic subsidies were eliminated, even if the elimination were prospective only and limited to future owners, because the value of the subsidies has been capitalized in the price of the properties.

Subsidies for owner-occupied housing include the deduction for home mortgage interest and the deduction for real property taxes. * * *

These deductions, if viewed as an encouragement to purchase a home, could be viewed as periodic subsidies. Elimination of these deductions would increase the after-tax cost of home ownership. * * *

Transition problems created by the elimination of the subsidies would not be solved merely by making the changes prospective and grandfathering current homeowners because the subsidies no longer would be reflected in the market prices that prospective purchasers of homes would be willing to pay. Even the prospective elimination of the subsidies would be likely to produce a reduction in single-family home prices and, in some cases, the elimination of the homeowner's built-up equity (the value of the home less the mortgage on it). Thus, regardless of how desirable in theoretical policy terms, the elimination of the "middle class" subsidies to home ownership may be, even the prospective elimination would cause considerable economic dislocation and financial hardship to current homeowners, absent compensation for the loss by the government. Such compensation, as a practical matter, would be unlikely because the elimination of the subsidies would have derived from the desire to eliminate the governmental expenditure through the tax system rather than out of some sense of theoretical tidiness, however laudable that latter goal may be.

* * *

Conclusion

* * * [E]nactment of periodic tax subsidies should be rejected unless Congress is willing to define, specifically limit and guarantee their duration. In the absence of such assurances, Congress should be prepared to live with periodic subsidies permanently or to compensate recipients if the subsidies are later removed. Use of certain periodic subsidies that involve the creation of transferable long-term benefits could require that the subsidy become a permanent part of the tax law if compensation is not politically viable.

As a practical matter, however, it is unlikely that Congress will be willing to retain every periodic subsidy enacted. Therefore, Congress should overcome the temptation to enact periodic tax subsidies.

Notes and Questions

40. Obviously, clarity is to be desired in any provision of law, including any provision of tax law. Do you agree with Bradley and Oliver that clarity is particularly important for incentive tax expenditures?

41. Professor Goldberg asserts a sharp dichotomy between one-time incentives and periodic incentives. Can a taxpayer never legitimately rely on the continuation of one-time incentives? Should a taxpayer always be entitled to rely on the continuation of periodic incentives?

42. As Goldberg recognizes, even if the incentive statute remains unaltered, changes in tax rates can materially affect the value of incentives. For example, some state-issued bonds are still outstanding that were issued before 1981, when the maximum rate on unearned income was 70 percent; clearly, the value of the tax exemption is worth much less today, with a maximum rate of 35 percent.

43. Would the logic of Professor Goldberg's argument lead one to conclude that Congress could not materially alter its basic form of taxation—for example, by instituting a consumption tax as a replacement for, or significant addition to, the income tax—without compensating all who entered the tax-preferred investment on the assumption that the income tax would continue as the dominant federal tax? (Here, many of the transition problems resemble those discussed in Chapter Seven, particularly in Notes #75-83 (at pages 488-90).)

44. As one example of a periodic tax preference, which perhaps never should have been enacted but cannot be ended without working an injustice, Goldberg highlights the home mortgage interest deduction. Importantly, present owners may have profited little if any from the deduction, because their purchase price was inflated by the existence of the tax preference. As Kay and King argued (see Chapter Three, Note #2 (at page 123)), this problem "demonstrates why tax capitalization is such a dangerous trap; although we believe it would be better if the system had never incorporated these concessions, it does not seem that it would now be either equitable or desirable to withdraw them."

45. Most observers would give high marks to the Tax Reform Act of 1986 as an example of true tax reform. Yet Professor Goldberg demonstrates the contribution of the 1986 Act—which not only removed preferences, but substituted tax penalties (or, in OMB's terminology, "negative tax preferences") in the form of passive loss limitation rules—to the savings and loan crisis of the late 1980s. That crisis ultimately cost taxpayers and investors hundreds of billions of dollars.

46. Professor Goldberg puts forward full compensation to present beneficiaries of preferences as an acceptable alternative to keeping the tax preferences on the books, but he acknowledges that such compensation would be difficult to compute, and highly unlikely as a political matter. His primary message is that Congress should not start down the periodic preference route.

47. But what are we to do once Congress places an unwise periodic preference in the law? Given that full compensation of present beneficiaries is not realistically in the cards, does Professor Goldberg's logic doom us to keep an inefficient and unwise preference forever?

48. Professor Michael Graetz, whose work is frequently referred to (and disputed) by Professor Goldberg, argues that the risk of legal change is simply one more risk for investors to take into account, and should not deter Congress from changing the law: "The tax law must remain a flexible instrument of public policy. When a provision has outlived its usefulness, it should be eliminated without the delay and windfall gains inherent in grandfathering prior transactions. People should make investments with the expectation that political policies may change."[p]

49. Is there anything special about tax provisions? Governments frequently change the law, upsetting expectations. What if a state where

---

[p]. Michael J. Graetz, *Legal Transitions: The Case of Retroactivity in Income Tax Revision*, 126 U. PA. L. REV. 47, 87 (1977).

gambling was legal changed its law after investors had spent billions of dollars building casinos in the reasonable expectation that the state would continue to allow gambling? What of producers and sellers of alcoholic beverages, many in business for decades, when Prohibition was instituted in 1919? What of the holders of billions of dollars worth of slaves when the Thirteenth Amendment[q] freed all slaves without compensation of their owners?

It is easy to understand a moral imperative to end slavery, and less weighty moral and practical arguments can be advanced against gambling and alcoholic beverages. It is less obvious that society should advance its moral and other policy judgments without any compensation to those who lawfully relied on the earlier societal view. Yet, the lesson of history, which Professor Goldberg does not dispute in the tax context, is that compensation will not be forthcoming from the political system. Barring compensation, should society implement its current views of policy, or refrain from doing so on the basis that such a change would be unfair to those who relied on earlier law?

E. A CASE STUDY:
THE EARNED INCOME TAX CREDIT

The earned income tax credit ("EITC") is perhaps the most interesting tax preference provided by current law. It is the one "refundable" credit, meaning that persons without income tax liability can still benefit from the credit. (Indeed, the EITC would be of limited significance were it not refundable, because most beneficiaries have little or no income tax liability.) The EITC thus may provide a working model of a system advocated, in many forms, by writers whose work appears in this book—some combination of the tax and transfer systems.

The EITC represents a politically popular attempt to use the tax system as a major component of delivering welfare payments to the working poor, especially those with children.   The appeal of EITC has always been obvious—on the surface, at least, it both aids poor people who need help, and encourages them to help themselves by working. (This combination of factors also helps to explain its appeal to members of Congress in both parties.)

The problems in the EITC are perhaps more obvious now than initially. The program may create perverse incentives regarding work and marriage. In terms of program structure and administration, the Internal Revenue Service may be ill-suited to administer what is, in substance, a massive welfare program.

---

q. President Lincoln's Emancipation Proclamation of 1862 (effective January 1, 1863) clearly did not free all slaves. Leaving aside questions of Presidential authority and the practical problem of enforcement at a time when the United States Government was not in control of the states where most slaves lived, the proclamation was wholly inapplicable to the northern tier of slave states, from Delaware to Missouri, which had not seceded. Only with the post-war Thirteenth Amendment were all slaves freed.

In the first excerpt, Professor Ann Alstott addresses policy issues regarding the incentive effects of the EITC and issues raised by use of the tax system to deliver welfare benefits. In the final excerpt, Yin, Scholz, Forman, and Mazur (two law professors and two economists) suggest reforms designed to improve the efficiency and efficacy of the EITC, assuming that the benefit is to be continued and that it will be administered through the tax system.

THE EARNED INCOME TAX CREDIT AND THE LIMITATIONS OF TAX-BASED WELFARE REFORM

Ann L. Alstott[*]

108 Harvard Law Review 533, 533-37, 540-41, 543-92 (1995)

Introduction

The federal earned income tax credit (EITC), which provides cash payments to low-income workers, has recently assumed a central role in U.S. social welfare policy. Under legislation enacted in 1993, by 1997 the EITC will pay annual aggregate benefits as large as those paid under Aid to Families with Dependent Children (AFDC), the nation's principal cash welfare program. * * *

Although the EITC is styled a "refundable tax credit," in fact it is a kind of welfare program—or, in economists' terms, an income-transfer program. It uses the rules and procedures of the federal income tax system to make payments to low-income workers based on their earnings and total income. As a refundable tax credit, the EITC not only reduces or eliminates federal income tax liability, but also pays cash to low-income taxpayers whose EITC exceeds the tax they owe.

For many years, the EITC was a relatively small program, viewed principally as a means of offsetting the adverse distributional and incentive effects of federal income and payroll taxes on low-income workers. In recent years, however, the EITC's advocates have increasingly promoted the EITC as a solution to two central and recurring concerns of welfare policy. First, proponents claim, the EITC promotes work and family responsibility among the poor, unlike traditional welfare programs, which have long attracted criticism for their putative effects on work and family structure. Second, advocates argue, because the EITC is part of the federal tax system, it is simpler and cheaper to administer than programs run by the welfare bureaucracy and affords greater dignity and privacy to beneficiaries.

A close examination of the two central claims made for the EITC reveals that the EITC is neither the radical departure from welfare that its advocates claim, nor the duplicate of welfare that its opponents depict. In this Article, I argue that current debates over the EITC are seriously incomplete in two

---

*. At time of original publication, Associate Professor, Columbia University School of Law.

ways. First, both advocates and opponents of the program give undue weight to its potential effects on work and marriage among EITC recipients. * * *

Second, both proponents and opponents of the EITC have overlooked the important point that, because the EITC is a tax-based transfer program, it faces significant institutional constraints that are not present in traditional welfare programs. Tax-based transfer programs may be cheaper and less stigmatizing than welfare, although advocates typically assert these claims without empirical support. Nevertheless, this Article shows that the tax system's limitations render the EITC inherently inaccurate, unresponsive, and vulnerable to fraud and error in ways that traditional welfare programs are not. * * * [I]mproving the performance of the EITC or other tax-based transfer programs requires either compromising the benefits of tax-based administration or undertaking a major restructuring of basic institutions of the federal tax system. Absent large-scale (and politically unlikely) reform of the federal income tax, the EITC and similar tax-based transfer programs are likely to prove acceptable only if we radically revise our expectations about accuracy, responsiveness, and compliance in income-transfer programs.

This second point is particularly important because the prospect of a unified tax-transfer system has fascinated economists and other public policy analysts at least since discussions of the negative income tax in the 1960s. This Article challenges the simple case for integrating the tax and transfer systems by showing the institutional dilemmas inherent in such an approach. Ultimately, this analysis suggests greater tolerance of separate tax and transfer systems. * * *

This Article uses a study of the EITC to illustrate some of the core dilemmas of income redistribution through tax-based transfer programs. * * *

The Case for the EITC as Welfare Reform

In one respect, the EITC represents an important liberalization of American social welfare policy. The EITC embodies a recognition that hard work may not lift a family out of poverty when wages are low and that the working poor as well as the nonworking poor need and deserve income transfers to support their families. Traditional welfare programs provide little aid to the working poor. Categorical eligibility restrictions exclude many families, and high benefit reduction rates quickly deny benefits even to workers with low earnings. In contrast, the EITC has grown in recent years to provide substantial levels of assistance to the working poor. Table 1 documents the EITC's growth since its enactment in 1975.

* * * [T]he EITC's redistributive function is cloaked in anti-welfare rhetoric to attract maximum political support.[11] * * *

---

11. A similar strategy linking work and benefits underlies the success of Social Security. Social Security's redistributive effects have been obscured by the promotion of the program as one in which each person gets only the benefits he or she has "earned."

The EITC is a complex hybrid of an earnings subsidy, a traditional income-transfer program, and a tax credit program. Understanding these features and the tensions they create lays the groundwork for the subsequent analysis of the EITC's effects on behavior and its institutional limitations.

Traditional income transfers provide a useful benchmark for comprehending the EITC. A traditional income-transfer program that tailors benefits to need pays the largest benefits to families with the lowest incomes and reduces benefits as income rises. * * *

TABLE 1: THE EXPANSION OF THE EITC, 1975-1995

Year	Earnings Subsidy Rate	Maximum Credit	Income Cutoff
1975	10%	$ 400	$ 8,000
1980	10%	$ 500	$ 10,000
1985	11%	$ 550	$ 11,000
1988	14%	$ 874	$ 18,576
1994	30%	$ 2528	$ 25,300
1996*	40%	$ 3370	$ 27,700

*. The 1996 figures show the fully-phased-in effects of the 1993 amendments to the EITC. All figures are in nominal dollars, except that the EITC benefit and income cutoff for 1996 are stated in 1994 dollars.

The EITC produces a pattern of benefits that at first seems entirely different. For workers with earnings and total income between one dollar and $8425, the EITC provides an earnings subsidy equal to an extra forty cents for every dollar of earnings. In this income range, the EITC appears to be a "backwards" income-transfer program, because it provides greater dollar benefits to those with higher earnings and no benefits at all to those without wages, regardless of need.

The EITC begins to tailor benefits to need through an income test at slightly higher levels of earnings. When earnings reach $8425, the earnings subsidy is capped. Above that threshold, the dollar amount of EITC benefits remains constant up to an earnings level of $11,000 and then is reduced by twenty-one cents for every dollar of earnings over $11,000. Under this schedule, EITC benefits are reduced to zero at $27,000 of earnings.[r] Thus, between $11,000 and $27,000 in earnings, the EITC resembles a traditional income-transfer program, which reduces benefits as earnings increase. * * *

---

r. All dollar figures in this article are different under present law, primarily due to inflation adjustments mandated by section 32(j). In more general terms, however, Professor Alstott's article is descriptive of EITC under current law. (Ed.)

The EITC also differs from traditional transfers in administration. Traditional welfare programs use government workers to collect and verify information about applicants and recipients. In contrast, the EITC is administered through the federal income tax system as a refundable tax credit. In theory, workers eligible for the EITC need never see a bureaucratic face. They simply attach a special schedule to their federal income tax returns.

The IRS awards the EITC based on the information provided in the tax return. The EITC first offsets federal income tax liability (if any), and the balance is refunded in cash. The unusual refund feature makes it possible for the EITC to provide cash benefits to workers who are too poor to owe any tax or whose tax liability is less than their EITC benefit.

How the EITC Debate Overstates the Importance of Behavioral Disincentives

Conventional policy debates over the EITC, like debates over welfare policy, are donominated by economic analyses that focus on potential disincentives for work and marriage. * * *

In the following discussion, it is essential to distinguish disincentives from the effects of those disincentives on behavior. Economic theory can establish the existence of disincentives to work or to marry, but empirical study is needed to establish whether and how those disincentives actually affect people's decisions to work or to marry. * * * I will refer to "potential" disincentives to emphasize the tentative nature of theoretical predictions. * * *

A Critical Evaluation of the Significance of Potential and Actual Work Disincentives in the EITC

One classic dilemma of redistribution is the potential trade off between redistribution and labor supply. Redistributive programs may decrease total economic output if they reduce work effort by income-transfer recipients or by taxpayers who finance the program. Thus, reductions in work effort raise the economic cost of redistributive programs. * * * Empirical studies suggest that redistributive programs on balance probably have a small but nontrivial negative effect on work effort. * * *

Contrary to EITC advocates' claims, microeconomic theory shows that the EITC does not necessarily increase work effort among the poor, and may actually reduce it. * * *

The standard analysis assumes that workers and potential workers understand how the EITC, the tax system, and the welfare system affect their earnings. Because the EITC is complex, however, EITC recipients may not understand the connection between work and the EITC benefits they receive. This informational gap may blunt both the EITC's potential incentives and its potential disincentives.

Standard economic analysis suggests that the EITC creates competing potential work incentives and disincentives that vary among groups of workers. * * * [T]he EITC combines three distinct elements: an earnings subsidy, a "stationary" range, and a "phase-out" or income test. For workers with earnings in the earnings subsidy range, the EITC acts as a proportional pay increase, which provides up to four dollars for every ten dollars of earnings. A casual observer might suppose that a pay raise necessarily increases work effort, but economic theory suggests that the earnings subsidy may either increase or decrease work by a worker who is already employed. The earnings subsidy increases the return to work relative to other activities (for example, leisure), and this "substitution effect" may increase people's proclivity to work rather than to consume leisure. On the other hand, EITC benefits provide extra money, which allows the worker to consume as much as before with less work. This "income effect" may lead the worker to consume more leisure, depending on her preferences. The net impact on work depends on the relative magnitudes of these competing effects. Importantly, however, the EITC's potential incentives are different for a nonworker contemplating entering the workforce. For her, the EITC is an unambiguous potential work incentive; she receives no income support from the EITC unless she goes to work and so the income effect is absent.

In contrast, workers with incomes in the stationary range, who receive an EITC benefit that does not vary with earnings, face a potential work disincentive. The earnings subsidy is no longer available with respect to extra earnings, so the EITC substitution effect neither encourages nor discourages work relative to leisure. Further, the income effect (or the feeling of being better off with less work) may discourage work.

For workers with earnings in the EITC phase-out range, additional earnings reduce EITC benefits, just as in a traditional income-transfer program. This incremental benefit reduction as income rises is analogous to a tax on income. * * * This benefit reduction, like any actual tax, reduces the net monetary reward for extra work. EITC recipients who also pay income and payroll taxes or who participate in other income-transfer programs can find that multiple marginal tax rates apply to the same dollars of earnings, and cumulative potential work disincentives can be quite large. For example, the EITC's benefit reduction rate is twenty-one percent, but EITC recipients who also pay federal income and payroll taxes face a cumulative marginal tax rate as high as forty-four percent, without taking into account state taxes or benefit reductions in other income-transfer programs.
  * * *

For workers in the EITC phase-out range, the EITC creates an unambiguous potential work disincentive. In this income range, the EITC's substitution effect may discourage work effort because the phase-out of EITC benefits, like a tax, reduces the net wage. Further, an EITC recipient in the phase-out range has a higher total income than a worker with no EITC benefit, and thus the EITC's income effect also may discourage work effort.

Although microeconomic theory can make limited predictions about the EITC's potential effects on different groups of workers, only empirical evidence can determine whether the EITC on balance encourages or discourages work. In theory, the EITC might do either. Early estimates of the EITC's impact on work effort suggest that the EITC reduces work effort in the aggregate, but probably by a smaller amount than do traditional welfare programs. * * *

Although potential work disincentives are inherent in the EITC and other income-tested transfer programs, it might appear that such disincentives could be reduced by lowering benefit reduction rates. The success of such changes in EITC design may be limited, however, by two dilemmas that also constrain welfare program design. First, reducing marginal tax rates creates difficult and politically troublesome trade offs. In an income-tested transfer program such as the EITC, it is impossible simultaneously to provide generous benefits, to keep program costs low by paying benefits only to the poor, and to keep benefit reduction rates low. Reducing the marginal tax rate means that benefits decline at a slower rate as income rises and thus become available to a larger and relatively richer group. The only way to reduce marginal tax rates without expanding the pool of eligible recipients is to reduce benefits.
     * * *

As the EITC has outgrown its traditional role as tax relief for the poor to become an expensive, large-scale income-transfer program, opponents have used the theoretical and empirical charge of work disincentives to attack the EITC. For example, one prominent critic of the EITC, economist Marvin Kosters, argues that the 1993 expansion of the credit was misguided.[73] Kosters contends that the effects on total economic output of the EITC's potential work disincentives are likely to be large, because many more EITC recipients fall in the EITC's phase-out range than in the earnings subsidy range, and workers in the phase-out range are more productive. Kosters argues, in effect, that it makes little sense to provide a potential work incentive for a relatively small number of welfare recipients at the cost of creating potentially large reductions in the work effort of many more poor workers who are already working.

The EITC's advocates respond with two arguments. First, some commentators claim that the EITC is a desirable policy, because its aggregate work disincentives are likely to be smaller than those of traditional welfare programs. * * * Second, other proponents say, the EITC's aggregate effects on labor supply, whatever they may be, do not tell the whole story: the effects of the EITC on work by different groups of EITC recipients are also important for social policy. Estimates of the EITC's labor-supply effects suggest that it increases work effort by a small amount, on net, for the very poor workers in the earnings subsidy range. EITC advocates argue that this effect is crucial, because the credit provides the greatest potential work incentives to the

---

73. *See* Marvin H. Kosters, *The Earned Income Tax Credit and the Working Poor*, AM. ENTERPRISE, May/June 1993, at 64, 68-70.

poorest recipients and to nonworkers, who begin with the weakest attachment to the labor force. At the same time, the EITC's income test concentrates potential disincentives on slightly higher-income workers who already are in the work force instead of on all program participants. These features may improve labor-force participation over time by easing the transition from welfare to work. Thus, EITC proponents characterize it as an "anti-underclass" program—a way of moving the poorest and most disadvantaged potential workers into the labor force. These arguments concede that potential and actual work disincentives are properly viewed as undesirable features of the EITC but argue that incentives for some groups are more important than disincentives for others.

The central problem with the conventional debate is that it focuses too narrowly on work disincentives. First, the "work disincentive" label carries a pejorative weight in the writings of both advocates and opponents of the EITC that is unjustified in conventional economic analysis. Even if the EITC leads some recipients to work fewer hours, these workers would be making a rational choice to use the extra dollars added to their wages by the EITC to buy a few hours of leisure or time for nonmarket work (for example, child care). * * * Further, if EITC recipients use their additional time for nonmarket work, such as care for children, the elderly, and the sick, their choice benefits these other people and, potentially, society as a whole. Thus, the potential labor-supply reductions that some policy analysts find so troubling actually would increase the well-being of the poor. In economists' terms, these free and rational choices between work and leisure maximize utility, which is the central norm that animates traditional economic analysis.

* * *

EITC recipients, unlike welfare recipients, cannot stop working altogether if they want to continue receiving EITC benefits. They can only choose to work fewer hours. * * * [W]orking less is quite different from not working at all. * * *

Another explanation for the peculiarity of debates over the EITC and work is that such dabates actually reflect unacknowledged normative tensions. Is the goal of the EITC to increase the well-being of the poor, to get the poor to work (even if they are worse off), or to increase gross domestic product (GDP)? * * * Although proponents of the latter two goals are likely to find the EITC preferable to traditional welfare programs, * * * no redistribution at all, or redistribution combined with mandatory work would seem to serve these goals even better. * * *

Finally, any comparison of the economic effects of the EITC and alternative policies should also consider the distributional and incentive effects of the taxes levied to finance the programs. For example, potential reductions in labor supply by taxpayers in response to higher taxes may reduce both total economic output and taxpayers' well-being. These changes represent additional costs of redistribution. * * *

The EITC "Marriage Penalty": Facing the Realities of Program Design

Debates over the EITC also reflect concerns about potential marital disincentives in income-transfer programs. Single-parent families, particularly those headed by women, tend to be disproportionately poor and constitute a growing segment of the population. The causes of poverty among female-headed families are complex, as are the causes of the declining marriage rate. However, if redistributive programs bolster an existing social trend that contributes to pre-transfer poverty, once again behavioral effects may raise the cost of redistribution. Despite popular stereotypes, empirical studies suggest that welfare has contributed little to the growth in the number of single-parent families. Nevertheless, the perceived effects of marital disincentives in welfare programs continue to play a significant role in both popular and academic discussions of welfare policy.

* * *

Further, critiques of the EITC's marital disincentives fail to confront the policy trade offs inherent in designing the EITC or any other redistributive program. Marriage penalties are a virtually unavoidable characteristic of income transfers that tailor benefits to need. * * *

Theorists generally agree that the aggregate income of the family provides a better measure of economic status than individual income. * * *

Although measuring family income tends to promote (relatively) accurate income measurement, it typically does so at the expense of marriage neutrality in the EITC and in other income-transfer programs tailored to need. * * * Only a system of constant (flat) marginal tax rates could achieve both equal treatment of families and marriage neutrality. In essence, aggregation of family income in an income-tested transfer program makes marriage neutrality impossible. Critics of the EITC's marriage penalty typically overlook the roots of such penalties in the very structure of income-transfer programs.

* * *

In theory, the EITC or any income-tested transfer program could be restructured so that it awarded only marriage bonuses and never marriage penalties. The resulting pattern of benefits, however, would probably strike many as undesirable. For example, one of the strangest consequences would be the payment of EITC benefits to relatively high-income married couples. To understand why, imagine a middle-class couple with two children and total earnings of $50,000. In a hypothetical worst-case scenario (worst case for the Treasury, that is), if this couple divorced, one would gain custody of both children and would have earnings that qualify for the maximum EITC. To avoid creating any incentive to divorce, we would have to award the maximum EITC to the intact couple, reduced to reflect the loss of the federal income tax marriage bonus for couples with disparate earnings. Many policymakers would probably accept some EITC marriage penalty in order to keep the program targeted more closely to the poor.

A similar but analytically distinct alternative is to award the EITC to each worker based on her earnings alone, regardless of marital status. Under this system, by definition, a change in marital status would not decrease (or increase) EITC benefits. This proposal, however, simply illustrates once again the trade off described above: awarding the EITC based on individual income avoids creating a marriage penalty but does so by eliminating the tailoring of benefits to need based on family income. As a consequence, even high-income families could qualify for the EITC. For example, a family in which the husband earns $10,000 and the wife earns $200,000 could qualify for the maximum EITC benefit.[120] * * *

Institutional Limitations of the EITC and Other Tax-based Transfer Programs

The conceptual link between income-transfer programs and the income tax has fascinated economists and policy analysts for years. Advocates of the negative income tax and, more recently, of the EITC have proposed administrative integration of the tax and transfer systems as a route to welfare reform. These analysts point to two principal advantages of tax-transfer integration. First, proponents argue, the EITC and other tax-based transfers can enhance administrative efficiency by reducing bureaucratic cost and complexity. Welfare administration is labor-intensive, expensive, and heavily dependent on "street-level" bureaucrats.* * * [125]

Second, advocates claim, tax-based transfers can reduce the stigma and social isolation associated with welfare. * * *

The idea of tax-transfer integration thus combines administrative, humanitarian, and political goals. * * * [T]he case for tax-transfer integration is less compelling than its proponents claim. The EITC illustrates the institutional dilemmas that inevitably arise in tax-based transfer programs that tailor benefits to need. * * *

Understanding the Inherent Limitations of Tax-Based Programs: The Importance of Income Measurement in the EITC

The task of income measurement is fundamental to both income tax and income-transfer systems. Both systems seek to assess economic well-being, using income as a proxy, in order to apportion tax burdens and income-transfer benefits appropriately. Much legal scholarship on tax policy addresses ways to make more precise the definition of income. Analogous issues confront social scientists who attempt to measure income for statistical purposes.

---

120. The exact dollar benefit would depend on the number of children in the family and how they were grouped with the two parents for EITC purposes.

125. In 1992, the costs of administering the federal income tax were around one percent of revenue raised, compared to administrative costs of 13% of benefits in the case of AFDC and 10% of benefits in the case of SSI.

Analytically, the problem of income measurement consists of at least four issues: How should income be defined? How should we group individuals into families for purposes of measuring income? Over what period should we measure income? What steps should we take to ensure compliance with the income measurement rules we establish? Answering each question requires some compromise among important objectives, and, not surprisingly, the existing income tax and transfer systems often strike different balances.

The divergence between the two systems may at first seem unwarranted: why should the tax and transfer systems adopt different measures of income? * * *

This view is too simple, however. * * * [T]he different approaches to income measurement in the tax and transfer systems may well be defensible, even productive, responses to the different goals and characteristics of each system. This argument challenges the easy case for tax-transfer integration by showing that there may be reasons to maintain separate systems. Traditional transfer programs and tax-based transfer programs face similar trade offs among important goals in measuring income. Each system, for example, must balance the desirability of a comprehensive definition of income against the cost of administering such a definition. The tax and transfer systems have, over time, struck different compromises in response to these trade offs. Consequently, any transfer program that adopts the tax system's rules and procedures necessarily strikes a different balance than traditional transfer programs do. Further, these different institutional choices make tax-based programs less accurate in tailoring benefits to need, less responsive to changing needs, and less capable of enforcing compliance than their traditional counterparts. The fundamental dilemma of tax-transfer integration is that reforms to alleviate these limitations necessarily require either compromising tax-transfer integration or undertaking wholesale reform of the tax system. For example, although in theory the tax system might adopt the more comprehensive definitions of income characteristic of traditional income transfer programs, such a change in the tax law would be disruptive, expensive, and probably politically unacceptable. Alternatively, the tax system might adopt separate, welfare-like rules and procedures solely for purposes of a tax-based transfer program, but that approach would tend to undermine the purported advantages of integration.

A recognition of these dilemmas does not require the rejection of the EITC or other tax-based transfer programs, but it does caution against assuming that tax-based programs are uncomplicated or unquestionably desirable. Implementing the "simple" vision of an integrated tax and transfer system would require radical and costly changes in the tax system—changes the advocates of tax-transfer integration rarely discuss.

One might question whether these income-measurement criteria are appropriate for evaluating the EITC. If we view the EITC as an earnings subsidy—intended only to "make work pay"—rather than as a traditional transfer program, perhaps these limitations are unimportant. For example, inaccuracy in awarding EITC benefits may be less troubling if the goal is to encourage work rather than to provide benefits to a sharply defined group of very poor recipients, as with welfare. * * *

The EITC, as we now know it, serves more than one purpose. It is an earnings subsidy, intended to encourage work among the poor. The EITC is simultaneously, however, a redistributive program that provides income support for the working poor, under income-testing rules that purport to target the assistance to low-income families. This dual aim is, ostensibly, the EITC's advantage over the minimum wage and other broadly-targeted policies: the EITC holds out the promise of stimulating work while providing extra earnings only to those who really need them. * * * Particularly in the 1990s, as the EITC has expanded beyond its traditional role as an offset to payroll taxes, its income-support function has become increasingly significant.

* * *

The Conflict Between Tax-Transfer Integration and Accurate Measurement of Need

Definitions of "income" and "family" are fundamental to the task of income measurement. The income definition determines which items are counted. The more comprehensive the income definition, the better a proxy "income" is for "economic resources." The family definition controls whose income is counted in evaluating the economic resources of a household. Completely accurate definitions of either "income" or "family" would require individualized determinations, which would be prohibitively costly. Consequently, both income tax and income-transfer systems adopt standardized definitions and sacrifice some precision for administrative savings. The federal income tax system adopts definitions of income and family that are narrower than those used in income-transfer programs and so tends to measure income with less accuracy. * * * Thus, the claimed pecuniary and dignitary advantages of tax-transfer integration come at the expense of adopting the inaccurate rules of the federal income tax.

1. Defining "Income." — Income as reported for federal income tax purposes understates "economic" income in important ways. For example, the income definition excludes certain fringe benefits, imputed income from property and services, interest on obligations of state and local governments, and a significant portion of income from capital investments. In addition, the income tax does not measure wealth and so cannot comprehensively assess total economic resources. * * * As a consequence, taxpayers with significant wealth or excludable capital income may qualify, quite legally, for EITC benefits. * * *

In contrast, traditional income-transfer programs tailored to need make relatively comprehensive assessments of income and wealth. Most programs attempt to measure all sources of cash available to meet the living expenses of a family, with limited deductions for expenses. The programs typically consider the value of assets as well as income to assess accurately the need for benefits.

* * * Adopting an expanded income definition solely for EITC purposes is likely to compromise the benefits of tax-transfer integration. Separate rules would increase the administrative cost and complexity of the program and could reduce the dignitary advantages of uniform procedures. This trade off creates a continuum of possible solutions. At one extreme lies a completely integrated EITC that fully incorporates the tax system's limited definitions; at the other extreme, a separate set of rules and procedures for the EITC could come to resemble a "mini-welfare program" run by the IRS.

In the middle are numerous possible compromises between integration and separation. * * *

Major reforms of the federal income tax could reconcile tax-transfer integration with more accurate income measurement, but such changes pose a formidable political challenge. The Tax Reform Act of 1986 probably illustrates the outer boundaries of feasible expansions of the federal income tax base. * * *

If the conflict between accurate income redistribution and tax-transfer integration in the EITC were unimportant in practical terms, we might well ignore it. * * *

Available data suggest that the problem of income mismeasurement is not large but not insignificant. * * *

Preliminary evidence also suggests that the absence of an EITC wealth test may have a significant effect. A study based on 1988 IRS data shows that up to ten percent of EITC benefits in that year were paid to taxpayers who apparently held investment assets in significant amounts.[160] * * *

The problem of income measurement may grow as the EITC program grows. * * *

2. Defining the "Family." — The definition of "family" creates similar institutional dilemmas. The federal income tax rules adopt a narrow definition of the family. * * * [I]ncome-transfer programs typically adopt a broader definition of family that includes most relatives who live together.

The EITC follows the federal income tax in treating the married couple as the basic family unit and in disregarding the income of other household members. * * *

Whether the EITC's rather narrow family definition distorts the desired pattern of income redistribution to any significant degree is an empirical question. Unfortunately, no publicly available data shed light on the

---

160. *See* Cherie J. O'Neil & Linda B. Nelsestuen, *The Earned Income Credit: The Need For a Wealth Restriction for Eligibility Determination*, 63 TAX NOTES 1189, 1190 (1994). The authors use total investment income (taxable and non-taxable), as reported on the tax return, as a proxy for wealth. In 1988, 10% of EITC benefits were paid to taxpayers reporting investment income of $300 or more. * * * This study probably understates the problem, because it takes into account only income-producing investment assets.

magnitude of the problem. In principle, however, the failure to define family in a realistic way is as troubling as the exclusion of certain sources of income. Careful program design might mitigate but cannot eliminate the potential inaccuracy. For example, the EITC pays the largest benefits to working families with children and provides benefits for childless workers only between the ages of twenty-five and sixty-five. These rules tend to improve accurate targeting in a rough way, by excluding elderly people and teenagers—two groups who are particularly likely to live in households in which they receive support from others.

Adopting truly precise family definition rules for purposes of the EITC would, even if desirable, be administratively difficult. * * *

The Conflict Between Tax-Transfer Integration and Responsiveness to Changing Circumstances

Because incomes fluctuate—sometimes dramatically—as jobs are won and lost, wages and hours worked change, and marriages form and dissolve, the measurement interval is important. The length of the accounting period affects the aggregate amount of taxes collected or transfers paid in any system in which marginal tax rates vary. Under the regressive marginal tax rate structure characteristic of the EITC and other income-tested transfer programs, shorter accounting periods tend to favor those with fluctuating incomes: their benefits are likely to be higher, in the aggregate, than those of individuals with steady incomes.[177] Under the federal income tax, in contrast, marginal tax rates rise with income and produce a progressive marginal income tax rate structure, which tends to impose higher total tax burdens on those with fluctuating incomes than on those with steady incomes.

Ideally, a tax or transfer system would both respond quickly to changing circumstances and react only to real changes in economic well-being. In practice, however, the two goals conflict. Responsiveness implies immediate adjustment to short-term changes, but accurate income measurement implies waiting to evaluate the permanency of the change in circumstances. * * *

The EITC, as a tax-based program, is thus inherently unresponsive relative to traditional transfer programs. Is this unresponsiveness a problem? One might argue that a degree of sluggishness in traditional income transfers

---

177. For example, suppose there are two periods (one and two), and the taxpayer earns $10 in period one and $25 in period two. A hypothetical transfer program provides a maximum benefit of five dollars, a benefit reduction rate of 33%, and an income cutoff of $15. Incomes greater than $15 but no greater than $30 are subject to income tax at a marginal tax rate of 10%. If income is measured (and benefits are awarded) for each period, the taxpayer will receive a benefit of $1.70 in period one. She will receive no transfer benefits in period two and will owe positive income tax of one dollar. Her net transfer for the two periods would be $0.70. In contrast, a taxpayer with steady income ($17.50 in each period) would receive no benefits and would pay income tax of $0.25 in each period, for a net tax of $0.50. If income were measured (and benefits were awarded) only at the end of period two (and the income cutoff, income tax threshold, and maximum benefit levels were doubled), both individuals would report income of $35, neither would receive benefits, and each would owe total income tax of $0.50.

could be beneficial, because it encourages work effort. Delays in awarding traditional benefits may discourage voluntary decisions to leave employment, and delays in eliminating benefits may reward initial efforts to find and hold a job. Unresponsiveness may impose real hardship on those for whom unemployment is involuntary, however, and may expend scarce resources on those who are no longer needy. In addition, unresponsiveness in the EITC, in contrast to traditional transfer programs, could, in some cases, discourage work by delaying transmittal of the EITC's earnings subsidy. * * *

Congress attempted in 1978 to enhance the responsiveness of the EITC by enacting the "advance payment" rules, which permit periodic payment of the EITC by employers throughout the year. * * * [T]he advance payment option is rarely used. A 1992 General Accounting Office study shows that fewer than one-half of one percent of EITC recipients chose the advance payment option in 1989. * * *

The basic problem is that the advance payment system (even if successfully implemented) cannot avoid the underlying institutional dilemma. Advance payment creates the illusion of responsiveness, but it cannot deliver true responsiveness as long as the EITC remains linked to the annual accounting interval of the federal income tax. The fear of EITC recipients that the advance payment system will leave them owing money to the government at the end of the year is well-founded. * * *

Only structural change would enhance the EITC's responsiveness. The EITC could adopt a shorter accounting period without year-end reconciliation, which is the approach used in traditional transfer programs. This solution would require a separate set of rules that is likely to compromise tax-transfer integration, however, because the tax system itself continues to operate on an annual basis. * * *

Tax-Transfer Integration and the Trade off Between Compliance and Participation

Compliance and participation are two important objectives of any tax or transfer program. Compliance is essential because rules for assessing taxes or awarding benefits based on income or other criteria are useless unless those rules are enforced.[198] Participation is critical because income-transfer programs cannot improve the economic situation of families unless the benefits are claimed. Income tax systems also typically seek maximum participation in order to spread the tax burden fairly among taxpayers. Income-transfer programs encounter a familiar trade off between compliance and participation: efforts to increase compliance can reduce eligible beneficiaries' willingness to come forward and claim the benefits to which they are entitled.[199]

---

198. Rational policymakers, of course, assume a certain level of noncompliance when designing a program, but compliance efforts remain necessary to contain compliance within anticipated boundaries.

199. For example, efforts to verify information about income, employment, and children can require long and complicated forms and certifications from third parties. In the early 1980s, for

The EITC encounters a similar trade off. It seems likely to achieve impressive participation rates, because participation in a tax-based program appears easier and more attractive than participation in a traditional welfare program. A tax-based program requires only the filing of a tax return—recipients need not travel to a welfare office, wait in line, confront brusque or overworked caseworkers, or register for work or training programs. On the other hand, the poor typically do not have to file tax returns except to claim the EITC. Ironically, the traditional tax policy goal of exempting the poor from income taxation tends to undermine automatic EITC participation. In response, the IRS and a number of private groups have undertaken community outreach efforts in recent years to spread information about the EITC.

Despite potential information failures, available data confirm that the EITC has * * * participation rates * * * substantially higher than participation rates in traditional income-transfer programs.

Enforcing compliance with EITC rules is more difficult. The EITC presents two intrinsic problems of compliance and enforcement: the unusual problem of incentives for income overstatement, and the disproportionate cost of collecting erroneous overpayments from EITC recipients. First, existing compliance mechanisms generally attempt to detect or prevent the understatement of earnings, which is the normal compliance problem faced by the IRS. The EITC, however, tends to encourage overstatement of earnings, at least by nonworkers and workers with earnings in the subsidy range. A poor nonworker with two children, for example, might receive a $3370 EITC simply by increasing the earned income she reports to $8425. The economist Eugene Steuerle terms the problem of exaggerated earnings the "superterranean economy" and argues that " bluntly stated, the IRS cannot enforce the EITC as it is currently designed, much less as it would be expanded in the 1993 legislation."[208]

The EITC also presents a second potential problem: collection of overpayments. EITC noncompliance may result in overpayments that are large relative to the taxpayers' income but that are small dollar amounts in absolute terms (no more than $3370 per taxpayer). Several thousand dollars can be an attractive windfall for an individual but is a relatively small amount

---

example, estimates indicate that efforts to crack down on welfare cheating reduced the welfare rolls significantly—in part by turning away eligible applicants who could or would not cope with the complex procedures designed to ensure compliance with eligibility requirements. * * *

However, not all compliance efforts necessarily reduce participation, and numerous factors other than compliance efforts—including, for example, pride or lack of information—may affect participation rates.

208. Gene Steuerle, *The IRS Cannot Control the New Superterranean Economy*, 59 TAX NOTES 1839, 1839 (1993).

Gaps in coordination between the tax and transfer systems may allow an EITC recipient to overstate her earnings in order to maximize her EITC benefit without suffering a reduction in other income-tested transfer benefits.

for the IRS to seek to collect from one person, particularly if investigation and collection require audit rather than computerized correspondence. The IRS might rationally choose to focus on higher-return cases, particularly given the difficulty of actually recovering the money from low-income households.

Current estimates of noncompliance in the EITC program are widely cited but probably flawed. In 1990, Congress received IRS data showing that ineligible taxpayers received thirty-nine percent of EITC benefits paid in 1985.[211] These data sparked newspaper reports and congressional concern, but the IRS methodology may have exaggerated error rates.[212] In response to the EITC's perceived problem of EITC noncompliance, the 1990 amendments to the EITC took steps to improve compliance. Anecdotal evidence continues to provoke concern about noncompliance in the EITC, however. * * *

Although some policy makers may be willing to accept noncompliance in the EITC as the price of obtaining its advantages, the potential for noncompliance inherent in a tax-based program is likely to be a matter of recurring public concern. The strong negative public and political reaction to EITC error rates reported in 1990 and more recent criticisms of EITC fraud suggest that persuading policymakers to accept noncompliance as a cost of tax-based administration may not be easy.

Conclusions and Directions for Further Research

This Article raises serious questions about the validity of the over-simplified claims made for—and against—the EITC. Claims that the EITC promotes work and responsibility are exaggerated, but EITC opponents' attempts to equate the EITC with welfare are equally unsound. The EITC may have certain advantages as a tax-based program, including greater accessibility, cheaper administration, and reduced stigma for recipients. But policy analysts should also consider the inherent disadvantages of a tax-based program: less accurate targeting, less responsiveness to changing needs, and vulnerability to noncompliance. * * *

Understanding these trade offs does not require a rejection of the EITC or tax-based administration. * * *

---

211. *See* Spencer Rich, *For Working Poor, a Tough Program to Figure*, WASH. POST, Aug. 14, 1990, at A19; Spencer Rich, *IRS: 40% of Recipients Of Child Aid Ineligible*, WASH. POST, June 22, 1990, at A10.

212. The source of the data was the 1985 Taxpayer Compliance Measurement Program (TCMP), drawn from a comprehensive audit of 50,000 taxpayers conducted every three years. In a TCMP audit, which occurs several years after the filing of the original return, taxpayers are required to provide verification for every item claimed. Failure to provide verification results in a determination that the taxpayer was ineligible for the claimed benefit. Thus, some EITC recipients classified as ineligible in the TCMP audit may have been eligible but simply could not satisfy the exacting verification requirements, particularly after the fact.

IMPROVING THE DELIVERY OF BENEFITS TO THE WORKING POOR: PROPOSALS TO REFORM THE EARNED INCOME TAX CREDIT PROGRAM

George K. Yin[*], John Karl Scholz[**]
Jonathan Barry Forman[***] & Mark J. Mazur[****]

11 American Journal of Tax Policy 225, 228-30, 252-53, 258-60, 279-94 (1994)

Introduction

At the urging of the Clinton Administration, Congress approved as part of the Omnibus Budget Reconciliation Act of 1993 (1993 Act) a significant expansion of the earned income tax credit (EITC), the federal program intended to provide cash assistance to low-income, working families with children. The new law came on top of other, major expansions to the program enacted by Congress over the last eight years. With the new law, the estimated annual cost of the program will be almost $25 billion by FY 1998, or approximately one-and-one-half times the entire federal contribution to the aid to families with dependent children (AFDC) program.

The expansion of the EITC program heightens concerns about the effectiveness with which the program's benefits are being delivered to its intended recipients. The concerns relate to both the level of participation and compliance in the program. * * *

This paper has two objectives. First, it analyzes the latest available empirical data relating to the "participation rate" of the EITC program, that is, the percentage of intended beneficiaries who in fact are receiving the benefit, as well as the program's rate of compliance. * * *

Second, the paper sets forth and evaluates a number of options for improving delivery of the benefit to its intended recipients. The focus is on increasing both participation and compliance and ensuring that the benefit is received in a timely fashion. We consider administrative and legal changes to the existing EITC program as well as alternative methods of achieving the program's goals. The paper generally does not directly address other important policy issues concerning the program, including the coverage and adequacy of the credit, its impact as a work incentive or on the decision to marry, and its interaction with other subsidies for low-income households. In addition, the paper assumes that the tax system will continue to be the vehicle through which the benefit is provided to its targeted group. Thus, for example, we do not consider the possibility of having the EITC benefit administered by a single, non-tax agency of the federal government responsible for all anti-poverty initiatives.

---

[*]. At time of original publication, Professor of Law, University of Virginia.

[**]. At time of original publication, Assistant Professor of Economics, University of Wisconsin-Madison.

[***]. At time of original publication, Professor of Law, University of Oklahoma.

[****]. At time of original publication, Senior Economist, Council of Economic Advisers.

* * *

Possible Reasons for EITC
Participation and Compliance Problems
Comparison of EITC Participation and Compliance Rates with Those of Other Government Transfer Programs for the Poor

EITC participation rates in the range of 75 to 86 percent compare quite favorably to those of other federal programs directed toward low-income households. For example, food stamp participation was estimated to be 56 percent in 1989. An older study estimated food stamp and SSI participation to be between 50 to 60 percent in the late 1970s, and AFDC participation varying from 95 percent in the District of Columbia to 56 percent in Arizona in 1975-76. A more recent estimate indicates a 62-72 percent AFDC participation rate and a 54-66 percent food stamp participation rate using data from the 1986 and 1987 SIPP panels.

From the standpoint of facilitating participation, however, the design of the EITC program provides it with many advantages over those other programs. There is little or no stigma associated with the EITC, whereas stigma is thought to discourage participation in other government transfer programs. The EITC program does not involve any bureaucracy that the claimant must encounter face-to-face in order to obtain the benefit. Further, although there are EITC eligibility conditions, they are all past conditions; a participant need not promise, for example, to undertake job training or assume some other future obligation to obtain the assistance. The EITC benefit also is in the form of cash, in contrast to a benefit like food stamps. Finally, the pool of EITC eligibles must all be in the labor force to receive the benefit, and therefore may be a little better educated and have a little greater familiarity with available government benefits than those eligible for other government transfer programs for the poor. For these reasons, expectations for the rate of EITC participation should be ambitious.

Although the EITC participation rate is comparatively high, EITC noncompliance is also high. A 42 percent rate of excessive claims and an ineligibility rate of 32.3 percent are considerably higher than excessive claim rates of 6.0 percent for AFDC and 7.3 percent for food stamps in FY 1990. Finally, * * * the overwhelming majority of participants obtain their benefits in lump sums at the end of the tax year. The next section explores some of the principal impediments to full, accurate, and timely participation in the EITC program.

Reasons for EITC Delivery Problems
Noncompliance and Related Concerns

* * * [T]he self-certification feature of the tax system deters participation in the EITC program on the part of some eligible participants. Somewhat paradoxically, the same feature facilitates receipt of the EITC benefit by others not eligible for it. Furthermore, due to the small amounts of money typically involved, there is little chance of detection of errors in advance by the Service and collection of erroneous payments after-the-fact. To be sure, much noncompliance may be inadvertent because of the complexity of the claims process. But noncompliance may also result from an overstatement of the amount of earned income, including self-employment income, an exaggeration of family responsibilities, and other errors. Moreover, according to the GAO, almost one-half of the individuals filing returns who had received an advance payment failed to report it, leading to the possibility of duplicate credits being obtained, one during the year and another at the end of the year.

The peculiar and difficult compliance problems presented by the EITC program are exacerbated by the increases in the size of the EITC benefit beyond any relationship to an individual's tax liability. Individuals in the phase-in range of the credit (or with no income whatsoever) are provided with the incentive to report fictitious amounts of earned income, such as self-employment income.[121] Alternatively, superfluous work may be generated, resulting in a legal EITC claim which is surely contrary to the spirit of the program. For example, two neighbors presently taking care of their own homes may begin taking care of each other's and pay each other an equal wage for that service. The consequences of a legal or illegal claim are additional Social Security retirement credit for the claimant plus a cash benefit from the Treasury equal to the excess of the EITC benefit over any Social Security and income taxes due.

The Service is, and will be, hard pressed to deal with these types of situations. The tax laws and administrative procedures are generally designed to ferret out income under statement cases, not the reverse. * * *

Possible Alternative Designs for the Program
* * *

In this section, we discuss two other methods of using the tax system to accomplish the general goals of the EITC program, but in a manner fundamentally different from the existing program. These proposals have the potential of significantly enhancing both participation and compliance, as well as the timeliness of participation. The first proposal involves enactment of a Social Security tax exemption and a family allowance credit in lieu of the EITC. The second proposal would provide the assistance to low-income workers indirectly, rather than directly, by means of a tax benefit directed to the employers of such workers.
* * *

Replace EITC Program with Social Security Tax Exemption and Family Allowance Credit

At its core, the EITC program provides financial support to two groups: low-income individuals who work and those with family responsibilities. This first alternative would redesign the program to provide separate subsidies for

---

121. We found that ineligible families obtaining the benefit had more self-employment income, and less wage income, than the average EITC eligible family.

each of those two groups: a benefit for the working poor, and a family benefit that takes into account the presence of children living in the home. The following sections summarize this idea.

A Benefit for the Working Poor

The goal of the working poor benefit would be to ensure that a family unit without children but headed by a full-time worker has an income above the poverty line. A step towards meeting that goal would be to exempt low-income workers from paying the employee's portion of Social Security taxes or income taxes. Currently, a childless two-person household supported by a single worker who is employed full-time for the full year and paid the minimum wage has $8,840 in annual earnings (52 wks x 40 hrs/wk x $4.25/hr). Even with no EITC benefit, the household is already exempt from paying any income taxes. If the worker were also exempt from paying the employee's share of Social Security taxes, the household would be within $590 of the 1993 poverty guideline for a two-person family unit, $9,430.[s]

A Social Security tax exemption is also consistent with one of the original rationales for the EITC program, to rebate the Social Security taxes of low-income workers. The current system of first collecting such taxes and then refunding them by means of the EITC is administratively unwieldy. It would be simpler not to collect the Social Security taxes in the first instance.

If the Social Security tax exemption were available only to low-income workers, however, there would be little improvement in the administration of the benefit. Workers eligible for the exemption would need first to identify themselves, creating the possibility of nonparticipation. In addition, they would then need to inform their employers of their eligibility, a procedure that might stigmatize them and therefore further reduce participation. Also, workers benefiting from the exemption might later be found to be ineligible due to their income level or other reasons. That possibility might necessitate the filing of a Social Security tax return, surely no improvement from the standpoint of simplification.

A better solution would be to exempt all workers from the payment of the employee's portion of Social Security taxes, but make the exemption only applicable up to a certain level of wages. Such a benefit could be recaptured from higher paid workers by imposing a higher Social Security tax rate on wages in excess of the exemption amount, raising the current earnings cap for the old-age and survivors and disability insurance (OASDI) portions of the tax, or both. Those alternatives and some of the general revenues currently dedicated to the EITC program could be used to pay for the exemption, so that there would be no need to change the amount of Social Security benefits available to any future beneficiary.

* * *

---

s. The dollar amounts in this article are outdated, but the authors' observations and proposals are still fully relevant. (Ed.)

A Family Allowance Benefit

Supplementing the working poor subsidy would be a family allowance benefit to provide additional income security for low-income families with children. The theory of the benefit would be to take account of the extra, nonconsumption, expenses incurred by families with children living in the home. The benefit would also be consistent with the theory of current poverty guidelines, which take into account family size.

The simplest method of delivering the family allowance benefit would be to provide a refundable income tax credit to any family with children living in the home, regardless of its work or income status. Up to some level, the size of the credit might vary with the number of children in the family living at home. Such a credit would be universally available to both low-and high-income families. If provided as a substitute for the existing dependency exemption, however, the credit would produce a shift in benefits from current law in favor of lower-income families. Various legislators, groups, and commentators have advocated similar proposals on policy grounds quite apart from administrability concerns, and a number of industrialized nations already have such a benefit in place.

Analysis

The combination of a Social Security tax exemption and a family allowance credit would offer many potential advantages over the current system. First, the working poor benefit would automatically be received by all eligible families in a timely manner in each paycheck. In that sense, it would be a much more visible benefit than the current credit. Beneficiaries would no longer need to obtain information, determine or assert eligibility, or even file a return. Voluntary nonparticipation would not be an issue, nor would the possibility of stigma. Employers would not be burdened except for the slight change to adjust for the exemption amount in calculating the amount of Social Security taxes to withhold. The simplicity of the proposal and the relative absence of any self-certifying features would assure a high level of compliance. Finally, by limiting the benefit to an exemption from taxes, the proposal would not provide an incentive for the performance of superfluous work or the reporting of fictitious income.

The universal availability of the family allowance credit should also make it far easier to administer than the EITC, which is targeted for only a portion of the population. All employees would simply need to complete a form, similar to the existing IRS Form W-4, indicating the number of children in their households.[199] The family allowance benefit would then automatically be provided to middle-and upper-income taxpayers during the year through adjustments to the withholding amount. Low-income families who work could also obtain the benefit during the course of the year through advance payments. The problems with advance payments under current law, including

---

199. An alternative procedure would have to be devised for nonworkers.

the lack of awareness of the option, the complexity in utilizing it, and the possible stigmatizing effect of claiming eligibility for it, would not be present because all employees would be required to fill out the same, simple form. Noncompliance issues would be limited to exaggerations of family responsibilities and the possible double claiming of the benefit by those with more than one job. The former could be alleviated by continuing the practice of requiring Social Security numbers for all children claimed. The latter could be addressed by calculating the advance payment amount in a very conservative manner.

An important disadvantage of the alternative is that it would not target the poor as well as the current program. Workers with low wage income but high capital income could nevertheless benefit from the Social Security tax exemption without any recapture. Examples include affluent teenagers or college students working at summer jobs and low-wage or part-time workers with wealthy spouses. One way to address some of this problem would be to implement the exemption on a weekly (or periodic) basis rather than on an annual one. For example, the exemption might be limited to the first $170 in wages per week ($4.25/hr minimum wage x 40 hrs/wk) rather than an annual exemption amount. A weekly exemption of this sort would tend to prevent much of the benefit from going to high-paid workers who have low annual wages because they only work a portion of the year, e.g., high-paid summer employees. A weekly (or periodic) exemption would also be easier for employers to implement than an annual one.

Another possibility is to impose some age limitation on the availability of the exemption. For example, the new EITC benefit for childless, low-income workers is available only to those who are at least 25 years of age but are less than 65 years old, effectively precluding teenagers and most college students as well as senior citizens from getting any benefit. A similar rule could be adopted to improve the targeting of the Social Security tax exemption.

Like the family allowance credit, a technical problem with the Social Security tax exemption involves the possible double claiming of the exemption amount by wage earners with multiple jobs. It might be necessary for workers to certify the absence of other exempt wages in order to qualify for the exemption. If the certification were keyed to the worker's Social Security number, there might be expected to be a high degree of compliance.

A final potential disadvantage of the alternative is that it will result in an erosion of the political support now behind the EITC program. Some legislators might be concerned with substantial federal benefits being provided to nonworking families with children. Others might object to benefits being directed towards those who work but who have no family responsibilities. Much of the strength and durability of the EITC program may well be attributable to its ability to satisfy many different political constituencies at the same time. On the other hand, if the credit is overburdened to the point of losing its effectiveness, that feature may prove to be its undoing.

Replace EITC with Indirect Assistance to Low-Income Workers Through a Tax Benefit Directed to Their Employers
Introduction

* * * The employer is a valuable link between the Service and the program beneficiary. One problem with significant employer participation, however, is the absence of adequate incentives for employer involvement. * * *

One way of insuring greater employer involvement is to provide the assistance to low-income workers indirectly by means of a tax benefit directed to their employers. For example, a tax credit could be awarded to the employer of certain qualifying workers. The theory is that the same general transaction—the hiring and compensation of a qualifying worker—can be subsidized by providing a direct benefit to either the employer or the worker in that transaction if the benefit is capitalized in the compensation arrangement and thereby shared by the parties to the transaction. Thus, whether provided directly or indirectly, the benefit to the worker would, in theory, be the same. The policy design question of whether to subsidize directly the employer or the employee has arisen elsewhere in the tax system[205] and is likely to arise again in connection with future tax subsidies.[206] With an employer-based subsidy, the adminstrative burden of the program could more easily be shifted to the firm and away from the worker because the subsidy itself would be provided directly to the firm.

A benefit awarded directly to employers should be easier to administer than one directed towards workers. First, the smaller number of firms than workers should reduce the information dissemination task. Further, firms could be expected to cope better than workers with the applicable rules for obtaining the benefit. Both of those differences, as well as the fact that there would be greater dollar amounts at stake per firm than per worker, could also enhance compliance. Finally, firms already deal with the Service so that fear of that agency would not be a rational reason for nonparticipation in the program. Accordingly, an employer benefit might have lower administrative costs than the current EITC program and, therefore, could result in higher levels of participation and compliance.

---

205. Several examples include the targeted jobs tax credit, I.R.C. § 51, a tax subsidy provided to employers to induce the hiring of individuals who are members of certain groups; the possessions tax credit, I.R.C. § 936, a benefit available to businesses with certain operations in a possession of the United States which is intended to promote employment in those areas; the new empowerment zone employment credit, I.R.C. § 1396, a benefit for businesses that employ workers who live and work in certain economically distressed areas; and the new Indian employment credit, I.R.C. § 45A, a tax subsidy for certain employers located on Indian reservations. These programs generally could have been designed with the subsidy going directly to the workers instead of the employers of those workers.

206. For example, any future tax benefit subsidizing the health care costs of low-income workers may raise the same issue.

Design of the Employer Benefit
Tax Credit Based on Level
of Wages Paid by Firm

Due to privacy concerns, it would not be feasible to implement a tax benefit to employers based on the sum of all sources of income of its workers. On the other hand, an employer subsidy based upon the level of wages paid by the employer to its workers would be an easy to administer program directed towards the same general population now targeted by the EITC. A tax benefit in the form of an employer credit could be calculated as a percentage of wages paid to low-wage (as opposed to low-income) employees. If desired, the same structure as the current EITC program could be implemented: a larger credit could be awarded to firms as the wage rate paid to a worker increases up to some level, and then the credit could gradually be taken away as the wage rate increases beyond some even higher level.

In certain respects, a wage subsidy program would be more desirable than an income subsidy approach such as the existing EITC program. The principal advantage is that unlike the current EITC, a wage subsidy would not benefit high-paid workers who simply choose to work part-time. For example, under current law, a worker whose entire income is derived from 500 hours of work during the year at $20/hour is subsidized to the same extent as one whose entire income is derived from 2000 hours of work at $5/hour. Another advantage is that a wage subsidy could avoid the penalty for marriage present under the existing EITC. Furthermore, in contrast to workers in the phase-out range of the EITC, a person willing to work more hours, or at multiple jobs, at the same rate of pay would not experience a loss of benefit under a wage subsidy program. Finally, there should be little stigma problem presented by an employer subsidy determined by wage rates. The only identifying characteristic for a worker under such a scheme is the low wage rate, a piece of information known to the employer and presumably not the basis for negative stereotyping by it.

A wage subsidy, if directed to the worker through the tax system, would be infeasible because wage rate information is not typically reported for income tax purposes. A wage subsidy granted directly to firms , however, should involve minor administrative difficulties. A credit could be granted to firms based upon wage rate information available from the normal books and records of the firm.

Exemption from Payment of Employer's
Share of Social Security Taxes

Alternatively, the subsidy could take the form of an exemption from the payment of the employer's share of Social Security taxes, applicable up to a certain level of wages paid to each employee. Indeed, the exemption could be paired with an abatement of the employee's share of such taxes, as described previously, so that up to some level of wages, neither portion of the tax would need to be paid. * * * If, as is widely believed, workers in competitive labor markets bear through lower wages the cost of all payroll taxes, including the employer's share, then relief from such taxes should redound to the benefit of those same workers. An additional advantage of this proposal is that it may reduce the filing burden of many employers of low-paid employees, such as domestic workers. Congress is actively searching for an acceptable solution in that area.

Analysis

The principal objection to an employer-based subsidy is that it would not have the same economic effect as the EITC program. There is doubt that bargaining between the firm and the worker would produce the same economic outcome regardless of whether the tax benefit is granted directly to one party or the other. Little, if any, of the tax benefit granted to a firm may end up in the hands of the low-income worker.

* * *

Another objection to an employer-based alternative is that it would not target the poor as well as the existing EITC program. Teenagers from affluent families as well as low-paid workers with wealthy spouses would benefit from the subsidy. A partial answer might be to place some type of limitation on the age of the worker whose wages entitle the employer to the tax benefit. Another possibility is to limit the subsidy to the employment of low-paid but full-time employees who work throughout the year. The latter rule would exclude, for example, teenagers employed only during the summer.

* * *

A related concern is the possibility of collusion between employers and workers in reporting lower wages and greater hours than actually worked in order to maximize the available tax benefit.

In any event, regardless of the relative merits of an employer-versus worker-based subsidy program, the transition costs of changing from the current system would likely outweigh any advantage obtained from the change. But if ineffective administration of the EITC program becomes an even greater concern, consideration could be given to initiating an employer-based option in lieu of further increases to the existing EITC program.

Notes and Questions

Behavioral effects of the EITC

50. As Professor Alstott notes (disapprovingly), the effects of EITC on marriage and work (and, less frequently, on childbearing) have been much debated. Professor Alstott wisely cautions us that any such effects largely depend upon an understanding of the law's economic effects. Given the broad lack of understanding of this complex law, behavioral effects may be less than might be expected by tax scholars who do understand the law.

Possible effects on marriage

51. One behavioral effect might be a disinclination to marriage. Assume two unmarried individuals, each supporting at least one child and earning

$15,000 annually. Separately, each would receive a substantial EITC. Married, they would be evaluated as a couple with $30,000 income, and would receive little or no EITC. This is another form of "marriage penalty," a topic discussed in Chapter Five. Especially when viewed as a percentage of income, the marriage penalty for EITC recipients can be substantial.

52. An alternative to avoiding marriage could be a fraudulent effort to conceal marriage from the Service.

53. Prior to 2001, the marriage penalty in the EITC was particularly sharp, because the same dollar limitations were applied to either unmarried individuals or married couples (who, under section 32(d), must file jointly to claim the EITC). Congress softened the EITC marriage penalty in 2001, providing that the phaseout range (at both the low and high end) for married couples would be increased, initially by $1,000, ultimately (starting in 2008) by $3,000. (Like the rest of the 2001 Act, this provision "sunsets" in 2011.)

Possible effects on work

54. Supporters of the EITC contend that it helps to "make work pay." Indeed, at first glance the EITC appears unambiguously to encourage work. Upon closer analysis, however, the incentive is far more complex than initially appears; for many workers, the EITC may actually discourage work effort.

55. Professor Alstott divides EITC beneficiaries into three categories. What might be the effect on work effort by individuals (or couples) in the lowest range, in which the credit increases with income? By those in the mid-range, in which the credit is unaffected by increases in income? By those in the higher, phase-out range, in which the credit falls as income rises?

56. Suppose it were established that the disincentives to workers in the higher phaseout range exceeded the incentives to workers in the lowest range, in which the credit increases with income. The EITC could still be defended because it gives the positive incentive to those who need it most—those who are not working at all, or whose relationship with the work force is most tenuous. Would you regard this as sufficient justification if the program discourages work by low-income persons as a group?

57. Should welfare programs in general, and the EITC in particular, be tied to individual income or to family income? If the latter, how should "family" be defined?

58. Most welfare programs take account of wealth, a factor considered by the income tax only to the degree that wealth generates income. The EITC, tied to the income tax, ignores wealth, meaning that low-income persons can

qualify even if they have substantial wealth not generating current income. Should the EITC take wealth into account?

59.   Professor Alstott points up the tension between designing programs to respond quickly to those in need, and designing programs to assure that a potential beneficiary's current economic problem is not transient. This relates to the length of time over which income should be measured, and the effects of this timing decision on individuals with steady, or with fluctuating, incomes. For an illustration, examine footnote 177 of Alstott's article with care.

Should income support programs look at an entire year, or at a shorter period?

60.   Are you concerned that less than one percent of EITC recipients take advantage of advance payments in the form of "negative withholding"?

61.   The Internal Revenue Service administers the EITC. While the Service's record in enforcing the tax laws is less than perfect, it obviously has expertise and techniques designed to detect those who report *less* income than they actually receive. Rarely does the Service need to worry about taxpayers intentionally reporting *more* income than they receive, and therefore, in this area, it may lack such expertise and techniques.

In the lowest, phase-in range, however, the EITC constitutes a significant negative income tax. As income rises, the credit increases much more than any associated increase in tax (primarily the Social Security tax).   Thus, a nonworker, for example, could claim to be earning self-employment income, and receive a credit of 40 percent in exchange for paying a Social Security tax of 15.3 percent (while receiving credit toward future Social Security benefits in the bargain). Can the Service be expected to police this provision?

62.   The Service reported to Congress in 1990 that ineligible recipients received some 39 percent of EITC benefits. (Professor Alstott questions the Service's methodology, but all agree that the number is high.) It may be expected that the liberalization of the EITC since 1990 could attract even more fraudulent claims.

63.   Yin, Scholz, Forman, and Mazur note that, as compared to other welfare programs, the EITC delivery mechanism results in high participation (desirable claims by those who legally qualify) but also high rates of noncompliance (undesirable claims by those who do not legally qualify). Given that no program can be perfect in either respect, which is more important?

64.   The four authors point out the possibility of intentionally (but legally) generating taxable income from an activity that would usually be expected to lead to untaxed imputed income. They raise the possibility of two neighbors

who stop cleaning their own homes, and each clean the house of the other, to generate income and thus obtain EITC. (In theory, it would not even be necessary for the neighbors to pay each other. A staple of the basic tax course is examination of Treas. Reg. § 1.61-2(d), generally coupled with the observation that an exchange of services by neighbors should, in theory, result in income. One supposes the Government receives little revenue from such transactions.)

65. Yin, Scholz, Forman, and Mazur suggest that EITC might be improved if we recognized that it consists of two components—aid for the working poor, and aid for families—and disaggregated the two benefits. They would aid the working poor by exempting from Social Security taxation an amount equal to the minimum wage (perhaps computed on an annual basis, perhaps hourly, the authors noting problems with either approach). The lost revenue to the Social Security system would be offset by higher taxes on earnings above the exemption level, or by an infusion of general revenue. There would be little incentive to claim extra income fraudulently, because the resulting EITC would be offset by Social Security tax.

66. Aid to families would be achieved by a family allowance, ideally a "refundable income tax credit to any family with children living in the home, regardless of its work or income status." Similar programs are widely used abroad and frequently advocated by writers whose work is excerpted in this book. Recall, however, the political assessment of Professors Zelenak and Moreland, in their discussion of optimal taxation excerpted in Chapter Four (at page 220): "In a political climate in which even need-based welfare-as-we-know-it has been drastically curtailed, a system of universal non-need based transfers has no chance."

67. The fusion of the work requirement and family need under the present structure of the EITC can produce questionable results. Professor Allan Samansky observes that "the extra benefit [under the EITC, using 1996 figures] when a person is supporting a second child is $80 when adjusted gross income and earned income are $4000, and $1016 when adjusted gross income and earned income are $9000. This result seems perverse because the first family presumably needs the extra support more than the second family."[t]

68. Under a second, completely different alternative, Yin, Scholz, Forman, and Mazur suggest giving a credit to employers of low-income persons rather than to the low-income persons themselves. How would this program be structured? How might it help the poor? Do you think, in fact, that it would

---

t. Allan J. Samansky, *Tax Policy and the Obligation to Support Children*, 57 OHIO STATE L.J. 329, 380 (1996).

primarily benefit low-income workers or their employers? What problems of administration would you envision?

69. Upon consideration, do you regard the EITC as a model for future programs that would use the tax system as a means of effecting income transfers? Or, is the EITC a program that should itself be curtailed or ended?

CHAPTER TWELVE

PERSONAL INJURY AWARDS

*The difficulty in interpreting section 104(a)(2) and the
inconsistent court holdings and Revenue Rulings of the past seven
decades probably comes from the lack of any cohesive tax theory or
social policy justifying the exemption. The Service, the courts, and the
commentators have failed to find any entirely satisfactory explanation
of section 104(a)(2)'s* raison d'etre.[a]

A. INTRODUCTION AND HISTORICAL DEVELOPMENT

Section 104(a)(2) excludes from gross income most tort awards for
personal injury—"any damages (other than punitive damages) received
(whether by suit or agreement and whether as lump sums or as periodic
payments) on account of personal physical injuries or physical sickness."
Other provisions in sections 104 and 105 exclude similar financial payments
related to personal injury, such as workers' compensation payments,[b] but
section 104(a)(2) has always been the focus of interest.

Though language similar to section 104(a)(2) has been in the Code since
1918, the exclusion has been in flux in recent years. For decades, the provision
received a broad reading administratively and in the courts. More recently,
concerned that the provision was unduly generous, Congress has moved to
narrow the exclusion. In 1996, section 104(a)(2) was amended, so that it no
longer protects either punitive damages or damages from non-physical
personal injuries (such as defamation of the plaintiff's personal reputation).
Among the questions we shall examine in this chapter is whether Congress has
established unworkable distinctions.

Apart from the recent amendments, section 104(a)(2) has attracted
increased interest in recent years. Torts is a growth industry, and section
104(a)(2) is no longer a peripheral provision that merely excludes the
occasional modest award. The heightened interest in the tax treatment of
personal injury awards makes this an interesting time to review the
theoretical underpinning of allowing an exclusion, and to consider the proper
scope of the exclusion. For example, should damages that compensate accident
victims for lost earnings be excluded, as under present law, given that the
earnings would have been taxed? Is the present exclusion of awards for pain

---

a. Margaret Henning, *Recent Developments in the Tax Treatment of Personal Injury and
Punitive Damage Recoveries,* 45 TAX LAW. 783, 795-96 (1992).

b. Section 104(a)(1).

and suffering appropriate, given the absence of a deduction for those who suffer pain without compensation?

Theoretical considerations must be tempered with practicality. If, for example, it were decided that some elements of personal injury recoveries should be taxed and others not, how should the law allocate amounts received in settlement? This question is significant, because the overwhelming majority of receipts come as a result of settlement before trial, or even before suit is filed.

In addition to illuminating an area of tax policy of considerable importance in its own right, the materials in this chapter offer valuable guidance into the nature of income—a fundamental issue for the student of tax policy.

In the immediately following article, Professors Burke and Friel discuss the historical origins of the exclusion, as well as some of the theories upon which the exclusion has been justified. Evaluation of these theories, which is the central theme of this chapter, is expanded in Subchapter B. In Subchapter C, Professor Griffith challenges traditional methods of tax policy analysis, using the tax treatment of personal injury awards as a case study.

Finally, Subchapter D considers tax complications arising from timing issues. These issues arise when a lump sum award replaces many years of future expected earnings and expected freedom from pain. Particular attention is given to the tax consequences of "structured settlements," under which, instead of a lump sum, the injured taxpayer receives compensation in a series of payments.

TAX TREATMENT OF EMPLOYMENT-RELATED PERSONAL INJURY AWARDS: THE NEED FOR LIMITS
J. Martin Burke[*] & Michael K. Friel[**]

50 Montana Law Review 13, 14-15, 42-47 (1989)

Section 104(a)(2) dates back to Section 213(b)(6) of the Revenue Act of 1918. The history of that original section suggests that Congress intended it to codify then-recent administrative decisions. Treasury regulations promulgated early in 1918 under the Revenue Acts of 1916 and 1917 provided specifically that damages were taxable, stating that an "[a]mount received as the result of a suit or compromise for personal injury, being similar to the proceeds of accident insurance, is to be accounted for as income." However, in June 1918, in response to a Treasury inquiry, an Attorney General's opinion held that accident insurance proceeds were not taxable, based on the theory that the "human body is a kind of capital" and the insurance proceeds represented a "conversion of the capital lost through the injury." Shortly thereafter, based on that Attorney General's opinion, the Treasury determined

---

[*]. At time of original publication, Dean and Professor of Law, University of Montana.
[**]. At time of original publication, Professor of Law and Director, Graduate Tax Program, University of Florida.

"upon similar principles that an amount received . . . as a result of a suit or compromise for personal injuries sustained . . . through accident" was not taxable and revoked its prior regulation to the contrary. Against this background Congress enacted Section 213(b)(6) of the Revenue Act of 1918, which provided that the term "gross income" did not include: "(6) [a]mounts received, through accident or health insurance or under workmen's compensation acts, as compensation for personal injuries or sickness, plus the amount of any damages received whether by suit or agreement on account of such injuries or sickness."

* * *

Given the history of Section 104(a)(2), only the return-of-capital concept should have any validity today, and even that concept suffers from severe limitations. Under traditional tax principles, application of the return-of-capital theory requires that the taxpayer establish an investment of capital in the asset in question, recognized by the tax code as basis. In the case of a person's corporal and noncorporal attributes—one's body, reputation, mental health, and the like—one presumes that the tax code, ordinarily at least, recognizes no investment of capital, and so no basis. * * *

If the receipt of a personal injury award constitutes realization of gain—which, by traditional tax standards, it must—the exclusion of the gain from income can be justified only by substantial policy considerations. One might presume that the involuntariness of the injury sustained is a factor underlying the exclusion, for the taxpayer who consents in advance to the "injury" apparently removes the compensation received from the protection of Section 104(a)(2). Commentators and courts have suggested that personal injury awards are excluded for humanitarian reasons. * * *

But if humanitarian concerns underlie the exclusion of damages from income, the obvious objection is that not all damages on account of involuntary personal injuries—and perhaps relatively few—warrant such tender treatment. It may, for example, be "heartless" to tax damage awards received on account of severe physical injuries, such as brain damage, paralysis, loss of sight or numerous other terrible injuries. But few conceivable humanitarian reasons exist to exclude damages received for a sprained ankle or a bruised arm. * * * Moreover, why is it only the compensated victim to whom humanitarian tax relief is extended? The uncompensated victim is presumably even more deserving of compassion, and surely administrative burdens could be satisfactorily taken into account in fashioning some tax relief program—an allowance of certain personal injury losses, perhaps—for the uncompensated. The conclusion one is finally driven to is that humanitarian reasons supply a woefully inadequate justification for the breadth of injuries encompassed by Section 104(a)(2).

* * *

The Code is replete with provisions that carve out exceptions to general tax rules. There would likely be little quarrel with a Congressional decision to exclude from income for humanitarian reasons a limited category of personal injury awards.[133] * * * Any special treatment provided must be seen as equitable, must be administratively feasible, and must be drafted so that clear guidance is given to taxpayers and the Service as to the specific circumstances that give rise to the favored treatment. The design of the special provisions should also hew as closely as possible to general tax principles underlying the income tax code. For example, increased personal exemptions could be granted to persons with objectively verifiable disabilities; the exemption could vary depending on the degree of disability, and could be phased out beyond certain income levels. Consistent with existing preferences for the blind and elderly, such an approach would have the further advantage of treating disabled persons equally for tax purposes, regardless of the cause of the disability (tortious injury, birth defect, etc.) and regardless of whether compensation had been received for the disability. Under such an approach, all recoveries for personal injuries would be taxable, except reimbursement of nondeductible medical expenses. As an alternative approach, the lost wages component of a damage award could be specifically subject to tax, along with any amount of punitive damages awarded. Such an approach would be consistent with the general tax principle that substitutes for ordinary income shall be taxed as ordinary income, and also with the *Glenshaw Glass* view of income. Where an award compensated for lost wages over a number of years, an income-averaging rule could be adopted to mitigate the bunching effect. As another alternative, an exclusion could be patterned on Section 105(c) and limited to what are presumably the most serious injuries—those that cause permanent disability or disfigurement.

The final suggestion might offer the most promise of a policy-based tax treatment of damages for personal injuries or sickness. The fundamental difficulty with Section 104(a)(2) is that it is not grounded in any sound tax policy. One solution would be to simply eliminate Section 104(a)(2), so that all such damages are taxed in full, as ordinary income in the year received. Such a solution may lack political appeal; it definitely lacks consistency with companion provisions in Section 104 and 105. The major problems with Section 104(a)(2) can successfully be addressed by narrowing its scope in a manner generally consistent with Sections 104 and 105. The Section 104(a)(2) exclusion for personal injuries or sickness should be no greater than that

---

133. Even among its related provisions in Sections 104 and 105, Section 104(a)(2) is noteworthy in its breadth. Section 104(a)(1) is limited to workers' compensation awards. Section 104(a)(3) excludes employee-financed accident or health insurance. Exclusions under Section 105 for employer-financed insurance are limited to medical expenses incurred by the employee and to certain permanent disability or disfigurement payments. Whatever the merits of such exclusions—and they are admittedly debatable—embedding them in the context of workers' compensation, or accident or health insurance, surely restrains their expansion and the ease with which they may be manipulated. Section 104(a)(4), as limited by Section 104(b), and Section 104(a)(5) provide exclusions only for certain military disability pensions and certain victims of terrorist attacks, and are clearly quite narrow in their application.

provided by other provisions of Section 104 and Section 105. Section 104(a)(3) and Section 105 distinguish between the tax treatment of proceeds of health and accident insurance based on whether the insurance is employer-provided or employee-provided. As between the two, the damages received by a tort victim may be better analogized to employer-provided insurance, since in both instances the recipient has no after-tax "investment" attributable to the amounts received. If the analogy is accepted, then consistent with Section 104(a)(3) and 105, the damages received under Section 104(a)(2) should be includable in income—except to the extent they are attributable to amounts expended for medical care in a manner similar to Section 105(b), and except to the extent they are attributable to permanent disability or disfigurement in a manner similar to Section 105(c). Such an approach would end the exclusion for non-physical injuries and for physical injuries that are not serious ones, yet would maintain a compassionate response for recoveries on account of the most serious physical injuries. It remains true, of course, that Section 104(a)(1) would continue to exclude amounts received under workers' compensation acts without limitations such as those contained in Section 105, and workers' compensation may be viewed as employer-provided insurance. Nonetheless, the tax treatment of workers' compensation may reflect its historic concern for employment conditions in or related to the workplace, and the favorable tax treatment is circumscribed by the requirement that compensation be under a workers' compensation act. Whether the distinction warrants different tax treatment may be debatable, but the distinction itself is apparent. The Section 104(a)(2) exclusion may thus be limited in a fashion consistent with Section 104(a)(3) and Section 105, and as a result may achieve a consistency, rationality, and policy basis that it sorely lacks now.

Notes and Questions

1.   What was the background to the initial adoption of the statutory exclusion of personal injury awards?

Nonphysical personal injuries

2.   In a portion of the article not excerpted, Professors Burke and Friel discuss the varying interpretation of "personal injury" for purposes of the exclusion. Immediately after the predecessor to section 104(a)(2) was enacted in 1918, the Service took the position that, despite statutory language that lent itself to a broader construction, "the term 'personal injuries', as used therein means physical injuries only."[c]

Following the Supreme Court's decision in *Eisner v. Macomber*,[d] with its restrictive language indicating that income was generally limited to gain obtained "from capital, from labor, or from both combined," the Revenue

---

c. 50 MONT. L. REV. at 15 (quoting Solicitor's Memorandum 957 (1919)).
d. 252 U.S. 189 (1920).

Service ultimately conceded that nonphysical personal injuries, such as defamation of the taxpayer's personal reputation, were excludable. The Service—erroneously, in the view of Burke and Friel—did not reexamine this view after the Supreme Court effectively repudiated *Eisner v. Macomber*'s restrictive view of income in cases such as *Glenshaw Glass*,[e] in which the Court indicated that "accessions to wealth," regardless of source, were presumptively income.

3. In 1996, Congress limited the exclusion to cases of *physical* injury or sickness. Assuming the exclusion for physical personal injury is to be continued, eliminating nonphysical personal injuries from the scope of the exclusion raises practical and theoretical problems.

Many tort actions involve both physical and nonphysical injuries, meaning that allocation of a lump-sum award or settlement will be difficult. In many instances, a single injury has physical and nonphysical components. Consider a female taxpayer who is pinched by a man, the pinch causing minor and temporary pain and discoloration, and continuing feelings of consternation and outrage. Clearly, this fits within the definition of a harmful battery. At the same time, it seems likely that the bulk of the plaintiff's compensatory damages is attributable to the plaintiff's emotional and psychological harm. (It is difficult to imagine that this minimal amount of physical harm, if caused negligently rather than intentionally—and therefore not causing a feeling of violation or outrage—would result in litigation.)

4. More broadly, as we learn more of the interrelationship between mind and body, it may be that the physical/nonphysical distinction will prove increasingly slippery. What if "physical" pain from an injured leg, for example, is actually a response of the brain to stimuli communicated to the brain through the nervous system? Is it a sufficient response to say, in effect, "we know physical injury when we see it"?

5. What policy basis supports a rule that grants an exclusion for *all* physical personal injury awards and *no* nonphysical personal injury awards? An obvious defense of present law might be that this supposedly bright-line test (but see Notes #3 and #4 above) is generally correct, because physical injuries are generally more serious than nonphysical injury. But is this a determination best made through tax law, or through tort law? Tort law has, over the centuries, developed a mechanism, however imperfect, for quantifying damages in cases of both physical and nonphysical injury. If tort law finds a physical injury more serious and thus allows a larger award, tax law can ratify that decision even if it excludes both awards. The exclusion will be worth more

---

e. Commissioner v. Glenshaw Glass Co., 348 U.S. 426 (1955).

to the physically injured plaintiff, because that plaintiff has received more damages.

But what if the tort system comes to the conclusion—manifested by a large award for compensatory damages—that a particular nonphysical injury is an extremely serious matter, more serious than most physical injuries? Is it appropriate for the tax system—which, unlike the tort system, has not considered the facts of this individual case—to make a blanket determination that the nonphysical injury is not very serious after all?

6.   A leading justification of section 104(a)(2) is return of capital: the plaintiff has no gain, but merely a restoration (in the form of a monetary equivalent, rather than in well-being). Does the return-of-capital justification support or undermine a distinction between physical and nonphysical personal injury?

In a portion of their article not excerpted,[f] Burke and Friel quote from Solicitor's Memorandum 1384, issued in 1920 prior to the Supreme Court's decision in *Eisner v. Macomber*. That Memorandum concluded that damages for alienation of affection were not excludable under the predecessor to section 104(a)(2), arguing: "From no ordinary conception of the term can a wife's affections be regarded as constituting capital."

Clearly, the Solicitor's observation is correct. On the other hand, pain and suffering is a major component of damages in cases of physical injury, and freedom from pain is not a capital asset by any "ordinary conception of the term."

7.   Assuming section 104(a)(2) is to be continued in some form, should the exclusion be limited to physical injuries? How would you analyze this question in terms of return of capital? In terms of humanitarian relief? In terms of administrative simplicity? Combining these considerations?

8.   *Attorneys' fees.* Suppose a plaintiff receives $300,000 in damages for nonphysical injury, of which $100,000 goes to the plaintiff's attorney. Obviously, the attorney has $100,000 income, but what of the client? Assuming the award is taxed (as present law provides), should the plaintiff be treated as having income of $200,000, or income of $300,000 and a deduction of $100,000? The Service asserts the latter, which can make a significant difference in some cases, primarily due to application of the alternative minimum tax.

---

f. 50 MONT. L. REV. at 15.

792   CHAPTER 12. PERSONAL INJURY AWARDS

B. HUMAN CAPITAL AND OTHER TRADITIONAL JUSTIFICATIONS FOR THE EXCLUSION

The purpose of this subchapter is to examine in detail the justifications for section 104(a)(2), and, assuming there is to be an exclusion, to consider its proper scope. As Professors Burke and Friel indicated in Subchapter A, from the earliest days of the income tax, even before the 1918 enactment of the predecessor to section 104(a)(2), the principal justification for exclusion has been that there is no gain, because the taxpayer's lost capital—his healthy self—has simply been restored by payment of its monetary equivalent. Professor Stephan examines the notion of human capital, giving particular attention to a problem largely ignored when the restoration-of-capital idea first appeared—the taxpayer has no obvious basis in his body, and recoveries for damage to capital usually are tax-free only to the extent of basis.

Perhaps the most questionable aspect of the section 104(a)(2) exclusion is that it protects from tax damages that replace lost earnings, even though the earnings themselves would have been taxed. Professor Brooks defends section 104(a)(2)'s favorable treatment of recoveries for lost earnings.

Professor Kahn regards the return-of-capital argument as insufficient to support the exclusion, but argues that section 104(a)(2) is justified by a combination of factors. In particular, he emphasizes the noncommercial nature of the transaction, and the popular perception of the Government taxing tort recoveries.

Professor Dodge examines various rationales for section 104(a)(2), with particular consideration of damages to compensate for severe pain and disfigurement. Even in this most appealing case, he finds the justifications for exclusion inadequate. He argues that the tax system should look to material resources with a market value, not to a subjective notion of utility, as its measure of income.

FEDERAL INCOME TAXATION AND HUMAN CAPITAL
Paul B. Stephan III[*]

70 Virginia Law Review 1357, 1358-60, 1388-99, 1402-03 (1984)

Human capital, in economic terms, is equivalent to the present value of the flow of future satisfactions that an individual can command in the course of his life. Some portion of this capital constitutes endowment, the biological and social inheritance that accompanies a person into the world. The remainder is acquired through individual action, such as education, on-the-job training, migration, and health care, or stems from exogenous changes such as technological or social transformation.[1] When one talks of human capital as

---

[*]. At time of original publication, Associate Professor, University of Virginia School of Law.

[1]. For the classical treatment of labor inputs to the production process, *see* A. MARSHALL, PRINCIPLES OF ECONOMICS 680-88 (8th ed. 1920); 2 J.S. MILL, PRINCIPLES OF POLITICAL ECONOMY 346-81 (5th ed. 1901); 1 A. SMITH, THE WEALTH OF NATIONS 5-18, 104-24 (J.E.T. Rogers ed. 1880).

a variety of income for taxation purposes, the discussion centers on net changes in the value of human capital over an accounting period rather than the value of capital possessed at any one time.[2]

For example, assume that a college graduate can expect to earn a constant annual income of $20,000 for fifty years. Using a ten percent discount rate (for simplicity more than for realism), these future earnings have a present value of $198,200 (if the salary is paid at the end of each year). Assume also that if the student goes to law school for three years instead of immediately entering the work force, he can earn $40,000 annually for the remaining forty-seven years of his working life. If the student wishes to maximize his wealth and if no other considerations apply, he would attend law school as long as the present value of its costs (forgone earnings plus direct expenses) were less than the present value of the increase in expected earnings. If the only direct expense were annual tuition of $10,000, the student would "pay" $30,000 a year (because he cannot collect earnings while in law school) for the right to increase his subsequent earnings by $20,000 annually. Because the present value of the return ($148,600) exceeds that of cost ($74,000), he will go to law school unless he has an even more profitable means of investing his time and effort. The increase in human capital produced by his schooling and measured by future earnings constitutes income during the period of acquisition, just as if the student owns securities that grow by a similar amount over the same period.

Under a comprehensive tax on economic income, increases in future earning power of the sort experienced by the law student should produce liability and decreases should produce deductions, even though the investor will also pay tax on earnings when received. Compare changes in human capital to a bond that increases in value as market interest rates decline: under current law the bond's gain will not be taxed unless the holder realizes it by selling the bond, but in theory realization is an administrative concern rather than an essential element of income. Similarly, changes in the value of human capital also constitute economic gain, albeit unrealized.

* * *

For more recent discussions of human capital, *see* G. BECKER, HUMAN CAPITAL (2d ed. 1975); M. FRIEDMAN & S. KUZNETS, INCOME FROM INDEPENDENT PROFESSIONAL PRACTICE (1945); L. Thurow, Investment in Human Capital (1970); Schultz, *Investment in Human Capital*, 51 AM. ECON. REV. 1 (1961); Schultz, *Capital Formation by Education*, 68 J. POL. ECON. 571 (1960).

2. Economic income is generally held to comprise consumption (measured in dollar terms) plus net changes in the value of savings (also reduced to dollar values), during the relevant accounting period (typically one year). *See* H. SIMONS, PERSONAL INCOME TAXATION 50 (1938). Using this equation, consumption can be defined as income (receipts less the cost of producing current receipts) minus savings (or plus disinvestment). *See* Andrews, *A Consumption-Type or Cash Flow Personal Income Tax*, 87 HARV. L. REV. 1113, 1120 (1974).

Exclusions for Injury Compensation
Current Law and Early Rationalizations
* * *

In the early years of the federal tax the government had difficulty treating any type of capital recovery as income, especially in cases where segregating the portion of gain accrued before adoption of the sixteenth amendment was impracticable. Characterization of the human body as a "kind of capital," albeit based more on analogies to physical goods than on any abstract notion of future income flows, thus led to exclusion of proceeds from the conversion of any part of this asset. When the Revenue Act of 1918 ratified this result by expressly excluding personal injury compensation from taxation, the Solicitor of Internal Revenue explained that Congress meant to endorse the analogy of the human body to a tangible capital asset.

The Concept of Basis Applied to Human Capital

Today the conceptual framework for taxing capital recoveries seems clearer. Unless some nonrecognition provision applies, conversion of a capital asset produces income to the extent that the amount realized exceeds adjusted basis. Adjusted basis, though sometimes dauntingly complex in its calculation, normally equals those acquisition costs not already deducted. Significant exceptions exist for inherited property, which under Section 1014 normally has a basis equal to the property's value at the time of the previous owner's death. * * *

Society might wish to follow this pattern by treating human capital as investment property and by specifying a basis for it. Two problems immediately arise. Should human capital basis reflect the inherited property * * * rules of Sections 1014? * * * To what extent should partial liquidations constitute basis recovery? Answering these formal tax structure questions will suggest a solution to the problem of taxing personal injury recoveries.

The Basis of Endowment

Human capital can be described as having two components: endowment inherited at birth and changes resulting from lifetime events. The endowment component is analogous to inherited property, and therefore might have imputed to it a basis equal to its value at birth. Of course, the rule embodied in Section 1014, generally although not completely accurately described as one of stepped-up basis, has been the target of tax reformers for many years. Its critics see the rule as a loophole through which large amounts of accumulated gain escape income taxation, permitting the small portion of the population that inherits substantial wealth to escape its fair share of the tax burden. It may seem perverse to extend such a principle, under fire in its own domain, to the context of human capital.

An important difference between the two contexts, however, is that for transactions to which Section 1014 applies there exists an alternative rule, by which the recipient of inherited property assumes the previous owner's basis. For the endowment or "inherited" portion of human capital, the alternative of carryover basis is unavailable because no method exists for imputing an individual's biological and social inheritance to a previous owner. As a result, the endowment portion of human capital must have a basis equal either to its value or to zero.

One argument for using a zero basis points to the problem of calculating depreciation. Human capital has an ascertainable useful life, and the normal pattern of capital cost recovery would permit an annual deduction to amortize the taxpayer's basis. If everyone's human capital had a nonzero basis, then separate calculations of these values for depreciation purposes would be necessary. A few ingenious taxpayers have attempted to do just this, but taxing authorities have shown no sympathy for their arguments.

It is possible, however, to accord a positive basis to the endowment portion of human capital while dispensing with a depreciation deduction. We might decide that some combination of the technical obstacles to valuing human capital and the moral difficulties engendered by imputing different opportunities to individuals from birth justifies assigning a uniform value to everyone's endowment. If we then used straight-line methods and a standard, rather than individualized, life expectancy, everyone would have the same deduction every year, in which case the deduction could be ignored. A cruder, but perhaps more satisfying version of this point is that individual differences among ideal human capital depreciation deductions are too small to warrant their calculation, but that large variations caused by abnormal disruptions in life patterns might command our attention.

* * *

The Basis of Accumulated Human Capital

As with the endowment component, the rules governing recovery of lifetime human capital investments could try to identify major departures from the normal career path without adjusting for minor variations in taxpayers' gains and losses. The normal pattern for attributing basis to a capital good is to sum undeducted acquisition costs and other undeducted capital expenditures. * * *

So far we have established the plausibility of treating human capital as a kind of investment with a positive but nonamortizable basis. In conventional business environments, the law usually requires taxpayers to document the basis of intangible assets and treats all recoveries as gain if no basis is proved. For the more universal but more complex phenomenon of human capital, however, the system might appropriately assume the existence of some basis and hold in abeyance the issue of value. The assumption that everyone starts with the same endowment, even though it beggars reality, both simplifies the problem and avoids the need for otherwise useless record keeping by the mass of taxpayers who might anticipate accidents. Businesses, by contrast, keep track of costs for reasons besides taxpaying, and hence can more easily bear a documentation requirement.

Timing of Basis Recovery in Partial Liquidations

Only the problem of basis allocation in partial liquidations remains. Life insurance benefits and wrongful death recoveries aside, most injury compensation involves partial impairments of human capital. In the analogous area of incomplete sales of property, a range of rules exists for allocation proceeds between basis and profit. When the transferor separates income interests from remainders, the system often allocates no basis to the income interests. In the case of part-gifts, part-sales to charities, and partial conversions of an asset, it imposes a pro-rata rule that imputes to the sale proceeds the same fraction of basis recovery as the ratio of total basis to the property value. For many transactions, however, the rules treat all proceeds as nontaxable capital recoveries until the basis is exhausted.

The early case of Burnet v. Logan[81] typifies this basis-first rule. * * *

The variety of allocation rules used by the tax system makes impossible the designation of one rule as a norm and disparagement of all others as departures from ideal income taxation. At one time or another Congress has applied variations on all three rules—income-first, pro-rata allocation, and basis-first—to annuities, an important standardized transaction. In view of the enormous valuation problems, the basis-first rule makes as much sense as any for partial liquidation of human capital.

A marriage of the presumption that all taxpayers have a substantial basis in their human capital to a rule allocating the proceeds from partial liquidations first to capital recovery supports the exclusion of most, if not all, individual injury compensation awards. The award, whether a tort or insurance recovery, simply replaces basis, and so as a matter of income definition should fall outside the tax base.

The Problem of Imputed Profit in Human Capital Recoveries

Saying that some, perhaps even the majority, of awards constitute nontaxable capital recoveries does not explain in comprehensive income taxation terms the failure to identify those awards that do exceed whatever basis we might impute to human capital. Recall the hypothetical law student. Half of his human capital upon graduation can be attributed to his law course, and about four-fifths of this component can be attributed either to subsidies or to forgone earnings, neither of which usually produces additions to basis. If a compensable injury suddenly reduced the student's earning potential by two-thirds, a significant portion of the recovery, in the make-believe world where we measure such things, would constitute gain. Yet the present tax system excludes the recovery from income.

Some of this apparent gain is a cashing in of the value of subsidized education, and its taxation might run contrary to the general pattern of not

---

81. 283 U.S. 404 (1931).

taxing in-kind government transfers. On the other hand, converting an in-kind benefit (education) into cash may eliminate the obvious administrative obstacle of valuation, and there may be no other reason for not taxing the conversion of the subsidy into cash.[86] Just as the recipient of free cheese who turns around and sells his handout theoretically should include the proceeds in income, the realized value of subsidized education embodied in injury compensation might be characterized as a taxable gain.

The dilemma is that identifying the gain portion of a recovery for injury is prohibitively costly in most circumstances. The problem is similar to that of mixed-motive business expenses such as entertainment, business clothing, and commuting, where segregation of personal consumption (nondeductible) and investment (deductible) may be impossible. The choice is between over taxation and under taxation, and one can only guess which rule errs more frequently or more dramatically. Under the basis-first approach it is consistent to assume that a substantial portion of most injury compensation represents a tax-free capital recovery. This presumption of nonincludibility produces fewer "wrong" results—those inconsistent with the model of human capital recovery—than would the opposite rule.

Some Special Cases

Although the difficulty of identifying profit in human capital recoveries makes a nonincludibility presumption very powerful, it need not be irrebuttable. The next section deals with categories of injuries where the profit element seems strong enough to suggest an opposite presumption. Here I will discuss some forms of recovery that might trigger tax liability regardless of the injury that they compensate.

* * *

Earnings Replacements

Distinguishing sudden losses of human capital from normal erosion is a more difficult problem. As argued above, a depreciation deduction for normal human capital loss is too costly to implement given the relatively small variance it would produce in individual tax liabilities. Large, lump-sum losses, however, produce greater variations, and employing the presumptions described above, cost little to measure. But when disability payments are contingent on continuing inability to work and extend for roughly the same period in roughly the same amounts as the salary replaced, then the victim may not have suffered a loss. His situation resembles that of an uninjured person, whose human capital erodes gradually with age.

Prolonged earnings replacement payments, however, do not always fully compensate human capital losses. Injuries may affect both the ability to earn and the ability to enjoy. Although market analogues provide less help for

---

86. Cf. Haverly v. United States, 513 F.2d 224 (7th Cir.), cert. denied, 423 U.S. 912 (1975) (free sample of books not included in income until "converted" through charitable contribution).

measuring the latter than the former, each has a capital value. The victims of such injuries might treat some portion of earnings replacements as recovery of lost future enjoyment even though the payments purport to substitute for earning abilities.

Without a suitable mechanism to assign money value to single-injury losses of earnings and enjoyment capital, it is impossible to develop a tax rule that accurately identifies the capital recovery, and hence the excludible portion of periodic compensation payments. A few rules of thumb might be practicable, however. We could distinguish injuries that affect only working life expectancy, but not life expectancy, as an admittedly rough way to distinguish between earnings and enjoyment capital. * * *

Deductions for the Costs of Injuries

Not all injuries result in compensation. Gaps in insurance or tort coverage will force some individuals to absorb the cost of sudden losses. If the pattern of taxation for injuries to property carried over to human capital, a taxpayer would be entitled to deduct whatever basis he might have in the lost asset. Without a direct method of measuring human capital and its basis, however, the tax system must account for these losses indirectly, if at all. Two costs that may coincide with human capital losses, and so may act as proxies for properly allowable deductions, are insurance and medical expenses. To the extent that deductions for these two items fulfill this function, they are consistent with, rather than departures from, a broad-based tax on income.

Insurance Costs

One way to look at insurance is as a gambling pool where gross "winnings" (compensation for injuries) are something less than total "wagers" (insurance premiums). Although gambling and insurance are opposites in how they distribute risk, they are similar (and formally distinguishable from all other investments) in that they are designed only to distribute risk, and not to seek other gains from trade. It is critical to the comparison that, aside from the service charge levied by the industry, the pool is a zero-sum game. In other words, insurance, like gambling, invites the tax collector to ignore individual risk preferences and to look only at the expected value of the investor's return, which unlike almost all profit-seeking contexts, is invariably a figure less than the investment.

If winnings and losses are distributed randomly across income and marginal-tax-rate levels, a hypothesis that is as plausible as any, and if premium payments are deductible profit-seeking expenses, * * * then absent transaction costs the government will be indifferent between a rule that deducts premium payments and includes compensation in income, and one that does not deduct payments but excludes payments from income. If the enterprise involves only risk distribution, the rules will produce equivalent revenues and will have equivalent distributional effects among income classes, although not among particular individuals. When transaction costs are considered, the no-deduction, no-income rule seems superior. It dispenses with two difficult tax issues that otherwise would increase record keeping, uncertainty, and dispute-resolution costs for many taxpayers.[g]

* * *

Medical Expenses

Medical expenses can not only be investments in future well-being, but can also replace something lost. The amount of medical care may measure, albeit imprecisely, the extent of this loss. One way to look at these expenses is as self-compensation in the absence of insurance or tort remedies. A deduction for outlays puts the self-compensator on the same footing as the person who excludes injury compensation provided by others.

* * * [T]he actual deductibility of medical expenses turns on who pays for them. Insurance reimbursements produce no income for the purchaser, and employer-obtained insurance generates deductible premiums. The patient's out-of-pocket payments, whether for medical services or for insurance to cover them, do not qualify for deduction except to the extent that they exceed a sum that grows in proportion to the taxpayer's income.

The rationale for structuring the deduction this way is similar to that for the tax treatment of insurance costs. Expenses covered by an employer more often involve serious injuries rather than self-indulgence, and serious injuries more likely entail human capital losses, especially losses of job-specific capital. If a person is unable to get his employer to pay his expenses, the tax rules in effect insist that he pay for a large portion out of his own pocket to demonstrate the seriousness of the loss. Furthermore, the amount that he must pay to signal seriousness grows with his income, because we believe either that money means less to wealthier people or that their medical expenses tend to involve a larger element of self-indulgence.

* * * [C]urrent law generally conforms to the pattern of human capital taxation outlined in this article. Taxpayers can deduct medical expenses when especially good reasons exist to believe that outlays correspond to a loss of human capital to which we most easily can assign a positive basis. Viewed from this perspective, the medical expense deduction looks less like a departure from a norm of comprehensive income taxation, and more like a refinement of the concept of taxable income to reflect losses of human capital.

* * *

DEVELOPING A THEORY OF
DAMAGE RECOVERY TAXATION
Jennifer J.S. Brooks[*]

14 William Mitchell Law Review 759, 769-70, 775-80 (1988)

Excludability of compensatory recoveries makes sense if the payment is

---

g. Compare the discussion in Chapter Eight, especially Note #3 (page 532). (Ed.)

*. At time of original publication, Associate Professor, William Mitchell College of Law.

a pecuniary restoration of either (1) something the taxpayer had acquired with after-tax dollars (a recovery of basis), or (2) a nontaxable "something" the taxpayer had and lost (a return of nonincludible value). Consider an analogy to recovery for tortious conversion of plaintiff's newly-purchased graphite tennis racket. Because the plaintiff paid $400 in after-tax dollars for the racket, she has a basis of $400, and her recovery of $400 is a nontaxable return of capital. The payment is not a substitute for ordinary income, and because it exactly replaces a racket valued at $400 there is no "accession to wealth;" plaintiff has not received anything more than she had. Her original acquisition of the racket was by a purchase with tax-paid dollars, so the recovery is not a substitute for ordinary income.

Now consider a plaintiff who is injured in an automobile accident and loses the use of his left leg. For simplicity, assume that the injury did not result in lost wages or loss of earning capacity. He accepts a settlement of $500,000. The return of basis analysis that made the previous example easy to resolve does not help this plaintiff. Yet, just as clearly, he has been "restored," if only by a monetary payment, to the status quo. He has not received anything more than he had. The taxpayer did not have a tax-paid basis in the leg, so the question is whether the recovery substitutes for ordinary income or instead for some nonincludible value. It appears that the recovery is a substitute for the nonincludible value of being physically whole—the value of having the leg, the value of its use, and the value of being free from pain.

* * *

The Problem of "Lost Earnings"

A replacement for nonincludible values may not be income, but what if part of a recovery is said to be for lost earnings? Is that part of the payment includible? A case can be made for inclusion. A payment for past lost wages is an accession to wealth that compensates the plaintiff for earnings he did not receive while away from his job during convalescence. If the earnings had been received, they would have been taxable as ordinary income. Thus, the past earnings portion of the settlement appears to be an includable substitute for ordinary income. The same analysis could apply to a payment for lost future earnings: the settlement does not replace something the plaintiff had, but instead confers something new upon him, so he has an accession to wealth; the future earnings would have been includable, so the substitute should be.

There is another way of thinking about this problem. If the "earnings" part of the settlement is conceived of as a recompense for loss of earning *capacity*, then the monetary payment restores the taxpayer to his previous status as a person with income earning potential. Economists have considered whether imputed income derived from the capitalized value of personal earning power should be included in the definition of income. In a nonslave state, personal earning power cannot be bought or sold and is not valued in market terms. Because the imputed income flowing from the earning capacity (as opposed to actual income from the exercise of that capacity) is not capable of objective measure, it is not generally included in the economic definition of income. Human capital does exist as a value; it produces imputed income; but the imputed income is ignored in the measure of taxable capacity until "actual" income occurs from the performance of labor. Other people are not taxed on either the capital value of having income-earning potential or the imputed income that flows from the capacity to earn; neither should the plaintiff in a personal injury case. The tax system really has not dealt with the problem of nonservices exchanges between human capital and market capital, but the fact that the *measure* of human capital loss may be expected future earnings should not alter the result.

A response to this argument might be that most people are taxed indirectly on their earning capacity because they pay tax every year on the monetary income produced by the exercise of their earning capacity in the performance of services. The plaintiff in a personal injury suit could be said to exercise his "earning capacity" by winning a judgment against the defendant (although payment may be in a lump sum rather than in annual increments over the plaintiff's working life). Loss of earning capacity is measured by expected future earnings because this part of the judgment is intended to substitute for ordinary income. Under this analysis, the "lost earnings" portion of an award or settlement should be includable in the plaintiff's income.

It does not seem a satisfactory answer to say that the plaintiff should be taxed on the recovery for lost earning capacity because the pursuit of his claim is the equivalent of the performance of services for another. Suppose it is possible to identify a part of the recovery as representing only the lost capital value of capacity to earn income. People normally enjoy this value tax-free, incurring tax only when the capacity is exercised by work. If an individual chooses not to work, and therefore not to transform the capacity into includable income, the unexercised capacity is not taxable. Put another way, the choice of leisure is not taxable. The capital value of earning capacity can be thought to produce both includable income from labor, and nonincludible imputed income from the choice of leisure. The plaintiff who is injured so that part of his human capital is lost, and who sues for replacement, may be pursuing the only possible course to recover the nonincludible capital values that were damaged. It does not seem to correct to equate the decision to sue with the choice of earning when a person with intact human capital has imputed income from all the human capital values, including earning capacity, and remains untaxed.

* * *

It is possible to argue that excluded capital and income values ought to be includable when the damage recovery transforms them into monetary terms. The argument is * * * based on the idea that imputed income is excluded only because it is hard to measure. Once the income is reduced to monetary values, it ought to be included. This convenience notion of income measurement has some place in the tax law; the realization requirement operates to cause income inclusion only when accretions to income are rendered fairly certain by the happening [of some] event, like a sale or exchange, that clearly identifies an accession to wealth. In the example of the tennis racket, income from the $400 is taxable if it is received as interest on investment of the funds, but excludible if received as imputed income from the use of a consumer durable. It is difficult to measure imputed income from the tennis racket, so it is excluded; the parallel income, interest from the investment, is easy to measure and so is included. Thus, the argument goes, the tax system should include cash recoveries for personal injuries on the theory that cash is includable no matter what its origin.

It is a flaw in the tax system's implementation of the accretion model that easily measured accretions to wealth are included and more difficult to measure values are excluded. An ideal accretion-type tax may be impractical; as long as accretion is a model, adjustments for practical problems of measurement are only to be expected. But the need to adapt the accretion model to everyday use does not compel inclusion of amounts simply because they are there. Returns of basis, for example, may be paid in cash but are not for that reason subject to inclusion. Substantial cash gifts to family members are not includable even though they are easy to measure. Cash payments of child support are not includable. Reference to income theory suggests reasons why these easy-to-reach transfers are excludible; convenience is not the sole arbiter of the tax base.

Exclusion of the imputed annual income from human capital until it has been translated into monetary terms by the performance of services for another provides a consistent basis for the measure of income. * * *

The plaintiff who recovers a personal injury damage award has not received a windfall that ought to be taxed. Nor is the transformation of human capital into money via the judgment a substitute for the performance of services. The injured plaintiff has lost a value that cannot be replaced like a tennis racket, because it is not a value that the economy measures in market terms. Failure to include imputed income from consumer durables is a flaw in the measurement of income that results from practical considerations, but the imputed income from human capital is outside the measurement of income. The plaintiff who recovers for lost human capital and lost imputed income from human capital is recompensed for values that lie without the market. Use of money to replace what is lost does not justify imposing tax on a person who has merely been restored (if that) to a status other taxpayers enjoy tax-free.

    * * *

COMPENSATORY AND PUNITIVE DAMAGES FOR A PERSONAL INJURY: TO TAX OR NOT TO TAX?

Douglas A. Kahn[*]

2 Florida Tax Review 327, 340-49, 351-52 (1995)

Return of Human Capital

While there is uncertainty as to precisely what considerations led Congress to adopt the antecedent to section 104(a)(2), the background history of the provision suggests that Congress focused on a "return of human capital" theory. * * *

The human capital theory has recently been criticized by courts and by commentators. Moreover, even if the theory was the original rationale for the statutory exclusion, it is not necessary to accept the theory as the justification for *retaining* the exclusion. A statute may be adopted for a reason that is later abandoned, but the statute may be retained for quite different reasons. Also, legislators may have a strong visceral belief that a remedy is needed, but not be able to ascertain the principles upon which that belief is founded. Thus, even when the legislative history sets forth a rationale for a provision, the rationale actually underlying the legislation may be something quite different because the legislators are then unable to articulate the true rationale.

* * *

For several reasons, the human capital theory, standing alone, does not adequately justify section 104(a)(2). First, a basic premise of the theory—that personal injury recoveries should not be taxed because they merely replace the unascertainable value of what the victim lost—is inconsistent with the rules generally applied to dispositions of property. On a disposition of property, gain or loss is measured as the difference between the amount realized and the taxpayer's basis for the property. The *value* of the asset when sold or destroyed is irrelevant for this purpose. * * *

Second, justification for the exclusion does not flow from the difficulties of determining the basis (if any) that a tort victim has in the body parts or personal rights that were damaged. A taxpayer has the burden of establishing basis, and if none can be established, basis is deemed to be zero. Since people do not anticipate having parts of their bodies (or personal rights) converted into cash, they do not keep records of any capital expenditures that may have been made in connection therewith, and it might seem appropriate to accord them relief by excluding all or part of their recoveries. However, it is highly unlikely that a person has any basis in body parts. * * *

Third, some courts and commentators have suggested that the human capital theory is undercut by the fact that the section 104(a)(2) exclusion extends to damages in substitution for lost income. * * *

---

[*]. At time of original publication, Paul G. Kauper Professor, University of Michigan Law School.

Finally, and most significantly, the human capital rationale does not jibe with the tax law's treatment of voluntary dispositions of human capital. The section 104(a)(2) exclusion applies only to damages (or to a settlement of a claim for damages) received on account of a personal injury or sickness. It has no application to an individual's voluntary sale of a body part or personal right. Federal law prohibits the sale of human organs.[67] But, if such a sale were permitted or were made in violation of the law (if, for example, a kidney were sold to a person needing a transplant), the entire amount received by the seller would be taxed as gain. It would not matter that the amount realized merely replaced a part of the seller's human capital or that the organ's basis is unascertainable. The prohibition against the sale of a human organ does not apply to the sale of blood, and it is well established that an amount realized by an individual on a sale of blood is ordinary income. * * *

Involuntary Conversion

Another rationale suggested for section 104(a)(2) is that since the taxpayer did not choose to dispose of the damaged personal right or body part, it seems rapacious to tax damages received as compensation for such a personal loss. Relief is provided when damages are received to compensate for a destruction of tangible property. * * * Section 1033 provides relief for a taxpayer in that predicament. * * * The taxpayer's investment in the destroyed item is rolled over and becomes part of the taxpayer's basis in the replacement property. In effect, the taxpayer's realized gain is deferred. * * *

Involuntariness alone is not a sufficient justification for this extraordinary exclusionary treatment since the involuntary conversion of tangible property is not treated so gently.

Combination of Considerations

Given the sympathy that a personal injury engenders, the section 104(a)(2) exclusion is perhaps warranted by the combination of the fact that a personal right or body part was destroyed (the return of human capital theory) and the involuntariness of the conversion. That is, even though neither factor alone is sufficient, the cumulative effect of the combination of the factors may be sufficient. The whole may well be greater than the sum of its parts.

The author believes that there are two additional factors that color the combination of the human capital theory and the involuntariness of the conversion of a body part, and the addition of that coloration makes a compelling case for the exclusion of such damages when given for a physical injury.

Noncommercial Zone

The tax law is aimed at market transactions. Gain on a sale of an item held for personal use, such as a residence or a piece of jewelry, is taxed, but, in such cases, the taxpayer has chosen to place the item into the commercial

---

67. National Organ Transplant Act, § 301, 42 U.S.C. § 274e(a) (1988).

market by putting it up for sale. Moreover, those types of property are commonly bought and sold in the market place and are properly regarded as commercial items. In contrast, noncommercial personal attributes are not traded in the market and lie far outside the zone of properties and activities that comprise the sphere of the tax laws' operation.

For example, if two persons exchange their services, each must typically include in income an amount equal to the value of the services received from the other.[72] However, when a husband and wife exchange their services by splitting household chores between them, neither recognizes income.[73] Similarly, if several persons living in Manhattan, each of whom owns a small piece of land on Long Island on which vegetables are grown, agree to take turns travelling to Long Island and watering the gardens owned by all of them, they are exchanging services, but they should not be taxed on that exchange because it occurs outside the market. Another example of activities within a noncommercial zone is a baby-sitting club in which parents sit for each other's children under a kind of barter arrangement. On the other hand, bartered exchanges can become so structured and substantial that they represent more than joint activities, in which case the parties have moved into the commercial sphere and their bartered exchange should be taxable.

When a part of an individual's body is damaged or destroyed, what has been taken from the individual is predominantly of a noncommercial nature. Since humans are engaged in commercial activities, their bodies and personal attributes are inexorably entwined with those activities. However, an individual's body and personal attributes are merely used in commercial activities; they are not detached and sold in the market place. It is a rare person who would contemplate the sale of body parts to be removed from him while still alive. If such a transaction were to take place, the individual would have committed the sale of that body part to a commercial venture; there is no reason for the tax law to exempt from taxation the gain from such a sale, and it does not do so. However, if a body part is destroyed or injured, the compensation that the victim receives is not the product of having voluntarily committed that part to a commercial sale. Although the victim must actively seek reparations in order to be compensated, that is the consequence of the injury and is not a voluntary entrance into the commercial market.

Vulturous Behavior

Perhaps, the most important consideration that weighs against taxing such damages is the heartlessness of the government profiting from the tort law's attempt to soften the blow that a victim has suffered. Monetary damages

---

72. Regs. § 1.61-2(d)(1).

73. No statute or regulation expressly exempts a spousal exchange of services from taxation. Under § 1041, which was added in 1984, no gain or loss is recognized on an interspousal transfer of property, but the provision does not address the tax consequences of exchanging services. The Service has never sought to tax interspousal exchanges of services, and the exclusion of such exchanges is part of the unwritten law of taxation.

are not [true] substitutes for a victim's loss, but, at most, some mitigation of it. Much of the loss is not monetary, but only monetary damages can be given because no substitute is available to replace what was lost. If the government were to tax damages for the loss of a body part (or for the death of a relative), it would seem to many to have engaged in a vulturous act—analogous to feeding off of the flesh of a dismembered arm or leg or off of the corpse of a recently departed.

> * * *

Our self-assessment system of taxation relies on a willingness of the populace to report honestly to the government, and that willingness rests on a popular belief that the government's system of taxation is fair. The government should therefore take into account not only whether the taxation of such damages would be vulturous, but also whether it would appear to the general population to be so. While the appearance of fairness is not always a strong enough consideration to control the tax treatment of an item, it should be taken into account, especially in a case such as this where the view that such damages have a noncompensatory nature rests on an opinion that is not widely shared.

Author's Conclusions

In the author's view, the noncommercial and nonmonetary nature of a destroyed or injured body part and the vulturous portrait that would be painted by the government's profiting from a personal tragedy explain why a suggestion that the damages for such an injury be taxed is typically met with a vigorous renunciation. * * *

TAXES AND TORTS
Joseph M. Dodge[*]
77 Cornell Law Review 143, 180-88 (1992)

This Part discusses the policy issue of whether punitive damages and "noneconomic" damages, encompassing both pain-and-suffering damages in physical-injury cases and nonphysical, noneconomic torts, *should* be excludible from income.

Punitive Damages

As a matter of policy, there is little doubt that punitive damages should be included in gross income. Such damages represent an economic windfall, and do not compensate for any loss whatsoever. Punitive damages represent a pure accretion to wealth.

One argument advanced in favor of excluding punitive damages is that the exclusion might compensate the plaintiff for legal fees and other expenses, and thereby truly make the plaintiff whole. However, punitive damages have no relation, under tort law, to legal fees. The argument for excludibility would

---

[*]. At time of original publication, William H. Francis, Jr. Professor, University of Texas School of Law.

be better directed toward reforming tort law to award legal fees to plaintiffs and to create standards for punitive damages. No justification exists for excluding punitive damages in excess of legal fees.

The only other plausible argument for excluding punitive damages is that their inclusion, while retaining exclusions for compensatory damages, would create an administrative problem of distinguishing includable from excludible damages, especially when the case was settled or went to judgment without specification of the punitive damages amount. However, one could also advance this argument in favor of the proposition that compensatory damages should be included in gross income. An allocation by the parties should not control, because their "tax" interests are not necessarily opposed. Nor should the plaintiff's allocation of damages in the complaint control,[177] because tax law should not unnecessarily dictate the behavior of personal-injury lawyers. With no external reference, such as a judicial decree or findings, the allocation must be made on the basis of an independent "tax" examination of the cause of action.

* * *

Recoveries for Noneconomic Harms

Section 104 currently excludes damages for pain and suffering, as well as for purely personal injuries, such as loss of privacy, loss of consortium, intentional infliction of emotional distress, and deprivation of rights.[h] Conceptually, the damages represent a conversion of some nonmaterial benefit, such as lost "normality," peace of mind, or dignity, into cash. This is not a situation in which an exclusion could be justified as maintaining the tax status quo with respect to income from human capital. Since no "basis" exists in any recovery of this type, such damages seemingly should be fully includable as pure accessions to material wealth. The burden of persuasion in the policy sense lies with the proponents of exclusion.

Some argue that these damages should not be taxed because they are a substitute for goods of a nontaxable nature, such as pleasure, pain, or normalcy. However, the "substitute for" analysis is not a policy tool. Rather, it is a doctrinal device employed to ascertain the substance of a receipt in order to determine which statutory category to apply. Moreover, in the doctrinal context, the "substitute for" analysis has limits. * * *

If one were to apply this doctrinal device to the policy arena, it would lead nowhere, because damages for noneconomic harm are not a "substitute for" any other kind of receipt that has tax significance. They are simply damages for noneconomic harm. Nonpecuniary damages are not computed with reference

---

177. If better evidence of a proper allocation cannot be found, the IRS looks to the complaint. Rev. Rul. 58-418, 1958-2 C.B. 18.

h. Professor Dodge wrote before Congress amended section 104(a)(2) to end the exclusion in the case of personal injuries that are not physical in nature. His analysis is still fully applicable to pain and suffering, an important element of tort recovery in almost every tort case involving physical injury. (Ed.)

to foregone consumption which would have been purchased in the market. If they were so computed, computing foregone consumption on an after-tax basis would subject the taxpayer to an implicit tax that would be preserved by an exclusion. In fact, pain-and-suffering damages compensate that which cannot be purchased. Thus, it is fundamentally misleading to call these damages "compensation"; they "replace" the irreplaceable.

A variation of the "substitute for" argument is that recoveries for noneconomic harms are mere restorations of a status quo which, in itself, would have been nontaxable as imputed income. Appeals to imputed income, however, are fruitless, because imputed income, by definition, refers to economic benefits that have not been converted to cash or property. In contrast, noneconomic damages result from a conversion to cash. It is also misleading to consider imputed income as nontaxable in the sense of being "excluded"; rather, it is simply ignored. The difference lies in the fact that excluded items are capable of creating a basis. To argue that conversions of imputed income to cash should be excluded is essentially the same as arguing that wages, which involve a conversion of leisure to labor, should be excluded. This argument actually cuts in favor of includibility; noneconomic damages are like wages for a miserable job.

One could argue that damages for noneconomic harms should not be taxed because the recovery merely replaces a loss of intangible benefits. This argument is equivalent to stating that wages are not income because they do not result in "gain," the laborer having "given up" leisure and other psychic goods to obtain wages. Of course, wages are the result of voluntary transactions, whereas pain-and-suffering damages are not. The question squarely raised, then, is whether the involuntariness of the transaction justifies not taxing the accession to wealth. One could argue for no taxation by analogy to the argument for taxing recovery of lost earning capacity like wages rather than like investments. Involuntariness may be a legitimate rationale for deferral of income or perhaps deductibility of outlay, but not for total and permanent exclusion of a clearly-realized accession to wealth.

* * *

[Another] argument for excluding noneconomic recoveries is simply that the transaction, as a whole, represents a net decrease in the taxpayer's "utility." That is, the plaintiff would be in a worse, not better, position if the recovery for nonpecuniary loss were taxed. Even working in an awful job presumably entails some increase in taxpayer utility; otherwise the employment would not have been undertaken. People do not risk life and limb in the hope of obtaining noneconomic damage recoveries, presumably because such transactions are acknowledged to be "losers" or, at least too risky.

One reason for taxing transactions which generate a utility gain is that the tax, if designed properly, will not unduly inhibit socially desirable activity. It does not follow, however, that involuntary transactions should be exempt from tax. Taxing plaintiffs on noneconomic damages will, if anything, increase deterrence and net social utility, especially if courts and juries shift plaintiff taxes to defendants.

The no-utility-gain argument raises the fundamental issue of the role of "utility" in taxation. Utility in taxation must be distinguished from utility in social welfare. Progressive rates in taxation, for example, have been justified on the theory that sacrificing dollars is less burdensome, in utility terms, on the rich than it is on the poor. Similarly, the desirability of excluding employee fringe benefits can be questioned on economic efficiency grounds. Excluding nonpecuniary damage recoveries has the effect of enriching personal injury plaintiffs relative to taxpayers generally. This kind of subsidy is subject to classic "tax expenditure" analysis, but apparently no welfare economist has undertaken to justify a discrete subsidy to plaintiffs receiving noneconomic damages. Any "economic incentive" justification for the exclusion is totally implausible. A social welfare claim based, at most, on a "hunch" is not a persuasive justification for this aspect of the section 104 exclusion. Finally, the tax rule for nonpecuniary loss recoveries does not ultimately solve the social welfare equation. Even if such recoveries are taxed to plaintiffs, the legal (tort) system can compensate plaintiffs for the incremental tax burden by shifting it to defendants.

We are left with the question of whether the core concept of "income" is ultimately tied to that of "utility." In practice, and ignoring "tax expenditure" provisions, the concept of income is *not* systematically tied to subjective utility, as opposed to changes in objective net wealth. Imputed income from consumer durables, as well as the value of self-provided services and leisure, is ignored. Income is taxed to the person who earns and controls it, not the person who enjoys it. Amounts includable are measured by market transactions, not subjective worth. Deductions, like medical expenses and casualty loss, can be rationalized on a non-utility basis. Other deductions, such as those for charitable contributions and taxes, are allowed despite substantial utility to the taxpayer.[208]

It is not obvious that the income tax *base*, as opposed to government policy in general, *should* be tied to utility in any normative sense, though influential commentators operating out of the tradition of Utilitarian welfare economics have made the connection. Though government policy may rely on utility analysis, and although virtually all items considered to be gross income potentially yield utility to the taxpayer (or to the taxpayer's family and friends), it does not logically follow that the tax base should be equated with utility. The tax base should be equated with material resources that can be appropriated by government for redistributive purposes, or, perhaps, with material resources that represent a claim against society's store of scarce

---

208. Utility plays a marginal role in distinguishing "personal" from "business" expenses. *See* Treas. Reg. § 1.183-2(b)(9) (1972) (personal pleasure is one factor in determining whether activity is "not for profit").

resources. These concepts of the tax base are objective *in principle*, not merely as an expedient. Government, which is supported mostly by taxes, has no interest in appropriating utility directly from taxpayers. Utility is subjective; that is, the utility "curves" of various individuals differ. Therefore, the government cannot transfer utility; it can only deal in money and property. Finally, as a normative concept, "income" is rendered much weaker by burdening it with goals that are unobtainable for practical or political reasons.

* * *

Wrongful Death Recoveries

Recoveries that accelerate tax-free receipts of money or property are *prima facie* candidates for exclusion. The best examples are wrongful death actions, where the recovery is for the lost tax-free support, gifts, and inheritance, which would have derived from the *decedent's* human capital. However, the amount of such support actually received would have been "after-tax" amounts; that is, such sums would have been reduced by the decedent's own income taxes before given to the recipients. Therefore, wrongful death recoveries should be treated like recoveries for other personal injuries.

If the survivor of a deceased plaintiff succeeds to the plaintiff's cause of action, any recovery by the survivor should not be treated as a tax-free bequest or inheritance. Instead, the recovery should be treated as "income in respect of a decedent," meaning that the survivor would step into the decedent's shoes for tax purposes.

* * *

Notes and Questions

Return of capital

9.   Numerous arguments beyond tradition are advanced in support of the exclusion of personal injury awards, although critics claim an answer to each. As noted by Burke and Friel in Subchapter A, as early as 1918 the return-of-capital theory was put forward by the Attorney General, and this theory remains one of the most-cited justifications for the exclusion. Personal injury awards, it is argued, constitute a return of capital, not a gain but restoration of something the taxpayer already had.

10.   In the usual case, if a taxpayer's capital asset is damaged or destroyed, the loss being compensated by insurance or a tortfeasor, the taxpayer would recognize gain to the extent that the amount received exceeded the taxpayer's basis in the asset. (Recognition of gain might be avoided through a statutory nonrecognition provision, such as section 1033; see Note #15.) Assuming the taxpayer received fair market value, which is the usual measure of insurance or tort recovery, the taxpayer would not have gained by the conversion of the capital asset to its monetary equivalent. Nevertheless, the conversion would constitute an occasion for taxing unrealized appreciation (value in excess of basis). Given the importance of basis in the normal scheme,

what are the implications for the return-of-capital theory as applied to personal injury awards?

11.   Normally, basis equals cost, and taxpayers are usually not regarded as having a basis in their own bodies. Professor Stephan argues that a novel application of accepted principles can lead to a determination that such a basis exists. What role is afforded inherited endowment under Professor Stephan's approach? Once he argues for a basis in a wasting asset (the human body and endowment), what is Professor Stephan's justification for ignoring depreciation? Do you agree that serious moral questions would attach to giving one taxpayer a higher basis than another in the taxpayer's *self*?

12.   If one accepts the human capital concept, yet agrees to ignore depreciation because, in part, of an assumption of a standard life expectancy, should an adjustment be made for taxpayers who die prematurely? Who live longer than expected? Compare Code section 72(b)(2) and (3), which make adjustments in the tax treatment of annuitants depending upon their *ex post* individualized longevity.

13.   Given the difficulty (impossibility?) of computing the taxpayer's basis in his human capital, and given the usual rule that a taxpayer can exclude damages only to the extent of basis, how can Professor Stephan argue that most personal injury awards should be fully excluded?

14.   Do you find Professor Stephan's sophisticated approach to the basis problem appealing, or can his arguments be swept aside by the following no-nonsense language of Professor Mark Cochran?:

> The return of capital argument is appealing, especially in the case of damages awarded for loss of a limb or organ. This type of injury graphically illustrates the concept of "human capital." The problem with this analogy is that a return of capital is excluded from gross income only to the extent of the taxpayer's basis. * * * However, in the personal injury context, the taxpayer's basis is zero, because a taxpayer generally does not pay for his limb or organs. * * * Actually, it is unnecessary to speculate about whether a taxpayer has a basis in the various parts of his body. A personal injury award does not pay a taxpayer for the damage to his or her body per se; rather, the taxpayer is compensated for consequent economic loss (i.e., lost earnings) and, in some instances, pain and suffering. Such compensation clearly falls outside the scope of the return of capital concept, since no capital is being exchanged for the award.[i]

---

i. Mark W. Cochran, *Should Personal Injury Damage Awards Be Taxed?*, 38 CASE WEST. L.

15. *Involuntary conversion.* To what degree should we be willing to bend usual rules of taxable income because of the involuntary nature of the conversion of well being into money. Contrast, for example, the voluntary conversion of leisure into earned income.

As discussed in Note #10 above, even in the case of involuntary conversion the usual rule is that income must be recognized if the amount realized from the conversion exceeds the taxpayer's basis in the asset converted. There are some relief provisions—notably section 1033—but the relief is conditioned on replacement of the converted property plus carryover of basis.   These limitations suggest that Congress envisioned a postponement of tax rather than a complete forgiveness, such as that granted by section 104(a)(2). Professor Lawrence Frolik has observed:

> One simply does not purchase a new spouse to replace an injured one, and therefore, section 104(a)(2) might be seen as an extension of the principle exemplified in section 1033. * * * Still, * * * [w]hile section 1033 merely postpones recognition of the gain, * * * section 104(a)(2) permanently excludes the gain. * * *
>
> The expectation that lost consortium or lost parenting will not be replaced evokes two, almost paradoxical, observations. On one hand, it symbolizes the reason for section 104(a)(2). The involuntary nature of the conversion, the lack of satisfactory in-kind replacement services, and the tax-free nature of the services for which a damage award substitutes, all argue the wisdom, if not the necessity, of section 104(a)(2). Conversely, the receipt of a tax-free damage award presents the claimant with the complete panoply of available consumption choices.[j]

Lost earnings

16. Many tort recoveries compensate the victim for lost past or future earnings. As contrasted with other elements of damage, such as pain and suffering, the compensation takes the place of something that would have been taxed had the injury not occurred. Taxpayers are not taxed on being free from pain, and therefore arguably should not be taxed on receiving the monetary equivalent of this state of well being; by contrast, taxpayers are taxed on earnings, and arguably should be taxed when they receive as tort damages the monetary equivalent.[k] Section 104(a)(2) excludes such damages, but should it?

REV. 43, 45-46 (1987).

j. Lawrence A. Frolik, *Personal Injury Compensation as a Tax Preference*, 37 ME. L. REV. 1, 20-21 (1985).

k. For a forceful repudiation of the "in lieu of what" test in interpreting section 104(a)(2), *see* Patricia T. Morgan, *Old Torts, New Torts and Taxes: The Still Uncertain Scope of Section 104(a)(2)*, 48 LA. L. REV. 875 (1988).

17. Professor Douglas Chapman repudiates the suggestion that damages for lost earnings should be protected from tax on humanitarian grounds: "[I]t seems only too logical that a plaintiff, fully compensated for injuries not based on earnings, needs no more humanitarianism than any other taxpayer who is required to pay his annual extraction on his earnings."[1]

18. Professor Brooks, in her article excerpted above, argues that recoveries for lost earnings can be thought of as recoveries for harm done to earning capacity, measured by expected future earnings. An uninjured taxpayer has a choice concerning whether this capacity is to be converted into taxable earnings; the tort victim, by contrast, receives monetary damages or nothing. How might this analysis lead one to conclude that a tort recovery for lost earnings merits exclusion? Do you find Professor Brooks' analysis persuasive?

19. Professor Kahn finds that the usual justifications for the section 104(a)(2) exclusion, such as return of capital and the involuntary nature of the conversion to money, do not justify the section 104(a)(2) exclusion when subjected to traditional analysis. Nonetheless, he supports the exclusion. Why?

20. Kahn emphasizes that the noncommercial nature of tort awards suggests that they should lie outside the tax system. Does that argument hold in light of the broad conception of income since *Glenshaw Glass*?

21. Professor Kahn compares tort awards to untaxed exchange of services (intrafamily exchange of services, neighbors watering gardens for each other, exchange of babysitting services). He contrasts such noncommercial exchanges to "bartered exchanges [that have] become so structured and so substantial" that they should be taxed. Professor Kahn's analysis raises at least two questions.

First, if a plaintiff receives a tort settlement or judgment for a million dollars, enforced with the power of law (and received only by the power of law), is the transaction now "so structured and so substantial" that even Kahn's analysis may suggest that the award should be taxed?

Second, the examples of untaxed exchanges of services that Kahn offers are transactions that will not be taxed, whatever theory may say. Do you agree with Professor Kahn that the best explanation for non-taxation is that these transactions are noncommercial, or, instead, do you think that taxes are not asserted for practical reasons—the *de minimis* amounts involved, and the

---

1. Douglas K. Chapman, *No Pain—No Gain? Should Personal Injury Damages Keep Their Tax Exempt Status?*, 9 U. ARK. LITTLE ROCK L.J. 407, 428 (1986-87).

administrative difficulty of valuation and enforcement? If the latter, what implications does this have for taxation of personal injury awards?

22. Much of the population, no doubt, views the Internal Revenue Code and the Internal Revenue Service in their entirety as "vulturous." Do you find particular force in Professor Kahn's argument that taxing personal injury awards would undercut the self-assessment system?

23. *Humanitarian considerations.* An oft-cited observation of a half century ago—still applicable today—is that "the treatment of lost earnings is rooted in emotional and traditional, rather than logical, factors. * * * [I]t is contended * * * that the taxation of recoveries carved from pain and suffering is offensive, and the victim is more to be pitied rather than taxed."[m] Is favorable tax treatment justified on humanitarian grounds, as is frequently contended? Does it matter what sort of injury is being compensated? For example, should favorable tax treatment be reserved for those who suffer severe and permanent physical injury (as Burke & Friel suggested in Subchapter A)? Or should the severity of injury merely affect the amount of damages awarded, not their tax treatment? Note that an exclusion based on humanitarian grounds should be viewed as a tax expenditure, while an exclusion based on the return-of-capital theory could be viewed as neutral application of tax principles.

24. It can be argued very plausibly that victims of personal injury, even after receiving monetary compensation as determined by the tort system, are worse off than before the injury. Does Professor Dodge think that such a decline in the taxpayer's "utility" justifies excluding the monetary damages received?

The uncompensated victim

25. Assume that one concludes that section 104(a)(2) strikes the proper balance between uninjured taxpayers and tort victims who receive monetary compensation. Nevertheless, one is left with the paradox that favorable tax treatment is made available to the compensated tort victim but not to the uncompensated victim.

If the explanation for section 104(a)(2) is tax-free return of capital, the logic of the argument would lead us to expect a deduction for the uncompensated victim's loss of capital. After all, such a deduction need not be limited to income-producing assets; for example, casualty and theft losses of non-income-producing property are deductible.[n]

---

m. Bertram Harnett, *Torts and Taxes*, 37 N.Y.U. L. REV. 614, 626-27 (1952).

n. Section 165(c)(3). This is an itemized deduction. Even for taxpayers who itemize, a full deduction is not allowed due to the limitations of section 165(h); indeed, most taxpayers who suffer a casualty loss can claim no deduction due to these limitations.

26. If the explanation for section 104(a)(2) is humanitarian concern—that is, if the provision is a tax expenditure—it is extraordinary that this concern should be limited to the most fortunate subset of injury victims, those who are compensated. If one takes into account the vagaries of the tort system, and recognizes that extraneous factors may lead to vastly differing compensation amounts for similarly injured persons,[o] present law becomes even more difficult to defend: The biggest tax benefit goes to the subset of the subset who receive a *large* tort recovery. At the other extreme, tort victims injured by a "judgment proof" defendant—no matter how seriously—not only receive no damages, but also no tax benefit.

27. The argument of the preceding note leads us to ask why a tax expenditure based on humanitarian concerns should be limited to accident victims. What of those who suffer as a result of birth defects or illness?

28. Is the objection to allowing tax benefits to the uncompensated victim only administrative simplicity? Certainly an unlimited deduction for personal injury would be unthinkable. (How much deduction for a headache? For tennis elbow?)

29. Do you find attractive the Burke & Friel approach, discussed in subchapter A, which attempts to tie the tax benefit to the disability, regardless of how it arose?

Punitive damages
30. Congress ended a period of legal uncertainty by amending section 104(a)(2) in 1996 to provide that the exclusion does not apply to punitive damages, meaning that presumptively such damages are included in income. No less than under prior law, when the status of punitive damages was uncertain, it is appropriate to consider whether limiting the exclusion to compensatory damages is wise and workable.

31. Almost all commentators agree with Professor Dodge that punitive damages *should* be taxed, even if compensatory damages are excluded. Such damages, he argues in the excerpt above, "represent an economic windfall, and do not compensate for any loss whatever."

32. Professor Patricia Morgan, on the other hand, emphasizes that tort damages defy ready division into damages to make the plaintiff whole and those that punish the defendant. With regard to punitive damages, Professor Morgan points to an American Bar Association commission, which

---

o. *See, e.g.*, Philip D. Oliver, *Once Is Enough: A Proposed Bar of the Injured Employee's Cause of Action Against a Third Party*, 58 FORDHAM L. REV. 117, 159-71 (1989).

recommended that punitive damages in excess of "a reasonable portion of the punitive damages award to compensate the plaintiff and counsel for bringing the action and prosecuting the punitive damages claim" be "allocated to public purposes."[p]   Professor Morgan asserts that if the ABA proposal were universally adopted, "the Service would agree that the portion of the 'punitive damages' that is allocated to the plaintiff is compensatory and therefore excludable."[q]

An alternative view might be that the ABA proposal contemplates compensating the plaintiff not for personal injuries, but for industry in prosecuting a claim that benefits the public. (The public benefit is both direct, through obtaining a portion of the punitive award for the public fisc, and indirect, through punishment and deterrence of bad actors.) By this analysis, the punitive award is similar to earned income, and the exclusion of section 104(a)(2) would not be merited.

Which treatment of punitive damages awarded under the ABA proposal would constitute better tax policy?

33.   What account should be taken of differences in state tort law? At the time of the 1995 amendments, Congress enacted section 104(c) to accommodate Alabama's unusual tort law governing wrongful death. Under Alabama's law, all wrongful death awards are exclusively punitive; in other states, punitive damages are available in wrongful death actions only for the same type of egregious conduct by the defendant that allows for punitive damages in any tort action.

Without section 104(c), Alabama plaintiffs in a routine wrongful death action arising from the defendant's simple negligence would be denied the section 104(a)(2) exclusion available to similarly situated plaintiffs in other states. On this basis, section 104(c) seems fair.

Note, however, that in a case where an Alabama jury allowed a very large recovery because of the defendant's especially egregious conduct, the Alabama plaintiff is actually better off, because the entirety of the award is excluded. An increased award in another state would be denominated as including punitive damages, and would be taxed to that extent.

Was Congress right to accommodate Alabama law? Was Congress right to limit the application of section 104(c) to states that already had this particular form of wrongful death law in effect?

Had section 104(c) not been enacted, Alabama could have responded to the taxation of punitive damages by amending its wrongful death statute to provide for compensatory damages. Would this have demonstrated undue federal pressure on an area of law traditionally reserved to states?

---

p. Report to the House of Delegates of the American Bar Association Action Commission to Improve the Tort Liability System, 18-19 (February, 1987), *quoted in* Patricia T. Morgan, *supra* note k, at 929.

q. *Id.*

34. As Professor Dodge points out, serious administrative problems arise from an attempt to tax punitive damages while exempting compensatory damages. Most personal injury cases are resolved through settlement. Should the parties' allocations between compensatory and punitive damages be controlling? In that case, we can suppose that all payments would be classified as compensatory, because the compensatory label would save the plaintiff money while costing the defendant nothing; the resulting tax savings would figure into the bargaining, and presumably be divided between the parties.[r]

Should we pay close attention to the pleadings?[s] By this approach, if the plaintiff in a personal injury case requested $1 million compensatory damages and $1 million punitive damages, then half of whatever was received would be subject to tax. But what do such pleadings prove if the plaintiff subsequently settles for $20,000? What if the case is settled before suit is filed, or if the pleadings simply ask for relief to be determined by the court?

35. Generally, a tortfeasor can deduct damages under section 162(a), because most tort payments are made for injuries caused in the course of business. Would denial of a deduction for punitive damages be appropriate? Neither fines nor the punitive two thirds of antitrust awards are deductible.[t]

C. TRADITIONAL ANALYSIS CHALLENGED: EVALUATING THE EXCLUSION OF PERSONAL INJURY AWARDS BY NORMATIVE CRITERIA

Subchapter B is typical of most policy discussion of section 104(a)(2) in its analysis of the exclusion by reference to well established tax rules in analogous areas. For example, analysis of "human capital" is derived from rules governing capital assets, with the concept of basis given corresponding prominence. Similarly, it is argued that immediate inclusion of personal injury awards is inappropriate due to the involuntary nature of the conversion of well being to money, drawing comparison to the nonrecognition rule of section 1033. The exclusion for damages replacing lost earnings is questionable precisely because the most comparable situation—receipt of the earnings themselves—clearly would be subject to tax.

In this subchapter, Professor Griffith takes issue with this mode of analysis for tax policy generally, using as his example the taxation of personal

---

r. Randall Barkan, Comment, *Tax Treatment of Post-Termination Personal Injury Agreements*, 61 CAL. L. REV. 1237, 1252 (1973) criticizes the Tax Court's decision in *Seay v. Com'r.*, 58 T.C. 32 (1972), because it allows favorable tax treatment without a determination that the payment was in fact made for personal injury.

s. *See* Mark W. Cochran, *1989 Tax Act Compounds Confusion Over Tax Status of Personal Injury Damages*, 49 TAX LAW. 1565 (1990).

t. Section 162 (f) and (g).

injury awards. He argues that we should structure tax law to achieve an optimal outcome, which should be determined by reference to explicitly acknowledged ethical or normative criteria, without concern for whether the result appears inconsistent with tax principles applicable in other areas.

SHOULD "TAX NORMS" BE ABANDONED?
RETHINKING TAX POLICY ANALYSIS AND
THE TAXATION OF PERSONAL INJURY RECOVERIES
Thomas D. Griffith[*]

1993 Wisconsin Law Review 1115,

1116-23, 1125-27, 1129-34, 1142, 1145, 1148, 1150-52, 1155-58

Traditional tax policy analysis has focused on whether the particular tax provision under examination is consistent with basic "tax norms" such as horizontal equity, vertical equity, ability to pay and the ideal tax base, typically Haig-Simons income. These norms are not grounded, however, in more general ethical principles. This Article will argue that this is a fundamental flaw and, thus, special tax principles should be discarded as a method of evaluating tax policy. Instead, this Article recommends that the likely consequences of the policies under consideration should be determined and then judged under explicitly stated general normative principles. This approach can lead to tax policy recommendations quite different from those generated by traditional methods.

In order to explore the differences between the traditional and suggested approaches to tax policy, the analysis of the taxation of personal injury recoveries will be examined under both approaches. Under current law, damage awards for personal injuries generally are excluded from an individual's gross income. The exclusion applies to damages received for monetary losses from increased medical expenses and lost earnings, and to damages received for non-monetary losses such as pain and suffering and permanent bodily injury.

The exclusion for personal injury recoveries is a departure from the tax rule applied to business injury claims. For business injuries, courts apply an "in lieu of" test, which looks to the nature of the claim to determine the tax treatment of damages received.

If an "in lieu of" test were applied to personal recoveries, damage awards received for lost earnings presumably would be taxed as ordinary income because they replace taxable wages or salary. The proper treatment of recoveries of medical expenses under such a test, however, is less obvious. Perhaps the recipient should be taxed on the amount received and then granted a medical expense deduction. On the other hand, medical expenses arguably should be given tax-free treatment on the grounds that they replace

---

*. At time of original publication, Professor of Law, University of Southern California.

exempt employer-provided medical services, or because they do not constitute gain because they simply restore the recipients to their pre-injury status.

Damage awards received for pain and suffering also raise thorny problems under an "in lieu of" test. Full taxation might be proper on the theory that individuals have no tax basis in their body parts, so that all amounts received constitute gain. On the other hand, an exemption might be appropriate under a return of human capital theory or simply because the recipients are no better off than they were before the injury. Excluding pain and suffering recoveries from the tax base also might be supported under an "in lieu of" test on the view that amounts received replace imputed income from good health that ordinarily is received tax free.

Tax scholars have generated a large literature exploring these issues. In general, these commentators have analyzed how personal injury recoveries would be treated under "tax principles" such as the "in lieu of" test mentioned previously, and then have considered whether any "non-tax" reasons exist for departing from these principles. There is a consensus in this literature that personal injury recoveries received as compensation for lost earnings should be fully taxed and that recoveries received for medical expenses should be tax exempt. Scholars are divided, however, regarding the proper tax treatment of recoveries for pain and suffering.

The central theme of this Article is that the basic approach to tax policy taken in the existing literature should be discarded because it is not based on any attractive general normative principles. Instead, a two-step method should be adopted. First, the consequences of alternative tax policies should be considered. Second, those consequences should be evaluated under explicitly stated ethical principles.

* * *

The conclusions reached in this Article regarding the proper treatment of personal injury recoveries are less significant than the methodology. Personal injury recoveries have been chosen not primarily because of their independent importance, but because the existing tax literature on such recoveries provides a good analysis of tax policy under the widely respected tax norms of horizontal equity and the ideal tax base. * * *

Developing a Model of Personal Injury Recoveries

Tax Exemptions as Insurance

The tax exemption for personal injury recoveries can be viewed as a form of insurance which provides additional income to an individual who is injured, at the expense of higher overall rates for individuals not injured. Such insurance provided by the tax exemption is mandatory, since an individual may not choose to forego this tax benefit in exchange for lower rates.

* * *

Viewing tax provisions as a form of insurance is appropriate for many provisions of the Internal Revenue Code. The deductions for casualty losses and for extraordinary medical expenses provide partial insurance against such losses. * * *

The basic function of insurance is to provide additional consumption to an individual in circumstances in which it is more valuable. Additional consumption will be more valuable to an individual in two cases. First, in general, income is worth more to an individual who has a lower level of current consumption. Maintaining a family's normal consumption level, for example, is the primary function of disability and term life insurance. Second, additional consumption is more valuable to an individual who has greater needs. Providing additional consumption in times of greater need is the central purpose of medical insurance.

The model applies these principles to the tax exemption for personal injury recoveries and determines whether the tax exemption allocates additional income to those circumstances in which it is more valuable. Application of the model leads to the conclusion that exempting recoveries for accident-related medical expenses reallocates income to more valuable states, but that exempting recoveries for lost wages and pain and suffering does not.

Normative Criteria

The model incorporates several simplifying assumptions regarding the nature of personal injury recoveries and the way that consumption and other factors influence personal welfare. The model then is used to calculate the impact of alternative tax policies on personal welfare in light of those assumptions.

The main normative criterion adopted is *ex ante* Pareto superiority. A tax policy is *ex ante* Pareto superior if, prior to the time any taxpayer knows his particular circumstances, each taxpayer would prefer that policy. In the context of personal injury recoveries, the *ex ante* perspective means that each individual must choose the tax treatment of such recoveries without knowing whether or not he will be injured.

> * * *

Assumptions of the Model

Individual welfare is assumed to be a function of two variables: (1) consumption of goods and services and (2) all other factors that affect individual well-being, such as good health, leisure and job satisfaction. * * * Consumption is assumed to have declining marginal utility, so that the value of additional consumption to an individual falls as the individual's total consumption increases.

It also is assumed that some individuals will suffer personal injuries for which they will recover damages, but the identities of the injured individuals are unknown. Finally, it is assumed that the government has constant revenue needs.

Application of the Model

The model will be applied to three types of personal injury recoveries: (1) lost wages, (2) medical expenses, and (3) pain and suffering. Each will be considered separately.

Lost Wages

The analysis in this section concludes that, for any rate structure and distribution of income, each individual can be made better off *ex ante* by switching from a tax system which provides tax-free recovery of lost earnings to one which taxes lost earnings but which has lower overall rates.

* * *

Imagine a society with two identical individuals each of whom has a pre-tax wage income of $50,000 per year. * * * If $40,000 in tax revenue must be raised, each individual will pay a tax of 40% [or] $20,000, leaving consumption of $30,000. * * *

Now suppose that one of the individuals suffers a personal injury resulting in $50,000 of lost wages for which the individual suffers compensatory damages. If the recovery is taxed, the combined tax base from both individuals will remain at $100,000. Each individual again will pay a tax of $20,000 and will have an after-tax consumption of $30,000. * * *

A different result occurs if recoveries for lost wages are exempt from income. The tax base will be reduced from $100,000 to $50,000, since the $50,000 received by the injured individual for lost wages will not be taxed. To raise the same $40,000 of revenue from this smaller base, the tax rate must be increased from 40% to 80%. The uninjured individual then will be taxed at an 80% rate on an income of $50,000, leading to a tax of $40,000, consumption of $10,000. * * * The uninjured individual will pay no tax and will enjoy after-tax consumption of $50,000. * * *

In sum, providing a tax exemption for wage recoveries has the effect of increasing the injured individual's consumption from $30,000 to $50,000 and reducing the consumption of the uninjured individual from $30,000 to $10,000. A net welfare loss results because $20,000 of consumption is comparatively less valuable in the range of $30,000 to $50,000 than in the range of $10,000 to $30,000. * * *

Medical Expenses

Medical expense recoveries differ from lost wages in that increased medical needs change the marginal value of consumption. Accident victims frequently require expensive medical treatment and receive damage awards to cover these costs. If, as seems reasonable, medical treatment is important enough to an accident victim's welfare that the individual could not be made better off by purchasing something other than medical care, then the marginal value of consumption will vary with an individual's level of consumption *after payment of accident-related medical expenses*. * * * Under these assumptions, it can be shown that it is *ex ante* Pareto superior to exempt medical expense recoveries from taxation.

* * *

Assume there are two individuals, each of whom earns $50,000 in wages. One of the individuals incurs $50,000 of medical expenses as a result of a personal injury and receives compensatory damages. If damages for injury-related medical expenses are fully taxed, the injured taxpayer will have a taxable income [of] $100,000 and the total tax base will increase to $150,000.

If the government must raise $40,000 of tax revenues, a tax rate of 26.67% will be required. The uninjured taxpayer will pay a tax of $13,333 on $50,000 of taxable income and enjoy an after-tax consumption of $36,667. * * * The injured taxpayer will pay a tax of $26,667 on $100,000 of taxable income, leaving consumption of $73,333, allocated between $50,000 for medical expenses and $23,333 for non-medical consumption. * * *

If damage recoveries for medical expenses are tax exempt, the injured and uninjured taxpayer each will [pay $20,000 in tax and] enjoy $30,000 of non-medical consumption [thereby increasing total welfare, again due to the declining marginal utility of money.]

Pain and Suffering

Pain and suffering damages include compensation both for actual pain and for any reduction in welfare due to permanent bodily impairment. Unlike recoveries for lost wages and for injury-related medical expenses, pain and suffering damages compensate individuals for non-monetary losses. Application of the model shows that expected utility is maximized if pain and suffering recoveries are fully taxed.

Pain and suffering recoveries are assumed to compensate an injured party precisely for any harm incurred; that is, the amount received, if not taxed, is assumed to make an injured individual as well-off as before the injury. This assumption is not essential, however, to the results; it is optimal to tax damages for pain and suffering, even if doing so means that injured individuals will not be fully compensated for their losses.

* * *

Assume a society with two individuals, each of whom earns $50,000 in wages. One individual receives a $50,000 recovery for pain and suffering. If total tax revenues of $40,000 are required by the government and pain and suffering recoveries are not taxed, each individual will pay a 40% tax of $20,000 on a taxable income of $50,000. The uninjured individual will have an after-tax consumption of $30,000 * * * while the injured taxpayer will have consumption of $80,000. * * *

If recoveries for pain and suffering are taxed, the injured individual's income will increase from $50,000 to $100,000 and the tax base will increase from $100,000 to $150,000. The necessary revenue could then be raised by a tax rate of 26.67%. At this rate, the uninjured taxpayer will pay a tax of $13,333 and will enjoy an after-tax consumption of $36,667 * * * while the injured taxpayer will pay a tax of $26,667 and consume $73,333. * * * Thus, elimination of the tax exemption for pain and suffering damages increases expected utility. * * *

The preceding analysis does not take into account any reduction in the welfare of the injured party from the pain and suffering. This omission is appropriate because the welfare loss from pain and suffering is identical whether or not recoveries are taxed. Including the welfare loss from pain and suffering in the calculation would lower expected utility under each tax regime by an identical amount, but would not affect the *marginal* utility of additional consumption and, thus, would not alter any individual's *ex ante* utility maximizing choice.

* * *

Tax Policy and Personal Injury Recoveries

This Part will examine the various ways in which the taxation of personal injury recoveries has been analyzed by courts, the Treasury, and, especially, by tax scholars. In particular, this Part will look at the application of two important traditional tax norms: the ideal tax base and horizontal equity.

The literature on the taxation of personal injury recoveries applies the norm of an ideal tax base by analyzing whether compensatory tort damages constitute "gain." To determine this, commentators often consider whether a basis exists in human ability. Attempts to determine the proper taxation of personal injury recoveries by looking at the treatment of "similar" transactions such as involuntary conversions of property, voluntary sales of personal rights, and the exclusion of imputed income from good health reflect the horizontal equity norm.

Ideal tax base and horizontal equity arguments are viewed as attempts to support the tax exemption for personal injury recoveries on "tax principles." If a tax provision cannot be justified under tax norms, traditional analysis then considers "non-tax" policy justifications. For personal injury recoveries, the most common non-tax justification is sympathy for the victim.

This Article argues that evaluating tax policy in terms of special tax norms that can, perhaps, be overridden by other ethical principles in unusual cases is inappropriate. Instead, * * * the policy maker should determine the likely consequences of the tax policies under consideration and then choose the policy whose consequences are most consistent with explicitly-stated general normative principles.

* * *

Gain, Horizontal Equity and the Ideal Tax Base

Tax commentators generally agree that lost wage recoveries and punitive damages arising from personal injuries cannot be excluded from taxation on a "no-gain" rationale. Punitive damages, they observe, place injured individuals in a better position than if they had never been hurt, while recoveries for lost wages replace gains from labor which ordinarily are taxed.

It is not clear, however, why "gain" should be the touchstone of taxation. A better rationale for taxing punitive damages and lost wages recoveries is that given in this Article—taxing such gains and lowering tax rates to maintain revenue neutrality will increase each taxpayer's *ex ante* expected welfare.

Tax commentators generally support the exclusion for unreimbursed medical expense recoveries. The remainder of this Part, then, will focus on the more controversial issue of the proper taxation of damages received for pain and suffering.

* * *

The Ideal Tax Base

Evaluating tax policies in terms of their conformity with an ideal tax base is common in tax policy discussions. The two most prominent ideal tax bases are the "normal tax base" and Haig-Simons income.

* * *

The Normal Tax Structure

The tax exemption for personal injury recoveries generally is viewed as a deviation from the "normal tax structure" and thus is characterized as a tax expenditure. * * *

The inability of tax commentators to develop a satisfactory method of assigning basis to human capital does not arise from measurement problems alone; there is also no consensus on how such basis should be assessed in theory. * * *

Analogies to the taxation of business assets do not seem helpful in answering these questions. * * * Conforming the taxation of human capital to standard basis recovery rules is valuable only if it serves the normative principles underlying traditional basis rules. * * *

Haig-Simons Income

Haig-Simons income is defined as consumption plus change in wealth during a specified period. It is not clear, however, how personal injury recoveries should be taxed under this standard. The argument in favor of taxation is straightforward—if an individual receives a damage award it will increase either her consumption, if spent, or her wealth, if saved. It is less certain whether a personal injury generates an offsetting reduction in consumption or wealth.

A loss of earning capacity from a personal injury might be viewed as a reduction in wealth. Nevertheless, it seems likely that no deduction for lost earning capacity would be permitted under a Haig-Simons standard; no depreciation deduction, for example, presumably is permitted for the decline in an individual's earning capacity over time due to aging. Instead, reduced earning capacity would be reflected by a reduction in Haig-Simons income in future years.

A loss in Haig-Simons income arguably also might be created by pain and suffering associated with an injury. A permanent physical disability might be viewed as a decline in wealth, and temporary discomfort during treatment might be characterized as a reduction in the consumption of imputed income from good health. Similarly, amounts spent on medical expenses might not be viewed as consumption under a Haig-Simons standard because they only restore the injured individual to a baseline level of good health.

* * * Henry Simons, however, saw his definition of income as measuring an individual's control over societal goods and services. He rejected the idea that the tax base should consider mental states. It is unlikely that he would favor a deduction for pain and suffering or physical disabilities.

More broadly, it is not clear why it is relevant, as a matter of tax policy, whether an item is included within the Haig-Simons definition of income. Conforming the tax system to Haig-Simons income or any other tax base is desirable only to the extent such conformity advances more general normative principles. * * *

Horizontal Equity Claims

Horizontal equity is, perhaps, the most widespread norm underlying traditional tax policy analysis. It is also the least helpful. This section argues that horizontal equity cannot provide the answer to the proper tax treatment of personal injury recoveries or, in fact, to any other important tax policy question.

Horizontal equity generally is defined as the principle that "individuals who are in equal positions should bear an equal tax burden." The problem is that all individuals are alike in some respects and different in others. The principle of horizontal equity cannot determine which differences justify different tax treatment.

* * * Consider the application of the horizontal equity principle to the following three taxpayers:

(1) Alice, who earns $50,000 in wages and suffers no injury.

(2) Bob, who earns $50,000 in wages, is injured, and receives damages of $10,000 which precisely compensate him for pain and suffering.

(3) Carol, who earns $60,000 in wages and suffers no injury.

Should Bob be considered equal to Alice, or to Carol? Horizontal equity does not tell us the answer. Rather, the correct comparison depends on which of the following normative principles one finds attractive.

Principle one: Individuals should be taxed in accordance with their utility levels.

Principle two: Individuals should be taxed in accordance with their monetary income.

It is necessary to choose one of these principles *before* one can determine which of the two taxpayers are "equal." If principle one is adopted and utility levels provide the basis for comparison, then Bob is in the same position as Alice, since the welfare he gets from the extra $10,000 of income exactly matches the welfare loss from his pain and suffering. Such "utility level" horizontal equity is implicit in arguments that pain and suffering damages should be tax exempt because they replace imputed income from good health which otherwise would be received tax-free. More broadly, utility level horizontal equity underlies arguments for the exclusion of damages on the ground that such damages do not constitute gain.

On the other hand, if principle two is adopted and cash income levels are the basis for comparison, then Bob is in the same position as Carol because each has an income of $60,000. "Cash income level" horizontal equity underlies the view that an individual who receives damages for the tortious invasion of personal rights should be taxed like an individual who voluntarily sells personal rights (such as privacy rights) because both have reduced those rights to cash.

Horizontal equity is of no help in deciding which comparison is the correct one. Moreover, horizontal equity analysis obscures the underlying principle of decision. Utility level horizontal equity implies that "individuals should be taxed on the basis of their utility levels," while income level horizontal equity implies the principle that "individuals should be taxed according to their level of cash income." It is interesting to note that although horizontal equity arguments implying taxation according to utility levels or cash income levels are common in the tax literature, few, if any, commentators explain why a tax structure based on either principle would be desirable. This is not surprising because neither tax base is appealing. Taxation according to cash income levels would ignore differences in needs. Taxation according to utility levels would require taxing non-monetary factors which affect utility, such as good health and a cheerful disposition. Neither tax base is consistent with any widely-held ethical theory.

$$* * *$$

Notes and Questions

36. Professor Griffith argues that "the basic approach to tax policy taken in the existing literature"—which would probably include most of the materials in this chapter—is simply the wrong way to go about analyzing tax policy questions in general and the tax treatment of personal injury awards in particular. Instead of attempting to analogize the particular tax problem to other situations for which the proper treatment seems relatively settled and clear—for example, analogizing personal injury recoveries to property damage recoveries—the policy maker should consider consequences of alternatives, and evaluate the alternatives "under explicitly stated ethical principles."

37. In what sense can a provision such as section 104(a)(2) be viewed as compulsory taxpayer "insurance"? What is the taxpayer's "premium" payment?

38. What is meant by *"ex ante* Pareto superiority" in the tax policy context?

39. The theory of declining marginal utility of money is basic to Professor Griffith's analysis.[u] This theory, which is generally accepted, assumes that each additional dollar of income is worth less to a given individual than the preceding dollar. (As Professor Griffith points out in a portion of the article not excerpted,[29] the theory is much weaker when used for interpersonal comparisons. That is, while we may readily assume that *A*'s tenth dollar has less utility than his first *to A*, it does not necessarily follow that *A*'s tenth dollar has less utility *to A* than *B*'s first dollar has *to B*.)

40. Assuming *ex ante* Pareto superiority as the primary target in structuring tax policy, and assuming declining marginal utility of money, Professor Griffith argues that—viewed *ex ante*, before any taxpayer knows whether he will become an accident victim—every taxpayer should prefer that damages compensating pain and suffering be taxed. A pain and suffering award does not actually replace freedom from pain, of course; the effect of the monetary award is additional marginal dollars for the victim's consumption. These additional dollars have lower marginal utility to the injured taxpayer than the dollars he already had. Suppose, for example, that a taxpayer with income of $25,000 knows that there is one chance in 1,000 that he will be injured and receive $1,000 for pain and suffering. Would he be better off with a system that excluded $1 from the taxable income of everyone, or a system that would exclude his extra $1,000 award if he were injured? It is crucial to the analysis that the 25,000th dollar is assumed to be of greater utility than dollars 25,001-26,000. Thus, he would prefer the certainty of protecting from tax the more valuable 25,000th dollar than the one-in-1,000 chance of protecting 1,000 less valuable dollars.

41. The same assumptions lead Professor Griffith to conclude that awards for medical expenses, unlike awards for pain and suffering, should be excluded from income. Suppose our hypothetical taxpayer with income of $25,000 had one chance in a thousand of receiving a $1,000 award to compensate for accident-induced unanticipated medical expenses. Would he prefer the certain $1 exclusion (as he would in the case of pain and suffering) or the exclusion of the $1,000 if he turned out to be the accident victim? Professor Griffith argues that awards compensating the victim for medical expenses, unlike pain and suffering awards, do not free up additional dollars for general (i.e., non-medical) consumption. The hypothetical taxpayer would therefore be faced with a system that either protected the 25,000th dollar *available for general consumption* from tax, or that offered one chance in one thousand of protecting dollars 24,001-25,000—dollars that have greater utility

---

u. This theory, which is an important element in justifying progressive taxation, is discussed in Chapter Four.

29. 1993 WIS. L. REV., at 1135-37.

than the 25,000th dollar. The rational taxpayer should choose the exclusion this time.

42. Does Professor Griffith's analysis take account of the risk-adverse person who might prefer exclusion of even the pain and suffering award, perhaps reasoning along these lines:

> Even in those cases in which I receive full compensation as measured by the tort system, I am going to be worse off after the accident than before, although perhaps not in monetary terms. Even at the cost of lowering my average *expected* return, I am willing to make a small certain sacrifice (forgoing the $1 exclusion) in order to get a significant tax benefit (exclusion of the $1,000 for pain and suffering) if I am an accident victim.

Does Professor Griffith's analysis take account of the good Samaritan who is willing to sacrifice his own best interest to protect those less fortunate than himself, even at some cost of efficiency?

Note, however, that section 104(a)(2) provides relief only to the compensated accident victim. Risk-adverse persons or good Samaritans might be more concerned with accidents or sickness in which the victim received no compensation.

43. Why does Professor Griffith think it unclear whether personal injury awards are income under the Haig-Simons definition? Why does he think it essentially irrelevant whether such awards fall within that definition?

44. Why does Professor Griffith find the principles of horizontal equity useless—indeed, worse than useless—not only in determining the proper tax treatment of personal injury awards but in tax policy generally?

45. Do you think that Professor Griffith's analysis offers useful insight into how personal injury awards should be taxed?

46. In common with other commentators whose views were discussed in Subchapter B, Professor Griffith suggests that some elements of tort awards should be taxed, and others exempted. Is this a practical suggestion?

Let us ignore punitive damages and focus only on compensatory damages. Suppose that we wished to tax only the portion of personal injury awards that represented compensation for lost earnings, and allow exclusion of other compensatory damages. If a jury returns a general verdict for $1 million, how are we to know how much of this total was for lost earnings? This problem might be reduced if state courts began using special verdict forms in all personal injury cases, but even then, we would be left with the overwhelming majority of cases, which are settled without trial.

The problems are comparable to those involved in separating punitive and compensatory damages (discussed in Note #34, at page 817). Actually, the problem dealt with here is more serious, because many tort cases present no issue of punitive damages, but most big-dollar tort cases involve both lost earnings and other damages.

D. STRUCTURED SETTLEMENTS AND OTHER TIMING PROBLEMS

Typically, tort law contemplates payment of a lump sum settlement or award in compensation for all past and future losses. To the extent attributable to future losses, such as future earnings lost to disability, the lump sum is reduced to present value to reflect the potential for investing it. The lump sum is exempt under section 104(a)(2), but the investment income it generates is taxable. This lump-sum method of payment and associated investment income raise timing issues for tax law.

In recent years, settlements—and, more rarely, judgments following trials—of large cases have frequently been paid out over a period of years (perhaps the lifetime of the victim) rather than in a lump sum. The total amount paid is higher than the lump sum would have been, reflecting the fact that the payor (the defendant or insurance company), and not the victim, will have use of the money. This increased total payment can be viewed as the economic equivalent of an investment return on a lump sum. Under present section 104(a)(2), all payments, including those made over a period of many years and representing significant investment income, are exempt from tax. Professor Frolik criticizes this tax treatment of "structured settlements:"

THE CONVERGENCE OF I.R.C. § 104(a)(2), *NORFOLK & WESTERN RAILWAY CO. V. LIEPELT* AND STRUCTURED TORT SETTLEMENTS: TAX POLICY "DERAILED"

Lawrence A. Frolik[*]

51 Fordham Law Review 565, 572-83 (1983)

The above-discussed inequities engendered by section 104(a)(2) might be borne as an unfortunate, but unavoidable consequence of an understandable congressional desire to assist personal injury victims. Other inequities, however—horizontal inequities—exist among personal injury claimants because of the current tax treatment of deferred payment arrangements (structured settlements), which are frequently used to settle personal injury claims. Those claimants who accept a deferred payment arrangement receive more favorable tax treatment than those claimants who accept a lump-sum settlement.

---

[*]. At time of original publication, Professor of Law, University of Pittsburgh.

The term structured settlement refers to the practice by which the claimant agrees to be paid over a number of years or to be paid an annuity for life rather than accepting a fixed, lump-sum amount. Expenses incurred by the claimant prior to the settlement are usually reimbursed by a lump-sum payment, while future anticipated damages are compensated by subsequent periodic payments. The payments may be a fixed amount, a fixed amount adjustable for inflation, or an amount varying according to the future needs of the claimant. In some instances, the parties may ignore any total calculation of damages and merely agree to a monthly or annual figure sufficient to meet the projected financial needs of the victim.

Once the parties have agreed on the amount of the periodic payment, the defendant is free to seek out the least expensive way to fulfill his obligation. Although some use is made of irrevocable, funded trusts (the claimant being the beneficiary), the preferred method is to purchase an annuity payable to the claimant for the prescribed period of time. Defendants generally hide the actual cost of the annuity from the claimant since it is often considerably less than anticipated by the claimant or less than the lump-sum amount that it supplanted.[v] The cost of a lifetime annuity may be surprisingly low if the claimant's life expectancy was severely diminished by the accident. However, because of this secretiveness, the parties, and the claimant's counsel in particular, are free to publicly ascribe a large value to the settlement and thereby garner the attendant publicity.

Amended Section 104(a)(2) Fosters Horizontal Inequity

On January 14, 1983, section 104(a)(2) was amended to provide that damage awards received as periodic payments on account of personal injuries are excluded from gross income. The amendment merely codified, rather than changed, the current interpretation of the law. Prior to the amendment, the IRS had held that periodic payments, including the portion of the deferred payments that represents interest earned on the deferred principal, are nontaxable. Thus, the total amount of a deferred settlement payment escapes taxation even though every periodic payment is comprised of a mix of principal and investment income arising from the deferred portion of the principal.[43]

An equitable and consistent income tax should treat a claimant's decision to receive an annuity (or the income from an irrevocable trust) in lieu of outright receipt of the principal sum as providing comparable economic benefit and, therefore, necessitating comparable taxation. Yet this is not the case. If, for example, rather than a deferred payment, the claimant accepted a

---

v. By "the lump-sum amount that [the structured settlement] supplanted," the author presumably refers to a tentative lump-sum settlement of a tort action, followed by further negotiation resulting in the substitution of a structured settlement for the lump sum. (Ed.)

43. That a deferred payment consists of both principal and interest is most clear in the event that the defendant purchases an annuity, payable to the claimant, as an insured method of payment. Annuities, almost by definition, are a return of principal together with interest.

lump-sum settlement and then invested it, the subsequent interest income would be included in gross income. If the claimant used the lump sum to purchase an annuity, he would be taxed on that portion of the proceeds that represented interest income. In short, section 104(a)(2) does not extend its protection to the income earned on invested damage awards, even though the parties are likely to have anticipated such earnings and calculated the amount of the settlement accordingly.

For purposes of consistency and equity, Congress should tax interest income that is paid to the claimant even though the interest is earned on principal that was not received by the claimant, but rather held or invested for his benefit under a deferred payment plan.[46] The principal need not be retained by the defendant-payor, because the interest is exempt even though earned by and paid through the use of an annuity, or by a funded irrevocable trust.[47] Given the inconsistent taxation of the interest income, the current tax system impels wise claimants to accept a deferred payout of the settlement, thereby obtaining the benefits of the section 104(a)(2) tax exemption for the interest income earned upon the principal sum of the settlement.

Imagine two sixty-year old tort victims, X and Y, both of whom suffer $100,000 in lost future earnings, the $100,000 figure being the discounted value of their lost earnings for the next five years. If X settles for a lump sum of $100,000 and invests it in 10% corporate bonds which mature in 5 years, X would have $10,000 a year taxable income and a return of the $100,000 at the end of the fifth year. X would have consumable income of $150,000 less the income taxes on the interest. If we assume a tax rate of 25%, X will pay $12,500 in taxes ($10,000 x 5 x 25%), leaving net income of $137,500. (A comparable result would occur if X had used the $100,000 to purchase a five-year annuity). If Y, on the other hand, chooses to accept deferred payments of $10,000 per year for five years with a payment of $100,000 at the end of the fifth year, Y's gross income would be $150,000, all of which is tax

---

46. Nor is tax exemption of the interest [consistent] with the treatment of interest arising from other deferred payment arrangements. The interest portion of a taxpayer purchased annuity is taxable. I.R.C. § 72(a) (1976). Any interest resulting from deferred payments of life insurance proceeds are taxable. The exemption for life insurance proceeds applies only to the amount of the at-death benefit. I.R.C. § 101(d) (1976).

47. Deferred payments of damage awards may assume various forms. The purchase of an annuity payable to the claimant is the most widely used form. Moore, *The Use of Annuities in the Settlement of Personal Injury Cases*, 49 INS. COUNS. J. 50, 50 (1982); Sedgwick & Judge, *The Use of Annuities in Settlement of Personal Injury Cases*, 41 INS. COUNS. J. 584, 584 (1974). Another method is an irrevocable funded trust usually with a bank trustee. When the obligation to pay the claimant terminates, usually at the death of the claimant, the trust terminates. The balance of the trust fund then reverts to the defendant or his insurer. Fuller, *Paying Tomorrow's Claims with Tomorrow's Dollars*, 3 LITIG. 27, 29 (Fall 1976). A third possibility is to have the defendant's casualty insurer underwrite its own annuity plan. The insurer would set aside and invest a lump sum, the income from which would be used to fulfill the periodic payment obligation. Verbeck & Michaels, *Structured Settlements and the Uniform Periodic Payments Act*, 29 FED'N INS. COUNS. Q. 17, 19 (1978).

free. (Again, the same result would occur if Y had accepted a five-year annuity purchased at a cost of $100,000).

Obviously, such disparate tax treatment finds little justification in economic realities. The chief difference in the above example between X and Y is the retention by X of the power to consume the principal or to choose the form of its investment. X also retained the ability to change investments or to terminate the investment and consume the principal. This "freedom of choice," however, might not exist if X purchased an annuity, or had invested in some similarly restrictive investment. Even an apparently flexible investment might be subject to any number of restraints that would discourage the recipient, as a practical matter, from exercising the freedom of investment that was apparently obtained by the acceptance of a lump-sum settlement. If, for example, the recipient purchased long-term bonds as a means of providing a stable income, and if interest rates subsequently rose, the bonds would decline in value. To change investments, the recipient would have to absorb a loss of principal; something he might not be willing to accept. Still, in our example, X does have continuing "dominion and control" over the damage award, while Y surrendered that control upon agreeing to a deferred payment arrangement. Does that modest difference in control warrant such a difference in tax treatment?

The doctrine of constructive receipt might seem to apply because it calls for taxation based upon underlying economic realities rather than the mere surface arrangements. The relevant Revenue Rulings, however, which seem to be correct, hold that the doctrine of constructive receipt is not applicable to periodic payments of tort settlements. The Regulations define constructive receipt of income as income "not actually reduced to a taxpayer's possession," but which "is credited to his account, set apart for him, or otherwise made available so that he may draw upon it at any time, or so that he could have drawn upon it during the taxable year if notice of intention to withdraw had been given."[51] In short, the taxpayer "may not deliberately turn his back on income and select his year of reporting."[52]

Returning to our example, one might argue that Y constructively received the $100,000 settlement at the moment in the negotiations when, rather than agreeing to deferred periodic payments he could have demanded immediate payment of the $100,000. The argument, although appealing, must be rejected in light of the cases that have considered when and how constructive receipt should apply to deferred compensation arrangements.[53] Suffice it to say that the cases, and the subsequent Revenue Rulings, have decisively concluded that the doctrine of constructive receipt does not govern the transaction merely

---

51. Treas. Reg. §1.451-2(a) (1979).

52. Metzer, *Constructive Receipt, Economic Benefit and Assignment of Income: A Case Study in Deferred Compensation*, 29 TAX L. REV. 525, 532 (1974).

53. For an exhaustive discussion of the application of the doctrine of constructive receipt to the various forms of deferred compensation, *see id.*, at 538-50.

because the taxpayer negotiated a deferred compensation agreement. Although deferred compensation is not completely analogous to a deferred payment damage award, the two are conceptually close enough to allow the former to be instructive as to the latter. Hence, the constructive receipt doctrine does not seem to justify taxation of periodic payments in the year of settlement.

A Proposed Solution–The "Economic Benefit Doctrine"

A better solution to the inequities of section 104(a)(2) would be the repeal of the 1983 amendment and the application of the doctrine of economic benefit, which arose in the context of employee compensation,[57] to structured settlements. The doctrine originated in Old Colony Trust Co. v. Commissioner,[58] which established that the predecessor to section 61 included as income any economic or financial benefit conferred upon the employee as compensation, whatever the form or mode by which it is effected. * * *

Beginning with *Burnet v. Logan*,[65] the economic benefit doctrine has been used to determine the year of taxation for deferred payments from the sale of property. In *Burnet*, the sale price for stock included deferred payments keyed to the tonnage of iron ore extracted from a mine by the purchaser of the stock. The Court held that no income was realized in the year of the sale because the "promise [of future money payments] was in no proper sense equivalent to cash. It had no ascertainable fair market value." Hence, the transaction was "held open" to await the actual receipt of the future payments before a determination was made as to whether the seller had realized any income.

Although the government lost under the particular facts of *Burnet*, in dicta the court did approve the government's contention that under appropriate conditions deferred payments were taxable in the year of sale. Taxation could precede receipt of the income because the taxpayer received economic benefit equal to the discounted value of the deferred payments.

In the wake of *Burnet*, deferred payment sales agreements are classified either as "open" or "closed" transactions. If the deferred payments have an ascertainable fair market value, the transaction is "closed" and the gain or loss is recognized in the year of sale. * * * IRS regulations hold that "only in rare and extraordinary cases will property be considered to have no fair market

---

57. The concept was not formally recognized until the 1945 case of Commissioner v. Smith, 324 U.S. 177, 181 (1945), but its antecedents extend at least to Old Colony Trust Co. v. Commissioner, 279 U.S. 716 (1929). The leading case is Sproull v. Commissioner, 16 T.C. 244 (1951), aff'd per curiam, 194 F.2d 541 (6th Cir. 1952) in which the employer in 1945 paid a bank trustee $10,500 in consideration for the services performed by the taxpayer/employee. The trustee was to pay out approximately one-half the principal and accumulated interest in 1946 and the remainder in 1947. Id., at 245. In holding that the $10,500 was taxable in 1945, the court conceded that it was not a case of constructive receipt. Instead the court held it taxable in the year that the taxpayer received the economic benefit in the form of a cash equivalent. Id. at 247; see Rev. Rul. 62-74, 1962-1 C.B. 68.

58. 279 U.S. 716 (1929).

65. 283 U.S. 404 (1931).

value"[74] and therefore, deferred payment sales are in overwhelming numbers deemed "closed" transactions.

Applying the Doctrine to Structured Settlements

The doctrine of economic benefit has been addressed and surprisingly rejected by the IRS in the context of periodic payment of damage awards.[76] Surely, however, the claimant who agrees to periodic payments does in fact receive economic benefit at the time of the agreement. The transaction must be considered "closed" because the periodic payments have an ascertainable fair market value, particularly if the payments are secured by an annuity or funded irrevocable trust. Thus, applying the doctrine of economic benefit to structured settlements, the claimant would realize income in the year of settlement equal to the discounted value—the ascertainable fair market value—of the future payments.

Generally, the claimant will demand the protection of a fully funded trust (or escrow account) or will require the defendant to purchase an annuity from a financially responsible third party such as an insurance company. In the case of an annuity, the claimant would have income equal to the cost of the annuity to the defendant.[78] If, rather than an annuity, the parties rely upon a funded irrevocable trust or an unsecured promise to pay, valuation would be more speculative, but still determinable. A funded, irrevocable trust, which is required to pay all its income to the claimant, would complicate the valuation problem because the rate of return is uncertain. Nevertheless, a solution might be found by analogy to the field of estate and gift tax, which relies upon valuation tables to determine the present value of future trust income. Even an unsecured promise to pay would have a fair market value, albeit deeply discounted to reflect the risk factor.

The failure of the IRS and Congress to apply the doctrine of economic benefit to periodic payments becomes even more confusing upon examination of applications of the doctrine in analogous contexts. For example, one Revenue Ruling held that the discounted value of prize payments were taxable in the year they were won, even though before the winner was chosen the contest sponsor had placed the prize money in an escrow account to be paid over a two-year period.[80] A similar result was reached in a case in which a father bought a winning Irish Sweepstakes ticket in the names of his minor

---

74. Treas. Reg. § 1.1001-1(a) (1960).

76. *E.g.*, Rev. Rul. 79-220, 1979-2 C.B. 74.

78. Disclosure to the claimant of the cost of the annuity could cause some problems, however. The issuer of the annuity may be unhappy about the release of its price; disclosure of that information may cost the issuer a competitive advantage if other issuers should learn of the price because the price of an annuity varies from company to company. Defendants also may not appreciate disclosing the price of the annuity because it may have cost less than what the claimant demanded as a lump-sum settlement. The cost of the annuity is keyed to the claimant's life expectancy, concerning which the parties may have quite different opinions.

80. Rev. Rul. 62-74, 1962-1 C.B. 68.

children.[81] Pursuant to Irish law, the cash prize was held by the Bank of Ireland until the children reached age 21 or until the bank received an application for release of the funds. The Tax Court held that under the doctrine of economic benefit the prize was taxable in the year it was won, rather than in the year(s) that the children turned twenty-one or in the year in which application was made for the money.

The argument for applying the doctrine of economic benefit to structured settlements is even more compelling than in the above examples. In those situations, the deferred nature of the payments was fortuitous—they could not have resulted from conscious tax planning on the part of the recipient. By contrast, the personal injury claimant plays a major role in determining the nature of the payments he will receive. * * *

Proposed Methods of Taxing Structured Settlements

If deferred payment damage awards were deemed income in the year of the settlement, section 104(a)(2) would come into play, with the result that the fair market value of the settlement would be tax exempt. Thereafter, the tax effect of the later receipt of the periodic payments could take either of two routes. The claimant could be treated as if he had purchased an annuity at a cost equal to present value of the future payments, i.e., the amount exempted by section 104(a)(2). The periodic payments would then be taxed according to section 72. Under that section, each periodic payment would be allocated between a tax-free return of capital—the cost of the annuity—and a taxable investment interest component.

In the alternative, the periodic payments would be taxed as are other closed transactions; the payments would be received tax-free until they totaled the fair market value of the settlement amount. Payments in excess of the amount exempted by section 104(a)(2) would represent taxable income. * * *

Depending on the particular circumstances and the bargaining power of the parties, structured settlements will confer the section 104(a)(2) tax savings upon either the claimant, the defendant or both. To the extent the claimant garners a portion of the tax savings, a horizontal inequity is created among personal injury award recipients. Moreover, the potential shift of some or all of the section 104(a)(2) tax savings to defendants was certainly not one of the purposes behind the section's enactment. By divesting structured settlements of their favored tax treatment both of these effects could be remedied. Deferred periodic payments should be treated as either "closed transactions" or as section 72 annuities.

* * *

---

81. Pulsifer v. Commissioner, 64 T.C. 245, 245 (1975).

Notes and Questions

Structured settlements

47. What are "structured settlements"? What is the tax advantage offered by structured settlements? Who benefits from this advantage?

48. Professor Frolik proposes application of the "economic benefit doctrine" to structured settlements. What effect would this have?

49. Present law clearly encourages structured settlements. What non-tax goals are furthered by this favorable tax treatment? Do the non-tax goals justify present law?

50. The importance of "structured settlements" is growing, in part because tort law is increasingly incorporating the approach even where the parties have not agreed to it in a settlement. Particularly in medical malpractice actions, statutes in a number of states allow a party to move to have payments structured over time, even if the opposing party objects.[w]

Timing issues in lump-sum awards

51. Time-value-of-money issues arise not only in the case of structured settlements, but with lump-sum awards as well. Under tort law, awards that compensate for future losses are "discounted to present value." Thus, an award that compensates for future earnings or future medical expenses is reduced to reflect the fact that a lump-sum award can be invested until the time of the element of loss it is supposed to compensate. The investment earnings of the lump-sum award are taxed.

If section 104(a)(2) were repealed, would taxing both the lump-sum award and the earnings generated by the award constitute double taxation?

52. If section 104(a)(2) is to be narrowed or repealed, *when* should the taxes be levied? Suppose a taxpayer receives $1,000,000 to compensate for thirty future years of lost earnings and pain. Assuming the decision to tax the lump-sum award, should it be taxed on receipt or over the thirty-year period? There are at least two aspects of this problem. First, does taxing on receipt improperly accelerate tax liability?

Second, does levying all taxes in a single year unfairly tax the tort plaintiff by "bunching" his income, because the lump sum is subjected to high progressive rates? The seriousness of the bunching argument depends on the degree of progressivity. For example, the problem would have been far more severe in the 1950s, when marginal rates exceeded ninety percent. According to one commentator of that era, if a plaintiff received a taxable award of

---

w. For example, California (Cal. Civ. Proc. Code §667.7 (West 1987)) and Illinois (735 Ill. Comp. Stat. § 5/2-1705 et seq.) have statutes authorizing this procedure.

$50,000 to take the place of five years of earning $10,000 per year: "The plaintiff will lose 20% of the full amount of his judgment *simply* because it was all taxable in the year judgment was received. (Actually 74% of the judgment would go for taxes, but only 20% is caused by the bunching effect.)"[x]

Should special relief provisions—income averaging, for example—accompany repeal or substantial limitation of section 104(a)(2)? Professor Malcolm Morris, for example, might combat the bunching problem by levying a tax "equal to five times the tax which would be imposed * * * on one-fifth of the amount."[y]

Effect of tax law on tort law

53. If section 104(a)(2) is left intact, should juries be informed that the award is tax-free? If section 104(a)(2) were repealed, should they be told that the award is taxable? Who would benefit in each case, as between plaintiff and defendant? The United States Supreme Court, in a personal injury case brought under the Federal Employers' Liability Act, struck a pro-defendant blow in holding that such an instruction should be given.[z] The majority position among states, however, continues to be that juries should not be informed that the award is tax-free. Under the *Erie* doctrine,[aa] this view is usually held to bind federal courts deciding diversity cases, which constitute the bulk of tort litigation in federal courts.

54. Might repeal of section 104(a)(2), or limitation of its application to certain elements of damage, have the unintended effect of increasing the fees of plaintiffs' attorneys? If one supposed that juries would be informed of the tax bite and make allowance by increasing the amounts awarded plaintiffs, a lawyer receiving a percentage contingency fee might see his income rise. Would this be likely to occur? Would this be undesirable?

55. In conclusion: In what way, if any, would you change section 104(a)(2)? Why?

---

x. Charles R. Cutler, *Taxation of the Proceeds of Litigation*, 57 COLUM. L. REV. 470, 477 (1957). [From a modern vantage point, perhaps the most striking part of the statement is the overall tax of 74%, rather than the bunching problem. (Ed.)]

y. Malcolm M. Morris, *Taxing Economic Loss Recovered in Personal Injury Actions: Towards a Capital Idea?*, 38 U. FLA. L. REV. 735, 758 (1986).

z. Norfolk & Western Railway v. Liepelt, 444 U.S. 490, *reh'g. denied*, 445 U.S. 972 (1980).

aa. Erie Railroad v. Tompkins, 304 U.S. 64 (1938), requires federal courts to apply substantive state law in diversity cases.

CHAPTER THIRTEEN

FEDERAL TAX TREATMENT OF STATE AND LOCAL TAXES

If, among deductions allowed under the Federal income tax, veneration is a function of age, then State and local taxes constitute the most venerable of all deductions. Together with Federal taxes, they were the only deductions specifically provided for in the Income Tax Act of 1861. Every income tax statute enacted since 1861 has continued their deductibility.[a]

A. INTRODUCTION

The language above should not lead the reader to conclude that the scope of the deduction for state and local taxes (S-L taxes) has remained unchanged. In the pre-1913 income tax statutes, and in the first years of the income tax under the Sixteenth Amendment, virtually all taxes were deductible. Prior to 1917, even the federal income tax itself was deductible.[b] Until 1964, all taxes were deductible unless specifically barred; in the Revenue Act of 1964, Congress reversed this approach so that taxes were not deductible unless specified allowed. The 1964 Act substantively narrowed the deduction, principally by not including S-L "sin" taxes (excise taxes on alcoholic beverages and tobacco products) in the list of deductible taxes. In 1978, motivated in part by petroleum shortages, Congress ended the deduction for gasoline taxes. The most recent change, and the most important, is the provision in the Tax Reform Act of 1986 that ended the deductibility of S-L sales taxes. At present, the only deductible S-L taxes are income taxes, real property taxes, and ad valorem personal property taxes.[c] (Other S-L taxes are deductible if they constitute expenses "in carrying on a trade or business or an activity described in section 212."[d] This chapter, however, deals with the deductibility of S-L taxes outside the business/income-producing context.)

---

a. Harvey E. Brazer, *The Deductibility of State and Local Taxes Under the Individual Income Tax, in* HOUSE COMM. ON WAYS & MEANS, 86TH CONG., 1ST SESS., 1 TAX REVISION COMPENDIUM 407 (1959).

b. For example, payment of 1915 taxes would have been made in 1916, and, under the cash method, would have been deductible in computing 1916 taxes.

c. Section 164(a)(1)-(3).

d. Section 164(a). S-L taxes that constitute business expenses are above-the-line deductions available even to taxpayers who do not itemize. Section 62(a)(1).

B. DEDUCTION OF STATE AND LOCAL TAXES

While previous restrictions on the deductibility of S-L taxes might be regarded as "tinkering," the 1986 Act went to the heart of the deduction. Prior to that act, the "big three" sources of S-L revenues—income taxes, property taxes, and sales taxes—were deductible; the 1986 Act ended the deductibility of sales taxes while leaving the other taxes fully deductible. All of the excerpts in this subchapter were published within a few years of this fundamental change, and the views expressed run the gamut. The drafters of Treasury I argued that none of the taxes should be deductible. The Senate Finance Committee's report justified the route ultimately chosen. Writing from an economic perspective, Noto and Zimmerman evaluated elimination of the sales tax deduction with other equal-revenue restrictions on deductibility of S-L taxes. The final two excerpts, both written by law professors (William Turnier and JB McCombs), examine from an academic perspective the conceptual question of the proper scope of the deduction.

TAX REFORM FOR FAIRNESS, SIMPLICITY, AND ECONOMIC GROWTH ["TREASURY I"]
United States Department of the Treasury
Vol. 1, at 78, 80; vol. 2, at 66-67 (1984)

Itemized deduction[s] for State and local taxes are not required for the accurate measurement of income. Many years ago, with top rates in the neighborhood of 90 percent, the deduction was perceived to be necessary to prevent the sum of the marginal tax rates for Federal and State income taxes from exceeding 100 percent. Given the present levels of tax rates, such an argument is no longer relevant. The deduction is sometimes defended as a subsidy that is required to reduce the taxpayer's net cost of paying State and local taxes. Some would argue that the deduction has the advantage of encouraging greater expenditures by State and local governments.

Expenditures by State and local governments provide benefits primarily for residents of the taxing jurisdiction. To the extent that State and local taxes merely reflect the benefits of services provided to taxpayers, there is no more reason for a Federal subsidy for spending by State and local governments than for private spending. Both equity and neutrality dictate that State and local services should be financed by taxes levied on residents or on businesses operating in the jurisdiction, in the absence of evidence that substantial benefits of such expenditures spill over into other jurisdictions. There is no reason to believe that most expenditures of State and local governments have such strong spillover effects that they would be greatly under-provided in the absence of the deduction for State and local taxes. There is no reason to have high Federal tax rates and provide implicit Federal subsidies to spending of State and local governments by allowing deduction for their taxes. It would be better—fairer, simpler, and more neutral—to have lower Federal tax rates and have State and local government services—like private purchases—funded from after-tax dollars.

* * *

The three most important sources of State and local tax revenue in the United States are the general sales tax, the personal income tax, and the property tax. There may be a tendency to believe that itemized deductions should be eliminated for some of these taxes, but retained for others. The Treasury Department rejects this view, because the degree of reliance on these three tax bases varies widely from state to state. Five States have no general sales tax, and six have no personal income tax. Moreover, local governments in various States make widely different use of the property tax; in 1982 the tax represented from below 40 percent to almost 100 percent of total local tax collections in various states. To allow itemized deductions for some of these revenue sources, but not others, would unfairly benefit residents of the States levying the deductible taxes, relative to those who live elsewhere. Moreover, it would distort tax policy at the State and local level away from the non-deductible revenue source. Current law does this by allowing deductions for certain taxes but not for many fees and other taxes.

Moreover, because the deduction for State and local taxes leads to higher federal tax rates for all, there is a net benefit only for States (and localities) that levy above-average taxes. Residents of States (and localities) with below-average taxes are worse off than if there were no deduction.

* * *

Reasons for Change

The current deduction for State and local taxes in effect provides a Federal subsidy for the public services provided by State and local governments, such as public education, road construction and repair, and sanitary services. When taxpayers acquire similar services by private purchase (for example, when taxpayers pay for water or sewer services), no deduction is allowed for the expenditure. Allowing a deduction for State and local taxes simply permits taxpayers to finance personal consumption expenditures with pre-tax dollars.

Many of the benefits provided by State and local governments, such as police and fire protection, judicial and administrative services, and public welfare or relief, are not directly analogous to privately purchased goods or services. They nevertheless provide substantial personal benefits to State and local taxpayers, whether directly or by enhancing the general quality of life in State and local communities. * * *

It is argued by some that State and local taxes should be deductible because they are not voluntarily paid. The argument is deficient in a number of respects. First, State and local taxes are voluntary in the sense that State and local taxpayers control their rates of taxation through the electoral process. Recent State and local tax reduction initiatives underline the importance of this process. Just as importantly, taxpayers are free to locate in the jurisdiction which provides the most amenable combination of public services and tax rates. Taxpayers have increasingly "voted with their feet" in recent years by moving to new localities to avoid high rates of taxation. Indeed, taxpayers have far greater control over the amount of State and local taxes they pay than over the level of Federal income taxes. Nevertheless, Federal income taxes are nondeductible.

The subsidy provided through the current deduction for State and local taxes is distributed in an uneven and unfair manner. Taxpayers in high-tax States receive disproportionate benefits, while those in low-tax States effectively subsidize the public service benefits received by taxpayers in neighboring States. Even within a single State or locality, the deduction of State and local taxes provides unequal benefits. Most State and local taxes are deductible only by taxpayers who itemize, and among itemizers, those with high incomes and high marginal tax rates receive a disproportionate benefit.

* * *

Proposal

The itemized deduction for State and local income taxes and other taxes that are not incurred in carrying on a trade or business or income-producing activity would be phased out over a two-year period. * * *

SENATE COMMITTEE ON FINANCE

Senate Report No. 99-313, 99th Cong., 2d Sess., at 56-57 (1986)

Reasons for Change

The committee believes that, as part of the approach of its bill to reduce tax rates through base-broadening, it is appropriate to disallow the itemized deduction for State and local sales taxes. A number of additional considerations support the committee's decision.

First, itemized deductions already are not allowed under present law for various types of State and local sales taxes—such as selective sales taxes on telephone and other utility services, admissions, and sales of alcoholic beverages, tobacco, and gasoline. Also, present law does not allow consumers any deduction to reflect the inclusion in selling price of taxes levied at the wholesale or manufacturers' level. The committee believes that extending nondeductibility to all State and local sales taxes will improve the consistency of Federal tax policy by not providing an income tax benefit for any type of consumption.

Further, to the extent that sales taxes are voluntary costs of purchasing the consumer product or other items to which the taxes apply, the deduction is unfair because it favors taxpayers with particular consumption patterns, and is inconsistent with the general rule that costs of personal consumption by individuals are nondeductible.

Second, although the committee is aware of arguments that eliminating the sales tax deduction will provide unwarranted encouragement for States to shift away from these taxes and will be unfair to States that retain them, the committee did not find persuasive evidence for this view. On the contrary, it is significant how small a portion of general sales taxes paid by individuals actually are claimed as itemized deductions. Data from 1984 show that less than one-quarter of all such taxes levied are claimed as itemized deductions. By contrast, well over one-half of State and local income taxes paid by individuals are claimed as itemized deductions. The fact that the large majority of sales tax payments already are not claimed as itemized deductions under present law alleviates any effect of repealing the deduction on the regional distribution of Federal income tax burdens or on the willingness of State and local governments to use general sales taxes as revenue sources.

Third, for itemizers who do not rely on the IRS-published tables to estimate their deductible sales taxes, the deduction for sales taxes involves substantial recordkeeping and computational burdens, since the taxpayer must determine which sales taxes are deductible, must keep receipts or invoices showing the tax paid on each purchase, and must calculate the total of all deductible sales taxes paid. * * * Thus, repealing the deduction advances the committee's goal of simplifying the tax system for individuals.

For itemizers who do rely on the IRS tables, the amount of deductions that individuals can take without challenge from the IRS may vary significantly in particular instances from the amount of general sales taxes actually paid to State and local governments. The tables do not provide accurate estimates for individuals who have either lower or higher levels of consumption than the average, and do not reflect the fact that an individual may purchase items in several States having different general sales tax rates. Accordingly, use of the tables neither accurately measures the amount of disposable income an individual retains after paying general sales taxes, nor accurately provides an appropriate Federal tax benefit to residents of States that use general sales taxes.

* * *

LIMITING STATE-LOCAL TAX DEDUCTIBILITY: EFFECTS AMONG THE STATES
Nonna A. Noto & Dennis Zimmerman[*]
37 National Tax Journal 539, 542, 546 (1984)

This paper starts from the premise that the Congress has decided to raise a specified amount of additional revenue from the federal individual income tax by limiting the deductibility of state and local (S-L) taxes through one of four proposals which surfaced in the discussions surrounding TEFRA[e] and subsequent to it. One proposal would completely eliminate the deductibility of the general sales tax. A second would treat all eligible S-L tax deductions in combination and impose a floor, set as a percent of AGI: only S-L tax payments

---

*. At the time of original publication, both authors were affiliated with the Congressional Research Service.
e. Tax Equity and Fiscal Reform Act of 1982. (Ed.)

in excess of the floor would remain deductible. A third proposal would impose a ceiling on the combined tax deductions, set as a percent of AGI: S-L taxes in excess of that ceiling amount would no longer be deductible. A fourth proposal would disallow from deduction a percentage of otherwise deductible tax payments.

    * * *

The precise dollar and percentage limits were calculated so as to make the floor, ceiling, and percent disallowance proposals revenue-equivalent to the sales tax proposal, which would have raised approximately $3.7 billion in additional federal revenue in 1980. Accordingly, the floor in proposal two would be 1.08 percent of adjusted gross income. The ceiling in proposal three would be 6.32 percent of AGI. The disallowance in proposal four would be 14.6 percent of taxes currently eligible for deductions.

    * * *

Policy Conclusions

Drawing upon all of the above theoretical and empirical considerations, our conclusion is that if S-L tax deductibility is to be limited, the preferred alternative is the percent of AGI floor.

The proposal to repeal the deductibility of the sales tax, the alternative most frequently mentioned in popular and political discussions, is unattractive on all of the grounds considered. First, this approach to raising federal revenue is anticipated to create unnecessary variability among the states in its effect on after-tax income, and consequently on S-L revenues, because of the differing dependence on the sales tax as a S-L revenue source. Second, it is expected to have income *and* substitution effects and consequently cause a greater S-L revenue loss per dollar of federal revenue gain than the floor approach, which is expected to have just an income effect.[f] Furthermore, as a result of the substitution effect anticipated if deductibility were repealed, S-L revenue officials could be expected to reduce their reliance on sales taxes relative to other taxes remaining eligible for deduction. This would be an unnecessary federal influence on S-L revenue choice. The foregoing conclusions are not unique to the sales tax. They would apply to any proposal to repeal the deductibility of a particular S-L tax.

It is difficult to have a "fair" ceiling if it must be expressed uniformly nationwide. Because of the tremendous variation among states in the S-L tax

---

f. The authors explain that the "income effect" reduces S-L tax revenues simply because S-L taxpayers, having lost a federal deduction, have less after-federal-tax money available to "spend" on "S-L goods and services." 47 NAT'L TAX J. at 540. All limitations on federal deductibility of S-L taxes would increase federal taxes, and therefore would have an adverse effect on S-L revenues due to the income effect.

    The "substitution effect" results in S-L taxpayers spending less on S-L services because those services, to the extent no longer deductible in computing federal taxes, have become more expensive relative to other goods and services. *Id.* at 540-41. The authors argue that the substitution effect would be applicable if the deductibility of S-L sales taxes were ended, but (as explained in the next footnote) not if the "floor" approach were used. (Ed.)

burden as a percent of AGI, a ceiling set at a given percent of AGI might not affect taxpayers in some jurisdictions at all but might affect taxpayers in other jurisdictions by a substantial amount. Another consequence of these differences in tax burdens is that the ceiling proposal has by far the greatest variability among the states in terms of expected effect on after-tax income and therefore S-L revenue. * * *

The percent disallowance proposal sounds evenhanded in the sense of disallowing the same fraction of deductions for all itemizers, unlike either the floor, ceiling, or sales tax proposals. In practice, however, it resembles the ceiling proposal in imposing a greater increase in federal tax liability on itemizers in states with high tax effort. * * *

A floor emerges as the preferred alternative. The floor approach is expected to have a less damaging effect on S-L own-source tax revenue than the sales tax, ceiling, or percent disallowance approaches because it is expected to have only an income effect, and not a substitution effect, if the floor is set below the S-L tax burden in even the lowest-tax jurisdiction.[g] Furthermore the floor proposal ranked as most evenhanded among the states in terms of federal impact on after-tax incomes.

* * *

EVALUATING PERSONAL DEDUCTIONS IN AN INCOME TAX—THE IDEAL

William J. Turnier[*]

66 Cornell Law Review 262, 262-63, 294-95 (1981)

The role of personal deductions in our income tax system has generated considerable debate among individuals who have criticized personal deductions as unwarranted erosions of the tax base. * * *

This dim view of personal deductions is unwarranted for a number of reasons. First, although critics generally agree on the definition of income, they have failed to define its key components. As a result, they leave unresolved the question of whether personal deductions are necessary to assure that only income is taxed. Moreover, in focusing exclusively on the extensiveness of an income tax, these critics overlook the role that our society intends this tax to play. Consequently, critics ignore the capacity of deductions to insure that the base is compatible with the principal reasons underlying society's adopting the income tax. Finally, critics also ignore the role that personal deductions can play in insuring the primacy of fundamental social,

---

g. "S-L tax deductions exceeded the proposed floor of 1.08 percent of itemizers' AGI for all states in 1980. Thus, if a floor of 1.08 percent were imposed, virtually all itemizers in all states would lose deductions equal to 1.08 percent of their AGI." *Id.* at 543. Because the limited loss of federal deductibility under the floor approach would have no effect on federal tax liability at the margin, the authors anticipated no substitution effect. (Ed.)

*. At time of original publication, Associate Professor of Law, University of North Carolina at Chapel Hill.

economic, and political values. In so doing, these critics elevate values implicit in a comprehensive income tax above all other values.

This Article proposes a three-tiered test to evaluate the propriety of personal deductions. First, one should measure all deductions against a generally accepted definition of income to determine if they are essential in arriving at the goal of taxing income. Second, an examination of deductions is necessary to determine whether their continued existence is related to the basic reasons why our society adopted and maintains an income tax. Third, one should ascertain whether deductions are required to insure the primacy of fundamental social, economic, and political values. Judging the validity of a given deduction involves balancing all the above factors; none of them alone should be determinative.

* * *

Personal deductions exempt from taxation expenditures or losses that do not constitute consumption; receipts, so adjusted, equal [Haig-Simons] income. The deduction for state and local income taxes represents such an essential adjustment. On the other hand, the deduction for state and local gasoline taxes is an example of a deduction that was unwarranted: these expenditures constituted consumption. The deductions for state and local sales and property taxes are not easily categorized. Although such taxes represent funds that are not consumed by the taxpayer, but rather by the general public, they are arguably incidents of consumption. As such, they are similar to many other taxes that are indirectly borne by consumers. * * *

Considering the principal reasons for adopting and maintaining an income tax system, one recognizes the need to insure that our tax structure is geared toward an individual's ability to pay. As a result, the involuntary nature of state and local income taxes makes them ideal candidates for deduction. Both property and sales taxes are involuntary only to the extent they are imposed on true essentials; therefore the deductibility of a vast majority of these taxes cannot be justified on the ground that they impair one's ability to pay. * * * Although at least two other reasons support an income tax—its role as an economic stabilizer and its capacity to raise substantial amounts of revenue in an efficient fashion—neither suggests that a further erosion of the tax base is required to accommodate the base to these considerations. A deduction for income, sales, and property taxes does not present substantial administrative and compliance burdens and their continued deductibility cannot be rejected on that ground. Moreover, the continued deductibility of these taxes probably has a mild positive impact on the role of the income tax as an economic stabilizer.

Considering the role of section 164 in a federal system, one must conclude that complete repeal of section 164 would produce a neutral environment in which the states could shape their legislative programs. However, because the existence of section 164 facilitates the states' revenue raising efforts, repeal would probably impair the ability of a number of states to fund programs adequately, thus placing more of the burden of funding programs on the federal government. Partial repeal of the deduction would render some of the states' principal sources of revenue nondeductible and others deductible. Arguably, states should not be subject to this indirect form of pressure in determining the composition of their revenue raising programs. However, because * * * repeal of the sales tax deduction would probably not produce a significant shift away from this tax toward the income tax, this consideration may merit little weight. * * *

After weighing the above competing considerations, this author suggests retaining the deduction for state and local income taxes. Moreover, because it is unclear whether the state sales and property taxes represent nonconsumption expenditures, and because state finances would be adversely affected if the taxes were repealed, one might conclude that the deduction for sales and property taxes should continue. Ultimate resolution of that issue, however, should hinge on whether another adequate accommodation to the revenue interests of the states can be found. If such an accommodation exists, repeal of the deduction for either the sales or property taxes would probably be desirable. * * *

A NEW FEDERAL TAX TREATMENT
OF STATE AND LOCAL TAXES
JB McCombs[*]

19 Pacific Law Journal 747, 748-50, 753-55, 759-62, 764 (1988)

The Haig-Simons definition of income is widely accepted as describing the theoretically ideal income tax base. It defines income as the sum of the taxpayer's consumption of goods and services plus the net increase in his or her savings and investments during the year. There is no serious argument that state and local tax payments represent any form of savings or investment by the individual taxpayer. Therefore, the focus throughout this article is on their possible characterization as a form of consumption by the taxpayer.

One plausible view of a sales tax is that it is an integral part of the cost of consumption. Because consumption is one component of the Haig-Simons definition of income, that view leads to the conclusion that sales tax payments are part of one's income, and should not be deductible for federal income tax purposes. In other words, the sales tax on a new stereo is no different, economically, than the actual purchase price of the stereo. From this viewpoint, the recent change[h] improves the theoretical soundness of the law.

The foregoing argument appears to be correct, if one views the issue through a close-up lens. This author looks at the big picture and comes to a different conclusion.

---

*. At time of original publication, Assistant Professor of Law, University of Nebraska.

h. Professor McCombs is referring to the repeal of the deduction for S-L sales taxes made by the Tax Reform Act of 1986. (Ed.)

In a world where the average individual taxpayer spends ninety-eight percent of his earnings, there is very little practical difference between an income tax that takes five percent from the taxpayer as he earns it, and a sales tax that takes five percent from the taxpayer as he spends it. The taxing government receives an essentially identical pound of flesh under either system. In both cases, the taxpayer has the same amount of after tax income remaining to purchase the goods and services he desires to consume. Although the two systems as found in practice have somewhat different impacts due to their differing deductions and exemptions, as a general proposition sales tax and income tax are more alike than different in their real economic effect. They represent government attempts to take water from the same stream, but simply at different points along its course. The theoretical argument to distinguish them breaks down when transferred to the real world where saving approaches zero and income virtually equals consumption.

The similarity between sales and income tax increases when a consideration of the property tax is added to the analysis. One major difference between the economic impact of an income tax and that of a sales tax is that the dollars used to buy[8] or rent a home are subjected to the income tax, but are not normally reached by the sales tax. The real property tax, by taxing those dollars at the expenditure end of the stream, fills this gap left by the sales tax structure. A property tax can be viewed as a massive sales tax on the construction and sale of a new home, which is collected (with interest) over the life of the home. Sales and property taxes, viewed together, tax nearly all dollars as they are spent. The income tax reaches nearly all dollars as they are received. An income tax dips from the taxpayers stream of money at one point, while the sales and property taxes together take from the same stream at a different location. Therefore, any federal distinction between these three types of general revenue taxes is not well founded in theory.

The foregoing argument is not meant to imply that all forms of state and local taxes are economically equivalent and should receive consistent federal tax treatment. The basic similarity between the three principal types of tax systems does not carry over to a sales or excise tax imposed on a narrow category of goods or services. The taxes imposed on liquor and cigarettes are not at all comparable to an income tax, because a class of people who all have the same income will spend widely varying amounts on alcohol and tobacco. * * *

Furthermore, the separate treatment of gasoline taxes is similarly defensible. In addition to the preceding analysis of narrow based sales taxes, which does apply to the gas tax, another difference between the gas tax and the three principal types of taxes is the fact that a gas tax is intended as, and has the effect of, a toll for the use of the roads. The more one drives, the more

---

8. I am referring here to the actual purchase price, to the extent paid in cash, or principal payments on a home loan.

one pays. It is economically equivalent to having a toll booth on every road in the state, but is much simpler and more efficient. * * *

A Closer Scrutiny of State and Local Tax Payments, In Light of Benefits from State and Local Governments

Professor Turnier states that "economists are in wide agreement that payments of state income taxes do not provide taxpayers with benefits which are in any way commensurate with the tax paid."[17] Nevertheless, each taxpayer does receive some level of direct benefits from state and local government programs, and it seems fair to presume that such direct benefits were funded with a portion of that particular individual's state and local tax payments. The fact that the payment is often much greater than the benefit is not sufficient reason to totally ignore the benefit.

* * *

A more appropriate test is the directness of the benefit. When Mr. and Ms. Taxpayer pay their state and local taxes, and some of those dollars are used to provide assistance to the handicapped, Mr. and Ms. Taxpayer have a benefit, which is the satisfaction of living in a compassionate society. That benefit is extremely indirect. The government's primary intention in making that particular expenditure was to benefit the handicapped persons who qualify for the particular program. On the other hand, if some of the dollars paid by Mr. and Ms. Taxpayer are used to educate their children, the benefit to them is extremely direct. * * *

This argument is leading, first, to the point that the value of goods and services provided by a state or local government to a direct beneficiary should be included in the definition of consumption, as that term is used in the Haig-Simons definition of income. From that conclusion, this author makes the argument that, as a theoretical ideal, tax payments to state and local governments should not be deducted for federal income tax purposes to the extent of the taxpayer's receipt of direct benefits from those governments. * * *

If one can assume that taxpayers who itemize their deductions are found primarily in the middle class and above, the scope of inquiry into direct benefits can be narrowed.

The task is to identify the major state and local government programs from which the middle class and above (hereinafter, for simplicity, the middle class) receive at least their pro rata share of the benefits. For example, if a city of 1,000 residents spends $40,000 to provide police protection, it is fair to say that the average middle class resident enjoys approximately $40 of police protection. If this city spends $15,000 for its symphony, one would be certain that the average middle class resident will enjoy more than $15 of symphonic performance, because the poor generally do not partake of such services in proportion to their numbers. * * * Finally, if this city spends $25,000 on its

---

17. Turnier, *Personal Deductions and Tax Reform: The High Road and the Low Road*, 31 VILL. L. REV. 1703, 1717 (1986).

welfare program, it is neither accurate [nor] fair to say that the average middle class resident receives $25 in direct benefits from that program. * * *

Some fairly obvious nominees to the category of programs that directly benefit the middle class are education,[i] roads, health and hospitals, police protection, and fire protection. * * *

This approach can now be applied to some actual figures for government spending. In 1984 the state and local governments of America spent a combined total of $145.3 billion (from their sales, property, and individual income tax revenues) on the following programs: education, roads, health and hospitals, police protection, and fire protection. Based on a population of 236 million, this translates into an expenditure of $616 per capita. * * * Until some rigorous empirical study and statistical analysis are conducted, let us assume that at least 80% of the itemizing taxpayers receive direct state and local government benefits in the amount of $500 or more each year.
* * *

[T]his article is proposing that a minimum floor of $500 in state and local tax payments be nondeductible, with any excess remaining deductible. * * *

Progressivity

Another possible modification is to calculate the proposed floor as a percentage of adjusted gross income (AGI), as is currently done with the medical, casualty, and "miscellaneous itemized" deductions. That would eliminate the admittedly regressive effect of the proposal made by this article.
* * *

Notes and Questions

1.   Is the deduction for S-L taxes, or some of them, necessary for accurate measurement of income, or is section 164 best viewed as a subsidy? Would you give the same answer for all types of S-L taxes?

2.   Is the deduction for S-L income taxes justified on the theory that the taxes are essentially indistinguishable from "ordinary and necessary" income-producing expenses deductible under sections 162 and 212?

3.   Is it sufficient answer to the preceding question to note that federal income taxes are even harder for the taxpayer to avoid than S-L income taxes, yet federal taxes have not been deductible since 1917? Or is Professor Turnier correct in arguing that "one can characterize the 1917 changes as nothing more than a significant increase in the tax rate,"[j] which therefore tell us nothing about the propriety of a deduction for S-L income taxes?

---

i. Professor McCombs acknowledged, and discussed at some length, the possible distortions in computation arising from the fact that most S-L taxes are spent on public education, which is utilized at widely varying rates by itemizing taxpayers. (Ed.)

j. The quoted language, which is not part of the excerpt reprinted above, is found at 66 CORNELL L. REV., at 267.

4.   A generation ago, marginal federal income tax rates stood at 91 percent. With some states imposing income tax rates of 10 percent or more, the deduction was thought to be necessary to prevent confiscatory taxation. Assuming this problem arose in the future, is the more appropriate solution for the federal government to allow deduction of S-L taxes, or vice versa? (Either route avoids the possibility of combined tax rates in excess of 100 percent.) At present, some states allow deduction of federal income taxes in computing state income tax liability.

5.   Assuming that the deduction for S-L taxes is viewed as a subsidy, who are the beneficiaries—high-tax states and localities, or high-bracket taxpayers who itemize deductions?   Section 103's exclusion from federal income tax of interest received by holders of S-L bonds is generally viewed as a boon for the issuers of the bonds, not their holders. Does section 164 lend itself to the same analysis?

6.   Or might the beneficiaries be low-income people in high-tax states, who receive higher welfare benefits from S-L taxes made politically possible by the deduction?

7.   How would you expect the elimination of the federal deduction for gasoline taxes to have affected consumption? In 1978, Congress ended the deductibility of S-L gasoline taxes, in part because "in view of the pressing national need to conserve energy and reduce oil imports, the Federal government should not in effect partially subsidize nonbusiness consumption of motor fuels through a deduction for State-local taxes on such fuels."[k] Fourteen years earlier, however, the Senate Finance Committee had defended the deductibility of the gasoline tax, in part arguing that "to deny the deduction of [the gasoline] tax while allowing the deduction of property, income, and general sales taxes tends to encourage States to use other than automotive taxes as their more important revenue sources."[l] If removing the deduction for S-L gasoline taxes had no effect on S-L tax policies, then ending federal deductibility would increase the after-tax cost of gasoline and discourage its consumption. But if states and localities reacted to the removal of federal deductibility by lowering gasoline taxes (or, much more likely in the real world, by refraining from increasing those taxes), then the removal of deductibility might have had the unintended effect of making gasoline consumption cheaper than it otherwise would have been.

8.   Quite apart from energy and environmental concerns, deductibility of gasoline taxes is almost uniformly condemned because the taxes are viewed

---

k. H. Rep. No. 1445, 95th Cong., 2d Sess., at 42 (1978); S. Rep. No. 1263, 95th Cong., 2d Sess., at 58 (1978).

l. S. Rep. No. 830, 88th Cong., 2d Sess., at 54 (1964).

as user fees, and are usually earmarked for highway construction and maintenance. But if one state finances its highways with income taxes while another employs gasoline taxes, should that difference mean that the first state, but not the second, should be able to shift part of its burden to the federal government? Or, if a state should choose to adopt high gasoline taxes to finance, let us say, education, why should the form of the tax bar the deduction?

9.   Congress has been solicitous of the homeowner in the tax laws, through provisions such as section 163(h)(2)(D) (excluding most home mortgage interest from the definition of nondeductible personal interest) and section 121 (excluding from income up to $500,000 of gain from the sale of a principal residence under certain circumstances). Moreover, the imputed income arising from home ownership goes untaxed. See Chapter Three. Is the deduction for property taxes on owner-occupied residences an additional subsidy for homeowners vis-à-vis renters?[m] Could one argue instead that the renter automatically gets the benefit of the landlord's deduction for property taxes in the form of lower rent—and without the requirement of itemizing deductions?

10. Is the problem one of economic efficiency rather than equity? Perhaps the housing market has adjusted to the property tax deduction with the result that housing is overvalued, as compared to its value in a non-tax world. It might be argued that home buyers are not really benefitted by the deduction, because they have paid for it in the form of higher purchase prices. Is the principal problem that the deduction artificially increases housing values and thus diverts resources to housing of all types?

11. On the other hand, perhaps it is the S-L real estate taxes themselves, rather than the federal deduction for those taxes, that distort the allocation of resources, and distort it *against* real estate investment. Real estate taxes tend to be much heavier than property taxes on other forms of wealth, such as securities and other types of intangible wealth. Real estate taxes owe much to tradition, and to the fact that real estate is very difficult to conceal either from the assessor or the collector. It may be that such taxes distort resources away from real estate investment, and that the federal income tax deduction of those taxes has the salutary effect of reducing that distortion. Do you find this argument persuasive?

---

m. There may be historical irony to the S-L tax deduction, now thought to favor homeowners. Professor Turnier, in a portion of his article that is not excerpted, suggested that the original deduction for taxes may have been designed to avoid unfairly favoring renters vis-à-vis homeowners. Congress allowed a deduction for rent in tax statutes enacted to finance the War Between the States, and Professor Turnier concluded that "the personal deduction for taxes probably arose out of a desire to equalize the tax treatment of renters and nonrenters." 66 CORNELL L. REV., at 269.

12. In general, should the form of the S-L tax be as important as it is under present federal tax law, which allows full deductibility of some S-L taxes and no deduction for others?

13. Writing before the federal deduction for S-L sales taxes was repealed in 1986, Dr. Noto and Dr. Zimmerman identified several revenue-neutral alternatives to abolition of the sales tax deduction. What were these alternatives? Which alternative did they prefer? Do you agree with their conclusions?

14. There is considerable difference of opinion concerning whether principles of federalism suggest that the federal government should allow deduction either of all major S-L taxes—income, property and general sales taxes—or of none. For example, in the Revenue Act of 1964, both the Ways and Means Committee and the Finance Committee concluded that if income and property taxes were to be deductible, the deductibility of sales taxes should be continued, because "it is important for the Federal Government to remain neutral as to the relative use made of these three forms of State and local taxation."[n] In 1986, Congress changed this policy. Is Congress improperly favoring states that rely on income and property taxes rather than sales taxes?

15. Assuming Congress' denial of a deduction for sales taxes is viewed as interference with S-L decision making, can such interference be justified as a federal attempt to discourage S-L use of regressive taxes?

On the other hand, note the antiprogressive effect of making S-L income taxes deductible. The ostensible degree of progressivity in S-L income taxes is reduced by the federal deduction. For example, a nine percent state income tax amounts to only six percent if the taxpayer itemizes and is in a 33 percent federal bracket.

16. If you agree that the federal government should "remain neutral," by treating major S-L taxes the same, should this be extended to *all* S-L taxes? In the recent past, S-L taxes such as "sin" taxes and gasoline taxes were deductible.

17. How much weight should be given to administrative concerns? It is relatively easy for taxpayers and the Internal Revenue Service to ascertain the amount of S-L income and property taxes paid. At the other extreme, it would be almost impossible to keep track of "sin" taxes and amusement taxes, and one might expect liberal guesses (a kinder, gentler term for fraud) from taxpayers, with the amounts being so small that the Service would rarely challenge them. Even the most conscientious taxpayer would have difficulty

n. H. Rep. No. 749, 88th Cong., 1st Sess., at 49 (1963); S. Rep. No. 830, 88th Cong., 2d Sess., at 54 (1964).

keeping track of gasoline taxes, except by reference to tables corresponding to mileage driven during the year, or of sales taxes, except by reference to tables based on income and family size.

18.   The primary motivation for restricting S-L deductibility was typical of the basic policy trade-off that the "revenue-neutral" 1986 Act embodied. In order to reduce rates substantially without cutting federal revenues, it was necessary to expand the tax base.   Limiting or eliminating the federal deduction for S-L sales taxes was a way to broaden the base.

However, the tax policy issues concerning deductibility of S-L taxes become enmeshed in broader issues about the proper scope of government and the means of financing it.   For example, if only some S-L taxes are to be deductible (and thus encouraged by federal law), one might expect liberals to encourage deductibility of the income tax, which is typically progressive, and to argue against deductibility of the sales tax, which is typically regressive with respect to income.   In the same vein, it may not be surprising that the Reagan Administration, which is identified with a preference for lower taxes at all levels of government, proposed an end to the deductibility of all S-L taxes. Treasury I argued that this would end an inappropriate subsidy to high-tax states, and an improper bias in favor of taxes rather than user fees. Critics of Treasury I saw it as an indirect method of attacking the social spending of high-tax states. If section 164 makes raising S-L taxes easier politically, does this argue in favor of retaining or repealing the provision?

19.   Perhaps a federal subsidy to high-tax states can be justified if the high taxes are a means of dealing with a national problem that impacts some states more severely than others.   Consider the following argument from Professor Edward Yorio:

Whenever a state imposes an above-average tax burden on its citizens, the excess may be due to one (or more) of the following factors: (1) the state provides more goods and services to its citizens than do other states; (2) the state is less efficient than other states; * * * (3) the cost of living in that state and hence the cost of government goods and services is higher; (4) citizens of that state endorse a higher level of government responsibility for solving social problems than citizens of other states; or (5) the state has been forced—or has chosen—to expend tax monies to alleviate a national social problem.

Of these explanations for variations in tax burdens among the states, only the last justifies a deduction for state and local taxes. * * *

[A]bove average rates of taxation in a particular state may be due to the state's assumption of a national burden, such as the costs of providing for an unusually large number of illegal aliens. Where

state spending produces spillover benefits for the rest of the nation,
the case for a deduction for state taxes is strong.[o] * * *
Assuming one accepts Professor Yorio's argument, how does one separate
factor 4 from factor 5 if, for example, a high-tax/high-social-benefit state
attracts, and provides for, a disproportionate share of the nation's homeless?
In addition, keep in mind that costs and benefits are usually more complex
than they initially appear. For example, employers in states with large
numbers of illegal aliens (the example chosen by Professor Yorio) benefit from
a supply of low-cost labor.

20. Do you agree with Treasury I's characterization of S-L taxes as a
form of consumption? Does it matter?

21. Do you agree with Treasury I's assertion that S-L taxes should not
be viewed as involuntary assessments because of the taxpayers' collective
control over the political machinery that levies the taxes? Professor Turnier
(not in the article excerpted above) ridiculed this suggestion: "On the basis of
that sort of reasoning, one can conclude that military conscription in a
democracy results in an all volunteer army or that the victims of capital
punishment in a democracy have committed suicide."[p] Professor Due, on the
other hand, argued that the taxes are "mandatory payments, and particular
individuals may strongly object. * * * But for the community as a whole, state
and local tax payments constitute voluntary payments for services rendered
and are as discretionary as the purchase of new cars or suits of clothes."[q]

22. Do you agree that the ability of S-L taxpayers to relocate to a
different taxing jurisdiction means that their S-L taxes should not be regarded
as involuntary?

23. Canada allows no deduction for provincial taxes. For a comparison
of Canadian and U.S. practice, including a brief discussion of "equalization
payments * * * paid by the Canadian federal government to the poorer
provinces," *see* Gordon Bale, *The Treasury's Proposals for Tax Reform: A
Canadian Perspective,* 48 LAW & COMTEMP. PROBS. 151, 157-67 (1985).

C. A FEDERAL CREDIT FOR STATE AND LOCAL TAXES?

Virtually all debate on the federal tax treatment of S-L taxes has centered
on whether payment of such taxes should give rise to a *deduction*. A

---

o. Edward Yorio, *The President's Tax Proposals: A Major Step in the Right Direction,* 53
FORDHAM L. REV. 1255, 1279-80 (1985).

p. William J. Turnier, *Personal Deductions and Tax Reform: The High Road and the Low
Road,* 31 VILL. L. REV. 1703, 1735 (1986).

q. John F. Due, *Personal Deductions, in* COMPREHENSIVE INCOME TAXATION 37, 51 (Joseph
A. Pechman ed., 1977).

deduction, however, merely reduces the sting of S-L taxes. On the other hand, it is certainly possible to envision a federal *credit* for S-L taxes. To the extent a federal credit were available, a taxpayer would be indifferent to the level of S-L taxes, because the burden would be offset by a dollar-for-dollar reduction in federal taxes. For example, under a ten percent credit, a taxpayer with pre-credit federal income tax liability of $5,000 might be allowed a credit of the lesser of $500 or his state income tax liability. An immediate consequence of such a system would be that all states would enact income taxes sufficient to absorb the credit, because this would give the states additional tax revenue without additional cost to their taxpayers. In 1959, Professor Walter Heller, while arguing that S-L taxes other than income taxes should not even be deductible, offered the Ways and Means Committee a detailed proposal for a limited federal income tax credit for state income taxes:

DEDUCTIONS AND CREDITS
FOR STATE INCOME TAXES
Walter W. Heller[*]

House Committee on Ways and Means, 86th Congress, 1st Session

1 Tax Revision Compendium 419, 423-27 (1959)

The Case for a Federal Credit

The case for a Federal credit for State income taxes paid does not rest on the removal of income tax deductibility. Retention or removal will affect the form which the credit should take, but not the underlying case for it. That case rests on (1) the need for drawing on the superior taxing power of the Federal Government to undergird the strenuous State tax efforts required to meet the severe financial strains on State and local budgets today and in the years ahead; (2) the need to reduce interstate differentials in income taxation and thereby to allay the fears of interstate migration of industry and wealth which plague the States in their efforts to make full use of their tax potential; (3) the need for Federal fiscal support in a form that will reduce rather than increase income inequalities among the States.

* * *

The Fear of Interstate Competition

Another important cause of favorable action on a Federal tax credit is the impact that fears of driving out industry and wealth have in choking off the full use of State tax resources. Although every unbiased study of location factors ranks taxes well below such considerations as skill and productivity of the labor force, closeness to markets, availability of plentiful water and low-cost power, the fear of interstate competition continues to be a major, even a growing, influence in the politics of State taxation. And the State income tax movement bears the full brunt of taxpayer threats to seek haven in friendlier tax territory. This process of playing off one State against another has the net

---

[*]. At time of original publication, Professor, University of Minnesota.

effect of weakening the financial base of responsible self-government and striking hard at the tax which responds most readily to economic growth. * * *

Congress should follow the precedent it established 35 years ago when it enacted a Federal estate tax credit to bring to an end the vicious competitive rate cutting which had threatened to run State death taxes into the ground. A Federal income tax credit averaging 5 or 10 percent would not remove the interstate competition threat entirely, but it would put a substantial noncompetitive floor under State income taxes and reduce the struggle for competitive advantage which has retarded the use of the outstanding growth tax in the State revenue system.

Interstate Equalization

Either substitution of a Federal credit for deductibility, whether as a flat percentage of the Federal tax or on a sliding-scale basis, or supplementation of deductibility by a sliding-scale credit would serve to reduce somewhat the existing interstate inequalities of income. * * * [T]he protective impact of deductibility is greater, the wealthier the state; the higher the brackets a State's taxpayers are in, on the average, the larger the percentage of the State income tax burden that can be "exported" to the Federal Government.
* * *

[S]ubstitution of a flat credit would materially improve the distribution of benefits by income groups in the sense of sharing a larger portion of the benefits with the lower bracket taxpayers than they receive at present under deductibility. * * * A corresponding improvement in the interstate impact of the allowance for State income taxes would also take place with the substitution of the credit for the deduction. Proportionately, the residents of the poorer States would get a substantially larger part of any given benefit in the form of a tax credit than they now get in the form of a deduction from income. The net effect would be a shift in Federal support from the wealthier to the poorer States.

This shift could be magnified by the adoption of a sliding-scale credit of the type illustrated in table 3. Here, the credit would be 20 percent of the first $200 of Federal income tax, 10 percent of the next $300, and 1 percent of the remainder. If Federal deductibility were retained, it would be imperative to put a Federal credit in this negatively graduated form in order to balance somewhat the bias of deductibility in favor of high incomes. Even if the deduction were eliminated, the desire to build a positive interstate equalizing effect into the credit for State income taxes might well lead to some form of the sliding scale.

Table 3 demonstrates the equalizing effect. The central column shows that State taxpayers in Mississippi and Montana would get almost twice as large an average credit against their Federal tax as those in Delaware, and about one-third more than those in New York, Michigan, and Illinois. Since the average credit allowed in each State depends on both the average size and the distribution of income, the suggested sliding-scale credit would not accomplish the perfect inverse correlation between size of credit and per capita income that might be desired. But its general effect would be the desired one: to provide more fiscal support to the poorer, and less fiscal support to the wealthier, States.

Table 3 – *Allowable Credit Against Federal Income Tax Under a Sliding-scale Credit Plan: 20 percent against the first $200 of Federal tax, 10 percent against the next $300, and 1 percent against tax in excess of $500, Selected States, 1956*

[dollar amounts in thousands]

States	1956 Federal individual income tax liability	Total Federal tax credit allowable to residents of each State under sliding scale credit plan	
		Amount	As percent of Federal liability
Arkansas	$133,344	$13,228	9.9
California	3,373,902	269,593	8.0
Delaware	161,748	8,600	5.3
Florida	644,329	51,198	7.9
Georgia	385,097	36,781	9.6
Illinois	2,611,643	203,751	7.8
Kansas	303,256	29,435	9.7
Louisiana	388,475	32,513	8.4
Maryland	646,807	57,981	9.0
Michigan	1,839,256	143,024	7.8
Minnesota	526,262	50,349	9.6
Mississippi	119,728	12,010	10.0
Missouri	746,046	65,349	8.8
Montana	97,412	9,790	10.1
New York	4,232,431	327,914	7.7
Ohio	2,149,144	181,794	8.5
Pennsylvania	2,373,040	207,911	8.8
Rhode Island	166,319	15,313	9.2
Tennessee	377,869	35,355	9.4
Texas	1,404,530	114,278	8.1
Wisconsin	686,386	63,210	9.2

Concluding Comments

* * *

As to the Federal revenue loss, this would depend on the size of the credit and the action taken on other State and local tax deductions. Removal of all such deductions would make possible a Federal credit averaging 5 percent without any appreciable revenue loss. * * *

Finally, what of the coercion issue? The crediting device represents a paradoxical combination of freedom and coercion. Its most fundamental purpose is to protect the power of the purse underlying State sovereignty and local independence. Moreover, Federal credits, while certain to bring about greater uniformity not only in income tax burdens but also in the structure of income taxation at the State level, leave ample room for variations in State definitions of income, exemptions, and tax rates. At the same time, the credit would strongly induce if not force [states without an income tax] to adopt at least minimum, credit-absorbing personal income taxes. On balance, it seems fair to conclude that the Federal tax credit, particularly if substituted for the present deduction for state income taxes, offers the States a large gain in fiscal integrity and independence in exchange for a relatively small loss in freedom of taxation.

Notes and Questions

24. It is important to remember that Professor Heller wrote more than 40 years ago. Obviously, the dollar amounts must be updated for inflation. More important may be the political and policy implications of large federal deficits. In developing the idea that the federal government should use its "superior taxing power" in support of the states, Professor Heller pointed to "[p]rojections for the next decade [that] generally forecast rising surpluses for the Federal Government, rising deficits for State-local governments." This same projection seems currently accurate for many financially strapped S-L governments, but is not descriptive of a federal budget running dozen-digit deficits.

25. The Internal Revenue Code provides taxpayers their choice of a deduction (section 164) or a credit (section 901) for income taxes paid to a foreign country. Normally, the credit proves more beneficial. Thus, if a U.S. citizen owns stock in a British company that pays dividends taxable by Great Britain, the taxpayer must include the dividends in U.S. income, but receives a credit for British tax paid or withheld (not to exceed the U.S. tax attributable to the British-source income). Presumably, Congress allows the credit in order to avoid double taxation—the same income being taxed by both Great Britain and the United States. Why do considerations of equity lead us to allow a credit with respect to foreign income taxes, but not for S-L income taxes? (Superficially, it might appear that a New York resident taxed by both New York and the federal government was being subjected to double taxation on the

same income, in the same way as the U.S.-citizen recipient of British dividends.)

26. States *inter se* normally provide a credit comparable to the federal foreign tax credit, for income taxes paid to another state. For example, if an Arkansas resident works part of the year in Missouri and is subjected to Missouri income tax, Arkansas requires inclusion of the Missouri-source income but then allows a credit for the Missouri tax paid (not to exceed the Arkansas tax attributable to the Missouri-source income).

27. Why would an unlimited federal credit for state income taxes be completely unworkable?

28. In part, Professor Heller justified his proposal as an effort to discourage both relocation by taxpayers, and actions by states and localities to affect relocation decisions. Why might enactment of his proposal have that effect? Does your answer depend upon whether the state's income tax is imposed at a rate in excess of the allowable federal credit?

29. Do you agree with Professor Heller that S-L efforts to attract industry with preferential tax rates are objectionable? Professor Heller states that tax considerations are less important than factors such as "skill and productivity of the labor force, closeness to markets, availability of plentiful water and low-cost power." Should states with less able labor forces, and less favorable locations and resources, be able to compete for industry by offering lower taxes?

30. Interstate tax competition is not limited to S-L *income* taxes, of course. Indeed, Professor Heller referred to the early competition among states for the wealthy elderly, who might be attracted by a low rate of death taxes. Congress responded by allowing a credit against the federal estate tax for state death taxes up to a certain level. This level became the minimum state death tax, because a state could no longer provide an advantage to its decedents by lowering the state death tax below the level that would be fully offset by the federal credit. See section 2011. For further discussion of this credit, see Chapter Nine, Note #17 (page 568).

31. What of competition arising from other preferential tax treatment, notably the property tax? And what of a state or locality providing a free building, such as a stadium to attract (or retain) a professional sports franchise?

32. Enactment of Professor Heller's proposal would mean that all states not having an income tax, or not having a tax high enough to absorb the

federal credit, would immediately change their laws to take advantage of the federal credit. In this sense, Professor Heller acknowledged that his proposal entailed, "a large measure of federal coercion." On the other hand, he argued that his proposal "represents a paradoxical combination of freedom and coercion." In what sense might a state find greater freedom of action under this proposal?

33. Focusing on individuals rather than states, a federal tax benefit structured as a credit probably would be of more value than an itemized deduction to low-income taxpayers, and of less value to high-income taxpayers. Does this argue in favor of the credit?

34. Professor Heller would prefer a sliding-scale credit, which would allow low-income taxpayers a relatively higher credit. For example (writing a generation ago), he suggested a credit of 20 percent of first $200 of federal income tax, 10 percent of the next $300, and one percent of the remainder. What justifications did he offer? Do you agree?

Professor Heller appeared to focus at least as much on high- and low-income *states* as on high- and low-income *individuals*. Obviously, some rich individuals live in poor states, and vice versa. Should our focus be on an equitable distribution of burden among rich and poor states, or among rich and poor individuals?

PART V

TAXATION OF BUSINESS AND INVESTMENT INCOME

For decades, issues relating to the proper income taxation of business and investment income have remained among the most politically contentious tax policy issues facing Congress. Chapter Fourteen covers issues involving corporations and dividends. Initially, we face the fundamental question of who bears the corporate income tax—shareholders, employees, customers, the return on capital in the economy generally, or the corporations themselves. Assuming that the corporate income tax is borne primarily by shareholders, who are also taxed on dividends distributed by the corporation and on capital gains attributable to retained earnings, the next question is what, if anything, should be done about this "double tax." The numerous solutions that have been offered to the double tax—including the temporary compromise enacted as part of the Jobs and Growth Tax Relief Reconciliation Act of 2003—are described. The economic implications of the tax treatment of debt and interest are considered. The chapter concludes with a political analysis of the double tax issue.

Chapter Fifteen deals with a perennial high-profile issue, the treatment of capital gains and losses. The unsettled history of their treatment is described. Consideration of unique features of capital gains, and of the related issue of whether there is a "true" capital asset, leads to consideration of peripheral areas where capital gain treatment is accorded to income that may appear to be "ordinary." The central topic considered in the chapter is the large number of asserted policy justifications for taxing capital gains more gently than ordinary income. The realization rule figures prominently in this discussion, and even more centrally in the issue of restrictions on the deductibility of losses. Finally, the politically-charged assertion that the tax treatment of capital gain is an important factor in determining national rates of saving and investment is explored.

Chapter Sixteen addresses the important issue of accurately measuring taxable income in a climate of changing price levels. Present inflation adjustments, through which tax brackets and a number of other key figures in the Internal Revenue Code are "indexed" against the Consumer Price Index, are described. Greater attention is given to the more complex—and more important—issues of whether, and how, to apply inflation adjustments to the measurement of gains, losses, interest deductions, and debt (from the perspective of borrowers as well as lenders). Because the distorting influence of inflation is closely linked to the passage of time, policy issues related to inflation are significantly affected by the tension between the realization rule and the mark-to-market approach, which adheres to the Haig-Simons definition of income. Chapter Sixteen closes with a detailed examination of the relationship between indexation and the realization rule.

CHAPTER FOURTEEN

CORPORATIONS AND DIVIDENDS

> *Commentators frequently criticize the double taxation of corporate income as contrary to the tax policy goals of equity and efficiency. An income tax is equitable when individuals with equal incomes bear equal tax burdens, irrespective of the sources from which their incomes are derived. Critics of double taxation claim that double taxation is inequitable because individuals receiving corporate income bear a heavier tax burden than similarly situated persons deriving their incomes from noncorporate sources. An efficient tax does not change the economic decisions that individuals would make in the absence of the tax. Critics claim that double taxation is inefficient because it causes taxpayers to avoid those alternatives that are subject to double taxation. The implications of double taxation on equity and efficiency have led many to conclude that distributed corporate income should be relieved from the burden of the corporate tax.*[a]

A. INTRODUCTION

For decades, the treatment of corporations and shareholders has been a leading question of tax policy, but of less political prominence than others, such as capital gains. The corporate/shareholder issue leaped to the front of the line in 2003, with President Bush's proposal to exempt most dividends from taxation. The compromise resolution of the issue in the Jobs and Growth Tax Relief Reconciliation Act of 2003 (the "2003 Act") assures that the issue will remain a high-profile issue for the foreseeable future.

In general, Congressional Republicans supported the President's proposal, while Democrats opposed it. A few Republicans—whose support in the closely divided Congress was crucial—concerned about revenue loss, refused to support full abolition of taxes on dividends. The compromise will tax dividends at the same rate as capital gains (a maximum rate of 15 percent under the 2003 Act), rather than exemption as the President proposed or as ordinary income, as prior law had provided. Thus, President Bush contends that the 2003 Act stopped short, while Democrats, observing that high-income taxpayers are the primary individual recipients of dividends, deride the reduced rate as a giveaway to the rich.

The temporary nature of the present compromise is emphasized by the

---

a. Jeffrey L. Kwall, *The Uncertain Case Against the Double Taxation of Corporate Income*, 68 N.C. L. REV. 613, 615 (1990).

sunset provisions of the rate reductions in the 2003 Act. The 15 percent rate will last through 2008, after which—on the doubtful assumption that Congress takes no action in the interval—dividends will again be taxed as ordinary income. (For taxpayers in the 10 and 15 percent brackets for ordinary income, the 2003 Act sets even lower rates for dividends—five percent in 2003-07, and zero in 2008, before returning to ordinary income rates in 2009.)

The tax treatment of corporations and shareholders is not only topical, but also of substantial economic importance. The taxes considered in this chapter generate significant revenue. The corporate income tax currently yields more than 10 percent of total federal tax revenues, as compared to 49 percent from individual income taxes and 36 percent from social insurance taxes.[b] Moreover, dividends paid by C corporations and taxed to individual shareholders have accounted for over three percent of taxable income under the individual income tax,[c] though the revenue yield from taxing dividends will be reduced in the future, at least through 2008, due to the application of capital gains rates to dividend income.

The preeminent policy issues in the taxation of corporations and shareholders relate to the degree to which tax law should follow nontax law to treat corporations and their shareholders as separate taxable entities. C corporations are taxable entities, separate from their shareholders, in contrast to partnerships[d] and S corporations.[e] Because corporations are not allowed a deduction for dividends paid, and the dividends are subject to tax in the hands of individual shareholders—traditionally, at ordinary income rates—the result is a double tax on income earned by a corporation and distributed as dividends to its individual owners.

The second tax cannot necessarily be avoided by a corporate policy of not paying dividends, even if one ignores the slight possibility of imposition of the accumulated earnings tax.[f] To the extent that common stock of a corporation appreciates in value because of undistributed income that has been earned and

---

b. In 2002, federal receipts from corporate income taxes were an estimated $201 billion, individual income tax receipts $949 billion, and social insurance tax receipts $708 billion. Total federal receipts amounted to approximately $1.946 trillion. U.S. BUREAU OF THE CENSUS, STATISTICAL ABSTRACT OF THE UNITED STATES: 2002, tbl. 454, at 308 (122nd ed. 2003).

c. In 1999, dividends included in the adjusted gross income of individuals amounted to $132 billion; total taxable income of individuals was $4.136 trillion. *Id.* tbl. 473, at 314. (Not all adjusted gross income becomes taxable income, of course, because some is offset by deductions and personal and dependency exemptions. Nevertheless, it is the case for most individuals that if dividends were not included in the tax base, taxable income would be reduced by the amount of the dividends.)

d. Some publicly traded partnerships are treated as taxable entities under the same provisions that apply to corporations and their shareholders. Section 7704. See Note #12 at page 870.

e. Hereinafter, the term "corporation" should be understood to refer to a C corporation unless otherwise indicated.

f. Sections 531 et seq. impose a tax on "accumulated taxable income," which usually means accumulated earnings of more than $250,000 that are "beyond the reasonable needs of the business."

taxed to the corporation, sale of the stock by the shareholders at a gain produces a second tax, generally in the form of a capital gain.[g] The portion of a capital gain tax that is a second tax due to accumulated earnings is difficult to isolate and measure because the market value of common stock is affected by many other factors.

Corporate shareholders have long been largely exempt from the tax on dividends. The dividends-received deduction in section 243 reflects a decision largely to exempt the passage of earnings from one corporation to another until distribution is finally made to a noncorporate shareholder, who normally would be fully taxed. Dividends received by corporations are entirely tax free if both the corporation paying the dividend and the corporation receiving the dividend are members of an "affiliated group." Under the consolidated returns provisions, this requires an 80-percent-ownership relationship while the earnings are accumulated and distributed. Otherwise, 80 percent of deductions can be deducted by a corporate shareholder that owns at least 20 percent of the stock of the dividend-paying corporation, and 70 percent of dividends are deductible if the corporate shareholder owns less than 20 percent of the payor.[h]

Similar to the individual income tax, the corporate rate structure of section 11 is graduated.[i] A corporation is taxed at 15 percent on the first $50,000 of income, 25 percent on income between $50,000 and $75,000, and 34 percent on income between $75,000 and $10 million. When a corporation's taxable income exceeds $100,000, however, a tax of five percentage points in addition to the 34 percent standard rate is applied to its income until this five-percentage-point tax amounts to $11,750. At this point, when the corporation's taxable income is $335,000, the five-percentage-point "notch" tax rate has absorbed all the advantage from the 15 percent rate and the 25 percent rate on the corporation's first $75,000 of income. The tax rate on income in excess of $10 million is 35 percent. Another notch rate of three additional percentage points, or a total rate of 38 percent, is applied to income in excess of $15 million until (when the corporation's income amounts to $18,333,333) it absorbs the advantage of the 34 percent rate. Thus, as a general rule, large, publicly-traded corporations face a flat rate of 35 percent, while smaller, closely-held corporations pay a lower effective rate.

---

g. The second tax is avoided if the shareholder dies while owning the appreciated stock, and the heir receives a stepped-up basis. The income tax treatment of property passing at death is in flux.; see Chapter Ten and sections 1014 and 1022.

h. Section 246A reduces the dividends-received deduction to the extent that "portfolio stock" is debt-financed. The apparent reason for this provision is to block a corporation's using debt financing to combine an interest deduction with dividend income taxed at preferential rates.

i. Certain personal service corporations are subjected to a flat rate of 35%. See Note #7, at page 869.

Notes and Questions

1.   While the 2003 Act is most realistically viewed as a political compromise, the approach of taxing dividends at capital gains rates can be defended in policy terms. If a corporation distributes its earnings, they are to be taxed at capital gains rates. If, on the other hand, the corporation retains its earnings and reinvests them in the business, presumably the corporation, and its outstanding shares of stock, become more valuable. A shareholder who sells shares at a gain (let us assume the gain is attributable to retained earnings) will also be taxed at capital gains rates.

One policy goal of ending the double tax on dividends—the primary focus of this Chapter, addressed in Subchapter C—is removing the bias against dividends and in favor of retaining earnings. The 2003 Act is reasonably effective in achieving that goal. (The shareholder of the corporation retaining earnings still enjoys a benefit of deferral not available to the shareholder receiving dividends. If the first shareholder's stock appreciates due to retained earnings, the capital gains tax is imposed only when that shareholder chooses to sell his stock. The dividend recipient is taxed immediately, even if the dividends are reinvested.)

2.   The favorable treatment (*i.e.*, taxation at capital gains rates) of dividends under the 2003 Act is conditioned on the shareholder owning the dividend-paying stock for at least 60 days during the 120-day period starting 60 days before the ex-dividend date.[j] (Thus, the shareholder can sell the stock immediately after the dividend is declared, if the shareholder has already owned the stock for 60 days, or can acquire the stock immediately before the ex-dividend date, so long as the shareholder continues to own the stock for an additional 60 days.) Is this rule justified? Is it a rough parallel to the capital gains tax rule, which affords favorable tax rates on sale only to those who are "long-term" owners of the capital asset?

Corporate income tax rates

3. Unlike the individual income tax rates of section 1, the corporate rates of section 11 have been relatively stable since the Tax Reform Act of 1986 reduced the top corporate rate from 46 percent. (The sole change was the addition of the 35 percent rate in 1993; the 1986 Act had set a top corporate rate of 34 percent.) The relationship—or lack of a relationship—between the individual and corporate rates is interesting. Prior to the 1986 Act, the top corporate rate (46 percent) was lower than the top individual rate (50 percent); the 1986 Act reversed this relationship, lowering both rates, but bringing the

---

j. These periods are doubled in the case of preferred stock.

top individual rate (28 percent) lower than the top corporate rate. By 1993, the top individual rate, 39.6 percent, again exceeded the top rate applicable to corporations. For the years 2003-10, the top rate faced by both corporations and individuals is the same—35 percent.[k] This temporary identity seems not to have resulted from any policy decision that the rates should be equal. Assuming that corporations should be taxable entities, what relationship (if any) should be maintained between corporate income tax rates and individual income tax rates?

4. There is no connection between a corporation's tax rate and the tax rates of its individual shareholders. Should there be such a connection?

5. In addition to the regular income tax, section 59A imposes an "environmental tax" of 0.12 percent on income in excess of $2 million. The tax is designed to finance the fund to clean up the environment.

6. Should the corporate income tax have progressive rates, as section 11 generally provides?

7. All income of some personal service corporations is taxed at a flat 35 percent rate. Section 11(b)(2). These corporations perform health, law, engineering, architectural, accounting, actuarial, art performance, or consulting services. Such corporations are viewed as the alter egos of their typically high-income owner/employees, and the high flat rate prevents these individuals from benefitting from the graduated corporate tax structure. Sections 11(b)(2), 448(d)(2).

8. *Dividends received by corporations.* As noted above, corporate shareholders qualify for a 100 percent dividends-received deduction only if the payor corporation and the recipient corporation are members of an affiliated group. Otherwise, the deduction is limited to 70 or 80 percent.

Arguably, this can lead to *triple* taxation. A corporation earns money, is taxed under section 11, and distributes a dividend to its shareholders. Assume that some of these dividends are paid to a corporate shareholder that qualifies for only a 70 percent dividends-received deduction, meaning it is taxed on 30 percent of the dividend. Then the shareholder corporation declares a dividend payable to an individual shareholder, who is taxed on the entire dividend (though now at capital gains rates). Indeed, depending on the number of corporations between the corporation earning the income and the individual

---

k. Under the sunset provisions of present law, the top individual rate is scheduled to increase to 39.6 percent in 2011.

shareholder, there could be four or more levels of tax.

9.   Is the policy basis for dividend relief, for either corporate or individual shareholders, dependent on the income having been taxed by the corporation that originally earned it?   Under the present statutory arrangements, it is possible that income not taxed to the corporation paying the dividend could nonetheless qualify for favorable treatment by the shareholder. (The favorable treatment for individuals is that the dividend is taxed at capital gains rates, and for corporations is the dividends-received deduction.)

Affiliated corporations

10. Groups of affiliated corporations are permitted to file consolidated income tax returns instead of reporting income or loss separately. Dividends are eliminated when paid within an affiliated group of corporations filing a consolidated return.   Treatment of consolidated returns is governed by extensive "legislative" regulations issued pursuant to section 1501.

11. Even if a consolidated return is not filed, if a corporation owns 80 percent or more of the stock of one or more other corporations, these corporations are combined for purposes of applying the graduated income tax rates. Section 1561. Corporations that are owned by the same small group of individuals also are combined for purposes of applying the graduated tax rates. Section 1563(a)(2). What is the purpose of these provisions?

12. *Entities taxable as corporations*. A corporation may have only one shareholder. Professional associations organized under a state's corporate laws can qualify as C corporations for tax purposes. Associations can be taxable as corporations even though they are not incorporated. Section 7701(a)(3). Among the associations taxable as corporations are trusts with transferable interests. So long as they are not "publicly traded partnerships" described in section 7704, partnerships, even limited partnerships, generally do not fall in the category of associations taxable as corporations. Nor do organizations set up as limited liability companies.   After decades of uncertainty concerning whether certain entities should be classified as corporations or as partnerships for tax purposes, the Treasury Department moved in 1995 to allow many associations to choose which tax classification they preferred.[1]

In some instances dummy corporations set up to facilitate title transfers

---

1. Notice, 95-14, 1995-1 C.B. 297.

and the like are disregarded for tax purposes. If a corporation engages in any substantial activity, however, it is required to file a corporate income tax return and is treated as a separate taxable entity.

Limitations on deductions by corporations

13. *Interest.* In general, the limits placed on interest deductions by individual taxpayers do not apply to corporations, because interest paid by corporations is considered paid in the course of trade or business. There are, however, some limits on interest deductions by corporations. In some instances, interest in excess of $5 million a year on subordinated indebtedness incurred to permit the debtor corporation to acquire stock or a substantial majority of the operating assets of another corporation may not be deducted. Section 279. Interest on debt between related corporations and between corporations and their over-50-percent owners may not be deducted until reported in income by the related creditor. Section 267. Also, corporations—as is the case with individuals—may not deduct interest on loans used to finance investments in tax-exempt bonds. Section 265(a)(2).

14. *Charitable contributions.* Section 170(b)(2) permits corporations to deduct charitable contributions in amounts up to 10 percent of taxable income.

15. *Losses.* Losses on transactions with over-50-percent shareholders are denied by section 267.

16. This Chapter does not discuss the alternative minimum tax, which applies lower tax rates to a broader base. Section 55 et seq.

B. WHO BEARS THE CORPORATE TAX?

FEDERAL TAX POLICY
Joseph A. Pechman[*]
Pages 135-37, 141-45, 151-54 (5th ed. 1987)

The corporation income tax was enacted in 1909, four years before the introduction of the individual income tax. To avoid a constitutional issue, Congress levied the tax as an excise on the privilege of doing business as a corporation. The law was challenged, but the Supreme Court upheld the authority of the federal government to impose such a tax and ruled that the privilege of doing corporate business could be measured by the corporation's profits.

---

[*]. At time of original publication, Senior Fellow, The Brookings Institution.

The corporation income tax produced more revenue than the individual income tax in seventeen of the twenty-eight years before 1941, when the latter was greatly expanded as a source of wartime revenue. From 1941 through 1967 corporation income tax receipts were second only to those of the individual income tax, but they were overtaken by payroll taxes in fiscal year 1968 and have since been declining in importance. The corporation income tax accounted for about 8 percent of federal receipts in 1986, compared with 28 percent in 1956. Since the end of World War II, the corporate tax rate has been reduced from a peak of 52 percent in 1952-63 to 34 percent beginning July 1, 1987. Corporate tax receipts should increase as a share of total tax collections as a result of the reforms enacted in 1986, but the share will remain significantly lower than it was in earlier postwar years.

   * * *

Despite its long history in the United States, the corporation income tax is the subject of considerable controversy. In the first place, there is no general agreement about who really pays it. Some believe the tax is borne by the corporations and hence by their stockholders. Others believe it depresses the rate of return to capital throughout the economy and is therefore borne by owners of capital in general. Still others argue that the tax is passed on to consumers through higher prices or may be shifted back to the workers in lower wages. Some believe that it is borne by all three groups—stockholders, consumers, and wage earners—in varying proportions. This uncertainty about the incidence of the tax makes strange bedfellows of individuals holding diametrically opposed views and often puts them in inconsistent positions. Some staunch opponents of a sales tax vigorously support the corporation income tax even though they profess to believe it is shifted to the consumer, while many who say that the corporation tax is "just another cost" (and is consequently shifted) demand that the tax be reduced and some form of consumption tax substituted for all or part of it.

   * * *

Shifting and Incidence of the Tax

There is no more controversial issue in taxation than the question, "Who bears the corporation income tax?" On this question, both economists and businessmen differ among themselves. The following quotations are representative of these divergent views:

> Corporate taxes are simply costs, and the method of their assessment does not change this fact. Costs must be paid by the public in prices, and corporate taxes are thus, in effect, concealed sales taxes. (Enders M. Voorhees, chairman of the Finance Committee, U.S. Steel Corporation, address before the Controllers'

Institute of America, New York, September 21, 1943.)

The initial or short-run incidence of the corporate income tax seems to be largely on corporations and their stockholders.... There seems to be little foundation for the belief that a large part of the corporate tax comes out of wages or is passed on to consumers in the same way that a selective excise [tax] tends to be shifted to buyers. (Richard Goode, *The Corporation Income Tax*, Wiley, 1951, pp. 71-72.)

. . . The corporation profits tax is almost entirely shifted; the government simply uses the corporation as a tax collector. (Kenneth E. Boulding, *The Organizational Revolution*, Harper, 1953, p. 277.)

It is hard to avoid the conclusion that plausible alternative sets of assumptions about the relevant elasticities all yield results in which capital bears very close to 100 percent of the [corporate] tax burden. (Arnold C. Harberger, "The Incidence of the Corporation Income Tax," *Journal of Political Economy*, vol. 70, June 1962, p. 234.)

. . . An increase in the [corporate] tax is shifted fully through short-run adjustments to prevent a decline in the net rate of return [on corporate investment], and . . . these adjustments are maintained subsequently. (Marian Krzyzaniak and Richard A. Musgrave, *The Shifting of the Corporation Income Tax*, Johns Hopkins Press, 1963, p. 65.)

. . . There is no inter-sector inefficiency resulting from the imposition of the corporate profits tax with the interest deductibility provision. Nor is there any misallocation between safe and risky industries. From an efficiency point of view, the whole corporate profits tax structure is just like a lump sum tax on corporations. (Joseph E. Stiglitz, "Taxation, Corporate Financial Policy, and the Cost of Capital," *Journal of Public Economics*, vol. 2, February 1973, p. 33.)

. . . If the net rate of return is given in the international market place, the burden of a tax on the income from capital in one country will not (in the middle or long run) end up being borne by capital (which can flee) but by other factors of production (land, labor, and to a degree, perhaps, old fixed capital). (Arnold C. Harberger, "The State of the Corporate Tax: Who Pays It? Should It Be Replaced?" in Charls E. Walker and Mark A. Bloomfield, eds., *New Directions in Federal Tax Policy for the 1980s*, Ballinger, 1983.)

Unfortunately, economics has not yet provided a scientific basis for accepting or rejecting one side or the other. This section presents the logic of each view and summarizes the evidence.

The Shifting Mechanism

One reason for the sharply divergent views is that the opponents frequently do not refer to the same type of shifting. It is important to distinguish between short- and long-run shifting and the mechanisms through which they operate. The "short run" is defined by economists as a period too short for firms to adjust their capital to changing demand and supply conditions. The "long run" is a period in which capital can be adjusted.

The Short Run

The classical view in economics is that the corporation income tax cannot be shifted in the short run. The argument is as follows: all business firms, whether they are competitive or monopolistic, seek to maximize net profits. This maximum occurs when output and prices are set at the point where the cost of producing an additional unit is exactly equal to the additional revenue obtained from the sale of that unit. In the short run, a tax on economic profit should make no difference in this decision. The output and price that maximized the firm's profits before the tax will continue to maximize profits after the tax is imposed. (This follows from simple arithmetic. If a series of figures is reduced by the same percentage, the figure that was highest before will be the highest after.)

The opposite view is that today's markets are characterized neither by perfect competition nor by monopoly; instead, they show considerable imperfection and mutual interdependence or oligopoly. In such markets, business firms may set their prices at the level that covers their full cost *plus* a margin for profits. Alternatively, the firms are described as aiming at an after-tax target rate of return on their invested capital. Under the cost-plus behavior, the firm treats the tax as an element of cost and raises its price to recover the tax. (Public utilities are usually able to shift the tax in this way, because state rate-making agencies treat the corporation tax as a cost.) Similarly, if the firm's objective is the after-tax target rate of return, imposition of a tax or an increase in the tax rate—by reducing the rate of return on invested capital—will have to be accounted for in making output and price decisions. To preserve the target rate of return, the tax must be shifted forward to consumers or backward to the workers or partly forward and partly backward.

It is also argued that the competitive models are irrelevant in most markets where one or a few large firms exercise a substantial degree of leadership. In such markets, efficient producers raise their prices to recover the tax, and the tax merely forms an "umbrella" that permits less efficient or marginal producers to survive.

When business managers are asked about their pricing policies, they often say that they shift the corporation income tax. However, even if business firms intend to shift the tax, there is some doubt about their ability to shift it fully in the short run. In the first place, the tax depends on the outcome of business operations during an entire year. Businessmen can only guess the ratio of the tax to their gross receipts, and it is hard to conceive of their setting a price that would recover the precise amount of tax they will eventually pay. (If shifting were possible, there would be some instances of firms shifting more than 100 percent of the tax, but few economists believe that overshifting actually occurs.)

Second, businessmen know that should they attempt to recover the corporation income tax through higher prices (or lower wages), other firms would not necessarily do the same. Some firms make no profit or have large loss carry-overs and thus pay no tax; among other firms, the ratio of tax to gross receipts differs. In multi product firms, the producer has even less basis for judging the ratio of tax to gross receipts for each product. All these possibilities increase the uncertainty of response by other firms and make the attempt to shift part or all of the corporation income tax hazardous.

The Long Run

In the long run, the corporation income tax influences investment by reducing the rate of return on corporate equity. If the corporation income tax is not shifted in the short run, net after-tax rates of return are depressed, and the incentive to undertake corporate investment is thereby reduced. After-tax rates of return tend to be equalized with those in the noncorporate sector, but in the process corporate capital and output will have been permanently reduced. Thus, if there is no short-run shifting and if the supply of capital is fixed, the burden of the tax falls on the owners of capital in general. If the depressed rate of return on capital reduces investment, productivity of labor decreases and at least part of the tax may be borne by workers.

Where investment is financed by borrowing, the corporation tax cannot affect investment decisions because interest on debt is a deductible expense. If the marginal investment of a firm is fully financed by debt, the corporation tax becomes a lump-sum tax on profits generated by previous investments and is borne entirely by the owners of the corporation, the stockholders. In view of the recent large increase in debt financing (see the section on equity and debt finance below), a substantial proportion of the corporation income tax may now rest on stockholders and not be diffused to owners of capital in general through the shifting process just described.

The Corporation Tax in an Open Economy

The foregoing analysis assumed that the corporation tax was imposed in a closed economy. In an open economy, the rate of return on capital is set in the international marketplace. If the tax in one country is higher than it is elsewhere, capital will move to other countries until the rate of return is raised to the international level. Thus the burden of the tax would not be borne by capital but by other factors of production (land, labor, and old fixed capital) that cannot move. Since labor is the largest input into corporate products, wage earners would bear most of the burden of the corporation tax through lower real wages.

In the years immediately after World War II, most countries imposed tight capital controls and currencies were not convertible. As capital controls were dismantled and many foreign currencies other than the U.S. dollar became acceptable in international transactions, the open economy model became more realistic. During this later period, the effective corporation tax rates have been declining in the United States. It follows that recent U.S. tax policy has probably reduced any adverse effect of the corporation income tax on real wages, not increased it as some allege.

* * *

Equity and Debt Finance

Corporations are allowed to deduct interest payments on borrowed capital from taxable income, but there is no corresponding deduction for dividends paid out to stockholders in return for the use of their funds as equity capital. At the 34 percent tax rate, a corporation must earn $1.52 before tax to be able to pay $1 in dividends, but it needs to earn only $1 to pay $1 interest. This asymmetry makes the cost of equity more expensive for the corporation than an equal amount of borrowed capital. In fact, in combination with the accelerated cost recovery system and the investment tax credit, the allowance of an interest deduction provided a substantial subsidy to investment in the early 1980s.

* * *

Financial experts discourage large amounts of debt financing by corporations. Debt makes good business sense if there is a safe margin for paying fixed interest charges. But business firms may be tightly squeezed when business falls off, and the margin will evaporate rapidly. At such times, defaults on interest and principal payments and bankruptcies begin to occur. Even though borrowed capital may increase returns to stockholders, corporations try to finance a major share of their capital requirements through equity capital (mainly retained earnings) to avoid these risks.

* * *

Resource Allocation

If the corporation income tax is not shifted in the short run, it becomes in effect a special tax on corporate capital. This does not necessarily mean that the tax permanently reduces rates of return on capital in the corporate sector relative to returns in the noncorporate sector. Capital may flow out of the taxed industries into the untaxed industries, and rates of return will tend to equalize. In the process, the allocation of capital between corporate and noncorporate business will be altered from the pattern that would have prevailed in the absence of the tax.

How much capital, if any, has left the corporate sector as a result of the corporation income tax is not known. It is possible that the corporate form of doing business is so advantageous for nontax reasons that, for the most part, capital remains in the corporate sector despite the tax. To the extent that corporate investment is financed by debt, the corporation income tax does not affect investment incentives because interest on debt is deductible as a business expense. The same is true if the capital-consumption allowances are so liberal as to be the equivalent of expensing (as they were before the Tax Reform Act of 1986 was passed). In addition, the preferential treatment of capital gains under the individual income tax provided an offsetting incentive to invest in the securities of corporations that retained earnings for reinvestment in the business. These earnings showed up as increases in the price of common stock rather than as regular income. In any case, the corporate sector has been getting larger, both relatively and absolutely, for decades. The discouragement of investment in the corporate form induced by the tax system, if any, must have been comparatively small. * * *

Distortions may also take place if the tax is shifted in the short run. If prices increase in response to an increase in the tax, they rise in proportion to the use of corporate equity capital in the various industries. Consumers will buy fewer goods and services produced by industries using a great deal of corporate capital because the prices of these products will have risen most, and they will buy more goods and services produced by industries with less corporate capital. Within the corporate sector, profits will fall in the "capital-intensive" industries as a result of the decline in sales and will rise in the "labor-intensive" industries. In the end, not only will less capital be attracted to the corporate sector, but less will be attracted to the capital-intensive industries in that sector, and the economy will suffer a loss in efficiency as a result. The quantitative effect of this process is heavily dependent, of course, on the degree to which the noncorporate form of doing business can be substituted for the corporate form and production can be transferred from capital-intensive to labor-intensive industries. As in the nonshifting case, even a shifted corporate tax would tend to distort the composition of output.

Major distortions were introduced by the pre-1986 allowances for investment and the deduction for interest on borrowed capital. The depreciation allowances under the accelerated cost recovery system (ACRS) plus the investment credit were equivalent on average to expensing of capital equipment, which can be shown to be equivalent to a zero tax on investment under certain conditions. If the investment was financed by debt, the tax was actually converted to a subsidy. Moreover, the investment tax credit was allowed only for equipment, and the depreciation allowances under ACRS were much less generous for buildings than for equipment. The result was that machinery was treated much more favorably than plant and other structures, inventories, and intangibles. Thus the effect of the capital allowances and the interest deduction differed greatly among different assets and industries. * * * These distortions were greatly reduced, though not entirely eliminated, by the tax reforms enacted in 1986.

Notes and Questions

17. In deciding who bears the corporate income tax, consider the possibility that the incidence of the tax might be changed by changing the structure of the tax or the tax treatment of other business entities, such as partnerships.

18. Is a business corporation an appropriate taxable entity in its own right? Is the decision to tax it based on anything more than tradition, and perhaps administrative feasibility?

19. What different categories of people might conceivably bear all or a portion of the burden of the corporate income tax?

20. Despite a recent trend toward deregulation, many privately-owned public utilities are subject to considerable regulation of rates charged to consumers. State regulators allow public utilities to pass on their corporate income taxes to their ratepayers as a cost of operations. Who bears the corporate tax imposed on regulated public utilities?

21. What is the incidence of the tax on corporations that are in direct competition with individual proprietors, partnerships, limited liability companies, and S corporations that do not pay corporate tax?

22. In the long run, who bears the burden of income tax imposed on

corporations for which capital is not a significant income-producing factor?

23. Dr. Pechman stated that the corporate tax will not adversely affect investment incentives if capital investments can be "expensed," or fully deducted when made, "as they were before the Tax Reform Act of 1986 was passed." This assertion requires explanation on two points. First, although pre-1986 law did not allow capital expenditures to be expensed (except for relatively small amounts under section 179), Pechman apparently agrees with economists who argued that the combination of the short depreciation periods and the 10 percent investment tax credit then in effect were as favorable as expensing.

The second point is to recall that immediate expensing of capital expenditures is said to completely eliminate, and not merely reduce, the impact on investment incentives of any income tax. See Chapter Two, Subchapter A.

C. THE DOUBLE TAX ISSUE

The six excerpts of this subchapter discuss varying answers to the same core question: Assuming the present "double tax" system imposed on corporations and their individual shareholders to be improper, what tax treatment should replace it? (As noted in Subchapter A, the 2003 Act gives partial relief from double taxation—but only through 2008—by levying the shareholder-level tax at capital gains rates.)

The mechanics of the various alternatives for ending or reducing double taxation of corporate earnings can be illustrated by examining how each would tax this simple corporate/shareholder situation: A corporation is started by a single shareholder who contributes $1,000 for stock. In the first year the corporation has $100 of taxable income. After paying any corporate tax due, the corporation distributes all of its after-tax earnings to the shareholder, who then pays any tax due at the individual level. For clarity of presentation, it will be assumed throughout that the corporate-level tax is 30 percent and that the individual tax is 40 percent.

Under the classic double-tax model—which very closely resembles U.S. law prior to 2003 and after 2008—the corporation pays $30 in tax, and distributes the remaining $70 to its shareholder. The shareholder then pays $28 in tax ($70 x 40 percent), leaving a net after both taxes of $42. Total taxes amount to $58, or 58 percent of the $100 earned by the corporation. (The 2003 Act reduces but does not eliminate the double tax during the years 2003-08. Two levels of tax are still applicable, though the shareholder-level tax is at preferential capital gains rates.)

"Pure integration" would eliminate double taxation by taxing corporations like partnerships—*i.e.*, income and deductions of the corporation would be completely integrated with those of the shareholder. If the corporation described above were so taxed, the entire $100 of corporate taxable income, whether or not distributed, would be taxed at the individual shareholder's 40 percent tax rate, for a total tax of $40. (If the corporation had a loss for the year, presumably the shareholder could deduct it currently—a privilege not now available to shareholders of C corporations.)

Another technique for integration of distributed income is to treat the corporate tax apportioned to dividends as a tax withheld from the shareholder's dividend, similar to the wage withholding tax. In the example, if the entire $100 were declared as a dividend, the entire $30 of corporation tax would be treated as withheld tax. The shareholder would report as income the $70 net amount received in cash plus the $30 "withheld" (corporate tax paid by the corporation), or a total of $100. (This treatment of the amount of tax paid by the corporation on the shareholder's behalf as part of the dividend is referred to as a "grossed-up" dividend.) The shareholder's tax on $100 at 40 percent would be $40, and the shareholder would claim a credit of $30 (the amount withheld at the corporate level) against this tax liability. (If the shareholder's marginal tax rate were below 30 percent, the additional tax withheld could be allowed as a credit against the shareholder's tax on other income or refunded to the shareholder.)

A simpler alternative would be to allow corporations to deduct dividends, much as they deduct interest now. In the example, payment of a $100 dividend would reduce corporate taxable income to zero, shareholder income would be $100, and tax on that amount at 40 percent would be $40. In this example, the result would be the same as partnership treatment, but if a corporation did not pay out all its earnings as dividends the result would be significantly different because, under partnership treatment, the shareholder would be taxed whether earnings are distributed or not.

Another alternative would exclude dividends from the individual shareholder's income; thus, the sole tax would be paid by the corporation. To assure that the dividends bear a full tax at one level, the exclusion could be limited to dividends paid from corporate earnings that have borne tax at the top *corporate* rate. In the example, a dividend of $100 paid from earnings that have been taxed at 30 percent would be excluded from the shareholder's income, so the total tax would be $30.

Yet another alternative would also exclude dividends from the individual shareholder's income; again, the sole tax would be paid by the corporation. But under this alternative, to assure that the dividends bear a full tax at one level, the exclusion would be limited in the case of dividends that have not borne a corporate tax equal to the top *individual* rate. In the example, the corporation would pay $30 tax on income of $100. The top individual rate on $100 of income is $40. Therefore, 30/40, or 75 percent, of the $100 dividend would be regarded as paid from earnings that have been taxed at 40 percent, and therefore would be excluded from the shareholder's income. The shareholder would be allowed to exclude $75, and would be taxed on the remaining $25. This would result in a corporate tax of $30 and a shareholder tax of $10 ($25 x 40 percent), so the total tax would be $40.

What all these alternatives have in common is that the total tax would not exceed the maximum statutory rate at one level—either the corporate or shareholder level. The classic model—even with the substantial relief temporarily afforded by the 2003 Act—levies a combined rate that exceeds the statutory rate for either the corporation or the shareholder.

There is no shortage of detailed proposals. The first excerpt of this subchapter is the 2003 proposal of the Bush administration, which ultimately led to the present compromise described in Subchapter A. Two additional Treasury studies, Treasury I in 1984 and a 1992 study focusing on corporate integration, are also excerpted. Also included are studies produced by Professor Alvin Warren as Reporter for the American Law Institute, and by the American Institute of Certified Public Accountants. The final excerpt is from a law review article by Professor Fred Peel, one of many academics to have suggested a way out of the classic double-tax model.

GENERAL EXPLANATIONS OF THE ADMINISTRATION'S FISCAL YEAR 2004 REVENUE PROPOSALS
United States Department of the Treasury
Pages 11-17, 19-22 (2003)

Current Law

Income earned by a corporation is taxed at the corporate level, generally at the rate of 35 percent. If the corporation distributes earnings to shareholders in the form of dividends, the income generally is taxed a second time at the shareholder level. * * * If a corporation instead retains its earnings, the value of corporate stock will reflect the retained earnings. When shareholders sell their stock, that additional value will be taxed as capital gains. * * * The combined rate of tax on corporate income can be as high as 60 percent, far in excess of rates of tax imposed on other types of income.

Reasons for Change

The double taxation of corporate profits creates significant economic distortions.

- First, double taxation creates a bias in favor of debt as compared to equity, because payments of interest by the corporation are deductible while returns on equity in the form of dividends and retained earnings are not. Excessive debt increases the risks of bankruptcy during economic downturns.

- Second, double taxation of corporate profits creates a bias in favor of unincorporated entities (such as partnerships and limited liability companies), which are not subject to the double tax.

- Third, because dividends are taxed at a higher rate than are capital gains, double taxation of corporate profits encourages a corporation to retain its earnings rather than distribute them in the form of dividends. This lessens the pressure on corporate managers to undertake only the most productive investments because corporate investments funded by retained earnings may receive less scrutiny than investments funded by outside equity or debt financing.

- Fourth, double taxation encourages corporations to engage in transactions such as share repurchases rather than to pay dividends because share repurchases permit the corporation to distribute earnings at reduced capital gains tax rates.

- Fifth, double taxation increases incentives for corporations to engage in transactions for the sole purpose of minimizing their tax liability.

By eliminating double taxation, the proposal will reduce tax-induced distortions that, in the current tax system, encourage firms to use debt rather than equity finance and to adopt noncorporate rather than corporate structures. Because shareholders will be exempt from tax only on distributions of previously taxed corporate income, the proposal will reduce incentives for certain types of corporate tax planning. In addition, the proposal will enhance corporate governance by eliminating the current bias against the payment of dividends. Dividends can provide evidence of a corporation's underlying financial health and enable investors to evaluate more readily a corporation's financial condition. This, in turn, increases the accountability of corporate management to its investors.

Proposal

Overview

The proposal would integrate the corporate and individual income taxes so that corporate earnings generally will be taxed once and only once. Under the proposal, public and private corporations would be permitted to distribute nontaxable dividends to their shareholders to the extent that those dividends are paid out of income previously taxed at the corporate level. The proposal generally would be effective for distributions made on or after January 1, 2003, with respect to corporate earnings after 2000.

To calculate the amount that can be distributed to its shareholders without further tax, a corporation will compute an excludable dividend amount

(EDA) for each year. The EDA reflects income of the corporation that has been fully taxed. Thus, for example, a corporation with $100 of income that pays $35 of U.S. income taxes will have an EDA of $65 that can be distributed as excludable dividends.

If an amount would be a dividend under current law, it will be treated as an excludable dividend to the extent of EDA. Excludable dividends will not be taxed to shareholders. If a corporation's distributions during a calendar year exceed its EDA, only a proportionate amount of each distribution will be treated as an excludable dividend. * * *

The capital gains tax on the sale of stock will be retained. Without further change, this would create an incentive for corporations to distribute previously taxed income as excludable dividends rather than retaining earnings for future investment. This is because excludable dividends would not be taxed to the shareholders but capital gains that represent retained earnings would be taxed to the shareholders when they sell their shares.

To ensure that distributions and retentions of previously taxed earnings are treated similarly, shareholders will be permitted to increase their basis in their shares to reflect that the retained earnings have already been taxed at the corporate level. As an alternative to distributing excludable dividends, corporations generally may allocate throughout the year all or a portion of the EDA to provide these basis increases. The basis increases will not be taxable. The effect of the basis increases will be to reduce the capital gains realized when shareholders sell their stock to the extent that the sales price reflects the corporation's retained, previously taxed earnings.

Technical Explanation

Corporate Level

In General

Corporations will continue to calculate their income under current law rules and will pay tax according to the existing graduated rate schedule. The corporate alternative minimum tax (AMT) will continue to apply.

The rules for computing earnings and profits will be retained. The rules for treating corporate level transactions, such as acquisitive and divisive reorganizations, liquidations, and taxable acquisitions will generally be the same as under current law. Corporations may continue to file consolidated returns as under current law. The consolidated return regulations will be amended to reflect the dividend exclusion.

* * *

Retained Earnings Basis Adjustments

As an alternative to distributing excludable dividends, corporations will be permitted to allocate throughout the year all or a portion of their EDA to increase their shareholders' basis in their stock.

* * * [B]asis increases will be permitted only to the extent that the total dividend distributions during the year do not exceed EDA. * * *

The basis increases will not be taxable. Basis increases will reduce the EDA and earnings and profits.

* * *

Allocated basis increases reflecting retained earnings are referred to as REBAs. A corporation will maintain records of the total REBAs made with respect to its stock in prior years. The cumulative amount of REBAs for all years is referred to as the CREBA.

From time to time, a corporation's EDA for a calendar year may be less than the distributions it intends to make. Instead of treating distributions in excess of EDA as taxable dividends, as described below, the proposal treats those distributions as effectively reversing basis adjustments that were allocated in prior years. These distributions reduce CREBA. This flexibility reflects the fact that, even though a corporation's taxable income may fluctuate, it may maintain a stable dividend payout.

Distributions

For a distribution to be an excludable dividend, it must be a dividend under current law, i.e., out of earnings and profits.

If a distribution is a dividend under current law, it will be treated as an excludable dividend to the extent of EDA. Distributions that are excludable dividends reduce EDA and earnings and profits.

If dividend distributions are less than EDA, a corporation may permit its shareholders to increase their basis in their stock as discussed above.

If a corporation's distributions during a calendar year exceed its EDA, only a proportionate amount will be treated as an excludable dividend.

Distributions that are not excludable dividends generally will be treated as:

- first a return of basis and then capital gain to the extent of the CREBA,
- then a taxable dividend to the extent of the corporation's earnings and profits,
- then a return of capital to the extent of the shareholder's remaining basis, and
- then capital gain.

* * *

Carryback of Net Operating Losses

The rules governing the carryback of net operating losses will be revised to ensure that EDA for a year in which shareholders have already derived a benefit is not affected. Accordingly, under the proposal, net operating losses of corporations may be carried back one year. For example, a net operating loss attributable to a taxable year ending during 2003 may be carried back one year to the taxable year ending in 2002. If a net operating loss is carried back, however, the EDA for the current year must be recomputed. That recomputed EDA will be used to determine the character of distributions made, and the amount of basis adjustments allocated, during the entire year.

* * *

Reorganizations and Liquidations

The proposal retains current law rules that treat a qualifying corporate reorganization and certain corporate liquidations as tax-free at the shareholder level and at the corporate level. Under current law, the acquired corporation's tax attributes, including its asset basis, carry over to the acquiror. These rules will be amended to provide for the carryover of the acquired corporation's EDA and CREBA.

The proposal retains current law rules governing tax-free spin-offs. Under the proposal, rules will be provided to divide the CREBA, if any, of the distributing and controlled corporations between the distributing and controlled corporations based on the relative fair market values of their assets and to ensure that duplicate CREBA is eliminated.

Consolidated Returns

The Secretary of the Treasury will amend the consolidated return regulations to effect the provisions of the proposal. For example, regulations might provide that, in a consolidated group, EDA will be calculated on a consolidated group basis based on U.S. income taxes of the group, and then apportioned among the entities that were members of the group during the taxable year based on each member's separate taxable income. No EDA will be allocated to members that generated a loss during the taxable year. * * *

Accumulated Earnings Tax and
Personal Holding Company Tax

The accumulated earnings tax and personal holding company tax will be repealed because they are of diminished importance in a system that does not impose a shareholder level of tax on dividends. Their repeal will simplify compliance with the tax laws.

* * *

Shareholder Level
Distributions

In General

Under the proposal, shareholders generally will exclude from gross income dividends that are characterized as excludable dividends. Each year, shareholders will receive a Form 1099 from the corporation setting forth which portions of their distributions are excludable dividends, taxable dividends, or returns of capital. In addition, the statement will show the amount by which shareholders are entitled to increase their basis in their stock as a result of

REBAs.

Special Rules for Dividend Exclusion and REBAS

Under current section 246(c), corporate shareholders must hold their stock for more than 45 days * * * during the 90-day period * * * beginning 45 days * * * before the ex-dividend date to be eligible to claim a dividends received deduction. A rule similar to section 246(c), with the same holding period requirements, will apply to excludable dividends received and REBAs allocated to both corporate and noncorporate shareholders.

* * *

Capital Gains

Shareholders will be taxed on sales of their stock, as under current law. REBAs should largely prevent shareholders from being taxed on the portion of appreciation in the value of their shares that is attributable to previously taxed income that the corporation has chosen to retain rather than pay out as dividends. The capital loss limitation will remain as under current law.

* * *

Shareholder Level Debt

Section 246A, which prohibits the dividends received deduction for debt-financed portfolio stock, will be modified to require that otherwise excludable dividends received by corporations be included in income if attributable to debt-financed stock. Additionally, because under section 163(d) excludable dividends will not be treated as investment income, excludable dividends will not increase the amount deductible as investment interest.

* * *

Pension Plans, 401(k) Plans, and Individual Retirement Accounts (Retirement Plans)

In a Retirement Plan, all investment income, including all dividend income, is effectively free from tax. The proposal's treatment of Retirement Plans will not change current law.

Generally, under current law, amounts contributed to a Retirement Plan are not subject to tax when contributed. Income of the Retirement Plan is not subject to tax when earned. Instead, contributions and earnings are subject to tax when distributed. In contrast, contributions to a Roth-IRA are made with after-tax dollars. However, both the after-tax contributions and income earned on those contributions are free from tax when distributed.

All investment income, including dividend income, earned by a Roth-IRA is free from tax. The tax treatment of other retirement plans is economically equivalent to Roth-IRA treatment. A plan with tax-free contributions and no tax until withdrawal produces the same after-tax benefit for an individual as a plan with after-tax contributions and tax-free investment returns.[m]

Because all investment income is effectively free from tax in Retirement Plans, investments in these plans will remain tax advantaged relative to investments outside of these plans.

* * *

Revenue Estimate

Fiscal Years							
2003	2004	2005	2006	2007	2008	2004-08	2004-13
$'s in millions							
-2,665	-24,224	-25,962	-31,501	-33,996	-36,983	-152,666	-385,429

TAX REFORM FOR FAIRNESS, SIMPLICITY, AND ECONOMIC GROWTH ("TREASURY I")
United States Department of the Treasury
Vol. 1, at 118-19 (1984)

With a comprehensive corporate income tax base, income derived from equity investment in the corporate sector would be taxed twice—once when earned by a corporation and again when distributed to shareholders. The double taxation of dividends has several undesirable effects. It encourages corporations to rely too heavily on debt, rather than equity finance. By increasing the risk of bankruptcy, this artificial inducement for debt finance increases the incidence of bankruptcies during business downturns.

The double taxation of dividends also creates an inducement for firms to retain earnings, rather than pay them out as dividends. There is however, no reason to believe that firms with retained earnings are necessarily those with the best investment opportunities. Instead, they may have more funds than they can invest productively, while new enterprises lack capital. If retained earnings are used to finance relatively low productivity investments, including uneconomic acquisitions of other firms, the quality of investment suffers. In addition, both corporate investment and aggregate saving are discouraged, because the double taxation of dividends increases the cost of capital to corporations and reduces the return to individual investors.

These problems cannot be solved by simply eliminating the corporate income tax. If there were no corporate tax, dividends would be taxed properly, at the tax rates of the shareholders who receive them, but earnings retained

---

m. See Subchapter A of Chapter Two. (Ed.)

by the corporations would not be taxed until distributed, and thus would be allowed to accumulate tax-free. As a result, there would be a substantial incentive to conduct business in corporate form, in order to take advantage of these benefits of tax exemption and deferral.

Nor can the corporate and individual income taxes be fully integrated by treating the corporation as a partnership for tax purposes. Technical difficulties * * * preclude adoption of this approach. The Treasury Department thus proposes that the United States, following the practice of many other developed countries, continue to levy the corporate income tax on earnings that are retained, but provide partial relief from double taxation of dividends.

There are two alternative ways to provide dividend relief. The approach more commonly employed in other countries is to allow shareholders a credit for a portion of the corporate tax attributable to the dividends they receive. The credit is generally available only to residents, although it is sometimes extended to foreigners by treaty. The credit can be denied tax-exempt organizations, if that is desired.

The simpler method, and the one proposed by the Treasury Department, will allow corporations a deduction for dividends paid similar to the deduction for interest expense. Dividends paid to nonresident shareholders will be subject to a compensatory withholding tax, equivalent to the reduction in tax at the corporate level. The proposal will not impose such a compensatory tax where it would be contrary to a U.S. tax treaty; nor will the compensatory tax apply to dividends paid to U.S. tax-exempt organizations. However, the initial decision to extend the benefits of dividend relief to these two groups of shareholders will be subject to continuing review.

Despite the advantages of full relief from double taxation of dividends, the Treasury Department proposal would provide a deduction of only one-half of dividends paid from income taxed to the corporation. This decision is based primarily on considerations of revenue loss, and can be reconsidered once the proposal is fully phased in.

The deduction would not be allowed for dividends paid from income that had not been subject to corporate tax; firms wishing to pay out tax-preferred income will not receive a deduction, but dividends will be presumed to be paid first from fully taxed income. For this purpose, income that did not bear a corporate tax because of allowable credits, including foreign tax credits, will not be eligible for the deduction.

Reduction of the double taxation of corporate equity income will tend to increase initially the market value of existing corporate shares of companies that distribute an above-average proportion of current earnings as dividends. It will reduce the current tax bias against equity finance in the corporate sector and make equity securities more competitive with debt. Because dividend relief will also reduce the tax bias against distributing earnings, corporations will be likely to pay greater dividends and to seek new funds in financial markets. Corporations will therefore, be more subject to the discipline of the marketplace and less likely to make relatively unproductive investments simply because they have available funds. Similarly, the pool of funds available to new firms with relatively high productivity investment opportunities will be larger. As a result, the productivity of investment should be improved substantially.

Dividend relief will be phased in gradually in order to match the phase-in of the correct rules for measurement of corporate income and to minimize unjustified windfall profits to current shareholders. Moreover, phasing in dividend relief will prevent a large loss of tax revenue and any associated reduction in the tax burden of high-income shareholders.

* * *

AMERICAN LAW INSTITUTE
REPORTER'S STUDY OF CORPORATE TAX
INTEGRATION:
SUMMARY AND PROPOSALS
Alvin C. Warren,[*] Reporter

Pages 1-8, 12 (1993)

The United States has long had what is usually called a classical income tax system, under which income is taxed to shareholders and corporations as distinct taxpayers. As a result, taxable income earned by a corporation and then distributed to individual shareholders as a dividend is taxed twice, once to the corporation and once to the shareholder on receipt of the dividend. Corporate taxable income distributed as dividends to exempt shareholders is taxed only at the corporate level. In contrast, earnings on corporate debt capital are nontaxable at the corporate level to the extent they are distributed as deductible interest payments. Whether interest is taxed to the recipient depends on the recipient's status, with foreign and tax-exempt lenders generally nontaxable on such receipts.

Integration of the individual and corporate income taxes refers to various means of eliminating the separate, additional burden of the corporate income tax, in favor of a system in which investor and corporate taxes are interrelated so as to produce a more uniform levy on capital income, whether earned through corporate enterprise or not. *The integration proposals in this study would convert the separate U. S. corporate income tax into a withholding tax with respect to income ultimately distributed to shareholders.*

---

[*]. At time of original publication, Professor of Law, Harvard University.

There are two principal reasons for studying this subject. First, the current system has long been the subject of criticism, for which integration has often been offered as a solution. * * *

The second reason for studying the subject is that most other major developed countries have in recent decades adopted various forms of integration. As the American economy becomes less separable from these other economies, it becomes more important to understand the potential advantages and disadvantages of integration for the United States and for U.S. companies.

* * *

The approach throughout the study is to develop proposals that provide as complete a response as possible to the defects of current law by converting the corporate tax into a withholding device. * * *

Defects in Current Law

In general, the classical system can (a) discourage individual investors from investing in new corporate equity; (b) encourage corporations to finance new projects with retained earnings and debt, rather than by issuing new stock; and (c) encourage corporations to distribute earnings in tax preferred transactions, such as redemptions, rather than by paying dividends. Whether the classical system encourages retention or distribution of corporate earnings depends on the rate relationships among corporate, shareholder, and capital gains rates, as well as assumptions about the operation of the capital markets. The tax-induced distortions of current law are undesirable to the extent they have deleterious economic effects (such as over reliance on debt finance by corporations) or create unadministrable legal distinctions (such as that between debt and equity). Integration would reduce or eliminate these undesirable effects.

System of Integration

There are a variety of ways in which the individual and corporate income taxes could be integrated to reduce the distortions of current law. The corporate tax could, for example, be repealed and shareholders taxed currently on all corporate earnings, but that approach would require annual attribution of undistributed corporate income to a myriad of complex capital interests. Alternatively, the corporate tax could be repealed and shareholders taxed annually on changes in stock values, which would require abandonment of the realization criterion of income taxation. Another approach would be for shareholders simply to exclude corporate dividends from their taxable income, but that approach would preclude application of graduated shareholder tax rates to dividend income. Finally, on receipt of a dividend, shareholders could receive a tax credit for corporate taxes previously paid with respect to that dividend. Shareholder credit integration along these lines is the approach most widely adopted abroad and is the system developed in this study. If withholding on dividend payments is considered desirable for compliance purposes, a corporate deduction for dividend payments is essentially equivalent to the recommended form of shareholder credit integration.

The proposed approach would convert the separate corporate income tax into a withholding tax with respect to dividends. Because some dividends will not have borne a corporate tax prior to distribution, an auxiliary dividend withholding tax is necessary to assure that shareholders do not receive tax credits for taxes that have never been paid at the corporate level. No double tax would result, because payments of regular corporate tax would be considered prepayments of this auxiliary tax. On the other hand, certain dividends may be free of corporate tax as a result of deliberately enacted corporate tax preferences that should be passed through to shareholders. Finally, in order to minimize differential treatment of debt and equity, a withholding tax on corporate interest payments would be desirable. Four proposals implement this basic system of integration:

1. A withholding tax will be levied on dividend distributions; payments of corporate tax will be fully creditable against this withholding tax.
2. Shareholders will receive a refundable tax credit for the dividend withholding tax.
3. Certain corporate tax preferences can be passed through to shareholders.
4. A withholding tax will be levied on payments of corporate interest; that tax will be fully creditable by and refundable to the recipients of such interest payments.

Retained Earnings

If the corporate income tax became part of a withholding system, retained earnings would present two problems. First, shareholders whose marginal tax rates were below the corporate rate would be disadvantaged by corporate retentions, creating a tax incentive for distributions of corporate earnings. Second, taxation of shareholder capital gains due to retained corporate earnings could, as under current law, constitute multiple taxation of the same gain. The second problem could be eliminated by preferential taxation of gains on corporate stock, but such a preference would be overbroad because not all gains on corporate stock are due to taxable corporate earnings. Both problems would be addressed by a constructive dividend option, under which shareholder tax credits would be available to shareholders without the requirement of an actual dividend distribution. If the withholding and corporate tax rates were equal to the highest individual rate, such constructive dividends could only benefit shareholders, who would either pay no taxes or receive a refund. The increase in shareholder basis due to the constructive reinvestment would eliminate the potential of double taxation on sale of the stock. These ideas are implemented by Proposals 5 and 6, which can be summarized as follows:

5. Corporations could make shareholder credits available to shareholders at any time through constructive dividends and reinvestments.

6. Sales of stock will be fully taxable to shareholders, with deductions for stock losses limited to dividends, realized stock gains, and the excess of realized stock losses over net unrealized stock gains.

* * *

Exempt Shareholders and Creditors

Nominally exempt suppliers of corporate capital, such as charitable organizations and pension funds, do not always receive their share of corporate income free of tax under current law. The portion of corporate income distributed to such investors is sometimes taxed (due to the corporate tax on income distributed as dividends) and sometimes not (due to the corporate deduction for interest payments and to corporate preferences for some income distributed as dividends). Because one of the goals of integration is elimination of such discontinuities, any comprehensive system of integration will necessarily affect currently exempt shareholders. The approach of these proposals is to maintain a single level of tax on corporate income received by such investors, and to rationalize that tax to eliminate tax-induced distortions in investment decisions. Accordingly, entities that are nominally exempt under current law would be subject to an explicit tax on corporate investment income, against which the shareholder and creditor withholding credits could be used, with any excess refundable. The basic idea of this proposal is that the rate of tax on income from corporate investment received by an exempt entity should be uniform and explicitly determined as a matter of tax policy. That rate could be set to maintain the same level of revenue that is currently collected on corporate income distributed to exempt shareholders, or at a higher or lower rate. The resulting proposal can be summarized as follows:

9. A new tax will be imposed on the corporate investment income of exempt organizations, which will be allowed credits for corporate taxes on the same basis as other investors.

* * *

The net effect of the * * * proposals summarized above is that the US corporate income tax would no longer function as a separate, additional tax. Rather, it would be part of an integrated system under which investors in corporate enterprise would be taxed once, but only once, on income from investment in corporate capital. The only rate of tax ultimately applicable to corporate income distributed to a shareholder or creditor would be that investor's rate. * * *

[W]hat follows is a long and complicated study,[n] but it is based on a simple and straightforward idea: *conversion of the separate U.S. corporate income tax into a withholding tax would reduce economic distortions and troublesome legal distinctions that arise under current law.*

STATEMENT OF TAX POLICY: INTEGRATION OF THE CORPORATE AND SHAREHOLDER TAX SYSTEMS
American Institute of Certified Public Accountants
Pages 18-19, 63-67 (1993)

The Objectives of Integration

A system of integration would lower the cost of capital and mitigate many of the distortions and inequities created by the present classical system by taxing corporate income only once. There are several methods or approaches available to relieve the double taxation of corporate profits.

In evaluating the alternative methods available, the AICPA has identified five basic objectives that an integrated system should seek to achieve:

* A more uniform taxation of income earned in the corporate and noncorporate sectors
* A reduction in the tax bias favoring debt financing
* A reduction of tax incentives for corporations to retain rather than distribute their profits
* An easy interface with foreign integrated tax systems
* No significant additional complexity for the tax system

Brief Overview of Alternative Methods

This study analyzes the three principal alternative methods of implementing an integration system: (1) the flow-through method; (2) the dividends-paid deduction method; and (3) the shareholder-credit method. * * *

Flow-Through Method

The flow-through integration method achieves complete integration of all corporate earnings by allocating all items of income to shareholders in a manner similar to the allocation of partnership and S corporation income under the current system. This method taxes all income at the shareholder level when earned, whether or not distributed. The flow-through method represents the purest form of integration because it subjects all corporate income to only one level of tax, at the shareholder rates.

Dividends-Paid Deduction Method

The dividends-paid deduction method allows a corporation to deduct all or part of dividends paid from taxable income. Under this method, the benefits

---

n. Professor Warren is referring to the entire Reporter's Study. Only the Summary and Proposals are excerpted. (Ed.)

of integration inure to the corporation, since shareholders still report dividends received as income. To the extent that corporations make fully deductible distributions, one level of tax at the shareholder's tax rate should result. This method does not extend integration benefits to retained earnings.

Shareholder-Credit Method

The shareholder-credit method imposes a corporate-level tax on all earnings, but grants a credit to shareholders for a portion of the corporate tax paid that is allocated or imputed to dividends. This method generally requires shareholders to "gross up" their dividend income by the amount of credit allowed. Integration is achieved by eliminating or reducing the tax on dividends at the shareholder level. Therefore, the benefits of integration inure to the shareholder. As with the dividends-paid deduction method, double-tax relief applies only to distributed income. Therefore, integration benefits are not granted to retained income.

* * *

Conclusions and Recommendations

Each of the three principal methods has been evaluated to determine whether it achieves five basic objectives for an integrated system and whether and how easily it can be designed to handle certain key issues. Each of these principal methods would achieve more neutral taxation by (1) providing more uniform taxation of income between the corporate and noncorporate sectors; (2) reducing the tax bias favoring debt investment; and (3) reducing the incentives to retain rather than distribute earnings. Accordingly, the AICPA believes that an integration method must be chosen primarily on the basis of its ease of administration, its compatibility with foreign integrated systems, and its flexibility in addressing the key issues of tax preferences, tax-exempt investors, and international transactions.

Theoretically, the flow-through method is the purest form of integration; however, it would be considerably more difficult to administer and implement. Broadening the eligibility of the S corporation election by expanding the number of allowable shareholders would offer one alternative to the use of the flow-through method, but the use of the S corporation rules would not be practical for large, widely held corporations. Moreover, if policy makers were to decide not to extend integration benefits to tax-exempt and foreign shareholders, the flow-through method would need to include an appropriate withholding mechanism, further complicating implementation of the method. After careful review, the flow-through method was not chosen as a viable option because of the numerous problems in administering the method, its lack of flexibility in dealing with the key issues, and its incompatibility with foreign integrated systems.

Both of the other two alternatives, the dividends-paid deduction and the shareholder-credit methods, would offer a more practical and realistic means of achieving integration. The public's perception of the equity of each method may be an important factor in determining whether either is adopted. The public may perceive that the dividends-paid deduction method would confer all of the benefits on the corporation. The shareholder-credit method is likely to be more acceptable, since the public may perceive that the shareholder would receive a greater benefit than under the current system or the dividends-paid deduction method. On the other hand, the public may perceive that integration benefits only high-income taxpayers.

The United States could adopt either the deduction or the credit method with substantially the same tax results.[99] However, to achieve this equality, it must be assumed that the corporate-dividend policy would be comparable under both methods. In addition, the deduction method would be assumed to include a withholding mechanism and credits under both methods would be refundable.

Proponents of the dividends-paid deduction method argue that (1) it is simpler and easier to administer than the shareholder-credit system, (2) it handles the debt-equity problem more effectively, and (3) it can more easily restrict integration benefits to new equity. The simplicity and ease of administration of the dividends-paid deduction method is its most significant advantage. However, the modifications (including withholding) required to implement adjustments for foreign and tax-exempt shareholders, credits, and tax preferences would complicate this method greatly. Without these modifications, greater revenue loss, reduced compliance, and a decrease in the value of tax preferences could result. Consequently, such a modified deduction method would provide no significant advantages over a shareholder-credit

---

99. For example:

	Credit	Deductions
Corporate Level		
Net income	$1,000	$1,000
Cash dividend	660	1,000
Dividend deduction	0	1,000
Taxable income	1,000	0
Corporate tax (34%)	340	0
Withholding tax (31%)	0	310
Shareholder Level		
Cash dividend received	$660	$690
Gross-up inclusion	340	310
Shareholder income	1,000	1,000
Tax before credit	310	310
Credit	340	310
Refundable credit	(30)	0
Net Cash to Shareholder	$690	$690

method.

Another advantage of the dividends-paid deduction method is that it would provide for more neutral tax treatment of debt and equity. The shareholder-credit method would not achieve the same result, since the shareholders, not the corporation, would receive the benefits of integration. Therefore, under the credit method, corporations may continue to prefer debt because interest would be deductible, whereas dividends would not.

Proponents of the shareholder-credit method argue that it is preferable to the dividends-paid deduction method because (1) it would achieve a higher level of compliance with less effort, (2) it would be more flexible in dealing with foreign and tax-exempt shareholders and corporate tax preferences, (3) it would more easily conform to the integrated systems of other countries, and (4) it would not affect the corporation's financial statements.

The shareholder-credit method should have a higher level of compliance than the dividends-paid deduction method, unless the deduction method includes a withholding mechanism. The level of compliance would be higher under the credit method because taxpayers would report dividend income before receiving the benefit of the credit, whereas under the deduction method, the corporation would be permitted to take a deduction for dividends even if some shareholders failed to report the dividend income.

The shareholder-credit method can more easily be designed either to extend or to limit benefits for foreign and tax-exempt shareholders, and either to pass through or to limit the pass-through of tax preferences to shareholders. Although the deduction method, too, can be designed to address these issues, the credit system would handle them with far less complexity. A special provision for corporate tax preferences would make both methods more complex, but implementation of rules relating to tax preferences would be more difficult under the dividends-paid deduction method.

If policy makers decide not to extend integration benefits to tax-exempt shareholders, the shareholder-credit method could make the credit nonrefundable to tax-exempt organizations, whereas the dividends-paid deduction method would have to tax dividends as unrelated trade or business income (or include a withholding mechanism) to achieve the same result. Making the credit nonrefundable is easier to implement, and certainly less complex, than requiring withholding or taxing dividends as unrelated trade or business income.

The shareholder-credit method also can be more easily tailored to other specific types of shareholders. This feature is especially important when determining the proper treatment of foreign shareholders, and may be the reason why other countries have preferred the shareholder-credit instead of the deduction method. Conversely, the main drawback to the dividends-paid deduction method is that it would apply to all categories of shareholders equally. Under the credit method, the United States could make the credit nonrefundable to foreign shareholders and extend integration benefits to foreign shareholders only through bilateral treaty negotiations. The only way to prevent the granting of integration benefits to foreign shareholders under the deduction method would be to increase the withholding rate on dividends paid to such shareholders. However, such an increase could be very difficult, if not impossible, to achieve under the provisions of many existing tax treaties.

Another advantage of the shareholder-credit system is that it would not change the amount of net income a corporation reports in its financial statements. Because the corporate income tax liability would not change under this method, there would be no consistency problems with reporting the prior year's operations and cash flows, such as those that would occur under the deduction method.

International conformity, however, may be the most important advantage of the shareholder-credit method. All other major industrialized nations that have adopted integration use this method. This international experience not only would benefit the United States in designing and implementing an integration system, it also would make it easier to interface the U.S. system with foreign systems. Adopting the shareholder-credit method also would facilitate bilateral treaty negotiations on providing reciprocal integration benefits.

    * * *

On balance, the AICPA concludes that the shareholder-credit method best achieves the objectives of an integrated system, and therefore recommends its adoption by the United States.

REPORT ON INTEGRATION OF THE INDIVIDUAL AND CORPORATE TAX SYSTEMS
United States Department of the Treasury
Pages vii-x (1992)

Currently, our tax system taxes corporate profits distributed to shareholders at least twice—once at the shareholder level and once at the corporate level. If the distribution is made through multiple unrelated corporations, profits may be taxed more than twice. If, on the other hand, the corporation succeeds in distributing profits in the form of interest on bonds to a tax-exempt or foreign lender, no U.S. tax at all is paid.

The two-tier tax system (i.e., imposing tax on distributed profits in the hands of shareholders after taxation at the corporate level) is often referred to as a classical tax system. Over the past two decades, most of our trading partners have modified their corporate tax systems to "integrate" the corporate and shareholder taxes to mitigate the impact of imposing two levels of tax on distributed corporate profits. Most typically, this has been accomplished by providing the shareholder with a full or partial credit for taxes paid at the corporate level.

Integration would reduce three distortions inherent in the classical system:

    (a)   *The incentive to invest in noncorporate rather than corporate businesses.* Current law's double tax on corporations creates a higher effective tax rate on corporate equity than on noncorporate equity. The additional tax burden encourages "self-help" integration through disincorporation.

    (b)   *The incentive to finance corporate investments with debt rather than new equity.* Particularly in the 1980s, corporations issued substantial amounts of debt. By 1990, net interest expense reached a postwar high of 19 percent of corporate cash flow.

    (c)   *The incentive to retain earnings or to structure distributions of corporate profits in a manner to avoid the double tax.* Between 1970 and 1990, corporations' repurchases of their own shares grew from $1.2 billion (or 5.4 percent of dividends) to $47.9 billion (or 34 percent of dividends). By 1990, over one-quarter of corporate interest payments were attributable to the substitution of debt for equity through share repurchases.

These distortions raise the cost of capital for corporate investments; integration could be expected to reduce it. To the extent that an integrated system reduces incentives for highly-leveraged corporate capital structures, it would provide important non-tax benefits by encouraging the adoption of capital structures less vulnerable to instability in times of economic downturn. The Report contains estimates of substantial potential economic gains from integration. Depending on its form, the Report estimates that integration could increase the capital stock in the corporate sector by $125 billion to $500 billion, could decrease the debt-asset ratio in the corporate sector by 1 to 7 percentage points and could produce an annual gain to the U.S. economy as a whole from $2.5 billion to $25 billion.

Prototypes

This Report defines four integration prototypes and provides specifications for how each would work. Three prototypes are described in Part II: (1) the dividend exclusion prototype, (2) the shareholder allocation prototype, and (3) the Comprehensive Business Income Tax (CBIT) prototype. * * * For administrative reasons that the Report details, we have not recommended the shareholder allocation prototype (a system in which all corporate income is allocated to shareholders and taxed in a manner similar to partnership income under current law). Simplification concerns led us to prefer the dividend exclusion to any form of the imputation credit prototype.

In the dividend exclusion prototype, shareholders exclude dividends from income because they have already been taxed at the corporate level. Dividend exclusion provides significant integration benefits and requires little structural change in the Internal Revenue Code. When fully phased in, dividend exclusion would cost approximately $13.1 billion per year.

CBIT is, as its name implies, a much more comprehensive and larger scale prototype and will require significant statutory revision. CBIT represents a long-term, comprehensive option for equalizing the tax treatment of debt and equity. It is not expected that implementation of CBIT would begin in the short term, and full implementation would likely be phased in over a period of about 10 years. In CBIT, shareholders and bondholders exclude dividends and interest received from corporations from income, but neither type of payment is deductible by the corporation. Because debt and equity receive identical treatment in CBIT, CBIT better achieves tax neutrality goals than does the dividend exclusion prototype. CBIT is self-financing and would permit lowering the corporate rate to the maximum individual rate of 31 percent[o] on a revenue neutral basis, even if capital gains on corporate stock were fully exempt from tax to shareholders.

Policy Recommendations

In addition to describing prototypes, the Report makes several basic policy recommendations which we believe should apply to any integration proposal ultimately adopted:

(a) *Integration should not result in the extension of corporate tax preferences to shareholders*. This stricture is grounded in both policy and revenue concerns and has been adopted by every country with an integrated system. The mechanism for preventing passthrough of preferences varies; some countries utilize a compensatory tax mechanism and others simply tax preference-sheltered income when distributed (as we recommend in the dividend exclusion prototype). Both of these mechanisms are discussed in the Report.

(b) *Integration should not reduce the total tax collected on corporate income allocable to tax-exempt investors*. Absent this restriction, business profits paid to tax-exempt entities could escape all taxation in an integrated system. This revenue loss would prove difficult to finance and would exacerbate distortions between taxable and tax-exempt investors.

---

o. The top corporate rate no longer exceeds the top individual rate. Until 2010, the maximum rates for both corporations and individuals is 35%. After 2010, the top individual rate is scheduled to rise above the top corporate rate. (Ed.)

COMPARISON OF THE FOUR PRINCIPAL INTEGRATION PROTOTYPES

	DIVIDEND EXCLUSION	SHAREHOLDER ALLOCATION	CBIT	IMPUTATION CREDIT
Rates a) Distributed Income	Corporate rate	Shareholder rate[1]	CBIT rate (31 percent)	Shareholder rate[1]
b) Retained Income	Corporate rate (additional shareholder level tax depends on the treatment of capital gains)	Shareholder rate[1]	CBIT rate (additional investor level tax depends on the treatment of capital gains)	Corporate rate (additional shareholder level tax depends on the treatment of capital gains)
Treatment of non-corporate businesses	Unaffected	Unaffected	CBIT applies to non-corporate businesses as well as corporations, except for very small businesses.	Unaffected
Corporate tax preferences	Does not extend preferences to shareholders. Preference income is subject to shareholder tax when distributed.	Extends preferences to shareholders.	Does not extend preferences to investors. Preference income is subject to compensatory tax or investor level tax when distributed.	Does not extend preferences to shareholders. Preference income is subject to shareholder tax when distributed.
Tax-exempt investors	Corporate equity income continues to bear one level of tax.	Corporate equity income continues to bear one level of tax.	A CBIT entity's equity income and income used to pay interest bear one level of tax.	Corporate equity income continues to bear one level of tax.
Treatment of debt	Unaffected	Unaffected	Equalizes treatment of debt and equity	Unaffected (unless bondholder credit system adopted)

---

1. Plus 3 percentage points of corporate level tax not creditable because the prototype retains the 34 percent corporate rate but provides credits at the 31 percent shareholder rate. [The 34% and 31% rates were the maximum corporate and individual rates when this report was published. (Ed.)]

(c) *Integration should be extended to foreign shareholders only through treaty negotiations, not by statute.* This is required to assure that U.S. shareholders receive reciprocal concessions from foreign tax jurisdictions.

(d) *Foreign taxes paid by U.S. corporations should not be treated, by statute, identically to taxes paid to the U.S. Government.* Absent this limitation, integration could eliminate all U.S. taxes on foreign source profits in many cases.

A table summarizing the characteristics of each of the prototypes [is on the preceding page].

A PROPOSAL FOR ELIMINATING DOUBLE TAXATION OF CORPORATE DIVIDENDS
Fred W. Peel, Jr.[*]

39 Tax Lawyer 1, 1-6 (1985)

Introduction

This article develops in detail a proposal for eliminating double taxation of corporate dividends by excluding dividends from gross income at the individual shareholder level if the dividends are paid from income previously taxed at the corporate level. In brief, the proposal is to adopt a single corporate income tax rate equal to the maximum individual tax rate and permit shareholders to exclude from income dividends paid out of corporate earnings that have been taxed at the single corporate rate. It is submitted that the proposal would advance tax simplification, while taxing corporate profits on a more rational basis.

The past decade has seen wide discussion of methods [for] integrating the corporate and individual income taxes—either completely or partially. Full integration would treat corporate income as though it had been earned initially by the shareholders as individuals. Partial integration plans are designed to achieve that result for all or part of the dividends distributed to individual shareholders, either by crediting the shareholders with the corporate tax or by allowing corporations to deduct all or part of their dividends.

Exclusion of dividends from the income of individual shareholders heretofore has generally been dismissed out-of-hand.[5] There appear to have been three reasons for the lack of interest in the dividend exclusion approach. First, until the maximum individual tax rate on investment income was reduced to 50%, the wide disparity between the corporate tax rate and the higher individual rates would have meant that exclusion of dividends would discriminate unacceptably in favor of corporate income. With a maximum

---

[*]. At time of original publication, Professor of Law, University of Arkansas at Little Rock.

5. *See, e.g.*, C. McLure, Must Corporate Income Be Taxed Twice? 5 (1979).

individual tax rate of 50%, however, the gap has been narrowed significantly. Now it is feasible to suggest that the two rates be made the same, at some rate between 46% and 50%, or perhaps at some lower rate if one of the current base-broadening plans is enacted.[p] Regardless of the adjustment, the proposed dividend exclusion requires a nonprogressive corporate tax rate that equals the maximum individual rate.

Second, because some dividends, defined in terms of earnings and profits, may not have been taxed at the corporate level, exclusion of all dividends would permit some corporate income to escape tax altogether. The proposal here will exclude dividends at the individual shareholder level only when distributed from previously taxed income, and only from income earned by the corporation after the proposal has been put into effect.

Third, there has been widespread confusion between two different policy objectives—integration of corporate and shareholder taxes, on the one hand, and elimination of double taxation of dividends, on the other hand. Although their consequences overlap to some degree, the objectives of integration and of elimination of double taxation differ sharply. For example, full integration, by treating corporate income as though earned directly by the shareholders, would not merely eliminate the double tax but also all tax when the shareholder is an exempt organization (unless the tax is reimposed on exempt organizations as a corollary to the tax on unrelated business income, or as an extension of the tax now imposed on investment income of some exempt organizations, such as social clubs). In essence, integration assumes that the corporation is not an appropriate taxpayer and that its role should be, at most, that of a tax withholding agent for its shareholders. In contrast, eliminating double taxation of dividends treats the corporation as a viable and appropriate taxpayer. After the corporate tax has been imposed, however, no further tax should be imposed on the same income when, diminished by the corporate tax, it is distributed to the shareholders

The Objections to Double Taxation

Put simply, the double tax on corporate dividends is unfair. It violates the principle of horizontal equity. A shareholder who is taxed on a dividend out of earnings that already have been taxed at the corporate level is bearing a heavier tax burden than an individual in the same tax bracket receiving equivalent income through an S corporation, through a partnership, or directly as a sole proprietor.

---

p. This article appeared just before the Tax Reform Act of 1986 lowered both corporate and individual rates. At present (until 2011), the maximum rate applicable to both individuals and corporations is 35%. After 2010, the top individual rate is scheduled to rise to 39.6%. The logic of Professor Peel's argument calls for making the equivalence of corporate and top individual rates permanent, at 35 percent or some other figure. (Ed.)

It is true that in some circumstances the C corporation shareholder may be treated better than his counterparts, at least when the income is initially earned. This occurs when the corporation's earnings are not distributed as dividends and the tax paid at the corporate level is at a lower rate than the shareholder would pay if he or she had received the income directly. For this reason, the present system has been described as biased in favor of retained corporate earnings. This bias * * * would be eliminated altogether under the proposal by taxing corporate income in full at the maximum individual rate.

In addition to its unfairness, the incidence of the double tax is inconsistent because of the escape routes open to some shareholders in lieu of receiving taxable dividends. For example, the second tax can be cut * * * by selling the stock at a capital gain equivalent to the accumulated corporate earnings. The same result can be achieved by liquidating the corporation or by stock redemptions within the bounds of section 302(b). Some publicly held corporations have combined tender offers for, or market purchases of, their own stock with a policy of declaring little or no cash dividends.[15] In addition, if a shareholder holds stock in a corporation until his death and the value of the stock reflects the accumulated earnings, the basis of the stock will be stepped up by the amount of the accumulated earnings so that the stock can be sold or redeemed by the heirs without any second tax on earnings accumulated during the decedent's ownership.

Individual shareholders of publicly held corporations can sell their stock and attempt to realize a capital gain equivalent to their share of the accumulated earnings. If, however, the stock is sold to other individuals who are no better positioned to extract the accumulated earnings without dividend tax, the stock price will be discounted by the potential of an eventual dividend tax. Individual investors who hold stock in publicly held corporations and have chosen dividend-paying stocks in order to have current income are the principal victims of the double tax. There is no compelling policy reason for penalizing these people as a class.

The dividend tax, therefore, seriously distorts the pricing mechanism for stock in publicly held corporations. In essence, there are at least two markets for the stock, with widely divergent prices. One market is made up of individual investors, who must discount the value of the dividend income stream by the individual income tax they will have to pay. The second market is comprised of corporations that, at most, must discount the value of the dividend income stream by a tax on only 15%.[q] (Exempt organizations, such as

---

15. For example, Teledyne, Incorporated, a corporation that does not pay dividends, repurchased 8.66 million shares of its own common stock for $200 a share under a June 1984 tender offer.

q. When this article was written, corporations could deduct 85 percent of dividends received from other corporations (100 percent if the corporations were affiliated.) Under present law, the pension trusts, might be considered as composing another market.)

If a corporate buyer acquires 80% or more of the stock of a target corporation, it may elect a 100% dividends-received deduction on distributions of future earnings of the target. Alternatively, the acquiring corporation may file a consolidated return with the target, eliminating all dividends from it, or liquidate the target and receive the earnings from its operations directly thereafter. The corporate buyer can recover the cost of stock of a target corporation tax free through dividends paid by the target corporation out of the latter's earnings, whereas an individual buying and holding stock must recover his or her investment out of after-tax dollars from dividends. A takeover bid by another corporation lifts the stock out of the low-priced market of individual investors who must pay tax on their dividends and places it in the market of corporate buyers who can recover the price of the shares out of tax free dividends. For this reason, among others, we have the phenomenon of sudden increases in the price of stocks when corporations become takeover candidates. This possibility, in turn, encourages investors to seek out corporations that are likely to become takeover candidates.

The double tax clearly discourages dividends by publicly held corporations.
* * *

The additional corporate tax on unreasonable accumulations is designed to curb corporate retention of earnings and to force dividend payments. It applies only to accumulations that cannot be justified by the needs of a new or existing business, however, and in any event a business corporation may accumulate $250,000 without penalty.[r] In the vast majority of cases, a business use can be found for accumulated earnings. The postponement or eventual avoidance of the double tax, however, is as real and advantageous as for the shareholder of a corporation that accumulates earnings without a business use. Meanwhile, the Service is saddled with the tremendous administrative job of finding and penalizing the corporations that cannot adequately excuse their accumulations. Although in the past the tax on unreasonable accumulations was applied only to closely held corporations, it may now apply to publicly held corporations as well.

The double tax on dividends also distorts the corporate choice between debt and equity financing. Because interest on debt is deductible, corporate earnings applied to payment for the use of borrowed capital are taxed only once—to the lender. Debt and equity capital are by no means interchangeable when the debt is owed to persons other than shareholders, so the choice in that case between the two types of financing is not based merely on tax considerations. Moreover, the tax differential can be minimized by not paying out dividends. Nonetheless,

---

general deduction is 70 percent. Section 243. (Ed.)

   r. See section 535(c)(2). (Ed.)

for a corporation that *must* pay dividends for use of its equity capital, the double tax on dividends favors raising capital by borrowing.

It might be thought that the bias would remain under the proposal because dividends still will not be deductible by the corporation. If there is a sufficiently close identity between corporate management and shareholders, however, exclusion by the shareholder is as good as deduction by the corporation. Even in the absence of identity between management and ownership, the cost of equity capital will be reduced as a result of the dividend exclusion, balancing the ability to deduct interest paid on indebtedness.

In addition to distortion of the debt-equity ratio for corporations borrowing from persons other than their shareholders, the present tax treatment of corporate debt and equity has created an apparently insuperable problem of distinguishing between debt and equity owned by the same persons. It is advantageous for shareholders in closely held corporations to hold as much of their investment as possible in the form of debt to avoid double tax on payments for the use of the capital and to permit additional withdrawals to be characterized as repayment of debt. Short of treating all debt owed to controlling shareholders as equity, there does not seem to be any workable (or logical) standard that can be applied to distinguish shareholder-owned debt from equity. Congress' attempt in 1969 to delegate authority to draw the line by regulation so far has failed.[26] The problem appears to be unavoidable so long as interest is taxed once and earnings paid out as dividends are taxed twice.

* * *

Notes and Questions

24. The most obvious difference in the 2003 Act and President Bush's proposal is that the statute taxes dividends at a preferential rate, rather than exempting them as the President had proposed.

Less obvious, but of critical importance, is that the 2003 Act does not limit the favorable treatment to dividends paid out of earnings previously subjected to the corporate tax. Under section 316, a "dividend" is any payment made from a corporation's current or accumulated earnings and profits. Due to discrepancies between a corporation's taxable income and its earnings and profits, it is possible that a dividend is being paid from funds never subjected to a corporate tax. As the proposal argued, limiting the favorable treatment for dividends to earnings subjected to corporate tax would have "reduce[d] incentives for certain types of corporate tax planning." In a broader sense, it

---

26. The Treasury Department has so far been unsuccessful under section 385, added by section 415(a) of the Tax Reform Act of 1969, Pub. L. No. 91-172, 83 Stat. 613, in issuing regulations to distinguish stock from indebtedness. Regs. § 1.385-1 to -10 were finally adopted in 1980, but were later withdrawn by T.D. 7920, 1983-2 C.B. 69.

would mean that a proposal aimed at elimination of double taxation could not be converted into elimination of all tax.

25.   A dividend exclusion might seem to change a corporate bias against paying dividends into a corporate bias against retaining earnings. Distributions from corporate earnings would be tax-free at the shareholder level.   By contrast, if corporate earnings were retained and share values increased as a result, a selling shareholder would be taxed on the resulting capital gain.

How did the Bush proposal address this perceived problem?

26.   Under the Bush proposal, a corporation's "excludable dividend amount" would become an important corporate tax attribute, such as earnings and profits or operating loss carryforwards.   The proposal envisioned a corporation's EDA being combined with that of another corporation in case of merger, or being separated into two parts in case of a spin-off.

27.   Under both the Bush proposal and the 2003 Act, the tax treatment of retirement funds would be unaltered. Consider, for example, a traditional IRA that is deductible when made and that is invested in common stocks. As under prior law, the initial contribution gives rise to the same tax saving (deduction), and the distributions are subjected to ordinary income tax rates.

Would you expect that either the Bush proposal or the 2003 Act would reduce incentives to contribute to retirement plans? Why, or why not? If so, do you view this as a problem?

28.   Tax rate changes in recent years, by bringing the top rates for individuals and for corporations closer together, have made ending the double tax on dividends more acceptable.

29.   Is a double tax eventually imposed on corporate earnings that are retained and reinvested? Is the capital gains tax on sale of corporate stock a double tax where reinvested earnings have increased the market price of a corporation's stock?

30.   How can the double tax be avoided or minimized by closely held C corporations?

31.   Treasury I asserts that by encouraging use of debt rather than equity, present law leads to increased numbers of bankruptcies during recessions. Why might this be so?

32. If the double tax were ended, would the attitude of stockholders be changed toward management's choice between retaining earnings and paying them out as dividends?

33. If corporations could deduct dividends, as they can deduct interest now, could corporate management resist pressure to distribute earnings?

34. Adoption of any of the proposals would be likely to encourage more liberal dividend policies, because corporate directors could no longer point to the double taxation of dividends as a reason to retain earnings. Corporate expansions would more often be financed by issuing new debt or equity rather than through retained earnings. Would these developments be desirable, as Treasury I asserts?

35. Professor Warren writes that adoption of his proposals "would convert the separate U.S. corporate income tax into a withholding tax with respect to income ultimately distributed to shareholders." What does this mean?

36. If shareholders were allowed to credit corporate income tax allocable to their dividends, why should the shareholders be required to "gross up," or increase, the dividends they receive by the amount credited? For example, if a corporation earned $100, paid $35 in tax, and distributed the remaining $65 in dividends, the shareholders would be required to report $100 of dividends, rather than $65, and would be granted a $35 credit against tax.

37. Why does Professor Warren propose that corporations that have not distributed dividends be allowed to make "constructive distributions," which then would be deemed to have been reinvested in the stock of the corporation?

38. The AICPA asserts that addressing the double tax problem through the shareholder-credit method would result in a higher level of taxpayer compliance than would the dividend-deduction method. Why?

39. According to the AICPA, what is the most important reason to prefer the shareholder-credit method over the dividend-deduction method?

40. The first paragraph of the excerpt from the 1992 Treasury proposal refers to the distribution of profits in the form of interest on bonds. This is overly broad. Interest paid to bondholders is a cost, not a distribution of profits, unless the bondholders also own the equity interest in the distributing

corporation—in which case the distinction between profit and interest expense can be considered artificial.

41. Should dividends paid from income that has been subject to foreign corporate income tax be eligible for whatever shareholder credit or exclusion is provided? What is the view of the 1992 Treasury proposal?

42. Peel argues that the double tax on dividends makes it possible for another corporation to offer a higher price for stock of a target corporation than individual stockholders would offer. Why might this be so?

43. Like other proponents of change, Peel argues that the present double-tax system leads to various economic problems. He also asserts, however, that the classic treatment of dividends—separate taxes at the corporate and shareholder level—is "unfair." Do you agree?

44. How should tax-exempt organizations be treated if the double tax system is ended? Under present law, if Irene Individual and the First Methodist Church each owns 100 shares of AT&T stock, each bears the same portion of the corporate tax, but only Irene pays a shareholder-level tax. Should integration or dividend relief result in the church being relieved of all tax with respect to AT&T earnings?

45. Under the shareholder-credit model, the corporation would pay the corporate income tax, which would generate a credit for shareholders. If this model were adopted, should a tax-exempt shareholder receive a refundable credit (and thus a check from the government, because it presumably would not have any tax liability to absorb the credit)? Professor Warren would impose a tax on dividends (as well as interest) received by tax-exempt organizations, then allow the credit with any excess credit being refundable.

46. Can a fully integrated system—taxing shareholders on all corporate income, distributed or undistributed—be devised that is practical? Would it help to make the corporation a withholding agent for its shareholders?

47. One consequence of the Hall-Rabushka flat tax proposal, which is excerpted in Chapter Seven (page 450), would be to eliminate tax on dividends. Unlike the Bush proposal (but in accord with the approach actually taken in the 2003 Act), Hall-Rabushka would not condition the shareholder-level exclusion on the dividend having been paid from earnings previously taxed at the corporate level.

48. Can it be argued that present stockholders are not penalized by the double tax because the price they paid for their stock already reflects a discount for the double tax? Would a change in the law be a windfall for such shareholders?

49. Of the various reform proposals to address the problem of double taxation, which do you find most attractive? Why?

D. INTEREST DEDUCTIONS AND RETAINED EARNINGS

Throughout the preceding subchapter, proponents of ending the double tax on corporate earnings referred to the debt-equity issue. They argue that because corporations are entitled to deduct interest but not dividends, while the recipients are taxed on both, the tax system influences corporations toward the use of debt. This subchapter focuses on the debt-equity aspect of the problem.

Professor William Andrews, Reporter for the American Law Institute's Subchapter C Project, argued that the bias in favor of debt could be addressed by integrating corporate and individual taxes by one of the various techniques discussed earlier in this chapter. But this result could be obtained only "at a substantial cost in revenue and progressivity, since a high proportion of dividends flow to high-income, wealthy individuals." (This is an academic formulation of the Democrats' claim that the 2003 reduction in dividend taxes is a "giveaway to the rich.") Andrews, therefore, makes the more limited argument that the tax law's preference for debt should be ended only with respect to new equity.

The shift from equity to debt in corporate financial structures was of particular concern to Professor Michael Graetz (Assistant Secretary of the Treasury for Tax Policy under the elder President Bush) because such a large share of corporate bonds is owned by organizations that pay little or no tax on their interest income. Thus, the corporate deduction for interest expense is not compensated for by tax at the creditor level. The net result is no tax, as contrasted to the double tax on corporate earnings paid out as dividends to taxed shareholders. Professor Graetz proposes implementing a single-level corporate tax on all earnings, whether attributable to debt or equity.

Finally, Professor Sappideen argues that the tax system is not to "blame" for corporations' preference for debt finance. He argues that this preference is due to financial incentives independent of the tax system.

AMERICAN LAW INSTITUTE REPORTER'S STUDY OF THE TAXATION OF CORPORATE DISTRIBUTIONS, APPENDIX TO SUBCHAPTER C PROPOSALS

William D. Andrews,[*] Reporter

Pages 327-33 (1982)

Throughout this century the United States has pursued the classical system of taxing corporate earnings, in which corporations and shareholders are treated effectively as separate income taxpayers. Corporations are taxed as such on corporate income, whether or not distributed. Shareholders, on the other hand, are taxed on their dividends without any significant credit for corporate taxes paid on the earnings from which they come. Distributed corporate earnings are therefore said to be doubly taxed, first to the corporation that earns them and then to the shareholders to whom they are distributed.

This treatment of dividend income is to be contrasted with the treatment of corporate interest payments. * * * Interest on corporate debt is fully taxable to the recipient, but it is deductible by the corporate payor; corporate revenue distributed as interest is therefore only taxed once, to the investor-distributee, not to the corporation. * * *

These differences in tax treatment generate both economic distortions and legal problems. The deductibility of interest and nondeductibility of dividends create an inducement to raise money by issuing debt instruments rather than stock, and they generate a legal problem of differentiating between debt and equity interests. * * *

One approach to these problems would be to accept as given the treatment described for each of these modes of distribution, but try to provide a better definition of the boundary lines between them. In particular, this would involve constructing a better way to differentiate between debt and equity for tax purposes. * * *

This approach has been taken in much valuable prior work. The trouble with this approach, however, is that it cannot eliminate or even much mitigate the disparities in treatment with which it deals; wherever the lines are drawn, substantial disparities will persist along with the economic and legal pressures they generate.

A bolder approach, widely discussed in the recent past, would seek to temper these disparities by eliminating or reducing double taxation of distributed earnings through integration of corporate and individual shareholder taxes. * * *

Any of these methods of integration would indeed reduce disparities

---

[*]. At time of original publication, Professor of Law, Harvard University.

among modes of distribution, by eliminating or reducing the double taxation of dividend income.   But that objective would only be accomplished at a substantial cost in revenue and progressivity, since a high proportion of dividends flow to high-income, wealthy individuals.   The initial effect of complete dividend relief would be almost to double the after-tax income of shareholders from dividends if aggregate corporate disbursements for taxes and dividends were held constant.

The approach explored in this Study runs along less familiar lines somewhere in between more general integration and mere refinement of existing boundaries.   The basic distribution of tax burdens imposed by the existing classical system has been taken as given, and there is no proposal, therefore, to eliminate or even reduce the burden of double taxation on dividend income from existing equity investment.   On the other hand, it has not been taken as given that the existing disparity in treatment between debt and equity * * * should be maintained.   Rather than redefining boundaries between debt and equity, * * * this Study proposes that disparities in treatment be reduced by making substantive changes.   Specifically, it is proposed to reduce or eliminate the disparity between debt and equity by giving particular limited relief for dividends on newly issued shares.   * * *

The proposals in this Study * * * are published here solely as a Reporter's Study.   * * *

Summary of Reporter's Distribution Proposals
   * * *

1) *Newly contributed equity capital.*   Existing law discriminates in favor of debt over newly issued equity by allowing a deduction for interest payments but not for dividends. This bias is familiar in theory and in practice, and it lies at the root of the seemingly intractable legal problem of differentiating satisfactorily between debt and equity for tax purposes.

Less obviously, perhaps, existing law also discriminates in favor of internally generated equity capital over contributed capital, by deferring individual income taxes on accumulation of the former. The effect of that deferral is similar to the benefit that would be conferred if individuals were allowed a deduction for purchasing newly issued shares. This bias is less familiar, stated this way, than the bias in favor of debt, but it is equally consistent with common experience. The main source of equity capital for most corporations other than regulated utilities is accumulation of earnings.

Because of this second bias, the existing discrimination in favor of debt can be defined more narrowly than at first appears.   In effect, it is only a discrimination against newly contributed equity capital, not all equity, since accumulated earnings enjoy the compensatory advantage of individual tax deferral.

Reporter's Proposal R1 is to relieve this discrimination, thus narrowly defined, by treating newly contributed equity capital like debt, allowing a deduction for dividends paid up to some specified rate on the amount of capital contributed. In effect, the proposal is to treat all newly contributed debt and equity capital alike by making its cost largely deductible.

This proposal bears some resemblance to schemes for partially integrating corporate and individual taxes by allowing some deduction or credit for all dividends. But the focus of this proposal is narrower, and its revenue cost and redistributional impact are very much less, since it would not permit any deduction for dividends attributable to income from capital accumulated by retention of earnings. Moreover, it is not even proposed to allow any deduction for dividends from earnings on contributed capital invested prior to the proposal's effective date. The primary aim of the proposal is simply to remove the bias against future equity contributions; it is too late to pursue that objective with respect to past contributions.

By mitigating or eliminating the bias against new issues of stock, the proposal would go a long way toward resolving the legal problem of differentiating between debt and equity. * * *

THE TAX ASPECTS OF LEVERAGED BUYOUTS AND OTHER CORPORATE FINANCIAL RESTRUCTURING TRANSACTIONS
Michael J. Graetz[*]
42 Tax Notes 721, 721-26 (1989)

There apparently is little evidence that recent mergers and acquisitions have been predominantly motivated by tax reasons. * * * The tax aspects of leveraged buyouts (LBOs) and other corporate financial restructuring, however, play a very significant role in how the transactions are structured, and are a worthy subject for congressional attention for both long- and short-term reasons.

Corporate Tax Base Problems

The immediate fiscal problem is the potential erosion of the corporate tax base. * * *

From both an immediate and a longer term, or structural, perspective of the corporate income tax, the most serious problem seems to be the long-lamented fact that the tax burden on income earned by a corporation and distributed to shareholders as dividends bears a heavier tax burden than corporate income distributed in other forms or to other suppliers of capital —most importantly, amounts distributed to bondholders as interest. Unlike

---

*. At time of original publication, Justice S. Hotchkiss Professor of Law, Yale University.

dividends, interest is deductible at the corporate level and, therefore, bears no corporate income tax. This disparity creates tax incentives for raising corporate capital through debt rather than equity and for substituting debt for equity. * * * [D]uring the period 1984 through 1987, corporate equity apparently decreased by more than $300 billion, while corporate debt increased in excess of $600 billion. These numbers alone obviously portend major revenue effects from substitutions of corporate debt for equity and, potentially, from restructuring the corporate income tax law.

 * * *

Needless to say, this number of potential variables, coupled with great flexibility in structuring corporate finance, make it extremely difficult either to obtain and maintain a firm grasp of the matters at stake or to devise a solution that cannot readily be undone by tax planners for the corporate and investment communities. These difficulties are further compounded by our general reliance on similar tax rules to govern the taxation of huge multinational corporations and small corporate businesses.

Substituting Debt for Equity

Such complexities, however, should not be permitted to obscure the potential impact of corporate financial restructuring on the Federal revenues. A back-of-the-envelope calculation demonstrates the critical points. The corporate income tax today generates nearly $100 billion of revenues, and additional revenues are produced by shareholder and creditor level taxes on dividends, interest, and stock and bond sales. These also are significant potential sources of revenues for state governments, many of which are confronting fiscal crises of their own.

At the extreme, $100 of corporate income distributed as dividends to a shareholder taxed at the top 33-percent marginal rate can produce as much as $55.78 of Federal income taxes ($34 at the corporate level plus $21.78 at the shareholder level (33 percent of the distributed $66 of after-tax income)). If the dividends are distributed to * * * a tax-exempt shareholder, the government collects only the $34 of corporate income taxes. By comparison, $100 of corporate income distributed as interest to bondholders bears no tax at the corporate level and is subject to a maximum of $33 of total Federal tax if distributed to the highest marginal bracket individual, * * * and no tax at all if distributed to a tax-exempt creditor. Corporate income that is retained at the corporate level normally bears a 34-percent corporate income tax.[s]

Depending on the corporation's method of raising capital, therefore, the Federal government's taxes on corporate-source income can range from zero to nearly 56 percent. If a single level tax were levied either in the form of a

---

s. As discussed in Subchapter A, the 2003 Act significantly, if temporarily, reduces the shareholder-level tax on distributed corporate earnings, by (generally) taxing dividends at 15%.

corporate income tax or at the top marginal rate applicable to individuals, the Federal government's tax would be roughly equal to one-third of the income, while about two-thirds would stay in private hands.

In 1985, the last year for which IRS data is available, corporate taxable income before interest deductions for domestic nonfinancial corporations totaled nearly $440 billion. A single Federal tax imposed at a 33-percent rate on such income would have produced about $145 billion of revenues, a number that seems to be at least as great as that year's combined corporate and individual level income taxes on all corporate-source income (by which I mean, simply, the net pretax income earned by corporations before it is divided among those who have contributed to the corporation the capital with which the income was earned, *viz.* the creditors and shareholders).

Federal Reserve estimates suggest that about one-half of corporate equity at the end of 1987 was held by individuals, while the other half was held by charitable organizations, pension funds, foreign investors, or life insurance companies, which are likely to receive favorable Federal income tax treatment. By contrast, only about five percent of corporate bonds are thought to be owned by individuals. Thus, a shift from equity to debt as a source of corporate capital will serve to avoid corporate income taxes and, in addition, will tend to reduce or eliminate individual income tax revenues. * * *

Inadequate Solutions

It is no small irony that this year marks the twentieth anniversary of two well-known "solutions" to the kinds of problems we are discussing here today. The first is section 385, added to the Internal Revenue Code in 1969, which, as every schoolchild knows, delegated to Treasury regulatory authority to resolve the question how to distinguish between debt and equity. The Treasury Department failed to produce as much as a whimper in this regard until it issued proposed regulations in 1980 that ultimately were withdrawn in 1983 when the enterprise attempting to distinguish debt from equity based on their economic substance once again returned to a moribund state.

The 1969 Tax Reform Act also added section 279 to the Code in an effort to restrict deductibility of interest on acquisition indebtedness, apparently on the view that, like construction period interest, such interest is in the nature of a capital expenditure. Corporate financiers, however, apparently have not found section 279 to be even a tiny barrier to corporate financial restructuring or LBOs.

The two decades of experience with these laws suggest great caution in attempting to enact solutions that require the recharacterization of debt as equity or that attempt to limit a disallowance of interest to indebtedness incurred for a particular purpose, such as a hostile (or even any) takeover. The past two decades also teach that there is little gain and no stability to be had from such marginal tinkering as opposed to beginning to address the underlying fundamental income tax problems. One cannot help but wonder where we would be today if Congress in 1969 or even in 1978—when Congressman Ullman, then chair of the House Ways and Means Committee, advanced such a proposal—had begun to phase in an integrated corporate tax that eliminated, or at least narrowed, the corporate income tax treatment of debt and equity.

* * *

A Single Tax on Corporate Income

* * *

What needs to be done, I think, is to begin now to move toward a single tax on corporate-source income—by which I again simply mean a single tax on the net pretax income earned by a corporation before it is divided among the creditors and shareholders who have contributed to the corporation the capital with which the income was earned. As indicated earlier, such a single tax should produce revenues at least equal to the combined corporate and individual income taxes now imposed on all corporate-source income, and, in addition, would ensure that the Federal government would share in any future growth in such income.

I do not mean to suggest by this observation that this is an appropriate occasion for raising additional revenues from taxes on corporate income, although it does seem the proper moment to halt the ongoing disappearance of the corporate tax base. There are a variety of revenue-neutral ways to begin to move toward the goal of a single tax on corporate income, and I think that it is important that steps be taken clearly in this direction now, indeed, far more important than the precise contours of such steps. My preferred solution, however, would be to phase in a shareholder-credit type integration of corporate dividends, financed through an identical bondholder-credit approach to interest payments. This would be an important first step toward equal treatment for corporate debt and equity.

Such a proposal is grounded in the lessons learned from thinking in some detail about corporate tax integration. In particular, we have learned that a dividend and interest deduction or, as an alternative, a shareholder and bondholder credit are essentially equivalent methods of eliminating the corporate tax burden on distributed earnings with respect to debt or equity contributed or owned by shareholders or bondholders who are allowed the credit.

In brief outline, a tax credit could be provided to shareholders for some portion or all of the corporate tax paid with respect to corporate earnings distributed to shareholders as dividends. Likewise, in lieu of the interest deduction, a similar tax credit could be provided to bondholders for some portion or all of the corporate tax paid with respect to corporate earnings distributed to bondholders as interest. The shareholder or bondholder would include both the amount of the tax and the cash dividend or interest in income and receive a tax credit for the amount of the tax.

* * *

To be sure, if the credit were not refundable, much of the burden of shifting from an interest deduction to a bondholder credit system would be borne by foreign creditors and tax-exempt bondholders, while the benefits of the shareholder credit would tend to accrue to individual shareholders who now bear the burden of the double corporate tax. However, many of the benefits of elimination of the corporate tax from substitution of debt for equity in leveraged buyouts and other corporate recapitalization transactions are now accruing to those same nontaxable persons and entities. * * *

[T]his idea merits the serious attention of Congress, because it implies a corporate income tax that would not distinguish between debt and equity and that, by providing such equal treatment, would eliminate the potential provided by current law to erode the corporate tax by substituting debt for equity. It has the additional advantage of abandoning the fruitless quest of the past two decades for a workable distinction between debt and equity. It would represent an important step toward neutrality between corporate and noncorporate investments, neutrality between debt and equity finance at the corporate level, and neutrality between retention and distribution of corporate earnings. At the same time, it avoids any effort to permit or disallow interest deductions based on the purpose of incurring a debt; such an enterprise is inevitably complex and ultimately will prove unsuccessful. If some basic structural change along these lines suggested here is not begun now, I fear that we simply can look forward to future years and perhaps decades of half-solutions or nonsolutions.

* * *

IMPUTATION OF THE CORPORATE AND PERSONAL INCOME TAX: IS IT CHASING ONE'S TAIL?
Razeen Sappideen[*]

15 American Journal of Tax Policy 167, 171, 174-83 (1998)

The Issue of Neutrality

* * *

The Preference for Debt

The corporation income tax is said to encourage debt financing rather than equity financing because interest is ordinarily deductible under most tax systems, whereas dividends are not. The over reliance on debt financing is

---

[*]. At time of original publication, Foundation Professor, School of Law, University of Western Sydney Nepean, Australia.

claimed to cause a welfare loss by increasing the vulnerability of corporations to bankruptcy. In other words, the elimination of the double taxation of dividends, it is claimed, will reduce the occurrence of bankruptcy not only by making equity financing more attractive vis-à-vis debt financing, but also by making equity holdings more attractive in their own right. * * *

The evidence as to whether the corporate tax significantly alters the debt-equity ratio is in itself inconclusive. A German study, for example, has found that the proportion of corporate capital investment financed by new equity dropped in that country despite the passage of a reduced tax rate on dividend distributions.[27] Further, a comparison of the debt-equity ratios of firms in the United States revealed no significant change between the 1920s and the 1950s, despite a quintupling of the corporate tax rate.[28] A study of corporate behaviour in the United Kingdom, on the other hand, concluded that the tax advantages of debt financing explained more than 80 percent of the variation in the debt to equity ratio during the years studied.[29] * * * Despite the economic literature on the subject being open ended, the discussion in this Article accepts as fact that the interest deduction makes borrowings extremely attractive compared to new share capital, and that the additional tier of taxation under the classical system makes corporate retentions attractive to shareholders subject to the additional tax.

    * * *

[T]here is no reason to believe that the shortcomings identified with the classical model will cease to exist under integration, as leverage is just as attractive under integration as it is under the classical model. * * *

Shareholders as Beneficiaries of Debt

Implied in the arguments of integrationists advancing equity against debt is the assumption that the preference for debt is egregious if for no other reason than it increases the occurrence of bankruptcy. A primary difficulty with this attempted rationalisation is that despite the very many efforts to draw up models (accounting, financial, and statistical) that would successfully predict the likelihood of corporate failure, none has been found reliable. * * * Corporations for their part make skilful use of debt and equity to enhance the value of the corporation, a practice commonly referred to as leverage. Those who stand to benefit by the product of such corporate alchemy are its shareholders, a fact that may be illustrated by the following example.

Assume a corporation with a single paid-up share of $100, bringing

---

27. Harry G. Gourevitch, *Corporate Income Tax Integration: The European Experience*, 31 TAX LAW. 65, 81 (1977).

28. *See* Merton H. Miller, *Debt and Taxes*, 32 J. Fin. 261, 264 (1977).

29. *See* J. GREGORY BALLENTINE, EQUITY, EFFICIENCY, AND THE U.S. CORPORATION INCOME TAX 62 (1980).

in a pretax profit of 20% on the investment, and subject to corporate tax at a flat rate of 40%. The after-tax profit of this corporation will be $12. Now if the corporation borrows another $100 at an interest rate of 6%, which generates a further return of 20% on which the corporation pays 40% tax, it will have an additional $8.40 of after-tax profit. The pretax return will now be $34, on the investment of $200, which includes the borrowed $100, and the after-tax return $20.40 ($40 − $6 (interest) = $34 − $13.60 tax = $20.40). Subject to the risks associated with bankruptcy and its cash flow restraints, a corporation can borrow as much as it can profitably use to minimise its tax liability. From the corporation's point of view, it has by this combination of equity and debt made an after-tax profit for itself of $20.40 compared to the equity only profit of $12.

Two points follow from the above illustration. The first is that, if the corporation had issued $200 worth of shares only (instead of $100 worth of shares and $100 of debt), it would have a surplus of $24 (instead of $20.40 in the 50 percent debt example above, as there is no interest expense), and each shareholder would have an after-tax stake in the corporation worth only $12. This contrasts with the combined debt and equity example ($100 shares and $100 debt) where the shareholder stake in the corporation is worth $20.40. The point then is that the expected gains for shareholders, whether in the form of dividends or capital appreciation, is far greater when share capital is combined with debt than when share capital is used alone. The theoretical literature on the benefits flowing from debt to shareholders is divided. Some view the results of corporate debt in negative terms, namely, as increasing shareholder risk because creditor claims now take priority. In contrast, debt may be seen as providing, in addition to the tax advantage, a spread of risk that shareholders alone would otherwise have to bear. Thus instead of risking $200 for a possible return of $24, the shareholder can limit the risk to $100 for a possible return of $20.40. This strategy of capital risk diversification by the corporation complements its other strategy of product diversification. * * *

The second, and perhaps more important point flowing from the above example is that this benefit of leverage will continue to be available to both shareholders and the corporation under integration, as well it is under the classical system. In other words, imputation does not eliminate the benefits of debt accruing to the corporation, or to shareholders borrowing in their own right. It also means that imputation will not abate the desire for debt financing by either the corporation or the investor for the simple reason that while returns on equity are capable of being enhanced by combining debt, the converse is not possible. Hence, there will always be a built-in preference by corporations for debt as against new equity under both tax models. * * *

Windfall Gains and the Cost of New Equity

The claim that integration will result in new equity being cheaper, thereby eliminating the preference for debt under the classic model is equally flawed, as it ignores the way markets price securities. Matters taken into account in the pricing of securities include the asset backing of the share, cash flow and liquidity, leverage, return on investment (being net income divided by total assets), and most importantly, the price/earnings ratio. The latter is calculated on the basis of the market price per share divided by the earnings per share. What is important is that the higher after-tax income that results from the tax credit under integration, will cause the price of shares to increase correspondingly. In other words, if the expected return on an investment is 8 percent, an anticipated return of 12 percent following a changeover to imputation will attract market participants to bid the share price up (other things being equal) until it equalizes with returns from other comparable investments with similar returns. Consequently, the price of already issued shares of the corporation will increase to accommodate this increased rate of earnings. This market adaptation to new information has been explained in terms of rational expectations theory, according to which markets, particularly financial markets, respond to anticipated events including fiscal reform and institutional changes.

Furthermore, as new issues are priced near enough to the market price of existing stock (for if not, the corporation will be making a gift of its shares), there will be no bargains offered on these shares by reason of integration. For this reason, it appears incorrect to assume that new issues under integration will continue to be available at prices that would have prevailed under the classical system. Consequently, integration will not result in new shares becoming a more attractive alternative to debt. In other words the benefits expected of integration will have been undone by individuals and by markets in anticipation of the event. Despite the institutional change effected through the switchover from one model to the other, no worthwhile results flow from the change itself. What will result from integration then, is a windfall gain to existing shareholders who benefit by the increase in their share prices.

* * *

It may be argued that the so-called windfall gain is nothing more than just compensation for past double taxation. Such an argument, based on the notion of initial entitlements, is flawed as it ignores the role of the marketplace as a decisionmaker on commercial matters. Since, absent transaction costs, investments move in the direction of highest returns, returns received by shareholders whether under the classical system or imputation, will always be relative to returns available from other comparable investments at any given point of time. For this reason, the argument of just compensation for past double taxation, would seem not to hold.

There are then difficulties with both the new and traditional views, and policymakers need to adopt both an eclectic and pragmatic approach here as elsewhere. In the real world corporations do pay dividends, raise share capital in the market, and make extensive use of debt and retained earnings, although not all of these at the same time. Further, corporations are influenced by clientele requirements as to returns, and markets do have a bearing on corporations holding on to free cash flow. In other words investors, influenced by their after-tax returns, shop around for returns (dividends, capital gains, and interest), and corporations try to please them. * * *

Notes and Questions

50. Corporations postpone the double tax by retaining and reinvesting earnings and, for most years, pay a single income tax at a rate lower than the top individual income tax rate. Does this justify imposing an additional corporate tax when corporations distribute their accumulated earnings in liquidation?

51. How does present law discriminate in favor of debt financing as contrasted with equity financing?

52. Professor Andrews is concerned with potential avenues of escape from a full tax on corporate earnings at the shareholder level. His concern arises from the ability of corporations to reinvest their accumulated earnings without their having been subjected to a second tax at the shareholder level.

53. Should discrimination against corporate equity compared to corporate debt be ended by denying corporations the right to deduct bond interest as well as dividends, and perhaps allowing credit to both bondholders and stockholders for corporate tax paid? Would such treatment have to be extended to interest on other types of corporate debt as well? Would similar treatment have to be given to partnerships? To sole proprietorships?

54. If corporations were denied a deduction for interest payments, would it also be necessary to deny a deduction for rent? After all, interest is simply rent for one category of property—money. What would prevent shareholders who wanted to keep personal ownership of property used by the corporation, and remove money from the corporation in a form deductible by the corporation, from achieving these ends by renting property to a corporation rather than lending it money at interest?

55. Professor Graetz proposes "a single tax on corporate-source income." What does he mean by this?

56. Professor Graetz asserts that his proposal could be implemented in a revenue-neutral manner, but prevent continued erosion of the corporate tax base. A corporation's interest payments would no longer be deductible, while equity would be treated better (through some form of integration to avoid double taxation).

Suppose the creditors of a corporation are unrelated to its owners. If the corporation's interest expense exceeds its income before interest—meaning that the corporation has actually incurred a loss—is it appropriate to tax the corporation on its "profit" ignoring interest?

57. Would any unfairness from taxing the corporation on illusory "profit," as the preceding question suggests, be adequately addressed by allowing the creditors a tax credit for taxes paid at the corporate level? Graetz asserts that "a dividend and interest deduction or, as an alternative, a shareholder and bondholder credit are essentially equivalent methods of eliminating corporate tax burden on distributed earnings with respect to debt or equity contributed or owned by shareholders or bondholders who are allowed the credit." Why might this be so?

58. The treatment of tax-exempt creditors is crucial, because a large proportion of debt is held by such entities. (Graetz states that only about five percent of corporate bonds are held by individuals.) Under present law, frequently the corporation's interest deduction is *not* offset by tax imposed on the creditor (because the creditor is tax-exempt).

If we adopted a plan of taxing corporations without a deduction for interest, but then allowed creditors (like shareholders) a credit for taxes paid at the corporate level, how should tax-exempt creditors be treated? If allowed a "refundable" credit, they would receive a check from the Government. If not, they would, in a sense, bear a portion of tax at the corporate level, which may seem inconsistent with their tax-exempt status.

59. Professor Sappideen takes issue with the frequent claim that present law influences corporations to prefer debt financing as opposed to additional equity financing. The claim is facially plausible, because the corporation can deduct payments to providers of debt financing (interest), but cannot deduct payments to providers of equity (dividends).

From this, arguably, it follows that the corporation is put at greater risk of bankruptcy, because a board of directors cannot suspend debt service during a difficult period, but can suspend dividends. The risk of bankruptcy, in turn, it said to prejudice the interests of shareholders, whose stock becomes worthless in case of bankruptcy.

Sappideen rejects this analysis, and claims that shareholders are the primary beneficiaries of corporate debt. Why might this be so?

60. Professor Sappideen argues that the advantages of debt to shareholders—the opportunity of higher risks while sharing risks with creditors—would lead corporations to utilize debt even if the tax treatment of debt and equity were equalized.

Obviously, debt would not disappear from corporate finance if interest were no longer deductible, or if dividends were not subject to a double tax. But would the use of debt be significantly reduced?

61. Sappideen argues that existing shareholders would receive a windfall if double taxation of corporate earnings were ended, and rejects the notion that "the so-called windfall gain is nothing more than just compensation for past double taxation." He rejects this argument, because "it ignores the role of the marketplace as a decisionmaker on commercial matters."

Do you agree with Sappideen? Or, would it be accurate to observe that the marketplace bases prices and yields based on perceptions of risks and opportunities, and that reduction or end of the double tax is one of the opportunities to be considered?

When Congress considers changing the tax rules after investment decisions have been made, is the issue different when the change is favorable to the taxpayer (as in the elimination of double taxation) as contrasted to an unfavorable change (for example, the effect on existing homeowners of ending the mortgage interest deduction)?

62. As discussed in Note #13 (page 871), present law contains several limitations on interest deductions by corporations.

E. THE POLITICS OF CORPORATE INTEGRATION

As we have seen throughout this chapter, there is a solid policy basis for ending the double taxation of corporate earnings. Yet—notwithstanding the substantial relief granted by the 2003 Act—double taxation endures. This can hardly be explained by Congressional deference to populist public opinion, because Congress regularly enacts tax preferences favoring corporations, such as accelerated depreciation.

Professors Jennifer Arlen and Deborah Weiss argue that the leaders of corporate America—managers of large, publicly held corporations—pursue interests that significantly differ from those of their companies' shareholders. Arlen and Weiss explain how these differences explain corporations' use of political capital, and suggest political strategies for proponents of ending double taxation.

A POLITICAL THEORY OF CORPORATE TAXATION
Jennifer Arlen[*] & Deborah M. Weiss[**]
105 Yale Law Journal 325, 326-31, 333-42, 346-50, 352, 355-63, 365-69 (1995)

Introduction

The American tax system imposes a double tax on the profits of corporations. This two-tier taxation is unusual, unfair, and inefficient. * * *

The persistence of the double-level tax is puzzling. To be sure, the tax code contains many provisions in desperate need of revision. Typically, though, these provisions are supported by a well-organized interest group that lobbies vigorously to retain its cherished preference. The corporate tax, in contrast, appears to benefit no one directly and to hurt the corporate sector, which is large, well organized, and generally able to defend its own interests. * * *

In this Article, we argue that the resilience of the corporate tax is a manifestation of the most enduring source of problems in corporate law, the separation between ownership and control of large corporations. * * *

Why a Corporate Tax?

Under the Internal Revenue Code, the profits of most corporations are, in theory, subject to a two-tier tax. * * *

The corporate tax creates significant efficiency losses. * * *

The double tax, moreover, is inconsistent with currently accepted views of tax equity. Most contemporary academics regard the corporation as simply a conduit of profits to shareholders and thus see it as an inappropriate unit of taxation.

Integration would considerably reduce many of the problems created by double taxation. It thus has long had the enthusiastic backing of academic observers, professional groups, various Treasury Department reports, and several presidential administrations. Members of both houses of Congress have introduced a steady stream of bills to integrate the tax system. Nonetheless, the double tax persists.

* * * Any theory of corporate taxation, we believe, must explain three facts. First, public corporations are subject to a double tax. Second, although

---

[*]. At time of original publication, Professor of Law, University of Southern California Law Center.
[**]. At time of original publication, Associate Professor, Stanford Law School.

Congress has not integrated the tax system, it regularly enacts other tax measures that reduce the tax burden on corporations. Finally, publicly held corporations have not lobbied for integration. * * *

Populist Entity Theory

Many scholars have suggested that the double tax persists because the public supports it. * * *

Some Empirical Evidence on Public Opinion
* * *

The public unquestionably supports the imposition of a significant corporate tax. Indeed, public opinion polls reveal that between 65% and 80% of those polled favored increasing the corporate tax. Respondents showed only somewhat more support for reducing dividend taxes than for reducing corporate taxes. * * *

But support for corporate taxation and dividend taxation does not translate into support for double taxation. At one time the public may have endorsed two-tier taxation. More recent polls, however, show that no more than 37% and as little as 29% of the public supports double taxation. The apparent contradiction between opposition to double taxation and support for each tax separately probably results from a framing problem. Until pressed, respondents interpret questions about corporate and dividend taxation as general questions about taxing capital.

* * *

Summary

Neither populist nor hidden-tax arguments can explain the failure of previous efforts to integrate the tax system. In the next two parts, we will examine the motives and behavior of corporate managers, a group ignored by the populist and hidden-tax theories.

What Managers Want in a Tax Cut

Most wealth in corporate form is held by large, publicly traded corporations. In these corporations, ownership is separated from control: The firms are controlled by professional managers, while firm owners—the shareholders—are largely passive. But although managers are entrusted with guarding shareholder interests, their own interests do not always coincide with those of shareholders. Where the interests of these two groups conflict, managers will attempt to pursue their own interests, even at shareholders' expense.

In this part, we argue that shareholders and managers will often have divergent views on tax policy. The principal difference between them results from their different views on subsidies to existing capital. Shareholders invariably favor policies that increase the return to existing capital; they sometimes, but not always, support policies that stimulate investment. In contrast, managers are primarily concerned with stimulating new investment. They have little interest in increasing the return to existing capital, though they do not actively oppose measures that do this. Managers therefore attach a low priority to integration, which provides a large windfall to existing capital, and only a small stimulus to new investment. Managers prefer to lobby for other tax measures, such as ACRS [accelerated cost recovery system] and ITCs [investment tax credits], that may be less advantageous to shareholders but are more cost-effective in stimulating investment.

Shareholders and Managers

Much of the conflict between shareholders and managers arises from the different portfolios they hold. Most shareholders hold fully diversified portfolios and are thus not overly dependent on any one firm. Managers, by contrast, have most of their wealth tied to their corporate employer, largely in the form of firm-specific human capital. These different portfolios produce different attitudes towards the risk of firm failure. Because most shareholders hold fully diversified portfolios, they are effectively risk-neutral with respect to the risk of firm failure. Accordingly, shareholders want managers to maximize each firm's expected profits without regard to risk. Managers, however, are heavily dependent on the fortunes of the firm they manage and thus are risk-averse with respect to the risk of firm failure.

* * * Managers may pursue investment strategies designed not to maximize profits but to secure their positions and increase their salaries. They may, for example, make their skills more valuable to the firm through irreversible investments in their areas of expertise. Similarly, managers of firms in declining industries may attempt to preserve their positions by expanding the firm into new businesses, even though shareholder wealth maximization might dictate shrinkage or liquidation.

Tax Policy

Because their interests differ, managers and shareholders have different views on tax policy. Congress can reduce the taxes paid by firms and their shareholders through a number of mechanisms, including integration, reduced corporate tax rates, and increased business tax preferences such as ACRS and ITCs. Congress is unlikely to grant more than a few of these benefits, however, and managers and shareholders differ on the priority that they assign to various policies.

Windfalls Versus Benefits to New Investments

Shareholders and managers have divergent views on integration largely because they differ in their taste for tax cuts that create windfalls. Virtually any cut in capital taxes will increase the return on new investments, and thus will stimulate investment. This stimulus always helps managers but may or may not help shareholders. Some cuts also increase the return to assets that firms have already purchased. These tax cuts therefore confer a windfall on existing assets, and thereby help existing shareholders. Managers, in contrast, have little to gain from tax cuts that produce windfalls, because windfalls do little to stimulate new investment.

Integration, corporate rate cuts, and capital gains cuts all confer windfalls on existing shareholders. The windfalls result from the fact that the price of any asset reflects expected after-tax returns. * * * When taxes on the asset are cut, the price of the asset rises, giving its owner a windfall. * * * In contrast, tax incentives such as ACRS and TTCs generally apply only to new assets. * * *

The effect of a tax cut on existing shareholders will depend on the type of cut that Congress chooses. A tax break limited to new investment, such as ACRS or an ITC, will lower the tax rate only on income from additional investment. The marginal cost of production will therefore fall, increasing the corporate sector's marginal supply of output to consumers. Equilibrium output will rise to the intersection of this new output supply curve with the existing output demand curve. The price of output will fall. The stimulus effect of this tax cut will actually harm old shareholders. The fall in output prices will depress the pretax return to all shares, while the tax treatment of old capital will stay constant. The value of old shares will therefore decline. * * *

Although an increase in ITCs or ACRS helps only new capital, a rate cut or integration plan will lower the burden on all capital. This reduction in tax rates will confer a windfall on existing equity, although the windfall will be partially offset by the drop in output prices. * * *

Because shareholders and managers have different attitudes towards windfalls and investment stimulus, they have different views on tax policy. Shareholders, by definition, own portfolios of existing equity. They therefore gain from policies, such as integration, that provide windfalls to existing equity. * * *

Most managers, in contrast, have much to gain from incentives for new investment, and little to gain from windfalls to existing equity. Most managers thus support stimulus measures, such as integration, that provide subsidies to both new and old capital, but generally prefer incentives, such as ACRS and ITCs, that subsidize only new capital. * * *

Indeed, to protect existing tax preferences for new capital, some managers may actively oppose integration. The windfall profits from integration would reduce tax revenues. Managers might reasonably fear that the tax revenues lost as a result of integration would be financed by reducing other corporate tax preferences, or by raising the tax rate on the richest individuals. * * *

A Few Managers Prefer Integration

A few managers may nonetheless actively support integration. Some businesses, by their nature, cannot benefit from tax provisions such as ACRS and ITCs. These include firms, such as high technology companies, that have relatively little physical capital. Like other managers, managers of these firms will advocate preferences, such as tax subsidies for research and development, that benefit new investments that their firms might make. Because such preferences are often not available, managers should support integration and lower rates as the only avenues through which their tax burden can be reduced.

The Legislative Record

Integration Versus ACRS and ITCs

The history of tax reform is consistent with our analysis of what policies managers should prefer. Managers have testified in favor of integration, but they have generally reserved their active lobbying efforts for tax preferences for new investments, such as ACRS and ITCs.

* * *

Closely Held Firms

In closely held firms, control and ownership are linked. The managers of these firms therefore have the same tax policy objectives as shareholders.

* * * A closely held firm can lower the double tax in a variety of ways. Shareholders of closely held corporations are often also employees of the firm. The firm thus can organize as a Subchapter C corporation and still largely avoid the double tax by paying these shareholder/employees substantial salaries. * * *

Closely held firms also can choose an organizational form that is not subject to two-tier taxation. * * *

Congress has steadily expanded the scope of Subchapter S, while retaining the restrictions that limit its applicability to closely held corporations. In contrast, in 1986 Congress reclassified publicly traded partnerships as corporations for tax purposes. * * *

The so-called corporate tax is therefore paid by virtually all publicly held entities, even those that are not corporations, and is not paid by closely held entities, even those organized as corporations. This evolution suggests that owner-managers have successfully pressed for a single-level tax, while public managers have not.

* * *

The Retained Earnings Trap

Most managers support integration but have not lobbied on behalf of it. A small group of managers, however, has actively opposed integration, including proposals that would not reduce incentives to new capital. In this part, we will examine the reason for their opposition.

Managers of publicly held firms often want to pursue suboptimal investment policies. They cannot make suboptimal investments, however, if shareholders can monitor effectively the firm's investment policy. Retained earnings are accompanied by less monitoring than other forms of finance, and managers consequently prefer them to other sources of capital. * * *

The double tax raises the cost to shareholders of dividend distributions, thus increasing shareholders' taste for retained earnings. Some managers therefore may prefer a double tax. * * *

Capital Structure

The investment objectives of managers of publicly held firms differ from those of shareholders. Shareholders accordingly attempt to monitor the managers' investment decisions to prevent investments that do not maximize shareholder profits. Managers, in turn, often seek to avoid this monitoring.

The monitoring to which firms are subject depends in large part on how the firm's capital needs are financed. Firms can obtain capital to finance new investments from three sources: retained earnings, new equity, or debt. Managers generally are subject to less monitoring when they employ retained earnings financing than when they use external financing from debt or new equity.

External financing facilitates monitoring through several mechanisms. To obtain external financing, managers must disclose substantial amounts of information and subject the firm's operations to the scrutiny of the capital markets. Managers will have trouble obtaining external financing for a suboptimal project. * * *

In many respects, then, external financing shifts the final decision to pursue an investment from managers to outsiders. To preserve their decisionmaking power, managers can finance projects with retained earnings. Shareholders cannot easily monitor managers' use of these earnings. Even if shareholders learn of a suboptimal project, they have, under the Business Judgment Rule,[99] almost no right to prevent managers from pursuing it. * * *

Managers' preference for retained earnings financing often will be reinforced by managerial compensation schemes. An executive stock option plan will generally induce managers to reduce corporate dividends because payment of a dividend decreases the per-share price and thus decreases the value of the unexercised stock option. * * *

---

99. Under the Business [Judgment] Rule, courts generally will not review the substantive merits of managers' decisions, particularly investment decisions, unless the shareholder can prove that the managers had a conflict of interest or failed to exercise due care in the process of making the decision (i.e., failed to obtain sufficient information). In practice, absent self-dealing, poor investment decisions thus generally cannot be challenged. *See* WILLIAM A. KLEIN & JOHN C. COFFEE, JR., BUSINESS ORGANIZATION AND FINANCE: LEGAL AND ECONOMIC PRINCIPLES 150-54 (5th ed. 1993).

How the Double Tax Can Trap Earnings
* * *

[E]ven if the personal tax rate is below the corporate rate, the double tax will trap retained earnings if shareholders plan to reinvest dividend distributions in the corporate sector. In fact, many shareholders will reinvest in the corporate sector. In this situation the "double tax" imposes a triple tax on earnings reinvested in another corporation. * * *

The double tax therefore can bring shareholders' tastes closer to those of managers by increasing shareholder desire for internal financing and firm expansion. * * *

Do Managers Support the Double Tax to Trap Earnings?

Managers will not necessarily support the double tax simply because it traps earnings. A manager will oppose integration in order to keep the retained earnings trap only if the double tax traps earnings in his firm and he benefits from the trap. In this section, we argue that both criteria are met in only a relatively small number of cases. Although the double tax traps earnings in most firms, most managers do not benefit from the trap.

Does the Double Tax Trap Earnings?

Throughout the history of the income tax, the double tax has trapped the earnings of a significant number of firms. Earnings are trapped whenever the personal tax rate exceeds the corporate rate, and the trap increases as the gap between the personal and corporate rates widens. * * * Between 1939 and 1986, top personal rates exceeded corporate rates, and the percentage of taxpayers whose marginal rates exceeded the marginal corporate rate steadily increased. Since 1986, however, the corporate and individual rates have been much closer together, and until 1993, the corporate rate exceeded the top individual rate.

The statutory rate structure, however, is not an accurate guide to the retained-earnings-trap effect. The retained earnings trap depends not on the relative statutory tax rates on personal and corporate income, but on the relative effective marginal rates. Many firms face effective marginal tax rates that are substantially below the statutory corporate rate. The Internal Revenue Code provides a variety of tax preferences, such as ACRS, that lower the effective tax rate on new capital far below the statutory rate. Under current law, tax preferences are not passed through to shareholders, and so they lower the corporate rate relative to the personal rate. * * *

Perhaps more importantly, not all taxpayers face the top statutory rate assumed by the previous analysis.   Top bracket taxpayers hold a disproportionate share of common stock but far from all of it. Indeed, with the growth of pension funds, tax-exempt organizations hold significant amounts of corporate equity. Low-tax-bracket shareholders are more likely than high bracket shareholders to want dividend distributions. These different preferences for dividends produce a "clientele effect": Each corporation will tend to attract shareholders with similar characteristics who prefer a similar payout ratio. To attract shareholders, some firms must appeal to lower-bracket investors with a strong preference for dividends, while others appeal to high-bracket investors who prefer retained earnings. Managers of firms with a low-bracket clientele will not be motivated by the trap to support double taxation. For them, the double tax not only fails to trap earnings, it also raises their cost of capital and can even create pressure to distribute earnings. Accordingly, managers of such firms should favor integration.

Why Most Managers Will Not Support the Double Tax

Even managers of firms that do face a retained earnings trap will not necessarily favor double taxation. Managers support the double tax only if their interests diverge from those of shareholders. This divergence will be common in publicly held firms. Most corporations, however, are closely held, and the manager-owners of these firms have a direct stake in firm projects. They thus have every incentive to maximize firm profits and little or no incentive to pursue non-profit-maximizing expansionist policies.

Even many managers of publicly held firms should not support the double tax. For many managers, the costs of the double tax will exceed the benefits of the retained earnings trap. Managers benefit from the double tax if they can finance new projects with retained earnings; they do not benefit if their firm's investment projects exceed available earnings, so that external financing is required anyway. * * * [T]he double tax does not enable these managers to avoid the monitoring of new investments by the capital markets.

        * * *

Finally, managers of firms dependent on external financing may find that the double tax exacerbates a conflict with shareholders that would exist even in the absence of taxes. The deductibility of interest on corporate debt obligations increases shareholder pressure to debt finance these additional projects. Debt creates the risk of default and bankruptcy. Consequently, risk-neutral shareholders have a greater taste for debt financing than do risk-averse managers.

The importance of each of these factors will vary widely between firms. Firms differ greatly in their ability to issue debt. Large, mature firms can readily obtain debt financing at competitive rates. * * * Debt financing, however, substantially increases the risk of insolvency for emerging firms, undiversified firms, firms with highly variable income streams, and firms with few tangible assets. Managers of such companies are therefore unlikely to support the double tax.

A given level of debt will also subject different firms to different levels of monitoring. Managers of firms with substantial physical assets can avoid much of the monitoring associated with debt by having their firms issue secured debt. * * *

Evidence

The historical pattern of effective tax rates suggests that some firms have faced a retained earnings trap for most of the last fifty years. Firms in this position have produced a small but influential group of managers who have opposed integration in order to preserve the earnings trap.

These managers have expressed concerns about pressure to pay dividends from the time the first integration measures were introduced by Secretary Simon and Representative Ullman. Each successive iteration of the 1986 reform bill reduced the amount of integration proposed, and the final version that emerged from conference contained none at all. Many observers believe that the behind-the-scenes intervention of the Business Roundtable killed the 1986 integration measure. * * * Managerial desire to preserve the earnings trap was expressed in the response to the recent Treasury integration study. For the corporate community to support integration, one executive said that "corporate managers' decisions to retain or distribute earnings should not be unduly burdened."

An influential segment of managers clearly wishes to trap earnings. At the same time, most managers do not seem to regard the retained earnings trap as a sufficient reason to oppose integration, and managers whose fear of excessive debt more than offsets any desire for the retained earnings trap actually support it. During congressional hearings on both the Simon and Ullman proposals, managers who testified—always in favor of integration—invariably gave as their principal reason the problem of excessive leverage. * * *

Implications for Reform

Integration is more likely to succeed if reformers have at least one major interest group as an ally. To this end, we propose that reformers adopt a three-part strategy. First, they should support corporate governance proposals that empower shareholders. Second, they should consider endorsing plans that make integration more attractive to managers. Finally, reformers should deny support to proposals that enable a select group of firms to avoid the double tax, as this would reduce the political pressure for integration of corporate sector taxes.

Shareholders

Shareholders have never played an active role in the debates on corporate taxation. * * * Still, tax reformers hoping for integration should support policies to increase shareholders' independent political power. * * *

Managers

Absent significant change in corporate governance laws, tax reformers cannot rely on shareholder pressure for integration. For integration to succeed, therefore, reformers will probably need the support of the only interest group with the ability and the inclination to lobby Congress on this issue: corporate managers.

Reformers can gain managerial support for integration by advancing integration plans that serve managers' interests. Most managers of publicly held firms are not opposed to integration in principle. Rather, they have little enthusiasm for tax reforms, such as conventional integration schemes, that provide windfalls to old capital. But windfalls are not an inevitable consequence of all integration plans. In particular, Congress might minimize windfalls by implementing integration in stages, as suggested by some integration proponents. Phase-in would concentrate the tax benefits from integration on new investments. Most managers thus should support such a proposal.

Phased-in integration also makes sense from a policy perspective. Tax analysts are perhaps even less enthusiastic than managers about windfalls, since they, like managers, prefer measures that stimulate new investment. * * *

While many managers will support an integration plan as long as it concentrates its tax benefits on new capital, confining the benefits of integration to new capital will not win the support of all managers. Managers who benefit from the retained earnings trap may oppose even phased-in integration plans if those plans would reduce the trap. Whether an integration plan that favors new investments could succeed despite this opposition is an open question. The group of managers who benefits on net from the retained earnings trap is relatively small. Nevertheless, this group includes managers of some very large and established firms. Reformers may find that this group is simply too influential to challenge, in which case they should consider supporting integration plans that would trap earnings. These integration plans would, it is true, fail to remove one of the principal inefficiencies associated with the double tax, the retained earnings trap. Nonetheless, these plans would reduce or eliminate two other problems: the excess tax burden on the corporate sector and the bias towards debt financing. Half a loaf may be better than none, and so reformers might find it necessary to support integration plans that do not eliminate the retained earnings trap. * * *

Tax reformers can increase managerial support for integration by opposing reforms that would permit selective avoidance of double taxation by some firms. Such reforms will only weaken political pressure to integrate. * * * We therefore believe that reformers should consider opposing the gradual extension of Subchapter S and related innovations.

Conclusion

* * *

[W]e believe that the history of integration efforts holds a lesson for those who seek to reform other aspects of the tax code. Effective reform requires a grasp of the flaws in current law and a plan to remedy those flaws. Reformers, however, must devise not only solutions, but solutions that can realistically be enacted as law. In this effort, they would do well to invest effort in understanding why the problem they seek to solve has persisted.

Notes and Questions

63. Many provisions of law are unwise, but endure due to popular misunderstanding or popular support. One can imagine some members of Congress who might support ending double taxation of corporate earnings, but fear 30-second attack advertisements in the coming election in which they are depicted as preferring the interests of large corporations over those of "ordinary people." Professors Arlen and Weiss reject this populist explanation for the enduring double tax, noting that members of Congress have not declined to vote for a range of corporate-friendly tax measures.

64. In what ways do the interests of managers of corporations differ from those of their shareholders? Why is this problem most severe in the case of large corporations?

65. In approaching a corporation's financial and investment policies, Arlen and Weiss assert that managers are more risk-averse than are shareholders. Why might this be so?

66. Professors Arlen and Weiss state that most managers support an end to double taxation, but find that other tax goals—accelerated depreciation, investment tax credits, provisions supporting research and development—are more important. Some, however, actively oppose ending double taxation. (But never publicly—a corporate manager could hardly advertise that his interests differ from those of his company's shareholders.)

Arlen and Weiss assert that ending the double tax could release "trapped" retained earnings—earnings that a corporation retains, likely with approval of the shareholders, who do not wish to pay the double tax.

67. Arlen and Weiss assert that trapped retained earnings can benefit a manager who wants to pursue suboptimal investments. Why might a manager

ever intentionally pursue a suboptimal investment? And why would it be easier to do so with retained earnings than with funds obtained by borrowing or issuing new equity?

68.   Professor James Repetti explains that giving relatively favorable tax treatment to retained earnings is likely to result not only in shareholder acquiescence to suboptimal investment policies, but in more general "abdication" of control by shareholders to corporate managers. Writing prior to 2003 (*i.e.*, when dividends were subjected to taxation at ordinary rates while increases in stock values attributable to retained earnings would be taxed at capital gains rates upon eventual sale), Repetti observed:

[As previously discussed,] taxpayers will be more predisposed to permit management to retain earnings so long as they can realize the value of those retained earnings at the preferential rate by selling their stock. This may exacerbate stockholder abdication in two ways. First, the preferential tax rate for capital gains motivates taxable stockholders to be more tolerant of management inefficiency in investing retained earnings. Recall an earlier example in which we assumed that all corporate and individual ordinary income was subject to the same tax rate of 30 percent while capital gain was subject to a lower tax rate of 20 percent. We saw that where a corporation distributes as a dividend $100 of its after-tax income to a noncorporate stockholder, the stockholder will have $70 after tax. If the stockholder invests that $70 amount in an investment yielding 10 percent pretax (7 percent after tax), the stockholder will have $98.17 after tax at the end of five years.

Contrast the $98.17 result with the amount the stockholder would receive if the corporation, instead of distributing the $100 as a dividend, retained the $100 and invested it on a project that has the same level of risk as the 10 percent yielding investment available to the stockholder, but that yields only 8 percent pretax (5.6 percent after tax). The corporation will have $132.32 after tax to distribute at the end of five years. If the distribution qualifies for capital gain treatment,[t] the stockholder would pay a tax at the rate of 20 percent and have $105.05 after tax. * * *

The fact that noncorporate stockholders will benefit from an inefficient management's retention of earnings with a capital gain preference may reinforce the reluctance of noncorporate stockholders

---

t. Even if there were no distribution, the shareholder could sell the shares at a price reflecting the retained earnings, and be taxed on the resulting gain at capital gains rates. (Ed.)

to incur significant costs in monitoring management's investment of retained earnings. * * *

The second way in which a capital gains preference may contribute to stockholder abdication is the manner in which a capital gains preference motivates stockholders to realize corporate profits. The incentive created by the preference to sell stock rather than receive dividends over a period of time is not conducive to encouraging stockholders to view the relationship with the corporation as long-term. Rather, the buy-sell investment strategy may reinforce the view that stock is merely another commodity to be traded, rather than part ownership of a business whose activity should be monitored.[u]

69. Professors Arlen and Weiss suggest that reformers focus on phased-in relief from double taxation—relief focused on new equity, rather than already-outstanding stock. Why might this be good policy? Why is this focus more likely to garner active support from managers of publicly held companies?

70. Most closely held corporations can avoid double taxation; one major technique is the election of Subchapter S status. It might seem that an advocate of ending double taxation of corporate earnings would applaud the extension of Subchapter S. Arlen and Weiss, however, suggest that reformers oppose this extension, because it reduces the political pressure for broader reform that would also apply to publicly held corporations.

71. Observe that the 2003 Act can be viewed as either consistent or inconsistent with the political explanations of corporate tax policy offered by Professors Arlen and Weiss. Supporting the "inconsistent" side of the argument, the 2003 Act represents broad-based, significant relief of double taxation, which is fully applicable to holders of previously-issued shares of stock.

On the other hand, perhaps the 2003 Act can be viewed as consistent with the arguments of Arlen and Weiss. Congress—with both houses in Republican control—did *not* repeal double taxation, as President Bush had asked. Double taxation continues, though in a gentler form until 2009 (assuming no further Congressional action). The explanation for this half-loaf approach is no doubt attributable in large part to the revenue cost of entirely ending the tax on

---

u. James R. Repetti, *Corporate Governance and Stockholder Abdication: Missing Factors in Tax Policy Analysis*, 67 NOTRE DAME L. REV. 971, 1007-09 (1992).

dividends. This may not be a complete explanation, however, because in the same 2003 Act Congress expanded accelerated depreciation—a pro-business measure more consistent with the predictions of Arlen and Weiss.

72. *International and historical U.S. practice.* Proponents of integration can point to international practice as a reason to change. Writing several years before the 2003 Act, Professor Joseph Dodge observed: "The United States is virtually alone among the major industrialized nations in imposing tax in full both on the net income of C corporations and again * * * when such income is distributed to shareholders."[v]

Less well known is that fact that levying only one level of tax on corporate earnings also has early American roots. In the pre-Sixteenth Amendment income tax statutes, the U.S. did *not* follow the "classic" model of double taxation. Instead, Professor Jeffrey Kwall informs us that, by one route or another, only one level of tax was imposed on corporate income:

> From 1861 to 1873, no discrete corporate tax was imposed. Instead, corporate income was included in the tax base of shareholders and subjected immediately to the individual income tax, irrespective of whether dividends were paid.

> Although the next round of tax legislation did treat the corporation as a separate entity, these laws continued to ensure that corporate income was not taxed twice. From 1894 to 1985, individuals and corporations paid taxes at a uniform rate of two percent. Dividends, however, were excluded from the individual income tax base.[w]

While it is doubtful that this Nineteenth Century precedent has political import today, the history tells us that the issue is of very long standing.

---

v. Joseph M. Dodge, *A Combined Mark-to-Market and Pass-Through Corporate-Shareholder Integration Proposal*, 50 TAX L. REV. 265, 268 (1995).

w. Kwall, *supra* note a, at 618.

CHAPTER FIFTEEN

CAPITAL GAINS AND LOSSES

Capital gains is viewed as religion by one side for whom it is a sure-fire cure for the economy, and as the embodiment of the devil by the other side for whom it is the sure-fire assurance that the wealthy will get all the money in America.[a]

A. HISTORY, DEFINITIONS, AND TAX TREATMENT

The proper tax treatment of capital gains and losses is a staple of any course in tax policy. Perhaps more frequently than in the case of any other area of tax law, the policy debate on this issue has gone beyond academic disputes to become a significant political issue. Since the Tax Reform Act of 1986, when Congress almost eliminated the favorable treatment of capital gain vis-à-vis ordinary income that had prevailed for the preceding 65 years, the issue has made its way into television newscasts and presidential campaigns. As this book goes to print, the ink is scarcely dry on the Jobs and Growth Tax Relief Reconciliation Act of 2003, which significantly reduced capital gains rates, approximating the favorable differential treatment that obtained before 1986.

Treating capital assets differently from other items generates complexity in the income tax. Intricate statutory and regulatory provisions are necessary to describe differential treatment and to limit its exploitation. These rules often are difficult to understand. Significant amounts of time and resources have long been spent searching for the rewards from achieving capital gain or ordinary loss treatment. Moreover, the capital gains and losses rules are difficult for the Revenue Service to police and to administer. In 1973, Professor Boris Bittker called the treatment of capital gains and losses "perhaps the single most complicating aspect of existing law."[b]

Capital gains and capital losses are gains and losses from the sale or exchange of capital assets. Section 1221 defines capital assets to be all assets not excluded by that section. The two major categories of assets that are excluded from the definition of capital assets are (1) stock in trade or inventory of taxpayers and (2) property used in taxpayers' trades or businesses that is either depreciable property or real property. Most other assets are capital

---

a. Ken Gideon, Discussion by CCH Tax Advisory Board Roundtable, Vol. 79, Number 26, Part 2, May 27, 1992, p. 5.

b. *General Tax Reform: Panel Discussions before the House Comm. on Ways and Means*, 93rd Cong., 1st Sess. 118 (1973).

assets. Capital assets include stocks and bonds (except where these securities represent the inventory of a brokerage firm), land held for investment purposes, and property held for personal use, such as a taxpayer's home, automobile, jewelry, and clothing.

In general, Congress has sought to give capital gain and loss treatment to most sales of property, while denying such treatment to sales where the proceeds represent earned income or income from ordinary business operations. For a variety of policy and political reasons, however, Congress has not been reluctant to depart from this general pattern. Even when Congress has not intentionally deviated from the general pattern, it has been difficult to draw lines consistently.

For example, section 1235 provides that gain by inventors on the sale of their patents is to be treated as capital gain. On the other hand, sections 1221(a)(3) and 1231(b)(1)(C) require that gain by authors on sale of their copyrights be treated as ordinary income.

Although corporate stock ordinarily is a capital asset, section 341 provides that if a taxpayer owns more than five percent of the stock of a "collapsible" corporation, gain on sale or exchange of the stock will be treated as ordinary income. In general terms, a collapsible corporation is one formed or used with a view to liquidating it or selling its stock before it has realized at least two-thirds of the anticipated income from its business operations.

An interest in a partnership is a capital asset, but the portion of a taxpayer's gain from sale of a partnership interest that is attributable to "unrealized receivables" is treated as ordinary income under section 751. Unrealized receivables primarily consist of the right to compensation for services the partnership has rendered or will render, and the right to payment for goods delivered or to be delivered by the partnership.

Although depreciable business assets and real property used in business are not capital assets, section 1231 generally treats gains on these assets that have been held for more than a year as capital gains if these gains exceed losses from similar assets. Section 1231 does not extend to "property of a kind that would properly be included in the inventory of the taxpayer," but does provide capital gain treatment to income from timber sales, coal and iron ore royalties, and some livestock sales, as well as gains from sale of unharvested crops sold along with land that has been held for more than a year.

The scope of capital gain treatment under section 1231 is narrowed substantially by sections 1245 and 1250. These "recapture" provisions may require ordinary income treatment of realized gain to the extent of deductions taken against ordinary income in earlier years.

The primary question to be addressed in this chapter is whether favorable treatment of capital gains is justified. Even if favorable treatment were justified, however, the scope of the transactions that should qualify is far from clear. Without endorsing the favorable treatment of capital gains in any setting, Professor Calvin Johnson identified seventeen areas in which the provision of capital gains treatment is not warranted by the general policy that appears to underlie the overall statutory scheme. The following excerpt from his article, covering only seven of his seventeen proposed "culls," suggests the range of peripheral problem areas in classifying the transactions that should qualify for capital gain treatment.

SEVENTEEN CULLS FROM CAPITAL GAINS
Calvin H. Johnson[*]
48 Tax Notes 1285, 1285-87, 1293-98 (1990)

Congress needs to simplify the law of capital gains to clean out some of the deadwood. The common understanding of "capital gain" is that it represents appreciation over time of investment property, such as land or corporate stock. * * * The existing law of capital gains has anomalies and complexities unrelated to any policy for giving special rates to capital gains.

* * * When the cows are crossed over the river to the land of low rate capital gains, there are some things that need to be culled from the herd. Following are seventeen reforms that need to be made to the law of capital gain. * * * None of the proposals is intended to endorse preferential rates for capital gains nor to imply the case for any preference has been made.

* * * Some of the proposals have important revenue impact; some just foreclose future abuses or achieve academic neatness. But for almost all, if not all, of the proposals, there is or would be a strong consensus within the academic community that these items should be culled from the definition of capital gains. The list is not, however, exhaustive.
        * * *

Proposal 1: Self-Produced Assets

Current law. Capital gain is understood to arise from the market appreciation of capital invested by the taxpayer rather than from value added by the personal efforts of the taxpayer or taxpayer's agents, but literally any "property" is a capital asset unless the property is "held primarily for sale to customers in ordinary course of a trade or business." IRC section 1221(3) (withdrawing capital asset treatment from assets created by personal efforts of the taxpayer) applies only to literary or artistic works.

Proposal. Exclude all self-produced assets from the definition of "capital asset" by amending now section 1221(3) to read:

---

[*]. At time of original publication, Arnold, White & Durkee Centennial Professor of Law, University of Texas.

"(3) property, whether real or intangible, where the personal efforts of the taxpayer or the taxpayer's agents created or substantially enhanced the value of the property."

Conform IRC section 1231 by replacing IRC section 1231(b)(1)(C) with the above language.

Reasons for the Change. A taxpayer who makes or improves an asset with his or her own personal efforts receives compensation for services when the asset is sold at a profit. Thus, for example, the sale of furniture made by an amateur cabinet maker is salary or compensation and not capital gain as a matter of economics, even if the cabinet maker does not have enough activity to be in a trade or business.

* * *

Section 1221(3) was adopted "to close the loophole," recognizing that gain on self-produced assets was supposed to be ordinary (S. Rep. No. 2375, 81st Cong., 2 Sess. 43 (1950), but the exclusion was narrowly drawn to cover only literary or artistic works. Under the proposal here, "capital asset" would exclude all real and intangible property created or improved by the taxpayer, not just artistic works.

* * *

Proposal 9: Open Transactions

Current Law. In *Burnet v. Logan*, 283 U.S. 404 (1931), the Supreme Court held that sales of property for assets that had no ascertainable value would not be taxed in the year of the sale based upon mere conjecture, but that the transaction would be kept "open" and taxed only when the seller received the cash (or property that had ascertainable value.) Once the open transaction doctrine applies, the first cash is tax-exempt recovery of basis up to seller's original basis and gain thereafter is generally considered to be capital gain. * * * The regulations claim open transactions are available only in rare and extraordinary circumstances involving contingent payments, but the courts are sometimes more generous. *See*, e.g., *Gralapp v. United States*, 458 F.2d 1158 (10th Cir. 1972).

Proposal. Make amounts taxed under the open transaction doctrine ordinary income, by adding a new subsection (b) to IRC section 1222: "(b) Sale or Exchange. The term 'sale or exchange' shall not include amounts received in a year after the year of sale reported under the open transaction doctrine." Conform IRC section 1222.

Reasons for the Change. The open transaction doctrine reduces the effective tax on the sale of property by allowing the tax to be deferred until cash (or property of ascertainable value) is received. * * *

Gain under the open transaction doctrine is also appropriately excluded from gain from a sale or exchange for independent reasons. The taxpayer receiving open transaction payments has not liquidated his or her interest. Instead the taxpayer is receiving amounts, spread out over many years, that are usually contingent upon normal business operations or interest or other normally ordinary income events. For instance, in *Burnet v. Logan*, a shareholder sold stock by liquidation of her corporation in exchange for a royalty interest in a mine distributed by the corporation. Because the royalty interest had no ascertainable value, the sale of stock was "open." Although *Logan* itself involved a year before capital gains were taxed at a lower rate, it is assumed that now the gain would be taxed as capital gain. But the royalty income would normally have been ordinary income, and there was no policy reason why the fact that the taxpayer had originally received the interest in a transaction accounted for in an advantageous way should have also converted the character of the ordinary royalty income into capital gain. The character of the income from the asset should be determined independently of whether it was possible to value the asset when received. * * *

Proposal 11: Corporate Distributions Not from E&P

Current Law. Current law provides that a corporate distribution on stock in excess of its earnings and profits and the shareholder's basis will be treated as a sale or exchange by the shareholder, even when the distribution effects neither a liquidation nor a meaningful reduction in the shareholder interest. IRC section 301(c)(3).

Proposal. Repeal IRC section 301(c)(3)(A) so that corporate distributions not out of earnings and profits would have to qualify under the redemption or liquidation rules to qualify as capital gain.

Reasons for the Change. Corporate distributions on stock are normally ordinary income rather than capital gain because "(t)he shareholder retains his underlying investment interest, and neither his voting power or rights to future income have been altered." Cohen, Surrey, Tarleau & Warren, *A Technical Revision of the Federal Income Tax Treatment of Corporate Distributions to Shareholders*, 52 COLUM. L. REV. 1, 5 (1952). Distributions described by section 301(c)(3) (but no other sale or exchange rule) are not sales or exchanges in fact nor reductions in the shareholder's interest in the corporation.

The fact that a distribution exceeds corporate earnings and profits and shareholder basis provides no independent reason for the capital gain advantage. Distributions falling under section 301(c)(3) are not subject to double tax on corporate income: If the corporation had paid corporate tax on the amounts distributed, the corporate income would have increased earnings and profits and made section 301(c)(3) inapplicable to the distribution.

* * *

The shareholder has recovered all of his capital before section 301(c)(3) can apply so that the shareholder has no capital that needs to be indexed for inflation. Since the shareholder has withdrawn and recovered all his capital for section 301(c)(3) to apply, the distribution cannot fairly be attributed to a return on or appreciation of the shareholder's already-taxed capital. * * *

Proposal 12: Incentive Stock Options

Current Law. Nontransferable "incentive stock options" issued to executives as compensation are not taxable to the executives when issued nor when exercised [if certain conditions are satisfied]. The executive's gains are taxed as capital gains only if and when the stock is sold. The corporate employer gets no compensation deduction. IRC section 422A [now section 422].

Proposal. Repeal IRC section 422A [now section 422.]

Reasons for the Change. Under general law, an executive must pay ordinary income tax on property received in connection with the performance of services. IRC section 83. * * * As a fundamental principle, "capital gain" does not encompass compensation (see Proposal 1) and stock options given in return for the employee services are compensation.

> * * *

Proposal 13: Sales of Patents

Current Law. An inventor whose efforts created a patent and an individual (other than employer or related party) who paid for an interest before the invention was reduced to practice has capital gain on sale of the patent, even though the sale price is contingent on future actual use of the patent. IRC section 1235. * * *

Proposal. Repeal IRC section 1235.

Reasons for the Change. For the inventor whose personal effort created the patent, the gain from the sale of the patent is salary or compensation. Lower tax rates on some kinds of compensation received by some kinds of taxpayers create a special caste or status system inconsistent with the equality of all people before the law. In a free market system, incentives for compensation come from pretax income—paid by the people who understand and can value the services provided—and not from government subsidies.

> * * *

Proposal 15: Coal and Iron Ore

Current Law. Sale of coal and iron ore by an owner (who does not mine the coal or ore) is capital gain, even if it is inventory and even if the lease by which it is sold would not otherwise be a sale or exchange. IRC sections 631(c), 1231(b)(2). Exploration expenses are expensed, even if investments, although they are recaptured from sale or production. IRC section 617. Development expenses, incurred after commercially marketable quantities have been disclosed, are expenses, and not recaptured, even though they would otherwise be inventoried or capitalized costs. IRC section 616.

Proposal. Repeal sections 616, 617, and 1232(b)(2), so as to treat coal and iron ore as inventory.

Reasons for the Change. Capital gain for the coal and iron industry is an off-budget hidden government subsidy because it gives capital gain to inventory, which is ordinary income under normal principles, and because it gives capital gain to leases, which do not qualify as sales or exchanges under normal principles. * * * There has never been any attempt to justify the capital gain for coal and iron in terms of normal tax doctrine or wise expenditure of government costs.

* * *

Proposal 16: Livestock and Crops

Current Law. Sale of livestock (but not poultry) held for draft, breeding, dairy or sporting purposes will be capital gain. Cattle and horses must have been held for 2 years, other livestock for 1 year. Costs of feed, seed and fertilizer are expenses when made by a farmer, even if otherwise inventoried costs (IRC section 180, Treas. Reg. section 1.162-12(1972), section 1.471-6(a)), but nonfarmers face an array of barriers to access to the benefits of expensing that farmers can get. * * *

Proposal. Repeal section 1231(b)(3) and (4).

Reasons for the Change. Capital gain for sale of livestock converts ordinary deductions into capital gain because the costs of feeding livestock are ordinary expenses, while the gain from sale of the livestock [is] capital gain. Capital gain under IRC section 1231(b)(3) is not available for livestock raised for sale or slaughter, but it does apply to livestock even though held "for sale to customers" because of the amount of the activity. Treas. Reg. section 1.1232-2(b)(2) Ex. (3)(1971). The mismatch between ordinary deductions for the inputs and capital gain for the revenue remains within the scope allowed. Assuming the capital gain rate drops to 15 percent, a farmer could plan to lose 27 percent of his or her costs economically on transactions benefitting from the mismatch of ordinary deductions and capital gain and still break even after tax.

The tax advantages mean that farmers face an onslaught of outside capital which drives up the price of feed and farm labor and drives down the sale price of livestock. Farmers who are not in high enough tax brackets to use the negative tax fully are then driven into failure. On the other hand, the current attempts to block outside capital, while retaining the advantages for true farmers with mud on their boots, if successful, blocks whatever benefit the economy might get from the negative tax. It is only by driving down the pretax profit from farming that the public at large gets any benefit from the farm subsidies.

Expensing of farm investments first arose under Treasury regulations issued in 1915. The most plausible historical explanation for the expensing of farm costs that would otherwise be inventoried or capitalized is that the regulation drafters thought that the timing did not make any difference. Johnson, *Soft Money Investing Under the Income Tax*, 1989 ILL. L. REV. 1019, 1089 (1990). But when combined with capital gain for the product of the expense, expensing has the impact of less than no tax.

The proposal would also repeal IRC section 1231(b)(4), which now provides that sale of an unharvested crop with the underlying farmland is capital gain. Crops are expiring assets that must be sold or left to rot, so there is no possibility of causing significantly earlier realizations of crop gain by reducing the tax rate. Absent IRC section 1231(b)(4), the crop would be an ordinary asset even though sold with the land. *Watson v. Commissioner*, 345 U.S. 544 (1953).

* * *

Notes and Questions

1.   Although Professor Johnson explicitly declines to endorse the idea of preferential tax treatment for any capital gains income, his approach may imply that there is such a thing as a true, or ideal, capital asset. The concept of the ideal capital asset—corporate stock is the classic example—is pervasive among professionals and in tax literature. It may have its basis in the distinction in property law and trust law between capital and income. While essential there to draw a line between the rights of income beneficiaries and the rights of remaindermen, it is not necessarily relevant to tax treatment. Leaving aside personal consumption assets and assets considered to have intrinsic value in and of themselves (such as art objects), the market value of capital assets reflects present value of capitalized future income streams. Such future income will be taxed as ordinary income. To justify favorable treatment of capital gains would require finding a conceptual basis for treating advance realization of income differently because it is accomplished by sale of assets that are expected to produce ordinary income, rather than by holding the assets and receiving the ordinary income they generate.

2.   Professor Johnson's list of potential "culls" suggests that sometimes the favorable treatment conflicts with the supposed norm of denying capital gain treatment to earned income (Proposals 1, 12, and 13); sometimes the favorable treatment conflicts with the supposed norm that earnings from ordinary business operations are not to be taxed as capital gains (Proposals 15

and 16); and sometimes the proposals derive from unclear historical roots and serve elusive policy goals (Proposals 9 and 11).

3.   Johnson's analysis in Proposal 16 suggests that sometimes Congress intends to help an industry by unwarranted (under general principles) capital gains treatment, but in fact distorts and indirectly injures the industry.

4.   Professor Johnson's other proposed "culls" included:
    #2.   Property without substantial investment
        • Professor Johnson would require substantial investment as a part of the definition of capital asset.
    #3.   Sale of name, likeness, or waiver of privacy of living or dead person
        • Johnson would codify *Miller v. Commissioner*, 299 F.2d 706 (2d Cir. 1962), to assure that the outcome does not turn on state law.
    #4.   Expensed asset is an ordinary asset
        • Johnson would exclude expensed assets from the definition of capital asset.
    #5.   Recapture of S corporation losses
        • Johnson suggests a new provision to tax gains on sale of S stock as ordinary income to extent of prior losses passed through.
    #6.   Recapture prior expenses
        • This would avoid the "negative tax" that can result from ordinary deduction coupled with subsequent income taxed as capital gain.
    #7.   Conversion into capital asset by gift or contribution
        • Johnson would exclude from capital gain treatment literary and artistic works, which are not capital assets in the hands of their creators, after contribution to another taxpayer.
    #8.   The installment method
        • Johnson would block "the combining of tax reductions" to deny capital gain treatment if the taxpayer has reported a sale under the installment method.
    #10.   Limitation to fair market value
        • Johnson would limit capital gain treatment for forgiven nonrecourse debt to the value of the asset at time of sale.
    #14.   Timber
        • Johnson would repeal section 1231(b)(2).

#17. Section 1231
> •   Johnson would repeal Section 1231.

In support of the final proposal, Johnson's broadest, he argues:

> Section 1231 is no longer very important as to depreciable property
> because rapid depreciation now makes it unusual that depreciable
> property will be sold below basis and depreciation recapture of
> depreciation usually makes the gain ordinary. Gain or loss on
> unimproved land (i.e., nondepreciable real estate) is market
> fluctuation that should be capital gain or capital loss in theory. * * *
> Section 1231 is complicated; it has a convoluted form (Form 4797) all
> its own. The tax effects it accomplishes are not worth the complexity
> it generates.[c]

5.   It might be argued that the broader lesson to be learned from
Professor Johnson's article is that with so many exceptions to the general rule,
one may question whether a general rule actually exists.

6.   While corporate stock is the quintessential capital asset, other
categories are of comparable importance. Writing in 1988 (prior to the stock
market boom, or bubble, of the 1990s), Jane Gravelle of the Congressional
Research Service and Professor (of Economics) Lawrence Lindsey observed
that corporate stocks represented only 20 percent of the value of assets in the
household sector, and 27 percent of "tradable household wealth" at the end of
1986.[d] In 1981, Gravelle and Lindsey reported, sales of corporate stock and of
personal residences each accounted for approximately 25 percent of net capital
gain. Note that while gains from corporate stock are taxed at preferential
rates, most gains from personal residences are not taxed at all.

7.   Gravelle and Lindsey note that corporate stock has attributes that
distinguish it from other capital assets:

> Although corporate stock comprises only about a quarter of all
> capital gains, such stock has a unique attribute. The reinvestment
> of after-tax profits in a corporate enterprise does not increase the
> basis * * * of the investor's asset. This reinvestment becomes subject
> to capital gains taxation when the corporate shares are sold.
> Although the taxpayer did not pay personal income tax on the
> profits, the corporate tax rate on the reinvested earnings is at least
> equivalent to the personal rate that would be paid on a similar

---

c. 48 TAX NOTES at 1298-99.
d. Jane G. Gravelle & Lawrence B. Lindsey, *Capital Gains*, 38 TAX NOTES 397, 398 (1988).

reinvestment in an unincorporated enterprise. The capital gains taxation on this reinvestment of corporate retained earnings constitutes, in our view, an important distinction between corporate stock and other types of assets.[e]

In Chapter Fourteen, we considered a number of possibilities for ending the double taxation of corporate earnings. (Partial relief was enacted in 2003, which provided that dividends, though not regarded as capital gains, would be taxed at the capital gains rate.) Would enactment of relief from the double taxation of corporate income undercut the case for taxing gains on the sale of corporate stock at preferential rates?

8. *Historical development.* In the years since the present federal income tax was first imposed in 1913, Congress has frequently legislated substantial change in the tax treatment of capital gains. This note explains some of these historical changes.

Prior to the Revenue Act of 1921, capital gains were taxed the same as ordinary income. Under the 1921 Act, short-term capital gains continued to be taxed as ordinary income, but a maximum tax of 12.5 percent was set for long-term capital gains. In the Revenue Act of 1934, a set of five graduated holding periods was enacted, with 100 percent of gain taxed on disposition of assets held for one year or less, 80 percent taxed for assets held from one to two years, 60 percent taxed for assets held from two to five years, 40 percent taxed for assets held five to 10 years, and only 30 percent taxed for assets held over 10 years. In the 1938 Act, the number of holding periods was cut to three, with a maximum tax rate of 15 percent on assets held more than 24 months.

The Revenue Act of 1942—which was passed within months of the attack on Pearl Harbor, and was designed to nearly triple the yield of the income tax to support the war effort—allowed individuals to deduct half of net long-term capital gain and set a maximum tax of 25 percent for gain on capital assets held longer than six months. Primarily in response to the Government's seizure of assets for war purposes, Congress also enacted the first version of what is now section 1231.

The Internal Revenue Code of 1954 initially provided for deduction of 50 percent of net long-term capital gains. In 1976, the holding period for long-term capital gains and losses was increased from six months to one year. In 1978, the deduction from net long-term capital gains was increased to 60 percent.

The Tax Reform Act of 1986 taxed net long-term capital gains at the same rates as other income, ending 65 years of favorable treatment for long-term

---

e. *Id.* at 399.

capital gains. The statutory rules defining capital assets and computing capital gain were left intact in the 1986 Code, however, apparently as a token of the sincerity of the promise by Congress (codified in section 1(h)) that the tax rate on long-term capital gains would not be increased if ordinary income tax rates subsequently were raised above their level under the 1986 Act. Consequently, when the top bracket income tax rate was increased above 28 percent in 1990, and still higher in 1993, the maximum tax on net long-term capital gains was kept at 28 percent. Because the statutory rules had been left intact, return to more favorable treatment of capital gains was very simple technically and did not require reexamination of the various special types of capital gains, such as those described by Professor Johnson.

In 2001 and 2003, as part of substantial tax cut measures that included reductions in ordinary income tax rates, Congress directly cut the capital gains rates. For the years 2003-08, the top rate applicable to capital gains is 15 percent, compared to a top rate of 35 percent for ordinary income. In the case of taxpayers in the 10 percent or 15 percent bracket for ordinary income, the top rate for capital gains is only five percent (zero for the year 2008).

B. SHOULD CAPITAL GAINS BE TAXED AT PREFERENTIAL RATES?

The central policy issue addressed in this chapter is not which transactions merit capital gains treatment, or how much differential should exist between the rates applied to capital gains and ordinary income. Rather, it is whether *any* special capital gains rate is justified. The burden of proof should be on the proponents of special treatment, given the obvious argument for equal treatment—in Professor Fred Peel's words, "the economic benefit from a dollar of capital gain is the same as the economic benefit from a dollar of ordinary income."[f]

Much has been written about the capital gains preference. At a minimum, it is fair to say that academics are less convinced of the merits of a preference than Congress has demonstrated for more than 80 years, almost without break, and than it continues to demonstrate today.

A group of scholars considered, and debated, the merits of the preference in the *Tax Law Review* in 1993. In the first excerpt below, Professors Cunningham and Schenk reconsider the arguments for the preference made over the years. They conclude that a generalized capital gains preference would not be part of an ideal income tax, and that every problem supposedly addressed by the capital gain preference could be better addressed by other

---

f. Fred W. Peel, Jr., *Capital Gains: Falling Short on Fairness and Simplicity*, 17 U. BALT. L. REV. 418, 418 (1988).

means. Nevertheless, given other major imperfections in current law, (notably, the realization rule, which is discussed in Chapter Two, and the step-up in basis at death, which is discussed in Chapter Ten), they reluctantly conclude that a preference may be warranted under the "theory of the second best."

Professor Halperin disagrees, arguing that a preference for capital gains is unwarranted even under the assumption (of no other possible reform) on which Cunningham and Schenk based their argument. More fundamentally, perhaps, Halperin is concerned that a capital gains preference reduces the likelihood of better solutions being enacted.

Professor Shaviro unenthusiastically endorses a preference, though he arrives at this conclusion by different reasoning than that of Cunningham and Schenk. Like Professor Halperin, Professor Shaviro is wary of the possible political effects of supporting a preference—once a preference is given legitimacy, Congress may "overdo it," giving a larger preference than the argument could support.

The final excerpt, from Professor of Economics George Zodrow, examines the key empirical question of whether taxing capital gains at a rate lower than that applied to ordinary income will, as proponents of the preference assert, result in increased revenues. As will be clear after examining this brief excerpt (which has been edited for simplification), providing an answer to this straightforward question is extremely complex, and may prove impossible.

THE CASE FOR A CAPITAL GAINS PREFERENCE
Noël B. Cunningham[*] and Deborah H. Schenk[**]
48 Tax Law Review 319, 320-32, 334, 336-41, 343-47, 350-66, 368, 370-75 (1993)

Introduction

For years, the authors have taught their students that we could identify no substantial argument to support a preference for capital gains in a tax system with Haig-Simons income as the normative tax base. Indeed, the arguments against the preference were so strong that it was hard to construct a competing claim. Although we acknowledged serious flaws in the current treatment of capital gains, we asserted that a preference appeared to be a very poor solution to any of these problems.

This Article undertakes to examine that conclusion. The arguments we consider were first and ably catalogued by Professor Walter Blum more than 35 years ago.[2] His "handy summary" remains a classic, and makes a persuasive case that the arguments in favor of a preference are weak.

---

[*]. At time of original publication, Professor of Law, New York University School of Law.
[**]. At time of original publication, Professor of Law, New York University School of Law.
2. Walter J. Blum, *A Handy Summary of the Capital Gains Arguments*, 35 TAXES 247 (1957).

Nevertheless, a capital gains preference continues to garner much support in political circles. We re-examine those arguments taking into account the learning of the last three decades. On one level, our analysis confirmed our intuition. We found all arguments favoring the preference wanting. * * * In each case, there is a solution that is far superior to a capital gains preference.

These solutions are well known and have been debated for years. Their adoption by Congress, however, does not appear to be imminent. This reality prompted us to analyze each argument on a second level. We considered whether, if the optimal solution were unavailable, a capital gains preference would be a sound second-best approach.[3] In all cases, save one, we find that a preference is not a tolerable second-best alternative. However, as a second-best response to lock-in—the incentive created by the tax law to retain assets, preferably until death—a capital gains preference may be acceptable.

Undoubtedly, there is a tax rate on capital gains that maximizes federal revenue. Imperfections in current law make it relatively easy to avoid paying tax on capital gains. Thus, one might expect the revenue-maximizing rate on capital gains to be below the general rate imposed on ordinary income in order to induce taxpayers to realize gains that they otherwise might easily avoid. Most empirical studies addressing this issue imply that there is a rate that would maximize revenues by increasing realizations and that it is probably below the general rate. Thus, taxing capital gains at a rate below the rate on ordinary income is likely to raise more revenue than taxing all income at the same rate. We reject, however, the premise that a tax is per se acceptable because it raises the needed amount of revenue, and instead, we evaluate the preference on efficiency and equity grounds.

Although complexity attributable to the preference is a significant offsetting factor, the preference might be efficient if it resulted in taxation of capital income at the revenue-maximizing rate. Whether a preference is unambiguously equitable is a much more difficult question. Although a preference could never be supported on equity grounds in designing a tax system, we find a stronger case can be made for the equity of a preference as a reform proposal. While we accept the classic standard of equity—equal incomes should bear equal burdens—as necessarily following from vertical equity in designing an income tax, we suggest that such a standard should not

---

3. Throughout this Article, we are required to consider possible application of the theory of second best. *See* R.G. Lipsey & Kelvin Lancaster, *The General Theory of Second Best*, 24 REV. ECON. STUD. 11 (1956). In general, the theory (or paradox) of second best is that the perfect solution in an ideal world may be a very poor solution in a less than ideal world. Furthermore, a poor solution in an ideal world may be the best solution in a less than ideal world. In the context of this article, this theory would hold that, even though an ideal income tax clearly would give no preference to capital gains, deviations from the norm require the preference to offset these other imperfections.

be the sole determinant in evaluating a reform proposal. Rather we assert that the proper inquiry is whether the distribution of the tax burden after the reform would be more in accord with how the tax burden would be distributed under an ideal income tax. We believe a strong case can be made that, on certain assumptions, a capital gains preference is an equitable reform proposal. Therefore, we argue that a capital gains preference might be supported both because it is efficient and because, in a second-best world, it promotes equity.

* * *

The Origin of the Problem: The Imperfect Treatment of Capital Gains under Current Law

In large measure, the arguments proffered for preferential treatment of capital gains derive from their imperfect treatment under current law. Under the Haig-Simons formulation of the normative base, income is a taxpayer's consumption plus change in wealth for a particular period. The normative treatment of the income produced by an asset for any tax period is an ex post accounting of its change in value. The tax is levied at the same rate as that applied to all other types of income.

There are at least four major ways in which the current treatment of capital gains diverges from this ideal—all attributable to the realization requirement. First, gains and losses generally are not taken into account as they accrue, but only when they are realized. Although the realization rule theoretically defers both gains and losses, as a practical matter, its primary impact is to defer gains. Taxpayers control the timing of realization, and they tend to realize losses as they accrue while deferring gains. * * *

A second divergence greatly magnifies the impact of the realization rule. The current rules that death is not a realization event and that a beneficiary takes a fair market value basis in property acquired from a decedent effectively exempt most capital gains from taxation.[12] Both rules are extraordinarily beneficial to taxpayers. For example, if the nominal rate of tax is 28%, and the taxpayer is able to defer tax on a capital gain for 10 years, the effective rate of tax is reduced to 19%.[13] If the asset is held until death, the effective rate is zero. A taxpayer can obtain this advantage even if he economically enjoys the value of the appreciation during life, for example, by borrowing against the security of an asset that is held until death.

Two other departures from the Haig-Simons ideal partially offset the benefits produced by these two divergences. First, because basis is not indexed

---

12. Approximately one-half of all accrued capital gains are held until death and are never taxed. Mervyn A. King & Don Fullerton, THE TAXATION OF INCOME FROM CAPITAL 221 (1984).

13. This assumes a 4% real after-tax rate of return.

for inflation, nominal gains always exceed economic gains. This factor can be quite important, especially during periods of high inflation such as the late 1970's. The failure to index requires many taxpayers to pay tax on inflationary gains that actually represent an economic loss.[16] The second deviation stems from the imposition of a double tax on corporate earnings. Under current law, corporate income is taxed twice, first at the corporate level, and again when the income is distributed (or in the case of retained earnings, when the underlying stock is sold or redeemed).

Taken together, these aberrations result in almost total mismeasurement of income from capital assets. * * *

Capital Gains in a Normative Income Tax

Most of the plausible arguments in favor of a capital gains preference are directed at one or more of the flaws in the current treatment of capital assets. In this Section, we carefully consider the arguments advanced in favor of a capital gains preference as a means of addressing the problems caused by deviations from the base. Several of the arguments are specious and we address them briefly in the next Section. We find no need to examine possible solutions because we find no problem.

The subsequent Sections detail more serious arguments. In each case where a problem actually exists, it is clear that it arises from the failure to treat capital gains in the theoretically correct manner. In designing an income tax system, conformity to the Haig-Simons ideal always would be preferred; that is, there is no case for a capital gains preference as a design choice. A capital gains preference is, however, a *tax reform* rather than a *design* proposal. Thus, it only arises as a serious option once the decision has been made to vary the definition of income in ways contrary to the Haig-Simons ideal.

The usual discussion of capital gains treats the preference as an original design question and assumes a multiplicity of choices. We presume, however, that prior choices have been made: Bowing to pragmatism and political reality, we accept that the optimal solutions are not forthcoming. That is, we take as given the realization rule, § 1014, the failure to index for inflation and the absence of integration, and we address only one option. If the *only* reform option were a capital gains preference, would it be supportable and preferable to current law? Taking the Haig-Simons formulation as normative, the issue is whether a capital gains preference—as a second-best alternative—would move the tax system closer to the norm. The current treatment of accrued

---

16. Another mistake partially compensates a seller who originally borrowed to fund the purchase of the asset. The taxpayer will have enjoyed inflated interest deductions that are offset only on the sale by the inclusion of an equally inflated sum in his amount realized with respect to the outstanding principal amount of the debt.

gain is a "mistake," but it does not follow that another mistake, the capital gains preference, necessarily would move the system further from the ideal. * * *

Thus, in each case we evaluate the preference not from the perspective of normative first principles, but rather from the perspective of whether it would bring an already defective system closer to the ideal. As a solution to all problems save one, the capital gains preference, as currently structured, is unsuitable. As a solution to lock-in, however, a capital gains preference may be tolerable.

Capital Gains Are Not Income

Several of the traditional arguments in favor of a preference essentially are definitional. They range from the conclusive ("capital gains are not income") to the completely specious ("people do not regard capital gains as income") to the slightly serious. Their gist is that capital gains are unexpected, nonrecurring receipts, wholly unlike wages or other payments for productive effort.

This view is misplaced. * * * It is based on an unsophisticated view of income and ignores Simons' admonition against taking the source of income into account. Furthermore, for most taxpayers, capital gains are expected and recurrent. Moreover, even assuming that capital gains were nonrecurrent and unexpected, those attributes do not call for special tax treatment. In fact, in the classic case of a one-time extraordinary receipt, such as treasure trove or windfall, the tax system subjects the recipient to tax at ordinary rates. Furthermore, to the extent this argument relies on the "unexpected" nature of the receipt, it is particularly weak because imposition of the tax could not affect behavior. In short, nothing inheres in the nature of a capital gain that warrants treating it differently from other sources of income.

Consumption and Not Income Should be Taxed

Commentators sometimes argue that because the ideal tax base is consumption, and not income, a preference comes fairly close to the correct treatment of capital gains. * * *

Obviously, if one advocates a consumption tax, the only truly satisfactory solution is to change the base. It is clear, however, that Congress nominally has chosen a tax based on income and that deviations from that base are the source of much inefficiency and complexity. * * * In sum, if consumption tax treatment is not extended universally, this movement in "the right direction" may produce worse results than no movement at all.

Bunching

Essentially, the bunching argument is that the realization rule forces a taxpayer to report in one year capital gains that have accrued over several years and may subject the gains to a higher marginal rate than would have applied had the gains been reported each year as they accrued. A preference acts as a crude averaging device to offset the telescoping effect of the realization requirement. To illustrate, consider the following:

> T purchased X stock 10 years ago for $10. During each of those 10 years, T was in the 25% tax bracket. This year T sold the stock for $510, recognizing a gain of $500. As a result of this gain, T is pushed into a higher bracket and must pay taxes on the gain at a 40% rate.

Bunching is a potential problem only in a system with graduated tax rates and only if the taxpayer is in a higher bracket on the disposition date than she was when the income accrued. Thus, for example, if the $500 gain is taxed at a 40% rate, T would owe $200 in taxes, compared to the $125 she would have owed if the gain had accrued at $50 a year for 10 years and had been subjected to a 25% rate.

The chief flaw with the bunching argument is that it fails to take into account the benefit T enjoys from deferral. While it is true that T's tax liability in absolute dollars is higher than it would have been if the gain had been taxed on an annual basis, T has deferred the liability throughout the period her economic income accrued. Depending on the assumptions, the deferral resulting from the realization requirement may offset the bunching effect completely.

Bunching currently is not a significant problem. Most capital gains are realized by taxpayers already in the highest bracket; therefore, at least for these taxpayers, taxing capital gains on realization rather than accrual does not force them into a higher bracket. * * *

On the other hand, there are taxpayers who experience bunching. A taxpayer below the highest bracket may incur an irregular capital gain—for example, the once-in-a-lifetime sale of stock to fund a college education—that will be taxed at the top marginal rate. * * *

A capital gains preference, however, deals very poorly with those few cases in which bunching presents a problem because it is not targeted. It applies in the extreme to cases involving no bunching; it offers the same preference to capital assets held for two years as those held for 10 years; and it applies to taxpayers whose top marginal bracket remains constant. In most cases, the preference simply compounds the advantage of deferral.

Double Taxation of Corporate Earnings

Under our current income tax system, corporate income is taxed twice, once at the corporate level when earned, and again at the shareholder level when distributed. This "classical system" of taxation is inconsistent with an ideal Haig-Simons income tax and has been the subject of much criticism. For decades, reformers have called for its elimination by integrating the corporate and individual income taxes.

* * *

Proponents of the preference for capital gains argue that, in the absence of integration, the preference can be justified as a second-best solution to the inefficiencies created by the double taxation of corporate earnings. Although a preference would not completely eliminate the problem created by the classical system, it would reduce its impact. Because this argument for the preference is premised on the inefficiency of the classical system and the concomitant importance of integration, it is persuasive only to the extent these premises are valid and then only with respect to subchapter C stock. * * *

The degree to which the classical system is inefficient depends on the extent to which corporations actually must seek a greater pretax rate of return on their investments than must other entities, or stated somewhat differently, the extent to which corporations have a higher marginal cost of capital than do other entities. The marginal cost of capital to a corporation depends upon its source, of which three are possible: borrowed funds, retained earnings and new issues of equity. Each is discussed directly below.

Borrowed Funds. The classical system does not distort investment decisions of a corporation that borrows. Because interest is deductible by the borrowing corporation, interest payments do not bear a corporate tax burden; only a single level of tax is imposed, at the lender's rates. As a lender's rate of return is unaffected by the tax rates of its borrowers, holding risk constant, corporations can borrow on the same terms as other entities. Therefore, double taxation does not create economic distortion when a corporation borrows funds to invest and no inefficiency results.

Retained Earnings. Similarly, no (or very little) economic distortion stems from double taxation when a corporation invests its retained earnings. * * *

New Issues. Where a corporation raises capital by issuing new stock, however, investors will require the corporation's expected rate of return to be higher than market to offset the effect of double taxation. * * *

The source of a corporation's marginal capital is inextricably related to a conundrum that has puzzled scholars for years: Why do corporations pay dividends? * * *

The new view results in far less support for integration and virtually no support for the current capital gains preference. Proponents believe that nontax factors do not explain corporate distributions adequately. Since retaining earnings costs so much less than issuing new equity, they do not believe that a corporation in need of additional capital would make distributions; that corporations do make distributions is strong evidence that more than sufficient equity capital already exists in corporate solution. To the extent there is sufficient equity capital in corporate solution, the classical system is not inefficient. * * *

Inflation

One of the principal arguments used to support the preference is that capital gains are largely inflationary. To that extent, they do not represent economic income and should not be included in a base with Haig-Simons income as the norm. The optimal solution, indexation, is discussed in detail elsewhere,[64] but the general conclusion appears to be that indexation may be achieved only with distorting simplifications.[65]

Even proponents of a preference as a substitute for indexation concede that it is a "rough justice" alternative.[67] That it would not account accurately for inflation is obvious in that a capital gains exclusion bears no relation either to the actual amount of inflation or the time the asset is held. The preference might be supported if it coincidentally approximated the results of indexing, but, in fact, exclusion of a fixed percentage of the gain almost never will. It provides the wrong results for assets held for both short and long periods of time, although for slightly different reasons.

For assets held for a long period of time, a preference provides the wrong outcome simply because there may be no problem. * * * The advantage of deferral increases over time and ultimately exceeds the disadvantage of taxing inflationary gains. If the asset were held long enough, therefore, a preference would not be necessary.

For assets held a short time, deferral offers little offset to the inflation component and thus inflation is more of a problem. * * *

Wholly apart from the advantage of deferral, a fixed percentage exclusion does an extremely poor job of addressing long-term inflation. * * *

In summary, the historically designed capital gains preference is so rough as to provide no justice; in many cases it would exclude real gain and in almost all cases would account for inflation on a purely random basis. Furthermore, any attempt to design an exclusion that would provide an accurate inflation adjustment is probably doomed to failure.

Risk

Proponents argue that a preference is necessary to offset the negative effects on risk taking of an income tax, especially one with limitations on the

---

64. *See, e.g.*, Michael C. Durst, *Inflation and the Tax Code: Guidelines for Policymaking*, 73 MINN. L. REV. 1217 (1989); Reed H. Shuldiner, *Indexing the Code*, 48 TAX L. REV. 537 (1993).

65. *See, e.g.*, Jerome Kurtz, *Comments on "Indexing for Inflation and the Interest Deduction,"* 30 WAYNE L. REV. 969, 970 (1984).

67. *See, e.g.,* Edward Yorio, *The President's Tax Proposals: A Major Step in the Right Direction*, 53 FORDHAM L. REV. 1255, 1269-70 (1985) (noting that a capital gains preference can be justified as an "admittedly crude" method of excluding inflationary gains).

deduction of realized losses. * * * There are at least two problems with this argument. First, as a general proposition, it is not clear that the existence of the income tax significantly discourages risk taking; second, even if it does, the definition of capital asset is not well designed to remedy this bias.
* * *

Assuming arguendo, that loss limitations create an unacceptable bias against risk taking, the problem is most appropriately addressed by modifying these limitations directly. A capital gains preference, however, is a very poor second-best solution. The definition of capital asset is not in any way targeted toward "risky" investments. There is no reason to think that financial investments in stocks and bonds are any riskier than a direct investment in a new business. Indeed, because an investor can diversify, existing financial instruments may be among the least risky investments available. * * *

Lock-In Effect
The Lock-in Phenomenon

The most serious argument in favor of a capital gains preference is premised upon the so-called lock-in effect. The lock-in effect describes an investor's reluctance to incur a tax on realization of gains; it is a direct consequence of prior decisions to impose a realization requirement and not to tax gains at death. An investor who is not taxed until realization and who can avoid tax altogether by holding an asset until death, tends not to change investments, even though he may believe that higher returns are available elsewhere. For example, suppose T holds Asset #1 with a basis of $100 and a value of $500 in a world with a flat 25% tax on income. The expected yield on this investment is 10%, or $50. T has the opportunity to invest in Asset #2, which has an expected yield of 12%. If T sold Asset #1, he would pay $100 in taxes, leaving only $400 to invest in Asset #2. Because a $400 investment in Asset #2 has an expected yield of only $48, T will not change investments. The toll charge prevents T from diversifying his portfolio.

Although studies differ as to the extent of realizations, they all agree that a large percentage (approximately one-half) of capital gains are never subject to tax. This lock-in of accrued gains is said to create inefficiency that impedes the flow of capital to its most productive uses. An individual who wishes to diversify her portfolio or to sell to fund consumption may be unwilling to do so, thus reducing her utility. * * *

Whether the lock-in effect attributable to the tax burden imposes a significant onus on the economy as a whole is less clear. Although an individual may benefit greatly by changing her portfolio, it is not clear that it matters much to society who owns IBM stock. * * * Even if lock-in does not significantly burden the economy as a whole, it certainly burdens those holding appreciated assets and those not holding assets at all because they must pay higher taxes than they otherwise would have.[105]

Optimal Solutions to Lock-in

* * * The lock-in effect would not exist if gains were taxed as they accrued. Thus, adoption of a mark-to-market system would eliminate distortions caused by lock-in. The consensus, however, is that the cost of implementing an accrual system would be so high as to make it infeasible. We disagree. While practical obstacles to an accrual system remain, it is likely that, in the long run, they can be surmounted.[106] In the meantime, a mark-to-market system already exists for assets that can be valued easily[107] and could be applied much more widely.[108] Because the primary obstacle to a mark-to-market system is valuation, scholars have proposed a variety of surrogates for accrual taxation and others could be developed.[g] * * *

Even if accrual taxation on a large scale is impractical, it is still possible to address lock-in by attacking its most significant cause head on: the step up of basis at death. Whereas the realization requirement offers deferral, § 1014 offers permanent exclusion and, thus, absent accrual taxation, is the root cause of lock-in. Hence, the optimal reform solution is to repeal § 1014. But, then, what should replace it?[h]

* * *

In summary, * * * if we were *designing* a tax system based upon a Haig-Simons definition of income, we would never seriously consider a preference for capital gain because lock-in would not be an issue. A tax base that distinguished receipts based on source would result in inefficiencies and inequities. Nevertheless, we are not designing an ideal tax and must consider second-best solutions, such as a capital gains preference. The remainder of this Section considers how the efficiency and equity aspects of the preference

---

105. * * * [T]he rate of tax on ordinary income is higher than it would be if accrued capital gains were realized, producing additional tax revenues.

106. *See* David J. Shakow, *Taxation Without Realization: A Proposal for Accrual Taxation*, 134 U. PA. L. REV. 1111 (1986) (describing a partial accrual tax system); Jeff Strnad, *Periodicity and Accretion Taxation: Norms and Implementation*, 99 YALE L.J. 1817, 1891-1903 (1990) (practical method of implementing accretion tax); *see also* Thomas L. Evans, *The Realization Doctrine After Cottage Savings*, 70 TAXES 897, 909-10 (1992).

One significant obstacle is the failure to index. Adoption of a mark-to-market system without indexation would result in very high effective tax rates. Currently, deferral offsets the negative effect of inflation.

107. IRC §§ 1092, 1256.

108. *See, e.g.,* Note, *Realizing Appreciation Without Sale: Accrual Taxation of Capital Gains on Marketable Securities*, 34 STAN. L. REV. 857, 871-76 (1982); David Slawson, *Taxing as Ordinary Income the Appreciation of Publicly Held Stock*, 76 YALE L.J. 623, 644-47 (1967).

g. The issues raised in this paragraph are the focus of Chapter Two. (Ed.)

h. Chapter Ten discusses section 1014 and proposals for its replacement. (Ed.)

should be framed and evaluated in the context of a *reform* proposal to eliminate lock-in.

Capital Gains Preference as a Second-Best Solution
Efficiency
Would a Cut Raise Revenue?

There is general agreement that a preference for capital gains would ameliorate the lock-in problem, and would result in increased realizations. The extent of the increase is controversial. Because the lock-in effect presents the strongest argument favoring a preference, it is important to try to determine the relationship between tax rates and realizations. In large part, a capital gains preference as a second-best solution to lock-in appears attractive because it actually might produce additional revenue from increased realizations. * * *

The starting point of the argument is the well-accepted notion that taxes affect behavior. Any tax, except a head tax, imposed on any item or activity, prompts taxpayers to investigate alternatives or substitutes to avoid the tax. As the tax rate increases, the avoidance incentive also increases. It long has been recognized that there is a revenue maximizing rate for most taxes, a point at which, if the tax rate were increased, the tax would generate less revenue than if it were left unchanged. Revenues would decline because taxpayers would engage in less of the activity or would find alternative ways to conduct it so as to avoid the tax.

The revenue maximizing rate for any tax is a function of many factors, the most important of which is how easy it is for taxpayers to avoid it. The revenue maximizing rate declines with the ease of avoidance. Under current law, the tax on capital gains is remarkably easy to avoid. Avoidance can be accomplished, first, by simply holding the asset, since the tax is imposed only upon a sale or exchange. Second, a taxpayer can realize the value of an asset without incurring the toll charge by resorting to nonrecognition provisions, such as §§ 1031, 1034 and 368, or borrowing, using the asset as security. Finally, and most important, taxpayers can avoid the tax altogether simply by holding the asset until death. * * *

Because the tax is often avoidable, it is not surprising that taxpayers are sensitive to rates. The only question is how sensitive. Economists measure this sensitivity by the "realizations elasticity." * * *

The actual realizations elasticity (and its implicit revenue maximizing rate) obviously is very important for political, economic and fiscal reasons. As a result, extensive empirical research over the last 15 years has sought its value. Nevertheless, nothing close to a consensus has developed. Researchers do not even agree on a theoretical model of capital gains realization behavior, which is the cornerstone for most empirical work. * * * Although all studies have found realizations responsive to capital gains rates, to date the models have produced wildly inconsistent elasticities ranging from 0.5 to more than 3.

Despite the chaotic state of the empirical evidence, most research indicates that the revenue maximizing rate for capital gains is likely to be less than the ordinary income rate, although even this is not entirely free from doubt. Despite political and fiscal importance, the actual revenue maximizing rate is not essential to evaluate the preference as a reform measure. While it is clear that the conclusions drawn from the econometric work are quite tenuous, the issue that we, as lawyers, wish to pursue is the policy implications if the empirical work ultimately coalesced on a realizations elasticity that implied a revenue maximizing capital gains rate less than the ordinary rate.

Implications for Capital Gains Preference

Although the principal reason for our income tax is to raise revenue, revenue production alone does not justify a particular provision. That is, simply because taxing capital gains more favorably than ordinary income would raise additional revenue does not of itself justify the preference. Like other commentators, we agree that revenue should be raised in as fair and efficient manner as possible. Therefore, even if a preference for capital gains raised revenue, we would evaluate the preference on efficiency and equity grounds.

The relevant issues raised by this inquiry are crystallized by consideration of two alternate proposals that raise precisely the same revenue. Assume that all income is taxed currently at 28%, regardless of source, but that, for whatever reason, additional revenue must be raised. Which of the following two proposals represents better tax policy, assuming the evaluative criteria are efficiency and equity?

* No Preference Proposal: Raise the top tax rates on all income to 42%, regardless of source.

* Preference Proposal: Leave the top rate on capital gains at 28% and raise the top rate on all other income to 40%.

In examining the efficiency of each proposal, it is useful to distinguish between tax burden and taxes paid. Assuming the revenue maximizing rate for capital gains were 28%, as the capital gains rate rose beyond 28%, the burden of the tax would increase, although the total revenues would decline. The difference between the burden imposed and revenue raised is the excess burden, or the deadweight loss of the tax. This burden can be regarded as the lost opportunities that those with capital gains have forgone. The larger the excess burden, the less efficient the tax, as it represents a decline in social welfare not gained by the government in the form of revenue. It is important to note that, as the rates increase from 28% to 42% in this example, the burden of the tax on holders of capital assets would go up substantially, while, at the same time, the amount of taxes they actually pay would go down considerably. That they would pay far less in taxes does not mean they are better off; it simply means that, at the proposed 42% rate, the lock-in effect would be so great that realizations would decrease substantially compared to their level at a 28% rate.

When asked to evaluate whether one proposal is better than another, economists and social choice theorists often resort to the Pareto efficiency standard. Under this standard, a given allocation of resources is said to be Pareto efficient if the only way to make one individual better off is to make another individual worse off. A reallocation of resources is a Pareto improvement if it makes at least one person better off without making anyone worse off. * * *

Using this standard, the Preference Proposal is undoubtedly a Pareto improvement over the No Preference Proposal and probably is Pareto optimal. At least initially, the Preference Proposal appears to be a Pareto improvement because by its adoption, everyone is better off financially than they would be under the No Preference Proposal. Capitalists (that is, those with capital gains) clearly would be better off, for they would be taxed at a lower rate (that is, 28%) under the Preference Proposal. Although, as a class, they would pay more taxes, they would benefit from the reduced tax burden on their property. Laborers (that is, those who do not hold capital gains) would be better off because they, too, would pay a lower rate (that is, 40%) under the Preference Proposal. Finally, the government would be no worse off because it would raise an identical amount of revenue.
* * *

This analysis is flawed in one respect. * * * [A] focus simply on the tax burden may ignore the enormous complexity created by the rate differential. This complexity has costs that may affect the financial positions of laborers and capitalists alike and thus must be weighed in evaluating the efficiency gains of the preference proposal.

A capital gains preference creates several types of complexity that appear to be universally disdained. First, rule complexity increases; because the preferential rates apply only to certain categories of income, congressional line drawing is essential. A substantial effort by the Service and the private sector to learn and interpret the rules usually follows. When rate differentials are meaningful, there is an increased likelihood of disputes over various eligibility requirements, often resulting in litigation and a secondary body of case law. Second, transactional complexity of a significant magnitude arises. Because the tax treatment is often contingent on the structure of a transaction, a staggering amount of time is devoted to converting ordinary income into capital gains.[166] * * *

Although there seems to be almost universal agreement that the capital gains rules account for a significant portion of the Code's complexity, there does not appear to have been any serious attempt to quantify this cost. This, however, is essential if the efficiency aspects of the preference are to be evaluated. The issue is whether all of the efficiency gains from taxing capital gains at a lower rate than ordinary income are offset by the complexity losses. Our sense is that it has not been weighed heavily enough, if at all. If the complexity losses are large enough and therefore the efficiency gains are small enough, any equity argument assumes far more importance.
      * * *

Thus, from an efficiency perspective, the choice between the two proposals is clouded by the lack of empirical work on the complexity costs of the preference. Nevertheless, it seems likely that the Preference Proposal is efficient (in terms of being a Pareto improvement). In order to explore equity as an independent standard and its relationship to efficiency, we assume in the next Section, that the Preference Proposal is efficient. That is, even considering the complexity costs, we assume for the sake of argument that everyone is better off under the Preference Proposal than under the No Preference Proposal.

Equity

Opponents of a capital gains preference traditionally attack it on the ground that it is inequitable. The thrust of the argument is that, in the Haig-Simons formulation of income, source is irrelevant and "a dollar of capital gain is like any other dollar of economic gain."[176] We do not think this to be so simple a proposition and find that it needs some explication.

An initial inquiry is why if the Preference Proposal were actually efficient (that is, a Pareto improvement), we would want to evaluate it using an additional standard. The simple answer is that we may not want a Pareto optimal economy. * * * In fact, although not essential to this debate, we always would weigh equity even if the efficiency gains, by any standard, were clear.

Most commonly, the criterion that is given some or equal weight is "fairness." While the literature has paid increased attention to what is meant by fairness, scholars have devoted very little discussion to the relative weight

---

166. David F. Bradford, Untangling the Income Tax 273 (1986) ("It is sometimes said that one-half of the practice of a tax lawyer is finding ways to convert ordinary income into long-term capital gains, the other half being the conversion of long-term capital losses into ordinary [losses].")

176. Blum, note 2, at 261 (argument 1).

to be given to fairness and, when it conflicts with efficiency, which factor controls.

In evaluating the equity of a particular proposal, commentators usually speak of both horizontal and vertical equity. * * * In an income tax, horizontal equity is said to require that those with equal incomes bear equal tax burdens.

* * *

Thus, the first step in providing an equitable tax system is to define the tax base: How do we determine that two people are alike? Most commentators believe that the base should reflect relative ability to pay. The two most commonly offered bases are income and consumption. Our somewhat tentative view is that economic income is a good yardstick against which to rank individuals. Income best measures ability to pay. * * * While the choice between economic income and consumption is a close one (and other standards such as wealth are less attractive), we proceed using income as the standard for the simple reason that the case for a capital gains preference need not be pursued if consumption is the criterion, and it is important, given the durability of the preference in our current "income" tax, to evaluate the arguments seriously.

The second step, given Haig-Simons income as the tax base, is the determination of whether a particular proposal to reform the base enhances equity. If a particular proposal would enhance equity, but be inefficient (or vice versa), the final step is to balance these two competing considerations. The following two Sections explore these two issues. The first applies the traditional method of determining whether a proposal promotes equity to the capital gains preference and then weighs that standard against efficiency. The succeeding Section offers an alternative for assessing the impact on equality.

Efficiency and the Classic Definition of Equality

The classic formulation of horizontal equity is the proposition that those with equal incomes should be treated equally, that is, bear equal tax burdens. The operative question in evaluating a reform proposal is whether it moves the system closer to that standard. This requires a comparison of the tax burden in the absence of the reform proposal with the burden when the reform is in place.

Even in the absence of a preference, because of the realization requirement, capital gains receive favored treatment. The No Preference Proposal would not eliminate this treatment, but it would not exacerbate it. Furthermore, by raising the tax on all income, no matter what its source, all taxpayers would bear approximately the same burden on their income. Although the burden on capital gains might not translate into additional federal revenue, it nevertheless burdens the income in a similar manner as the tax on labor income. Therefore, the No Preference Proposal would not be rejected as inequitable under the classic formulation.

On the contrary, the Preference Proposal, by reducing the tax burden on already favored income, a fortiori would be inequitable. Increasing the tax on labor income to 40% without increasing the tax on capital income would result in a burden on labor income exceeding that on capital income. If, however, the tax preference were completely capitalized into the price of capital assets, no horizontal inequity would result, even under the classic formulation. We note that this is consistent with a view that a statutorily created unequal treatment of income from capital raises no substantial question of horizontal inequity. Because the capital markets are thought to be quite efficient, whatever inequalities are created will be short-lived, and the after-tax yields will converge. Thus, for example, an exemption from tax on the yield of one type of capital will cause its yield to fall until it is equal with the after-tax yield on capital not eligible for the preference. The favored asset is said to bear an implicit tax and therefore has an equal tax burden. Therefore, although nominally unequal treatment of capital income might be inefficient, it is not inequitable, at least among the holders of capital. Thus, a proposal to provide preferential treatment for some kinds of capital but not others does not raise a substantial question of horizontal equity.

Assuming the preference is not completely capitalized, the Preference Proposal would violate the classic formulation of horizontal equity. Should it be rejected automatically? We think not. This requires a balancing of equity and efficiency. In general, there is no consensus as to which consideration should control. * * *

If the efficiency gains were marginal, we would permit equity to trump for two reasons. First, adoption of the Preference Proposal might decrease the pressure to get the system right. Recall that this analysis is based on a second-best approach and that in all cases we prefer the first-best alternative. If very little advantage is to be gained from the second-best approach, it should be rejected.

Another reason that the equity standard might be permitted to trump a somewhat uncertain efficiency gain with regard to the Preference Proposal is what we call perceptional equity. By that we mean that a proposal probably should be rejected if it is perceived as inequitable. * * *

[A] tax that is perceived to be inequitable may be difficult or impossible to administer. Perceived inequity may lead to diminished compliance and increase the likelihood of outright cheating. This, in turn, will decrease efficiency gains.

        * * *

In summary, given the uncertain effects of complexity costs on efficiency gains and a violation of the classic equity standard that compares ex ante and ex post tax burdens, the case for the preference as a solution to lock-in may be unconvincing, even as a second-best solution.

Efficiency and a Reformulated Determination of Equality

* * * Evaluating a reform proposal, * * * the utility of horizontal equity is, at best, marginal and its use actually may produce inequitable results. By definition, a reform proposal arises only in the context of a tax system that is "wrong," that is, a system that has at least one deviation from the ideal base and in which taxpayers are bearing inappropriate burdens. In reforming an imperfect system, "fixing" one of the imperfections does not necessarily result in an improvement and may actually increase inequity.

* * *

Even a reform proposal that would treat all equals equally might be undesirable. Consider the following example: Assume that using the appropriate standard of distributive justice, the tax burden under an income tax should be allocated in descending order as follows: A and B (equal incomes) followed by C, D and E. In fact, the actual burden is distributed in the following descending order: A, C, D, E and B. The reform proposal is to reduce the tax on A so that A and B are treated equally. Although this reform would result in "horizontal equity," it also would result in A and B being taxed in a way diametrically opposed to the standard of distributive justice. Whereas they should bear the highest tax burden, they both would bear the lowest.

We reject the proposition that a reform proposal should be either accepted or rejected as equitable solely depending on whether it would result in the equal treatment of equals. Rather, the essential question is whether the distribution of the tax burden after the reform would be more in accord with how the tax burden would be distributed under an ideal tax. A reform measure that moved the tax burden closer to the ideal distribution would enhance equity (even though it did not result in vertical equity).

This approach, while conceptually preferable, is admittedly harder to apply. It does not have the simplicity of the classic definition of horizontal equity that apparently would support any reform proposal that resulted in the equal treatment of equals and would reject any proposal that resulted in the unequal treatment of equals. Whether equals would bear equal tax burdens is only one factor to be weighed in evaluating the equity of a reform proposal because getting one person in the right position does not necessarily enhance equity. The key factor is the relative burdens post-reform. Whether they are closer to the ideal burdens is a question of judgment (or even perhaps aesthetics).

In making this judgment, a relevant factor is the effective rate of taxes paid, both before and after the reform. More specifically, a reform proposal that reduced the disparity between the effective rate of tax and the nominal statutory rate would be strong (although not conclusive) evidence that the proposal would move the system closer to the ideal. * * *

An evaluation of the Preference Proposal is an example where our approach to equity might result in a quite different judgment than the classical approach. The Preference Proposal would increase the disparity of tax burdens and thus would not result in equal tax burdens on taxpayers with equal income. It therefore would violate the traditional horizontal equity standard. We would not reject the Preference Proposal on equity grounds, however, solely because it did not result in equal tax burdens.

The reduced burden on capital income is one that restricts the choices of those holding capital assets without generating any revenue or benefitting anyone else, either directly or indirectly. Because, however, the Preference Proposal would reduce the disparity between the effective tax rate and the nominal statutory rate on capital gains, our judgment is that it would more closely conform to the appropriate distribution of the tax burden. The benefit of deferral reduces the rate on capital income below the rate on labor. But by lowering the nominal rate, the effective rate rises, thus actually reducing the disparity between the effective and statutory rates. Adoption of the Preference Proposal would bring the system closer to imposing the same effective rate of taxation on all income. Thus, in our view the Preference Proposal would be equitable. Even though the effective rate on capital would not be exactly the same as that on labor because the taxpayer can continue to hold the capital asset, this reform proposal should not be rejected simply because it fails to impose an identical tax burden on two taxpayers with equal economic income or because it does not conform to the standard chosen for *designing* an income tax.

The effects of this approach are not limited to capital gains. Consider, for example, a proposal to repeal the penalty for early withdrawal of funds from tax-favored individual retirement accounts (IRAs). The reformulation would produce a different gauge of equality. Under the classic formulation, one might oppose the penalty's repeal because it would reduce further the tax burden on an already favored asset. Under our formulation, however, the repeal would not be opposed on the basis of equity. Existence of the penalty creates a type of lock-in effect. Removal of the penalty undoubtedly would increase withdrawals from IRAs. Indeed, it is quite possible that repeal of the penalty would generate more revenue than the penalty itself and have the result of increasing the rate of tax on those with IRAs. If this were so, although we might object to the repeal on other bases (undercutting retirement policies), we would not object to the repeal on equitable grounds because it would have the effect of decreasing the disparity of effective tax rates on funds invested in an IRA and those invested in other capital.

Conclusion

All serious arguments in support of a capital gains preference can be traced to deviations from the appropriate taxation of capital gains in a Haig-Simons income tax. In each case, the optimal solution is significantly better than a capital gains preference. In order to evaluate the preference, however, we have assumed that the optimal resolution of the problem is unavailable. Nevertheless, in almost all cases, the current form of a capital gains preference is an extremely poor second-best alternative.

    * * *

Even considering these problems in conjunction rather than separately, we conclude that a preference cannot be supported. Admittedly, inflation and the double taxation of corporate earnings present serious problems; bunching and risk may be problems. In combination, they present a threat to a realization-based income tax. But an untargeted capital gains preference does not accurately solve any of these difficulties and in some cases exacerbates them. The attractiveness of the preference is not increased simply because it is throwing stones at multiple targets and missing them all.

Lock-in often is perceived to be the most significant problem, but that may be because the preferable alternatives are thought to be unobtainable. Repealing § 1014 and taxing gains at death is better theoretically and less complex than a capital gains preference. It is only in the context of the lock-in effect, however, that a capital gains preference might be an acceptable second-best solution. If a capital gains preference pays for itself, it may very well promote efficiency, particularly if it were structured to eliminate some of its complexity. * * *

Ultimately, whether or not a capital gains preference, as a second-best alternative, is desirable depends on the resolution of two issues. First, the preference is only acceptable if, in fact, it promoted efficiency by increasing realizations to the level that permitted a rate reduction on ordinary income. As noted elsewhere, the empirical evidence is ambiguous. * * * Second, the preference is only a second-best alternative, and any support for an inferior solution may weaken the resolve for optimal solutions. Thus, a willingness to accept a capital gains preference should be linked directly to one's predictions about the political likelihood that Congress will repeal § 1014 or adopt an accretion tax.

    * * *

A CAPITAL GAINS PREFERENCE IS
NOT *EVEN* A SECOND-BEST SOLUTION
Daniel Halperin[*]

48 Tax Law Review 381, 381-391 (1993)

In their Article, Professors Cunningham and Schenk present an interesting challenge. Assuming no other changes in the law are possible, they ask whether, under the law as it exists today, a capital gains preference is desirable.[2] In other words, would a lower rate of tax on capital gains be an appropriate "second-best" solution given the discrepancies between the current system and a more perfect income tax?

My first reaction is that this is an inappropriate question. As Professors Cunningham and Schenk note, most of the arguments raised in favor of a capital gains preference have little force, and where a problem can be identified, "there is always a solution that is far superior to a capital gains preference." Why should we alleviate some of the pressure that might force such a superior solution by reducing the tax burden on capital gains? I turn first, therefore, to a discussion of the possibility of a more direct solution to the supposed problems of current law. Then, I will indicate why, even on the terms set by Professors Cunningham and Schenk, I would reject a capital gains preference as a tolerable solution to the lock-in problem, and further, as a solution at all.

Direct Solutions

I find, as apparently do Professors Cunningham and Schenk, only two arguments for special treatment of capital gains to be even remotely appropriate. These relate to the impact of current law on investment or risk taking and on the willingness to dispose of assets, the so-called lock-in effect.

* * *

A related argument, frequently made, advances a capital gains preference as a means of facilitating risky investments. I agree with Professors Cunningham and Schenk that if risk taking is a problem, by far the better solution is to explore more complete allowance of losses. If losses were fully allowable, the tax system would not impose any greater burden on risky investments. Limitations on losses are thought necessary to prevent taxpayers, particularly highly diversified wealthy taxpayers, from avoiding their fair share of taxes by "cherrypicking," namely, selling investments that have declined in value (in sufficient volume to offset wages, interest, dividends and other recurring income), while retaining assets that have appreciated.

---

[*]. At time of original publication, Professor of Law, Georgetown University.

2. Noël B. Cunningham & Deborah H. Schenk, *The Case for a Capital Gains Preference*, 48 TAX L. REV. 319 (1993) [the immediately preceding excerpt].

Nevertheless, a significant loosening of current law appears viable. For example, perhaps the limitation on capital losses could apply instead to losses on marketable securities, which present the greatest likelihood of cherrypicking. In the case of other assets, there ordinarily would be economic restraints on tax-motivated sales, at least if the denial of losses on sales between related parties is strengthened. Furthermore, it should be possible to allow taxpayers to claim losses on marketable securities to the extent they have losses in excess of unrealized gains on such property.

In fact, it would be preferable to permit fuller allowance of losses, without fear of cherrypicking, by shifting as much as possible to an accrual or Haig-Simons system of taxation that would take account of changes in value without regard to realization (generally referred to as mark-to-market). This approach would have the additional advantage of mitigating the lock-in problem as well. While, because of political reasons as well as the difficulties of measurement, I do not expect a mark-to-market system ever to include small businesses or farms, I think annual accrual for most assets is not only feasible (as Professors Cunningham and Schenk acknowledge) but also enormously simplifying. * * *

In recent years, the tax system has made some limited moves toward mark-to-market taxation. * * *

I recognize that the system I envision requires drawing a line between assets subject to a realization system and those subject to an annual accounting of changes in value. Besides the line drawing difficulties, economic distortions may arise as taxpayers seek to avoid the accrual system (at least for gains). We need further research and study to see if we can develop a system which, despite these difficulties, would be preferable to current law, with or without a capital gains preference. As far as I know, none of that work is being done. I would not assume that such changes, which have far more promise in mitigating both the complexity and economic distortion of current law, are impossible.

Capital Gains Preference

I turn now to the problem posed by Professors Cunningham and Schenk: Assuming that none of the above changes are possible, would a preference for capital gains improve the system? As Professors Cunningham and Schenk suggest, the strongest and perhaps the only plausible argument for the preference is that it mitigates the so-called lock-in effect. The lower the rate applicable to capital gains, the less chance that investors will be locked into holdings they would sell were it not for the tax burden that would be imposed. As I understand it, the authors' contention that a preferential rate may be both equitable and efficient is based on the fact that such a rate most likely would derive more revenue from wealthy holders of capital assets than would be generated if the current rates applicable to ordinary income applied to capital gain as well.

In response I argue two points: First, that lock-in does not merit as much attention as it is given; and, second, and more importantly, that regardless of the problem for which the preference is touted as a remedy, the costs of preserving the preference are simply too large to justify it. In other words, I believe that the "complexity," which Professors Cunningham and Schenk recognize to be a significant offsetting factor, more than offsets the claimed "efficiency" gains.

In determining how much one should be concerned about the lock-in effect, it is critical to distinguish between the impact on the overall investment pattern of society and the welfare (utility) loss to individual investors. It is likely, as the authors recognize, that lock-in affects only the ownership of assets, not the deployment thereof. The fact that A decides to hold X, even though she would prefer to own Y, because the tax costs of selling X are too great, does not have a great deal of impact on the total amount of Y stock outstanding. Someone else will buy Y. What is involved for the most part, is the welfare loss to individuals, not society as a whole.

Since people who do not sell because of the potential capital gains tax on the sale are less diversified than they would prefer to be, their welfare can be improved by reducing the rate on capital gains, thereby increasing the chance that they will sell assets. But it is important to recognize that the would-be beneficiaries of such a reduction already are better off than they would be under what, in my mind, is the fairest system of taxation, namely, a pure accrual system that would tax gains (or at least real gains) annually, whether or not there was a sale. Obviously, people with unrealized gain could sell their assets every year and approximate an accrual system. If they do not do so, they have decided that they are better off holding perhaps less desirable assets than they would be if they sold such assets and paid the tax.

Consider the following example. A has purchased stock in X for $200, and it is now worth $300. A believes stock in Y is more valuable than stock in X, but does not shift because she would have to pay tax of $28. While A prefers $300 of Y to $300 of X, she would rather hold on to her $300 investment in X when the alternative is only $272 of Y. But in an ideal tax system, A would have been required to pay tax on unrealized gains, reducing her net assets to $272. While A might not be as well off as she could be if she could change investments without paying tax, she is better off than she should be. By refusing to sell, she shows that she values X at more than $272.

Of course, A's welfare could be improved still further if we reduced the rate on capital gains. For example, if the tax rate were 15%, A might sell if she preferred $285 of Y to $300 of X. On the other hand, the tax impact on sales could be mitigated by full accrual, a deemed realization at death or elimination of basis step-up at death. *A* likely would oppose all these changes even though they may free her to diversify. I would rather maintain the pressure to make those changes, which I believe are inevitable, or at least inevitable if the tax system is ever going to be rationalized, rather than reduce the pressure by a capital gain differential.

* * * [H]olders of capital assets have the advantage of deferral, whether or not there is a preferential rate. If a lower rate leads to greater realizations, it follows that holders of capital assets are even better off, compared to other taxpayers, because they voluntarily chose to pay more tax in order to diversify their holdings or increase consumption. In these circumstances, I am not inclined to give much weight to the argument that the increase in realizations, and thus in taxes paid, makes for a more equitable distribution of the tax burden because it narrows the difference between effective and actual rates of tax. This may be true in some sense. Nevertheless, I am troubled by the proposition that when *A* is treated better than *B*, a move which increases the welfare of *A* alone can narrow the gap between *A* and *B*.

The lock-in rationale for a capital gains preference, therefore, arises not from concern about lock-in's harmful effects on either *A* or society, but from the argument that there is a free lunch: A preference can help *A*, while, at the same time, improving the lot of the rest of society. Congress might as well make *A* better off by lowering the capital gains rate (thus, allowing her to diversify), because otherwise *A* will hold *X* until death and pay no tax; if she needs money, she can always borrow using *X* as security. By helping *A*, Congress also can make the rest of society better off. This occurs if a reduced rate of tax leads to a sufficient increase in realizations, so that *A* and others like her actually may pay more taxes despite the lower rate. The additional collections could permit deficit reduction or even a tax cut for the middle class. * * *

In my view, however, the lunch is not free.

This leads me to my second argument. I believe that the distortions, particularly in administration and planning, caused by a rate differential are far more serious than is sometimes suggested. Part of the problem is that most of the information concerning the costs of the capital gains preference is in the heads of practicing lawyers, not in the heads of academic tax lawyers and certainly not in the heads of economists. Economists are, of course, aware of the potential distortion caused by favoring one form of investment over another. But the more important thing, to my mind, is the impact the preference has on tax planning to convert ordinary income to capital gain. I also continue to believe that a substantial simplification of the tax system and greater allowance of capital losses would be possible with permanent equal treatment for capital gain and ordinary income.

The changes in 1986 reduced transactional planning, but they did not begin to scratch the surface of what could have been accomplished were there agreement that the rate differential would not reappear. For example, at least some of the complexity in the partnership, trust, and corporate provisions derive from the distinction between capital gains and ordinary income. Also, without the differential, many of the recapture rules would be superfluous. I may be wrong about the ability to simplify, but I would not give up the opportunity to try in return for the supposed advantages claimed by Professors Cunningham and Schenk. * * * There are real costs in a differential rate. The goal should be to make policymakers understand the cost of the preference. * * *

So, what can be done to eliminate the existing preference? I think in the long run, the rates on ordinary income must be brought down from where they are today by broadening the base. Items that cost significant revenue, like stepped-up basis at death, the mortgage interest deduction for up to $1 million of acquisition indebtedness, or the failure to tax inside build-up on annuity contracts and life insurance may not yield much revenue in the short run because we are likely to protect existing holdings. This also may prove true as to any effort to change the current system of realization substantially in order to tax more gains as they accrue. Therefore, we may need to think about legislation with a 10- or 15-year phase-in as the only way to make the higher rates on ordinary income and the resulting tax preference for capital gains "temporary."
  * * *

In short, a capital gains preference creates significant transactional complexity and forecloses the possibility of substantial simplification of the income tax. It should be eliminated as soon as feasible. Lock-in can be mitigated through increased use of mark-to-market, more frequent imputation of income annually and elimination of basis step-up at death. This promises a tax system that is both simpler and more neutral than a system with a rate preference for capital gains.

UNEASINESS AND CAPITAL GAINS
Daniel N. Shaviro[*]

48 Tax Law Review 393, 393-94, 396-400, 402-04, 411-17 (1993)

Introduction

The capital gains preference presents two main questions, the first difficult and the second easy. The difficult question is whether the preference will raise revenue over the long term—considering not only the standard estimating issues of realizations elasticity, the effects of conversion and arbitrage, and the like, but also how Congress, a political decisionmaker, will behave over time if its menu of choices includes establishing a preferential rate for capital gains. The easy question is whether the preference would be desirable if one could stipulate that it would raise revenue long term. To this, the answer is clearly yes. Genuinely revenue-raising rate reduction is nearly always desirable, absent greater external effects than any that seem present here.

In their Article,[1] Professors Cunningham and Schenk acknowledge the difficulty of the first question, but they ignore its political dimension. Apart from the second-best constraint they impose on adopting more desirable changes, their analysis does not adjust for the fact that tax laws are enacted by the House and Senate and not, say, by the Brookings Institution and the American Enterprise Institute. Legal academics all too often assume that tax policy can be divorced from messy politics, but the assumption is particularly crucial and contestable here.

Professors Cunningham and Schenk mainly emphasize the second question, which they strive energetically to show is difficult. In this, despite their best efforts, they do not succeed. On efficiency grounds, the case for a genuinely revenue-raising rate cut that does not impose significant external costs is simply too strong. On equity grounds, the claim that one should forgo a revenue-raising rate cut, and thereby make everyone worse off—those with capital gains, by increasing their tax rate, and those without capital gains, by requiring them to pay more tax to replace the lost revenue—is simply too weak. Professors Cunningham and Schenk's discussion of the tradeoff between equity and efficiency falls short, in my estimation, just where it needs to be most persuasive: in explaining why equity, as they define it, is important.

Often equity is an important offset to allocative efficiency for reasons of redistribution. This is not the issue here, however, if a revenue-raising capital gain preference would make everyone, rich and poor alike, better off. Professors Cunningham and Schenk rely instead on horizontal and vertical

---

[*]. At time of original publication, Professor of Law, University of Chicago.

[1]. Noël B. Cunningham & Deborah H. Schenk, The Case for a Capital Gains Preference, 48 Tax L. Rev. 319 (1993) [the first excerpt of this subchapter].

equity, a closely related pair of traditional tax standards that focus on the relationships between different people's tax burdens, and that therefore could mandate, in the name of abstract justice, making everyone worse off in absolute terms.

* * * Once one moves beyond formalism to substance, these traditional tax policy norms cannot plausibly support a proposal to make everyone worse off by rejecting a revenue-raising rate cut.

The ultimately most interesting and important capital gains question is a third one: What should be done given the uncertainty about the preference's long-term revenue effects? My own view is that, as the maximum statutory rate for tax on ordinary income increases, at some point the argument for the preference becomes irresistible, despite the danger that Congress will set the preferential capital gains rate well below the point of revenue maximization. Yet, what would be clear at a 70% ordinary income rate is far from clear at, say, the 28% rate that applied briefly after 1986. Taking as given the present maximum nominal rate of 39.6%, it is plausible, particularly given the political risks inherent in reopening the issue, that the current capital gains rate of 28% should be kept in place.

* * *

Efficiency
The Lock-In Effect

This brings us to the capital gains arguments relating to the lock-in effect, which Professors Cunningham and Schenk rightly regard as at the core of the capital gains issue. As they suggest, the efficiency of a capital gains preference is closely related to the question of how it affects tax revenues. While conceding the lack of empirical consensus on the revenue question, Professors Cunningham and Schenk note evidence suggesting that the revenue-maximizing rate for capital gains is likely to be less than the ordinary income rate. * * *

[T]he decision whether to recognize gain by disposing of a durable appreciated asset tends to be far more tax-elastic than, say, deciding whether to perform services in exchange for earned income. This gives rise to the argument for a capital gains rate below the rate for earned income, even where it is below the revenue-maximizing capital gains rate, and notwithstanding the line drawing difficulties, along with the distortion of taxpayer behavior, that result from crudely shoehorning everything into the two stylized categories of ordinary income and capital gain. The increased complexity simply becomes a cost that needs to be weighed against the benefit of reducing the tax system's effects on taxpayer behavior.

While Professors Cunningham and Schenk do not extensively discuss optimal taxation as such, their analysis of lock-in generally is consistent with it. They recognize that, where the tax rate for capital gains otherwise would be above the revenue-maximizing point, a revenue increase from reducing the rate tends to be desirable, because it indicates reduced lock-in. Fewer gain-recognition transactions would be tax-deterred.[15] Professors Cunningham and Schenk then ask how the efficiency gain from reducing lock-in compares to the efficiency losses of complexity, including rule and transaction complexity, along with added uncertainty where the classification of an item as capital or ordinary is unclear.

They conclude that the efficiency gain seems likely to exceed the efficiency loss, based in part on the hope that rule complexity could be reduced by changes in the structural design of the preference. I find this hope quite slender, yet strongly endorse the conclusion on alternative grounds—again, assuming overall revenue gain.

The hope of efficiency gain due to the potential for simplifying the definition of a capital gain is slender for both a small reason and a big reason. The small reason is that simplifying incremental changes, such as those proposed by Professor Calvin Johnson[18] may not be enacted. * * *

The big reason that the claim of efficiency gain from simplification is problematic is that, even if sensible improvements such as those proposed by Professor Johnson were enacted, the definition of a capital gain would continue to be problematic. The core concept of distinguishing between capital and ordinary assets is inherently fuzzy at best, and incoherent at worst. * * *

For these reasons, the hope of simplification provides little support for assuming efficiency gain from a revenue-maximizing capital gains preference. Yet, one could argue powerfully for efficiency gain on alternative grounds. The argument goes as follows: Where a tax preference for capital gains increases revenues, it must reduce the directly affected taxpayers' lock-in costs by more than it increases their complexity costs. For example, say that, as a result of the capital gains preference, *A* decides to recognize gain more frequently, and therefore deliberately increases her overall capital gains tax by $20,000. Assuming her behavior is both rationally self-interested and well-informed, the change must leave her more than $20,000 better off, disregarding taxes. * * *

The most obvious response to this argument for the efficiency of a revenue-raising capital gains tax preference is that it mistakenly assumes that the directly affected taxpayers bear all of the added complexity costs. Certainly the government (on behalf of all current and future taxpayers) bears

---

15. Of course, a zero tax rate would deter the fewest transactions (none). Assuming revenue needs are fixed, however, it would require imposing higher taxes elsewhere, presumably causing their own set of distortions.

18. Calvin H. Johnson, Seventeen Culls from Capital Gains, 48 Tax Notes 1285 (Sept. 3, 1990). [This article is excerpted in Subchapter A, at page 939. (Ed.)]

added costs as well, for example, from auditing and litigating capital gains issues. Yet, this objection can be met if the capital gains preference raises revenue net of the government's added costs from administering it. The preference would seem to impose few complexity costs other than those borne by the directly affected taxpayers and the government.

* * * One should recognize, however, that the danger of setting the preferential rate too low is not just one of estimating error, but of politics. Once Congress heads down the path of setting special capital gains rates, interest group pressures and the general popularity of tax cuts give it powerful motivations to go too far. Well-organized and well-connected taxpayers welcome reduced tax liabilities no less than reduced lock-in. Such taxpayers often operate without effective political opposition even though, if their taxes are reduced and government spending remains the same, others in the society (now or in the future) can be expected to pay more.

This political perspective—which legal commentators on taxation all too often, with unjustifiable myopia, ignore—is extremely important to the merits of the capital gains issue. Even beyond the danger of setting the capital gains rate too low, there is a broader problem with relying on optimal taxation principles in the political process. Flawed decisionmakers such as Congress may create better tax rules when their operating premise, requiring special justification for a departure, is that everything should be taxed alike, than if the premise is that each item should be taxed in accordance with its own unique (and highly debatable) characteristics.

* * *

I therefore reach the following conclusions. First, the efficiency case for a particular capital gains tax preference that is known to increase revenue long term is quite strong. Second, from the design standpoint of whether the tax system should be structured to include a capital gains preference that Congress will specify, the efficiency case is considerably less strong, given both the difficulty of estimating revenue effects accurately and the problems with political decisionmaking. The conflict between these two perspectives—the institutionally abstract and the political—helps to make the long-term efficiency consequences of a capital gains preference perennially interesting, yet perhaps unresolvable.

* * *

Perceptional Equity

An additional aspect of Professors Cunningham and Schenk's equity analysis is their discussion of what they call "perceptional equity." Admittedly, they do not treat this principle as much more than a tie-breaker, to be consulted if the advantages of the capital gains preference should otherwise prove small or nil. * * *

Nevertheless, because the principle of perceptional equity superficially sounds so plausible, and recently has been popular in the tax policy literature, and yet, in my view, is poorly conceived, I regard it as worth addressing here.

* * * For several reasons, however, I suspect that the presence or absence of the capital gains preference would have only a vanishingly trivial effect, if that, on people's good feelings about the tax system and the level of compliance, even if there were greater public consensus one way or the other about the capital gains issue.

Those of us in the legal community like to think that our debates are of great importance to, and are closely followed by, the society as a whole. In practice, however, these debates not only are too complex and arcane for the public to follow more than minimally—or to know, in most cases, whether or why the outcome might matter—but are overwhelmed by all the other societal information that busy people, often with jobs and families, encounter and must try to grasp. The outside information to which people do give significant attention tends to be salient and anecdotal, and better still, in the age of television, pleasingly visual.

* * *

As to compliance, I see no evidence that the Service, which one would hope knows best about these matters, sees eliminating the preference, in order to restore faith in equal treatment of all taxpayers—or, alternatively, expanding the preference if the public opinion polls so dictate—as an important compliance initiative. This is not surprising. To a large extent, compliance or noncompliance is a rational choice that turns on one's understanding of the odds that obtain in the "audit lottery." Concededly, however, people's beliefs about the tax system's fairness also may affect the level of compliance. Noncompliance can be a form of protest, having expressive value to the angry taxpayer, whether or not it is monetarily rational. The Service appears to agree with this view, but it makes its stand elsewhere, rather than on issues such as capital gains. Its prime tactic on the perception front seems to be enforcement actions against prominent and wealthy taxpayers such as Leona Helmsley, whose reported claim that only the "little people" pay taxes surely contributed to her punishment. Prosecuting Helmsley, rather than making any particular proposal regarding capital gains, is precisely the sort of compliance initiative on the perceptual front that one would expect, given the public's disproportionately strong response to salient, anecdotal and televisual information.

I conclude, therefore, that the perceptional equity issues raised by the capital gains preference are simply too trivial to be worth considering. * * *

Little that I have said thus far would indicate that focusing on perceptional equity is anything worse than a waste of time. I believe, however, that the notion can be actively harmful. The problem goes beyond the mushiness and manipulability of perceptional equity, to the fact that casual public opinion about tax matters tends to be systematically biased by fiscal illusion. For example, taxpayers tend not to realize the extent to which tax benefits enjoyed by others shift the costs of government to themselves. They often confuse the amount due at tax time with their real tax costs net of withholding. They tend to think that corporations (rather than some group of people such as shareholders, employees or customers) somehow really bear the corporate income tax. In addition, due to rational ignorance and collective action problems, too often only the proponents and beneficiaries of a special tax provision understand or even know about it.

Participants in the scholarly debate about tax policy ought to try, however ineffectually, given the level of wider attention they receive, to address and combat the effects of rational ignorance and fiscal illusion. Perceptional equity harms any such effort, by in effect embracing people's systematic misunderstanding, and encouraging the public to live in a fool's paradise. * * *

To illustrate the significance of the fool's paradise problem of deferring factual questions to public opinion, consider the increase in 1993 of the highest explicit marginal tax rate from 33% to 39.6%. President Clinton heralded this change as ensuring that the "wealthy" would bear a greater share of the national tax burden. As I have discussed elsewhere, however, the dynastically wealthy whom his rhetoric seemed principally to target were little affected by this change, given their continuing benefit from the realization requirement and the 28% capital gains rate. Rather, the rate increase fell principally on professional and other high wage earners whom many would classify as merely upper middle class. Assuming that the public understood and supported the rate change as a way of requiring the dynastically wealthy to bear a larger tax burden, is the erroneous perception of increased fairness that thereby was created a good thing?

I would leave the management of public perceptions to the politicians, without importing it to the specialists' tax policy debate as a significant independent value. Even this probably leaves perception management with too great a role, the consequences of which may include a tendency to be self defeating over the long run. Contemporary government is the most responsive in our history. Presidents and members of Congress seem scarcely to act or speak without responding to what they learn from focus groups and daily tracking polls. This heightened level of moment-by-moment responsiveness has been accompanied by the growth of unprecedented public cynicism about government. Perhaps, after all is said and done, the best way to seem fair is simply to try as best one can to be fair.

More generally, we should stick to real effects and leave perceptions to take care of themselves. If tax rules do a good enough job of collecting adequate tax revenues, distributing the tax burden reasonably, and minimizing excess burden costs to the society, one is entitled to hope that most taxpayers, to the extent that they base their compliance decisions on their general good or ill feeling, will view the system as sufficiently fair to merit voluntary compliance.

Conclusion

Despite any differences that we may have concerning particular issues, I agree with Professors Cunningham and Schenk's core conclusion that a revenue-raising capital gains tax preference probably is better than no tax preference. * * *

The core problem, however, which cannot be assumed away, is whether and when the preference raises revenue relative to no preference. Concern about ineradicable revenue-estimating problems ought to be compounded by concern about whether Congress will consistently try to set a revenue-increasing preferential rate. The risk that, once the tax preference is accepted, it will lead in practice both to reduced efficiency and to a regressive redistribution of tax burdens, causes justifiable uneasiness.

Given the underlying uncertainty, academic scruples incline me to want to avoid taking a clear position on the capital gains preference, on the ground that nothing can be asserted with confidence. I recognize, however, that such scruples are of little use to decisionmakers. That being so, my tentative bottom-line answer is that the existing tax preference—resulting from the spread between the 28% and 39.6% maximum rates that apply, respectively, to capital gains and ordinary income—should be kept in place, assuming the political impossibility of more dramatic change to the tax system. * * * Thus, whether or not we are at the precise optimum point, the chance that significant change would only make things worse is great enough that perhaps, in a less than wholly trustworthy political environment, the issue is best not raised.

The difficulty of knowing what to do about the capital gains preference helps to illuminate a central dilemma in tax policy. We often face a choice between two different kinds of tax systems: one that treats its components as equally as possible (for example, by implementing the Haig-Simons income definition), and one that differentiates between its components based on principles of optimal taxation. The choice cannot adequately be made without considering tax politics. While the optimal tax approach tends to be better in theory (at least, from the efficiency standpoint of minimizing excess burden), one can powerfully argue that the equal tax approach often is better in practice.

ECONOMIC ANALYSES OF CAPITAL GAINS TAXATION: REALIZATIONS, REVENUES, EFFICIENCY AND EQUITY

George R. Zodrow[*]

48 Tax Law Review 419, 429-31, 433-43, 445, 492 (1993)

Realizations and Revenue Effects

Much of the controversy surrounding the effects of income taxation of capital gains has focused on whether reductions in capital gains taxes might induce an increase in realizations sufficiently large that an increase in revenues would result. Unfortunately, despite a voluminous literature examining the relationship between tax rates and capital gains realizations, this issue is far from settled. In particular, there is considerable disagreement regarding the long-run effect on realizations, and empirical estimates of the long-run elasticity of realizations with respect to tax rates vary considerably. Policymakers no doubt are frustrated that such a large volume of research has not yet produced a consensus regarding the effects on realizations and revenues of changes in rates from current levels. Unfortunately, the existence of a significant number of serious problems that plague empirical work on this issue suggests that this state of affairs will continue, at least to some extent, into the foreseeable future.

This Section reviews the many issues that complicate estimating the effects of tax changes on capital gains realizations and revenues. It describes the four general empirical approaches that have been used to investigate this issue—time-series studies, cross section analyses, panel studies, and approaches that pool cross section and time-series data. * * *

Types of Empirical Studies

Time-series studies use regression analysis to explain annual data on aggregate capital gains realizations as a function of some measure of the marginal tax rate on capital gains. These studies control for the effects of other "explanatory" variables also believed to affect realizations, such as income, the age distribution of the population, some measure of wealth or the stock of accrued gains, and macroeconomic variables, such as the level of or changes in gross national product and the price level. These analyses examine the post-war experience on capital gains taxes and realizations, and typically are based on roughly 30-35 years of data.

In contrast, a cross section study examines a single year of data obtained from individual taxpayer returns. Since all taxpayers face the same tax system in a given year, the variation in marginal tax rates is due to differences in individual circumstances at a single point in time, rather than to the

---

[*]. At time of original publication, Professor of Economics, Rice University.

evolution of the tax system over time, which provides the variation in tax rates in a time-series study. A cross section analysis attempts to explain the capital gains realizations behavior of individual taxpayers as a function of an estimate of the individual tax rate on capital gains, controlling for other individual characteristics, such as income, deductions, marital status and family size, that might be expected to affect realizations and are available from tax return data. These data are often supplemented with information from other sources (including supplementary data collected by the Service) on other taxpayer attributes, especially age and wealth, to the extent that such data can be either matched or imputed to the taxpayers in the sample. Sample sizes in cross section studies are usually very large, often including many thousands of taxpayers.

The two remaining types of analyses are combinations of the time-series and cross section approaches. A panel study examines the behavior of a fixed sample of individual taxpayers over several years; that is, the data consist of several consecutive cross sections for the same group of taxpayers. By comparison, a "pooled time-series cross section" analysis also combines several years of cross sectional data; however, no attempt is made to track the behavior of individual taxpayers over time. * * *

Problems Common to All Empirical Studies

A number of problems are common to all four types of empirical studies. Although considerable progress has been made in recent years in addressing many of these difficulties, they all, to varying degrees, plague attempts to determine empirically the relationship between capital gains tax rates, realizations and revenue.

Absence of a Widely Accepted Theoretical Model of Realizations Behavior

In most empirical investigations of microeconomic issues, econometric analysis is based to a fairly large extent on a well-developed theoretical model of individual or firm decisionmaking that specifies the objectives of the decisionmaking agent and then solves for the behavioral implications of optimizing behavior. Unfortunately, despite some very interesting efforts in this area, there currently is no widely accepted model of capital gains realization behavior. Accordingly, the economic factors motivating the decision to realize gains are not well specified, and theory provides few predictions about how and why capital gains are realized. Indeed, a primary implication of one strand of the theoretical literature—the "tax avoidance" model—is that gains should seldom, if ever, be realized.

The scope of the problem can be seen by considering the wide variety of features that, in principle, should be included in a comprehensive model (in addition to a modeling of tax avoidance strategies and the limits to such strategies posed by transactions costs, various Code provisions designed to limit avoidance, imperfect capital markets and other factors). Such a model presumably would have a multi-period life cycle structure. It would have to cope simultaneously with modeling realization behavior and with many other issues that to varying degrees are still unresolved in the public finance literature. These include the modeling of life cycle consumption/saving decisions, precautionary saving, saving for bequests, risk taking, and portfolio reallocation in response to changes in market prices and in expectations of future returns—all in the context of a model that properly accounts for both income and estate and gift taxes. Not surprisingly, such a model has yet to be fully articulated.

The absence of a widely-accepted behavioral model implies that theory will offer relatively little guidance in interpreting conflicting empirical evidence regarding the relationship between tax rates and capital gains realizations. * * *

Uncertainty Regarding the Best Empirical Approach

There is still considerable uncertainty as to whether time-series or cross section analysis is better suited to determining the effects of taxation on realizations. This is not surprising since both approaches suffer from serious econometric difficulties. Nevertheless, this is a serious problem because the results of most time-series studies suggest that capital gains are significantly less sensitive to tax rates than do most cross section studies. There is, however, a fair degree of consensus that the use of panel data—especially if the data extend over a number of years—is a promising approach, because it combines most of the advantages of both techniques (although to some degree it also shares the problems of both approaches). * * *

Absence of Reliable Data on Several Key Variables

Another serious problem confronting empirical researchers is that little reliable data exist for several variables that would be critical to realization decisions under any reasonable behavioral model. In particular, realization decisions presumably are strongly affected by the stock of accrued gains, the stock of total wealth, the amount of gains transferred at death (and thus eliminated from the stock of accrued gains that are potentially taxable) and by the level of transactions costs, but data on these variables are unreliable. * * *

In addition, accurate estimation of the effects of capital gains taxes, in principle, requires disaggregation of realizations by asset type. Realization responsiveness (and transactions costs) presumably vary according to the type of asset, realizations of various types of assets presumably are affected by different variables (for example, different indices of asset values), and any given change in the tax treatment of capital gains is likely to have differential effects on the incentives to realize gains on various types of assets. Again, data limits generally preclude such disaggregation. The 1985 Treasury Report is the prime exception, and its results suggest that this point is, in fact, an important one.

* * * Another problem is that virtually all of the early studies had no data on marginal capital gains rates at the state level. Since there is considerable variation in such rates, the tax rate used in the studies was subject to measurement error. State capital gains taxes have played an important role in several recent studies.

Additional measurement error is introduced by the fact that the realizations data for a given year include realizations reported in that year on late returns from previous years. Finally, almost all empirical studies ignore transactions costs, despite the fact that such costs—like the capital gains tax—discourage realizations.

Difficulties in Relating Changes in Tax Structure to Changes in Revenues

* * *

Another complicating factor is that changes in the tax treatment of capital gains generally do not take the simple form of changes in marginal tax rates, but instead appear in alternative forms, such as changes in the entire rate structure, in the maximum rate applied to gains, or in exclusion or inclusion percentages. These changes in tax treatment must be translated into changes in marginal and average rates before revenue effects can be approximated. * * *

Accounting for Complex Feedback Revenue Effects

Although many studies have examined the revenue effects of changes in capital gains rates, most have focused narrowly on revenues from capital gains taxes. Such an approach may be highly misleading, however, if feedback effects on other components of income tax revenue are significant. For example, a reduction in the tax rate on capital gains might cause income tax revenues to decline to the extent that (1) firms reduced dividend payouts because the effective tax rate on retained earnings declined, (2) * * *.

On the other hand, a lower capital gains rate might cause positive revenue feedback effects if (1) individual portfolio reallocations involved moving resources from relatively low-taxed housing and consumer durables to the moderately taxed noncorporate business sector or to the relatively heavily taxed corporate sector (a reallocation from the noncorporate to the corporate sector would have the same result), (2) * * *. Moreover, a reduction in capital gains taxes might result in an increase in stock prices that would in turn spur additional realizations. * * *

Several studies have attempted to incorporate such revenue feedback effects into their empirical models of the revenue effects of capital gains taxes, but the results of these studies are mixed. * * *

Uncertainty About the Dynamics of the Realizations Response

Both the short-run and the long-run responses to changes in capital gains rates are of considerable interest to policymakers. Although the short- to medium-term response may be of more direct concern to revenue estimators and those concerned with five-year budget forecasts, most policy discussions have focused on the nature of the long-run response. Although several studies have attempted to separate long-run from short-run responses, this issue is still controversial.

Most observers argue that the short-run realizations response to a capital gains tax reduction will exceed the long-run response. The intuition underlying this argument is as follows. At any given tax rate, some individuals are deferring realizations because the marginal tax cost of an asset sale exceeds the marginal gain obtained by selling the asset. This is the so-called lock-in effect. By reducing the tax penalty for asset sales, a rate cut reduces this lock-in effect for the entire stock of assets held by the investor; thus, it is likely to cause an immediate surge in realizations. As these sales occur, however, the stock of locked-in accrued gains declines and the investor moves toward a new long-run equilibrium level of realizations (or ratio of realizations to assets) that is permanently higher, but not as high as that required to eliminate the stock of newly unlocked gains during the transition. In addition, an increase in current realizations, to at least some extent, implies a reduction in future realizations (and revenues), since the basis of the asset is increased to the sales price so that future reported gains are less than they would have been in the absence of the sale.

Separating the short-run and long-run responses to a change in capital gains taxes represents a significant problem in all empirical (and theoretical) analyses of realizations behavior. * * *

Difficulties in Modeling Expectations of Future Tax Rates

* * * [R]ealizations can be affected significantly by expected future tax rates. For example, if investors anticipate a future rate cut, they will defer current realizations. * * *

Of course, estimating expected future tax rates is inevitably problematic. * * * Some recent results suggest that expected future tax rates can play an important role in predicting realizations behavior, which in turn implies that estimates of realization elasticities that ignore future tax rates are suspect.

The Econometric Problem of Simultaneity

Although each methodology has its own econometric problems, one serious problem is common to all four types of analysis. Specifically, a variety of "simultaneity" problems exist in all analyses of capital gains tax rates and realizations.

A brief intuitive description of the simultaneity problem is as follows. Econometric analysis requires that the various explanatory variables in a regression equation (for example, capital gains rates and all the other variables thought to affect realizations) must be determined independently of the variable being explained (for example, realizations). Accordingly, the explanatory variables are referred to as "independent" and the variable being explained is described as the "dependent" variable.

* * *

Violation of this independence assumption results in the problem of "simultaneity." * * *

Unfortunately, simultaneity problems are quite common in capital gains regression equations. The most obvious example is that the explanatory variable of most policy interest—the marginal tax rate on gains—depends positively on the level of capital gains realizations, since individuals with large realizations will be in higher rate brackets under a progressive rate structure. * * *

All investigators have recognized this particular simultaneity problem and attempted to correct for it by substituting an alternative measure of the capital gains rate that does not depend on the level of realizations. These corrections, however, have not always been successful in removing all elements of endogeneity from the tax rate variable. More importantly, the simultaneity problem in capital gains equations is much more pervasive than just the relationship between rates and realizations, and greatly complicates the estimation problem for all four empirical approaches.

* * *

Difficulties in Measuring
Disequilibrium Relationships

Yet another issue related to difficulties in identifying the dynamic aspects of the realizations response is that standard econometric techniques assume that the economy is at an equilibrium, so that the regression coefficients measure the effects of changes in the independent variables from that equilibrium. As the above discussion suggests, however, changes in capital gains rates will have effects that last for several years. Although the models estimated in several recent empirical studies make modest attempts to capture the effects of past tax rate changes, none can capture even moderately complex time paths of adjustment. Consequently, estimated regression coefficients may reflect the effects of several past rate regimes, making it very difficult to disentangle the effects of various policy changes.

　　　　* * *

Conclusion

　　* * *   [T]here appears to be an increased awareness that all of the empirical results in this area are quite tenuous, and that one should be exceedingly careful in attempting to draw policy implications from this literature. * * *

Notes and Questions

9.　Professors Cunningham and Schenk find the realization rule (in various forms) to be the primary "culprit"—the root of most of the distortions that, in turn, the capital gains preference supposedly addresses. As we saw in Chapter Two, considerable effort has been expended in devising methods that avoid the distortions of the realization rule without encountering the two significant problems that any form of mark-to-market seems to entail—valuation and liquidity. In Congress, however, despite a bit of nibbling at the edges, the realization rule seems not to be under serious challenge.

10.　The realization rule means that taxpayers can delay gains until sale. If the taxpayer never sells, but dies while still owning the appreciated property, the gain is permanently excluded from income by section 1014. As discussed in Chapter Ten, Congress in 2001 voted to end stepped-up basis at death and substitute a rule of carryover basis (though the change will be effective only for the year 2010, absent further congressional action). If this change became permanent, would the analysis of Cunningham and Schenk be affected significantly?

11.　Cunningham and Schenk point to two deviations from Haig-Simons income that are adverse to taxpayers enjoying capital gains. First, they are taxed on nominal gains, which may be reduced or eliminated, in real terms, by inflation. This applies to all capital assets. The issue of inflation is addressed in Chapter Sixteen.

　　The final distortion is applicable to one important category of capital assets—stock in C corporations. Because of the double tax on corporate income—the primary subject of Chapter Fourteen—a tax on the sale of appreciated corporate stock, even at capital gains rates, can be viewed as a "double tax," to the degree the gain represents retained earnings already taxed to the corporation.

Traditional arguments for the preference

12. What do Cunningham and Schenk think of the argument that capital gains should be taxed favorably because they are unexpected and nonrecurring? Do you agree with them?

13. Should advocates of consumption taxation as a broad replacement for the income tax advocate a capital gains preference as moving closer to their ideal?

14. Why is the problem of "bunching" seen as unfairly burdening taxpayers realizing gains from long-held assets? Why is bunching a problem only under a progressive rate structure? Why do Cunningham and Schenk generally reject the argument (even under a progressive rate structure)?

15. As noted above (see Note #11), the failure to account for inflation—as by allowing holders of capital assets to index their tax basis—results in capital gains taxes being levied on nominal gains rather than real gains. Where the nominal gain is entirely attributable to inflation, a taxpayer will be taxed in the absence of a real gain, or even where the transaction has resulted in a real loss. Proponents of the capital gains preference assert that the preference works "rough justice," by taxing too much gain (nominal rather than real gain), but taxing it at lower rates.

Professors Cunningham and Schenk acknowledge that the failure to account for inflation represents a serious challenge to the capital gains tax. While the problem is real, however, they find no answer in the present preference, or in any likely future capital gains preference.

For long holding periods, there is little problem, because the advantage of tax deferral may largely offset, or more than offset, the overtaxation resulting from inflation. For shorter holding periods, Cunningham and Schenk see a greater possibility that the benefit of deferral will not offset the adverse effect of taxing illusory gain attributable to inflation. (It should be noted that both deferral and inflation become less important as the holding period is shortened.) Cunningham and Schenk conclude that the capital gains preference "account[s] for inflation on a purely random basis," and thus "is so rough as to provide no justice."

16. The capital gains tax is said to adversely affect taxpayers' willingness to undertake risky investments. Here, the primary problem is likely to be the unbalanced treatment of gains and losses. While gains are taxed (albeit at a reduced rate), losses are allowed only as an offset to gains (and, in the case of individuals, against up to $3,000 per year of ordinary income). Thus, the

investor may see the risky investment as a gamble in which "heads the Government and I win together, tails I lose (alone)." The sharp limits on deductibility of losses, discussed further in Subchapter C, is directly attributable to the realization rule.

Professors Cunningham and Schenk argue that not only is a capital gains preference not the best solution, it is "a very poor second best solution," because it is not targeted to risky investments. What is the best solution to the issue of risk?

17. Professor Halperin suggests that a better solution to the limitation on capital loss deductions is politically feasible. What is the basis for his suggestion that it might be appropriate to remove the loss limitation rules outside the area of marketable securities?

The problem of "lock-in"

18. Professors Cunningham and Schenk devote most attention to the problem of "lock-in." Why might the present tax structure tend to lock investors in to investments with unrealized appreciation? (Are investors locked in to investments that have declined in value?)

19. "Lock-in" is clearly a burden on the holders of capital assets, who, by hypothesis, would prefer to sell but for the capital gains tax. Their welfare is reduced. The effect of lock-in on the broader society and economy is less clear. In theory, assets should be worth more to their most efficient users, suggesting that lock-in leads to inefficiency. But Professor Shaviro asserts that "[w]hat is involved for the most part, is the welfare loss to individuals, not society as a whole." Or, as Cunningham and Schenk put it, "it is not clear that it matters much to society who owns IBM stock."

Do you think lock-in harms only the owners of appreciated property, or does it have broader effect? Is your answer the same for marketable securities and for other capital assets, such as land and closely-held business interests?

20. Although Cunningham and Schenk ultimately accept a capital gains preference as a second-best solution to the problem of lock-in, clearly it is not their preference. What are better solutions to the problem of "lock-in," according to Cunningham and Schenk?

21. The revenue issue is crucial in this debate, and, as the excerpt from Professor Zodrow's article demonstrates, almost impossible to resolve. It seems obvious that with any tax, there will come a point at which an increase in the tax will yield less revenue, because taxpayers will generate less

economic income, or will take measures of avoidance or evasion. Even with regard to personal service income, it is likely that a tax rate of 99 percent would yield less revenue than a tax rate of 50 percent. At a 99 percent rate, taxpayers might decide to spend more time on leisure and activities generating untaxed imputed income, and take strenuous efforts to avoid taxation on their market activities. However, avoidance of taxation on personal service income entails significant costs, such as quitting work or committing tax fraud.

The revenue problem, however, is particularly severe with capital gains, because lawful avoidance of the tax is so simple. The taxpayer need *not* refrain from generating economic income in the market—the investment can continue in place. The taxpayer need *not* take burdensome or illegal measures to avoid taxation—simply doing nothing, holding the investment, is sufficient. With avoidance this simple, the tax seems almost optional, and taxpayers will be reluctant to pay a significant capital gains tax.

22. Professors Cunningham and Schenk argue that taxing capital gains at a lower rate than that applied to ordinary income may be beneficial not only to taxpayers who realize capital gains, but to those who do not. Why might this be so?

23. If reducing the rate on capital gains means that owners of capital gains will pay more taxes, why do Cunningham and Schenk assert that their "burden" of taxation would be reduced?

24. Professors Cunningham and Schenk assert that it is possible that reducing the tax on capital gains could leave all taxpayers better off, yet still be inequitable. Ultimately, they conclude that any inequity would be short-lived, because of tax capitalization—the market would adjust the price of capital assets to account for the favorable tax treatment.

"Perceptional equity"
25. Cunningham and Schenk also address the notion of "perceptional equity," by which they mean "that a proposal probably should be rejected if it is perceived as inequitable."

26. Consider the two following scenarios—one actual, the other hypothetical—from legal realms far removed from taxation. In each case, consider whether the arrangement is equitable, inequitable, or actually equitable but should be rejected because it flunks the "perceptional equity" test.

During the War Between the States, the Union employed a military draft, but allowed men who were drafted to hire replacements. This was "efficient," in that both the men hired and those who hired them must have thought their situation improved, and no one was adversely affected, at least in any obvious way.

Suppose a billionaire needed a replacement heart, for which he would pay one billion dollars. One thousand healthy individuals, each possessing characteristics that would allow the transplant to succeed, volunteered for the following arrangement: each would receive one million dollars in exchange for running one chance in a thousand of being selected by lottery as the donor. The recipient is better off. The potential donors voluntarily run one chance in a million of death to receive a million dollars—a risk smaller than that run routinely by many people, for smaller rewards. And no poor potential recipient is denied a heart, because these healthy people were not potential donors under normal donor programs.

27. Should we pay any attention to perceptional equity in taxation? Or, do you agree with Professor Shaviro that "after all is said and done, the best way to seem fair is simply to try as best one can to be fair"?

28. Indeed, Shaviro argues that the notion of perceptional equity is worse than a waste of time—instead, "the notion can be actively harmful." What is the basis for his argument on this point? Do you agree?

29. All agree that capital gains provisions make tax law more complex, and that as a result more resources are devoted to planning transactions, and to compliance and enforcement, than would be the case absent the preference. The questions concerning complexity costs relate not to their existence but to their magnitude. Professor Halperin asserts that the costs of the "distortions, particularly in administration and planning, caused by a rate differential are far more serious than is sometimes suggested." Should we reject a preferential rate on these grounds?

30. Professor Shaviro fears that even if a small preference for capital gains were justified, Congress would likely grant a significantly larger preference. Writing in 1993, he argued that perhaps it was best to leave in place a preferential rate of 28 percent (compared to a top rate of 39.6 percent for ordinary income) "given the political risks inherent in reopening the issue." Obviously, the issue was reopened (if it had ever closed). What would Shaviro think of the current 15 percent top rate?

31. All agree that the question of revenues—whether a preferential rate for capital gains increases or decreases revenue—is extremely important. As Professor Zodrow explains, researchers have attempted to develop economic models to determine revenue issues, but their resolution is extremely difficult. One thing this complexity explains is how Republicans are able to summons reputable economists to testify that a proposed cut in capital gains rates will boost revenues, while Democrats can call on equally reputable economists to testify that revenues will fall.

32. Professor Zodrow's article demonstrates a pervasive difficulty with applying scientific methodology to social and economic research: It is impossible to hold other variables constant while testing the variable in question (here, capital gains rates).

33. If a revenue-enhancing capital gains rate preferential is deemed desirable, but a revenue-losing preference is not, what should we do when the data are as unclear as Zodrow suggests?

34. Professor Alan Auerbach was generally complimentary of Professor Zodrow's article, but suggested that our focus should move from the difficult revenue question toward changes in the realization rule:

> In addition to being thorough, Professor Zodrow is sensible and evenhanded as well. * * * My main criticism is of the article's choice of topics. * * *
>
> In a sense, this choice reflects the nature of the debate. Professor Zodrow focuses on the issues that have received the most attention. Indeed, this is one of the problems with the existing policy debate: There has been so much discussion about revenues and realizations elasticities, and so little about changes in capital gains taxation beyond whether the rate should be raised or lowered. Yet, it is now known that moving toward a system of accrual taxation, or its equivalent—and eliminating the lock-in effect and timing arbitrage entirely—would not be especially difficult for the bulk of investments. It strikes me that there is probably a bigger social payoff in trying to work out details of a transition to such a system than in getting more reliable estimates of realizations elasticities."[i]

---

i. Alan A. Auerbach, *Commentary*, 48 TAX L. REV. 529, 529 (1993).

C. TREATMENT OF CAPITAL LOSSES

Capital losses may be deducted in full against capital gains. For this purpose, there is no distinction between long-term and short-term capital gains and between long-term and short-term capital losses. For a year in which capital losses exceed capital gains, individuals, estates, and trusts are allowed to deduct up to $3,000 of the excess capital loss against ordinary income ($1,500 by a married individual filing separately). Corporations may deduct capital losses only to the extent of capital gains. Section 1211.

Unused capital losses of individuals, estates, and trusts may be carried forward to succeeding years until they are exhausted. Unused capital losses of corporations may be carried back three years and carried forward five years. Section 1212.

When special treatment of capital gains was terminated (temporarily) by the Tax Reform Act of 1986, the limits on deduction of capital losses were not changed. In the first excerpt below, Professor Martin Ginsburg and former Assistant Secretary of the Treasury for Tax Policy Kenneth Gideon discuss an area of concern in allowing unlimited deduction of capital losses—"cherry-picking." Due to taxpayer control over realization of capital gains and losses, taxpayers may let their potential capital gains ride without realization while realizing their capital losses to avoid tax on ordinary income. In the second excerpt, Professor Fred Peel argues against limiting capital losses, even if capital gains are taxed at preferential rates (which Peel opposes).

DISCUSSION BY CCH TAX ADVISORY BOARD ROUNDTABLE

Vol. 79, Number 26, Part 2, May 27, 1992, pp. 5-6

Martin Ginsburg: A common concern or shared objective in what has been said so far is tax simplification. Certainly I am a great believer, as who is not. But it struck me that neither in Ken's opening, ground-laying discussion nor in any of the comments that followed did I hear a reference to the taxation of capital gains. Does this reticence reflect a general belief that a taxing regime that awards special treatment to capital gains and losses cannot earn the simplification merit badge? * * * We have already seen the return of a rate preference, albeit a small one. Is more to come?

Ken Gideon: * * *

As long as we have the fundamental rule in the Code—which we are not about to abandon because we can't afford to—that we are going to classify capital losses and limit them so that we've got to keep track of what's a capital item already, it's hard for me to see that there is a significant complication added by giving a preferential rate for capital gains. And this is wholly apart from whether a capital gains cut would be good, bad, or indifferent. I'm simply saying I don't see that on the simplification scale you really can put much weight on one side or the other.

Martin Ginsburg: * * * Ken's reference to capital losses urges the question, isn't there something more sensible we can do with the tax treatment of capital losses, more sensible than the present arrangement of limiting deductibility to offsetting capital gains plus $3,000 of ordinary income? I do agree that in allowing greater deductibility of capital losses, the revenue concern is the real one but the problem is not amorphous or abstract, it is a problem of cherry picking which, essentially, centers on property for which there is a quoted price and a ready market.

If I have enough money, a surplus $400 million say, I will probably never have to pay taxes again if there is unlimited deductibility of capital losses. I will invest $1,000,000 in each of 400 different publicly traded stocks. With good luck 360 of them will go up in value, 20 will stay the same, and 20 will go down in value. Then, abusing our realization system, I will sell the 20 depressed stocks to generate a large loss while retaining the 360 good ones with their appreciated value unrecognized and intact. Permitted freely to do so, I will offset [all ordinary income by] the large cherry-picked loss. * * *

CAPITAL GAINS: FALLING SHORT ON FAIRNESS AND SIMPLICITY
Fred W. Peel, Jr.*

17 University of Baltimore Law Review 418, 418-19 (1988)

Fair treatment of capital gain and loss requires that each be treated the same as ordinary income and loss, respectively, because the economic benefit from a dollar of capital gain is the same as the economic benefit from a dollar of ordinary income, and a dollar of capital loss has the same effect as a dollar of ordinary loss. There is no intrinsic difference between capital assets and other assets that justifies special treatment for either capital gains or capital losses. Taxpayers invest in capital assets to profit from their use or their eventual disposition. Such assets may yield current income through rents, royalties, dividends, or interest. Even those assets held for personal use—homes, pleasure boats, etc.—yield imputed income to their owners. Capital assets held for eventual profit through sale at a gain really are being held for sale even though they escape the narrower classification of inventory or property held for sale to customers in the ordinary course of a trade or business. The thinness of the distinction between capital assets and business assets is demonstrated by the anomalous treatment in section 1231 of the

---

*. At time of original publication, Ben J. Altheimer Professor of Law Emeritus, University of Arkansas at Little Rock.

Internal Revenue Code of depreciable assets and land used in a trade or business.

Unlimited allowance of capital losses may be justified in theory even when net capital gains are given favorable tax treatment.[2] Certainly, theoretical justification exists for unlimited allowance of capital losses when capital gains are fully taxed at the same rate as ordinary income. It is no longer possible to defend restrictions on the allowance of capital losses by arguing that such treatment is justified because it is parallel to the treatment given capital gains.[3]

The parallel treatment argument was specious from its outset except in the case of gains and losses realized by the same taxpayer. Restriction of one taxpayer's use of an economic loss cannot be justified by pointing to another taxpayer's benefit from special treatment of capital gains. An extreme example is the unfortunate individual who has one large capital loss in a lifetime and no present or foreseeable capital gains. Even if this taxpayer should live long enough to recoup the loss through small annual deductions of the unused capital loss carry forward each year, such recoupment will not accurately reflect the current cost of the initial loss to the taxpayer.

* * *

Notes and Questions

35. Treatment of capital losses has varied wildly over the years. Under the 1913 Act, losses were allowed in full if incurred in trade—otherwise, no losses were allowed. In the 1918 Act, all losses were allowed on transactions entered into for profit. Under the 1924 Act, the tax saved by using capital losses to offset ordinary income was limited to 12.5 percent of the losses, matching the maximum tax rate then imposed on long-term capital gains. The 1932 Act limited deduction of short-term losses to short-term gains. Under the 1934 Act, only $2,000 of capital losses in excess of capital gains were allowed to offset ordinary income. Under the 1938 Act, only 30 percent of capital losses could be used to offset tax on ordinary income. Under the 1942 Act, individuals were allowed to deduct only $1,000 of capital losses from ordinary income. The present limitations date from 1986.

36. Why might the potential for "cherry-picking" have led Congress to limit deduction of capital losses?

---

2. *See* Warren, *The Deductibility by Individuals of Capital Losses under the Federal Income Tax*, 40 U. CHI. L. REV. 291, 295 (1973).

3. The parallel treatment argument was used by the Committee on Ways and Means in its Report on the Revenue Act of 1924. *See* H.R. Rep. No. 179, 68th Cong., 1st Sess. 57 (1924).

36. Consider Peel's argument in the final paragraph of the excerpt of his article. Must the tax system be fair on a taxpayer-by-taxpayer basis, or is it sufficient to be fair to investors as a group? Is the tax system unjust if it limits cherry-picking through a statutory device that penalizes a taxpayer who experienced only loss, and never had a chance to realize losses while letting gains ride?

38. One longstanding provision, abandoned in 1986, provided that two dollars of long-term capital loss were required to offset one dollar of ordinary income. Interestingly, the 1995 Republican proposal excepted in Subchapter D at page 1001 (see final paragraph of excerpt) would have reinstated this anti-taxpayer provision as part of a generally pro-taxpayer capital gains proposal (which was not enacted). This provision was presumably included to reduce the revenue loss of the proposal.

A policy basis for more strictly limiting the deductibility of long-term capital losses than of short-term capital losses is elusive. The thinking was apparently that if only a portion of long-term capital gain is taxed, then only a portion of long-term capital losses should be deducted. This ignores the fact that different taxpayers will be reporting gains and losses. (Indeed, if the same taxpayer reports them in a single year, the gains and losses will be netted before being included in income or being deducted against ordinary income.) It also ignores the fact that a long-term capital loss is even worse than it seems, because the longer holding period means that the real loss has been reduced, in nominal terms, by the effects of inflation.

D. EFFECT OF TAXING CAPITAL GAINS ON INCENTIVES

Commentators have advanced various economic theories to support favorable tax treatment of capital gains. As discussed in Subchapter B, proponents of preferential treatment for capital gains argue that taxing them at ordinary income rates deters risk-taking. A 1990 study by the Congressional Budget Office (at a time when Democrats controlled Congress and a Republican, the first President Bush, was in the White House), the first excerpt below, discussed the impact on risk-taking of the tax treatment of capital gains and losses. The focus of this excerpt is a comparison of a preference in the form of a partial exclusion of capital gains and some form of indexing for inflation, so that only *real* capital gains would be taxed.

In order to stimulate investment, the first President Bush consistently, and without success, sought modifications of the income tax provisions governing capital gains. His administration's case for special treatment of capital gains as an incentive for increased saving and investment was made by Michael J. Boskin, Chairman of the President's Council of Economic Advisers, before the Senate Finance Committee in 1990.

Both increased savings and more efficient capital markets were given as reasons for a deduction of 50 percent of net capital gains in the excerpt from the Ways and Means Committee report on the Contract with America Tax Relief Act of 1995. This proposal (from the newly Republican-majority House), though never enacted, is typical of the argument favoring preferential treatment of capital gains.

In contrast to broad, generalized arguments that lower taxes on capital gains stimulate savings and investment, James M. Poterba's analysis of sources of venture capital concluded that across-the-board reductions in individual capital gains tax rates would have little effect on the tax burden on venture capital financiers, while providing large benefits to owners of many other assets. Mr. Poterba explains his position in the final excerpt of this subchapter.

INDEXING CAPITAL GAINS
Congressional Budget Office
Pages 39-42 (1990)

Capital Gains Taxes and Risk-Sharing

A tax on capital gains lowers the after-tax return from investing in risky assets. By itself this would discourage risk-taking. So long as capital losses are also deductible, however, a capital gains tax also lowers the variability of returns, which makes risky assets relatively more attractive.

Under current law, capital losses are fully deductible against capital gains, and up to $3,000 of capital losses in excess of capital gains may be deducted against ordinary income. For investors with both gains and losses, or only small net capital losses, current law amounts to taxation of capital gains with full loss offsets. Thus, the net effect on risk-taking of current law is ambiguous, and the presumption that current law deters risk-taking may be unwarranted. Furthermore, current law favors assets that pay returns in the form of capital gains over income-producing assets because of the ability to defer taxes. Since risky assets are more likely to pay their returns in the form of capital gains, current law taxes the gain to risky investments relatively favorably, although less so than before the 1986 tax reform.

A capital gains tax preference such as indexing or an exclusion is sometimes rationalized as a subsidy to encourage risk-taking by raising expected after-tax returns on risky investments. However, the two forms of tax preference would have much different incentive effects. As compared with present law, an exclusion would reduce risk less than an otherwise equivalent indexing scheme because it would reduce the effective marginal tax rate on capital gains, whereas indexing does not affect the marginal rate. For example, for assets held for the same length of time, a 30 percent exclusion at a 28 percent statutory tax rate on capital gains would increase the variance of return by 25 percent as compared with indexing or present law. An exclusion that fully offset inflation (on average) would be larger and it would increase variance even more. Thus, in the absence of loss limitations, indexing would encourage risk-taking more than an equivalent (on average) exclusion.

In addition, a major source of risk in investment is inflation. The effective tax rate under an exclusion increases with inflation whereas under indexing the effective tax rate is invariant with respect to inflation (for a given holding period). Thus, the variance in after-tax returns resulting from unexpected inflation is much smaller under indexing than under an exclusion.

One qualification must be made. Since indexing would treat yield assets much more favorably than would an exclusion, indexing might shift investment away from growth assets into yield assets. If yield assets are inherently less risky than growth assets, indexing might result in less aggregate risk-taking than a similar exclusion. However, it is important to note that this would occur because yield assets would be penalized less, not because risky assets would be penalized more.

Effect of Loss Limitations

As noted above, current law limits deductions for realized capital losses in excess of realized capital gains. Under a capital gains tax based on realization, a limitation on the deductibility of losses is needed. Otherwise, taxpayers with diversified portfolios could achieve negative effective tax rates on capital gains by realizing capital losses and deferring capital gains whenever possible. However, a loss limitation, when it was binding, would affect riskier investments much more than less risky investments since the former would be more likely to produce losses.

* * *

Diversified investors can often avoid current loss limitations by using capital losses to offset other capital gains. The loss limitation would be a serious constraint primarily on undiversified investors—for example, on those who invest heavily in their own businesses. However the special indexing loss limitation would affect any risky investment that faced a possibility of real losses. Such a limitation would discourage risk-taking even more than full taxation of capital gains and losses.

To see this, consider two investments: one is safe and always yields a gain of $100; the other is risky and yields no gain or a gain of $200 with equal likelihood. Both have the same expected (average) return of $100. Under present law, both would also face the same average tax of $28 at a 28 percent rate. An investor who was not concerned about risk (risk-neutral) would be indifferent between the two investments. Now suppose that inflation erodes the initial investment by $50, so the real return is $50 for the certain investment. Because of inflation, the risky asset produces a real loss of $50 and a real gain of $150 with equal probability. The tax on the safe investment under indexing would be $14 (28 percent of the real gain of $50). The loss limitation would disallow the real loss on the risky investment, if it occurred, so the tax would be $0 or $42 with equal probability. The average tax for the risky asset would thus be $21, or 50 percent higher than the tax for the riskless investment. The risky asset would be relatively penalized by the indexing loss limitation, even though its average tax liability would fall relative to full taxation. The penalty would arise because the tax on the riskless investment would fall by more than the tax on the risky investment.

Notice that the disincentive effect of the indexing loss limitation occurs because of the asymmetric treatment of gains and losses. Since partial indexing—for example, allowing only $25 of inflation indexing in the preceding example—treats gains and losses symmetrically, it would not produce this bias against risk-taking.

TAX INCENTIVES FOR INCREASING SAVINGS AND INVESTMENTS
Testimony of Michael J. Boskin[*]

Hearings before the Senate Committee on Finance, 101st Congress, 2d Session 40-43 (1990)

I appreciate the opportunity to present the Administration's views on the capital gains tax provisions of the Savings and Economic Growth Act of 1990.[j] The key component of that Act is the restoration of the capital gains tax differential which existed prior to the Tax Reform Act of 1986. This proposal is an important part of a package of Administration initiatives designed to remove impediments to savings and investment, to encourage innovation and entrepreneurship, and to enhance economic growth.

    * * *

The Administration's foremost priority is to sustain the highest possible rate of economic growth. That goal, sir, is not just an abstraction, it is how we create rising living standards for the bulk of the population, how we develop the resources to uplift those most in need, how we provide economic and social mobility to our citizens, how we leave a better legacy to our children, and how we maintain America's leadership in the world.

The faster economic growth is going to require movement on several fronts, but it will make more social and private goals attainable. Increasing

---

[*]. At time of original testimony, Chairman of the President's Council of Economic Advisors.

j. This proposed Act was not enacted. (Ed.)

the rate of growth of living standards will require higher rates of savings and investment. Longstanding Government policies * * * such as the budget deficit, as well as tax policies, impede national savings and investment.

Partly because of these policies Americans save and invest a smaller fraction of gross national product than their counterparts in other industrialized countries. According to the World Bank the United States' investment rate ranks last among the 22 Western industrialized economies.

A major reason for the relatively low rate of investment in the United States is the high cost of capital. Some studies estimate the cost of capital in the United States is almost twice that in Germany or Japan. Taxes, a large component of the cost of capital, produce a bias against equity finance in the United States. Taxes on capital gains increase capital costs for equity finance while reducing the returns to investors.

Lowering the capital gains tax rate will lower the cost of capital. As a result of the Tax Reform Act of 1986, the overwhelming bulk of which was quite favorable, the United States unfortunately now taxes capital gains at the same rate as other income for the first time since 1921. The United States is burdened with a higher capital gains tax rate than almost every one of our major competitors. Most of them tax capital gains at a lower rate than ordinary income. Many of them do not tax capital gains at all—for example, West Germany, Italy, and most of the newly industrialized economies of the Pacific Rim.

Most of these nations also have numerous other tax provisions—such as partial or complete integration of personal and corporate income taxes—that reduce the overall taxation of capital income. The high cost of capital is a particularly onerous problem for new ventures and small businesses that have only limited access to traditional sources of finance.

Much of the return to entrepreneurs who bring new products to market, particularly through new business formation, comes through increasing the value of the business. Reducing the tax rate on capital gains will reward those who bring successful ideas to market and will help improve the climate to invest in new technologies and products, thereby creating jobs.

During the current record breaking expansion, as throughout U.S. history, most new jobs have been created by small and medium size firms. Lowering the capital gains tax rate will encourage entrepreneurs to start new businesses, to develop new products for new markets here and abroad. Lower capital gains tax rates will encourage risk taking, raise investment, improve competitiveness and spur economic growth.

These important issues, notwithstanding, much discussion has been focused on the more narrow question—how will the President's proposal or any other proposal affect Federal revenues?

* * *

A capital gains tax rate reduction affects revenues in five ways. Therefore, one has to estimate each of these five to get an estimate of the total impact of the capital gains tax rate reduction on Federal revenues.

First, the lower capital gains tax rate will induce greater realization of capital gains, as investors sell after they become unlocked from the higher capital gains rate. Many of these gains would escape taxation completely or at least defer it substantially. It is well documented that lowering the capital gains tax rate will reduce this lock-in effect, freeing investors to find more productive investments, increasing realizations of capital gains and raising revenue due to higher voluntary tax payments.

The second effect reduces revenue, as the tax rates on capital gains that would have been realized anyway are lower.

Third, over time there will be some restructuring of return to investments from ordinary income into capital gains. And with the reduced tax rate, that will reduce revenue.

Fourth, * * *.

Fifth, and most important, the capital gains rate reduction will spur growth, increase incomes and GNP, leading to additional revenues.

While opinions can differ on each of these five factors, our best estimate of the bottom line is that the Administration's proposal to reduce capital gains tax rates is likely to raise Federal revenues in both the short run and over the longer horizon. The Office of Tax Analysis of the Treasury estimates that the President's proposal will gain $12.5 billion over the next 5 years. The Joint Committee on Taxation estimates that the President's proposal will lose $11.4 billion.

Neither of these estimates captures the favorable effects of economic growth on Federal receipts which would offset JCT's estimated losses or enhance OTA's estimated gains.

* * *

Let me turn now for a few moments to discuss the impact of capital gains tax rate reductions on economic performance. The United States is faced with challenges to increase saving and investment, raise technical innovation and productivity growth, and improve our international competitiveness. The President's proposal on capital gains is one part—a central, important part—of a program to lower the barriers to meeting these goals.

Reducing the tax rate on capital gains will foster more rapid economic growth. To estimate the likely size of this effect, the CEA [Council of Economic Advisors] has done a standard computation of the impact of lower capital gains tax rates on the economy. The computation traces through the effect of lower tax rates on the cost of capital, capital formation and the resulting increase in productivity and GNP.

This computation may well be conservative since it ignores some important effects of capital gains, such as the reallocation of capital to higher productivity uses as the result of the reduced lock-in, increased entrepreneurial activity and so on.

Despite its limitations, it provides a rough, useful estimate of the magnitude of the likely effect and is comparable to other estimates. Over the past 2 years there have been a variety of estimates to the effect of reducing capital gains tax rates on national output and other costs of capital.

Put on a basis consistent with the Administration's proposal, a survey of these suggested that GNP will ultimately rise by between two-tenths of a percent and 1.2 percent per year.

The Council of Economic Advisers' estimate is that the effect lies roughly in the middle of this range, with GNP ultimately rising by about six-tenths of a percent as the result of adopting the Administration's proposal, which would amount to about $60 billion per year in the year 2000. This would be a rise equivalent to current Federal spending on education, training, employment and social services combined and roughly four times private sector spending on basic research.

Over the next 5 years, cumulatively, we estimate the President's proposal would increase GNP by roughly speaking $60 billion, over the next 10, cumulatively, by about $280 billion.

As I stressed in my opening remarks, increases in GNP represent new jobs, better opportunities and better standards of living for Americans. It also means higher Federal revenues. The estimated revenue dividend from the growth induced by the capital gains proposal would be roughly $12 billion over the next 5 years and probably over $50 billion over the next 10 years.

* * *

HOUSE REPORT 104-84

H.R. Report No. 84, 104th Congress, 1st Session, part 1, at 35-37 (1995)

The Committee believes it is important that tax policy be conducive to economic growth. Economic growth cannot occur without saving, investment, and the willingness of individuals to take risks and exploit new market opportunities. The greater the pool of savings, the greater the monies available for business investment in equipment and research. It is through such investment in equipment and new products and services that the United States economy can increase output and productivity. It is through increases in productivity that workers earn higher real wages. Hence, greater saving is necessary for all Americans to benefit through a higher standard of living.

The net personal saving rate in the United States averaged 4.8 percent of gross domestic product (GDP) in the 1980s, below the 5.5 percent rate of the 1970s, and far below the rates of Japan, Germany, Canada and other major trading partners. The net personal saving rate reported by the Department of Commerce for 1990 through 1992 averaged only 3.5 percent of GDP. The Committee believes such saving is inadequate to finance the investment that is needed to equip the country's businesses with the equipment and research dollars necessary to create the higher productivity that results in higher real wages for working Americans. A reduction in the taxation of capital gains increases the rate of return on household saving. Testimony by many economists before the Committee generally concluded that increasing the after-tax return to saving should increase the saving rate of American households.

American technological leadership has been enhanced by the willingness of individuals to take the risk of pursuing new businesses exploiting new technologies. Risk taking is stifled if the taxation of any resulting gain is high and the ability to claim losses is limited. The Committee believes it is important to encourage risk taking and believes a reduction in the taxation of capital gains will have that effect.

Reduction in the taxation of capital gains also should improve the efficiency of the capital markets. The taxation of capital gains upon realization encourages investors who have accrued past gains to keep their monies "locked in" to such investments even when better investment opportunities present themselves. All economists that testified before the Committee agreed that reducing the rate of taxation of capital gains would encourage investors to unlock many of these gains. This unlocking will permit more monies to flow to new, highly valued uses in the economy. When monies flow freely, the efficiency of the capital market is improved.

The unlocking effect also has the short-term and long-term effect of increasing revenues to the Federal Government.   * * *   [C]urrent Congressional estimates project that revenue losses to the Federal Government will arise from the reduction in the tax rate on capital gains beginning in fiscal year 1997. The Committee observes, however, that the conservative approach embodied in such estimates does not attempt to account for the potential for increased growth in GDP that can result from increased saving and risk taking. Many macro economists have concluded that reductions in the taxation of capital gains will increase GDP and wage growth sufficiently that future tax revenues from the taxation of wages and business profits will offset the losses forecast from the sale of capital assets. * * *

The Committee rejects the narrow view that reductions in the taxation of capital gains benefit primarily higher-income Americans.   Traditional attempts to measure the benefit of a tax reduction for capital gains are deficient. Typically, the classification of individuals in such studies measure the individuals' incomes including any capital gains realized. Many Americans realize only one or two capital gains during their lifetime, for example upon the sale of family business upon retirement. Including the gain on such a one-time sale in the income of the individual makes the individual appear, for that one year, to be a higher-income taxpayer when, in other years, the taxpayer would appear to be solidly middle class. Another deficiency is that such studies classify taxpayers only by their current economic condition. Studies show that there is substantial economic mobility in the United States. An individual who might be counted as lower income now may in a decade be higher income.

* * *

Explanation of Provision

The bill allows individuals a deduction equal to 50 percent of net capital gain for the taxable year. * * * Thus, under the bill, the effective rate on the net capital gain of an individual in the highest (i.e., 39.6 percent) marginal rate bracket is 19.8 percent.

* * *

The bill reinstates the rule in effect prior to the 1986 Tax Reform Act that required two dollars of the long-term capital loss of an individual to offset one dollar of ordinary income. The $3,000 limitation on the deduction of capital losses against ordinary income continues to apply.

* * *

CAPITAL GAINS TAX POLICY
TOWARD ENTREPRENEURSHIP
James M. Poterba[*]

42 National Tax Journal 375, 375-85 (1989)

The need to subsidize risky new ventures is frequently cited as a reason for taxing capital gains at rates below other types of income. This paper investigates the efficacy of lowering individual capital gains tax rates as a device for subsidizing such ventures, particularly those which are funded through the organized venture capital process.

The paper makes two central points. First, more than three quarters of the funds that are invested in start-up firms are provided by investors *who are not subject to the individual capital gains tax*. Funds committed by untaxed investors, notably pension funds, have expanded more rapidly than funds from

---

    *. At time of original publication, Massachusetts Institute of Technology and National Bureau for Economic Research.

taxable investors in the years since the 1978 capital gains tax cut. A significant fraction of the funds supplied to venture firms is therefore unaffected by the individual capital gains tax.

Second, the overwhelming majority of taxable capital gains results from investments in activities *other* than start-up firms. Less than one third of reported gains are the result of appreciation of corporate equity, and only a small fraction of the gains on equity are related to venture capital investments. An across-the-board capital gains tax cut is therefore a relatively blunt device for encouraging venture investment. If policy makers wish to subsidize venture investments, some form of targeted capital gains reduction would be a more attractive option.

* * *

Capital Gains Taxation and the Supply of Venture Capital Funds

The source of funds for start-up enterprises is a central issue in assessing the importance of capital gains tax changes. Start-up firms receive capital from many sources. The corporate founder and other employees usually contribute capital, much of this in the form of equity that is ultimately subject to individual capital gains taxation. * * * In 1976, organized venture capitalists accounted for less than 15 percent of total funding. By comparison, equity from insiders and unaffiliated individuals amounted to 24.9 percent of the initial capital for technology-based firms. Approximately 54 percent of the funds for these small firms was supplied as equity. For non-technology firms, the equity share was 29.7 percent with insiders and other individuals supplying 20.7 percent of total capitalization.

The importance of organized venture capital has almost surely grown since the 1976 survey. Nevertheless, the common view that start-up enterprises rely exclusively on equity finance seems incorrect. Although small firms appear to use relatively more equity than their larger counterparts, many start-ups rely heavily on debt finance. One recent study commissioned by the Small Business Administration found that 57.8 percent of start-up businesses did not use *any* of the founders' saving. Debt, either from banks or from friends and relatives, accounted for more than 80 percent of capitalization in 24.8 percent of the start-ups.

The "bottleneck theory" of equity finance may apply to some classes of start-up firms, although the importance of this view remains to be demonstrated. This theory implies that without a certain amount of equity finance at a critical early stage, many firms would never be viable. If the suppliers of this equity capital, who may be the corporate founder or friends and relatives of the founder, are discouraged by high capital gains tax rates, then the amount of start-up activity could decline in response to higher capital gains tax rate even if most of the funds flowing to more mature start-up firms are unaffected[2]. There is some evidence, however, that the organized venture capital market can be used to avoid this bottleneck: 45 percent of commitments by organized venture capital firms in 1985 were to firms in the start-up or pre-start-up stages.

The rapid growth in organized venture capital funding during the last decade has been widely cited as demonstrating the sensitivity of the supply of venture funds to capital gains tax policy. The evidence traditionally used to bolster this view, namely the rapid growth in organized venture capital partnerships, is not particularly supportive of this view. Taxable individual investors have supplied relatively little of the capital these funds have invested.

Organized venture capital consists of three classes of institutions: independent venture capital funds, Small Business Investment Companies (SBICs), and corporate subsidiaries. Independent venture funds are the most important financing channel. They usually involve a general partner or partners who screen potential investments and assist the management teams the partnership has invested in, as well as limited partners who provide financial capital. At the end of 1988, the total capitalization of the venture industry was $31 billion, with almost $25 billion of the total supplied through independent venture partnerships. Commitments to such partnerships have increased fifteen-fold during the last decade, while funds channeled through SBICs and corporate subsidiaries have not even doubled.

Small Business Investment Companies are licensed and regulated by the Small Business Administration (SBA). They are essentially closed-end investment trusts which provide both capital and managerial assistance to start-up firms. The 1958 legislation authorizing SBICs allowed these entities to borrow three dollars at Treasury interest rates for each dollar of equity capital they raised. Because the investment income of SBICs is not taxable until it is distributed to shareholders, SBICs provide an attractive investment vehicle for banks or insurance companies wishing to defer taxable income. Individuals may invest through SBICs, but they have not been primary suppliers of capital through this channel.

Corporate subsidiaries enable large corporations to become involved in developments at start-up firms. They are designed to provide diversification or innovation for their corporate parents. Venture capital investments through corporate subsidiaries face corporate tax rates, so they should be much less sensitive to changes in the individual income tax treatment of capital gains than investments though independent venture partnerships.

---

2. None of the available data sets on startup firms are adequate for determining whether, and in what circumstances, the bottleneck theory is correct.

* * * Individual investors account for less than one quarter of the capital invested in the organized venture capital industry. Moreover, their share of the *new investment* flow has declined through time, from more than one third at the end of the 1970s to only 8 percent in 1988. Although individuals supplied less capital to independent venture funds after the 1986 capital gains tax increases took effect, it is difficult to attribute this decline to changes in their tax burdens. Individuals committed $392 million in new capital in 1986. This amount *increased* to $501 million in 1987 (after the new higher rates were in effect), and then declined by fifty percent—to $236 million—in 1988. This decline cannot be traced solely to capital gains tax burdens on capital suppliers, however, since commitments by pension funds also declined by 20 percent, those by foundations by 25 percent, and those by foreign investors declined by 33 percent between 1987 and 1988.

Corporations emerge as the single most important category of capital supplier. * * * Of the 37.2 percent of the venture capital pool supplied by firms at the end of 1988, 20.5 percent was due to insurance companies and 16.7 percent was from nonfinancial corporations.

After corporations, the second most important group of capital suppliers are tax-exempt investors such as pension funds and foundations. They accounted for 32.5 percent of the stock of funds in 1988, and were even more significant (59 percent) in the flow of new money in that year. The importance of untaxed investors in this market suggests that pretax returns have not been reduced by the favorable tax treatment of venture capital gains to individuals. If this subsidy were central in this market, then untaxed investors would be paying an implicit tax by investing in venture projects. These investors avoid other assets with substantial implicit taxes (such as tax-exempt debt) and their presence in this market suggests that the current tax subsidies are not overwhelming. Finally, 13 percent of the venture funding pool in 1988 was supplied by foreign investors. These investors are unaffected by the United States' capital gains tax.[3]

The finding that more than 80 percent of the funding for venture capital projects is from investors who are not affected by the personal income tax casts doubt on the view that changes in the capital gains tax rate affect the supply of funds to new ventures. * * *

There may be an important link between capital gains tax rates and the *demand* for venture capital funds operating through the occupational decisions of potential entrepreneurs. These individuals can work as middle or high-level managers for large firms, or they can start their own firms with a senior

---

3. Several nations that account for substantial inflows of equity investment to the U.S., notably Japan, the Netherlands, and West Germany, do not tax long-term capital gains on corporate equities.

management position. A given worker's compensation package is likely to involve a larger share of capital gains at a start-up firm than at a larger, more established firm. By altering the relative tax burdens on wage and capital gains income, reductions in the capital gains tax make entrepreneurship more attractive.

* * *

The Small World of Venture Capital

An across-the-board cut in capital gains tax cut is a relatively blunt instrument for encouraging venture activity. Most of the benefits of such a tax reduction would accrue to investors in assets besides venture capital firms. In 1981, for example, the most recent year for which the IRS published detailed tabulations, only one third of taxable capital gains reflects appreciation on common stock. Venture activity is only a small share of this equity component. Real property accounts for a larger share of net gains than does common stock in each of the survey years. This underscores an important point for capital-gains policy making: a systematic reduction in capital gains tax rates will benefit many investments besides equity-financed venture capital activity.

The pool of venture capital funds under management in 1988 totaled approximately $31 billion, or approximately one percent of the value of U.S. equity markets. * * *

On Targeting a Venture Capital Subsidy

The relatively small amount of realized venture gains suggests that if one were to design a policy to aid high-risk start-up firms, the policy should be targeted so as to avoid substantial revenue loss without substantial benefit to start-up firms.[4] A number of issues of practical tax design arise in crafting such a targeted policy.

Targeting by Enterprise Size

One option is to design tax policies to provide lower capital gains burdens on investments in small firms. It may be difficult, however, to distinguish between genuine new ventures and pre-existing ventures that have been spun-off into new enterprises. A lower tax rate on capital gains in start-up firms would distort organizational structure away from large firms and toward many small enterprises. Many of the same problems that arise in policing transfer pricing between multinational subsidiaries would arise in transfers between existing firms and start-ups in which they owned equity. There would be strong incentives for established firms to transfer patents or other valuable assets to startup firms that would qualify for more favorable tax treatment.

---

4. Any targeted policy will have adverse incentive effects in distorting the organization of economic activity. The efficiency costs of such distortions would need to be far larger than reasonable calculations would suggest in order to offset the revenue losses from an untargeted capital gain reduction.

The case for encouraging small firms at the expense of larger enterprises is not clear. Several indicators suggest that workers fare better at large than small firms. * * * [S]maller firms tend to pay lower wages. Workers at larger firms are less likely to be injured in the workplace, and they are more likely to be covered by a pension plan and health insurance. Offsetting these disadvantages for employees are the potentially greater flexibility of smaller firms and the higher research and development intensity of smaller firms. It is likely to be very difficult to compare these various aspects of industrial structure in deciding what constitutes optimal governmental policy.

Targeting by Enterprise Risk

A second possibility is to target high risk ventures. As the difficulty in designing regulations for debt versus equity securities suggests, it is difficult to objectively measure the riskiness of an investment. A risk-based targeting scheme might encourage many individuals providing services, such as doctors, lawyers, and tradesmen, to incorporate and find ways to bear risk in order to take advantage of favorable tax rates. Many of the implementation problems which would arise in this case have strong parallels in existing contexts such as the design of rules for personal holding companies.

Lower tax rates on capital gains may not be the most effective way of subsidizing high risk ventures. If it were possible to distinguish risky activities, some attention should also be devoted to current loss-offset provisions, since these might have substantial value to potential entrepreneurs. Phillips and Kirchoff (1989) report that 23.7 percent of start-up firms fail within two years, 51.7 percent within four years, and 62.7 percent in six years. The implementation problems associated with more generous subsidies for large losses may be smaller than the corresponding problems with lower tax rates on certain classes of gains, so these options may warrant exploration.

Conclusions

The policy debate concerning the links between capital gains tax rates and venture capital activity has been largely misplaced. It is simply not credible to argue that a substantial fraction of the growth in organized venture capital markets since the late 1970s is the result of lower capital gains tax rates on investors, since most of the funds have come from investors who do not face the personal capital gains tax. Across-the-board reductions in individual capital gains tax rates would have a small effect on the total tax burden on venture capital financiers, while conveying large benefits on many assets other than venture capital investments.

While the links between the supply of venture capital funds and the level of capital gains tax rates has been much discussed, two issues which are central for policy evaluation have received very limited attention. First, there is very limited evidence on the extent to which the supply of entrepreneurial activity responds to the relative tax burdens on capital gains and labor income. Interviews suggest that taxes may affect employment venue, which in turn could link capital gains tax rates with the *demand* for venture capital funds by potential entrepreneurs. Economists understand very little about the entrepreneurial process, and this makes it difficult to analyze the potential effects of tax changes.

A second neglected issue is the feasibility of designing a targeted tax subsidy for the high-risk start-up sector. Neither the practical tax issues nor the more theoretical questions of whether policy *should* subsidize small or risky firms have been resolved. Policy discussion has focused almost exclusively on the rate of capital gains taxation, while other instruments such as loss offset rules or change in estate and gift tax provisions on equity in start-up firms should also be explored.

Notes and Questions

39. Notwithstanding the capital loss limitations (discussed in Subchapter C), the Internal Revenue Code contains provisions designed to cushion taxpayers from the possible adverse consequences of risky investments. Section 1244 allows an individual shareholder in a small business corporation to deduct $50,000 of losses on the corporation's stock from ordinary income each year ($100,000 if the shareholder files a joint return). Also, election of Subchapter S treatment permits losses of corporations to be passed through to individual shareholders without the losses being transmuted into capital losses.

40. The CBO Report argues that indexing for inflation would be more supportive of risk-taking than would a partial exclusion of nominal capital gains. Ironically, the Report notes that such a change might lead investors toward less-risky yield assets, but only "because yield assets would be penalized less, not because risky assets would be penalized more." The issue of accounting for inflation in the tax system is considered more fully in Chapter Sixteen.

41. Any proposal to index basis for inflation raises the prospect not only of reduced gains for tax purposes, but of increased losses as well. The CBO Report notes that the capital loss limitation rules would become more important. Why would the combination of indexing and loss limitations tend to discourage risky investments?

42. Dr. Boskin states that the U.S. practice (in 1990) of taxing capital gains at the same rates applied to ordinary income was in marked contrast to "almost every one of our major competitors," which either do not tax capital gain or tax it more gently than ordinary income. Of what importance is foreign practice?

43. Speculation on the effect of capital gains taxes on the flow of capital for investment tends to ignore the role of retained earnings and of tax-exempt entities, such as pension and profit-sharing funds. Dr. Boskin concedes that established corporations rely largely on debt or retained earnings for new investment.

44. Are Dr. Boskin's conclusions as to the economic effect of lower capital gains taxes predicated on increased savings or increased investment?

45. Note Dr. Boskin's reference to the revenue effects of a capital gains preference. As we have seen in Subchapter B, this important question is extremely difficult to answer. Respectable economists can be found to support widely differing interpretations. (Economists working for Democrats who oppose broad-based preferential treatment for capital gains generally forecast long-term revenue losses, while economists working for Republicans who support such preferential treatment tend to forecast long-term revenue gains. This result accords with the favorable projection from the Republican administration's Office of Tax Analysis of the Treasury, and with the unfavorable projection from the Democratic Congress' Joint Committee on Taxation.)

It must be noted that the revenue argument has two components. The first is applicable to tax rates on any form of income. Lower taxes can always be expected to stimulate increased economic activity. While lower capital gains rates may stimulate more investment and more willingness to realize gains, it is also true that lower tax rates on ordinary income will make taxpayers willing to take second jobs, work longer hours, etc. So the question is whether there is something special about capital gains tax rates that is not present in taxation of ordinary income.

The key, as Professors Cunningham and Schenk argued in Subchapter B, is the realization rule. It is difficult to utilize labor without currently realizing income. Thus, taxpayers in the labor force are likely to continue working and generating taxable income, with any marginal impact from variations in tax rates being relatively minor. A decision not to utilize labor means the income is lost, not postponed.

Income from unrealized capital gains that is not realized, however, is not lost. The asset, with its value in excess of basis, can be kept, and the tax postponed. Under present law, if the asset is held until death, the tax is not merely postponed but permanently avoided. (See Chapter Ten.) The decision to realize and pay taxes is much more likely to be sensitive to tax rates than is the decision to work more. Lower capital gains tax rates, therefore, may stimulate greater increases in realization of capital gain than would lower rates on ordinary income stimulate additional labor. The extra realizations could generate sufficient additional revenue to pay for the capital gains tax cut. It is generally agreed that revenue would increase initially; as noted above, economists disagree concerning long-term revenue effects.

46. Critics of preferential treatment argue that any significant favorable revenue effect will be temporary, and that thereafter lower capital gains rates will translate into lower tax revenues. Why might this be the case?

47. Capital gains constitute a disproportional share of the income of higher-income taxpayers, prompting critics to assert that an exclusion or rate preference unfairly favors the rich. What is the basis for the Republican Ways and Means Committee's 1995 rejection of this "narrow view"? Is the committee report persuasive on this point?

48. Mr. Poterba's article is an attempt, using the limited data available, to measure the actual effect of capital gains taxes on the flow of funds from investors to new ventures. This is a refreshing contrast to generalized, and typically politicized, arguments over the effect of capital gains taxation.

49. Is an across-the-board capital gains tax cut a cost-effective way to encourage investment in new ventures?

50. The Poterba article points to evidence that workers are better off in large firms. Does this counter the frequently-asserted view that it is desirable for the income tax to be structured to favor small businesses?

51. First, assume that you are persuaded that fairness should lead us to tax capital gains income at the same rate as ordinary income. Second, assume that you are persuaded that the Government would get as much revenue, over the long term, if it lowered capital gains tax rates and kept rates on ordinary income the same (but not if it lowered rates on both types of income). Under this pair of assumptions, do you think that Congress should enact preferential

tax treatment of capital gains, or tax capital gains and ordinary income equally?

Personal residences

52. For millions of taxpayers, a residence is the biggest "investment" they will ever make. A personal residence is a capital asset, but its purchase is not deemed a transaction entered into for profit. Accordingly, losses are not deductible. Gains on principal residences are seldom taxed, because section 121 excludes up to $250,000 of gain ($500,000 of gain on a joint return), if certain conditions are met. Is this treatment justifiable?

Professor Gerard Brannon suggests that it may be:

> In a well-ordered tax system, the provision of housing services would be regarded as a business in which the taxpayer provides housing services to himself. The rental value of the home would be included in income and the costs of providing these services would be a deduction. Among the costs would be, of course, depreciation.
>
> * * *
>
> The complication in the sale of a home in the system that we have is that the taxpayer has not maintained a depreciation account. Assume a taxpayer buys a house for $50,000 and assume that we know for sure that the useful life of the house is exactly 50 years. If our taxpayer sells the house for $40,000 after he has lived in it for 40 years, then certainly he has had a substantial capital gain. He has not lost anything. He used up 4/5th of his investment living in the house. The cost less depreciation should be down to $10,000 and the sale should represent a $30,000 gain.
>
> * * *
>
> If we had depreciation accounts for homes, it would be logical to allow capital losses on sale when the house is sold for less than cost adjusted for depreciation.
>
> * * *
>
> Given the practical problem of no depreciation accounts, the tax law takes a very broad swipe at the problem. The tax law solution is to deliberately understate the gain (by not requiring a depreciation adjustment) and to deny any "loss" that may be indicated by this peculiar calculation. This solution may not be elegant but, by God, it's simple! (Remember that the next time somebody yaks at you about how complicated the tax law is.)[k]

---

k. Gerard M. Brannon, *Bringing Taxes Home: Capital Gains on Residences in* THE CAPITAL GAINS CONTROVERSY: A TAX ANALYSTS READER 413 (1974).

53. Is there a logical basis for distinguishing the loss on the sale of a taxpayer's home from the situation in which a taxpayer buys a suit of clothes for $400, uses it until it wears out, and then sells it for two dollars?

CHAPTER SIXTEEN

RESPONDING TO
PRICE LEVEL CHANGES

*It is conventionally accepted that modest inflation—2% to 3% per year—safely can be neglected in the tax system. * * * [T]he real rate of return to pure waiting (as opposed to risk taking) in U.S. financial markets over the past few decades has been about 0.5% per year. (This is the average real rate of return on U.S. Treasury bills.) If this is a reasonably close approximation to the pure intertemporal return, a very modest income tax rate applied to nominal interest of 2.5% to 3.5% renders the real, after-tax return negative. It is somewhat ironic that great effort is applied to assure that all transactions are treated equally badly.*[a]

A. INTRODUCTION

Since the Great Depression of the 1930s, overall changes in price levels have invariably been upward. Conceivably price levels might drop, but for practical purposes responding to price level changes means responding to price level increases. In common parlance and in most of the literature, this is called inflation.

Inflation affects an income tax in two ways. First, it changes the meaning in real terms of the amounts expressed in the law as specific dollar figures. Thus, personal exemptions and standard deductions expressed as specific dollar amounts become less valuable to the taxpayer as a result of inflation. Also, the upper and lower limits on tax brackets apply to smaller real income amounts than originally intended.

In many instances, Congress has implemented *structural indexation*, which addresses the effect of inflation on tax brackets, exemptions, and various other dollar amounts specified in the Code. Annual adjustments to the tax rate tables are provided to correct for changes in the cost of living, measured by the Consumer Price Index, so that inflation will not result in tax increases in real terms. Similarly, the dollar amounts of dependency exemptions, the standard deduction, and limits on contributions and benefits under qualified pension plans are adjusted for estimated changes in the cost of living. Structural indexation is not total; in many instances, dollar amounts specified in the Code are not indexed. (For example, the tax brackets for the

---

a. David F. Bradford, *Fixing Realization Accounting: Symmetry, Consistency and Correctness in the Taxation of Financial Instruments*, 50 TAX L. REV. 731, 737 (1995).

graduated corporate income tax are not indexed. Section 11.) There appears to be no pattern to explain why some amounts are indexed and others are not.

The second major effect of inflation on the income tax is to distort measurement of gains and losses and of income and deduction items. The typical example is the taxpayer who sells stock (or any other asset) for more than she paid for it, but finds that the dollar proceeds from the sale are worth no more (and possibly worth less) than the purchasing power of the dollars she paid for the stock originally. Another example, less frequently recognized, is a lender-taxpayer who lends money to a borrower-taxpayer. When the loan is repaid in a subsequent year in dollars that have less buying power than the dollars originally lent, the detriment to the lender is equaled by a benefit to the borrower.

Price level changes distort the measurement of interest income, interest deductions, debt repayment, capital gains and losses, and depreciation deductions. By and large, taxable income from service activities is calculated in current dollars and consequently is not affected by price level changes. *Tax basis indexation* has been proposed, and is discussed in this chapter, but has not been implemented.

Inflation also distorts income from sales of inventory for taxpayers who use the FIFO convention, because the gain is based on the acquisition price, without adjustment for subsequent inflation. A taxpayer can elect to use the LIFO convention, however, under which a taxpayer who maintains inventory levels is measuring income using current dollar costs. If inventory levels fall, however, so that the taxpayer is drawing down inventory bought in earlier years at lower price levels, part of the inventory profit will be due to inflation that occurred after the inventory was acquired.

Tax basis indexation is far more complex than structural indexation. Thus far, Congress has not attempted to deal explicitly with the distortion that price level changes cause in the measurement of gains, losses, income items, and deductions. Most of the discussion of the distorting effect of inflation on measurement of taxable income has focused on capital gains, as discussed in Subchapter B. Debt, the subject of Subchapter C, may prove a greater obstacle to implementing systematic adjustments to account for inflation.

The issue of tax basis indexation is closely tied to the realization rule, which is the central topic of Chapter Two, and which is closely tied to the issue of the proper taxation of capital gains considered in Chapter Fifteen. Were the realization rule generally replaced by a mark-to-market system, the problems caused by inflation would be much more manageable. Subchapter D discusses the interplay of indexation and the realization rule.

INFLATION AND THE INCOME TAX
Henry J. Aaron,[*] ed.

Pages 5-6 (1976)

All tax systems distort economic decisions. Indexing makes these distortions the same regardless of the rate of inflation. An inflation-free, or indexed, income tax system is one that imposes the same real tax burden on a particular amount of real before-tax income regardless of the rate of inflation. For given real before-tax income the real tax base and the rate structure must be unaffected by inflation. Whether indexing is desirable depends on whether in its absence inflation improves or worsens the particular set of distortions a tax system contains. Indexing the tax system cannot eradicate, although it may offset, consequences of inflation not related directly to the tax system, such as the reduction in the demand for money and the consequent effects on interest rates, savings, and investment.

Inflation affects income tax liabilities in two distinct ways. First, inflation distorts the tax base—the measures of current-dollar business and personal income from which personal exemptions and deductions are subtracted and to which personal and corporate income tax rates are applied in order to compute tax liabilities. Second, inflation changes the rate structure, loosely defined to include the real value of all nominal quantities in the Internal Revenue Code, most notably personal exemptions and dollar-limited credits, the standard deduction, * * * the refundable credit on earnings, and the size of the income brackets to which the personal income tax applies. * * *

In general the distorting effects of inflation on the tax base are important because they cause a taxpayer to pay a different amount of tax than he would pay on the same real income in a noninflationary world. Moreover, this distortion will vary among taxpayers. In contrast, the distorting effects of inflation on the rate structure are important principally because they change the relative tax liabilities of taxpayers who would be in different brackets in a noninflationary world.

Tax Base

Economists generally define income as the sum of consumption plus additions to real net worth (for individuals) or as the excess of receipts over costs, where costs include the replacement of capital consumed (for businesses). Some individuals receive both business income—in the form of dividends, profits, rents, interest, or capital gains—and earnings, in the form of salaries and wages.

Inflation negligibly distorts the measurement of earned income but creates serious problems in the measurement of business income. Business income is the residual after subtracting from receipts a variety of expenses. Since receipts and associated expenses may occur at widely separated times,

---

*. At time of original publication, Director, Economic Studies Program, The Brookings Institution.

the purchasing power of the dollars in which they are measured may differ widely. When inflation is occurring, earnings received at the beginning and end of the year also are denominated in dollars of different purchasing power and are not strictly comparable; but in most cases these effects are relatively small. Earnings paid evenly throughout the year are denominated *on the average* in midyear dollars. Unless some earners are paid mostly at the beginning of the year or mostly at the end, *relative* earnings will not be affected by inflation.

In principle, the definition of income just enunciated requires that all changes in real net worth be taxed as accrued. In fact, the Internal Revenue Code generally requires realization of gains or losses on capital assets before they become subject to tax, but permits (and generally requires) businesses to accrue receipts and expenses in measuring business net income. Whether this distinction should be preserved if adjustments are made for inflation (or if they are not) raises difficult questions, because inflation simultaneously affects current expenses and receipts and the value of capital assets.

Inflation-sensitive elements of income include (1) capital gains and losses and interest payments and (2) business deductions for depreciation and the cost of materials used.

　＊ ＊ ＊

Notes and Questions

1.   Aaron identifies two types of distortions introduced into the tax system by inflation. What are these? Which can be more easily addressed in the Code?

2.   The "great leap forward" toward structural indexation came in the Economic Recovery Tax Act of 1981, though the concept has been considerably broadened since then. What do you think accounts for the opposition expressed in Congress to the system of automatic adjustments to tax brackets, exemption amounts, etc. to correct for inflation?

3.   Structural indexation under the Internal Revenue Code is generally tied to section 1(f), which provides only for upward adjustments. Should price levels drop, there is no provision for downward adjustments.

4.   It is generally thought by economists that the Consumer Price Index, which is the most common benchmark for indexing for inflation, overstates the effect of inflation. Revision of the means of computing the CPI, or abandoning the CPI for some other inflation measuring stick, might result in smaller adjustments for tax purposes and with respect to important nontax matters such as cost-of-living adjustments (COLAs) in payments to retirees and others.

5.   An additional complicating factor is that the impact of inflation varies according to consumption patterns, and thus varies greatly by age, income level, geographic location, and individual tastes in consumption. The process of revision of the CPI would be likely to cause sharp divisions among affected interest groups.

6.   How does application of structural indexation affect the countercyclical influence of the individual income tax?

7.   Wages, like the value of capital assets, rise with inflation. Why, then, does Aaron say that inflation only negligibly distorts the measurement of earned income?

8.   It is unclear that indexing need lead to a reappraisal of the present requirement that capital gains and losses be realized before they are taken into account in computing taxable income, as Aaron implies. On the other hand, if gains had to be taken into account before realization, as adherence to the Haig-Simons standard would require, it seems likely that pressure to correct the definition of gain for inflation would be intensified. Why?

B. INFLATION AND CAPITAL GAIN

TAXATION OF CAPITAL GAINS—LET'S BE FAIR
Calvin Engler* & Mitchell L. Engler**
50 Tax Notes 1303, 1303-04 (1991)

[I]t is appropriate to examine the need for capital gains tax relief. The relief thus far granted fails to consider the effects of inflation during the period of time property is held. Inflation will have a markedly different effect on property held for a short period of time, say a year or two, compared to property held for a long period of time—20 or more years. In contrast, the * * * rate reduction applies equally to property held for a short period or long period of time.

A cure for this inequity in taxation would be to index capital gains. * * * Indexing of personal exemptions and the standard deduction are already a part of income tax law, and the need for indexing capital gains is illustrated by the following example.

Example 1: Assume a taxpayer purchases shares of capital stock for $100,000 and sells the shares a year later for $110,000. The inflation rate during this holding period—the time between the purchase and sale of the property—was 10 percent. Under present tax law the taxpayer would be taxed on a capital gain of $10,000. The imposition of a tax on these facts is unjust

     *. At time of original publication, Professor of Accounting, Iona College.
     **. At time of original publication, recent recipient of LL.M. in Taxation, New York University Law School.

to the taxpayer because the taxpayer merely maintained his/her purchasing power and did not have a real economic gain of $10,000; rather, the differential was all due to inflation. Indexing capital gains would correct this inequity by limiting the tax on capital gains to the true economic gain. This would be accomplished by adjusting the taxpayer's basis (i.e., cost of the asset) for the amount of inflation during the holding period. On the facts of Example 1, the taxpayer's original basis of $100,000 would be multiplied by 110 percent giving the taxpayer an adjusted basis of $110,000. Therefore, the taxpayer would not be subject to any tax since the sales proceeds would be equal to the taxpayer's adjusted basis.

However, this indexing of capital gains would create a windfall to the taxpayer if any part of the $100,000 purchase price was financed through borrowed funds. This can be illustrated by the following example.

Example 2: Assume the same facts as in Example 1 except that the taxpayer borrowed the full $100,000 purchase price at an interest rate of 10 percent. When the taxpayer sells the stock for $110,000, he/she uses the full $110,000 to pay off the lender ($100,000 toward principal and $10,000 toward interest). Indexing only the gain side of the transaction would allow the taxpayer a net deduction of $10,000. Once again the taxpayer would have no taxable gain on the sales proceeds because the adjusted basis would be $110,000, but the taxpayer would be allowed an interest deduction of $10,000 (assuming for the moment that it is qualifying interest). Therefore, the taxpayer would have a net deduction of $10,000 from a transaction that was an economic wash. Bear in mind that the taxpayer did not use any personal funds to achieve the $10,000 tax deduction. * * * Indexing only the gain side of the transaction irrespective of the source of the funds used to purchase property would merely substitute one inequity for another inequity.

Since many taxpayers purchase stock securities on margin and almost all purchases of real estate are financed in part through the use of mortgages, the failure of existing proposals to consider the interaction of borrowed funds with purchases raises substantial concerns of equity in taxation. * * * Henry Aaron, of the Brookings Institution, * * * suggests that all loan transactions should be adjusted for inflation to prevent a taxpayer from earning a tax arbitrage by using borrowed funds to acquire property.

An alternate solution would be to allow a taxpayer the benefits of indexing capital gains only to the extent that the taxpayer's basis is attributable to nonborrowed funds. This proposal would accomplish the goal of providing indexation where needed and would avoid the complexity of adjusting all loan transactions for inflation.

At the simplest level our proposal would work as follows:

Example 3: Assume the same facts as in Example 2 except that only the portion of basis attributable to nonborrowed funds is indexed for inflation. Since the purchase price was financed entirely by borrowed funds, none of the basis is indexed and remains at $100,000. Therefore, when the taxpayer sells the securities for $110,000 he/she will have a taxable gain of $10,000 and a tax deduction of $10,000 for interest. Thus, the taxpayer will not have a tax benefit from a transaction that is an economic wash. Of course, this proposal, if enacted, would require that the * * * rate differential [between capital gains and ordinary income] be eliminated.

Our proposals also would achieve the same equitable result in more realistic scenarios. For example:

Example 4: A taxpayer purchases a building on January 1, 1990 for $500,000 using a down payment of $100,000 and assumes a mortgage of $400,000. Principal payments for 1990 and 1991 amount to $20,000 and are payable at the end of each year. The inflation index at January 1, 1990 is 100; at January 1, 1991 it is 110; and at January 1, 1992 it is 121. The taxpayer sells the property for $700,000 on January 1, 1992. If the basis of the property is indexed, the taxable gain would be:

Selling price	$700,000
Basis ($ 500,000 x 121%)	$605,000
Taxable gain	$95,000

As described earlier, this would create an inequity for fairness in taxation. The way to avoid this inequity is to index only nonborrowed funds. This would be accomplished as follows:

Example 5:

Average Invested Funds			Indexed Amount
$100,000	x	21%	$21,000
20,000	x	10%	2,000
20,000	x	0%	0
			$23,000

Under this approach, the taxpayer's basis would be $523,000 ($500,000 + $23,000) leaving a taxable gain of $177,000 ($700,000 – $523,000). Thus, a taxpayer would be prevented from reaping an arbitrage windfall from leveraging (borrowing) against purchased property.

Some observers undoubtedly will argue that it is difficult to separate borrowed basis from nonborrowed basis. In the case of stock securities purchased on margin or real estate purchased with a mortgage, however, this separation can be accomplished easily. Since most real estate transactions and many purchases of stock fall within these categories, the source of the purchase price will be obvious. For those transactions where tracing the borrowed funds would be necessary, existing regulations of the Internal Revenue Code already provide a method for allocating borrowed funds to various expenditures.

In sum, while the indexation of only nonborrowed basis would not eliminate all inequities in the Internal Revenue Code arising from inflation, our proposal would be a relatively simple procedure to alleviate inequities in connection with the taxation of capital gains.

REPORT ON INFLATION ADJUSTMENTS TO THE BASIS OF CAPITAL ASSETS
New York State Bar Association Section on Taxation
Ad Hoc Committee
48 Tax Notes 759, 759-60, 773-75 (1990)

Introduction

In the ongoing debate regarding the implementation of some form of preferential taxation of capital gain income, many legislative alternatives will be considered. One such alternative is adjusting or "indexing" the basis of certain capital assets to reflect general price level inflation, thereby attempting to tax only "real" as opposed to inflationary gains. This Report discusses the issues, problems, and other considerations raised by the indexing of the basis of capital assets.

* * *

The Weak Theoretical Basis for Indexing

All the complexity and exposure to significant erosion of the revenue base would be problematic even under a perfect indexation system, because the primary theoretical bases supporting indexation of the tax system are themselves problematic.

Inexact Nature of Adjustments

The main premise underlying any indexing proposal, i.e., that indexing the basis of an asset will result in the taxation of only real appreciation, is highly questionable. The four factors discussed below contribute to this conclusion. Given the reality that any inflation adjustment would be imprecise at best, we believe * * * that any form of indexation would be extremely bad tax policy.

First, the use of any particular inflation index will offer inexact relief to the owner of any particular asset. For example, if the consumer price index is used, exact relief will be given only to an owner who plans to use the income from the asset for consumption, as opposed to business or investment purposes, and then only if the composition of the owner's planned or actual consumption matches that of the basket of goods whose price level is measured in composing the index. Although it may be said that consumption is the ultimate goal or at least use for all income, it nevertheless is true that for certain periods, investment goals may predominate. This has caused some to question whether use of an index other than the consumer price index would be appropriate.

Second, the price of an asset and the returns available from that asset already may be adjusted to account for inflation. For example, if a lessor charges higher rents to compensate for the overtaxation attributable to inflation, basis adjustments would provide the lessor with redundant relief. For this reason, it is unclear whether it would be preferable to index basis for actual or expected inflation.

Third, deferring basis indexation adjustments until disposition creates arbitrary results where income-producing property generates periodic returns in excess of the "real" rate of return. For example, if the current income generated by property were sufficiently high, there would be relatively little real or nominal appreciation in that property. All the currently received income would be treated as ordinary income to the recipient, notwithstanding the fact that in an inflationary environment, a portion of that income in economic terms would represent a return of principal. Thus, indexing basis would be of limited usefulness to the holder of this type of property for whom property appreciation attributable to inflation would be recognized as ordinary income over the period the property is held, accompanied by a capital loss (if losses are allowed) or diminution of capital gain on disposition.[58] Ironically, the benefit of basis indexation is greater for property that does not generate current income and that as a result already enjoys the benefit of tax deferral.

Finally, even assuming that the proper measure of inflation in an asset can be determined with reasonable precision, it can be demonstrated that in most cases actual basis adjustments will match inflationary increases only by happenstance. This unfortunate result occurs because in the absence of gain realization, annual adjustments are made to the basis of the asset without regard to its fair market value. Nevertheless, inflation in any period by its nature will increase the nominal price of an asset relative to its value at the beginning of the measurement period.

For example, assume that *Ms. A* purchased an asset for $1,000. After one year the asset is still worth $1,000. After two years, *Ms. A* sells the asset for $1,300. Inflation in each year is 10 percent. Under an indexation system, *Ms. A* would have a basis in the asset at the time of sale of $1,210 (i.e., $1,000 plus $100 for the first year and $110 for the second year). Although *Ms. A*'s inflation adjustment of $100 for the first year is appropriate, her inflation adjustment for the second year should be limited to $100. Price level increases in the second year only inflated the actual value of her asset, not the asset's adjusted basis. *Ms. A*'s taxable gain is $10 less than her "real" gain. By comparison, *Mr. B* purchases an asset for $1,000. The asset is worth $1,200

---

58. This result is most easily understood in the context of an investment in nonparticipating preferred stock. For example, individual Investor A pays $1,000 for $1,000 face amount of XYZ Corp. preferred stock, which has a 10 percent annual dividend. Inflation of five percent is anticipated in determining the dividend rate and inflation actually occurs at that rate. A's stock is redeemed after 10 years for $1,000. At that time, A's indexed basis in the stock is $1,629, resulting in a capital (and economic) loss of $629. This loss occurs because each unindexed dividend payment represents economically a return of capital in part. Cf. section 1059(f). The same phenomenon occurs with respect to depreciable property if basis is indexed only on disposition and depreciation deductions are not indexed.

after one year and is sold for $1,300 after two years. At the time of sale, *Mr. B*'s basis also would be $1,210, but his inflation adjustment for the second year should have been $120 rather than $110, resulting in tax of $10 of gain in excess of real gain.

Accordingly, the basis adjustment for an asset will exactly equal the measure of its price inflation (assuming that the exact amount of price inflation can be measured in any event) only where the asset appreciates at exactly the rate of inflation. Basis adjustments will be inadequate to adjust for inflation where an asset appreciates faster than the rate of inflation, and basis adjustments will be excessive where an asset appreciates at a rate slower than inflation.

* * *

Neutral Taxation of Capital Income

Another often-stated premise underlying indexation proposals is that indexation is needed to achieve neutral taxation of income from capital as compared to other sources, i.e., to prevent capital income from being taxed more heavily than other income by reason of including inflationary as well as real gains in the tax base. This premise too is false. It is well understood that the current system taxes income from capital more favorably than income from other sources because gain from the appreciation of capital is not taxed unless realized and avoids tax altogether if the asset is held at death. Other advantages include accelerated depreciation, the availability of interest deductions on related indebtedness, and LIFO inventories. Thus, unless these other benefits are eliminated, indexing of basis will allow income from capital to enjoy an even more favored tax status relative to income from other sources than it now enjoys.

Conclusion

It is our position that the implementation of any indexation system as a part of a modification of the present tax system would be highly inadvisable.

* * *

Notes and Questions

9.   The Engler and Engler article illustrates the complexity of indexing gains and losses without taking into account the distorting effects of inflation on the use of borrowed money to finance the purchase of assets. Does inflation not distort *any* debtor-creditor relationship? If a taxpayer borrows $1,000 in 1995 for 10 years and repays the loan in 2005 with $1,000 that have purchasing power equal to only 60 percent of 1995 dollars, has not the borrower enjoyed a gain, and the lender suffered a loss, of $400 in real terms?

10.   Engler and Engler argue that indexing capital gains would result in a windfall for the taxpayer who acquired an asset with borrowed funds. Consider whether the effect of inflation on taxes could better be broken down into two problems: what to do about debt repaid with cheap dollars and what

to do about assets whose real value is eroded by inflation. For example, suppose *A* borrows $5,000 to finance a trip to Europe (using a home equity loan secured by his personal residence) and repays the loan in later years with cheap dollars. Also suppose *B* borrows $5,000 that he invests in common stocks and repays his loan in later years with cheap dollars. Both *A* and *B* have benefitted from repaying their debts with cheap dollars. If *A* does not have income from the transaction, would it be fair, as Engler and Engler propose, to deny *B* an inflation adjustment to his stock market gain?

11. Engler and Engler state that their proposed inflation adjustment for gain derived from nonborrowed funds would "of course" require the elimination of any capital gain rate differential. Does this conclusion follow as a matter of course?

12. Are Engler and Engler correct in concluding that their proposal would be a relatively simple procedure?

13. Apart from the substance of the argument, the New York State Bar Committee report is interesting because, rather than attempting a balanced discussion, the committee appears to have produced a thinly veiled brief against indexation.

14. The critique by the New York State Bar Committee points up the fallibility of all inflation indices. Neither the Consumer Price Index nor any other index reflects precisely the change in purchasing power of a dollar over time to any particular person. In addition to subjective differences, problems lurk in the composition of each price index. One common failure arises from the difficulty in adjusting price indices to account for quality changes and the introduction of new products.

The committee's approach appears to be that imprecision in measuring inflation means that it should be ignored. Do you agree? (Professor Daniel Halperin does not agree: "The New York State Bar supported its argument by the claim that the inflation adjustment would inevitably be inexact. However, of the *four* reasons given for this conclusion, *three* are wrong and the fourth * * * can be mitigated, or even eliminated if there is a move to mark-to-market."[b])

15. Is the New York State Bar Committee Report correct in characterizing accelerated depreciation, interest deductions on related indebtedness, and LIFO inventory treatment as tax advantages for income from capital compared with income from other sources?

---

b. Daniel Halperin, *Saving the Income Tax: An Agenda for Research*, 24 OHIO N.U. L. REV. 493, 509 (1998).

16. Assuming the New York State Bar Committee is correct in its assertion that income from capital is generally more favorably taxed than income from other sources (principally, labor), does it follow that taxing nominal gains attributable to inflation is an appropriate response?

17. The New York State Bar Committee Report asserts that, for purposes of determining gain or loss upon disposition of an asset, an inflation adjustment should be made on an asset-by-asset basis, to take account of that particular asset's inflation experience. Read again with care the example involving *Ms. A* and *Mr. B*.

The Committee's description of indexing appears to be flawed, and thereby to exaggerate the difficulties in indexing the basis of capital assets. The Committee appears to have forgotten the purpose of indexing for inflation, which, at least for capital assets sold at gain or loss, is to measure the gain or loss in a manner that accounts for inflation. Inflation adjustments during the period of ownership are irrelevant. Thus, *A* and *B* each started into their transactions with 1,000 *dollars* and finished up with 1,300 *dollars*. The question is, how much are the dollars received at time of sale worth in comparison to the dollars expended at time of purchase. The answer must be the same for *A* and *B*. What the assets were worth at any time during the holding period sheds no light on the problem.

18. The closest the United States has come to tax basis indexation was in the proposed Contract with America Tax Relief Act of 1995, which passed the House of Representatives but never became law. That bill contained a provision for indexing the basis of assets for purposes of computing gain (but not loss). The adjustment was based on quarterly changes in the Gross Domestic Product (GDP) deflator. The bill applied only to assets acquired after 1994. The indexed assets were common stock of C corporations and tangible property, including both capital assets and property used in trade or business. Benefits flowed through to the owners of S corporations, partnerships, and common trust funds. To be eligible, assets must have been held for at least three years.

No adjustments were provided for the basis of debt obligations, and there were no offsets against indexing benefits when the taxpayer's eligible assets were debt financed. Indexing benefits were not made available to C corporations, perhaps because gain on sale of their common stock was eligible for indexing. This explanation is not entirely satisfactory, however, because C corporations are taxpayers in their own right.

19. Recall, from discussion in Chapter Seven of Professor Andrews' proposed consumption-style income tax, that one asserted advantage of that form of tax was that it appropriately and automatically handled the problem of nominal gains attributable to inflation. See, in particular, Note #23 (page 414).

C. INFLATION AND DEBT

Most discussion of the tax effect of inflation has centered on overstatement of profit upon sale of assets. In addition, there is concern over the failure of depreciation reserves to cover the cost of replacement assets. Relatively little attention has been given to the failure of the income tax to reflect gain or loss on repayment of indebtedness. This omission by political figures is understandable, and only in part because accounting for inflation is more complex in debt transactions. The more serious political problem is that unlike the cases of capital gain or depreciation, a proper accounting for inflation in debt transactions would generate tax losers (debtors) as well as winners (creditors).

The two excerpts of this subchapter address this important, complex, and neglected aspect of the inflation problem. The 1984 Treasury I proposal, in addition to indexing gains on sale of assets, treated the impact of inflation on debt as a separate issue. Treasury I, instead of treating borrowers as having income as a result of inflation, reduced deductible interest payments by a price inflation adjustment and excluded corresponding amounts from the interest income of creditors. Professor Durst's article is largely a commentary on, and evaluation of, the Treasury I proposal.

TAX REFORM FOR FAIRNESS, SIMPLICITY, AND ECONOMIC GROWTH ["TREASURY I"]
United States Department of the Treasury
Vol. 2, pp. 190-97 (1984)

Reasons for Change

Over time inflation erodes the value of a creditor's claim for repayment of an indebtedness with a fixed principal amount, and the debtor's liability to repay principal is correspondingly reduced. Debtors and creditors routinely take account of the anticipated effects of inflation on a lending transaction by adjusting the rate of interest charged. Thus, nominal interest rates typically include an inflation component which compensates the lender for the anticipated reduction in the real value of an obligation of a fixed dollar amount; as to the borrower, this payment is an offsetting charge for the inflationary reduction in the value of the principal amount of the borrowing.

Because the inflation component of nominal interest payments is, in effect, a repayment of principal, the current treatment of nominal interest payments as fully deductible by the debtor and fully taxable to the creditor mismeasures the income of each. These inaccuracies in the measurement of income distort a variety of investment decisions, greatly increasing the significance of tax considerations in such matters as the allocation of investment funds between debt and equity and between long-term and short-term financing. Moreover, in a progressive tax system, overstatement of interest expense and income accentuates the existing incentive for lower tax-bracket taxpayers (including tax-exempt institutions) to be net creditors and higher tax-bracket taxpayers to be net borrowers. This so-called "clientele effect" occurs because the tax savings from interest deductions is greater for high-bracket borrowers than is the increased tax liability from interest income to low-bracket lenders. This clientele effect is aggravated during times of high inflation and corresponding high nominal interest rates.

The failure of the current tax system to recognize and measure the inflation component of nominal interest payments also accentuates the economic effects of variable inflation on debtors and creditors. If the rate of inflation increases unexpectedly, a creditor with fixed-interest indebtedness suffers an economic loss, and the debtor has a corresponding economic gain. These changes in economic position are compounded by the treatment of interest under current law, since the entire amount of nominal interest payments remains deductible or includible in income regardless of changes in the inflation rate. The resulting mismeasurement of income in an economy with variable inflation spawns economic uncertainty. Such uncertainty likely contributes to reduced levels of savings, investment and risk-taking.

Finally, the overstatement of interest under current law encourages borrowing for investments in which income is tax exempt or tax deferred. For example, the investment of borrowed funds in capital assets produces a current deduction for interest expense but no realization of the increase in value of the capital asset until its sale or disposition. This mismatching of income and expense from related transactions understates current income and thus permits the deferral of tax. Overstatement of interest expense thus increases the extent to which debt-financed tax shelter investments can be used to offset taxable income from other sources.

Proposal

Interest would be indexed for tax purposes by excluding a fractional amount of interest receipts from income and denying a deduction for a corresponding fraction of interest payments. For example, with a fractional exclusion rate of 25 percent, taxpayers would include in income only 75 percent of otherwise taxable interest receipts and deduct only 75 percent of otherwise deductible interest payments. The fractional exclusion rate would be based on the annual inflation rate, as explained below.

In general, the proposal would apply the fractional exclusion rate to a taxpayer's net interest income or net interest expense, subject to the following exceptions. First, an individual would deduct any mortgage interest on indebtedness secured by or allocable to his or her principal residence. Qualifying mortgage indebtedness for this purpose could not exceed the fair market value of the principal residence. Next, an individual would net aggregate gross interest expenses (excluding home mortgage interest) against aggregate gross interest income (excluding tax-exempt interest). An individual with net interest expense would apply the fractional exclusion rate to the amount of interest expense. * * * An individual with net interest income would apply the fractional exclusion rate to such net interest income. Interest income, after reduction by the fractional rate would be includible in income.

All of a corporation's interest income and expense would be subject to the fractional exclusions. Interest incurred by a partnership or other pass-through entity would be treated as incurred by the partner or other person to whom the payments are allocable.

Interest received by a partnership or other pass-through entity would be treated as received by the partner or other person reporting such payments.

Tax-favored retirement plans, such as an individual retirement account or qualified pension plan, which earn interest income would not be able to pass on the benefit of the fractional exclusion to the plan beneficiaries. Thus, the fractional exclusion rate could not be claimed with respect to distributions from tax-favored retirement plans. * * *

The fractional exclusion rate would be modified annually to reflect changes in the rate of inflation, as measured by the Bureau of Labor Statistics' Consumer Price Index. The proposed relationship between fractional exclusion rates and inflation rates is set forth in Table 1. The proposed relationship set forth in Table 1 is based on an assumption of a constant six percent real, before-tax interest rate. Assumption of lower real interest rates would result in higher exclusion rates for any given inflation rate. The fractional exclusion rate for a taxpayer that uses a functional currency other than the U.S. dollar should be based on the inflation rate in the foreign currency.

The proposal would not alter the current law definition of interest. The current law rules which impute interest income in certain transactions would also be retained.

    * * *

Analysis
Indexing Interest Rather than Principal

An ideal measure of real economic income for tax purposes would recognize the inflationary reduction in principal on a loan as creating loss for the creditor and income for the debtor on an annual basis. That ideal system departs from the realization doctrine of current law, however, under which mere changes in the value of an asset, including a debt instrument, do not trigger income or loss. Abandonment of the realization doctrine in this context would introduce substantial costs in complexity and recordkeeping.

Inflation's impact on indebtedness may be indirectly accounted for, however, without departing from the realization doctrine. Instead of computing inflationary gain or loss on principal, the effects of inflation can be approximated by indexing interest payments and receipts through application of the proposed fractional exclusion rate.

Table 1
Fractional Exclusion Rule Rate

InflationRate (Percent)	Fractional Exclusion Rates (Percent)[1]
0	0
1	14
2	25
3	33
4	40
5	45
6	50
7	54
8	57
9	60
10	62
11	65
12	67

For example, A borrows $100 from B on January 1, agreeing to pay back the principal plus ten percent interest on December 31. Over the course of the year, there is four percent inflation and the real, pre-tax rate of return is six percent. On December 31, A satisfies its indebtedness by repaying the $100 principal and $10 in interest. B's receipt of the $100 in principal actually represents a loss of $4 in real purchasing power. B's receipt of $10 in nominal interest, however, actually represents a $6 real return on the loan, plus a $4 inflationary component which offsets the reduction in the value of the $100 principal. Thus, in this example, a fractional exclusion rate of 40 percent would be appropriate.

---

1. Fractional exclusion rate is determined by assuming a constant, six percent real interest rate (rate of return).

The example demonstrates that, in theory, the effects of inflation on indebtedness may be reflected for tax purposes either by indexing principal or indexing interest. Indexing interest retains the realization rules of current law, and is a much more administrable system.

Determining the Fractional Exclusion Rate

In a world with but one nominal interest rate, real interest income and expense would be accurately measured by a fractional exclusion rate equal to the ratio of the inflation rate to the nominal interest rate. With such an exclusion rate, the excluded interest payments and receipts would correspond to the inflationary component of nominal interest.

The proposal's single fractional exclusion rate for each inflation rate obviously oversimplifies the relationships between inflation and nominal interest rates in a diverse economy. The real rate of return earned on indebtedness will differ from lender to lender. The proposal's economy-wide fractional exclusion rate, however, allows a more accurate measurement of real economic income than does current law, which implicitly provides a zero fractional exclusion rate for all interest.

Effects on Nominal Interest Rates

The proposal would likely result in lower nominal interest rates than would prevail under current law for any given set of economic conditions. For any expected inflation rate, lenders would not demand as high an inflation premium since the inflation component of nominal interest receipts would not be taxed. Similarly, borrowers would be less willing to pay a high inflation premium, since the inflation component of nominal interest payments would not be tax deductible. Accordingly, nominal interest rates would likely fall, relative to levels that would prevail under current law for any given economic conditions. * * *

The proposal also likely would result in reduced volatility of interest rates with respect to changes in inflation. Under the proposal, a change in inflation should induce a smaller change in nominal rates than would occur under current law.

Effects of the Exceptions
to Fractional Exclusion Rate

The proposal would not apply the fractional exclusion rate to all deductible interest payments, resulting in some asymmetric treatment of borrowers and lenders. Homeowners would be permitted full deduction of mortgage interest on a principal residence, while mortgagees would be entitled to apply the fractional exclusion rate to interest received on home mortgages. All individuals would be allowed full deduction (without indexing) of the first $5,000 of other net interest expense. Although these exceptions depart from theoretical symmetry for all interest payments and receipts, their retention facilitates the transition from an unindexed to an indexed tax system. The exception for home mortgages, however, would create an incentive for taxpayers both to mortgage the existing equity in their homes, and to disguise consumer, investment or business indebtedness as increases in home mortgages. These opportunities for tax arbitrage present serious revenue concerns, and it may be necessary to develop strict rules to prevent such schemes from circumventing the intent of the exception.

* * *

INFLATION AND THE TAX CODE: GUIDELINES FOR POLICYMAKING
Michael C. Durst[*]

73 Minnesota Law Review 1217, 1251-56 (1989)

The Basic Effects of Inflation on the Tax Burdens of Lenders and Borrowers[117]

Consider first the very simple situation of a person, whether or not an asset holder, who borrows $100 for a period of one year. In the absence of anticipated inflation, the lender will charge the borrower annual interest equivalent to the lender's "time value of money"—the price the lender will demand for forgoing alternative uses of the borrowed funds during the year. For example, in the absence of anticipated inflation, the annual interest rate charged to a reasonably creditworthy borrower might amount to five percent.

Adding inflation to the equation complicates the picture. The lender will demand, in addition to compensation for the time value of money, compensation for the erosion that inflation will cause in the value of the borrower's repayment obligation during the course of the year. If inflation occurs during the year at an annual rate of ten percent, the real value of the borrower's repayment obligation would shrink at the rate of ten percent during the year, a result that would enrich the borrower at the expense of the lender. To compensate for this enrichment and to make the lender "whole," the parties must find some way of effectively increasing the amount of the repayment obligation during the year.

To accomplish this adjustment in practice, lenders commonly require that interest payments include compensation for the time value of money (as well as for any risk of default), and an additional amount designed to compensate for the erosion of the value of the loan principal anticipated from inflation. Thus, in the above example, if the parties expected inflation to occur at a rate of ten percent per year, the borrower would be responsible for interest not of five but of fifteen percent: five percent to compensate the lender for the time value of money, plus ten percent to compensate the lender for the erosion in the value of the borrower's repayment obligation. Interest thus commonly includes two components: a "real" component designed to compensate the lender for the time value of money and for bearing any risk of nonpayment,

---

[*]. At time of original publication, Associate Professor, Notre Dame Law School.

117. The discussion in this subsection follows, in substance, the analysis in 1 U.S. TREASURY DEP'T, TAX REFORM FOR FAIRNESS, SIMPLICITY, AND ECONOMIC GROWTH (1984), at 77, and 2 *id.* at 193-200.

and an "inflation" component designed to offset the effects of inflation on the value of the principal.

To measure net income properly under an accretion-model tax system, Congress should permit a borrower who uses loan proceeds for income-producing purposes to deduct the true economic cost of maintaining the loan. In periods of inflation, the borrower's economic cost of maintaining the loan is the *difference* between the borrower's total interest expense (including both the time value of money and inflation components of interest, as well as any risk premium charged by the lender) and the economic benefit the borrower receives from the erosion of the real value of the repayment obligation. Thus, under a pure accretion system, if Congress permitted the borrower of a loan for income-producing purposes to deduct in full all interest paid on the loan, Congress also should require the borrower to include in gross income the amount by which inflation lowers the real value of the borrower's repayment obligation.

The proper tax treatment of the lender, under an accretion-model system, mirrors that of the borrower. Congress should require the lender to include in gross income all interest payments received from the borrower. In addition, as the borrower receives an economic benefit from inflation's erosion of the real value of the repayment obligation, the lender suffers an economic detriment. Congress should permit the lender to deduct the amount of this detriment.

In actual operation, the tax laws depart radically from the accretion model in their treatment of debt. Although the tax code does not include in gross income the economic benefit the borrower enjoys from the erosion in the value of the repayment obligation, the Code generally does allow the taxpayer to deduct the entire amount of interest payments made, including the inflation premium. As a result, the borrower can deduct inflation-related costs without paying an offsetting tax on inflation-related benefits. Conversely, the lender must include all interest payments in gross income, but does not receive any deduction for inflation's erosion of the value of the repayment obligation.

These imperfections in the tax treatment of debt would have no significant consequences if the borrower and lender shared the same marginal tax rate. The Code's undertaxing of the borrower as a result of inflation then would match precisely the overtaxing of the lender. In a competitive market for loans, lenders would pass their tax costs to borrowers in the form of additional interest, so that the cost of borrowing would be the same as it would be under a tax system that adjusted both interest deductions and receipts for inflation. The borrower and lender would be left in the same economic positions they would occupy if the Code conformed to the accretion model.

Borrowers and lenders, however, often do not face the same marginal tax rates. In many loan transactions, the lender faces an unusually low marginal rate or is entirely tax-exempt. Thus, in many instances, the borrower's tax advantage from deducting the inflation component of interest will not match the corresponding tax detriment to the lender and inflation will result in an overall tax reduction.

In keeping with Treasury I's policy of adhering closely to the accretion model, the proposal would have implemented for the first time a system of explicit indexation for debt. On grounds of feasibility, Treasury I rejected the theoretically exact approach of computing the outstanding balance of each loan on an annual basis, and of including in the borrower's gross income, and excluding from the lender's gross income, the amount by which inflation had caused the real value of the loan principal to decline during the year. Treasury I instead employed the admittedly rough assumption that the "real" component of interest on long-term debt averages approximately six percent per year, and that interest paid in excess of six percent constitutes an inflation premium.[126] Treasury I would have used this assumption to estimate the proportion of interest payments and receipts during the year that was attributable to inflation.

For example, if the average long-term interest rate in the economy during the year was thirteen percent, Treasury I would have assumed that six percent represented real interest, and seven percent represented an inflation component. Based on this assumption, Treasury I would have permitted borrowers to deduct only six-thirteenths of any interest payments made during the year, and would have excluded from gross income an equivalent proportion of lenders' interest receipts.

The Administration dropped Treasury I's debt-indexation proposal from the Treasury II reform plan, thus rendering interest indexation an early casualty of the legislative process that led to the 1986 Act. In large measure, the failure of the interest indexation proposal resulted from its sheer novelty to many participants in the tax reform process, as well as from opposition from the real estate industry, which relies heavily on debt financing. * * *

A concern over prospective revenue losses also contributed to the rejection of interest indexation in the 1986 Act. A significant portion of interest paid consists of interest on federal government debt. The payer of this interest—the government—is tax-exempt, but the recipients comprise a mixture of taxable and tax-exempt entities. The indexation plan's reduction of interest deductions therefore would not have raised tax revenue from this interest, but the exclusion from gross income of a portion of receipts would have reduced tax revenue. As the principal author of Treasury I subsequently has pointed out, the net effect on government revenues probably would have been limited, because the partial exclusion from gross income of receipts probably would have permitted the government to lower the rate of interest

---

126. 2 U.S. TREASURY DEP'T, *supra* note 117, at 194-98. "The formula's use of 6 percent—a rate that is high relative to historical real interest rates—was chosen to err on the side of a smaller than appropriate disallowance of interest deductions (although this decision also implied a relatively small interest income exclusion)." McLure & Zodrow, *Treasury I and the Tax Reform Act of 1986: The Economics and Politics of Tax Reform*, 1 J. ECON. PERSP. 37, 52 (1987).

paid on its debt. Despite this argument, however, revenue concerns apparently helped to account for the rejection of Treasury I's interest indexation proposals.

    * * *

Notes and Questions

20. Indexing bases to measure gain for tax purposes is complex, perhaps too complex to use to respond to low or moderate inflation. (But see Professor Bradford's observation in this chapter's opening quotation.) Do present levels of inflation justify the imposition of indexing? If not, should we wait for higher inflation before acting? But might indexing prove politically easier (because less costly to the Government) in periods of low inflation?

21. Treasury I proposes an inflation adjustment based on the assumption of a "real" interest rate of six percent, noting that "assumption of lower real interest rates would result in higher exclusion rates." Why?

22. Assume an inflation rate of six percent. Treasury I's adjustment mechanism would assume that nominal rates would be about 12 percent (six percent real interest plus six percent inflation), and that therefore 50 percent of all interest payments were attributable to inflation. By contrast, if real interest rates were assumed to be only two percent, an inflation rate of six percent would imply nominal rates of eight percent, with the result that 75 percent of all interest payments would be attributed to inflation—a result markedly more favorable to creditors and more unfavorable to debtors.

23. Six percent is an extremely high rate of real interest, assuming the benchmark is a safe investment, such as Treasury bonds. Footnote 126 of Professor Durst's article suggests that Treasury may have intentionally overstated the real interest rate in an attempt to err on the side of understating, rather than overstating, the portion of interest attributable to inflation.

24. Alternatively, perhaps Treasury I used a higher real rate of return because it was attempting to use a single inflation adjustment for all interest payments, not just those on the most secure investments. Suppose prevailing interest rates—which incorporate inflationary expectations—are five percent for Treasury bonds, but 18 percent on credit card debt. A one-size-fits-all inflation adjustment, in the form proposed by Treasury I, will have to understate the share of Treasury interest attributable to inflation, overstate the share of credit card interest attributable to inflation, or (most likely) some combination of the two. Stated differently, the Treasury I adjustment is inadequate for creditors and favorable to debtors in loan transactions where

real interest is less than six percent, but is generous to creditors and punitive to debtors where real interest is more than six percent.

25. Given that Treasury I either understates or overstates the portion of interest due to inflation (save in the rare case in which the nominal interest rate happens to exceed the inflation rate by exactly six percent), why did the proposal not use varying adjustments for each debt transaction?

26. Another aspect of the problems inherent in Treasury I's one-size-fits-all inflation adjustment for debt is demonstrated by the following example offered by Professor Reed Shuldiner. In reading this example, remember that in case of five percent inflation, Treasury I would have attributed 45 percent of interest to inflation, thus excluding that fraction of interest (for both income and deduction purposes).

> *Bank Co.* has deposits of $1 million on which it pays 3% interest and has consumer loans outstanding of $1 million on which it is paid 18% interest. The inflation rate is 5%. In nominal terms, *Bank Co.* has interest income of $180,000, interest expense of $30,000, and net income of $150,000. In real terms, moreover, its income is also $150,000, because its inflationary loss of $50,000 on its assets is exactly offset by its inflationary gain of $50,000 on its liabilities.
>
> Under a fraction exclusion of 45%, however, *Bank Co.* would be able to exclude 45% of its gross income, or $81,000, but would lose only 45% of its interest expense, or $13,500. In net terms, it would be able to exclude $67,500 of its net income. Its taxable income, therefore, would be only $82,500, rather than $150,000.
>
> * * * [T]he bank's real income would be underreported by 45%, the full amount of the fractional exclusion.[c]

27. Professor Shuldiner states that "[o]ne possible solution to the financial institution problem would be to require financial institutions to use exact indexing, while permitting other taxpayers to use a fractional exclusion. Any such proposal would require distinguishing between financial and nonfinancial institutions."

Still more problems might await such a proposal. As Yoram Margalioth observes:

> [I]f financial institutions are required to use exact indexing, then the financial institution's calculations can be used by the other parties to the transaction, *i.e.*, the taxpayer that lends money to the bank and the taxpayer that borrows money from the bank. Since substantially all lending transactions are done through the

---

c. Reed Shuldiner, *Indexing the Tax Code*, 48 TAX L. REV. 537, 632 (1993). Professor Shuldiner's article is excerpted in Subchapter D.

intermediation of financial institutions, I think that it is pointless not to require all the taxpayers to use exact indexing and shift the burden of calculating it to the financial institutions.[d]

28. Interest rates are set with regard to prospective inflation. Treasury I, however, ties the inflation adjustment to actual inflation. Which is the better adjustment?

29. In a portion of his article not excerpted, Professor Durst proposed a "safety-valve" inflation adjustment to be allowed in computing depreciation allowances. The basis for Professor Durst's proposal is that Congress had a given level of moderate inflation—Professor Durst argues this was four percent—in mind as one reason for allowing depreciation write-offs that otherwise were too generous to reflect economic depreciation. Only if inflation significantly exceeded that anticipated amount would any adjustment at all be appropriate:

> The safety value would compensate for the effects of inflation only to the extent that inflation *exceeds* the rate assumed in setting the 1986 Act's depreciation schedules. Thus, unless inflation accelerates to unforeseen levels, the safety-valve adjustment would have no revenue cost at all. The safety value would have some revenue cost in periods of high inflation, but the revenue cost very likely would be lower than the costs of other measures that Congress would implement if high inflation were to recur and Congress had not previously set in place protections against its effects.[e]

> Professor Durst's safety valve proposal—which he acknowledges to be a "compromise"[f]—is no panacea. The proposal assumes that the accelerated depreciation schedules adopted by Congress in fact constitute an adequate response to moderate, anticipated levels of inflation. This is not self-evident. Moreover, while accelerated depreciation is available to borrowers and non-borrowers alike, Professor Durst's proposal would apply only to borrower-owners of depreciable assets. Finally, accelerated depreciation does nothing to meet the problem of lenders who are repaid in dollars cheapened even by moderate inflation.

30. Note that the Internal Revenue Code contains provisions that limit to some degree the ability of taxpayers to generate current interest deductions that result in mismatching of income and expense. See sections 163(d) and 265(a)(2).

---

d. Yoram Margalioth, *The Case for Tax Indexation of Debt*, 15 Am. J. Tax Pol. 205, 267 (1998).

e. 73 Minn. L. Rev. at 1266.

f. *Id.* at 1267.

31. Professor Durst observes that under present law, "the borrower can deduct inflation-related costs without paying an offsetting tax on inflation-related benefits." What does he mean by this?

32. In proposing to reduce interest deductions by an inflation quotient, Treasury I generally balanced benefit for creditors with detriment to debtors (in both cases, attempting to track the economic effect of inflation). But individual debtors were to be allowed a full deduction, without inflation adjustment, for interest on mortgage indebtedness secured by a taxpayer's principal residence, and for $5,000 of other interest. Is there a policy justification for these exceptions, or is the explanation purely political?

33. Professor Durst implies that the only difficulty with the failure of the market to produce interest rates that will compensate for the effect of inflation on borrowers and lenders is the overall loss of revenue to the Government, a problem that would disappear "if the borrower and lender shared the same marginal tax rate."

In one sense, this is true. For example, assume a tax system that makes no allowance for inflation, and that imposes a flat income tax rate of 20 percent. Assume further that all interest income is taxable to creditors and that all interest expense is deductible by debtors. If the market anticipates inflation of four percent, presumably the market will build into interest rates an inflation premium of *five* percent (not four percent)—because five percent before tax becomes four percent after tax, for both creditors and debtors. If a real interest rate of six percent were desired in a loan from C to D, the nominal rate should be set at 11 percent. In effect, the inflation adjustment would be washed out for both C and D, while the six percent of real interest would be taxed to C and deducted by D. Arguably, the market would have made appropriate adjustment for the tax system's failure to adjust for inflation.

34. In another sense, however, an inflation adjustment might still seem necessary to achieve an appropriate outcome. Take the hypothetical in the preceding question, but add the assumption that inflation during the life of the loan actually amounted to 11 percent—with the result that the real interest rate worked out to be zero. Is it enough that the bargain was fair and that the tax system was applied neutrally, or does fairness require that the tax system accurately tax the result of the transaction? Generally, of course, taxes are levied based on outcomes, not expectations.

35. Would the Treasury I proposal result in more or less revenue, or be revenue neutral? Is your answer the same for private-sector debt and Treasury debt? (Consider the last paragraph of the Durst excerpt.)

36. As the last paragraph of the Durst excerpt points out, however, the effect on the Government of adopting the Treasury I proposal would not be limited to tax receipts. What effect would adoption of the Treasury I proposal have on interest rates? What effect would this have on the world's largest borrower, the United States Government?

D. INDEXATION AND THE REALIZATION RULE

Inflation causes problems in the accurate measurement of income. Assuming the Haig-Simons definition of income to be the ideal, the realization rule causes significant problems as well. In the first excerpt below, Professor Engler argues that indexation could precisely deal with both problems—not just the distortion of inflation, but that arising from the realization rule as well. Furthermore, he argues that an appropriate adjustment can be made without encountering the politically contentious matter of indexing debt.

Professor Shuldiner's article considers several ways in which inflation can cause a divergence between nominal income and real income. Across-the-board imposition of mark-to-market, even if feasible, would not deal with all of these problems. Instead, the proper response is indexation. Note, in particular, Shuldiner's reservations about excluding debt from an indexation regime.

PARTIAL BASIS INDEXATION: AN IMPLICIT
RESPONSE TO TAX DEFERRAL
Mitchell L. Engler[*]

53 Tax Law Review 177, 178-89, 199-202 (2000)

Introduction

The current Code contains two significant deviations from the Haig-Simons ideal income tax base. First, the interest-free deferral of tax on unrealized gains results in the undertaxation of assets held beyond a single taxable period. Second, the failure to adjust capital outlays for inflation results in the overtaxation of real economic gains. A response to either deviation could be made independent of the other; that is, imposition of an interest charge on gains when realized would respond to deferral, and indexation of asset basis would respond to inflation. One might conclude, however, that correcting only one of the two deviations would lead to further distortion since the two roughly offset each other. Thus, much thoughtful analysis has concluded that notwithstanding the generally-accepted theoretical appeal of basis indexation, adoption of any indexation proposal should be coupled with adoption of an anti-deferral mechanism.

A conclusion that any indexation proposal must contain additional

---

*. At time of original publication, Associate Professor, Benjamin N. Cardozo School of Law, Yeshiva University.

adjustments for deferral might lead to rejection of basis indexation on the grounds that the combined complexity of the two proposals would exceed acceptable thresholds or attempts at crafting a workable anti-deferral regime have proven unsuccessful.

[As demonstrated below, however,] a system of partial basis indexation (that is, a system in which debt instruments would not be indexed for inflation) implicitly supplies a charge for the deferral of taxes. [This discussion] highlights the attractiveness of partial basis indexation as an anti-deferral mechanism since, unlike other anti-deferral measures that have been considered, the deferral charge for each period is based on the exact amount of deferred gain. In addition, based on historical data, the charge is a reasonable approximation of the short-term government rate. I further demonstrate that a deferral charge at the short-term government rate should be reasonably fair in a significant number of circumstances. While this charge might be understated in certain circumstances, it nonetheless significantly improves current law.

[The final section of the excerpt] continues the analysis by focusing on the two key components of the form of indexation considered by this Article. I first explain how maintenance of the anti-deferral charge requires consideration of indexation as a replacement for, rather than a supplement to, the current capital gains preference. I then revisit the decision to exclude debt from indexation in order to address tax arbitrage,[14] a potential ancillary issue raised by the exclusion.

 * * *

Indexation as Self-Contained Anti-Deferral Regime

This Section analyzes the impact of deferral on the implementation of partial basis indexation. First, it provides a brief overview of two key issues that have hindered acceptance of standard anti-deferral regimes—allocation of gain to specific tax periods and selection of an appropriate charge for deferral.

The remainder of this Section demonstrates how partial basis indexation implicitly responds to these two issues without any incremental complexity. First, I describe how basis indexation automatically allocates gain on realization to the precise accrual period without any annual valuation or calculation. I then describe how the implicit deferral charge imposed on the allocated gain approximates the short-term government rate and why this is appropriate.

Problems With Anti-Deferral Regimes

While an annual mark-to-market (or accrual) system of taxation would eliminate the deferral problem, it raises ongoing complexity, valuation, and liquidity concerns. Therefore, standard responses to the deferral problem have suggested continuation of deferral until realization coupled with an 'interest-

---

14. By tax arbitrage, I mean the possibility that a leveraged acquisition of an equity asset could provide taxpayers with a positive after-tax yield even where the transaction was an economic wash.

type' charge for the benefits of such deferral.[17] The appeal of an interest charge stems from the recognition that in a current realization-based system, deferral of taxes from one period to the next is the equivalent of an interest-free loan.

Perhaps the most troubling aspect of the interest-charge approach is that such a system requires an arbitrary allocation of the overall gain to specific tax periods (unless annual calculations with the complexity and valuation concerns that impede accrual-based taxation are undertaken). Rules have been suggested or considered, such as pro rata or constant accrual allocations, that appear reasonably fair on average.

Such rules, however, are only estimates at best and could result in significant overtaxation where a disproportionate percentage of the gain accrues late in the holding period or significant undertaxation where a disproportionate percentage of the gain accrues early in the holding period. Although it could be argued that such instances of over- and undertaxation generally will "even out" for each taxpayer over the course of time and his portfolio, this general offset will not be true in all cases, possibly resulting in instances of significant over- or undertaxation.

The second issue that has generated debate under the standard anti-deferral proposal is the appropriate deferral charge.

Precision of Allocation of Gain Under Basis Indexation

Partial basis indexation's implicit response to deferral derives from the fact that each year's indexation adjustment is based on the asset's basis rather than its fair market value. When compared to the Haig-Simons accrual regime, this appears unfair and arbitrary to taxpayers who own appreciated assets since their indexation adjustment will be less than the correct amount: that is, the inflation factor times the asset's fair market value.

This basis shortfall can be stated, for each taxable year, as an amount equal to the product of (1) the excess of the asset's fair market value over its basis and (2) the inflation percentage for the year. This highlights the unique anti-deferral attribute of a basis-indexed tax system. In particular, an implicit charge is imposed on the exact amount of the deferred tax for each taxable period. This occurs since the basis shortfall arises only on assets whose value exceeds basis at the start of the tax year, and only in an amount based on such excess.

Some relatively simple illustrations demonstrate the precise workings of this feature of basis indexation. First, assume A purchased stock for $10,000 on January 1, 1997 and continued to hold it as of December 31, 1997 when the stock had a value of $11,000. Assume that A sold the stock for $12,100 on December 31, 1998 and that the annual inflation for each year was 3%. Under a basis-indexed Code, since A did not sell at the end of 1997, A's indexed basis

---

17. * * * For a thorough discussion of the issues raised by anti-deferral proposals, see Stephen B. Land, Defeating Deferral: A Proposal for Retrospective Taxation, 52 Tax L. Rev. 45, 65-73 (1996).

at the end of 1998 would be only 10,609.[32] *A* therefore would report $1,491 of taxable income[33] in 1998, resulting in a $596.40 tax liability.[34]

Compare the results under an accrual regime. At the end of 1997, *A*'s indexed basis would have been $10,300,[35] resulting in taxable income of $700,[36] and a 1997 tax liability of $280.[37] *A*'s basis as of December 31, 1997 would increase to $11,000 since the asset was marked to market. At the end of 1998, *A*'s indexed basis would have been $11,330,[38] resulting in $770 of taxable gain[39] and $308 of tax liability for 1998.[40]

In sum, under the accrual tax, *A* would have owed $280 in 1997 and $308 in 1998 for a total of $588; under indexation, *A* would owe $596.40 in 1998. Thus, in comparison to the accrual tax, the 1997 tax liability of $280 was deferred to 1998 under indexation and an additional payment of $8.40[41] was imposed on *A*. The $8.40 additional charge equals the inflation factor of 3% for the period of deferral (one year) times the amount of the 1997 deferred tax ($280).

The following examples further illustrate the precision with which indexation can be viewed as implicitly allocating the deferred gain for purposes of the interest charge. First, assume that *A* sold the stock from the earlier example (purchased on January 1, 1997 for $10,000) for $26,000 on December 31, 2006. Assume again that inflation for each year was 3%. Finally, assume in the first instance that the asset experienced all of its real gain in Year 10 (that is, the nominal appreciation for each of the first nine years was only 3%). Since *A* has not deferred recognition of any real gain, no interest should be imposed.

Under a basis-indexed system, *A* would have taxable income in Year 10 of $12,561,[43] and a $5,024.40 tax liability.[44] This is the identical answer that would be reached in an accrual system with annual inflation adjustments since (1) the 3% annual nominal gain for each of Years 1 through 9 would be offset exactly by the inflation adjustment, and (2) the $12,952 of nominal gain in Year 10[45] would be reduced by the $391 indexation adjustment,[46] leaving a real gain of $12,561 (once again generating $5,024.40 of tax liability).

---

32. $10,000 x (1.03)^2.

33. $12,100 – $10,609.

34. 40% x $1,491. Consistent with the current law's top bracket of 39.6%, IRC § 1, unless explicitly stated otherwise, the examples throughout this Article assume that the taxpayer is subject to tax at the top marginal rate of 40% (rounded up from 39.6% for ease of calculation).

35. $10,000 x 1.03.

36. $11,000 – $10,300.

37. $700 x .4.

38. $11,000 x 1.03.

39. $12,100 – $11,330.

40. $770 x .4.

41. $596.40 – ($280 + $308) = $8.40.

43. $26,000 – [$10,000 x (1.03)^{10}].

44. $12,561 x .4.

45. $26,000 – [$10,000 x (1.03)^9].

46. [$10,000 x (1.03)^9] x .03.

At the other extreme, assume that all of the real gain accrued in Year 1 such that the value at the end of Year 1 was $19,927.[47] Under an annual accrual system, there would be $9,627 of taxable income in Year 1,[48] and a tax liability of $3,850.80.[49] Imposing interest on the $3,850.80 for the nine years of deferral at the rate of 3% would result in a tax liability of $5,024.40 in Year 10.[50] Indexation provides an identical answer. In fact, regardless of when the real gain occurred during the 10 years, the $5,024.40 tax liability under an indexation system exactly equals the result that would occur under an accrual system (with a precise annual valuation mechanism) that allowed each year's tax liability to be deferred until disposition with interest imposed at the rate of 3%.

This relationship holds even where an asset experiences a real loss for one or more periods, since any real decline in asset value during a tax year should be viewed as a loan by the taxpayer to the government. Table 1 illustrates a sample case where the asset value randomly increased and decreased during the course of a five-year holding period.[53] Table 1 illustrates the results under a mark-to-market regime with a 40% tax rate and interest charged at the inflation rate (assumed to be 3% per annum). The asset is purchased for $10,000 on January 1, 2001 and is sold for $18,000 on December 31, 2005.

---

47. $19,927 x $(1.03)^9$ = $26,000.

48. $19,927 – ($10,000 x 1.03).

49. $9,627 x .4.

50. $3,850.80 x $(1.03)^9$ = $5,024.42 (the .02 differential is attributable to rounding).

53. Interest always is charged on the tax deferral loan even if the taxpayer has no gain or loss on realization, as the following example illustrates.

Example 1: A buys stock for $10,000 on January 1, 1997 and sells it for $10,609 on December 31, 1998, although its intermediary value on December 31, 1997 was $20,000. It may appear at first blush that the government is denied any interest or principal on the tax deferral loan from December 31, 1997 since A reports no gain or loss on the sale of the stock under an indexed system [$10,609 – ($10,000 x $(1.03)^2$) = 0]. A closer look at the indexed system, through a comparison to an accrual system that taxes only real, rather than nominal, gains illustrates how interest and principal are "collected." Under the accrual system, A would have a tax deferral loan of $3,880 on December 31, 1997 (.4 x [$20,000 – ($10,000 x 1.03)]). When A sells for $10,609 on December 31, 1998, A would have a tax loss of $9,991 [$10,609 – ($20,000 x 1.03)] or tax savings of $3,996.40 (40% of $9,991). A, however, would owe the $3,880 of tax-deferred loan plus $116.40 ($3,880 x .03) of interest. Thus, the tax-deferred loan of $3,880 and interest of $116.40 are "collected" as an offset against the $3,996.40 of tax savings to which A would have been entitled under accrual taxation. The gain and loss automatically were placed in the correct periods (that is, gain in 1997, loss in 1998) and interest automatically was imposed on the deferral of the 1997 gain.

Table 1

Year	(1) 1/1 FMV	(2) 12/31 FMV	(3)[54] 12/31 Indexed Basis	(4)[55] Taxable Gain or \<Loss>	(5)[56] Tax at 40%	(6)[57] Charge
1	$10,000	$12,000	$10,300	$1,700	$680	-0-
2	12,000	16,000	12,360	3,640	1,456	20.40
3	16,000	20,000	16,480	3,520	1,408	64.69
4	20,000	8,000	20,600	\<12,600>	\<5,040>	108.87
5	8,000	18,000	8,240	9,760	3,904	\<39.06>
Total					$2,408	$154.90

Interest Charge Under Partial Basis Indexation

Having established that basis indexation implicitly imposes a charge on deferred taxes at the inflation rate, this Section discusses the sufficiency of the deferral charge. The next Subsection demonstrates that the indexation charge can serve as a sufficient proxy for the short-term government rate. The following Subsection then considers the sufficiency of an interest charge at that rate.

Partial Indexation Charge as Proxy for Short-Term Government Rate

Initially, interest imposed at the rate of inflation might appear insufficient even in comparison to the short-term government rate benchmark since the government rate encompasses both inflation and the risk-free rate of return.[61] Under partial, rather than full, basis indexation, however, the full amount of a taxpayer's explicit investment interest expense (including the inflationary component) generally remains deductible since debt is excluded from indexation.[62]

By virtue of the interest deduction under partial basis indexation, a

---

54. This is computed as Column 1 x 1.03.

55. This is computed as Column 2 – Column 3.

56. This is computed as Column 4 x .4.

57. This is the deferral charge and is computed as 3% of the aggregate sum of all amounts from Columns 5 and 6 for all prior years. Thus, for example, the interest charge during Year 2 is .03 x $680 (or $20.40) and Year 5 is .03 x ($680 + $1,456 + $1,408 – $5,040 + $20.40 + $64.69 + $108.87), which equals <$39.06>.

61. The third component of interest—compensation for risk—is not taken into account for the government rate since it is considered to be risk-free.

62. * * * The full deductibility of investment interest assumes that the taxpayer has sufficient qualifying investment income. IRC § 163(d).

taxpayer's actual cost on explicit borrowing from third parties is only the interest rate x (1 – the tax rate). Similarly, since the implicit indexation charge at the inflation rate is the after-tax cost, the real pretax charge under partial indexation is inflation/(1 – tax rate) or $I/(1 - t)$. Thus, the attractiveness of partial indexation increases since it generally raises the deferral charge from merely inflation to the more acceptable $I/(1 - t)$.[65]

Deductibility of the inflation component of interest under partial indexation might be viewed as a mere windfall to the debtor. Deductibility of the inflation component of debt, however, is appropriate on a systemic basis since the lender includes the inflationary component.[66] Furthermore, on an individual basis, deductibility of the inflation component is justified to the extent the taxpayer has creditor positions (including likely bank interest, money market accounts, Treasury securities, and the like) on which the inflationary component is included.

How does an interest rate of $I/(1 - t)$ measure up against the government short-term borrowing rate? Not surprisingly, given that the real pretax risk-free rate over approximately the last 70 years has been less than 1% and that the real after-tax rate is often negative, charging tax deferral loan interest at $I/(1 - t)$ would have resulted in greater interest than utilization of the one-month Treasury rate for each of the following 10-year periods: 1987-1996, 1977-1986, 1967-1976, 1947-1956 and 1937-1946. In addition, for the most recent 10-year period, where $I/(1 - t)$ did not exceed the one-month T-bill rate, dating back to (1957-1966), $I/(1 - T)$ would have provided an interest charge in excess of 96% of the T-bill rate.[72]

* * *

Partial Indexation in Lieu
of Capital Gains Preference

This Section furthers the analysis by focusing on the two critical characteristics of the form of indexation considered by this Article. First, it explains why indexation should be considered as a replacement for the capital gains preference. Second, it revisits the consideration of partial, rather than full, indexation to address a potential ancillary concern raised by the exclusion of debt from indexation (that is, tax arbitrage).

---

65. Thus, the pretax interest rate in the examples in the previous Section was a more reasonable 5% $(.03/(1 - .4))$.

66. Since the lender on tax deferral loans is the government, it might appear that this inclusion is inconsequential. These tax deferral loans, however, should be considered in tandem with the significant debt issued by the government where the recipient—if not tax-exempt—must include the inflationary component even though the excess deduction to the government borrower is inconsequential.

72. * * * The T-bill return was 3.05%. Inflation was 1.77%; thus $I/(1 - t)$ equaled 2.95%. Note that I/(1– t) is more likely to understate the government rate in times of lower inflation.

Indexation as a Replacement for the Capital Gains Preference

In order to maintain its strong theoretical appeal, basis indexation should be considered as a replacement for, rather than a supplement to, the current capital gains preference. As shown [above,] basis indexation operates to impose a reasonable interest charge for deferral. Combining basis indexation with a lower tax rate for qualifying capital assets would reduce, if not eliminate, the interest charge.

Consider again the example * * * where A purchased stock on January 1, 1997 for $10,000 and sold the stock on December 31, 2006 for $26,000. Annual inflation was 3%. [It was] demonstrated that A would owe $5024.40 in the year of disposition (2006) under an accrual-based system that allowed deferral of payment until disposition with interest imposed at the after-tax rate of 3%. [It was] further demonstrated that partial indexation would provide an identical result, assuming the taxable income of $12,561 was subject to the same tax rate of 40%.[118] If the indexed gain of $12,561 qualified for a reduced long-term capital gains rate of less than 40%, the implicit charge would be reduced or even eliminated.

In addition, the rationale for a capital gains preference—already on somewhat shaky grounds—in a basis-indexed Code would be weakened further. First, one of the often-cited justifications for the preferential rate is that it provides some kind of rough relief for the effects of inflation in an unindexed Code. Second, while an unindexed Code fails to provide any relief for the lock-in problem (that is, the continued holding of appreciated assets by investors who would sell in a tax-free world since payment of the taxes can be deferred interest free), a basis-indexed Code does address the lock-in problem.

Consideration of Partial Rather Than Full Indexation

As discussed earlier, partial rather than full basis indexation increases the pretax deferral charge from I to $I/(1-t)$, thereby approximating the short-term government rate. The exclusion of debt instruments from indexation, however, might lead to tax arbitrage concerns—the possibility that leveraged acquisitions of nondebt assets would result in after-tax positive yields even where the transactions generated zero cash flow. This would arise because the tax system would be too generous in allowing a full deduction for the nominal interest expense while the inflationary component of gains from the asset would be excluded.

Similar potential exists under the current law's preference regime since taxpayers can make leveraged acquisitions of capital assets and use the interest deductions to offset other ordinary investment income while the gains are subject to tax at lower capital gains rates. Since this Article considers partial basis indexation as a replacement for, rather than as a supplement to,

---

118. See notes 43-46 and accompanying text.

the preference regime, the relevant question thus becomes whether the arbitrage (and other related tax-advantaged) potential would be exacerbated under partial indexation as compared to current law with a capital gains preference. While it is difficult to draw absolute conclusions, an in-depth comparative analysis indicates that the arbitrage (and related) potential under partial indexation and the preference is quite similar. Thus, the increased potential under partial indexation, if any, does not appear to be meaningful.

Finally, in addition to providing a more reasonable deferral charge, the exclusion of debt from indexation is justified as a response to the most consistent criticism of basis indexation; that is, its complexity makes it administratively unworkable.

* * *

INDEXING THE TAX CODE
Reed Shuldiner[*]

48 Tax Law Review 537, 540-43, 547-50, 552-54, 556,

558, 563, 595-99, 613-17, 621-28, 634-45, 650-51 (1993)

Indexing the Tax Structure
The Need to Index the Tax Structure

It is important to understand that the structural problems caused by inflation are not due to the fact that inflation increases nominal taxes, but rather to the fact that inflation increases nominal taxes by more or less than the rate of inflation. In other words, problems arise when inflation increases or decreases real and not merely nominal tax burdens. Compare, for example, the effect of inflation on a sales tax with the effect on a per unit excise tax. Assume a city imposes a 5% tax on all sales and sales total $1 million. The city would collect $50,000 in taxes. If 10% inflation causes sales to increase to $1.1 million, the city would collect $55,000 in taxes. The 10% increase in tax collections would offset exactly the effects of inflation. In real or constant dollar terms, tax revenues would be unchanged. By contrast, consider the effect of a $1 per unit excise tax. Assume that prior to the inflation, the $1 million in sales is generated by the sale of 50,000 units at $20 per unit. The city would collect $50,000 from the excise tax. If 10% inflation increased the per unit price to $22 and sales volume were unchanged, the tax revenue would remain at $50,000. While the tax would have stayed constant in nominal dollars, it would have decreased in real dollars. If the city wished to maintain its excise tax revenues in real terms, it could adjust the excise tax each year to compensate for the effects of inflation. In the example, the city could maintain its real tax revenues by increasing the excise rate from $1 to $1.10 per unit, thereby raising its revenues from $50,000 to $55,000. The adjustment could be made by revising the tax law each year or it could be

---

*. At time of original publication, Assistant Professor, University of Pennsylvania Law School.

automatic. Such an automatic adjustment for inflation is referred to as "indexation."

Similarly, an income tax may or may not be affected by inflation. Consider first a strictly proportional income tax. Assume that there is a 20% income tax and that in Year 1 a taxpayer has income of $40,000. The taxpayer would be liable for $8,000 in taxes. If, as part of a general 10% inflation, her income increased to $44,000 in Year 2, her tax liability would increase to $8,800. * * * While her nominal tax has increased in proportion to her nominal income, her real tax has remained a constant proportion of her real income. Thus, in the case of a strictly proportional income tax, indexing is unnecessary.

Like a sales tax, the structure of an income tax becomes sensitive to inflation when it diverges from a strictly proportional tax. Thus, for example, when an income tax has features such as floors, ceilings, deductions, exemptions and brackets that are specified in fixed dollar amounts, the structure of the tax is sensitive to inflation. * * *

In addition to reducing the real value of fixed deductions, inflation has the effect of reducing the size of tax brackets expressed in fixed dollar amounts. For example, consider an income tax of 10% on the first $10,000 of income and 20% on all income in excess of $10,000. Under such a structure, a taxpayer earning $40,000 would owe $7,000. If, however, as a result of 10% inflation, her income increased to $44,000, her tax liability would increase to $7,800. The increase from $7,000 to $7,800 represents a nominal increase of 11.4% and a real increase of 1.3%.

Current Indexation of the Code

The Code contains many significant features specified as fixed dollar amounts, including the rate brackets, the standard deduction (or zero bracket amount) and the personal exemptions. Prior to the indexation of the Code as part of the Economic Recovery Tax Act of 1981 (ERTA), the Joint Committee on Taxation estimated that a 10% inflation rate caused a 16% increase in tax revenues. ERTA indexed the rate brackets, the personal exemptions and the standard deduction. In addition to these principal structural features, Congress has indexed a variety of other Code provisions including, for example, the earned income credit, the threshold for the phaseout of itemized deductions, and, at least in part, the phaseout of personal exemptions.

The structural indexation enacted to date has not imposed a significant administrative burden on the tax system because the Service can perform the necessary computations and publish them along with the appropriate tax forms and publications. * * *

Despite the relative ease of indexing the tax structure, there remain a large number of instances where it has not been indexed. * * *

Choice of Index
* * *

Regardless of the particular price index selected, it is important to note that indexing the tax structure in terms of a general price index does not compensate for increases in real income.   Given a fully price-indexed progressive income tax, aggregate tax revenue will increase by more than the percentage increase in real income as real growth forces taxpayers into higher brackets. At least one country, Denmark, has chosen to index its tax structure on the basis of changes in average earnings of industrial workers, thus limiting the extent to which increases in real income will cause disproportionate increases in real taxes.

Indexing Capital Gains
Introduction

The discussion of indexing the income tax structure in the previous section is based on the assumption that the tax base has been measured accurately.   Even where the income tax structure has been completely indexed, however, inflation can cause serious problems in the measurement of the income tax base.

The most familiar instance of inflation induced mismeasurement of income is with capital gains. Consider, for example, *T* who purchases an asset for $1,000 in 1990, holds onto the asset for 10 years and then sells the asset for $1,500 in the year 2000.   Under conventional methods of income measurement, *T* has taxable income (a capital gain) of $500. In fact, without knowing the amount of intervening inflation, it is impossible to determine whether, in a real sense, *T* is better or worse off for having owned the asset. In other words, whether *T*'s command over goods and services, her ability to pay, has increased or decreased since she first purchased the asset is unknown. If, for instance, there has been a total of 80% inflation over the 10-year period, *T* would need approximately $1,800 in 2000 to purchase the same bundle of goods and services that she was able to purchase with $1,000 in 1990.   Therefore, in a real sense, *T* has a loss of $300, rather than a gain of $500. Fundamentally, the mismeasurement of income is caused by the fact that gain or loss, which is computed in current dollars, is determined by reference to basis stated in terms of historical dollars. Although the problem may be somewhat harder to see, a similar mismeasurement of income is caused any time that a historical basis figure is used to compute current income.   Thus, for example, absent indexing or a similar adjustment, net income derived from ownership of depreciable property or from the sale of inventory is also mismeasured.

Similarly, inflation will cause the mismeasurement of (negative) income from liabilities. For example, assume that *T* borrows $1,000, promising to repay $1,100 in one year. Under conventional income accounting, $1,000 of the repayment would be denominated as principal and have no tax consequences and the remaining $100 of the repayment would be denominated as interest and potentially would be deductible. Economically, however, the amount of real principal T repays would depend on the level of inflation. If, during the intervening year, there had been 6% inflation, in real terms she would owe principal of [$1,060] and, therefore, would be paying only [$40] in interest. Thus, inflation would have caused her to overstate her interest by [150%].

Specific Issues in Indexing Capital Gains

As discussed above, one of the primary areas where inflation causes the mismeasurement of income is capital gains. The error in measurement arises out of the fact that to determine income from the disposition of a capital asset, it is necessary to compare dollars from two distinct periods of time. In particular, gain (or loss) is defined as the difference between the amount realized from the sale or other disposition of an asset and the taxpayer's basis in the asset. Since the taxpayer's basis generally represents the taxpayer's historical investment in the asset, it is measured in historical dollars, while the amount realized, measured by a current receipt, is measured in current dollars. The resulting computation with historical and current dollars is inaccurate. The simplest solution is to index the taxpayer's basis, thus converting the historical basis of the asset into current dollars that can be compared meaningfully with the proceeds from the sale of the asset to compute gain or loss.

* * *

The Relationship Between Indexing and Holding Period

Since inflation compounds over time, it is natural to conclude that inflation causes a greater problem the longer the holding period of the asset. In fact, with respect to assets that have real gains, inflation is in certain ways a greater problem the shorter the holding period. It is, of course, true that the size of the inflation adjustment increases with the cumulative amount of inflation and, therefore, generally with time. The significance of the inflation adjustment, however, declines with time in two ways. First, assuming a constant inflation rate and a constant real growth rate, the correction for inflation as a percentage of nominal gains decreases rather than increases with time. Second, because gain generally is not taxed until realization, a longer holding period offers the advantage of deferral, which can offset the overtaxation due to inflation.

It is easiest to demonstrate that the correction for inflation decreases over time with a numerical example.

> *Example 1: David* purchases an asset for $1,000. The asset has real annual growth of 5% and inflation is 5%. At the end of the first year, the asset is worth $1,102 and has an indexed basis of $1,050. At the end of 20 years, the asset is worth $7,040 and has an indexed basis of $2,653.

If the asset is sold after one year, the nominal gain on the asset is $102 of which $50, or approximately one-half, is properly excluded. If the asset is sold after 20 years, the nominal gain is $6,040, of which $1,653, or approximately one-quarter, is properly excluded. The fact that the fraction of gain that should be excluded decreases over time is one argument against using a capital gains exclusion in lieu of indexing.

The second reason that indexation of capital gains becomes less important the longer the holding period is that while inflation causes the overtaxation of capital gains, deferral causes the undertaxation of such gains. By "deferral," I refer to the fact that under the realization doctrine, gains and losses on capital assets generally are not taxed on a current basis, but rather only upon disposition. The ability to defer the payment of tax on gains has the effect of lowering the burden of the tax. The longer the holding period, the greater the extent to which deferral compensates for the failure to index for inflation.

      * * *

[T]o some extent, the desirability of indexing depends on the length of the holding period. For brief holding periods, indexing can be critical to prevent excessive tax rates. For long holding periods, the failure to index may merely offset the benefit of deferral. In fact, it is arguable that for long holding periods, it is inappropriate to index given the value of deferral.

Second, accrual or mark-to-market taxation often is recommended as the appropriate method for taxing income from capital assets because it solves the problem of deferral. As a result, in recent years Congress has shown an increasing willingness to impose either mark-to-market taxation or taxation that approximates mark-to-market treatment. In the absence of inflation, accrual taxation eliminates deferral and guarantees that the effective tax rate is the same as the statutory tax rate. With inflation and without indexation, however, accrual taxation means that the effective rate on income from capital may far exceed the statutory rate because the offsetting benefit of deferral has been eliminated.

      * * *

Indexation of Loss Assets

In the previous section, I argue that because, as a percentage of real gain, the indexation correction becomes smaller the longer the holding period and because deferral compensates for the failure to index, indexing real gain is less important the longer the holding period. In the case of losses, however, neither of these conditions hold and indexing becomes more critical the longer the holding period. Consider first the size of the inflation adjustment relative to the amount of nominal gain or loss. Where there is a loss in real terms, the size of the inflation adjustment relative to the amount of loss increases with the length of the holding period. Thus, the indexation adjustment becomes more necessary with holding period. Second, in the case of losses, deferral represents a burden to the taxpayer, not an advantage. Just as deferral of gains is equivalent to an interest-free loan from the government to the taxpayer, deferral of losses is equivalent to an interest-free loan from the taxpayer to the government. The fact that indexing is, in certain ways, more important for loss assets than it is for gain assets makes it particularly odd that indexing proposals often are limited to gain assets.

* * *

The Failure to Index Capital Assets
as a Proxy Tax on Wealth

Another argument against indexation of capital assets is that inflation in an unindexed tax system may have beneficial effects on the tax base. It is possible to view an unindexed tax on capital gains as a combination of a wealth tax and an income tax. In a world in which all nominal gains and losses were taxable annually, the failure to index would be equivalent to a tax on wealth levied at a rate approximately equal to the taxpayer's marginal income tax rate times the rate of inflation. Even under the assumption of full accrual taxation, it would be a very peculiar wealth tax whose rate was proportional to the rate of inflation. Without regard to the income tax, inflation has the effect of redistributing income. For example, people with assets paying a fixed rate are hurt by increases in inflation, while people with fixed-rate liabilities are helped. It is not at all clear that it is desirable to compound this implicit redistribution with a variable rate tax on wealth. Finally, it is a wealth tax that is levied only upon realization.

* * *

Indexing Depreciable Property
In General

As with any other asset purchased in one period and accounted for in another period, depreciable property must be indexed for inflation in order to measure income properly. The effect of failing to index depreciation can be seen by comparing two simple examples, one without inflation and the other with moderate inflation.

Example 19: *David* purchases a machine that without additional costs produces one widget a year for two years. The widgets can be sold immediately and costlessly for $100. Given the prevailing interest rate of 5%, *David* pays $186 for the machine. Once the machine has produced its first widget, its value falls to $95, reflecting the fact that it is now expected to generate $100 in one year. The machine, therefore, depreciates $91 in its first year. Once the machine has produced its second widget it becomes worthless, depreciating an additional $95.

For his first year of operation, *David* reports gross income of $100 from the sale of the widget, takes a depreciation deduction of $91, and has taxable income of $9. For his second year of operation,

David reports gross income of $100, depreciation of $95 and taxable income of $5.

Example 20 shows the effect of moderate inflation on *Example 19*:

Example 20: Assume the same facts as in *Example 19* except that there is 5% inflation between the first and second year. Thus, the second widget is sold for $105, rather than $100.

For his first year of operation, *David* again reports gross income of $100, depreciation of $91, and taxable income of $9. In the second year of operation, given the change in the price level, *David* reports gross income of $105 from the sale of widgets. Assuming that *David* is still permitted an unindexed depreciation deduction of $95, *David*'s taxable income is $10.

Thus, in *Example 20*, a modest 5% inflation causes a 100% increase in taxable income, showing that the failure to index depreciation can have dramatic effects on the taxation of business profits.

A preliminary question in indexing depreciable assets is whether the adjustment should be made annually or only upon final disposition of the asset. Given the general assumption that the nominal income generated by a depreciable asset is included in income currently, it is appropriate for the indexation adjustment also to be made currently.

Once the decision has been made to index currently, there are a variety of equivalent techniques that can be used to compute the amount of indexed depreciation. Economic depreciation is the decline in the real value of the asset over the taxable period. In the absence of inflation, depreciation, therefore, is equal to the difference between the value of the property at the beginning and end of the period. In the presence of inflation, it is necessary to measure the decline in value in constant dollars. Thus, stated in terms of end-of-period dollars, depreciation for the period is equal to the value at the beginning of the period, adjusted upwards for inflation, minus the value at the end of the period.

Example 21: *Emily* purchases an asset for $1,000 to use in her business. The asset depreciates in real terms at the rate of 30% per year. In the absence of inflation, the asset would be worth $700 at the end of the first year. Accordingly, *Emily* should be entitled to a depreciation deduction of $300 for the first year.

Assuming 10% inflation, however, at the end of the first year, the asset would be worth $770. *Emily*'s indexed basis for the asset, however, would be $1,100. Accordingly, *Emily* should be entitled to a depreciation deduction of $330. Her remaining indexed basis in the asset should be $770.

Equivalently, depreciation could be indexed simply by first indexing the taxpayer's basis and then multiplying the taxpayer's indexed basis by the depreciation rate.

Example 22: In the absence of inflation, *Emily*'s depreciation deduction in *Example 21* could be determined by multiplying *Emily*'s basis, $1,000, by the depreciation rate, 30%. Thus, *Emily* would be entitled to $300 of depreciation.

With 10% inflation, *Emily*'s depreciation deduction could be determined by multiplying *Emily*'s indexed basis, $1,100, by the real depreciation rate, 30%. Thus, *Emily* would be entitled to $330 of depreciation. Her remaining basis of $770 would be determined by subtracting her indexed depreciation from her indexed basis.

The marginal information and other administrative costs of indexing depreciation would be small because computing depreciation deductions under current law already requires keeping careful track of the basis of assets.

Accelerated Depreciation

* * *

There are, however, a variety of problems with using accelerated depreciation in lieu of indexing. The primary problem is that accelerated depreciation can at best compensate for expected, not actual inflation. * * *

Indexing Inventories

As is generally the case with buying and selling assets, income from transactions in inventory is mismeasured under inflation. The effects of inflation on inventory can be seen from a simple example.

Example 26: A hardware store purchases a hammer for $2 on June 1, 1994, and sells the hammer on June 1, 1995 for $3. Under conventional accounting, the hardware store would be considered to have $1 in gross profit from the purchase and sale of the hammer.

If inflation were 10% during the year that the hammer was in inventory, the store's profit would be overstated. Properly stated in 1995 dollars, the store would have an indexed cost of goods sold of $2.20 and would have an indexed gross profit of only $.80.

The failure to index inventories has had a significant effect on the amount of taxes collected from the business sector.

While Treasury has recommended indexing inventories, Congress has been unwilling to do so. In part, the pressure to index inventories has been reduced by the existence of the last-in, first-out (LIFO) method of accounting for inventories which acts as an ad hoc method of indexation. Under first-in, first-out (FIFO) inventory accounting a taxpayer treats sales of inventories as coming out of the oldest inventory on hand. Under LIFO a taxpayer is permitted to treat sales of inventory as occurring from the most recently purchased inventory. In periods of rising costs, FIFO tends to minimize costs of goods sold and hence maximize taxable income. Similarly, LIFO tends to maximize cost of goods sold and, hence, minimize taxable income. The operation of LIFO can be seen from a simple example.

> *Example 27*: Assume that the hardware store in *Example 26* purchased an additional hammer in 1995 for $2.20. Under LIFO, the store would be permitted to treat the hammer sold during 1995 as being the hammer that was purchased during 1995. As a result, the store would have a cost of goods sold of $2.20 and would have gross profits of $.80.

As illustrated in *Example 27*, LIFO can produce results that are the same as indexed inventory accounting. There are, however, a variety of problems with the use of LIFO in lieu of indexation. First, particularly in the case of small firms, LIFO's complexity is believed to discourage its use. Second, the conformity requirement, which prohibits the use of LIFO unless the taxpayer uses it for financial accounting purposes, also discourages its use. Because LIFO depresses profits, firms may be reluctant to use it for reporting profits to shareholders. Third, LIFO is not available to all taxpayers. For example, security dealers are required to mark their inventories to market and thus are unable to use LIFO. Whatever the cause, Treasury has estimated that as of 1981, 70% of inventories were valued using FIFO, rather than LIFO or some other method.

Additionally, LIFO is not a perfect substitute for indexed depreciation. To begin with, LIFO does not exclude inflationary gains, but merely defers the realization of inflationary gains. When overall levels of inventory are reduced, taxpayers using LIFO effectively are required to take their deferred inflationary gains into income. The taxation of deferred inflationary gains when inventories contract provides a noneconomic incentive to maintain inventories. * * *

Finally, because LIFO generally operates based on changes in the price of the inventory, rather than changes in the overall price level, LIFO either will overcorrect or undercorrect for inflation to the extent that prices have risen more quickly or slowly in the inventoried goods than overall. * * *

In summary, LIFO provides only a partial solution to the problem of inflation. Moreover, given the complexity of the LIFO method, it is not clear that explicitly indexing inventories would pose greater administrative burdens than does LIFO.

Indexing Debt

As with other investments, a holder's basis in a debt instrument must be indexed in order to measure income properly. Similarly, proper measurement of the borrower's income requires indexing the principal amount of a loan.

> *Example 30*: *B* borrows $100 from *L* and promises to pay back $115 in one year. In the absence of inflation, *B* would have a $15 interest deduction and *L* would have $15 in interest income. If, however, there was 10% inflation, the inflated principal amount of the debt would be $110 and when *B* repays $115, in economic terms she would be repaying $110 in inflated principal and $5 in interest. Therefore, *B* should have an interest deduction of only $5 and *L* should have corresponding interest income of $5.

* * *

Specific Issues Arising with Debt Indexation
* * *

Home Mortgages

The administrative problems of indexing home mortgage debt are not particularly severe. * * *

The real problem with indexing home mortgage debt is political. As the following example demonstrates, indexing home mortgage debt would limit the benefit of the home mortgage deduction significantly.

> *Example 36*: A taxpayer in the 36% bracket has a 30-year, $200,000 mortgage at 10%. Under current law, the after-tax cost of the interest on the mortgage in the first year is approximately $12,800. Assuming 5% inflation, if the mortgage were indexed, the after-tax cost would be approximately $16,400, a 28% increase.

Even if, as is likely, indexing applied only to new mortgages, by raising the after-tax cost to homebuyers, indexing mortgages might well depress housing prices causing existing homeowners to suffer losses. It is, of course, possible that mortgage interest rates would fall to reflect the lower taxes on lenders. It is not at all clear, however, that interest rates would fall enough to offset the entire burden of indexing. * * *

Is Debt Indexation Unnecessary?

The discussion of debt indexation so far essentially has ignored the effect of the failure to index debt on pretax interest rates. Opponents of debt indexation argue that because both lenders and borrowers understand that their tax liabilities are based on nominal, not real, interest payments, interest rates adjust to take into account the overtaxation and that, therefore, indexation becomes unnecessary. The theoretical ability of interest rates to adjust to take into account the failure to index interest is demonstrated by the following example.

> *Example 38*: Assume that both the real interest rate and the inflation rate are 5% and that all taxpayers face a 30% marginal rate. Well aware of monetary illusion, but blind to fiscal illusion, *Bank Co.* sets its lending rate at 10% to cover both the real cost of its funds and inflation. *Bank Co.* lends $1,000 to *Borrower* for one year. *Bank Co.* expects to earn an after-tax real return of $35.

> After one year, *Borrower* repays $1,100. *Bank Co.* pays taxes of $30 on the interest, leaving itself with $1,070 after taxes. Its accountant points out that after adjusting for the $50 loss in value in its principal, *Bank Co.* has earned only $20 in real terms, rather than $35 as expected.

> No longer subject to fiscal illusion, *Bank Co.* raises its lending rate to 12.2%, charging $122 interest on its $1,000 loan to *Borrower*. After paying $37 in taxes, *Bank Co.* is left with $85 after tax. Adjusting for its $50 inflationary loss, *Bank Co.* has an after-tax real return of $35 or 3.5%. Similarly, *Borrower* has an after-tax real interest cost of $35.

As shown by the example, in order to have an interest rate sufficient to compensate both for the effect of inflation and for the failure of the tax system to index debt, a lender must set an interest rate that is high enough to cover the real interest rate, expected losses due to inflation and the tax penalty on the inflation premium. * * *

Some argue that if interest rates fully adjust to compensate for the lack of indexation, debt indexation is unnecessary, and since debt indexation has a significant administrative cost, it should not be done. In essence, the argument is that since no one, including the fisc, is hurt by the failure to index, indexation is just an academic exercise not worth the administrative cost. * * *

Even if it were correct that borrowers and lenders take taxes into account, that is, there is no fiscal illusion, there remain strong arguments in favor of debt indexation. * * *

Second, the derivation of the tax-adjusted Fisher equation assumes that all borrowers and lenders have the same marginal tax rate, τ. As is well known, this assumption is false because different taxpayers generally face different marginal tax rates. * * *

If a borrower has a marginal tax rate less than τ^*, her ability to deduct nominal interest is of reduced value and, therefore, she faces a higher real borrowing cost than she would with indexation. Conversely, a borrower with a marginal tax rate greater than τ* faces a lower real borrowing cost without indexation. Similarly, lenders with marginal tax rates greater than τ* receive lower real returns than they would with indexation and lenders with marginal tax rates less than τ* receive higher real returns. These differences both raise issues of equity and create deadweight loss by distorting borrowing and lending decisions. For example, lower income individuals generally will have lower marginal tax rates than will higher income individuals. As a result, lower income individuals will face higher real borrowing costs than will higher income individuals with respect to deductible loans. Efficiency issues are raised by the fact that the tax penalty on interest income will encourage institutions and individuals with low marginal rates to become net lenders and institutions and individuals with high marginal rates to become net borrowers.

In addition to the theoretical critiques of the argument that debt indexation is unnecessary because market forces are able to adjust for the failure to index, there is also a strong empirical critique. The empirical work suggests that * * * market interest rates have not adjusted to take into account the payment of taxes on the inflation component of interest. * * *

If market rates have not adjusted to take the inflation tax penalty into account, then real after-tax interest rates are affected strongly by inflation. Therefore, the argument against indexing based on the fact that for every debt there is both a borrower and a lender becomes, at best, an argument about revenue neutrality: Borrowers are helped by the tax penalty, lenders are hurt by the tax penalty, but at least the fisc is kept whole. Even, however, the claim that there is no revenue cost from failing to index debt collapses when it is recognized that borrowers and lenders face different marginal rates. The failure to index debt has already put strong pressure on the tax treatment of debt and as a result, the rules concerning the tax treatment of interest already have been changed significantly to limit the ability to deduct the inflationary component of debt. Thus, for individual borrowers, the disallowance of consumer interest, the investment interest limitation, the at-risk rules, and the passive loss rules all can be seen as ad hoc measures necessary in part to cope with the overstatement of interest expense and the resulting tax arbitrage opportunities. In the case of corporations, much of the pressure on the debt-equity distinction is due to the failure to index interest deductions. Indexing debt would take significant pressure off the tax system by reducing both the value of the interest deduction and the cost of holding debt.

Indexing Assets but not Liabilities: The Problem of Arbitrage

Partial Indexation

While in many respects, the case for indexing liabilities is as strong, if not stronger, than the case for indexing assets, the political reality is that there is pressure to index assets without indexing liabilities. * * * The primary reason that indexing assets is more popular than indexing liabilities is that, for the most part, indexing assets creates only winners, while indexing liabilities creates losers as well as winners. The secondary reason is complexity. Opponents of indexing debt argue that the two-sided nature of debt makes indexing both less necessary and more complex. Indexing assets without liabilities, however, enhances arbitrage opportunities. Thus, while in isolation, asset indexation may be a good idea, asset indexation is less attractive in a system in which there is unindexed debt.

To put the arbitrage problem in stark relief, consider a taxpayer entering into an entirely debt-financed transaction. A fully leveraged taxpayer would have equal amounts of inflationary gain on the asset side and inflationary loss on the liability side. Therefore, ignoring timing differences caused by the realization requirement, her net income is as accurately measured by making no corrections for inflation as it is by fully correcting for inflation. Correcting for inflation on the asset side while failing to correct for inflation on the liability side causes her net income to be seriously understated. The following example provides a numerical demonstration of the problems caused by partial indexation.

> *Example 39*: *Margot* buys an asset for $100, fully financing the purchase with debt. The debt bears a 15% nominal interest rate and the inflation rate is 10%. One year later, *Margot* sells the asset for $120, repays the debt with $115, and is left with $5.

> *No indexing*: Without indexing, *Margot* has $20 of gain, a $15 interest deduction and net income of $5.

> *Comprehensive indexing*:   If both the debt and the asset were indexed, *Margot* would have gain on the asset of only $10 and an indexed interest deduction of only $5. Her net income again would be $5.

> *Indexing assets but not liabilities*: If only the asset were indexed, *Margot* would have a gain of $5 and an interest deduction of $15 and, therefore, a net loss of $10.

As *Example 39* demonstrates, under some circumstances, indexing assets without liabilities produces the least accurate measurement of net income.

Comprehensive indexing and no indexing are only equivalent when the taxpayer's basis in the indexed asset and the indexed liability are identical.
* * *

[A]s an empirical matter, both the assumption that the lender is paying a proxy tax and the assumption that interest rates will have risen to account for the proxy tax are questionable. As a result of the clientele effect, lenders tend to be in lower tax brackets than do borrowers. Therefore, in general, the taxes paid by the lender fail to compensate for the taxes avoided by the borrower. Moreover, empirical studies suggest that nominal interest rates have not risen to compensate for the taxation of the inflationary component of nominal interest. Therefore, not only are the wrong amount of taxes being paid, but, both as a matter of appearance and a matter of reality, they are being paid by the wrong party.

* * *

Conclusion

* * *

One problem with debt indexation is the deductibility of home mortgage interest. There are basically three approaches to home mortgage interest. First, it could be unindexed for both borrower and lender. Second, it could be indexed for lenders, but not borrowers. Third, it could be fully indexed. Of the three alternatives, the last is clearly the best. It represents perhaps the best opportunity to treat home ownership in a more rational fashion. The second is the second-best solution. It limits the damage to the homeowner and makes the revenue cost of the tax expenditure clear. The least attractive alternative is to create a class of unindexed debt in a world of indexation. The primary justification for the first approach over the second approach is revenue, but the revenue would be illusory because the vast majority of mortgage debt would end up in the hands of tax-exempt entities.

Notes and Questions

37.   Professor Engler begins by identifying two principal ways in which current law deviates from true, economic Haig-Simons income. What are these?

38.   Why does Professor Engler contend that correcting only one of these two distortions, without addressing the other, might actually make the overall distortion worse?

39.   Professor Engler reasonably acknowledges complexity as a concern, one which may seem particularly daunting when one contemplates simultaneously embracing both indexation and mark-to-market. Engler is not alone in finding the problems manageable, perhaps more easily managed in tandem than separately. Professor Daniel Halperin, for example, argues that "[m]ark-to-market * * * makes indexing simpler. * * * The most notorious example is stock held under a dividend reinvestment plan. Indexing would require not only keeping track of multiple bases, but also require different inflation adjustments to each, depending on the time of acquisition, even if the entire investment were liquidated at one time."[f]

---

f. Halperin, *supra* note b, at 513.

40. Engler begins with the proposition that, in theory, we would prefer to tax all gain as it accrued (*i.e.*, following Haig-Simons rather than the realization rule). As discussed in Chapter Two, we do not do this due to the burden of annual appraisal and because of liquidity problems that would arise from taxing unrealized appreciation. But without mark-to-market taxation, the taxpayer enjoys an interest-free loan from the Government measured by the uncollected tax on the unrealized appreciation.

The challenge, then, is to find a system that matches in economic effect, or at least approximates, the Haig-Simons ideal, while avoiding the problems of valuation and liquidity.

41. One set of proposals turns on taxing at realization, but including an interest charge to account for the delay in the imposition of the tax. To avoid appraisals, it would be assumed that the appreciation occurred at a uniform rate throughout the period of ownership. As Professor Engler points out, while this system would represent an improvement over present law, as compared to the Haig-Simons mark-to-market ideal it would tend to undertax investors where the gain was concentrated early in the taxpayer's period of ownership, and overtax them when the gain occurred late. Why would the rules have this effect?

42. Engler demonstrates that basis indexation coupled with taxation at realization exactly matches, in present-value terms, mark-to-market taxation, with the deferred tax being charged based on the rate of inflation. Surprisingly, perhaps, this relationship holds regardless of the pattern of growth of value, even when the asset dips in value (and mark-to-market taxation should provide a deductible loss).

43. Somewhat counterintuitively, Professor Engler argues that partial indexation—excluding debt instruments from the indexing regime—may make the indexing system work better. Initially, observe that removing debt from the indexing regime implies higher interest rates, because the lender must charge additional interest to cover not only inflation, but also the tax on the inflation component of the nominal interest rate. The borrower, in turn, pays a higher rate of interest (as compared to that which would obtain if the tax system indexed debt), but is allowed a deduction for the full nominal interest.

The effect of this, Professor Engler demonstrates, is that the taxpayer who is receiving a tax-free loan from the Government (by deferral of the tax on the unrealized appreciation) will now find that the implicit interest charge is higher—not merely the rate of inflation, but the interest rate that would be required to match the rate of inflation in a world with taxes. (Thus, if inflation were three percent and taxes were imposed at a flat rate of 40 percent, obtaining an after-tax yield of three percent would require an interest rate of five percent.)

As an empirical matter, Professor Shuldiner questions whether the interest rate in fact reacts to inflation as Professor Engler argues that it should in theory.

44. Engler suggests that the resulting implied interest rate would closely track the prevailing rates on short-term Government debt, and would frequently exceed it. Is this rate appropriate?

45. Professor Engler argues that adoption of his proposal should be accompanied by abolition of preferential capital gains tax rates. Why might the argument for ending the preference be stronger than under present law?

46. Interestingly, Professor Shuldiner begins by discussing an instance in which inflation reduces, rather than increases, the real tax. Why is the real burden of schedular (per-item) excise taxes reduced by inflation?

47. What is your reaction to the Danish approach, under which the income tax structure is indexed to changes in earnings, rather than to changes in prices? Assuming real economic growth, this provides a larger inflation adjustment. Which measure of inflation is more appropriate?

48. For Social Security *taxes*, increases in the tax base are tied to growth in earnings. Social Security *benefits*, by contrast, are tied to price increases. Is this appropriate? Assuming real growth, is the Government inconsistently imposing a heads-I-win-tails-you-lose set of inflation adjustments?

49. Professor Shuldiner makes the counterintuitive observation that inflation is a lesser problem for gains accruing over long periods of time than for gains accruing over short periods. Why?

50. Why, by contrast, does a longer holding period exacerbate the distortions of inflation in the case of loss assets?

51. Generally, the error of failure to index tends to be offset by the failure to mark to market. In what sense might mark-to-market without indexation be viewed as a tax on wealth? Why would Professor Shuldiner regard this as an unfortunate method of taxing wealth?

52. If a taxpayer purchases depreciable property for $1,000, the depreciation deduction is a form of allowing the taxpayer a deduction of $1,000 over time. Shuldiner asserts that the taxpayer should be entitled to a greater deduction to offset inflation during the period of ownership. Why?

53. We normally think about the effect of inflation on a capital asset held for a period of time. Why is ordinary business income—for example, that of a retailer—affected by inflation? Is LIFO an adequate answer to the problem of inflation? Why is LIFO not more widely used?

54. Professor Shuldiner notes that the Treasury has proposed indexing of inventories, but "Congress has been unwilling to do so." Is congressional acquiescence essential? Some commentators argue that indexation can be achieved administratively: "After conducting an analysis of the Code and its legislative history, as well as of the relevant general principles of administrative law, we concluded in August 1992, that the Treasury would have the authority to index capital gains without an amendment to the Code."[g] The Justice Department's Office of Legal Counsel, however, came to the opposite conclusion.[h]

55. Professor Engler went so far as to suggest that leaving debt out of an indexation system might make it work better. Clearly, Professor Shuldiner disagrees, asserting that in some instances indexing assets without indexing debt might be worse than no indexing at all. (See Example 39.)

56. Even if indexing were generally adopted, and even if indexing generally extended to debt, indexing home mortgages would be politically problematic. Presumably, indexing would lead to reduction of the borrower's interest deduction, and even if applied prospectively it might adversely affect housing values. Recall that Treasury I would have protected borrowers from indexing.

Shuldiner's excerpt closes with three options for indexing of home mortgages. How do you rank them in terms of desirability? In terms of political feasibility?

57. Both Engler and Shuldiner see dangers of "tax arbitrage" under a system of partial indexation (inapplicable to debt). Debtors could borrow, deducting nominal interest including the inflation premium, then invest in assets in which only the real return would be taxed. Engler suggests that his proposal would not be worse than present law, because his proposal, by ending the capital gains preference, would end the similar possibility for tax arbitrage of borrowing (deducting interest against ordinary income) to invest in capital assets (upon which gain would be taxed at preferential rates).

---

g. Charles J. Cooper, Michael A. Carvin & Vincent J. Colatriano, *The Legal Authority of the Department of the Treasury to Promulgate a Regulation Providing for the Indexation of Capital Gains*, 12 VA. TAX REV. 631, 636 (1993).

h. *Id. (citing* Memorandum for Jeanne S. Archibald Re: Legal Authority of the Department of the Treasury to Issue Regulations Indexing Capital Gains for Inflation, 16 Op. Off. Legal Counsel 145 (1992).)

58. Tax arbitrage has always been with us. Professor Bradford warns, however, that the stress placed on the system by tax arbitrage is likely to be increasing with the rise of phenomena such as low-cost on-line transactions:

Arguably, it is transactions costs that protect the income tax from much more extensive tax arbitrage than currently exists. * * *

One of the most striking developments in financial markets in recent years has been a steady decline in transactions costs, reflected in the proliferation of new instruments. [Bradford's] Article thus can be read as exploring problems that can be expected to get worse, absent redesign of the rules.[i]

---

i. Bradford, *supra* note a, at 736.

PART VI

ENACTING TAX LAW

This book has been concerned with the issue of what particular provisions of tax law *should* be. The book concludes, however, with a single-chapter part that explores how tax law is in fact made and changed. In evaluating the process, much depends on whether one views the glass as half full or half empty. Otto von Bismarck, Chancellor of the German Empire in the late Nineteenth Century, famously remarked that "The less people know about how sausages and laws are made, the better they'll sleep at night."[a] An even more eminent European statesman, Sir Winston Churchill, sounds a somewhat more encouraging note in his observation that "Democracy is the worst form of government except for all others that have been tried."[b]

---

a. Otto von Bismarck, *quoted in* George Anastaplo, *Legal Realism, The New Journalism, and* The Brethren,1983 DUKE L.J. 1045, 1066 n.44.

   People who quote Bismarck always do so in the course of commenting on the process of lawmaking, as your editor does here. However, perhaps we should pay attention to the other part of the statement, and exhibit more societal concern for the treatment of the hogs and other animals we confine and kill.

b. Winston S. Churchill, Address to the House of Commons (Nov. 11, 1947).

CHAPTER SEVENTEEN

TAXES AND THE
LEGISLATIVE PROCESS

At one time, the complexity and inequity in the tax law were attributed to tax policy. Now the proliferation of tax expenditures, exceptions to exceptions, targeted credits, specialized deductions, cascading definitions, bubbled tax rates, and the swamping of the Code with disguised appropriations provisions suggests that much of the morass that is the tax law is the product of electoral politics.[a]

A. INTRODUCTION

The primary goal of this chapter is an examination of how tax law comes into being. This requires some appreciation of the roles and motivations of at least the following: members of Congress, the President and other executive officials, congressional and executive staffs, affected taxpayers, organizations, lobbyists, media, and voters. The process is not simple—clearly, it is more complex than a generation ago—and it is not particularly pretty. It is important, however.

Attention is given to the important role in the budget process played by revenue estimates. Related to this is the attempt of Congress to control its tendencies toward spending without legislating taxes to pay for the spending, and the resulting increased involvement in tax policy of "spending" congressional committees and executive departments.

The Tax Reform Act of 1986 is treated as a case study, and we shall also examine explanations for the rapid demise of that act's vision of a broad tax base with relatively few special provisions. The chapter closes with an examination of the factors that seem likely to generate considerable legislative activity—certainly in the tax arena—for the foreseeable future.

B. THE ROLE OF ADMINISTRATIVE
AND CONGRESSIONAL STAFF

An understanding of the tax law process in Washington requires some appreciation of the key role played by congressional and Treasury Department staffs. While the focus of this chapter is on the legislative process, the staffs, especially at Treasury, also play key roles in shaping the law in other ways, such as issuance of regulations. The activities of the two staffs principally

---

a. James Edward Maule, *Point & Counterpoint: Tax Policy and Politics*, 20 A.B.A. SEC. TAX'N 16 (2001).

concerned are discussed in articles by Kenneth Gideon, former Assistant Secretary of the Treasury for Tax Policy, and Ronald Pearlman, who served as Assistant Secretary of the Treasury for Tax Policy and later as Chief of Staff of the Joint Committee on Taxation.

TAX POLICY AT THE TREASURY DEPARTMENT: A 20-YEAR PERSPECTIVE
Kenneth W. Gideon[*]
57 Tax Notes 889, 889-91 (1992)

The first assistant secretary for tax policy of the Treasury, Stanley Surrey, took office just over 30 years ago. * * * Institutional concern for tax policy at Treasury is much older. Joint Committee documents from the 1920s make references to Treasury's tax experts. The tax legislative counsel's position dates back to the 1930s, and a number of assistants to the secretary before 1961 had primary responsibility for tax issues. But the modern form of the Office of Tax Policy dates from Surrey's appointment by President Kennedy.

Initially, the single deputy assistant secretary was an economist and supervised the Office of Tax Analysis (OTA), the cadre of career economists who perform the critical tasks of economic studies and revenue estimating. Later, * * * a second deputy assistant secretary for tax policy was added on the legal side. These officials and the OTA economists have a fine reporting relationship to the assistant secretary.

In contrast, the lawyers on the tax policy staff report (in long honored tradition and theory) to the general counsel. In fact, they work for the assistant secretary. So long as everyone concerned understands this, the system works well as it has on most occasions over the past 30 years. * * *

Relationship to the Secretary

Officially described as the Treasury Department's spokesman on matters of tax policy, the assistant secretary's influence derives from serving as the secretary's principal adviser on tax issues. In contrast to my experience at the IRS, where contacts with the secretary's office outside regular staff meetings were limited and typically concerned issues such as the Service's budget, the assistant secretary is literally "on call" at any time. While technology has eliminated John Connolly's strolls down the hall (now there is a direct, push-button telephone line from the secretary's office that bypasses all other secretaries), the immediate and frequent nature of the contacts have not changed. When not at the office, the secretary's operators (who rival their White House counterparts in the ability to find anyone, anywhere, anytime) can always get the call through.

These ubiquitous contacts—ranging from two-minute phone calls to almost endless briefings or budget sessions—are the transmission system for

---

[*]. At time of original publication, partner, Fried, Frank, Harris, Shriver, & Jacobson, Washington, D.C.

tax policy concerns into the public policy decisionmaking process. Maintaining such direct access to the secretary and through him to the White House, is critical if the assistant secretary is to be a credible spokesperson within the administration for Treasury and for the administration before the taxwriting committees. Over the years, various proposals have been made to have the assistant secretary report to the secretary through one of the undersecretaries. It's a bad idea. Unless the undersecretary is prepared to function as the assistant secretary (in which case, the proposal amounts to a change in title, not function), regular and direct access must be maintained for the Tax Policy office to do its job.

Legislation

Perhaps no aspect of the work of the Office of Tax Policy has seen more change in the past 20 years than its role in the legislative process. In 1972, the office could look back on a primary role in the initiation and enactment of the Tax Reform Act of 1969. That participation was itself a function of a more compact legislative process in Congress. Chairman Mills headed a Ways and Means Committee of 25 members (compared to 36 today) with no subcommittees. His committee also served as the Committee on Committees and thus controlled committee assignments for the whole House. The Senate Finance Committee had 16 members then as compared to 20 today, and it, too, had no subcommittees. In that era, if the chairman of the Ways and Means Committee and the chairman of the Finance Committee and their staff at the Joint Committee on Taxation concurred with a Treasury proposal, it was virtually an accomplished fact.

Modern practice is very different, in part because there are so many more active participants in the process and, in part, because the politics of the process have become bitter, but more fundamentally because the issue of revenue has moved from an occasional concern of the Congress, usually left to its specialist committees, to a fundamental limitation in all congressional action. Exploring why this occurred would require a paper of its own (although elimination of the automatic revenue dividend that arose from bracket-creep before indexation of the brackets and the changes in congressional staffing after Watergate would be high on any list of causes).

Now there are many more players. Five active technical staffs on the Hill are engaged with any piece of tax legislation (a majority and minority staff for each tax-writing committee in addition to the Joint Committee staff). All are considerably larger now than they were in 1972 (the Treasury staff is larger, too—but Treasury staff growth has not matched congressional staff growth.) In addition, a member of either taxwriting committee is now likely to have a tax technician on their personal staff (who often takes issue with the committee staffs and Treasury). The organization of the tax writing committees into subcommittees has significantly multiplied the number of subjects that can be addressed at any given time (thereby forcing Treasury to devote time to those issues as well). Treasury finds itself, in this environment, one voice among many.

On a broader scale, Treasury and the taxwriting committees have found Congress and other executive departments less willing to cede authority over revenue issues to their expertise. Budgetary constraints drive other congressional committees and executive departments to seek "revenue offsets" for their programs. Deprived of the steadily increasing revenue base provided by bracket creep, the Congressional Budget Committees and the Office of Management and Budget must assert themselves in defining at least the size of revenue requirements to fulfill their budgetary responsibilities.

But Treasury's core legislative roles remain. Treasury remains a critical initiator of tax system revision, even if its ultimate influence on outcomes has diminished because there are more participants and because the politics of the moment from time to time exclude it from the final decisionmaking process. Treasury studies and initiatives have been precursors not only to major tax reform, but to a variety of less sweeping, but significant changes. Treasury views on legislation are always sought and often heeded. Treasury remains the tax system's primary gatekeeper on "member" issues, saying "no" when it needs to be said (often when others are politically unable to do so).[b]

Tax Administration

Organizationally, the relationship between the Office of Tax Policy and the IRS has changed little in the last 20 years. The commissioner and the assistant secretary each report directly to the secretary and not to each other. The precept of leaving individual case matters to the Service while focusing the Tax Policy staff on issues of general guidance remains intact (and indeed was recently strengthened by Treasury's withdrawal from formal participation in the letter ruling process). Both the commissioner and the assistant secretary must approve a regulation and Treasury staff reviews published rulings and revenue procedures.

But, within these bounds, there has been constant experimentation with the goal of making the guidance process work "better." The objective content of "better" has shifted from time to time. Often "better" means faster—issuing guidance as promptly as possible after significant legislation and avoiding long delays between "proposed" and "final" regulations. At other times, "better" has referred to the quality of the guidance. But what constitutes "quality" guidance has itself undergone cyclic variation. When I served as chief counsel from 1981 to 1983, we were urged to provide "meaningful" guidance (which meant answering as many questions as possible rather than providing broad, general rules). Products of the "meaningful guidance" era were criticized for "hyperlexis," bringing on the current era of "simplification." It will be no

---

b. This refers to a long-standing practice in the Ways and Means Committee of occasionally reporting out a bill containing one provision desired by each committee member and accepted by the whole committee with only cursory review. (Ed.)

surprise to find today's products criticized in the future as insufficiently "meaningful."

Issuing guidance faster is unambiguously desirable. The difficulty has been to balance the need for adequate review with the need for speed. From an institutional standpoint, this has led to an evolution from informal "policy" meetings between senior Treasury and IRS officials, which occurred on an "as needed" basis 20 years ago, to the current structure in which senior officials regularly set priorities for guidance projects and make general policy decisions in response to a staff-generated "issues memorandum" at the commencement of a regulation project. This assures that the general form of a regulation is likely to be acceptable to those who must ultimately approve it and prevents the waste of staff time on approaches having little chance of ultimate publication. * * *

Charting the boundaries between not interfering in individual cases at the Service and making general policy at Treasury may, however, become a significant issue for future tax policy staffs. Significant individual cases can drive policy results, particularly if they become engraved in stone as Supreme Court decisions. A recent case, *Arkansas Best*, illustrates the difficulty: Although the Supreme Court's decision in *Arkansas Best* was rendered with respect to a quite different set of facts, the language of the decision has proved to be a significant impediment to achieving an appropriate policy solution for liability hedges. A mechanism for better harmonizing the positions taken by government litigators, particularly before the Supreme Court, with policy positions of the Treasury Department would be a welcome development.

Revenue Estimating

Treasury has always made revenue estimates, but the significance of this task changed dramatically with the enactment of the Gramm-Rudman-Hollings budget reforms. Revenue neutrality became a legal requirement, enforceable by across-the-board sequester. As the official administration scorekeeper for revenues, OTA's estimates have become critical determinants of policy in the last decade. Because the revenue estimates have become so much more important, there has been increased focus on the revenue-estimating process.

Over time, the process has changed with both OTA and its Joint Committee counterpart seeking to improve their ability to make "dynamic" estimates (i.e., those that account for changes in taxpayer behavior caused by the proposed change rather than simply measuring the impact of the proposal on the current "static" bases). The most notable example has been in capital gains estimating and that example illustrates the difficulties of attempting to predict changes in behavior.

There has been substantial pressure in recent years to include "feedback" effects in the estimates as well (i.e., to estimate the expansion of the overall economy that would occur if a particular proposal were enacted). Thus far, "feedback" estimates have been resisted because the estimators doubt that economic measurements of the overall economy are sufficiently accurate to permit reasonable quantification of such impacts and because there is doubt that growth from a proposal can be distinguished from sector shifts involving little or no overall change in the economy. On a more practical level, "feedback" estimates could undermine budget discipline by providing pork barrel proponents with the argument that the cost of their projects should be offset by the "growth" they will produce.

Studies

Some of Treasury's best work over the past 20 years has arisen from integrating its economic and legal staffs to produce studies. Some are legendary: for examples *Blueprints* and the 1984 tax reform study.[c] But the range of studies has been very wide and their impact as precursors of legislative change is apparent. The principal change over the last 20 years has been the increasing tendency of Congress to award mandated studies as consolation prizes to disappointed legislative hopefuls. Good and worthwhile studies typically require substantial staff effort and a great deal of time (often two to three years). They cannot be mass produced and ought not to be trivialized.

Tax Treaties

The most noticeable change since 1972 with respect to treaties has been the heightened concern about treaty abuse. This concern has led to both legislative action and treaty renegotiations to limit treaty shopping and, in a few notable cases, to treaty terminations. The pace of substantive law legislative change has also created an environment in which treaty modernization, either through the negotiation of protocols or complete renegotiation (e.g., the German treaty), now consumes as much or more of the staff's time than the negotiation of new conventions. While the treaty process has benefited from the talents of a succession of talented lawyers on the ITC [International Tax Counsel] staff over the past 20 years, the senior Treasury economists who work in the treaty area have been in place during the entire period since 1972 and have furnished an invaluable store of knowledge, experience, and institutional memory.

Staffing

The professional staff of the Office of Tax Policy is approximately 30 percent larger today than it was in 1972. Career tenure for the economic staff is in transition. In 1972, most OTA professionals expected to make a career of government service. Significantly more attractive financial opportunities in the private sector have led to higher turnover in OTA in recent years and may in time cause recruiting for the OTA staff to more closely resemble recruiting for the legal staff. As was true in 1972, the legal staff is recruited by finding the best young lawyers in the country and attempting to lure them to Treasury

---

c. U.S. DEP'T OF TREASURY, BLUEPRINTS FOR BASIC TAX REFORM (1977); U.S. DEP'T OF TREASURY, REPORT ON TAX REFORM FOR FAIRNESS, SIMPLICITY, AND ECONOMIC GROWTH (1984) ("Treasury I"). Treasury I was the study that formed the basis for the Tax Reform Act of 1986. (Ed.)

for a two- to three-year tour. Unlike 1972, the invitation now almost invariably requires financial sacrifice since Treasury pay scales seldom allow the Office to match outside compensation.

* * *

THE TAX LEGISLATIVE PROCESS: 1972-1992
Ronald A. Pearlman[*]
57 Tax Notes 939, 939-43 (1992)

There are a number of possible explanations for the explosion in the volume and complexity of tax legislation. To an important extent, it may be attributable to changes in the tax legislative process. The following commentary focuses on several of the more significant changes in the process since 1972. They are: (1) the emergence of the budget deficit as an issue of intense public debate and the changes since the mid-1970s in the federal budget process; (2) changes in the size and organization of the taxwriting committees and the size, sophistication, and responsibilities of the various congressional tax staffs; and (3) at least since 1986, the diminution in the role of the Treasury Department in the tax legislative process.

The Deficit and the Budget Process

The fiscal year 1972 budget deficit was $ 23.4 billion. Although not very large when compared to $ 290.2 billion for fiscal year 1992, the fact of increasing annual budget deficits concerned congressional budget policymakers in the 1970s and particularly impacted the tax legislative process in the 1980s.[6] In fact, the deficit and changes in the budget process beginning in 1974 may well be the two developments that have resulted in a tax legislative process today that is so different than that of the early 1970s.

Three budget-related developments have influenced the tax legislative process: (1) changes in the budget process itself; (2) the refusal of the Reagan and Bush administrations to support tax-rate increases but a willingness to agree to loophole closures, base broadeners, and certain other "indirect" revenue increases; and (3) the indexing of tax brackets and personal exemptions in 1981, thereby eliminating the annual increase in federal revenues resulting from bracket creep. * * * [M]uch of the tax legislation of the 1970s was designed, at least in part, to offset bracket creep.[9]

Since 1972, three major pieces of budget legislation have been enacted: the Budget Act of 1974, the Gramm-Rudman-Hollings enforcement mechanisms,[11] and the expenditure caps and pay-as-you-go enforcement feature of the 1990 Budget Act. The impact on the tax legislative process,

---

[*]. At time of original publication, partner, Covington & Burling, Washington, D.C.

6. The first budget reconciliation legislation was enacted as the Omnibus Reconciliation Act of 1980, Pub. L. No. 96-499, 94 Stat. 2599 (1980).

9. Leonard, "Perspectives on the Tax Legislative Process," 38 *Tax Notes* 969, 971-72 (1988).

11. Balanced Budget and Emergency Deficit Control Act of 1985, Pub. L. No. 99-177, 99 Stat. 1037, section 200, et seq. (1985).

particularly during the 1980s, of the budget deficit and changes in the budget process is reflected in at least four developments during this period. First, in recent years, the budget process frequently has required the taxwriting committees to adopt revenue-increasing tax legislation in response to mandated budget reconciliation resolutions without regard to whether members of the committees thought that changes in the tax law were appropriate either as a matter of policy or timing.[13]

The second effect on tax legislation has been the relatively recent emergence of the concept of revenue neutrality. The Treasury Department adopted revenue neutrality as one of the benchmarks of its 1984 tax reform recommendations to the president as a means of constraining a process that easily could have turned into a massive deficit increasing exercise. President Reagan also adopted this standard in his 1985 tax reform recommendations to Congress and, since then, revenue neutrality has been honored informally as a legislative constraint by the taxwriting committees. A revenue neutrality restriction was formalized in the "pay-as-you-go" provisions of the 1990 Budget Act.

The revenue-neutrality constraint has been a double-edged sword. It has limited the number and size of revenue-losing changes in the tax law that might have further increased the deficit or represented bad tax policy. However, it also has restricted the ability to enact revenue-losing proposals that were considered to be economically sound or were designed merely to correct substantive defects in existing law. Revenue neutrality also has complicated the design of new substantive tax law changes, even those intended to increase revenues. This has been true particularly when such initiatives were included in a revenue-neutral tax package of revenue losers and revenue raisers as often occurred in the late 1980s. When a new proposal that was part of such a package initially was represented as raising a certain amount of revenue, it became very difficult to change the proposal during the course of the legislative process in response to public comment if the proposed change reduced the revenue raising potential of the proposal. This frequently was the case even if the change was intended merely to make the proposal more administrable or to provide appropriate transition relief. As a result, the ultimate substantive design of revenue proposals enacted during this period, even when grounded in sound tax policy, has been distorted by the revenue neutrality constraint.

The third effect of the current budget process on the development of tax legislation is the importance now attached to revenue estimates. In 1972, revenue estimates were more or less an afterthought, considered after policy decisions were made. The relative unimportance of revenue estimates at the time is evidenced by the minor resources devoted to revenue estimates by the

---

13. The 1974 Budget Act required the Congress to adopt annual budget reconciliation resolutions that directed the taxwriting committees to increase revenues by specified dollar amounts.

Joint Committee on Taxation, Congress' official revenue estimator. In 1972, the Joint Committee employed three revenue estimators and one revenue analyst. The Joint Committee estimators did not have access to a computer model and their data sources were very limited. (Treasury estimators had been using a computerized individual tax model since the mid-1960s.) Today, there are 14 revenue estimators and four computer analysts on the Joint Committee revenue estimating staff. Moreover, the estimating process is dependent on a greatly expanded data base and on sophisticated computer analyses. The revenue estimating staff serving in Treasury's Office of Tax Analysis (OTA) in the early 1970s was larger than that of the Joint Committee (in 1972, seven estimators and three statisticians) in large part because OTA had the responsibility to estimate receipts for budgeting purposes. However, even at Treasury, there has been a rather substantial growth in the size of the estimating staff. Today, there are 14 revenue estimators and 10 computer modeling specialists on the OTA staff.

A fourth outgrowth of changes in the budget process is the increase in the number of people on Capitol Hill who are indirectly involved in the tax legislative process. The 1974 Budget Act created the House and Senate Budget Committees and the Congressional Budget Office (CBO). The two budget committees are responsible for developing and implementing the annual congressional budget resolution and, therefore, have a direct interest in revenue legislation and an ability to influence the tax legislative process through revenue-raising reconciliation instructions. It also has become increasingly common for individual members of the budget committees to put forth specific tax legislative proposals. In addition, as an adjunct to CBO's responsibility to estimate annual budget receipts and the revenue effects of certain nonincome tax legislative proposals, its staff of 19 professional tax policy analysts have assumed an active role in the tax policy process through the publication of CBO's annual compendium of revenue options[17] and other periodic tax policy analyses.[18] Although these budget-related organizations have played a relatively modest role in effecting specific substantive changes in the tax law when compared to the role of the taxwriting committees and the traditional congressional tax staffs, their role in the budget process has enabled them to broadly influence the tax debate.

Changes in the Size and Composition of the Taxwriting Committees and Congressional Tax Staffs

The most dramatic changes since 1972 relating to people involved in the tax legislative process are reflected in the increased size of the taxwriting committees, the creation of subcommittees, the growth and increased

---

17. *See, e.g., Reducing the Deficit: Spending and Revenue Options* (Congressional Budget Office, 1992).

18. *See, e.g., The Changing Distribution of Federal Taxes: 1975-1990* (Congressional Budget Office, 1987) and *The Changing Distribution of Federal Taxes: A Closer Look at 1980* (Congressional Budget Office, 1988).

prominence of the taxwriting committee professional tax staffs, and the employment of tax legislative assistants on the taxwriting committee members' personal staffs.

In 1972, the Ways and Means Committee was comprised of 24 members. Today, the committee is almost 50 percent larger with a membership of 35. The Senate Finance Committee also has increased in size since 1972 (from 16 to 20 members), but not as dramatically as the Ways and Means Committee. In 1972, neither the Ways and Means Committee nor the Finance Committee had subcommittees.[19] In late 1974, the Ways and Means Committee formed the Oversight Subcommittee and, in 1977, the Miscellaneous Revenue Measures Subcommittee, the predecessor to the present Select Revenue Measures Subcommittee.   The Finance Committee first organized a Subcommittee on Administration of the Internal Revenue Code in 1975 and the Subcommittee on Taxation and Debt Management in 1977. Currently, among its eight subcommittees, two are primarily tax related, the Subcommittee on Taxation and the Subcommittee on Private Retirement Plans and Oversight of the IRS. * * * [T]he Ways and Means subcommittees, and particularly the Oversight Subcommittee, have played important roles in initiating certain tax legislation. The Finance Committee subcommittees, on the other hand, have no legislative authority and no separate staffs and, therefore, have played a less important role.

In examining the relative roles of the congressional tax staffs, it is clear that in 1972, the Joint Committee on Taxation was dominant both in terms of size and influence and that Dr. Lawrence Woodworth, the Joint Committee Chief of Staff since 1964, was the most influential tax staff member on Capitol Hill. The Joint Committee staff was comprised of 19 professional members, excluding the lawyers responsible for refund cases within the committee's jurisdiction. The Ways and Means Committee tax staff, on the other hand, was comprised of two individuals on the majority side and one on the minority side, and the Finance Committee tax staff was comprised of two individuals who served both the majority and minority members of the committee. Substantive responsibility for the design of tax legislative proposals and implementation of the committees' tax policy decisions rested almost exclusively with the staff of the Joint Committee and the House and Senate Legislative Counsel. As late as 1974, for example, the Ways and Means Committee tax staff did not attend legislative drafting sessions.

Although the Joint Committee staff has expanded during the 21-year period and presently numbers 51 professionals, the growth and increased influence of the taxwriting committee staffs and the employment of tax legislative assistants on the personal staffs of the members of the taxwriting committees are most noteworthy. Today, the Ways and Means Committee

---

19. The Ways and Means Committee previously had subcommittees until the early 1960s, when they were disbanded until the mid-1970s.

majority tax staff is comprised of eight individuals, and there are five professional members of the minority tax staff. In addition, the Ways and Means Oversight Subcommittee majority staff has seven professional members, and the minority staff has one professional member. The Finance Committee tax staff also has increased in size since the early 1970s. Today, the Democratic [majority] staff is comprised of seven individuals and the Republican [minority] staff, of four individuals.

In 1972, the taxwriting committee members did not employ tax legislative assistants on their personal staffs. Since the early 1980s, however, most Ways and Means Committee members have employed individuals who devote most of their time to tax matters,[20] and since the beginning of the 101st Congress, a portion of the salaries of committee members' tax legislative assistants has been paid out of the Ways and Means Committee budget, thereby enabling the committee members to hire more experienced individuals. Members of the Finance Committee began employing specialized personal staff members in 1977, after Senators received budget authority to increase the size of their personal staffs. Today, the House and Senate taxwriting committee members' legislative assistants often are directly involved in the development of legislation of particular interest to the members for whom they work. These legislative assistants look to, and expect support from, the taxwriting committee and Joint Committee staffs in implementing the members' objectives.

The General Accounting Office (GAO) and the Congressional Research Service (CRS) are not directly involved in the development of tax legislation but are indirectly involved in the tax policy process. The Tax Policy and Administration Division of GAO undertakes a large number of tax studies at the request of members of Congress, the taxwriting committees, and the congressional tax staffs and serves as a major investigative and data resource. Presently, the Division employs 75 professionals based both in Washington and in other locations; in 1972, the Division was not even in existence. The CRS employs approximately 20 economists and lawyers in its American Law and Economics Divisions (as compared to approximately five individuals in the early 1970s). These individuals, who are tax specialists, serve as legal and policy resources to members of Congress and regularly publish analyses of important current tax policy topics.

The increase in the size of the taxwriting committees, particularly on the House side, and the existence of subcommittees has resulted in a somewhat increased democratization of the committee legislative process during the past 21 years, although it would be inaccurate to understate the continued substantial influence of the committee chairmen. Compared to 1972, when the staff of the Joint Committee dominated the scene, the expanded size and

---

20. Previously, on occasion, several Ways and Means Committee members would pool resources to employ a professional tax legislative assistant.

increased quality of the taxwriting committee tax staffs, as well as the addition of tax legislative assistants on the committee members' personal staffs, has significantly increased the number of people involved in the development of tax legislation and has served to diffuse the decisionmaking process at the staff level. Some have suggested that the increases in the size of the taxwriting committees and the number of congressional tax staff have themselves contributed to the increased volume of tax legislation on the theory that the job of a legislature is to legislate.

Role of the Administration and the Treasury Department

The administrations of five presidents have had the opportunity to influence federal tax policy during the past 21 years. Surely, President Reagan's 1981 tax reduction initiatives and his 1985 tax reform initiatives put him at the forefront during this period in influencing the course of federal budget and tax policy.

The Treasury Department's Office of Tax Policy (OTP) has served as the administration's tax policy professional staff throughout the period. In 1972, the OTP was comprised of approximately 73 professionals; today, the professional staff, including members of the Office of Tax Analysis, numbers 93. It would be inaccurate to attribute the increase in the size of the OTP staff solely to its legislative responsibilities because a large part of the office's work relates to, among other things, regulatory and other interpretative responsibilities, the administration of the U.S. tax treaty network, and other international tax policy matters. However, there have been times during the past 21 years when pending tax legislation was the staff's highest priority and strained the office's resources.

One aspect of the structure of the Treasury Department generally, and of the OTP specifically, that largely goes unnoticed has been the relative lack of continuity, particularly when compared to the congressional tax leadership and tax staffs. * * *

The lack of continuity, * * * particularly among the lawyers who are active in the legislative process, puts Treasury at a disadvantage when dealing with the committee leadership and congressional staff. It simply is not possible to understand the inner workings of the legislative process and establish the necessary interpersonal relationships on Capitol Hill during a relatively brief tenure. In addition, many of the legislative initiatives that are active at any point in time have been considered previously. Yet, anyone new to the tax legislative process, whether at Treasury or on Capitol Hill, may not be familiar with recent history, let alone understand what happened five years ago.

* * *

Notes and Questions

1.   The Joint Committee on Taxation (JCT) was the first joint Congressional Committee established on a permanent basis with a professional staff. The Joint Congressional Budget Committee was modeled after it.

The JCT staff is not duplicative of the staffs of the House Ways and Means Committee and the Senate Finance Committee. Historically, the JCT staff has provided the advantage of continuity, because it did not change when control of Congress shifted from one party to the other. The JCT staff provides a different sort of continuity by following revenue bills from the House to the Senate. By custom, JCT staff members have been left to develop a level of professionalism and expertise that could not be duplicated in the staff of a House or Senate committee, who are more closely tied to the political fortunes of the chair and his party.

2.   Both the Tax Legislative Counsel (TLC) and the JCT have functions in addition to tax legislation, but these do not detract from the performance of legislative duties. The TLC staff reviews drafts of Treasury Regulations which ordinarily are written in the Internal Revenue Service. This review gives the TLC staff a broader perspective on tax issues. (Unfortunately, attention to tax legislative issues often results in inordinate delays in reviewing and clearing regulations.)

The JCT reviews large tax refunds before they are paid by the Revenue Service. While this requires final review by the Chief of Staff, most of the refund review work is carried out by a separate division of the staff that does not ordinarily work on legislation.

3.   Yet another function of staffs is the preparation of "studies." Mr. Gideon notes the danger of mandated studies being included in bills as "consolation prizes," thereby diverting limited staff resources.

4.   The importance of "bracket creep" and its elimination is discussed elsewhere in this book, from Chapter One to Chapter Sixteen. Mr. Gideon observes that because indexing deprives the Government of automatic "real" tax increases caused by inflation, Congress no longer has the periodic opportunity to enact politically easy tax cuts.

This development tends to expand the list of tax legislation "players" beyond the tax-writing congressional committees and Treasury. As Gideon observes, "the Congressional Budget Office and the Office of Management and Budget must assert themselves in defining at least the size of revenue requirements to fulfill their budgetary responsibilities."

More broadly, the end of bracket creep is one factor increasing the pressure on Congress to cut expenditures or to increase taxes. Other congressional committees and executive departments, seeking to protect spending programs, are likely to seek "revenue offsets."

5.   Mr. Pearlman identifies four developments over the past 30 years that have effected significant change in the tax legislative process. What are these four developments? Which is most important? Why?

6.   Professor Sheldon Pollack emphasizes the key role of "experts":
    Perhaps the most prominent example of this dynamic was the enactment of tax reform in 1986. The tax experts in Treasury, along with academic proponents, had been campaigning for tax reform for decades. The issue arose on the tax policy agenda only after the president and congressional leadership were prodded into action by congressional policy entrepreneurs. It is true that in the end, the traditional leadership of Congress was most responsible for assuring a legislative victory. The tax policy agenda, however, had been set well before the time congressional leadership became crucial. In addition, much of the real impact of tax reform was felt only later in the implmentation of particular policies through regulations devised by the experts and professionals in the tax bureaucracy.
    In many more mundane cases, the agenda may be set and controlled by tax experts, who in particularly technical matters may be the only ones in the federal government who are aware of and comprehend the specific abuses of the tax law that are to be corrected. Many of the more technical and highly arcane provisions enacted into the the tax law in the past decade found their way onto the tax agenda, and then into law, exclusively on account of the persistence of tax experts and professionals in the bureaucracy and on the staffs of the tax committees.[d]

C. THE ROLE OF BUDGET CONSTRAINTS AND REVENUE ESTIMATES

In Subchapter B, both Messrs. Gideon and Pearlman emphasized the role of budget constraints. These restraints have been particularly acute since enactment of the Economic Recovery Tax Act of 1981, which directly reduced revenues and, ultimately more important, eliminated future "bracket creep." Congress now operates under a self-imposed restriction that requires revenue-losing tax legislation to be accompanied by offsetting estimated revenue increases or expenditure reductions. Revenue estimates have acquired enormous importance.

Revenue estimating is not an exact science. There are two official sources of revenue estimates: the Office of Tax Analysis (OTA) in the Treasury Department, and the Staff of the Joint Committee on Taxation (JCT). Their estimates are based, respectively, on projections for the overall economy by the Office of Management and Budget (OMB) and the Congressional Budget Office

---

d. Sheldon D. Pollack, *A New Dynamics of Tax Policy?*, 12 AM. J. TAX POL'Y 61, 70 (1995).

(CBO). Even when the OTA and JCT estimates coincide, they are not always correct. When they are at variance with one another, the estimators find themselves involved in tax policy disputes. The revenue effect of a 1990 proposed cut in capital gains tax rates, discussed in the excerpt from Mr. Bopp's article, is a case in point. Professor Graetz, who served as Deputy Assistant Secretary of Treasury under the first President Bush, contends that revenue estimates have taken on a tail-wagging-the-dog quality, as inherently inaccurate revenue estimates are allowed unduly to constrain the policy choices of political actors.

THE ROLES OF REVENUE ESTIMATION AND SCORING IN THE FEDERAL BUDGET PROCESS
Michael D. Bopp[*]
56 Tax Notes 1629, 1645-47 (1992)

Problems With the Existing Revenue Estimation Processes

Though the revenue estimating process is challenged by a number of problems, this section focuses upon two—the inaccuracy and politicization that threaten the efficacy and integrity of revenue estimates. These two "problems" might also be thought of as symptoms of other, underlying difficulties, upon which the following discussion will elaborate. Both the OTA and the JCT, as well as private revenue estimators, are, in varying degrees, faced daily with these problems.

As a starting point for discussion, this section will focus upon the accuracy and politicization considerations raised by the recent controversy over capital gains revenue estimates. The controversy embraced elements of both problems and has helped incite efforts to reform the process.

When two government entities derive significantly different revenue estimates for the same legislative proposal, the controversy threatens an erosion of public confidence. Revenue estimation is the practical application of a social science—economics—to the inner workings of the U.S. tax system. Revenue estimation differs from more theoretical applications of economics in that the former practice demands quantification of behavioral assumptions. But, predicting and quantifying people's behavior is inherently speculative, and revenue estimators possess no particular clairvoyance into the minds of individuals. And when the JCT and the OTA derive different estimates of behavior effects, charges of politicization are inevitably raised.

The JCT and the OTA produced well-publicized, disparate estimates of President Bush's capital gains proposal in late 1990.[181] The JCT believed that the proposal would lose $11.4 billion in Treasury receipts over five years,

---

*. At time of original publication, associate, Kutak Rock, Washington, D.C.

181. The proposal afforded an exclusion from income for capital assets held for at least one year. The exclusion increased from 10 percent for assets held at least one year, but less than two years, to 30 percent for assets held three years or more.

whereas the OTA estimated a $12.5 billion revenue increase.[d] What explains the greatest share of the disparity between these estimates is a divergence in assumptions regarding the effect of the proposal on realizations, or the elasticity of realization response with respect to taxes. * * *

Problems of Inaccuracy

The different assumptions adopted by the JCT and the OTA might be explained by structural problems that plague government revenue estimation. One could reason that revenue estimation is inherently inaccurate and is unworthy of the imprimatur of science. Ironically, this position is bolstered by the JCT admission that "the choice of an elasticity is ultimately a judgment call,"[185] and by acknowledgments that both elasticity assumptions are reasonable. The effects of these acknowledgments are ironic, because they attempt to restore confidence in the revenue estimating process, though they ultimately betray the speculative nature of the undertaking.

The accuracy of both the JCT's and the OTA's elasticities has been called into question by a recent study. The study, conducted by Congressional Research Service economist Jane Gravelle, indicates that both government revenue estimating bodies adopted elasticities figures that are too high.[187] Gravelle's results "imply a revenue loss from a gains cut which is at least twice what the JCT projects, and probably more than five times as great."[188]

Gravelle's study, it might be argued, assumes particular importance in light of the difficulties associated with evaluating the accuracy of revenue estimates. These difficulties stem from an inability to hold constant all revenue influences other than the provision being examined; an inability to isolate a single tax law change. Only aggregate revenue figures are determined with certainty. Thus, when GAO analysts attempted to ascertain, on the basis of Statistics of Income data, the accuracy of prior OTA revenue estimates, they confessed an inability to "claim any added measure of accuracy for our projected baseline of what revenues might have been had tax provisions not been introduced or altered."[191] The authors nevertheless did attempt to measure the accuracy of a number of OTA estimates, including an estimate of the relaxation of IRA requirements in 1981. They found substantial inaccuracies in the OTA estimates, concluding that the OTA's revenue estimate of legislation providing for IRAs was off "by a factor of at least

---

d. In 1990, OTA was part of President Bush's Treasury Department. JCT, on the other hand, was a joint committee drawn from the two tax-writing committees, both controlled by Democrats who opposed the Republican President's capital gain tax proposal. (Ed.)

185. Staff of Joint Comm. on Taxation, 101st Cong., 2d Sess., *Explanation of Methodology Used to Estimate Proposals Affecting the Taxation of Income from Capital Gains* 7 (Comm. Print 1990).

187. Gravelle, *Can a Capital Gains Tax Cut Pay for Itself?* 14 (CRS Report for Congress, March 23, 1990).

188. Hoerner, "Treasury and JCT Both Off Mark in Estimating Revenue Effects of Capital Gains Cut, CRS Finds," 50 *Tax Notes* 1329 (March 25, 1991).

191. Dehorn, McColl, and Jantscher, "Revenue Estimating: A More Prominent Part of Tax Policy," *The GAO Journal* 64, 68 (Summer 1988).

four."[192] The GAO analysts concluded that "[w]hen a change in a provision allows taxpayers a number of alternative responses, economic models are less likely to yield an accurate prediction of how the change will play out in the 'real world.'"[193]

In contrast to this rather gloomy appraisal of government revenue estimation [stand] a number of arguments made in its defense. * * *

The GAO analysis is similarly subject to a criticism. The analysis is undermined by the argument that ex post facto analyses of revenue estimating accuracy are conjectural endeavors.[196] More specifically, it has been argued that it is impossible to quantify the decrease in tax revenues attributable to IRA provisions because "[t]here is no way to know whether monies placed into IRAs were fully taxable under prior law, partly taxable, or sheltered."[197] In short, there are too many variables imbedded in the Internal Revenue Code to know with certainty what a taxpayer would have done had one variable been added or taken away.

Some commentators and estimators have suggested that problems of revenue estimation inaccuracy can be ameliorated with fairly straightforward improvements. The chief explanation for the difference between Gravelle's and the government estimators' elasticity figures centers upon time, one former OTA estimator noted. Government revenue estimators do not possess enough of it to delve into all of the assumptions that they must determine. And the trend has been such that revenue estimators have increasingly less time to spend per estimate. A number of revenue estimators perceive that the solution to this predicament is to increase the resources of the JCT and the OTA. It seems not implausible that 550 revenue estimates is too heavy a burden for the Joint Committee's 10 estimators to shoulder in one year. Indeed, most revenue estimates engender complex and time consuming activities including data gathering, economic formulations, and computer modelling.[202]

Another possible, partial solution, is to improve the available data. Revenue estimators could better determine behavioral variables if they had access to different forms of data. This point is no more apparent than in the

---

192. *Id.*

193. *Id.* at 71.

196. It is also contradicted by another ex post facto assessment of revenue estimating accuracy, one performed by the CBO. The CBO's analysis attempted to assess the OTA's overall revenue estimating accuracy for the period, 1963-1978. It concluded that OTA receipts estimates were accurate "to within one percent of actual collections" after adjusting for inaccuracies in the economic forecast and the fact that proposed tax legislation was not enacted. A Review of the Accuracy of Treasury Revenue Forecasts, 1963-1978 17 (CBO Staff Working Paper, Feb. 1981).

197. Barry L. Dennis, Remarks at the Tax Executives Institute 41st Midyear Conference (March 26, 1991).

202. If adding to the staffs of JCT and OTA would not solve the problems of inaccuracy, perhaps a better solution is one suggested by commentator Rob Bennett. He posits that "[i]t might even be a good thing if lawmakers were told they could not obtain an unlimited number of estimates. The fact that JCT estimates are a 'free good' seems to have created an unquenchable thirst for ever more estimates." Bennett, "About Those 'Technical Differences,'" 50 Tax Notes 891, 892 (Feb. 25, 1991).

context of estimating the revenue effects of a change in the tax treatment of capital gains. Efforts to refine and improve revenue estimating data have focused mainly on creating a more complete, though static, picture of U.S. taxpayers. What is lacking is longitudinal data, data that traces the tax status of individuals over a number of years. One analyst, who helps disseminate and package data used by both government and private revenue estimators, has noted the need for longitudinal data in examining taxpayer behavior with respect to capital gains. He argues that:

> [T]he policy implications are quite different if, on the one hand, most people realize gains at only a few points in their lives (e.g., selling a home or a business, or cashing in assets post-retirement) or if, on the other hand, they typically realize gains every single year (e.g., stock market speculators). . . . [N]o amount of data analysis of single-shot, one-year tax returns can shed any light on this matter. . . . Thus, whether to analyze existing tax systems or to be ready to analyze future tax systems, it is imperative that we acquire more longitudinal information on taxpayers.[204]

But, better data and a heavier staff would not, by themselves, cause the JCT and the OTA to produce the same capital gains revenue estimate. A factor that accounts for $2 billion, or eight percent of the discrepancy between the existing JCT and OTA estimates, is the baseline amount of realizations assumed by each estimating body. The "baseline" figure predicts the amount of realizations that will occur over the next five years under current law. The OTA used OMB figures, which forecast $1,466 billion in realizations between 1990 and 1995. The JCT adopted the CBO baseline figure, which predicted $1,604 billion in realizations, or 9.4 percent more realizations than expected by OMB.

* * *

PAINT-BY-NUMBERS TAX LAWMAKING
Michael J. Graetz[*]

95 Columbia Law Review 609, 613-14, 668-82 (1995)

Congressional decisionmaking regarding both the revenue and distributional questions reveals a unitary weakness in the current tax legislative process: Congressional decisionmakers routinely suffer from illusions of precision. Congress today seems to want tax policymaking to turn on simple numerical answers, reminiscent of the supercomputer Deep Thought, who in the science fiction classic, The Hitchhiker's Guide to the Galaxy, revealed that the answer to the "great Question of Life, the Universe and Everything" was "42." Armed with mathematical answers to both revenue and distributional questions, tax policymakers routinely eschew the difficulties

---

204. Bristol, "Tax Modelling and the Policy Environment of the 1990s," 8 *SOI Bulletin* 115, 116 (Fall 1988).

*. At time of original publication, Justus S. Hotchkiss Professor of Law, Yale Law School.

of exercising judgment to strike an appropriate balance among ambiguous and often conflicting normative goals; in the process, they put aside the massive empirical uncertainties they inevitably face.   Instead, they constrain themselves to write laws that conform to misleading or wrongheaded mathematical straightjackets.

* * *   I do not mean to embrace an easy attack on the theoretical difficulties and limitations of data in order to conclude that nothing of any import can or should be said. That would be palpably false. There is much we know about the likely winners and losers from changes in tax policy. Decisionmakers need such information and are entitled to share in this knowledge. But current illusions of precision should be abandoned.

* * * With regard to revenue estimates, greater attention should be given to long-term and overall revenue consequences of legislation to estimate the current practice of structuring legislation to maximize revenue gains or minimize revenue losses within the budget period.   In addition, the reliability—or lack thereof—of these estimates should be identified for policymakers, for example, by providing a range of likely outcomes. * * *

Revenue Estimates

Overview of the Revenue Estimating Process

* * * My goals in this section are simply to demonstrate congressional willingness—even determination—to be bound by meaningless or, in some cases misleading, numbers, to illuminate the shortcomings of existing revenue estimating practices, and to identify proposed solutions.

In general, an estimate of the revenue consequences of a proposed change in tax law is simply a staff's best estimate of the difference between federal receipts with and without the changes in law for each year of the budget period. The estimate of receipts without the proposed change is the baseline receipts forecast, which is based upon an assumed level of certain macroeconomic variables, including Gross Domestic Product (GDP), the overall price level, interest rates, total employee compensation, total domestic investment, and the total level of state and local taxes.

Revenue estimates * * * hold these macroeconomic variables constant, but * * * take other relevant behavioral changes into account.   For example, revenue estimates are based upon estimates of the increase or decrease in tobacco consumption expected to occur in response to changes in tobacco tax rates; they take into account increases or decreases in capital gains realizations expected as a result of changes in capital gains tax rates. Holding macroeconomic variables constant when estimating revenue effects has long been controversial.   Holding such estimates constant eliminates a range of disputes over the consequences of proposed legislation, facilitates comparisons of various proposed changes, and makes tax projections consistent with budgetary estimates of spending proposals. The public finance economist, Alan Auerbach, who recently served as Deputy Chief of Staff of Joint Committee on Taxation, which is responsible for revenue estimating for the Congress, has remarked that the opposite course—incorporating estimates of macroeconomic effects of tax legislation—"places the estimator in the very uncomfortable position of having to claim confidence in an estimate in which no sensible person could have much confidence."[135]

Nevertheless, significant tax changes are likely to affect these macroeconomic variables, and if these effects are large, they could change the size of the revenue estimate and in some cases even whether the revenue estimate is predicted to raise or lose revenue. * * *

The seemingly straightforward starting point for revenue estimates—the baseline forecast of receipts without the proposed changes in law—is itself somewhat ambiguous, particularly when current law is in dispute or is otherwise unclear. The tax treatment of purchases of intangible assets, such as business goodwill or customer lists, offers a recent instance.[136] In 1993, when Congress was considering changing the tax treatment of purchases of intangibles, the Supreme Court decided *Newark Morning Ledger Co. v. United States*,[137] a case involving the taxation of newspaper subscription lists—a customer-based intangible asset. The Court's determination of the current law treatment of this intangible asset might have had a substantial effect on the estimate of baseline receipts and, as a result, caused a change in the revenue estimates of proposals for changing the law. Indeed, before the Court's decision in the case, a fourteen-year amortization period for purchases of intangible assets, including goodwill, had been estimated to be revenue-neutral; after the decision, enactment of the fourteen-year amortization was estimated to raise more than one billion dollars during the period 1994-1998. * * *

The most difficult aspect of revenue estimating is anticipating changes in behavior that will be induced by changes in the tax law. During 1989, 1990 and 1991, differences between the judgments of JCT and Treasury revenue estimators about the likely behavioral responses of people in realizing capital gains in response to lowered tax rates became a revenue estimating *cause celebré*. During the five-year budget period, relatively small differences in the two staffs' behavioral assumptions produced more than a twenty billion dollar swing in projected revenue effects of a proposed exclusion from income of thirty percent of capital gains. For the years 1990-1995, Treasury estimated in 1990 that the proposal would increase revenues by $12.5 billion, while JCT estimated a decrease of nearly $11.5 billion. Virtually all of this gap was due to differences in assumed behavioral responses: first, Treasury assumed a short-run elasticity of 1.2, JCT 1.1; second, Treasury assumed a long-run elasticity of 0.8, JCT 0.66; and finally, Treasury thought it would take three years to reach the long-run, JCT only two years. Most economists would not

---

135. See Alan J. Auerbach, Public Finance in Theory and Practice, 46 Nat'l Tax J. 519, 523 (1993).

136. See 26 U.S.C. § 167(a) (1988).

137. 113 S. Ct. 1670 (1993).

view the existing empirical evidence as sufficient to choose confidently between these assumptions, but such small differences in assumed behavioral responses can, and did, have large effects on the revenue estimates.

The anticipated revenue loss from the 1981 universalization of eligibility for tax-favored individual retirement accounts ("IRAs") has become a notorious example of a grossly underestimated change, attributed largely to the estimators' failure to anticipate the mass marketing of IRAs by banks and other financial institutions. When revenue estimators aggregate a large number of individual revenue estimates for specific changes to predict the overall revenue effect of a piece of tax legislation, they often claim to rely on their patron saint, "St. Offset," who they hope will assure that their errors are not all in the same direction but will instead tend to offset one another, resulting in an acceptable overall prediction and error rate.

Commentators have long recognized that revenue estimates differ in reliability, depending on both the quality of data available to the revenue estimators and the difficulty of predicting how the change will be perceived and acted upon by taxpayers. No one denies, for example, that a revenue projection for increases or decreases in the personal exemption for the blind is far more reliable than an estimate of the revenue change from enacting or repealing special tax allowances for particular kinds of investments.

* * *

Asking the Wrong Question

Routine congressional reliance on estimates of questionable reliability has been compounded by Congress' insistence on grounding parliamentary objections during consideration of legislation and, in some instances, even legal compliance with general budgetary requirements, on predictions of changes in revenues for each year of a five-year budget period. Beginning with the enactment in 1985 of the Gramm-Rudman-Hollings Budget Act, *estimates* of the annual revenue effects of legislation directly triggered sequestration, a series of across-the-board spending cuts. This central role for revenue estimating continued through the 1987 Amendments of Gramm-Rudman and was, if anything, enhanced by the so-called pay-go requirements of the 1990 Budget Act. * * * The amendments also required that any provisions that are estimated to lose revenue in any year of the budget period must be offset by revenue-gainers of a magnitude equal to the forecasted loss. This basic mechanism of the 1990 Act remains in force, but the Senate has expanded the relevant period for revenue estimates from five to ten years in some circumstances.

There is no need to describe further the arcana of this budget legislation, since my limited point is that Congress has mistakenly elevated the significance of estimates of annual revenue effects of tax legislation for each year of a five- or ten-year budget period by tying potentially serious spending and tax consequences to these numbers. A politician therefore is behaving quite reasonably—given these constraints—when her dominant concern in considering tax legislation is making the revenue numbers "come out right." The diminished capacity of the traditional normative concerns of taxation—fairness, economic efficiency, and simplicity—to influence legislation in this context is not surprising.

Nor should it be surprising that the revenue estimates themselves have taken on increased significance, or that legislators have become experts at playing revenue estimating games in an effort to achieve the legislative outcomes they desire. A few examples of such revenue estimate games should suffice to illustrate the potential aberrations from accounting for revenues on an annual cash-flow basis within a specified budget period. Generally, these games involve accepting long-term pain to achieve short-term gain.

First, cash-flow "budget window" revenue estimates greatly influence the design of tax provisions. For example, the close relationship between investment tax credits, expensing of assets, and accelerated depreciation is well known in the tax policy literature. Reasonably sophisticated analysts, for example, can construct proposals for accelerating depreciation, partial expensing of assets' costs, or investment tax credits that are equivalent tax reductions in terms of their present value, but that involve quite different timing of the tax reductions and therefore have very different impacts on annual revenue estimates during a budget period. * * *

A related phenomenon occurs with respect to the choice between "front-loaded" and "back-loaded" savings incentives. With respect to the former, the taxpayer deducts the cost of the investment when made, accumulates investment income tax-free, and pays taxes when the funds are withdrawn. In the latter case, the taxpayer gets no deduction for putting the funds in the savings account, accumulates investment income tax-free, and pays no tax when the funds are withdrawn. When interest and tax rates are constant over time, the present value of the revenue cost of these two approaches is the same, but the pattern of revenue effects is quite different. Front-loaded savings accounts have large revenue costs in the years of savings; back-loaded accounts cost substantial revenues in the years of withdrawal. During the period 1989-1994, proposals to restore the universal IRA, which had been repealed by the 1986 Tax Reform Act, often took the back-loaded form, principally because the delayed revenue costs did not occur in the budget window, and, therefore, under the Budget rules, neither triggered spending cuts nor required offsetting tax increases. * * *

Probably the most venerable technique for taking advantage of cash-flow revenue estimating is the "speed-up." A speed-up simply moves revenues that would otherwise be collected in a later year to an earlier year. * * * [R]ecently, Congress's favorite speed-up has been accelerating collections of required estimated tax payments from individuals and corporations. Extraordinarily complex individual estimated tax provisions were adopted in 1991 solely to accelerate revenues to "pay for" extensions of unemployment benefits. Here, the temporary revenue gain was used only to pay for a temporary increase in spending, but budget rules permit using such a temporary gain to pay for a permanent revenue loser. * * *

Probably the most egregious use of budget scorekeeping rules to finance permanent tax reductions with temporary revenues is the sale of government-owned assets to pay for permanent tax changes. It is obvious that the revenue losses from the tax reductions will continue to decrease receipts long after the proceeds from the asset sale have been spent.

As a final example of revenue estimating gamesmanship, consider the creative use of temporary (or expiring) provisions. Budget scorekeeping rules, along with revenue estimating conventions, allow Congress to enact "temporary" tax increase provisions and then to count as revenue gains subsequent extensions of the temporary provision. This occurs because the "baseline" estimate of receipts does not include revenues from the expiring tax increase. * * *

A variety of sensible proposals have been offered to make revenue estimates more meaningful. For example, estimating the effect of proposed changes on the present value of revenues collected from current taxpayers might limit the likelihood that Congress could offer taxpayers an overall tax reduction in exchange for accelerating their tax payments. Jane Gravelle of the Congressional Research Service has recently proposed "annuitizing" the revenue effects of alternative policy proposals to facilitate more appropriate comparisons of alternative proposals.[164] This approach would convert any tax proposal, regardless of its effects on the federal government's cash flow, into the equivalent of an annuity, thereby putting proposals with different cash patterns on an equal footing. * * *

To be sure, both of these suggestions offer potential improvements in the process and could be coupled with providing ranges of revenue estimates and classifying estimates according to their likely reliability.[165] * * *

But we should not be overconfident about the ability to specify procedures that will make revenue estimates routinely reliable or meaningful. * * * Whatever the scorekeeping rules, * * * opportunistic and creative legislators and their staff will work within and around them, structuring proposals to maximize the likelihood of outcomes they desire.

To be sure, legislators need to be aware generally of the size and direction of revenue effects of proposals under consideration and of enactments. But permitting uncertain and frequently meaningless revenue estimates to serve as a straightjacket on policy outcomes, as they have in the past decade, inhibits thoughtful tax policymaking and undermines public respect for both the laws that result and the lawmakers that enact them.

---

164. See Jane G. Gravelle, Estimating Long-Run Revenue Effects of Tax Law Changes, 19 E. Econ. J. 481, 490-94 (1993).

165. Emil M. Sunley & Randall D. Weiss, The Revenue Estimating Process, 11 Am. J. Tax Pol'y, 261, 265 n.6 (1992).

Conclusion

It seems impossibly difficult to communicate even the simplest facts about tax and fiscal policy to the American public. One cannot be entirely certain whether this is because politicians are engaged in willful distortions, because the politicians themselves simply do not know the facts or are misinformed, or because, as I have demonstrated here, the truth in matters of this sort is at best elusive, and often unknowable. * * *

My concerns expressed here should not be taken to imply that I believe distributional or revenue information to be unimportant or that policymakers should not be informed of the distributional or revenue consequences of their proposed actions. * * *

The current use of revenue estimates is, if anything, even more troubling. Protected by supposed budget scorekeeping safeguards, policy proposals are manipulated to produce revenue results in a five -year budget window when the longer-term revenue consequences are known to be quite different from that within the budget window. The process should be revised to make explicit long- run comparisons of the budgetary effects of proposals in an effort to make legislators accountable for the long-term consequences of their decisions. Moreover, a range of estimated revenue effects should be given to Congress and the Administration. * * *

[T]he current use of both distributional tables and revenue estimates in tax policymaking may prove extremely costly to sensible tax policy. To take only one recent example, the substantial increases in the marriage penalties under the 1993 legislation occurred as a consequence of an effort to make both revenue estimates and distributional tables come out in a certain manner. * * *

Addendum

On March 23, 1995, after this Article went to press, the Wall Street Journal reported that the Treasury Department (OTA) and the Joint Committee on Taxation (JCT) made substantial changes in their methodologies for distributing benefits of tax reductions advanced by the new Republican House of Representatives majority. Both OTA and JCT reversed their positions on distributing changes in taxes versus changes in burdens for proposed capital gains tax rate reductions. OTA distributed the static revenue cost of the change as an estimate of the change in tax burdens (JCT's prior practice) and JCT distributed the actual anticipated change in taxes (OTA's prior practice). JCT also abandoned its prior practice of allocating changes in corporate taxes to owners of capital and instead did not include any of the benefits of corporate tax reductions in its distribution tables. * * * As the Wall Street Journal accurately reported, "The result: The Treasury's changes make the Republican tax-cut bill look extremely generous to the rich. Changes by the congressional Joint Committee on Taxation make the same tax cuts look less generous to the wealthy."[180]

These methodological changes should shake anyone's remaining confidence that the various staffs' distributional tables discussed in this Article are–or even can be–driven by economic science rather than by politics. The mystery deepens as to why these distributional tables should be used to determine tax legislative outcomes.

I rest my case.

Notes and Questions

7.   Would it be better to insulate revenue estimating from both the Treasury and the JCT by creating a separate office of estimators? If so, should it be part of the executive branch, part of the legislative branch, or an "independent" body akin to, or conceivably part of, the Federal Reserve System?

8.   Professor Graetz identifies a number of "games" used to finesse the limitations imposed by revenue estimates and their role in the budget process. Some are a transparent decision to juggle the numbers in order to achieve a desired result (which result always entails an increased real deficit). Selling government assets, which cannot be sold again, to balance an ongoing expenditure increase or tax cut, represents an obvious decision to follow the budget rules in form but not in substance. Much the same could be said of moving up estimated tax payments by one day, from October 1 to September 30 (or delaying expenditures from September 30 to October 1). Either technique helps the numbers for the fiscal year ending September 30, but is a one-time "fix" that cannot be duplicated in future years.

Of greater interest is the more sophisticated use of tax law to hide real tax cuts (real, in present-value terms) by pushing the revenue loss into the future, ideally out of the relevant budgetary window. For example, the cost to the Government in present-value terms is the same for traditional IRAs and Roth IRAs. (See Chapter Two, Subchapter A.) The traditional IRA costs revenues on the front end, as does a typical qualified retirement plan, because contributions are made on a pre-tax basis; later, however, the Government will fully tax distributions. With a Roth IRA, by contrast, there is no revenue lost at the outset, because contributions are not deductible; many years later, however, the Government will receive substantially reduced revenues when the distributions are received tax-free.

How would Professor Graetz change the revenue estimating process to address this problem?

---

180. Lucinda Harper, Treasury, Congress Disagree How Much GOP's Gains-Tax Cut Benefits the Rich, Wall St. J., March 23, 1995, at A2.

9.   Professor Graetz does not suggest ending revenue estimates, because he recognizes that they have value, even though he thinks they are "driven [not] by economic science but by politics." Rather than a single number, he recommends that policymakers be given "a range of estimated revenue effects." Would this significantly improve the process?

10.   Is the primary problem the inherent inaccuracy of revenue estimates, the politicization of the revenue estimating process, the failure to provide present-value revenue estimates, or the weight placed on revenue estimates by the budget process?

11.   Professor Graetz's criticisms of the revenue estimating process, and of the weight placed upon "getting the numbers right" in the budget process, are persuasive. At the same time, it must be remembered that these processes were put into place in an attempt to place some limits on the natural tendency of Congress to spend money readily and impose taxes reluctantly.

Would the budgetary deficit be even more difficult to control if the processes were changed as Graetz suggests?

D. THE TAX REFORM ACT OF 1986: A CASE STUDY IN FUNDAMENTAL TAX REFORM (AND WHY IT DID NOT LAST)

The Tax Reform Act of 1986 was the most ambitious attempt in history to fundamentally reform the income tax. Unlike other revenue acts that focussed on a few specific segments of the tax system, the 1986 Act attempted to revise the whole system in one massive effort. Even if it failed to do all one might have hoped, and even though some of its changes were reversed in subsequent years, enacting a such sweeping tax revision was an enormous, and surprising, accomplishment.

Professor Witte's article, written just after a dramatic breakthrough in the Senate Finance Committee that ultimately was to lead to passage of the 1986 Act, puts that Act in the context of tax history and tax policy. Mr. Birnbaum, who observed the process from the vantage point of a *Wall Street Journal* reporter, gives what is probably the best explanation of how the 1986 Act came to pass. Dr. Brannon's article is a critical and cynical analysis of what the 1986 tax revision accomplished.

A LONG VIEW OF TAX REFORM
John F. Witte[*]
39 National Tax Journal 255, 255-59 (1986)

Beyond the simple excitement of tax politics, I also have a modest personal stake in the result, primarily because of a passage, written late in an

---

[*]. At time of original publication, Professor, University of Wisconsin-Madison.

evening during a particularly depressing period in tax politics following the 1981 tax cut. I committed that passage to print, and made the further error of italicizing it. It occurs at the end of a long, and perhaps tedious, but I think scholarly treatment of the politics, development, and consequences of the federal income tax. The passage follows a description of the then most popular tax reform proposals, Bradley-Gephardt, Kemp-Roth, and Hall-Rabushka. It reads as follows:

> There is nothing, absolutely nothing in the history or politics of the income tax that indicates that any of these schemes have the slightest hope of being enacted in the forms proposed.

Later, just before the book went to press in January 1985, I added an epilogue, which was a reaction to the first Treasury reform proposal. At this point I was facing the embarrassing prospect of having a prediction go to press which would already have been proven wrong. So I did what any intelligent person would do—I carefully waffled.

> The central argument of this book has been that our political system has, to this point, been incapable of producing such lasting reform. This time the chips seem about to fall, but that has happened before—in 1969 and 1976—and they did not. Instead, what followed the 1976 effort was wholesale retreat from tax reform. * * * [P]roposals are not laws and I remain highly skeptical that these proposals will become and remain law over the long run. More likely, I would predict some curtailing of tax expenditures (although elimination of very few), a reduction in the number of brackets (which simplifies nothing and will reduce progressivity), and then, in the years ahead, a return to the more natural political impulses of conferring both broad and specialized benefits through the tax system. Lasting tax reform will not come without lasting political reform.

Until about three weeks ago those passages looked pretty good . . . now I am not so certain. I have never claimed that these prognoses were very imaginative or analytically astute. A relatively quick reading of the major historical trends in tax policy, which I will render in very brief form today, suggests these results. Indeed I would offer them as an example of the deadly phrase used by social psychologists: "My mother could have told you that."

Today, however, I am faced with a dilemma: stick with the prognosis and argument and discuss why *lasting*, comprehensive tax reform will not become a reality given our present political process; or cave in and discuss what went wrong with my bleak analysis and what led to this potentially monumental reform which seems to be on the threshold. I chose the former approach, and leave to my respondents and the audience the opportunity to raise all the interesting and hopeful prospects of recent events.

I chose to remain with my basic argument. * * * First, it is very important, particularly for tax policy which undergoes continuous change (a very serious problem in its own right), to have some grasp of the longer-term factors and basic incentives that drive tax politics. Second, I still think I am basically correct. * * * [O]ne bill does not insure lasting tax reform. The political and financial incentives I conceive as so obvious and apparent in tax politics will not be changed; and the actors, including those legions whose lives and fortunes have come to be tied to our tax system, are not about to pack their bags and go home.

In what follows I will first sketch the long-term patterns in income tax policy, particularly as they relate to the prospects for tax reform. I then will discuss the deeper problem as it relates to the general structure of politics which nurtures the development of tax policy in directions that produce the litany of defects that we all know so well.

Historical Trends and Tax Reform

Two essential facts are critical to understanding the historical development of the income tax in the United States. The first is the importance of periods of war; and the second is the incremental process of change which shapes tax policy. * * * [T]he initial income tax enacted in 1913 was a modest piece of legislation. Given the exemption level of $4,000 for a family of four, and thus the very small number of people required to file, an irate Henry Cabot Lodge correctly labelled the act as "the pillage of a class." * * *

World War I radically changed the very modest provisions of that initial act. Those changes established the potential of the income tax as a major source of revenue and created the first truly progressive tax structure in our history. In the years 1914 and 1915, the percentage of federal revenue derived from income taxes was minuscule. However, by the end of the war the combined individual and corporate income taxes, including excess profits taxes, accounted for approximately 60 percent of all federal revenues. At the same time the nominal rate structure was ballooning from an initial top rate of 7 percent to a war-ending top bracket rate of 77 percent.

Between the wars, these dramatic increases were largely undone, as both the progressivity and the revenue capacity of the taxes were considerably reduced (although never to pre-war levels). However, with the onset of World War II, the income tax again became the mainstay of our tax system, accounting for over 75 percent of revenues. The magnitude of revenues far outstripped any other period in our history. In 1938 revenues from each income tax were less than 1 percent of GNP; by 1942 they each were approximately 8 percent of GNP. Progressivity was drastically altered not only by raising rates to an historical high of 94 percent, but more importantly by shifting the definition of bracket widths so that large numbers of people paid at these higher marginal rates.[1] Finally, and most importantly, the war

---

1. For example, the 77 percent rate during World War I only affected income over $1 million, and Roosevelt's famous Wealth Tax of 1935 had a top rate of 81 percent for incomes exceeding $5 million. On the other hand, the top World War II rate applied to incomes over $200,000.

eliminated the elite nature of the income tax. World War I produced an increase in the percentage of the work force paying income taxes from less than 1 percent to 13 percent. That percentage then declined throughout the 1920s, increasing in the 1930s to approximately 7 percent in 1938. By war's end, 70 percent of the labor force were paying taxes and almost 90 percent were filing returns. That wartime system, which was reenacted for the Korean War, was largely kept intact with the writing of Internal Revenue Act of 1954, to which all subsequent income tax laws are amendments.

Because the modern structure of the income tax, and thus the foundation of our system of public finance was created as a response to war, it is not implausible to suggest that the basic features of that system would not have resulted from the more normal political process that governs tax policy-making in other periods. I have argued that the normal process is an excellent example of the incremental model of decision-making as first set out in detail by Charles Lindblom. In non-war periods, and to some degree also in wartime, the legislative process produces an almost continuous series of marginal changes in the status quo, often presented as remedies for current problems either internal to the tax system ("abuses") or as an answer to the plight of specific groups. Provisions are endlessly tinkered with, with new provisions introduced modestly and over time rather than in one grand sweep orchestrated by an overall plan for tax revision or reform.

What is important for this discussion of the long-term prospects for tax reform are the results of this combination of rapid, almost uncontrolled change induced by outside forces, set against a "normal" process of incremental political bargaining. The first important result is that the high level of taxes and the progressivity of that system were induced under abnormal circumstances. Indeed, the normal result of peacetime tax legislation has been almost perfectly consistent in reversing this trend. Through 1981, only one major income tax bill in history legislated a total tax increase, and that was in 1932 as a response to an effort to balance the budget as a remedy for the depression. Beyond that, whether a reform bill or not, politicians of both parties have always been able to claim that their actions "cut taxes." Walter Mondale can attest to the political power of such claims.[e]

A second trend resulting from the incremental changes in tax policy that follow wartime periods—a trend which continues to this very day—is a constant downward ratcheting of marginal rates. Although there is severe difficulty in making accurate estimates of historical effective rates, the

---

e. During the 1984 Presidential campaign, former Vice President Mondale, the Democratic candidate, stated that tax increases were inevitable—he would raise taxes if elected, but President Reagan would also raise taxes if re-elected. President Reagan subsequently stated that tax increases would come "over my dead body." On election day, Reagan carried 49 states.

Certainly, it would be too broad a reading to attribute Reagan's re-election, or even his landslide victory, to the candidates' differences in tax policy. Reagan was personally and politically popular, and times were good. Nonetheless, the difference in the candidates' positions on tax increases clearly played to Mondale's disadvantage. (Ed.)

political intent again appears to be quite obvious; leading me to the conclusion that the often discussed national commitment to a progressive tax system was never a real commitment at all, but rather a backdoor result of war.

Finally, although incremental changes are by definition non-radical departures from the status quo, it is a major error to interpret the longterm result of this process as conservative or producing little change. The reason is that modifications are *cumulative*. This simple fact has produced the policy results with which we are all so familiar—a hopelessly large tax code, that is unbearably complex, and riddled with particularized sets of benefits for all ranges and types of taxpayers. The wealthy benefit from these cumulative changes in a greater proportion than those not as fortunately situated, but there is almost no group that is left without an important set of provisions which lower their tax burden.

* * * Tax politics is not simply, or even mainly, a welfare program for the rich. If it was, the task of reforming it would be substantially less difficult.

What these basic trends and patterns in tax history mean for the prospects of major, lasting tax reform, have to this point been relatively obvious. The prospects are not good. Major tax reforms implies radical, comprehensive change, which is anathema to the normal incremental process. However, the historical trends also suggest major problems even if the political process could be controlled to generate and sustain the power needed to overcome incremental impulses. It is very difficult to conceive of tax reform and overall tax increases at the same time. In the past, tax reform has been purchased, and thus sold on the back of tax reduction. In addition, tax reform must also contend with the counter-trends of reduction in marginal rates and continuous expansion of the tax expenditure system.

Additionally, the base political incentives producing each of these trends are very strong. A politician's perfect world is to deliver a speech that proclaims his or her efforts for overall tax reduction, lower tax rates, and an added particular benefit (or protection of a benefit) for the specific audience at hand (elderly, teachers, developers, farmers, military personnel, small businesses . . . the list is endless). Ironically, that same politician is very likely to end the speech with an attack on the tax system, which may vary depending on current conditions, but usually includes problems of complexity, fairness, and the drag of the tax system on the growth of the economy. * * * The speech may well end with a call for tax reform as an immediate priority . . . immediately after the election.

* * * If I was in their position, * * * I would do the same thing . . . and so would all but the most courageous, or perhaps the dimmest of you.

The Deeper Problem

The difficult road to tax reform rests on a larger set of political problems than simple extrapolations of historical trends or assumptions concerning political incentives. These problems have to do with the basic design and workings of our representative system. And while I believe these flaws directly affect tax policy and add to explanations of the obstacles to tax reform, they are also more general and affect other bases of public policy as well.

Our initial representative system, which has undergone remarkably little structural change in over two hundred years, was based on a notion of government as a necessary evil. Following the failure of the Articles of Confederation, a majority emerged in favor of a stronger central government and federal system that would establish uniformity in and enforcement of laws, particularly those involving parties in different states. Provisions were also made for rudimentary services such as the coining of money and postal services, that obviously made more sense on a national level. The intent was to use government only to the point of establishing some certainty in economic and social transactions, and of course protecting the rights of property and contract. A central government was also viewed as essential in protecting the nation and individual states from foreign aggression and possible internal insurrection.

Discussion during the Constitutional Convention, and afterward during the process of ratification, repeatedly returned to the dangers of government and the need to proceed with caution. States' rights extremists, such as Patrick Henry, did not even ascribe to the limited role of a central government as outlined above. Federalists, such as Madison and Hamilton, often couched their arguments in language that admitted the possibility of excessive government and the need to guard against it. The most famous of the federalist papers, number 10 written by James Madison, argues for an encompassing federal system because it would limit factions from coming together to form majorities which would then use government to tyrannize minorities. The design of our system of fragmented and divided powers, between branches of the federal government and between state and federal governments, followed from this fear of government and the need to limit its powers and actions.

Beginning in the latter part of the nineteenth and the early part of the twentieth century, and greatly accelerating during the depression, that conception of government changed in a dramatic way. Government began to be viewed as the answer to national problems as well as the problems of specific groups. * * * The transition from government as a necessary evil, to a much larger government, that is a much more necessary good, is the major political fact of our age.

Now what does all this have to do with the prospects for tax reform? I believe a great deal, because the system first established to protect against government, is not as effective in dealing with government as a benefactor. The issues, for tax policy and other matters, are two-fold. First, why are policies that clearly benefit only a narrow minority ever approved by a majority that must eventually bear at least a marginal cost? And second, why is it often impossible to radically restructure a policy, such as a tax code, when the vast majority agree on the basic designs for reform?

There are several plausible answers to the first question, which for tax politics explains the proliferation of specialized tax expenditures. The most often cited explanation is that because specialized benefits (such as tax expenditures) are of large value to a few, while costs are widely dispersed, opposition will be weak. This is a variant of Madison's original argument—if the countervailing interests are widely enough dispersed, it will be difficult to form a majority. The shift has come in what the majority is anticipated to be doing. In the original formulation, the system was designed to prevent the majority from damaging the minority. However, in the modern state, the absence of majority will allow minority factions to secure benefits for themselves. Madison's logic remains intact, but that he wrongly conceived the problem is taking its toll.

Additionally, the underlying assumption that majorities will form and act on a sole expression of self-interest is also questionable. People may listen with empathy to special pleadings, particularly when they can conceive of themselves affected at some point by similar pleas. The aged are vulnerable; small businesses can be victimized by large corporations; students may need aid as they advance their education; and even those involved in oil production may need help when the Arabs fail to cooperate.

This prospect is even more important for elites who represent constituents; constituents who may or may not be carefully watching the actions of government. The gain for an elected politician from opposing specialized benefits requested by colleagues is likely to be minimal, particularly if the request is relatively marginal, as most are. On the other hand, the cost of isolating oneself through opposition may be high particularly when it is their turn to propose or assume credit for a benefit. Thus empathy may force inaction either through genuine agreement or as a calculated strategy.

Last, the torturous path to governmental action, institutionalized as fragmented and divided power, provides a possible explanation for both of the problems. The obstacles imbedded in the system may work to the benefit of narrow interests because success requires a diligence and perseverance that intense gain will engender (repeal of the withholding of interest comes to mind). Additionally, the lack of majority opposition to narrow, marginal gains increases the likelihood of passage, particularly when considered over the long term.

On the other hand, appeals to widely shared majoritarian concerns, such as tax reform, are much more difficult when the cost is potential disruption of acquired benefits. If a majority is faced with a clear prospect of harm, one can easily imagine a consensual coalition. However, when confronted with a complicated, confusing and uncertain shift of benefits, that coalition is much harder to form and to hold. And all of the fragmentation, potential for delay, and devices to kill an action will be brought into play.

* * *

SHOWDOWN AT GUCCI GULCH
Jeffrey H. Birnbaum[*]
40 National Tax Journal 357, 357-61 (1987)

With Alan Murray, I have written a book for Random House that carries the same name as this speech: *Showdown at Gucci Gulch*. The title is meant to convey that taxwriting is NOT a bore. * * * The Tax Reform Act of 1986 proves that, and our book details it.

* * *

There is more than one Gucci Gulch. The term is simply the nickname for the hallways outside of the Ways and Means and Finance Committees where hundreds of people stood for two years waiting for the members of Congress and their aides to decide the fate of the nation's income tax. These denizens of the hallway, mostly lobbyists and journalists, believed that they were outsiders looking in, powerless to do anything about the decisions that were being made secretly inside. Our book chronicles these deliberations.

In fact, forces that were working well beyond even the people inside the room, were what was pushing tax reform forward. What I hope to describe to you today are the conclusions that Alan and I have reached about what propelled this very unlikely piece of legislation forward, and what forced so many of us to wear out our heels on those marble floors, in Gucci Gulch, for so long.

In brief, I believe tax reform passed not because anyone really wanted it. Indeed, it was the bill that nobody wanted. It succeeded because so few people were willing to kill it once it got rolling. Put another way, no one wanted the dog to die on his doorstep.

At the end of 1983, when the Reagan administration was debating whether to put tax reform at the top of the next year's agenda, White House Chief of Staff James Baker asked pollster Richard Wirthlin for his view. Wirthlin was decidedly unenthused. He knew that tax changes always create more anger among potential losers than gratitude among winners. Moreover, he said, "the words 'tax reform' for a lot of Americans mean 'tax increase.'"

The next three years proved Mr. Wirthlin's point. Despite soaring rhetoric and whistlestop tours around the country, neither President Reagan nor Senator Bill Bradley was ever able to excite audiences with their plans to overhaul the nation's income tax. Mr. Reagan boldly labeled the effort a "second American revolution." Senator Bradley used more restrained, but no less compelling terms. Some Republican analysts even predicted that tax reform would bring about a grand "realignment" of political loyalties. Sen. Bradley, and later Chairman Dan Rostenkowski of Ways and Means, warned about the Republicans' plan and prepared to fight back for the good of their own Democratic Party.

---

[*]. At time of original publication, reporter for *The Wall Street Journal*.

But, for the most part, absolutely none of that happened. The country reacted with a yawn. The parties remained pretty much aligned as they always had been.

Even after the new law was enacted and hailed as a legislative miracle of sorts the public remained ambivalent. When asked to name the most significant event of 1986, only 9 percent of those asked picked the passage of tax reform. Far more people chose the explosion of the space shuttle, the U.S. sale of arms to Iran, and the bombing of Libya.

Tax reform, as Chairman Rostenkowski put it, was "the bill that nobody wanted." It was opposed by armies of Washington lobbyists. Lawmakers were equally unimpressed; many of them feared that they would be forced to vote against groups that kept their campaign coffers filled. Even the men who shepherded the bill forward—Treasury Secretary James Baker, Senate Finance Committee Chairman Bob Packwood and Chairman Rostenkowski—approached the task reluctantly. The only natural constituency for reform was the great mass of voters who paid their taxes each year without the benefits of shelters and tax gimmicks—and even they were skeptical.

> * * *

To be sure, most polls taken in 1985 and 1986 showed that a majority of Americans favored reform. But their support tended to be uninformed and thin. Although the bill promised tax cuts to two-thirds of the nation's taxpayers, most people thought their own taxes would not be reduced. Moreover, when poll-takers explained which tax breaks were being threatened, support quickly evaporated. Most taxpayers were worried about losing deductions, even if lower tax rates more than made up for the loss.

Take the case of poor Ron Pearlman. Back in 1985, when he and others at the Treasury were putting together what would later be called Treasury II, he was paid a visit by an army of armed-services veterans. The group was led by Chad Colley, national commander of the Disabled American Veterans, who had lost both legs and one arm while fighting in Vietnam.

Pearlman started the meeting by asking the triple amputee, "Why should veterans' disability payments be treated differently than any other income?" The meeting went downhill from there. Pearlman's question was heresy to a world accustomed to lenient treatment by the income tax. The red-faced Treasury official tried to dig himself out of the hole he had dug for himself, but to no avail. The veterans left his office and went on the warpath.

They demanded a second meeting at Treasury, this time with Pearlman's boss, Jim Baker. They brought with them a full-page advertisement that they were planning to run in three national newspapers. It had a huge picture of Commander Colley in a wheelchair, his missing appendages painfully evident. At the top of the page, in large, bold letters, the copy read: "What's so special about disabled veterans?" And it continued: "That's what a top Treasury official said to Chad Colley."

Baker called Pearlman into his office a little later. He said, "I think we'll have to drop this one."

With few people actively supporting it, and lots of powerful groups lined up against it, how did tax reform become law? The answer requires a more complex understanding of taxes and the way the public and lawmakers view them. While polls showed no abiding interest in the bill, per se, they also showed profound dissatisfaction with the existing tax code, and the political system that brought it into being. Politicians with their ears to the ground feared a public backlash might engulf anyone who was perceived as opposing the effort. Few legislators wanted tax reform, but even fewer wanted to be responsible for killing it. It was this decidedly negative motivation that was largely responsible for the enactment of the most sweeping overhaul of the federal income tax in history.

As a result, once President Reagan put the bill into motion, and Chairman Rostenkowski joined him making the effort bipartisan, tax reform acquired supernatural momentum of its own. As Senator Alan Dixon of Illinois put it: "This thing breathes its own air."

Or put another way. No one wanted the dog to die on his doorstep.

The income tax was enacted three-quarters of a century ago in an attempt to bring fairness to the U.S. tax system. At the close of the nineteenth century, the government raised all of its revenue from tariffs and excise taxes, which placed a heavy burden on low-income Americans. "If taxation is a badge of freedom," declared William Jennings Bryan, an early income-tax advocate, "let me assure my friend that the poor people of this country are covered all over with the insignia of freedom."

* * *

The idea that the income tax is, by and large, a fair tax persevered for many decades. When a Fortune magazine survey asked people to name the most unjust tax in 1938, only 8 percent fingered the income tax. Even as late as 1972, when the Advisory Commission on Intergovernmental Relations asked Americans which tax was the most fair, the federal income tax came out on top.

The 1970s, however, saw a steady erosion of taxpayers' faith in the federal income tax. To a large degree, the decline reflected the effects of inflation, which distorted the tax system in many ways, and pushed the poor and the middle class into higher tax brackets. But the dissatisfaction also reflected a growing awareness of tax shelters and ever larger tax loopholes that were used by the wealthiest, and most advantaged among us.

* * *

Roscoe Egger, the commissioner of the Internal Revenue Service during the first five years of the Reagan administration, recognized this public frustration and saw that it posed a major threat. He said: "People were rapidly becoming disenchanted with the whole system. We began to see the emergence of tax protesters. Groups refused to file, backyard churches began to claim income as charitable contributions, and tax shelters reached entirely different proportions. One couldn't fail to recognize that this was a reflection of deepseated unhappiness with the entire tax system. By 1983, we even began to see people in the lower-income levels, with incomes of only $18,000 or $20,000 a year, buying into phony tax shelters. . . . They listened to this siren song and said: 'Gee, everybody else is doing it. Why not me?'"

Horror stories about millionaires and large corporations that paid no tax became commonplace. Many Americans began to perceive that the income tax was not very progressive. It sometimes seemed that the average man on the street paid a higher portion of his income than the typical millionaire, rather than the other way around.

Gary Hecht, an assistant principal for a school in New York City, reflected the sentiments of millions of Americans in a December 1984 discussion group conducted by the *Wall Street Journal*: "My feeling with the federal tax goes back to the same old story. The rich get richer, the poor stay poor, and the middle class gets poor too. Because of the loopholes, this is going to constantly occur."

By January 1984, when President Reagan called for his tax reform study, no one could doubt that the American people were harboring a huge reservoir of resentment toward the income tax. It promised to be a powerful political force if ever effectively tapped.

The problem, though, was that the American public was also deeply cynical. They were upset by the tax system, but doubted that the President or Congress could fix it. As pollster Wirthlin had predicted, many people feared that tax reform would, for them at least, be a tax increase in disguise.

The ambivalence over taxes was recognized by most of the members of the House Ways and Means Committee, who were forced to confront the issue in 1985. Tax reform was a hot topic in Washington, but in the members' districts it remained a sleeper. * * * [H]ardly anyone mentioned tax reform, and when they did it was to complain. * * *

Republican Representative Bill Frenzel concluded, "It's obvious that for every friend you make with tax reform, you are going to make a few enemies."

Even Speaker Tip O'Neill, a backer of the bill, noticed the trend. "I have found very little sentiment. The people in the street, they never mention it."

Members of the Ways and Means Committee began serious consideration of tax reform in the fall of 1985. Aware of the public's apathy, they proceeded to rip the measure apart. Heeding the requests of special-interest lobbyists, they voted to restore tax breaks, one after the other, that both the President and Ways and Means Chairman Rostenkowski had slated for elimination. With little public support, tax reform was headed for the rocks.

The turning point for the House bill came on Tuesday Oct. 15, 1985. An amendment was offered in the committee by Alabama Democrat Ronnie Flippo to expand the deduction for bad debt reserves—the biggest tax break enjoyed by financial institutions. Flippo's amendment was the antithesis of reform; it represented old-time tax legislation at its worst, giving out goodies to favored interests, rather than taking them away. And to the surprise of Chairman Rostenkowski, the amendment passed, 17-13. Out in the hallway, a jubilant bank lobbyist shouted triumphantly, "We won! We won!"

The next day, the national newspapers attacked the committee for the vote, and vividly reported the glee of the gloating lobbyist. Whether these reports made their way into the nation's heartland is unclear. But their message was obvious enough. If the Ways and Means members allowed tax reform to die, they would take a heavy beating in the press, and probably in public opinion as well. Reminded of that threat, lawmakers slowly began to turn. No one wanted the dog to die on his doorstep.

Rostenkowski discovered a new willingness to compromise among his members. Within a week, in fact, the bank vote was reversed and the bill was on its way to passage. One savvy aide said at the time: "The last thing that any of these guys want is for it to be written that tax reform dies in the Ways and Means Committee because sleazebag politicians want to take care of First National City Bank so the average public gets screwed."

At about this time, members who had opposed the chairman's drive began to worry that they would be left behind, and left out. Indeed, those who had battled against the chairman, like Sam Gibbons of Florida, had reason to fear they might be the subject of the chairman's revenge in the final bill. * * *

For his part, Chairman Rostenkowski spoke of the tax bill as the "Phoenix Project," after the mythological creature that rose from its own ashes. He understood that tax revision gained its greatest strength after it appeared to have failed.

In the Senate, the bill followed a similar course. Aware of scant public support, (and ample private opposition), members of the Senate Finance Committee at first ripped into the bill. Even the committee's chairman, Oregon Republican Bob Packwood, had little interest in the measure. He had hoped it would die in the House. When it didn't, he felt bound to make an attempt to pass it in the Senate. But clearly, his heart wasn't in it. He allowed his committee to vote to retain one tax break after another, until, by April 18, 1986, the bill was "in ruins," as Democratic Senator Daniel Patrick Moynihan so aptly put it.

Like the House Ways and Means Committee, the Senate Finance Committee took a beating in the press for its behavior. Packwood, in particular, felt the sting. A month away from what he knew would be a bruising primary race back in Oregon, Packwood was pounded by a political opponent for "floundering" in his first major test as chairman. Oregon newspapers chided him for taking huge campaign contributions from dozens of groups with an interest in the tax bill. He rapidly gained a reputation as "Mr. Special Interest." The *New Republic* magazine dubbed him "Senator Hackwood."

Worried about the potential damage to his career, Senator Packwood and his top aide, Bill Diefenderfer, retreated to a Capitol Hill saloon and began plotting a truly radical overhaul of the tax system—one that would bring tax rates even lower than the President's plan. This new approach was mostly a political ploy. Neither Packwood nor his aide, who downed two pitchers of beer at lunch, believed that the radical approach would do much more than call the bluffs of the other committee members who claimed they wanted "real reform" while voting for special interests.

Senator Packwood himself described the boozy lunch and its product as being like the end of the movie "The Wild Bunch." In the film, a gang of bandits sells out a young member of their crew to the other side, but later decides to undo the deed. As Packwood describes it, "The next morning they get up and look at each other and strap on their guns and go to get the kid. They know they're going to be killed, but they've got to do this, they've got to try it. Bill and I just felt, OK, this is something we've got to try. If we fail, we fail at a great enterprise. No guts, no glory."

But to the surprise of almost everyone, a small group of Packwood's colleagues, some of whom had suffered similar second thoughts due to the public outcry, decided to join in the radical new approach to tax reform that emerged from that desperate lunch. And again a bill began to take shape, born NOT out of a belief that the public would applaud such an effort, but rather out of fear that the public would punish failure.

They didn't want the dog to die on their doorstep.

SOME ECONOMICS OF TAX REFORM, 1986
Gerard M. Brannon[*]
39 National Tax Journal 277, 277-79 (1986)

My colleagues on the panel have analyzed the current tax reform efforts in political terms, the circumstances of Gramm-Rudman-Hollings, the effect of the Great Communicator,[f] etc. I would like to contribute an economic perspective to what explains the success of the present tax reform.

A key element in the current process is the outcome of some highly sophisticated economic analysis relating to effective marginal tax rates. This economic analysis story starts 30 years ago.

In the 1950s the views about investment among the prevailing Keynesian economists changed from the earlier concern with over-saving and pessimism about investment. The new view emphasized the importance of investment for economic growth. This shift to Neo-Keynesianism was critical to the adoption of the investment credit, an invention of the economic advisers to President Kennedy.

---

[*]. At time of original publication, Professor, Georgetown University.
f. A reference to President Reagan. (Ed.)

The view at that time was that the investment credit was a neutral way to improve the level of investment. The investment credit was thought to be uniform between various kinds of equipment. It particularly seemed more neutral than the gadgety changes in depreciation that were the alternatives for encouraging more investment.

After the adoption of the credit, something important happened back at the ranch called public finance theory. It was discovered that the investment credit was not very neutral after all. That credit operates like a uniform reduction in the price of equipment but in truth the price of equipment hasn't been reduced. Leading investors to think that equipment is cheaper than it is will distort investment toward more short-lived equipment. When capital seems very cheap one tends to waste it, to spend more on capital that wears out fast.

The critical economic discovery was that the important test of neutrality was not a uniform cost reduction for equipment, but a uniform effective marginal tax rate. An efficient tax incentive for investment should uniformly reduce the tax burden on investment. This led directly to the proposal to repeal the investment tax credit and lower the business tax rate. The efficiency gain involved made it possible to use less revenue on rate reduction than was gained by repeal of the investment credit and still generate enough capital investment to improve productivity over what it would be under present tax laws.

This different kind of fiscal dividend made it possible to package a reform program based on investment credit repeal which would contain individual tax reduction which Professor Witte regards as the *sine qua non* of non-emergency tax legislation. Treasury I and II built on this core by adding several other corporate reforms that had this efficiency bonus. These changes alone were enough to pay for substantial individual tax reduction but the Treasury plans went further by adding selected individual loophole closers (fringe benefits, State and local taxes etc.) to make the individual rate cuts quite spectacular.

The response to all this in the Democratic House was quite close to a standard political prediction. A proposal from a Republican Administration to raise business taxes and to provide substantial relief for low incomes was manna from heaven. The real problem was get some share of the credit. The House bill: rejected most of the individual reforms; used the business tax increase to pay for the full relief program at low incomes; and, adopted only modest tax rate reductions. Significantly the House bill had sufficient individual reforms to pay for a sharp cut in the top tax rate, the only rate that gets mentioned in the press summaries. Due to the juggling of the brackets, there was not much overall rate reduction. This was a neat bit of symbolism about which we will have more to say later.

One aggregate description of the Senate bill makes it close to the political tradition. The Republican Senate opted for less business tax increase and less individual tax reduction than the House bill. The Finance Committee took the easy investment credit repeal and some other business tax reforms, but rejected others (revision of mineral and timber taxation). The remarkable thing about the Finance Committee bill is that despite the lower individual tax relief, it accomplished more rate reduction than the House bill. This is the one part that doesn't fit any traditional formula.

When one looks closely at the loophole closers that the Finance Committee used to cover its rate reductions some familiar patterns re-emerge.

Denial of deduction for State and local sales taxes is an almost classic compromise. Sales tax was the safest of the big three taxes to pick on. Property tax runs into the homeownership lobbies. Income tax can be very large for some taxpayers and it can be a big thing for some powerful States.[g]

* * *

Increasing the capital gains rate, another Senate Committee bill feature, is a traditional tax change. We have diddled with this rate innumerable times. Significantly the bill says nothing about the serious loophole in the capital gains area, the tax free step up in basis at death. So long as this loophole remains, capital gains is virtually a voluntary tax. Ample research has demonstrated that increases in the capital gains rate will reduce realizations. The question is only whether there will be any appreciable increase in revenue.

The new limitation on the deduction of consumer interest is in the timid compromise pattern. Most consumers have the opportunity to finance consumer goods purchases by adding to their home mortgage the interest on which will still be deductible. There is reform here but a reform crafted to avoid hurting anybody very much.

The disallowance of passive tax shelter losses also fits into another established pattern, i.e., dealing with problem areas by increased complexification. There is good reason to argue that some business situations are allowed excessive deductions but the bill doesn't remove the excessive deductions, per se, it only disallows some deductions when they are packaged in a certain way, i.e., for outside investors. This provides a sporting challenge to tax lawyers and accountants to repackage the investments. My money is on the lawyers and accountants.

Another big revenue source for the Finance Committee is the minimum tax, a tax which is more reform by complexification. A variety of special tax benefits is provided in the law to encourage activities like mining. If a company concentrates in one or more favored activities its average rate will be low and it will be hit by minimum tax. The same benefits are there if a low tax company merges with a high tax company but then the minimum tax is avoided. Again we have a provision that hangs on how things are packaged

---

g. As discussed in Chapter Thirteen, immediately prior to 1986 three major categories of state and local taxes were deductible (outside the business or income-producing context)—income taxes, property taxes, and sales taxes. Treasury I proposed elimination of the deduction for all three. The compromise struck in 1986 was to end the deduction for sales taxes only. (Ed.)

and invites tax practitioners to repackage. This is in the historical tradition of tax reform.

In an economic vein, I worry about the solidity of revenue estimates from these reforms that don't go to fundamentals but leave so much room for taxpayer maneuvering.

In a political vein, I am struck by how much symbolism there is in this. The essence of the minimum tax and the tax shelter amendments is to deal with public perceptions of tax abuses. A specific minimum tax proposal in the Finance Committee bill goes to the very statistic, book profit, which is used to compute the headlines about low effective average tax rates of this or that company. There is no underlying analysis as to why this is a sensible tax base; the provision is only designed to deal with what some parts of the public consider to be a symbol of tax abuse.

The other anti-symbol reform, the limitations on tax shelter deductions, is in a logical sense the opposite of the minimum tax. In the minimum tax case, the taxpayer who gets punished is the one who concentrates in a favored activity, thereby reducing the average tax rate. In the tax shelter case the typical taxpayer who gets punished is the one already paying a high rate who finds it attractive to invest on the side in a tax favored activity. Any underlying economic theory escapes me. The indications are that our tax law in the future should be designed after consultation with public relations experts.

Notes and Questions

12. Professor Witte notes that U.S. tax policy has generally changed incrementally. What are the relative merits of an incremental approach to tax reform as compared to a convulsive, overall revision of the sort carried out in 1986?

13. Professor Witte observes that war has played an important role in tax policy. In general terms, rates rise sharply and the rate structure becomes more progressive. It is clear why rates rise—the Government needs money to finance the war—but why do rates also tend to become sharply progressive?

14. In times of peace, rates tend to fall and to flatten. Viewed in this light, the tax cuts of the past quarter century, and particularly the reductions in the top rate, can be seen as part of a predictable peacetime trend.

15. Why is Professor Witte pessimistic about the long-term prospects for tax reform?

16. Witte suggests that our Madisonian governmental structure was well designed to protect a unified and determined minority from exploitation by government. That structure, however, also facilitates such a minority in

obtaining unjustified largess from government. "Madison's logic remains intact, but that he wrongly conceived the problem is taking its toll."

17. According to Mr. Birnbaum, the Tax Reform Act of 1986 passed against all odds. Why?

18. Had you read Birnbaum's account when it was published in 1987, would it have led you to expect that the reforms of 1986 might prove short-lived?

19. According to Professor Brannon, what was the political effect of the economic conclusion that a cut in corporate income tax rates was a more efficient stimulus to investment than was the investment tax credit?

20. Do you agree that "individual tax reduction [is] the *sine qua non* of non-emergency tax legislation"?

E. INFLUENCES ON CONGRESS

When all is said and done, what causes Congress to act? The most obvious influences, in varying ratios for each member, would seem to be the desire to effect good policy and the desire to be reelected and otherwise to benefit politically.

Obviously, Congress is influenced by citizen input, especially that of constituents, political supporters, and contributors. Americans have a right to be heard by their lawmakers. The right "to petition the Government for a redress of grievances" is explicitly protected by the First Amendment. While many exercise this right individually, an alternative (or additional) route is to hire professionals to lobby on one's behalf, with the result that lobbyists are key players in shaping legislation.

Professor Surrey served as Tax Legislative Counsel during the Truman administration and Assistant Secretary of Treasury for Tax Policy during the Kennedy and Johnson administrations. In these positions, he observed, and influenced, the process first hand. The brief excerpt from his article focuses on the differences in American tax lawmaking as contrasted to that which might be expected under a more controlled parliamentary system of government.

Professor Shaviro's article asserts that traditional analysis of lawmaking is too shallow. "Public interest"—legislating to make society better—is generally dismissed as naive, the pablum we feed our grade-school children. The dominant view is that lawmaking is actually dominated by "public choice"—essentially, selling legislative action to the highest bidder (typically, not in a form as crass as an actual bribe). Shaviro asserts that legislators typically pursue self interest, but not in the shallow, monetary sense that public choice theory posits.

THE CONGRESS AND THE TAX LOBBYIST—
HOW SPECIAL TAX PROVISIONS GET ENACTED
Stanley S. Surrey[*]
70 Harvard Law Review 1145, 1153-55 (1957)

History and Politics

* * *

Political considerations naturally overhang this whole area, for taxation is a sensitive and volatile matter. Any major congressional action represents the compromises of the legislator as he weighs and balances the strong forces constantly focused on him by the pressure groups of the country. Many special provisions—capital gains, for one—are caught in these swirling pressures. The response of the legislator to issues raised by these provisions is like his response to the general level of tax rates or to personal exemptions, a political response of considerable significance. * * *

Separation of Executive and Legislative Branches of Government

But many of the tax provisions we are considering do not lie at this political level. They are simply a part of the technical tax law. They are not of major importance in their revenue impact. But they are of major importance to the group or individual benefited and they are glaring in their departure from tax fairness. The inquiry, therefore, must here be directed toward some of the institutional features in the tax-legislation process which may be responsible for special provisions of this technical variety. Lacking direct knowledge, I must leave to others the task of describing the types of pressure from constituents or other groups which may be operative in a particular case. While these pressures may explain why the congressman who is directly subject to the pressures may act and vote for a special provision, they do not explain why other congressmen, not so subject, go along with the proposal. We must look for reasons beyond these pressures if we are to understand the adoption of these special tax provisions. A number of these reasons lie in the institutional aspects of the tax legislative process.

Basic to a consideration of these institutional aspects are the nature of our governmental system and the relationship between the Congress and the executive. A different Governmental structure might give the legislator little or nothing to say about tax provisions. Under a parliamentary government, the revenue department retains tight control over the statutory development of tax law. It is responsive only to the broad political issues that require decisions of a party nature. Beyond these, the governmental tax technicians mold the structure, so that the tax lobbyist pressing for special legislative consideration or the legislator seeking to ease a constituent's problem by special tax relief is not a significant part of the tax scene. Thus, under the British practice, finance bills are framed by the Treasury and the Board of

---

*. At time of original publication, Professor of Law, Harvard Law School.

Inland Revenue. The bills are debated in the Committee of Ways and Means—the entire House of Commons sitting under another name and with different rules of procedure. Here is an opportunity for anyone sufficiently concerned, who can persuade a Member of Parliament to voice his proposals, to have these proposals considered in the debates on the bill. Such discussion may focus attention on weaknesses in the bill or law, and if the proposal is considered meritorious by the minister in charge of the bill a change will be made. But if the government does not accept a member's amendment, party discipline is such that the minister is always supported and the amendment defeated. In practice, consequently, finance bills generally emerge in about the same form as introduced.

The United States picture is quite different, for here Congress occupies the role of mediator between the tax views of the executive and the demands of the pressure groups. This is so whether the tax issue involved is a major political matter or a minor technical point. The Congress is zealous in maintaining this position in the tax field. A factor of special importance here is article I, section 7, Of the Constitution, which provides that "All Bills for raising Revenue shall originate in the House of Representatives." The House Committee on Ways and Means jealously guards this clause against possible inroads by the Senate. It also protects its jurisdiction over revenue legislation from encroachment by other House committees. When senators and other congressmen must toe the line, the executive is not likely to be permitted to occupy a superior position. Further, a legislator regards tax matters as politically very sensitive, and hence as having a significant bearing on elections. It is no accident that the tax committees are generally strong committees, whose membership is carefully controlled by the party leaders.

The Congress, consequently, regards the shaping of a revenue bill as very much its prerogative. It will seek the views of the executive, for there is a respect for the sustained labors of those in the executive departments and also a recognition, varying with the times, of the importance of presidential programs. But control over the legislation itself, both as to broad policies and as to details, rests with the Congress. Hence a congressman, and especially a member of the tax committees, is in a position to make the tax laws bend in favor of a particular individual or group despite strong objection from the executive branch. Under such a governmental system the importance to the tax structure of the institutional factors that influence a congressman's decision is obvious.

* * *

BEYOND PUBLIC CHOICE AND PUBLIC INTEREST: A STUDY OF THE LEGISLATIVE PROCESS AS ILLUSTRATED BY TAX LEGISLATION IN THE 1980s

Daniel Shaviro[*]

139 University of Pennsylvania Law Review 1,

3-10, 31, 36, 42-43, 64-67, 71-92, 94-98, 104-17, 120-23 (1990)

Introduction

Just as China in the 1960s had perpetual revolution, so the United States in the 1980s had perpetual income tax legislation. Congress passed historic watershed tax bills in 1981 and 1986. Important, though not historic, packages of tax legislation were enacted in 1982, 1984, and 1987. * * *

Even more peculiar than the rapid pace of 1980s tax legislation was the wildly erratic and cyclical nature of tax policy. In this country, tax policy tends to take either of two forms. First, under what I call an "instrumentalist" approach, tax law ostensibly serves social and economic policy goals (for example, increasing productivity, home ownership, or competitiveness) by providing preferential treatment for selected types of income. This approach is characterized not so much by a fixed agenda as by a willingness to use the tax system to pursue a broad array of goals. Second, the approach that in the last forty years has captured the label "tax reform" aims to tax different types of economic income more equally and to prevent high-income taxpayers from entirely avoiding significant tax liability.

Although tax legislation has shown cyclical tendencies since the early days of the federal income tax, the problem reached a new level in the 1980s. In the entire history of the income tax system, the 1981 Act was the high water mark of tax instrumentalism. It provided tax incentives on a previously unheard of scale, through provisions such as sharply accelerated depreciation for capital equipment, universal individual retirement accounts (IRAs) and other savings incentives for individuals, and a host of benefits for particular industries. By contrast, the 1986 Act was the all-time leading example of tax reform. It eliminated longstanding tax preferences such as the partial exclusion for capital gains (in existence since 1921) and the investment tax credit (in existence for all but two years since 1962). Moreover, it contained an array of provisions that impeded efforts by high-income taxpayers to eliminate entirely their tax liabilities through the use of remaining preferences. Now in 1990, Congress is considering a return to instrumentalism, through restoration of a capital gains preference and savings incentives similar to those eliminated in 1986.

The oscillating congressional approach would be less surprising if it had resulted from changes in the political landscape; for example, if tax instrumentalists had been defeated in the mid-1980s and then restored to power at the end of the decade. Yet, for the most part, this has not been the

---

[*]. At time of original publication, Assistant Professor, University of Chicago Law School.

case. For example, President Reagan and Congressman Rostenkowski (the chairman of the Ways and Means Committee) played critical roles in shaping both the 1981 and the 1986 legislation. Senator Packwood, in 1986 the chairman of the Senate Finance Committee, started out "sort of lik[ing]" the highly preferential post-1981 law just "the way it [was]."[15] He then spearheaded the dramatic 1986 changes, but more recently has championed the restoration of tax breaks that, as chairman, he helped eliminate.

How can such erratic behavior by both institutions and individuals be understood and explained? While the tax context may be important, the question also raises fundamental issues about politics and the legislative process. This Article will therefore examine various theories concerning why Congress legislates, evaluating them both in general and as explanations for the recent course of tax legislation. My goal is to provide both a specific case study and a broader positive account of the institutional forces that shape legislation, using each to illuminate the other.

To organize the discussion, I will focus on what are currently the two dominant approaches in the legal and economic literature. First, there is public interest theory, under which the government attempts to improve the general welfare, for example, by financing public goods and correcting instances of market failure. Conceived somewhat more broadly, the public interest view emphasizes the importance of ideology and the desire to make good policy, which are seen as motivating legislators to seek to improve society (according to their perhaps controversial notions of what is good). As I will show, public interest theory has been powerfully challenged in its narrow form as lacking a causal mechanism and failing to explain actual government behavior. In its broader form (relating to ideology), the view has received some empirical support, but seems to over-predict the coherence and stability of legislative policy-making.

Second, there is a branch of public choice theory called the economic theory of regulation.[18] This view holds, in brief, that legislation (along with other government action) is a product supplied to well-organized interest groups that are struggling to maximize the incomes of their members, often at the expense of the less well-organized. In effect, legislation is sold to the highest bidder, with bids being paid in the currency of votes, campaign contributions, and personal benefits such as honoraria. As I will show, this view has some explanatory power, but in its strongest form is not only theoretically implausible but has been empirically refuted in an extensive political science literature that public choice writers simply ignore. Public choice theory flattens the motivations and overlooks the independent influence

---

15. *See, e.g.*, J. BIRNBAUM & A. MURRAY, SHOWDOWN AT GUCCI GULCH: LAWMAKERS, LOBBYISTS, AND THE UNLIKELY TRIUMPH OF TAX REFORM (1987) at 19.

18. For convenience and following common usage, I will call this "public choice theory" although my comments will not apply to any branch thereof apart from the economic theory of regulation.

of both politicians and the general voting public. Its explanation of why interest groups often succeed in "rent seeking" (securing transfers from the general public that are negative-sum for society) turns out to be merely one application of a broader principle: that government policy tends to provide visible benefit in exchange for less visible (even if unduly high) cost. Finally, public choice theory fails to explain fully not only the 1986 Act, where special interest groups were generally the big losers, but also the 1981 Act, where such groups were unusually big winners.

The problems with public choice theory have recently begun to attract critical attention. Unfortunately, however, many of the theory's critics, unable to imagine any third alternative to public interest theory and public choice theory, have seemingly assumed that, to the extent one of the two theories is false, the other must be true. If and when legislation is not just rent seeking by interest groups, it must be altruistic, socially beneficial, or a source of immense public satisfaction. As I will show, however, this panglossianism is neither logically nor empirically supportable. The foes of public choice theory, like its friends, fail to understand how self-interested political behavior apart from wealth maximization shapes legislative outcomes.

Public interest and public choice writers, because of their shared failure to consider the implications of self-interest aside from wealth maximization, make an assumption that often turns out to be false. They assume that legislation is primarily directed to some substantive end and intended to have particular real world effects (whether improving society or enriching a particular group). In fact, politicians' claims to intend real world effects are often a pretext, rather than a serious effort. Even if legislation nonetheless has substantial real world effects, from a subjective standpoint these may be incidental.

In many cases, Congress legislates because its members and others who influence it value and benefit from the activity of legislating. The reasons for such behavior can be divided into two categories. First, proposing and enacting legislation is a means of symbolic communication with members of the general public, of causing them to like a politician without the inconvenience (and possible political inconsequence) of actually having to benefit them tangibly.[25] Thus, without regard to its actual effects, legislation can promote reelection. Second, succeeding legislatively is a means of exercising and demonstrating one's power. It is inherently gratifying (as when an emperor enjoys seeing statues of himself), and it increases one's prestige and status in political circles. Thus, without regard to its actual effects, legislation can promote self-interested goals apart from reelection.

To the extent that one seeks to legislate for reasons apart from anticipated real world effects, it may be enough that the stated goal of

---

25. The classic work concerning this type of political behavior is M. EDELMAN, THE SYMBOLIC USES OF POLITICS (1964); *see also* C. ELDER & R. COBB, THE POLITICAL USES OF SYMBOLS (1983) (describing the role of symbols in political activities).

legislation is superficially plausible and relates to areas of public concern. The proponent need not invest much effort in considering whether the legislation actually will do what it promises. Any such assessment is difficult in any case, but even where possible it may be politically unimportant. * * *

The various views of the legislative process that I have outlined are not mutually exclusive. Indeed, all can apply simultaneously, and only a complex multi-factored approach can begin to do justice to the underlying reality. I will argue, however, that the particular factors I emphasize—voters' taste for symbolism and politicians' taste for power and prestige—are extremely important yet have largely been ignored by previous commentators. These factors indeed are dominant as explanations of recent tax legislation, where other causal factors have reduced importance due to the muddiness of ideological cleavages in taxation and the severe limits to both the public's and politicians' understanding of tax issues.

Under the particular historical circumstances of the 1980s, the principal effect of the symbolic and prestige factors on tax legislation was to create the legislative equivalent of "churning" a portfolio account. Since both of the dominant opposing policies (tax instrumentalism and tax reform) sounded appealing, but only the one less recently tried could be presented as a bold new departure, Congress shuttled back and forth between them. I will suggest, however, that these factors need not always lead to alternating tax reform and tax instrumentalism. They can lead just as easily to one instrumentalist bill after another. * * *

The Public Interest Theory of Legislation
The Various Strands of Public Interest Theory

In contemporary law and economics literature, the public interest theory of legislation is little more than a strawman. Writers describe it as an old-fashioned and now universally rejected school of economic thought, discuss it very briefly, and then move on to the real (public choice-based) discussion. The term is nonetheless useful because it describes a basic attitude, involving optimism about the legislative process, that in sympathetic hands often has specific content. * * *

Criticisms of Public Interest Theory

One could not sensibly assert that the public interest view of American politics is wholly false. Surely the government does many things that increase social well-being, such as maintaining public roads, enforcing contracts, and deterring violent crime and foreign invasion. Moreover, the political system reflects and responds to the public's wishes, at least in the extreme sense that no one proposing the policies of a Pol Pot or a Nicolae Ceausescu would have good prospects of sustained electoral success. Disagreements with the public interest view are in part a matter of degree * * *, as well as of emotional predilection regarding whether to focus on the system's elements of success or failure.

Nonetheless, the public interest view has been criticized on theoretical and empirical grounds for misapprehending both the balance between good and bad and its underlying causation. * * *

(Largely Empirical) Criticisms by Political Scientists

In recent years many political scientists, like economists, have become skeptical of the pluralist/public interest view of legislation. This skepticism arises principally from empirical studies of who interest groups represent and how interest groups participate in the legislative process. The pluralists' optimism about the balance and universality of group representation in Washington is contradicted by substantial evidence. * * *

Schattschneider's * * * classic study of interest group lobbying on the Smoot-Hawley Tariff demonstrated that business groups seeking high tariffs were virtually unopposed by those (such as consumers) who would have benefitted from low tariffs. Instead of pluralist competition, he found a pattern of pervasive logrolling, whereby business lobbyists agreed to "reciprocal non-interference," or support for each other's high tariff demands. If one group sought a tariff on items that a second group needed to purchase, the second group would settle for a "compensatory duty" on its own products. Thus, the legislative process was a positive sum game for its participants, and probably a highly negative sum game for the country as a whole.

* * *

The Public Choice Theory of Legislation
Overview of Public Choice Theory

In the law and economics literature, the perennially favored alternative to public interest theory is public choice theory. In its broadest sense, public choice theory is simply the economic study of nonmarket (i.e., political) decision-making. At this level of generality, it requires no stronger assumption than that people act rationally in light of their objectives, whatever these may happen to be. Following common usage, however, I will use the term "public choice theory" to describe what is actually a sub-genre, sometimes called the economic theory of regulation. As we will see, this sub-genre makes considerably stronger and more questionable assumptions.

In the words of Fred McChesney, "[t]he essential insight of the economic model is that, like any other good or service, regulation [i.e., legislation] will be provided to the highest bidder."[295] The sellers are legislators, and they are paid in votes, campaign contributions, and personal benefits such as honoraria and free vacations. The buyers, drawing on the economic theory of groups, are organized interest groups seeking wealth transfers.

---

295. McChesney, *Regulation, Taxes, and Political Extortion, in* REGULATION AND THE REAGAN ERA: POLITICS, BUREAUCRACY, AND THE PUBLIC INTEREST, 223 (R. Meiners & B. Yandle eds. 1989).

McChesney's "essential insight" has a certain rhetorical force. If we assume that everything else in life works a certain way, why should politics be any different? As other public choice writers have put it:

> The point is that there is no bifurcation of personality as between our "political" and "private" selves. We do not seek to satisfy the "public interest" when we vote and the "private interest" when we buy groceries. We seek our "self-interests" in both cases.[298] * * *

Unfortunately, this argument is somewhat misleading. Public choice theory does not automatically follow from accepting the continuity between our public and private selves. Take the basic analogy to a market where people buy and sell items such as groceries. This market has two important attributes: specific goods to be bought and sold, and the use of money as a uniform medium of exchange. Standard economic analysis, such as the drawing of supply and demand curves, does not require making theoretical assumptions about what goods people want (i.e., what nonmonetary preferences they bring to market). It assumes only that, once in the market, they generally try to do as well as possible in monetary terms. All else being equal, buyers try to pay as little, and sellers to receive as much, as possible. This assumption seems eminently reasonable. Nonmonetary preferences are not being denied; they merely have little effect at this stage of the process. Thus, the economic model of a market does not (to quote a standard criticism of economists) "posit . . . [a] shallow and incomplete . . . caricature" of human nature[299] as concerned only with narrow material gain.

Now consider politics. Here we have a "market" where the goods are unspecified unless we make assumptions about people's preferences. Voters, for example, may care about ideological or symbolic issues that have no direct bearing on their monetary interests. In voting, they are deciding what to buy, not how much to pay, since each voter has but one vote and cash sales of votes are discouraged. Politicians similarly may care about ideological or symbolic issues that have no direct bearing on their monetary or professional interests. Although public choice classifies them as "sellers" of legislation, there is no theoretical reason why they may not want at times to "buy" particular outcomes. Even treating politicians purely as "sellers" who seek to maximize professional self-interest, we encounter a further difference between politics and the standard private market. In politics, despite the importance of money, there is no uniform medium of exchange, unless we simply assume that money is all that politicians want, as opposed to, say, power, prestige, and flattering press coverage (either as ends in themselves or as useful for reelection).

---

298. R. McCormick & R. Tollison, Politicians, Legislation, and the Economy: An Inquiry into the Interest-Group Theory of Government at 7 (1981) (comparing a market failure approach with a public choice approach in explaining the role of government in the economy).

299. M. Kelman, *On Democracy-Bashing: A Skeptical Look at the Theoretical and "Empirical" Practice of the Public Choice Movement*, 74 Va. L. Rev. 199, 206 (1988).

Public choice theory ignores these problems with the analogy to a private market, and treats monetary exchange between interest groups and politicians as all that matters. The public is not only ignorant but irrelevant. Interest groups are all-powerful and concerned purely with monetary wealth. Politicians are not only self-interested but narrowly so; they are literally for sale. By viewing politics so reductively, public choice theory begins to look like the "shallow and incomplete" caricature of human nature expected by critics of economists. Good economic analysis takes people's preferences as a given and asks what consequences will follow from them, assuming only means-ends rationality. Public choice theory instead makes crudely reductive assumptions about the preferences that people actually have. It is as if one predicted that people will buy only healthful and nutritious groceries, or will not pay anything extra for Cadillacs with tail fins.

I should clarify that this is much too harsh for the best public choice writers—who principally teach in economics departments rather than law schools. * * *

Much public choice writing, however, particularly from law schools, comes considerably closer to the "crude caricature." As we will see, it thereby falsifies not only human nature, but observable facts about the legislative process. * * *

What Public Choice Theory Omits

* * * [Public Choice Theory] needs to be supplemented, not abandoned. To improve public choice theory, we need a more systematic account of how and why it fails to explain legislative politics. This section will discuss the theory's shortcomings and the principal factors that it omits. Though only a complex and multi-faceted approach can achieve reasonable descriptive accuracy, two factors are particularly important: voters' taste for symbolic legislation and politicians' taste for power and prestige. Under circumstances of high publicity, these factors can easily outweigh interest group politics.

Voters

Public choice theory treats voters as narrow profit-maximizers who, due to information costs and collective action problems, remain rationally ignorant and thus politically irrelevant to the extent they are not organized into interest groups. The view, however, runs into an immediate logical problem. The rational voter that public choice theory posits would find the act of voting to be irrational, even assuming full knowledge about the candidates and issues. Given the arithmetical unimportance of any one vote, even if the election's outcome is very important, the expected monetary gain from voting in one's interest is almost infinitesimal and the costs of voting (such as the expenditure of time) seem clearly greater. In view of the adverse cost-benefit tradeoff, the fact that millions of people vote is paradoxical to many public choice writers, as is the fact that better-educated voters, whom one would think more likely to be aware that voting is "irrational," vote more than others.

As the best public choice writers have come to recognize, the paradox suggests that voting is based, not on narrow self-interest, but on consumption motives, typically involving symbolic or expressive behavior. Voters "buy" ideological, emotional, or moral satisfaction in the course of satisfying what they may regard as a civic duty, at an individually low cost even if voting conflicts directly against their narrow interests. The satisfaction is derived from the vote itself, as distinct from the electoral outcome, and thus is a strict private good unaffected by its arithmetical unimportance or by collective action problems.

The low value of a single vote provides only one reason for questioning the rational voter model. Consider as well the significance, described by Murray Edelman, of politics' status as a "spectator sport." * * * Emotional involvement is facilitated by the fact that, even if one's interest in politics remains low, much information (both true and false) may come one's way casually, as when one watches the local news during dinner or glances at newspaper headlines.
* * *

Given both the arithmetical unimportance of a single vote and voters' emotional involvement, politics evokes behavior far less centered on narrow wealth maximization than does a private market, even though voters, presumably without schizophrenic personalities, participate in both. Some critics of public choice theory see politics as a realm of greater altruism, where people sacrifice their own interests in order to act properly towards others. This conclusion does not necessarily follow, however, from the lesser importance of monetary self-interest. It depends on what preferences people substitute for wealth maximization. * * *

A further aspect of voter behavior apart from altruism arises from the pervasive role of television in bringing prominent national and local politicians into people's living rooms on a regular basis. The false intimacy created can lead voters to identify with and support a politician on much the same basis as the star of a dramatic television series. * * * Gary Orren thinks politics has "more in common with religion than with economics."[357] In an age of weak party allegiances and high focus on personality, with frequent ticket-splitting, numerous independent voters, and an increasingly fickle electorate, a better analogy may be to the entertainment industry.

In summary, the public choice model of voters as narrowly self- interested profit-maximizers seems inaccurate. It confuses low information with no information and ignores important motivations apart from narrow self-interest. To understand more fully the systematic implications of these inaccuracies, it is necessary to examine some of the other descriptive shortcomings of public choice theory.

---

357. Orren, *Beyond Self-Interest, in* THE POWER OF PUBLIC IDEAS at 27 (R. Reich ed. 1988).

Politicians

* * *

If politicians are as exclusively "money-mad" as McChesney posits, one wonders why they have chosen politics as their profession. Elected positions often pay less than the available private sector alternatives, in addition to bringing long hours and relative job instability. The politician who seeks to supplement her income through private arrangements may risk disgrace and even prison, as numerous congressmen and senators have learned in recent years. Moreover, while politics can pave the way to a more lucrative career (such as lobbying), many politicians remain in the business long past the point of maximizing their lifetime earnings potential.

This is not to deny the extreme importance of money in politics, as both a direct goal of politicians and a means of winning reelection. To replace the public choice account with one that is more realistic, however, we must look more closely at politicians' objectives.

Politicians' Varied Motives

To the extent that one can generalize, what sort of people are politicians? * * * Many contemporary observers agree that politicians approach "each new situation and each other [person] with the simplest question: What can this do for me?"[365]

One senses the voice of envy in some of this. Yet even more sympathetic observers agree that politicians generally are motivated to an unusual degree by what is variously described as a "desire for attention and adulation," "intense and ungratified craving for deference," "ache for applause and recognition," and an "urge for that warm feeling of importance." Thus, self-interest is agreed to be extremely important to politicians, but not primarily the narrow monetary self-interest emphasized by economists. (It is of course likely that some politicians fit the public choice model, and one would expect to find broad variation among individuals' motives.)

These impressionistic accounts of politicians' motives are confirmed by empirical studies of the U.S. Congress. Perhaps the best two such studies, based on extensive confidential interviews, are Richard Fenno's *Congressmen in Committees* [(1973)] and John Manley's *The Politics of Finance: The House Committee on Ways and Means* [(1970)]. Fenno found that three goals espoused by House members are "the most widely held and the most consequential for committee activity." They are (in no particular order of priority): (1) reelection, (2) "influence" within the House, meaning power and prestige, and (3) good public policy. Manley documented the preeminence of the second of these goals, power and prestige, among members of the Ways and Means Committee.[373] * * *

---

365. H. SMITH, THE POWER GAME: HOW WASHINGTON WORKS at 113 (quoting T. CRUISE, THE BOYS ON THE BUS 71 (1973) (quoting Richard Reeves)).

373. *See* J. MANLEY, THE POLITICS OF FINANCE, 53-58 (1970).

Of the three goals cited by Fenno, reelection, while obviously a prerequisite to all else, is not a serious problem for everyone. Incumbents win reelection well over 90 percent of the time (at least in the House), and some incumbents, being stronger than others, are particularly safe. While incumbents' success results in part from their doing what they have to do, the high success rate does suggest some freedom to pursue goals other than reelection. Such freedom is particularly great for many senior members in leadership positions. Their seniority is both evidence of electoral strength and a source of strength, while their leadership positions help make influence and policy both more important and more attainable as goals. * * *

Beginning with power and prestige, its implications obviously depend on the context. For a leader, such as the Speaker of the House or a committee chairman, it often depends on winning legislative victories. Wilbur Mills, the Chairman of the Ways and Means Committee from 1958 to 1974, who never lost a tax bill on the House floor, seemingly regarded his "aura of invincibility" as more important than the content of legislation. To this end, he practiced "followership," extensively consulting his colleagues so that he could supply the legislation that they wanted. * * *

For members not in leadership positions, the routes to power and prestige are more varied. A member can gain status by introducing ideas that become widely discussed, whether or not the ideas are enacted. Examples include tax reform, which benefitted Senator Bradley and Congressman Gephardt even before enactment became plausible. * * * With the increased popularity of TV talk shows such as "Nightline" and "20/20," along with C-SPAN's full-time coverage, one can pursue a career as a television celebrity, although at the risk of gaining an inside reputation as a "show horse" who is all talk and no action.

In the struggle for power and prestige, interest groups can help a member. They can provide the political support that is crucial to winning a legislative contest. * * * It seems clear, however, that interest groups are relatively less important in the quest for power and prestige than they are with regard to fund-raising. Ideas, for example, emanate far more from government insiders and academics than from interest groups. The political salience of an idea, as with tax reform, often varies positively with it being hostile to what the media perceives as the "special interests." Thus, interest groups are far less powerful and important in a world where members compete for power and prestige than in a world of McChesneyian money monsters.

Now consider the goal of making good policy or furthering one's ideology. This goal is so important, according to some studies, that ideology is a better predictor of legislative voting behavior than economic interest variables. Moreover, there is anecdotal evidence that members often derive great pleasure from putting ideas into action and having an effect on society. Again, while interest groups can help a member (for example, by exploiting an ideology that serves their purposes, or suggesting workable legislative proposals), their dominance is far less than in fund-raising.

* * * In today's Congress, seemingly everyone wants to be an influential policy-maker. As one member put it, "Congress exists to do things. There isn't much mileage in doing nothing."[400] Members often want to participate in making policy to a far greater extent than they know what they want to do. Moreover, those who favor activism in a particular area tend to be the ones who seek and get the committee assignments in that area. What results is a bias in favor of action over inaction, a reluctance to consider carefully the merits of legislation (which become subordinate to one's own or one's colleagues' personal investment in it), and a tendency to legislate for legislation's sake. * * *

What is true of members of Congress is true as well of a vast array of other "players" in the Washington political community. Like congressmen, congressional staffers, cabinet members and other executive branch political appointees, career bureaucrats, lobbyists, self-styled public interest advocates, journalists, academics, and intellectuals affiliated with think tanks often push for legislation motivated by both desire for influence and concern about policy, as well as sheer enjoyment of the political game. * * *

Politicians' Means of Pursuing Reelection

An important factor in support of the public choice writers' claim that Congress cares only about money is the vital link between campaign financing and reelection. Fund-raising has become increasingly important in recent years. * * *

[T]he inaccuracy of the claim that members literally sell legislation is by no means fatal to a claim of interest group dominance driven by campaign financing. For example, even if members honestly do what they think is right, the political equivalent of natural selection might ensure that only people who agree with interest groups win elections. We also should not underestimate the capacity of a human being to persuade herself that action in her self-interest also happens to be right—especially since members often only hear the interest group's side of the story, and even in good faith may be swayed by feelings of obligation or gratitude towards contributors.

Yet the implications of campaign financing for interest group politics can easily be overstated. Only a small fraction of the money spent on lobbying takes the form of contributions to candidates—suggesting surprising inefficiency or irrationality on the part of interest groups if campaign financing is the unique engine of legislative success. Moreover, PAC contributions (often an important vehicle of interest group influence) are but a part of the campaign financing universe. * * *

Even more significantly, campaign financing is only one factor among many that affects reelection and other factors may dilute or even counter interest groups' influence. Perhaps the most thorough study of how members

---

400. J. KINGDON, AGENDAS, ALTERNATIVES, AND PUBLIC POLICIES at 41 (1984).

pursue reelection is David Mayhew's *Congress: The Electoral Connection.*[415] Mayhew finds that members engage principally in three kinds of activities in pursuit of reelection. The first is *advertising*, or "disseminat[ing] one's name among constituents in such a fashion as to create a favorable image but in messages having little or no issue content." The second is *position taking*, or "the public enunciation of a judgmental statement on anything likely to be of interest" to one's audience, often without regard to actual legislation. Finally, members engage in *credit claiming*, or "acting so as to generate a belief . . . that one is personally responsible for causing the government, or some unit thereof, to do something . . . desirable." A variation of credit claiming is blame avoidance, or deflecting perceived responsibility for unpopular government action.

Each of these activities lends importance to factors apart from interest group influence. * * *

Organized Interest Groups

The public choice view of organized interest groups is as narrow and stereotyped as the public choice views of voters and politicians. An interest group ostensibly consists of rational profit-maximizers, cooperating to seek transfers from the rest of society because for each participating individual the expected marginal benefit of cooperating exceeds the expected marginal cost.

* * *

[S]everal empirical studies have revealed * * * that, like so much else in politics, the groups respond to more than narrow monetary motives. Interest group rank and file members are in some ways like voters. They join for a variety of reasons, including not only narrow self-interest (i.e., expected economic benefit from successful lobbying and demand for goods like trade magazines), but also what James Q. Wilson calls solidary and purposive incentives: the social and status pleasures of belonging to a cohesive group, and emotional attachment to a group's political goals. They do not closely monitor their leaders' activities, and can be kept in line through symbolic behavior such as position-taking. Interest group leaders exploit their own resulting freedom to pursue a combination of goals resembling those held by members of Congress, i.e., institutional survival (the equivalent of reelection), ideological goals that their members may not share, and the desire for power and prestige within the Washington political community. This observation suggests once again that legislation reflects considerably more than the narrowly economic goals emphasized by public choice theory.

The Media

* * *

The media is more than a passive purveyor of information, however. Its reporting tends to have various predictable biases, perceptual if not partisan.

---

415. D. MAYHEW, CONGRESS: THE ELECTORAL CONNECTION 5 (1974) (arguing that congressmen can usefully be viewed as "singleminded seekers of reelection").

For example, it focuses on personalities and political "horse races" to a far greater extent than on ideas. The media often portrays politicians as unprincipled power-seekers, and challenges front-runners and incumbents in particular. Perhaps most importantly, in the interest group context, the media has a longstanding populist and muckraking tradition, rooted in reporters' personal beliefs and professional self-images as well as in their sense of what makes a good story. This tradition includes both a love of political scandals and supporting the "little guy" over the establishment.

    * * *

Thus, the media is potentially a powerful ally of policy entrepreneurs who take positions against what are deemed special interests. Reformers like Bradley, and (once they adopted reform roles) Rostenkowski and Packwood, can develop a symbiotic relationship with the media: they give it a good story, and in return it both portrays them favorably and lends powerful support to their side of the struggle. * * *

Ideas and Ideology

The critical importance of ideas and ideology is one of the most difficult aspects of politics for most public choice writers to appreciate. A mechanical view of wealth maximization has the appeal of a pseudo-science, purporting to unmask underlying realities and ostensibly leading to testable theorems and predictions. Yet the truth, of course, is that people often like ideas, find them interesting, and believe in them, with the result that ideas matter a great deal.

    * * *

Implications of the Factors
Apart From Interest Group Influence

For the reasons described above, members of Congress in enacting legislation both have considerable leeway and are subject to significant constraints apart from interest group influence. Specifically, members of Congress seek reelection, power, prestige, and ideological goals in a world where ill-informed voters are subject to symbolic responses and where the media can exercise great and often populist influence. Beyond these broad generalizations, the details of legislative behavior are inherently unpredictable. In particular, the incentives for policy entrepreneurship can stimulate any number of responses. An example is taxation, in which one may gain either by being a reformer who opposes interest groups or by championing tax instrumentalism.

The choice of how to seek success as a policy entrepreneur is controlled by the individual legislator. Members of Congress may seek the approbation of their colleagues, the media, the Washington political establishment, or the voters in any number of ways. No abstract model, whether narrowly economic or otherwise, can predict in detail either what proposals will be made at any time or which ones will succeed. Fortuity and the choices made by a small number of idiosyncratic individuals simply play too large a role here.

    * * *

While the content of legislation is difficult to predict, the likelihood that there will be a lot of it seems clear. In particular, the sheer number of different persons and institutions seeking legislative influence, yet bearing little political accountability for the real effects of their actions, promotes a dangerous lack of restraint and discipline. As compared with the opposite extreme of a centralized parliamentary system, the current system may tend to yield more aggregate legislation, rather than less (as one might think from the need for more extended bargaining), because so many different "players" must get to do something. The resulting legislation may be less unified and coherent than under a centralized parliamentary system. * * *

Application of the Broader Model to Tax Legislation

By now, we have seen not only what is wrong with public choice theory, but how the 1986 Act won enactment. The public was known to be dissatisfied with the income tax system, largely due to increased real tax burdens (because of bracket creep), growing discontent with government performance, and widely publicized instances of tax avoidance by wealthy individuals and large corporations. The political benefits of responding to this dissatisfaction and the intellectual appeal of tax reform, attracted policy entrepreneurs in Congress and then (more fortuitously) in the Reagan Administration. Once Reagan had made tax reform a cornerstone of his second term, additional forces went to work. Congressional leaders such as Rostenkowski and Packwood found that as leaders in the public spotlight, they had powerful incentives to support tax reform vigorously. The media's populist reporting of the issue pressured committee members to fall in line. * * * The incentives of the Democratic and Republican parties first to claim credit for enacting tax reform and then to avoid the blame for killing it contributed to approval by both houses, and also helped ensure the success of an acrimonious House-Senate conference.

Fitting this analysis into the model of congressional behavior that we have developed, we find that the goals of enhancing reelection, prestige, and ideology all played a role.

* * *

Some Broader Implications of Going Beyond Public Interest Theory and Public Choice Theory

* * *

Electoral and Other Systemic Reform

* * *

To bring fundamental, not just marginal, improvement, there really is no substitute for the unlikely prospect of the voting population becoming significantly better educated, better informed, more public-spirited, and more interested in politics. Still, since law generally aims at the margin, it is worth considering a few possibilities.

Campaign Financing and Expenditure Reform

The understanding that legislation is not in a simple sense "for sale," and that campaign financing is only one of many potentially distorting pressures, does not contradict the need for limiting campaign financing or expenditures. * * *

It may well be that public financing of all campaigns for federal office, at a high enough dollar level to dilute incumbents' advantages and induce most candidates to renounce private financing, would improve the legislative process. The analysis in this Article suggests, however, that such a reform might change the process less than many people expect.

Power of Congressional Leadership and Parties

A second direction for reform would * * * enhance the power of the congressional leadership, on the theory that such a change will at least marginally improve the legislative process[.] John Witte has suggested reversing the 1974 congressional reforms, and in particular increasing the chairperson's power, reducing the size of key committees, reinstituting and extending closed rules (barring floor amendments) to the Senate, and restricting open committee sessions (where the public, which usually just means lobbyists, can observe the proceedings) to the early stages of legislation under consideration.[518] These proposals are supported by the analysis in this Article, despite the unpredictability of how leaders will exercise power.

A related type of reform would seek to increase the power exercised over members of Congress by their political parties by, for example, directing public financing to the parties or moving towards a parliamentary system. * * *

Both increasing the power of the congressional leadership and strengthening the parties would tend to centralize the exercise of legislative authority, and to remove some practical checks and balances that are Madisonian in principle although not constitutionally mandated. The logical endpoint of moving in this direction would be to reject even the constitutionally mandated separation of powers and adopt a parliamentary system of party government. * * *

Depoliticizing Particular Decisional Areas

A third direction for reform, also suggested by John Witte, reflects greater despair about the legislative process. Witte proposes that authority over the tax system be insulated from politics through delegation to administrative bodies or executive agencies. He notes that tariff law was similarly depoliticized in the 1930s through legislation empowering the President to negotiate tariff changes that could then be implemented through executive order. This proposal may raise concerns about elitism versus popular government as well as the danger that interest groups will "capture" the new decision-makers. If limited to areas where legislative parochialism seems

---

518. J. WITTE, THE POLITICS AND DEVELOPMENT OF THE FEDERAL INCOME TAX at 381-82 (1985) (arguing that the 1981 Act "was unique only because it was extreme, not because it established new trends in tax legislation").

particularly acute (for example, control over the placement of military bases), and if insulated from direct presidential control, it might, however, be beneficial.

For taxation, this delegation model is already followed interstitially. Congress often grants the Treasury extensive authority to prescribe regulations giving flesh to a vague and conceptual provision. Broader reliance on delegation seems unlikely. * * *

Notes and Questions

21.   In many ways Professor Surrey's 1957 article reads as though it were written last week, but it should be remembered that it was written in a different tax world. The top marginal individual income tax rate exceeded 90 percent at that time; by contrast, since 1986 the top nominal rate has continuously been less than 40 percent. Rate reduction has been the most important consequence of tax legislation during the past 40 years. This change not only reduces the equitable appeal of a taxpayer asking for relief, but it lowers the stakes: a taxpayer presumably is more concerned about petitioning Congress to avoid a tax of 90 percent than a tax of 35 percent.

22.   Is the "loophole" label a useful tool for tax policy analysis? Should the term be reserved for unintended glitches in the law, or should it encompass intentionally-enacted special interest provisions? (As Professor Surrey observed in a portion of his article not excerpted, the beneficiaries are likely to view the "loophole" as "relief from special hardship.")

23.   Is it reasonable to assume that tax provisions are unfair if they apply only to specified groups, particularly small groups?

24.   Professor Surrey compares the American system for legislating taxes to the British parliamentary system, where the executive branch and the legislative branch are not separate and revenue bills pass through Parliament virtually unscathed.   Would we have a better income tax if we had a parliamentary form of government?

Lobbying

25.   Most obviously, lobbying means attempting to influence legislation by dealing directly with members of Congress. But lobbying objectives also are accomplished by communicating with congressional staff, Treasury staff, and, occasionally, with Revenue Service personnel. In a broader use of the term, lobbying includes attempts to persuade the public directly—grassroots lobbying.

At least in theory, input from affected taxpayers and their representatives should improve the process. Citizen input informs legislators about political acceptability of proposals in the best sense of the term. Lobbying can also add to the knowledge of decsionmakers. For example, taxpayers who will be affected are likely to be better informed than members of Congress concerning the impact of a complex legislative proposal, and may make legislators and their staff aware of unintended consequences.

26. The expense of most lobbying activity—whether direct or grassroots—would fit within the broad ambit of "ordinary and necessary" business expenses. The deductibility of lobbying expenses has varied over the years, however. Originally, Congress did not deal explicitly with the issue. Deduction of expenditures to influence legislation was denied by regulation, which the Supreme Court upheld against a challenge that it was inconsistent with the Code provision allowing deduction of ordinary and necessary expenses.[g] In 1962, Congress responded with section 162(e), which allowed deduction of certain lobbying expenses as business expenses. No deduction was allowed for expenditures on grassroots lobbying.

In 1993, section 162(e) was amended to deny deduction of lobbying expenses even when they constitute ordinary and necessary business expenses. (Section 162(e)(5)(A) makes clear that business expenses of conducting the business of lobbying on behalf of others remain deductible.)

27. Is there any justification for treating lobbying expenses different from other expenses of carrying on a trade or business?

28. Suppose Ms. Macbeth, a real estate developer, lobbies the state legislature to repeal a law that blocks her plans to subdivide Burnham Wood into quarter-acre lots for single family dwellings. Suppose Mr. McDuff, an individual with no business interest in the matter, is dismayed by Ms. Macbeth's proposal because he likes to walk through Burnham Wood to escape the noise of the city. Clearly Mr. McDuff cannot deduct any expenses he has in lobbying the state legislature by using ecological arguments on the issue because, for him, the expenses are personal and not business-related. Should Ms. Macbeth be able to deduct her lobbying expenses?

29. What of the distinction between grassroots and direct lobbying? If expenses of grassroots lobbying were deductible, could the Service readily distinguish between deductible lobbying expense and nondeductible political contributions?

"Public interest" and "Public choice"
30. What is meant by the "public interest" theory and by the "public choice" theory as explanations of the legislative process?

---

g. Cammarano v. United States, 358 U.S. 498 (1959).

31. Do you agree that public interest theory gives a less satisfactory explanation of the legislative process than does the dominant public choice theory?

32. Professor Shaviro argues that government will consistently provide visible (especially if literally visible, on television) benefit in exchange for greater, but less visible, cost. Do you agree?

Is the post-9/11 response, in granting unlimited government compensation to all those injured or killed, an example of this reaction? (Obviously, the 9/11 victims were blameless and suffered, but could that not be said equally of most victims of crime? Of almost all victims of cancer? Of all victims of birth defect? Was the controlling difference in these cases the degree of suffering, or the degree of national attention to the suffering?)

33. Shaviro makes a strong argument that money cannot account for the actions of members of Congress, because many (probably almost all) could make more money, and work less, by leaving office to assume other positions (frequently, as lobbyists). This argues against acceptance of at least the more crass forms of public choice explanation for tax legislation.

34. If we reject the narrow public choice theory, must we accept the view that the process is run by disinterested statesmen acting in the public interest? Shaviro argues not, asserting that much legislative action is motivated not by a desire to achieve *any* substantive end—either to benefit the public (public interest theory) or to benefit financial supporters (public choice theory)—but simply by a desire to engage in the process of legislating. What benefits might flow to a legislator from simply engaging in this process?

35. Professor Shaviro argues that narrowly self-interested voters, even with much at stake in the outcome of a national election, would act rationally by not bothering to vote. Why not?

36. Do you agree with the characterization of politics as a form of "spectator sport," in which the media and the voters are more focused on scandal and competition itself (the "horse race") than on the substance? (As this is being written, more than a year prior to the 2004 election, television networks are already devoting a segment of each newscast to coverage of the "upcoming" Presidential election.)

37. Shaviro suggests a parallel between politics and the entertainment industry. It might be argued that one reason for President Clinton's popularity in the face of scandal was that his scandals entertained us—perhaps we would rather be outraged than bored.

38. Professor Shaviro notes the rapid vacillation between "instrumentalist" tax statutes, of which the Economic Recovery Tax Act of 1981 was the high-water mark, and "reform" measures, of which the Tax Reform Act of 1986 was the apogee. He concludes that "[w]hile the content of legislation is difficult to predict, the likelihood that there will be lots of it seems clear." Do you agree?

39. Professor Shaviro's analysis and that of Professor Surrey seem to converge on the point that our disparate set of power bases creates a less cohesive system, and a less stable law, than would be the case under a parliamentary system. In Britain, for example, the government by definition controls majority support in the House of Commons (otherwise the Commons would vote "no confidence" in the government, and depose it). When combined with strong party discipline, this means that it is likely that a British government can pass tax measures or other legislation in much "purer" form than can an American government.

Is this an argument for a parliamentary form of government? The contrasting view—that of Madisonian checks and balances—is that we do not want it to be easy for government to act. Perhaps a system that almost requires compromise is better than one that allows a single clear vision to be enacted.

40. A final observation is that the process of writing tax legislation, and the factors that influence it, reflect the legislative process in all areas. For example, the differences between the American system and a parliamentary system are present in all types of legislation.

APPENDIX I

PRESENT VALUE OF $1.00

years	1%	2%	3%	4%	5%	6%	7%	8%	9%	10%	12%	15%
1	.99010	.98039	.97087	.96154	.95238	.94340	.93458	.92593	.91743	.90909	.89286	.86957
2	.98030	.96117	.94260	.92456	.90703	.89000	.87344	.85734	.84168	.82645	.79719	.75614
3	.97059	.94232	.91514	.88900	.86384	.83962	.81630	.79383	.77218	.75131	.71178	.65752
4	.96098	.92385	.88849	.85480	.82270	.79209	.76290	.73503	.70843	.68301	.63552	.57175
5	.95147	.90573	.86261	.82193	.78353	.74726	.71299	.68058	.64993	.62092	.56743	.49718
6	.94205	.88797	.83748	.79031	.74622	.70496	.66634	.63017	.59627	.56447	.50663	.43233
7	.93272	.87056	.81309	.75992	.71068	.66506	.62275	.58349	.54703	.51316	.45235	.37594
8	.92348	.85349	.78941	.73069	.67684	.62741	.58201	.54027	.50187	.46651	.40388	.32690
9	.91434	.83676	.76642	.70259	.64461	.59190	.54393	.50025	.46043	.42410	.36061	.28426
10	.90529	.82035	.74409	.67556	.61391	.55839	.50835	.46319	.42241	.38554	.32197	.24718
11	.89632	.80426	.72242	.64958	.58468	.52679	.47059	.42288	.38753	.35049	.28748	.21494
12	.88745	.78849	.70138	.62460	.55684	.49697	.44401	.39711	.35553	.31863	.25668	.18691
13	.87866	.77303	.68095	.60057	.53032	.46884	.41496	.36770	.32618	.28966	.22917	.16253
14	.86996	.75788	.66112	.57748	.50507	.44230	.38782	.34046	.29925	.26333	.20462	.14133
15	.86135	.74301	.64186	.55526	.48102	.41727	.36245	.31524	.27454	.23939	.18270	.12289
16	.85282	.72845	.62317	.53391	.45811	.39365	.33873	.29189	.25187	.21763	.16312	.10686
17	.84438	.71416	.60502	.51337	.43630	.37136	.31657	.27027	.23107	.19784	.14564	.09293
18	.83602	.70016	.58739	.49363	.41552	.35034	.29586	.25025	.21199	.17986	.13004	.08081
19	.82774	.68643	.57029	.47464	.39573	.33051	.27651	.23171	.19499	.16351	.11611	.07027
20	.81954	.67297	.55368	.45639	.37689	.31180	.25842	.21455	.17843	.14864	.10367	.06110
22	.80340	.64684	.52189	.42196	.34185	.27751	.22571	.18394	.15018	.12285	.08264	.04620
24	.78757	.62172	.49193	.39012	.31007	.24698	.19715	.15770	.12640	.10153	.06588	.03493
26	.77205	.59758	.46369	.36069	.28124	.21981	.17220	.13520	.10639	.08391	.05252	.02642
28	.75684	.57437	.43708	.3348	.25509	.19563	.15040	.11591	.08955	.06934	.04187	.01997
30	.74192	.55207	.41199	.30832	.23138	.17411	.13137	.09938	.07537	.05731	.03338	.01510
32	.72730	.53063	.38834	.28506	.20987	.15496	.11474	.08520	.06344	.04736	.02661	.01142
34	.71297	.51003	.36604	.26355	.19035	.13791	.10022	.07305	.05339	.03914	.02121	.00864
36	.69892	.49022	.34503	.24367	.17266	.12274	.08754	.06262	.04494	.03235	.01691	.00653
38	.68515	.47119	.32523	.22529	.15661	.10924	.07646	.05369	.03783	.02673	.01348	.00494
40	.67165	.45289	.30656	.20829	.14295	.09722	.06678	.04603	.03184	.02209	.01075	.00373
50	.60804	.37153	.22811	.14071	.08720	.05429	.03395	.02132	.01345	.00852	.00346	.00092
100	.36971	.13803	.05203	.01980	.00760	.00295	.00115	.00045	.00018	.00007	.00001	.00000

Source: ALAN GUNN & LARRY D. WARD, FEDERAL INCOME TAXATION 799 (5th ed. 2002).

APPENDIX II

FUTURE VALUE OF $1.00

years	1%	2%	3%	4%	5%	6%	7%	8%	9%	10%	12%	15%
1	1.01000	1.02000	1.03000	1.04000	1.05000	1.06000	1.07000	1.08000	1.09000	1.10000	1.12000	1.15000
2	1.02010	1.04040	1.06090	1.08160	1.10250	1.12360	1.14490	1.16640	1.18810	1.21000	1.25440	1.32250
3	1.03030	1.06121	1.09273	1.12486	1.15763	1.19102	1.22504	1.25971	1.29503	1.33100	1.40493	1.52087
4	1.04060	1.08243	1.12551	1.16986	1.21551	1.26248	1.31080	1.36049	1.41158	1.46410	1.57352	1.74901
5	1.05101	1.10408	1.15927	1.21665	1.27628	1.33823	1.40255	1.46933	1.53862	1.61051	1.76234	2.01136
6	1.06152	1.12616	1.19405	1.26532	1.34010	1.41852	1.50073	1.58687	1.67710	1.77156	1.97382	2.31306
7	1.07214	1.14869	1.22987	1.31593	1.40710	1.50363	1.60578	1.71382	1.82804	1.94872	2.21068	2.66002
8	1.08286	1.17166	1.26677	1.36857	1.47746	1.59385	1.71819	1.85093	1.99256	2.14359	2.47596	3.05902
9	1.09369	1.19509	1.30477	1.42331	1.55133	1.68948	1.83846	1.99900	2.17189	2.35795	2.77308	3.51788
10	1.10462	1.21899	1.34392	1.48024	1.62889	1.79085	1.96715	2.15892	2.36736	2.59374	3.10585	4.04566
11	1.11567	1.24337	1.38423	1.53945	1.71034	1.89830	2.10485	2.33164	2.58043	2.85312	3.47855	4.65239
12	1.12683	1.26824	1.42576	1.60103	1.79586	2.01220	2.25219	2.51817	2.81266	3.13843	3.89598	5.35025
13	1.13809	1.29361	1.46853	1.66507	1.88565	2.13293	2.40985	2.71962	3.06580	3.45227	4.36349	6.15279
14	1.14947	1.31948	1.51259	1.73168	1.97993	2.26090	2.57853	2.93719	3.34173	3.79750	4.88711	7.07571
15	1.16097	1.34587	1.55797	1.80094	2.07893	2.39656	2.75903	3.17217	3.64248	4.17725	5.47357	8.13706
16	1.17258	1.37279	1.60471	1.87298	2.18287	2.54035	2.95260	3.42594	3.97031	4.59497	6.13039	9.35762
17	1.18430	1.40024	1.65285	1.94790	2.29202	2.69277	3.15882	3.70002	4.32763	5.05447	6.86604	10.76126
18	1.19615	1.42825	1.70243	2.02582	2.40662	2.85434	3.37993	3.99602	4.71712	5.55992	7.68997	12.37545
19	1.20811	1.45681	1.75351	2.10685	2.52695	3.02560	3.61653	4.31570	5.14166	6.11591	8.61276	14.23177
20	1.22019	1.48595	1.80611	2.19112	2.65330	3.20714	3.86968	4.66096	5.60441	6.72750	9.64629	16.36654
22	1.24472	1.54598	1.91610	2.36992	2.92526	3.60354	4.43040	5.43654	6.65860	8.14027	12.10031	21.64475
24	1.26973	1.60844	2.03279	2.56330	3.22510	4.04893	5.07237	6.34118	7.91108	9.84973	15.17863	28.62518
26	1.29526	1.67342	2.15659	2.77247	3.55567	4.54938	5.80735	7.39635	9.39960	11.91818	19.04007	37.85680
28	1.13129	1.74102	2.28793	2.99870	3.92013	5.11169	6.64884	8.62711	11.16714	14.42099	23.88387	50.06561
30	1.34785	1.81136	2.42726	3.24340	4.32194	5.74349	7.61226	10.06266	13.26768	17.44940	29.95992	66.21177
32	1.37494	1.84454	2.57508	3.50806	4.76494	6.45339	8.71527	11.73708	15.76333	21.11378	37.58173	87.56507
34	1.40258	1.96068	2.73191	3.79432	5.25335	7.25103	9.97811	13.69013	18.72841	25.54767	47.14252	115.8048
36	1.43077	2.03989	2.89829	4.10393	5.79182	8.14725	11.42394	15.96817	22.25123	30.91268	59.13557	153.1519
38	1.45953	2.12230	3.07478	4.43881	6.38548	9.15425	13.07927	18.62528	26.43668	37.40434	74.17966	202.5433
40	1.48886	2.20804	3.26204	4.80102	7.03999	10.28572	14.97446	21.72452	31.40942	45.25926	93.05097	267.8635
50	1.6463	2.69159	4.38391	7.10668	11.46740	18.42015	29.45703	46.90161	74.35752	117.3909	289.0022	1,083.66
100	2.70481	7.24465	19.21863	50.50495	131.5013	339.3021	867.7163	2199.76	5,529.04	13,780.6	83,522.3	117×10^4

Source: ALAN GUNN & LARRY D. WARD, FEDERAL INCOME TAXATION 798 (5th ed. 2002).

TABLE OF CASES

INTERNAL REVENUE CODE SECTIONS

References are to Pages.

INTERNAL REVENUE CODE SECTIONS

INDEX

References are to pages.

†